The Complete 70 Book Apocrypha including Writings of the Apostolic Fathers:

the Deuterocanon, Enoch 1-3, Pseudepigrapha, Jubilees, Giants, and The Gospel of Thomas

Compiled by Joseph Lumpkin

Joseph Lumpkin

**The Complete 70 Book Apocrypha Including Writings of the Apostolic Fathers:
the Deuterocanon, Enoch 1-3, Pseudepigrapha, Jubilees, Giants, and The Gospel of Thomas**

Fifth Estate Publishers, Blountsville, AL 35031.

First Printing, 2023

Printed on acid-free paper

ISBN 13: 9798851070365

Fifth Estate, 2009

Table of Contents

A Brief History of the Apocrypha

The official editions of the King James contained the books of the Apocrypha until 1796. Most printers did not clear inventories and change to the sixty-six book version we know today until the mid 1800's. Thus, most Bibles printed before 1840 still had the Apocrypha, or at least most of the Apocrypha. As it turns out, various religions have differing versions of the Bible, made up of divergent lists of books. The Protestant church has its sixty-six books, the Catholics have kept most of the Apocrypha. The Eastern Orthodox Church claims three more books than the Catholics, and the Ethiopic Church has a total of eighty-one books in its Bible.

Etymologically, the word "apocrypha" means "things that are hidden," but why they were hidden is not clear. Some have suggested that the books were "hidden" from common use because they contained esoteric knowledge, too profound to be communicated to any except the initiated (compare 2 Esd 14.45-46). Others have suggested that such books were hidden due to their spurious or heretical teaching.

According to traditional usage "Apocrypha" has been the designation applied to the fifteen books, or portions of books, listed below. (in many earlier editions of the Apocrypha, the Letter of Jeremiah is incorporated as the final chapter of the Book of Baruch; hence in these editions there are fourteen books.)

Tobit, Judith, The Additions to the Book of Esther (contained in the Greek version of Esther), The Wisdom of Solomon, Ecclesiasticus, The Wisdom of Jesus son of Sirach, Baruch, The Letter of Jeremiah, The Prayer of Azariah, The Song of the Three Jews ,"Susanna, Bel, and the Dragon", 1 Maccabees, 2 Maccabees, 1 Esdras, The Prayer of Manasseh, and 2 Esdras.

In addition, the present expanded edition includes the following three texts that are of special interest to Eastern Orthodox readers are 3 Maccabees, 4 Maccabees, and Psalm 151.

None of these books are included in the Hebrew canon of Holy Scripture. All of them, however, with the exception of 2 Esdras, are present in copies of the Greek version of the Old Testament known as the Septuagint. The Old Latin translations of the Old Testament, made from the Septuagint, also include them, along with 2 Esdras. The Eastern Orthodox Churches chose to include 1 Esdras, Psalm 151, the Prayer of Manasseh, and 3 Maccabees, and 4 Maccabees, which is placed in an appendix as a historical work.

At the end of the fourth century, Pope Damasus commissioned Jerome to prepare a standard Latin version of the Scriptures called the Latin Vulgate. Jerome wrote a note or preface, designating a separate category for the apocryphal books. However, copyists failed the include Jerome's prefaces. Thus, during the medieval period the Western Church generally regarded these books as part of the holy Scriptures.

In 1546 the Council of Trent decreed that the canon of the Old Testament includes the Apocrypha with the exception of the Prayer of Manasseh and 1 and 2 Esdras. Later, the church completed the decision by writing in its Roman Catholic Catechism, "Deuterocanonical does not mean Apocryphal, but simply 'later added to the canon."

But wait, there's more.
The canon of the Ethiopic church contains the following Old Testament books:

Genesis
Exodus
Leviticus
Numbers
Deuteronomy
Enoch
Jubilees
Joshua
Judges
Ruth
1 Samuel
2 Samuel
1 Kings
2 Kings
1 Chronicles
2 Chronicles
Ezra
Nehemiah
3rd Ezra
4rth Ezra
Tobit
Judith
Esther (includes additions to Esther)
1 Macabees
2 Macabees
3 Macabees
Job
Psalms (+ Psalm 151)
Proverbs (Proverbs 1-24)
Täagsas (Proverbs 25-31)
Wisdom of Solomon
Ecclesiastes
Song of Solomon
Sirach (Ecclesiasticus)
Isaiah
Jeremiah

Baruch (includes Letter of Jeremiah)
Lamentations
Ezekiel
Daniel
Hosea
Amos
Micah
Joel
Obadiah
Jonah
Nahum
Habakkuk
Zephaniah
Haggai
Zecariah

Additions to The Book of Esther

AddEsth.11

[1] In the fourth year of Ptolomeus and Cleopatra, Dositheus and Leuite, who claimed to be a priest brought the Epistle of Phurim that was in Jerusalem and had it interpreted.

[2] In the second year of the reign of Artaxerxes the Great, on the first day of Nisan, Mordecai the son of Jair, son of Shimei, son of Kish, of the tribe of Benjamin, had a dream.

[3] He was a Jew, dwelling in the city of Susa, a great man, serving in the court of the king.

[4] He was one of the captives whom Nebuchadnezzar king of Babylon had brought from Jerusalem with Jeconiah king of Judea. And this was his dream:

[5] Behold, noise and confusion, thunders and earthquake, tumult upon the earth!

[6] And behold, two great dragons came forward, both ready to fight, and they roared terribly.

[7] And at their roaring every nation prepared for war, to fight against the nation of the righteous.

[8] And behold, a day of darkness and gloom, tribulation and distress, affliction and great tumult upon the earth!

[9] And the whole righteous nation was troubled; they feared the evils that threatened them, and were ready to perish.

[10] Then they cried to God; and from their cry, as though from a tiny spring, there came a great river, with abundant water; [11] light came, and the sun rose, and the lowly were exalted and consumed those held in honor.

[12] Mordecai saw in this dream what God had determined to do, and after he awoke he had it on his mind and sought all day to understand it in every detail.

AddEsth.12

[1] Now Mordecai took his rest in the courtyard with Gabatha and Tharra, the two eunuchs of the king who kept watch in the courtyard.

[2] He overheard their conversation and inquired into their purposes, and learned that they were preparing to lay hands upon Artaxerxes the king; and he informed the king concerning them.

[3] Then the king examined the two eunuchs, and when they confessed they were led to execution.

[4] The king made a permanent record of these things, and Mordecai wrote an account of them.

[5] And the king ordered Mordecai to serve in the court and rewarded him for these things.

[6] But Haman, the son of Hammedatha, a Bougaean, was in great honor with the king, and he sought to injure Mordecai and his people because of the two eunuchs of the king.

AddEsth.13

[1] This is a copy of the letter: "The Great King, Artaxerxes, to the rulers of the hundred and twenty-seven provinces from India to Ethiopia and to the governors under them, writes thus:

[2] "Having become ruler of many nations and master of the whole world, not elated with presumption of authority but always acting reasonably and with kindness, I have determined to settle the lives of my subjects in lasting tranquillity and, in order to make my kingdom peaceable and open to travel throughout all its extent, to re-establish the peace which all men desire.

[3] "When I asked my counselors how this might be accomplished, Haman, who excels among us in sound judgment, and is distinguished for his unchanging good will and steadfast fidelity, and has attained the second place in the kingdom,

[4] pointed out to us that among all the nations in the world there is scattered a certain hostile people, who have laws contrary to those of every nation and continually disregard the ordinances of the kings, so that the unifying of the kingdom which we honorably intend cannot be brought about.

[5] We understand that this people, and it alone, stands constantly in opposition to all men, perversely following a strange manner of life and laws, and is ill-disposed to our government, doing all the harm they can so that our kingdom may not attain stability.

[6] "Therefore we have decreed that those indicated to you in the letters of Haman, who is in charge of affairs and is our second father, shall all, with their wives and children, be utterly destroyed by the sword of their enemies, without pity or mercy, on the fourteenth day of the twelfth month, Adar, of this present year,

[7] so that those who have long been and are now hostile may in one day go down in violence to Hades, and leave our government completely secure and untroubled hereafter."

[8] Then Mordecai prayed to the Lord, calling to remembrance all the works of the Lord. He said:

[9] "O Lord, Lord, King who rulest over all things, for the universe is in thy power and there is no one who can oppose thee if it is thy will to save Israel.

[10] For thou hast made heaven and earth and every wonderful thing under heaven,

[11] and thou art Lord of all, and there is no one who can resist thee, who art the Lord.

[12] Thou knowest all things; thou knowest, O Lord, that it was not in insolence or pride or for any love of glory that I did this, and refused to bow down to this proud Haman.

[13] For I would have been willing to kiss the soles of his feet, to save Israel!

[14] But I did this, that I might not set the glory of man above the glory of God, and I will not bow down to any one but to thee, who art my Lord; and I will not do these things in pride.

[15] And now, O Lord God and King, God of Abraham, spare thy people; for the eyes of our foes are upon us to annihilate us, and they desire to destroy the inheritance that has been your from the beginning.

[16] Do not neglect thy portion, which thou didst redeem for thyself out of the land of Egypt.

[17] Hear my prayer, and have mercy upon thy inheritance turn our mourning into feasting, that we may live and sing praise to thy name, O Lord; do not destroy the mouth of those who praise thee."

[18] And all Israel cried out mightily, for their death was before their eyes.

AddEsth.14

[1] And Esther the queen, seized with deathly anxiety, fled to the Lord;

[2] she took off her splendid apparel and put on the garments of distress and mourning, and instead of costly perfumes she covered her head with ashes and dung, and she utterly humbled her body, and every part that she loved to adorn she covered with her tangled hair.

[3] And she prayed to the Lord God of Israel, and said: Lord, thou only art our King; help me, who am alone and have no helper but thee,

[4] for my danger is in my hand.

[5] Ever since I was born I have heard in the tribe of my family that thou, O Lord, didst take Israel out of all the nations, and our fathers from among all their ancestors, for an everlasting inheritance, and that thou didst do for them all that thou didst promise.

[6] And now we have sinned before thee, and thou hast given us into the hands of our enemies,

[7] because we glorified their gods. Thou art righteous, O Lord!

[8] And now they are not satisfied that we are in bitter slavery, but they have covenanted with their idols

[9] to abolish what thy mouth has ordained and to destroy thy inheritance, to stop the mouths of those who praise thee and to quench thy altar and the glory of thy house,

[10] to open the mouths of the nations for the praise of vain idols, and to magnify for ever a mortal king.

[11] O Lord, do not surrender thy scepter to what has no being; and do not let them mock at our downfall; but turn their plan against themselves, and make an example of the man who began this against us.

[12] Remember, O Lord; make thyself known in this time of our affliction, and give me courage, O King of the gods and Master of all dominion!

[13] Put eloquent speech in my mouth before the lion, and turn his heart to hate the man who is fighting against us, so that there may be an end of him and those who agree with him.

[14] But save us by thy hand, and help me, who am alone and have no helper but thee, O Lord.

[15] Thou hast knowledge of all things; and thou knowest that I hate the splendor of the wicked and abhor the bed of the uncircumcised and of any alien.

[16] Thou knowest my necessity -- that I abhor the sign of my proud position, which is upon my head on the days when I appear in public. I abhor it like a menstruous rag, and I do not wear it on the days when I am at leisure.

[17] And thy servant has not eaten at Haman's table, and I have not honored the king's feast or drunk the wine of the libations.

[18] Your servant has had no joy since the day that I was brought here until now, except in thee, O Lord God of Abraham.

[19] O God, whose might is over all, hear the voice of the despairing, and save us from the hands of evildoers. And save me from my fear!"

AddEsth.15

[1] On the third day, when she ended her prayer, she took off the garments in which she had worshiped, and arrayed herself in splendid attire.

[2] Then, majestically adorned, after invoking the aid of the all-seeing God and Savior, she took her two maids with her,

[3] leaning daintily on one,

[4] while the other followed carrying her train.

[5] She was radiant with perfect beauty, and she looked happy, as if beloved, but her heart was frozen with fear.

[6] When she had gone through all the doors, she stood before the king. He was seated on his royal throne, clothed in the full array of his majesty, all covered with gold and precious stones. And he was most terrifying.

[7] Lifting his face, flushed with splendor, he looked at her in fierce anger. And the queen faltered, and turned pale and faint, and collapsed upon the head of the maid who went before her.

[8] Then God changed the spirit of the king to gentleness, and in alarm he sprang from his throne and took her in his arms until she came to herself. And he comforted her with soothing words, and said to her,

[9] "What is it, Esther? I am your brother. Take courage;

[10] you shall not die, for our law applies only to the people. Come near."

[11] Then he raised the golden scepter and touched it to her neck;

[12] and he embraced her, and said, "Speak to me."

[13] And she said to him, "I saw you, my lord, like an angel of God and my heart was shaken with fear at your glory.

[14] For you are wonderful, my lord, and your countenance is full of grace."

[15] But as she was speaking, she fell fainting.

[16] And the king was agitated, and all his servants sought to comfort her.

AddEsth.16

[1] The following is a copy of this letter: "The Great King, Artaxerxes, to the rulers of the provinces from India to Ethiopia, one hundred and twenty-seven satrapies, and to those who are loyal to our government, greeting.

[2] "The more often they are honored by the too great kindness of their benefactors, the more proud do many men become.

[3] They not only seek to injure our subjects, but in their inability to stand prosperity they even undertake to scheme against their own benefactors.

[4] They not only take away thankfulness from among men, but, carried away by the boasts of those who know nothing of goodness, they suppose that they will escape the evil-hating justice of God, who always sees everything.

[5] And often many of those who are set in places of authority have been made in part responsible for the shedding of innocent blood, and have been involved in irremediable calamities, by the persuasion of friends who have been entrusted with the administration of public affairs,

[6] when these men by the false trickery of their evil natures beguile the sincere good will of their sovereigns.

[7] "What has been wickedly accomplished through the pestilent behavior of those who exercise authority unworthily, can be seen not so much from the more ancient records which we hand on as from investigation of matters close at hand.

[8] For the future we will take care to render our kingdom quiet and peaceable for all men,

[9] by changing our methods and always judging what comes before our eyes with more equitable consideration.

[10] For Haman, the son of Hammedatha, a Macedonian (really an alien to the Persian blood, and quite devoid of our kindliness), having become our guest,

[11] so far enjoyed the good will that we have for every nation that he was called our father and was continually bowed down to by all as the person second to the royal throne.

[12] But, unable to restrain his arrogance, he undertook to deprive us of our kingdom and our life,

[13] and with intricate craft and deceit asked for the destruction of Mordecai, our savior and perpetual benefactor, and of Esther, the blameless partner of our kingdom, together with their whole nation.

[14] He thought that in this way he would find us undefended and would transfer the kingdom of the Persians to the Macedonians.

[15] "But we find that the Jews, who were consigned to annihilation by this thrice accursed man, are not evildoers but are governed by most righteous laws

[16] and are sons of the Most High, the most mighty living God, who has directed the kingdom both for us and for our fathers in the most excellent order.

[17] "You will therefore do well not to put in execution the letters sent by Haman the son of Hammedatha,

[18] because the man himself who did these things has been hanged at the gate of Susa, with all his household. For God, who rules over all things, has speedily inflicted on him the punishment he deserved.

[19] "Therefore post a copy of this letter publicly in every place, and permit the Jews to live under their own laws.

[20] And give them reinforcements, so that on the thirteenth day of the twelfth month, Adar, on that very day they may defend themselves against those who attack them at the time of their affliction.

[21] For God, who rules over all things, has made this day to be a joy to his chosen people instead of a day of destruction for them.

[22] "Therefore you shall observe this with all good cheer as a notable day among your commemorative festivals,

[23] so that both now and hereafter it may mean salvation for us and the loyal Persians, but that for those who plot against us it may be a reminder of destruction.

[24] "Every city and country, without exception, which does not act accordingly, shall be destroyed in wrath with spear and fire. It shall be made not only impassable for men, but also most hateful for all time to beasts and birds."

AddEsth.10

[1] And Mordecai said, "These things have come from God.

[2] For I remember the dream that I had concerning these matters, and none of them has failed to be fulfilled.

[3] The tiny spring which became a river, and there was light and the sun and abundant water -- the river is Esther, whom the king married and made queen.

[4] The two dragons are Haman and myself.

[5] The nations are those that gathered to destroy the name of the Jews.

[6] And my nation, this is Israel, who cried out to God and were saved. The Lord has saved his people; the Lord has delivered us from all these evils; God has done great signs and wonders, which have not occurred among the nations.

[7] For this purpose he made two lots, one for the people of God and one for all the nations.

[8] And these two lots came to the hour and moment and day of decision before God and among all the nations.

[9] And God remembered his people and vindicated his inheritance.

[10] So they will observe these days in the month of Adar, on the fourteenth and fifteenth of that month, with an assembly and joy and gladness before God, from generation to generation for ever among his people Israel."

AddEsth.11

[1] In the fourth year of the reign of Ptolemy and Cleopatra, Dositheus, who said that he was a priest and a Levite, and Ptolemy his son brought to Egypt the preceding Letter of Purim, which they said was genuine and had been translated by Lysimachus the son of Ptolemy, one of the residents of Jerusalem.

Additional Psalms

There are ten additional psalms found only in a few sources. Only Psalm 151 is included in the NRSV and Orthodox Study Bible. No other Bible accords Psalms 151 canon, and no mainline Christian denomination accepts Psalms 151 through 160 as canon accept ancient Syriac versions of the Bible. These ten psalms are found in the Peshitta and/or the Dead Sea Scrolls, with only Psalm 151 being found in many manuscripts of the Septuagint (LXX). The Peshitta is the ancient Syriac version of the Bible, used in Syriac-speaking Christian countries from the early 5th century and still the official Bible of the Syrian Christian Churches.

Canonicity

Psalm 151 was part of many manuscripts of the Septuagint, and some of the Peshitta. The Hebrew text of this Psalm from the Dead Sea Scrolls (11Q5) does differ slightly, in which verses 1-5 are considered to be a longer text designated 151A, and verses 6-8 are considered a separate fragmentary text designated 151B.

Psalms 152-155 were included in some manuscripts of the Syriac Peshitta. Psalms 154 and 155, in addition to their presence in the Syriac Peshitta, were also found among the Dead Sea Scrolls. (11Q5) The translation presented here from the Syriac has been compared with the Hebrew text found at Qumran and then rendered in to a modern English version.

Psalms 156-160 come exclusively from the Dead Sea Scrolls, (11Q5 and 4Q88) in which these Psalms are listed alongside many canonical Psalms from the Hebrew Bible.

Due to the antiquity of the scrolls containing texts of Psalms 156-160 there are places where damage made the texts unreadable. In some cases, serious gaps exists in the text. In these cases, words are placed according to reasonable syntax. Several of the most well-meaning scholars have attempted to restore the texts to the best of their abilities.

Psalm No.	Source
151	Peshitta, LXX, DSS (11Q5)
152	Peshitta
153	Peshitta
154	Peshitta, DSS (11Q5 XVIII)
155	Peshitta, DSS (11Q5 XXIV)
156	DSS (11Q5 XIX)
157	DSS (11Q5 XXII, 4Q88 VII)
158	DSS (4Q88 IX)
159	DSS (4Q88 X)
160	DSS (11Q5 XXVI)

Psalm 151

Ps151.1
[1] I was the smallest in my father's house and the youngest of my brothers. I took care of my father's sheep.
[2] My hands made a harp, my fingers fashioned a lyre.
[3] And who will declare it to my Lord? The Lord himself; it is he who hears.
[4] It was he who sent his messenger and took me from my father's sheep, and anointed me with his anointing oil.
[5] My brothers were handsome and tall, but the Lord was not pleased with them.
[6] I went out to meet the Philistine, and he cursed me by his idols.
[7] But I drew his own sword; I beheaded him, and removed reproach from the people of Israel.

Psalm 152
Spoken by David, when he was contending with the lion and the wolf which took a sheep from his flock.
1 O God, O God, come to my aid; help me, save me, and deliver my soul from the murderer. 2 Will I go down to Sheol (the place of the dead) by the mouth of the lion? Will the wolf be the end of me? 3 Was it not enough for those who lay in wait for my father's flock, and ripped apart a sheep of my father's flock–must they also wish the destruction of my own soul? 4 Have pity, O LORD, and save Your holy one from destruction, so that he may recount to all Your glories for all of his days, and may praise Your great name, 5 when You have delivered him from the hands of the destroying lion and of the ravening wolf, and when You have rescued me from being captured by the cunning of the wild beasts. 6 Quickly, my Lord, send a deliverer from Yourself, and pull me out of the gaping pit which imprisons me in its depths.

Psalm 153
Spoken by David, thanking God for deliverance from the lion and the wolf, after he had slain them both.
1 Praise the LORD, all you nations; glorify Him, and bless His name. 2 He has rescued the soul of His elect from the hands of death, and delivered His holy one from destruction. 3 He has saved me from the nets of Sheol (the underworld), and my soul from the pit that cannot be measured.
4 Before my deliverance could go forth from Him, I was very nearly tore in half by two wild beasts; 5 but He sent His angel, and closed up their mouths from me, and rescued my life from destruction. 6 My soul will glorify Him and exalt Him, because of all His kindnesses which He has done and will continue to do to me.

Psalm 154

A Prayer of Hezekiah, when he was surrounded by his enemies.

1 Glorify God with a loud voice, and proclaim His glory in the assembly of crowds. 2 Glorify His praise among the multitude of the upright, and speak about His glory with the righteous people. 3 Let your souls be fixed on the good and the perfect, to glorify the Most High God. 4 Gather yourselves together and proclaim His strength, and do not be slow in showing forth His deliverance and His strength, and His glory to all who are young.

5 Wisdom has been given so the honor of the LORD may be known, and it has been made known to men so they may tell of His works: 6 to make known to the children His strength, and to cause those who lack understanding to comprehend His glory, 7 who are far from His entrances and distant from His gates; 8 for the God of Jacob is exalted, and His glory is upon all His works.

9 He will take pleasure in a man who glorifies the Most High, like one who offers fine meal, 10 and like one who offers he-goats and calves, and like one who makes the altar full with a multitude of burnt offerings, and as the smell of incense from the hands of the just. 11 His voice will be heard from Your upright gates, and correction from the voice of the upright. 12 In their eating and their drinking, when they share together, they will be satisfied in truth. 13 Their mind dwells on the Law of the Most High God, and their speech is to make known His strength.

14 How far the wicked are from conversations about Him, and from all transgressors to know Him! 15 Behold; the eye of the LORD takes pity on the good! He will multiply mercy to those who glorify Him, and from the time of evil He will deliver their soul. 16 Blessed be the LORD, who has delivered the poor and broken-hearted from the hand of the wicked; who raises up a horn out of Jacob, and a judge of the nations out of Israel, 17 that He may prolong His dwelling in Zion, and may adorn our time (era / epoch) in Jerusalem.

Psalm 155

A prayer of thanksgiving, when the people obtained permission from Cyrus to return home.

1 O LORD, I have cried to You; hear me. 2 I have lifted up my hands to Your holy dwelling place; incline Your ear to me. 3 Grant me my request; do not withhold from me my request.

4 Build up my soul, and do not destroy it, and do not lay it bare before the wicked. 5 Those who reward evil things turn You away from me, O judge of truth. 6 O LORD, do not judge me according to my sins, because no flesh is innocent before You.

7 Make Your Law plain to me, O LORD, and teach me Your judgments. 8 Many will hear of Your works, and the nations will praise Your honor. 9 Remember me, and do not forget me; and do not lead me into difficulties I cannot overcome. 10 Cause the sins of my youth to pass away from me, and remember my punishments against me no longer. 11 Cleanse me, O LORD, from the evil leprosy, and do not let it come against me any longer. 12 Dry up its roots from within me, and do not let its leaves sprout within me. 13 You are great, O LORD; therefore, my request will be fulfilled in You. 14 To whom will I complain that can help me? What help can be found in the strength of men? 15 From You, O LORD, is my confidence; I cried to the LORD, and He heard me, and healed the breaking of my heart. 16 I slumbered and slept; I dreamed and was helped, and the LORD sustained me. 17 They sorely pained my heart; I will thanks again because the LORD delivered me. 18 Now will I rejoice in their shame; I have hoped in You, and I will not be ashamed.

19 May You be given honor forever, even for eternity. 20 Deliver Israel, Your chosen, and those of the house of Jacob, Your proved one.

Psalm 156 (Translated exclusively from the Dead Sea Scrolls: 11Q5 and 4Q88.

Note: significant gaps occur in these manuscripts and some words have been selectively added.)

A Plea for Deliverance.

1 A worm does not thank You, nor does a maggot tell of Your loving-kindness. 2 Only the living thank You, all they whose feet stumble thank You indeed, when You make Your loving-kindness known to them, and cause them to understand Your righteousness; 3 for the soul of all the living is in Your hand, and You have given breath to all flesh. 4 O LORD, do to us according to Your goodness, according to the greatness of Your mercies, and according to the greatness of Your righteous deeds.

5 The LORD listens to the voice of all who love His name, and He does not permit His loving-kindness to depart from them. 6 Blessed is the LORD who performs righteousness and who crowns His elect ones with loving-kindness and mercies.

7 My soul shouts out in praise of Your name, to praise Your mercies with rejoicing and to proclaim Your faithfulness. There is no limit to Your praises. 8 I belonged to death because of my sins, and my iniquities had sold me to Sheol; 9 but You saved me, O LORD, according to the greatness of Your mercies, and according to the greatness of Your righteous deeds. 10 I have truly loved Your name and have

taken refuge in Your shadow. 11 My heart is strengthened when I remember Your power, and I rely on Your mercies.

12 Forgive my sins, O LORD, and purify me of my iniquity. 13 Grant me a spirit of faithfulness and knowledge; let me not be dishonored in ruin. 14 Do not allow the wicked one or an unclean spirit to overtake me, and do not allow pain or the evil inclination to possess my bones; 15 for You, O LORD, are my praise, and I hope in You every day. 16 My brothers rejoice with me, and the household of my father is amazed by Your graciousness.

17 I will always rejoice in You.

Psalm 157 (Translated exclusively from the Dead Sea Scrolls: 11Q5 and 4Q88.

Note: significant gaps occur in these manuscripts and some words have been selectively added.)

A Hymn to Zion.

1 I will remember you, O Zion. You are a blessing. I love you with all My might; for your memory is to be blessed forever. 2 Your hope is strong, O Zion. Your peace and your awaited salvation will come. 3 Generation after generation shall dwell in you, and generations of the righteous shall be your ornament. 4 They who desire the day of your salvation shall rejoice in the greatness of your glory. 5 They shall be suckled on the fullness of your glory, and in your beautiful streets they shall make sounds of bells. 6 You shall remember the righteous deeds of your prophets, and shall glorify yourself in the deeds of your righteous ones.

7 Cleanse violence from among you. May lying and sin be cut off from you. 8 Your sons shall rejoice within you, and your cherished ones shall be joined to you. How much have they hoped in your salvation? 9 How much have your perfect ones mourned for you? 10 Your hope, O Zion, shall not perish, and your expectation will not be forgotten.

11 Is there a righteous man who has perished? Is there a man who has escaped his iniquity? 12 Man is tried according to his way, each is repaid according to his deeds. 13 Your oppressors shall be cut off from around you, O Zion, and all who hate you shall be scattered. 14 Your praise is pleasing, O Zion; it rises up in all the world. 15 I will remember you many times for a blessing, and I will bless you with all My heart. 16 You shall attain eternal righteousness, and shall receive blessings from the noble ones. 17 Take the vision which speaks of you, and the dreams of the prophets requested for you.

18 Be exalted and increase, O Zion, and praise the Most High, your Redeemer! May my soul rejoice in your glory!

Psalm 158 (Translated exclusively from the Dead Sea Scrolls: 11Q5 and 4Q88.

Note: significant gaps occur in these manuscripts and some words have been selectively added.)

A Hymn to the Name of the LORD.

1 In the midst of the congregation they shall praise the name of the LORD, 2 for He has come to judge every action, to remove the wicked from the earth, so that the children of iniquity shall not be found.

3 The heavens shall give their dew, and there shall be no drought within their boundaries. 4 The earth shall give its fruit in its time, and its produce shall not fail. 5 The fruit trees and vineyards shall give fruit, and the ground shall not cheat but it shall give its produce. 6 The poor shall eat, and those who fear God shall be filled.

Psalm 159 (Translated exclusively from the Dead Sea Scrolls: 11Q5 and 4Q88.

Note: significant gaps occur in these manuscripts and some words have been selectively added.)

A Hymn to Judah.

1 Heaven and earth shall give praise together. Let all the stars of the evening twilight give praise! 2 Rejoice, Judah. Rejoice! Rejoice, rejoice and be joyful with gladness! 3 Celebrate your feasts, and pay your vows; for there is no wickedness in your midst. 4 Raise your hand, and fortify your right hand! 5 Behold, the enemy shall perish, and all the workers of iniquity shall be scattered; 6 but You, O LORD, are forever, and Your glory shall be forever and ever. Hallelujah!

Psalm 160 (Translated exclusively from the Dead Sea Scrolls: 11Q5 and 4Q88.

Note: significant gaps occur in these manuscripts and some words have been selectively added.)

A Hymn to the Creator.

1 The LORD is great and holy. He is the holiest for generation after generation. 2 Majesty goes before Him, and abundance of many waters comes after Him. 3 Loving-kindness and truth surround His face; truth, judgment, and righteousness are the pedestal of His throne. 4 He divides light from the unknown, and He establishes the dawn by the knowledge of His heart. 5 All His angels sang when they saw it; for He showed them things they had not known. 6 He crowns the mountains with fruit, with good food for all the living.

7 May the Lord of the earth be blessed, along with His power; for He establishes the world by His wisdom. 8 He stretched out the heaven by His understanding, and brought forth wind from His storehouses. 9 He made lightnings for the rain, and raised mist from the ends of the earth.

Prayer of Azariah

[1] And they walked in the midst of the fire, praising God and blessing the Lord

[2] Then Azariah stood and offered this prayer; in the midst of the fire he opened his mouth and said:

[3] "Blessed art thou, O Lord, God of our fathers, and worthy of praise; and thy name is glorified for ever.

[4] For thou art just in all that thou hast done to us, and all thy works are true and thy ways right, and all thy judgments are truth.

[5] Thou has executed true judgments in all that thou hast brought upon us and upon Jerusalem, the holy city of our fathers, for in truth and justice thou hast brought all this upon us because of our sins.

[6] For we have sinfully and lawlessly departed from thee, and have sinned in all things and have not obeyed thy commandments;

[7] we have not observed them or done them, as thou hast commanded us that it might go well with us.

[8] So all that thou hast brought upon us, and all that thou hast done to us, thou hast done in true judgment.

[9] Thou hast given us into the hands of lawless enemies, most hateful rebels, and to an unjust king, the most wicked in all the world.

[10] And now we cannot open our mouths; shame and disgrace have befallen thy servants and worshipers.

[11] For thy name's sake do not give us up utterly, and do not break thy covenant,

[12] and do not withdraw thy mercy from us, for the sake of Abraham thy beloved and for the sake of Isaac thy servant and Israel thy holy one,

[13] to whom thou didst promise to make their descendants as many as the stars of heaven and as the sand on the shore of the sea.

[14] For we, O Lord, have become fewer than any nation, and are brought low this day in all the world because of our sins.

[15] And at this time there is no prince, or prophet, or leader, no burnt offering, or sacrifice, or oblation, or incense, no place to make an offering before thee or to find mercy.

[16] Yet with a contrite heart and a humble spirit may we be accepted, as though it were with burnt offerings of rams and bulls, and with tens of thousands of fat lambs;

[17] such may our sacrifice be in thy sight this day, and may we wholly follow thee, for there will be no shame for those who trust in thee.

[18] And now with all our heart we follow thee, we fear thee and seek thy face.

[19] Do not put us to shame, but deal with us in thy forbearance and in thy abundant mercy.

[20] Deliver us in accordance with thy marvelous works, and give glory to thy name, O Lord! Let all who do harm to thy servants be put to shame;
[21] let them be disgraced and deprived of all power and dominion, and let their strength be broken.
[22] Let them know that thou art the Lord, the only God, glorious over the whole world."
[23] Now the king's servants who threw them in did not cease feeding the furnace fires with naphtha, pitch, tow, and brush.
[24] And the flame streamed out above the furnace forty-nine cubits,
[25] and it broke through and burned those of the Chaldeans whom it caught about the furnace.
[26] But the angel of the Lord came down into the furnace to be with Azariah and his companions, and drove the fiery flame out of the furnace,
[27] and made the midst of the furnace like a moist whistling wind, so that the fire did not touch them at all or hurt or trouble them.
[28] Then the three, as with one mouth, praised and glorified and blessed God in the furnace, saying: [29] "Blessed art thou, O Lord, God of our fathers, and to be praised and highly exalted for ever; [30] And blessed is thy glorious, holy name and to be highly praised and highly exalted for ever; [31] Blessed art thou in the temple of thy holy glory and to be extolled and highly glorified for ever. [32] Blessed art thou, who sittest upon cherubim and lookest upon the deeps, and to be praised and highly exalted for ever. [33] Blessed art thou upon the throne of thy kingdom and to be extolled and highly exalted for ever. [34] Blessed art thou in the firmament of heaven and to be sung and glorified for ever. [35] "Bless the Lord, all works of the Lord, sing praise to him and highly exalt him for ever. [36] Bless the Lord, you heavens, sing praise to him and highly exalt him for ever. [37] Bless the Lord, you angels of the Lord, sing praise to him and highly exalt him for ever. [38] Bless the Lord, all waters above the heaven, sing praise to him and highly exalt him for ever. [39] Bless the Lord, all powers, sing praise to him and highly exalt him for ever. [40] Bless the Lord, sun and moon, sing praise to him and highly exalt him for ever. [41] Bless the Lord, stars of heaven, sing praise to him and highly exalt him for ever. [42] Bless the Lord, all rain and dew, sing praise to him and highly exalt him for ever. [43] Bless the Lord, all winds, sing praise to him and highly exalt him for ever. [44] Bless the Lord, fire and heat, sing praise to him and highly exalt him for ever. [45] Bless the Lord, winter cold and summer heat, sing praise to him and highly exalt him for ever. [46] Bless the Lord, dews and snows, sing praise to him and highly exalt him for ever. [47] Bless the Lord, nights and days, sing praise to him and highly exalt him for ever. [48] Bless the Lord, light and darkness, sing praise to him and highly exalt him for ever. [49] Bless the Lord, ice and cold, sing praise to him and highly exalt him for ever. [50] Bless the Lord, frosts and snows, sing praise to him and highly exalt him for ever. [51] Bless the Lord, lightnings and clouds, sing praise to him and highly exalt him for ever. [52] Let the earth bless the Lord; let it sing praise to him and highly exalt him for ever. [53] Bless the Lord, mountains and hills, sing praise to him and highly exalt him for ever. [54] Bless the Lord, all things that grow on the earth, sing praise to him and highly exalt him for ever. [55] Bless the Lord, you springs, sing praise to him and highly exalt him for ever. [56] Bless the Lord, seas and rivers, sing praise to him and highly exalt him for ever. [57] Bless the Lord, you whales and all creatures that move in the waters, sing praise to him and highly exalt him for ever. [58] Bless the Lord, all birds of the air, sing praise to him and highly exalt him for ever. [59] Bless the Lord, all beasts and cattle, sing praise to him and highly exalt him for ever. [60] Bless the Lord, you sons of men, sing praise to him and highly exalt him for ever. [61] Bless the Lord, O Israel, sing praise to him and highly exalt him for ever. [62] Bless the Lord, you priests of the Lord, sing praise to him and highly exalt him for ever. [63] Bless the Lord, you servants of the Lord sing praise to him and highly exalt him for ever. [64] Bless the Lord, spirits and souls of the righteous, sing praise to him and highly exalt him for ever. [65] Bless the Lord, you who are holy and humble in heart, sing praise to him and highly exalt him for ever. [66] Bless the Lord, Hananiah, Azariah, and Mishael, sing praise to him and highly exalt him for ever; for he has rescued us from Hades and saved us from the hand of death, and delivered us from the midst of the burning fiery furnace; from the midst of the fire he has delivered us.

[67] Give thanks to the Lord, for he is good, for his mercy endures for ever. [68] Bless him, all who worship the Lord, the God of gods, sing praise to him and give thanks to him, for his mercy endures for ever."

Susanna

Sus.1

[1] There lived a man in Babylon named Joacim:

[2] And he took a wife named Susanna, the daughter of Hilkiah, a very beautiful woman and one who feared the Lord.

[3] Her parents were righteous, and had taught their daughter according to the law of Moses.

[4] Joakim was very rich, and had a spacious garden adjoining his house; and the Jews used to come to him because he was the most honored of them all.

[5] In that year two elders from the people were appointed as judges. Concerning them the Lord had said: "Iniquity came forth from Babylon, from elders who were judges, who were supposed to govern the people."

[6] These men were frequently at Joakim's house, and all who had suits at law came to them.

[7] When the people departed at noon, Susanna would go into her husband's garden to walk.

[8] The two elders used to see her every day, going in and walking about, and they began to desire her.

[9] And they perverted their minds and turned away their eyes from looking to Heaven or remembering righteous judgments.

[10] Both were overwhelmed with passion for her, but they did not tell each other of their distress,

[11] for they were ashamed to disclose their lustful desire to possess her.

[12] And they watched eagerly, day after day, to see her.

[13] They said to each other, "Let us go home, for it is mealtime."

[14] And when they went out, they parted from each other. But turning back, they met again; and when each pressed the other for the reason, they confessed their lust. And then together they arranged for a time when they could find her alone.

[15] Once, while they were watching for an opportune day, she went in as before with only two maids, and wished to bathe in the garden, for it was very hot.

[16] And no one was there except the two elders, who had hid themselves and were watching her.

[17] She said to her maids, "Bring me oil and ointments, and shut the garden doors so that I may bathe."

[18] They did as she said, shut the garden doors, and went out by the side doors to bring what they had been commanded; and they did not see the elders, because they were hidden.

[19] When the maids had gone out, the two elders rose and ran to her, and said:

[20] "Look, the garden doors are shut, no one sees us, and we are in love with you; so give your consent, and lie with us.

[21] If you refuse, we will testify against you that a young man was with you, and this was why you sent your maids away."

[22] Susanna sighed deeply, and said, "I am hemmed in on every side. For if I do this thing, it is death for me; and if I do not, I shall not escape your hands.

[23] I choose not to do it and to fall into your hands, rather than to sin in the sight of the Lord."

[24] Then Susanna cried out with a loud voice, and the two elders shouted against her.

[25] And one of them ran and opened the garden doors.

[26] When the household servants heard the shouting in the garden, they rushed in at the side door to see what had happened to her.

[27] And when the elders told their tale, the servants were greatly ashamed, for nothing like this had ever been said about Susanna.

[28] The next day, when the people gathered at the house of her husband Joakim, the two elders came, full of their wicked plot to have Susanna put to death.

[29] They said before the people, "Send for Susanna, the daughter of Hilkiah, who is the wife of Joakim."

[30] So they sent for her. And she came, with her parents, her children, and all her kindred.

[31] Now Susanna was a woman of great refinement, and beautiful in appearance.

[32] As she was veiled, the wicked men ordered her to be unveiled, that they might feed upon her beauty.

[33] But her family and friends and all who saw her wept.

[34] Then the two elders stood up in the midst of the people, and laid their hands upon her head.

[35] And she, weeping, looked up toward heaven, for her heart trusted in the Lord.

[36] The elders said, "As we were walking in the garden alone, this woman came in with two maids, shut the garden doors, and dismissed the maids.

[37] Then a young man, who had been hidden, came to her and lay with her.

[38] We were in a corner of the garden, and when we saw this wickedness we ran to them.

[39] We saw them embracing, but we could not hold the man, for he was too strong for us, and he opened the doors and dashed out.

[40] So we seized this woman and asked her who the young man was, but she would not tell us. These things we testify."

[41] The assembly believed them, because they were elders of the people and judges; and they condemned her to death.

[42] Then Susanna cried out with a loud voice, and said, "O eternal God, who do discern what is secret, who art aware of all things before they come to be,

[43] thou knowest that these men have borne false witness against me. And now I am to die! Yet I have

done none of the things that they have wickedly invented against me!"

[44] The Lord heard her cry.

[45] And as she was being led away to be put to death, God aroused the holy spirit of a young lad named Daniel;

[46] and he cried with a loud voice, "I am innocent of the blood of this woman."

[47] All the people turned to him, and said, "What is this that you have said?"

[48] Taking his stand in the midst of them, he said, "Are you such fools, you sons of Israel? Have you condemned a daughter of Israel without examination and without learning the facts?

[49] Return to the place of judgment. For these men have borne false witness against her."

[50] Then all the people returned in haste. And the elders said to him, "Come, sit among us and inform us, for God has given you that right."

[51] And Daniel said to them, "Separate them far from each other, and I will examine them."

[52] When they were separated from each other, he summoned one of them and said to him, "You old relic of wicked days, your sins have now come home, which you have committed in the past,

[53] pronouncing unjust judgments, condemning the innocent and letting the guilty go free, though the Lord said, `Do not put to death an innocent and righteous person.'

[54] Now then, if you really saw her, tell me this: Under what tree did you see them being intimate with each other?" He answered, "Under a mastic tree."

[55] And Daniel said, "Very well! You have lied against your own head, for the angel of God has received the sentence from God and will immediately cut you in two."

[56] Then he put him aside, and commanded them to bring the other. And he said to him, "You offspring of Canaan and not of Judah, beauty has deceived you and lust has perverted your heart.

[57] This is how you both have been dealing with the daughters of Israel, and they were intimate with you through fear; but a daughter of Judah would not endure your wickedness.

[58] Now then, tell me: Under what tree did you catch them being intimate with each other?" He answered, "Under an evergreen oak."

[59] And Daniel said to him, "Very well! You also have lied against your own head, for the angel of God is waiting with his sword to saw you in two, that he may destroy you both."

[60] Then all the assembly shouted loudly and blessed God, who saves those who hope in him.

[61] And they rose against the two elders, for out of their own mouths Daniel had convicted them of bearing false witness;

[62] and they did to them as they had wickedly planned to do to their neighbor; acting in accordance with the law of Moses, they put them to death. Thus innocent blood was saved that day.

[63] And Hilkiah and his wife praised God for their daughter Susanna, and so did Joakim her husband and all her kindred, because nothing shameful was found in her.

[64] And from that day onward Daniel had a great reputation among the people.

Bel and the Dragon

Bel.1

[1] When King Astyages was laid with his fathers, Cyrus the Persian received his kingdom.

[2] And Daniel was a companion of the king, and was the most honored of his friends.

[3] Now the Babylonians had an idol called Bel, and every day they spent on it twelve bushels of fine flour and forty sheep and fifty gallons of wine.

[4] The king revered it and went every day to worship it. But Daniel worshiped his own God.

[5] And the king said to him, "Why do you not worship Bel?" He answered, "Because I do not revere man-made idols, but the living God, who created heaven and earth and has dominion over all flesh."

[6] The king said to him, "Do you not think that Bel is a living God? Do you not see how much he eats and drinks every day?"

[7] Then Daniel laughed, and said, "Do not be deceived, O king; for this is but clay inside and brass outside, and it never ate or drank anything."

[8] Then the king was angry, and he called his priests and said to them, "If you do not tell me who is eating these provisions, you shall die.

[9] But if you prove that Bel is eating them, Daniel shall die, because he blasphemed against Bel." And Daniel said to the king, "Let it be done as you have said."

[10] Now there were seventy priests of Bel, besides their wives and children. And the king went with Daniel into the temple of Bel.

[11] And the priests of Bel said, "Behold, we are going outside; you yourself, O king, shall set forth the food and mix and place the wine, and shut the door and seal it with your signet.

[12] And when you return in the morning, if you do not find that Bel has eaten it all, we will die; or else Daniel will, who is telling lies about us."

[13] They were unconcerned, for beneath the table they had made a hidden entrance, through which they used to go in regularly and consume the provisions.

[14] When they had gone out, the king set forth the food for Bel. Then Daniel ordered his servants to bring ashes and they sifted them throughout the whole temple in the presence of the king alone. Then they went out, shut the door and sealed it with the king's signet, and departed.

[15] In the night the priests came with their wives and children, as they were accustomed to do, and ate and drank everything.

[16] Early in the morning the king rose and came, and Daniel with him.

[17] And the king said, "Are the seals unbroken, Daniel?" He answered, "They are unbroken, O king."

[18] As soon as the doors were opened, the king looked at the table, and shouted in a loud voice, "You are great, O Bel; and with you there is no deceit, none at all."

[19] Then Daniel laughed, and restrained the king from going in, and said, "Look at the floor, and notice whose footsteps these are."

[20] The king said, "I see the footsteps of men and women and children."

[21] Then the king was enraged, and he seized the priests and their wives and children; and they showed him the secret doors through which they were accustomed to enter and devour what was on the table.

[22] Therefore the king put them to death, and gave Bel over to Daniel, who destroyed it and its temple.

[23] There was also a great dragon, which the Babylonians revered.

[24] And the king said to Daniel, "You cannot deny that this is a living god; so worship him."

[25] Daniel said, "I will worship the Lord my God, for he is the living God.

[26] But if you, O king, will give me permission, I will slay the dragon without sword or club." The king said, "I give you permission."

[27] Then Daniel took pitch, fat, and hair, and boiled them together and made cakes, which he fed to the dragon. The dragon ate them, and burst open. And Daniel said, "See what you have been worshiping!"

[28] When the Babylonians heard it, they were very indignant and conspired against the king, saying, "The king has become a Jew; he has destroyed Bel, and slain the dragon, and slaughtered the priests."

[29] Going to the king, they said, "Hand Daniel over to us, or else we will kill you and your household."

[30] The king saw that they were pressing him hard, and under compulsion he handed Daniel over to them.

[31] They threw Daniel into the lions' den, and he was there for six days.

[32] There were seven lions in the den, and every day they had been given two human bodies and two sheep; but these were not given to them now, so that they might devour Daniel.

[33] Now the prophet Habakkuk was in Judea. He had boiled pottage and had broken bread into a bowl, and was going into the field to take it to the reapers.

[34] But the angel of the Lord said to Habakkuk, "Take the dinner which you have to Babylon, to Daniel, in the lions' den."

[35] Habakkuk said, "Sir, I have never seen Babylon, and I know nothing about the den."

[36] Then the angel of the Lord took him by the crown of his head, and lifted him by his hair and set him down in Babylon, right over the den, with the rushing sound of the wind itself.

[37] Then Habakkuk shouted, "Daniel, Daniel! Take the dinner which God has sent you."

[38] And Daniel said, "Thou hast remembered me, O God, and hast not forsaken those who love thee."

[39] So Daniel arose and ate. And the angel of God immediately returned Habakkuk to his own place.

[40] On the seventh day the king came to mourn for Daniel. When he came to the den he looked in, and there sat Daniel.

[41] And the king shouted with a loud voice, "Thou art great, O Lord God of Daniel, and there is no other besides thee."

[42] And he pulled Daniel out, and threw into the den the men who had attempted his destruction, and they were devoured immediately before his eyes.

Tobit

Tob.1

[1] The book of the acts of Tobit the son of Tobiel, son of Ananiel, son of Aduel, son of Gabael, of the descendants of Asiel and the tribe of Naphtali,

[2] who in the days of Shalmaneser, king of the Assyrians, was taken into captivity from Thisbe, which is to the south of Kedesh Naphtali in Galilee above Asher.

[3] I, Tobit, walked in the ways of truth and righteousness all the days of my life, and I performed many acts of charity to my brethren and countrymen who went with me into the land of the Assyrians, to Nineveh.

[4] Now when I was in my own country, in the land of Israel, while I was still a young man, the whole tribe of Naphtali my forefather deserted the house of Jerusalem. This was the place which had been chosen from among all the tribes of Israel, where all the tribes should sacrifice and where the temple of the dwelling of the Most High was consecrated and established for all generations for ever.

[5] All the tribes that joined in apostasy used to sacrifice to the calf Baal, and so did the house of Naphtali my forefather.

[6] But I alone went often to Jerusalem for the feasts, as it is ordained for all Israel by an everlasting decree. Taking the first fruits and the tithes of my produce and the first shearings, I would give these to the priests, the sons of Aaron, at the altar.

[7] Of all my produce I would give a tenth to the sons of Levi who ministered at Jerusalem; a second tenth I would sell, and I would go and spend the proceeds each year at Jerusalem;

[8] the third tenth I would give to those to whom it was my duty, as Deborah my father's mother had commanded me, for I was left an orphan by my father.

[9] When I became a man I married Anna, a member of our family, and by her I became the father of Tobias.

[10] Now when I was carried away captive to Nineveh, all my brethren and my relatives ate the food of the Gentiles;

[11] but I kept myself from eating it,

[12] because I remembered God with all my heart.

[13] Then the Most High gave me favor and good appearance in the sight of Shalmaneser, and I was his buyer of provisions.

[14] So I used to go into Media, and once at Rages in Media I left ten talents of silver in trust with Gabael, the brother of Gabrias.

[15] But when Shalmaneser died, Sennacherib his son reigned in his place; and under him the highways were unsafe, so that I could no longer go into Media.

[16] In the days of Shalmaneser I performed many acts of charity to my brethren.

[17] I would give my bread to the hungry and my clothing to the naked; and if I saw any one of my people dead and thrown out behind the wall of Nineveh, I would bury him.

[18] And if Sennacherib the king put to death any who came fleeing from Judea, I buried them secretly. For in his anger he put many to death. When the bodies were sought by the king, they were not found.

[19] Then one of the men of Nineveh went and informed the king about me, that I was burying them; so I hid myself. When I learned that I was being searched for, to be put to death, I left home in fear.

[20] Then all my property was confiscated and nothing was left to me except my wife Anna and my son Tobias.

[21] But not fifty days passed before two of Sennacherib's sons killed him, and they fled to the mountains of Ararat. Then Esarhaddon, his son, reigned in his place; and he appointed Ahikar, the son of my brother Anael, over all the accounts of his kingdom and over the entire administration.

[22] Ahikar interceded for me, and I returned to Nineveh. Now Ahikar was cupbearer, keeper of the signet, and in charge of administration of the accounts, for Esarhaddon had appointed him second to himself. He was my nephew.

Tob.2

[1] When I arrived home and my wife Anna and my son Tobias were restored to me, at the feast of Pentecost, which is the sacred festival of the seven weeks, a good dinner was prepared for me and I sat down to eat.

[2] Upon seeing the abundance of food I said to my son, "Go and bring whatever poor man of our brethren you may find who is mindful of the Lord, and I will wait for you."

[3] But he came back and said, "Father, one of our people has been strangled and thrown into the market place."

[4] So before I tasted anything I sprang up and removed the body to a place of shelter until sunset.

[5] And when I returned I washed myself and ate my food in sorrow.

[6] Then I remembered the prophecy of Amos, how he said, "Your feasts shall be turned into mourning, and all your festivities into lamentation." And I wept.

[7] When the sun had set I went and dug a grave and buried the body.

[8] And my neighbors laughed at me and said, "He is no longer afraid that he will be put to death for doing this; he once ran away, and here he is burying the dead again!"

[9] On the same night I returned from burying him, and because I was defiled I slept by the wall of the courtyard, and my face was uncovered.

[10] I did not know that there were sparrows on the wall and their fresh droppings fell into my open eyes and white films formed on my eyes. I went to physicians, but they did not help me. Ahikar, however, took care of me until he went to Elymais.

[11] Then my wife Anna earned money at women's work.

[12] She used to send the product to the owners. Once when they paid her wages, they also gave her a kid;

[13] and when she returned to me it began to bleat. So I said to her, "Where did you get the kid? It is not stolen, is it? Return it to the owners; for it is not right to eat what is stolen."

[14] And she said, "It was given to me as a gift in addition to my wages." But I did not believe her, and told her to return it to the owners; and I blushed for her. Then she replied to me, "Where are your charities and your righteous deeds? You seem to know everything!"

Tob.3

[1] Then in my grief I wept, and I prayed in anguish, saying,

[2] "Righteous art thou, O Lord; all thy deeds and all they ways are mercy and truth, and thou do render true and righteous judgment for ever.

[3] Remember me and look favorably upon me; do not punish me for my sins and for my unwitting offences and those which my fathers committed before thee.

[4] For they disobeyed thy commandments, and thou gavest us over to plunder, captivity, and death; thou madest us a byword of reproach in all the nations among which we have been dispersed.

[5] And now thy many judgments are true in exacting penalty from me for my sins and those of my fathers, because we did not keep thy commandments. For we did not walk in truth before thee.

[6] And now deal with me according to thy pleasure; command my spirit to be taken up, that I may depart and become dust. For it is better for me to die than to live, because I have heard false reproaches, and great is the sorrow within me. Command that I now be released from my distress to go to the eternal abode; do not turn thy face away from me."

[7] On the same day, at Ecbatana in Media, it also happened that Sarah, the daughter of Raguel, was reproached by her father's maids,

[8] because she had been given to seven husbands, and the evil demon Asmodeus had slain each of them before he had been with her as his wife. So the maids said to her, "Do you not know that you strangle your husbands? You already have had seven and have had no benefit from any of them.

[9] Why do you beat us? If they are dead, go with them! May we never see a son or daughter of yours!"

[10] When she heard these things she was deeply grieved, even to the thought of hanging herself. But she said, "I am the only child of my father; if I do this, it will be a disgrace to him, and I shall bring his old age down in sorrow to the grave.

[11] So she prayed by her window and said, "Blessed art thou, O Lord my God, and blessed is thy holy and honored name for ever. May all thy works praise thee for ever.

[12] And now, O Lord, I have turned my eyes and my face toward thee.

[13] Command that I be released from the earth and that I hear reproach no more.

[14] Thou knowest, O Lord, that I am innocent of any sin with man,

[15] and that I did not stain my name or the name of my father in the land of my captivity. I am my father's only child, and he has no child to be his heir, no near kinsman or kinsman's son for whom I should keep myself as wife. Already seven husbands of mine are dead. Why should I live? But if it be not pleasing to thee to take my life, command that respect be shown to me and pity be taken upon me, and that I hear reproach no more."

[16] The prayer of both was heard in the presence of the glory of the great God.

[17] And Raphael was sent to heal the two of them: to scale away the white films of Tobit's eyes; to give Sarah the daughter of Raguel in marriage to Tobias the son of Tobit, and to bind Asmodeus the evil demon, because Tobias was entitled to possess her. At that very moment Tobit returned and entered his house and Sarah the daughter of Raguel came down from her upper room.

Tob.4

[1] On that day Tobit remembered the money which he had left in trust with Gabael at Rages in Media, and he said to himself;

[2] "I have asked for death. Why do I not call my son Tobias so that I may explain to him about the money before I die?"

[3] So he called him and said, "My son, when I die, bury me, and do not neglect your mother. Honor her all the days of your life; do what is pleasing to her, and do not grieve her.

[4] Remember, my son, that she faced many dangers for you while you were yet unborn. When she dies bury her beside me in the same grave.

[5] "Remember the Lord our God all your days, my son, and refuse to sin or to transgress his commandments. Live uprightly all the days of your life, and do not walk in the ways of wrongdoing.

[6] For if you do what is true, your ways will prosper through your deeds.

[7] Give alms from your possessions to all who live uprightly, and do not let your eye begrudge the gift when you make it. Do not turn your face away from any poor man, and the face of God will not be turned away from you.

[8] If you have many possessions, make your gift from them in proportion; if few, do not be afraid to give according to the little you have.

[9] So you will be laying up a good treasure for yourself against the day of necessity.

[10] For charity delivers from death and keeps you from entering the darkness;

[11] and for all who practice it charity is an excellent offering in the presence of the Most High.

[12] "Beware, my son, of all immorality. First of all take a wife from among the descendants of your fathers and do not marry a foreign woman, who is not of your father's tribe; for we are the sons of the prophets. Remember, my son, that Noah, Abraham, Isaac, and Jacob, our fathers of old, all took wives from among their brethren. They were blessed in their children, and their posterity will inherit the land.

[13] So now, my son, love your brethren, and in your heart do not disdain your brethren and the sons and daughters of your people by refusing to take a wife for yourself from among them. For in pride there is ruin and great confusion; and in shiftlessness there is loss and great want, because shiftlessness is the mother of famine.

[14] Do not hold over till the next day the wages of any man who works for you, but pay him at once; and if you serve God you will receive payment. "Watch yourself, my son, in everything you do, and be disciplined in all your conduct.

[15] And what you hate, do not do to any one. Do not drink wine to excess or let drunkenness go with you on your way.

[16] Give of your bread to the hungry, and of your clothing to the naked. Give all your surplus to charity, and do not let your eye begrudge the gift when you made it.

[17] Place your bread on the grave of the righteous, but give none to sinners.

[18] Seek advice from every wise man, and do not despise any useful counsel.

[19] Bless the Lord God on every occasion; ask him that your ways may be made straight and that all your paths and plans may prosper. For none of the nations has understanding; but the Lord himself gives all good things, and according to his will he humbles whomever he wishes. "So, my son, remember my commands, and do not let them be blotted out of your mind.

[20] And now let me explain to you about the ten talents of silver which I left in trust with Gabael the son of Gabrias at Rages in Media.

[21] Do not be afraid, my son, because we have become poor. You have great wealth if you fear God and refrain from every sin and do what is pleasing in his sight."

Tob.5
[1] Then Tobias answered him, "Father, I will do everything that you have commanded me;
[2] but how can I obtain the money when I do not know the man?"
[3] Then Tobit gave him the receipt, and said to him, "Find a man to go with you and I will pay him wages as long as I live; and go and get the money."
[4] So he went to look for a man; and he found Raphael, who was an angel,
[5] but Tobias did not know it. Tobias said to him, "Can you go with me to Rages in Media? Are you acquainted with that region?"
[6] The angel replied, "I will go with you; I am familiar with the way, and I have stayed with our brother Gabael."
[7] Then Tobias said to him, "Wait for me, and I shall tell my father."
[8] And he said to him, "Go, and do not delay." So he went in and said to his father, "I have found some one to go with me." He said, "Call him to me, so that I may learn to what tribe he belongs, and whether he is a reliable man to go with you."
[9] So Tobias invited him in; he entered and they greeted each other.
[10] Then Tobit said to him, "My brother, to what tribe and family do you belong? Tell me. "
[11] But he answered, "Are you looking for a tribe and a family or for a man whom you will pay to go with your son?" And Tobit said to him, "I should like to know, my brother, your people and your name."
[12] He replied, "I am Azarias the son of the great Ananias, one of your relatives."
[13] Then Tobit said to him, "You are welcome, my brother. Do not be angry with me because I tried to learn your tribe and family. You are a relative of mine, of a good and noble lineage. For I used to know Ananias and Jathan, the sons of the great Shemaiah, when we went together to Jerusalem to worship and offered the first-born of our flocks and the tithes of our produce. They did not go astray in the error of our brethren. My brother, you come of good stock.
[14] But tell me, what wages am I to pay you -- a drachma a day, and expenses for yourself as for my son?
[15] And besides, I will add to your wages if you both return safe and sound." So they agreed to these terms.
[16] Then he said to Tobias, "Get ready for the journey, and good success to you both." So his son made the preparations for the journey. And his father said to him, "Go with this man; God who dwells in heaven will prosper your way, and may his angel attend you." So they both went out and departed, and the young man's dog was with them.
[17] But Anna, his mother, began to weep, and said to Tobit, "Why have you sent our child away? Is he not the staff of our hands as he goes in and out before us?
[18] Do not add money to money, but consider it as rubbish as compared to our child.
[19] For the life that is given to us by the Lord is enough for us."
[20] And Tobit said to her, "Do not worry, my sister; he will return safe and sound, and your eyes will see him.
[21] For a good angel will go with him; his journey will be successful, and he will come back safe and sound." Tob 5:[22] So she stopped weeping.

Tob.6
[1] Now as they proceeded on their way they came at evening to the Tigris river and camped there.
[2] Then the young man went down to wash himself. A fish leaped up from the river and would have swallowed the young man;
[3] and the angel said to him, "Catch the fish." So the young man seized the fish and threw it up on the land.
[4] Then the angel said to him, "Cut open the fish and take the heart and liver and gall and put them away safely."
[5] So the young man did as the angel told him; and they roasted and ate the fish. And they both continued on their way until they came near to Ecbatana.
[6] Then the young man said to the angel, "Brother Azarias, of what use is the liver and heart and gall of the fish?"
[7] He replied, "As for the heart and liver, if a demon or evil spirit gives trouble to any one, you make a smoke from these before the man or woman, and that person will never be troubled again.
[8] And as for the gall, anoint with it a man who has white films in his eyes, and he will be cured."
[9] When they approached Ecbatana,
[10] the angel said to the young man, "Brother, today we shall stay with Raguel. He is your relative, and he has an only daughter named Sarah. I will suggest that she be given to you in marriage,
[11] because you are entitled to her and to her inheritance, for you are her only eligible kinsman.
[12] The girl is also beautiful and sensible. Now listen to my plan. I will speak to her father, and as soon as we return from Rages we will celebrate the marriage. For I know that Raguel, according to the law of Moses, cannot give her to another man without incurring the penalty of death, because you rather than any other man are entitled to the inheritance."
[13] Then the young man said to the angel, "Brother Azarias, I have heard that the girl has been given to

seven husbands and that each died in the bridal chamber.

[14] Now I am the only son my father has, and I am afraid that if I go in I will die as those before me did, for a demon is in love with her, and he harms no one except those who approach her. So now I fear that I may die and bring the lives of my father and mother to the grave in sorrow on my account. And they have no other son to bury them."

[15] But the angel said to him, "Do you not remember the words with which your father commanded you to take a wife from among your own people? Now listen to me, brother, for she will become your wife; and do not worry about the demon, for this very night she will be given to you in marriage.

[16] When you enter the bridal chamber, you shall take live ashes of incense and lay upon them some of the heart and liver of the fish so as to make a smoke.

[17] Then the demon will smell it and flee away, and will never again return. And when you approach her, rise up, both of you, and cry out to the merciful God, and he will save you and have mercy on you. Do not be afraid, for she was destined for you from eternity. You will save her, and she will go with you, and I suppose that you will have children by her." When Tobias heard these things, he fell in love with her and yearned deeply for her.

Tob.7

[1] When they reached Ecbatana and arrived at the house of Raguel, Sarah met them and greeted them. They returned her greeting, and she brought them into the house.

[2] Then Raguel said to his wife Edna, "How much the young man resembles my cousin Tobit!"

[3] And Raguel asked them, "Where are you from, brethren?" They answered him, "We belong to the sons of Naphtali, who are captives in Nineveh."

[4] So he said to them, "Do you know our brother Tobit?" And they said, "Yes, we do." And he asked them, "Is he in good health?"

[5] They replied, "He is alive and in good health." And Tobias said, "He is my father."

[6] Then Raguel sprang up and kissed him and wept.

[7] And he blessed him and exclaimed, "Son of that good and noble man!" When he heard that Tobit had lost his sight, he was stricken with grief and wept.

[8] And his wife Edna and his daughter Sarah wept. They received them very warmly; and they killed a ram from the flock and set large servings of food before them. Then Tobias said to Raphael, "Brother Azarias, speak of those things which you talked about on the journey, and let the matter be settled."

[9] So he communicated the proposal to Raguel. And Raguel said to Tobias, "Eat, drink, and be merry;

[10] for it is your right to take my child. But let me explain the true situation to you.

[11] I have given my daughter to seven husbands, and when each came to her he died in the night. But for the present be merry." And Tobias said, "I will eat nothing here until you make a binding agreement with me."

[12] So Raguel said, "Take her right now, in accordance with the law. You are her relative, and she is yours. The merciful God will guide you both for the best."

[13] Then he called his daughter Sarah, and taking her by the hand he gave her to Tobias to be his wife, saying, "Here she is; take her according to the law of Moses, and take her with you to your father." And he blessed them.

[14] Next he called his wife Edna, and took a scroll and wrote out the contract; and they set their seals to it.

[15] Then they began to eat.

[16] And Raguel called his wife Edna and said to her, "Sister, make up the other room, and take her into it."

[17] so she did as he said, and took her there; and the girl began to weep. But the mother comforted her daughter in her tears, and said to her,

[18] "Be brave, my child; the Lord of heaven and earth grant you joy in place of this sorrow of yours. Be brave, my daughter."

Tob.8

[1] When they had finished eating, they escorted Tobias in to her.

[2] As he went he remembered the words of Raphael, and he took the live ashes of incense and put the heart and liver of the fish upon them and made a smoke.

[3] And when the demon smelled the odor he fled to the remotest parts of Egypt, and the angel bound him.

[4] When the door was shut and the two were alone, Tobias got up from the bed and said, "Sister, get up, and let us pray that the Lord may have mercy upon us."

[5] And Tobias began to pray, "Blessed art thou, O God of our fathers, and blessed be thy holy and glorious name for ever. Let the heavens and all thy creatures bless thee.

[6] Thou madest Adam and gavest him Eve his wife as a helper and support. From them the race of mankind has sprung. Thou didst say, `It is not good that the man should be alone; let us make a helper for him like himself.'

[7] And now, O Lord, I am not taking this sister of mine because of lust, but with sincerity. Grant that I may find mercy and may grow old together with her."

[8] And she said with him, "Amen."

[9] Then they both went to sleep for the night. But Raguel arose and went and dug a grave,

[10] with the thought, "Perhaps he too will die."

[11] Then Raguel went into his house

[12] and said to his wife Edna, "Send one of the maids to see whether he is alive; and if he is not, let us bury him without any one knowing about it."

[13] So the maid opened the door and went in, and found them both asleep.

[14] And she came out and told them that he was alive.

[15] Then Raguel blessed God and said, "Blessed art thou, O God, with every pure and holy blessing. Let thy saints and all thy creatures bless thee; let all thy angels and thy chosen people bless thee for ever.

[16] Blessed art thou, because thou hast made me glad. It has not happened to me as I expected; but thou hast treated us according to thy great mercy.

[17] Blessed art thou, because thou hast had compassion on two only children. Show them mercy, O Lord; and bring their lives to fulfilment in health and happiness and mercy."

[18] Then he ordered his servants to fill in the grave.

[19] After this he gave a wedding feast for them which lasted fourteen days.

[20] And before the days of the feast were over, Raguel declared by oath to Tobias that he should not leave until the fourteen days of the wedding feast were ended,

[21] that then he should take half of Raguel's property and return in safety to his father, and that the rest would be his "when my wife and I die."

Tob.9

[1] Then Tobias called Raphael and said to him,

[2] "Brother Azarias, take a servant and two camels with you and go to Gabael at Rages in Media and get the money for me; and bring him to the wedding feast.

[3] For Raguel has sworn that I should not leave;

[4] but my father is counting the days, and if I delay long he will be greatly distressed."

[5] So Raphael made the journey and stayed over night with Gabael. He gave him the receipt, and Gabael brought out the money bags with their seals intact and gave them to him.

[6] In the morning they both got up early and came to the wedding feast. And Gabael blessed Tobias and his wife.

Tob.10

[1] Now his father Tobit was counting each day, and when the days for the journey had expired and they did not arrive,

[2] he said, "Is it possible that he has been detained? Or is it possible that Gabael has died and there is no one to give him the money?"

[3] And he was greatly distressed.

[4] And his wife said to him, "The lad has perished; his long delay proves it." Then she began to mourn for him, and said,

[5] "Am I not distressed, my child, that I let you go, you who are the light of my eyes?"

[6] But Tobit said to her, "Be still and stop worrying; he is well."

[7] And she answered him, "Be still and stop deceiving me; my child has perished." And she went out every day to the road by which they had left; she ate nothing in the daytime, and throughout the nights she never stopped mourning for her son Tobias, until the fourteen days of the wedding feast had expired which Raguel had sworn that he should spend there. At that time Tobias said to Raguel, "Send me back, for my father and mother have given up hope of ever seeing me again."

[8] But his father-in-law said to him, "Stay with me, and I will send messengers to your father, and they will inform him how things are with you."

[9] Tobias replied, "No, send me back to my father."

[10] So Raguel arose and gave him his wife Sarah and half of his property in slaves, cattle, and money.

[11] And when he had blessed them he sent them away, saying, "The God of heaven will prosper you, my children, before I die."

[12] He said also to his daughter, "Honor your father-in-law and your mother-in-law; they are now your parents. Let me hear a good report of you. " And he kissed her. And Edna said to Tobias, "The Lord of heaven bring you back safely, dear brother, and grant me to see your children by my daughter Sarah, that I may rejoice before the Lord. See, I am entrusting my daughter to you; do nothing to grieve her."

Tob.11

[1] After this Tobias went on his way, praising God because he had made his journey a success. And he blessed Raguel and his wife Edna. So he continued on his way until they came near to Nineveh.

[2] Then Raphael said to Tobias, "Are you not aware, brother, of how you left your father?

[3] Let us run ahead of your wife and prepare the house.

[4] And take the gall of the fish with you." So they went their way, and the dog went along behind them.

[5] Now Anna sat looking intently down the road for her son.

[6] And she caught sight of him coming, and said to his father, "Behold, your son is coming, and so is the man who went with him!"

[7] Raphael said, "I know, Tobias, that your father will open his eyes.

[8] You therefore must anoint his eyes with the gall; and when they smart he will rub them, and will cause the white films to fall away, and he will see you."

[9] Then Anna ran to meet them, and embraced her son, and said to him, "I have seen you, my child; now I am ready to die." And they both wept.

[10] Tobit started toward the door, and stumbled. But his son ran to him

[11] and took hold of his father, and he sprinkled the gall upon his father's eyes, saying, "Be of good cheer, father."

[12] And when his eyes began to smart he rubbed them,

[13] and the white films scaled off from the corners of his eyes.

[14] Then he saw his son and embraced him, and he wept and said, "Blessed art thou, O God, and blessed is thy name for ever, and blessed are all thy holy angels.

[15] For thou hast afflicted me, but thou hast had mercy upon me; here I see my son Tobias!" And his son went in rejoicing, and he reported to his father the great things that had happened to him in Media.

[16] Then Tobit went out to meet his daughter-in-law at the gate of Nineveh, rejoicing and praising God. Those who saw him as he went were amazed because he could see.

[17] And Tobit gave thanks before them that God had been merciful to him. When Tobit came near to Sarah his daughter-in-law, he blessed her, saying, "Welcome, daughter! Blessed is God who has brought you to us, and blessed are your father and your mother." So there was rejoicing among all his brethren in Nineveh.

[18] Ahikar and his nephew Nadab came,

[19] and Tobias' marriage was celebrated for seven days with great festivity.

Tob.12

[1] Tobit then called his son Tobias and said to him, "My son, see to the wages of the man who went with you; and he must also be given more."

[2] He replied, "Father, it would do me no harm to give him half of what I have brought back.

[3] For he has led me back to you safely, he cured my wife, he obtained the money for me, and he also healed you."

[4] The old man said, "He deserves it."

[5] So he called the angel and said to him, "Take half of all that you two have brought back."

[6] Then the angel called the two of them privately and said to them: "Praise God and give thanks to him; exalt him and give thanks to him in the presence of all the living for what he has done for you. It is good to praise God and to exalt his name, worthily declaring the works of God. Do not be slow to give him thanks.

[7] It is good to guard the secret of a king, but gloriously to reveal the works of God. Do good, and evil will not overtake you.

[8] Prayer is good when accompanied by fasting, almsgiving, and righteousness. A little with righteousness is better than much with wrongdoing. It is better to give alms than to treasure up gold.

[9] For almsgiving delivers from death, and it will purge away every sin. Those who perform deeds of charity and of righteousness will have fulness of life;

[10] but those who commit sin are the enemies of their own lives.

[11] "I will not conceal anything from you. I have said, `It is good to guard the secret of a king, but gloriously to reveal the works of God.'

[12] And so, when you and your daughter-in-law Sarah prayed, I brought a reminder of your prayer before the Holy One; and when you buried the dead, I was likewise present with you.

[13] When you did not hesitate to rise and leave your dinner in order to go and lay out the dead, your good deed was not hidden from me, but I was with you.

[14] So now God sent me to heal you and your daughter-in-law Sarah.

[15] I am Raphael, one of the seven holy angels who present the prayers of the saints and enter into the presence of the glory of the Holy One."

[16] They were both alarmed; and they fell upon their faces, for they were afraid.

[17] But he said to them, "Do not be afraid; you will be safe. But praise God for ever.

[18] For I did not come as a favor on my part, but by the will of our God. Therefore praise him for ever.

[19] All these days I merely appeared to you and did not eat or drink, but you were seeing a vision.

[20] And now give thanks to God, for I am ascending to him who sent me. Write in a book everything that has happened."

[21] Then they stood up; but they saw him no more.

[22] So they confessed the great and wonderful works of God, and acknowledged that the angel of the Lord had appeared to them.

Tob.13

[1] Then Tobit wrote a prayer of rejoicing, and said: "Blessed is God who lives for ever, and blessed is his kingdom. [2] For he afflicts, and he shows mercy; he leads down to Hades, and brings up again, and there is no one who can escape his hand. [3] Acknowledge him before the nations, O sons of Israel; for he has scattered us among them. [4] Make his greatness known there, and exalt him in the presence of all the living; because he is our Lord and God, he is our Father for ever. [5] He will afflict us for our iniquities; and again he will show mercy, and will gather us from all the nations among whom you have been scattered. [6] If you turn to him with all your heart and with all your soul, to do what is true before him, then he will turn to you and will not hide his face from you. But see what he will do with you; give thanks to him with your full voice. Praise the Lord of righteousness, and exalt the King of the ages. I give him thanks in the land of my captivity, and I show his power and majesty to a nation of sinners. Turn back,

you sinners, and do right before him; who knows if he will accept you and have mercy on you? [7] I exalt my God; my soul exalts the King of heaven, and will rejoice in his majesty. [8] Let all men speak, and give him thanks in Jerusalem. [9] O Jerusalem, the holy city, he will afflict you for the deeds of your sons, but again he will show mercy to the sons of the righteous.

[10] Give thanks worthily to the Lord, and praise the King of the ages, that his tent may be raised for you again with joy. May he cheer those within you who are captives, and love those within you who are distressed, to all generations for ever. [11] Many nations will come from afar to the name of the Lord God, bearing gifts in their hands, gifts for the King of heaven. Generations of generations will give you joyful praise. [12] Cursed are all who hate you; blessed for ever will be all who love you. [13] Rejoice and be glad for the sons of the righteous; for they will be gathered together, and will praise the Lord of the righteous. [14] How blessed are those who love you! They will rejoice in your peace. Blessed are those who grieved over all your afflictions; for they will rejoice for you upon seeing all your glory, and they will be made glad for ever. [15] Let my soul praise God the great King. [16] For Jerusalem will be built with sapphires and emeralds, her walls with precious stones, and her towers and battlements with pure gold. [17] The streets of Jerusalem will be paved with beryl and ruby and stones of Ophir; [18] all her lanes will cry `Hallelujah!' and will give praise, saying, `Blessed is God, who has exalted you for ever.'"

Tob.14
[1] Here Tobit ended his words of praise.
[2] He was fifty-eight years old when he lost his sight, and after eight years he regained it. He gave alms, and he continued to fear the Lord God and to praise him.
[3] When he had grown very old he called his son and grandsons, and said to him, "My son, take your sons; behold, I have grown old and am about to depart this life.
[4] Go to Media, my son, for I fully believe what Jonah the prophet said about Nineveh, that it will be overthrown. But in Media there will be peace for a time. Our brethren will be scattered over the earth from the good land, and Jerusalem will be desolate. The house of God in it will be burned down and will be in ruins for a time.
[5] But God will again have mercy on them, and bring them back into their land; and they will rebuild the house of God, though it will not be like the former one until the times of the age are completed. After this they will return from the places of their captivity, and will rebuild Jerusalem in splendor. And the house of God will be rebuilt there with a glorious building for all generations for ever, just as the prophets said of it.
[6] Then all the Gentiles will turn to fear the Lord God in truth, and will bury their idols.
[7] All the Gentiles will praise the Lord, and his people will give thanks to God, and the Lord will exalt his people. And all who love the Lord God in truth and righteousness will rejoice, showing mercy to our brethren.
[8] "So now, my son, leave Nineveh, because what the prophet Jonah said will surely happen.
[9] But keep the law and the commandments, and be merciful and just, so that it may be well with you.
[10] Bury me properly, and your mother with me. And do not live in Nineveh any longer. See, my son, what Nadab did to Ahikar who had reared him, how he brought him from light into darkness, and with what he repaid him. But Ahikar was saved, and the other received repayment as he himself went down into the darkness. Ahikar gave alms and escaped the deathtrap which Nadab had set for him; but Nadab fell into the trap and perished.
[11] So now, my children, consider what almsgiving accomplishes and how righteousness delivers." As he said this he died in his bed. He was a hundred and fifty-eight years old; and Tobias gave him a magnificent funeral.
[12] And when Anna died he buried her with his father. Then Tobias returned with his wife and his sons to Ecbatana, to Raguel his father-in-law.
[13] He grew old with honor, and he gave his father-in-law and mother-in-law magnificent funerals. He inherited their property and that of his father Tobit.
[14] He died in Ecbatana of Media at the age of a hundred and twenty-seven years.
[15] But before he died he heard of the destruction of Nineveh, which Nebuchadnezzar and Ahasuerus had captured. Before his death he rejoiced over Nineveh.

Judith

Jdt.1

[1] In the twelfth year of the reign of Nebuchadnezzar, who ruled over the Assyrians in the great city of Nineveh, in the days of Arphaxad, who ruled over the Medes in Ecbatana --

[2] he is the king who built walls about Ecbatana with hewn stones three cubits thick and six cubits long; he made the walls seventy cubits high and fifty cubits wide;

[3] at the gates he built towers a hundred cubits high and sixty cubits wide at the foundations;

[4] and he made its gates, which were seventy cubits high and forty cubits wide, so that his armies could march out in force and his infantry form their ranks --

[5] it was in those days that King Nebuchadnezzar made war against King Arphaxad in the great plain which is on the borders of Ragae.

[6] He was joined by all the people of the hill country and all those who lived along the Euphrates and the Tigris and the Hydaspes and in the plain where Arioch ruled the Elymaeans. Many nations joined the forces of the Chaldeans.

[7] Then Nebuchadnezzar king of the Assyrians sent to all who lived in Persia and to all who lived in the west, those who lived in Cilicia and Damascus and Lebanon and Antilebanon and all who lived along the seacoast,

[8] and those among the nations of Carmel and Gilead, and Upper Galilee and the great Plain of Esdraelon,

[9] and all who were in Samaria and its surrounding towns, and beyond the Jordan as far as Jerusalem and Bethany and Chelous and Kadesh and the river of Egypt, and Tahpanhes and Raamses and the whole land of Goshen,

[10] even beyond Tanis and Memphis, and all who lived in Egypt as far as the borders of Ethiopia.

[11] But all who lived in the whole region disregarded the orders of Nebuchadnezzar king of the Assyrians, and refused to join him in the war; for they were not afraid of him, but looked upon him as only one man, and they sent back his messengers empty-handed and shamefaced.

[12] Then Nebuchadnezzar was very angry with this whole region, and swore by his throne and kingdom that he would surely take revenge on the whole territory of Cilicia and Damascus and Syria, that he would kill them by the sword, and also all the inhabitants of the land of Moab, and the people of Ammon, and all Judea, and every one in Egypt, as far as the coasts of the two seas.

[13] In the seventeenth year he led his forces against King Arphaxad, and defeated him in battle, and overthrew the whole army of Arphaxad, and all his cavalry and all his chariots.

[14] Thus he took possession of his cities, and came to Ecbatana, captured its towers, plundered its markets, and turned its beauty into shame.

[15] He captured Arphaxad in the mountains of Ragae and struck him down with hunting spears; and he utterly destroyed him, to this day.

[16] Then he returned with them to Nineveh, he and all his combined forces, a vast body of troops; and there he and his forces rested and feasted for one hundred and twenty days.

Jdt.2

[1] In the eighteenth year, on the twenty-second day of the first month, there was talk in the palace of Nebuchadnezzar king of the Assyrians about carrying out his revenge on the whole region, just as he said.

[2] He called together all his officers and all his nobles and set forth to them his secret plan and recounted fully, with his own lips, all the wickedness of the region;

[3] and it was decided that every one who had not obeyed his command should be destroyed.

[4] When he had finished setting forth his plan, Nebuchadnezzar king of the Assyrians called Holofernes, the chief general of his army, second only to himself, and said to him,

[5] "Thus says the Great King, the lord of the whole earth: When you leave my presence, take with you men confident in their strength, to the number of one hundred and twenty thousand foot soldiers and twelve thousand cavalry.

[6] Go and attack the whole west country, because they disobeyed my orders.

[7] Tell them to prepare earth and water, for I am coming against them in my anger, and will cover the whole face of the earth with the feet of my armies, and will hand them over to be plundered by my troops,

[8] till their wounded shall fill their valleys, and every brook and river shall be filled with their dead, and overflow;

[9] and I will lead them away captive to the ends of the whole earth.

[10] You shall go and seize all their territory for me in advance. They will yield themselves to you, and you shall hold them for me till the day of their punishment.

[11] But if they refuse, your eye shall not spare and you shall hand them over to slaughter and plunder throughout your whole region.

[12] For as I live, and by the power of my kingdom, what I have spoken my hand will execute.

[13] And you -- take care not to transgress any of your sovereign's commands, but be sure to carry them out just as I have ordered you; and do not delay about it."

[14] So Holofernes left the presence of his master, and called together all the commanders, generals, and officers of the Assyrian army,

[15] and mustered the picked troops by divisions as his lord had ordered him to do, one hundred and twenty thousand of them, together with twelve thousand archers on horseback,

[16] and he organized them as a great army is marshaled for a campaign.

[17] He collected a vast number of camels and asses and mules for transport, and innumerable sheep and oxen and goats for provision;

[18] also plenty of food for every man, and a huge amount of gold and silver from the royal palace.

[19] So he set out with his whole army, to go ahead of King Nebuchadnezzar and to cover the whole face of the earth to the west with their chariots and horsemen and picked troops of infantry.

[20] Along with them went a mixed crowd like a swarm of locusts, like the dust of the earth -- a multitude that could not be counted.

[21] They marched for three days from Nineveh to the plain of Bectileth, and camped opposite Bectileth near the mountain which is to the north of Upper Cilicia.

[22] From there Holofernes took his whole army, his infantry, cavalry, and chariots, and went up into the hill country

[23] and ravaged Put and Lud, and plundered all the people of Rassis and the Ishmaelites who lived along the desert, south of the country of the Chelleans.

[24] Then he followed the Euphrates and passed through Mesopotamia and destroyed all the hilltop cities along the brook Abron, as far as the sea.

[25] He also seized the territory of Cilicia, and killed every one who resisted him, and came to the southern borders of Japheth, fronting toward Arabia.

[26] He surrounded all the Midianites, and burned their tents and plundered their sheepfolds.

[27] Then he went down into the plain of Damascus during the wheat harvest, and burned all their fields and destroyed their flocks and herds and sacked their cities and ravaged their lands and put to death all their young men with the edge of the sword.

[28] So fear and terror of him fell upon all the people who lived along the seacoast, at Sidon and Tyre, and those who lived in Sur and Ocina and all who lived in Jamnia. Those who lived in Azotus and Ascalon feared him exceedingly.

Jdt.3

[1] So they sent messengers to sue for peace, and said,

[2] "Behold, we the servants of Nebuchadnezzar, the Great King, lie prostrate before you. Do with us whatever you will.

[3] Behold, our buildings, and all our land, and all our wheat fields, and our flocks and herds, and all our sheepfolds with their tents, lie before you; do with them whatever you please.

[4] Our cities also and their inhabitants are your slaves; come and deal with them in any way that seems good to you."

[5] The men came to Holofernes and told him all this.

[6] Then he went down to the seacoast with his army and stationed garrisons in the hilltop cities and took picked men from them as his allies.

[7] And these people and all in the country round about welcomed him with garlands and dances and tambourines.

[8] And he demolished all their shrines and cut down their sacred groves; for it had been given to him to destroy all the gods of the land, so that all nations should worship Nebuchadnezzar only, and all their tongues and tribes should call upon him as god.

[9] Then he came to the edge of Esdraelon, near Dothan, fronting the great ridge of Judea;

[10] here he camped between Geba and Scythopolis, and remained for a whole month in order to assemble all the supplies for his army.

Jdt.4

[1] By this time the people of Israel living in Judea heard of everything that Holofernes, the general of Nebuchadnezzar the king of the Assyrians, had done to the nations, and how he had plundered and destroyed all their temples;

[2] they were therefore very greatly terrified at his approach, and were alarmed both for Jerusalem and for the temple of the Lord their God.

[3] For they had only recently returned from the captivity, and all the people of Judea were newly gathered together, and the sacred vessels and the altar and the temple had been consecrated after their profanation.

[4] So they sent to every district of Samaria, and to Kona and Beth-horon and Belmain and Jericho and to Choba and Aesora and the valley of Salem,

[5] and immediately seized all the high hilltops and fortified the villages on them and stored up food in preparation for war -- since their fields had recently been harvested.

[6] And Joakim, the high priest, who was in Jerusalem at the time, wrote to the people of Bethulia and Betomesthaim, which faces Esdraelon opposite the plain near Dothan,

[7] ordering them to seize the passes up into the hills, since by them Judea could be invaded, and it was easy to stop any who tried to enter, for the approach was narrow, only wide enough for two men at the most.

[8] So the Israelites did as Joakim the high priest and the senate of the whole people of Israel, in session at Jerusalem, had given order.

[9] And every man of Israel cried out to God with great fervor, and they humbled themselves with much fasting.

[10] They and their wives and their children and their cattle and every resident alien and hired laborer and purchased slave -- they all girded themselves with sackcloth.

[11] And all the men and women of Israel, and their children, living at Jerusalem, prostrated themselves before the temple and put ashes on their heads and spread out their sackcloth before the Lord.

[12] They even surrounded the altar with sackcloth and cried out in unison, praying earnestly to the God of Israel not to give up their infants as prey and their wives as booty, and the cities they had inherited to be destroyed, and the sanctuary to be profaned and desecrated to the malicious joy of the Gentiles.

[13] So the Lord heard their prayers and looked upon their affliction; for the people fasted many days throughout Judea and in Jerusalem before the sanctuary of the Lord Almighty.

[14] And Joakim the high priest and all the priests who stood before the Lord and ministered to the Lord, with their loins girded with sackcloth, offered the continual burnt offerings and the vows and freewill offerings of the people.

[15] With ashes upon their turbans, they cried out to the Lord with all their might to look with favor upon the whole house of Israel.

Jdt.5

[1] When Holofernes, the general of the Assyrian army, heard that the people of Israel had prepared for war and had closed the passes in the hills and fortified all the high hilltops and set up barricades in the plains,

[2] he was very angry. So he called together all the princes of Moab and the commanders of Ammon and all the governors of the coastland,

[3] and said to them, "Tell me, you Canaanites, what people is this that lives in the hill country? What cities do they inhabit? How large is their army, and in what does their power or strength consist? Who rules over them as king, leading their army?

[4] And why have they alone, of all who live in the west, refused to come out and meet me?"

[5] Then Achior, the leader of all the Ammonites, said to him, "Let my lord now hear a word from the mouth of your servant, and I will tell you the truth about this people that dwells in the nearby mountain district. No falsehood shall come from your servant's mouth.

[6] This people is descended from the Chaldeans.

[7] At one time they lived in Mesopotamia, because they would not follow the gods of their fathers who were in Chaldea.

[8] For they had left the ways of their ancestors, and they worshiped the God of heaven, the God they had come to know; hence they drove them out from the presence of their gods; and they fled to Mesopotamia, and lived there for a long time.

[9] Then their God commanded them to leave the place where they were living and go to the land of Canaan. There they settled, and prospered, with much gold and silver and very many cattle.

[10] When a famine spread over Canaan they went down to Egypt and lived there as long as they had food; and there they became a great multitude -- so great that they could not be counted.

[11] So the king of Egypt became hostile to them; he took advantage of them and set them to making bricks, and humbled them and made slaves of them.

[12] Then they cried out to their God, and he afflicted the whole land of Egypt with incurable plagues; and so the Egyptians drove them out of their sight.

[13] Then God dried up the Red Sea before them,

[14] and he led them by the way of Sinai and Kadesh-barnea, and drove out all the people of the wilderness.

[15] So they lived in the land of the Amorites, and by their might destroyed all the inhabitants of Heshbon; and crossing over the Jordan they took possession of all the hill country.

[16] And they drove out before them the Canaanites and the Perizzites and the Jebusites and the Shechemites and all the Gergesites, and lived there a long time.

[17] As long as they did not sin against their God they prospered, for the God who hates iniquity is with them.

[18] But when they departed from the way which he had appointed for them, they were utterly defeated in many battles and were led away captive to a foreign country; the temple of their God was razed to the ground, and their cities were captured by their enemies.

[19] But now they have returned to their God, and have come back from the places to which they were scattered, and have occupied Jerusalem, where their sanctuary is, and have settled in the hill country, because it was uninhabited.

[20] Now therefore, my master and lord, if there is any unwitting error in this people and they sin against their God and we find out their offense, then we will go up and defeat them.

[21] But if there is no transgression in their nation, then let my lord pass them by; for their Lord will defend them, and their God will protect them, and we shall be put to shame before the whole world."

[22] When Achior had finished saying this, all the men standing around the tent began to complain; Holofernes' officers and all the men from the seacoast and from Moab insisted that he must be put to death.

[23] "For," they said, "we will not be afraid of the Israelites; they are a people with no strength or power for making war.

[24] Therefore let us go up, Lord Holofernes, and they will be devoured by your vast army."

Jdt.6

[1] When the disturbance made by the men outside the council died down, Holofernes, the commander of the Assyrian army, said to Achior and all the Moabites in the presence of all the foreign contingents:

[2] "And who are you, Achior, and you hirelings of Ephraim, to prophesy among us as you have done today and tell us not to make war against the people of Israel because their God will defend them? Who is God except Nebuchadnezzar?

[3] He will send his forces and will destroy them from the face of the earth, and their God will not deliver them -- we the king's servants will destroy them as one man. They cannot resist the might of our cavalry.

[4] We will burn them up, and their mountains will be drunk with their blood, and their fields will be full of their dead. They cannot withstand us, but will utterly perish. So says King Nebuchadnezzar, the lord of the whole earth. For he has spoken; none of his words shall be in vain.

[5] "But you, Achior, you Ammonite hireling, who have said these words on the day of your iniquity, you shall not see my face again from this day until I take revenge on this race that came out of Egypt.

[6] Then the sword of my army and the spear of my servants shall pierce your sides, and you shall fall among their wounded, when I return.

[7] Now my slaves are going to take you back into the hill country and put you in one of the cities beside the passes,

[8] and you will not die until you perish along with them.

[9] If you really hope in your heart that they will not be taken, do not look downcast! I have spoken and none of my words shall fail."

[10] Then Holofernes ordered his slaves, who waited on him in his tent, to seize Achior and take him to Bethulia and hand him over to the men of Israel.

[11] So the slaves took him and led him out of the camp into the plain, and from the plain they went up into the hill country and came to the springs below Bethulia.

[12] When the men of the city saw them, they caught up their weapons and ran out of the city to the top of the hill, and all the slingers kept them from coming up by casting stones at them.

[13] However, they got under the shelter of the hill and they bound Achior and left him lying at the foot of the hill, and returned to their master.

[14] Then the men of Israel came down from their city and found him; and they untied him and brought him into Bethulia and placed him before the magistrates of their city,

[15] who in those days were Uzziah the son of Micah, of the tribe of Simeon, and Chabris the son of Gothoniel, and Charmis the son of Melchiel.

[16] They called together all the elders of the city, and all their young men and their women ran to the assembly; and they set Achior in the midst of all their people, and Uzziah asked him what had happened.

[17] He answered and told them what had taken place at the council of Holofernes, and all that he had said in the presence of the Assyrian leaders, and all that Holofernes had said so boastfully against the house of Israel.

[18] Then the people fell down and worshiped God, and cried out to him, and said,

[19] "O Lord God of heaven, behold their arrogance, and have pity on the humiliation of our people, and look this day upon the faces of those who are consecrated to thee."

[20] Then they consoled Achior, and praised him greatly.

[21] And Uzziah took him from the assembly to his own house and gave a banquet for the elders; and all that night they called on the God of Israel for help.

Jdt.7

[1] The next day Holofernes ordered his whole army, and all the allies who had joined him, to break camp and move against Bethulia, and to seize the passes up into the hill country and make war on the Israelites.

[2] So all their warriors moved their camp that day; their force of men of war was one hundred and seventy thousand infantry and twelve thousand cavalry, together with the baggage and the foot soldiers handling it, a very great multitude.

[3] They encamped in the valley near Bethulia, beside the spring, and they spread out in breadth over Dothan as far as Balbaim and in length from Bethulia to Cyamon, which faces Esdraelon.

[4] When the Israelites saw their vast numbers they were greatly terrified, and every one said to his neighbor, "These men will now lick up the face of the whole land; neither the high mountains nor the valleys nor the hills will bear their weight."

[5] Then each man took up his weapons, and when they had kindled fires on their towers they remained on guard all that night.

[6] On the second day Holofernes led out all his cavalry in full view of the Israelites in Bethulia,

[7] and examined the approaches to the city, and visited the springs that supplied their water, and seized them and set guards of soldiers over them, and then returned to his army.

[8] Then all the chieftains of the people of Esau and all the leaders of the Moabites and the commanders of the coastland came to him and said,

[9] "Let our lord hear a word, lest his army be defeated.

[10] For these people, the Israelites, do not rely on their spears but on the height of the mountains where they live, for it is not easy to reach the tops of their mountains.

[11] Therefore, my lord, do not fight against them in battle array, and not a man of your army will fall.

[12] Remain in your camp, and keep all the men in your forces with you; only let your servants take possession of the spring of water that flows from the foot of the mountain --

[13] for this is where all the people of Bethulia get their water. So thirst will destroy them, and they will give up their city. We and our people will go up to the tops of the nearby mountains and camp there to keep watch that not a man gets out of the city.

[14] They and their wives and children will waste away with famine, and before the sword reaches them they will be strewn about in the streets where they live.

[15] So you will pay them back with evil, because they rebelled and did not receive you peaceably."

[16] These words pleased Holofernes and all his servants, and he gave orders to do as they had said.

[17] So the army of the Ammonites moved forward, together with five thousand Assyrians, and they encamped in the valley and seized the water supply and the springs of the Israelites.

[18] And the sons of Esau and the sons of Ammon went up and encamped in the hill country opposite Dothan; and they sent some of their men toward the south and the east, toward Acraba, which is near Chusi beside the brook Mochmur. The rest of the Assyrian army encamped in the plain, and covered the whole face of the land, and their tents and supply trains spread out in great number, and they formed a vast multitude.

[19] The people of Israel cried out to the Lord their God, for their courage failed, because all their enemies had surrounded them and there was no way of escape from them.

[20] The whole Assyrian army, their infantry, chariots, and cavalry, surrounded them for thirty-four days, until all the vessels of water belonging to every inhabitant of Bethulia were empty;

[21] their cisterns were going dry, and they did not have enough water to drink their fill for a single day, because it was measured out to them to drink.

[22] Their children lost heart, and the women and young men fainted from thirst and fell down in the streets of the city and in the passages through the gates; there was no strength left in them any longer.

[23] Then all the people, the young men, the women, and the children, gathered about Uzziah and the rulers of the city and cried out with a loud voice, and said before all the elders,

[24] "God be judge between you and us! For you have done us a great injury in not making peace with the Assyrians.

[25] For now we have no one to help us; God has sold us into their hands, to strew us on the ground before them with thirst and utter destruction.

[26] Now call them in and surrender the whole city to the army of Holofernes and to all his forces, to be plundered.

[27] For it would be better for us to be captured by them; for we will be slaves, but our lives will be spared, and we shall not witness the death of our babes before our eyes, or see our wives and children draw their last breath.

[28] We call to witness against you heaven and earth and our God, the Lord of our fathers, who punishes us according to our sins and the sins of our fathers. Let him not do this day the things which we have described!"

[29] Then great and general lamentation arose throughout the assembly, and they cried out to the Lord God with a loud voice.

[30] And Uzziah said to them, "Have courage, my brothers! Let us hold out for five more days; by that time the Lord our God will restore to us his mercy, for he will not forsake us utterly.

[31] But if these days pass by, and no help comes for us, I will do what you say."

[32] Then he dismissed the people to their various posts, and they went up on the walls and towers of their city. The women and children he sent home. And they were greatly depressed in the city.

Jdt.8

[1] At that time Judith heard about these things: she was the daughter of Merari the son of Ox, son of Joseph, son of Oziel, son of Elkiah, son of Ananias, son of Gideon, son of Raphaim, son of Ahitub, son of Elijah, son of Hilkiah, son of Eliab, son of Nathanael, son of Salamiel, son of Sarasadai, son of Israel.

[2] Her husband Manasseh, who belonged to her tribe and family, had died during the barley harvest.

[3] For as he stood overseeing the men who were binding sheaves in the field, he was overcome by the burning heat, and took to his bed and died in Bethulia his city. So they buried him with his fathers in the field between Dothan and Balamon.

[4] Judith had lived at home as a widow for three years and four months.

[5] She set up a tent for herself on the roof of her house, and girded sackcloth about her loins and wore the garments of her widowhood.

[6] She fasted all the days of her widowhood, except the day before the sabbath and the sabbath itself, the day before the new moon and the day of the new moon, and the feasts and days of rejoicing of the house of Israel.

[7] She was beautiful in appearance, and had a very lovely face; and her husband Manasseh had left her gold and silver, and men and women slaves, and cattle, and fields; and she maintained this estate.

[8] No one spoke ill of her, for she feared God with great devotion.

[9] When Judith heard the wicked words spoken by the people against the ruler, because they were faint for lack of water, and when she heard all that Uzziah said to them, and how he promised them under oath to surrender the city to the Assyrians after five days,

[10] she sent her maid, who was in charge of all she possessed, to summon Chabris and Charmis, the elders of her city.

[11] They came to her, and she said to them, "Listen to me, rulers of the people of Bethulia! What you have said to the people today is not right; you have even sworn and pronounced this oath between God and you, promising to surrender the city to our enemies unless the Lord turns and helps us within so many days.

[12] Who are you, that have put God to the test this day, and are setting yourselves up in the place of God among the sons of men?

[13] You are putting the Lord Almighty to the test -- but you will never know anything!

[14] You cannot plumb the depths of the human heart, nor find out what a man is thinking; how do you expect to search out God, who made all these things, and find out his mind or comprehend his thought? No, my brethren, do not provoke the Lord our God to anger.

[15] For if he does not choose to help us within these five days, he has power to protect us within any time he pleases, or even to destroy us in the presence of our enemies.

[16] Do not try to bind the purposes of the Lord our God; for God is not like man, to be threatened, nor like a human being, to be won over by pleading.

[17] Therefore, while we wait for his deliverance, let us call upon him to help us, and he will hear our voice, if it pleases him.

[18] "For never in our generation, nor in these present days, has there been any tribe or family or people or city of ours which worshiped gods made with hands, as was done in days gone by --

[19] and that was why our fathers were handed over to the sword, and to be plundered, and so they suffered a great catastrophe before our enemies.

[20] But we know no other god but him, and therefore we hope that he will not disdain us or any of our nation.

[21] For if we are captured all Judea will be captured and our sanctuary will be plundered; and he will exact of us the penalty for its desecration.

[22] And the slaughter of our brethren and the captivity of the land and the desolation of our inheritance -- all this he will bring upon our heads among the Gentiles, wherever we serve as slaves; and we shall be an offense and a reproach in the eyes of those who acquire us.

[23] For our slavery will not bring us into favor, but the Lord our God will turn it to dishonor.

[24] "Now therefore, brethren, let us set an example to our brethren, for their lives depend upon us, and the sanctuary and the temple and the altar rest upon us.

[25] In spite of everything let us give thanks to the Lord our God, who is putting us to the test as he did our forefathers.

[26] Remember what he did with Abraham, and how he tested Isaac, and what happened to Jacob in Mesopotamia in Syria, while he was keeping the sheep of Laban, his mother's brother.

[27] For he has not tried us with fire, as he did them, to search their hearts, nor has he taken revenge upon us; but the Lord scourges those who draw near to him, in order to admonish them."

[28] Then Uzziah said to her, "All that you have said has been spoken out of a true heart, and there is no one who can deny your words.

[29] Today is not the first time your wisdom has been shown, but from the beginning of your life all the people have recognized your understanding, for your heart's disposition is right.

[30] But the people were very thirsty, and they compelled us to do for them what we have promised, and made us take an oath which we cannot break.

[31] So pray for us, since you are a devout woman, and the Lord will send us rain to fill our cisterns and we will no longer be faint."

[32] Judith said to them, "Listen to me. I am about to do a thing which will go down through all generations of our descendants.

[33] Stand at the city gate tonight, and I will go out with my maid; and within the days after which you have promised to surrender the city to our enemies, the Lord will deliver Israel by my hand.

[34] Only, do not try to find out what I plan; for I will not tell you until I have finished what I am about to do."

[35] Uzziah and the rulers said to her, "Go in peace, and may the Lord God go before you, to take revenge upon our enemies."

[36] So they returned from the tent and went to their posts.

Jdt.9

[1] Then Judith fell upon her face, and put ashes on her head, and uncovered the sackcloth she was

wearing; and at the very time when that evening's incense was being offered in the house of God in Jerusalem, Judith cried out to the Lord with a loud voice, and said,

[2] "O Lord God of my father Simeon, to whom thou gavest a sword to take revenge on the strangers who had loosed the girdle of a virgin to defile her, and uncovered her thigh to put her to shame, and polluted her womb to disgrace her; for thou hast said, `It shall not be done' -- yet they did it.

[3] So thou gavest up their rulers to be slain, and their bed, which was ashamed of the deceit they had practiced, to be stained with blood, and thou didst strike down slaves along with princes, and princes on their thrones;

[4] and thou gavest their wives for a prey and their daughters to captivity, and all their booty to be divided among thy beloved sons, who were zealous for thee, and abhorred the pollution of their blood, and called on thee for help -- O God, my God, hear me also, a widow.

[5] "For thou hast done these things and those that went before and those that followed; thou hast designed the things that are now, and those that are to come. Yea, the things thou didst intend came to pass,

[6] and the things thou didst will presented themselves and said, `Lo, we are here'; for all they ways are prepared in advance, and thy judgment is with foreknowledge.

[7] "Behold now, the Assyrians are increased in their might; they are exalted, with their horses and riders; they glory in the strength of their foot soldiers; they trust in shield and spear, in bow and sling, and know not that thou art the Lord who crushest wars; the Lord is thy name.

[8] Break their strength by thy might, and bring down their power in thy anger; for they intend to defile thy sanctuary, and to pollute the tabernacle where thy glorious name rests, and to cast down the horn of thy altar with the sword.

[9] Behold their pride, and send thy wrath upon their heads; give to me, a widow, the strength to do what I plan.

[10] By the deceit of my lips strike down the slave with the prince and the prince with his servant; crush their arrogance by the hand of a woman.

[11] "For thy power depends not upon numbers, nor thy might upon men of strength; for thou art God of the lowly, helper of the oppressed, upholder of the weak, protector of the forlorn, savior of those without hope.

[12] Hear, O hear me, God of my father, God of the inheritance of Israel, Lord of heaven and earth, Creator of the waters, King of all thy creation, hear my prayer!

[13] Make my deceitful words to be their wound and stripe, for they have planned cruel things against thy covenant, and against thy consecrated house, and against the top of Zion, and against the house possessed by thy children.

[14] And cause thy whole nation and every tribe to know and understand that thou art God, the God of all power and might, and that there is no other who protects the people of Israel but thou alone!"

Jdt.10
[1] When Judith had ceased crying out to the God of Israel, and had ended all these words,

[2] she rose from where she lay prostrate and called her maid and went down into the house where she lived on sabbaths and on her feast days;

[3] and she removed the sackcloth which she had been wearing, and took off her widow's garments, and bathed her body with water, and anointed herself with precious ointment, and combed her hair and put on a tiara, and arrayed herself in her gayest apparel, which she used to wear while her husband Manasseh was living.

[4] And she put sandals on her feet, and put on her anklets and bracelets and rings, and her earrings and all her ornaments, and made herself very beautiful, to entice the eyes of all men who might see her.

[5] And she gave her maid a bottle of wine and a flask of oil, and filled a bag with parched grain and a cake of dried fruit and fine bread; and she wrapped up all her vessels and gave them to her to carry.

[6] Then they went out to the city gate of Bethulia, and found Uzziah standing there with the elders of the city, Chabris and Charmis.

[7] When they saw her, and noted how her face was altered and her clothing changed, they greatly admired her beauty, and said to her,

[8] "May the God of our fathers grant you favor and fulfil your plans, that the people of Israel may glory and Jerusalem may be exalted." And she worshiped God.

[9] Then she said to them, "Order the gate of the city to be opened for me, and I will go out and accomplish the things about which you spoke with me." So they ordered the young men to open the gate for her, as she had said.

[10] When they had done this, Judith went out, she and her maid with her; and the men of the city watched her until she had gone down the mountain and passed through the valley and they could no longer see her.

[11] The women went straight on through the valley; and an Assyrian patrol met her

[12] and took her into custody, and asked her, "To what people do you belong, and where are you coming from, and where are you going?" She replied, "I am a daughter of the Hebrews, but I am fleeing

from them, for they are about to be handed over to you to be devoured.

[13] I am on my way to the presence of Holofernes the commander of your army, to give him a true report; and I will show him a way by which he can go and capture all the hill country without losing one of his men, captured or slain."

[14] When the men heard her words, and observed her face -- she was in their eyes marvelously beautiful -- they said to her,

[15] "You have saved your life by hurrying down to the presence of our lord. Go at once to his tent; some of us will escort you and hand you over to him.

[16] And when you stand before him, do not be afraid in your heart, but tell him just what you have said, and he will treat you well."

[17] They chose from their number a hundred men to accompany her and her maid, and they brought them to the tent of Holofernes.

[18] There was great excitement in the whole camp, for her arrival was reported from tent to tent, and they came and stood around her as she waited outside the tent of Holofernes while they told him about her.

[19] And they marveled at her beauty, and admired the Israelites, judging them by her, and every one said to his neighbor, "Who can despise these people, who have women like this among them? Surely not a man of them had better be left alive, for if we let them go they will be able to ensnare the whole world!"

[20] Then Holofernes' companions and all his servants came out and led her into the tent.

[21] Holofernes was resting on his bed, under a canopy which was woven with purple and gold and emeralds and precious stones.

[22] When they told him of her he came forward to the front of the tent, with silver lamps carried before him.

[23] And when Judith came into the presence of Holofernes and his servants, they all marveled at the beauty of her face; and she prostrated herself and made obeisance to him, and his slaves raised her up.

Jdt.11

[1] Then Holofernes said to her, "Take courage, woman, and do not be afraid in your heart, for I have never hurt any one who chose to serve Nebuchadnezzar, the king of all the earth.

[2] And even now, if your people who live in the hill country had not slighted me, I would never have lifted my spear against them; but they have brought all this on themselves.

[3] And now tell me why you have fled from them and have come over to us -- since you have come to safety.

[4] Have courage; you will live, tonight and from now on. No one will hurt you, but all will treat you well,

as they do the servants of my lord King Nebuchadnezzar."

[5] Judith replied to him, "Accept the words of your servant, and let your maidservant speak in your presence, and I will tell nothing false to my lord this night.

[6] And if you follow out the words of your maidservant, God will accomplish something through you, and my lord will not fail to achieve his purposes.

[7] Nebuchadnezzar the king of the whole earth lives, and as his power endures, who had sent you to direct every living soul, not only do men serve him because of you, but also the beasts of the field and the cattle and the birds of the air will live by your power under Nebuchadnezzar and all his house.

[8] For we have heard of your wisdom and skill, and it is reported throughout the whole world that you are the one good man in the whole kingdom, thoroughly informed and marvelous in military strategy.

[9] "Now as for the things Achior said in your council, we have heard his words, for the men of Bethulia spared him and he told them all he had said to you.

[10] Therefore, my lord and master, do not disregard what he said, but keep it in your mind, for it is true: our nation cannot be punished, nor can the sword prevail against them, unless they sin against their God.

[11] "And now, in order that my lord may not be defeated and his purpose frustrated, death will fall upon them, for a sin has overtaken them by which they are about to provoke their God to anger when they do what is wrong.

[12] Since their food supply is exhausted and their water has almost given out, they have planned to kill their cattle and have determined to use all that God by his laws has forbidden them to eat.

[13] They have decided to consume the first fruits of the grain and the tithes of the wine and oil, which they had consecrated and set aside for the priests who minister in the presence of our God at Jerusalem -- although it is not lawful for any of the people so much as to touch these things with their hands.

[14] They have sent men to Jerusalem, because even the people living there have been doing this, to bring back to them permission from the senate.

[15] When the word reaches them and they proceed to do this, on that very day they will be handed over to you to be destroyed.

[16] "Therefore, when I, your servant, learned all this, I fled from them; and God has sent me to accomplish with you things that will astonish the whole world, as many as shall hear about them.

[17] For your servant is religious, and serves the God of heaven day and night; therefore, my lord, I will remain with you, and every night your servant will

Joseph Lumpkin

go out into the valley, and I will pray to God and he will tell me when they have committed their sins.
[18] And I will come and tell you, and then you shall go out with your whole army, and not one of them will withstand you.
[19] Then I will lead you through the middle of Judea, till you come to Jerusalem; and I will set your throne in the midst of it; and you will lead them like sheep that have no shepherd, and not a dog will so much as open its mouth to growl at you. For this has been told me, by my foreknowledge; it was announced to me, and I was sent to tell you."
[20] Her words pleased Holofernes and all his servants, and they marveled at her wisdom and said,
[21] "There is not such a woman from one end of the earth to the other, either for beauty of face or wisdom of speech!"
[22] And Holofernes said to her, "God has done well to send you before the people, to lend strength to our hands and to bring destruction upon those who have slighted my lord.
[23] You are not only beautiful in appearance, but wise in speech; and if you do as you have said, your God shall be my God, and you shall live in the house of King Nebuchadnezzar and be renowned throughout the whole world."

Jdt.12
[1] Then he commanded them to bring her in where his silver dishes were kept, and ordered them to set a table for her with some of his own food and to serve her with his own wine.
[2] But Judith said, "I cannot eat it, lest it be an offense; but I will be provided from the things I have brought with me."
[3] Holofernes said to her, "If your supply runs out, where can we get more like it for you? For none of your people is here with us."
[4] Judith replied, "As your soul lives, my lord, your servant will not use up the things I have with me before the Lord carries out by my hand what he has determined to do."
[5] Then the servants of Holofernes brought her into the tent, and she slept until midnight. Along toward the morning watch she arose
[6] and sent to Holofernes and said, "Let my lord now command that your servant be permitted to go out and pray."
[7] So Holofernes commanded his guards not to hinder her. And she remained in the camp for three days, and went out each night to the valley of Bethulia, and bathed at the spring in the camp.
[8] When she came up from the spring she prayed the Lord God of Israel to direct her way for the raising up of her people.
[9] So she returned clean and stayed in the tent until she ate her food toward evening.

[10] On the fourth day Holofernes held a banquet for his slave only, and did not invite any of his officers.
[11] And he said to Bagoas, the eunuch who had charge of his personal affairs, "Go now and persuade the Hebrew woman who is in your care to join us and eat and drink with us.
[12] For it will be a disgrace if we let such a woman go without enjoying her company, for if we do not embrace her she will laugh at us."
[13] So Bagoas went out from the presence of Holofernes, and approached her and said, "This beautiful maidservant will please come to my lord and be honored in his presence, and drink wine and be merry with us, and become today like one of the daughters of the Assyrians who serve in the house of Nebuchadnezzar."
[14] And Judith said, "Who am I, to refuse my lord? Surely whatever pleases him I will do at once, and it will be a joy to me until the day of my death!"
[15] So she got up and arrayed herself in all her woman's finery, and her maid went and spread on the ground for her before Holofernes the soft fleeces which she had received from Bagoas for her daily use, so that she might recline on them when she ate.
[16] Then Judith came in and lay down, and Holofernes' heart was ravished with her and he was moved with great desire to possess her; for he had been waiting for an opportunity to deceive her, ever since the day he first saw her.
[17] So Holofernes said to her. "Drink now, and be merry with us!"
[18] Judith said, "I will drink now, my lord, because my life means more to me today than in all the days since I was born."
[19] Then she took and ate and drank before him what her maid had prepared.
[20] And Holofernes was greatly pleased with her, and drank a great quantity of wine, much more than he had ever drunk in any one day since he was born.

Jdt.13
[1] When evening came, his slaves quickly withdrew, and Bagoas closed the tent from outside and shut out the attendants from his master's presence; and they went to bed, for they all were weary because the banquet had lasted long.
[2] So Judith was left alone in the tent , with Holofernes stretched out on his bed, for he was overcome with wine.
[3] Now Judith had told her maid to stand outside the bedchamber and to wait for her to come out, as she did every day; for she said she would be going out for her prayers. And she had said the same thing to Bagoas.
[4] So every one went out, and no one, either small or great, was left in the bedchamber. Then Judith, standing beside his bed, said in her heart, "O Lord

36

God of all might, look in this hour upon the work of my hands for the exaltation of Jerusalem.

[5] For now is the time to help thy inheritance, and to carry out my undertaking for the destruction of the enemies who have risen up against us."

[6] She went up to the post at the end of the bed, above Holofernes' head, and took down his sword that hung there.

[7] She came close to his bed and took hold of the hair of his head, and said, "Give me strength this day, O Lord God of Israel!"

[8] And she struck his neck twice with all her might, and severed it from his body.

[9] Then she tumbled his body off the bed and pulled down the canopy from the posts; after a moment she went out, and gave Holofernes' head to her maid,

[10] who placed it in her food bag. Then the two of them went out together, as they were accustomed to go for prayer; and they passed through the camp and circled around the valley and went up the mountain to Bethulia and came to its gates.

[11] Judith called out from afar to the watchmen at the gates, "Open, open the gate! God, our God, is still with us, to show his power in Israel, and his strength against our enemies, even as he has done this day!"

[12] When the men of her city heard her voice, they hurried down to the city gate and called together the elders of the city.

[13] They all ran together, both small and great, for it was unbelievable that she had returned; they opened the gate and admitted them, and they kindled a fire for light, and gathered around them.

[14] Then she said to them with a loud voice, "Praise God, O praise him! Praise God, who has not withdrawn his mercy from the house of Israel, but has destroyed our enemies by my hand this very night!"

[15] Then she took the head out of the bag and showed it to them, and said, "See, here is the head of Holofernes, the commander of the Assyrian army, and here is the canopy beneath which he lay in his drunken stupor. The Lord has struck him down by the hand of a woman.

[16] As the Lord lives, who has protected me in the way I went, it was my face that tricked him to his destruction, and yet he committed no act of sin with me, to defile and shame me."

[17] All the people were greatly astonished, and bowed down and worshiped God, and said with one accord, "Blessed art thou, our God, who hast brought into contempt this day the enemies of thy people."

[18] And Uzziah said to her, "O daughter, you are blessed by the Most High God above all women on earth; and blessed be the Lord God, who created the heavens and the earth, who has guided you to strike the head of the leader of our enemies.

[19] Your hope will never depart from the hearts of men, as they remember the power of God.

[20] May God grant this to be a perpetual honor to you, and may he visit you with blessings, because you did not spare your own life when our nation was brought low, but have avenged our ruin, walking in the straight path before our God." And all the people said, "So be it, so be it!"

Jdt.14

[1] Then Judith said to them, "Listen to me, my brethren, and take this head and hang it upon the parapet of your wall.

[2] And as soon as morning comes and the sun rises, let every valiant man take his weapons and go out of the city, and set a captain over them, as if you were going down to the plain against the Assyrian outpost; only do not go down.

[3] Then they will seize their arms and go into the camp and rouse the officers of the Assyrian army; and they will rush into the tent of Holofernes, and will not find him. Then fear will come over them, and they will flee before you,

[4] and you and all who live within the borders of Israel shall pursue them and cut them down as they flee.

[5] But before you do all this, bring Achior the Ammonite to me, and let him see and recognize the man who despised the house of Israel and sent him to us as if to his death."

[6] So they summoned Achior from the house of Uzziah. And when he came and saw the head of Holofernes in the hand of one of the men at the gathering of the people, he fell down on his face and his spirit failed him.

[7] And when they raised him up he fell at Judith's feet, and knelt before her, and said, "Blessed are you in every tent of Judah! In every nation those who hear your name will be alarmed.

[8] Now tell me what you have done during these days." Then Judith described to him in the presence of the people all that she had done, from the day she left until the moment of her speaking to them.

[9] And when she had finished, the people raised a great shout and made a joyful noise in their city.

[10] And when Achior saw all that the God of Israel had done, he believed firmly in God, and was circumcised, and joined the house of Israel, remaining so to this day.

[11] As soon as it was dawn they hung the head of Holofernes on the wall, and every man took his weapons, and they went out in companies to the passes in the mountains.

[12] And when the Assyrians saw them they sent word to their commanders, and they went to the generals and the captains and to all their officers.

[13] So they came to Holofernes' tent and said to the steward in charge of all his personal affairs, "Wake up our lord, for the slaves have been so bold as to come

down against us to give battle, in order to be destroyed completely."

[14] So Bagoas went in and knocked at the door of the tent, for he supposed that he was sleeping with Judith.

[15] But when no one answered, he opened it and went into the bedchamber and found him thrown down on the platform dead, with his head cut off and missing.

[16] And he cried out with a loud voice and wept and groaned and shouted, and rent his garments.

[17] Then he went to the tent where Judith had stayed, and when he did not find her he rushed out to the people and shouted,

[18] "The slaves have tricked us! One Hebrew woman has brought disgrace upon the house of King Nebuchadnezzar! For look, here is Holofernes lying on the ground, and his head is not on him!"

[19] When the leaders of the Assyrian army heard this, they rent their tunics and were greatly dismayed, and their loud cries and shouts arose in the midst of the camp.

Jdt.15

[1] When the men in the tents heard it, they were amazed at what had happened.

[2] Fear and trembling came over them, so that they did not wait for one another, but with one impulse all rushed out and fled by every path across the plain and through the hill country.

[3] Those who had camped in the hills around Bethulia also took to flight. Then the men of Israel, every one that was a soldier, rushed out upon them.

[4] And Uzziah sent men to Betomasthaim and Bebai and Choba and Kola, and to all the frontiers of Israel, to tell what had taken place and to urge all to rush out upon their enemies to destroy them.

[5] And when the Israelites heard it, with one accord they fell upon the enemy, and cut them down as far as Choba. Those in Jerusalem and all the hill country also came, for they were told what had happened in the camp of the enemy; and those in Gilead and in Galilee outflanked them with great slaughter, even beyond Damascus and its borders.

[6] The rest of the people of Bethulia fell upon the Assyrian camp and plundered it, and were greatly enriched.

[7] And the Israelites, when they returned from the slaughter, took possession of what remained, and the villages and towns in the hill country and in the plain got a great amount of booty, for there was a vast quantity of it.

[8] Then Joakim the high priest, and the senate of the people of Israel who lived at Jerusalem, came to witness the good things which the Lord had done for Israel, and to see Judith and to greet her.

[9] And when they met her they all blessed her with one accord and said to her, "You are the exaltation of Jerusalem, you are the great glory of Israel, you are the great pride of our nation!

[10] You have done all this singlehanded; you have done great good to Israel, and God is well pleased with it. May the Almighty Lord bless you for ever!" And all the people said, "So be it!"

[11] So all the people plundered the camp for thirty days. They gave Judith the tent of Holofernes and all his silver dishes and his beds and his bowls and all his furniture; and she took them and loaded her mule and hitched up her carts and piled the things on them.

[12] Then all the women of Israel gathered to see her, and blessed her, and some of them performed a dance for her; and she took branches in her hands and gave them to the women who were with her;

[13] and they crowned themselves with olive wreaths, she and those who were with her; and she went before all the people in the dance, leading all the women, while all the men of Israel followed, bearing their arms and wearing garlands and with songs on their lips.

Jdt.16

[1] Then Judith began this thanksgiving before all Israel, and all the people loudly sang this song of praise.

[2] And Judith said, Begin a song to my God with tambourines, sing to my Lord with cymbals. Raise to him a new psalm; exalt him, and call upon his name.

[3] For God is the Lord who crushes wars; for he has delivered me out of the hands of my pursuers, and brought me to his camp, in the midst of the people.

[4] The Assyrian came down from the mountains of the north; he came with myriads of his warriors; their multitude blocked up the valleys, their cavalry covered the hills.

[5] He boasted that he would burn up my territory, and kill my young men with the sword, and dash my infants to the ground and seize my children as prey, and take my virgins as booty.

[6] But the Lord Almighty has foiled them by the hand of a woman.

[7] For their mighty one did not fall by the hands of the young men, nor did the sons of the Titans smite him, nor did tall giants set upon him; but Judith the daughter of Merari undid him with the beauty of her countenance.

[8] For she took off her widow's mourning to exalt the oppressed in Israel. She anointed her face with ointment and fastened her hair with a tiara and put on a linen gown to deceive him.

[9] Her sandal ravished his eyes, her beauty captivated his mind, and the sword severed his neck.

[10] The Persians trembled at her boldness, the Medes were daunted at her daring.

[11] Then my oppressed people shouted for joy; my weak people shouted and the enemy trembled; they lifted up their voices, and the enemy were turned back.

[12] The sons of maidservants have pierced them through; they were wounded like the children of fugitives, they perished before the army of my Lord.

[13] I will sing to my God a new song: O Lord, thou are great and glorious, wonderful in strength, invincible.

[14] Let all thy creatures serve thee, for thou didst speak, and they were made. Thou didst send forth thy Spirit, and it formed them; there is none that can resist thy voice.

[15] For the mountains shall be shaken to their foundations with the waters; at thy presence the rocks shall melt like wax, but to those who fear thee thou wilt continue to show mercy.

[16] For every sacrifice as a fragrant offering is a small thing, and all fat for burnt offerings to thee is a very little thing, but he who fears the Lord shall be great for ever.

[17] Woe to the nations that rise up against my people! The Lord Almighty will take vengeance on them in the day of judgment; fire and worms he will give to their flesh; they shall weep in pain for ever.

[18] When they arrived at Jerusalem they worshiped God. As soon as the people were purified, they offered their burnt offerings, their freewill offerings, and their gifts.

[19] Judith also dedicated to God all the vessels of Holofernes, which the people had given her; and the canopy which she took for herself from his bedchamber she gave as a votive offering to the Lord.

[20] So the people continued feasting in Jerusalem before the sanctuary for three months, and Judith remained with them.

[21] After this every one returned home to his own inheritance, and Judith went to Bethulia, and remained on her estate, and was honored in her time throughout the whole country.

[22] Many desired to marry her, but she remained a widow all the days of her life after Manasseh her husband died and was gathered to his people.

[23] She became more and more famous, and grew old in her husband's house, until she was one hundred and five years old. She set her maid free. She died in Bethulia, and they buried her in the cave of her husband Manasseh,

[24] and the house of Israel mourned for her seven days. Before she died she distributed her property to all those who were next of kin to her husband Manasseh, and to her own nearest kindred.

[25] And no one ever again spread terror among the people of Israel in the days of Judith, or for a long time after her death.

Wisdom of Solomon

Wis.1

[1] Love righteousness, you rulers of the earth, think of the Lord with uprightness, and seek him with sincerity of heart;

[2] because he is found by those who do not put him to the test, and manifests himself to those who do not distrust him.

[3] For perverse thoughts separate men from God, and when his power is tested, it convicts the foolish;

[4] because wisdom will not enter a deceitful soul, nor dwell in a body enslaved to sin.

[5] For a holy and disciplined spirit will flee from deceit, and will rise and depart from foolish thoughts, and will be ashamed at the approach of unrighteousness.

[6] For wisdom is a kindly spirit and will not free a blasphemer from the guilt of his words; because God is witness of his inmost feelings, and a true observer of his heart, and a hearer of his tongue.

[7] Because the Spirit of the Lord has filled the world, and that which holds all things together knows what is said;

[8] therefore no one who utters unrighteous things will escape notice, and justice, when it punishes, will not pass him by.

[9] For inquiry will be made into the counsels of an ungodly man, and a report of his words will come to the Lord, to convict him of his lawless deeds;

[10] because a jealous ear hears all things, and the sound of murmurings does not go unheard.

[11] Beware then of useless murmuring, and keep your tongue from slander; because no secret word is without result, and a lying mouth destroys the soul.

[12] Do not invite death by the error of your life, nor bring on destruction by the works of your hands;

[13] because God did not make death, and he does not delight in the death of the living.

[14] For he created all things that they might exist, and the generative forces of the world are wholesome, and there is no destructive poison in them; and the dominion of Hades is not on earth.

[15] For righteousness is immortal.

[16] But ungodly men by their words and deeds summoned death; considering him a friend, they pined away, and they made a covenant with him, because they are fit to belong to his party.

Wis.2

[1] For they reasoned unsoundly, saying to themselves, Short and sorrowful is our life, and there is no remedy when a man comes to his end, and no one has been known to return from Hades.

[2] Because we were born by mere chance, and hereafter we shall be as though we had never been;

because the breath in our nostrils is smoke, and reason is a spark kindled by the beating of our hearts.

[3] When it is extinguished, the body will turn to ashes, and the spirit will dissolve like empty air.

[4] Our name will be forgotten in time and no one will remember our works; our life will pass away like the traces of a cloud, and be scattered like mist that is chased by the rays of the sun and overcome by its heat.

[5] For our allotted time is the passing of a shadow, and there is no return from our death, because it is sealed up and no one turns back.

[6] "Come, therefore, let us enjoy the good things that exist, and make use of the creation to the full as in youth.

[7] Let us take our fill of costly wine and perfumes, and let no flower of spring pass by us.

[8] Let us crown ourselves with rosebuds before they wither.

[9] Let none of us fail to share in our revelry, everywhere let us leave signs of enjoyment, because this is our portion, and this our lot.

[10] Let us oppress the righteous poor man; let us not spare the widow nor regard the gray hairs of the aged.

[11] But let our might be our law of right, for what is weak proves itself to be useless.

[12] "Let us lie in wait for the righteous man, because he is inconvenient to us and opposes our actions; he reproaches us for sins against the law, and accuses us of sins against our training.

[13] He professes to have knowledge of God, and calls himself a child of the Lord.

[14] He became to us a reproof of our thoughts;

[15] the very sight of him is a burden to us, because his manner of life is unlike that of others, and his ways are strange.

[16] We are considered by him as something base, and he avoids our ways as unclean; he calls the last end of the righteous happy, and boasts that God is his father.

[17] Let us see if his words are true, and let us test what will happen at the end of his life;

[18] for if the righteous man is God's son, he will help him, and will deliver him from the hand of his adversaries.

[19] Let us test him with insult and torture, that we may find out how gentle he is, and make trial of his forbearance.

[20] Let us condemn him to a shameful death, for, according to what he says, he will be protected."

[21] Thus they reasoned, but they were led astray, for their wickedness blinded them,

[22] and they did not know the secret purposes of God, nor hope for the wages of holiness, nor discern the prize for blameless souls;

[23] for God created man for incorruption, and made him in the image of his own eternity,

[24] but through the devil's envy death entered the world, and those who belong to his party experience it.

Wis.3

[1] But the souls of the righteous are in the hand of God, and no torment will ever touch them.
[2] In the eyes of the foolish they seemed to have died, and their departure was thought to be an affliction,
[3] and their going from us to be their destruction; but they are at peace.
[4] For though in the sight of men they were punished, their hope is full of immortality.
[5] Having been disciplined a little, they will receive great good, because God tested them and found them worthy of himself;
[6] like gold in the furnace he tried them, and like a sacrificial burnt offering he accepted them.
[7] In the time of their visitation they will shine forth, and will run like sparks through the stubble.
[8] They will govern nations and rule over peoples, and the Lord will reign over them for ever.
[9] Those who trust in him will understand truth, and the faithful will abide with him in love, because grace and mercy are upon his elect, and he watches over his holy ones.
[10] But the ungodly will be punished as their reasoning deserves, who disregarded the righteous man and rebelled against the Lord;
[11] for whoever despises wisdom and instruction is miserable. Their hope is vain, their labors are unprofitable, and their works are useless.
[12] Their wives are foolish, and their children evil;
[13] their offspring are accursed. For blessed is the barren woman who is undefiled, who has not entered into a sinful union; she will have fruit when God examines souls.
[14] Blessed also is the eunuch whose hands have done no lawless deed, and who has not devised wicked things against the Lord; for special favor will be shown him for his faithfulness, and a place of great delight in the temple of the Lord.
[15] For the fruit of good labors is renowned, and the root of understanding does not fail.
[16] But children of adulterers will not come to maturity, and the offspring of an unlawful union will perish.
[17] Even if they live long they will be held of no account, and finally their old age will be without honor.
[18] If they die young, they will have no hope and no consolation in the day of decision.
[19] For the end of an unrighteous generation is grievous.

Wis.4

[1] Better than this is childlessness with virtue, for in the memory of virtue is immortality, because it is known both by God and by men.
[2] When it is present, men imitate it, and they long for it when it has gone; and throughout all time it marches crowned in triumph, victor in the contest for prizes that are undefiled.
[3] But the prolific brood of the ungodly will be of no use, and none of their illegitimate seedlings will strike a deep root or take a firm hold.
[4] For even if they put forth boughs for a while, standing insecurely they will be shaken by the wind, and by the violence of the winds they will be uprooted.
[5] The branches will be broken off before they come to maturity, and their fruit will be useless, not ripe enough to eat, and good for nothing.
[6] For children born of unlawful unions are witnesses of evil against their parents when God examines them.
[7] But the righteous man, though he die early, will be at rest.
[8] For old age is not honored for length of time, nor measured by number of years;
[9] but understanding is gray hair for men, and a blameless life is ripe old age.
[10] There was one who pleased God and was loved by him, and while living among sinners he was taken up.
[11] He was caught up lest evil change his understanding or guile deceive his soul.
[12] For the fascination of wickedness obscures what is good, and roving desire perverts the innocent mind.
[13] Being perfected in a short time, he fulfilled long years;
[14] for his soul was pleasing to the Lord, therefore he took him quickly from the midst of wickedness.
[15] Yet the peoples saw and did not understand, nor take such a thing to heart, that God's grace and mercy are with his elect, and he watches over his holy ones.
[16] The righteous man who had died will condemn the ungodly who are living, and youth that is quickly perfected will condemn the prolonged old age of the unrighteous man.
[17] For they will see the end of the wise man, and will not understand what the Lord purposed for him, and for what he kept him safe.
[18] They will see, and will have contempt for him, but the Lord will laugh them to scorn. After this they will become dishonored corpses, and an outrage among the dead for ever;
[19] because he will dash them speechless to the ground, and shake them from the foundations; they will be left utterly dry and barren, and they will suffer anguish, and the memory of them will perish.

[20] They will come with dread when their sins are reckoned up, and their lawless deeds will convict them to their face.

Wis.5
[1] Then the righteous man will stand with great confidence in the presence of those who have afflicted him, and those who make light of his labors.
[2] When they see him, they will be shaken with dreadful fear, and they will be amazed at his unexpected salvation.
[3] They will speak to one another in repentance, and in anguish of spirit they will groan, and say,
[4] "This is the man whom we once held in derision and made a byword of reproach -- we fools! We thought that his life was madness and that his end was without honor.
[5] Why has he been numbered among the sons of God? And why is his lot among the saints?
[6] So it was we who strayed from the way of truth, and the light of righteousness did not shine on us, and the sun did not rise upon us.
[7] We took our fill of the paths of lawlessness and destruction, and we journeyed through trackless deserts, but the way of the Lord we have not known.
[8] What has our arrogance profited us? And what good has our boasted wealth brought us?
[9] "All those things have vanished like a shadow, and like a rumor that passes by;
[10] like a ship that sails through the billowy water, and when it has passed no trace can be found, nor track of its keel in the waves;
[11] or as, when a bird flies through the air, no evidence of its passage is found; the light air, lashed by the beat of its pinions and pierced by the force of its rushing flight, is traversed by the movement of its wings, and afterward no sign of its coming is found there;
[12] or as, when an arrow is shot at a target, the air, thus divided, comes together at once, so that no one knows its pathway.
[13] So we also, as soon as we were born, ceased to be, and we had no sign of virtue to show, but were consumed in our wickedness."
[14] Because the hope of the ungodly man is like chaff carried by the wind, and like a light hoarfrost driven away by a storm; it is dispersed like smoke before the wind, and it passes like the remembrance of a guest who stays but a day.
[15] But the righteous live for ever, and their reward is with the Lord; the Most High takes care of them.
[16] Therefore they will receive a glorious crown and a beautiful diadem from the hand of the Lord, because with his right hand he will cover them, and with his arm he will shield them.
[17] The Lord will take his zeal as his whole armor, and will arm all creation to repel his enemies;

[18] he will put on righteousness as a breastplate, and wear impartial justice as a helmet;
[19] he will take holiness as an invincible shield,
[20] and sharpen stern wrath for a sword, and creation will join with him to fight against the madmen.
[21] Shafts of lightning will fly with true aim, and will leap to the target as from a well-drawn bow of clouds,
[22] and hailstones full of wrath will be hurled as from a catapult; the water of the sea will rage against them, and rivers will relentlessly overwhelm them;
[23] a mighty wind will rise against them , and like a tempest it will winnow them away. Lawlessness will lay waste the whole earth, and evil-doing will overturn the thrones of rulers.

Wis.6
[1] Listen therefore, O kings, and understand; learn, O judges of the ends of the earth.
[2] Give ear, you that rule over multitudes, and boast of many nations.
[3] For your dominion was given you from the Lord, and your sovereignty from the Most High, who will search out your works and inquire into your plans.
[4] Because as servants of his kingdom you did not rule rightly, nor keep the law, nor walk according to the purpose of God,
[5] he will come upon you terribly and swiftly, because severe judgment falls on those in high places.
[6] For the lowliest man may be pardoned in mercy, but mighty men will be mightily tested.
[7] For the Lord of all will not stand in awe of any one, nor show deference to greatness; because he himself made both small and great, and he takes thought for all alike.
[8] But a strict inquiry is in store for the mighty.
[9] To you then, O monarchs, my words are directed, that you may learn wisdom and not transgress.
[10] For they will be made holy who observe holy things in holiness, and those who have been taught them will find a defense.
[11] Therefore set your desire on my words; long for them, and you will be instructed.
[12] Wisdom is radiant and unfading, and she is easily discerned by those who love her, and is found by those who seek her.
[13] She hastens to make herself known to those who desire her.
[14] He who rises early to seek her will have no difficulty, for he will find her sitting at his gates.
[15] To fix one's thought on her is perfect understanding, and he who is vigilant on her account will soon be free from care,
[16] because she goes about seeking those worthy of her, and she graciously appears to them in their paths, and meets them in every thought.

[17] The beginning of wisdom is the most sincere desire for instruction, and concern for instruction is love of her,

[18] and love of her is the keeping of her laws, and giving heed to her laws is assurance of immortality,

[19] and immortality brings one near to God;

[20] so the desire for wisdom leads to a kingdom.

[21] Therefore if you delight in thrones and scepters, O monarchs over the peoples, honor wisdom, that you may reign for ever.

[22] I will tell you what wisdom is and how she came to be, and I will hide no secrets from you, but I will trace her course from the beginning of creation, and make knowledge of her clear, and I will not pass by the truth;

[23] neither will I travel in the company of sickly envy, for envy does not associate with wisdom.

[24] A multitude of wise men is the salvation of the world, and a sensible king is the stability of his people.

[25] Therefore be instructed by my words, and you will profit.

Wis.7

[1] I also am mortal, like all men, a descendant of the first-formed child of earth; and in the womb of a mother I was molded into flesh,

[2] within the period of ten months, compacted with blood, from the seed of a man and the pleasure of marriage.

[3] And when I was born, I began to breathe the common air, and fell upon the kindred earth, and my first sound was a cry, like that of all.

[4] I was nursed with care in swaddling cloths.

[5] For no king has had a different beginning of existence;

[6] there is for all mankind one entrance into life, and a common departure.

[7] Therefore I prayed, and understanding was given me; I called upon God, and the spirit of wisdom came to me.

[8] I preferred her to scepters and thrones, and I accounted wealth as nothing in comparison with her.

[9] Neither did I liken to her any priceless gem, because all gold is but a little sand in her sight, and silver will be accounted as clay before her.

[10] I loved her more than health and beauty, and I chose to have her rather than light, because her radiance never ceases.

[11] All good things came to me along with her, and in her hands uncounted wealth.

[12] I rejoiced in them all, because wisdom leads them; but I did not know that she was their mother.

[13] I learned without guile and I impart without grudging; I do not hide her wealth,

[14] for it is an unfailing treasure for men; those who get it obtain friendship with God, commended for the gifts that come from instruction.

[15] May God grant that I speak with judgment and have thought worthy of what I have received, for he is the guide even of wisdom and the corrector of the wise.

[16] For both we and our words are in his hand, as are all understanding and skill in crafts.

[17] For it is he who gave me unerring knowledge of what exists, to know the structure of the world and the activity of the elements;

[18] the beginning and end and middle of times, the alternations of the solstices and the changes of the seasons,

[19] the cycles of the year and the constellations of the stars,

[20] the natures of animals and the tempers of wild beasts, the powers of spirits and the reasonings of men, the varieties of plants and the virtues of roots;

[21] I learned both what is secret and what is manifest,

[22] for wisdom, the fashioner of all things, taught me. For in her there is a spirit that is intelligent, holy, unique, manifold, subtle, mobile, clear, unpolluted, distinct, invulnerable, loving the good, keen, irresistible,

[23] beneficent, humane, steadfast, sure, free from anxiety, all-powerful, overseeing all, and penetrating through all spirits
that are intelligent and pure and most subtle.

[24] For wisdom is more mobile than any motion; because of her pureness she pervades and penetrates all things.

[25] For she is a breath of the power of God, and a pure emanation of the glory of the Almighty; therefore nothing defiled gains entrance into her.

[26] For she is a reflection of eternal light, a spotless mirror of the working of God, and an image of his goodness.

[27] Though she is but one, she can do all things, and while remaining in herself, she renews all things; in every generation she passes into holy souls and makes them friends of God, and prophets;

[28] for God loves nothing so much as the man who lives with wisdom.

[29] For she is more beautiful than the sun, and excels every constellation of the stars. Compared with the light she is found to be superior,

[30] for it is succeeded by the night, but against wisdom evil does not prevail.

Wis.8

[1] She reaches mightily from one end of the earth to the other, and she orders all things well.

[2] I loved her and sought her from my youth, and I desired to take her for my bride, and I became enamored of her beauty.

[3] She glorifies her noble birth by living with God, and the Lord of all loves her.

[4] For she is an initiate in the knowledge of God, and an associate in his works.

[5] If riches are a desirable possession in life, what is richer than wisdom who effects all things?

[6] And if understanding is effective, who more than she is fashioner of what exists?

[7] And if any one loves righteousness, her labors are virtues; for she teaches self-control and prudence, justice and courage; nothing in life is more profitable for men than these.

[8] And if any one longs for wide experience, she knows the things of old, and infers the things to come; she understands turns of speech and the solutions of riddles; she has foreknowledge of signs and wonders and of the outcome of seasons and times.

[9] Therefore I determined to take her to live with me, knowing that she would give me good counsel and encouragement in cares and grief.

[10] Because of her I shall have glory among the multitudes and honor in the presence of the elders, though I am young.

[11] I shall be found keen in judgment, and in the sight of rulers I shall be admired.

[12] When I am silent they will wait for me, and when I speak they will give heed; and when I speak at greater length
they will put their hands on their mouths.

[13] Because of her I shall have immortality, and leave an everlasting remembrance to those who come after me.

[14] I shall govern peoples, and nations will be subject to me;

[15] dread monarchs will be afraid of me when they hear of me; among the people I shall show myself capable, and courageous in war.

[16] When I enter my house, I shall find rest with her, for companionship with her has no bitterness, and life with her has no pain, but gladness and joy.

[17] When I considered these things inwardly, and thought upon them in my mind, that in kinship with wisdom there is immortality,

[18] and in friendship with her, pure delight, and in the labors of her hands, unfailing wealth, and in the experience of her company, understanding, and renown in sharing her words, I went about seeking how to get her for myself.

[19] As a child I was by nature well endowed, and a good soul fell to my lot;

[20] or rather, being good, I entered an undefiled body.

[21] But I perceived that I would not possess wisdom unless God gave her to me -- and it was a mark of insight to know whose gift she was -- so I appealed to the Lord and besought him, and with my whole heart I said:

Wis.9

[1] "O God of my fathers and Lord of mercy, who hast made all things by thy word,

[2] and by thy wisdom hast formed man, to have dominion over the creatures thou hast made,

[3] and rule the world in holiness and righteousness, and pronounce judgment in uprightness of soul,

[4] give me the wisdom that sits by thy throne, and do not reject me from among thy servants.

[5] For I am thy slave and the son of thy maidservant, a man who is weak and short-lived, with little understanding of judgment and laws;

[6] for even if one is perfect among the sons of men, yet without the wisdom that comes from thee he will be regarded as nothing.

[7] Thou hast chosen me to be king of thy people and to be judge over thy sons and daughters.

[8] Thou hast given command to build a temple on thy holy mountain, and an altar in the city of thy habitation, a copy of the holy tent which thou didst prepare from the beginning.

[9] With thee is wisdom, who knows thy works and was present when thou didst make the world, and who understand what is pleasing in thy sight and what is right according to thy commandments.

[10] Send her forth from the holy heavens, and from the throne of thy glory send her, that she may be with me and toil,
and that I may learn what is pleasing to thee.

[11] For she knows and understands all things, and she will guide me wisely in my actions and guard me with her glory.

[12] Then my works will be acceptable, and I shall judge thy people justly, and shall be worthy of the throne of my father.

[13] For what man can learn the counsel of God? Or who can discern what the Lord wills?

[14] For the reasoning of mortals is worthless, and our designs are likely to fail,

[15] for a perishable body weighs down the soul, and this earthy tent burdens the thoughtful mind.

[16] We can hardly guess at what is on earth, and what is at hand we find with labor; but who has traced out what is in the heavens?

[17] Who has learned thy counsel, unless thou hast given wisdom and sent thy holy Spirit from on high?

[18] And thus the paths of those on earth were set right, and men were taught what pleases thee, and were saved by wisdom."

Wis.10

[1] Wisdom protected the first-formed father of the world, when he alone had been created; she delivered him from his transgression,

[2] and gave him strength to rule all things.

[3] But when an unrighteous man departed from her in his anger, he perished because in rage he slew his brother.

[4] When the earth was flooded because of him, wisdom again saved it, steering the righteous man by a paltry piece of wood.

[5] Wisdom also, when the nations in wicked agreement had been confounded, recognized the righteous man and preserved him blameless before God, and kept him strong in the face of his compassion for his child.

[6] Wisdom rescued a righteous man when the ungodly were perishing; he escaped the fire that descended on the Five Cities.

[7] Evidence of their wickedness still remains: a continually smoking wasteland, plants bearing fruit that does not ripen,

and a pillar of salt standing as a monument to an unbelieving soul.

[8] For because they passed wisdom by, they not only were hindered from recognizing the good, but also left for mankind a reminder of their folly, so that their failures could never go unnoticed.

[9] Wisdom rescued from troubles those who served her.

[10] When a righteous man fled from his brother's wrath, she guided him on straight paths; she showed him the kingdom of God, and gave him knowledge of angels; she prospered him in his labors, and increased the fruit of his toil.

[11] When his oppressors were covetous, she stood by him and made him rich.

[12] She protected him from his enemies, and kept him safe from those who lay in wait for him; in his arduous contest she gave him the victory, so that he might learn that godliness is more powerful than anything.

[13] When a righteous man was sold, wisdom did not desert him, but delivered him from sin. She descended with him into the dungeon,

[14] and when he was in prison she did not leave him, until she brought him the scepter of a kingdom and authority over his masters. Those who accused him she showed to be false, and she gave him everlasting honor.

[15] A holy people and blameless race wisdom delivered from a nation of oppressors.

[16] She entered the soul of a servant of the Lord, and withstood dread kings with wonders and signs.

[17] She gave holy men the reward of their labors; she guided them along a marvelous way, and became a shelter to them by day, and a starry flame through the night.

[18] She brought them over the Red Sea, and led them through deep waters;

[19] but she drowned their enemies, and cast them up from the depth of the sea.

[20] Therefore the righteous plundered the ungodly; they sang hymns, O Lord, to thy holy name, and praised with one accord thy defending hand,

[21] because wisdom opened the mouth of the dumb, and made the tongues of babes speak clearly.

Wis.11

[1] Wisdom prospered their works by the hand of a holy prophet.

[2] They journeyed through an uninhabited wilderness, and pitched their tents in untrodden places.

[3] They withstood their enemies and fought off their foes.

[4] When they thirsted they called upon thee, and water was given them out of flinty rock, and slaking of thirst from hard stone.

[5] For through the very things by which their enemies were punished, they themselves received benefit in their need.

[6] Instead of the fountain of an ever-flowing river, stirred up and defiled with blood

[7] in rebuke for the decree to slay the infants, thou gavest them abundant water unexpectedly,

[8] showing by their thirst at that time how thou didst punish their enemies.

[9] For when they were tried, though they were being disciplined in mercy, they learned how the ungodly were tormented

when judged in wrath.

[10] For thou didst test them as a father does in warning, but thou didst examine the ungodly as a stern

king does in condemnation.

[11] Whether absent or present, they were equally distressed,

[12] for a twofold grief possessed them, and a groaning at the memory of what had occurred.

[13] For when they heard that through their own punishments the righteous had received benefit, they perceived it was the Lord's doing.

[14] For though they had mockingly rejected him who long before had been cast out and exposed, at the end of the events they marveled at him, for their thirst was not like that of the righteous.

[15] In return for their foolish and wicked thoughts, which led them astray to worship irrational serpents and worthless animals, thou didst send upon them a multitude of irrational creatures to punish them,

[16] that they might learn that one is punished by the very things by which he sins.

[17] For thy all-powerful hand, which created the world out of formless matter, did not lack the means to send upon them a multitude of bears, or bold lions,
[18] or newly created unknown beasts full of rage, or such as breathe out fiery breath, or belch forth a thick pall of smoke, or flash terrible sparks from their eyes;
[19] not only could their damage exterminate men, but the mere sight of them could kill by fright.
[20] Even apart from these, men could fall at a single breath when pursued by justice and scattered by the breath of thy power. But thou hast arranged all things by measure and number and weight.
[21] For it is always in thy power to show great strength, and who can withstand the might of thy arm?
[22] Because the whole world before thee is like a speck that tips the scales, and like a drop of morning dew that falls upon the ground.
[23] But thou art merciful to all, for thou canst do all things, and thou do overlook men's sins, that they may repent.
[24] For thou lovest all things that exist, and hast loathing for none of the things which thou hast made, for thou wouldst not have made anything if thou hadst hated it.
[25] How would anything have endured if thou hadst not willed it? Or how would anything not called forth by thee
have been preserved?
[26] Thou sparest all things, for they are your, O Lord who lovest the living.

Wis.12
[1] For thy immortal spirit is in all things.
[2] Therefore thou do correct little by little those who trespass, and do remind and warn them of the things wherein they sin, that they may be freed from wickedness and put their trust in thee, O Lord.
[3] Those who dwelt of old in thy holy land
[4] thou didst hate for their detestable practices, their works of sorcery and unholy rites,
[5] their merciless slaughter of children, and their sacrificial feasting on human flesh and blood. These initiates from the midst of a heathen cult,
[6] these parents who murder helpless lives, thou didst will to destroy by the hands of our fathers,
[7] that the land most precious of all to thee might receive a worthy colony of the servants of God.
[8] But even these thou didst spare, since they were but men, and didst send wasps as forerunners of thy army, to destroy them little by little,
[9] though thou wast not unable to give the ungodly into the hands of the righteous in battle, or to destroy them at one blow by dread wild beasts or thy stern word.
[10] But judging them little by little thou gavest them a chance to repent, though thou wast not unaware

that their origin was evil and their wickedness inborn, and that their way of thinking would never change.
[11] For they were an accursed race from the beginning, and it was not through fear of any one that thou didst leave them unpunished for their sins.
[12] For who will say, "What hast thou done?" Or will resist thy judgment? Who will accuse thee for the destruction of
nations which thou didst make? Or who will come before thee to plead as an advocate for unrighteous men?
[13] For neither is there any god besides thee, whose care is for all men, to whom thou shouldst prove that thou hast not judged unjustly;
[14] nor can any king or monarch confront thee about those whom thou hast punished.
[15] Thou art righteous and rulest all things righteously, deeming it alien to thy power to condemn him who does not deserve to be punished.
[16] For thy strength is the source of righteousness, and thy sovereignty over all causes thee to spare all.
[17] For thou do show thy strength when men doubt the completeness of thy power, and do rebuke any insolence among those who know it.
[18] Thou who art sovereign in strength do judge with mildness, and with great forbearance thou do govern us; for thou hast power to act whenever thou do choose.
[19] Through such works thou has taught thy people that the righteous man must be kind, and thou hast filled thy sons with good hope, because thou givest repentance for sins.
[20] For if thou didst punish with such great care and indulgence the enemies of thy servants and those deserving of death,
granting them time and opportunity to give up their wickedness,
[21] with what strictness thou hast judged thy sons, to whose fathers thou gavest oaths and covenants full of good promises!
[22] So while chastening us thou scourgest our enemies ten thousand times more, so that we may meditate upon thy goodness when we judge, and when we are judged we may expect mercy.
[23] Therefore those who in folly of life lived unrighteously thou didst torment through their own abominations.
[24] For they went far astray on the paths of error, accepting as gods those animals which even their enemies despised;
they were deceived like foolish babes.
[25] Therefore, as to thoughtless children, thou didst send thy judgment to mock them.
[26] But those who have not heeded the warning of light rebukes will experience the deserved judgment of God.

[27] For when in their suffering they became incensed at those creatures which they had thought to be gods, being punished by means of them, they saw and recognized as the true God him whom they had before refused to know.
Therefore the utmost condemnation came upon them.

Wis.13
[1] For all men who were ignorant of God were foolish by nature; and they were unable from the good things that
are seen to know him who exists, nor did they recognize the craftsman while paying heed to his works;
[2] but they supposed that either fire or wind or swift air, or the circle of the stars, or turbulent water, or the luminaries of heaven were the gods that rule the world.
[3] If through delight in the beauty of these things men assumed them to be gods, let them know how much better than these is their Lord, for the author of beauty created them.
[4] And if men were amazed at their power and working, let them perceive from them how much more powerful is he who formed them.
[5] For from the greatness and beauty of created things comes a corresponding perception of their Creator.
[6] Yet these men are little to be blamed, for perhaps they go astray while seeking God and desiring to find him.
[7] For as they live among his works they keep searching, and they trust in what they see, because the things that are seen are beautiful.
[8] Yet again, not even they are to be excused;
[9] for if they had the power to know so much that they could investigate the world, how did they fail to find sooner the Lord of these things?
[10] But miserable, with their hopes set on dead things, are the men who give the name "gods" to the works of men's hands, gold and silver fashioned with skill, and likenesses of animals, or a useless stone, the work of an ancient hand.
[11] A skilled woodcutter may saw down a tree easy to handle and skilfully strip off all its bark, and then with pleasing workmanship make a useful vessel that serves life's needs,
[12] and burn the castoff pieces of his work to prepare his food, and eat his fill.
[13] But a castoff piece from among them, useful for nothing, a stick crooked and full of knots, he takes and carves with care in his leisure, and shapes it with skill gained in idleness; he forms it like the image of a man,
[14] or makes it like some worthless animal, giving it a coat of red paint and coloring its surface red and covering every blemish in it with paint;

[15] then he makes for it a niche that befits it, and sets it in the wall, and fastens it there with iron.
[16] So he takes thought for it, that it may not fall, because he knows that it cannot help itself, for it is only an image and has need of help.
[17] When he prays about possessions and his marriage and children, he is not ashamed to address a lifeless thing.
[18] For health he appeals to a thing that is weak; for life he prays to a thing that is dead; for aid he entreats a thing that is utterly inexperienced; for a prosperous journey, a thing that cannot take a step;
[19] for money-making and work and success with his hands he asks strength of a thing whose hands have no strength.

Wis.14
[1] Again, one preparing to sail and about to voyage over raging waves calls upon a piece of wood more fragile than the ship which carries him.
[2] For it was desire for gain that planned that vessel, and wisdom was the craftsman who built it;
[3] but it is thy providence, O Father, that steers its course, because thou hast given it a path in the sea, and a safe way through the waves,
[4] showing that thou canst save from every danger, so that even if a man lacks skill, he may put to sea.
[5] It is thy will that works of thy wisdom should not be without effect; therefore men trust their lives even to the smallest piece of wood, and passing through the billows on a raft they come safely to land.
[6] For even in the beginning, when arrogant giants were perishing, the hope of the world took refuge on a raft, and guided by thy hand left to the world the seed of a new generation.
[7] For blessed is the wood by which righteousness comes.
[8] But the idol made with hands is accursed, and so is he who made it; because he did the work, and the perishable thing was named a god.
[9] For equally hateful to God are the ungodly man and his ungodliness,
[10] for what was done will be punished together with him who did it.
[11] Therefore there will be a visitation also upon the heathen idols, because, though part of what God created, they became an abomination, and became traps for the souls of men and a snare to the feet of the foolish.
[12] For the idea of making idols was the beginning of fornication, and the invention of them was the corruption of life,
[13] for neither have they existed from the beginning nor will they exist for ever.
[14] For through the vanity of men they entered the world, and therefore their speedy end has been planned.

[15] For a father, consumed with grief at an untimely bereavement, made an image of his child, who had been suddenly

taken from him; and he now honored as a god what was once a dead human being, and handed on to his dependents secret rites and initiations.

[16] Then the ungodly custom, grown strong with time, was kept as a law, and at the command of monarchs graven images were worshiped.

[17] When men could not honor monarchs in their presence, since they lived at a distance, they imagined their appearance far away, and made a visible image of the king whom they honored, so that by their zeal they might flatter the absent one as though present.

[18] Then the ambition of the craftsman impelled even those who did not know the king to intensify their worship.

[19] For he, perhaps wishing to please his ruler, skilfully forced the likeness to take more beautiful form,

[20] and the multitude, attracted by the charm of his work, now regarded as an object of worship the one whom shortly before they had honored as a man.

[21] And this became a hidden trap for mankind, because men, in bondage to misfortune or to royal authority, bestowed on objects of stone or wood the name that ought not to be shared.

[22] Afterward it was not enough for them to err about the knowledge of God, but they live in great strife due to ignorance, and they call such great evils peace.

[23] For whether they kill children in their initiations, or celebrate secret mysteries, or hold frenzied revels with strange customs,

[24] they no longer keep either their lives or their marriages pure, but they either treacherously kill one another, or grieve one another by adultery,

[25] and all is a raging riot of blood and murder, theft and deceit, corruption, faithlessness, tumult, perjury,

[26] confusion over what is good, forgetfulness of favors, pollution of souls, sex perversion, disorder in marriage, adultery, and debauchery.

[27] For the worship of idols not to be named is the beginning and cause and end of every evil.

[28] For their worshipers either rave in exultation, or prophesy lies, or live unrighteously, or readily commit perjury;

[29] for because they trust in lifeless idols they swear wicked oaths and expect to suffer no harm.

[30] But just penalties will overtake them on two counts: because they thought wickedly of God in devoting themselves to idols, and because in deceit they swore unrighteously through contempt for holiness.

[31] For it is not the power of the things by which men swear, but the just penalty for those who sin, that always pursues the transgression of the unrighteous.

Wis.15
[1] But thou, our God, art kind and true, patient, and ruling all things in mercy.

[2] For even if we sin we are your, knowing thy power; but we will not sin, because we know that we are accounted your.

[3] For to know thee is complete righteousness, and to know thy power is the root of immortality.

[4] For neither has the evil intent of human art misled us, nor the fruitless toil of painters, a figure stained with varied colors,

[5] whose appearance arouses yearning in fools, so that they desire the lifeless form of a dead image.

[6] Lovers of evil things and fit for such objects of hope are those who either make or desire or worship them.

[7] For when a potter kneads the soft earth and laboriously molds each vessel for our service, he fashions out of the same clay both the vessels that serve clean uses and those for contrary uses, making all in like manner; but which shall be the use of each of these the worker in clay decides.

[8] With misspent toil, he forms a futile god from the same clay -- this man who was made of earth a short time before

and after a little while goes to the earth from which he was taken, when he is required to return the soul that was lent him.

[9] But he is not concerned that he is destined to die or that his life is brief, but he competes with workers in gold and silver, and imitates workers in copper; and he counts it his glory that he molds counterfeit gods.

[10] His heart is ashes, his hope is cheaper than dirt, and his life is of less worth than clay,

[11] because he failed to know the one who formed him and inspired him with an active soul and breathed into him a living spirit.

[12] But he considered our existence an idle game, and life a festival held for profit, for he says one must get money however one can, even by base means.

[13] For this man, more than all others, knows that he sins when he makes from earthy matter fragile vessels and graven images.

[14] But most foolish, and more miserable than an infant, are all the enemies who oppressed thy people.

[15] For they thought that all their heathen idols were gods, though these have neither the use of their eyes to see with, nor nostrils with which to draw breath, nor ears with which to hear, nor fingers to feel with, and their feet are of no use for walking.

[16] For a man made them, and one whose spirit is borrowed formed them; for no man can form a god which is like himself.

[17] He is mortal, and what he makes with lawless hands is dead, for he is better than the objects he worships, since he has life, but they never have.
[18] The enemies of thy people worship even the most hateful animals, which are worse than all others, when judged by their lack of intelligence;
[19] and even as animals they are not so beautiful in appearance that one would desire them, but they have escaped both the praise of God and his blessing.

Wis.16
[1] Therefore those men were deservedly punished through such creatures, and were tormented by a multitude of animals.
[2] Instead of this punishment thou didst show kindness to thy people, and thou didst prepare quails to eat, a delicacy to satisfy the desire of appetite;
[3] in order that those men, when they desired food, might lose the least remnant of appetite because of the odious creatures sent to them, while thy people, after suffering want a short time, might partake of delicacies.
[4] For it was necessary that upon those oppressors inexorable want should come, while to these it was merely shown how their enemies were being tormented.
[5] For when the terrible rage of wild beasts came upon thy people and they were being destroyed by the bites of writhing serpents, thy wrath did not continue to the end;
[6] they were troubled for a little while as a warning, and received a token of deliverance to remind them of thy law's command.
[7] For he who turned toward it was saved, not by what he saw, but by thee, the Savior of all.
[8] And by this also thou didst convince our enemies that it is thou who deliverest from every evil.
[9] For they were killed by the bites of locusts and flies, and no healing was found for them, because they deserved to be punished by such things;
[10] but thy sons were not conquered even by the teeth of venomous serpents, for thy mercy came to their help and healed them.
[11] To remind them of thy oracles they were bitten, and then were quickly delivered, lest they should fall into deep forgetfulness and become unresponsive to thy kindness.
[12] For neither herb nor poultice cured them, but it was thy word, O Lord, which heals all men.
[13] For thou hast power over life and death; thou do lead men down to the gates of Hades and back again.
[14] A man in his wickedness kills another, but he cannot bring back the departed spirit, nor set free the imprisoned soul.
[15] To escape from thy hand is impossible;
[16] for the ungodly, refusing to know thee, were scourged by the strength of thy arm, pursued by

unusual rains and hail and relentless storms, and utterly consumed by fire.
[17] For -- most incredible of all -- in the water, which quenches all things, the fire had still greater effect, for the universe defends the righteous.
[18] At one time the flame was restrained, so that it might not consume the creatures sent against the ungodly, but that seeing this they might know that they were being pursued by the judgment of God;
[19] and at another time even in the midst of water it burned more intensely than fire, to destroy the crops of the unrighteous land.
[20] Instead of these things thou didst give thy people food of angels, and without their toil thou didst supply them
from heaven with bread ready to eat, providing every pleasure and suited to every taste.
[21] For thy sustenance manifested thy sweetness toward thy children; and the bread, ministering to the desire of the one who took it, was changed to suit every one's liking.
[22] Snow and ice withstood fire without melting, so that they might know that the crops of their enemies were being destroyed by the fire that blazed in the hail and flashed in the showers of rain;
[23] whereas the fire, in order that the righteous might be fed, even forgot its native power.
[24] For creation, serving thee who hast made it, exerts itself to punish the unrighteous, and in kindness relaxes on behalf of those who trust in thee.
[25] Therefore at that time also, changed into all forms, it served thy all-nourishing bounty, according to the desire of those who had need,
[26] so that thy sons, whom thou didst love, O Lord, might learn that it is not the production of crops that feeds man, but that thy word preserves those who trust in thee.
[27] For what was not destroyed by fire was melted when simply warmed by a fleeting ray of the sun,
[28] to make it known that one must rise before the sun to give thee thanks, and must pray to thee at the dawning of the light;
[29] for the hope of an ungrateful man will melt like wintry frost, and flow away like waste water.

Wis.17
[1] Great are thy judgments and hard to describe; therefore uninstructed souls have gone astray.
[2] For when lawless men supposed that they held the holy nation in their power, they themselves lay as captives of darkness and prisoners of long night, shut in under their roofs, exiles from eternal providence.
[3] For thinking that in their secret sins they were unobserved behind a dark curtain of forgetfulness, they were scattered, terribly alarmed, and appalled by specters.

[4] For not even the inner chamber that held them protected them from fear, but terrifying sounds rang out around them,
and dismal phantoms with gloomy faces appeared.
[5] And no power of fire was able to give light, nor did the brilliant flames of the stars avail to illumine that hateful night.
[6] Nothing was shining through to them except a dreadful, self-kindled fire, and in terror they deemed the things which they saw to be worse than that unseen appearance.
[7] The delusions of their magic art lay humbled, and their boasted wisdom was scornfully rebuked.
[8] For those who promised to drive off the fears and disorders of a sick soul were sick themselves with ridiculous fear.
[9] For even if nothing disturbing frightened them, yet, scared by the passing of beasts and the hissing of serpents,
[10] they perished in trembling fear, refusing to look even at the air, though it nowhere could be avoided.
[11] For wickedness is a cowardly thing, condemned by its own testimony; distressed by conscience, it has always exaggerated the difficulties.
[12] For fear is nothing but surrender of the helps that come from reason;
[13] and the inner expectation of help, being weak, prefers ignorance of what causes the torment.
[14] But throughout the night, which was really powerless, and which beset them from the recesses of powerless Hades,
they all slept the same sleep,
[15] and now were driven by monstrous specters, and now were paralyzed by their souls' surrender, for sudden and unexpected fear overwhelmed them.
[16] And whoever was there fell down, and thus was kept shut up in a prison not made of iron;
[17] for whether he was a farmer or a shepherd or a workman who toiled in the wilderness, he was seized, and endured the inescapable fate; for with one chain of darkness they all were bound.
[18] Whether there came a whistling wind, or a melodious sound of birds in wide-spreading branches, or the rhythm of violently rushing water,
[19] or the harsh crash of rocks hurled down, or the unseen running of leaping animals, or the sound of the most savage roaring beasts, or an echo thrown back from a hollow of the mountains, it paralyzed them with terror.
[20] For the whole world was illumined with brilliant light, and was engaged in unhindered work,
[21] while over those men alone heavy night was spread, an image of the darkness that was destined to receive them;
but still heavier than darkness were they to themselves.

Wis.18
[1] But for thy holy ones there was very great light. Their enemies heard their voices but did not see their forms, and counted them happy for not having suffered,
[2] and were thankful that thy holy ones, though previously wronged, were doing them no injury; and they begged their pardon for having been at variance with them.
[3] Therefore thou didst provide a flaming pillar of fire as a guide for thy people's unknown journey, and a harmless sun for their glorious wandering.
[4] For their enemies deserved to be deprived of light and imprisoned in darkness, those who had kept thy sons imprisoned, through whom the imperishable light of the law was to be given to the world.
[5] When they had resolved to kill the babes of thy holy ones, and one child had been exposed and rescued, thou didst in punishment take away a multitude of their children; and thou didst destroy them all together by a mighty flood.
[6] That night was made known beforehand to our fathers, so that they might rejoice in sure knowledge of the oaths in which they trusted.
[7] The deliverance of the righteous and the destruction of their enemies were expected by thy people.
[8] For by the same means by which thou didst punish our enemies thou didst call us to thyself and glorify us.
[9] For in secret the holy children of good men offered sacrifices, and with one accord agreed to the divine law, that the saints would share alike the same things, both blessings and dangers; and already they were singing the praises of the fathers.
[10] But the discordant cry of their enemies echoed back, and their piteous lament for their children was spread abroad.
[11] The slave was punished with the same penalty as the master, and the common man suffered the same loss as the king;
[12] and they all together, by the one form of death, had corpses too many to count. For the living were not sufficient even to bury them, since in one instant their most valued children had been destroyed.
[13] For though they had disbelieved everything because of their magic arts, yet, when their first-born were destroyed,
they acknowledged thy people to be God's son.
[14] For while gentle silence enveloped all things, and night in its swift course was now half gone,
[15] thy all-powerful word leaped from heaven, from the royal throne, into the midst of the land that was doomed,
a stern warrior

[16] carrying the sharp sword of thy authentic command, and stood and filled all things with death, and touched heaven while standing on the earth.
[17] Then at once apparitions in dreadful dreams greatly troubled them, and unexpected fears assailed them;
[18] and one here and another there, hurled down half dead, made known why they were dying;
[19] for the dreams which disturbed them forewarned them of this, so that they might not perish without knowing
why they suffered.
[20] The experience of death touched also the righteous, and a plague came upon the multitude in the desert, but the wrath did not long continue.
[21] For a blameless man was quick to act as their champion; he brought forward the shield of his ministry, prayer and propitiation by incense; he withstood the anger and put an end to the disaster, showing that he was thy servant.
[22] He conquered the wrath not by strength of body, and not by force of arms, but by his word he subdued the punisher,
appealing to the oaths and covenants given to our fathers.
[23] For when the dead had already fallen on one another in heaps, he intervened and held back the wrath, and cut off its way to the living.
[24] For upon his long robe the whole world was depicted, and the glories of the fathers were engraved on the four rows of stones, and thy majesty on the diadem upon his head.
[25] To these the destroyer yielded, these he feared; for merely to test the wrath was enough.
Wis.19
[1] But the ungodly were assailed to the end by pitiless anger, for God knew in advance even their future actions,
[2] that, though they themselves had permitted thy people to depart and hastily sent them forth, they would change their minds and pursue them.
[3] For while they were still busy at mourning, and were lamenting at the graves of their dead, they reached another foolish decision, and pursued as fugitives those whom they had begged and compelled to depart.
[4] For the fate they deserved drew them on to this end, and made them forget what had happened, in order that they might fill up the punishment which their torments still lacked,
[5] and that thy people might experience an incredible journey, but they themselves might meet a strange death.
[6] For the whole creation in its nature was fashioned anew, complying with thy commands, that thy children might be kept unharmed.

[7] The cloud was seen overshadowing the camp, and dry land emerging where water had stood before, an unhindered way out of the Red Sea, and a grassy plain out of the raging waves,
[8] where those protected by thy hand passed through as one nation, after gazing on marvelous wonders.
[9] For they ranged like horses, and leaped like lambs, praising thee, O Lord, who didst deliver them.
[10] For they still recalled the events of their sojourn, how instead of producing animals the earth brought forth gnats,
and instead of fish the river spewed out vast numbers of frogs.
[11] Afterward they saw also a new kind of birds, when desire led them to ask for luxurious food;
[12] for, to give them relief, quails came up from the sea.
[13] The punishments did not come upon the sinners without prior signs in the violence of thunder, for they justly suffered because of their wicked acts; for they practiced a more bitter hatred of strangers.
[14] Others had refused to receive strangers when they came to them, but these made slaves of guests who were their benefactors.
[15] And not only so, but punishment of some sort will come upon the former for their hostile reception of the aliens;
[16] but the latter, after receiving them with festal celebrations, afflicted with terrible sufferings those who had already shared the same rights.
[17] They were stricken also with loss of sight -- just as were those at the door of the righteous man -- when, surrounded by yawning darkness, each tried to find the way through his own door.
[18] For the elements changed places with one another, as on a harp the notes vary the nature of the rhythm, while each note remains the same. This may be clearly inferred from the sight of what took place.
[19] For land animals were transformed into water creatures, and creatures that swim moved over to the land.
[20] Fire even in water retained its normal power, and water forgot its fire-quenching nature.
[21] Flames, on the contrary, failed to consume the flesh of perishable creatures that walked among them, nor did they melt the crystalline, easily melted kind of heavenly food.
[22] For in everything, O Lord, thou hast exalted and glorified thy people; and thou hast not neglected to help them at all times and in all places.

The Book of Sirach (or Ecclesiasticus)

Chapter 1

1 All wisdom is from the Lord God, and hath been always with him, and is before all time.

2 Who hath numbered the sand of the sea, and the drops of rain, and the days of the world? Who hath measured the height of heaven, and the breadth of the earth, and the depth of the abyss?

3 Who hath searched out the wisdom of God that goeth before all things?

4 Wisdom hath been created before all things, and the understanding of prudence from everlasting.

5 The word of God on high is the fountain of wisdom, and her ways are everlasting commandments.

6 To whom hath the root of wisdom been revealed, and who hath known her wise counsels?

7 To whom hath the discipline of wisdom been revealed and made manifest? and who hath understood the multiplicity of her steps?

8 There is one most high Creator Almighty, and a powerful king, and greatly to be feared, who sitteth upon his throne, and is the God of dominion.

9 He created her in the Holy Ghost, and saw her, and numbered her, and measured her.

10 And he poured her out upon all his works, and upon all flesh according to his gift, and hath given her to them that love him.

11 The fear of the Lord is honour, and glory, and gladness, and a crown of joy.

12 The fear of the Lord shall delight the heart, and shall give joy, and gladness, and length of days.

13 With him that feareth the Lord, it shall go well in the latter end, and in the day of his death he shall be blessed.

14 The love of God is honourable wisdom.

15 Ana they to whom she shall shew herself love her by the sight, and by the knowledge of her great works.

16 The fear of the Lord Is the beginning of wisdom, and was created with the faithful in the womb, it walketh with chosen women, and is known with the just and faithful.

17 The fear of the Lord is the religiousness of knowledge.

18 Religiousness shall keep and justify the heart, it shall give joy and gladness.

19 It shall go well with him that feareth the Lord, and in the days of his end he shall be blessed.

20 To fear God is the fulness of wisdom, and fulness is from the fruits thereof.

21 She shall fill all her house with her increase, and the storehouses with her treasures.

22 The fear of the Lord is a crown of wisdom, filling up peace and the fruit of salvation:

23 And it hath seen and numbered her: but both are the gifts of God.

24 Wisdom shall distribute knowledge and understanding of prudence: and exalteth the glory of them that hold her.

25 The root of wisdom is to fear the Lord: and the branches thereof are long-lived.

26 In the treasures of wisdom is understanding, and religiousness of knowledge: but to sinners wisdom is an abomination.

27 The fear of the Lord driveth out sin:

28 For he that is without fear, cannot be justified: for the wrath of his high spirits is his ruin.

29 A patient man shall bear for a time, and afterwards joy shall be restored to him.

30 A good understanding will hide his words for a time, and the lips of many shall declare his wisdom.

31 In the treasures of wisdom is the signification of discipline:

32 But the worship of God is an abomination to a sinner.

33 Son, if thou desire wisdom, keep justice, and God will give her to thee.

34 For the fear of the Lord is wisdom and discipline: and that which is agreeable to him,

35 Is faith, and meekness: and he will fill up his treasures.

36 Be not incredulous to the fear of the Lord: and come not to him with a double heart.

37 Be not a hypocrite in the sight of men, and let not thy lips be a stumblingblock to thee.

38 Watch over them, lest thou fall, and bring dishonour upon thy soul,

39 And God discover thy secrets, and cast thee down in the midst of the congregation.

40 Because thou camest to the Lord wickedly, and thy heart is full of guile and deceit.

Chapter 2

1 Son, when thou comest to the service of God, stand in justice and in fear, and prepare thy soul for temptation.

2 Humble thy heart, and endure: incline thy ear, and receive the words of understanding: and make not haste in the time of clouds.

3 Wait on God with patience: join thyself to God, and endure, that thy life may be increased in the latter end.

4 Take all that shall be brought upon thee: and in thy sorrow endure, and in thy humiliation keep patience.

5 For gold and silver are tried in the fire, but acceptable men in the furnace of humiliation.

6 Believe God, and he will recover thee: and direct thy way, and trust in him. Keep his fear, and grow old therein.

7 Ye that fear the Lord, wait for his mercy: and go not aside from him, lest ye fall. 8 Ye that fear the Lord, believe him: and your reward shall not be made void.

9 Ye that fear the Lord, hope in him: and mercy shall come to you for your delight.

10 Ye that fear the Lord, love him, and your hearts shall be enlightened.

11 My children behold the generations of men: and know ye that no one hath hoped in the Lord, and hath been confounded.

12 For who hath continued in his commandment, and hath been forsaken? or who hath called upon him, and he despised him?

13 For God is compassionate and merciful, and will forgive sins in the day of tribulation: and he is a protector to all that seek him in truth.

14 Woe to them that are of a double heart and to wicked lips, and to the hands that do evil, and to the sinner that goeth on the earth two ways.

15 Woe to them that are fainthearted, who believe not God: and therefore they shall not be protected by him.

16 Woe to them that have lost patience, and that have forsaken the right ways, and have gone aside into crooked ways.

17 And what will they do, when the Lord shall begin to examine?

18 They that fear the Lord, will not be incredulous to his word: and they that love him, will keep his way.

19 They that fear the Lord, will seek after the things that are well pleasing to him: and they that love him, shall be filled with his law.

20 They that fear the Lord, will prepare their hearts, and in his sight will sanctify their souls.

21 They that fear the Lord, keep his Commandments, and will have patience even until his visitation,

22 Saying: If we do not penance, we shall fall into the hands of the Lord, and not into the hands of men.

23 For according to his greatness, so also is his mercy with him.

Chapter 3

1 The sons of wisdom are the church of the just: and their generation, obedience and love.

2 Children, hear the judgment of your father, and so do that you may be saved.

3 For God hath made the father honourable to the children: and seeking the judgment of the mothers, hath confirmed it upon the children.

4 He that loveth God, shall obtain pardon for his sine by prayer, and shall refrain himself from them, and shall be heard in the prayer of days.

5 And he that honoureth his mother is as one that layeth up a treasure.

6 He that honoureth his father shall have joy in his own children, and in the day of his prayer he shall be heard.

7 He that honoureth his father shall enjoy a long life: and he that obeyeth the father, shall be a comfort to his mother.

8 He that feareth the Lord, honoureth his parents, and will serve them as his masters that brought him into the world.

9 Honour thy father, in work and word, and all patience,

10 That a blessing may come upon thee from him, and his blessing may remain in the latter end.

11 The father's blessing establisheth the houses of the children: but the mother's curse rooteth up the foundation.

12 Glory not in the dishonour of thy father: for his shame is no glory to thee.

13 For the glory of a man is from the honour of his father, and a father without honour is the disgrace of the son.

14 Son, support the old age of thy father, and grieve him not in his life;

15 And if his understanding fail, have patience with him, and despise him not when thou art in thy strength: for the relieving of the father shall not be forgotten.

16 For good shall be repaid to thee for the sin of thy mother.

17 And in justice thou shalt be built up, and in the day of affliction thou shalt be remembered: and thy sine shall melt away as the ice in the fair warm weather.

18 Of what an evil fame is he that forsaketh his father: and he is cursed of God that angereth his mother.

19 My son, do thy works in meekness, and thou shalt be beloved above the glory of men.

20 The greater thou art, the more humble thyself in all things, and thou shalt find grace before God:

21 For great is the power of God alone, and he is honoured by the humble.

22 Seek not the things that are too high for thee, and search not into things above thy ability: but the things that God hath commanded thee, think on them always, and in many of his works be not curious.

23 For it is not necessary for thee to see with thy eyes those things that are hid.

24 In unnecessary matters be not over curious, and in many of his works thou shalt not be inquisitive.

25 For many things are shewn to thee above the understanding of men.

26 And the suspicion of them hath deceived many, and hath detained their minds in vanity.

27 A hard heart shall fear evil at the last: and he that loveth danger shall perish in it.

28 A heart that goeth two ways shall not have success, and the perverse of heart shall be scandalized therein.

29 A wicked heart shall be laden with sorrows, and the sinner will add sin to sin.

30 The congregation of the proud shall not be healed: for the plant of wickedness shall take root in them, and it shall not be perceived.

31 The heart of the wise is understood in wisdom, and a good ear will hear wisdom with all desire.

32 A wise heart, and which hath under- standing, will abstain from sine, and in the works of justice shall have success.

33 Water quencheth a flaming fire, and alms resisteth sins:

34 And God provideth for him that sheweth favour: he remembereth him afterwards, and in the time of his fall he shall find a sure stay.

Chapter 4

1 Son, defraud not the poor of alms, and turn not away thy eyes from the poor.

2 Despise not the hungry soul: and provoke not the Boor in his want.

3 Afflict not the heart of the needy, and defer not to give to him that is in distress.

4 Reject not the petition of the afflicted: and turn not away thy face from the needy.

5 Turn not away thy eyes from the poor for fear of anger: and leave not to them that ask of thee to curse thee behind thy back.

6 For the prayer of him that curseth thee in the bitterness of his soul, shall be heard, for he that made him will hear him.

7 Make thyself affable to the congregation of the poor, and humble thy soul to the ancient, and bow thy head to a great man.

8 Bow down thy ear cheerfully to the poor, and pay what thou owest, and answer him peaceable words with mildness.

9 Deliver him that suffereth wrong out of the hand of the proud: and be not fainthearted in thy soul.

10 In judging be merciful to the fatherless as a father, and as a husband to their mother.

11 And thou shalt be as the obedient son of the most High, and he will have mercy on thee more than a mother.

12 Wisdom inspireth life into her children, and protecteth them that seek after her, and will go before them in the way of justice.

13 And he that loveth her, loveth life: and they that watch for her, shall embrace her sweetness.

14 They that hold her fast, shall inherit life: and whithersoever she entereth, God will give a blessing.

15 They that serve her, shall be servants to the holy one: and God loveth them that love her.

16 He that hearkeneth to her, shall judge nations: and he that looketh upon her, shall remain secure.

17 If he trust to her, he shall inherit her, and his generation shall be in assurance.

18 For she walketh with him in temptation, and at the first she chooseth him.

19 She will bring upon him fear and dread and trial: and she will scourge him with the affliction of her discipline, till she try him by her laws, and trust his soul.

20 Then she will strengthen him, and make a straight way to him, and give him joy,

21 And will disclose her secrets to him, and will heap upon him treasures of knowledge and understanding of justice.

22 But if he go astray, she will forsake him, and deliver him into the hands of his enemy.

23 Son, observe the time, and fly from evil.

24 For thy soul be not ashamed to say the truth.

25 For there is a shame that bringeth sin, and there is a shame that bringeth glory and grace.

26 Accept no person against thy own person, nor against thy soul a lie.

27 Reverence not thy neighbour in his fall:

28 And refrain not to speak in the time of salvation. Hide not thy wisdom in her beauty.

29 For by the tongue wisdom is discerned: and understanding, and knowledge, and learning by the word of the wise, and steadfastness in the works of justice.

30 In nowise speak against the truth, but be ashamed of the lie of thy ignorance.

31 Be not ashamed to confess thy sins, but submit not thyself to every man for sin.

32 Resist not against the face of the mighty, and do not strive against the stream of the river.

33 Strive for justice for thy soul, and even unto death fight for justice, and God will overthrow thy enemies for thee.

34 Be not hasty in thy tongue: and slack and remiss in thy works.

35 Be not as a lion in thy house, terrifying them of thy household, and oppressing them that are under thee.

36 Let not thy hand be stretched out to receive, and shut when thou shouldst give.

Chapter 5

1 Set not thy heart upon unjust possessions, and say not: I have enough to live on: for it shall be of no service in the time of vengeance and darkness.

2 Follow not in thy strength the desires of thy heart:

3 And say not: How mighty am I? and who shall bring me under for my deeds? for God will surely take revenge.

4 Say not: I have sinned, and whet harm hath befallen me? for the most High is a patient rewarder.

5 Be not without fear about sin forgiven, and add not sin upon sin:

6 And say not: The mercy of the Lord is great, he will have mercy on the multitude of my sins.

7 For mercy and wrath quickly come from him, and his wrath looketh upon sinners.

8 Delay not to be converted to the Lord, and defer it not from day to day.

9 For his wrath shall come on a sudden, and in the time of vengeance he will destroy thee.

10 Be not anxious for goods unjustly gotten: for they shall not profit thee in the day of calamity and revenge.

11 Winnow not with every wind, and go not into every

way: for so is every sinner proved by a double tongue.

12 Be steadfast in the way of the Lord, and in the truth of thy judgment, and in knowledge, and let the word of peace and justice keep with thee.

13 Be meek to hear the word, that thou mayst understand: and return a true answer with wisdom.

14 If thou have understanding, answer thy neighbour: but if not, let thy hand be upon thy mouth, lest thou be surprised in an unskilful word, and be confounded.

15 Honour and glory is in the word of the wise, but the tongue of the fool is his ruin.

16 Be not called a whisperer, and be not taken in thy tongue, and confounded.

17 For confusion and repentance is upon a thief, and an evil mark of disgrace upon the double tongued, but to the whisperer hatred, and enmity, and reproach.

18 Justify alike the small and the great.

Chapter 6

1 Instead of a friend become not an enemy to thy neighbour: for an evil man shall inherit reproach and shame, so shall every sinner that is envious and double tongued.

2 Extol not thyself in the thoughts of thy soul like a bull: lest thy strength be quashed by folly,

3 And it eat up thy leaves, and destroy thy fruit: and thou be left as a dry tree in the wilderness.

4 For a wicked soul shall destroy him that hath it, and maketh him to be a joy to his enemies, and shall lead him into the lot of the wicked.

5 A sweet word multiplieth friends, and appeaseth enemies, and a gracious tongue in a good man aboundeth.

6 Be in peace with many, but let one of a thousand be thy counsellor.

7 If thou wouldst get a friend, try him before thou takest him, and do not credit him easily.

8 For there is a friend for his own occasion, and he will not abide in the day of thy trouble.

9 And there is a friend that turneth to enmity; and there is a friend that will disclose hatred and strife and reproaches.

10 And there is a friend a companion at the table, and he will not abide in the day of distress.

11 A friend ii he continue steadfast, shall be to thee as thyself, and shall act with confidence among them of thy household.

12 If he humble himself before thee, and hide himself from thy face, thou shalt have unanimous friendship for good.

13 Separate thyself from thy enemies, and take heed of thy friends.

14 A faithful friend is a strong defence: and he that hath found him, hath found a treasure.

15 Nothing can be compared to a faithful friend, and no weight of gold and silver is able to countervail the goodness of his fidelity.

16 A faithful friend is the medicine of life and immortality: and they that fear the Lord, shall find him.

17 He that feareth God, shall likewise have good friendship: because according to him shall his friend be.

18 My son, from thy youth up receive instruction, and even to thy grey hairs thou shalt find wisdom.

19 Come to her as one that plougheth, and soweth, and wait for her good fruits:

20 For in working about her thou shalt labour a little, and shalt quickly eat of her fruits.

21 How very unpleasant is wisdom to the unlearned, and the unwise will not continue with her.

22 She shall be to them as a mighty stone of trial, and they will cast her from them before it be long.

23 For the wisdom of doctrine is according to her name, and she is not manifest unto many, but with them to whom she is known, she continueth even to the sight of God.

24 Give ear, my son, and take wise counsel, and cast not away my advice.

25 Put thy feet into her fetters, and thy neck into her chains:

26 Bow down thy shoulder, and bear her, and be not grieved with her bands.

27 Come to her with all thy mind, and keep her ways with all thy power.

28 Search for her, and she shall be made known to thee, and when thou hast gotten her, let her not go:

29 For in the latter end thou shalt find rest in her, and she shall be turned to thy joy.

30 Then shall her fetters be a strong defence for thee, and a firm foundation, and her chain a robe of glory:

31 For in her is the beauty of life, and her bands are a healthful binding.

32 Thou shalt put her on as a robe of glory, and thee shalt set her upon thee as a crown of joy. 3

3 My son, if thou wilt attend to me, thou shalt learn: and if thou wilt apply thy mind, thou shalt be wise.

34 If thou wilt incline thy ear, thou shalt receive instruction: and if thou love to hear, thou shalt be wise.

35 Stand in the multitude of ancients that are wise, and join thyself from thy heart to their wisdom, that thou mayst hear every discourse of God, and the sayings of praise may not escape thee.

36 And if thou see a man of understanding, go to him early in the morning, and let thy foot wear the steps of his doors.

37 Let thy thoughts be upon the precepts of God, and meditate continually on his commandments: and he will give thee a heart, and the desire of wisdom shall be given thee.

Chapter 7

1 Do no evils, and no evils shall lay hold of thee.

2 Depart from the unjust, and evils shall depart from thee.

3 My son, sow not evils in the furrows of injustice, and thou shalt not reap them sevenfold. 4 Seek not of the Lord a pre-eminence, nor of the king the seat of honour.

5 Justify not thyself before God, for he knoweth the heart: and desire not to appear wise before the king.

6 Seek not to be made a judge, unless thou have strength enough to extirpate iniquities: lest thou fear the person of the powerful, and lay a stumblingblock for thy integrity.

7 Offend not against the multitude of a city, neither cast thyself in upon the people,

8 Nor bind sin to sin: for even in one thou shalt not be unpunished.

9 Be not fainthearted in thy mind:

10 Neglect not to pray, and to give alms.

11 Say not: God will have respect to the multitude of my gifts, and when I offer to the most high God, he will accept my offerings.

12 Laugh no man to scorn in the bitterness of his soul: for there is one that humbleth and exalteth, God who seeth

13 Devise not a lie against thy brother: neither do the like against thy friend.

14 Be not willing to make any manner of lie: for the custom thereof is not good.

15 Be not full of words in a multitude of ancients, and repeat not the word in thy prayer.

16 Hate not laborious works, nor husbandry ordained by the most High.

17 Number not thyself among the multitude of the disorderly.

18 Remember wrath, for it will not tarry long.

19 Humble thy spirit very much: for the vengeance on the flesh of the ungodly is fire and worms.

20 Do not transgress against thy friend deferring money, nor despise thy dear brother for the sake of gold.

21 Depart not from a wise and good wife, whom thou best gotten in the fear of the Lord: for the grace of her modesty is above gold.

22 Hurt not the servant that worketh faithfully, nor the hired man that giveth thee his life.

23 Let a wise servant be dear to thee as thy own soul, defraud him not of liberty, nor leave him needy.

24 Hast thou cattle? have an eye to them: and if they be for thy profit, keep them with thee.

25 Hast thou children? instruct them, and bow down their neck from their childhood.

26 Hast thou daughters? have a care of their body, and shew not thy countenance gay towards them.

27 Marry thy daughter well, and then shalt do a great work, and give her to a wise man.

28 If thou hast a wife according to thy soul, cast her not off: and to her that is hateful, trust not thyself. With thy whole heart,

29 Honour thy father, and forget not the groanings of thy mother:

30 Remember that thou hadst not been born but through them: and make a return to them as they have done for thee.

31 With all thy soul fear the Lord, and reverence his priests.

32 With all thy strength love him that made thee: and forsake not his ministers.

33 Honour God with all thy soul, and give honour to the priests, and purify thyself with thy arms.

34 Give them their portion, as it is commanded thee, of the firstfruits and of purifications: and for thy negligences purify thyself with a few.

35 Offer to the Lord the gift of thy shoulders, and the sacrifice of sanctification, and the firstfruits of the holy things:

36 And stretch out thy hand to the poor, that thy expiation and thy blessing may be perfected.

37 A gift hath grace in the sight of all the living, and restrain not grace from the dead.

38 And stretch out thy hand to the poor, that thy expiation and thy blessing may be perfected.

38 Be not wanting in comforting them that weep, and walk with them that mourn.

39 Be not slow to visit the sick: for by these things thou shalt be confirmed in love.

40 In all thy works remember thy last end, and thou shalt never sin.

Chapter 8

1 Strive not with a powerful man, lest thou fall into his hands.

2 Contend not with a rich man, lest he bring an action against thee.

3 For gold and silver hath destroyed many, and hath reached even to the heart of kings, and perverted them.

4 Strive not with a man that is full of tongue, and heap not wood upon his fire.

5 Communicate not with an ignorant man, lest he speak ill of thy family.

6 Despise not a man that turneth away from sin, nor reproach him therewith: remember that we are all worthy of reproof.

7 Despise not a man in his old age; for we also shall become old.

8 Rejoice not at the death of thy enemy; knowing that we all die, and are not willing that others should rejoice at our death.

9 Despise not the discourse of them that are ancient and wise, but acquaint thyself with their proverbs.

10 For of them thou shalt learn wisdom, and instruction of understanding, and to serve great men without blame.

11 Let not the discourse of the ancients escape thee, for they have learned of their fathers:

12 For of them thou shalt learn understanding, and to give an answer in time of need.

13 Kindle not the coals of sinners by rebuking them, lest thou be burnt with the flame of the fire of their sins.

14 Stand not against the face of an injurious person, lest he sit as a spy to entrap thee in thy words.

15 Lend not to a man that is mightier than thyself: and if thou lendest, count it as lost.

16 Be not surety above thy power: and if thou be surety, think as if thou wert to pay it.

17 Judge not against a judge: for he judgeth according to that which is just.

18 Go not on the way with a bold man, lest he burden thee with his evils: for he goeth according to his own will, and thou shalt perish together with his folly.

19 Quarrel not with a passionate man, and go not into the desert with a bold man: for blood is as nothing in his sight, and where there is no help he will overthrow thee.

20 Advise not with fools, for they cannot love but such things as please them.

21 Before a stranger do no matter of counsel: for thou knowest not what he will bring forth.

22 Open not thy heart to every man: lest he repay thee with an evil turn, and speak reproachfully to thee.

Chapter 9

1 Be not jealous over the wife of thy bosom, lest she shew in thy regard the malice of a wicked lesson.

2 Give not the power of thy soul to a woman, lest she enter upon thy strength, and thou be confounded.

3 Look not upon a woman that hath a mind for many: lest thou fall into her snares.

4 Use not much the company of her that is a dancer, and hearken not to her, lest thou perish by the force of her charms.

5 Gaze not upon a maiden, lest her beauty be a stumblingblock to thee.

6 Give not thy soul to harlots in any point: lest thou destroy thyself and thy inheritance.

7 Look not round about thee in the of the city, nor wander up and down in the streets thereof.

8 Turn away thy face from a woman dressed up, and gaze not about upon another's beauty.

9 For many have perished by the beauty of a woman, and hereby lust is enkindled as a fire.

10 Every woman that is a harlot, shall be trodden upon as dung in the way.

11 Many by admiring the beauty of another man's wife, have become reprobate, for her conversation burneth as fire.

12 Sit not at all with another man's wife, nor repose upon the bed with her:

13 And strive not with her over wine, lest thy heart decline towards her, and by thy blood thou fall into destruction.

14 Forsake not an old friend, for the new will not be like to him.

15 A new friend is as new wine: it shall grow old, and thou shalt drink it with pleasure.

16 Envy not the glory and riches of a sinner: for thou knowest not what his ruin shall be.

17 Be not pleased with the wrong done by the unjust, knowing that even to hell the wicked shall not please.

18 Keep thee far from the man that hath power to kill, so thou shalt not suspect the fear of death.

19 And if thou come to him, commit no fault, lest he take away thy life.

20 Know it to be a communication with death: for thou art going in the midst of snares, and walking upon the arms of them that are grieved:

21 According to thy power beware of thy neighbor, and treat with the wise and prudent.

22 Let just men be thy guests, and let thy glory be in the fear of God.

23 And let the thought of God be in thy mind, and all thy discourse on the commandments of the Highest.

24 Works shall be praised for the hand of the artificers, and the prince of the people for the wisdom of his speech, but word of the ancients for the sense.

25 A man full of tongue is terrible in his city, and he that is rash in his word shall be hateful.

Chapter 10

1 There is not a more wicked thing than to love money: for such a one setteth even his own soul to sale: because while he liveth he hath cast away his bowels.

11 All power is of short life. A long sickness is troublesome to the physician.

12 The physician cutteth off it short sickness: so also a king is to day, and to morrow he shall die.

13 For when a man shall die, he shall inherit serpents, end beasts, and worms.

14 The beginning of the pride of man, is to fall off from God:

15 Because his heart is departed from him that made him: for pride is the beginning of all sin: be that holdeth it, shall be filled with maledictions, and it shall ruin him in the end.

16 Therefore hath the Lord disgraced the assemblies of the wicked, and hath utterly destroyed them.

17 God hath overturned the thrones of proud princes, and hath set up the meek in their stead.

18 God hath made the roots of proud nations to wither, and hath planted the humble of these nations.

19 The Lord hath overthrown the lands of the Gentiles, and hath destroyed them even to the foundation.

20 He hath made some of them to wither away, and hath destroyed them, and hath made the memory of them to cease from the earth.

21 God hath abolished the memory of the proud, and hath preserved the memory of them that are humble in mind.

22 Pride was not made for men: nor wrath for the race of women.

23 That seed of men shall be honoured, which feareth God: but that seed shall be dishonoured, which transgresseth the commandments of the Lord.

24 In the midst of brethren their chief is honourable: so shall they that fear the Lord, be in his eyes.

25 The fear of God is the glory of the rich, and of the honourable, and of the poor:

26 Despise not a just man that is poor, and do not magnify a sinful man that is rich.

27 The great man, and the judge, and the mighty is in honour: and there is none greater than he that feareth God.

28 They that are free shall serve a servant that is wise: and a man that is prudent and well instructed will not murmur when he is reproved; and he that is ignorant, shall not be honoured.

29 Extol not thyself in doing thy work, and linger not in the time of distress:

30 Better is he that laboureth, and aboundeth in all things, than he that boasteth himself and wanteth bread.

31 My son, keep thy soul in meekness, and give it honour according to its desert.

32 Who will justify him that sinneth against his own soul? and who will honour him that dishonoureth his own soul?

33 The poor man is glorified by his discipline and fear: and there is a man that is honoured for his wealth.

34 But he that is glorified in poverty, how much more in wealth? and he that is glorified in wealth, let him fear poverty.

Chapter 11

1 The wisdom of the humble shall exalt his head, and shall make him sit in the midst of great men.

2 Praise not a man for his beauty, neither despise a man for his look.

3 The bee is small among flying things, but her fruit hath the chiefest sweetness.

4 Glory not in apparel at any time, and be not exalted in the day of thy honour: for the works of the Highest only are wonderful, and his works are glorious, and secret, end hidden.

5 Many tyrants have sat on the throne, and he whom no man would think on, hath worn the crown.

6 Many mighty men have been greatly brought down, and the glorious have been delivered into the hand of others.

7 Before thou inquire, blame no man: and when thou hast inquired, reprove justly.

8 Before thou hear, answer not a word: and interrupt not others in the midst of their discourse.

9 Strive not in a matter which doth not concern thee, and sit not in judgment with sinners.

10 My son, meddle not with many matters: and if thou be rich, thou shalt not be free from sin: for if thou pursue after thou shalt not overtake: and if thou run before thou shalt not escape.

11 There is an ungodly man that laboureth, and maketh haste, and is in sorrow, and is so much the more in want.

12 Again, there is an inactive man that wanteth help, is very weak in ability, and full of poverty:

13 Yet the eye of God hath looked upon him for good, and hath lifted him up from his low estate, and hath exalted his head: and many have wondered at him, and have glorified God.

14 Good things and evil, life and death, poverty and riches, are from God.

15 Wisdom and discipline, and the knowledge of the law are with God. Love and the ways of good things are with him

16 Error and darkness are created with sinners: and they that glory in evil things, grow old in evil.

17 The gift of God abideth with the just, and his advancement shall have success for ever.

18 There is one that is enriched by living sparingly, and this is the portion of his reward.

19 In that he saith: I have found me rest, and now I will eat of my goods alone:

20 And he knoweth not what time shall pass, and that death approacheth, and that he must leave all to others, and shall die.

21 Be steadfast in thy covenant, and be conversant therein, and grow old in the work of thy commandments.

22 Abide not in the works of sinners. But trust in God, and stay in thy place.

23 For it is easy in the eyes of God on a sudden to make the poor man rich.

24 The blessing of God maketh haste to reward the just, and in a swift hour his blessing beareth fruit.

25 Say not: What need I, and what good shall I have by this?

26 Say not: I am sufficient for myself: and what shall I be made worse by this?

27 In the day of good things be not unmindful of evils: and in the day of evils be not unmindful of good things:

28 For it is easy before God in the day of death to reward every one according to his ways.

29 The affliction of an hour maketh one forget great delights, and in the end of a man is the disclosing of his works.

30 Praise not any man before death, for a man is known by his children.

31 Bring not every man into thy house: for many are the snares of the deceitful.

32 For as corrupted bowels send forth stinking breath, and as the partridge is brought into the cage, and as the roe into the snare: so also is the heart of the proud, and as a spy that looketh on the fall of his neighbour.

33 For he lieth in wait and turneth good into evil, and on the elect he will lay a blot.

34 Of one spark cometh a great fire, and of one deceitful man much blood: and a sinful man lieth in wait for blood.

35 Take heed to thyself of a mischievous man, for he worketh evils: lest he bring upon thee reproach for ever.

36 Receive a stranger in, and he shall overthrow thee with a whirlwind, and shall turn thee out of thy own.

Chapter 12

1 If thou do good, know to whom thou dost it, and there shall be much thanks for thy good deeds.

2 Do good to the just, and thou shalt find great recompense: and if not of him, assuredly of the Lord.

3 For there is no good for him that is always occupied in evil, and that giveth no alms: for the Highest hateth sinners, and hath mercy on the penitent.

4 Give to the merciful and uphold not the sinner: God will repay vengeance to the ungodly and to sinners, and keep them against the day of vengeance.

5 Give to the good, and receive not a sinner.

6 Do good to the humble, and give not to the ungodly: hold back thy bread, and give it not to him, lest thereby he overmaster thee.

7 For thou shalt receive twice as much evil for all the good thou shalt have done to him: for the Highest also hateth sinners, and will repay vengeance to the ungodly.

8 A friend shall not be known in prosperity, and an enemy shall not be hidden in adversity.

9 In the prosperity of a man, his enemies are grieved: and a friend is known in his adversity.

10 Never trust thy enemy: for as a brass pot his wickedness rusteth:

11 Though he humble himself and go crouching, yet take good heed and beware of him.

12 Set him not by thee, neither let him sit on thy right hand, lest he turn into thy place, and seek to take thy seat: and at the last thou acknowledge my words, and be pricked with my sayings.

13 Who will pity an enchanter struck by a serpent, or any that come near wild beasts? so is it with him that keepeth company with a wicked man, and is involved in his sins.

14 For an hour he will abide with thee: but if thou begin to decline, he will not endure it.

15 An enemy speaketh sweetly with his lips, but in his heart he lieth in wait, to throw thee into a pit.

16 An enemy weepeth with his eyes: but if he find an opportunity he will not be satisfied with blood:

17 And if evils come upon thee, thou shalt find him there first.

18 An enemy hath tears in his eyes, and while he pretendeth to help thee, will undermine thy feet.

19 He will shake his head, and clap his hands, and whisper much, and change his countenance.

Chapter 13

1 He that toucheth pitch, shall be defiled with it: and he that hath fellowship with the proud, shall put on pride.

2 He shall take a burden upon him that hath fellowship with one more honour- able than himself. And have no fellow- ship with one that is richer than thyself.

3 What agreement shall the earthen pot have with the kettle? for if they knock one against the other, it shall be broken.

4 The rich man hath done wrong, and yet he will fume: but the poor is wronged and must hold his peace.

5 If thou give, he will make use of thee: and if thou have nothing, he will forsake thee.

6 If thou have any thing, he will live with thee, and will make thee bare, and he will not be sorry for thee.

7 If he have need of thee he will deceive thee, and smiling upon thee will put thee in hope; he will speak thee fair, and will say: What wantest thou?

8 And he will shame thee by his meats, till he have drawn thee dry twice or thrice, and at last he will laugh at thee: and afterward when he seeth thee, he will forsake thee, and shake his head at thee.

9 Humble thyself to God, and wait for his hands.

10 Beware that thou be not deceived Into folly, and be humbled.

11 Be not lowly in thy wisdom, lest being humbled thou be deceived into folly.

12 If thou be invited by one that is mightier, withdraw thyself: for so he will invite thee the more.

13 Be not troublesome to him, lest thou be put back: and keep not far from him, lest thou be forgotten.

14 Affect not to speak with him as an equal: and believe not his many words: for by much talk he will sift thee, and smiling will examine thee concerning thy secrets.

15 His cruel mind will lay up thy words: and he will not spare to do thee hurt, and to cast thee into prison.

16 Take heed to thyself, and attend diligently to what thou hearest: for thou walkest in danger of thy ruin.

17 When thou hearest those things, see as it were in sleep, and thou shalt awake.

18 Love God all thy life, and call upon him for thy salvation.

19 Every beast loveth its like: so also every man him that is nearest to himself.

20 All flesh shall consort with the like to itself, and every man shall associate himself to his like.

21 If the wolf shall at any time have fellowship with the lamb, so the sinner with the just.

22 What fellowship hath a holy man with a dog, or what part hath the rich with the poor?

23 The wild ass is the lion's prey in the desert: so also the poor are devoured by the rich.

24 And as humility is an abomination to the proud: so also the rich man abhorreth the poor.

25 When a rich man is shaken, he is kept up by his friends: but when a poor man is fallen down, he is thrust away even by his acquaintance.

26 When a rich man hath been deceived, he hath many helpers: he hath spoken proud things, and they have justified him.

27 The poor man was deceived, and he is rebuked also: he hath spoken wisely, and could have no place.

28 The rich man spoke, and all held their peace, and what he said they extol even to the clouds.

29 The poor man spoke, and they say: Who is this? and if he stumble, they will overthrow him.

30 Riches are good to him that hath no sin in his conscience: and poverty is very wicked in the mouth of the ungodly.

31 The heart of a man changeth his countenance, either for good, or for evil.

32 The token of a good heart, and a good countenance thou shalt hardly find, and with labour.

Chapter 14

1 Blessed is the man that hath not slipped by a word out of his mouth, and is not pricked with the remorse of sin.

2 Happy is he that hath had no sadness of his mind, and who is not fallen from his hope.

3 Riches are not comely for a covetous man and a niggard, and what should an envious man do with gold?

4 He that gathereth together by wronging his own soul, gathereth for others, and another will squander away his goods in rioting.

5 He that is evil to himself, to whom will he be good? and he shall not take pleasure in his goods.

6 There is none worse than he that envieth himself, and this is the reward of his wickedness:

7 And if he do good, he doth it ignorantly, and unwillingly: and at the last he discovereth his wickedness.

8 The eye of the envious is wicked: and he turneth away his face, and despiseth his own soul.

9 The eye of the covetous man is insatiable in his portion of iniquity: he will not be satisfied till he consume his own soul, drying it up.

10 An evil eye is towards evil things: and he shall not have his fill of bread, but shall be needy and pensive at his own table.

11 My son, if thou have any thing, do good to thyself, and offer to God worthy offerings.

12 Remember that death is not slow, and that the covenant of hell hath been shewn to thee: for the covenant of this world shall surely die.

13 Do good to thy friend before thou die, and according to thy ability, stretching out thy hand give to the poor.

14 Defraud not thyself of the good day, and let not the part of a good gift over- pass thee.

15 Shalt thou not leave to others to divide by lot thy sorrows and labours?

16 Give and take, and justify thy soul.

17 Before thy death work justice: for in hell there is no finding food.

18 All flesh shall fade as grass, and as the leaf that springeth out on a green tree.

19 Some grow, and some fall off: so is the generation of flesh and blood, one cometh to an end, and another is born.

20 Every work that is corruptible shall fail in the end: and the worker thereof shall go with it.

21 And every excellent work shall be justified: and the worker thereof shall be honoured therein.

22 Blessed is the man that shall continue in wisdom, and that shall meditate in his justice, and in his mind shall think of the all seeing eye of God.

23 He that considereth her ways in his heart, and hath understanding in her secrets, who goeth after her as one that traceth, and stayeth in her ways:

24 He who looketh in at her windows, and hearkeneth at her door:

25 He that lodgeth near her house, and fastening a pin in her walls shall set up his tent nigh unto her, where good things shall rest in his lodging for ever.

26 He shall set his children under her shelter, and shall lodge under her branches:

27 He shall be protected under her covering from the heat, and shall rest in her glory.

Chapter 15

1 He that feareth God, will do good: and he that possesseth justice, shall lay hold on her,

2 And she will meet him as an honourable mother, and will receive him as a wife married of a virgin.

3 With the bread of life and understanding, she shall feed him, and give him the water of wholesome wisdom to drink: and she shall be made strong in him, and he shall not be moved:

4 And she shall hold him fast, and he shall not be confounded: and she shall exalt him among his neighbours.

5 And in the midst of the church she shall open his mouth, and shall fill him with the spirit of wisdom and understanding, and shall clothe him with a robe of glory.

6 She shall heap upon him a treasure of joy and gladness, and shall cause him to inherit an everlasting name.

7 But foolish men shall not obtain her, and wise men shall meet her, foolish men shall not see her: for she is far from pride and deceit.

8 Lying men shall not be mindful of her: but men that speak truth shall be found with her, and shall advance, even till they come to the sight of God.

9 Praise is not seemly in the mouth of a sinner:

10 For wisdom came forth from God: for praise shall be with the wisdom of God, and shall abound in a faithful mouth, and the sovereign Lord will give praise unto it.

11 Say not: It is through God, that she is not with me: for do not thou the things that he hateth.

12 Say not: He hath caused me to err: for he hath no need of wicked men.

13 The Lord hateth all abomination of error, and they that fear him shall not love it.

14 God made man from the beginning, and left him in the hand of his own counsel.

15 He added his commandments and precepts.

16 If thou wilt keep the commandments and perform acceptable fidelity for ever, they shall preserve thee.

17 He hath set water and fire before thee: stretch forth thy hand to which thou wilt.

18 Before man is life and death, good and evil, that which he shall choose shall be given him:

19 For the wisdom of God is great, and he is strong in power, seeing all men without ceasing.

20 The eyes of the Lord are towards them that fear him, and he knoweth all the work of man.

21 He hath commanded no man to do wickedly, and he hath given no man license to sin:

22 For he desireth not a multitude of faithless and unprofitable children.

Chapter 16

1 Rejoice not in ungodly children, if they be multiplied: neither be delighted in them, if the fear of God be not with them.

2 Trust not to their life, and respect not their labours.

3 For better is one that feareth God, than a thousand ungodly children.

4 And it is better to die without children, than to leave ungodly children.

5 By one that is wise a country shall be inhabited, the tribe of the ungodly shall become desolate.

6 Many such things hath my eyes seen, and greater things than these my ear hath heard.

7 In the congregation of sinners a fire shall be kindled, and in an unbelieving nation wrath shall dame out.

8 The ancient giants did not obtain pardon for their sine, who were destroyed trusting to their own strength:

9 And he spared not the place where Lot sojourned, but abhorred them for the pride of their word.

10 He had not pity on them, destroying the whole nation that extolled themselves in their sine.

11 So did he with the six hundred thousand footmen, who were gathered together in the hardness of their heart: and if one had been stiffnecked, it is a wonder if he had escaped unpunished:

12 For mercy and wrath are with him. He is mighty to forgive, and to pour out indignation:

13 According as his mercy is, so his correction judgeth a man according to his works.

14 The sinner shall not escape in his rapines, and the patience of him that sheweth mercy shall not be put off.

15 All mercy shall make a place for every man according to the merit of his works, and according to the wisdom of his sojournment.

16 Say not: I shall be hidden from God. and who shall remember me from on high?

17 In such a multitude I shall not be known: for what is my soul in such an immense creation?

18 Behold the heaven, and the heavens of heavens, the deep, and all the earth, and the things that are in them, shall be moved in his sight,

19 The mountains also, and the hills, end the foundations of the earth: when God shall look upon them, they shall be shaken with trembling.

20 And in all these things the heart is senseless: and every heart is understood by him:

21 And his ways who shall understand, and the storm, which no eye of man see?

22 For many of his works are hidden: hut the works of his justice who shall declare? or who shall endure? for the testament is far from some, and the examination of all is in the end.

23 He that wanteth understanding thinketh vain things: and the foolish, and erring man, thinketh foolish things.

24 Hearken to me, my son, and learn the discipline of understanding, and attend to my words in thy heart.

25 And I will shew forth good doctrine in equity, and will seek to declare wisdom: and attend to my words in thy heart, whilst with equity of spirit I tell thee the virtues that God hath put upon his works from the beginning, and I shew forth in truth his knowledge.

26 The works of God are done in judgment from the beginning, and from the making of them he distinguished their parts, and their beginnings in their generations.

27 He beautified their works for ever, they have neither hungered, nor laboured, and they have not ceased from their works.

28 Nor shall any of them straiten his neighbour at any time.

29 Be not thou incredulous to his word.

30 After this God looked upon the earth, and filled it with his goods.

31 The soul of every living thing hath shewn forth before the face thereof, and into it they return again.

Chapter 17

1 God created man of the earth, and made him after his own image.

2 And he turned him into it again, and clothed him with strength according to himself.

3 He gave him the number of his days and time, and gave him power over all things that are upon the earth.

4 He put the fear of him upon all flesh, and he had dominion over beasts and fowls.

5 He created of him a helpmate like to himself: he gave them counsel, and a tongue, and eyes, and ears, and a heart to devise: and he filled them with the knowledge of understanding.

6 He created in them the science of the spirit, he filled their heart with wisdom, and shewed them both good and evil.

7 He set his eye upon their hearts to shew them the greatness of his works:

8 That they might praise the name which he hath sanctified: and glory in his wondrous acts, that they might declare the glorious things of his works.

9 Moreover he gave them instructions, and the law of life for an inheritance.

10 He made an everlasting covenant with them, and he shewed them his justice and judgments.

11 And their eye saw the majesty of his glory. and their ears heard his glorious voice, and he said to them: Beware of all iniquity.

12 And he gave to every one of them commandment concerning his neighbour.

13 Their ways are always before him, they are not hidden from his eyes.

14 Over every nation he set a ruler.

15 And Israel was made the manifest portion of God.

16 And all their works are as the sun in the sight of God: and his eyes are continually upon their ways.

17 Their covenants were not hid by their iniquity, and all their iniquities are in the sight of God.

18 The alms of a man is as a signet with him, and shall preserve the grace of a man as the apple of the eye:

19 And afterward he shall rise up, and shall render them their reward, to every one upon their own head, and shall turn them down into the bowels of the earth.

20 But to the penitent he hath given the way of justice, and he hath strengthened them that were fainting in patience, and hath appointed to them the lot of truth.

21 Turn to the Lord, and forsake thy sins:

22 Make thy prayer before the face of the Lord, and offend less.

23 Return to the Lord, and turn away from thy injustice, and greatly hate abomination.

24 And know the justices and judgments of God, and stand firm in the lot set before thee, and in prayer to the most high God.

25 Go to the side of the holy age, with them that live and give praise to God.

26 Tarry not in the error of the ungodly, give glory before death. Praise perisheth from the dead as nothing.

27 Give thanks whilst thou art living, whilst thou art alive and in health thou shalt give thanks, and shalt praise God, and shalt glory in his mercies.

28 How great is the mercy of the Lord, and his forgiveness to them that turn to him I

29 For all things cannot be in men, because the son of man is not immortal, and they are delighted with the vanity of evil.

30 What is brighter than the sun; yet it shall be eclipsed. Or what is more wicked than that which flesh and blood hath invented? and this shall be reproved.

31 He beholdeth the power of the height of heaven: and all men are earth and ashes.

Chapter 18

1 He that liveth for ever created all things together. God only shall be justified, and he remaineth an invincible king for ever.

2 Who is able to declare his works?

3 For who shall search out his glorious acts?

4 And who shall shew forth the power of his majesty? or who shall be able to declare his mercy?

5 Nothing may be taken away, nor added, neither is it possible to find out the glorious works of God:

6 When a man hath done, then shall he begin: and when he leaveth off, he shall be at a loss.

7 What is man, and what is his grace? and what is his good, or what is his evil?

8 The number of the days of men at the most are a hundred years: as a drop of water of the sea are they esteemed: and as a pebble of the sand, so are a few years compared to eternity.

9 Therefore God is patient in them, and poureth forth his mercy upon them.

10 He hath seen the presumption of their heart that it is wicked, and hath known their end that it is evil.

11 Therefore bath he filled up his mercy in their favour, and hath shewn them the way of justice.

12 The compassion of man is toward his neighbour: but the mercy of God is upon all flesh.

13 He hath mercy, and teacheth, and correcteth, as a shepherd doth his hock.

14 He hath mercy on him that receiveth the discipline of mercy, and that maketh haste in his judgments. 15 My son, in thy good deeds, make no complaint, and when thou givest any thing, add not grief by an evil word. 16 Shall not the dew assuage the heat? so also the good word is better than the gift.

17 Lo, is not a word better than a gift? but both are with a justified man.

18 A fool will upbraid bitterly: and a gift of one ill taught consumeth the eyes.

19 Before judgment prepare thee justice, and learn before thou speak.

20 Before sickness take a medicine, and before judgment examine thyself, and thou shalt find mercy in the sight of God.

21 Humble thyself before thou art sick, and in the time of sickness shew thy conversation.

22 Let nothing hinder thee from praying always, and be not afraid to be justified even to death: for the reward of God continueth for ever.

23 Before prayer prepare thy soul: and be not as a man that tempteth God.

24 Remember the wrath that shall be at the last day, and the time of repaying when he shall turn away his face.

25 Remember poverty is the time of abundance, and the necessities of poverty in the day of riches.

26 From the morning until the evening the time shall be changed, and all these are swift in the eyes of God.

27 A wise man will fear in every thing, and in the days of sine will beware of sloth.

28 Every man of understanding knoweth wisdom, and will give praise to him that findeth her.

29 They that were of good understanding in words, have also done wisely themselves: and have understood truth and justice, and have poured forth pro- verbs and judgments.

30 Go not after thy lusts, but turn away from thy own will.

31 If thou give to thy soul her desires, she will make thee a joy to thy enemies.

32 Take no pleasure in riotous assemblies, be they ever so small: for their concertation is continual.

33 Make not thyself poor by borrowing to contribute to feasts when thou hast nothing in thy purse : for thou shalt be an enemy to thy own life.

Chapter 19

1 Hast thou heard a word against thy neighbour? let it die within thee, trusting that it will not burst thee.

11 At the hearing of a word the fool is in travail, as a woman groaning. in the bringing forth a child.

12 As an arrow that sticketh in a man's thigh: so is a word in the heart of a fool.

13 Reprove a friend, lest he may not have understood, and say : f did it not: or if he did it, that he may do it no more.

14 Reprove thy neighbour, for it may be he hath not said it: and if he hath said it, that he may not say it again.

15 Admonish thy friend: for there is often a fault committed.

16 And believe not every word. There is one, that slippeth with the tongue, but not from his heart.

17 For who is there that hath not offended with his tongue? Admonish thy neighbour before thou threaten him.

18 And give place to the fear of the most High: for the fear of God is all wisdom, and therein is to fear God, and the disposition of the law is in all wisdom.

19 But the learning of wickedness is not wisdom: and the device of sinners is not prudence.

20 There is a subtle wickedness, and the same is detestable: and there is a man that is foolish, wanting in wisdom.

21 Better is a man that hath less wisdom, and wanteth understanding, with the fear of God, than he that aboundeth in understanding, and transgresseth the law of the most High.

22 There is an exquisite subtilty, and the same is unjust.

23 And there is one that uttereth an exact word telling the truth. There is one that humbleth himself wickedly, and his interior is full of deceit:

24 And there is one that submitteth himself exceedingly with a great lowliness: and there is one that casteth down his countenance, and maketh as if he did not see that which is unknown:

25 And if he be hindered from sinning for want of power, if he shall find opportunity to do evil, he will do it.

26 A man is known by his look, and a wise man, when thou meetest him, is known by his countenance.

27 The attire of the body, and the laughter of the teeth, and the gait of the man, shew what he is.

28 There is a lying rebuke in the anger of an injurious man: and there is a judgment that is not allowed to be good: and there is one that holdeth his peace, he is wise.

Chapter 20

1 How much better is it to reprove, than to be angry, and not to hinder him that confesseth in prayer.

2 The lust of an eunuch shall devour a young maiden:

3 So is he that by violence executeth unjust judgment.

4 How good is it, when thou art reproved, to shew repentance! for so thou shalt escape wilful sin.

5 There is one that holdeth his peace, that is found wise: and there is another that is hateful, that is bold in speech.

6 There is one that holdeth his peace, because he knoweth not what to say: and there is another that holdeth his peace, knowing the proper time.

7 A wise man will hold his peace till he see opportunity: but a babbler, and a fool, will regard no time.

8 He that useth many words shall hurt his own soul: and he that taketh authority to himself unjustly shall be hated.

9 There is success in evil things to a man without discipline, and there is a finding that turneth to loss.

10 There is a gift that is not profitable: and there is a gift, the recompense of which is double.

11 There is an abasement because of glory: and there is one that shall lift up his head from a low estate.

12 There is that buyeth much for a small price, and restoreth the same sevenfold.

13 A man wise in words shall make himself beloved: but the graces of fools shall be poured out.

14 The gift of the fool shall do thee no good: for his eyes are sevenfold.

15 He will give a few things, and upbraid much: and the opening of his mouth is the kindling of a fire.

16 To day a man lendeth, and to morrow he asketh it again: such a man as this is hateful.

17 A fool shall have no friend, and there shall be no thanks for his good deeds.

18 For they that eat his bread, are of a false tongue. How often, and how many will laugh him to scorn!

19 For he doth not distribute with right understanding that which was to be had: in like manner also that which was not to be had.

20 The slipping of a false tongue is as one that falleth on the pavement: so the fall of the wicked shall come speedily.

21 A man without grace is as a vain fable, it shall be continually in the mouth of the unwise.

22 A parable coming out, of a fool's mouth shall be rejected: for he doth not speak it in due season.

23 There is that is hindered from sinning through want, and in his rest he shall be pricked.

24 There is that will destroy his own soul through shamefacedness, and by occasion of an unwise person he will destroy it: and by respect of person he will destroy himself.

25 There is that for bashfulness promiseth to his friend, and maketh him his enemy for nothing.

26 A lie is a foul blot in a man, and yet it will be continually in the mouth of men without discipline.

27 A thief is better than a man that is always lying: but both of them shall inherit destruction.

28 The manners of lying men are without honour: and their confusion is with them without ceasing.

29 A wise man shall advance himself with his words, and a prudent man shall please the great ones.

30 He that tilleth his land shall make a high heap of corn: and he that worketh justice shall be exalted: and he that pleaseth great men shall escape iniquity.

31 Presents and gifts blind the eyes of judges, and make them dumb in the mouth, so that they cannot correct.

32 Wisdom that is hid, and treasure that is not seen: what profit is there in them both?

33 Better is he that hideth his folly, than the man that hideth his wisdom.

Chapter 21

1 My son, hast thou sinned? do so no more: but for thy former sins also pray that they may be forgiven thee.

2 Flee from sins as from the face of a serpent: for if thou comest near them, they will take hold of thee.

3 The teeth thereof are the teeth of a lion, killing the souls of men.

4 All iniquity is like a two-edged sword, there is no remedy for the wound thereof.

5 Injuries and wrongs will waste riches: and the house that is very rich shall be brought to nothing by pride : so the substance of the proud shall be rooted out.

6 The prayer out of the mouth of the poor shall reach the ears of God, and judgment shall come for him speedily.

7 He that hateth to be reproved walketh in the trace of a sinner: and he that feareth God will turn to his own heart.

8 He that is mighty by a bold tongue is known afar off, but a wise man knoweth to slip by him.

9 He that buildeth his house at other men's charges, is as he that gathereth himself stones to build in the winter.

10 The congregation of sinners is like tow heaped together, and the end of them is a flame of fire.

11 The way of sinners is made plain with stones, and in their end is hell, and darkness, and pains.

12 He that keepeth justice shall get the understanding thereof.

13 The perfection of the fear of God is wisdom and understanding.

14 He that is not wise in good, will not be taught.

15 But there is a wisdom that aboundeth in evil : and there is no understanding where there is bitterness.

16 The knowledge of a wise man shall abound like a flood, and his counsel continueth like a fountain of life.

17 The heart of a fool is like a broken vessel, and no wisdom at all shall it hold.

18 A man of sense will praise every wise word he shall hear, and will apply it to himself: the luxurious man hath heard it, and it shall displease him, and he will cast it behind his back.

19 The talking of a fool is like a burden in the way: but in the lips of the wise, grace shall be found.

20 The mouth of the prudent is sought after in the church, and they will think upon his words in their hearts.

21 As a house that is destroyed, so is wisdom to a fool: and the knowledge of the unwise is as words without sense.

22 Doctrine to a fool is as fetters on the feet, and like manacles on the right hand.

23 A fool lifteth up his voice in laughter: but a wise man will scarce laugh low to himself.

24 Learning to the prudent is as an ornament of gold, and like a bracelet upon his right arm.

25 The foot of a fool is soon in his neighbour's house: but a man of experience will be abashed at the person of the mighty.

26 A fool will peep through the window into the house: but he that is well taught will stand without.

27 It is the folly of a man to hearken at the door: and a wise man will be grieved with the disgrace.

28 The lips of the unwise will be telling foolish things but the words of the wise shall be weighed in a balance.

29 The heart of fools is in their mouth: and the mouth of wise men is in their heart.

30 While the ungodly curseth the devil, he curseth his own soul.

31 The talebearer shall defile his own soul, and shall be hated by all: and he that shall abide with him shall be hateful: the silent and wise man shall be honoured.

Chapter 22

1 The sluggard is pelted with a dirty stone, and all men will speak of his disgrace.

2 The sluggard is pelted with the dung of oxen: and every one that toucheth him will shake his hands.

3 A son ill taught is the confusion of the father: and a foolish daughter shall be to his loss.

4 A wise daughter shall bring an inheritance to her husband: but she that confoundeth, becometh a disgrace to her father.

5 She that is bold shameth both her father and husband, and will not be inferior to the ungodly: and shall be disgraced by them both.

6 A tale out of time is like music in mourning: but the stripes and instruction of wisdom are never out of time.

7 He that teacheth a fool, is like one that glueth a potsherd together.

8 He that telleth a word to him that heareth not, is like one that waketh a man out of a deep sleep.

9 He speaketh with one that is asleep, who uttereth wisdom to a fool: and in the end of the discourse he saith: Who is this?

10 Weep for the dead, for his light hath failed: and weep for the fool, for his understanding faileth.

11 Weep but a little for the dead, for he is at rest.

12 For the wicked life of a wicked fool is worse than death.

13 The mourning for the dead is seven days: but for a fool and an ungodly man all the days of their life.

14 Talk not much with a fool, and go not with him that hath no sense.

15 Keep thyself from him, that thou mayst not have trouble, and thou shalt not be defiled with his sin.

16 Turn away from him, and thou shalt find rest, and shalt not be wearied out with his folly.

17 What is heavier than lead? and what other name hath he but fool?

18 Sand and salt, and a mass of iron is easier to bear, than a man without sense, that is both foolish and wicked.

19 A frame of wood bound together in the foundation of a building, shall not be loosed: so neither shall the heart that is established by advised counsel.

20 The thought of him that is wise at all times, shall not be depraved by fear.

21 As pales set in high places, and plasterings made without cost, will not stand against the face of the wind:

22 So also a fearful heart in the imagination of a fool shall not resist against the violence of fear.

23 As a fearful heart in the thought of a fool at all times will not fear, so neither shall he that continueth always in the commandments of God.

24 He that pricketh the eye, bringeth out tears: and he that pricketh the heart, bringeth forth resentment.

25 He that flingeth a stone at birds, shall drive them away: so he that upbraideth his friend, breaketh friendship.

26 Although thou hast drawn a sword at a friend, despair not: for there may be a returning. To a friend,

27 If thou hast opened a sad mouth, fear not, for there may be a reconciliation: except upbraiding, and reproach, and pride, and disclosing of secrets, or a treacherous wound: for in all these cases a friend will flee away.

28 Keep fidelity with a friend in his poverty, that in his prosperity also thou mayst rejoice.

29 In the time of his trouble continue faithful to him, that thou mayst also be heir with him in his inheritance.

30 As the vapour of a chimney, and the smoke of the fire goeth up before the fire: so also injurious words, and reproaches, and threats, before blood.

31 I will not be ashamed to salute a friend, neither will I hide myself from his face: and if any evil happen to me by him, I will bear it.

32 But every one that shall hear it, will beware of him.

33 Who will set a guard before my mouth, and a sure seal upon my lips, that I fall not by them, and that my tongue destroy me not?

Chapter 23

1 And let not the naming of God be usual in thy mouth, and meddle not with the names of saints, for thou shalt not escape free from them.

11 For as a slave daily put to the question, is never without a blue mark: so every one that sweareth, and nameth, shall not be wholly pure from sin.

12 A man that sweareth much, shall be filled with iniquity, and a scourge shall not depart from his house.

13 And if he make it void, his sin shall be upon him: and if he dissemble it, he offendeth double:

14 And if he swear in vain, he shall not be justified: for his house shall be filled with his punishment.

15 There is also another speech opposite to death, let it not be found in the inheritance of Jacob.

16 For from the merciful all these things shall be taken away, and they shall not wallow in sins.

17 Let not thy mouth be accustomed to indiscreet speech: for therein is the word of sin.

18 Remember thy father and thy mother, for thou sittest is the midst of great men:

19 Lest God forget thee in their sight, and thou, by thy daily custom, be infatuated and suffer reproach: and wish that thou hadst not been born, and curse the day of thy nativity.

20 The man that is accustomed to opprobrious words, will never be corrected all the days of his life.

21 Two sorts of men multiply sins, and the third bringeth wrath and destruction.

22 A hot soul is a burning fire, it will never be quenched, till it devour some thing.

23 And a man that is wicked in the mouth of his flesh, will not leave off till he hath kindled a fire.

24 To a man that is a fornicator all bread is sweet, he will not be weary of sinning unto the end.

25 Every man that passeth beyond his own bed, despising his own soul, and saying: Who seeth me?

26 Darkness compasseth me about, and the walls cover me, and no man seeth me: whom do I fear? the most High will not remember my sins.

27 And he understandeth not that his eye seeth all things, for such a man's fear driveth from him the fear of God, and the eyes of men fearing him:

28 And he knoweth not that the eyes of the Lord are far brighter than the sun, beholding round about all the ways of men, and the bottom of the deep, and looking into the hearts of men, into the most hidden parts.

29 For all things were known to the Lord God, before they were created: so also after they were perfected he beholdeth all things.

30 This man shall be punished in the streets of the city, and he shall be chased as a colt: and where he suspected not, he shall be taken.

31 And he shall be in disgrace with all men, because he understood not the fear of the Lord.

32 So every woman also that leaveth her husband, and bringeth in an heir by another :

33 For first she hath been unfaithful to the law of the most High: and secondly, she hath offended against her husband: thirdly, she hath fornicated in adultery, end hath gotten her children of another man.

34 This woman shall be brought into the assembly, and inquisition shall be made of her children.

35 Her children shall not take root, and her branches shall bring forth no fruit.

36 She shall leave her memory to be cursed, and her infamy shall not be blotted out.

37 And they that remain shall know. that there is nothing better than the fear of God: and that there is nothing sweeter than to have regard to the commandments of the Lord.

38 It is great glory to follow the Lord for length of days shall be received from him.

Chapter 24

1 Wisdom shall praise her own self, and shall be honoured in God, and shall glory in the midst of her people,

2 And shall open her mouth in the churches of the most High, and shall glorify herself in the sight of his power,

3 And in the midst of her own people she shall be exalted, and shall be admired in the holy assembly.

4 And in the multitude of the elect she shall have praise, and among the blessed she shall be blessed, saying:

5 I came out of the mouth of the most High, the firstborn before all creatures:

6 I made that in the heavens there should rise light that never faileth, and as a cloud I covered all the earth:

7 I dwelt in the highest places, and my throne is in a pillar of a cloud.

8 I alone have compassed the circuit of heaven, and have penetrated into the bottom of the deep, and have walked in the waves of the sea,

9 And have stood in all the earth: and in every people,

10 And in every nation I have had the chief rule:

11 And by my power I have trodden under my feet the hearts of all the high and low: and in all these I sought rest, and I shall abide in the inheritance of the Lord.

12 Then the creator of all things commanded, and said to me: and he that made me, rested in my tabernacle,

13 And he said to me: Let thy dwelling be in Jacob, and thy inheritance in Israel, and take root in my elect.

14 From the beginning, and before the world, was I created, and unto the world to come I shall not cease to be, and in the holy dwelling place I have ministered before him.

15 And so was I established in Sion, and in the holy city likewise I rested, and my power was in Jerusalem.

16 And I took root in an honourable people, and in the portion of mg God his inheritance, and my abode is in the full assembly of saints.

17 I was exalted like a cedar in Libanus, and as a cypress tree on mount Sion.

18 I was exalted like a palm tree in Cades, and as a rose plant in Jericho:

19 As a fair olive tree in the plains, and as a plane tree by the water in the streets, was I exalted.

20 I gave a sweet smell like cinnamon. and aromatical balm: I yielded a sweet odour like the best myrrh:

21 And I perfumed my dwelling as storax, and galbanum, and onyx, and aloes, and as the frankincense not cut, and my odour is as the purest balm.

22 I have stretched out my branches as the turpentine tree, and my branches are of honour and grace.

23 As the vine I have brought forth a pleasant odour: and my flowers are the fruit of honour and riches.

24 I am the mother of fair love, and of fear, and of knowledge, and of holy hope.

25 In me is all grace of the way and of the truth, in me is all hope of life and of virtue.

26 Come over to me, all ye that desire me, and be filled with my fruits.

27 For my spirit is sweet above honey, and my inheritance above honey and the honeycomb.

28 My memory is unto everlasting generations.

29 They that eat me, shall yet hunger: and they that drink me, shall yet thirst.

30 He that hearkeneth to me, shall not be confounded: and they that work by me, shall not sin.

31 They that explain me shall have life everlasting.

32 All these things are the book of life, and the covenant of the most High, and the knowledge of truth.

33 Moses commanded a law in the precepts of justices, and an inheritance to the house of Jacob, and the promises to Israel.

34 He appointed to David his servant to raise up of him a most mighty king, and sitting on the throne of glory for ever.

35 Who filleth up wisdom as the Phison, and as the Tigris in the days of the new fruits.

36 Who maketh understanding to abound as the Euphrates, who multiplieth it as the Jordan in the time of harvest.

37 Who sendeth knowledge as the light, and riseth up as Gehon in the time of the vintage.

38 Who first hath perfect knowledge of her, and a weaker shall not search her out.

39 For her thoughts are more vast than the sea, and her counsels more deep than the great ocean.

40 I, wisdom, have poured out rivers.

41 I, like a brook out of a river of a mighty water; I, like a channel of a river. and like an aqueduct, came out of paradise.

42 I said: I will water my garden of plants, and I will water abundantly the fruits of my meadow.

43 And behold my brook became a great river, and my river came near to a sea:

44 For I make doctrine to shine forth to all as the morning light, and I will declare it afar off.

45 I will penetrate to all the lower parts of the earth, and will behold all that sleep, and will enlighten all that hope in the Lord.

46 I will yet pour out doctrine as prophecy, and will leave it to them that seek wisdom, and will not cease to instruct their offspring even to the holy age.

47 See ye that I have not laboured for myself only, but for all that seek out the truth.

Chapter 25

1 With three things my spirit is pleased, which are approved before God and men:

2 The concord of brethren, and the love of neighbours, and mall and wife that agree well together.

3 Three sorts my soul hateth, and I am greatly grieved at their life:

4 A poor man that is proud: a rich man that is a liar: an old man that is a fool, and doting.

5 The things that thou hast not gathered in thy youth, how shalt thou find them in thy old age?

6 O how comely is judgment for a grey head, and for ancients to know counsel!

7 O how comely is wisdom for the aged, and understanding and counsel to men of honour!

8 Much experience is the crown of old men, and the fear of God is their glory.

9 Nine things that are not to be imagined by the heart have I magnified, and the tenth I will utter to men with my tongue.

10 A man that hath joy of his children: and he that liveth and seeth the fall of his enemies.

11 Blessed is he. that dwelleth with a wise woman, and that hath not slipped with his tongue, and that hath not served such as are unworthy of him.

12 Blessed is he that findeth a true friend, and that declareth justice to an ear that heareth.

13 How great is he that findeth wisdom and knowledge! but there is none above him that feareth the Lord.

14 The fear of God hath set itself above all things:

15 Blessed is the man, to whom it is given to have the fear of God: he that holdeth it, to whom shall he be likened?

16 The fear of God is the beginning of his love: and the beginning of faith is to be fast joined unto it.

17 The sadness of the heart is every plague: and the wickedness of a woman is all evil.

18 And a man will choose any plague, but the plague of the heart:

19 And ally wickedness, but the wickedness of a woman:

20 And any affliction, but the affliction from them that hate him:

21 And ally revenge, but the revenge of enemies.

22 There is no head worse than the head of a serpent:

23 And there is no anger above the anger of a woman. It will be more agreeable to abide with a lion and a dragon, than to dwell with a wicked woman.

24 The wickedness of a woman changeth her face: and she darkeneth her countenance as a bear: and sheweth it like sackcloth. In the midst of her neighbours,

25 Her husband groaned, and hearing he sighed a little.

26 All malice is shore to the malice of a woman, let the lot of sinners fall upon her.

27 As the climbing of a sandy way is to the feet of the aged, so is a wife full of tongue to a quiet man.

28 Look not upon a woman's beauty, and desire not a woman for beauty.

29 A woman's anger, and impudence, and confusion is great.

30 A woman, if she have superiority, is contrary to her husband.

31 A wicked woman abateth the courage, and maketh a heavy countenance, and a wounded heart.

32 Feeble hands, and disjointed knees, a woman that doth not make her husband happy.

33 From the woman came the beginning of sin, and by her we all die.

34 Give no issue to thy water, no, not a little: nor to a wicked woman liberty to gad abroad.

35 If she walk not at thy hand, she will confound thee in the sight of thy enemies.

36 Cut her off from thy flesh, lest she always abuse thee.

Chapter 26

1 Happy is the husband of a good wife: for the number of his years is double.

2 A virtuous woman rejoiceth her husband: and shall fulfil the years of his life in peace.

3 A good wife is a good portion, she shall be given in the portion of them that fear God, to a man for his good deeds.

4 Rich or poor, if his heart is good, his countenance shall be cheerful at all times.

5 Of three things my heart hath been afraid, and at the fourth my face hath trembled:

6 The accusation of a city, and the gathering together of the people:

7 And a false calumny, all are more grievous than death.

8 A jealous woman is the grief and mourning of the heart.

9 With a jealous woman is a scourge of the tongue which communicateth with all.

10 As a yoke of oxen that is moved to and fro, so also is a wicked woman: he that hath hold of her, is as he that taketh hold of a scorpion.

11 A drunken woman is a great wrath: and her reproach and shame shall not be hid.

12 The fornication of a woman shall be known by the haughtiness of her eyes, and by her eyelids.

13 On a daughter that turneth not away herself, set a strict watch: lest finding an opportunity she abuse herself.

14 Take heed of the impudence of her eyes, and wonder not if she slight thee.

15 She will open her mouth as a thirsty traveller to the fountain, and will drink of every water near her, and will sit down by every hedge, and open her quiver against every arrow, until she fail.

16 The grace of a diligent woman shall delight her husband, and shall fat his bones.

17 Her discipline is the gift of God.

18 Such is a wise and silent woman, and there is nothing so much worth as a well instructed soul.

19 A holy and shamefaced woman is grace upon grace.

20 And no price is worthy of a continent soul.

21 As the sun when it riseth to the world in the high places of God, so is the beauty of a good wife for the ornament of her house.

22 As the lamp shining upon the holy candlestick, so is the beauty of the face in a ripe age.

23 As golden pillars upon bases of silver, so are the firm feet upon the soles of a steady woman.

24 As everlasting foundations upon a solid rock, so the commandments of God In the heart of a holy woman.

25 At two things my heart is grieved, and the third bringeth anger upon me:

26 A man of was fainting through poverty: and a man of sense despised:

27 And he that passeth over from justice to sin, God hath prepared such an one for the sword.

28 Two sorts of callings have appeared to me hard and dangerous: a merchant is hardly free from negligence: and a huckster shall not be justified from the sins of the lips.

Chapter 27

1 Through poverty many have sinned: and he that seeketh to be enriched, turneth away his eye.

2 As a stake sticketh fast in the midst of the joining of stones, so also in the midst of selling and buying, sin shall stick fast.

3 Sin shall be destroyed with the sinner.

4 Unless thou hold thyself diligently in the fear of the Lord, thy house shall quickly be overthrown.

5 As when one sifteth with a sieve, the dust will remain: so will the perplexity of a man in his thoughts.

6 The furnace trieth the potter's vessels, and the trial of affliction just men.

7 Be the dressing of a tree sheweth the fruit thereof, so a word out of the thought of the heart of man.

8 Praise not a man before he speaketh, for this is the trial of men.

9 If thou followest justice, thou shalt obtain her: and shalt put her on as a long robe of honour, and thou shalt dwell with her: and she shall protect thee for ever, and in the day of acknowledgment thou shalt find a strong foundation.

10 Birds resort unto their like: so truth will return to them that practise her.

11 The lion always lieth in wait for prey: so do sine for them that work iniquities.

12 A holy man continueth in wisdom as the sun: but a fool is changed as the moon.

13 In the midst of the unwise keep in the word till its time: but be continually among men that think.

14 The discourse of sinners is hateful, and their laughter is at the pleasures of sin.

15 The speech that sweareth much shall make the hair of the head stand upright: and its irreverence shall make one stop his ears.

16 Is the quarrels of the proud is the shedding of blood: and their cursing is a grievous hearing.

17 He that discloseth the secret of a friend loseth his credit, and shall never find a friend to his mind.

18 Love thy neighbour, and be joined to him with fidelity.

19 But if thou discover his secrets, follow no more after him.

20 For as a man that destroyeth his friend, so also is he that destroyeth the friendship of his neighbour.

21 And as one that letteth a bird go out of his hand, so hast thou let thy neighbour go, and thou shalt not get him again.

22 Follow after him no more, for he is gone afar off, he is fled, as a roe escaped out of the snare: because his soul is wounded.

23 Thou canst no more bind him up. And of a curse there is reconciliation:

24 But to disclose the secrets of a friend, leaveth no hope to an unhappy soul.

25 He that winketh with the eye forgeth wicked things, and no man will cast him off:

26 In the sight of thy eyes he will sweeten his mouth, and will admire thy words: but at the last he will writhe his mouth, and on thy words he will lay a stumblingblock.

27 I have hated many things, but not like him, and the Lord will hate him.

28 If one cast a stone on high, it will fall upon his own head: and the deceitful stroke will wound the deceitful.

29 He that diggeth a pit, shall fall into it: and he that setteth a stone for his neighbour, shall stumble upon it: and he that layeth a snare for another, shall perish in it.

30 A mischievous counsel shall be rolled back upon the author, and he shall not know from whence it cometh to him.

31 Mockery and reproach are of the proud, and vengeance as a lion shall lie in wait for him.

32 They shall perish in a snare that are delighted with the fall of the just: and sorrow shall consume them before they die.

33 Anger and fury are both of them abominable, and the sinful man shall be subject to them.

Chapter 28

1 He that seeketh to revenge himself, shall find vengeance from the Lord, and he will surely keep his sins in remembrance.

2 Forgive thy neighbour if he hath hurl thee: and then shall thy sins be forgiven to thee when thou prayest.

3 Man to man reserveth anger, and doth he seek remedy of God?

4 He hath no mercy on a man like himself, and doth he entreat for his own sins?

5 He that is but flesh, nourisheth anger, and doth he ask forgiveness of God? who shall obtain pardon for his sins?

6 Remember thy last things, and let enmity cease:

7 For corruption and death hang over in his commandments.

8 Remember the fear of God, and be not angry with thy neighbour.

9 Remember the covenant of the most High, and overlook the ignorance of thy neighbour.

10 Refrain from strife, and thou shalt diminish thy sine:

11 For a passionate man kindleth strife, and a sinful man will trouble his friends, and bring in debate in the midst of them that are at peace.

12 For as the wood of the forest is, so the fire burneth: and as a man's strength is, so shall his anger be, and according to his riches he shall increase his anger.

13 A hasty contention kindleth a fire: and a hasty quarrel sheddeth blood: and a tongue that beareth witness bringeth death.

14 If thou blow the spark, it shall burn as a fire: and if thou spit upon it, it shall be quenched: both come out of the mouth.

15 The whisperer and the double tongued is accursed: for he hath troubled many that were at peace.

16 The tongue of a third person hath disquieted many, and scattered them from nation to nation.

17 It hath destroyed the strong cities of the rich, and hath overthrown the houses of great men.

18 It hath cut in pieces the forces of people, and undone strong nations.

19 The tongue of a third person hath cast out valiant women, and deprived them of their labours.

20 He that hearkeneth to it, shall never have rest, neither shall he have a friend in whom he may repose.

21 The stroke of a whip maketh a blue mark: but the stroke of the tongue will break the bones.

22 Many have fallen by the edge of the sword, but not so many as have perished by their own tongue.

23 Blessed is he that is defended from a wicked tongue, that hath not passed into the wrath thereof, and that hath not drawn the yoke thereof, and hath not been bound in its bands.

24 For its yoke is a yoke of iron: and its bands are bands of brass.

25 The death thereof is a most evil death: and hell is preferable to it.

26 Its continuance shall not be for a long time, but it shall possess the ways of the unjust: and the just shall not be burnt with its flame.

27 They that forsake God shall fall into it, and it shall burn in them, and shall not be quenched, and it shall

be sent upon them as a lion, and as a leopard it shall tear them.

28 Hedge in thy ears with thorns, hear not a wicked tongue, and make doors and bars to thy mouth.

29 Melt down thy gold and silver, and make a balance for thy words, and a just bridle for thy mouth:

30 And take heed lest thou slip with thy tongue, and fall in the sight of thy enemies who lie in wait for thee, and thy fall be incurable unto death.

Chapter 29

1 He that sheweth mercy, lendeth to his neighbour: and he that is stronger in hand, keepeth the commandments.

2 Lend to thy neighbour in the time of his need, and pay thou thy neighbour again in due time.

3 Reap thy word, and deal faithfully with him: and thou shalt always find that which is necessary for thee.

4 Many have looked upon a thing lent as a thing found, and have given trouble to them that helped them.

5 Till they receive, they kiss the hands of the lender, and in promises they humble their voice:

6 But when they should repay, they will ask time, and will return tedious and murmuring words, and will complain of the time:

7 And if he be able to pay, he will stand off, he will scarce pay one half, and will count it as if he had found it:

8 But if not, he will defraud him of his money, and he shall get him for an enemy without cause:

9 And he will pay him with reproaches and curses, and instead of honour and good turn will repay him injuries.

10 Many have refused to lend, not out of wickedness, but they were afraid to be defrauded without cause.

11 But yet towards the poor be thou more hearty, and delay not to shew him mercy.

12 Help the poor because of the commandment: and send him not away empty handed because of his poverty.

13 Lose thy money for thy brother and thy friend: and hide it not under a stone to be lost.

14 Place thy treasure in the commandments of the most High, and it shall bring thee more profit than gold.

15 Shut up alms in the heart of the poor, and it shall obtain help for thee against all evil.

16 Better than the shield of the mighty, and better than the spear:

17 It shall fight for thee against thy enemy.

18 A good man is surety for his neighbour: and he that hath lost shame, will leave him to himself.

19 Forget not the kindness of thy surety: for he hath given his life for thee.

20 The sinner and the unclean fleeth from his surety.

21 A sinner attributeth to himself the goods of his surety: and he that is of an unthankful mind will leave him that delivered him.

22 A man is surety for his neighbour: and when he hath lost all shame, he shall forsake him.

23 Evil suretyship hath undone many of good estate, and hath tossed them as a wave of the sea.

24 It hath made powerful men to go from place to place round about, and they have wandered in strange countries.

25 A sinner that transgresseth the commandment of the Lord, shall fall into an evil suretyship: and he that undertaketh many things, shall fall into judgment.

26 Recover thy neighbour according to thy power, and take heed to thyself that thou fall not.

27 The chief thing for man's life is water and bread, and clothing, and a house to cover shame.

28 Better is the poor man's fare under a roof of boards, than sumptuous cheer abroad in another man's house.

29 Be contented with little instead of much, and thou shalt not hear the reproach of going abroad.

30 It is a miserable life to go as a guest from house to house: for where a man is a stranger, he shall not deal confidently, nor open his mouth.

31 He shall entertain and feed, and give drink to the unthankful, and moreover he shall hear bitter words.

32 Go, stranger, and furnish the table, and give others to eat what thou hast in thy hand.

33 Give place to the honourable presence of my friends: for I want my house, my brother being to be lodged with me.

34 These things are grievous to a man of understanding: the upbraiding of houseroom, and the reproaching of the lender.

Chapter 30

1 He that loveth his son, frequently chastiseth him, that he may rejoice in his latter end, and not grope after the doors of his neighbours.

2 He that instructeth his son shall be praised in him, and shall glory in him in the midst of them of his household.

3 He that teacheth his son, maketh his enemy jealous, and in the midst of his friends he shall glory in him.

4 His father is dead, and he is as if he were not dead: for he hath left one behind him that is like himself.

5 While he lived he saw and rejoiced in him: and when he died he was not sorrowful, neither was he confounded before his enemies.

6 For he left behind him a defender of his house against his enemies, and one that will requite kindness to his friends.

7 For the souls of his sons he shall bind up his wounds, and at every cry his bowels shall be troubled.

8 A horse not broken becometh stubborn, and a child left to himself will become headstrong.

9 Give thy son his way, and he shall make thee afraid: play with him, and he shall make thee sorrowful.

10 Laugh not with him, lest thou have sorrow, and at the last thy teeth be set on edge.

11 Give him not liberty in his youth, and wink not at his devices.

12 Bow down his neck while he is young, and beat his sides while he is a child, lest he grow stubborn, and regard thee not, and so be a sorrow of heart to thee.

13 Instruct thy son, and labour about him, lest his lewd behaviour be an offence to thee.

14 Better is a poor man who is sound, and strong of constitution, than a rich man who is weak and afflicted with evils.

15 Health of the soul in holiness of justice, is better then all gold and silver: and a sound body, than immense revenues.

16 There is no riches above the riches of the health of the body: and there is no pleasure above the joy of the heart.

17 Better is death than a bitter life: and everlasting rest, than continual sickness.

18 Good things that are hidden in a mouth that is shut, are as masses of meat set about a grave.

19 What good shall an offering do to an idol? for it can neither eat, nor smell:

20 So is he that is persecuted by the Lord, bearing the reward of his iniquity:

21 He seeth with his eyes, and groaneth, as an eunuch embracing a virgin, and sighing.

22 Give not up thy soul to sadness, and afflict not thyself in thy own counsel.

23 The joyfulness of the heart, is the life of a man, and a never failing treasure of holiness: and the joy of a man is length of life.

24 Have pity on thy own soul, pleasing God, and contain thyself: gather up thy heart in his holiness: and drive away sadness far from thee.

25 For sadness hath killed many, and there is no profit in it.

26 Envy and anger shorten a man's days, and pensiveness will bring old age before the time.

27 A Cheerful and good heart is always feasting: for his banquets are prepared with diligence.

Chapter 31

1 Watching for riches consumeth the flesh, and the thought thereof driveth away sleep.

2 The thinking beforehand turneth away the understanding, and a grievous sickness maketh the soul sober.

3 The rich man hath laboured in gathering riches together, and when he resteth he shall be filled with his goods.

4 The poor man hath laboured in his low way of life, and in the end he is still poor.

5 He that loveth gold, shall not be justified: and he that followeth after corruption, shall be filled with it.

6 Many have been brought to fall for gold, and the beauty thereof hath been their ruin.

7 Gold is a stumblingblock to them that sacrifice to it: woe to them that eagerly follow after it, and every fool shall perish by it.

8 Blessed is the rich man that is found without blemish: and that hath not gone after gold, nor put his trust in money nor in treasures.

9 Who is he, and we will praise him? for he hath done wonderful things in his life.

10 Who hath been tried thereby, and made perfect, he shall have glory everlasting. He that could have transgressed, and hath not transgressed: and could do evil things, and hath not done them:

11 Therefore are his goods established in the Lord, and all the church of the saints shall declare his alms.

12 Art thou set at a great table? be not the first to open thy mouth upon it.

13 Say not: There are many things which are upon it.

14 Remember that a wicked eye is evil.

15 What is created more wicked than an eye? therefore shall it weep over all the face when it shall see.

16 Stretch not out thy hand first, lest being disgraced with envy thou be put to confusion.

17 Be not hasty in a feast.

18 Judge of the disposition of thy neighbour by thyself.

19 Use as a frugal man the things that are set before thee: lest if thou eatest much, thou be hated.

20 Leave off first, for manners' sake: and exceed not, lest thou offend.

21 And if thou sittest among many, reach not thy hand out first of all: and be not the first to ask for drink.

22 How sufficient is a little wine for a man well taught, and in sleeping thou shalt not be uneasy with it, and thou shalt feel no pain.

23 Watching, and choler, and gripes, are with an intemperate man:

24 Sound and wholesome sleep with a moderate man: he shall sleep till morning, and his soul shall be delighted with him.

25 And if thou hast been forced to eat much, arise, go out, and vomit: and it shall refresh thee, and thou shalt not bring sickness upon thy body.

26 Hear me, my son, and despise me not: and in the end thou shalt find my words.

27 In all thy works be quick, and no infirmity shall come to thee.

28 The lips of many shall bless him that is liberal of his bread, and the testimony of his truth is faithful.

29 Against him that is niggardly of his bread, the city will murmur, and the testimony of his niggardliness is true.

30 Challenge not them that love wine: for wine hath destroyed very many.

31 Fire trieth hard iron: so wine drunk to excess shall rebuke the hearts of the proud.

32 Wine taken with sobriety is equal lire to men: if thou drink it moderately, thou shalt be sober.

33 What is his life, who is diminished with wine?

34 What taketh away life? death.

35 Wine was created from the beginning to make men joyful, and not to make them drunk.

36 Wine drunken with moderation is the joy of the soul and the heart.

37 Sober drinking is health to soul and body.

38 Wine drunken with excess raiseth quarrels; and wrath, and many ruins.

39 Wine drunken with excess is bitterness of the soul.

40 The heat of drunkenness is the stumblingblock of the fool, lessening strength and causing wounds.

41 Rebuke not thy neighbour in a banquet of wine: and despise him not in hip mirth.

42 Speak not to him words of reproach: and press him not in demanding again.

Chapter 32

1 Have they made thee ruler? be not lifted up: be among them as one of them.

2 Have care of them, and so sit down, and when thou hast acquitted thyself of all thy charge, take thy place :

3 That thou mayst rejoice for them, and receive a crown as an ornament of grace, and get the honour of the contribution.

4 Speak, thou that art elder: for it becometh thee,

5 To speak the first word with care knowledge, and hinder not music.

6 Where there is no hearing, pour out words, and be not lifted up out season with thy wisdom.

7 A concert of music in a banquet wine is as a carbuncle set in gold.

8 As a signet of an emerald in a work of gold: so is the melody of music with pleasant and moderate wine.

9 Hear in silence, and for thy reverence good grace shall come to thee.

10 Young man, scarcely speak in thy own cause.

11 If thou be asked twice, let thy answer be short.

12 In many things be as if thou wert ignorant, and hear in silence and withal seeking.

13 In the company of great men bake not upon thee: and when the ancients are present, speak not much.

14 Before a storm goeth lightning: and before shamefacedness goeth favour: and for thy reverence good grace shall come to thee.

15 And at the time of rising be not slack: but be first to run home to thy house, and there withdraw thyself, and there take thy pastime.

16 And do what thou hast a mind, but not in sin or proud speech.

17 And for all these things bless the Lord, that made thee, and that replenisheth thee with all his good things.

18 He that feareth the Lord, will receive his discipline: and they that will seek him early, shall find a blessing.

19 He that seeketh the law, shall be filled with it: and he that dealeth deceitfully, shall meet with a stumblingblock therein.

20 They that fear the Lord, shall find just judgment, and shall kindle justice as a light.

21 A sinful man will flee reproof, and will find an excuse according to his will.

22 A man of counsel will not neglect understanding, a strange and proud man will not dread fear:

23 Even after he hath done with fear without counsel, he shall be controlled by the things of his own seeking.

24 My son, do thou nothing without counsel, and thou shalt not repent when thou hast done.

25 Go not in the way of ruin, and thou shalt not stumble against the stones; trust not thyself to a rugged may, lest thou set a stumblingblock to thy soul.

26 And beware of thy own children, and take heed of them of thy household.

27 In every work of thine regard thy soul in faith: for this is the keeping of the commandments.

28 He that believeth God, taketh heed to the commandments: and he that trusteth in him, shall fare never the worse.

Chapter 33

1 No evils shall happen to him that feareth the Lord, but in temptation God will keep him, and deliver him from evils.

2 A wise man hateth not the commandments and justices, and he shall not be dashed in pieces as a ship in a storm.

3 A man of understanding is faithful to the law of God, and the law is faithful to him.

4 He that cleareth up a question, shall prepare what to say, and so having prayed he shall be heard, and shall keep discipline, and then he shall answer.

5 The heart of a fool is as a wheel of a cart: and his thoughts are like a rolling axletree.

6 A friend that is a mocker, is like a stallion horse: he neigheth under every one that sitteth upon him.

7 Why doth one day excel another, and one light another, and one year another year, when all come of the sun?

8 By the knowledge of the Lord they were distinguished, the sun being made, and keeping his commandment.

9 And he ordered the seasons, and holidays of them, and in them they celebrated festivals at an hour.

10 Some of them God made high and great days, and some of them he put in the number of ordinary days. And all men are from the ground, and out of the earth, from whence Adam was created.

11 With much knowledge the Lord hath divided them and diversified their ways.

12 Some of them hath he blessed, and exalted: and some of them hath he sanctified, and set near himself:

and some of them hath he cursed and brought low, end turned them from their station.

13 As the potter's clay is in his hand, to fashion and order it:

14 All his ways are according to his ordering: so man is in the hand of him that made him, and he will render to him according to his judgment.

15 Good is set against evil, and life against death: so also is the sinner against a just man. And so look upon all the works of the most High. Two and two, and one against another.

16 And I awaked last of all, and as one that gathereth after the grapegatherers.

17 In the blessing of God I also have hoped: and as one that gathereth grapes, have I filled the winepress.

18 See that I have not laboured for myself only, but for all that seek discipline.

19 Hear me, ye great men, and all ye people, and hearken with your ears, ye rulers of the church.

20 Give not to son or wife, brother or friend, power over thee while thou livest; and give not thy estate to another, lest then repent, and thou entreat for the same.

21 As long as thou livest, and hast breath in thee, let no man change thee.

22 For it is better that thy children should ask of thee, than that thou look toward the hands of thy children.

23 In all thy works keep the pre-eminence.

24 Let no stain sully thy glory. In the time when thou shalt end the days of thy life, and in the time of thy decease, distribute thy inheritance.

25 Fodder, and a wand, and a burden are for an ass: bread, and correction, and work for a slave.

26 He worketh under correction, and seeketh to rest: let his hands be idle, and he seeketh liberty.

27 The yoke and the thong bend a stiff neck, and continual labours bow a slave.

28 Torture and fetters are for a malicious slave: send him to work, that he be not idle:

29 For idleness hath taught much evil.

30 Set him to work: for so it is fit for him. And if he be not obedient, bring him down with fetters, but be not excessive towards any one: and do no grievous thing without judgment.

31 If thou have a faithful servant, let him be to thee as thy own soul: treat him as a brother: because in the blood of thy soul thou hast gotten him.

32 If thou hurt him unjustly, he will run away:

33 And if he rise up and depart, thou knowest not whom to ask, and in what way to seek him.

Chapter 34

1 The hopes of a man that is void of understanding are vain and deceitful: and dreams lift up fools.

2 The man that giveth heed to lying visions, is like to him that catcheth at a shadow, and followeth after the wind.

3 The vision of dreams is the resemblance of one thing to another: as when a man's likeness is before the face of a man.

4 What can be made clean by the unclean? and what truth can come from that which is false?

5 Deceitful divinations and lying omens and the dreams of evildoers, are vanity:

6 And the heart fancieth as that of a woman in travail: except it be a vision sent forth from the most High, set no thy heart upon them.

7 For dreams have deceived many, and they have failed that put their trust in them.

8 The word of the law shall be fulfilled without a lie, and wisdom shall be made plain in the mouth of the faithful.

9 What doth he know, that hath not been tried? A man that hath much experience, shall think of many things: and he that hath learned many things, shall shew forth understanding.

10 He that hath no experience, knoweth little: and he that hath been experienced in many things, multiplieth prudence.

11 He that hath not been tried, what manner of things doth he know? he that hath been surprised, shall abound with subtlety.

12 I have seen many things by travelling, and many customs of things.

13 Sometimes I have been in danger of death for these things, and I have been delivered by the grace of God.

14 The spirit of those that fear God; is sought after, and by his regard shall be blessed.

15 For their hope is on him that saveth them, and the eyes of God are upon them that love him.

16 He that feareth the Lord shall tremble at nothing, and shall not be afraid for he is his hope.

17 The soul of him that feareth the Lord is blessed.

18 To whom doth he look, and who in his strength?

19 The eyes of the Lord are upon them that fear him, he is their powerful protector, and strong stay, a defence from the heat, and a cover from the sun at noon,

20 A preservation from stumbling, and a help from falling; he raiseth up the soul, and enlighteneth the eyes, and giveth health, and life, and blessing.

21 The offering of him that sacrificeth of a thing wrongfully gotten, is stained, and the mockeries of the unjust are not acceptable.

22 The Lord is only for them that wait upon him in the way of truth and justice.

23 The most High approveth not the gifts of the wicked: neither hath he respect to the oblations of the unjust, nor will he be pacified for sine by the multitude of their sacrifices.

24 He that offereth sacrifice of the goods of the poor, is as one that sacrificeth the son in the presence of his father.

25 The bread of the needy, is the life of the poor: he that defraudeth them thereof, is a man of blood.

26 He that taketh away the bread gotten by sweat, is like him that killeth his neighbour.

27 He that sheddeth blood, and he that defraudeth the labourer of his hire, are brothers.

28 When one buildeth up, and another pulleth down: what profit have they but the labour?

29 When one prayeth, and another curseth: whose voice will God hear?

30 He that washeth himself after touching the dead, if he toucheth him again, what doth his washing avail?

31 So a man that fasteth for his sins, and doth the same again, what doth his humbling himself profit him? who will hear his prayer?

Chapter 35

1 He that keepeth the law, multiplieth offerings.

2 It is a wholesome sacrifice to take heed to the commandments, and to depart from all iniquity. _J

3 And to depart from injustice, is to offer a propitiatory sacrifice for injustices, and a begging of pardon for sins.

4 He shall return thanks, that offereth fine flour: and he that doth mercy, offereth sacrifice.

5 To depart from iniquity is that which pleaseth the Lord, and to depart from injustice, is an entreaty for sins.

6 Thou shalt not appear empty in the sight of the Lord.

7 For all these things are to be done because of the commandment of God.

8 The oblation of the just maketh the altar fat, and is an odour of sweetness in the sight of the most High.

9 The sacrifice of the just is acceptable, and the Lord will not forget the memorial thereof.

10 Give glory to God with a good heart: and diminish not the firstfruits of thy hands.

11 In every gift shew a cheerful countenance, and sanctify thy tithes with joy.

12 Give to the most High according to what he hath given to thee, and with a good eye do according to the ability of thy hands:

13 For the Lord maketh recompense, and will give thee seven times as much.

14 Do not offer wicked gifts, for such he will not receive.

15 And look not upon an unjust sacrifice, for the Lord is judge, and there is not with him respect of person.

16 The Lord will not accept any person against a poor man, and he will hear the prayer of him that is wronged.

17 He will not despise the prayers of the fatherless; nor the widow, when she poureth out her complaint.

18 Do not the widow's tears run down the cheek, and her cry against him that causeth them to fall?

19 For from the cheek they go up even to heaven, and the Lord that heareth will not be delighted with them.

20 He that adoreth God with joy, shall be accepted, and his prayer shall approach even to the clouds.

21 The prayer of him that humbleth himself, shall pierce the clouds: and till it come nigh he will not be comforted: and he will not depart till the most High behold.

22 And the Lord will not be slack, but will judge for the just, and will do judgment: and the Almighty will not have patience with them, that he may crush their back:

23 And he will repay vengeance to the Gentiles, till he have taken away the multitude of the proud, and broken the sceptres of the unjust,

24 Till he have rendered to men according to their deeds: and according to the works of Adam, and according to his presumption,

25 Till he have judged the cause of his people, and he shall delight the just with his mercy.

26 The mercy of God is beautiful in the time of affliction, as a cloud of rain in the time of drought.

Chapter 36

1 Have mercy upon us, O God of all, and behold us, and shew us the light of thy mercies:

2 And send thy fear upon the nations, that have not sought after thee: that they may know that there is no God beside thee, and that they may shew forth thy wonders.

3 Lift up thy hand over the strange nations, that they may see thy power.

4 For as thou hast been sanctified in us in their sight, so thou shalt be magnified among them in our presence,

5 That they may know thee, as we also have known thee, that there is no God beside thee, O Lord.

6 Renew thy signs, and work new miracles.

7 Glorify thy hand, and thy right arm.

8 Raise up indignation, and pour out wrath.

9 Take away the adversary, and crush the enemy.

10 Hasten the time, and remember the end, that they may declare thy wonderful works.

11 Let him that escapeth be consumed by the rage of the fire: and let them perish that oppress thy people.

12 Crush the head of the princes of the enemies that say: There is no other beside us.

13 Gather together all the tribes of Jacob: that they may know that there is no God besides thee, and may declare thy great works: and thou shalt inherit them as from the beginning.

14 Have mercy on thy people, upon whom thy name is invoked: and upon Israel, m whom thou hast raised up to be thy firstborn.

15 Have mercy on Jerusalem, the city which thou hast sanctified, the city of thy rest.

16 Fill Sion with thy unspeakable words, and thy people with thy glory.

17 Give testimony to them that are thy creatures from the beginning, and raise up the prophecies which the former prophets spoke in thy name.

18 Reward them that patiently wait for thee, that thy prophets may be found faithful: and hear the prayers of thy servants,

19 According to the blessing of Aaron over thy people, and direct us into the way of justice, and let all know that dwell upon the earth, that thou art God the beholder of all ages.

20 The belly will devour all meat, yet one is better than another.

21 The palate tasteth venison and the wise heart false speeches.

22 A perverse heart will cause grief, and a man of experience will resist it.

23 A woman will receive every man: yet one daughter is better than another.

24 The beauty of a woman cheereth the countenance of her husband, and a man desireth nothing more.

25 If she have a tongue that can cure, and likewise mitigate and shew mercy: her husband is not like other men.

26 He that possesseth a good wife, beginneth a possession: she is a help like to himself, and a pillar of rest.

27 Where there is no hedge, the possession shall be spoiled: and where there is no wife, he mourneth that is in want.

28 Who will trust him that hath no rest, and that lodgeth wheresoever the night taketh him, as a robber well appointed, that skippeth from city to city.

Chapter 37

1 Every friend will say: I also am his friend: but there is a friend, that is only a friend in name. Is not this a grief even to death?

2 But a companion and a friend shall be turned to an enemy.

3 O wicked presumption, whence camest thou to cover the earth with thy malice, and deceitfulness?

4 There is a companion who rejoiceth with his friend in his joys, but in the time of trouble, he will be against him.

5 There is a companion who condoleth with his friend for his belly's sake, and he will take up a shield against enemy.

6 Forget not thy friend in thy mind, and be not unmindful of him in thy riches.

7 Consult not with him that layeth a snare for thee, and hide thy counsel from them that envy thee.

8 Every counsellor giveth out counsel, but there is one that is a counsellor for himself.

9 Beware of a counsellor. And know before what need he hath: for he will devise to his own mind:

10 Lest he thrust a stake into the ground, and say to thee:

11 Thy way is good; and then stand on the other side to see what shall befall thee.

12 Treat not with a man without religion concerning holiness, nor with an unjust man concerning justice, nor with a woman touching her of whom she is jealous, nor with a coward concerning war, nor with a merchant about traffic, nor with a buyer of selling, nor with an envious man of giving thanks,

13 Nor with the ungodly of piety, nor with the dishonest of honesty, nor with the held labourer of every work

14 Nor with him that worketh by the year of the finishing of the year, nor with an idle servant of much business: give no heed to these in any matter of counsel.

15 But be continually with a holy man, whomsoever thou shalt know to observe the fear of God,

16 Whose soul is according to thy own soul: and who, when thou shalt stumble in the dark, will be sorry for thee.

17 And establish within thyself a heart of good counsel: for there is no other thing of more worth to thee than it.

18 The soul of a holy man discovereth sometimes true things, more than seven watchmen that sit in a high piece to watch.

19 But above all these things pray to the most High, that he may direct thy way in truth.

20 In all thy works let the true word go before thee, and steady counsel before every action.

21 A wicked word shall change the beast: out of which four manner of things arise, good and evil, life and death: and the tongue is continually the ruler of them. There is a man that is subtle and a teacher of many, and yet is unprofitable to his own soul.

22 A skilful man hath taught many, and is sweet to his own soul.

23 He that speaketh sophistically, is hateful: he shall be destitute of every thing.

24 Grace is not given him from the Lord: for he is deprived of all wisdom.

25 There is a wise man that is wise to his own soul: and the fruit of his understanding is commendable.

26 A wise man instructeth his own people, and the fruits of his understanding are faithful.

27 A wise man shall be filled with blessings, and they that see shall praise him.

28 The life of a man is in the number of his days: but the days of Israel are innumerable.

29 A wise man shall inherit honour among his people, and his name shall live for ever.

30 My son, prove thy soul in thy life: and if it be wicked, give it no power:

31 For all things are not expedient for all, and every kind pleaseth not every soul.

32 Be not greedy in any feasting, and pour not out thyself upon any meat:

33 For in many meats there will be sickness, and greediness will turn to choler.

34 By surfeiting many have perished: but he that is temperate, shall prolong life.

Chapter 38

1 Honour the physician for the need thou hast of him: for the most High hath created him.

2 For all healing is from God, and he shall receive gifts of the king.

3 The skill of the physician shall lift up his head, and in the sight of great men he shall be praised.

4 The most High hath created medicines out of the earth, and a wise man will not abhor them.

5 Was not bitter water made sweet with wood?

6 The virtue of these things is come to the knowledge of men, and the meet High hath given knowledge to men, that he may be honoured in his wonders.

7 By these he shall cure and shall allay their pains, and of these the apothecary shall make sweet confections, and shall make up ointments of health, and of his works there shall be no end.

8 For the peace of God is over all the face of the earth.

9 My son, in thy sickness neglect not thyself, but pray to the Lord, and he shall heal thee.

10 Turn away from sin and order thy hands aright, and cleanse thy heart from all offence.

11 Give a sweet savour, and a memorial of fine flour, and make a fat offering, and then give place to the physician.

12 For the Lord created him: and let him not depart from thee, for his works are necessary.

13 For there is a time when thou must fall into their hands:

14 And they shall beseech the Lord, that he would prosper what they give for ease and remedy, for their conversation.

15 He that sinneth in the sight of his Maker, shall fall into the hands of the physician.

16 My son, shed tears over the dead, and begin to lament as if thou hadst suffered some great harm, and according to judgment cover his body, and neglect not his burial.

17 And for fear of being ill spoken of weep bitterly for a, day, and then comfort thyself in thy sadness.

18 And make mourning for him according to his merit for a day, or two, for fear of detraction.

19 For of sadness cometh death, and it overwhelmeth the strength, and the sorrow of the heart boweth down the neck.

20 In withdrawing aside sorrow remaineth: and the substance of the poor is according to his heart.

21 Give not up thy heart to sadness, but drive it from thee: and remember the latter end.

22 Forget it not: for there is no returning, and thou shalt do him no good, and shalt hurt thyself.

23 Remember my judgment: for also shall be so: yesterday for me, and to day for thee.

24 When the dead is at rest, let his remembrance rest, and comfort him in the departing of his spirit.

25 The wisdom of a scribe cometh by his time of leisure: and he that is less in action, shall receive wisdom.

26 With what wisdom shall he be furnished that holdeth the plough, and that glorieth in the goad, that driveth the oxen therewith, and is occupied in their labours, and his whole talk is about the offspring of bulls?

27 He shall give his mind to turn up furrows, and his care is to give the kine fodder.

28 So every craftsman and workmaster that laboureth night and day, he who maketh graven seals, and by his continual diligence varieth the figure: he shall give his mind to the resemblance of the picture, and by his watching shall finish the work.

29 So doth the smith sitting by the anvil and considering the iron work. The vapour of the fire wasteth his flesh, and he fighteth with the heat of the furnace.

30 The noise of the hammer is always in his ears, and his eye is upon the pat tern of the vessel he maketh.

31 He setteth his mind to finish his work, and his watching to polish them, to perfection.

32 So doth the potter sitting at his work, turning the wheel about with his feet, who is always carefully set to his work, and maketh all his work by number:

33 He fashioneth the clay with his arm, and boweth down his strength before his feet:

34 He shall give his mind to finish the glazing, and his watching to make clean the furnace.

35 All these trust to their hands, and every one is wise in his own art.

36 Without these a city is not built.

37 And they shall not dwell, nor walk about therein, and they shall not go up into the assembly.

38 Upon the judges' seat they shall not sit, and the ordinance of judgment they shall not understand, neither shall they declare discipline and judgment, and they shall not be found where parables are spoken:

39 But they shall strengthen the state of the world, and their prayer shall be in the work of their craft, applying their soul, and searching in the law of the most High.

Chapter 39

1 The wise men will seek out the wisdom of all the ancients and will be occupied in the prophets.

2 He will keep the sayings of renowned men, and will enter withal into the subtilties of parables.

3 He will search out the hidden meanings of proverbs, and will be conversant in the secrets of parables.

4 He shall serve among great men, and: appear before the governor.

5 He shall pass into strange countries: for he shall try good and evil among men.

6 He will give his heart to resort early to the Lord that made him, and he will pray in the sight of the most High.

7 He will open his mouth in prayer, and will make supplication for his sins.

8 For if it shall please the great Lord, he will fill him with the spirit of understanding:

9 And he will pour forth the words of his wisdom as showers, and in his prayer he will confess to the Lord.

10 And he shall direct his counsel, and his knowledge, and in his secrets shall he meditate.

11 He shall shew forth the discipline he hath learned, and shall glory in the law of the covenant of the Lord.

12 Many shall praise his wisdom, and it shall never be forgotten.

13 The memory of him shall not depart away, and his name shall be in request from generation to generation.

14 Nations shall declare his wisdom, and the church shall shew forth his praise.

15 If he continue, he shall leave a name above a thousand: and if he rest, it shall be to his advantage.

16 I will yet meditate that I may declare: for I am filled as with a holy transport.

17 By a voice he saith: Hear me, ye divine offspring, and bud forth as the rose planted by the brooks of waters.

18 Give ye a sweet odour as frankincense.

19 Send forth flowers, as the lily, and yield a smell, and bring forth leaves in grace, and praise with canticles, and bless the Lord in his works.

20 Magnify his name, and give glory to him with the voice of your lips, and with the canticles of your mouths, and with harps, and in praising him, you shall say in this manner:

21 All the works of the Lord are exceeding good.

22 At his word the waters stood as a heap: and at the words of his mouth the receptacles of waters:

23 For at his commandment favour is shewn, and there is no diminishing of his salvation.

24 The works of all flesh are before him, and there is nothing hid from his eyes.

25 He seeth from eternity to eternity, and there is nothing wonderful before him.

26 There is no saying: What is this, or what is that? for all things shall be sought in their time.

27 His blessing hath overflowed like a river.

28 And as a flood hath watered the earth; so shall his wrath inherit the nations, that have not sought after him:

29 Even as he turned the waters into a dry land, and the earth was made dry: and his ways were made plain for their journey: so to sinners they are stumbling blocks in his wrath.

30 Good things were created for the good from the beginning, so for the wicked, good and evil things.

31 The principal things necessary for the life of men, are water, fire, and iron, salt, milk, and bread of flour, and honey, and the cluster of the grape, and oil, and clothing.

32 All these things shall be for good to the holy, so to the sinners and the ungodly they shall be turned into evil.

33 There are spirits that are created for vengeance, and in their fury they lay on grievous torments.

34 In the time of destruction they shall pour out their force: and they shall appease the wrath of him that made them.

35 Fire, hail, famine, and death, all these were created for vengeance.

36 The teeth of beasts, and scorpions, and serpents, and the sword taking vengeance upon the ungodly unto destruction.

37 In his commandments they shall feast, and they shall be ready upon earth when need is, and when their time is come they shall not transgress his word.

38 Therefore from the beginning I was resolved, and I have meditated, and thought on these things and left them in writing.

39 All the works of the Lord are good, and he will furnish every work in due time.

40 It is not to be said: This is worse than that: for all shall be well approved in their time.

41 Now therefore with the whole heart and mouth praise ye him, and bless the name of the Lord.

Chapter 40

1 Great labour is created for all men, and a heavy yoke is upon the children of Adam, from the day of their coming out of their mother's womb, until the day of their burial into the mother of all.

2 Their thoughts, and fears of the heart, their imagination of things to come, and the day of their end:

3 From him that sitteth on a glorious throne, unto him that is humbled in earth and ashes:

4 From him that weareth purple, and beareth the crown, even to him that is covered with rough linen: wrath, envy, trouble, unquietness, and the fear of death, continual anger, and strife,

5 And in the time of rest upon his bed, the sleep of the night changeth his knowledge.

6 A little and as nothing is his rest, and afterward in sleep, as in the day of keeping watch.

7 He is troubled in the vision of his heart, as if he had escaped in the day of battle. In the time of his safety he rose up, and wondereth that there is no fear:

8 Such things happen to all flesh, from man even to beast, and upon sinners are sevenfold more.

9 Moreover, death, and bloodshed, strife, and sword, oppressions, famine, and affliction, and scourges:

10 All these things are created for the wicked, and for their sakes came the flood.

11 All things that are of the earth, shall return to the earth again, and all waters shall return to the sea.

12 All bribery, and injustice shall blotted out, and fidelity shall stand for ever.

13 The riches of the unjust shall be dried up like a river, and shall pass sway a noise like a great thunder in rain.

14 While he openeth his hands he shall rejoice: but transgressors shall pine away in the end.

15 The offspring of the ungodly shall not bring forth many branches, and make a noise as unclean roots upon the top of a rock.

16 The weed growing over every water, and at the bank of the river, shall be pulled up before all grass.

17 Grace is like a paradise in blessings, and mercy remaineth for ever.

18 The life of a labourer that is content with what he hath, shall be sweet, and in it thou shalt find a treasure.

19 Children, and the building of a city shall establish a name, but a blameless wife shall be counted above them both.

20 Wine and music rejoice the heart, but the love of wisdom is above them both.

21 The flute and the psaltery make a sweet melody, but a pleasant tongue is above them both.

22 Thy eye desireth favour and beauty, but more than these green sown fields.

23 A friend and companion meeting together in season, but above them both is a wife with her husband.

24 Brethren are a help in the time of trouble, but mercy shall deliver more than they.

25 Gold and silver make the feet stand sure: but wise counsel is above them both.

26 Riches and strength lift up the heart: but above these is the fear of the Lord.

27 There is no want in the fear of the Lord, and it needeth not to seek for help.

28 The fear of the Lord is like a paradise of blessing, and they have covered it above all glory.

29 My son, in thy lifetime be not indigent: for it is better to die than to want.

30 The life of him that looketh toward another man's table is not to be counted a life: for he feedeth his soul with another man's meat.

31 But a man, well instructed and taught, will look to himself.

32 Begging will be sweet in the mouth of the unwise, but in his belly there shall burn a fire.

Chapter 41

1 The children will complain of an ungodly father, because for his sake they are in reproach.

11 Woe to you, ungodly men, who have forsaken the law of the most high Lord.

12 And if you be born, you shall be born in malediction: and if you die, in malediction shall be your portion.

13 All things that are of the earth, shall return into the earth: so the ungodly shall from malediction to destruction.

14 The mourning of men is about their body, but the name of the ungodly shall be blotted out.

15 Take care of a good name: for this shall continue with thee, more than a thousand treasures precious and great.

16 A good life hath its number of days: but a good name shall continue for ever.

17 My children, keep discipline in peace: for wisdom that is hid, and a treasure that is not seen, what profit is there in them both? 18 Better is the man that hideth his folly, then the man that hideth his wisdom.

19 Wherefore have a shame of these things I am now going to speak of.

20 For it is not good to keep all shamefacedness: and all things do not please all men in opinion.

21 Be ashamed of fornication before father and mother: and of a lie before a governor and a man in power:

22 Of an offence before a prince, and a judge: of iniquity before a congregation and a people:

23 Of injustice before a companion and friend: and in regard to the place where thou dwellest,

24 Of theft, and of the truth of God, and the covenant: of leaning with thy elbow over meat, and of deceit in giving and taking:

25 Of silence before them that salute thee: of looking upon a harlot: and of turning away thy face from thy kinsman.

26 Turn not sway thy face from thy neighbour, and of taking away a portion and not restoring.

27 Gaze not upon another man's wife, and be not inquisitive after his handmaid, and approach not her bed.

28 Be ashamed of upbraiding speeches before friends: and after thou hast given, upbraid not.

Chapter 42

1 Repeat not the word which thou hast heard, and disclose not the thing that is secret; so shalt thou be truly without confusion, and shah find favour before all men: be not ashamed of any of these things, and accept no person to sin thereby:

2 Of the law of the most High, and of his covenant, and of judgment to justify the ungodly:

3 Of the affair of companions and travellers, and of the gift of the inheritance of friends:

4 Of exactness of balance and weights, of getting much or little:

5 Of the corruption of buying, and of merchants, and of much correction of children, and to make the side of a wicked slave to bleed.

6 Sure keeping is good over a wicked wife.

7 Where there are many hands, shut up, and deliver all things in number, and weight: and put all in writing that thou givest out or receivest in.

8 Be not ashamed to inform the unwise and foolish, and the aged, that are judged I by young men: and thou shalt be well instructed in all things, and well approved in the sight of all men living.

9 The father waketh for the daughter when no man knoweth, and the care for her taketh away his sleep, when she is young, lest she pass away the flower of her age, and when she is married, lest she should be hateful:

10 In her virginity, lest she should be corrupted, and be found with child in her father's house: and having a husband, lest she should misbehave herself, or at the least become barren.

11 Keep a sure watch over a shameless daughter: lest at any time she make thee become a laughingstock to thy enemies, and a byword in the city, and a reproach among the people, and she make thee ashamed before all the multitude.

12 Behold not everybody's beauty: and tarry not among women.

13 For from garments cometh a moth, end from a woman the iniquity of a man.

14 For better is the iniquity of a man, than a woman doing a good turn, and a woman bringing shame and reproach.

15 I will now remember the works of the Lord, and I will declare the things I have seen. By the words of the Lord are his works.

16 The sun giving light hath looked upon all things, and full of the glory of the Lord is his work.

17 Hath not the Lord made the saints to declare all his wonderful works, which the Lord Almighty hath firmly settled to be established for his glory?

18 He hath searched out the deep, and the heart of men: and considered their crafty devices.

19 For the Lord knoweth all knowledge, and hath beheld the signs of the world, he declareth the things that are past, and the things that are to come, and revealeth the traces of hidden things.

20 No thought escapeth him, and no word can hide itself from him.

21 He hath beautified the glorious works of his wisdom: and he Is from eternity to eternity, and to him nothing may be added,

22 Nor can he be diminished, and he hath no need of any counsellor.

23 O how desirable are all his works, and what we can know is but as a spark!

24 All these things live, and remain for ever, and for every use all things obey him.

25 All things are double, one against another, and he hath made nothing defective.

26 He hath established the good things of every one. And who shall be filled with beholding his glory?

Chapter 43

1 The firmament on high is his beauty, the beauty of heaven with its glorious shew.

2 The sun when he appeareth shewing forth at his rising, an admirable instrument, the work of the most High.

3 At noon he burneth the earth, and who can abide his burning heat? As one keeping a furnace in the works of heat:

4 The sun three times as much, burneth the mountains, breathing out fiery vapours, and shining with his beams, he blindeth the eyes.

5 Great is the Lord that made him, and at his words he hath hastened his course.

6 And the moon in all in her season, is for a declaration of times and a sign of the world.

7 From the moon is the sign of the festival day, a light that decreaseth in her perfection.

8 The month is called after her name, increasing wonderfully in her perfection

9 Being an instrument of the armies on high, shining gloriously in the Armament of heaven.

10 The glory of the stars is the beauty of heaven; the Lord enlighteneth the world on high.

11 By the words of the holy one they shall stand in judgment, and shall never fail in their watches.

12 Look upon the rainbow, and bless him that made it: it is very beautiful in its brightness.

13 It encompasseth the heaven about with the circle of its glory, the hands of the most High have displayed it.

14 By his commandment he maketh the snow to fall apace, and sendeth forth swiftly the lightnings of his judgment.

15 Through this are the treasures opened, and the clouds fly out like birds.

16 By his greatness he hath fixed the clouds, and the hailstones are broken.

17 At his sight shall the mountains be shaken, and at his will the south wind shall blow.

18 The noise of his thunder shall strike the earth, so doth the northern storm, and the whirlwind:

19 And as the birds lighting upon the earth, he scattereth snow, and the falling thereof, is as the coming down of locusts.

20 The eye admireth at the beauty of the whiteness thereof, and the heart is astonished at the shower thereof.

21 He shall pour frost as salt upon the earth: and when it freezeth, it shall become like the tops of thistles.

22 The cold north wind bloweth, and the water is congealed into crystal; upon every gathering together of waters it shall rest, and shall clothe the waters as a breastplate.

23 And it shall devour the mountains, and burn the wilderness, and consume all that is green as with fire.

24 A present remedy of all is the speedy coming of a cloud, and a dew that meeteth it, by the heat that cometh, shall overpower it.

25 At his word the wind is still, and with his thought he appeaseth the deep, and the Lord hath planted islands therein.

26 Let them that sail on the sea, tell the dangers thereof: and when we hear with our ears, we shall admire.

27 There are great and wonderful works: a variety of beasts, and of all living things, and the monstrous creatures of whales.

28 Through him is established the end of their journey, and by his word all things are regulated.

29 We shall say much, and yet shall want words: but the sum of our words is, He is all.

30 What shall we be able to do to glorify him? for the Almighty himself is above all his works.

31 The Lord is terrible, and exceeding great, and his power is admirable.

32 Glorify the Lord as much as ever you can, for he will yet far exceed, and his magnificence is wonderful.

33 Blessing the Lord, exalt him as much as you can: for he is above all praise.

34 When you exalt him put forth all your strength, and be not weary: for you can never go far enough.

35 Who shall see him, and declare him? and who shall magnify him as he is from the beginning?

36 There are many things hidden from us that are greater than these: for we have seen but a few of his works.

37 But the Lord hath made all things, and to the godly he hath given wisdom.

Chapter 44

1 Let us now praise men of renown, and our fathers in their generation.

2 The Lord hath wrought great glory through his magnificence from the beginning.

3 Such as have borne rule in their dominions, men of great power, and endued with their wisdom, shewing forth in the prophets the dignity of prophets,

4 And ruling over the present people, and by the strength of wisdom instructing the people in most holy words.

5 Such as by their skill sought out musical tunes, and published canticles of the scriptures.

6 Rich men in virtue, studying beautifulness: living at peace in their houses.

7 All these have gained glory in their generations, and were praised in their days.

8 They that were born of them have left a name behind them, that their praises might be related:

9 And there are some, of whom there is no memorial: who are perished, as if they had never been: and are become as if they had never been born, and their children with them.

10 But these were men of mercy, whose godly deeds have not failed:

11 Good things continue with their seed,

12 Their posterity are a holy inheritance, and their seed hath stood in the covenants.

13 And their children for their sakes remain for ever: their seed and their glory shall not be forsaken.

14 Their bodies are buried in peace, and their name liveth unto generation and generation.

15 Let the people shew forth their wisdom, and the church declare their praise.

16 Henoch pleased God, and was translated into paradise, that he may give repentance to the nations.

17 Noe was found perfect, just, and in the time of wrath he was made a reconciliation.

18 Therefore was there a remnant left to the earth, when the flood came.

19 The covenants of the world were made with him, that all flesh should no more be destroyed with the hood.

20 Abraham was the great father of a multitude of nations, and there was not found the like to him in glory, who kept the law of the most High, and was in covenant with him.

21 In his flesh he established the covenant, and in temptation he was found faithful.

22 Therefore by an oath he gave him glory in his posterity, that he should increase as the dust of the earth,

23 And that he would exalt his seed as the stars, and they should inherit from sea to sea, and from the river to the ends of the earth.

24 And he did in like manner with Isaac for the sake of Abraham his father.

25 The Lord gave him the blessing of all nations, and confirmed his covenant upon the head of Jacob.

26 He acknowledged him in his blessings, and gave him an inheritance, and divided him his portion in twelve tribes.

27 And he preserved for him men of mercy, that found grace in the eyes of all flesh.

Chapter 45

1 Moses was beloved of God, and men: whose memory is in benediction.

2 He made him like the saints in glory, and magnified him in the fear of his enemies, and with his words he made prodigies to cease.

3 He glorified him in the sight of kings, and gave him commandments in the sight of his people, and shewed him his glory.

4 He sanctified him in his faith, and meekness, and chose him out of all flesh.

5 For he heard him, and his voice, and brought him into a cloud.

6 And he gave him commandments before his face, and a law of life and instruction, that he might teach Jacob his covenant, and Israel his judgments.

7 He exalted Aaron his brother, and like to himself of the tribe of Levi:

8 He made an everlasting covenant with him, and gave him the priesthood of the nation, and made him blessed in glory,

9 And he girded him about with a glorious girdle, and clothed him with a robe of glory, and crowned him with majestic attire.

10 He put upon him a garment to the feet, and breeches, and as ephod, and he compassed him with many little bells of gold all round about,

11 That as he went there might be a sound, and a noise made that might be heard in the temple, for a memorial to the children of his people.

12 He gave him a holy robe of gold, and blue, and purple, a woven work of a wise man, endued with judgment and truth:

13 Of twisted scarlet the work of an artist, with precious stones cut and set in gold, and graven by the work of a lapidary for a memorial, according to the number of the tribes of Israel.

14 And a crown of gold upon his mitre wherein was engraved Holiness, an ornament of honour: a work of power, and delightful to the eyes for its beauty.

15 Before him there were none so beautiful, even from the beginning.

16 No stranger was ever clothed with them, but only his children alone, and his grandchildren for ever.

17 His sacrifices were consumed with fire every day.

18 Moses filled his hands and anointed him with holy oil.

19 This was made to him for an everlasting testament, and to his seed as the days of heaven, to execute the office of the priesthood, and to have praise, and to glorify his people in his name.

20 He chose him out of all men living, to offer sacrifice to God, incense, and a good savour, for a memorial to make reconciliation for his people:

21 And he gave him power in his commandments, in the covenants of his judgments, that he should teach Jacob his testimonies, and give light to Israel in his law.

22 And strangers stood up against him, and through envy the men that were with Dathan and Abiron, compassed him about in the wilderness, and the congregation of Core in their wrath.

23 The Lord God saw and it pleased him not, and they were consumed in his wrathful indignation.

24 He wrought wonders upon them, and consumed them with a flame of fire.

25 And he added glory to Aaron, and gave him an inheritance, and divided unto him the firstfruits of the increase of the earth.

26 He prepared them bread in the first place unto fulness: for the sacrifices also of the Lord they shall eat, which he gave to him, and to his seed.

27 But he shall not inherit among the people in the land, and he hath no portion among the people: for he himself is his portion and inheritance.

28 Phinees the son of Eleazar is the third in glory, by imitating him in the fear of the Lord:

29 And he stood up in the shameful fall of the people: in the goodness and readiness of his soul he appeased God for Israel.

30 Therefore he made to him a covenant of peace, to be the prince of the sanctuary, and of his people, that the dignity of priesthood should be to him and to his seed for ever.

31 And a covenant to David the king, the son of Jesse of the tribe of Juda, an inheritance to him and to his seed, that he might give wisdom into our heart to judge his people in justice, that their good things might not be abolished, and he made their glory in their nation everlasting.

Chapter 46

1 Valiant in war was Jesus the son of Nave, who was successor of Moses among the prophets, who was great according to his name,

2 Very great for the saving the elect of God, to overthrow the enemies that rose up against them, that he might get the inheritance for Israel.

3 How great glory did he gain when he lifted up his hands, and stretched out swords against the cities?

4 Who before him hath so resisted? for the Lord himself brought the enemies.

5 Was not the sun stopped in his anger, and one day made as two?

6 He called upon the most high Sovereign when the enemies assaulted him on every side, and the great and holy God heard him by hailstones of exceeding great force.

7 He made a violent assault against the nation of his enemies, and in the descent he destroyed the adversaries.

8 That the nations might know his power, that it is not easy to fight against God. And he followed the mighty one:

9 And in the days of Moses he did a work of mercy, he and Caleb the son of Jephone, in standing against the enemy, and withholding the people from sins, and appeasing the wicked murmuring.

10 And they two being appointed, were delivered out of the danger from among the number of six hundred thousand men on foot, to bring them into their inheritance, into the land that floweth with milk and honey.

11 And the Lord gave strength also to Caleb, and his strength continued even to his old age, so that he went up to the high places of the land, and his seed obtained it for an inheritance:

12 That all the children of Israel might see, that it is good to obey the holy God.

13 Then all the judges, every one by name, whose heart was not corrupted: who turned not away from the Lord,

14 That their memory might be blessed, and their bones spring up out of their place,

15 And their name continue for ever, the glory of the holy men remaining unto their children.

16 Samuel the prophet of the Lord, the beloved of the Lord his God, established a new government, and anointed princes over his people.

17 By the law of the Lord he judged the congregation, and the God of Jacob beheld, and by his fidelity he was proved a prophet.

18 And he was known to be faithful in his words, because he saw the God of light:

19 And called upon the name of the Lord Almighty, in fighting against the enemies who beset him on every side, when he offered a lamb without blemish.

20 And the Lord thundered from heaven, and with a great noise made his voice to be heard.

21 And he crushed the princes of the Tyrians, and all the lords of the Philistines:

22 And before the time of the end of his life in the world, he protested before the Lord, and his anointed: money, or any thing else, even to a shoe, he had not taken of any man, and no mall did accuse him.

23 And after this he slept, and he made known to the king, and shewed him the end of his life, and he lifted up his voice from the earth in prophecy to blot out the wickedness of the nation.

Chapter 47

1 Then Nathan the prophet arose in the days of David.

1 the Lord the Almighty, and he gave strength in his right hand, to take away the mighty warrior, and to set up the horn of his nation.

2 And as the fat taken away from the flesh, so was David chosen from among the children of Israel.

3 He played with lions as with lambs: and with bears he did in like manner as with the lambs of the flock, in his youth.

4 Did not he kill the giant, and take away reproach from his people?

5 In lifting up his hand, with the stone in the sling he beat down the boasting of Goliath:

6 For he called upon the Almighty Lord and he gave him strength in his right hand to kill a man mighty in war, to exalt the horn of his people

7 So in ten thousand did he glorify him, and praised him in the blessings of the Lord, in offering to him a crown of glory:

8 For he destroyed the enemies on every side, and extirpated the Philistines the adversaries unto this day: he broke their horn for ever.

9 In all his works he gave thanks to the holy one, and to the most High, with words of glory.

10 With his whole heart he praised the Lord, and loved God that made him: and he gave him power against his enemies:

11 And he set singers before the altar, and by their voices he made sweet melody.

12 And to the festivals he added beauty, and set in order the solemn times even to the end of his life, that they should praise the holy name of the Lord, and magnify the holiness of God in the morning.

13 The Lord took away his sine, and exalted his horn for ever: and he gave him a covenant of the kingdom, and a throne of glory in Israel.

14 After him arose up a wise son, and for his sake he cast down all the power of the enemies.

15 Solomon reigned in days of peace, and God brought all his enemies under him, that he might build a house in his name, and prepare a sanctuary for ever: O how wise wast thou in thy youth!

16 And thou wast filled as a river with wisdom, and thy soul covered the earth.

17 And thou didst multiply riddles in parables: thy name went abroad to the islands far off, and thou wast beloved in thy peace.

18 The countries wondered at thee for thy canticles, and proverbs, and parables, and interpretations,

19 And at the name of the Lord God, whose surname is, God of Israel.

20 Thou didst gather gold as copper, and didst multiply silver as lead,

21 And thou didst bow thyself to women: and by thy body thou wast brought under subjection.

22 Thou hast stained thy glory, and defiled thy seed so as to bring wrath upon thy children, and to have thy folly kindled,

23 That thou shouldst make the kingdom to be divided, and out of Ephraim a rebellious kingdom to rule.

24 But God will not leave off his mercy, and he will not destroy, nor abolish his own works, neither will he out up by the roots the offspring of his elect: and he will not utterly take away the seed of him that loveth the Lord.

25 Wherefore he gave a remnant to Jacob, and to David of the same stock.

26 And Solomon had an end with his fathers.

27 And he left behind him of his seed, the folly of the nation,

28 Even Roboam that had little wisdom, who turned away the people through his counsel:

29 And Jeroboam the son of Nabat, who caused Israel to sin, and shewed Ephraim the way of sin, and their sins were multiplied exceedingly.

30 They removed them far away from their land.

31 And they sought out all iniquities, till vengeance came upon them, and put an end to all their sine.

Chapter 48

1 And Elias the prophet stood up, as a fire, and his word burnt like a torch.

2 He brought a famine upon them, and they that provoked him in their envy, were reduced to a small number, for they could not endure the commandments of the Lord.

3 By the word of the Lord he shut up the heaven, and he brought down fire from heaven thrice.

4 Thus was Elias magnified in his wondrous works. And who can glory like to thee?

5 Who raisedst up a dead man from below, from the lot of death, by the word of the Lord God.

6 Who broughtest down kings to destruction, and brokest easily their power in pieces, and the glorious from their bed.

7 Who heardest judgment in Sina, and in Horeb the judgments of vengeance.

8 Who anointedst kings to penance, and madest prophets successors after thee.

9 Who wast taken up in a whirlwind of fire, in a chariot of fiery horses.

10 Who art registered in the judgments of times to appease the wrath of the Lord, to reconcile the heart of the father to the son, and to restore the tribes of Jacob.

11 Blessed are they that saw thee, and were honoured with thy friendship.

12 For we live only in our life, but after death our name shall not be such.

13 Elias was indeed covered with the whirlwind, and his spirit was filled up in Eliseus: in his days he feared not the prince, and no man was more powerful than he.

14 No word could overcome him, and after death his body prophesied.

15 In his life he did great wonders, and is death he wrought miracles.

16 For all this the people repented not, neither did they depart from their sins till they were cast out of their land, and were scattered through all the earth.

17 And there was left but a small people, and a prince in the house of David.

18 Some of these did that which pleased God: but others committed many sine.

19 Ezechias fortified his city, and brought in water into the midst thereof, and he digged a rock with iron, and made a well for water.

20 In his days Sennacherib came up, and sent Rabsaces, and lifted up his hand against them, and he stretched out his hand against Sion, and became proud through his power.

21 Then their hearts and hands trembled, and they were in pain as women in travail.

22 And they called upon the Lord who is merciful, and spreading their hands, they lifted them up to heaven: and the holy Lord God quickly heard their voice.

23 He was not mindful of their sins, neither did he deliver them up to their enemies, but he purified them by the hand of Isaias, the holy prophet.

24 He overthrew the army of the Assyrians, and the angel of the Lord destroyed them.

25 For Ezechias did that which pleased God, and walked valiantly in the way of David his father, which Isaias, the great prophet, and faithful in the sight of God, had commanded him.

26 In his days the sun went backward, and he lengthened the king's life.

27 With a great spirit he saw the things that are to come to pass at last, and comforted the mourners in Sion.

28 He shewed what should come to pass for ever, and secret things before they came.

Chapter 49

1 The memory of Josias is like the composition of a sweet smell made by the art of a perfumer:

2 His remembrance shall be sweet as honey in every mouth, and as music at a banquet of wine.

3 He was directed by God unto the repentance of the nation, and he took away the abominations of wickedness.

4 And he directed his heart towards the Lord, and in the days of sinners he strengthened godliness.

5 Except David, and Ezechias, and Josias, all committed sin.

6 For the kings of Juda forsook the law of the most High, and despised the fear of God.

7 So they gave their kingdom to others, and their glory to a strange nation.

8 They burnt the chosen city of holiness, and made the streets thereof desolate according to the prediction of Jeremias.

9 For they treated him evil, who was consecrated a prophet from his mother's womb, to overthrow, and pluck up, and destroy, and to build again, and renew.

10 It was Ezechiel that saw the glorious vision, which was shewn him upon the chariot of cherubims.

11 For he made mention of the enemies under the figure of rain, and of doing good to them that shewed right ways.

12 And may the bones of the twelve prophets spring up out of their place: for they strengthened Jacob, and re- deemed themselves by strong faith.

13 How shall we magnify Zorobabel? for he was as a signet on the right hand;

14 In like manner Jesus the son of Josedec? who in their days built the house, and set up a holy temple to the Lord, prepared for everlasting glory.

15 And let Nehemias be a long time remembered, who raised up for us our walls that were cast down, and set up the gates and the bars, who rebuilt our houses.

16 No man was born upon earth like Henoch: for he also was taken up from the earth.

17 Nor as Joseph, who was a man born prince of his brethren, the support of his family, the ruler of his brethren, the stay of the people:

18 And his bones were visited, and after death they prophesied.

19 Seth and Sem obtained glory among men: and above every soul Adam in the beginning.

Chapter 50

1 Simon the high priest, the son of Onias, who in his life propped up the house, and in his days fortified the temple.

2 By him also the height of the temple was founded, the double building and the high walls of the temple.

3 In his days the wells of water flowed out, and they were filled as the sea above measure.

4 He took care of his nation, and delivered it from destruction.

5 He prevailed to enlarge the city, and obtained glory in his conversation with the people: and enlarged the entrance of the house and the court.

6 He shone in his days as the morning star in the midst of a cloud, and as the moon at the full.

7 And as the sun when it shineth, so did he shine in the temple of God.

8 And as the rainbow giving light in the bright clouds, and as the flower of roses in the days of the spring, and as the lilies that are on the brink of the water, and as the sweet smelling frankincense in the time of summer.

9 As a bright Are, and frankincense burning in the fire.

10 As a massy vessel of gold, adorned with every precious stone.

11 As an olive tree budding forth, and a cypress tree rearing itself on high, when he put on the robe of glory, and was clothed with the perfection of power.

12 When he went up to the holy altar, he honoured the vesture of holiness.

13 And when he took the portions out of the hands of the priests, he himself stood by the altar. And about him was the ring of his brethren: and as the cedar planted in mount Libanus,

14 And as branches of palm trees, they stood round about him, and all the sons of Aaron in their glory.

15 And the oblation of the Lord was in their hands, before all the congregation of Israel: and finishing his service, on the altar, to honour the offering of the most high Ring,

16 He stretched forth his hand to make a libation, and offered of the blood of the grape.

17 He poured out at the foot of the altar a divine odour to the most high Prince.

18 Then the sons of Aaron shouted, they sounded with beaten trumpets, and made a great noise to be heard for a remembrance before God.

19 Then all the people together made haste, and fell down to the earth upon their faces, to adore the Lord their God, and to pray to the Almighty God the most High.

20 And the singers lifted up their voices. and in the great house the sound of sweet melody was increased.

21 And the people in prayer besought the Lord the most High, until the worship of the Lord was perfected, and they had finished their office.

22 Then coming down, he lifted up his hands over all the congregation of the children of Israel, to give glory to God with his lips, and to glory in his name:

23 And he repeated his prayer, willing to shew the power of God.

24 And now pray ye to the God of all, who hath done great things in all the earth, who hath increased our days from our mother's womb, and hath done with us according to his mercy.

25 May he grant us joyfulness of heart, and that there be peace in our days in Israel for ever:

26 That Israel may believe that the mercy of God is with us, to deliver us in his days.

27 There are two nations which my soul abhorreth: and the third is no nation, which I hate:

28 They that sit on mount Seir, and the Philistines, and the foolish people that dwell in Sichem.

29 Jesus the son of Sirach, of Jerusalem, hath written in this book the doctrine of wisdom and instruction, who renewed wisdom from his heart.

30 Blessed is he that is conversant in these good things: and he that layeth them up in his heart, shall be wise always.

31 For if he do them, he shall be strong to do all things: because the light of God guideth his steps.

Chapter 51

1 They compassed me on every side, and there was no one that would help me. I looked for the succour of men, and there was none.

11 I remembered thy mercy, O Lord, and thy works, which are from the beginning of the world.

12 How thou deliverest them that wait for thee, O Lord, and savest them out of the hands of the nations.

13 Thou hast exalted my dwelling place upon the earth and I have prayed for death to pass away.

14 I called upon the Lord, the father of my Lord, that he would not leave me in the day of my trouble, and in the time of the proud without help.

15 I will praise thy name continually, and will praise it with thanksgiving, and my prayer was heard.

16 And thou hast saved me from destruction, and hast delivered me from the evil time.

17 Therefore I will give thanks, and praise thee, and bless the name of the Lord.

18 When I was yet young, before I wandered about, I sought for wisdom openly in my prayer.

19 I prayed for her before the temple, and unto the very end I will seek after her, and she flourished as a grape soon ripe.

20 My heart delighted in her, my foot walked in the right way, from my youth up I sought after her.

21 I bowed down my ear a little, and received her.

22 I found much wisdom in myself, and I profited much therein.

23 To him that giveth me wisdom, will I give glory.

24 For I have determined to follow her: I have had a zeal for good, and shall not be confounded.

25 My soul hath wrestled for her, and in doing it I have been confirmed.

26 I stretched forth my hands on high, and I bewailed my ignorance of her.

27 I directed my soul to her, and in knowledge I found her.

28 I possessed my heart with her from the beginning: therefore I shall not be forsaken.

29 My entrails were troubled in seeking her: therefore shall I possess a good possession.

30 The Lord hath given me a tongue for my reward: and with it I will praise him.

31 Draw near to me, ye unlearned, and gather yourselves together into the house of discipline.

32 Why are ye slow? and what do you say of these things? your souls are exceeding thirsty.

33 I have opened my mouth, and have spoken: buy her for yourselves without silver,

34 And submit your neck to the yoke, and let your soul receive discipline: for she is near at hand to be found.

35 Behold with your eyes how I have laboured a little, and have found much rest to myself.

36 Receive ye discipline as a great sum of money, and possess abundance of gold by her.

37 Let your soul rejoice in his mercy, and you shall not be confounded in his praise.

38 Work your work before the time, and he will give you your reward in his time.

Wisdom of Jesus Son of Sirach

Sir.0

[1-14] Whereas many great teachings have been given to us through the law and the prophets and the others that followed them, on account of which we should praise Israel for instruction and wisdom; and since it is necessary not only that the readers themselves should acquire understanding but also that those who love learning should be able to help the outsiders by both speaking and writing, my grandfather Jesus, after devoting himself especially to the reading of the law and the prophets and the other books of our fathers, and after acquiring considerable proficiency in them, was himself also led to write something pertaining to instruction and wisdom, in order that, by becoming conversant with this also, those who love learning should make even greater progress in living according to the law.

[15-26]
You are urged therefore to read with good will and attention, and to be indulgent in cases where, despite out diligent labor in translating, we may seem to have rendered some phrases imperfectly. For what was originally expressed in Hebrew does not have exactly the same sense when translated into another language. Not only this work, but even the law itself, the prophecies, and the rest of the books differ not a little as originally expressed.

[27-36]
When I came to Egypt in the thirty-eighth year of the reign of Euergetes and stayed for some time, I found opportunity for no little instruction. It seemed highly necessary that I should myself devote some pains and labor to the translation of the following book, using in that period of time great watchfulness and skill in order to complete and publish the book for those living abroad who wished to gain learning, being prepared in character to live according to the law.

Sir.1

[1] All wisdom comes from the Lord and is with him for ever.
[2] The sand of the sea, the drops of rain, and the days of eternity -- who can count them?
[3] The height of heaven, the breadth of the earth, the abyss, and wisdom -- who can search them out?
[4] Wisdom was created before all things, and prudent understanding from eternity.
[5] The root of wisdom -- to whom has it been revealed? Her clever devices -- who knows them?
[6] There is One who is wise, greatly to be feared, sitting upon his throne.
[7] The Lord himself created wisdom; he saw her and apportioned her, he poured her out upon all his works.

[8] She dwells with all flesh according to his gift, and he supplied her to those who love him.
[9] The fear of the Lord is glory and exultation, and gladness and a crown of rejoicing.
[10] The fear of the Lord delights the heart, and gives gladness and joy and long life.
[11] With him who fears the Lord it will go well at the end; on the day of his death he will be blessed.
[12] To fear the Lord is the beginning of wisdom; she is created with the faithful in the womb.
[13] She made among men an eternal foundation, and among their descendants she will be trusted.
[14] To fear the Lord is wisdom's full measure; she satisfies men with her fruits;
[15] she fills their whole house with desirable goods, and their storehouses with her produce.
[16] The fear of the Lord is the crown of wisdom, making peace and perfect health to flourish.
[17] He saw her and apportioned her; he rained down knowledge and discerning comprehension, and he exalted the glory of those who held her fast.
[18] To fear the Lord is the root of wisdom, and her branches are long life.
[22] Unrighteous anger cannot be justified, for a man's anger tips the scale to his ruin.
[23] A patient man will endure until the right moment, and then joy will burst forth for him.
[24] He will hide his words until the right moment, and the lips of many will tell of his good sense.
[25] In the treasuries of wisdom are wise sayings, but godliness is an abomination to a sinner.
[26] If you desire wisdom, keep the commandments, and the Lord will supply it for you.
[27] For the fear of the Lord is wisdom and instruction, and he delights in fidelity and meekness.
[28] Do not disobey the fear of the Lord; do not approach him with a divided mind.
[29] Be not a hypocrite in men's sight, and keep watch over your lips.
[30] Do not exalt yourself lest you fall, and thus bring dishonor upon yourself. The Lord will reveal your secrets
and cast you down in the midst of the congregation, because you did not come in the fear of the Lord, and your heart was full of deceit.

Sir.2

[1] My son, if you come forward to serve the Lord, prepare yourself for temptation.
[2] Set your heart right and be steadfast, and do not be hasty in time of calamity.
[3] Hold fast to him and do not depart, that you may be honored at the end of your life.
[4] Accept whatever is brought upon you, and in changes that humble you be patient.
[5] For gold is tested in the fire, and acceptable men in the furnace of humiliation.

[6] Trust in him, and he will help you; make your ways straight, and hope in him.

[7] You who fear the Lord, wait for his mercy; and turn not aside, lest you fall.

[8] You who fear the Lord, trust in him, and your reward will not fail;

[9] you who fear the Lord, hope for good things, for everlasting joy and mercy.

[10] Consider the ancient generations and see: who ever trusted in the Lord and was put to shame? Or who ever persevered in the fear of the Lord and was forsaken? Or who ever called upon him and was overlooked?

[11] For the Lord is compassionate and merciful; he forgives sins and saves in time of affliction.

[12] Woe to timid hearts and to slack hands, and to the sinner who walks along two ways!

[13] Woe to the faint heart, for it has no trust! Therefore it will not be sheltered.

[14] Woe to you who have lost your endurance! What will you do when the Lord punishes you?

[15] Those who fear the Lord will not disobey his words, and those who love him will keep his ways.

[16] Those who fear the Lord will seek his approval, and those who love him will be filled with the law.

[17] Those who fear the Lord will prepare their hearts, and will humble themselves before him.

[18] Let us fall into the hands of the Lord, but not into the hands of men; for as his majesty is, so also is his mercy.

Sir.3

[1] Listen to me your father, O children; and act accordingly, that you may be kept in safety.

[2] For the Lord honored the father above the children, and he confirmed the right of the mother over her sons.

[3] Whoever honors his father atones for sins,

[4] and whoever glorifies his mother is like one who lays up treasure.

[5] Whoever honors his father will be gladdened by his own children, and when he prays he will be heard.

[6] Whoever glorifies his father will have long life, and whoever obeys the Lord will refresh his mother;

[7] he will serve his parents as his masters.

[8] Honor your father by word and deed, that a blessing from him may come upon you.

[9] For a father's blessing strengthens the houses of the children, but a mother's curse uproots their foundations.

[10] Do not glorify yourself by dishonoring your father, for your father's dishonor is no glory to you.

[11] For a man's glory comes from honoring his father, and it is a disgrace for children not to respect their mother.

[12] O son, help your father in his old age, and do not grieve him as long as he lives;

[13] even if he is lacking in understanding, show forbearance; in all your strength do not despise him.

[14] For kindness to a father will not be forgotten, and against your sins it will be credited to you;

[15] in the day of your affliction it will be remembered in your favor; as frost in fair weather, your sins will melt away.

[16] Whoever forsakes his father is like a blasphemer, and whoever angers his mother is cursed by the Lord.

[17] My son, perform your tasks in meekness; then you will be loved by those whom God accepts.

[18] The greater you are, the more you must humble yourself; so you will find favor in the sight of the Lord.

[20] For great is the might of the Lord; he is glorified by the humble.

[21] Seek not what is too difficult for you, nor investigate what is beyond your power.

[22] Reflect upon what has been assigned to you, for you do not need what is hidden.

[23] Do not meddle in what is beyond your tasks, for matters too great for human understanding have been shown you.

[24] For their hasty judgment has led many astray, and wrong opinion has caused their thoughts to slip.

[26] A stubborn mind will be afflicted at the end, and whoever loves danger will perish by it.

[27] A stubborn mind will be burdened by troubles, and the sinner will heap sin upon sin.

[28] The affliction of the proud has no healing, for a plant of wickedness has taken root in him.

[29] The mind of the intelligent man will ponder a parable, and an attentive ear is the wise man's desire.

[30] Water extinguishes a blazing fire: so almsgiving atones for sin.

[31] Whoever requites favors gives thought to the future; at the moment of his falling he will find support.

Sir.4

[1] My son, deprive not the poor of his living, and do not keep needy eyes waiting.

[2] Do not grieve the one who is hungry, nor anger a man in want.

[3] Do not add to the troubles of an angry mind, nor delay your gift to a beggar.

[4] Do not reject an afflicted suppliant, nor turn your face away from the poor.

[5] Do not avert your eye from the needy, nor give a man occasion to curse you;

[6] for if in bitterness of soul he calls down a curse upon you, his Creator will hear his prayer.

[7] Make yourself beloved in the congregation; bow your head low to a great man.

[8] Incline your ear to the poor, and answer him peaceably and gently.

[9] Deliver him who is wronged from the hand of the wrongdoer; and do not be fainthearted in judging a case.

[10] Be like a father to orphans, and instead of a husband to their mother; you will then be like a son of the Most High,

and he will love you more than does your mother.

[11] Wisdom exalts her sons and gives help to those who seek her.

[12] Whoever loves her loves life, and those who seek her early will be filled with joy.

[13] Whoever holds her fast will obtain glory, and the Lord will bless the place she enters.

[14] Those who serve her will minister to the Holy One; the Lord loves those who love her.

[15] He who obeys her will judge the nations, and whoever gives heed to her will dwell secure.

[16] If he has faith in her he will obtain her; and his descendants will remain in possession of her.

[17] For at first she will walk with him on tortuous paths, she will bring fear and cowardice upon him, and will torment him by her discipline until she trusts him, and she will test him with her ordinances.

[18] Then she will come straight back to him and gladden him, and will reveal her secrets to him.

[19] If he goes astray she will forsake him, and hand him over to his ruin.

[20] Observe the right time, and beware of evil; and do not bring shame on yourself.

[21] For there is a shame which brings sin, and there is a shame which is glory and favor.

[22] Do not show partiality, to your own harm, or deference, to your downfall.

[23] Do not refrain from speaking at the crucial time, and do not hide your wisdom.

[24] For wisdom is known through speech, and education through the words of the tongue.

[25] Never speak against the truth, but be mindful of your ignorance.

[26] Do not be ashamed to confess your sins, and do not try to stop the current of a river.

[27] Do not subject yourself to a foolish fellow, nor show partiality to a ruler.

[28] Strive even to death for the truth and the Lord God will fight for you.

[29] Do not be reckless in your speech, or sluggish and remiss in your deeds.

[30] Do not be like a lion in your home, nor be a faultfinder with your servants.

[31] Let not your hand be extended to receive, but withdrawn when it is time to repay.

Sir.5
[1] Do not set your heart on your wealth, nor say, "I have enough."

[2] Do not follow your inclination and strength, walking according to the desires of your heart.

[3] Do not say, "Who will have power over me?" for the Lord will surely punish you.

[4] Do not say, "I sinned, and what happened to me?" for the Lord is slow to anger.

[5] Do not be so confident of atonement that you add sin to sin.

[6] Do not say, "His mercy is great, he will forgive the multitude of my sins," for both mercy and wrath are with him,

and his anger rests on sinners.

[7] Do not delay to turn to the Lord, nor postpone it from day to day; for suddenly the wrath of the Lord will go forth,

and at the time of punishment you will perish.

[8] Do not depend on dishonest wealth, for it will not benefit you in the day of calamity.

[9] Do not winnow with every wind, nor follow every path: the double-tongued sinner does that.

[10] Be steadfast in your understanding, and let your speech be consistent.

[11] Be quick to hear, and be deliberate in answering.

[12] If you have understanding, answer your neighbor; but if not, put your hand on your mouth.

[13] Glory and dishonor come from speaking, and a man's tongue is his downfall.

[14] Do not be called a slanderer, and do not lie in ambush with your tongue; for shame comes to the thief, and severe condemnation to the double-tongued.

[15] In great and small matters do not act amiss,

Sir.6
[1] and do not become an enemy instead of a friend; for a bad name incurs shame and reproach: so fares the double-tongued sinner.

[2] Do not exalt yourself through your soul's counsel, lest your soul be torn in pieces like a bull.

[3] You will devour your leaves and destroy your fruit, and will be left like a withered tree.

[4] An evil soul will destroy him who has it, and make him the laughingstock of his enemies.

[5] A pleasant voice multiplies friends, and a gracious tongue multiplies courtesies.

[6] Let those that are at peace with you be many, but let your advisers be one in a thousand.

[7] When you gain a friend, gain him through testing, and do not trust him hastily.

[8] For there is a friend who is such at his own convenience, but will not stand by you in your day of trouble.

[9] And there is a friend who changes into an enemy, and will disclose a quarrel to your disgrace.

[10] And there is a friend who is a table companion, but will not stand by you in your day of trouble.

[11] In prosperity he will make himself your equal, and be bold with your servants;

[12] but if you are brought low he will turn against you, and will hide himself from your presence.

[13] Keep yourself far from your enemies, and be on guard toward your friends.

[14] A faithful friend is a sturdy shelter: he that has found one has found a treasure.

[15] There is nothing so precious as a faithful friend, and no scales can measure his excellence.

[16] A faithful friend is an elixir of life; and those who fear the Lord will find him.

[17] Whoever fears the Lord directs his friendship aright, for as he is, so is his neighbor also.

[18] My son, from your youth up choose instruction, and until you are old you will keep finding wisdom.

[19] Come to her like one who plows and sows, and wait for her good harvest. For in her service you will toil a little while, and soon you will eat of her produce.

[20] She seems very harsh to the uninstructed; a weakling will not remain with her.

[21] She will weigh him down like a heavy testing stone, and he will not be slow to cast her off.

[22] For wisdom is like her name, and is not manifest to many.

[23] Listen, my son, and accept my judgment; do not reject my counsel.

[24] Put your feet into her fetters, and your neck into her collar.

[25] Put your shoulder under her and carry her, and do not fret under her bonds.

[26] Come to her with all your soul, and keep her ways with all your might.

[27] Search out and seek, and she will become known to you; and when you get hold of her, do not let her go.

[28] For at last you will find the rest she gives, and she will be changed into joy for you.

[29] Then her fetters will become for you a strong protection, and her collar a glorious robe.

[30] Her yoke is a golden ornament, and her bonds are a cord of blue.

[31] You will wear her like a glorious robe, and put her on like a crown of gladness.

[32] If you are willing, my son, you will be taught, and if you apply yourself you will become clever.

[33] If you love to listen you will gain knowledge, and if you incline your ear you will become wise.

[34] Stand in the assembly of the elders. Who is wise? Hold fast to him.

[35] Be ready to listen to every narrative, and do not let wise proverbs escape you.

[36] If you see an intelligent man, visit him early; let your foot wear out his doorstep.

[37] Reflect on the statutes of the Lord, and meditate at all times on his commandments. It is he who will give insight to your mind, and your desire for wisdom will be granted.

Sir.7

[1] Do no evil, and evil will never befall you.

[2] Stay away from wrong, and it will turn away from you.

[3] My son, do not sow the furrows of injustice, and you will not reap a sevenfold crop.

[4] Do not seek from the Lord the highest office, nor the seat of honor from the king.

[5] Do not assert your righteousness before the Lord, nor display your wisdom before the king.

[6] Do not seek to become a judge, lest you be unable to remove iniquity, lest you be partial to a powerful man, and thus put a blot on your integrity.

[7] Do not offend against the public, and do not disgrace yourself among the people.

[8] Do not commit a sin twice; even for one you will not go unpunished.

[9] Do not say, "He will consider the multitude of my gifts, and when I make an offering to the Most High God he will accept it."

[10] Do not be fainthearted in your prayer, nor neglect to give alms.

[11] Do not ridicule a man who is bitter in soul, for there is One who abases and exalts.

[12] Do not devise a lie against your brother, nor do the like to a friend.

[13] Refuse to utter any lie, for the habit of lying serves no good.

[14] Do not prattle in the assembly of the elders, nor repeat yourself in your prayer.

[15] Do not hate toilsome labor, or farm work, which were created by the Most High.

[16] Do not count yourself among the crowd of sinners; remember that wrath does not delay.

[17] Humble yourself greatly, for the punishment of the ungodly is fire and worms.

[18] Do not exchange a friend for money, or a real brother for the gold of Ophir.

[19] Do not deprive yourself of a wise and good wife, for her charm is worth more than gold.

[20] Do not abuse a servant who performs his work faithfully, or a hired laborer who devotes himself to you.

[21] Let your soul love an intelligent servant; do not withhold from him his freedom.

[22] Do you have cattle? Look after them; if they are profitable to you, keep them.

[23] Do you have children? Discipline them, and make them obedient from their youth.

[24] Do you have daughters? Be concerned for their chastity, and do not show yourself too indulgent with them.

[25] Give a daughter in marriage; you will have finished a great task. But give her to a man of understanding.

[26] If you have a wife who pleases you, do not cast her out; but do not trust yourself to one whom you detest.

[27] With all your heart honor your father, and do not forget the birth pangs of your mother.

[28] Remember that through your parents you were born; and what can you give back to them that equals their gift to you?

[29] With all your soul fear the Lord, and honor his priests.

[30] With all your might love your Maker, and do not forsake his ministers.

[31] Fear the Lord and honor the priest, and give him his portion, as is commanded you: the first fruits, the guilt offering, the gift of the shoulders, the sacrifice of sanctification, and the first fruits of the holy things.

[32] Stretch forth your hand to the poor, so that your blessing may be complete.

[33] Give graciously to all the living, and withhold not kindness from the dead.

[34] Do not fail those who weep, but mourn with those who mourn.

[35] Do not shrink from visiting a sick man, because for such deeds you will be loved.

[36] In all you do, remember the end of your life, and then you will never sin.

Sir.8

[1] Do not contend with a powerful man, lest you fall into his hands.

[2] Do not quarrel with a rich man, lest his resources outweigh yours; for gold has ruined many, and has perverted the minds of kings.

[3] Do not argue with a chatterer, nor heap wood on his fire.

[4] Do not jest with an ill-bred person, lest your ancestors be disgraced.

[5] Do not reproach a man who is turning away from sin; remember that we all deserve punishment.

[6] Do not disdain a man when he is old, for some of us are growing old.

[7] Do not rejoice over any one's death; remember that we all must die.

[8] Do not slight the discourse of the sages, but busy yourself with their maxims; because from them you will gain instruction and learn how to serve great men.

[9] Do not disregard the discourse of the aged, for they themselves learned from their fathers; because from them you will gain understanding and learn how to give an answer in time of need.

[10] Do not kindle the coals of a sinner, lest you be burned in his flaming fire.

[11] Do not get up and leave an insolent fellow, lest he lie in ambush against your words.

[12] Do not lend to a man who is stronger than you; but if you do lend anything, be as one who has lost it.

[13] Do not give surety beyond your means, but if you give surety, be concerned as one who must pay.

[14] Do not go to law against a judge, for the decision will favor him because of his standing.

[15] Do not travel on the road with a foolhardy fellow, lest he be burdensome to you; for he will act as he pleases, and through his folly you will perish with him.

[16] Do not fight with a wrathful man, and do not cross the wilderness with him; because blood is as nothing in his sight,
and where no help is at hand, he will strike you down.

[17] Do not consult with a fool, for he will not be able to keep a secret.

[18] In the presence of a stranger do nothing that is to be kept secret, for you do not know what he will divulge.

[19] Do not reveal your thoughts to every one, lest you drive away your good luck.

Sir.9

[1] Do not be jealous of the wife of your bosom, and do not teach her an evil lesson to your own hurt.

[2] Do not give yourself to a woman so that she gains mastery over your strength.

[3] Do not go to meet a loose woman, lest you fall into her snares.

[4] Do not associate with a woman singer, lest you be caught in her intrigues.

[5] Do not look intently at a virgin, lest you stumble and incur penalties for her.

[6] Do not give yourself to harlots lest you lose your inheritance.

[7] Do not look around in the streets of a city, nor wander about in its deserted sections.

[8] Turn away your eyes from a shapely woman, and do not look intently at beauty belonging to another; many have been misled by a woman's beauty, and by it passion is kindled like a fire.

[9] Never dine with another man's wife, nor revel with her at wine; lest your heart turn aside to her, and in blood you be plunged into destruction.

[10] Forsake not an old friend, for a new one does not compare with him. A new friend is like new wine; when it has aged you will drink it with pleasure.

[11] Do not envy the honors of a sinner, for you do not know what his end will be.

[12] Do not delight in what pleases the ungodly; remember that they will not be held guiltless as long as they live.

[13] Keep far from a man who has the power to kill, and you will not be worried by the fear of death. But

if you approach him, make no misstep, lest he rob you of your life. Know that you are walking in the midst of snares, and that you are going about on the city battlements.

[14] As much as you can, aim to know your neighbors, and consult with the wise.

[15] Let your conversation be with men of understanding, and let all your discussion be about the law of the Most High.

[16] Let righteous men be your dinner companions, and let your glorying be in the fear of the Lord.

[17] A work will be praised for the skill of the craftsmen; so a people's leader is proved wise by his words.

[18] A babbler is feared in his city, and the man who is reckless in speech will be hated.

Sir.10

[1] A wise magistrate will educate his people, and the rule of an understanding man will be well ordered.

[2] Like the magistrate of the people, so are his officials; and like the ruler of the city, so are all its inhabitants.

[3] An undisciplined king will ruin his people, but a city will grow through the understanding of its rulers.

[4] The government of the earth is in the hands of the Lord, and over it he will raise up the right man for the time.

[5] The success of a man is in the hands of the Lord, and he confers his honor upon the person of the scribe.

[6] Do not be angry with your neighbor for any injury, and do not attempt anything by acts of insolence.

[7] Arrogance is hateful before the Lord and before men, and injustice is outrageous to both.

[8] Sovereignty passes from nation to nation on account of injustice and insolence and wealth.

[9] How can he who is dust and ashes be proud? for even in life his bowels decay.

[10] A long illness baffles the physician; the king of today will die tomorrow.

[11] For when a man is dead, he will inherit creeping things, and wild beasts, and worms.

[12] The beginning of man's pride is to depart from the Lord; his heart has forsaken his Maker.

[13] For the beginning of pride is sin, and the man who clings to it pours out abominations. Therefore the Lord brought upon them extraordinary afflictions, and destroyed them utterly.

[14] The Lord has cast down the thrones of rulers, and has seated the lowly in their place.

[15] The Lord has plucked up the roots of the nations, and has planted the humble in their place.

[16] The Lord has overthrown the lands of the nations, and has destroyed them to the foundations of the earth.

[17] He has removed some of them and destroyed them, and has extinguished the memory of them from the earth.

[18] Pride was not created for men, nor fierce anger for those born of women.

[19] What race is worthy of honor? The human race. What race is worthy of honor? Those who fear the Lord. What race is unworthy of honor? The human race. What race is unworthy of honor? Those who transgress the commandments.

[20] Among brothers their leader is worthy of honor, and those who fear the Lord are worthy of honor in his eyes.

[22] The rich, and the eminent, and the poor -- their glory is the fear of the Lord.

[23] It is not right to despise an intelligent poor man, nor is it proper to honor a sinful man.

[24] The nobleman, and the judge, and the ruler will be honored, but none of them is greater than the man who fears the Lord.

[25] Free men will be at the service of a wise servant, and a man of understanding will not grumble.

[26] Do not make a display of your wisdom when you do your work, nor glorify yourself at a time when you are in want.

[27] Better is a man who works and has an abundance of everything, than one who goes about boasting, but lacks bread.

[28] My son, glorify yourself with humility, and ascribe to yourself honor according to your worth.

[29] Who will justify the man that sins against himself? And who will honor the man that dishonors his own life?

[30] A poor man is honored for his knowledge, while a rich man is honored for his wealth.

[31] A man honored in poverty, how much more in wealth! And a man dishonored in wealth, how much more in poverty!

Sir.11

[1] The wisdom of a humble man will lift up his head, and will seat him among the great.

[2] Do not praise a man for his good looks, nor loathe a man because of his appearance.

[3] The bee is small among flying creatures, but her product is the best of sweet things.

[4] Do not boast about wearing fine clothes, nor exalt yourself in the day that you are honored; for the works of the Lord are wonderful, and his works are concealed from men.

[5] Many kings have had to sit on the ground, but one who was never thought of has worn a crown.

[6] Many rulers have been greatly disgraced, and illustrious men have been handed over to others.

[7] Do not find fault before you investigate; first consider, and then reprove.

[8] Do not answer before you have heard, nor interrupt a speaker in the midst of his words.

[9] Do not argue about a matter which does not concern you, nor sit with sinners when they judge a case.

[10] My son, do not busy yourself with many matters; if you multiply activities you will not go unpunished, and if you pursue you will not overtake, and by fleeing you will not escape.

[11] There is a man who works, and toils, and presses on, but is so much the more in want.

[12] There is another who is slow and needs help, who lacks strength and abounds in poverty; but the eyes of the Lord look upon him for his good; he lifts him out of his low estate

[13] and raises up his head, so that many are amazed at him.

[14] Good things and bad, life and death, poverty and wealth, come from the Lord.

[17] The gift of the Lord endures for those who are godly, and what he approves will have lasting success.

[18] There is a man who is rich through his diligence and self-denial, and this is the reward allotted to him:

[19] when he says, "I have found rest, and now I shall enjoy my goods!" he does not know how much time will pass

until he leaves them to others and dies.

[20] Stand by your covenant and attend to it, and grow old in your work.

[21] Do not wonder at the works of a sinner, but trust in the Lord and keep at your toil; for it is easy in the sight of the Lord to enrich a poor man quickly and suddenly.

[22] The blessing of the Lord is the reward of the godly, and quickly God causes his blessing to flourish.

[23] Do not say, "What do I need, and what prosperity could be mine in the future?"

[24] Do not say, "I have enough, and what calamity could happen to me in the future?"

[25] In the day of prosperity, adversity is forgotten, and in the day of adversity, prosperity is not remembered.

[26] For it is easy in the sight of the Lord to reward a man on the day of death according to his conduct.

[27] The misery of an hour makes one forget luxury, and at the close of a man's life his deeds will be revealed.

[28] Call no one happy before his death; a man will be known through his children.

[29] Do not bring every man into your home, for many are the wiles of the crafty.

[30] Like a decoy partridge in a cage, so is the mind of a proud man, and like a spy he observes your weakness;

[31] for he lies in wait, turning good into evil, and to worthy actions he will attach blame.

[32] From a spark of fire come many burning coals, and a sinner lies in wait to shed blood.

[33] Beware of a scoundrel, for he devises evil, lest he give you a lasting blemish.

[34] Receive a stranger into your home and he will upset you with commotion, and will estrange you from your family.

Sir.12

[1] If you do a kindness, know to whom you do it, and you will be thanked for your good deeds.

[2] Do good to a godly man, and you will be repaid -- if not by him, certainly by the Most High.

[3] No good will come to the man who persists in evil or to him who does not give alms.

[4] Give to the godly man, but do not help the sinner.

[5] Do good to the humble, but do not give to the ungodly; hold back his bread, and do not give it to him, lest by means of it he subdue you; for you will receive twice as much evil for all the good which you do to him.

[6] For the Most High also hates sinners and will inflict punishment on the ungodly.

[7] Give to the good man, but do not help the sinner.

[8] A friend will not be known in prosperity, nor will an enemy be hidden in adversity.

[9] A man's enemies are grieved when he prospers, and in his adversity even his friend will separate from him.

[10] Never trust your enemy, for like the rusting of copper, so is his wickedness.

[11] Even if he humbles himself and goes about cringing, watch yourself, and be on your guard against him; and you will be to him like one who has polished a mirror, and you will know that it was not hopelessly tarnished.

[12] Do not put him next to you, lest he overthrow you and take your place; do not have him sit at your right, lest he try to take your seat of honor, and at last you will realize the truth of my words, and be stung by what I have said.

[13] Who will pity a snake charmer bitten by a serpent, or any who go near wild beasts?

[14] So no one will pity a man who associates with a sinner and becomes involved in his sins.

[15] He will stay with you for a time, but if you falter, he will not stand by you.

[16] An enemy will speak sweetly with his lips, but in his mind he will plan to throw you into a pit; an enemy will weep with his eyes, but if he finds an opportunity his thirst for blood will be insatiable.

[17] If calamity befalls you, you will find him there ahead of you; and while pretending to help you, he will trip you by the heel;

[18] he will shake his head, and clap his hands, and whisper much, and change his expression.

Sir.13

[1] Whoever touches pitch will be defiled, and whoever associates with a proud man will become like him.

[2] Do not lift a weight beyond your strength, nor associate with a man mightier and richer than you. How can the clay pot associate with the iron kettle? The pot will strike against it, and will itself be broken.

[3] A rich man does wrong, and he even adds reproaches; a poor man suffers wrong, and he must add apologies.

[4] A rich man will exploit you if you can be of use to him, but if you are in need he will forsake you.

[5] If you own something, he will live with you; he will drain your resources and he will not care.

[6] When he needs you he will deceive you, he will smile at you and give you hope. He will speak to you kindly and say, "What do you need?"

[7] He will shame you with his foods, until he has drained you two or three times; and finally he will deride you. Should he see you afterwards, he will forsake you, and shake his head at you.

[8] Take care not to be led astray, and not to be humiliated in your feasting.

[9] When a powerful man invites you, be reserved; and he will invite you the more often.

[10] Do not push forward, lest you be repulsed; and do not remain at a distance, lest you be forgotten.

[11] Do not try to treat him as an equal, nor trust his abundance of words; for he will test you through much talk, and while he smiles he will be examining you.

[12] Cruel is he who does not keep words to himself; he will not hesitate to injure or to imprison.

[13] Keep words to yourself and be very watchful, for you are walking about with your own downfall.

[15] Every creature loves its like, and every person his neighbor;

[16] all living beings associate by species, and a man clings to one like himself.

[17] What fellowship has a wolf with a lamb? No more has a sinner with a godly man.

[18] What peace is there between a hyena and a dog? And what peace between a rich man and a poor man?

[19] Wild asses in the wilderness are the prey of lions; likewise the poor are pastures for the rich.

[20] Humility is an abomination to a proud man; likewise a poor man is an abomination to a rich one.

[21] When a rich man totters, he is steadied by friends, but when a humble man falls, he is even pushed away by friends.

[22] If a rich man slips, his helpers are many; he speaks unseemly words, and they justify him. If a humble man slips, they even reproach him; he speaks sensibly, and receives no attention.

[23] When the rich man speaks all are silent, and they extol to the clouds what he says. When the poor man speaks they say, "Who is this fellow?" And should he stumble, they even push him down.

[24] Riches are good if they are free from sin, and poverty is evil in the opinion of the ungodly.

[25] A man's heart changes his countenance, either for good or for evil.

[26] The mark of a happy heart is a cheerful face, but to devise proverbs requires painful thinking.

Sir.14

[1] Blessed is the man who does not blunder with his lips and need not suffer grief for sin.

[2] Blessed is he whose heart does not condemn him, and who has not given up his hope.

[3] Riches are not seemly for a stingy man; and of what use is property to an envious man?

[4] Whoever accumulates by depriving himself, accumulates for others; and others will live in luxury on his goods.

[5] If a man is mean to himself, to whom will he be generous? He will not enjoy his own riches.

[6] No one is meaner than the man who is grudging to himself, and this is the retribution for his baseness;

[7] even if he does good, he does it unintentionally, and betrays his baseness in the end.

[8] Evil is the man with a grudging eye; he averts his face and disregards people.

[9] A greedy man's eye is not satisfied with a portion, and mean injustice withers the soul.

[10] A stingy man's eye begrudges bread, and it is lacking at his table.

[11] My son, treat yourself well, according to your means, and present worthy offerings to the Lord.

[12] Remember that death will not delay, and the decree of Hades has not been shown to you.

[13] Do good to a friend before you die, and reach out and give to him as much as you can.

[14] Do not deprive yourself of a happy day; let not your share of desired good pass by you.

[15] Will you not leave the fruit of your labors to another, and what you acquired by toil to be divided by lot?

[16] Give, and take, and beguile yourself, because in Hades one cannot look for luxury.

[17] All living beings become old like a garment, for the decree from of old is, "You must surely die!"

[18] Like flourishing leaves on a spreading tree which sheds some and puts forth others, so are the generations of flesh and blood: one dies and another is born.

[19] Every product decays and ceases to exist, and the man who made it will pass away with it.
[20] Blessed is the man who meditates on wisdom and who reasons intelligently.
[21] He who reflects in his mind on her ways will also ponder her secrets.
[22] Pursue wisdom like a hunter, and lie in wait on her paths.
[23] He who peers through her windows will also listen at her doors;
[24] he who encamps near her house will also fasten his tent peg to her walls;
[25] he will pitch his tent near her, and will lodge in an excellent lodging place;
[26] he will place his children under her shelter, and will camp under her boughs;
[27] he will be sheltered by her from the heat, and will dwell in the midst of her glory.

Sir.15
[1] The man who fears the Lord will do this, and he who holds to the law will obtain wisdom.
[2] She will come to meet him like a mother, and like the wife of his youth she will welcome him.
[3] She will feed him with the bread of understanding, and give him the water of wisdom to drink.
[4] He will lean on her and will not fall, and he will rely on her and will not be put to shame.
[5] She will exalt him above his neighbors, and will open his mouth in the midst of the assembly.
[6] He will find gladness and a crown of rejoicing, and will acquire an everlasting name.
[7] Foolish men will not obtain her, and sinful men will not see her.
[8] She is far from men of pride, and liars will never think of her.
[9] A hymn of praise is not fitting on the lips of a sinner, for it has not been sent from the Lord.
[10] For a hymn of praise should be uttered in wisdom, and the Lord will prosper it.
[11] Do not say, "Because of the Lord I left the right way"; for he will not do what he hates.
[12] Do not say, "It was he who led me astray"; for he had no need of a sinful man.
[13] The Lord hates all abominations, and they are not loved by those who fear him.
[14] It was he who created man in the beginning, and he left him in the power of his own inclination.
[15] If you will, you can keep the commandments, and to act faithfully is a matter of your own choice.
[16] He has placed before you fire and water: stretch out your hand for whichever you wish.
[17] Before a man are life and death, and whichever he chooses will be given to him.
[18] For great is the wisdom of the Lord; he is mighty in power and sees everything;

[19] his eyes are on those who fear him, and he knows every deed of man.
[20] He has not commanded any one to be ungodly, and he has not given any one permission to sin.

Sir.16
[1] Do not desire a multitude of useless children, nor rejoice in ungodly sons.
[2] If they multiply , do not rejoice in them, unless the fear of the Lord is in them.
[3] Do not trust in their survival, and do not rely on their multitude; for one is better than a thousand, and to die childless is better than to have ungodly children.
[4] For through one man of understanding a city will be filled with people, but through a tribe of lawless men it will be made desolate.
[5] Many such things my eye has seen, and my ear has heard things more striking than these.
[6] In an assembly of sinners a fire will be kindled, and in a disobedient nation wrath was kindled.
[7] He was not propitiated for the ancient giants who revolted in their might.
[8] He did not spare the neighbors of Lot, whom he loathed on account of their insolence.
[9] He showed no pity for a nation devoted to destruction, for those destroyed in their sins;
[10] nor for the six hundred thousand men on foot, who rebelliously assembled in their stubbornness.
[11] Even if there is only one stiff-necked person, it will be a wonder if he remains unpunished. For mercy and wrath are with the Lord; he is mighty to forgive, and he pours out wrath.
[12] As great as his mercy, so great is also his reproof; he judges a man according to his deeds.
[13] The sinner will not escape with his plunder, and the patience of the godly will not be frustrated.
[14] He will make room for every act of mercy; every one will receive in accordance with his deeds.
[17] Do not say, "I shall be hidden from the Lord, and who from on high will remember me? Among so many people I shall not be known, for what is my soul in the boundless creation?
[18] Behold, heaven and the highest heaven, the abyss and the earth, will tremble at his visitation.
[19] The mountains also and the foundations of the earth shake with trembling when he looks upon them.
[20] And no mind will reflect on this. Who will ponder his ways?
[21] Like a tempest which no man can see, so most of his works are concealed.
[22] Who will announce his acts of justice? Or who will await them? For the covenant is far off."
[23] This is what one devoid of understanding thinks; a senseless and misguided man thinks foolishly.
[24] Listen to me, my son, and acquire knowledge, and pay close attention to my words.

[25] I will impart instruction by weight, and declare knowledge accurately.
[26] The works of the Lord have existed from the beginning by his creation, and when he made them, he determined their divisions.
[27] He arranged his works in an eternal order, and their dominion for all generations; they neither hunger nor grow weary, and they do not cease from their labors.
[28] They do not crowd one another aside, and they will never disobey his word.
[29] After this the Lord looked upon the earth, and filled it with his good things;
[30] with all kinds of living beings he covered its surface, and to it they return.

Sir.17
[1] The Lord created man out of earth, and turned him back to it again.
[2] He gave to men few days, a limited time, but granted them authority over the things upon the earth.
[3] He endowed them with strength like his own, and made them in his own image.
[4] He placed the fear of them in all living beings, and granted them dominion over beasts and birds.
[6] He made for them tongue and eyes; he gave them ears and a mind for thinking.
[7] He filled them with knowledge and understanding, and showed them good and evil.
[8] He set his eye upon their hearts to show them the majesty of his works.
[10] And they will praise his holy name, to proclaim the grandeur of his works.
[11] He bestowed knowledge upon them, and allotted to them the law of life.
[12] He established with them an eternal covenant, and showed them his judgments.
[13] Their eyes saw his glorious majesty, and their ears heard the glory of his voice.
[14] And he said to them, "Beware of all unrighteousness." And he gave commandment to each of them concerning
his neighbor.
[15] Their ways are always before him, they will not be hid from his eyes.
[17] He appointed a ruler for every nation, but Israel is the Lord's own portion.
[19] All their works are as the sun before him, and his eyes are continually upon their ways.
[20] Their iniquities are not hidden from him, and all their sins are before the Lord.
[22] A man's almsgiving is like a signet with the Lord and he will keep a person's kindness like the apple of his eye.
[23] Afterward he will arise and requite them, and he will bring their recompense on their heads.

[24] Yet to those who repent he grants a return, and he encourages those whose endurance is failing.
[25] Turn to the Lord and forsake your sins; pray in his presence and lessen your offenses.
[26] Return to the Most High and turn away from iniquity, and hate abominations intensely.
[27] Who will sing praises to the Most High in Hades, as do those who are alive and give thanks?
[28] From the dead, as from one who does not exist, thanksgiving has ceased; he who is alive and well sings the Lord's praises.
[29] How great is the mercy of the Lord, and his forgiveness for those who turn to him!
[30] For all things cannot be in men, since a son of man is not immortal.
[31] What is brighter than the sun? Yet its light fails. So flesh and blood devise evil.
[32] He marshals the host of the height of heaven; but all men are dust and ashes.

Sir.18
[1] He who lives for ever created the whole universe;
[2] the Lord alone will be declared righteous.
[4] To none has he given power to proclaim his works; and who can search out his mighty deeds?
[5] Who can measure his majestic power? And who can fully recount his mercies?
[6] It is not possible to diminish or increase them, nor is it possible to trace the wonders of the Lord.
[7] When a man has finished, he is just beginning, and when he stops, he will be at a loss.
[8] What is man, and of what use is he? What is his good and what is his evil?
[9] The number of a man's days is great if he reaches a hundred years.
[10] Like a drop of water from the sea and a grain of sand so are a few years in the day of eternity.
[11] Therefore the Lord is patient with them and pours out his mercy upon them.
[12] He sees and recognizes that their end will be evil; therefore he grants them forgiveness in abundance.
[13] The compassion of man is for his neighbor, but the compassion of the Lord is for all living beings. He rebukes and trains and teaches them, and turns them back, as a shepherd his flock.
[14] He has compassion on those who accept his discipline and who are eager for his judgments.
[15] My son, do not mix reproach with your good deeds, nor cause grief by your words when you present a gift.
[16] Does not the dew assuage the scorching heat? So a word is better than a gift.
[17] Indeed, does not a word surpass a good gift? Both are to be found in a gracious man.
[18] A fool is ungracious and abusive, and the gift of a grudging man makes the eyes dim.

[19] Before you speak, learn, and before you fall ill, take care of your health.

[20] Before judgment, examine yourself, and in the hour of visitation you will find forgiveness.

[21] Before falling ill, humble yourself, and when you are on the point of sinning, turn back.

[22] Let nothing hinder you from paying a vow promptly, and do not wait until death to be released from it.

[23] Before making a vow, prepare yourself; and do not be like a man who tempts the Lord.

[24] Think of his wrath on the day of death, and of the moment of vengeance when he turns away his face.

[25] In the time of plenty think of the time of hunger; in the days of wealth think of poverty and need.

[26] From morning to evening conditions change, and all things move swiftly before the Lord.

[27] A wise man is cautious in everything, and in days of sin he guards against wrongdoing.

[28] Every intelligent man knows wisdom, and he praises the one who finds her.

[29] Those who understand sayings become skilled themselves, and pour forth apt proverbs.

[30] Do not follow your base desires, but restrain your appetites.

[31] If you allow your soul to take pleasure in base desire, it will make you the laughingstock of your enemies.

[32] Do not revel in great luxury, lest you become impoverished by its expense.

[33] Do not become a beggar by feasting with borrowed money, when you have nothing in your purse.

Sir.19

[1] A workman who is a drunkard will not become rich; he who despises small things will fail little by little.

[2] Wine and women lead intelligent men astray, and the man who consorts with harlots is very reckless.

[3] Decay and worms will inherit him, and the reckless soul will be snatched away.

[4] One who trusts others too quickly is lightminded, and one who sins does wrong to himself.

[5] One who rejoices in wickedness will be condemned,

[6] and for one who hates gossip evil is lessened.

[7] Never repeat a conversation, and you will lose nothing at all.

[8] With friend or foe do not report it, and unless it would be a sin for you, do not disclose it;

[9] for some one has heard you and watched you, and when the time comes he will hate you.

[10] Have you heard a word? Let it die with you. Be brave! It will not make you burst!

[11] With such a word a fool will suffer pangs like a woman in labor with a child.

[12] Like an arrow stuck in the flesh of the thigh, so is a word inside a fool.

[13] Question a friend, perhaps he did not do it; but if he did anything, so that he may do it no more.

[14] Question a neighbor, perhaps he did not say it; but if he said it, so that he may not say it again.

[15] Question a friend, for often it is slander; so do not believe everything you hear.

[16] A person may make a slip without intending it. Who has never sinned with his tongue?

[17] Question your neighbor before you threaten him; and let the law of the Most High take its course.

[20] All wisdom is the fear of the Lord, and in all wisdom there is the fulfilment of the law.

[22] But the knowledge of wickedness is not wisdom, nor is there prudence where sinners take counsel.

[23] There is a cleverness which is abominable, but there is a fool who merely lacks wisdom.

[24] Better is the God-fearing man who lacks intelligence, than the highly prudent man who transgresses the law.

[25] There is a cleverness which is scrupulous but unjust, and there are people who distort kindness to gain a verdict.

[26] There is a rascal bowed down in mourning, but inwardly he is full of deceit.

[27] He hides his face and pretends not to hear; but where no one notices, he will forestall you.

[28] And if by lack of strength he is prevented from sinning, he will do evil when he finds an opportunity.

[29] A man is known by his appearance, and a sensible man is known by his face, when you meet him.

[30] A man's attire and open-mouthed laughter, and a man's manner of walking, show what he is.

Sir.20

[1] There is a reproof which is not timely; and there is a man who keeps silent but is wise.

[2] How much better it is to reprove than to stay angry! And the one who confesses his fault will be kept from loss.

[3] Like a eunuch's desire to violate a maiden is a man who executes judgments by violence.

[5] There is one who by keeping silent is found wise, while another is detested for being too talkative.

[6] There is one who keeps silent because he has no answer, while another keeps silent because he knows when to speak.

[7] A wise man will be silent until the right moment, but a braggart and fool goes beyond the right moment.

[8] Whoever uses too many words will be loathed, and whoever usurps the right to speak will be hated.

[9] There may be good fortune for a man in adversity, and a windfall may result in a loss.

[10] There is a gift that profits you nothing, and there is a gift that brings a double return.

[11] There are losses because of glory, and there are men who have raised their heads from humble circumstances.

[12] There is a man who buys much for a little, but pays for it seven times over.

[13] The wise man makes himself beloved through his words, but the courtesies of fools are wasted.

[14] A fool's gift will profit you nothing, for he has many eyes instead of one.

[15] He gives little and upbraids much, he opens his mouth like a herald; today he lends and tomorrow he asks it back;

such a one is a hateful man.

[16] A fool will say, "I have no friend, and there is no gratitude for my good deeds; those who eat my bread speak unkindly."

[17] How many will ridicule him, and how often!

[18] A slip on the pavement is better than a slip of the tongue; so the downfall of the wicked will occur speedily.

[19] An ungracious man is like a story told at the wrong time, which is continually on the lips of the ignorant.

[20] A proverb from a fool's lips will be rejected, for he does not tell it at its proper time.

[21] A man may be prevented from sinning by his poverty, so when he rests he feels no remorse.

[22] A man may lose his life through shame, or lose it because of his foolish look.

[23] A man may for shame make promises to a friend, and needlessly make him an enemy.

[24] A lie is an ugly blot on a man; it is continually on the lips of the ignorant.

[25] A thief is preferable to a habitual liar, but the lot of both is ruin.

[26] The disposition of a liar brings disgrace, and his shame is ever with him.

[27] He who speaks wisely will advance himself, and a sensible man will please great men.

[28] Whoever cultivates the soil will heap up his harvest, and whoever pleases great men will atone for injustice.

[29] Presents and gifts blind the eyes of the wise; like a muzzle on the mouth they avert reproofs.

[30] Hidden wisdom and unseen treasure, what advantage is there in either of them?

[31] Better is the man who hides his folly than the man who hides his wisdom.

Sir.21

[1] Have you sinned, my son? Do so no more, but pray about your former sins.

[2] Flee from sin as from a snake; for if you approach sin, it will bite you. Its teeth are lion's teeth, and destroy the souls of men.

[3] All lawlessness is like a two-edged sword; there is no healing for its wound.

[4] Terror and violence will lay waste riches; thus the house of the proud will be laid waste.

[5] The prayer of a poor man goes from his lips to the ears of God, and his judgment comes speedily.

[6] Whoever hates reproof walks in the steps of the sinner, but he that fears the Lord will repent in his heart.

[7] He who is mighty in speech is known from afar; but the sensible man, when he slips, is aware of it.

[8] A man who builds his house with other people's money is like one who gathers stones for his burial mound.

[9] An assembly of the wicked is like tow gathered together, and their end is a flame of fire.

[10] The way of sinners is smoothly paved with stones, but at its end is the pit of Hades.

[11] Whoever keeps the law controls his thoughts, and wisdom is the fulfilment of the fear of the Lord.

[12] He who is not clever cannot be taught, but there is a cleverness which increases bitterness.

[13] The knowledge of a wise man will increase like a flood, and his counsel like a flowing spring.

[14] The mind of a fool is like a broken jar; it will hold no knowledge.

[15] When a man of understanding hears a wise saying, he will praise it and add to it; when a reveler hears it, he dislikes it

and casts it behind his back.

[16] A fool's narration is like a burden on a journey, but delight will be found in the speech of the intelligent.

[17] The utterance of a sensible man will be sought in the assembly, and they will ponder his words in their minds.

[18] Like a house that has vanished, so is wisdom to a fool; and the knowledge of the ignorant is unexamined talk.

[19] To a senseless man education is fetters on his feet, and like manacles on his right hand.

[20] A fool raises his voice when he laughs, but a clever man smiles quietly.

[21] To a sensible man education is like a golden ornament, and like a bracelet on the right arm.

[22] The foot of a fool rushes into a house, but a man of experience stands respectfully before it.

[23] A boor peers into the house from the door, but a cultivated man remains outside.

[24] It is ill-mannered for a man to listen at a door, and a discreet man is grieved by the disgrace.

[25] The lips of strangers will speak of these things, but the words of the prudent will be weighed in the balance.

[26] The mind of fools is in their mouth, but the mouth of wise men is in their mind.

[27] When an ungodly man curses his adversary, he curses his own soul.

[28] A whisperer defiles his own soul and is hated in his neighborhood.

Sir.22

[1] The indolent may be compared to a filthy stone, and every one hisses at his disgrace.

[2] The indolent may be compared to the filth of dunghills; any one that picks it up will shake it off his hand.

[3] It is a disgrace to be the father of an undisciplined son, and the birth of a daughter is a loss.

[4] A sensible daughter obtains her husband, but one who acts shamefully brings grief to her father.

[5] An impudent daughter disgraces father and husband, and will be despised by both.

[6] Like music in mourning is a tale told at the wrong time, but chastising and discipline are wisdom at all times.

[7] He who teaches a fool is like one who glues potsherds together, or who rouses a sleeper from deep slumber.

[8] He who tells a story to a fool tells it to a drowsy man; and at the end he will say, "What is it?"

[11] Weep for the dead, for he lacks the light; and weep for the fool, for he lacks intelligence; weep less bitterly for the dead, for he has attained rest; but the life of the fool is worse than death.

[12] Mourning for the dead lasts seven days, but for a fool or an ungodly man it lasts all his life.

[13] Do not talk much with a foolish man, and do not visit an unintelligent man; guard yourself from him to escape trouble,

and you will not be soiled when he shakes himself off; avoid him and you will find rest, and you will never be wearied by his madness.

[14] What is heavier than lead? And what is its name except "Fool"?

[15] Sand, salt, and a piece of iron are easier to bear than a stupid man.

[16] A wooden beam firmly bonded into a building will not be torn loose by an earthquake; so the mind firmly fixed on a reasonable counsel will not be afraid in a crisis.

[17] A mind settled on an intelligent thought is like the stucco decoration on the wall of a colonnade.

[18] Fences set on a high place will not stand firm against the wind; so a timid heart with a fool's purpose will not stand firm against any fear.

[19] A man who pricks an eye will make tears fall, and one who pricks the heart makes it show feeling.

[20] One who throws a stone at birds scares them away, and one who reviles a friend will break off the friendship.

[21] Even if you have drawn your sword against a friend, do not despair, for a renewal of friendship is possible.

[22] If you have opened your mouth against your friend, do not worry, for reconciliation is possible; but as for reviling, arrogance, disclosure of secrets, or a treacherous blow -- in these cases any friend will flee.

[23] Gain the trust of your neighbor in his poverty, that you may rejoice with him in his prosperity; stand by him in time of affliction, that you may share with him in his inheritance.

[24] The vapor and smoke of the furnace precede the fire; so insults precede bloodshed.

[25] I will not be ashamed to protect a friend, and I will not hide from him;

[26] but if some harm should happen to me because of him, whoever hears of it will beware of him.

[27] O that a guard were set over my mouth, and a seal of prudence upon my lips, that it may keep me from falling, so that my tongue may not destroy me!

Sir.23

[1] O Lord, Father and Ruler of my life, do not abandon me to their counsel, and let me not fall because of them!

[2] O that whips were set over my thoughts, and the discipline of wisdom over my mind! That they may not spare me in my errors, and that it may not pass by my sins;

[3] in order that my mistakes may not be multiplied, and my sins may not abound; then I will not fall before my adversaries, and my enemy will not rejoice over me.

[4] O Lord, Father and God of my life, do not give me haughty eyes,

[5] and remove from me evil desire.

[6] Let neither gluttony nor lust overcome me, and do not surrender me to a shameless soul.

[7] Listen, my children, to instruction concerning speech; the one who observes it will never be caught.

[8] The sinner is overtaken through his lips, the reviler and the arrogant are tripped by them.

[9] Do not accustom your mouth to oaths, and do not habitually utter the name of the Holy One;

[10] for as a servant who is continually examined under torture will not lack bruises, so also the man who always swears and utters the Name will not be cleansed from sin.

[11] A man who swears many oaths will be filled with iniquity, and the scourge will not leave his house; if he offends, his sin remains on him, and if he disregards it, he sins doubly; if he has sworn needlessly, he will not be justified, for his house will be filled with calamities.

[12] There is an utterance which is comparable to death; may it never be found in the inheritance of

Jacob! For all these errors will be far from the godly, and they will not wallow in sins.

[13] Do not accustom your mouth to lewd vulgarity, for it involves sinful speech.

[14] Remember your father and mother when you sit among great men; lest you be forgetful in their presence, and be deemed a fool on account of your habits; then you will wish that you had never been born, and you will curse the day of your birth.

[15] A man accustomed to use insulting words will never become disciplined all his days.

[16] Two sorts of men multiply sins, and a third incurs wrath. The soul heated like a burning fire will not be quenched until it is consumed; a man who commits fornication with his near of kin will never cease until the fire burns him up.

[17] To a fornicator all bread tastes sweet; he will never cease until he dies.

[18] A man who breaks his marriage vows says to himself, "Who sees me? Darkness surrounds me, and the walls hide me, and no one sees me. Why should I fear? The Most High will not take notice of my sins."

[19] His fear is confined to the eyes of men, and he does not realize that the eyes of the Lord are ten thousand times brighter than the sun; they look upon all the ways of men, and perceive even the hidden places.

[20] Before the universe was created, it was known to him; so it was also after it was finished.

[21] This man will be punished in the streets of the city, and where he least suspects it, he will be seized.

[22] So it is with a woman who leaves her husband and provides an heir by a stranger.

[23] For first of all, she has disobeyed the law of the Most High; second, she has committed an offense against her husband; and third, she has committed adultery through harlotry and brought forth children by another man.

[24] She herself will be brought before the assembly, and punishment will fall on her children.

[25] Her children will not take root, and her branches will not bear fruit.

[26] She will leave her memory for a curse, and her disgrace will not be blotted out.

[27] Those who survive her will recognize that nothing is better than the fear of the Lord, and nothing sweeter than to heed the commandments of the Lord.

Sir.24

[1] Wisdom will praise herself, and will glory in the midst of her people.

[2] In the assembly of the Most High she will open her mouth, and in the presence of his host she will glory:

[3] "I came forth from the mouth of the Most High, and covered the earth like a mist.

[4] I dwelt in high places, and my throne was in a pillar of cloud.

[5] Alone I have made the circuit of the vault of heaven and have walked in the depths of the abyss.

[6] In the waves of the sea, in the whole earth, and in every people and nation I have gotten a possession.

[7] Among all these I sought a resting place; I sought in whose territory I might lodge.

[8] "Then the Creator of all things gave me a commandment, and the one who created me assigned a place for my tent.
And he said, `Make your dwelling in Jacob, and in Israel receive your inheritance.'

[9] From eternity, in the beginning, he created me, and for eternity I shall not cease to exist.

[10] In the holy tabernacle I ministered before him, and so I was established in Zion.

[11] In the beloved city likewise he gave me a resting place, and in Jerusalem was my dominion.

[12] So I took root in an honored people, in the portion of the Lord, who is their inheritance.

[13] "I grew tall like a cedar in Lebanon, and like a cypress on the heights of Hermon.

[14] I grew tall like a palm tree in En-ge'di, and like rose plants in Jericho; like a beautiful olive tree in the field, and like a plane tree I grew tall.

[15] Like cassia and camel's thorn I gave forth the aroma of spices, and like choice myrrh I spread a pleasant odor, like galbanum, onycha, and stacte, and like the fragrance of frankincense in the tabernacle.

[16] Like a terebinth I spread out my branches, and my branches are glorious and graceful.

[17] Like a vine I caused loveliness to bud, and my blossoms became glorious and abundant fruit.

[19] "Come to me, you who desire me, and eat your fill of my produce.

[20] For the remembrance of me is sweeter than honey, and my inheritance sweeter than the honeycomb.

[21] Those who eat me will hunger for more, and those who drink me will thirst for more.

[22] Whoever obeys me will not be put to shame, and those who work with my help will not sin."

[23] All this is the book of the covenant of the Most High God, the law which Moses commanded us as an inheritance for the congregations of Jacob.

[25] It fills men with wisdom, like the Pishon, and like the Tigris at the time of the first fruits.

[26] It makes them full of understanding, like the Euphrates, and like the Jordan at harvest time.

[27] It makes instruction shine forth like light, like the Gihon at the time of vintage.

[28] Just as the first man did not know her perfectly, the last one has not fathomed her;

[29] for her thought is more abundant than the sea, and her counsel deeper than the great abyss.

[30] I went forth like a canal from a river and like a water channel into a garden.

[31] I said, "I will water my orchard and drench my garden plot"; and lo, my canal became a river, and my river became a sea.

[32] I will again make instruction shine forth like the dawn, and I will make it shine afar;

[33] I will again pour out teaching like prophecy, and leave it to all future generations.

[34] Observe that I have not labored for myself alone, but for all who seek instruction.

Sir.25

[1] My soul takes pleasure in three things, and they are beautiful in the sight of the Lord and of men; agreement between brothers, friendship between neighbors, and a wife and a husband who live in harmony.

[2] My soul hates three kinds of men, and I am greatly offended at their life: a beggar who is proud, a rich man who is a liar, and an adulterous old man who lacks good sense.

[3] You have gathered nothing in your youth; how then can you find anything in your old age?

[4] What an attractive thing is judgment in gray-haired men, and for the aged to possess good counsel!

[5] How attractive is wisdom in the aged, and understanding and counsel in honorable men!

[6] Rich experience is the crown of the aged, and their boast is the fear of the Lord.

[7] With nine thoughts I have gladdened my heart, and a tenth I shall tell with my tongue: a man rejoicing in his children;

a man who lives to see the downfall of his foes;

[8] happy is he who lives with an intelligent wife, and he who has not made a slip with his tongue, and he who has not served a man inferior to himself;

[9] happy is he who has gained good sense, and he who speaks to attentive listeners.

[10] How great is he who has gained wisdom! But there is no one superior to him who fears the Lord.

[11] The fear of the Lord surpasses everything; to whom shall be likened the one who holds it fast?

[13] Any wound, but not a wound of the heart! Any wickedness, but not the wickedness of a wife!

[14] Any attack, but not an attack from those who hate! And any vengeance, but not the vengeance of enemies!

[15] There is no venom worse than a snake's venom, and no wrath worse than an enemy's wrath.

[16] I would rather dwell with a lion and a dragon than dwell with an evil wife.

[17] The wickedness of a wife changes her appearance, and darkens her face like that of a bear.

[18] Her husband takes his meals among the neighbors, and he cannot help sighing bitterly.

[19] Any iniquity is insignificant compared to a wife's iniquity; may a sinner's lot befall her!

[20] A sandy ascent for the feet of the aged -- such is a garrulous wife for a quiet husband.

[21] Do not be ensnared by a woman's beauty, and do not desire a woman for her possessions.

[22] There is wrath and impudence and great disgrace when a wife supports her husband.

[23] A dejected mind, a gloomy face, and a wounded heart are caused by an evil wife. Drooping hands and weak knees

are caused by the wife who does not make her husband happy.

[24] From a woman sin had its beginning, and because of her we all die.

[25] Allow no outlet to water, and no boldness of speech in an evil wife.

[26] If she does not go as you direct, separate her from yourself.

Sir.26

[1] Happy is the husband of a good wife; the number of his days will be doubled.

[2] A loyal wife rejoices her husband, and he will complete his years in peace.

[3] A good wife is a great blessing; she will be granted among the blessings of the man who fears the Lord.

[4] Whether rich or poor, his heart is glad, and at all times his face is cheerful.

[5] Of three things my heart is afraid, and of a fourth I am frightened: The slander of a city, the gathering of a mob, and false accusation -- all these are worse than death.

[6] There is grief of heart and sorrow when a wife is envious of a rival, and a tongue-lashing makes it known to all.

[7] An evil wife is an ox yoke which chafes; taking hold of her is like grasping a scorpion.

[8] There is great anger when a wife is drunken; she will not hide her shame.

[9] A wife's harlotry shows in her lustful eyes, and she is known by her eyelids.

[10] Keep strict watch over a headstrong daughter, lest, when she finds liberty, she use it to her hurt.

[11] Be on guard against her impudent eye, and do not wonder if she sins against you.

[12] As a thirsty wayfarer opens his mouth and drinks from any water near him, so will she sit in front of every post and open her quiver to the arrow.

[13] A wife's charm delights her husband, and her skill puts fat on his bones.

[14] A silent wife is a gift of the Lord, and there is nothing so precious as a disciplined soul.

[15] A modest wife adds charm to charm, and no balance can weigh the value of a chaste soul.

[16] Like the sun rising in the heights of the Lord, so is the beauty of a good wife in her well-ordered home.
[17] Like the shining lamp on the holy lampstand, so is a beautiful face on a stately figure.
[18] Like pillars of gold on a base of silver, so are beautiful feet with a steadfast heart.
[28] At two things my heart is grieved, and because of a third anger comes over me: a warrior in want through poverty,
and intelligent men who are treated contemptuously; a man who turns back from righteousness to sin -- the Lord will prepare him for the sword!
[29] A merchant can hardly keep from wrongdoing, and a tradesman will not be declared innocent of sin.

Sir.27
[1] Many have committed sin for a trifle, and whoever seeks to get rich will avert his eyes.
[2] As a stake is driven firmly into a fissure between stones, so sin is wedged in between selling and buying.
[3] If a man is not steadfast and zealous in the fear of the Lord, his house will be quickly overthrown.
[4] When a sieve is shaken, the refuse remains; so a man's filth remains in his thoughts.
[5] The kiln tests the potter's vessels; so the test of a man is in his reasoning.
[6] The fruit discloses the cultivation of a tree; so the expression of a thought discloses the cultivation of a man's mind.
[7] Do not praise a man before you hear him reason, for this is the test of men.
[8] If you pursue justice, you will attain it and wear it as a glorious robe.
[9] Birds flock with their kind; so truth returns to those who practice it.
[10] A lion lies in wait for prey; so does sin for the workers of iniquity.
[11] The talk of the godly man is always wise, but the fool changes like the moon.
[12] Among stupid people watch for a chance to leave, but among thoughtful people stay on.
[13] The talk of fools is offensive, and their laughter is wantonly sinful.
[14] The talk of men given to swearing makes one's hair stand on end, and their quarrels make a man stop his ears.
[15] The strife of the proud leads to bloodshed, and their abuse is grievous to hear.
[16] Whoever betrays secrets destroys confidence, and he will never find a congenial friend.
[17] Love your friend and keep faith with him; but if you betray his secrets, do not run after him.
[18] For as a man destroys his enemy, so you have destroyed the friendship of your neighbor.

[19] And as you allow a bird to escape from your hand, so you have let your neighbor go, and will not catch him again.
[20] Do not go after him, for he is too far off, and has escaped like a gazelle from a snare.
[21] For a wound may be bandaged, and there is reconciliation after abuse, but whoever has betrayed secrets is without hope.
[22] Whoever winks his eye plans evil deeds, and no one can keep him from them.
[23] In your presence his mouth is all sweetness, and he admires your words; but later he will twist his speech and with your own words he will give offense.
[24] I have hated many things, but none to be compared to him; even the Lord will hate him.
[25] Whoever throws a stone straight up throws it on his own head; and a treacherous blow opens up wounds.
[26] He who digs a pit will fall into it, and he who sets a snare will be caught in it.
[27] If a man does evil, it will roll back upon him, and he will not know where it came from.
[28] Mockery and abuse issue from the proud man, but vengeance lies in wait for him like a lion.
[29] Those who rejoice in the fall of the godly will be caught in a snare, and pain will consume them before their death.
[30] Anger and wrath, these also are abominations, and the sinful man will possess them.

Sir.28
[1] He that takes vengeance will suffer vengeance from the Lord, and he will firmly establish his sins.
[2] Forgive your neighbor the wrong he has done, and then your sins will be pardoned when you pray.
[3] Does a man harbor anger against another, and yet seek for healing from the Lord?
[4] Does he have no mercy toward a man like himself, and yet pray for his own sins?
[5] If he himself, being flesh, maintains wrath, who will make expiation for his sins?
[6] Remember the end of your life, and cease from enmity, remember destruction and death, and be true to the commandments.
[7] Remember the commandments, and do not be angry with your neighbor; remember the covenant of the Most High, and overlook ignorance.
[8] Refrain from strife, and you will lessen sins; for a man given to anger will kindle strife,
[9] and a sinful man will disturb friends and inject enmity among those who are at peace.
[10] In proportion to the fuel for the fire, so will be the burning, and in proportion to the obstinacy of strife will be the burning; in proportion to the strength of the man will be his anger, and in proportion to his wealth he will heighten his wrath.

[11] A hasty quarrel kindles fire, and urgent strife sheds blood.

[12] If you blow on a spark, it will glow; if you spit on it, it will be put out; and both come out of your mouth.

[13] Curse the whisperer and deceiver, for he has destroyed many who were at peace.

[14] Slander has shaken many, and scattered them from nation to nation, and destroyed strong cities, and overturned the houses of great men.

[15] Slander has driven away courageous women, and deprived them of the fruit of their toil.

[16] Whoever pays heed to slander will not find rest, nor will he settle down in peace.

[17] The blow of a whip raises a welt, but a blow of the tongue crushes the bones.

[18] Many have fallen by the edge of the sword, but not so many as have fallen because of the tongue.

[19] Happy is the man who is protected from it, who has not been exposed to its anger, who has not borne its yoke,

and has not been bound with its fetters;

[20] for its yoke is a yoke of iron, and its fetters are fetters of bronze;

[21] its death is an evil death, and Hades is preferable to it.

[22] It will not be master over the godly, and they will not be burned in its flame.

[23] Those who forsake the Lord will fall into its power; it will burn among them and will not be put out. It will be sent out against them like a lion; like a leopard it will mangle them.

[24] See that you fence in your property with thorns, lock up your silver and gold,

[25] make balances and scales for your words, and make a door and a bolt for your mouth.

[26] Beware lest you err with your tongue, lest you fall before him who lies in wait.

Sir.29

[1] He that shows mercy will lend to his neighbor, and he that strengthens him with his hand keeps the commandments.

[2] Lend to your neighbor in the time of his need; and in turn, repay your neighbor promptly.

[3] Confirm your word and keep faith with him, and on every occasion you will find what you need.

[4] Many persons regard a loan as a windfall, and cause trouble to those who help them.

[5] A man will kiss another's hands until he gets a loan, and will lower his voice in speaking of his neighbor's money;

but at the time for repayment he will delay, and will pay in words of unconcern, and will find fault with the time.

[6] If the lender exert pressure, he will hardly get back half, and will regard that as a windfall. If he does not,

the borrower has robbed him of his money, and he has needlessly made him his enemy; he will repay him with curses and reproaches,

and instead of glory will repay him with dishonor.

[7] Because of such wickedness, therefore, many have refused to lend; they have been afraid of being defrauded needlessly.

[8] Nevertheless, be patient with a man in humble circumstances, and do not make him wait for your alms.

[9] Help a poor man for the commandment's sake, and because of his need do not send him away empty.

[10] Lose your silver for the sake of a brother or a friend, and do not let it rust under a stone and be lost.

[11] Lay up your treasure according to the commandments of the Most High, and it will profit you more than gold.

[12] Store up almsgiving in your treasury, and it will rescue you from all affliction;

[13] more than a mighty shield and more than a heavy spear, it will fight on your behalf against your enemy.

[14] A good man will be surety for his neighbor, but a man who has lost his sense of shame will fail him.

[15] Do not forget all the kindness of your surety, for he has given his life for you.

[16] A sinner will overthrow the prosperity of his surety,

[17] and one who does not feel grateful will abandon his rescuer.

[18] Being surety has ruined many men who were prosperous, and has shaken them like a wave of the sea; it has driven men of power into exile, and they have wandered among foreign nations.

[19] The sinner who has fallen into suretyship and pursues gain will fall into lawsuits.

[20] Assist your neighbor according to your ability, but take heed to yourself lest you fall.

[21] The essentials for life are water and bread and clothing and a house to cover one's nakedness.

[22] Better is the life of a poor man under the shelter of his roof than sumptuous food in another man's house.

[23] Be content with little or much.

[24] It is a miserable life to go from house to house, and where you are a stranger you may not open your mouth;

[25] you will play the host and provide drink without being thanked, and besides this you will hear bitter words:

[26] "Come here, stranger, prepare the table, and if you have anything at hand, let me have it to eat."

[27] "Give place, stranger, to an honored person; my brother has come to stay with me; I need my house."

[28] These things are hard to bear for a man who has feeling: scolding about lodging and the reproach of the moneylender.

Sir.30

[1] He who loves his son will whip him often, in order that he may rejoice at the way he turns out.

[2] He who disciplines his son will profit by him, and will boast of him among acquaintances.

[3] He who teaches his son will make his enemies envious, and will glory in him in the presence of friends.

[4] The father may die, and yet he is not dead, for he has left behind him one like himself;

[5] while alive he saw and rejoiced, and when he died he was not grieved;

[6] he has left behind him an avenger against his enemies, and one to repay the kindness of his friends.

[7] He who spoils his son will bind up his wounds, and his feelings will be troubled at every cry.

[8] A horse that is untamed turns out to be stubborn, and a son unrestrained turns out to be wilful.

[9] Pamper a child, and he will frighten you; play with him, and he will give you grief.

[10] Do not laugh with him, lest you have sorrow with him, and in the end you will gnash your teeth.

[11] Give him no authority in his youth, and do not ignore his errors.

[12] Bow down his neck in his youth, and beat his sides while he is young, lest he become stubborn and disobey you,

and you have sorrow of soul from him.

[13] Discipline your son and take pains with him, that you may not be offended by his shamelessness.

[14] Better off is a poor man who is well and strong in constitution than a rich man who is severely afflicted in body.

[15] Health and soundness are better than all gold, and a robust body than countless riches.

[16] There is no wealth better than health of body, and there is no gladness above joy of heart.

[17] Death is better than a miserable life, and eternal rest than chronic sickness.

[18] Good things poured out upon a mouth that is closed are like offerings of food placed upon a grave.

[19] Of what use to an idol is an offering of fruit? For it can neither eat nor smell. So is he who is afflicted by the Lord;

[20] he sees with his eyes and groans, like a eunuch who embraces a maiden and groans.

[21] Do not give yourself over to sorrow, and do not afflict yourself deliberately.

[22] Gladness of heart is the life of man, and the rejoicing of a man is length of days.

[23] Delight your soul and comfort your heart, and remove sorrow far from you, for sorrow has destroyed many, and there is no profit in it.

[24] Jealousy and anger shorten life, and anxiety brings on old age too soon.

[25] A man of cheerful and good heart will give heed to the food he eats.

Sir.31

[1] Wakefulness over wealth wastes away one's flesh, and anxiety about it removes sleep.

[2] Wakeful anxiety prevents slumber, and a severe illness carries off sleep.

[3] The rich man toils as his wealth accumulates, and when he rests he fills himself with his dainties.

[4] The poor man toils as his livelihood diminishes, and when he rests he becomes needy.

[5] He who loves gold will not be justified, and he who pursues money will be led astray by it.

[6] Many have come to ruin because of gold, and their destruction has met them face to face.

[7] It is a stumbling block to those who are devoted to it, and every fool will be taken captive by it.

[8] Blessed is the rich man who is found blameless, and who does not go after gold.

[9] Who is he? And we will call him blessed, for he has done wonderful things among his people.

[10] Who has been tested by it and been found perfect? Let it be for him a ground for boasting. Who has had the power to transgress and did not transgress, and to do evil and did not do it?

[11] His prosperity will be established, and the assembly will relate his acts of charity.

[12] Are you seated at the table of a great man? Do not be greedy at it, and do not say, "There is certainly much upon it!"

[13] Remember that a greedy eye is a bad thing. What has been created more greedy than the eye? Therefore it sheds tears from every face.

[14] Do not reach out your hand for everything you see, and do not crowd your neighbor at the dish.

[15] Judge your neighbor's feelings by your own, and in every matter be thoughtful.

[16] Eat like a human being what is set before you, and do not chew greedily, lest you be hated.

[17] Be the first to stop eating, for the sake of good manners, and do not be insatiable, lest you give offense.

[18] If you are seated among many persons, do not reach out your hand before they do.

[19] How ample a little is for a well-disciplined man! He does not breathe heavily upon his bed.

[20] Healthy sleep depends on moderate eating; he rises early, and feels fit. The distress of sleeplessness and of nausea

and colic are with the glutton.

[21] If you are overstuffed with food, get up in the middle of the meal, and you will have relief.

[22] Listen to me, my son, and do not disregard me, and in the end you will appreciate my words. In all your work be industrious, and no sickness will overtake you.

[23] Men will praise the one who is liberal with food, and their testimony to his excellence is trustworthy.

[24] The city will complain of the one who is niggardly with food, and their testimony to his niggardliness is accurate.

[25] Do not aim to be valiant over wine, for wine has destroyed many.

[26] Fire and water prove the temper of steel, so wine tests hearts in the strife of the proud.

[27] Wine is like life to men, if you drink it in moderation. What is life to a man who is without wine? It has been created to make men glad.

[28] Wine drunk in season and temperately is rejoicing of heart and gladness of soul.

[29] Wine drunk to excess is bitterness of soul, with provocation and stumbling.

[30] Drunkenness increases the anger of a fool to his injury, reducing his strength and adding wounds.

[31] Do not reprove your neighbor at a banquet of wine, and do not despise him in his merrymaking; speak no word of reproach to him, and do not afflict him by making demands of him.

Sir.32

[1] If they make you master of the feast, do not exalt yourself; be among them as one of them; take good care of them and then be seated;

[2] when you have fulfilled your duties, take your place, that you may be merry on their account and receive a wreath for your excellent leadership.

[3] Speak, you who are older, for it is fitting that you should, but with accurate knowledge, and do not interrupt the music.

[4] Where there is entertainment, do not pour out talk; do not display your cleverness out of season.

[5] A ruby seal in a setting of gold is a concert of music at a banquet of wine.

[6] A seal of emerald in a rich setting of gold is the melody of music with good wine.

[7] Speak, young man, if there is need of you, but no more than twice, and only if asked.

[8] Speak concisely, say much in few words; be as one who knows and yet holds his tongue.

[9] Among the great do not act as their equal; and when another is speaking, do not babble.

[10] Lightning speeds before the thunder, and approval precedes a modest man.

[11] Leave in good time and do not be the last; go home quickly and do not linger.

[12] Amuse yourself there, and do what you have in mind, but do not sin through proud speech.

[13] And for these things bless him who made you and satisfies you with his good gifts.

[14] He who fears the Lord will accept his discipline, and those who rise early to seek him will find favor.

[15] He who seeks the law will be filled with it, but the hypocrite will stumble at it.

[16] Those who fear the Lord will form true judgments, and like a light they will kindle righteous deeds.

[17] A sinful man will shun reproof, and will find a decision according to his liking.

[18] A man of judgment will not overlook an idea, and an insolent and proud man will not cower in fear.

[19] Do nothing without deliberation; and when you have acted, do not regret it.

[20] Do not go on a path full of hazards, and do not stumble over stony ground.

[21] Do not be overconfident on a smooth way,

[22] and give good heed to your paths.

[23] Guard yourself in every act, for this is the keeping of the commandments.

[24] He who believes the law gives heed to the commandments, and he who trusts the Lord will not suffer loss.

Sir.33

[1] No evil will befall the man who fears the Lord, but in trial he will deliver him again and again.

[2] A wise man will not hate the law, but he who is hypocritical about it is like a boat in a storm.

[3] A man of understanding will trust in the law; for him the law is as dependable as an inquiry by means of Urim.

[4] Prepare what to say, and thus you will be heard; bind together your instruction, and make your answer.

[5] The heart of a fool is like a cart wheel, and his thoughts like a turning axle.

[6] A stallion is like a mocking friend; he neighs under every one who sits on him.

[7] Why is any day better than another, when all the daylight in the year is from the sun?

[8] By the Lord's decision they were distinguished, and he appointed the different seasons and feasts;

[9] some of them he exalted and hallowed, and some of them he made ordinary days.

[10] All men are from the ground, and Adam was created of the dust.

[11] In the fullness of his knowledge the Lord distinguished them and appointed their different ways;

[12] some of them he blessed and exalted, and some of them he made holy and brought near to himself; but some of them he cursed and brought low, and he turned them out of their place.

[13] As clay in the hand of the potter -- for all his ways are as he pleases -- so men are in the hand of him who made them, to give them as he decides.

[14] Good is the opposite of evil, and life the opposite of death; so the sinner is the opposite of the godly.

[15] Look upon all the works of the Most High; they likewise are in pairs, one the opposite of the other.

[16] I was the last on watch; I was like one who gleans after the grape-gatherers; by the blessing of the Lord I excelled,
and like a grape-gatherer I filled my wine press.
[17] Consider that I have not labored for myself alone, but for all who seek instruction.
[18] Hear me, you who are great among the people, and you leaders of the congregation, hearken.
[19] To son or wife, to brother or friend, do not give power over yourself, as long as you live; and do not give your property to another, lest you change your mind and must ask for it.
[20] While you are still alive and have breath in you, do not let any one take your place.
[21] For it is better that your children should ask from you than that you should look to the hand of you sons.
[22] Excel in all that you do; bring no stain upon your honor.
[23] At the time when you end the days of your life, in the hour of death, distribute your inheritance.
[24] Fodder and a stick and burdens for an ass; bread and discipline and work for a servant.
[25] Set your slave to work, and you will find rest; leave his hands idle, and he will seek liberty.
[26] Yoke and thong will bow the neck, and for a wicked servant there are racks and tortures.
[27] Put him to work, that he may not be idle, for idleness teaches much evil.
[28] Set him to work, as is fitting for him, and if he does not obey, make his fetters heavy.
[29] Do not act immoderately toward anybody, and do nothing without discretion.
[30] If you have a servant, let him be as yourself, because you have bought him with blood.
[31] If you have a servant, treat him as a brother, for as your own soul you will need him. If you ill-treat him, and he leaves and runs away, which way will you go to seek him?

Sir.34
[1] A man of no understanding has vain and false hopes, and dreams give wings to fools.
[2] As one who catches at a shadow and pursues the wind, so is he who gives heed to dreams.
[3] The vision of dreams is this against that, the likeness of a face confronting a face.
[4] From an unclean thing what will be made clean? And from something false what will be true?
[5] Divinations and omens and dreams are folly, and like a woman in travail the mind has fancies.
[6] Unless they are sent from the Most High as a visitation, do not give your mind to them.
[7] For dreams have deceived many, and those who put their hope in them have failed.
[8] Without such deceptions the law will be fulfilled, and wisdom is made perfect in truthful lips.

[9] An educated man knows many things, and one with much experience will speak with understanding.
[10] He that is inexperienced knows few things, but he that has traveled acquires much cleverness.
[11] I have seen many things in my travels, and I understand more than I can express.
[12] I have often been in danger of death, but have escaped because of these experiences.
[13] The spirit of those who fear the Lord will live, for their hope is in him who saves them.
[14] He who fears the Lord will not be timid, nor play the coward, for he is his hope.
[15] Blessed is the soul of the man who fears the Lord! To whom does he look? And who is his support?
[16] The eyes of the Lord are upon those who love him, a mighty protection and strong support, a shelter from the hot wind and a shade from noonday sun, a guard against stumbling and a defense against falling.
[17] He lifts up the soul and gives light to the eyes; he grants healing, life, and blessing.
[18] If one sacrifices from what has been wrongfully obtained, the offering is blemished; the gifts of the lawless are not acceptable.
[19] The Most High is not pleased with the offerings of the ungodly; and he is not propitiated for sins by a multitude of sacrifices.
[20] Like one who kills a son before his father's eyes is the man who offers a sacrifice from the property of the poor.
[21] The bread of the needy is the life of the poor; whoever deprives them of it is a man of blood.
[22] To take away a neighbor's living is to murder him; to deprive an employee of his wages is to shed blood.
[23] When one builds and another tears down, what do they gain but toil?
[24] When one prays and another curses, to whose voice will the Lord listen?
[25] If a man washes after touching a dead body, and touches it again, what has he gained by his washing?
[26] So if a man fasts for his sins, and goes again and does the same things, who will listen to his prayer? And what has he gained by humbling himself?

Sir.35
[1] He who keeps the law makes many offerings; he who heeds the commandments sacrifices a peace offering.
[2] He who returns a kindness offers fine flour, and he who gives alms sacrifices a thank offering.
[3] To keep from wickedness is pleasing to the Lord, and to forsake unrighteousness is atonement.
[4] Do not appear before the Lord empty-handed,
[5] for all these things are to be done because of the commandment.
[6] The offering of a righteous man anoints the altar, and its pleasing odor rises before the Most High.

[7] The sacrifice of a righteous man is acceptable, and the memory of it will not be forgotten.

[8] Glorify the Lord generously, and do not stint the first fruits of your hands.

[9] With every gift show a cheerful face, and dedicate your tithe with gladness.

[10] Give to the Most High as he has given, and as generously as your hand has found.

[11] For the Lord is the one who repays, and he will repay you sevenfold.

[12] Do not offer him a bribe, for he will not accept it; and do not trust to an unrighteous sacrifice; for the Lord is the judge, and with him is no partiality.

[13] He will not show partiality in the case of a poor man; and he will listen to the prayer of one who is wronged.

[14] He will not ignore the supplication of the fatherless, nor the widow when she pours out her story.

[15] Do not the tears of the widow run down her cheek as she cries out against him who has caused them to fall?

[16] He whose service is pleasing to the Lord will be accepted, and his prayer will reach to the clouds.

[17] The prayer of the humble pierces the clouds, and he will not be consoled until it reaches the Lord; he will not desist until the Most High visits him, and does justice for the righteous, and executes judgment.

[18] And the Lord will not delay, neither will he be patient with them, till he crushes the loins of the unmerciful and repays vengeance on the nations; till he takes away the multitude of the insolent, and breaks the scepters of the unrighteous;

[19] till he repays the man according to his deeds, and the works of men according to their devices; till he judges the case of his people and makes them rejoice in his mercy.

[20] Mercy is as welcome when he afflicts them as clouds of rain in the time of drought.

Sir.36

[1] Have mercy upon us, O Lord, the God of all, and look upon us,

[2] and cause the fear of thee to fall upon all the nations.

[3] Lift up thy hand against foreign nations and let them see thy might.

[4] As in us thou hast been sanctified before them, so in them be thou magnified before us;

[5] and let them know thee, as we have known that there is not God but thee, O Lord.

[6] Show signs anew, and work further wonders; make thy hand and thy right arm glorious.

[7] Rouse thy anger and pour out thy wrath; destroy the adversary and wipe out the enemy.

[8] Hasten the day, and remember the appointed time, and let people recount thy mighty deeds.

[9] Let him who survives be consumed in the fiery wrath, and may those who harm thy people meet destruction.

[10] Crush the heads of the rulers of the enemy, who say, "There is no one but ourselves."

[11] Gather all the tribes of Jacob, and give them their inheritance, as at the beginning.

[12] Have mercy, O Lord, upon the people called by thy name, upon Israel, whom thou hast likened to a first-born son.

[13] Have pity on the city of thy sanctuary, Jerusalem, the place of thy rest.

[14] Fill Zion with the celebration of thy wondrous deeds, and thy temple with thy glory.

[15] Bear witness to those whom thou didst create in the beginning, and fulfil the prophecies spoken in thy name.

[16] Reward those who wait for thee, and let thy prophets be found trustworthy.

[17] Hearken, O Lord, to the prayer of thy servants, according to the blessing of Aaron for thy people, and all who are on the earth will know that thou art the Lord, the God of the ages.

[18] The stomach will take any food, yet one food is better than another.

[19] As the palate tastes the kinds of game, so an intelligent mind detects false words.

[20] A perverse mind will cause grief, but a man of experience will pay him back.

[21] A woman will accept any man, but one daughter is better than another.

[22] A woman's beauty gladdens the countenance, and surpasses every human desire.

[23] If kindness and humility mark her speech, her husband is not like other men.

[24] He who acquires a wife gets his best possession, a helper fit for him and a pillar of support.

[25] Where there is no fence, the property will be plundered; and where there is no wife, a man will wander about and sigh.

[26] For who will trust a nimble robber that skips from city to city? So who will trust a man that has no home,

and lodges wherever night finds him?

Sir.37

[1] Every friend will say, "I too am a friend"; but some friends are friends only in name.

[2] Is it not a grief to the death when a companion and friend turns to enmity?

[3] O evil imagination, why were you formed to cover the land with deceit?

[4] Some companions rejoice in the happiness of a friend, but in time of trouble are against him.

[5] Some companions help a friend for their stomach's sake, and in the face of battle take up the shield.

[6] Do not forget a friend in your heart, and be not unmindful of him in your wealth.

[7] Every counselor praises counsel, but some give counsel in their own interest.

[8] Be wary of a counselor, and learn first what is his interest -- for he will take thought for himself -- lest he cast the lot against you

[9] and tell you, "Your way is good," and then stand aloof to see what will happen to you.

[10] Do not consult the one who looks at you suspiciously; hide your counsel from those who are jealous of you.

[11] Do not consult with a woman about her rival or with a coward about war, with a merchant about barter or with a buyer about selling, with a grudging man about gratitude or with a merciless man about kindness, with an idler about any work or with a man hired for a year about completing his work, with a lazy servant about a big task -- pay no attention to these in any matter of counsel.

[12] But stay constantly with a godly man whom you know to be a keeper of the commandments, whose soul is in accord with your soul, and who will sorrow with you if you fail.

[13] And establish the counsel of your own heart, for no one is more faithful to you than it is.

[14] For a man's soul sometimes keeps him better informed than seven watchmen sitting high on a watchtower.

[15] And besides all this pray to the Most High that he may direct your way in truth.

[16] Reason is the beginning of every work, and counsel precedes every undertaking.

[17] As a clue to changes of heart

[18] four turns of fortune appear, good and evil, life and death; and it is the tongue that continually rules them.

[19] A man may be shrewd and the teacher of many, and yet be unprofitable to himself.

[20] A man skilled in words may be hated; he will be destitute of all food,

[21] for grace was not given him by the Lord, since he is lacking in all wisdom.

[22] A man may be wise to his own advantage, and the fruits of his understanding may be trustworthy on his lips.

[23] A wise man will instruct his own people, and the fruits of his understanding will be trustworthy.

[24] A wise man will have praise heaped upon him, and all who see him will call him happy.

[25] The life of a man is numbered by days, but the days of Israel are without number.

[26] He who is wise among his people will inherit confidence, and his name will live for ever.

[27] My son, test your soul while you live; see what is bad for it and do not give it that.

[28] For not everything is good for every one, and not every person enjoys everything.

[29] Do not have an insatiable appetite for any luxury, and do not give yourself up to food;

[30] for overeating brings sickness, and gluttony leads to nausea.

[31] Many have died of gluttony, but he who is careful to avoid it prolongs his life.

Sir.38

[1] Honor the physician with the honor due him, according to your need of him, for the Lord created him;

[2] for healing comes from the Most High, and he will receive a gift from the king.

[3] The skill of the physician lifts up his head, and in the presence of great men he is admired.

[4] The Lord created medicines from the earth, and a sensible man will not despise them.

[5] Was not water made sweet with a tree in order that his power might be known?

[6] And he gave skill to men that he might be glorified in his marvelous works.

[7] By them he heals and takes away pain;

[8] the pharmacist makes of them a compound. His works will never be finished; and from him health is upon the face of the earth.

[9] My son, when you are sick do not be negligent, but pray to the Lord, and he will heal you.

[10] Give up your faults and direct your hands aright, and cleanse your heart from all sin.

[11] Offer a sweet-smelling sacrifice, and a memorial portion of fine flour, and pour oil on your offering, as much as you can afford.

[12] And give the physician his place, for the Lord created him; let him not leave you, for there is need of him.

[13] There is a time when success lies in the hands of physicians,

[14] for they too will pray to the Lord that he should grant them success in diagnosis and in healing, for the sake of preserving life.

[15] He who sins before his Maker, may he fall into the care of a physician.

[16] My son, let your tears fall for the dead, and as one who is suffering grievously begin the lament. Lay out his body with the honor due him, and do not neglect his burial.

[17] Let your weeping be bitter and your wailing fervent; observe the mourning according to his merit, for one day, or two, to avoid criticism; then be comforted for your sorrow.

[18] For sorrow results in death, and sorrow of heart saps one's strength.

[19] In calamity sorrow continues, and the life of the poor man weighs down his heart.

[20] Do not give your heart to sorrow; drive it away, remembering the end of life.

[21] Do not forget, there is no coming back; you do the dead no good, and you injure yourself.

[22] "Remember my doom, for yours is like it: yesterday it was mine, and today it is yours."

[23] When the dead is at rest, let his remembrance cease, and be comforted for him when his spirit is departed.

[24] The wisdom of the scribe depends on the opportunity of leisure; and he who has little business may become wise.

[25] How can he become wise who handles the plow, and who glories in the shaft of a goad, who drives oxen and is occupied with their work, and whose talk is about bulls?

[26] He sets his heart on plowing furrows, and he is careful about fodder for the heifers.

[27] So too is every craftsman and master workman who labors by night as well as by day; those who cut the signets of seals, each is diligent in making a great variety; he sets his heart on painting a lifelike image, and he is careful to finish his work.

[28] So too is the smith sitting by the anvil, intent upon his handiwork in iron; the breath of the fire melts his flesh, and he wastes away in the heat of the furnace; he inclines his ear to the sound of the hammer, and his eyes are on the pattern of the object. He sets his heart on finishing his handiwork, and he is careful to complete its decoration.

[29] So too is the potter sitting at his work and turning the wheel with his feet; he is always deeply concerned over his work, and all his output is by number.

[30] He moulds the clay with his arm and makes it pliable with his feet; he sets his heart to finish the glazing, and he is careful to clean the furnace.

[31] All these rely upon their hands, and each is skilful in his own work.

[32] Without them a city cannot be established, and men can neither sojourn nor live there.

[33] Yet they are not sought out for the council of the people, nor do they attain eminence in the public assembly.

They do not sit in the judge's seat, nor do they understand the sentence of judgment; they cannot expound discipline or judgment, and they are not found using proverbs.

[34] But they keep stable the fabric of the world, and their prayer is in the practice of their trade.

Sir.39

[1] On the other hand he who devotes himself to the study of the law of the Most High will seek out the wisdom of all the ancients, and will be concerned with prophecies;

[2] he will preserve the discourse of notable men and penetrate the subtleties of parables;

[3] he will seek out the hidden meanings of proverbs and be at home with the obscurities of parables.

[4] He will serve among great men and appear before rulers; he will travel through the lands of foreign nations, for he tests the good and the evil among men.

[5] He will set his heart to rise early to seek the Lord who made him, and will make supplication before the Most High; he will open his mouth in prayer and make supplication for his sins.

[6] If the great Lord is willing, he will be filled with the spirit of understanding; he will pour forth words of wisdom and give thanks to the Lord in prayer.

[7] He will direct his counsel and knowledge aright, and meditate on his secrets.

[8] He will reveal instruction in his teaching, and will glory in the law of the Lord's covenant.

[9] Many will praise his understanding, and it will never be blotted out; his memory will not disappear, and his name will live through all generations.

[10] Nations will declare his wisdom, and the congregation will proclaim his praise;

[11] if he lives long, he will leave a name greater than a thousand, and if he goes to rest, it is enough for him.

[12] I have yet more to say, which I have thought upon, and I am filled, like the moon at the full.

[13] Listen to me, O you holy sons, and bud like a rose growing by a stream of water;

[14] send forth fragrance like frankincense, and put forth blossoms like a lily. Scatter the fragrance, and sing a hymn of praise; bless the Lord for all his works;

[15] ascribe majesty to his name and give thanks to him with praise, with songs on your lips, and with lyres; and this you shall say in thanksgiving:

[16] "All things are the works of the Lord, for they are very good, and whatever he commands will be done in his time."

[17] No one can say, "What is this?" "Why is that?" for in God's time all things will be sought after. At his word the waters stood in a heap, and the reservoirs of water at the word of his mouth.

[18] At his command whatever pleases him is done, and none can limit his saving power.

[19] The works of all flesh are before him, and nothing can be hid from his eyes.

[20] From everlasting to everlasting he beholds them, and nothing is marvelous to him.

[21] No one can say, "What is this?" "Why is that?" for everything has been created for its use.

[22] His blessing covers the dry land like a river, and drenches it like a flood.

[23] The nations will incur his wrath, just as he turns fresh water into salt.

[24] To the holy his ways are straight, just as they are obstacles to the wicked.

[25] From the beginning good things were created for good people, just as evil things for sinners.

[26] Basic to all the needs of man's life are water and fire and iron and salt and wheat flour and milk and honey, the blood of the grape, and oil and clothing.
[27] All these are for good to the godly, just as they turn into evils for sinners.
[28] There are winds that have been created for vengeance, and in their anger they scourge heavily; in the time of consummation they will pour out their strength and calm the anger of their Maker.
[29] Fire and hail and famine and pestilence, all these have been created for vengeance;
[30] the teeth of wild beasts, and scorpions and vipers, and the sword that punishes the ungodly with destruction;
[31] they will rejoice in his commands, and be made ready on earth for their service, and when their times come they will not transgress his word.
[32] Therefore from the beginning I have been convinced, and have thought this out and left it in writing:
[33] The works of the Lord are all good, and he will supply every need in its hour.
[34] And no one can say, "This is worse than that," for all things will prove good in their season.
[35] So now sing praise with all your heart and voice, and bless the name of the Lord.

Sir.40
[1] Much labor was created for every man, and a heavy yoke is upon the sons of Adam, from the day they come forth from their mother's womb till the day they return to the mother of all.
[2] Their perplexities and fear of heart -- their anxious thought is the day of death,
[3] from the man who sits on a splendid throne to the one who is humbled in dust and ashes,
[4] from the man who wears purple and a crown to the one who is clothed in burlap;
[5] there is anger and envy and trouble and unrest, and fear of death, and fury and strife. And when one rests upon his bed, his sleep at night confuses his mind.
[6] He gets little or no rest, and afterward in his sleep, as though he were on watch, he is troubled by the visions of his mind like one who has escaped from the battle-front;
[7] at the moment of his rescue he wakes up, and wonders that his fear came to nothing.
[8] With all flesh, both man and beast, and upon sinners seven times more,
[9] are death and bloodshed and strife and sword, calamities, famine and affliction and plague.
[10] All these were created for the wicked, and on their account the flood came.
[11] All things that are from the earth turn back to the earth, and what is from the waters returns to the sea.

[12] All bribery and injustice will be blotted out, but good faith will stand for ever.
[13] The wealth of the unjust will dry up like a torrent, and crash like a loud clap of thunder in a rain.
[14] A generous man will be made glad; likewise transgressors will utterly fail.
[15] The children of the ungodly will not put forth many branches; they are unhealthy roots upon sheer rock.
[16] The reeds by any water or river bank will be plucked up before any grass.
[17] Kindness is like a garden of blessings, and almsgiving endures for ever.
[18] Life is sweet for the self-reliant and the worker, but he who finds treasure is better off than both.
[19] Children and the building of a city establish a man's name, but a blameless wife is accounted better than both.
[20] Wine and music gladden the heart, but the love of wisdom is better than both.
[21] The flute and the harp make pleasant melody, but a pleasant voice is better than both.
[22] The eye desires grace and beauty, but the green shoots of grain more than both.
[23] A friend or a companion never meets one amiss, but a wife with her husband is better than both.
[24] Brothers and help are for a time of trouble, but almsgiving rescues better than both.
[25] Gold and silver make the foot stand sure, but good counsel is esteemed more than both.
[26] Riches and strength lift up the heart, but the fear of the Lord is better than both. There is no loss in the fear of the Lord, and with it there is no need to seek for help.
[27] The fear of the Lord is like a garden of blessing, and covers a man better than any glory.
[28] My son, do not lead the life of a beggar; it is better to die than to beg.
[29] When a man looks to the table of another, his existence cannot be considered as life. He pollutes himself with another man's food, but a man who is intelligent and well instructed guards against that.
[30] In the mouth of the shameless begging is sweet, but in his stomach a fire is kindled.

Sir.41
[1] O death, how bitter is the reminder of you to one who lives at peace among his possessions, to a man without distractions, who is prosperous in everything, and who still has the vigor to enjoy his food!
[2] O death, how welcome is your sentence to one who is in need and is failing in strength, very old and distracted over everything; to one who is contrary, and has lost his patience!

[3] Do not fear the sentence of death; remember your former days and the end of life; this is the decree from the Lord for all flesh,

[4] and how can you reject the good pleasure of the Most High? Whether life is for ten or a hundred or a thousand years,

there is no inquiry about it in Hades.

[5] The children of sinners are abominable children, and they frequent the haunts of the ungodly.

[6] The inheritance of the children of sinners will perish, and on their posterity will be a perpetual reproach.

[7] Children will blame an ungodly father, for they suffer reproach because of him.

[8] Woe to you, ungodly men, who have forsaken the law of the Most High God!

[9] When you are born, you are born to a curse; and when you die, a curse is your lot.

[10] Whatever is from the dust returns to dust; so the ungodly go from curse to destruction.

[11] The mourning of men is about their bodies, but the evil name of sinners will be blotted out.

[12] Have regard for your name, since it will remain for you longer than a thousand great stores of gold.

[13] The days of a good life are numbered, but a good name endures for ever.

[14] My children, observe instruction and be at peace; hidden wisdom and unseen treasure, what advantage is there in either of them?

[15] Better is the man who hides his folly than the man who hides his wisdom.

[16] Therefore show respect for my words: For it is good to retain every kind of shame, and not everything is confidently esteemed by every one.

[17] Be ashamed of immorality, before your father or mother; and of a lie, before a prince or a ruler;

[18] of a transgression, before a judge or magistrate; and of iniquity, before a congregation or the people; of unjust dealing, before your partner or friend;

[19] and of theft, in the place where you live. Be ashamed before the truth of God and his covenant. Be ashamed of selfish behavior at meals, of surliness in receiving and giving,

[20] and of silence, before those who greet you; of looking at a woman who is a harlot,

[21] and of rejecting the appeal of a kinsman; of taking away some one's portion or gift, and of gazing at another man's wife;

[22] of meddling with his maidservant -- and do not approach her bed; of abusive words, before friends -- and do not upbraid after making a gift;

[23] of repeating and telling what you hear, and of revealing secrets. Then you will show proper shame, and will find favor with every man.

Sir.42

[1] Of the following things do not be ashamed, and do not let partiality lead you to sin:

[2] of the law of the Most High and his covenant, and of rendering judgment to acquit the ungodly;

[3] of keeping accounts with a partner or with traveling companions, and of dividing the inheritance of friends;

[4] of accuracy with scales and weights, and of acquiring much or little;

[5] of profit from dealing with merchants, and of much discipline of children, and of whipping a wicked servant severely.

[6] Where there is an evil wife, a seal is a good thing; and where there are many hands, lock things up.

[7] Whatever you deal out, let it be by number and weight, and make a record of all that you give out or take in.

[8] Do not be ashamed to instruct the stupid or foolish or the aged man who quarrels with the young. Then you will be truly instructed, and will be approved before all men.

[9] A daughter keeps her father secretly wakeful, and worry over her robs him of sleep; when she is young, lest she do not marry, or if married, lest she be hated;

[10] while a virgin, lest she be defiled or become pregnant in her father's house; or having a husband, lest she prove unfaithful, or, though married, lest she be barren.

[11] Keep strict watch over a headstrong daughter, lest she make you a laughingstock to your enemies, a byword in the city and notorious among the people, and put you to shame before the great multitude.

[12] Do not look upon any one for beauty, and do not sit in the midst of women;

[13] for from garments comes the moth, and from a woman comes woman's wickedness.

[14] Better is the wickedness of a man than a woman who does good; and it is a woman who brings shame and disgrace.

[15] I will now call to mind the works of the Lord, and will declare what I have seen. By the words of the Lord his works are done.

[16] The sun looks down on everything with its light, and the work of the Lord is full of his glory.

[17] The Lord has not enabled his holy ones to recount all his marvelous works, which the Lord the Almighty has established that the universe may stand firm in his glory.

[18] He searches out the abyss, and the hearts of men, and considers their crafty devices. For the Most High knows all that may be known, and he looks into the signs of the age.

[19] He declares what has been and what is to be, and he reveals the tracks of hidden things.

[20] No thought escapes him, and not one word is hidden from him.

[21] He has ordained the splendors of his wisdom, and he is from everlasting and to everlasting. Nothing can be added or taken away, and he needs no one to be his counselor.

[22] How greatly to be desired are all his works, and how sparkling they are to see!

[23] All these things live and remain for ever for every need, and are all obedient.

[24] All things are twofold, one opposite the other, and he has made nothing incomplete.

[25] One confirms the good things of the other, and who can have enough of beholding his glory?

Sir.43

[1] The pride of the heavenly heights is the clear firmament, the appearance of heaven in a spectacle of glory.

[2] The sun, when it appears, making proclamation as it goes forth, is a marvelous instrument, the work of the Most High.

[3] At noon it parches the land; and who can withstand its burning heat?

[4] A man tending a furnace works in burning heat, but the sun burns the mountains three times as much; it breathes out fiery vapors, and with bright beams it blinds the eyes.

[5] Great is the Lord who made it; and at his command it hastens on its course.

[6] He made the moon also, to serve in its season to mark the times and to be an everlasting sign.

[7] From the moon comes the sign for feast days, a light that wanes when it has reached the full.

[8] The month is named for the moon, increasing marvelously in its phases, an instrument of the hosts on high shining forth in the firmament of heaven.

[9] The glory of the stars is the beauty of heaven, a gleaming array in the heights of the Lord.

[10] At the command of the Holy One they stand as ordered, they never relax in their watches.

[11] Look upon the rainbow, and praise him who made it, exceedingly beautiful in its brightness.

[12] It encircles the heaven with its glorious arc; the hands of the Most High have stretched it out.

[13] By his command he sends the driving snow and speeds the lightnings of his judgment.

[14] Therefore the storehouses are opened, and the clouds fly forth like birds.

[15] In his majesty he amasses the clouds, and the hailstones are broken in pieces.

[16] At his appearing the mountains are shaken; at his will the south wind blows.

[17] The voice of his thunder rebukes the earth; so do the tempest from the north and the whirlwind. He scatters the snow like birds flying down, and its descent is like locusts alighting.

[18] The eye marvels at the beauty of its whiteness, and the mind is amazed at its falling.

[19] He pours the hoarfrost upon the earth like salt, and when it freezes, it becomes pointed thorns.

[20] The cold north wind blows, and ice freezes over the water; it rests upon every pool of water, and the water puts it on like a breastplate.

[21] He consumes the mountains and burns up the wilderness, and withers the tender grass like fire.

[22] A mist quickly heals all things; when the dew appears, it refreshes from the heat.

[23] By his counsel he stilled the great deep and planted islands in it.

[24] Those who sail the sea tell of its dangers, and we marvel at what we hear.

[25] for in it are strange and marvelous works, all kinds of living things, and huge creatures of the sea.

[26] Because of him his messenger finds the way, and by his word all things hold together.

[27] Though we speak much we cannot reach the end, and the sum of our words is: "He is the all."

[28] Where shall we find strength to praise him? For he is greater than all his works.

[29] Terrible is the Lord and very great, and marvelous is his power.

[30] When you praise the Lord, exalt him as much as you can; for he will surpass even that. When you exalt him, put forth all your strength, and do not grow weary, for you cannot praise him enough.

[31] Who has seen him and can describe him? Or who can extol him as he is?

[32] Many things greater than these lie hidden, for we have seen but few of his works.

[33] For the Lord has made all things, and to the godly he has granted wisdom.

Sir.44

[1] Let us now praise famous men, and our fathers in their generations.

[2] The Lord apportioned to them great glory, his majesty from the beginning.

[3] There were those who ruled in their kingdoms, and were men renowned for their power, giving counsel by their understanding, and proclaiming prophecies;

[4] leaders of the people in their deliberations and in understanding of learning for the people, wise in their words of instruction;

[5] those who composed musical tunes, and set forth verses in writing;

[6] rich men furnished with resources, living peaceably in their habitations --

[7] all these were honored in their generations, and were the glory of their times.

[8] There are some of them who have left a name, so that men declare their praise.

[9] And there are some who have no memorial, who have perished as though they had not lived; they

have become as though they had not been born, and so have their children after them.

[10] But these were men of mercy, whose righteous deeds have not been forgotten;

[11] their prosperity will remain with their descendants, and their inheritance to their children's children.

[12] Their descendants stand by the covenants; their children also, for their sake.

[13] Their posterity will continue for ever, and their glory will not be blotted out.

[14] Their bodies were buried in peace, and their name lives to all generations.

[15] Peoples will declare their wisdom, and the congregation proclaims their praise.

[16] Enoch pleased the Lord, and was taken up; he was an example of repentance to all generations.

[17] Noah was found perfect and righteous; in the time of wrath he was taken in exchange; therefore a remnant was left to the earth when the flood came.

[18] Everlasting covenants were made with him that all flesh should not be blotted out by a flood.

[19] Abraham was the great father of a multitude of nations, and no one has been found like him in glory;

[20] he kept the law of the Most High, and was taken into covenant with him; he established the covenant in his flesh, and when he was tested he was found faithful.

[21] Therefore the Lord assured him by an oath that the nations would be blessed through his posterity; that he would multiply him like the dust of the earth, and exalt his posterity like the stars, and cause them to inherit from sea to sea and from the River to the ends of the earth.

[22] To Isaac also he gave the same assurance for the sake of Abraham his father.

[23] The blessing of all men and the covenant he made to rest upon the head of Jacob; he acknowledged him with his blessings, and gave him his inheritance; he determined his portions, and distributed them among twelve tribes.

Sir.45

[1] From his descendants the Lord brought forth a man of mercy, who found favor in the sight of all flesh and was beloved by God and man, Moses, whose memory is blessed.

[2] He made him equal in glory to the holy ones, and made him great in the fears of his enemies.

[3] By his words he caused signs to cease; the Lord glorified him in the presence of kings. He gave him commands for his people, and showed him part of his glory.

[4] He sanctified him through faithfulness and meekness; he chose him out of all mankind.

[5] He made him hear his voice, and led him into the thick darkness, and gave him the commandments face to face, the law of life and knowledge, to teach Jacob the covenant, and Israel his judgments.

[6] He exalted Aaron, the brother of Moses, a holy man like him, of the tribe of Levi.

[7] He made an everlasting covenant with him, and gave him the priesthood of the people. He blessed him with splendid vestments, and put a glorious robe upon him.

[8] He clothed him with superb perfection, and strengthened him with the symbols of authority, the linen breeches, the long robe, and the ephod.

[9] And he encircled him with pomegranates, with very many golden bells round about, to send forth a sound as he walked, to make their ringing heard in the temple as a reminder to the sons of his people;

[10] with a holy garment, of gold and blue and purple, the work of an embroiderer; with the oracle of judgment, Urim and Thummim;

[11] with twisted scarlet, the work of a craftsman; with precious stones engraved like signets, in a setting of gold, the work of a jeweler, for a reminder, in engraved letters, according to the number of the tribes of Israel;

[12] with a gold crown upon his turban, inscribed like a signet with "Holiness," a distinction to be prized, the work of an expert, the delight of the eyes, richly adorned.

[13] Before his time there never were such beautiful things. No outsider ever put them on, but only his sons and his descendants perpetually.

[14] His sacrifices shall be wholly burned twice every day continually.

[15] Moses ordained him, and anointed him with holy oil; it was an everlasting covenant for him and for his descendants all the days of heaven, to minister to the Lord and serve as priest and bless his people in his name.

[16] He chose him out of all the living to offer sacrifice to the Lord, incense and a pleasing odor as a memorial portion, to make atonement for the people.

[17] In his commandments he gave him authority and statutes and judgments, to teach Jacob the testimonies, and to enlighten Israel with his law.

[18] Outsiders conspired against him, and envied him in the wilderness, Dathan and Abiram and their men and the company of Korah, in wrath and anger.

[19] The Lord saw it and was not pleased, and in the wrath of his anger they were destroyed; he wrought wonders against them to consume them in flaming fire.

[20] He added glory to Aaron and gave him a heritage; he allotted to him the first of the first fruits, he prepared bread of first fruits in abundance;

[21] for they eat the sacrifices to the Lord, which he gave to him and his descendants.

[22] But in the land of the people he has no inheritance, and he has no portion among the people; for the Lord himself is his portion and inheritance.
[23] Phinehas the son of Eleazar is the third in glory, for he was zealous in the fear of the Lord, and stood fast, when the people turned away, in the ready goodness of his soul, and made atonement for Israel.
[24] Therefore a covenant of peace was established with him, that he should be leader of the sanctuary and of his people,
that he and his descendants should have the dignity of the priesthood for ever.
[25] A covenant was also established with David, the son of Jesse, of the tribe of Judah: the heritage of the king is from son to son only; so the heritage of Aaron is for his descendants.
[26] May the Lord grant you wisdom in your heart to judge his people in righteousness, so that their prosperity may not vanish, and that their glory may endure throughout their generations.

Sir.46
[1] Joshua the son of Nun was mighty in war, and was the successor of Moses in prophesying. He became, in accordance with his name, a great savior of God's elect, to take vengeance on the enemies that rose against them, so that he might give Israel its inheritance.
[2] How glorious he was when he lifted his hands and stretched out his sword against the cities!
[3] Who before him ever stood so firm? For he waged the wars of the Lord.
[4] Was not the sun held back by his hand? And did not one day become as long as two?
[5] He called upon the Most High, the Mighty One, when enemies pressed him on every side,
[6] and the great Lord answered him with hailstones of mighty power. He hurled down war upon that nation, and at the descent of Beth-horon he destroyed those who resisted, so that the nations might know his armament, that he was fighting in the sight of the Lord; for he wholly followed the Mighty One.
[7] And in the days of Moses he did a loyal deed, he and Caleb the son of Jephunneh: they withstood the congregation,
restrained the people from sin, and stilled their wicked murmuring.
[8] And these two alone were preserved out of six hundred thousand people on foot, to bring them into their inheritance,
into a land flowing with milk and honey.
[9] And the Lord gave Caleb strength, which remained with him to old age, so that he went up to the hill country, and his children obtained it for an inheritance;
[10] so that all the sons of Israel might see that it is good to follow the Lord.

[11] The judges also, with their respective names, those whose hearts did not fall into idolatry and who did not turn away from the Lord -- may their memory be blessed!
[12] May their bones revive from where they lie, and may the name of those who have been honored live again in their sons!
[13] Samuel, beloved by his Lord, a prophet of the Lord, established the kingdom and anointed rulers over his people.
[14] By the law of the Lord he judged the congregation, and the Lord watched over Jacob.
[15] By his faithfulness he was proved to be a prophet, and by his words he became known as a trustworthy seer.
[16] He called upon the Lord, the Mighty One, when his enemies pressed him on every side, and he offered in sacrifice a sucking lamb.
[17] Then the Lord thundered from heaven, and made his voice heard with a mighty sound;
[18] and he wiped out the leaders of the people of Tyre and all the rulers of the Philistines.
[19] Before the time of his eternal sleep, Samuel called men to witness before the Lord and his anointed: "I have not taken any one's property, not so much as a pair of shoes." And no man accused him.
[20] Even after he had fallen asleep he prophesied and revealed to the king his death, and lifted up his voice out of the earth in prophecy, to blot out the wickedness of the people.

Sir.47
[1] And after him Nathan rose up to prophesy in the days of David.
[2] As the fat is selected from the peace offering, so David was selected from the sons of Israel.
[3] He played with lions as with young goats, and with bears as with lambs of the flock.
[4] In his youth did he not kill a giant, and take away reproach from the people, when he lifted his hand with a stone in the sling and struck down the boasting of Goliath?
[5] For he appealed to the Lord, the Most High, and he gave him strength in his right hand to slay a man mighty in war, to exalt the power of his people.
[6] So they glorified him for his ten thousands, and praised him for the blessings of the Lord, when the glorious diadem was bestowed upon him.
[7] For he wiped out his enemies on every side, and annihilated his adversaries the Philistines; he crushed their power even to this day.
[8] In all that he did he gave thanks to the Holy One, the Most High, with ascriptions of glory; he sang praise with all his heart, and he loved his Maker.
[9] He placed singers before the altar, to make sweet melody with their voices.

[10] He gave beauty to the feasts, and arranged their times throughout the year, while they praised God's holy name, and the sanctuary resounded from early morning.

[11] The Lord took away his sins, and exalted his power for ever; he gave him the covenant of kings and a throne of glory in Israel.

[12] After him rose up a wise son who fared amply because of him;

[13] Solomon reigned in days of peace, and God gave him rest on every side, that he might build a house for his name and prepare a sanctuary to stand for ever.

[14] How wise you became in your youth! You overflowed like a river with understanding.

[15] Your soul covered the earth, and you filled it with parables and riddles.

[16] Your name reached to far-off islands, and you were loved for your peace.

[17] For your songs and proverbs and parables, and for your interpretations, the countries marveled at you.

[18] In the name of the Lord God, who is called the God of Israel, you gathered gold like tin and amassed silver like lead.

[19] But you laid your loins beside women, and through your body you were brought into subjection.

[20] You put stain upon your honor, and defiled your posterity, so that you brought wrath upon your children and they were grieved at your folly,

[21] so that the sovereignty was divided and a disobedient kingdom arose out of Ephraim.

[22] But the Lord will never give up his mercy, nor cause any of his works to perish; he will never blot out the descendants of his chosen one, nor destroy the posterity of him who loved him; so he gave a remnant to Jacob, and to David a root of his stock.

[23] Solomon rested with his fathers, and left behind him one of his sons, ample in folly and lacking in understanding, Rehoboam, whose policy caused the people to revolt. Also Jeroboam the son of Nebat, who caused Israel to sin and gave to Ephraim a sinful way.

[24] Their sins became exceedingly many, so as to remove them from their land.

[25] For they sought out every sort of wickedness, till vengeance came upon them.

Sir.48

[1] Then the prophet Elijah arose like a fire, and his word burned like a torch.

[2] He brought a famine upon them, and by his zeal he made them few in number.

[3] By the word of the Lord he shut up the heavens, and also three times brought down fire.

[4] How glorious you were, O Elijah, in your wondrous deeds! And who has the right to boast which you have?

[5] You who raised a corpse from death and from Hades, by the word of the Most High;

[6] who brought kings down to destruction, and famous men from their beds;

[7] who heard rebuke at Sinai and judgments of vengeance at Horeb;

[8] who anointed kings to inflict retribution, and prophets to succeed you.

[9] You who were taken up by a whirlwind of fire, in a chariot with horses of fire;

[10] you who are ready at the appointed time, it is written, to calm the wrath of God before it breaks out in fury, to turn the heart of the father to the son, and to restore the tribes of Jacob.

[11] Blessed are those who saw you, and those who have been adorned in love; for we also shall surely live.

[12] It was Elijah who was covered by the whirlwind, and Elisha was filled with his spirit; in all his days he did not tremble before any ruler, and no one brought him into subjection.

[13] Nothing was too hard for him, and when he was dead his body prophesied.

[14] As in his life he did wonders, so in death his deeds were marvelous.

[15] For all this the people did not repent, and they did not forsake their sins, till they were carried away captive from their land and were scattered over all the earth; the people were left very few in number, but with rulers from the house of David.

[16] Some of them did what was pleasing to God, but others multiplied sins.

[17] Hezekiah fortified his city, and brought water into the midst of it; he tunneled the sheer rock with iron and built pools for water.

[18] In his days Sennacherib came up, and sent the Rabshakeh; he lifted up his hand against Zion and made great boasts in his arrogance.

[19] Then their hearts were shaken and their hands trembled, and they were in anguish, like women in travail.

[20] But they called upon the Lord who is merciful, spreading forth their hands toward him; and the Holy One quickly heard them from heaven, and delivered them by the hand of Isaiah.

[21] The Lord smote the camp of the Assyrians, and his angel wiped them out.

[22] For Hezekiah did what was pleasing to the Lord, and he held strongly to the ways of David his father, which Isaiah the prophet commanded, who was great and faithful in his vision.

[23] In his days the sun went backward, and he lengthened the life of the king.

[24] By the spirit of might he saw the last things, and comforted those who mourned in Zion.

[25] He revealed what was to occur to the end of time, and the hidden things before they came to pass.

Sir.49

[1] The memory of Josiah is like a blending of incense prepared by the art of the perfumer; it is sweet as honey to every mouth, and like music at a banquet of wine.

[2] He was led aright in converting the people, and took away the abominations of iniquity.

[3] He set his heart upon the Lord; in the days of wicked men he strengthened godliness.

[4] Except David and Hezekiah and Josiah they all sinned greatly, for they forsook the law of the Most High; the kings of Judah came to an end;

[5] for they gave their power to others, and their glory to a foreign nation,

[6] who set fire to the chosen city of the sanctuary, and made her streets desolate, according to the word of Jeremiah.

[7] For they had afflicted him; yet he had been consecrated in the womb as prophet, to pluck up and afflict and destroy,

and likewise to build and to plant.

[8] It was Ezekiel who saw the vision of glory which God showed him above the chariot of the cherubim.

[9] For God remembered his enemies with storm, and did good to those who directed their ways aright.

[10] May the bones of the twelve prophets revive from where they lie, for they comforted the people of Jacob and delivered them with confident hope.

[11] How shall we magnify Zerubbabel? He was like a signet on the right hand,

[12] and so was Jeshua the son of Jozadak; in their days they built the house and raised a temple holy to the Lord,

prepared for everlasting glory.

[13] The memory of Nehemiah also is lasting; he raised for us the walls that had fallen, and set up the gates and bars and rebuilt our ruined houses.

[14] No one like Enoch has been created on earth, for he was taken up from the earth.

[15] And no man like Joseph has been born, and his bones are cared for.

[16] Shem and Seth were honored among men, and Adam above every living being in the creation.

Sir.50

[1] The leader of his brethren and the pride of his people was Simon the high priest, son of Onias, who in his life repaired the house, and in his time fortified the temple.

[2] He laid the foundations for the high double walls, the high retaining walls for the temple enclosure.

[3] In his days a cistern for water was quarried out, a reservoir like the sea in circumference.

[4] He considered how to save his people from ruin, and fortified the city to withstand a seige.

[5] How glorious he was when the people gathered round him as he came out of the inner sanctuary!

[6] Like the morning star among the clouds, like the moon when it is full;

[7] like the sun shining upon the temple of the Most High, and like the rainbow gleaming in glorious clouds;

[8] like roses in the days of the first fruits, like lilies by a spring of water, like a green shoot on Lebanon on a summer day;

[9] like fire and incense in the censer, like a vessel of hammered gold adorned with all kinds of precious stones;

[10] like an olive tree putting forth its fruit, and like a cypress towering in the clouds.

[11] When he put on his glorious robe and clothed himself with superb perfection and went up to the holy altar, he made the court of the sanctuary glorious.

[12] And when he received the portions from the hands of the priests, as he stood by the hearth of the altar with a garland of brethren around him, he was like a young cedar on Lebanon; and they surrounded him like the trunks of palm trees,

[13] all the sons of Aaron in their splendor with the Lord's offering in their hands, before the whole congregation of Israel.

[14] Finishing the service at the altars, and arranging the offering to the Most High, the Almighty,

[15] he reached out his hand to the cup and poured a libation of the blood of the grape; he poured it out at the foot of the altar, a pleasing odor to the Most High, the King of all.

[16] Then the sons of Aaron shouted, they sounded the trumpets of hammered work, they made a great noise to be heard

for remembrance before the Most High.

[17] Then all the people together made haste and fell to the ground upon their faces to worship their Lord, the Almighty, God Most High.

[18] And the singers praised him with their voices in sweet and full-toned melody.

[19] And the people besought the Lord Most High in prayer before him who is merciful, till the order of worship of the Lord was ended; so they completed his service.

[20] Then Simon came down, and lifted up his hands over the whole congregation of the sons of Israel, to pronounce the blessing of the Lord with his lips, and to glory in his name;

[21] and they bowed down in worship a second time, to receive the blessing from the Most High.

[22] And now bless the God of all, who in every way does great things; who exalts our days from birth, and deals with us according to his mercy.

[23] May he give us gladness of heart, and grant that peace may be in our days in Israel, as in the days of old.

[24] May he entrust to us his mercy! And let him deliver us in our days!

[25] With two nations my soul is vexed, and the third is no nation:

[26] Those who live on Mount Seir, and the Philistines, and the foolish people that dwell in Shechem.

[27] Instruction in understanding and knowledge I have written in this book, Jesus the son of Sirach, son of Eleazar, of Jerusalem, who out of his heart poured forth wisdom.

[28] Blessed is he who concerns himself with these things, and he who lays them to heart will become wise.

[29] For if he does them, he will be strong for all things, for the light of the Lord is his path.

Sir.51

[1] I will give thanks to thee, O Lord and King, and will praise thee as God my Savior. I give thanks to thy name,

[2] for thou hast been my protector and helper and hast delivered my body from destruction and from the snare of a slanderous tongue, from lips that utter lies. Before those who stood by thou wast my helper,

[3] and didst deliver me, in the greatness of thy mercy and of thy name, from the gnashings of teeth about to devour me,
from the hand of those who sought my life, from the many afflictions that I endured,

[4] from choking fire on every side and from the midst of fire which I did not kindle,

[5] from the depths of the belly of Hades, from an unclean tongue and lying words --

[6] the slander of an unrighteous tongue to the king. My soul drew near to death, and my life was very near to Hades beneath.

[7] They surrounded me on every side, and there was no one to help me; I looked for the assistance of men, and there was none.

[8] Then I remembered thy mercy, O Lord, and thy work from of old, that thou do deliver those who wait for thee and do save them from the hand of their enemies.

[9] And I sent up my supplication from the earth, and prayed for deliverance from death.

[10] I appealed to the Lord, the Father of my lord, not to forsake me in the days of affliction, at the time when there is no help against the proud.

[11] I will praise thy name continually, and will sing praise with thanksgiving. My prayer was heard,

[12] for thou didst save me from destruction and rescue me from an evil plight. Therefore I will give thanks to thee and praise thee, and I will bless the name of the Lord.

[13] While I was still young, before I went on my travels, I sought wisdom openly in my prayer.

[14] Before the temple I asked for her, and I will search for her to the last.

[15] From blossom to ripening grape my heart delighted in her; my foot entered upon the straight path; from my youth I followed her steps.

[16] I inclined my ear a little and received her, and I found for myself much instruction.

[17] I made progress therein; to him who gives wisdom I will give glory.

[18] For I resolved to live according to wisdom, and I was zealous for the good; and I shall never be put to shame.

[19] My soul grappled with wisdom, and in my conduct I was strict; I spread out my hands to the heavens, and lamented my ignorance of her.

[20] I directed my soul to her, and through purification I found her. I gained understanding with her from the first,
therefore I will not be forsaken.

[21] My heart was stirred to seek her, therefore I have gained a good possession.

[22] The Lord gave me a tongue as my reward, and I will praise him with it.

[23] Draw near to me, you who are untaught, and lodge in my school.

[24] Why do you say you are lacking in these things, and why are your souls very thirsty?

[25] I opened my mouth and said, Get these things for yourselves without money.

[26] Put your neck under the yoke, and let your souls receive instruction; it is to be found close by.

[27] See with your eyes that I have labored little and found myself much rest.

[28] Get instruction with a large sum of silver, and you will gain by it much gold.

[29] May your soul rejoice in his mercy, and may you not be put to shame when you praise him.

[30] Do your work before the appointed time, and in God's time he will give you your reward.

Baruch

Bar.1

[1] These are the words of the book which Baruch the son of Neraiah, son of Mahseiah, son of Zedekiah, son of Hasadiah, son of Hilkiah, wrote in Babylon,

[2] in the fifth year, on the seventh day of the month, at the time when the Chaldeans took Jerusalem and burned it with fire.

[3] And Baruch read the words of this book in the hearing of Jeconiah the son of Jehoiakim, king of Judah, and in the hearing of all the people who came to hear the book,

[4] and in the hearing of the mighty men and the princes, and in the hearing of the elders, and in the hearing of all the people, small and great, all who dwelt in Babylon by the river Sud.

[5] Then they wept, and fasted, and prayed before the Lord;

[6] and they collected money, each giving what he could;

[7] and they sent it to Jerusalem to Jehoiakim the high priest, the son of Hilkiah, son of Shallum, and to the priests, and to all the people who were present with him in Jerusalem.

[8] At the same time, on the tenth day of Sivan, Baruch took the vessels of the house of the Lord, which had been carried away from the temple, to return them to the land of Judah -- the silver vessels which Zedekiah the son of Josiah, king of Judah, had made,

[9] after Nebuchadnezzar king of Babylon had carried away from Jerusalem Jeconiah and the princes and the prisoners and the mighty men and the people of the land, and brought them to Babylon.

[10] And they said: "Herewith we send you money; so buy with the money burnt offerings and sin offerings and incense, and prepare a cereal offering, and offer them upon the altar of the Lord our God;

[11] and pray for the life of Nebuchadnezzar king of Babylon, and for the life of Belshazzar his son, that their days on earth may be like the days of heaven.

[12] And the Lord will give us strength, and he will give light to our eyes, and we shall live under the protection of Nebuchadnezzar king of Babylon, and under the protection of Belshazzar his son, and we shall serve them many days and find favor in their sight.

[13] And pray for us to the Lord our God, for we have sinned against the Lord our God, and to this day the anger of the Lord and his wrath have not turned away from us.

[14] And you shall read this book which we are sending you, to make your confession in the house of the Lord on the days of the feasts and at appointed seasons.

[15] "And you shall say: `Righteousness belongs to the Lord our God, but confusion of face, as at this day, to us, to the men of Judah, to the inhabitants of Jerusalem,

[16] and to our kings and our princes and our priests and our prophets and our fathers,

[17] because we have sinned before the Lord,

[18] and have disobeyed him, and have not heeded the voice of the Lord our God, to walk in the statutes of the Lord which he set before us.

[19] From the day when the Lord brought our fathers out of the land of Egypt until today, we have been disobedient to the Lord our God, and we have been negligent, in not heeding his voice.

[20] So to this day there have clung to us the calamities and the curse which the Lord declared through Moses his servant at the time when he brought our fathers out of the land of Egypt to give to us a land flowing with milk and honey.

[21] We did not heed the voice of the Lord our God in all the words of the prophets whom he sent to us, but we each followed the intent of his own wicked heart by serving other gods and doing what is evil in the sight of the Lord our God.

Bar.2

[1] "`So the Lord confirmed his word, which he spoke against us, and against our judges who judged Israel, and against our kings and against our princes and against the men of Israel and Judah.

[2] Under the whole heaven there has not been done the like of what he has done in Jerusalem, in accordance with what is written in the law of Moses,

[3] that we should eat, one the flesh of his son and another the flesh of his daughter.

[4] And he gave them into subjection to all the kingdoms around us, to be a reproach and a desolation among all the surrounding peoples, where the Lord has scattered them.

[5] They were brought low and not raised up, because we sinned against the Lord our God, in not heeding his voice.

[6] "`Righteousness belongs to the Lord our God, but confusion of face to us and our fathers, as at this day.

[7] All those calamities with which the Lord threatened us have come upon us.

[8] Yet we have not entreated the favor of the Lord by turning away, each of us, from the thoughts of his wicked heart.

[9] And the Lord has kept the calamities ready, and the Lord has brought them upon us, for the Lord is righteous in all his works which he has commanded us to do.

[10] Yet we have not obeyed his voice, to walk in the statutes of the Lord which he set before us.

[11] "`And now, O Lord God of Israel, who didst bring thy people out of the land of Egypt with a

mighty hand and with signs and wonders and with great power and outstretched arm, and hast made thee a name, as at this day,

[12] we have sinned, we have been ungodly, we have done wrong, O Lord our God, against all thy ordinances.

[13] Let thy anger turn away from us, for we are left, few in number, among the nations where thou hast scattered us.

[14] Hear, O Lord, our prayer and our supplication, and for thy own sake deliver us, and grant us favor in the sight of those who have carried us into exile;

[15] that all the earth may know that thou art the Lord our God, for Israel and his descendants are called by thy name.

[16] O Lord, look down from thy holy habitation, and consider us. Incline thy ear, O Lord, and hear;

[17] open thy eyes, O Lord, and see; for the dead who are in Hades, whose spirit has been taken from their bodies, will not ascribe glory or justice to the Lord,

[18] but the person that is greatly distressed, that goes about bent over and feeble, and the eyes that are failing, and the person that hungers, will ascribe to thee glory and righteousness, O Lord.

[19] For it is not because of any righteous deeds of our fathers or our kings that we bring before thee our prayer for mercy, O Lord our God.

[20] For thou hast sent thy anger and thy wrath upon us, as thou didst declare by thy servants the prophets, saying:

[21] "Thus says the Lord: Bend your shoulders and serve the king of Babylon, and you will remain in the land which I gave to your fathers.

[22] But if you will not obey the voice of the Lord and will not serve the king of Babylon,

[23] I will make to cease from the cities of Judah and from the region about Jerusalem the voice of mirth and the voice of gladness, the voice of the bridegroom and the voice of the bride, and the whole land will be a desolation without inhabitants."

[24] "`But we did not obey thy voice, to serve the king of Babylon; and thou hast confirmed thy words, which thou didst speak by thy servants the prophets, that the bones of our kings and the bones of our fathers would be brought out of their graves;

[25] and behold, they have been cast out to the heat of day and the frost of night. They perished in great misery, by famine and sword and pestilence.

[26] And the house which is called by thy name thou hast made as it is today, because of the wickedness of the house of Israel and the house of Judah.

[27] "`Yet thou hast dealt with us, O Lord our God, in all thy kindness and in all thy great compassion,

[28] as thou didst speak by thy servant Moses on the day when thou didst command him to write thy law in the presence of the people of Israel, saying,

[29] "If you will not obey my voice, this very great multitude will surely turn into a small number among the nations, where I will scatter them.

[30] For I know that they will not obey me, for they are a stiff-necked people. But in the land of their exile they will come to themselves,

[31] and they will know that I am the Lord their God. I will give them a heart that obeys and ears that hear;

[32] and they will praise me in the land of their exile, and will remember my name,

[33] and will turn from their stubbornness and their wicked deeds; for they will remember the ways of their fathers, who sinned before the Lord.

[34] I will bring them again into the land which I swore to give to their fathers, to Abraham and to Isaac and to Jacob, and they will rule over it; and I will increase them, and they will not be diminished.

[35] I will make an everlasting covenant with them to be their God and they shall be my people; and I will never again remove my people Israel from the land which I have given them."

Bar.3

[1] "`O Lord Almighty, God of Israel, the soul in anguish and the wearied spirit cry out to thee.

[2] Hear, O Lord, and have mercy, for we have sinned before thee.

[3] For thou art enthroned for ever, and we are perishing for ever.

[4] O Lord Almighty, God of Israel, hear now the prayer of the dead of Israel and of the sons of those who sinned before thee, who did not heed the voice of the Lord their God, so that calamities have clung to us.

[5] Remember not the iniquities of our fathers, but in this crisis remember thy power and thy name.

[6] For thou art the Lord our God, and thee, O Lord, will we praise.

[7] For thou hast put the fear of thee in our hearts in order that we should call upon thy name; and we will praise thee in our exile, for we have put away from our hearts all the iniquity of our fathers who sinned before thee.

[8] Behold, we are today in our exile where thou hast scattered us, to be reproached and cursed and punished for all the iniquities of our fathers who forsook the Lord our God.'"

[9] Hear the commandments of life, O Israel; give ear, and learn wisdom!

[10] Why is it, O Israel, why is it that you are in the land of your enemies, that you are growing old in a foreign country, that you are defiled with the dead,

[11] that you are counted among those in Hades?

[12] You have forsaken the fountain of wisdom. [13] If you had walked in the way of God, you would be dwelling in peace for ever. [14] Learn where there is wisdom, where there is strength, where there is

understanding, that you may at the same time discern where there is length of days, and life, where there is light for the eyes, and peace. [15] Who has found her place? And who has entered her storehouses? [16] Where are the princes of the nations, and those who rule over the beasts on earth; [17] those who have sport with the birds of the air, and who hoard up silver and gold, in which men trust, and there is no end to their getting; [18] those who scheme to get silver, and are anxious, whose labors are beyond measure? [19] They have vanished and gone down to Hades, and others have arisen in their place. [20] Young men have seen the light of day, and have dwelt upon the earth; but they have not learned the way to knowledge, nor understood her paths, nor laid hold of her. [21] Their sons have strayed far from her way. [22] She has not been heard of in Canaan, nor seen in Teman; [23] the sons of Hagar, who seek for understanding on the earth, the merchants of Merran and Teman, the story-tellers and the seekers for understanding, have not learned the way to wisdom, nor given thought to her paths. [24] O Israel, how great is the house of God! And how vast the territory that he possesses! [25] It is great and has no bounds; it is high and immeasurable. [26] The giants were born there, who were famous of old, great in stature, expert in war. [27] God did not choose them, nor give them the way to knowledge; [28] so they perished because they had no wisdom, they perished through their folly. [29] Who has gone up into heaven, and taken her, and brought her down from the clouds? [30] Who has gone over the sea, and found her, and will buy her for pure gold? [31] No one knows the way to her, or is concerned about the path to her. [32] But he who knows all things knows her, he found her by his understanding. He who prepared the earth for all time filled it with four-footed creatures; [33] he who sends forth the light, and it goes, called it, and it obeyed him in fear; [34] the stars shone in their watches, and were glad; he called them, and they said, "Here we are!" They shone with gladness for him who made them. [35] This is our God; no other can be compared to him! [36] He found the whole way to knowledge, and gave her to Jacob his servant and to Israel whom he loved. [37] Afterward she appeared upon earth and lived among men.

Bar.4

[1] She is the book of the commandments of God, and the law that endures for ever. All who hold her fast will live, and those who forsake her will die.
[2] Turn, O Jacob, and take her; walk toward the shining of her light.

[3] Do not give your glory to another, or your advantages to an alien people.
[4] Happy are we, O Israel, for we know what is pleasing to God.
[5] Take courage, my people, O memorial of Israel!
[6] It was not for destruction that you were sold to the nations, but you were handed over to your enemies because you angered God.
[7] For you provoked him who made you, by sacrificing to demons and not to God.
[8] You forgot the everlasting God, who brought you up, and you grieved Jerusalem, who reared you.
[9] For she saw the wrath that came upon you from God, and she said: "Hearken, you neighbors of Zion, God has brought great sorrow upon me;
[10] for I have seen the captivity of my sons and daughters, which the Everlasting brought upon them.
[11] With joy I nurtured them, but I sent them away with weeping and sorrow.
[12] Let no one rejoice over me, a widow and bereaved of many; I was left desolate because of the sins of my children, because they turned away from the law of God.
[13] They had no regard for his statutes; they did not walk in the ways of God's commandments, nor tread the paths of discipline in his righteousness.
[14] Let the neighbors of Zion come; remember the capture of my sons and daughters, which the Everlasting brought upon them.
[15] For he brought against them a nation from afar, a shameless nation, of a strange language, who had no respect for an old man, and had no pity for a child.
[16] They led away the widow's beloved sons, and bereaved the lonely woman of her daughters.
[17] "But I, how can I help you?
[18] For he who brought these calamities upon you will deliver you from the hand of your enemies.
[19] Go, my children, go; for I have been left desolate.
[20] I have taken off the robe of peace and put on the sackcloth of my supplication; I will cry to the Everlasting all my days.
[21] "Take courage, my children, cry to God, and he will deliver you from the power and hand of the enemy.
[22] For I have put my hope in the Everlasting to save you, and joy has come to me from the Holy One, because of the mercy which soon will come to you from your everlasting Savior.
[23] For I sent you out with sorrow and weeping, but God will give you back to me with joy and gladness for ever.
[24] For as the neighbors of Zion have now seen your capture, so they soon will see your salvation by God, which will come to you with great glory and with the splendor of the Everlasting.
[25] My children, endure with patience the wrath that has come upon you from God. Your enemy has

overtaken you, but you will soon see their destruction and will tread upon their necks.

[26] My tender sons have traveled rough roads; they were taken away like a flock carried off by the enemy.

[27] "Take courage, my children, and cry to God, for you will be remembered by him who brought this upon you.

[28] For just as you purposed to go astray from God, return with tenfold zeal to seek him.

[29] For he who brought these calamities upon you will bring you everlasting joy with your salvation."

[30] Take courage, O Jerusalem, for he who named you will comfort you.

[31] Wretched will be those who afflicted you and rejoiced at your fall.

[32] Wretched will be the cities which your children served as slaves; wretched will be the city which received your sons.

[33] For just as she rejoiced at your fall and was glad for your ruin, so she will be grieved at her own desolation.

[34] And I will take away her pride in her great population, and her insolence will be turned to grief.

[35] For fire will come upon her from the Everlasting for many days, and for a long time she will be inhabited by demons.

[36] Look toward the east, O Jerusalem, and see the joy that is coming to you from God!

[37] Behold, your sons are coming, whom you sent away; they are coming, gathered from east and west, at the word of the Holy One, rejoicing in the glory of God.

Bar.5

[1] Take off the garment of your sorrow and affliction, O Jerusalem, and put on for ever the beauty of the glory from God.

[2] Put on the robe of the righteousness from God; put on your head the diadem of the glory of the Everlasting.

[3] For God will show your splendor everywhere under heaven.

[4] For your name will for ever be called by God, "Peace of righteousness and glory of godliness."

[5] Arise, O Jerusalem, stand upon the height and look toward the east, and see your children gathered from west and east, at the word of the Holy One, rejoicing that God has remembered them.

[6] For they went forth from you on foot, led away by their enemies; but God will bring them back to you, carried in glory, as on a royal throne.

[7] For God has ordered that every high mountain and the everlasting hills be made low and the valleys filled up, to make level ground, so that Israel may walk safely in the glory of God.

[8] The woods and every fragrant tree have shaded Israel at God's command.

[9] For God will lead Israel with joy, in the light of his glory, with the mercy and righteousness that come from him.

1 Maccabees

1Mac.1

[1] After Alexander son of Philip, the Macedonian, who came from the land of Kittim, had defeated Darius, king of the Persians and the Medes, he succeeded him as king. (He had previously become king of Greece.)

[2] He fought many battles, conquered strongholds, and put to death the kings of the earth.

[3] He advanced to the ends of the earth, and plundered many nations. When the earth became quiet before him, he was exalted, and his heart was lifted up.

[4] He gathered a very strong army and ruled over countries, nations, and princes, and they became tributary to him.

[5] After this he fell sick and perceived that he was dying.

[6] So he summoned his most honored officers, who had been brought up with him from youth, and divided his kingdom among them while he was still alive.

[7] And after Alexander had reigned twelve years, he died.

[8] Then his officers began to rule, each in his own place.

[9] They all put on crowns after his death, and so did their sons after them for many years; and they caused many evils on the earth.

[10] From them came forth a sinful root, Antiochus Epiphanes, son of Antiochus the king; he had been a hostage in Rome. He began to reign in the one hundred and thirty-seventh year of the kingdom of the Greeks.

[11] In those days lawless men came forth from Israel, and misled many, saying, "Let us go and make a covenant with the Gentiles round about us, for since we separated from them many evils have come upon us."

[12] This proposal pleased them,

[13] and some of the people eagerly went to the king. He authorized them to observe the ordinances of the Gentiles.

[14] So they built a gymnasium in Jerusalem, according to Gentile custom,

[15] and removed the marks of circumcision, and abandoned the holy covenant. They joined with the Gentiles and sold themselves to do evil.

[16] When Antiochus saw that his kingdom was established, he determined to become king of the land of Egypt, that he might reign over both kingdoms.

[17] So he invaded Egypt with a strong force, with chariots and elephants and cavalry and with a large fleet.

[18] He engaged Ptolemy king of Egypt in battle, and Ptolemy turned and fled before him, and many were wounded and fell.

[19] And they captured the fortified cities in the land of Egypt, and he plundered the land of Egypt.

[20] After subduing Egypt, Antiochus returned in the one hundred and forty-third year. He went up against Israel and came to Jerusalem with a strong force.

[21] He arrogantly entered the sanctuary and took the golden altar, the lampstand for the light, and all its utensils.

[22] He took also the table for the bread of the Presence, the cups for drink offerings, the bowls, the golden censers, the curtain, the crowns, and the gold decoration on the front of the temple; he stripped it all off.

[23] He took the silver and the gold, and the costly vessels; he took also the hidden treasures which he found.

[24] Taking them all, he departed to his own land. He committed deeds of murder, and spoke with great arrogance.

[25] Israel mourned deeply in every community,

[26] rulers and elders groaned, maidens and young men became faint, the beauty of women faded.

[27] Every bridegroom took up the lament; she who sat in the bridal chamber was mourning.

[28] Even the land shook for its inhabitants, and all the house of Jacob was clothed with shame.

[29] Two years later the king sent to the cities of Judah a chief collector of tribute, and he came to Jerusalem with a large force.

[30] Deceitfully he spoke peaceable words to them, and they believed him; but he suddenly fell upon the city, dealt it a severe blow, and destroyed many people of Israel.

[31] He plundered the city, burned it with fire, and tore down its houses and its surrounding walls.

[32] And they took captive the women and children, and seized the cattle.

[33] Then they fortified the city of David with a great strong wall and strong towers, and it became their citadel.

[34] And they stationed there a sinful people, lawless men. These strengthened their position;

[35] they stored up arms and food, and collecting the spoils of Jerusalem they stored them there, and became a great snare.

[36] It became an ambush against the sanctuary, an evil adversary of Israel continually.

[37] On every side of the sanctuary they shed innocent blood; they even defiled the sanctuary.

[38] Because of them the residents of Jerusalem fled; she became a dwelling of strangers; she became strange to her offspring, and her children forsook her.

[39] Her sanctuary became desolate as a desert; her feasts were turned into mourning, her sabbaths into a reproach,
her honor into contempt.
[40] Her dishonor now grew as great as her glory; her exaltation was turned into mourning.
[41] Then the king wrote to his whole kingdom that all should be one people,
[42] and that each should give up his customs.
[43] All the Gentiles accepted the command of the king. Many even from Israel gladly adopted his religion; they sacrificed to idols and profaned the sabbath.
[44] And the king sent letters by messengers to Jerusalem and the cities of Judah; he directed them to follow customs strange to the land,
[45] to forbid burnt offerings and sacrifices and drink offerings in the sanctuary, to profane sabbaths and feasts,
[46] to defile the sanctuary and the priests,
[47] to build altars and sacred precincts and shrines for idols, to sacrifice swine and unclean animals,
[48] and to leave their sons uncircumcised. They were to make themselves abominable by everything unclean and profane,
[49] so that they should forget the law and change all the ordinances.
[50] "And whoever does not obey the command of the king shall die."
[51] In such words he wrote to his whole kingdom. And he appointed inspectors over all the people and commanded the cities of Judah to offer sacrifice, city by city.
[52] Many of the people, every one who forsook the law, joined them, and they did evil in the land;
[53] they drove Israel into hiding in every place of refuge they had.
[54] Now on the fifteenth day of Chislev, in the one hundred and forty-fifth year, they erected a desolating sacrilege upon the altar of burnt offering. They also built altars in the surrounding cities of Judah,
[55] and burned incense at the doors of the houses and in the streets.
[56] The books of the law which they found they tore to pieces and burned with fire.
[57] Where the book of the covenant was found in the possession of any one, or if any one adhered to the law, the decree of the king condemned him to death.
[58] They kept using violence against Israel, against those found month after month in the cities.
[59] And on the twenty-fifth day of the month they offered sacrifice on the altar which was upon the altar of burnt offering.
[60] According to the decree, they put to death the women who had their children circumcised,

[61] and their families and those who circumcised them; and they hung the infants from their mothers' necks.
[62] But many in Israel stood firm and were resolved in their hearts not to eat unclean food.
[63] They chose to die rather than to be defiled by food or to profane the holy covenant; and they did die.
[64] And very great wrath came upon Israel.
1Mac.2
[1] In those days Mattathias the son of John, son of Simeon, a priest of the sons of Joarib, moved from Jerusalem and settled in Modein.
[2] He had five sons, John surnamed Gaddi,
[3] Simon called Thassi,
[4] Judas called Maccabeus,
[5] Eleazar called Avaran, and Jonathan called Apphus.
[6] He saw the blasphemies being committed in Judah and Jerusalem,
[7] and said, "Alas! Why was I born to see this, the ruin of my people, the ruin of the holy city, and to dwell there when it was given over to the enemy, the sanctuary given over to aliens?
[8] Her temple has become like a man without honor;
[9] her glorious vessels have been carried into captivity. Her babes have been killed in her streets, her youths by the sword of the foe.
[10] What nation has not inherited her palaces and has not seized her spoils?
[11] All her adornment has been taken away; no longer free, she has become a slave.
[12] And behold, our holy place, our beauty, and our glory have been laid waste; the Gentiles have profaned it.
[13] Why should we live any longer?"
[14] And Mattathias and his sons rent their clothes, put on sackcloth, and mourned greatly.
[15] Then the king's officers who were enforcing the apostasy came to the city of Modein to make them offer sacrifice.
[16] Many from Israel came to them; and Mattathias and his sons were assembled.
[17] Then the king's officers spoke to Mattathias as follows: "You are a leader, honored and great in this city, and supported by sons and brothers.
[18] Now be the first to come and do what the king commands, as all the Gentiles and the men of Judah and those that are left in Jerusalem have done. Then you and your sons will be numbered among the friends of the king, and you and your sons will be honored with silver and gold and many gifts."
[19] But Mattathias answered and said in a loud voice: "Even if all the nations that live under the rule of the king obey him, and have chosen to do his commandments, departing each one from the religion of his fathers,

[20] yet I and my sons and my brothers will live by the covenant of our fathers.

[21] Far be it from us to desert the law and the ordinances.

[22] We will not obey the king's words by turning aside from our religion to the right hand or to the left."

[23] When he had finished speaking these words, a Jew came forward in the sight of all to offer sacrifice upon the altar in Modein, according to the king's command.

[24] When Mattathias saw it, be burned with zeal and his heart was stirred. He gave vent to righteous anger; he ran and killed him upon the altar.

[25] At the same time he killed the king's officer who was forcing them to sacrifice, and he tore down the altar.

[26] Thus he burned with zeal for the law, as Phinehas did against Zimri the son of Salu.

[27] Then Mattathias cried out in the city with a loud voice, saying: "Let every one who is zealous for the law and supports the covenant come out with me!"

[28] And he and his sons fled to the hills and left all that they had in the city.

[29] Then many who were seeking righteousness and justice went down to the wilderness to dwell there,

[30] they, their sons, their wives, and their cattle, because evils pressed heavily upon them.

[31] And it was reported to the king's officers, and to the troops in Jerusalem the city of David, that men who had rejected the king's command had gone down to the hiding places in the wilderness.

[32] Many pursued them, and overtook them; they encamped opposite them and prepared for battle against them on the sabbath day.

[33] And they said to them, "Enough of this! Come out and do what the king commands, and you will live."

[34] But they said, "We will not come out, nor will we do what the king commands and so profane the sabbath day."

[35] Then the enemy hastened to attack them.

[36] But they did not answer them or hurl a stone at them or block up their hiding places,

[37] for they said, "Let us all die in our innocence; heaven and earth testify for us that you are killing us unjustly."

[38] So they attacked them on the sabbath, and they died, with their wives and children and cattle, to the number of a thousand persons.

[39] When Mattathias and his friends learned of it, they mourned for them deeply.

[40] And each said to his neighbor: "If we all do as our brethren have done and refuse to fight with the Gentiles for our lives and for our ordinances, they will quickly destroy us from the earth."

[41] So they made this decision that day: "Let us fight against every man who comes to attack us on the sabbath day; let us not all die as our brethren died in their hiding places."

[42] Then there united with them a company of Hasideans, mighty warriors of Israel, every one who offered himself willingly for the law.

[43] And all who became fugitives to escape their troubles joined them and reinforced them.

[44] They organized an army, and struck down sinners in their anger and lawless men in their wrath; the survivors fled to the Gentiles for safety.

[45] And Mattathias and his friends went about and tore down the altars;

[46] they forcibly circumcised all the uncircumcised boys that they found within the borders of Israel.

[47] They hunted down the arrogant men, and the work prospered in their hands.

[48] They rescued the law out of the hands of the Gentiles and kings, and they never let the sinner gain the upper hand.

[49] Now the days drew near for Mattathias to die, and he said to his sons: "Arrogance and reproach have now become strong; it is a time of ruin and furious anger.

[50] Now, my children, show zeal for the law, and give your lives for the covenant of our fathers.

[51] "Remember the deeds of the fathers, which they did in their generations; and receive great honor and an everlasting name.

[52] Was not Abraham found faithful when tested, and it was reckoned to him as righteousness?

[53] Joseph in the time of his distress kept the commandment, and became lord of Egypt.

[54] Phinehas our father, because he was deeply zealous, received the covenant of everlasting priesthood.

[55] Joshua, because he fulfilled the command, became a judge in Israel.

[56] Caleb, because he testified in the assembly, received an inheritance in the land.

[57] David, because he was merciful, inherited the throne of the kingdom for ever.

[58] Elijah because of great zeal for the law was taken up into heaven.

[59] Hannaniah, Azariah, and Mishael believed and were saved from the flame.

[60] Daniel because of his innocence was delivered from the mouth of the lions.

[61] "And so observe, from generation to generation, that none who put their trust in him will lack strength.

[62] Do not fear the words of a sinner, for his splendor will turn into dung and worms.

[63] Today he will be exalted, but tomorrow he will not be found, because he has returned to the dust, and his plans will perish.

[64] My children, be courageous and grow strong in the law, for by it you will gain honor.

[65] "Now behold, I know that Simeon your brother is wise in counsel; always listen to him; he shall be your father.

[66] Judas Maccabeus has been a mighty warrior from his youth; he shall command the army for you and fight the battle against the peoples.

[67] You shall rally about you all who observe the law, and avenge the wrong done to your people.

[68] Pay back the Gentiles in full, and heed what the law commands."

[69] Then he blessed them, and was gathered to his fathers.

[70] He died in the one hundred and forty-sixth year and was buried in the tomb of his fathers at Modein. And all Israel mourned for him with great lamentation.

1Mac.3

[1] Then Judas his son, who was called Maccabeus, took command in his place.

[2] All his brothers and all who had joined his father helped him; they gladly fought for Israel.

[3] He extended the glory of his people. Like a giant he put on his breastplate; he girded on his armor of war and waged battles, protecting the host by his sword.

[4] He was like a lion in his deeds, like a lion's cub roaring for prey.

[5] He searched out and pursued the lawless; he burned those who troubled his people.

[6] Lawless men shrank back for fear of him; all the evildoers were confounded; and deliverance prospered by his hand.

[7] He embittered many kings, but he made Jacob glad by his deeds, and his memory is blessed for ever.

[8] He went through the cities of Judah; he destroyed the ungodly out of the land; thus he turned away wrath from Israel.

[9] He was renowned to the ends of the earth; he gathered in those who were perishing.

[10] But Apollonius gathered together Gentiles and a large force from Samaria to fight against Israel.

[11] When Judas learned of it, he went out to meet him, and he defeated and killed him. Many were wounded and fell, and the rest fled.

[12] Then they seized their spoils; and Judas took the sword of Apollonius, and used it in battle the rest of his life.

[13] Now when Seron, the commander of the Syrian army, heard that Judas had gathered a large company, including a body of faithful men who stayed with him and went out to battle,

[14] he said, "I will make a name for myself and win honor in the kingdom. I will make war on Judas and his companions, who scorn the king's command."

[15] And again a strong army of ungodly men went up with him to help him, to take vengeance on the sons of Israel.

[16] When he approached the ascent of Beth-horon, Judas went out to meet him with a small company.

[17] But when they saw the army coming to meet them, they said to Judas, "How can we, few as we are, fight against so great and strong a multitude? And we are faint, for we have eaten nothing today."

[18] Judas replied, "It is easy for many to be hemmed in by few, for in the sight of Heaven there is no difference between saving by many or by few.

[19] It is not on the size of the army that victory in battle depends, but strength comes from Heaven.

[20] They come against us in great pride and lawlessness to destroy us and our wives and our children, and to despoil us;

[21] but we fight for our lives and our laws.

[22] He himself will crush them before us; as for you, do not be afraid of them."

[23] When he finished speaking, he rushed suddenly against Seron and his army, and they were crushed before him.

[24] They pursued them down the descent of Beth-horon to the plain; eight hundred of them fell, and the rest fled into the land of the Philistines.

[25] Then Judas and his brothers began to be feared, and terror fell upon the Gentiles round about them.

[26] His fame reached the king, and the Gentiles talked of the battles of Judas.

[27] When king Antiochus heard these reports, he was greatly angered; and he sent and gathered all the forces of his kingdom, a very strong army.

[28] And he opened his coffers and gave a year's pay to his forces, and ordered them to be ready for any need.

[29] Then he saw that the money in the treasury was exhausted, and that the revenues from the country were small because of the dissension and disaster which he had caused in the land by abolishing the laws that had existed from the earliest days.

[30] He feared that he might not have such funds as he had before for his expenses and for the gifts which he used to give more lavishly than preceding kings.

[31] He was greatly perplexed in mind, and determined to go to Persia and collect the revenues from those regions and raise a large fund.

[32] He left Lysias, a distinguished man of royal lineage, in charge of the king's affairs from the river Euphrates to the borders of Egypt.

[33] Lysias was also to take care of Antiochus his son until he returned.

[34] And he turned over to Lysias half of his troops and the elephants, and gave him orders about all that he wanted done. As for the residents of Judea and Jerusalem,

[35] Lysias was to send a force against them to wipe out and destroy the strength of Israel and the remnant of Jerusalem; he was to banish the memory of them from the place,

[36] settle aliens in all their territory, and distribute their land.

[37] Then the king took the remaining half of his troops and departed from Antioch his capital in the one hundred and forty-seventh year. He crossed the Euphrates river and went through the upper provinces.

[38] Lysias chose Ptolemy the son of Dorymenes, and Nicanor and Gorgias, mighty men among the friends of the king,

[39] and sent with them forty thousand infantry and seven thousand cavalry to go into the land of Judah and destroy it, as the king had commanded.

[40] so they departed with their entire force, and when they arrived they encamped near Emmaus in the plain.

[41] When the traders of the region heard what was said to them, they took silver and gold in immense amounts, and fetters, and went to the camp to get the sons of Israel for slaves. And forces from Syria and the land of the Philistines joined with them.

[42] Now Judas and his brothers saw that misfortunes had increased and that the forces were encamped in their territory. They also learned what the king had commanded to do to the people to cause their final destruction.

[43] But they said to one another, "Let us repair the destruction of our people, and fight for our people and the sanctuary."

[44] And the congregation assembled to be ready for battle, and to pray and ask for mercy and compassion.

[45] Jerusalem was uninhabited like a wilderness; not one of her children went in or out.The sanctuary was trampled own,

and the sons of aliens held the citadel; it was a lodging place for the Gentiles. Joy was taken from Jacob; the flute and the harp ceased to play.

[46] So they assembled and went to Mizpah, opposite Jerusalem, because Israel formerly had a place of prayer in Mizpah.

[47] They fasted that day, put on sackcloth and sprinkled ashes on their heads, and rent their clothes.

[48] And they opened the book of the law to inquire into those matters about which the Gentiles were consulting the images of their idols.

[49] They also brought the garments of the priesthood and the first fruits and the tithes, and they stirred up the Nazirites who had completed their days;

[50] and they cried aloud to Heaven, saying, "What shall we do with these? Where shall we take them?

[51] Your sanctuary is trampled down and profaned, and thy priests mourn in humiliation.

[52] And behold, the Gentiles are assembled against us to destroy us; thou knowest what they plot against us.

[53] How will we be able to withstand them, if thou do not help us?"

[54] Then they sounded the trumpets and gave a loud shout.

[55] After this Judas appointed leaders of the people, in charge of thousands and hundreds and fifties and tens.

[56] And he said to those who were building houses, or were betrothed, or were planting vineyards, or were fainthearted, that each should return to his home, according to the law.

[57] Then the army marched out and encamped to the south of Emmaus.

[58] And Judas said, "Gird yourselves and be valiant. Be ready early in the morning to fight with these Gentiles who have assembled against us to destroy us and our sanctuary.

[59] It is better for us to die in battle than to see the misfortunes of our nation and of the sanctuary.

[60] But as his will in heaven may be, so he will do."

1Mac.4

[1] Now Gorgias took five thousand infantry and a thousand picked cavalry, and this division moved out by night

[2] to fall upon the camp of the Jews and attack them suddenly. Men from the citadel were his guides.

[3] But Judas heard of it, and he and his mighty men moved out to attack the king's force in Emmaus

[4] while the division was still absent from the camp.

[5] When Gorgias entered the camp of Judas by night, he found no one there, so he looked for them in the hills, because he said, "These men are fleeing from us."

[6] At daybreak Judas appeared in the plain with three thousand men, but they did not have armor and swords such as they desired.

[7] And they saw the camp of the Gentiles, strong and fortified, with cavalry round about it; and these men were trained in war.

[8] But Judas said to the men who were with him, "Do not fear their numbers or be afraid when they charge.

[9] Remember how our fathers were saved at the Red Sea, when Pharaoh with his forces pursued them.

[10] And now let us cry to Heaven, to see whether he will favor us and remember his covenant with our fathers and crush this army before us today.

[11] Then all the Gentiles will know that there is one who redeems and saves Israel."

[12] When the foreigners looked up and saw them coming against them,

[13] they went forth from their camp to battle. Then the men with Judas blew their trumpets

[14] and engaged in battle. The Gentiles were crushed and fled into the plain,

[15] and all those in the rear fell by the sword. They pursued them to Gazara, and to the plains of Idumea, and to Azotus and Jamnia; and three thousand of them fell.

[16] Then Judas and his force turned back from pursuing them,

[17] and he said to the people, "Do not be greedy for plunder, for there is a battle before us;

[18] Gorgias and his force are near us in the hills. But stand now against our enemies and fight them, and afterward seize the plunder boldly."

[19] Just as Judas was finishing this speech, a detachment appeared, coming out of the hills.

[20] They saw that their army had been put to flight, and that the Jews were burning the camp, for the smoke that was seen showed what had happened.

[21] When they perceived this they were greatly frightened, and when they also saw the army of Judas drawn up in the plain for battle,

[22] they all fled into the land of the Philistines.

[23] Then Judas returned to plunder the camp, and they seized much gold and silver, and cloth dyed blue and sea purple, and great riches.

[24] On their return they sang hymns and praises to Heaven, for he is good, for his mercy endures for ever.

[25] Thus Israel had a great deliverance that day.

[26] Those of the foreigners who escaped went and reported to Lysias all that had happened.

[27] When he heard it, he was perplexed and discouraged, for things had not happened to Israel as he had intended, nor had they turned out as the king had commanded him.

[28] But the next year he mustered sixty thousand picked infantrymen and five thousand cavalry to subdue them.

[29] They came into Idumea and encamped at Beth-zur, and Judas met them with ten thousand men.

[30] When he saw that the army was strong, he prayed, saying, "Blessed art thou, O Savior of Israel, who didst crush the attack of the mighty warrior by the hand of thy servant David, and didst give the camp of the Philistines into the hands of Jonathan, the son of Saul, and of the man who carried his armor.

[31] So do thou hem in this army by the hand of thy people Israel, and let them be ashamed of their troops and their cavalry.

[32] Fill them with cowardice; melt the boldness of their strength; let them tremble in their destruction.

[33] Strike them down with the sword of those who love thee, and let all who know thy name praise thee with hymns."

[34] Then both sides attacked, and there fell of the army of Lysias five thousand men; they fell in action.

[35] And when Lysias saw the rout of his troops and observed the boldness which inspired those of Judas, and how ready they were either to live or to die

nobly, he departed to Antioch and enlisted mercenaries, to invade Judea again with an even larger army.

[36] Then said Judas and his brothers, "Behold, our enemies are crushed; let us go up to cleanse the sanctuary and dedicate it."

[37] So all the army assembled and they went up to Mount Zion.

[38] And they saw the sanctuary desolate, the altar profaned, and the gates burned. In the courts they saw bushes sprung up as in a thicket, or as on one of the mountains. They saw also the chambers of the priests in ruins.

[39] Then they rent their clothes, and mourned with great lamentation, and sprinkled themselves with ashes.

[40] They fell face down on the ground, and sounded the signal on the trumpets, and cried out to Heaven.

[41] Then Judas detailed men to fight against those in the citadel until he had cleansed the sanctuary.

[42] He chose blameless priests devoted to the law,

[43] and they cleansed the sanctuary and removed the defiled stones to an unclean place.

[44] They deliberated what to do about the altar of burnt offering, which had been profaned.

[45] And they thought it best to tear it down, lest it bring reproach upon them, for the Gentiles had defiled it. So they tore down the altar,

[46] and stored the stones in a convenient place on the temple hill until there should come a prophet to tell what to do with them.

[47] Then they took unhewn stones, as the law directs, and built a new altar like the former one.

[48] They also rebuilt the sanctuary and the interior of the temple, and consecrated the courts.

[49] They made new holy vessels, and brought the lampstand, the altar of incense, and the table into the temple.

[50] Then they burned incense on the altar and lighted the lamps on the lampstand, and these gave light in the temple.

[51] They placed the bread on the table and hung up the curtains. Thus they finished all the work they had undertaken.

[52] Early in the morning on the twenty-fifth day of the ninth month, which is the month of Chislev, in the one hundred and forty-eighth year,

[53] they rose and offered sacrifice, as the law directs, on the new altar of burnt offering which they had built.

[54] At the very season and on the very day that the Gentiles had profaned it, it was dedicated with songs and harps and lutes and cymbals.

[55] All the people fell on their faces and worshiped and blessed Heaven, who had prospered them.

[56] So they celebrated the dedication of the altar for eight days, and offered burnt offerings with gladness; they offered a sacrifice of deliverance and praise.

[57] They decorated the front of the temple with golden crowns and small shields; they restored the gates and the chambers for the priests, and furnished them with doors.

[58] There was very great gladness among the people, and the reproach of the Gentiles was removed.

[59] Then Judas and his brothers and all the assembly of Israel determined that every year at that season the days of dedication of the altar should be observed with gladness and joy for eight days, beginning with the twenty-fifth day of the month of Chislev.

[60] At that time they fortified Mount Zion with high walls and strong towers round about, to keep the Gentiles from coming and trampling them down as they had done before.

[61] And he stationed a garrison there to hold it. He also fortified Beth-zur, so that the people might have a stronghold that faced Idumea.

1Mac.5

[1] When the Gentiles round about heard that the altar had been built and the sanctuary dedicated as it was before, they became very angry,

[2] and they determined to destroy the descendants of Jacob who lived among them. So they began to kill and destroy among the people.

[3] But Judas made war on the sons of Esau in Idumea, at Akrabattene, because they kept lying in wait for Israel. He dealt them a heavy blow and humbled them and despoiled them.

[4] He also remembered the wickedness of the sons of Baean, who were a trap and a snare to the people and ambushed them on the highways.

[5] They were shut up by him in their towers; and he encamped against them, vowed their complete destruction, and burned with fire their towers and all who were in them.

[6] Then he crossed over to attack the Ammonites, where he found a strong band and many people with Timothy as their leader.

[7] He engaged in many battles with them and they were crushed before him; he struck them down.

[8] He also took Jazer and its villages; then he returned to Judea.

[9] Now the Gentiles in Gilead gathered together against the Israelites who lived in their territory, and planned to destroy them. But they fled to the stronghold of Dathema,

[10] and sent to Judas and his brothers a letter which said, "The Gentiles around us have gathered together against us to destroy us.

[11] They are preparing to come and capture the stronghold to which we have fled, and Timothy is leading their forces.

[12] Now then come and rescue us from their hands, for many of us have fallen,

[13] and all our brethren who were in the land of Tob have been killed; the enemy have captured their wives and children and goods, and have destroyed about a thousand men there."

[14] While the letter was still being read, behold, other messengers, with their garments rent, came from Galilee and made a similar report;

[15] they said that against them had gathered together men of Ptolemais and Tyre and Sidon, and all Galilee of the Gentiles, "to annihilate us."

[16] When Judas and the people heard these messages, a great assembly was called to determine what they should do for their brethren who were in distress and were being attacked by enemies.

[17] Then Judas said to Simon his brother, "Choose your men and go and rescue your brethren in Galilee; I and Jonathan my brother will go to Gilead."

[18] But he left Joseph, the son of Zechariah, and Azariah, a leader of the people, with the rest of the forces, in Judea to guard it;

[19] and he gave them this command, "Take charge of this people, but do not engage in battle with the Gentiles until we return."

[20] Then three thousand men were assigned to Simon to go to Galilee, and eight thousand to Judas for Gilead.

[21] so Simon went to Galilee and fought many battles against the Gentiles, and the Gentiles were crushed before him.

[22] He pursued them to the gate of Ptolemais, and as many as three thousand of the Gentiles fell, and he despoiled them.

[23] Then he took the Jews of Galilee and Arbatta, with their wives and children, and all they possessed, and led them to Judea with great rejoicing.

[24] Judas Maccabeus and Jonathan his brother crossed the Jordan and went three days' journey into the wilderness.

[25] They encountered the Nabateans, who met them peaceably and told them all that had happened to their brethren in Gilead:

[26] "Many of them have been shut up in Bozrah and Bosor, in Alema and Chaspho, Maked and Carnaim" -- all these cities were strong and large--

[27] "and some have been shut up in the other cities of Gilead; the enemy are getting ready to attack the strongholds tomorrow and take and destroy all these men in one day."

[28] Then Judas and his army quickly turned back by the wilderness road to Bozrah; and he took the city, and killed every male by the edge of the sword; then he seized all its spoils and burned it with fire.

[29] He departed from there at night, and they went all the way to the stronghold of Dathema.

[30] At dawn they looked up, and behold, a large company, that could not be counted, carrying ladders and engines of war to capture the stronghold, and attacking the Jews within.

[31] So Judas saw that the battle had begun and that the cry of the city went up to Heaven with trumpets and loud shouts,

[32] and he said to the men of his forces, "Fight today for your brethren!"

[33] Then he came up behind them in three companies, who sounded their trumpets and cried aloud in prayer.

[34] And when the army of Timothy realized that it was Maccabeus, they fled before him, and he dealt them a heavy blow. As many as eight thousand of them fell that day.

[35] Next he turned aside to Alema, and fought against it and took it; and he killed every male in it, plundered it, and burned it with fire.

[36] From there he marched on and took Chaspho, Maked, and Bosor, and the other cities of Gilead.

[37] After these things Timothy gathered another army and encamped opposite Raphon, on the other side of the stream.

[38] Judas sent men to spy out the camp, and they reported to him, "All the Gentiles around us have gathered to him; it is a very large force.

[39] They also have hired Arabs to help them, and they are encamped across the stream, ready to come and fight against you." And Judas went to meet them.

[40] Now as Judas and his army drew near to the stream of water, Timothy said to the officers of his forces, "If he crosses over to us first, we will not be able to resist him, for he will surely defeat us.

[41] But if he shows fear and camps on the other side of the river, we will cross over to him and defeat him."

[42] When Judas approached the stream of water, he stationed the scribes of the people at the stream and gave them this command, "Permit no man to encamp, but make them all enter the battle."

[43] Then he crossed over against them first, and the whole army followed him. All the Gentiles were defeated before him, and they threw away their arms and fled into the sacred precincts at Carnaim.

[44] But he took the city and burned the sacred precincts with fire, together with all who were in them. Thus Carnaim was conquered; they could stand before Judas no longer.

[45] Then Judas gathered together all the Israelites in Gilead, the small and the great, with their wives and children and goods, a very large company, to go to the land of Judah.

[46] So they came to Ephron. This was a large and very strong city on the road, and they could not go round it to the right or to the left; they had to go through it.

[47] But the men of the city shut them out and blocked up the gates with stones.

[48] And Judas sent them this friendly message, "Let us pass through your land to get to our land. No one will do you harm; we will simply pass by on foot." But they refused to open to him.

[49] Then Judas ordered proclamation to be made to the army that each should encamp where he was.

[50] So the men of the forces encamped, and he fought against the city all that day and all the night, and the city was delivered into his hands.

[51] He destroyed every male by the edge of the sword, and razed and plundered the city. Then he passed through the city over the slain.

[52] And they crossed the Jordan into the large plain before Beth-shan.

[53] And Judas kept rallying the laggards and encouraging the people all the way till he came to the land of Judah.

[54] So they went up to Mount Zion with gladness and joy, and offered burnt offerings, because not one of them had fallen before they returned in safety.

[55] Now while Judas and Jonathan were in Gilead and Simon his brother was in Galilee before Ptolemais,

[56] Joseph, the son of Zechariah, and Azariah, the commanders of the forces, heard of their brave deeds and of the heroic war they had fought.

[57] So they said, "Let us also make a name for ourselves; let us go and make war on the Gentiles around us."

[58] And they issued orders to the men of the forces that were with them, and they marched against Jamnia.

[59] And Gorgias and his men came out of the city to meet them in battle.

[60] Then Joseph and Azariah were routed, and were pursued to the borders of Judea; as many as two thousand of the people of Israel fell that day.

[61] Thus the people suffered a great rout because, thinking to do a brave deed, they did not listen to Judas and his brothers.

[62] But they did not belong to the family of those men through whom deliverance was given to Israel.

[63] The man Judas and his brothers were greatly honored in all Israel and among all the Gentiles, wherever their name was heard.

[64] Men gathered to them and praised them.

[65] Then Judas and his brothers went forth and fought the sons of Esau in the land to the south. He struck Hebron and its villages and tore down its strongholds and burned its towers round about.

[66] Then he marched off to go into the land of the Philistines, and passed through Marisa.

[67] On that day some priests, who wished to do a brave deed, fell in battle, for they went out to battle unwisely.

[68] But Judas turned aside to Azotus in the land of the Philistines; he tore down their altars, and the graven images of their gods he burned with fire; he plundered the cities and returned to the land of Judah.

1Mac.6

[1] King Antiochus was going through the upper provinces when he heard that Elymais in Persia was a city famed for its wealth in silver and gold.

[2] Its temple was very rich, containing golden shields, breastplates, and weapons left there by Alexander, the son of Philip, the Macedonian king who first reigned over the Greeks.

[3] So he came and tried to take the city and plunder it, but he could not, because his plan became known to the men of the city

[4] and they withstood him in battle. So he fled and in great grief departed from there to return to Babylon.

[5] Then some one came to him in Persia and reported that the armies which had gone into the land of Judah had been routed;

[6] that Lysias had gone first with a strong force, but had turned and fled before the Jews; that the Jews had grown strong from the arms, supplies, and abundant spoils which they had taken from the armies they had cut down;

[7] that they had torn down the abomination which he had erected upon the altar in Jerusalem; and that they had surrounded the sanctuary with high walls as before, and also Beth-zur, his city.

[8] When the king heard this news, he was astounded and badly shaken. He took to his bed and became sick from grief, because things had not turned out for him as he had planned.

[9] He lay there for many days, because deep grief continually gripped him, and he concluded that he was dying.

[10] So he called all his friends and said to them, "Sleep departs from my eyes and I am downhearted with worry.

[11] I said to myself, `To what distress I have come! And into what a great flood I now am plunged! For I was kind and beloved in my power.'

[12] But now I remember the evils I did in Jerusalem. I seized all her vessels of silver and gold; and I sent to destroy the inhabitants of Judah without good reason.

[13] I know that it is because of this that these evils have come upon me; and behold, I am perishing of deep grief in a strange land."

[14] Then he called for Philip, one of his friends, and made him ruler over all his kingdom.

[15] He gave him the crown and his robe and the signet, that he might guide Antiochus his son and bring him up to be king.

[16] Thus Antiochus the king died there in the one hundred and forty-ninth year.

[17] And when Lysias learned that the king was dead, he set up Antiochus the king's son to reign. Lysias had brought him up as a boy, and he named him Eupator.

[18] Now the men in the citadel kept hemming Israel in around the sanctuary. They were trying in every way to harm them and strengthen the Gentiles.

[19] So Judas decided to destroy them, and assembled all the people to besiege them.

[20] They gathered together and besieged the citadel in the one hundred and fiftieth year; and he built siege towers and other engines of war.

[21] But some of the garrison escaped from the siege and some of the ungodly Israelites joined them.

[22] They went to the king and said, "How long will you fail to do justice and to avenge our brethren?

[23] We were happy to serve your father, to live by what he said and to follow his commands.

[24] For this reason the sons of our people besieged the citadel and became hostile to us; moreover, they have put to death as many of us as they have caught, and they have seized our inheritances.

[25] And not against us alone have they stretched out their hands, but also against all the lands on their borders.

[26] And behold, today they have encamped against the citadel in Jerusalem to take it; they have fortified both the sanctuary and Beth-zur;

[27] and unless you quickly prevent them, they will do still greater things, and you will not be able to stop them."

[28] The king was enraged when he heard this. He assembled all his friends, the commanders of his forces and those in authority.

[29] And mercenary forces came to him from other kingdoms and from islands of the seas.

[30] The number of his forces was a hundred thousand foot soldiers, twenty thousand horsemen, and thirty-two elephants accustomed to war.

[31] They came through Idumea and encamped against Beth-zur, and for many days they fought and built engines of war; but the Jews sallied out and burned these with fire, and fought manfully.

[32] Then Judas marched away from the citadel and encamped at Beth-zechariah, opposite the camp of the king.

[33] Early in the morning the king rose and took his army by a forced march along the road to Beth-zechariah, and his troops made ready for battle and sounded their trumpets.

[34] They showed the elephants the juice of grapes and mulberries, to arouse them for battle.

[35] And they distributed the beasts among the phalanxes; with each elephant they stationed a thousand men armed with coats of mail, and with brass helmets on their heads; and five hundred picked horsemen were assigned to each beast.

[36] These took their position beforehand wherever the beast was; wherever it went they went with it, and they never left it.

[37] And upon the elephants were wooden towers, strong and covered; they were fastened upon each beast by special harness, and upon each were four armed men who fought from there, and also its Indian driver.

[38] The rest of the horsemen were stationed on either side, on the two flanks of the army, to harass the enemy while being themselves protected by the phalanxes.

[39] When the sun shone upon the shields of gold and brass, the hills were ablaze with them and gleamed like flaming torches.

[40] Now a part of the king's army was spread out on the high hills, and some troops were on the plain, and they advanced steadily and in good order.

[41] All who heard the noise made by their multitude, by the marching of the multitude and the clanking of their arms, trembled, for the army was very large and strong.

[42] But Judas and his army advanced to the battle, and six hundred men of the king's army fell.

[43] And Eleazar, called Avaran, saw that one of the beasts was equipped with royal armor. It was taller than all the others, and he supposed that the king was upon it.

[44] So he gave his life to save his people and to win for himself an everlasting name.

[45] He courageously ran into the midst of the phalanx to reach it; he killed men right and left, and they parted before him on both sides.

[46] He got under the elephant, stabbed it from beneath, and killed it; but it fell to the ground upon him and he died.

[47] And when the Jews saw the royal might and the fierce attack of the forces, they turned away in flight.

[48] The soldiers of the king's army went up to Jerusalem against them, and the king encamped in Judea and at Mount Zion.

[49] He made peace with the men of Beth-zur, and they evacuated the city, because they had no provisions there to withstand a siege, since it was a sabbatical year for the land.

[50] So the king took Beth-zur and stationed a guard there to hold it.

[51] Then he encamped before the sanctuary for many days. He set up siege towers, engines of war to throw fire and stones, machines to shoot arrows, and catapults.

[52] The Jews also made engines of war to match theirs, and fought for many days.

[53] But they had no food in storage, because it was the seventh year; those who found safety in Judea from the Gentiles had consumed the last of the stores.

[54] Few men were left in the sanctuary, because famine had prevailed over the rest and they had been scattered, each to his own place.

[55] Then Lysias heard that Philip, whom King Antiochus while still living had appointed to bring up Antiochus his son to be king,

[56] had returned from Persia and Media with the forces that had gone with the king, and that he was trying to seize control of the government.

[57] So he quickly gave orders to depart, and said to the king, to the commanders of the forces, and to the men, "We daily grow weaker, our food supply is scant, the place against which we are fighting is strong, and the affairs of the kingdom press urgently upon us.

[58] Now then let us come to terms with these men, and make peace with them and with all their nation,

[59] and agree to let them live by their laws as they did before; for it was on account of their laws which we abolished that they became angry and did all these things."

[60] The speech pleased the king and the commanders, and he sent to the Jews an offer of peace, and they accepted it.

[61] So the king and the commanders gave them their oath. On these conditions the Jews evacuated the stronghold.

[62] But when the king entered Mount Zion and saw what a strong fortress the place was, he broke the oath he had sworn and gave orders to tear down the wall all around.

[63] Then he departed with haste and returned to Antioch. He found Philip in control of the city, but he fought against him, and took the city by force.

1Mac.7

[1] In the one hundred and fifty-first year Demetrius the son of Seleucus set forth from Rome, sailed with a few men to a city by the sea, and there began to reign.

[2] As he was entering the royal palace of his fathers, the army seized Antiochus and Lysias to bring them to him.

[3] But when this act became known to him, he said, "Do not let me see their faces!"

[4] So the army killed them, and Demetrius took his seat upon the throne of his kingdom.

[5] Then there came to him all the lawless and ungodly men of Israel; they were led by Alcimus, who wanted to be high priest.

[6] And they brought to the king this accusation against the people: "Judas and his brothers have destroyed all your friends, and have driven us out of our land.

[7] Now then send a man whom you trust; let him go and see all the ruin which Judas has brought upon us and upon the land of the king, and let him punish them and all who help them."

[8] So the king chose Bacchides, one of the king's friends, governor of the province Beyond the River; he was a great man in the kingdom and was faithful to the king.

[9] And he sent him, and with him the ungodly Alcimus, whom he made high priest; and he commanded him to take vengeance on the sons of Israel.

[10] So they marched away and came with a large force into the land of Judah; and he sent messengers to Judas and his brothers with peaceable but treacherous words.

[11] But they paid no attention to their words, for they saw that they had come with a large force.

[12] Then a group of scribes appeared in a body before Alcimus and Bacchides to ask for just terms.

[13] The Hasideans were first among the sons of Israel to seek peace from them,

[14] for they said, "A priest of the line of Aaron has come with the army, and he will not harm us."

[15] And he spoke peaceable words to them and swore this oath to them, "We will not seek to injure you or your friends."

[16] So they trusted him; but he seized sixty of them and killed them in one day, in accordance with the word which was written,

[17] "The flesh of thy saints and their blood they poured out round about Jerusalem, and there was none to bury them."

[18] Then the fear and dread of them fell upon all the people, for they said, "There is no truth or justice in them, for they have violated the agreement and the oath which they swore."

[19] Then Bacchides departed from Jerusalem and encamped in Beth-zaith. And he sent and seized many of the men who had deserted to him, and some of the people, and killed them and threw them into a great pit.

[20] He placed Alcimus in charge of the country and left with him a force to help him; then Bacchides went back to the king.

[21] Alcimus strove for the high priesthood,

[22] and all who were troubling their people joined him. They gained control of the land of Judah and did great damage in Israel.

[23] And Judas saw all the evil that Alcimus and those with him had done among the sons of Israel; it was more than the Gentiles had done.

[24] So Judas went out into all the surrounding parts of Judea, and took vengeance on the men who had deserted, and he prevented those in the city from going out into the country.

[25] When Alcimus saw that Judas and those with him had grown strong, and realized that he could not withstand them, he returned to the king and brought wicked charges against them.

[26] Then the king sent Nicanor, one of his honored princes, who hated and detested Israel, and he commanded him to destroy the people.

[27] So Nicanor came to Jerusalem with a large force, and treacherously sent to Judas and his brothers this peaceable message,

[28] "Let there be no fighting between me and you; I shall come with a few men to see you face to face in peace."

[29] So he came to Judas, and they greeted one another peaceably. But the enemy were ready to seize Judas.

[30] It became known to Judas that Nicanor had come to him with treacherous intent, and he was afraid of him and would not meet him again.

[31] When Nicanor learned that his plan had been disclosed, he went out to meet Judas in battle near Caphar-salama.

[32] About five hundred men of the army of Nicanor fell, and the rest fled into the city of David.

[33] After these events Nicanor went up to Mount Zion. Some of the priests came out of the sanctuary, and some of the elders of the people, to greet him peaceably and to show him the burnt offering that was being offered for the king.

[34] But he mocked them and derided them and defiled them and spoke arrogantly,

[35] and in anger he swore this oath, "Unless Judas and his army are delivered into my hands this time, then if I return safely I will burn up this house." And he went out in great anger.

[36] Then the priests went in and stood before the altar and the temple, and they wept and said,

[37] "Thou didst choose this house to be called by thy name, and to be for thy people a house of prayer and supplication.

[38] Take vengeance on this man and on his army, and let them fall by the sword; remember their blasphemies, and let them live no longer."

[39] Now Nicanor went out from Jerusalem and encamped in Beth-horon, and the Syrian army joined him.

[40] And Judas encamped in Adasa with three thousand men. Then Judas prayed and said,

[41] "When the messengers from the king spoke blasphemy, thy angel went forth and struck down one hundred and eighty-five thousand of the Assyrians.

[42] So also crush this army before us today; let the rest learn that Nicanor has spoken wickedly against the sanctuary, and judge him according to this wickedness."

[43] So the armies met in battle on the thirteenth day of the month of Adar. The army of Nicanor was crushed, and he himself was the first to fall in the battle.

[44] When his army saw that Nicanor had fallen, they threw down their arms and fled.

[45] The Jews pursued them a day's journey, from Adasa as far as Gazara, and as they followed kept sounding the battle call on the trumpets.

[46] And men came out of all the villages of Judea round about, and they out-flanked the enemy and drove them back to their pursuers, so that they all fell by the sword; not even one of them was left.

[47] Then the Jews seized the spoils and the plunder, and they cut off Nicanor's head and the right hand which he so arrogantly stretched out, and brought them and displayed them just outside Jerusalem.

[48] The people rejoiced greatly and celebrated that day as a day of great gladness.

[49] And they decreed that this day should be celebrated each year on the thirteenth day of Adar.

[50] So the land of Judah had rest for a few days.

1Mac.8

[1] Now Judas heard of the fame of the Romans, that they were very strong and were well-disposed toward all who made an alliance with them, that they pledged friendship to those who came to them,

[2] and that they were very strong. Men told him of their wars and of the brave deeds which they were doing among the Gauls, how they had defeated them and forced them to pay tribute,

[3] and what they had done in the land of Spain to get control of the silver and gold mines there,

[4] and how they had gained control of the whole region by their planning and patience, even though the place was far distant from them. They also subdued the kings who came against them from the ends of the earth, until they crushed them and inflicted great disaster upon them; the rest paid them tribute every year.

[5] Philip, and Perseus king of the Macedonians, and the others who rose up against them, they crushed in battle and conquered.

[6] They also defeated Antiochus the Great, king of Asia, who went to fight against them with a hundred and twenty elephants and with cavalry and chariots and a very large army. He was crushed by them;

[7] they took him alive and decreed that he and those who should reign after him should pay a heavy tribute and give hostages and surrender some of their best provinces,

[8] the country of India and Media and Lydia. These they took from him and gave to Eumenes the king.

[9] The Greeks planned to come and destroy them,

[10] but this became known to them, and they sent a general against the Greeks and attacked them. Many of them were wounded and fell, and the Romans took captive their wives and children; they plundered them, conquered the land, tore down their strongholds, and enslaved them to this day.

[11] The remaining kingdoms and islands, as many as ever opposed them, they destroyed and enslaved;

[12] but with their friends and those who rely on them they have kept friendship. They have subdued kings far and near, and as many as have heard of their fame have feared them.

[13] Those whom they wish to help and to make kings, they make kings, and those whom they wish they depose; and they have been greatly exalted.

[14] Yet for all this not one of them has put on a crown or worn purple as a mark of pride,

[15] but they have built for themselves a senate chamber, and every day three hundred and twenty senators constantly deliberate concerning the people, to govern them well.

[16] They trust one man each year to rule over them and to control all their land; they all heed the one man, and there is no envy or jealousy among them.

[17] So Judas chose Eupolemus the son of John, son of Accos, and Jason the son of Eleazar, and sent them to Rome to establish friendship and alliance,

[18] and to free themselves from the yoke; for they saw that the kingdom of the Greeks was completely enslaving Israel.

[19] They went to Rome, a very long journey; and they entered the senate chamber and spoke as follows:

[20] "Judas, who is also called Maccabeus, and his brothers and the people of the Jews have sent us to you to establish alliance and peace with you, that we may be enrolled as your allies and friends."

[21] The proposal pleased them,

[22] and this is a copy of the letter which they wrote in reply, on bronze tablets, and sent to Jerusalem to remain with them there as a memorial of peace and alliance:

[23] "May all go well with the Romans and with the nation of the Jews at sea and on land for ever, and may sword and enemy be far from them.

[24] If war comes first to Rome or to any of their allies in all their dominion,

[25] the nation of the Jews shall act as their allies wholeheartedly, as the occasion may indicate to them.

[26] And to the enemy who makes war they shall not give or supply grain, arms, money, or ships, as Rome has decided; and they shall keep their obligations without receiving any return.

[27] In the same way, if war comes first to the nation of the Jews, the Romans shall willingly act as their allies, as the occasion may indicate to them.

[28] And to the enemy allies shall be given no grain, arms, money, or ships, as Rome has decided; and they shall keep these obligations and do so without deceit.

[29] Thus on these terms the Romans make a treaty with the Jewish people.

[30] If after these terms are in effect both parties shall determine to add or delete anything, they shall do so

at their discretion, and any addition or deletion that they may make shall be valid.

[31] "And concerning the wrongs which King Demetrius is doing to them we have written to him as follows, `Why have you made your yoke heavy upon our friends and allies the Jews?

[32] If now they appeal again for help against you, we will defend their rights and fight you on sea and on land.'"

1Mac.9

[1] When Demetrius heard that Nicanor and his army had fallen in battle, he sent Bacchides and Alcimus into the land of Judah a second time, and with them the right wing of the army.

[2] They went by the road which leads to Gilgal and encamped against Mesaloth in Arbela, and they took it and killed many people.

[3] In the first month of the one hundred and fifty-second year they encamped against Jerusalem;

[4] then they marched off and went to Berea with twenty thousand foot soldiers and two thousand cavalry.

[5] Now Judas was encamped in Elasa, and with him were three thousand picked men.

[6] When they saw the huge number of the enemy forces, they were greatly frightened, and many slipped away from the camp, until no more than eight hundred of them were left.

[7] When Judas saw that his army had slipped away and the battle was imminent, he was crushed in spirit, for he had no time to assemble them.

[8] He became faint, but he said to those who were left, "Let us rise and go up against our enemies. We may be able to fight them."

[9] But they tried to dissuade him, saying, "We are not able. Let us rather save our own lives now, and let us come back with our brethren and fight them; we are too few."

[10] But Judas said, "Far be it from us to do such a thing as to flee from them. If our time has come, let us die bravely for our brethren, and leave no cause to question our honor."

[11] Then the army of Bacchides marched out from the camp and took its stand for the encounter. The cavalry was divided into two companies, and the slingers and the archers went ahead of the army, as did all the chief warriors.

[12] Bacchides was on the right wing. Flanked by the two companies, the phalanx advanced to the sound of the trumpets; and the men with Judas also blew their trumpets.

[13] The earth was shaken by the noise of the armies, and the battle raged from morning till evening.

[14] Judas saw that Bacchides and the strength of his army were on the right; then all the stouthearted men went with him,

[15] and they crushed the right wing, and he pursued them as far as Mount Azotus.

[16] When those on the left wing saw that the right wing was crushed, they turned and followed close behind Judas and his men.

[17] The battle became desperate, and many on both sides were wounded and fell.

[18] Judas also fell, and the rest fled.

[19] Then Jonathan and Simon took Judas their brother and buried him in the tomb of their fathers at Modein,

[20] and wept for him. And all Israel made great lamentation for him; they mourned many days and said,

[21] "How is the mighty fallen, the savior of Israel!"

[22] Now the rest of the acts of Judas, and his wars and the brave deeds that he did, and his greatness, have not been recorded, for they were very many.

[23] After the death of Judas, the lawless emerged in all parts of Israel; all the doers of injustice appeared.

[24] In those days a very great famine occurred, and the country deserted with them to the enemy.

[25] And Bacchides chose the ungodly and put them in charge of the country.

[26] They sought and searched for the friends of Judas, and brought them to Bacchides, and he took vengeance on them and made sport of them.

[27] Thus there was great distress in Israel, such as had not been since the time that prophets ceased to appear among them.

[28] Then all the friends of Judas assembled and said to Jonathan,

[29] "Since the death of your brother Judas there has been no one like him to go against our enemies and Bacchides, and to deal with those of our nation who hate us.

[30] So now we have chosen you today to take his place as our ruler and leader, to fight our battle."

[31] And Jonathan at that time accepted the leadership and took the place of Judas his brother.

[32] When Bacchides learned of this, he tried to kill him.

[33] But Jonathan and Simon his brother and all who were with him heard of it, and they fled into the wilderness of Tekoa and camped by the water of the pool of Asphar.

[34] Bacchides found this out on the sabbath day, and he with all his army crossed the Jordan.

[35] And Jonathan sent his brother as leader of the multitude and begged the Nabateans, who were his friends, for permission to store with them the great amount of baggage which they had.

[36] But the sons of Jambri from Medeba came out and seized John and all that he had, and departed with it.

[37] After these things it was reported to Jonathan and Simon his brother, "The sons of Jambri are

celebrating a great wedding, and are conducting the bride, a daughter of one of the great nobles of Canaan, from Nadabath with a large escort."

[38] And they remembered the blood of John their brother, and went up and hid under cover of the mountain.

[39] They raised their eyes and looked, and saw a tumultuous procession with much baggage; and the bridegroom came out with his friends and his brothers to meet them with tambourines and musicians and many weapons.

[40] Then they rushed upon them from the ambush and began killing them. Many were wounded and fell, and the rest fled to the mountain; and they took all their goods.

[41] Thus the wedding was turned into mourning and the voice of their musicians into a funeral dirge.

[42] And when they had fully avenged the blood of their brother, they returned to the marshes of the Jordan.

[43] When Bacchides heard of this, he came with a large force on the sabbath day to the banks of the Jordan.

[44] And Jonathan said to those with him, "Let us rise up now and fight for our lives, for today things are not as they were before.

[45] For look! the battle is in front of us and behind us; the water of the Jordan is on this side and on that, with marsh and thicket; there is no place to turn.

[46] Cry out now to Heaven that you may be delivered from the hands of our enemies."

[47] So the battle began, and Jonathan stretched out his hand to strike Bacchides, but he eluded him and went to the rear.

[48] Then Jonathan and the men with him leaped into the Jordan and swam across to the other side, and the enemy did not cross the Jordan to attack them.

[49] And about one thousand of Bacchides' men fell that day.

[50] Bacchides then returned to Jerusalem and built strong cities in Judea: the fortress in Jericho, and Emmaus, and Beth-horon, and Bethel, and Timnath, and Pharathon, and Tephon, with high walls and gates and bars.

[51] And he placed garrisons in them to harass Israel.

[52] He also fortified the city of Beth-zur, and Gazara, and the citadel, and in them he put troops and stores of food.

[53] And he took the sons of the leading men of the land as hostages and put them under guard in the citadel at Jerusalem.

[54] In the one hundred and fifty-third year, in the second month, Alcimus gave orders to tear down the wall of the inner court of the sanctuary. He tore down the work of the prophets!

[55] But he only began to tear it down, for at that time Alcimus was stricken and his work was hindered; his mouth was stopped and he was paralyzed, so that he could no longer say a word or give commands concerning his house.

[56] And Alcimus died at that time in great agony.

[57] When Bacchides saw that Alcimus was dead, he returned to the king, and the land of Judah had rest for two years.

[58] Then all the lawless plotted and said, "See! Jonathan and his men are living in quiet and confidence. So now let us bring Bacchides back, and he will capture them all in one night."

[59] And they went and consulted with him.

[60] He started to come with a large force, and secretly sent letters to all his allies in Judea, telling them to seize Jonathan and his men; but they were unable to do it, because their plan became known.

[61] And Jonathan's men seized about fifty of the men of the country who were leaders in this treachery, and killed them.

[62] Then Jonathan with his men, and Simon, withdrew to Bethbasi in the wilderness; he rebuilt the parts of it that had been demolished, and they fortified it.

[63] When Bacchides learned of this, he assembled all his forces, and sent orders to the men of Judea.

[64] Then he came and encamped against Bethbasi; he fought against it for many days and made machines of war.

[65] But Jonathan left Simon his brother in the city, while he went out into the country; and he went with only a few men.

[66] He struck down Odomera and his brothers and the sons of Phasiron in their tents.

[67] Then he began to attack and went into battle with his forces; and Simon and his men sallied out from the city and set fire to the machines of war.

[68] They fought with Bacchides, and he was crushed by them. They distressed him greatly, for his plan and his expedition had been in vain.

[69] So he was greatly enraged at the lawless men who had counseled him to come into the country, and he killed many of them. Then he decided to depart to his own land.

[70] When Jonathan learned of this, he sent ambassadors to him to make peace with him and obtain release of the captives.

[71] He agreed, and did as he said; and he swore to Jonathan that he would not try to harm him as long as he lived.

[72] He restored to him the captives whom he had formerly taken from the land of Judah; then he turned and departed to his own land, and came no more into their territory.

[73] Thus the sword ceased from Israel. And Jonathan dwelt in Michmash. And Jonathan began to judge the people, and he destroyed the ungodly out of Israel. 1Mac.10

[1] In the one hundred and sixtieth year Alexander Epiphanes, the son of Antiochus, landed and occupied Ptolemais. They welcomed him, and there he began to reign.

[2] When Demetrius the king heard of it, he assembled a very large army and marched out to meet him in battle.

[3] And Demetrius sent Jonathan a letter in peaceable words to honor him;

[4] for he said, "Let us act first to make peace with him before he makes peace with Alexander against us,

[5] for he will remember all the wrongs which we did to him and to his brothers and his nation."

[6] So Demetrius gave him authority to recruit troops, to equip them with arms, and to become his ally; and he commanded that the hostages in the citadel should be released to him.

[7] Then Jonathan came to Jerusalem and read the letter in the hearing of all the people and of the men in the citadel.

[8] They were greatly alarmed when they heard that the king had given him authority to recruit troops.

[9] But the men in the citadel released the hostages to Jonathan, and he returned them to their parents.

[10] And Jonathan dwelt in Jerusalem and began to rebuild and restore the city.

[11] He directed those who were doing the work to build the walls and encircle Mount Zion with squared stones, for better fortification; and they did so.

[12] Then the foreigners who were in the strongholds that Bacchides had built fled;

[13] each left his place and departed to his own land.

[14] Only in Beth-zur did some remain who had forsaken the law and the commandments, for it served as a place of refuge.

[15] Now Alexander the king heard of all the promises which Demetrius had sent to Jonathan, and men told him of the battles that Jonathan and his brothers had fought, of the brave deeds that they had done, and of the troubles that they had endured.

[16] So he said, "Shall we find another such man? Come now, we will make him our friend and ally."

[17] And he wrote a letter and sent it to him, in the following words:

[18] "King Alexander to his brother Jonathan, greeting.

[19] We have heard about you, that you are a mighty warrior and worthy to be our friend.

[20] And so we have appointed you today to be the high priest of your nation; you are to be called the king's friend" (and he sent him a purple robe and a golden crown) "and you are to take our side and keep friendship with us."

[21] So Jonathan put on the holy garments in the seventh month of the one hundred and sixtieth year,

at the feast of tabernacles, and he recruited troops and equipped them with arms in abundance.

[22] When Demetrius heard of these things he was grieved and said,

[23] "What is this that we have done? Alexander has gotten ahead of us in forming a friendship with the Jews to strengthen himself.

[24] I also will write them words of encouragement and promise them honor and gifts, that I may have their help."

[25] So he sent a message to them in the following words: "King Demetrius to the nation of the Jews, greeting.

[26] Since you have kept your agreement with us and have continued your friendship with us, and have not sided with our enemies, we have heard of it and rejoiced.

[27] And now continue still to keep faith with us, and we will repay you with good for what you do for us.

[28] We will grant you many immunities and give you gifts.

[29] "And now I free you and exempt all the Jews from payment of tribute and salt tax and crown levies,

[30] and instead of collecting the third of the grain and the half of the fruit of the trees that I should receive, I release them from this day and henceforth. I will not collect them from the land of Judah or from the three districts added to it from Samaria and Galilee, from this day and for all time.

[31] And let Jerusalem and her environs, her tithes and her revenues, be holy and free from tax.

[32] I release also my control of the citadel in Jerusalem and give it to the high priest, that he may station in it men of his own choice to guard it.

[33] And every one of the Jews taken as a captive from the land of Judah into any part of my kingdom, I set free without payment; and let all officials cancel also the taxes on their cattle.

[34] "And all the feasts and sabbaths and new moons and appointed days, and the three days before a feast and the three after a feast -- let them all be days of immunity and release for all the Jews who are in my kingdom.

[35] No one shall have authority to exact anything from them or annoy any of them about any matter.

[36] "Let Jews be enrolled in the king's forces to the number of thirty thousand men, and let the maintenance be given them that is due to all the forces of the king.

[37] Let some of them be stationed in the great strongholds of the king, and let some of them be put in positions of trust in the kingdom. Let their officers and leaders be of their own number, and let them live by their own laws, just as the king has commanded in the land of Judah.

[38] "As for the three districts that have been added to Judea from the country of Samaria, let them be so annexed to Judea that they are considered to be under one ruler and obey no other authority but the high priest.

[39] Ptolemais and the land adjoining it I have given as a gift to the sanctuary in Jerusalem, to meet the necessary expenses of the sanctuary.

[40] I also grant fifteen thousand shekels of silver yearly out of the king's revenues from appropriate places.

[41] And all the additional funds which the government officials have not paid as they did in the first years, they shall give from now on for the service of the temple.

[42] Moreover, the five thousand shekels of silver which my officials have received every year from the income of the services of the temple, this too is canceled, because it belongs to the priests who minister there.

[43] And whoever takes refuge at the temple in Jerusalem, or in any of its precincts, because he owes money to the king or has any debt, let him be released and receive back all his property in my kingdom.

[44] "Let the cost of rebuilding and restoring the structures of the sanctuary be paid from the revenues of the king.

[45] And let the cost of rebuilding the walls of Jerusalem and fortifying it round about, and the cost of rebuilding the walls in Judea, also be paid from the revenues of the king."

[46] When Jonathan and the people heard these words, they did not believe or accept them, because they remembered the great wrongs which Demetrius had done in Israel and how he had greatly oppressed them.

[47] They favored Alexander, because he had been the first to speak peaceable words to them, and they remained his allies all his days.

[48] Now Alexander the king assembled large forces and encamped opposite Demetrius.

[49] The two kings met in battle, and the army of Demetrius fled, and Alexander pursued him and defeated them.

[50] He pressed the battle strongly until the sun set, and Demetrius fell on that day.

[51] Then Alexander sent ambassadors to Ptolemy king of Egypt with the following message:

[52] "Since I have returned to my kingdom and have taken my seat on the throne of my fathers, and established my rule -- for I crushed Demetrius and gained control of our country;

[53] I met him in battle, and he and his army were crushed by us, and we have taken our seat on the throne of his kingdom --

[54] now therefore let us establish friendship with one another; give me now your daughter as my wife, and

I will become your son-in-law, and will make gifts to you and to her in keeping with your position."

[55] Ptolemy the king replied and said, "Happy was the day on which you returned to the land of your fathers and took your seat on the throne of their kingdom.

[56] And now I will do for you as you wrote, but meet me at Ptolemais, so that we may see one another, and I will become your father-in-law, as you have said."

[57] So Ptolemy set out from Egypt, he and Cleopatra his daughter, and came to Ptolemais in the one hundred and sixty-second year.

[58] Alexander the king met him, and Ptolemy gave him Cleopatra his daughter in marriage, and celebrated her wedding at Ptolemais with great pomp, as kings do.

[59] Then Alexander the king wrote to Jonathan to come to meet him.

[60] So he went with pomp to Ptolemais and met the two kings; he gave them and their friends silver and gold and many gifts, and found favor with them.

[61] A group of pestilent men from Israel, lawless men, gathered together against him to accuse him; but the king paid no attention to them.

[62] The king gave orders to take off Jonathan's garments and to clothe him in purple, and they did so.

[63] The king also seated him at his side; and he said to his officers, "Go forth with him into the middle of the city and proclaim that no one is to bring charges against him about any matter, and let no one annoy him for any reason."

[64] And when his accusers saw the honor that was paid him, in accordance with the proclamation, and saw him clothed in purple, they all fled.

[65] Thus the king honored him and enrolled him among his chief friends, and made him general and governor of the province.

[66] And Jonathan returned to Jerusalem in peace and gladness.

[67] In the one hundred and sixty-fifth year Demetrius the son of Demetrius came from Crete to the land of his fathers.

[68] When Alexander the king heard of it, he was greatly grieved and returned to Antioch.

[69] And Demetrius appointed Apollonius the governor of Coelesyria, and he assembled a large force and encamped against Jamnia. Then he sent the following message to Jonathan the high priest:

[70] "You are the only one to rise up against us, and I have become a laughingstock and reproach because of you. Why do you assume authority against us in the hill country?

[71] If you now have confidence in your forces, come down to the plain to meet us, and let us match strength with each other there, for I have with me the power of the cities.

[72] Ask and learn who I am and who the others are that are helping us. Men will tell you that you cannot stand before us, for your fathers were twice put to flight in their own land.

[73] And now you will not be able to withstand my cavalry and such an army in the plain, where there is no stone or pebble, or place to flee."

[74] When Jonathan heard the words of Apollonius, his spirit was aroused. He chose ten thousand men and set out from Jerusalem, and Simon his brother met him to help him.

[75] He encamped before Joppa, but the men of the city closed its gates, for Apollonius had a garrison in Joppa.

[76] So they fought against it, and the men of the city became afraid and opened the gates, and Jonathan gained possession of Joppa.

[77] When Apollonius heard of it, he mustered three thousand cavalry and a large army, and went to Azotus as though he were going farther. At the same time he advanced into the plain, for he had a large troop of cavalry and put confidence in it.

[78] Jonathan pursued him to Azotus, and the armies engaged in battle.

[79] Now Apollonius had secretly left a thousand cavalry behind them.

[80] Jonathan learned that there was an ambush behind him, for they surrounded his army and shot arrows at his men from early morning till late afternoon.

[81] But his men stood fast, as Jonathan commanded, and the enemy's horses grew tired.

[82] Then Simon brought forward his force and engaged the phalanx in battle (for the cavalry was exhausted); they were overwhelmed by him and fled,

[83] and the cavalry was dispersed in the plain. They fled to Azotus and entered Beth-dagon, the temple of their idol, for safety.

[84] But Jonathan burned Azotus and the surrounding towns and plundered them; and the temple of Dagon, and those who had taken refuge in it he burned with fire.

[85] The number of those who fell by the sword, with those burned alive, came to eight thousand men.

[86] Then Jonathan departed from there and encamped against Askalon, and the men of the city came out to meet him with great pomp.

[87] And Jonathan and those with him returned to Jerusalem with much booty.

[88] When Alexander the king heard of these things, he honored Jonathan still more;

[89] and he sent to him a golden buckle, such as it is the custom to give to the kinsmen of kings. He also gave him Ekron and all its environs as his possession.

1Mac.11

[1] Then the king of Egypt gathered great forces, like the sand by the seashore, and many ships; and he tried to get possession of Alexander's kingdom by trickery and add it to his own kingdom.

[2] He set out for Syria with peaceable words, and the people of the cities opened their gates to him and went to meet him, for Alexander the king had commanded them to meet him, since he was Alexander's father-in-law.

[3] But when Ptolemy entered the cities he stationed forces as a garrison in each city.

[4] When he approached Azotus, they showed him the temple of Dagon burned down, and Azotus and its suburbs destroyed, and the corpses lying about, and the charred bodies of those whom Jonathan had burned in the war, for they had piled them in heaps along his route.

[5] They also told the king what Jonathan had done, to throw blame on him; but the king kept silent.

[6] Jonathan met the king at Joppa with pomp, and they greeted one another and spent the night there.

[7] And Jonathan went with the king as far as the river called Eleutherus; then he returned to Jerusalem.

[8] So King Ptolemy gained control of the coastal cities as far as Seleucia by the sea, and he kept devising evil designs against Alexander.

[9] He sent envoys to Demetrius the king, saying, "Come, let us make a covenant with each other, and I will give you in marriage my daughter who was Alexander's wife, and you shall reign over your father's kingdom.

[10] For I now regret that I gave him my daughter, for he has tried to kill me."

[11] He threw blame on Alexander because he coveted his kingdom.

[12] So he took his daughter away from him and gave her to Demetrius. He was estranged from Alexander, and their enmity became manifest.

[13] Then Ptolemy entered Antioch and put on the crown of Asia. Thus he put two crowns upon his head, the crown of Egypt and that of Asia.

[14] Now Alexander the king was in Cilicia at that time, because the people of that region were in revolt.

[15] And Alexander heard of it and came against him in battle. Ptolemy marched out and met him with a strong force, and put him to flight.

[16] So Alexander fled into Arabia to find protection there, and King Ptolemy was exalted.

[17] And Zabdiel the Arab cut off the head of Alexander and sent it to Ptolemy.

[18] But King Ptolemy died three days later, and his troops in the strongholds were killed by the inhabitants of the strongholds.

[19] So Demetrius became king in the one hundred and sixty-seventh year.

[20] In those days Jonathan assembled the men of Judea to attack the citadel in Jerusalem, and he built many engines of war to use against it.

[21] But certain lawless men who hated their nation went to the king and reported to him that Jonathan was besieging the citadel.

[22] When he heard this he was angry, and as soon as he heard it he set out and came to Ptolemais; and he wrote Jonathan not to continue the siege, but to meet him for a conference at Ptolemais as quickly as possible.

[23] When Jonathan heard this, he gave orders to continue the siege; and he chose some of the elders of Israel and some of the priests, and put himself in danger,

[24] for he went to the king at Ptolemais, taking silver and gold and clothing and numerous other gifts. And he won his favor.

[25] Although certain lawless men of his nation kept making complaints against him,

[26] the king treated him as his predecessors had treated him; he exalted him in the presence of all his friends.

[27] He confirmed him in the high priesthood and in as many other honors as he had formerly had, and made him to be regarded as one of his chief friends.

[28] Then Jonathan asked the king to free Judea and the three districts of Samaria from tribute, and promised him three hundred talents.

[29] The king consented, and wrote a letter to Jonathan about all these things; its contents were as follows:

[30] "King Demetrius to Jonathan his brother and to the nation of the Jews, greeting.

[31] This copy of the letter which we wrote concerning you to Lasthenes our kinsman we have written to you also, so that you may know what it says.

[32] `King Demetrius to Lasthenes his father, greeting.

[33] To the nation of the Jews, who are our friends and fulfil their obligations to us, we have determined to do good, because of the good will they show toward us.

[34] We have confirmed as their possession both the territory of Judea and the three districts of Aphairema and Lydda and Rathamin; the latter, with all the region bordering them, were added to Judea from Samaria. To all those who offer sacrifice in Jerusalem, we have granted release from the royal taxes which the king formerly received from them each year, from the crops of the land and the fruit of the trees.

[35] And the other payments henceforth due to us of the tithes, and the taxes due to us, and the salt pits and the crown taxes due to us -- from all these we shall grant them release.

[36] And not one of these grants shall be canceled from this time forth for ever.

[37] Now therefore take care to make a copy of this, and let it be given to Jonathan and put up in a conspicuous place on the holy mountain.'"

[38] Now when Demetrius the king saw that the land was quiet before him and that there was no opposition to him, he dismissed all his troops, each man to his own place, except the foreign troops which he had recruited from the islands of the nations. So all the troops who had served his fathers hated him.

[39] Now Trypho had formerly been one of Alexander's supporters. He saw that all the troops were murmuring against Demetrius. So he went to Imalkue the Arab, who was bringing up Antiochus, the young son of Alexander,

[40] and insistently urged him to hand Antiochus over to him, to become king in place of his father. He also reported to Imalkue what Demetrius had done and told of the hatred which the troops of Demetrius had for him; and he stayed there many days.

[41] Now Jonathan sent to Demetrius the king the request that he remove the troops of the citadel from Jerusalem, and the troops in the strongholds; for they kept fighting against Israel.

[42] And Demetrius sent this message to Jonathan, "Not only will I do these things for you and your nation, but I will confer great honor on you and your nation, if I find an opportunity.

[43] Now then you will do well to send me men who will help me, for all my troops have revolted."

[44] So Jonathan sent three thousand stalwart men to him at Antioch, and when they came to the king, the king rejoiced at their arrival.

[45] Then the men of the city assembled within the city, to the number of a hundred and twenty thousand, and they wanted to kill the king.

[46] But the king fled into the palace. Then the men of the city seized the main streets of the city and began to fight.

[47] So the king called the Jews to his aid, and they all rallied about him and then spread out through the city; and they killed on that day as many as a hundred thousand men.

[48] They set fire to the city and seized much spoil on that day, and they saved the king.

[49] When the men of the city saw that the Jews had gained control of the city as they pleased, their courage failed and they cried out to the king with this entreaty,

[50] "Grant us peace, and make the Jews stop fighting against us and our city."

[51] And they threw down their arms and made peace. So the Jews gained glory in the eyes of the king and of all the people in his kingdom, and they returned to Jerusalem with much spoil.

[52] So Demetrius the king sat on the throne of his kingdom, and the land was quiet before him.

[53] But he broke his word about all that he had promised; and he became estranged from Jonathan and did not repay the favors which Jonathan had done him, but oppressed him greatly.

[54] After this Trypho returned, and with him the young boy Antiochus who began to reign and put on the crown.

[55] All the troops that Demetrius had cast off gathered around him, and they fought against Demetrius, and he fled and was routed.

[56] And Trypho captured the elephants and gained control of Antioch.

[57] Then the young Antiochus wrote to Jonathan, saying, "I confirm you in the high priesthood and set you over the four districts and make you one of the friends of the king."

[58] And he sent him gold plate and a table service, and granted him the right to drink from gold cups and dress in purple and wear a gold buckle.

[59] Simon his brother he made governor from the Ladder of Tyre to the borders of Egypt.

[60] Then Jonathan set forth and traveled beyond the river and among the cities, and all the army of Syria gathered to him as allies. When he came to Askalon, the people of the city met him and paid him honor.

[61] From there he departed to Gaza, but the men of Gaza shut him out. So he beseiged it and burned its suburbs with fire and plundered them.

[62] Then the people of Gaza pleaded with Jonathan, and he made peace with them, and took the sons of their rulers as hostages and sent them to Jerusalem. And he passed through the country as far as Damascus.

[63] Then Jonathan heard that the officers of Demetrius had come to Kadesh in Galilee with a large army, intending to remove him from office.

[64] He went to meet them, but left his brother Simon in the country.

[65] Simon encamped before Beth-zur and fought against it for many days and hemmed it in.

[66] Then they asked him to grant them terms of peace, and he did so. He removed them from there, took possession of the city, and set a garrison over it.

[67] Jonathan and his army encamped by the waters of Gennesaret. Early in the morning they marched to the plain of Hazor,

[68] and behold, the army of the foreigners met him in the plain; they had set an ambush against him in the mountains, but they themselves met him face to face.

[69] Then the men in ambush emerged from their places and joined battle.

[70] All the men with Jonathan fled; not one of them was left except Mattathias the son of Absalom and Judas the son of Chalphi, commanders of the forces of the army.

[71] Jonathan rent his garments and put dust on his head, and prayed.

[72] Then he turned back to the battle against the enemy and routed them, and they fled.

[73] When his men who were fleeing saw this, they returned to him and joined him in the pursuit as far as Kadesh, to their camp, and there they encamped.

[74] As many as three thousand of the foreigners fell that day. And Jonathan returned to Jerusalem.

1Mac.12

[1] Now when Jonathan saw that the time was favorable for him, he chose men and sent them to Rome to confirm and renew the friendship with them.

[2] He also sent letters to the same effect to the Spartans and to other places.

[3] So they went to Rome and entered the senate chamber and said, "Jonathan the high priest and the Jewish nation have sent us to renew the former friendship and alliance with them."

[4] And the Romans gave them letters to the people in every place, asking them to provide for the envoys safe conduct to the land of Judah.

[5] This is a copy of the letter which Jonathan wrote to the Spartans:

[6] "Jonathan the high priest, the senate of the nation, the priests, and the rest of the Jewish people to their brethren the Spartans, greeting.

[7] Already in time past a letter was sent to Onias the high priest from Arius, who was king among you, stating that you are our brethren, as the appended copy shows.

[8] Onias welcomed the envoy with honor, and received the letter, which contained a clear declaration of alliance and friendship.

[9] Therefore, though we have no need of these things, since we have as encouragement the holy books which are in our hands,

[10] we have undertaken to send to renew our brotherhood and friendship with you, so that we may not become estranged from you, for considerable time has passed since you sent your letter to us.

[11] We therefore remember you constantly on every occasion, both in our feasts and on other appropriate days, at the sacrifices which we offer and in our prayers, as it is right and proper to remember brethren.

[12] And we rejoice in your glory.

[13] But as for ourselves, many afflictions and many wars have encircled us; the kings round about us have waged war against us.

[14] We were unwilling to annoy you and our other allies and friends with these wars,

[15] for we have the help which comes from Heaven for our aid; and we were delivered from our enemies and our enemies were humbled.

[16] We therefore have chosen Numenius the son of Antiochus and Antipater the son of Jason, and have sent them to Rome to renew our former friendship and alli ance with them.

[17] We have commanded them to go also to you and greet you and deliver to you this letter from us concerning the renewal of our brotherhood.
[18] And now please send us a reply to this."
[19] This is a copy of the letter which they sent to Onias:
[20] "Arius, king of the Spartans, to Onias the high priest, greeting.
[21] It has been found in writing concerning the Spartans and the Jews that they are brethren and are of the family of Abraham.
[22] And now that we have learned this, please write us concerning your welfare;
[23] we on our part write to you that your cattle and your property belong to us, and ours belong to you. We therefore command that our envoys report to you accordingly."
[24] Now Jonathan heard that the commanders of Demetrius had returned, with a larger force than before, to wage war against him.
[25] So he marched away from Jerusalem and met them in the region of Hamath, for he gave them no opportunity to invade his own country.
[26] He sent spies to their camp, and they returned and reported to him that the enemy were being drawn up in formation to fall upon the Jews by night.
[27] So when the sun set, Jonathan commanded his men to be alert and to keep their arms at hand so as to be ready all night for battle, and he stationed outposts around the camp.
[28] When the enemy heard that Jonathan and his men were prepared for battle, they were afraid and were terrified at heart; so they kindled fires in their camp and withdrew.
[29] But Jonathan and his men did not know it until morning, for they saw the fires burning.
[30] Then Jonathan pursued them, but he did not overtake them, for they had crossed the Eleutherus river.
[31] So Jonathan turned aside against the Arabs who are called Zabadeans, and he crushed them and plundered them.
[32] Then he broke camp and went to Damascus, and marched through all that region.
[33] Simon also went forth and marched through the country as far as Askalon and the neighboring strongholds. He turned aside to Joppa and took it by surprise,
[34] for he had heard that they were ready to hand over the stronghold to the men whom Demetrius had sent. And he stationed a garrison there to guard it.
[35] When Jonathan returned he convened the elders of the people and planned with them to build strongholds in Judea,
[36] to build the walls of Jerusalem still higher, and to erect a high barrier between the citadel and the city to separate it from the city, in order to isolate it so that its garrison could neither buy nor sell.
[37] So they gathered together to build up the city; part of the wall on the valley to the east had fallen, and he repaired the section called Chaphenatha.
[38] And Simon built Adida in the Shephelah; he fortified it and installed gates with bolts.
[39] Then Trypho attempted to become king in Asia and put on the crown, and to raise his hand against Antiochus the king.
[40] He feared that Jonathan might not permit him to do so, but might make war on him, so he kept seeking to seize and kill him, and he marched forth and came to Beth-shan.
[41] Jonathan went out to meet him with forty thousand picked fighting men, and he came to Beth-shan.
[42] When Trypho saw that he had come with a large army, he was afraid to raise his hand against him.
[43] So he received him with honor and commended him to all his friends, and he gave him gifts and commanded his friends and his troops to obey him as they would himself.
[44] Then he said to Jonathan, "Why have you wearied all these people when we are not at war?
[45] Dismiss them now to their homes and choose for yourself a few men to stay with you, and come with me to Ptolemais. I will hand it over to you as well as the other strongholds and the remaining troops and all the officials, and will turn round and go home. For that is why I am here."
[46] Jonathan trusted him and did as he said; he sent away the troops, and they returned to the land of Judah.
[47] He kept with himself three thousand men, two thousand of whom he left in Galilee, while a thousand accompanied him.
[48] But when Jonathan entered Ptolemais, the men of Ptolemais closed the gates and seized him, and all who had entered with him they killed with the sword.
[49] Then Trypho sent troops and cavalry into Galilee and the Great Plain to destroy all Jonathan's soldiers.
[50] But they realized that Jonathan had been seized and had perished along with his men, and they encouraged one another and kept marching in close formation, ready for battle.
[51] When their pursuers saw that they would fight for their lives, they turned back.
[52] So they all reached the land of Judah safely, and they mourned for Jonathan and his companions and were in great fear; and all Israel mourned deeply.
[53] And all the nations round about them tried to destroy them, for they said, "They have no leader or helper. Now therefore let us make war on them and blot out the memory of them from among men."
1Mac.13

[1] Simon heard that Trypho had assembled a large army to invade the land of Judah and destroy it,

[2] and he saw that the people were trembling and fearful. So he went up to Jerusalem, and gathering the people together

[3] he encouraged them, saying to them, "You yourselves know what great things I and my brothers and the house of my father have done for the laws and the sanctuary; you know also the wars and the difficulties which we have seen.

[4] By reason of this all my brothers have perished for the sake of Israel, and I alone am left.

[5] And now, far be it from me to spare my life in any time of distress, for I am not better than my brothers.

[6] But I will avenge my nation and the sanctuary and your wives and children, for all the nations have gathered together out of hatred to destroy us."

[7] The spirit of the people was rekindled when they heard these words,

[8] and they answered in a loud voice, "You are our leader in place of Judas and Jonathan your brother.

[9] Fight our battles, and all that you say to us we will do."

[10] So he assembled all the warriors and hastened to complete the walls of Jerusalem, and he fortified it on every side.

[11] He sent Jonathan the son of Absalom to Joppa, and with him a considerable army; he drove out its occupants and remained there.

[12] Then Trypho departed from Ptolemais with a large army to invade the land of Judah, and Jonathan was with him under guard.

[13] And Simon encamped in Adida, facing the plain.

[14] Trypho learned that Simon had risen up in place of Jonathan his brother, and that he was about to join battle with him, so he sent envoys to him and said,

[15] "It is for the money that Jonathan your brother owed the royal treasury, in connection with the offices he held, that we are detaining him.

[16] Send now a hundred talents of silver and two of his sons as hostages, so that when released he will not revolt against us, and we will release him."

[17] Simon knew that they were speaking deceitfully to him, but he sent to get the money and the sons, lest he arouse great hostility among the people, who might say,

[18] "Because Simon did not send him the money and the sons, he perished."

[19] So he sent the sons and the hundred talents, but Trypho broke his word and did not release Jonathan.

[20] After this Trypho came to invade the country and destroy it, and he circled around by the way to Adora. But Simon and his army kept marching along opposite him to every place he went.

[21] Now the men in the citadel kept sending envoys to Trypho urging him to come to them by way of the wilderness and to send them food.

[22] So Trypho got all his cavalry ready to go, but that night a very heavy snow fell, and he did not go because of the snow. He marched off and went into the land of Gilead.

[23] When he approached Baskama, he killed Jonathan, and he was buried there.

[24] Then Trypho turned back and departed to his own land.

[25] And Simon sent and took the bones of Jonathan his brother, and buried him in Modein, the city of his fathers.

[26] All Israel bewailed him with great lamentation, and mourned for him many days.

[27] And Simon built a monument over the tomb of his father and his brothers; he made it high that it might be seen, with polished stone at the front and back.

[28] He also erected seven pyramids, opposite one another, for his father and mother and four brothers.

[29] And for the pyramids he devised an elaborate setting, erecting about them great columns, and upon the columns he put suits of armor for a permanent memorial, and beside the suits of armor carved ships, so that they could be seen by all who sail the sea.

[30] This is the tomb which he built in Modein; it remains to this day.

[31] Trypho dealt treacherously with the young king Antiochus; he killed him

[32] and became king in his place, putting on the crown of Asia; and he brought great calamity upon the land.

[33] But Simon built up the strongholds of Judea and walled them all around, with high towers and great walls and gates and bolts, and he stored food in the strongholds.

[34] Simon also chose men and sent them to Demetrius the king with a request to grant relief to the country, for all that Trypho did was to plunder.

[35] Demetrius the king sent him a favorable reply to this request, and wrote him a letter as follows,

[36] "King Demetrius to Simon, the high priest and friend of kings, and to the elders and nation of the Jews, greeting.

[37] We have received the gold crown and the palm branch which you sent, and we are ready to make a general peace with you and to write to our officials to grant you release from tribute.

[38] All the grants that we have made to you remain valid, and let the strongholds that you have built be your possession.

[39] We pardon any errors and offenses committed to this day, and cancel the crown tax which you owe; and whatever other tax has been collected in Jerusalem shall be collected no longer.

[40] And if any of you are qualified to be enrolled in our bodyguard, let them be enrolled, and let there be peace between us."

[41] In the one hundred and seventieth year the yoke of the Gentiles was removed from Israel,

[42] and the people began to write in their documents and contracts, "In the first year of Simon the great high priest and commander and leader of the Jews."

[43] In those days Simon encamped against Gazara and surrounded it with troops. He made a siege engine, brought it up to the city, and battered and captured one tower.

[44] The men in the siege engine leaped out into the city, and a great tumult arose in the city.

[45] The men in the city, with their wives and children, went up on the wall with their clothes rent, and they cried out with a loud voice, asking Simon to make peace with them;

[46] they said, "Do not treat us according to our wicked acts but according to your mercy."

[47] So Simon reached an agreement with them and stopped fighting against them. But he expelled them from the city and cleansed the houses in which the idols were, and then entered it with hymns and praise.

[48] He cast out of it all uncleanness, and settled in it men who observed the law. He also strengthened its fortifications and built in it a house for himself.

[49] The men in the citadel at Jerusalem were prevented from going out to the country and back to buy and sell. So they were very hungry, and many of them perished from famine.

[50] Then they cried to Simon to make peace with them, and he did so. But he expelled them from there and cleansed the citadel from its pollutions.

[51] On the twenty-third day of the second month, in the one hundred and seventy-first year, the Jews entered it with praise and palm branches, and with harps and cymbals and stringed instruments, and with hymns and songs, because a great enemy had been crushed and removed from Israel.

[52] And Simon decreed that every year they should celebrate this day with rejoicing. He strengthened the fortifications of the temple hill alongside the citadel, and he and his men dwelt there.

[53] And Simon saw that John his son had reached manhood, so he made him commander of all the forces, and he dwelt in Gazara.

1Mac.14

[1] In the one hundred and seventy-second year Demetrius the king assembled his forces and marched into Media to secure help, so that he could make war against Trypho.

[2] When Arsaces the king of Persia and Media heard that Demetrius had invaded his territory, he sent one of his commanders to take him alive.

[3] And he went and defeated the army of Demetrius, and seized him and took him to Arsaces, who put him under guard.

[4] The land had rest all the days of Simon. He sought the good of his nation; his rule was pleasing to them, as was the honor shown him, all his days.

[5] To crown all his honors he took Joppa for a harbor, and opened a way to the isles of the sea.

[6] He extended the borders of his nation, and gained full control of the country.

[7] He gathered a host of captives; he ruled over Gazara and Beth-zur and the citadel, and he removed its uncleanness from it; and there was none to oppose him.

[8] They tilled their land in peace; the ground gave its increase, and the trees of the plains their fruit.

[9] Old men sat in the streets; they all talked together of good things; and the youths donned the glories and garments of war.

[10] He supplied the cities with food, and furnished them with the means of defense, till his renown spread to the ends of the earth.

[11] He established peace in the land, and Israel rejoiced with great joy.

[12] Each man sat under his vine and his fig tree, and there was none to make them afraid.

[13] No one was left in the land to fight them, and the kings were crushed in those days.

[14] He strengthened all the humble of his people; he sought out the law, and did away with every lawless and wicked man.

[15] He made the sanctuary glorious, and added to the vessels of the sanctuary.

[16] It was heard in Rome, and as far away as Sparta, that Jonathan had died, and they were deeply grieved.

[17] When they heard that Simon his brother had become high priest in his place, and that he was ruling over the country and the cities in it,

[18] they wrote to him on bronze tablets to renew with him the friendship and alliance which they had established with Judas and Jonathan his brothers.

[19] And these were read before the assembly in Jerusalem.

[20] This is a copy of the letter which the Spartans sent: "The rulers and the city of the Spartans to Simon the high priest and to the elders and the priests and the rest of the Jewish people, our brethren, greeting.

[21] The envoys who were sent to our people have told us about your glory and honor, and we rejoiced at their coming.

[22] And what they said we have recorded in our public decrees, as follows, `Numenius the son of Antiochus and Antipater the son of Jason, envoys of the Jews, have come to us to renew their friendship with us.

[23] It has pleased our people to receive these men with honor and to put a copy of their words in the public archives, so that the people of the Spartans

may have a record of them. And they have sent a copy of this to Simon the high priest.'"

[24] After this Simon sent Numenius to Rome with a large gold shield weighing a thousand minas, to confirm the alliance with the Romans.

[25] When the people heard these things they said, "How shall we thank Simon and his sons?

[26] For he and his brothers and the house of his father have stood firm; they have fought and repulsed Israel's enemies and established its freedom."

[27] So they made a record on bronze tablets and put it upon pillars on Mount Zion. This is a copy of what they wrote: "On the eighteenth day of Elul, in the one hundred and seventy-second year, which is the third year of Simon the great high priest,

[28] in Asaramel, in the great assembly of the priests and the people and the rulers of the nation and the elders of the country, the following was proclaimed to us:

[29] "Since wars often occurred in the country, Simon the son of Mattathias, a priest of the sons of Joarib, and his brothers, exposed themselves to danger and resisted the enemies of their nation, in order that their sanctuary and the law might be perserved; and they brought great glory to their nation.

[30] Jonathan rallied the nation, and became their high priest, and was gathered to his people.

[31] And when their enemies decided to invade their country and lay hands on their sanctuary,

[32] then Simon rose up and fought for his nation. He spent great sums of his own money; he armed the men of his nation's forces and paid them wages.

[33] He fortified the cities of Judea, and Beth-zur on the borders of Judea, where formerly the arms of the enemy had been stored, and he placed there a garrison of Jews.

[34] He also fortified Joppa, which is by the sea, and Gazara, which is on the borders of Azotus, where the enemy formerly dwelt. He settled Jews there, and provided in those cities whatever was necessary for their restoration.

[35] "The people saw Simon's faithfulness and the glory which he had resolved to win for his nation, and they made him their leader and high priest, because he had done all these things and because of the justice and loyalty which he had maintained toward his nation. He sought in every way to exalt his people.

[36] And in his days things prospered in his hands, so that the Gentiles were put out of the country, as were also the men in the city of David in Jerusalem, who had built themselves a citadel from which they used to sally forth and defile the environs of the sanctuary and do great damage to its purity.

[37] He settled Jews in it, and fortified it for the safety of the country and of the city, and built the walls of Jerusalem higher.

[38] "In view of these things King Demetrius confirmed him in the high priesthood,

[39] and he made him one of the king's friends and paid him high honors.

[40] For he had heard that the Jews were addressed by the Romans as friends and allies and brethren, and that the Romans had received the envoys of Simon with honor.

[41] "And the Jews and their priests decided that Simon should be their leader and high priest for ever, until a trustworthy prophet should arise,

[42] and that he should be governor over them and that he should take charge of the sanctuary and appoint men over its tasks and over the country and the weapons and the strongholds, and that he should take charge of the sanctuary,

[43] and that he should be obeyed by all, and that all contracts in the country should be written in his name, and that he should be clothed in purple and wear gold.

[44] "And none of the people or priests shall be permitted to nullify any of these decisions or to oppose what he says, or to convene an assembly in the country without his permission, or to be clothed in purple or put on a gold buckle.

[45] Whoever acts contrary to these decisions or nullifies any of them shall be liable to punishment."

[46] And all the people agreed to grant Simon the right to act in accord with these decisions.

[47] So Simon accepted and agreed to be high priest, to be commander and ethnarch of the Jews and priests, and to be protector of them all.

[48] And they gave orders to inscribe this decree upon bronze tablets, to put them up in a conspicuous place in the precincts of the sanctuary,

[49] and to deposit copies of them in the treasury, so that Simon and his sons might have them.

1Mac.15

[1] Antiochus, the son of Demetrius the king, sent a letter from the islands of the sea to Simon, the priest and ethnarch of the Jews, and to all the nation;

[2] its contents were as follows: "King Antiochus to Simon the high priest and ethnarch and to the nation of the Jews, greeting.

[3] Whereas certain pestilent men have gained control of the kingdom of our fathers, and I intend to lay claim to the kingdom so that I may restore it as it formerly was, and have recruited a host of mercenary troops and have equipped warships,

[4] and intend to make a landing in the country so that I may proceed against those who have destroyed our country and those who have devastated many cities in my kingdom,

[5] now therefore I confirm to you all the tax remissions that the kings before me have granted you, and release from all the other payments from which they have released you.

[6] I permit you to mint your own coinage as money for your country,

[7] and I grant freedom to Jerusalem and the sanctuary. All the weapons which you have prepared and the strongholds which you have built and now hold shall remain yours.

[8] Every debt you owe to the royal treasury and any such future debts shall be canceled for you from henceforth and for all time.

[9] When we gain control of our kingdom, we will bestow great honor upon you and your nation and the temple, so that your glory will become manifest in all the earth."

[10] In the one hundred and seventy-fourth year Antiochus set out and invaded the land of his fathers. All the troops rallied to him, so that there were few with Trypho.

[11] Antiochus pursued him, and he came in his flight to Dor, which is by the sea;

[12] for he knew that troubles had converged upon him, and his troops had deserted him.

[13] So Antiochus encamped against Dor, and with him were a hundred and twenty thousand warriors and eight thousand cavalry.

[14] He surrounded the city, and the ships joined battle from the sea; he pressed the city hard from land and sea, and permitted no one to leave or enter it.

[15] Then Numenius and his companions arrived from Rome, with letters to the kings and countries, in which the following was written:

[16] "Lucius, consul of the Romans, to King Ptolemy, greeting.

[17] The envoys of the Jews have come to us as our friends and allies to renew our ancient friendship and alliance. They had been sent by Simon the high priest and by the people of the Jews,

[18] and have brought a gold shield weighing a thousand minas.

[19] We therefore have decided to write to the kings and countries that they should not seek their harm or make war against them and their cities and their country, or make alliance with those who war against them.

[20] And it has seemed good to us to accept the shield from them.

[21] Therefore if any pestilent men have fled to you from their country, hand them over to Simon the high priest, that he may punish them according to their law."

[22] The consul wrote the same thing to Demetrius the king and to Attalus and Ariarathes and Arsaces,

[23] and to all the countries, and to Sampsames, and to the Spartans, and to Delos, and to Myndos, and to Sicyon, and to Caria, and to Samos, and to Pamphylia, and to Lycia, and to Halicarnassus, and to Rhodes, and to Phaselis, and to Cos, and to Side, and to Aradus and Gortyna and Cnidus and Cyprus and Cyrene.

[24] They also sent a copy of these things to Simon the high priest.

[25] Antiochus the king besieged Dor anew, continually throwing his forces against it and making engines of war; and he shut Trypho up and kept him from going out or in.

[26] And Simon sent to Antiochus two thousand picked men, to fight for him, and silver and gold and much military equipment.

[27] But he refused to receive them, and he broke all the agreements he formerly had made with Simon, and became estranged from him.

[28] He sent to him Athenobius, one of his friends, to confer with him, saying, "You hold control of Joppa and Gazara and the citadel in Jerusalem; they are cities of my kingdom.

[29] You have devastated their territory, you have done great damage in the land, and you have taken possession of many places in my kingdom.

[30] Now then, hand over the cities which you have seized and the tribute money of the places which you have conquered outside the borders of Judea;

[31] or else give me for them five hundred talents of silver, and for the destruction that you have caused and the tribute money of the cities, five hundred talents more. Otherwise we will come and conquer you."

[32] So Athenobius the friend of the king came to Jerusalem, and when he saw the splendor of Simon, and the sideboard with its gold and silver plate, and his great magnificence, he was amazed. He reported to him the words of the king,

[33] but Simon gave him this reply: "We have neither taken foreign land nor seized foreign property, but only the inheritance of our fathers, which at one time had been unjustly taken by our enemies.

[34] Now that we have the opportunity, we are firmly holding the inheritance of our fathers.

[35] As for Joppa and Gazara, which you demand, they were causing great damage among the people and to our land; for them we will give you a hundred talents." Athenobius did not answer him a word,

[36] but returned in wrath to the king and reported to him these words and the splendor of Simon and all that he had seen. And the king was greatly angered.

[37] Now Trypho embarked on a ship and escaped to Orthosia.

[38] Then the king made Cendebeus commander-in-chief of the coastal country, and gave him troops of infantry and cavalry.

[39] He commanded him to encamp against Judea, and commanded him to build up Kedron and fortify its gates, and to make war on the people; but the king pursued Trypho.

[40] So Cendebeus came to Jamnia and began to provoke the people and invade Judea and take the people captive and kill them.

[41] He built up Kedron and stationed there horsemen and troops, so that they might go out and make raids along the highways of Judea, as the king had ordered him.

1Mac.16

[1] John went up from Gazara and reported to Simon his father what Cendebeus had done.

[2] And Simon called in his two older sons Judas and John, and said to them: "I and my brothers and the house of my father have fought the wars of Israel from our youth until this day, and things have prospered in our hands so that we have delivered Israel many times.

[3] But now I have grown old, and you by His mercy are mature in years. Take my place and my brother's, and go out and fight for our nation, and may the help which comes from Heaven be with you."

[4] So John chose out of the country twenty thousand warriors and horsemen, and they marched against Cendebeus and camped for the night in Modein.

[5] Early in the morning they arose and marched into the plain, and behold, a large force of infantry and horsemen was coming to meet them; and a stream lay between them.

[6] Then he and his army lined up against them. And he saw that the soldiers were afraid to cross the stream, so he crossed over first; and when his men saw him, they crossed over after him.

[7] Then he divided the army and placed the horsemen in the midst of the infantry, for the cavalry of the enemy were very numerous.

[8] And they sounded the trumpets, and Cendebeus and his army were put to flight, and many of them were wounded and fell; the rest fled into the stronghold.

[9] At that time Judas the brother of John was wounded, but John pursued them until Cendebeus reached Kedron, which he had built.

[10] They also fled into the towers that were in the fields of Azotus, and John burned it with fire, and about two thousand of them fell. And he returned to Judea safely.

[11] Now Ptolemy the son of Abubus had been appointed governor over the plain of Jericho, and he had much silver and gold,

[12] for he was son-in-law of the high priest.

[13] His heart was lifted up; he determined to get control of the country, and made treacherous plans against Simon and his sons, to do away with them.

[14] Now Simon was visiting the cities of the country and attending to their needs, and he went down to Jericho with Mattathias and Judas his sons, in the one hundred and seventy-seventh year, in the eleventh month, which is the month of Shebat.

[15] The son of Abubus received them treacherously in the little stronghold called Dok, which he had built; he gave them a great banquet, and hid men there.

[16] When Simon and his sons were drunk, Ptolemy and his men rose up, took their weapons, and rushed in against Simon in the banquet hall, and they killed him and his two sons and some of his servants.

[17] So he committed an act of great treachery and returned evil for good.

[18] Then Ptolemy wrote a report about these things and sent it to the king, asking him to send troops to aid him and to turn over to him the cities and the country.

[19] He sent other men to Gazara to do away with John; he sent letters to the captains asking them to come to him so that he might give them silver and gold and gifts;

[20] and he sent other men to take possession of Jerusalem and the temple hill.

[21] But some one ran ahead and reported to John at Gazara that his father and brothers had perished, and that "he has sent men to kill you also."

[22] When he heard this, he was greatly shocked; and he seized the men who came to destroy him and killed them, for he had found out that they were seeking to destroy him.

[23] The rest of the acts of John and his wars and the brave deeds which he did, and the building of the walls which he built, and his achievements,

[24] behold, they are written in the chronicles of his high priesthood, from the time that he became high priest after his father.

2 Maccabees

2Mac.1
[1] The Jewish brethren in Jerusalem and those in the land of Judea, To their Jewish brethren in Egypt, Greeting, and good peace.
[2] May God do good to you, and may he remember his covenant with Abraham and Isaac and Jacob, his faithful servants.
[3] May he give you all a heart to worship him and to do his will with a strong heart and a willing spirit.
[4] May he open your heart to his law and his commandments, and may he bring peace.
[5] May he hear your prayers and be reconciled to you, and may he not forsake you in time of evil.
[6] We are now praying for you here.
[7] In the reign of Demetrius, in the one hundred and sixty-ninth year, we Jews wrote to you, in the critical distress which came upon us in those years after Jason and his company revolted from the holy land and the kingdom
[8] and burned the gate and shed innocent blood. We besought the Lord and we were heard, and we offered sacrifice and cereal offering, and we lighted the lamps and we set out the loaves.
[9] And now see that you keep the feast of booths in the month of Chislev, in the one hundred and eighty-eighth year.
[10] Those in Jerusalem and those in Judea and the senate and Judas, To Aristobulus, who is of the family of the anointed priests, teacher of Ptolemy the king, and to the Jews in Egypt, Greeting, and good health.
[11] Having been saved by God out of grave dangers we thank him greatly for taking our side against the king.
[12] For he drove out those who fought against the holy city.
[13] For when the leader reached Persia with a force that seemed irresistible, they were cut to pieces in the temple of Nanea by a deception employed by the priests of Nanea.
[14] For under pretext of intending to marry her, Antiochus came to the place together with his friends, to secure most of its treasures as a dowry.
[15] When the priests of the temple of Nanea had set out the treasures and Antiochus had come with a few men inside the wall of the sacred precinct, they closed the temple as soon as he entered it.
[16] Opening the secret door in the ceiling, they threw stones and struck down the leader and his men, and dismembered them and cut off their heads and threw them to the people outside.
[17] Blessed in every way be our God, who has brought judgment upon those who have behaved impiously.
[18] Since on the twenty-fifth day of Chislev we shall celebrate the purification of the temple, we thought it necessary to notify you, in order that you also may celebrate the feast of booths and the feast of the fire given when Nehemiah, who built the temple and the altar, offered sacrifices.
[19] For when our fathers were being led captive to Persia, the pious priests of that time took some of the fire of the altar and secretly hid it in the hollow of a dry cistern, where they took such precautions that the place was unknown to any one.
[20] But after many years had passed, when it pleased God, Nehemiah, having been commissioned by the king of Persia, sent the descendants of the priests who had hidden the fire to get it. And when they reported to us that they had not found fire but thick liquid, he ordered them to dip it out and bring it.
[21] And when the materials for the sacrifices were presented, Nehemiah ordered the priests to sprinkle the liquid on the wood and what was laid upon it.
[22] When this was done and some time had passed and the sun, which had been clouded over, shone out, a great fire blazed up, so that all marveled.
[23] And while the sacrifice was being consumed, the priests offered prayer -- the priests and every one. Jonathan led, and the rest responded, as did Nehemiah.
[24] The prayer was to this effect:
"O Lord, Lord God, Creator of all things, who art awe-inspiring and strong and just and merciful, who alone art King and art kind, [25] who alone art bountiful, who alone art just and almighty and eternal, who do rescue Israel from every evil, who didst choose the fathers and consecrate them, [26] accept this sacrifice on behalf of all thy people Israel and preserve thy portion and make it holy. [27] Gather together our scattered people, set free those who are slaves among the Gentiles, look upon those who are rejected and despised, and let the Gentiles know that thou art our God. [28] Afflict those who oppress and are insolent with pride. [29] Plant thy people in thy holy place, as Moses said." [30] Then the priests sang the hymns. [31] And when the materials of the sacrifice were consumed, Nehemiah ordered that the liquid that was left should be poured upon large stones. [32] When this was done, a flame blazed up; but when the light from the altar shone back, it went out. [33] When this matter became known, and it was reported to the king of the Persians that, in the place where the exiled priests had hidden the fire, the liquid had appeared with which Nehemiah and his associates had burned the materials of the sacrifice, [34] the king investigated the matter, and enclosed the place and made it sacred.
[35] And with those persons whom the king favored he exchanged many excellent gifts. [36] Nehemiah and his associates called this "nephthar," which means purification, but by most people it is called naphtha.

2Mac.2

[1] One finds in the records that Jeremiah the prophet ordered those who were being deported to take some of the fire, as has been told,

[2] and that the prophet after giving them the law instructed those who were being deported not to forget the commandments of the Lord, nor to be led astray in their thoughts upon seeing the gold and silver statues and their adornment.

[3] And with other similar words he exhorted them that the law should not depart from their hearts.

[4] It was also in the writing that the prophet, having received an oracle, ordered that the tent and the ark should follow with him, and that he went out to the mountain where Moses had gone up and had seen the inheritance of God.

[5] And Jeremiah came and found a cave, and he brought there the tent and the ark and the altar of incense, and he sealed up the entrance.

[6] Some of those who followed him came up to mark the way, but could not find it.

[7] When Jeremiah learned of it, he rebuked them and declared: "The place shall be unknown until God gathers his people together again and shows his mercy.

[8] And then the Lord will disclose these things, and the glory of the Lord and the cloud will appear, as they were shown in the case of Moses, and as Solomon asked that the place should be specially consecrated."

[9] It was also made clear that being possessed of wisdom Solomon offered sacrifice for the dedication and completion of the temple.

[10] Just as Moses prayed to the Lord, and fire came down from heaven and devoured the sacrifices, so also Solomon prayed, and the fire came down and consumed the whole burnt offerings.

[11] And Moses said, "They were consumed because the sin offering had not been eaten."

[12] Likewise Solomon also kept the eight days.

[13] The same things are reported in the records and in the memoirs of Nehemiah, and also that he founded a library and collected the books about the kings and prophets, and the writings of David, and letters of kings about votive offerings.

[14] In the same way Judas also collected all the books that had been lost on account of the war which had come upon us, and they are in our possession.

[15] So if you have need of them, send people to get them for you.

[16] Since, therefore, we are about to celebrate the purification, we write to you. Will you therefore please keep the days?

[17] It is God who has saved all his people, and has returned the inheritance to all, and the kingship and priesthood and consecration,

[18] as he promised through the law. For we have hope in God that he will soon have mercy upon us and will gather us from everywhere under heaven into his holy place, for he has rescued us from great evils and has purified the place.

[19] The story of Judas Maccabeus and his brothers, and the purification of the great temple, and the dedication of the altar,

[20] and further the wars against Antiochus Epiphanes and his son Eupator,

[21] and the appearances which came from heaven to those who strove zealously on behalf of Judaism, so that though few in number they seized the whole land and pursued the barbarian hordes,

[22] and recovered the temple famous throughout the world and freed the city and restored the laws that were about to be abolished, while the Lord with great kindness became gracious to them --

[23] all this, which has been set forth by Jason of Cyrene in five volumes, we shall attempt to condense into a single book.

[24] For considering the flood of numbers involved and the difficulty there is for those who wish to enter upon the narratives of history because of the mass of material,

[25] we have aimed to please those who wish to read, to make it easy for those who are inclined to memorize, and to profit all readers.

[26] For us who have undertaken the toil of abbreviating, it is no light matter but calls for sweat and loss of sleep,

[27] just as it is not easy for one who prepares a banquet and seeks the benefit of others. However, to secure the gratitude of many we will gladly endure the uncomfortable toil,

[28] leaving the responsibility for exact details to the compiler, while devoting our effort to arriving at the outlines of the condensation.

[29] For as the master builder of a new house must be concerned with the whole construction, while the one who undertakes its painting and decoration has to consider only what is suitable for its adornment, such in my judgment is the case with us.

[30] It is the duty of the original historian to occupy the ground and to discuss matters from every side and to take trouble with details,

[31] but the one who recasts the narrative should be allowed to strive for brevity of expression and to forego exhaustive treatment.

[32] At this point therefore let us begin our narrative, adding only so much to what has already been said; for it is foolish to lengthen the preface while cutting short the history itself.

2Mac.3

[1] While the holy city was inhabited in unbroken peace and the laws were very well observed because

of the piety of the high priest Onias and his hatred of wickedness,

[2] it came about that the kings themselves honored the place and glorified the temple with the finest presents,

[3] so that even Seleucus, the king of Asia, defrayed from his own revenues all the expenses connected with the service of the sacrifices.

[4] But a man named Simon, of the tribe of Benjamin, who had been made captain of the temple, had a disagreement with the high priest about the administration of the city market;

[5] and when he could not prevail over Onias he went to Apollonius of Tarsus, who at that time was governor of Coelesyria and Phoenicia.

[6] He reported to him that the treasury in Jerusalem was full of untold sums of money, so that the amount of the funds could not be reckoned, and that they did not belong to the account of the sacrifices, but that it was possible for them to fall under the control of the king.

[7] When Apollonius met the king, he told him of the money about which he had been informed. The king chose Heliodorus, who was in charge of his affairs, and sent him with commands to effect the removal of the aforesaid money.

[8] Heliodorus at once set out on his journey, ostensibly to make a tour of inspection of the cities of Coelesyria and Phoenicia, but in fact to carry out the king's purpose.

[9] When he had arrived at Jerusalem and had been kindly welcomed by the high priest of the city, he told about the disclosure that had been made and stated why he had come, and he inquired whether this really was the situation.

[10] The high priest explained that there were some deposits belonging to widows and orphans,

[11] and also some money of Hyrcanus, son of Tobias, a man of very prominent position, and that it totaled in all four hundred talents of silver and two hundred of gold. To such an extent the impious Simon had misrepresented the facts.

[12] And he said that it was utterly impossible that wrong should be done to those people who had trusted in the holiness of the place and in the sanctity and inviolability of the temple which is honored throughout the whole world.

[13] But Heliodorus, because of the king's commands which he had, said that this money must in any case be confiscated for the king's treasury.

[14] So he set a day and went in to direct the inspection of these funds. There was no little distress throughout the whole city.

[15] The priests prostrated themselves before the altar in their priestly garments and called toward heaven upon him who had given the law about deposits, that he should keep them safe for those who had deposited them.

[16] To see the appearance of the high priest was to be wounded at heart, for his face and the change in his color disclosed the anguish of his soul.

[17] For terror and bodily trembling had come over the man, which plainly showed to those who looked at him the pain lodged in his heart.

[18] People also hurried out of their houses in crowds to make a general supplication because the holy place was about to be brought into contempt.

[19] Women, girded with sackcloth under their breasts, thronged the streets. Some of the maidens who were kept indoors ran together to the gates, and some to the walls, while others peered out of the windows.

[20] And holding up their hands to heaven, they all made entreaty.

[21] There was something pitiable in the prostration of the whole populace and the anxiety of the high priest in his great anguish.

[22] While they were calling upon the Almighty Lord that he would keep what had been entrusted safe and secure for those who had entrusted it,

[23] Heliodorus went on with what had been decided.

[24] But when he arrived at the treasury with his bodyguard, then and there the Sovereign of spirits and of all authority caused so great a manifestation that all who had been so bold as to accompany him were astounded by the power of God, and became faint with terror.

[25] For there appeared to them a magnificently caparisoned horse, with a rider of frightening mien, and it rushed furiously at Heliodorus and struck at him with its front hoofs. Its rider was seen to have armor and weapons of gold.

[26] Two young men also appeared to him, remarkably strong, gloriously beautiful and splendidly dressed, who stood on each side of him and scourged him continuously, inflicting many blows on him.

[27] When he suddenly fell to the ground and deep darkness came over him, his men took him up and put him on a stretcher

[28] and carried him away, this man who had just entered the aforesaid treasury with a great retinue and all his bodyguard but was now unable to help himself; and they recognized clearly the sovereign power of God.

[29] While he lay prostrate, speechless because of the divine intervention and deprived of any hope of recovery,

[30] they praised the Lord who had acted marvelously for his own place. And the temple, which a little while before was full of fear and disturbance, was filled with joy and gladness, now that the Almighty Lord had appeared.

[31] Quickly some of Heliodorus' friends asked Onias to call upon the Most High and to grant life to one who was lying quite at his last breath.

[32] And the high priest, fearing that the king might get the notion that some foul play had been perpetrated by the Jews with regard to Heliodorus, offered sacrifice for the man's recovery.

[33] While the high priest was making the offering of atonement, the same young men appeared again to Heliodorus dressed in the same clothing, and they stood and said, "Be very grateful to Onias the high priest, since for his sake the Lord has granted you your life.

[34] And see that you, who have been scourged by heaven, report to all men the majestic power of God." Having said this they vanished.

[35] Then Heliodorus offered sacrifice to the Lord and made very great vows to the Savior of his life, and having bidden Onias farewell, he marched off with his forces to the king.

[36] And he bore testimony to all men of the deeds of the supreme God, which he had seen with his own eyes.

[37] When the king asked Heliodorus what sort of person would be suitable to send on another mission to Jerusalem, he replied,

[38] "If you have any enemy or plotter against your government, send him there, for you will get him back thoroughly scourged, if he escapes at all, for there certainly is about the place some power of God.

[39] For he who has his dwelling in heaven watches over that place himself and brings it aid, and he strikes and destroys those who come to do it injury."

[40] This was the outcome of the episode of Heliodorus and the protection of the treasury.

2Mac.4

[1] The previously mentioned Simon, who had informed about the money against his own country, slandered Onias, saying that it was he who had incited Heliodorus and had been the real cause of the misfortune.

[2] He dared to designate as a plotter against the government the man who was the benefactor of the city, the protector of his fellow countrymen, and a zealot for the laws.

[3] When his hatred progressed to such a degree that even murders were committed by one of Simon's approved agents,

[4] Onias recognized that the rivalry was serious and that Apollonius, the son of Menestheus and governor of Coelesyria and Phoenicia, was intensifying the malice of Simon.

[5] So he betook himself to the king, not accusing his fellow citizens but having in view the welfare, both public and private, of all the people.

[6] For he saw that without the king's attention public affairs could not again reach a peaceful settlement, and that Simon would not stop his folly.

[7] When Seleucus died and Antiochus who was called Epiphanes succeeded to the kingdom, Jason the brother of Onias obtained the high priesthood by corruption,

[8] promising the king at an interview three hundred and sixty talents of silver and, from another source of revenue, eighty talents.

[9] In addition to this he promised to pay one hundred and fifty more if permission were given to establish by his authority a gymnasium and a body of youth for it, and to enrol the men of Jerusalem as citizens of Antioch.

[10] When the king assented and Jason came to office, he at once shifted his countrymen over to the Greek way of life.

[11] He set aside the existing royal concessions to the Jews, secured through John the father of Eupolemus, who went on the mission to establish friendship and alliance with the Romans; and he destroyed the lawful ways of living and introduced new customs contrary to the law.

[12] For with alacrity he founded a gymnasium right under the citadel, and he induced the noblest of the young men to wear the Greek hat.

[13] There was such an extreme of Hellenization and increase in the adoption of foreign ways because of the surpassing wickedness of Jason, who was ungodly and no high priest,

[14] that the priests were no longer intent upon their service at the altar. Despising the sanctuary and neglecting the sacrifices, they hastened to take part in the unlawful proceedings in the wrestling arena after the call to the discus,

[15] disdaining the honors prized by their fathers and putting the highest value upon Greek forms of prestige.

[16] For this reason heavy disaster overtook them, and those whose ways of living they admired and wished to imitate completely became their enemies and punished them.

[17] For it is no light thing to show irreverence to the divine laws -- a fact which later events will make clear.

[18] When the quadrennial games were being held at Tyre and the king was present,

[19] the vile Jason sent envoys, chosen as being Antiochian citizens from Jerusalem, to carry three hundred silver drachmas for the sacrifice to Hercules. Those who carried the money, however, thought best not to use it for sacrifice, because that was inappropriate, but to expend it for another purpose.

[20] So this money was intended by the sender for the sacrifice to Hercules, but by the decision of its carriers it was applied to the construction of triremes.

[21] When Apollonius the son of Menestheus was sent to Egypt for the coronation of Philometor as king, Antiochus learned that Philometor had become hostile to his government, and he took measures for his own security. Therefore upon arriving at Joppa he proceeded to Jerusalem.

[22] He was welcomed magnificently by Jason and the city, and ushered in with a blaze of torches and with shouts. Then he marched into Phoenicia.

[23] After a period of three years Jason sent Menelaus, the brother of the previously mentioned Simon, to carry the money to the king and to complete the records of essential business.

[24] But he, when presented to the king, extolled him with an air of authority, and secured the high priesthood for himself, outbidding Jason by three hundred talents of silver.

[25] After receiving the king's orders he returned, possessing no qualification for the high priesthood, but having the hot temper of a cruel tyrant and the rage of a savage wild beast.

[26] So Jason, who after supplanting his own brother was supplanted by another man, was driven as a fugitive into the land of Ammon.

[27] And Menelaus held the office, but he did not pay regularly any of the money promised to the king.

[28] When Sostratus the captain of the citadel kept requesting payment, for the collection of the revenue was his responsibility, the two of them were summoned by the king on account of this issue.

[29] Menelaus left his own brother Lysimachus as deputy in the high priesthood, while Sostratus left Crates, the commander of the Cyprian troops.

[30] While such was the state of affairs, it happened that the people of Tarsus and of Mallus revolted because their cities had been given as a present to Antiochis, the king's concubine.

[31] So the king went hastily to settle the trouble, leaving Andronicus, a man of high rank, to act as his deputy.

[32] But Menelaus, thinking he had obtained a suitable opportunity, stole some of the gold vessels of the temple and gave them to Andronicus; other vessels, as it happened, he had sold to Tyre and the neighboring cities.

[33] When Onias became fully aware of these acts he publicly exposed them, having first withdrawn to a place of sanctuary at Daphne near Antioch.

[34] Therefore Menelaus, taking Andronicus aside, urged him to kill Onias. Andronicus came to Onias, and resorting to treachery offered him sworn pledges and gave him his right hand, and in spite of his suspicion persuaded Onias to come out from the place of sanctuary; then, with no regard for justice, he immediately put him out of the way.

[35] For this reason not only Jews, but many also of other nations, were grieved and displeased at the unjust murder of the man.

[36] When the king returned from the region of Cilicia, the Jews in the city appealed to him with regard to the unreasonable murder of Onias, and the Greeks shared their hatred of the crime.

[37] Therefore Antiochus was grieved at heart and filled with pity, and wept because of the moderation and good conduct of the deceased;

[38] and inflamed with anger, he immediately stripped off the purple robe from Andronicus, tore off his garments, and led him about the whole city to that very place where he had committed the outrage against Onias, and there he dispatched the bloodthirsty fellow. The Lord thus repaid him with the punishment he deserved.

[39] When many acts of sacrilege had been committed in the city by Lysimachus with the connivance of Menelaus, and when report of them had spread abroad, the populace gathered against Lysimachus, because many of the gold vessels had already been stolen.

[40] And since the crowds were becoming aroused and filled with anger, Lysimachus armed about three thousand men and launched an unjust attack, under the leadership of a certain Auranus, a man advanced in years and no less advanced in folly.

[41] But when the Jews became aware of Lysimachus' attack, some picked up stones, some blocks of wood, and others took handfuls of the ashes that were lying about, and threw them in wild confusion at Lysimachus and his men.

[42] As a result, they wounded many of them, and killed some, and put them all to flight; and the temple robber himself they killed close by the treasury.

[43] Charges were brought against Menelaus about this incident.

[44] When the king came to Tyre, three men sent by the senate presented the case before him.

[45] But Menelaus, already as good as beaten, promised a substantial bribe to Ptolemy son of Dorymenes to win over the king.

[46] Therefore Ptolemy, taking the king aside into a colonnade as if for refreshment, induced the king to change his mind.

[47] Menelaus, the cause of all the evil, he acquitted of the charges against him, while he sentenced to death those unfortunate men, who would have been freed uncondemned if they had pleaded even before Scythians.

[48] And so those who had spoken for the city and the villages and the holy vessels quickly suffered the unjust penalty.

[49] Therefore even the Tyrians, showing their hatred of the crime, provided magnificently for their funeral.

[50] But Menelaus, because of the cupidity of those in power, remained in office, growing in wickedness, having become the chief plotter against his fellow citizens.

2Mac.5

[1] About this time Antiochus made his second invasion of Egypt.

[2] And it happened that over all the city, for almost forty days, there appeared golden-clad horsemen charging through the air, in companies fully armed with lances and drawn swords --

[3] troops of horsemen drawn up, attacks and counterattacks made on this side and on that, brandishing of shields, massing of spears, hurling of missiles, the flash of golden trappings, and armor of all sorts.

[4] Therefore all men prayed that the apparition might prove to have been a good omen.

[5] When a false rumor arose that Antiochus was dead, Jason took no less than a thousand men and suddenly made an assault upon the city. When the troops upon the wall had been forced back and at last the city was being taken, Menelaus took refuge in the citadel.

[6] But Jason kept relentlessly slaughtering his fellow citizens, not realizing that success at the cost of one's kindred is the greatest misfortune, but imagining that he was setting up trophies of victory over enemies and not over fellow countrymen.

[7] He did not gain control of the government, however; and in the end got only disgrace from his conspiracy, and fled again into the country of the Ammonites.

[8] Finally he met a miserable end. Accused before Aretas the ruler of the Arabs, fleeing from city to city, pursued by all men, hated as a rebel against the laws, and abhorred as the executioner of his country and his fellow citizens, he was cast ashore in Egypt;

[9] and he who had driven many from their own country into exile died in exile, having embarked to go to the Lacedaemonians in hope of finding protection because of their kinship.

[10] He who had cast out many to lie unburied had no one to mourn for him; he had no funeral of any sort and no place in the tomb of his fathers.

[11] When news of what had happened reached the king, he took it to mean that Judea was in revolt. So, raging inwardly, he left Egypt and took the city by storm.

[12] And he commanded his soldiers to cut down relentlessly every one they met and to slay those who went into the houses.

[13] Then there was killing of young and old, destruction of boys, women, and children, and slaughter of virgins and infants.

[14] Within the total of three days eighty thousand were destroyed, forty thousand in hand-to-hand fighting; and as many were sold into slavery as were slain.

[15] Not content with this, Antiochus dared to enter the most holy temple in all the world, guided by Menelaus, who had become a traitor both to the laws and to his country.

[16] He took the holy vessels with his polluted hands, and swept away with profane hands the votive offerings which other kings had made to enhance the glory and honor of the place.

[17] Antiochus was elated in spirit, and did not perceive that the Lord was angered for a little while because of the sins of those who dwelt in the city, and that therefore he was disregarding the holy place.

[18] But if it had not happened that they were involved in many sins, this man would have been scourged and turned back from his rash act as soon as he came forward, just as Heliodorus was, whom Seleucus the king sent to inspect the treasury.

[19] But the Lord did not choose the nation for the sake of the holy place, but the place for the sake of the nation.

[20] Therefore the place itself shared in the misfortunes that befell the nation and afterward participated in its benefits; and what was forsaken in the wrath of the Almighty was restored again in all its glory when the great Lord became reconciled.

[21] So Antiochus carried off eighteen hundred talents from the temple, and hurried away to Antioch, thinking in his arrogance that he could sail on the land and walk on the sea, because his mind was elated.

[22] And he left governors to afflict the people: at Jerusalem, Philip, by birth a Phrygian and in character more barbarous than the man who appointed him;

[23] and at Gerizim, Andronicus; and besides these Menelaus, who lorded it over his fellow citizens worse than the others did. In his malice toward the Jewish citizens,

[24] Antiochus sent Apollonius, the captain of the Mysians, with an army of twenty-two thousand, and commanded him to slay all the grown men and to sell the women and boys as slaves.

[25] When this man arrived in Jerusalem, he pretended to be peaceably disposed and waited until the holy sabbath day; then, finding the Jews not at work, he ordered his men to parade under arms.

[26] He put to the sword all those who came out to see them, then rushed into the city with his armed men and killed great numbers of people.

[27] But Judas Maccabeus, with about nine others, got away to the wilderness, and kept himself and his companions alive in the mountains as wild animals do; they continued to live on what grew wild, so that they might not share in the defilement.

2Mac.6

[1] Not long after this, the king sent an Athenian senator to compel the Jews to forsake the laws of their fathers and cease to live by the laws of God,

[2] and also to pollute the temple in Jerusalem and call it the temple of Olympian Zeus, and to call the one in Gerizim the temple of Zeus the Friend of Strangers, as did the people who dwelt in that place.

[3] Harsh and utterly grievous was the onslaught of evil.

[4] For the temple was filled with debauchery and reveling by the Gentiles, who dallied with harlots and had intercourse with women within the sacred precincts, and besides brought in things for sacrifice that were unfit.

[5] The altar was covered with abominable offerings which were forbidden by the laws.

[6] A man could neither keep the sabbath, nor observe the feasts of his fathers, nor so much as confess himself to be a Jew.

[7] On the monthly celebration of the king's birthday, the Jews were taken, under bitter constraint, to partake of the sacrifices; and when the feast of Dionysus came, they were compelled to walk in the procession in honor of Dionysus, wearing wreaths of ivy.

[8] At the suggestion of Ptolemy a decree was issued to the neighboring Greek cities, that they should adopt the same policy toward the Jews and make them partake of the sacrifices,

[9] and should slay those who did not choose to change over to Greek customs. One could see, therefore, the misery that had come upon them.

[10] For example, two women were brought in for having circumcised their children. These women they publicly paraded about the city, with their babies hung at their breasts, then hurled them down headlong from the wall.

[11] Others who had assembled in the caves near by, to observe the seventh day secretly, were betrayed to Philip and were all burned together, because their piety kept them from defending themselves, in view of their regard for that most holy day.

[12] Now I urge those who read this book not to be depressed by such calamities, but to recognize that these punishments were designed not to destroy but to discipline our people.

[13] In fact, not to let the impious alone for long, but to punish them immediately, is a sign of great kindness.

[14] For in the case of the other nations the Lord waits patiently to punish them until they have reached the full measure of their sins; but he does not deal in this way with us,

[15] in order that he may not take vengeance on us afterward when our sins have reached their height.

[16] Therefore he never withdraws his mercy from us. Though he disciplines us with calamities, he does not forsake his own people.

[17] Let what we have said serve as a reminder; we must go on briefly with the story.

[18] Eleazar, one of the scribes in high position, a man now advanced in age and of noble presence, was being forced to open his mouth to eat swine's flesh.

[19] But he, welcoming death with honor rather than life with pollution, went up to the the rack of his own accord, spitting out the flesh,

[20] as men ought to go who have the courage to refuse things that it is not right to taste, even for the natural love of life.

[21] Those who were in charge of that unlawful sacrifice took the man aside, because of their long acquaintance with him, and privately urged him to bring meat of his own providing, proper for him to use, and pretend that he was eating the flesh of the sacrificial meal which had been commanded by the king,

[22] so that by doing this he might be saved from death, and be treated kindly on account of his old friendship with them.

[23] But making a high resolve, worthy of his years and the dignity of his old age and the gray hairs which he had reached with distinction and his excellent life even from childhood, and moreover according to the holy God-given law, he declared himself quickly, telling them to send him to Hades.

[24] "Such pretense is not worthy of our time of life," he said, "lest many of the young should suppose that Eleazar in his ninetieth year has gone over to an alien religion,

[25] and through my pretense, for the sake of living a brief moment longer, they should be led astray because of me, while I defile and disgrace my old age.

[26] For even if for the present I should avoid the punishment of men, yet whether I live or die I shall not escape the hands of the Almighty.

[27] Therefore, by manfully giving up my life now, I will show myself worthy of my old age

[28] and leave to the young a noble example of how to die a good death willingly and nobly for the revered and holy laws." When he had said this, he went at once to the rack.

[29] And those who a little before had acted toward him with good will now changed to ill will, because the words he had uttered were in their opinion sheer madness.

[30] When he was about to die under the blows, he groaned aloud and said: "It is clear to the Lord in his holy knowledge that, though I might have been saved from death, I am enduring terrible sufferings in my body under this beating, but in my soul I am glad to suffer these things because I fear him."

[31] So in this way he died, leaving in his death an example of nobility and a memorial of courage, not only to the young but to the great body of his nation. 2Mac.7

[1] It happened also that seven brothers and their mother were arrested and were being compelled by the king, under torture with whips and cords, to partake of unlawful swine's flesh.

[2] One of them, acting as their spokesman, said, "What do you intend to ask and learn from us? For we are ready to die rather than transgress the laws of our fathers."

[3] The king fell into a rage, and gave orders that pans and caldrons be heated.

[4] These were heated immediately, and he commanded that the tongue of their spokesman be cut out and that they scalp him and cut off his hands and feet, while the rest of the brothers and the mother looked on.

[5] When he was utterly helpless, the king ordered them to take him to the fire, still breathing, and to fry him in a pan. The smoke from the pan spread widely, but the brothers and their mother encouraged one another to die nobly, saying,

[6] "The Lord God is watching over us and in truth has compassion on us, as Moses declared in his song which bore witness against the people to their faces, when he said, `And he will have compassion on his servants.'"

[7] After the first brother had died in this way, they brought forward the second for their sport. They tore off the skin of his head with the hair, and asked him, "Will you eat rather than have your body punished limb by limb?"

[8] He replied in the language of his fathers, and said to them, "No." Therefore he in turn underwent tortures as the first brother had done.

[9] And when he was at his last breath, he said, "You accursed wretch, you dismiss us from this present life, but the King of the universe will raise us up to an everlasting renewal of life, because we have died for his laws."

[10] After him, the third was the victim of their sport. When it was demanded, he quickly put out his tongue and courageously stretched forth his hands,

[11] and said nobly, "I got these from Heaven, and because of his laws I disdain them, and from him I hope to get them back again."

[12] As a result the king himself and those with him were astonished at the young man's spirit, for he regarded his sufferings as nothing.

[13] When he too had died, they maltreated and tortured the fourth in the same way.

[14] And when he was near death, he said, "One cannot but choose to die at the hands of men and to cherish the hope that God gives of being raised again

by him. But for you there will be no resurrection to life!"

[15] Next they brought forward the fifth and maltreated him.

[16] But he looked at the king, and said, "Because you have authority among men, mortal though you are, you do what you please. But do not think that God has forsaken our people.

[17] Keep on, and see how his mighty power will torture you and your descendants!"

[18] After him they brought forward the sixth. And when he was about to die, he said, "Do not deceive yourself in vain. For we are suffering these things on our own account, because of our sins against our own God. Therefore astounding things have happened.

[19] But do not think that you will go unpunished for having tried to fight against God!"

[20] The mother was especially admirable and worthy of honorable memory. Though she saw her seven sons perish within a single day, she bore it with good courage because of her hope in the Lord.

[21] She encouraged each of them in the language of their fathers. Filled with a noble spirit, she fired her woman's reasoning with a man's courage, and said to them,

[22] "I do not know how you came into being in my womb. It was not I who gave you life and breath, nor I who set in order the elements within each of you.

[23] Therefore the Creator of the world, who shaped the beginning of man and devised the origin of all things, will in his mercy give life and breath back to you again, since you now forget yourselves for the sake of his laws."

[24] Antiochus felt that he was being treated with contempt, and he was suspicious of her reproachful tone. The youngest brother being still alive, Antiochus not only appealed to him in words, but promised with oaths that he would make him rich and enviable if he would turn from the ways of his fathers, and that he would take him for his friend and entrust him with public affairs.

[25] Since the young man would not listen to him at all, the king called the mother to him and urged her to advise the youth to save himself.

[26] After much urging on his part, she undertook to persuade her son.

[27] But, leaning close to him, she spoke in their native tongue as follows, deriding the cruel tyrant: "My son, have pity on me. I carried you nine months in my womb, and nursed you for three years, and have reared you and brought you up to this point in your life, and have taken care of you.

[28] I beseech you, my child, to look at the heaven and the earth and see everything that is in them, and recognize that God did not make them out of things that existed. Thus also mankind comes into being.

[29] Do not fear this butcher, but prove worthy of your brothers. Accept death, so that in God's mercy I may get you back again with your brothers."

[30] While she was still speaking, the young man said, "What are you waiting for? I will not obey the king's command, but I obey the command of the law that was given to our fathers through Moses.

[31] But you, who have contrived all sorts of evil against the Hebrews, will certainly not escape the hands of God.

[32] For we are suffering because of our own sins.

[33] And if our living Lord is angry for a little while, to rebuke and discipline us, he will again be reconciled with his own servants.

[34] But you, unholy wretch, you most defiled of all men, do not be elated in vain and puffed up by uncertain hopes, when you raise your hand against the children of heaven.

[35] You have not yet escaped the judgment of the almighty, all-seeing God.

[36] For our brothers after enduring a brief suffering have drunk of everflowing life under God's covenant; but you, by the judgment of God, will receive just punishment for your arrogance.

[37] I, like my brothers, give up body and life for the laws of our fathers, appealing to God to show mercy soon to our nation and by afflictions and plagues to make you confess that he alone is God,

[38] and through me and my brothers to bring to an end the wrath of the Almighty which has justly fallen on our whole nation."

[39] The king fell into a rage, and handled him worse than the others, being exasperated at his scorn.

[40] So he died in his integrity, putting his whole trust in the Lord.

[41] Last of all, the mother died, after her sons.

[42] Let this be enough, then, about the eating of sacrifices and the extreme tortures.

2Mac.8

[1] But Judas, who was also called Maccabeus, and his companions secretly entered the villages and summoned their kinsmen and enlisted those who had continued in the Jewish faith, and so they gathered about six thousand men.

[2] They besought the Lord to look upon the people who were oppressed by all, and to have pity on the temple which had been profaned by ungodly men,

[3] and to have mercy on the city which was being destroyed and about to be leveled to the ground, and to hearken to the blood that cried out to him,

[4] and to remember also the lawless destruction of the innocent babies and the blasphemies committed against his name, and to show his hatred of evil.

[5] As soon as Maccabeus got his army organized, the Gentiles could not withstand him, for the wrath of the Lord had turned to mercy.

[6] Coming without warning, he would set fire to towns and villages. He captured strategic positions and put to flight not a few of the enemy.

[7] He found the nights most advantageous for such attacks. And talk of his valor spread everywhere.

[8] When Philip saw that the man was gaining ground little by little, and that he was pushing ahead with more frequent successes, he wrote to Ptolemy, the governor of Coelesyria and Phoenicia, for aid to the king's government.

[9] And Ptolemy promptly appointed Nicanor the son of Patroclus, one of the king's chief friends, and sent him, in command of no fewer than twenty thousand Gentiles of all nations, to wipe out the whole race of Judea. He associated with him Gorgias, a general and a man of experience in military service.

[10] Nicanor determined to make up for the king the tribute due to the Romans, two thousand talents, by selling the captured Jews into slavery.

[11] And he immediately sent to the cities on the seacoast, inviting them to buy Jewish slaves and promising to hand over ninety slaves for a talent, not expecting the judgment from the Almighty that was about to overtake him.

[12] Word came to Judas concerning Nicanor's invasion; and when he told his companions of the arrival of the army,

[13] those who were cowardly and distrustful of God's justice ran off and got away.

[14] Others sold all their remaining property, and at the same time besought the Lord to rescue those who had been sold by the ungodly Nicanor before he ever met them,

[15] if not for their own sake, yet for the sake of the covenants made with their fathers, and because he had called them by his holy and glorious name.

[16] But Maccabeus gathered his men together, to the number six thousand, and exhorted them not to be frightened by the enemy and not to fear the great multitude of Gentiles who were wickedly coming against them, but to fight nobly,

[17] keeping before their eyes the lawless outrage which the Gentiles had committed against the holy place, and the torture of the derided city, and besides, the overthrow of their ancestral way of life.

[18] "For they trust to arms and acts of daring," he said, "but we trust in the Almighty God, who is able with a single nod to strike down those who are coming against us and even the whole world."

[19] Moreover, he told them of the times when help came to their ancestors; both the time of Sennacherib, when one hundred and eighty-five thousand perished,

[20] and the time of the battle with the Galatians that took place in Babylonia, when eight thousand in all went into the affair, with four thousand Macedonians; and when the Macedonians were hard pressed, the

eight thousand, by the help that came to them from heaven, destroyed one hundred and twenty thousand and took much booty.

[21] With these words he filled them with good courage and made them ready to die for their laws and their country; then he divided his army into four parts.

[22] He appointed his brothers also, Simon and Joseph and Jonathan, each to command a division, putting fifteen hundred men under each.

[23] Besides, he appointed Eleazar to read aloud from the holy book, and gave the watchword, "God's help"; then, leading the first division himself, he joined battle with Nicanor.

[24] With the Almighty as their ally, they slew more than nine thousand of the enemy, and wounded and disabled most of Nicanor's army, and forced them all to flee.

[25] They captured the money of those who had come to buy them as slaves. After pursuing them for some distance, they were obliged to return because the hour was late.

[26] For it was the day before the sabbath, and for that reason they did not continue their pursuit.

[27] And when they had collected the arms of the enemy and stripped them of their spoils, they kept the sabbath, giving great praise and thanks to the Lord, who had preserved them for that day and allotted it to them as the beginning of mercy.

[28] After the sabbath they gave some of the spoils to those who had been tortured and to the widows and orphans, and distributed the rest among themselves and their children.

[29] When they had done this, they made common supplication and besought the merciful Lord to be wholly reconciled with his servants.

[30] In encounters with the forces of Timothy and Bacchides they killed more than twenty thousand of them and got possession of some exceedingly high strongholds, and they divided very much plunder, giving to those who had been tortured and to the orphans and widows, and also to the aged, shares equal to their own.

[31] Collecting the arms of the enemy, they stored them all carefully in strategic places, and carried the rest of the spoils to Jerusalem.

[32] They killed the commander of Timothy's forces, a most unholy man, and one who had greatly troubled the Jews.

[33] While they were celebrating the victory in the city of their fathers, they burned those who had set fire to the sacred gates, Callisthenes and some others, who had fled into one little house; so these received the proper recompense for their impiety.

[34] The thrice-accursed Nicanor, who had brought the thousand merchants to buy the Jews,

[35] having been humbled with the help of the Lord by opponents whom he regarded as of the least account, took off his splendid uniform and made his way alone like a runaway slave across the country till he reached Antioch, having succeeded chiefly in the destruction of his own army!

[36] Thus he who had undertaken to secure tribute for the Romans by the capture of the people of Jerusalem proclaimed that the Jews had a Defender, and that therefore the Jews were invulnerable, because they followed the laws ordained by him.

2Mac.9

[1] About that time, as it happened, Antiochus had retreated in disorder from the region of Persia.

[2] For he had entered the city called Persepolis, and attempted to rob the temples and control the city. Therefore the people rushed to the rescue with arms, and Antiochus and his men were defeated, with the result that Antiochus was put to flight by the inhabitants and beat a shameful retreat.

[3] While he was in Ecbatana, news came to him of what had happened to Nicanor and the forces of Timothy.

[4] Transported with rage, he conceived the idea of turning upon the Jews the injury done by those who had put him to flight; so he ordered his charioteer to drive without stopping until he completed the journey. But the judgment of heaven rode with him! For in his arrogance he said, "When I get there I will make Jerusalem a cemetery of Jews."

[5] But the all-seeing Lord, the God of Israel, struck him an incurable and unseen blow. As soon as he ceased speaking he was seized with a pain in his bowels for which there was no relief and with sharp internal tortures --

[6] and that very justly, for he had tortured the bowels of others with many and strange inflictions.

[7] Yet he did not in any way stop his insolence, but was even more filled with arrogance, breathing fire in his rage against the Jews, and giving orders to hasten the journey. And so it came about that he fell out of his chariot as it was rushing along, and the fall was so hard as to torture every limb of his body.

[8] Thus he who had just been thinking that he could command the waves of the sea, in his superhuman arrogance, and imagining that he could weigh the high mountains in a balance, was brought down to earth and carried in a litter, making the power of God manifest to all.

[9] And so the ungodly man's body swarmed with worms, and while he was still living in anguish and pain, his flesh rotted away, and because of his stench the whole army felt revulsion at his decay.

[10] Because of his intolerable stench no one was able to carry the man who a little while before had thought that he could touch the stars of heaven.

[11] Then it was that, broken in spirit, he began to lose much of his arrogance and to come to his senses under the scourge of God, for he was tortured with pain every moment.

[12] And when he could not endure his own stench, he uttered these words: "It is right to be subject to God, and no mortal should think that he is equal to God."

[13] Then the abominable fellow made a vow to the Lord, who would no longer have mercy on him, stating

[14] that the holy city, which he was hastening to level to the ground and to make a cemetery, he was now declaring to be free;

[15] and the Jews, whom he had not considered worth burying but had planned to throw out with their children to the beasts, for the birds to pick, he would make, all of them, equal to citizens of Athens;

[16] and the holy sanctuary, which he had formerly plundered, he would adorn with the finest offerings; and the holy vessels he would give back, all of them, many times over; and the expenses incurred for the sacrifices he would provide from his own revenues;

[17] and in addition to all this he also would become a Jew and would visit every inhabited place to proclaim the power of God.

[18] But when his sufferings did not in any way abate, for the judgment of God had justly come upon him, he gave up all hope for himself and wrote to the Jews the following letter, in the form of a supplication. This was its content:

[19] "To his worthy Jewish citizens, Antiochus their king and general sends hearty greetings and good wishes for their health and prosperity.

[20] If you and your children are well and your affairs are as you wish, I am glad. As my hope is in heaven,

[21] I remember with affection your esteem and good will. On my way back from the region of Persia I suffered an annoying illness, and I have deemed it necessary to take thought for the general security of all.

[22] I do not despair of my condition, for I have good hope of recovering from my illness,

[23] but I observed that my father, on the occasions when he made expeditions into the upper country, appointed his successor,

[24] so that, if anything unexpected happened or any unwelcome news came, the people throughout the realm would not be troubled, for they would know to whom the government was left.

[25] Moreover, I understand how the princes along the borders and the neighbors to my kingdom keep watching for opportunities and waiting to see what will happen. So I have appointed my son Antiochus to be king, whom I have often entrusted and commended to most of you when I hastened off to the upper provinces; and I have written to him what is written here.

[26] I therefore urge and beseech you to remember the public and private services rendered to you and to maintain your present good will, each of you, toward me and my son.

[27] For I am sure that he will follow my policy and will treat you with moderation and kindness."

[28] So the murderer and blasphemer, having endured the more intense suffering, such as he had inflicted on others, came to the end of his life by a most pitiable fate, among the mountains in a strange land.

[29] And Philip, one of his courtiers, took his body home; then, fearing the son of Antiochus, he betook himself to Ptolemy Philometor in Egypt.

2Mac.10

[1] Now Maccabeus and his followers, the Lord leading them on, recovered the temple and the city;

[2] and they tore down the altars which had been built in the public square by the foreigners, and also destroyed the sacred precincts.

[3] They purified the sanctuary, and made another altar of sacrifice; then, striking fire out of flint, they offered sacrifices, after a lapse of two years, and they burned incense and lighted lamps and set out the bread of the Presence.

[4] And when they had done this, they fell prostrate and besought the Lord that they might never again fall into such misfortunes, but that, if they should ever sin, they might be disciplined by him with forbearance and not be handed over to blasphemous and barbarous nations.

[5] It happened that on the same day on which the sanctuary had been profaned by the foreigners, the purification of the sanctuary took place, that is, on the twenty-fifth day of the same month, which was Chislev.

[6] And they celebrated it for eight days with rejoicing, in the manner of the feast of booths, remembering how not long before, during the feast of booths, they had been wandering in the mountains and caves like wild animals.

[7] Therefore bearing ivy-wreathed wands and beautiful branches and also fronds of palm, they offered hymns of thanksgiving to him who had given success to the purifying of his own holy place.

[8] They decreed by public ordinance and vote that the whole nation of the Jews should observe these days every year.

[9] Such then was the end of Antiochus, who was called Epiphanes.

[10] Now we will tell what took place under Antiochus Eupator, who was the son of that ungodly man, and will give a brief summary of the principal calamities of the wars.

[11] This man, when he succeeded to the kingdom, appointed one Lysias to have charge of the government and to be chief governor of Coelesyria and Phoenicia.

[12] Ptolemy, who was called Macron, took the lead in showing justice to the Jews because of the wrong that had been done to them, and attempted to maintain peaceful relations with them.

[13] As a result he was accused before Eupator by the king's friends. He heard himself called a traitor at every turn, because he had abandoned Cyprus, which Philometor had entrusted to him, and had gone over to Antiochus Epiphanes. Unable to command the respect due his office, he took poison and ended his life.

[14] When Gorgias became governor of the region, he maintained a force of mercenaries, and at every turn kept on warring against the Jews.

[15] Besides this, the Idumeans, who had control of important strongholds, were harassing the Jews; they received those who were banished from Jerusalem, and endeavored to keep up the war.

[16] But Maccabeus and his men, after making solemn supplication and beseeching God to fight on their side, rushed to the strongholds of the Idumeans.

[17] Attacking them vigorously, they gained possession of the places, and beat off all who fought upon the wall, and slew those whom they encountered, killing no fewer than twenty thousand.

[18] When no less than nine thousand took refuge in two very strong towers well equipped to withstand a siege,

[19] Maccabeus left Simon and Joseph, and also Zacchaeus and his men, a force sufficient to besiege them; and he himself set off for places where he was more urgently needed.

[20] But the men with Simon, who were money-hungry, were bribed by some of those who were in the towers, and on receiving seventy thousand drachmas let some of them slip away.

[21] When word of what had happened came to Maccabeus, he gathered the leaders of the people, and accused these men of having sold their brethren for money by setting their enemies free to fight against them.

[22] Then he slew these men who had turned traitor, and immediately captured the two towers.

[23] Having success at arms in everything he undertook, he destroyed more than twenty thousand in the two strongholds.

[24] Now Timothy, who had been defeated by the Jews before, gathered a tremendous force of mercenaries and collected the cavalry from Asia in no small number. He came on, intending to take Judea by storm.

[25] As he drew near, Maccabeus and his men sprinkled dust upon their heads and girded their loins with sackcloth, in supplication to God.

[26] Falling upon the steps before the altar, they besought him to be gracious to them and to be an enemy to their enemies and an adversary to their adversaries, as the law declares.

[27] And rising from their prayer they took up their arms and advanced a considerable distance from the city; and when they came near to the enemy they halted.

[28] Just as dawn was breaking, the two armies joined battle, the one having as pledge of success and victory not only their valor but their reliance upon the Lord, while the other made rage their leader in the fight.

[29] When the battle became fierce, there appeared to the enemy from heaven five resplendent men on horses with golden bridles, and they were leading the Jews.

[30] Surrounding Maccabeus and protecting him with their own armor and weapons, they kept him from being wounded. And they showered arrows and thunderbolts upon the enemy, so that, confused and blinded, they were thrown into disorder and cut to pieces.

[31] Twenty thousand five hundred were slaughtered, besides six hundred horsemen.

[32] Timothy himself fled to a stronghold called Gazara, especially well garrisoned, where Chaereas was commander.

[33] Then Maccabeus and his men were glad, and they besieged the fort for four days.

[34] The men within, relying on the strength of the place, blasphemed terribly and hurled out wicked words.

[35] But at dawn of the fifth day, twenty young men in the army of Maccabeus, fired with anger because of the blasphemies, bravely stormed the wall and with savage fury cut down every one they met.

[36] Others who came up in the same way wheeled around against the defenders and set fire to the towers; they kindled fires and burned the blasphemers alive. Others broke open the gates and let in the rest of the force, and they occupied the city.

[37] They killed Timothy, who was hidden in a cistern, and his brother Chaereas, and Apollophanes.

[38] When they had accomplished these things, with hymns and thanksgivings they blessed the Lord who shows great kindness to Israel and gives them the victory.

2Mac.11

[1] Very soon after this, Lysias, the king's guardian and kinsman, who was in charge of the government, being vexed at what had happened,

[2] gathered about eighty thousand men and all his cavalry and came against the Jews. He intended to make the city a home for Greeks,

[3] and to levy tribute on the temple as he did on the sacred places of the other nations, and to put up the high priesthood for sale every year.

[4] He took no account whatever of the power of God, but was elated with his ten thousands of infantry, and his thousands of cavalry, and his eighty elephants.

[5] Invading Judea, he approached Beth-zur, which was a fortified place about five leagues from Jerusalem, and pressed it hard.

[6] When Maccabeus and his men got word that Lysias was besieging the strongholds, they and all the people, with lamentations and tears, besought the Lord to send a good angel to save Israel.

[7] Maccabeus himself was the first to take up arms, and he urged the others to risk their lives with him to aid their brethren. Then they eagerly rushed off together.

[8] And there, while they were still near Jerusalem, a horseman appeared at their head, clothed in white and brandishing weapons of gold.

[9] And they all together praised the merciful God, and were strengthened in heart, ready to assail not only men but the wildest beasts or walls of iron.

[10] They advanced in battle order, having their heavenly ally, for the Lord had mercy on them.

[11] They hurled themselves like lions against the enemy, and slew eleven thousand of them and sixteen hundred horsemen, and forced all the rest to flee.

[12] Most of them got away stripped and wounded, and Lysias himself escaped by disgraceful flight.

[13] And as he was not without intelligence, he pondered over the defeat which had befallen him, and realized that the Hebrews were invincible because the mighty God fought on their side. So he sent to them

[14] and persuaded them to settle everything on just terms, promising that he would persuade the king, constraining him to be their friend.

[15] Maccabeus, having regard for the common good, agreed to all that Lysias urged. For the king granted every request in behalf of the Jews which Maccabeus delivered to Lysias in writing.

[16] The letter written to the Jews by Lysias was to this effect: "Lysias to the people of the Jews, greeting.

[17] John and Absalom, who were sent by you, have delivered your signed communication and have asked about the matters indicated therein.

[18] I have informed the king of everything that needed to be brought before him, and he has agreed to what was possible.

[19] If you will maintain your good will toward the government, I will endeavor for the future to help promote your welfare.

[20] And concerning these matters and their details, I have ordered these men and my representatives to confer with you.

[21] Farewell. The one hundred and forty-eighth year, Dioscorinthius twenty-fourth."

[22] The king's letter ran thus: "King Antiochus to his brother Lysias, greeting.

[23] Now that our father has gone on to the gods, we desire that the subjects of the kingdom be undisturbed in caring for their own affairs.

[24] We have heard that the Jews do not consent to our father's change to Greek customs but prefer their own way of living and ask that their own customs be allowed them.

[25] Accordingly, since we choose that this nation also be free from disturbance, our decision is that their temple be restored to them and that they live according to the customs of their ancestors.

[26] You will do well, therefore, to send word to them and give them pledges of friendship, so that they may know our policy and be of good cheer and go on happily in the conduct of their own affairs."

[27] To the nation the king's letter was as follows: "King Antiochus to the senate of the Jews and to the other Jews, greeting.

[28] If you are well, it is as we desire. We also are in good health.

[29] Menelaus has informed us that you wish to return home and look after your own affairs.

[30] Therefore those who go home by the thirtieth day of Xanthicus will have our pledge of friendship and full permission

[31] for the Jews to enjoy their own food and laws, just as formerly, and none of them shall be molested in any way for what he may have done in ignorance.

[32] And I have also sent Menelaus to encourage you.

[33] Farewell. The one hundred and forty-eighth year, Xanthicus fifteenth."

[34] The Romans also sent them a letter, which read thus: "Quintus Memmius and Titus Manius, envoys of the Romans, to the people of the Jews, greeting.

[35] With regard to what Lysias the kinsman of the king has granted you, we also give consent.

[36] But as to the matters which he decided are to be referred to the king, as soon as you have considered them, send some one promptly, so that we may make proposals appropriate for you. For we are on our way to Antioch.

[37] Therefore make haste and send some men, so that we may have your judgment.

[38] Farewell. The one hundred and forty-eighth year, Xanthicus fifteenth."

2Mac.12

[1] When this agreement had been reached, Lysias returned to the king, and the Jews went about their farming.

[2] But some of the governors in various places, Timothy and Apollonius the son of Gennaeus, as well as Hieronymus and Demophon, and in addition to

these Nicanor the governor of Cyprus, would not let them live quietly and in peace.

[3] And some men of Joppa did so ungodly a deed as this: they invited the Jews who lived among them to embark, with their wives and children, on boats which they had provided, as though there were no ill will to the Jews;

[4] and this was done by public vote of the city. And when they accepted, because they wished to live peaceably and suspected nothing, the men of Joppa took them out to sea and drowned them, not less than two hundred.

[5] When Judas heard of the cruelty visited on his countrymen, he gave orders to his men

[6] and, calling upon God the righteous Judge, attacked the murderers of his brethren. He set fire to the harbor by night, and burned the boats, and massacred those who had taken refuge there.

[7] Then, because the city's gates were closed, he withdrew, intending to come again and root out the whole community of Joppa.

[8] But learning that the men in Jamnia meant in the same way to wipe out the Jews who were living among them,

[9] he attacked the people of Jamnia by night and set fire to the harbor and the fleet, so that the glow of the light was seen in Jerusalem, thirty miles distant.

[10] When they had gone more than a mile from there, on their march against Timothy, not less than five thousand Arabs with five hundred horsemen attacked them.

[11] After a hard fight Judas and his men won the victory, by the help of God. The defeated nomads besought Judas to grant them pledges of friendship, promising to give him cattle and to help his people in all other ways.

[12] Judas, thinking that they might really be useful in many ways, agreed to make peace with them; and after receiving his pledges they departed to their tents.

[13] He also attacked a certain city which was strongly fortified with earthworks and walls, and inhabited by all sorts of Gentiles. Its name was Caspin.

[14] And those who were within, relying on the strength of the walls and on their supply of provisions, behaved most insolently toward Judas and his men, railing at them and even blaspheming and saying unholy things.

[15] But Judas and his men, calling upon the great Sovereign of the world, who without battering-rams or engines of war overthrew Jericho in the days of Joshua, rushed furiously upon the walls.

[16] They took the city by the will of God, and slaughtered untold numbers, so that the adjoining lake, a quarter of a mile wide, appeared to be running over with blood.

[17] When they had gone ninety-five miles from there, they came to Charax, to the Jews who are called Toubiani.

[18] They did not find Timothy in that region, for he had by then departed from the region without accomplishing anything, though in one place he had left a very strong garrison.

[19] Dositheus and Sosipater, who were captains under Maccabeus, marched out and destroyed those whom Timothy had left in the stronghold, more than ten thousand men.

[20] But Maccabeus arranged his army in divisions, set men in command of the divisions, and hastened after Timothy, who had with him a hundred and twenty thousand infantry and two thousand five hundred cavalry.

[21] When Timothy learned of the approach of Judas, he sent off the women and the children and also the baggage to a place called Carnaim; for that place was hard to besiege and difficult of access because of the narrowness of all the approaches.

[22] But when Judas' first division appeared, terror and fear came over the enemy at the manifestation to them of him who sees all things; and they rushed off in flight and were swept on, this way and that, so that often they were injured by their own men and pierced by the points of their swords.

[23] And Judas pressed the pursuit with the utmost vigor, putting the sinners to the sword, and destroyed as many as thirty thousand men.

[24] Timothy himself fell into the hands of Dositheus and Sosipater and their men. With great guile he besought them to let him go in safety, because he held the parents of most of them and the brothers of some and no consideration would be shown them.

[25] And when with many words he had confirmed his solemn promise to restore them unharmed, they let him go, for the sake of saving their brethren.

[26] Then Judas marched against Carnaim and the temple of Atargatis, and slaughtered twenty-five thousand people.

[27] After the rout and destruction of these, he marched also against Ephron, a fortified city where Lysias dwelt with multitudes of people of all nationalities. Stalwart young men took their stand before the walls and made a vigorous defense; and great stores of war engines and missiles were there.

[28] But the Jews called upon the Sovereign who with power shatters the might of his enemies, and they got the city into their hands, and killed as many as twenty-five thousand of those who were within it.

[29] Setting out from there, they hastened to Scythopolis, which is seventy-five miles from Jerusalem.

[30] But when the Jews who dwelt there bore witness to the good will which the people of Scythopolis had

shown them and their kind treatment of them in times of misfortune,

[31] they thanked them and exhorted them to be well disposed to their race in the future also. Then they went up to Jerusalem, as the feast of weeks was close at hand.

[32] After the feast called Pentecost, they hastened against Gorgias, the governor of Idumea.

[33] And he came out with three thousand infantry and four hundred cavalry.

[34] When they joined battle, it happened that a few of the Jews fell.

[35] But a certain Dositheus, one of Bacenor's men, who was on horseback and was a strong man, caught hold of Gorgias, and grasping his cloak was dragging him off by main strength, wishing to take the accursed man alive, when one of the Thracian horsemen bore down upon him and cut off his arm; so Gorgias escaped and reached Marisa.

[36] As Esdris and his men had been fighting for a long time and were weary, Judas called upon the Lord to show himself their ally and leader in the battle.

[37] In the language of their fathers he raised the battle cry, with hymns; then he charged against Gorgias' men when they were not expecting it, and put them to flight.

[38] Then Judas assembled his army and went to the city of Adullam. As the seventh day was coming on, they purified themselves according to the custom, and they kept the sabbath there.

[39] On the next day, as by that time it had become necessary, Judas and his men went to take up the bodies of the fallen and to bring them back to lie with their kinsmen in the sepulchres of their fathers.

[40] Then under the tunic of every one of the dead they found sacred tokens of the idols of Jamnia, which the law forbids the Jews to wear. And it became clear to all that this was why these men had fallen.

[41] So they all blessed the ways of the Lord, the righteous Judge, who reveals the things that are hidden;

[42] and they turned to prayer, beseeching that the sin which had been committed might be wholly blotted out. And the noble Judas exhorted the people to keep themselves free from sin, for they had seen with their own eyes what had happened because of the sin of those who had fallen.

[43] He also took up a collection, man by man, to the amount of two thousand drachmas of silver, and sent it to Jerusalem to provide for a sin offering. In doing this he acted very well and honorably, taking account of the resurrection.

[44] For if he were not expecting that those who had fallen would rise again, it would have been superfluous and foolish to pray for the dead.

[45] But if he was looking to the splendid reward that is laid up for those who fall asleep in godliness, it was a holy and pious thought. Therefore he made atonement for the dead, that they might be delivered from their sin.

2Mac.13

[1] In the one hundred and forty-ninth year word came to Judas and his men that Antiochus Eupator was coming with a great army against Judea,

[2] and with him Lysias, his guardian, who had charge of the government. Each of them had a Greek force of one hundred and ten thousand infantry, five thousand three hundred cavalry, twenty-two elephants, and three hundred chariots armed with scythes.

[3] Menelaus also joined them and with utter hypocrisy urged Antiochus on, not for the sake of his country's welfare, but because he thought that he would be established in office.

[4] But the King of kings aroused the anger of Antiochus against the scoundrel; and when Lysias informed him that this man was to blame for all the trouble, he ordered them to take him to Beroea and to put him to death by the method which is the custom in that place.

[5] For there is a tower in that place, fifty cubits high, full of ashes, and it has a rim running around it which on all sides inclines precipitously into the ashes.

[6] There they all push to destruction any man guilty of sacrilege or notorious for other crimes.

[7] By such a fate it came about that Menelaus the lawbreaker died, without even burial in the earth.

[8] And this was eminently just; because he had committed many sins against the altar whose fire and ashes were holy, he met his death in ashes.

[9] The king with barbarous arrogance was coming to show the Jews things far worse than those that had been done in his father's time.

[10] But when Judas heard of this, he ordered the people to call upon the Lord day and night, now if ever to help those who were on the point of being deprived of the law and their country and the holy temple,

[11] and not to let the people who had just begun to revive fall into the hands of the blasphemous Gentiles.

[12] When they had all joined in the same petition and had besought the merciful Lord with weeping and fasting and lying prostrate for three days without ceasing, Judas exhorted them and ordered them to stand ready.

[13] After consulting privately with the elders, he determined to march out and decide the matter by the help of God before the king's army could enter Judea and get possession of the city.

[14] So, committing the decision to the Creator of the world and exhorting his men to fight nobly to the

death for the laws, temple, city, country, and commonwealth, he pitched his camp near Modein.

[15] He gave his men the watchword, "God's victory," and with a picked force of the bravest young men, he attacked the king's pavilion at night and slew as many as two thousand men in the camp. He stabbed the leading elephant and its rider.

[16] In the end they filled the camp with terror and confusion and withdrew in triumph.

[17] This happened, just as day was dawning, because the Lord's help protected him.

[18] The king, having had a taste of the daring of the Jews, tried strategy in attacking their positions.

[19] He advanced against Beth-zur, a strong fortress of the Jews, was turned back, attacked again, and was defeated.

[20] Judas sent in to the garrison whatever was necessary.

[21] But Rhodocus, a man from the ranks of the Jews, gave secret information to the enemy; he was sought for, caught, and put in prison.

[22] The king negotiated a second time with the people in Beth-zur, gave pledges, received theirs, withdrew, attacked Judas and his men, was defeated;

[23] he got word that Philip, who had been left in charge of the government, had revolted in Antioch; he was dismayed, called in the Jews, yielded and swore to observe all their rights, settled with them and offered sacrifice, honored the sanctuary and showed generosity to the holy place.

[24] He received Maccabeus, left Hegemonides as governor from Ptolemais to Gerar,

[25] and went to Ptolemais. The people of Ptolemais were indignant over the treaty; in fact they were so angry that they wanted to annul its terms.

[26] Lysias took the public platform, made the best possible defense, convinced them, appeased them, gained their good will, and set out for Antioch. This is how the king's attack and withdrawal turned out.

2Mac.14

[1] Three years later, word came to Judas and his men that Demetrius, the son of Seleucus, had sailed into the harbor of Tripolis with a strong army and a fleet,

[2] and had taken possession of the country, having made away with Antiochus and his guardian Lysias.

[3] Now a certain Alcimus, who had formerly been high priest but had wilfully defiled himself in the times of separation, realized that there was no way for him to be safe or to have access again to the holy altar,

[4] and went to King Demetrius in about the one hundred and fifty-first year, presenting to him a crown of gold and a palm, and besides these some of the customary olive branches from the temple. During that day he kept quiet.

[5] But he found an opportunity that furthered his mad purpose when he was invited by Demetrius to a meeting of the council and was asked about the disposition and intentions of the Jews. He answered:

[6] "Those of the Jews who are called Hasideans, whose leader is Judas Maccabeus, are keeping up war and stirring up sedition, and will not let the kingdom attain tranquillity.

[7] Therefore I have laid aside my ancestral glory -- I mean the high priesthood -- and have now come here,

[8] first because I am genuinely concerned for the interests of the king, and second because I have regard also for my fellow citizens. For through the folly of those whom I have mentioned our whole nation is now in no small misfortune.

[9] Since you are acquainted, O king, with the details of this matter, deign to take thought for our country and our hard-pressed nation with the gracious kindness which you show to all.

[10] For as long as Judas lives, it is impossible for the government to find peace."

[11] When he had said this, the rest of the king's friends, who were hostile to Judas, quickly inflamed Demetrius still more.

[12] And he immediately chose Nicanor, who had been in command of the elephants, appointed him governor of Judea, and sent him off

[13] with orders to kill Judas and scatter his men, and to set up Alcimus as high priest of the greatest temple.

[14] And the Gentiles throughout Judea, who had fled before Judas, flocked to join Nicanor, thinking that the misfortunes and calamities of the Jews would mean prosperity for themselves.

[15] When the Jews heard of Nicanor's coming and the gathering of the Gentiles, they sprinkled dust upon their heads and prayed to him who established his own people for ever and always upholds his own heritage by manifesting himself.

[16] At the command of the leader, they set out from there immediately and engaged them in battle at a village called Dessau.

[17] Simon, the brother of Judas, had encountered Nicanor, but had been temporarily checked because of the sudden consternation created by the enemy.

[18] Nevertheless Nicanor, hearing of the valor of Judas and his men and their courage in battle for their country, shrank from deciding the issue by bloodshed.

[19] Therefore he sent Posidonius and Theodotus and Mattathias to give and receive pledges of friendship.

[20] When the terms had been fully considered, and the leader had informed the people, and it had appeared that they were of one mind, they agreed to the covenant.

[21] And the leaders set a day on which to meet by themselves. A chariot came forward from each army; seats of honor were set in place;

[22] Judas posted armed men in readiness at key places to prevent sudden treachery on the part of the enemy; they held the proper conference.

[23] Nicanor stayed on in Jerusalem and did nothing out of the way, but dismissed the flocks of people that had gathered.

[24] And he kept Judas always in his presence; he was warmly attached to the man.

[25] And he urged him to marry and have children; so he married, settled down, and shared the common life.

[26] But when Alcimus noticed their good will for one another, he took the covenant that had been made and went to Demetrius. He told him that Nicanor was disloyal to the government, for he had appointed that conspirator against the kingdom, Judas, to be his successor.

[27] The king became excited and, provoked by the false accusations of that depraved man, wrote to Nicanor, stating that he was displeased with the covenant and commanding him to send Maccabeus to Antioch as a prisoner without delay.

[28] When this message came to Nicanor, he was troubled and grieved that he had to annul their agreement when the man had done no wrong.

[29] Since it was not possible to oppose the king, he watched for an opportunity to accomplish this by a stratagem.

[30] But Maccabeus, noticing that Nicanor was more austere in his dealings with him and was meeting him more rudely than had been his custom, concluded that this austerity did not spring from the best motives. So he gathered not a few of his men, and went into hiding from Nicanor.

[31] When the latter became aware that he had been cleverly outwitted by the man, he went to the great and holy temple while the priests were offering the customary sacrifices, and commanded them to hand the man over.

[32] And when they declared on oath that they did not know where the man was whom he sought,

[33] he stretched out his right hand toward the sanctuary, and swore this oath: "If you do not hand Judas over to me as a prisoner, I will level this precinct of God to the ground and tear down the altar, and I will build here a splendid temple to Dionysus."

[34] Having said this, he went away. Then the priests stretched forth their hands toward heaven and called upon the constant Defender of our nation, in these words:

[35] "O Lord of all, who hast need of nothing, thou wast pleased that there be a temple for thy habitation among us;

[36] so now, O holy One, Lord of all holiness, keep undefiled for ever this house that has been so recently purified."

[37] A certain Razis, one of the elders of Jerusalem, was denounced to Nicanor as a man who loved his fellow citizens and was very well thought of and for his good will was called father of the Jews.

[38] For in former times, when there was no mingling with the Gentiles, he had been accused of Judaism, and for Judaism he had with all zeal risked body and life.

[39] Nicanor, wishing to exhibit the enmity which he had for the Jews, sent more than five hundred soldiers to arrest him;

[40] for he thought that by arresting him he would do them an injury.

[41] When the troops were about to capture the tower and were forcing the door of the courtyard, they ordered that fire be brought and the doors burned. Being surrounded, Razis fell upon his own sword,

[42] preferring to die nobly rather than to fall into the hands of sinners and suffer outrages unworthy of his noble birth.

[43] But in the heat of the struggle he did not hit exactly, and the crowd was now rushing in through the doors. He bravely ran up on the wall, and manfully threw himself down into the crowd.

[44] But as they quickly drew back, a space opened and he fell in the middle of the empty space.

[45] Still alive and aflame with anger, he rose, and though his blood gushed forth and his wounds were severe he ran through the crowd; and standing upon a steep rock,

[46] with his blood now completely drained from him, he tore out his entrails, took them with both hands and hurled them at the crowd, calling upon the Lord of life and spirit to give them back to him again. This was the manner of his death.

2Mac.15

[1] When Nicanor heard that Judas and his men were in the region of Samaria, he made plans to attack them with complete safety on the day of rest.

[2] And when the Jews who were compelled to follow him said, "Do not destroy so savagely and barbarously, but show respect for the day which he who sees all things has honored and hallowed above other days,"

[3] the thrice-accursed wretch asked if there were a sovereign in heaven who had commanded the keeping of the sabbath day.

[4] And when they declared, "It is the living Lord himself, the Sovereign in heaven, who ordered us to observe the seventh day,"

[5] he replied, "And I am a sovereign also, on earth, and I command you to take up arms and finish the king's business." Nevertheless, he did not succeed in carrying out his abominable design.

[6] This Nicanor in his utter boastfulness and arrogance had determined to erect a public monument of victory over Judas and his men.

[7] But Maccabeus did not cease to trust with all confidence that he would get help from the Lord.

[8] And he exhorted his men not to fear the attack of the Gentiles, but to keep in mind the former times when help had come to them from heaven, and now to look for the victory which the Almighty would give them.

[9] Encouraging them from the law and the prophets, and reminding them also of the struggles they had won, he made them the more eager.

[10] And when he had aroused their courage, he gave his orders, at the same time pointing out the perfidy of the Gentiles and their violation of oaths.

[11] He armed each of them not so much with confidence in shields and spears as with the inspiration of brave words, and he cheered them all by relating a dream, a sort of vision, which was worthy of belief.

[12] What he saw was this: Onias, who had been high priest, a noble and good man, of modest bearing and gentle manner, one who spoke fittingly and had been trained from childhood in all that belongs to excellence, was praying with outstretched hands for the whole body of the Jews.

[13] Then likewise a man appeared, distinguished by his gray hair and dignity, and of marvelous majesty and authority.

[14] And Onias spoke, saying, "This is a man who loves the brethren and prays much for the people and the holy city, Jeremiah, the prophet of God."

[15] Jeremiah stretched out his right hand and gave to Judas a golden sword, and as he gave it he addressed him thus:

[16] "Take this holy sword, a gift from God, with which you will strike down your adversaries."

[17] Encouraged by the words of Judas, so noble and so effective in arousing valor and awaking manliness in the souls of the young, they determined not to carry on a campaign but to attack bravely, and to decide the matter, by fighting hand to hand with all courage, because the city and the sanctuary and the temple were in danger.

[18] Their concern for wives and children, and also for brethren and relatives, lay upon them less heavily; their greatest and first fear was for the consecrated sanctuary.

[19] And those who had to remain in the city were in no little distress, being anxious over the encounter in the open country.

[20] When all were now looking forward to the coming decision, and the enemy was already close at hand with their army drawn up for battle, the elephants strategically stationed and the cavalry deployed on the flanks,

[21] Maccabeus, perceiving the hosts that were before him and the varied supply of arms and the savagery of the elephants, stretched out his hands toward heaven and called upon the Lord who works wonders; for he knew that it is not by arms, but as the Lord decides, that he gains the victory for those who deserve it.

[22] And he called upon him in these words: "O Lord, thou didst send thy angel in the time of Hezekiah king of Judea, and he slew fully a hundred and eighty-five thousand in the camp of Sennacherib.

[23] So now, O Sovereign of the heavens, send a good angel to carry terror and trembling before us.

[24] By the might of thy arm may these blasphemers who come against thy holy people be struck down." With these words he ended his prayer.

[25] Nicanor and his men advanced with trumpets and battle songs;

[26] and Judas and his men met the enemy in battle with invocation to God and prayers.

[27] So, fighting with their hands and praying to God in their hearts, they laid low no less than thirty-five thousand men, and were greatly gladdened by God's manifestation.

[28] When the action was over and they were returning with joy, they recognized Nicanor, lying dead, in full armor.

[29] Then there was shouting and tumult, and they blessed the Sovereign Lord in the language of their fathers.

[30] And the man who was ever in body and soul the defender of his fellow citizens, the man who maintained his youthful good will toward his countrymen, ordered them to cut off Nicanor's head and arm and carry them to Jerusalem.

[31] And when he arrived there and had called his countrymen together and stationed the priests before the altar, he sent for those who were in the citadel.

[32] He showed them the vile Nicanor's head and that profane man's arm, which had been boastfully stretched out against the holy house of the Almighty;

[33] and he cut out the tongue of the ungodly Nicanor and said that he would give it piecemeal to the birds and hang up these rewards of his folly opposite the sanctuary.

[34] And they all, looking to heaven, blessed the Lord who had manifested himself, saying, "Blessed is he who has kept his own place undefiled."

[35] And he hung Nicanor's head from the citadel, a clear and conspicuous sign to every one of the help of the Lord.

[36] And they all decreed by public vote never to let this day go unobserved, but to celebrate the thirteenth day of the twelfth month -- which is called Adar in the Syrian language -- the day before Mordecai's day.

[37] This, then, is how matters turned out with Nicanor. And from that time the city has been in the possession of the Hebrews. So I too will here end my story.

[38] If it is well told and to the point, that is what I myself desired; if it is poorly done and mediocre, that was the best I could do.

[39] For just as it is harmful to drink wine alone, or, again, to drink water alone, while wine mixed with water is sweet and delicious and enhances one's enjoyment, so also the style of the story delights the ears of those who read the work. And here will be the end.

3 Maccabees

3Mac.1

[1] When Philopator learned from those who returned that the regions which he had controlled had been seized by Antiochus, he gave orders to all his forces, both infantry and cavalry, took with him his sister Arsinoe, and marched out to the region near Raphia, where Antiochus's supporters were encamped.
[2] But a certain Theodotus, determined to carry out the plot he had devised, took with him the best of the Ptolemaic arms that had been previously issued to him, and crossed over by night to the tent of Ptolemy, intending single-handed to kill him and thereby end the war.
[3] But Dositheus, known as the son of Drimylus, a Jew by birth who later changed his religion and apostatized from the ancestral traditions, had led the king away and arranged that a certain insignificant man should sleep in the tent; and so it turned out that this man incurred the vengeance meant for the king.
[4] When a bitter fight resulted, and matters were turning out rather in favor of Antiochus, Arsinoe went to the troops with wailing and tears, her locks all disheveled, and exhorted them to defend themselves and their children and wives bravely, promising to give them each two minas of gold if they won the battle.
[5] And so it came about that the enemy was routed in the action, and many captives also were taken.
[6] Now that he had foiled the plot, Ptolemy decided to visit the neighboring cities and encourage them.
[7] By doing this, and by endowing their sacred enclosures with gifts, he strengthened the morale of his subjects.
[8] Since the Jews had sent some of their council and elders to greet him, to bring him gifts of welcome, and to congratulate him on what had happened, he was all the more eager to visit them as soon as possible.
[9] After he had arrived in Jerusalem, he offered sacrifice to the supreme God and made thank-offerings and did what was fitting for the holy place. Then, upon entering the place and being impressed by its excellence and its beauty,
[10] he marveled at the good order of the temple, and conceived a desire to enter the holy of holies.
[11] When they said that this was not permitted, because not even members of their own nation were allowed to enter, nor even all of the priests, but only the high priest who was pre-eminent over all, and he only once a year, the king was by no means persuaded.
[12] Even after the law had been read to him, he did not cease to maintain that he ought to enter, saying,

"Even if those men are deprived of this honor, I ought not to be."
[13] And he inquired why, when he entered every other temple, no one there had stopped him.
[14] And someone heedlessly said that it was wrong to take this as a sign in itself.
[15] "But since this has happened," the king said, "why should not I at least enter, whether they wish it or not?"
[16] Then the priests in all their vestments prostrated themselves and entreated the supreme God to aid in the present situation and to avert the violence of this evil design, and they filled the temple with cries and tears;
[17] and those who remained behind in the city were agitated and hurried out, supposing that something mysterious was occurring.
[18] The virgins who had been enclosed in their chambers rushed out with their mothers, sprinkled their hair with dust, and filled the streets with groans and lamentations.
[19] Those women who had recently been arrayed for marriage abandoned the bridal chambers prepared for wedded union, and, neglecting proper modesty, in a disorderly rush flocked together in the city.
[20] Mothers and nurses abandoned even newborn children here and there, some in houses and some in the streets, and without a backward look they crowded together at the most high temple.
[21] Various were the supplications of those gathered there because of what the king was profanely plotting.
[22] In addition, the bolder of the citizens would not tolerate the completion of his plans or the fulfillment of his intended purpose.
[23] They shouted to their fellows to take arms and die courageously for the ancestral law, and created a considerable disturbance in the holy place; and being barely restrained by the old men and the elders, they resorted to the same posture of supplication as the others.
[24] Meanwhile the crowd, as before, was engaged in prayer,
[25] while the elders near the king tried in various ways to change his arrogant mind from the plan that he had conceived.
[26] But he, in his arrogance, took heed of nothing, and began now to approach, determined to bring the aforesaid plan to a conclusion.
[27] When those who were around him observed this, they turned, together with our people, to call upon him who has all power to defend them in the present trouble and not to overlook this unlawful and haughty deed.
[28] The continuous, vehement, and concerted cry of the crowds resulted in an immense uproar;

[29] for it seemed that not only the men but also the walls and the whole earth around echoed, because indeed all at that time preferred death to the profanation of the place.

3Mac.2

[1] Then the high priest Simon, facing the sanctuary, bending his knees and extending his hands with calm dignity, prayed as follows:

[2] "Lord, Lord, king of the heavens, and sovereign of all creation, holy among the holy ones, the only ruler, almighty, give attention to us who are suffering grievously from an impious and profane man, puffed up in his audacity and power.

[3] For you, the creator of all things and the governor of all, are a just Ruler, and you judge those who have done anything in insolence and arrogance.

[4] You destroyed those who in the past committed injustice, among whom were even giants who trusted in their strength and boldness, whom you destroyed by bringing upon them a boundless flood.

[5] You consumed with fire and sulphur the men of Sodom who acted arrogantly, who were notorious for their vices; and you made them an example to those who should come afterward.

[6] You made known your mighty power by inflicting many and varied punishments on the audacious Pharaoh who had enslaved your holy people Israel.

[7] And when he pursued them with chariots and a mass of troops, you overwhelmed him in the depths of the sea, but carried through safely those who had put their confidence in you, the Ruler over the whole creation.

[8] And when they had seen works of your hands, they praised you, the Almighty.

[9] You, O King, when you had created the boundless and immeasurable earth, chose this city and sanctified this place for your name, though you have no need of anything; and when you had glorified it by your magnificent manifestation, you made it a firm foundation for the glory of your great and honored name.

[10] And because you love the house of Israel, you promised that if we should have reverses, and tribulation should overtake us, you would listen to our petition when we come to this place and pray.

[11] And indeed you are faithful and true.

[12] And because oftentimes when our fathers were oppressed you helped them in their humiliation, and rescued them from great evils,

[13] see now, O holy King, that because of our many and great sins we are crushed with suffering, subjected to our enemies, and overtaken by helplessness.

[14] In our downfall this audacious and profane man undertakes to violate the holy place on earth dedicated to your glorious name.

[15] For your dwelling, the heaven of heavens, is unapproachable by man.

[16] But because you graciously bestowed your glory upon your people Israel, you sanctified this place.

[17] Do not punish us for the defilement committed by these men, or call us to account for this profanation, lest the transgressors boast in their wrath or exult in the arrogance of their tongue, saying,

[18] `We have trampled down the house of the sanctuary as offensive houses are trampled down.'

[19] Wipe away our sins and disperse our errors, and reveal your mercy at this hour.

[20] Speedily let your mercies overtake us, and put praises in the mouth of those who are downcast and broken in spirit, and give us peace."

[21] Thereupon God, who oversees all things, the first Father of all, holy among the holy ones, having heard the lawful supplication, scourged him who had exalted himself in insolence and audacity.

[22] He shook him on this side and that as a reed is shaken by the wind, so that he lay helpless on the ground and, besides being paralyzed in his limbs, was unable even to speak, since he was smitten by a righteous judgment.

[23] Then both friends and bodyguards, seeing the severe punishment that had overtaken him, and fearing lest he should lose his life, quickly dragged him out, panic-stricken in their exceedingly great fear.

[24] After a while he recovered, and though he had been punished, he by no means repented, but went away uttering bitter threats.

[25] When he arrived in Egypt, he increased in his deeds of malice, abetted by the previously mentioned drinking companions and comrades, who were strangers to everything just.

[26] He was not content with his uncounted licentious deeds, but he also continued with such audacity that he framed evil reports in the various localities; and many of his friends, intently observing the king's purpose, themselves also followed his will.

[27] He proposed to inflict public disgrace upon the Jewish community, and he set up a stone on the tower in the courtyard with this inscription:

[28] "None of those who do not sacrifice shall enter their sanctuaries, and all Jews shall be subjected to a registration involving poll tax and to the status of slaves. Those who object to this are to be taken by force and put to death;

[29] those who are registered are also to be branded on their bodies by fire with the ivy-leaf symbol of Dionysus, and they shall also be reduced to their former limited status."

[30] In order that he might not appear to be an enemy to all, he inscribed below: "But if any of them prefer to join those who have been initiated into the mysteries, they shall have equal citizenship with the Alexandrians."

[31] Now some, however, with an obvious abhorrence of the price to be exacted for maintaining the religion of their city, readily gave themselves up, since they expected to enhance their reputation by their future association with the king.

[32] But the majority acted firmly with a courageous spirit and did not depart from their religion; and by paying money in exchange for life they confidently attempted to save themselves from the registration.

[33] They remained resolutely hopeful of obtaining help, and they abhorred those who separated themselves from them, considering them to be enemies of the Jewish nation, and depriving them of common fellowship and mutual help.

3Mac.3

[1] When the impious king comprehended this situation, he became so infuriated that not only was he enraged against those Jews who lived in Alexandria, but was still more bitterly hostile toward those in the countryside; and he ordered that all should promptly be gathered into one place, and put to death by the most cruel means.

[2] While these matters were being arranged, a hostile rumor was circulated against the Jewish nation by men who conspired to do them ill, a pretext being given by a report that they hindered others from the observance of their customs.

[3] The Jews, however, continued to maintain good will and unswerving loyalty toward the dynasty;

[4] but because they worshiped God and conducted themselves by his law, they kept their separateness with respect to foods. For this reason they appeared hateful to some;

[5] but since they adorned their style of life with the good deeds of upright people, they were established in good repute among all men.

[6] Nevertheless those of other races paid no heed to their good service to their nation, which was common talk among all;

[7] instead they gossiped about the differences in worship and foods, alleging that these people were loyal neither to the king nor to his authorities, but were hostile and greatly opposed to his government. So they attached no ordinary reproach to them.

[8] The Greeks in the city, though wronged in no way, when they saw an unexpected tumult around these people and the crowds that suddenly were forming, were not strong enough to help them, for they lived under tyranny. They did try to console them, being grieved at the situation, and expected that matters would change;

[9] for such a great community ought not be left to its fate when it had committed no offense.

[10] And already some of their neighbors and friends and business associates had taken some of them aside privately and were pledging to protect them and to exert more earnest efforts for their assistance.

[11] Then the king, boastful of his present good fortune, and not considering the might of the supreme God, but assuming that he would persevere constantly in his same purpose, wrote this letter against them:

[12] "King Ptolemy Philopator to his generals and soldiers in Egypt and all its districts, greetings and good health.

[13] I myself and our government are faring well.

[14] When our expedition took place in Asia, as you yourselves know, it was brought to conclusion, according to plan, by the gods' deliberate alliance with us in battle,

[15] and we considered that we should not rule the nations inhabiting Coele-Syria and Phoenicia by the power of the spear but should cherish them with clemency and great benevolence, gladly treating them well.

[16] And when we had granted very great revenues to the temples in the cities, we came on to Jerusalem also, and went up to honor the temple of those wicked people, who never cease from their folly.

[17] They accepted our presence by word, but insincerely by deed, because when we proposed to enter their inner temple and honor it with magnificent and most beautiful offerings,

[18] they were carried away by their traditional conceit, and excluded us from entering; but they were spared the exercise of our power because of the benevolence which we have toward all.

[19] By maintaining their manifest ill-will toward us, they become the only people among all nations who hold their heads high in defiance of kings and their own benefactors, and are unwilling to regard any action as sincere.

[20] "But we, when we arrived in Egypt victorious, accommodated ourselves to their folly and did as was proper, since we treat all nations with benevolence.

[21] Among other things, we made known to all our amnesty toward their compatriots here, both because of their alliance with us and the myriad affairs liberally entrusted to them from the beginning; and we ventured to make a change, by deciding both to deem them worthy of Alexandrian citizenship and to make them participants in our regular religious rites.

[22] But in their innate malice they took this in a contrary spirit, and disdained what is good. Since they incline constantly to evil,

[23] they not only spurn the priceless citizenship, but also both by speech and by silence they abominate those few among them who are sincerely disposed toward us; in every situation, in accordance with their infamous way of life, they secretly suspect that we may soon alter our policy.

[24] Therefore, fully convinced by these indications that they are ill-disposed toward us in every way, we have taken precautions lest, if a sudden disorder

should later arise against us, we should have these impious people behind our backs as traitors and barbarous enemies.

[25] Therefore we have given orders that, as soon as this letter shall arrive, you are to send to us those who live among you, together with their wives and children, with insulting and harsh treatment, and bound securely with iron fetters, to suffer the sure and shameful death that befits enemies.

[26] For when these all have been punished, we are sure that for the remaining time the government will be established for ourselves in good order and in the best state.

[27] But whoever shelters any of the Jews, old people or children or even infants, will be tortured to death with the most hateful torments, together with his family.

[28] Any one willing to give information will receive the property of the one who incurs the punishment, and also two thousand drachmas from the royal treasury, and will be awarded his freedom.

[29] Every place detected sheltering a Jew is to be made unapproachable and burned with fire, and shall become useless for all time to any mortal creature."

[30] The letter was written in the above form.

3Mac.4

[1] In every place, then, where this decree arrived, a feast at public expense was arranged for the Gentiles with shouts and gladness, for the inveterate enmity which had long ago been in their minds was now made evident and outspoken.

[2] But among the Jews there was incessant mourning, lamentation, and tearful cries; everywhere their hearts were burning, and they groaned because of the unexpected destruction that had suddenly been decreed for them.

[3] What district or city, or what habitable place at all, or what streets were not filled with mourning and wailing for them?

[4] For with such a harsh and ruthless spirit were they being sent off, all together, by the generals in the several cities, that at the sight of their unusual punishments, even some of their enemies, perceiving the common object of pity before their eyes, reflected upon the uncertainty of life and shed tears at the most miserable expulsion of these people.

[5] For a multitude of gray-headed old men, sluggish and bent with age, was being led away, forced to march at a swift pace by the violence with which they were driven in such a shameful manner.

[6] And young women who had just entered the bridal chamber to share married life exchanged joy for wailing, their myrrh-perfumed hair sprinkled with ashes, and were carried away unveiled, all together raising a lament instead of a wedding song, as they were torn by the harsh treatment of the heathen.

[7] In bonds and in public view they were violently dragged along as far as the place of embarkation.

[8] Their husbands, in the prime of youth, their necks encircled with ropes instead of garlands, spent the remaining days of their marriage festival in lamentations instead of good cheer and youthful revelry, seeing death immediately before them.

[9] They were brought on board like wild animals, driven under the constraint of iron bonds; some were fastened by the neck to the benches of the boats, others had their feet secured by unbreakable fetters,

[10] and in addition they were confined under a solid deck, so that with their eyes in total darkness, they should undergo treatment befitting traitors during the whole voyage.

[11] When these men had been brought to the place called Schedia, and the voyage was concluded as the king had decreed, he commanded that they should be enclosed in the hippodrome which had been built with a monstrous perimeter wall in front of the city, and which was well suited to make them an obvious spectacle to all coming back into the city and to those from the city going out into the country, so that they could neither communicate with the king's forces nor in any way claim to be inside the circuit of the city.

[12] And when this had happened, the king, hearing that the Jews' compatriots from the city frequently went out in secret to lament bitterly the ignoble misfortune of their brothers,

[13] ordered in his rage that these men be dealt with in precisely the same fashion as the others, not omitting any detail of their punishment.

[14] The entire race was to be registered individually, not for the hard labor that has been briefly mentioned before, but to be tortured with the outrages that he had ordered, and at the end to be destroyed in the space of a single day.

[15] The registration of these people was therefore conducted with bitter haste and zealous intentness from the rising of the sun till its setting, and though uncompleted it stopped after forty days.

[16] The king was greatly and continually filled with joy, organizing feasts in honor of all his idols, with a mind alienated from truth and with a profane mouth, praising speechless things that are not able even to communicate or to come to one's help, and uttering improper words against the supreme God.

[17] But after the previously mentioned interval of time the scribes declared to the king that they were no longer able to take the census of the Jews because of their innumerable multitude,

[18] although most of them were still in the country, some still residing in their homes, and some at the place; the task was impossible for all the generals in Egypt.

[19] After he had threatened them severely, charging that they had been bribed to contrive a means of escape, he was clearly convinced about the matter

[20] when they said and proved that both the paper and the pens they used for writing had already given out.

[21] But this was an act of the invincible providence of him who was aiding the Jews from heaven.

3Mac.5

[1] Then the king, completely inflexible, was filled with overpowering anger and wrath; so he summoned Hermon, keeper of the elephants,

[2] and ordered him on the following day to drug all the elephants -- five hundred in number -- with large handfuls of frankincense and plenty of unmixed wine, and to drive them in, maddened by the lavish abundance of liquor, so that the Jews might meet their doom.

[3] When he had given these orders he returned to his feasting, together with those of his friends and of the army who were especially hostile toward the Jews.

[4] And Hermon, keeper of the elephants, proceeded faithfully to carry out the orders.

[5] The servants in charge of the Jews went out in the evening and bound the hands of the wretched people and arranged for their continued custody through the night, convinced that the whole nation would experience its final destruction.

[6] For to the Gentiles it appeared that the Jews were left without any aid,

[7] because in their bonds they were forcibly confined on every side. But with tears and a voice hard to silence they all called upon the Almighty Lord and Ruler of all power, their merciful God and Father, praying

[8] that he avert with vengeance the evil plot against them and in a glorious manifestation rescue them from the fate now prepared for them.

[9] So their entreaty ascended fervently to heaven.

[10] Hermon, however, when he had drugged the pitiless elephants until they had been filled with a great abundance of wine and satiated with frankincense, presented himself at the courtyard early in the morning to report to the king about these preparations.

[11] But the Lord sent upon the king a portion of sleep, that beneficence which from the beginning, night and day, is bestowed by him who grants it to whomever he wishes.

[12] And by the action of the Lord he was overcome by so pleasant and deep a sleep that he quite failed in his lawless purpose and was completely frustrated in his inflexible plan.

[13] Then the Jews, since they had escaped the appointed hour, praised their holy God and again begged him who is easily reconciled to show the might of his all-powerful hand to the arrogant Gentiles.

[14] But now, since it was nearly the middle of the tenth hour, the person who was in charge of the invitations, seeing that the guests were assembled, approached the king and nudged him.

[15] And when he had with difficulty roused him, he pointed out that the hour of the banquet was already slipping by, and he gave him an account of the situation.

[16] The king, after considering this, returned to his drinking, and ordered those present for the banquet to recline opposite him.

[17] When this was done he urged them to give themselves over to revelry and to make the present portion of the banquet joyful by celebrating all the more.

[18] After the party had been going on for some time, the king summoned Hermon and with sharp threats demanded to know why the Jews had been allowed to remain alive through the present day.

[19] But when he, with the corroboration of his friends, pointed out that while it was still night he had carried out completely the order given him,

[20] the king, possessed by a savagery worse than that of Phalaris, said that the Jews were benefited by today's sleep, "but," he added, "tomorrow without delay prepare the elephants in the same way for the destruction of the lawless Jews!"

[21] When the king had spoken, all those present readily and joyfully with one accord gave their approval, and each departed to his own home.

[22] But they did not so much employ the duration of the night in sleep as in devising all sorts of insults for those they thought to be doomed.

[23] Then, as soon as the cock had crowed in the early morning, Hermon, having equipped the beasts, began to move them along in the great colonnade.

[24] The crowds of the city had been assembled for this most pitiful spectacle and they were eagerly waiting for daybreak.

[25] But the Jews, at their last gasp, since the time had run out, stretched their hands toward heaven and with most tearful supplication and mournful dirges implored the supreme God to help them again at once.

[26] The rays of the sun were not yet shed abroad, and while the king was receiving his friends, Hermon arrived and invited him to come out, indicating that what the king desired was ready for action.

[27] But he, upon receiving the report and being struck by the unusual invitation to come out -- since he had been completely overcome by incomprehension -- inquired what the matter was for which this had been so zealously completed for him.

[28] This was the act of God who rules over all things, for he had implanted in the king's mind a forgetfulness of the things he had previously devised.

[29] Then Hermon and all the king's friends pointed out that the beasts and the armed forces were ready, "O king, according to your eager purpose."

[30] But at these words he was filled with an overpowering wrath, because by the providence of God his whole mind had been deranged in regard to these matters; and with a threatening look he said,

[31] "Were your parents or children present, I would have prepared them to be a rich feast for the savage beasts instead of the Jews, who give me no ground for complaint and have exhibited to an extraordinary degree a full and firm loyalty to my ancestors.

[32] In fact you would have been deprived of life instead of these, were it not for an affection arising from our nurture in common and your usefulness."

[33] So Hermon suffered an unexpected and dangerous threat, and his eyes wavered and his face fell.

[34] The king's friends one by one sullenly slipped away and dismissed the assembled people, each to his own occupation.

[35] Then the Jews, upon hearing what the king had said, praised the manifest Lord God, King of kings, since this also was his aid which they had received.

[36] The king, however, reconvened the party in the same manner and urged the guests to return to their celebrating.

[37] After summoning Hermon he said in a threatening tone, "How many times, you poor wretch, must I give you orders about these things?

[38] Equip the elephants now once more for the destruction of the Jews tomorrow!"

[39] But the officials who were at table with him, wondering at his instability of mind, remonstrated as follows:

[40] "O king, how long will you try us, as though we are idiots, ordering now for a third time that they be destroyed, and again revoking your decree in the matter?

[41] As a result the city is in a tumult because of its expectation; it is crowded with masses of people, and also in constant danger of being plundered."

[42] Upon this the king, a Phalaris in everything and filled with madness, took no account of the changes of mind which had come about within him for the protection of the Jews, and he firmly swore an irrevocable oath that he would send them to death without delay, mangled by the knees and feet of the beasts,

[43] and would also march against Judea and rapidly level it to the ground with fire and spear, and by burning to the ground the temple inaccessible to him would quickly render it forever empty of those who offered sacrifices there.

[44] Then the friends and officers departed with great joy, and they confidently posted the armed forces at the places in the city most favorable for keeping guard.

[45] Now when the beasts had been brought virtually to a state of madness, so to speak, by the very fragrant draughts of wine mixed with frankincense and had been equipped with frightful devices, the elephant keeper

[46] entered at about dawn into the courtyard -- the city now being filled with countless masses of people crowding their way into the hippodrome -- and urged the king on to the matter at hand.

[47] So he, when he had filled his impious mind with a deep rage, rushed out in full force along with the beasts, wishing to witness, with invulnerable heart and with his own eyes, the grievous and pitiful destruction of the aforementioned people.

[48] And when the Jews saw the dust raised by the elephants going out at the gate and by the following armed forces, as well as by the trampling of the crowd, and heard the loud and tumultuous noise,

[49] they thought that this was their last moment of life, the end of their most miserable suspense, and giving way to lamentation and groans they kissed each other, embracing relatives and falling into one another's arms -- parents and children, mothers and daughters, and others with babies at their breasts who were drawing their last milk.

[50] Not only this, but when they considered the help which they had received before from heaven they prostrated themselves with one accord on the ground, removing the babies from their breasts,

[51] and cried out in a very loud voice, imploring the Ruler over every power to manifest himself and be merciful to them, as they stood now at the gates of death.

3Mac.6

[1] Then a certain Eleazar, famous among the priests of the country, who had attained a ripe old age and throughout his life had been adorned with every virtue, directed the elders around him to cease calling upon the holy God and prayed as follows:

[2] "King of great power, Almighty God Most High, governing all creation with mercy,

[3] look upon the descendants of Abraham, O Father, upon the children of the sainted Jacob, a people of your consecrated portion who are perishing as foreigners in a foreign land.

[4] Pharaoh with his abundance of chariots, the former ruler of this Egypt, exalted with lawless insolence and boastful tongue, you destroyed together with his arrogant army by drowning them in the sea, manifesting the light of your mercy upon the nation of Israel.

[5] Sennacherib exulting in his countless forces, oppressive king of the Assyrians, who had already

gained control of the whole world by the spear and was lifted up against your holy city, speaking grievous words with boasting and insolence, you, O Lord, broke in pieces, showing your power to many nations.

[6] The three companions in Babylon who had voluntarily surrendered their lives to the flames so as not to serve vain things, you rescued unharmed, even to a hair, moistening the fiery furnace with dew and turning the flame against all their enemies.

[7] Daniel, who through envious slanders was cast down into the ground to lions as food for wild beasts, you brought up to the light unharmed.

[8] And Jonah, wasting away in the belly of a huge, sea-born monster, you, Father, watched over and restored unharmed to all his family.

[9] And now, you who hate insolence, all-merciful and protector of all, reveal yourself quickly to those of the nation of Israel -- who are being outrageously treated by the abominable and lawless Gentiles.

[10] Even if our lives have become entangled in impieties in our exile, rescue us from the hand of the enemy, and destroy us, Lord, by whatever fate you choose.

[11] Let not the vain-minded praise their vanities at the destruction of your beloved people, saying, `Not even their god has rescued them.'

[12] But you, O Eternal One, who have all might and all power, watch over us now and have mercy upon us who by the senseless insolence of the lawless are being deprived of life in the manner of traitors.

[13] And let the Gentiles cower today in fear of your invincible might, O honored One, who have power to save the nation of Jacob.

[14] The whole throng of infants and their parents entreat you with tears.

[15] Let it be shown to all the Gentiles that you are with us, O Lord, and have not turned your face from us; but just as you have said, `Not even when they were in the land of their enemies did I neglect them,' so accomplish it, O Lord."

[16] Just as Eleazar was ending his prayer, the king arrived at the hippodrome with the beasts and all the arrogance of his forces.

[17] And when the Jews observed this they raised great cries to heaven so that even the nearby valleys resounded with them and brought an uncontrollable terror upon the army.

[18] Then the most glorious, almighty, and true God revealed his holy face and opened the heavenly gates, from which two glorious angels of fearful aspect descended, visible to all but the Jews.

[19] They opposed the forces of the enemy and filled them with confusion and terror, binding them with immovable shackles.

[20] Even the king began to shudder bodily, and he forgot his sullen insolence.

[21] The beasts turned back upon the armed forces following them and began trampling and destroying them.

[22] Then the king's anger was turned to pity and tears because of the things that he had devised beforehand.

[23] For when he heard the shouting and saw them all fallen headlong to destruction, he wept and angrily threatened his friends, saying,

[24] "You are committing treason and surpassing tyrants in cruelty; and even me, your benefactor, you are now attempting to deprive of dominion and life by secretly devising acts of no advantage to the kingdom.

[25] Who is it that has taken each man from his home and senselessly gathered here those who faithfully have held the fortresses of our country?

[26] Who is it that has so lawlessly encompassed with outrageous treatment those who from the beginning differed from all nations in their goodwill toward us and often have accepted willingly the worst of human dangers?

[27] Loose and untie their unjust bonds! Send them back to their homes in peace, begging pardon for your former actions!

[28] Release the sons of the almighty and living God of heaven, who from the time of our ancestors until now has granted an unimpeded and notable stability to our government."

[29] These then were the things he said; and the Jews, immediately released, praised their holy God and Savior, since they now had escaped death.

[30] Then the king, when he had returned to the city, summoned the official in charge of the revenues and ordered him to provide to the Jews both wines and everything else needed for a festival of seven days, deciding that they should celebrate their rescue with all joyfulness in that same place in which they had expected to meet their destruction.

[31] Accordingly those disgracefully treated and near to death, or rather, who stood at its gates, arranged for a banquet of deliverance instead of a bitter and lamentable death, and full of joy they apportioned to celebrants the place which had been prepared for their destruction and burial.

[32] They ceased their chanting of dirges and took up the song of their fathers, praising God, their Savior and worker of wonders. Putting an end to all mourning and wailing, they formed choruses as a sign of peaceful joy.

[33] Likewise also the king, after convening a great banquet to celebrate these events, gave thanks to heaven unceasingly and lavishly for the unexpected rescue which he had experienced.

[34] And those who had previously believed that the Jews would be destroyed and become food for birds, and had joyfully registered them, groaned as they

themselves were overcome by disgrace, and their fire-breathing boldness was ignominiously quenched.

[35] But the Jews, when they had arranged the aforementioned choral group, as we have said before, passed the time in feasting to the accompaniment of joyous thanksgiving and psalms.

[36] And when they had ordained a public rite for these things in their whole community and for their descendants, they instituted the observance of the aforesaid days as a festival, not for drinking and gluttony, but because of the deliverance that had come to them through God.

[37] Then they petitioned the king, asking for dismissal to their homes.

[38] So their registration was carried out from the twenty-fifth of Pachon to the fourth of Epeiph, for forty days; and their destruction was set for the fifth to the seventh of Epeiph, the three days

[39] on which the Lord of all most gloriously revealed his mercy and rescued them all together and unharmed.

[40] Then they feasted, provided with everything by the king, until the fourteenth day, on which also they made the petition for their dismissal.

[41] The king granted their request at once and wrote the following letter for them to the generals in the cities, magnanimously expressing his concern:

3Mac.7

[1] "King Ptolemy Philopator to the generals in Egypt and all in authority in his government, greetings and good health.

[2] We ourselves and our children are faring well, the great God guiding our affairs according to our desire.

[3] Certain of our friends, frequently urging us with malicious intent, persuaded us to gather together the Jews of the kingdom in a body and to punish them with barbarous penalties as traitors;

[4] for they declared that our government would never be firmly established until this was accomplished, because of the ill-will which these people had toward all nations.

[5] They also led them out with harsh treatment as slaves, or rather as traitors, and, girding themselves with a cruelty more savage than that of Scythian custom, they tried without any inquiry or examination to put them to death.

[6] But we very severely threatened them for these acts, and in accordance with the clemency which we have toward all men we barely spared their lives. Since we have come to realize that the God of heaven surely defends the Jews, always taking their part as a father does for his children,

[7] and since we have taken into account the friendly and firm goodwill which they had toward us and our ancestors, we justly have acquitted them of every charge of whatever kind.

[8] We also have ordered each and every one to return to his own home, with no one in any place doing them harm at all or reproaching them for the irrational things that have happened.

[9] For you should know that if we devise any evil against them or cause them any grief at all, we always shall have not man but the Ruler over every power, the Most High God, in everything and inescapably as an antagonist to avenge such acts. Farewell."

[10] Upon receiving this letter the Jews did not immediately hurry to make their departure, but they requested of the king that at their own hands those of the Jewish nation who had willfully transgressed against the holy God and the law of God should receive the punishment they deserved.

[11] For they declared that those who for the belly's sake had transgressed the divine commandments would never be favorably disposed toward the king's government.

[12] The king then, admitting and approving the truth of what they said, granted them a general license so that freely and without royal authority or supervision they might destroy those everywhere in his kingdom who had transgressed the law of God.

[13] When they had applauded him in fitting manner, their priests and the whole multitude shouted the Hallelujah and joyfully departed.

[14] And so on their way they punished and put to a public and shameful death any whom they met of their fellow-countrymen who had become defiled.

[15] In that day they put to death more than three hundred men; and they kept the day as a joyful festival, since they had destroyed the profaners.

[16] But those who had held fast to God even to death and had received the full enjoyment of deliverance began their departure from the city, crowned with all sorts of very fragrant flowers, joyfully and loudly giving thanks to the one God of their fathers, the eternal Savior of Israel, in words of praise and all kinds of melodious songs.

[17] When they had arrived at Ptolemais, called "rose-bearing" because of a characteristic of the place, the fleet waited for them, in accord with the common desire, for seven days.

[18] There they celebrated their deliverance, for the king had generously provided all things to them for their journey, to each as far as his own house.

[19] And when they had landed in peace with appropriate thanksgiving, there too in like manner they decided to observe these days as a joyous festival during the time of their stay.

[20] Then, after inscribing them as holy on a pillar and dedicating a place of prayer at the site of the festival, they departed unharmed, free, and overjoyed, since at the king's command they had been brought safely by land and sea and river each to his own place.

[21] They also possessed greater prestige among their enemies, being held in honor and awe; and they were not subject at all to confiscation of their belongings by any one.

[22] Besides they all recovered all of their property, in accordance with the registration, so that those who held any restored it to them with extreme fear. So the supreme God perfectly performed great deeds for their deliverance.

[23] Blessed be the Deliverer of Israel through all times! Amen.

4 Maccabees

4Mac.1

[1] The subject that I am about to discuss is most philosophical, that is, whether devout reason is sovereign over the emotions. So it is right for me to advise you to pay earnest attention to philosophy.

[2] For the subject is essential to everyone who is seeking knowledge, and in addition it includes the praise of the highest virtue -- I mean, of course, rational judgment.

[3] If, then, it is evident that reason rules over those emotions that hinder self-control, namely, gluttony and lust,

[4] it is also clear that it masters the emotions that hinder one from justice, such as malice, and those that stand in the way of courage, namely anger, fear, and pain.

[5] Some might perhaps ask, "If reason rules the emotions, why is it not sovereign over forgetfulness and ignorance?" Their attempt at argument is ridiculous!

[6] For reason does not rule its own emotions, but those that are opposed to justice, courage, and self-control; and it is not for the purpose of destroying them, but so that one may not give way to them.

[7] I could prove to you from many and various examples that reason is dominant over the emotions,

[8] but I can demonstrate it best from the noble bravery of those who died for the sake of virtue, Eleazar and the seven brothers and their mother.

[9] All of these, by despising sufferings that bring death, demonstrated that reason controls the emotions.

[10] On this anniversary it is fitting for me to praise for their virtues those who, with their mother, died for the sake of nobility and goodness, but I would also call them blessed for the honor in which they are held.

[11] For all people, even their torturers, marveled at their courage and endurance, and they became the cause of the downfall of tyranny over their nation. By their endurance they conquered the tyrant, and thus their native land was purified through them.

[12] I shall shortly have an opportunity to speak of this; but, as my custom is, I shall begin by stating my main principle, and then I shall turn to their story, giving glory to the all-wise God.

[13] Our inquiry, accordingly, is whether reason is sovereign over the emotions.

[14] We shall decide just what reason is and what emotion is, how many kinds of emotions there are, and whether reason rules over all these.

[15] Now reason is the mind that with sound logic prefers the life of wisdom.

[16] Wisdom, next, is the knowledge of divine and human matters and the causes of these.

[17] This, in turn, is education in the law, by which we learn divine matters reverently and human affairs to our advantage.

[18] Now the kinds of wisdom are rational judgment, justice, courage, and self-control.

[19] Rational judgment is supreme over all of these, since by means of it reason rules over the emotions.

[20] The two most comprehensive types of the emotions are pleasure and pain; and each of these is by nature concerned with both body and soul.

[21] The emotions of both pleasure and pain have many consequences.

[22] Thus desire precedes pleasure and delight follows it.

[23] Fear precedes pain and sorrow comes after.

[24] Anger, as a man will see if he reflects on this experience, is an emotion embracing pleasure and pain.

[25] In pleasure there exists even a malevolent tendency, which is the most complex of all the emotions.

[26] In the soul it is boastfulness, covetousness, thirst for honor, rivalry, and malice;

[27] in the body, indiscriminate eating, gluttony, and solitary gormandizing.

[28] Just as pleasure and pain are two plants growing from the body and the soul, so there are many offshoots of these plants,

[29] each of which the master cultivator, reason, weeds and prunes and ties up and waters and thoroughly irrigates, and so tames the jungle of habits and emotions.

[30] For reason is the guide of the virtues, but over the emotions it is sovereign. Observe now first of all that rational judgment is sovereign over the emotions by virtue of the restraining power of self-control.

[31] Self-control, then, is dominance over the desires.

[32] Some desires are mental, others are physical, and reason obviously rules over both.

[33] Otherwise how is it that when we are attracted to forbidden foods we abstain from the pleasure to be had from them? Is it not because reason is able to rule over appetites? I for one think so.

[34] Therefore when we crave seafood and fowl and animals and all sorts of foods that are forbidden to us by the law, we abstain because of domination by reason.

[35] For the emotions of the appetites are restrained, checked by the temperate mind, and all the impulses of the body are bridled by reason.

4Mac.2

[1] And why is it amazing that the desires of the mind for the enjoyment of beauty are rendered powerless?

[2] It is for this reason, certainly, that the temperate Joseph is praised, because by mental effort he overcame sexual desire.

[3] For when he was young and in his prime for intercourse, by his reason he nullified the frenzy of the passions.

[4] Not only is reason proved to rule over the frenzied urge of sexual desire, but also over every desire.

[5] Thus the law says, "You shall not covet your neighbor's wife...or anything that is your neighbor's."

[6] In fact, since the law has told us not to covet, I could prove to you all the more that reason is able to control desires. Just so it is with the emotions that hinder one from justice.

[7] Otherwise how could it be that someone who is habitually a solitary gormandizer, a glutton, or even a drunkard can learn a better way, unless reason is clearly lord of the emotions?

[8] Thus, as soon as a man adopts a way of life in accordance with the law, even though he is a lover of money, he is forced to act contrary to his natural ways and to lend without interest to the needy and to cancel the debt when the seventh year arrives.

[9] If one is greedy, he is ruled by the law through his reason so that he neither gleans his harvest nor gathers the last grapes from the vineyard. In all other matters we can recognize that reason rules the emotions.

[10] For the law prevails even over affection for parents, so that virtue is not abandoned for their sakes.

[11] It is superior to love for one's wife, so that one rebukes her when she breaks the law.

[12] It takes precedence over love for children, so that one punishes them for misdeeds.

[13] It is sovereign over the relationship of friends, so that one rebukes friends when they act wickedly.

[14] Do not consider it paradoxical when reason, through the law, can prevail even over enmity. The fruit trees of the enemy are not cut down, but one preserves the property of enemies from the destroyers and helps raise up what has fallen.

[15] It is evident that reason rules even the more violent emotions: lust for power, vainglory, boasting, arrogance, and malice.

[16] For the temperate mind repels all these malicious emotions, just as it repels anger -- for it is sovereign over even this.

[17] When Moses was angry with Dathan and Abiram he did nothing against them in anger, but controlled his anger by reason.

[18] For, as I have said, the temperate mind is able to get the better of the emotions, to correct some, and to render others powerless.

[19] Why else did Jacob, our most wise father, censure the households of Simeon and Levi for their irrational slaughter of the entire tribe of the Shechemites, saying, "Cursed be their anger"?

[20] For if reason could not control anger, he would not have spoken thus.

[21] Now when God fashioned man, he planted in him emotions and inclinations,

[22] but at the same time he enthroned the mind among the senses as a sacred governor over them all.

[23] To the mind he gave the law; and one who lives subject to this will rule a kingdom that is temperate, just, good, and courageous.

[24] How is it then, one might say, that if reason is master of the emotions, it does not control forgetfulness and ignorance?

4Mac.3

[1] This notion is entirely ridiculous; for it is evident that reason rules not over its own emotions, but over those of the body.

[2] No one of us can eradicate that kind of desire, but reason can provide a way for us not to be enslaved by desire.

[3] No one of us can eradicate anger from the mind, but reason can help to deal with anger.

[4] No one of us can eradicate malice, but reason can fight at our side so that we are not overcome by malice.

[5] For reason does not uproot the emotions but is their antagonist.

[6] Now this can be explained more clearly by the story of King David's thirst.

[7] David had been attacking the Philistines all day long, and together with the soldiers of his nation had slain many of them.

[8] Then when evening fell, he came, sweating and quite exhausted, to the royal tent, around which the whole army of our ancestors had encamped.

[9] Now all the rest were at supper,

[10] but the king was extremely thirsty, and although springs were plentiful there, he could not satisfy his thirst from them.

[11] But a certain irrational desire for the water in the enemy's territory tormented and inflamed him, undid and consumed him.

[12] When his guards complained bitterly because of the king's craving, two staunch young soldiers, respecting the king's desire, armed themselves fully, and taking a pitcher climbed over the enemy's ramparts.

[13] Eluding the sentinels at the gates, they went searching throughout the enemy camp

[14] and found the spring, and from it boldly brought the king a drink.

[15] But David, although he was burning with thirst, considered it an altogether fearful danger to his soul to drink what was regarded as equivalent to blood.

[16] Therefore, opposing reason to desire, he poured out the drink as an offering to God.

[17] For the temperate mind can conquer the drives of the emotions and quench the flames of frenzied desires;

[18] it can overthrow bodily agonies even when they are extreme, and by nobility of reason spurn all domination by the emotions.

[19] The present occasion now invites us to a narrative demonstration of temperate reason.

[20] At a time when our fathers were enjoying profound peace because of their observance of the law and were prospering, so that even Seleucus Nicanor, king of Asia, had both appropriated money to them for the temple service and recognized their commonwealth --

[21] just at that time certain men attempted a revolution against the public harmony and caused many and various disasters.

4Mac.4

[1] Now there was a certain Simon, a political opponent of the noble and good man, Onias, who then held the high priesthood for life. When despite all manner of slander he was unable to injure Onias in the eyes of the nation, he fled the country with the purpose of betraying it.

[2] So he came to Apollonius, governor of Syria, Phoenicia, and Cilicia, and said,

[3] "I have come here because I am loyal to the king's government, to report that in the Jerusalem treasuries there are deposited tens of thousands in private funds, which are not the property of the temple but belong to King Seleucus."

[4] When Apollonius learned the details of these things, he praised Simon for his service to the king and went up to Seleucus to inform him of the rich treasure.

[5] On receiving authority to deal with this matter, he proceeded quickly to our country accompanied by the accursed Simon and a very strong military force.

[6] He said that he had come with the king's authority to seize the private funds in the treasury.

[7] The people indignantly protested his words, considering it outrageous that those who had committed deposits to the sacred treasury should be deprived of them, and did all that they could to prevent it.

[8] But, uttering threats, Apollonius went on to the temple.

[9] While the priests together with women and children were imploring God in the temple to shield the holy place that was being treated so contemptuously,

[10] and while Apollonius was going up with his armed forces to seize the money, angels on horseback with lightning flashing from their weapons appeared from heaven, instilling in them great fear and trembling.

[11] Then Apollonius fell down half dead in the temple area that was open to all, stretched out his hands toward heaven, and with tears besought the

Hebrews to pray for him and propitiate the wrath of the heavenly army.

[12] For he said that he had committed a sin deserving of death, and that if he were delivered he would praise the blessedness of the holy place before all people.

[13] Moved by these words, Onias the high priest, although otherwise he had scruples about doing so, prayed for him lest King Seleucus suppose that Apollonius had been overcome by human treachery and not by divine justice.

[14] So Apollonius, having been preserved beyond all expectations, went away to report to the king what had happened to him.

[15] When King Seleucus died, his son Antiochus Epiphanes succeeded to the throne, an arrogant and terrible man,

[16] who removed Onias from the priesthood and appointed Onias's brother Jason as high priest.

[17] Jason agreed that if the office were conferred upon him he would pay the king three thousand six hundred and sixty talents annually.

[18] So the king appointed him high priest and ruler of the nation.

[19] Jason changed the nation's way of life and altered its form of government in complete violation of the law,

[20] so that not only was a gymnasium constructed at the very citadel of our native land, but also the temple service was abolished.

[21] The divine justice was angered by these acts and caused Antiochus himself to make war on them.

[22] For when he was warring against Ptolemy in Egypt, he heard that a rumor of his death had spread and that the people of Jerusalem had rejoiced greatly. He speedily marched against them,

[23] and after he had plundered them he issued a decree that if any of them should be found observing the ancestral law they should die.

[24] When, by means of his decrees, he had not been able in any way to put an end to the people's observance of the law, but saw that all his threats and punishments were being disregarded,

[25] even to the point that women, because they had circumcised their sons, were thrown headlong from heights along with their infants, though they had known beforehand that they would suffer this --

[26] when, then, his decrees were despised by the people, he himself, through torture, tried to compel everyone in the nation to eat defiling foods and to renounce Judaism.

4Mac.5

[1] The tyrant Antiochus, sitting in state with his counselors on a certain high place, and with his armed soldiers standing about him,

[2] ordered the guards to seize each and every Hebrew and to compel them to eat pork and food sacrificed to idols.

[3] If any were not willing to eat defiling food, they were to be broken on the wheel and killed.

[4] And when many persons had been rounded up, one man, Eleazar by name, leader of the flock, was brought before the king. He was a man of priestly family, learned in the law, advanced in age, and known to many in the tyrant's court because of his philosophy.

[5] When Antiochus saw him he said,

[6] "Before I begin to torture you, old man, I would advise you to save yourself by eating pork,

[7] for I respect your age and your gray hairs. Although you have had them for so long a time, it does not seem to me that you are a philosopher when you observe the religion of the Jews.

[8] Why, when nature has granted it to us, should you abhor eating the very excellent meat of this animal?

[9] It is senseless not to enjoy delicious things that are not shameful, and wrong to spurn the gifts of nature.

[10] It seems to me that you will do something even more senseless if, by holding a vain opinion concerning the truth, you continue to despise me to your own hurt.

[11] Will you not awaken from your foolish philosophy, dispel your futile reasonings, adopt a mind appropriate to your years, philosophize according to the truth of what is beneficial,

[12] and have compassion on your old age by honoring my humane advice?

[13] For consider this, that if there is some power watching over this religion of yours, it will excuse you from any transgression that arises out of compulsion."

[14] When the tyrant urged him in this fashion to eat meat unlawfully, Eleazar asked to have a word.

[15] When he had received permission to speak, he began to address the people as follows:

[16] "We, O Antiochus, who have been persuaded to govern our lives by the divine law, think that there is no compulsion more powerful than our obedience to the law.

[17] Therefore we consider that we should not transgress it in any respect.

[18] Even if, as you suppose, our law were not truly divine and we had wrongly held it to be divine, not even so would it be right for us to invalidate our reputation for piety.

[19] Therefore do not suppose that it would be a petty sin if we were to eat defiling food;

[20] to transgress the law in matters either small or great is of equal seriousness,

[21] for in either case the law is equally despised.

[22] You scoff at our philosophy as though living by it were irrational,

[23] but it teaches us self-control, so that we master all pleasures and desires, and it also trains us in courage, so that we endure any suffering willingly;

[24] it instructs us in justice, so that in all our dealings we act impartially, and it teaches us piety, so that with proper reverence we worship the only real God.

[25] "Therefore we do not eat defiling food; for since we believe that the law was established by God, we know that in the nature of things the Creator of the world in giving us the law has shown sympathy toward us.

[26] He has permitted us to eat what will be most suitable for our lives, but he has forbidden us to eat meats that would be contrary to this.

[27] It would be tyrannical for you to compel us not only to transgress the law, but also to eat in such a way that you may deride us for eating defiling foods, which are most hateful to us.

[28] But you shall have no such occasion to laugh at me,

[29] nor will I transgress the sacred oaths of my ancestors concerning the keeping of the law,

[30] not even if you gouge out my eyes and burn my entrails.

[31] I am not so old and cowardly as not to be young in reason on behalf of piety.

[32] Therefore get your torture wheels ready and fan the fire more vehemently!

[33] I do not so pity my old age as to break the ancestral law by my own act.

[34] I will not play false to you, O law that trained me, nor will I renounce you, beloved self-control.

[35] I will not put you to shame, philosophical reason, nor will I reject you, honored priesthood and knowledge of the law.

[36] You, O king, shall not stain the honorable mouth of my old age, nor my long life lived lawfully.

[37] The fathers will receive me as pure, as one who does not fear your violence even to death.

[38] You may tyrannize the ungodly, but you shall not dominate my religious principles either by word or by deed."

4Mac.6

[1] When Eleazar in this manner had made eloquent response to the exhortations of the tyrant, the guards who were standing by dragged him violently to the instruments of torture.

[2] First they stripped the old man, who remained adorned with the gracefulness of his piety.

[3] And after they had tied his arms on each side they scourged him,

[4] while a herald opposite him cried out, "Obey the king's commands!"

[5] But the courageous and noble man, as a true Eleazar, was unmoved, as though being tortured in a dream;

[6] yet while the old man's eyes were raised to heaven, his flesh was being torn by scourges, his blood flowing, and his sides were being cut to pieces.

[7] And though he fell to the ground because his body could not endure the agonies, he kept his reason upright and unswerving.

[8] One of the cruel guards rushed at him and began to kick him in the side to make him get up again after he fell.

[9] But he bore the pains and scorned the punishment and endured the tortures.

[10] And like a noble athlete the old man, while being beaten, was victorious over his torturers;

[11] in fact, with his face bathed in sweat, and gasping heavily for breath, he amazed even his torturers by his courageous spirit.

[12] At that point, partly out of pity for his old age,

[13] partly out of sympathy from their acquaintance with him, partly out of admiration for his endurance, some of the king's retinue came to him and said,

[14] "Eleazar, why are you so irrationally destroying yourself through these evil things?

[15] We will set before you some cooked meat; save yourself by pretending to eat pork."

[16] But Eleazar, as though more bitterly tormented by this counsel, cried out:

[17] "May we, the children of Abraham, never think so basely that out of cowardice we feign a role unbecoming to us!

[18] For it would be irrational if we, who have lived in accordance with truth to old age and have maintained in accordance with law the reputation of such a life, should now change our course

[19] become a pattern of impiety to the young, in becoming an example of the eating of defiling food.

[20] It would be shameful if we should survive for a little while and during that time be a laughing stock to all for our cowardice,

[21] and if we should be despised by the tyrant as unmanly, and not protect our divine law even to death.

[22] Therefore, O children of Abraham, die nobly for your religion!

[23] And you, guards of the tyrant, why do you delay?"

[24] When they saw that he was so courageous in the face of the afflictions, and that he had not been changed by their compassion, the guards brought him to the fire.

[25] There they burned him with maliciously contrived instruments, threw him down, and poured stinking liquids into his nostrils.

[26] When he was now burned to his very bones and about to expire, he lifted up his eyes to God and said,

[27] "You know, O God, that though I might have saved myself, I am dying in burning torments for the sake of the law.

[28] Be merciful to your people, and let our punishment suffice for them.

[29] Make my blood their purification, and take my life in exchange for theirs."

[30] And after he said this, the holy man died nobly in his tortures, and by reason he resisted even to the very tortures of death for the sake of the law.

[31] Admittedly, then, devout reason is sovereign over the emotions.

[32] For if the emotions had prevailed over reason, we would have testified to their domination.

[33] But now that reason has conquered the emotions, we properly attribute to it the power to govern.

[34] And it is right for us to acknowledge the dominance of reason when it masters even external agonies. It would be ridiculous to deny it.

[35] And I have proved not only that reason has mastered agonies, but also that it masters pleasures and in no respect yields to them.

4Mac.7

[1] For like a most skilful pilot, the reason of our father Eleazar steered the ship of religion over the sea of the emotions,

[2] and though buffeted by the stormings of the tyrant and overwhelmed by the mighty waves of tortures,

[3] in no way did he turn the rudder of religion until he sailed into the haven of immortal victory.

[4] No city besieged with many ingenious war machines has ever held out as did that most holy man. Although his sacred life was consumed by tortures and racks, he conquered the besiegers with the shield of his devout reason.

[5] For in setting his mind firm like a jutting cliff, our father Eleazar broke the maddening waves of the emotions.

[6] O priest, worthy of the priesthood, you neither defiled your sacred teeth nor profaned your stomach, which had room only for reverence and purity, by eating defiling foods.

[7] O man in harmony with the law and philosopher of divine life!

[8] Such should be those who are administrators of the law, shielding it with their own blood and noble sweat in sufferings even to death.

[9] You, father, strengthened our loyalty to the law through your glorious endurance, and you did not abandon the holiness which you praised, but by your deeds you made your words of divine philosophy credible.

[10] O aged man, more powerful than tortures; O elder, fiercer than fire; O supreme king over the passions, Eleazar!

[11] For just as our father Aaron, armed with the censer, ran through the multitude of the people and conquered the fiery angel,

[12] so the descendant of Aaron, Eleazar, though being consumed by the fire, remained unmoved in his reason.

[13] Most amazing, indeed, though he was an old man, his body no longer tense and firm, his muscles flabby, his sinews feeble, he became young again

[14] in spirit through reason; and by reason like that of Isaac he rendered the many-headed rack ineffective.

[15] O man of blessed age and of venerable gray hair and of law-abiding life, whom the faithful seal of death has perfected!

[16] If, therefore, because of piety an aged man despised tortures even to death, most certainly devout reason is governor of the emotions.

[17] Some perhaps might say, "Not every one has full command of his emotions, because not every one has prudent reason."

[18] But as many as attend to religion with a whole heart, these alone are able to control the passions of the flesh,

[19] since they believe that they, like our patriarchs Abraham and Isaac and Jacob, do not die to God, but live in God.

[20] No contradiction therefore arises when some persons appear to be dominated by their emotions because of the weakness of their reason.

[21] What person who lives as a philosopher by the whole rule of philosophy, and trusts in God,

[22] and knows that it is blessed to endure any suffering for the sake of virtue, would not be able to overcome the emotions through godliness?

[23] For only the wise and courageous man is lord of his emotions.

4Mac.8

[1] For this is why even the very young, by following a philosophy in accordance with devout reason, have prevailed over the most painful instruments of torture.

[2] For when the tyrant was conspicuously defeated in his first attempt, being unable to compel an aged man to eat defiling foods, then in violent rage he commanded that others of the Hebrew captives be brought, and that any who ate defiling food should be freed after eating, but if any were to refuse, these should be tortured even more cruelly.

[3] When the tyrant had given these orders, seven brothers -- handsome, modest, noble, and accomplished in every way -- were brought before him along with their aged mother.

[4] When the tyrant saw them, grouped about their mother as if in a chorus, he was pleased with them. And struck by their appearance and nobility, he smiled at them, and summoned them nearer and said,

[5] "Young men, I admire each and every one of you in a kindly manner, and greatly respect the beauty and the number of such brothers. Not only do I advise you not to display the same madness as that of the old man who has just been tortured, but I also exhort you to yield to me and enjoy my friendship.

[6] Just as I am able to punish those who disobey my orders, so I can be a benefactor to those who obey me.

[7] Trust me, then, and you will have positions of authority in my government if you will renounce the ancestral tradition of your national life.

[8] And enjoy your youth by adopting the Greek way of life and by changing your manner of living.

[9] But if by disobedience you rouse my anger, you will compel me to destroy each and every one of you with dreadful punishments through tortures.

[10] Therefore take pity on yourselves. Even I, your enemy, have compassion for your youth and handsome appearance.

[11] Will you not consider this, that if you disobey, nothing remains for you but to die on the rack?"

[12] When he had said these things, he ordered the instruments of torture to be brought forward so as to persuade them out of fear to eat the defiling food.

[13] And when the guards had placed before them wheels and joint-dislocators, rack and hooks and catapults and caldrons, braziers and thumbscrews and iron claws and wedges and bellows, the tyrant resumed speaking:

[14] "Be afraid, young fellows, and whatever justice you revere will be merciful to you when you transgress under compulsion."

[15] But when they had heard the inducements and saw the dreadful devices, not only were they not afraid, but they also opposed the tyrant with their own philosophy, and by their right reasoning nullified his tyranny.

[16] Let us consider, on the other hand, what arguments might have been used if some of them had been cowardly and unmanly. Would they not have been these?

[17] "O wretches that we are and so senseless! Since the king has summoned and exhorted us to accept kind treatment if we obey him,

[18] why do we take pleasure in vain resolves and venture upon a disobedience that brings death?

[19] O men and brothers, should we not fear the instruments of torture and consider the threats of torments, and give up this vain opinion and this arrogance that threatens to destroy us?

[20] Let us take pity on our youth and have compassion on our mother's age;

[21] and let us seriously consider that if we disobey we are dead!

[22] Also, divine justice will excuse us for fearing the king when we are under compulsion.

[23] Why do we banish ourselves from this most pleasant life and deprive ourselves of this delightful world?

[24] Let us not struggle against compulsion nor take hollow pride in being put to the rack.

[25] Not even the law itself would arbitrarily slay us for fearing the instruments of torture.

[26] Why does such contentiousness excite us and such a fatal stubbornness please us, when we can live in peace if we obey the king?"

[27] But the youths, though about to be tortured, neither said any of these things nor even seriously considered them.

[28] For they were contemptuous of the emotions and sovereign over agonies,

[29] so that as soon as the tyrant had ceased counseling them to eat defiling food, all with one voice together, as from one mind, said:

4Mac.9

[1] "Why do you delay, O tyrant? For we are ready to die rather than transgress our ancestral commandments;

[2] we are obviously putting our forefathers to shame unless we should practice ready obedience to the law and to Moses our counselor.

[3] Tyrant and counselor of lawlessness, in your hatred for us do not pity us more than we pity ourselves.

[4] For we consider this pity of yours which insures our safety through transgression of the law to be more grievous than death itself.

[5] You are trying to terrify us by threatening us with death by torture, as though a short time ago you learned nothing from Eleazar.

[6] And if the aged men of the Hebrews because of their religion lived piously while enduring torture, it would be even more fitting that we young men should die despising your coercive tortures, which our aged instructor also overcame.

[7] Therefore, tyrant, put us to the test; and if you take our lives because of our religion, do not suppose that you can injure us by torturing us.

[8] For we, through this severe suffering and endurance, shall have the prize of virtue and shall be with God, for whom we suffer;

[9] but you, because of your bloodthirstiness toward us, will deservedly undergo from the divine justice eternal torment by fire."

[10] When they had said these things the tyrant not only was angry, as at those who are disobedient, but also was enraged, as at those who are ungrateful.

[11] Then at his command the guards brought forward the eldest, and having torn off his tunic, they bound his hands and arms with thongs on each side.

[12] When they had worn themselves out beating him with scourges, without accomplishing anything, they placed him upon the wheel.

[13] When the noble youth was stretched out around this, his limbs were dislocated,

[14] and though broken in every member he denounced the tyrant, saying,

[15] "Most abominable tyrant, enemy of heavenly justice, savage of mind, you are mangling me in this manner, not because I am a murderer, or as one who acts impiously, but because I protect the divine law."

[16] And when the guards said, "Agree to eat so that you may be released from the tortures,"

[17] he replied, "You abominable lackeys, your wheel is not so powerful as to strangle my reason. Cut my limbs, burn my flesh, and twist my joints.

[18] Through all these tortures I will convince you that sons of the Hebrews alone are invincible where virtue is concerned."

[19] While he was saying these things, they spread fire under him, and while fanning the flames they tightened the wheel further.

[20] The wheel was completely smeared with blood, and the heap of coals was being quenched by the drippings of gore, and pieces of flesh were falling off the axles of the machine.

[21] Although the ligaments joining his bones were already severed, the courageous youth, worthy of Abraham, did not groan,

[22] but as though transformed by fire into immortality he nobly endured the rackings.

[23] "Imitate me, brothers," he said. "Do not leave your post in my struggle or renounce our courageous brotherhood.

[24] Fight the sacred and noble battle for religion. Thereby the just Providence of our ancestors may become merciful to our nation and take vengeance on the accursed tyrant."

[25] When he had said this, the saintly youth broke the thread of life.

[26] While all were marveling at his courageous spirit, the guards brought in the next eldest, and after fitting themselves with iron gauntlets having sharp hooks, they bound him to the torture machine and catapult.

[27] Before torturing him, they inquired if he were willing to eat, and they heard this noble decision.

[28] These leopard-like beasts tore out his sinews with the iron hands, flayed all his flesh up to his chin, and tore away his scalp. But he steadfastly endured this agony and said,

[29] "How sweet is any kind of death for the religion of our fathers!"

[30] To the tyrant he said, "Do you not think, you most savage tyrant, that you are being tortured more than I, as you see the arrogant design of your tyranny being defeated by our endurance for the sake of religion?

[31] I lighten my pain by the joys that come from virtue,

[32] but you suffer torture by the threats that come from impiety. You will not escape, most abominable tyrant, the judgments of the divine wrath."

4Mac.10

[1] When he too had endured a glorious death, the third was led in, and many repeatedly urged him to save himself by tasting the meat.

[2] But he shouted, "Do you not know that the same father begot me and those who died, and the same mother bore me, and that I was brought up on the same teachings?

[3] I do not renounce the noble kinship that binds me to my brothers."

[4]

[5] Enraged by the man's boldness, they disjointed his hands and feet with their instruments, dismembering him by prying his limbs from their sockets,

[6] and breaking his fingers and arms and legs and elbows.

[7] Since they were not able in any way to break his spirit, they abandoned the instruments and scalped him with their fingernails in a Scythian fashion.

[8] They immediately brought him to the wheel, and while his vertebrae were being dislocated upon it he saw his own flesh torn all around and drops of blood flowing from his entrails.

[9] When he was about to die, he said,

[10] "We, most abominable tyrant, are suffering because of our godly training and virtue,

[11] but you, because of your impiety and bloodthirstiness, will undergo unceasing torments."

[12] When he also had died in a manner worthy of his brothers, they dragged in the fourth, saying,

[13] "As for you, do not give way to the same insanity as your brothers, but obey the king and save yourself."

[14] But he said to them, "You do not have a fire hot enough to make me play the coward.

[15] No, by the blessed death of my brothers, by the eternal destruction of the tyrant, and by the everlasting life of the pious, I will not renounce our noble brotherhood.

[16] Contrive tortures, tyrant, so that you may learn from them that I am a brother to those who have just been tortured."

[17] When he heard this, the bloodthirsty, murderous, and utterly abominable Antiochus gave orders to cut out his tongue.

[18] But he said, "Even if you remove my organ of speech, God hears also those who are mute.

[19] See, here is my tongue; cut it off, for in spite of this you will not make our reason speechless.

[20] Gladly, for the sake of God, we let our bodily members be mutilated.

[21] God will visit you swiftly, for you are cutting out a tongue that has been melodious with divine hymns."

4Mac.11

[1] When this one died also, after being cruelly tortured, the fifth leaped up, saying,

[2] "I will not refuse, tyrant, to be tortured for the sake of virtue.

[3] I have come of my own accord, so that by murdering me you will incur punishment from the heavenly justice for even more crimes.

[4] Hater of virtue, hater of mankind, for what act of ours are you destroying us in this way?

[5] Is it because we revere the Creator of all things and live according to his virtuous law?

[6] But these deeds deserve honors, not tortures."

[7]

[9] While he was saying these things, the guards bound him and dragged him to the catapult;

[10] they tied him to it on his knees, and fitting iron clamps on them, they twisted his back around the wedge on the wheel, so that he was completely curled back like a scorpion, and all his members were disjointed.

[11] In this condition, gasping for breath and in anguish of body,

[12] he said, "Tyrant, they are splendid favors that you grant us against your will, because through these noble sufferings you give us an opportunity to show our endurance for the law."

[13] After he too had died, the sixth, a mere boy, was led in. When the tyrant inquired whether he was willing to eat and be released, he said,

[14] "I am younger in age than my brothers, but I am their equal in mind.

[15] Since to this end we were born and bred, we ought likewise to die for the same principles.

[16] So if you intend to torture me for not eating defiling foods, go on torturing!"

[17] When he had said this, they led him to the wheel.

[18] He was carefully stretched tight upon it, his back was broken, and he was roasted from underneath.

[19] To his back they applied sharp spits that had been heated in the fire, and pierced his ribs so that his entrails were burned through.

[20] While being tortured he said, "O contest befitting holiness, in which so many of us brothers have been summoned to an arena of sufferings for religion, and in which we have not been defeated!

[21] For religious knowledge, O tyrant, is invincible.

[22] I also, equipped with nobility, will die with my brothers,

[23] and I myself will bring a great avenger upon you, you inventor of tortures and enemy of those who are truly devout.

[24] We six boys have paralyzed your tyranny!

[25] Since you have not been able to persuade us to change our mind or to force us to eat defiling foods, is not this your downfall?

[26] Your fire is cold to us, and the catapults painless, and your violence powerless.

[27] For it is not the guards of the tyrant but those of the divine law that are set over us; therefore, unconquered, we hold fast to reason."

4Mac.12

[1] When he also, thrown into the caldron, had died a blessed death, the seventh and youngest of all came forward.

[2] Even though the tyrant had been fearfully reproached by the brothers, he felt strong compassion for this child when he saw that he was already in fetters. He summoned him to come nearer and tried to console him, saying,

[3] "You see the result of your brothers' stupidity, for they died in torments because of their disobedience.

[4] You too, if you do not obey, will be miserably tortured and die before your time,

[5] but if you yield to persuasion you will be my friend and a leader in the government of the kingdom."

[6] When he had so pleaded, he sent for the boy's mother to show compassion on her who had been bereaved of so many sons and to influence her to persuade the surviving son to obey and save himself.

[7] But when his mother had exhorted him in the Hebrew language, as we shall tell a little later,

[8] he said, "Let me loose, let me speak to the king and to all his friends that are with him."

[9] Extremely pleased by the boy's declaration, they freed him at once.

[10] Running to the nearest of the braziers,

[11] he said, "You profane tyrant, most impious of all the wicked, since you have received good things and also your kingdom from God, were you not ashamed to murder his servants and torture on the wheel those who practice religion?

[12] Because of this, justice has laid up for you intense and eternal fire and tortures, and these throughout all time will never let you go.

[13] As a man, were you not ashamed, you most savage beast, to cut out the tongues of men who have feelings like yours and are made of the same elements as you, and to maltreat and torture them in this way?

[14] Surely they by dying nobly fulfilled their service to God, but you will wail bitterly for having slain without cause the contestants for virtue."

[15] Then because he too was about to die, he said,

[16] "I do not desert the excellent example of my brothers,

[17] and I call on the God of our fathers to be merciful to our nation;

[18] but on you he will take vengeance both in this present life and when you are dead."

[19] After he had uttered these imprecations, he flung himself into the braziers and so ended his life.

4Mac.13

[1] Since, then, the seven brothers despised sufferings even unto death, everyone must concede that devout reason is sovereign over the emotions.

[2] For if they had been slaves to their emotions and had eaten defiling food, we would say that they had been conquered by these emotions.

[3] But in fact it was not so. Instead, by reason, which is praised before God, they prevailed over their emotions.

[4] The supremacy of the mind over these cannot be overlooked, for the brothers mastered both emotions and pains.

[5] How then can one fail to confess the sovereignty of right reason over emotion in those who were not turned back by fiery agonies?

[6] For just as towers jutting out over harbors hold back the threatening waves and make it calm for those who sail into the inner basin,

[7] so the seven-towered right reason of the youths, by fortifying the harbor of religion, conquered the tempest of the emotions.

[8] For they constituted a holy chorus of religion and encouraged one another, saying,

[9] "Brothers, let us die like brothers for the sake of the law; let us imitate the three youths in Assyria who despised the same ordeal of the furnace.

[10] Let us not be cowardly in the demonstration of our piety."

[11] While one said, "Courage, brother," another said, "Bear up nobly,"

[12] and another reminded them, "Remember whence you came, and the father by whose hand Isaac would have submitted to being slain for the sake of religion."

[13] Each of them and all of them together looking at one another, cheerful and undaunted, said, "Let us with all our hearts consecrate ourselves to God, who gave us our lives, and let us use our bodies as a bulwark for the law.

[14] Let us not fear him who thinks he is killing us,

[15] for great is the struggle of the soul and the danger of eternal torment lying before those who transgress the commandment of God.

[16] Therefore let us put on the full armor of self-control, which is divine reason.

[17] For if we so die, Abraham and Isaac and Jacob will welcome us, and all the fathers will praise us."

[18] Those who were left behind said to each of the brothers who were being dragged away, "Do not put us to shame, brother, or betray the brothers who have died before us."

[19] You are not ignorant of the affection of brotherhood, which the divine and all-wise Providence has bequeathed through the fathers to their descendants and which was implanted in the mother's womb.

[20] There each of the brothers dwelt the same length of time and was shaped during the same period of

time; and growing from the same blood and through the same life, they were brought to the light of day.
[21] When they were born after an equal time of gestation, they drank milk from the same fountains. For such embraces brotherly-loving souls are nourished;
[22] and they grow stronger from this common nurture and daily companionship, and from both general education and our discipline in the law of God.
[23] Therefore, when sympathy and brotherly affection had been so established, the brothers were the more sympathetic to one another.
[24] Since they had been educated by the same law and trained in the same virtues and brought up in right living, they loved one another all the more.
[25] A common zeal for nobility expanded their goodwill and harmony toward one another,
[26] because, with the aid of their religion, they rendered their brotherly love more fervent.
[27] But although nature and companionship and virtuous habits had augmented the affection of brotherhood, those who were left endured for the sake of religion, while watching their brothers being maltreated and tortured to death.

4Mac.14

[1] Furthermore, they encouraged them to face the torture, so that they not only despised their agonies, but also mastered the emotions of brotherly love.
[2] O reason, more royal than kings and freer than the free!
[3] O sacred and harmonious concord of the seven brothers on behalf of religion!
[4] None of the seven youths proved coward or shrank from death,
[5] but all of them, as though running the course toward immortality, hastened to death by torture.
[6] Just as the hands and feet are moved in harmony with the guidance of the mind, so those holy youths, as though moved by an immortal spirit of devotion, agreed to go to death for its sake.
[7] O most holy seven, brothers in harmony! For just as the seven days of creation move in choral dance around religion,
[8] so these youths, forming a chorus, encircled the sevenfold fear of tortures and dissolved it.
[9] Even now, we ourselves shudder as we hear of the tribulations of these young men; they not only saw what was happening, yes, not only heard the direct word of threat, but also bore the sufferings patiently, and in agonies of fire at that.
[10] What could be more excruciatingly painful than this? For the power of fire is intense and swift, and it consumed their bodies quickly.
[11] Do not consider it amazing that reason had full command over these men in their tortures, since the mind of woman despised even more diverse agonies,

[12] for the mother of the seven young men bore up under the rackings of each one of her children.
[13] Observe how complex is a mother's love for her children, which draws everything toward an emotion felt in her inmost parts.
[14] Even unreasoning animals, like mankind, have a sympathy and parental love for their offspring.
[15] For example, among birds, the ones that are tame protect their young by building on the housetops,
[16] and the others, by building in precipitous chasms and in holes and tops of trees, hatch the nestlings and ward off the intruder.
[17] If they are not able to keep him away, they do what they can to help their young by flying in circles around them in the anguish of love, warning them with their own calls.
[18] And why is it necessary to demonstrate sympathy for children by the example of unreasoning animals,
[19] since even bees at the time for making honeycombs defend themselves against intruders as though with an iron dart sting those who approach their hive and defend it even to the death?
[20] But sympathy for her children did not sway the mother of the young men; she was of the same mind as Abraham.

4Mac.15

[1] O reason of the children, tyrant over the emotions! O religion, more desirable to the mother than her children!
[2] Two courses were open to this mother, that of religion, and that of preserving her seven sons for a time, as the tyrant had promised.
[3] She loved religion more, religion that preserves them for eternal life according to God's promise.
[4] In what manner might I express the emotions of parents who love their children? We impress upon the character of a small child a wondrous likeness both of mind and of form. Especially is this true of mothers, who because of their birthpangs have a deeper sympathy toward their offspring than do the fathers.
[5] Considering that mothers are the weaker sex and give birth to many, they are more devoted to their children.
[6] The mother of the seven boys, more than any other mother, loved her children. In seven pregnancies she had implanted in herself tender love toward them,
[7] and because of the many pains she suffered with each of them she had sympathy for them;
[8] yet because of the fear of God she disdained the temporary safety of her children.
[9] Not only so, but also because of the nobility of her sons and their ready obedience to the law she felt a greater tenderness toward them.
[10] For they were righteous and self-controlled and brave and magnanimous, and loved their brothers

and their mother, so that they obeyed her even to death in keeping the ordinances.

[11] Nevertheless, though so many factors influenced the mother to suffer with them out of love for her children, in the case of none of them were the various tortures strong enough to pervert her reason.

[12] Instead, the mother urged them on, each child singly and all together, to death for the sake of religion.

[13] O sacred nature and affection of parental love, yearning of parents toward offspring, nurture and indomitable suffering by mothers!

[14] This mother, who saw them tortured and burned one by one, because of religion did not change her attitude.

[15] She watched the flesh of her children consumed by fire, their toes and fingers scattered on the ground, and the flesh of the head to the chin exposed like masks.

[16] O mother, tried now by more bitter pains than even the birth-pangs you suffered for them!

[17] O woman, who alone gave birth to such complete devotion!

[18] When the first-born breathed his last it did not turn you aside, nor when the second in torments looked at you piteously nor when the third expired;

[19] nor did you weep when you looked at the eyes of each one in his tortures gazing boldly at the same agonies, and saw in their nostrils the signs of the approach of death.

[20] When you saw the flesh of children burned upon the flesh of other children, severed hands upon hands, scalped heads upon heads, and corpses fallen on other corpses and when you saw the place filled with many spectators of the torturings, you did not shed tears.

[21] Neither the melodies of sirens nor the songs of swans attract the attention of their hearers as did the voices of the children in torture calling to their mother.

[22] How great and how many torments the mother then suffered as her sons were tortured on the wheel and with the hot irons!

[23] But devout reason, giving her heart a man's courage in the very midst of her emotions, strengthened her to disregard her temporal love for her children.

[24] Although she witnessed the destruction of seven children and the ingenious and various rackings, this noble mother disregarded all these because of faith in God.

[25] For as in the council chamber of her own soul she saw mighty advocates -- nature, family, parental love, and the rackings of her children --

[26] this mother held two ballots, one bearing death and the other deliverance for her children.

[27] She did not approve the deliverance which would preserve the seven sons for a short time,

[28] but as the daughter of God-fearing Abraham she remembered his fortitude.

[29] O mother of the nation, vindicator of the law and champion of religion, who carried away the prize of the contest in your heart!

[30] O more noble than males in steadfastness, and more manly than men in endurance!

[31] Just as Noah's ark, carrying the world in the universal flood, stoutly endured the waves,

[32] so you, O guardian of the law, overwhelmed from every side by the flood of your emotions and the violent winds, the torture of your sons, endured nobly and withstood the wintry storms that assail religion.

4Mac.16

[1] If, then, a woman, advanced in years and mother of seven sons, endured seeing her children tortured to death, it must be admitted that devout reason is sovereign over the emotions.

[2] Thus I have demonstrated not only that men have ruled over the emotions, but also that a woman has despised the fiercest tortures.

[3] The lions surrounding Daniel were not so savage, nor was the raging fiery furnace of Mishael so intensely hot, as was her innate parental love, inflamed as she saw her seven sons tortured in such varied ways.

[4] But the mother quenched so many and such great emotions by devout reason.

[5] Consider this also. If this woman, though a mother, had been fainthearted, she would have mourned over them and perhaps spoken as follows:

[6] "O how wretched am I and many times unhappy! After bearing seven children, I am now the mother of none!

[7] O seven childbirths all in vain, seven profitless pregnancies, fruitless nurturings and wretched nursings!

[8] In vain, my sons, I endured many birth-pangs for you, and the more grievous anxieties of your upbringing.

[9] Alas for my children, some unmarried, others married and without offspring. I shall not see your children or have the happiness of being called grandmother.

[10] Alas, I who had so many and beautiful children am a widow and alone, with many sorrows.

[11] Nor when I die, shall I have any of my sons to bury me."

[12] Yet the sacred and God-fearing mother did not wail with such a lament for any of them, nor did she dissuade any of them from dying, nor did she grieve as they were dying,

[13] but, as though having a mind like adamant and giving rebirth for immortality to the whole number of

her sons, she implored them and urged them on to death for the sake of religion.

[14] O mother, soldier of God in the cause of religion, elder and woman! By steadfastness you have conquered even a tyrant, and in word and deed you have proved more powerful than a man.

[15] For when you and your sons were arrested together, you stood and watched Eleazar being tortured, and said to your sons in the Hebrew language,

[16] "My sons, noble is the contest to which you are called to bear witness for the nation. Fight zealously for our ancestral law.

[17] For it would be shameful if, while an aged man endures such agonies for the sake of religion, you young men were to be terrified by tortures.

[18] Remember that it is through God that you have had a share in the world and have enjoyed life,

[19] and therefore you ought to endure any suffering for the sake of God.

[20] For his sake also our father Abraham was zealous to sacrifice his son Isaac, the ancestor of our nation; and when Isaac saw his father's hand wielding a sword and descending upon him, he did not cower.

[21] And Daniel the righteous was thrown to the lions, and Hananiah, Azariah, and Mishael were hurled into the fiery furnace and endured it for the sake of God.

[22] You too must have the same faith in God and not be grieved.

[23] It is unreasonable for people who have religious knowledge not to withstand pain."

[24] By these words the mother of the seven encouraged and persuaded each of her sons to die rather than violate God's commandment.

[25] They knew also that those who die for the sake of God live in God, as do Abraham and Isaac and Jacob and all the patriarchs.

4Mac.17

[1] Some of the guards said that when she also was about to be seized and put to death she threw herself into the flames so that no one might touch her body.

[2] O mother, who with your seven sons nullified the violence of the tyrant, frustrated his evil designs, and showed the courage of your faith!

[3] Nobly set like a roof on the pillars of your sons, you held firm and unswerving against the earthquake of the tortures.

[4] Take courage, therefore, O holy-minded mother, maintaining firm an enduring hope in God.

[5] The moon in heaven, with the stars, does not stand so august as you, who, after lighting the way of your star-like seven sons to piety, stand in honor before God and are firmly set in heaven with them.

[6] For your children were true descendants of father Abraham.

[7] If it were possible for us to paint the history of your piety as an artist might, would not those who first beheld it have shuddered as they saw the mother of the seven children enduring their varied tortures to death for the sake of religion?

[8] Indeed it would be proper to inscribe upon their tomb these words as a reminder to the people of our nation:

[9] "Here lie buried an aged priest and an aged woman and seven sons, because of the violence of the tyrant who wished to destroy the way of life of the Hebrews.

[10] They vindicated their nation, looking to God and enduring torture even to death."

[11] Truly the contest in which they were engaged was divine,

[12] for on that day virtue gave the awards and tested them for their endurance. The prize was immortality in endless life.

[13] Eleazar was the first contestant, the mother of the seven sons entered the competition, and the brothers contended.

[14] The tyrant was the antagonist, and the world and the human race were the spectators.

[15] Reverence for God was victor and gave the crown to its own athletes.

[16] Who did not admire the athletes of the divine legislation? Who were not amazed?

[17] The tyrant himself and all his council marveled at their endurance,

[18] because of which they now stand before the divine throne and live through blessed eternity.

[19] For Moses says, "All who are consecrated are under your hands."

[20] These, then, who have been consecrated for the sake of God, are honored, not only with this honor, but also by the fact that because of them our enemies did not rule over our nation,

[21] the tyrant was punished, and the homeland purified -- they having become, as it were, a ransom for the sin of our nation.

[22] And through the blood of those devout ones and their death as an expiation, divine Providence preserved Israel that previously had been afflicted.

[23] For the tyrant Antiochus, when he saw the courage of their virtue and their endurance under the tortures, proclaimed them to his soldiers as an example for their own endurance,

[24] and this made them brave and courageous for infantry battle and siege, and he ravaged and conquered all his enemies.

4Mac.18

[1] O Israelite children, offspring of the seed of Abraham, obey this law and exercise piety in every way,

[2] knowing that devout reason is master of all emotions, not only of sufferings from within, but also of those from without.

[3] Therefore those who gave over their bodies in suffering for the sake of religion were not only admired by men, but also were deemed worthy to share in a divine inheritance.

[4] Because of them the nation gained peace, and by reviving observance of the law in the homeland they ravaged the enemy.

[5] The tyrant Antiochus was both punished on earth and is being chastised after his death. Since in no way whatever was he able to compel the Israelites to become pagans and to abandon their ancestral customs, he left Jerusalem and marched against the Persians.

[6] The mother of seven sons expressed also these principles to her children:

[7] "I was a pure virgin and did not go outside my father's house; but I guarded the rib from which woman was made.

[8] No seducer corrupted me on a desert plain, nor did the destroyer, the deceitful serpent, defile the purity of my virginity.

[9] In the time of my maturity I remained with my husband, and when these sons had grown up their father died. A happy man was he, who lived out his life with good children, and did not have the grief of bereavement.

[10] While he was still with you, he taught you the law and the prophets.

[11] He read to you about Abel slain by Cain, and Isaac who was offered as a burnt offering, and of Joseph in prison.

[12] He told you of the zeal of Phineas, and he taught you about Hananiah, Azariah, and Mishael in the fire.

[13] He praised Daniel in the den of the lions and blessed him.

[14] He reminded you of the scripture of Isaiah, which says, `Even though you go through the fire, the flame shall not consume you.'

[15] He sang to you songs of the psalmist David, who said, `Many are the afflictions of the righteous.'

[16] He recounted to you Solomon's proverb, `There is a tree of life for those who do his will.'

[17] He confirmed the saying of Ezekiel, `Shall these dry bones live?'

[18] For he did not forget to teach you the song that Moses taught, which says,

[19] `I kill and I make alive: this is your life and the length of your days.'"

[20] O bitter was that day -- and yet not bitter -- when that bitter tyrant of the Greeks quenched fire with fire in his cruel caldrons, and in his burning rage brought those seven sons of the daughter of Abraham to the catapult and back again to more tortures,

[21] pierced the pupils of their eyes and cut out their tongues, and put them to death with various tortures.

[22] For these crimes divine justice pursued and will pursue the accursed tyrant.

[23] But the sons of Abraham with their victorious mother are gathered together into the chorus of the fathers, and have received pure and immortal souls from God,

[24] to whom be glory for ever and ever. Amen.

1 Esdras

[1] Josiah kept the passover to his Lord in Jerusalem; he killed the passover lamb on the fourteenth day of the first month,

[2] having placed the priests according to their divisions, arrayed in their garments, in the temple of the Lord.

[3] And he told the Levites, the temple servants of Israel, that they should sanctify themselves to the Lord and put the holy ark of the Lord in the house which Solomon the king, the son of David, had built;

[4] and he said, "You need no longer carry it upon your shoulders. Now worship the Lord your God and serve his people Israel; and prepare yourselves by your families and kindred,

[5] in accordance with the directions of David king of Israel and the magnificence of Solomon his son. Stand in order in the temple according to the groupings of the fathers' houses of you Levites, who minister before your brethren the people of Israel,

[6] and kill the passover lamb and prepare the sacrifices for your brethren, and keep the passover according to the commandment of the Lord which was given to Moses."

[7] And Josiah gave to the people who were present thirty thousand lambs and kids, and three thousand calves; these were given from the king's possessions, as he promised, to the people and the priests and Levites.

[8] And Hilkiah, Zechariah, and Jehiel, the chief officers of the temple, gave to the priests for the passover two thousand six hundred sheep and three hundred calves. [9] And Jeconiah and Shemaiah and Nethanel his brother, and Hashabiah and Ochiel and Joram, captains over thousands, gave the Levites for the passover five thousand sheep and seven hundred calves. [10] And this is what took place. The priests and the Levites, properly arrayed and having the unleavened bread, stood according to kindred

[11] and the grouping of the fathers' houses, before the people, to make the offering to the Lord as it is written in the book of Moses; this they did in the morning. [12] They roasted the passover lamb with fire, as required; and they boiled the sacrifices in brass pots and caldrons, with a pleasing odor, [13] and carried them to all the people. Afterward they prepared the passover for themselves and for their brethren the priests, the sons of Aaron, [14] because the priests were offering the fat until night; so the Levites prepared it for themselves and for their brethren the priests, the sons of Aaron. [15] And the temple singers, the sons of Asaph, were in their place according to the arrangement made by David, and also Asaph, Zechariah, and Eddinus, who represented the king. [16] The gatekeepers were at each gate; no one needed to depart from his duties, for their brethren the Levites prepared the passover for them.

[17] So the things that had to do with the sacrifices to the Lord were accomplished that day: the passover was kept

[18] and the sacrifices were offered on the altar of the Lord, according to the command of King Josiah. [19] And the people of Israel who were present at that time kept the passover and the feast of unleavened bread seven days. [20] No passover like it had been kept in Israel since the times of Samuel the prophet; [21] none of the kings of Israel had kept such a passover as was kept by Josiah and the priests and Levites and the men of Judah and all of Israel who were dwelling in Jerusalem. [22] In the eighteenth year of the reign of Josiah this passover was kept. [23] And the deeds of Josiah were upright in the sight of the Lord, for his heart was full of godliness. [24] The events of his reign have been recorded in the past, concerning those who sinned and acted wickedly toward the Lord beyond any other people or kingdom, and how they grieved the Lord deeply, so that the words of the Lord rose up against Israel.

[25] After all these acts of Josiah, it happened that Pharaoh, king of Egypt, went to make war at Carchemish on the Euphrates, and Josiah went out against him.

[26] And the king of Egypt sent word to him saying, "What have we to do with each other, king of Judea? [27] I was not sent against you by the Lord God, for my war is at the Euphrates. And now the Lord is with me! The Lord is with me, urging me on! Stand aside, and do not oppose the Lord." [28] But Josiah did not turn back to his chariot, but tried to fight with him, and did not heed the words of Jeremiah the prophet from the mouth of the Lord.

[29] He joined battle with him in the plain of Megiddo, and the commanders came down against King Josiah. [30] And the king said to his servants, "Take me away from the battle, for I am very weak." And immediately his servants took him out of the line of battle. [31] And he got into his second chariot; and after he was brought back to Jerusalem he died, and was buried in the tomb of his fathers. [32] And in all Judea they mourned for Josiah. Jeremiah the prophet lamented for Josiah, and the principal men, with the women, have made lamentation for him to this day; it was ordained that this should always be done throughout the whole nation of Israel. [33] These things are written in the book of the histories of the kings of Judea; and every one of the acts of Josiah, and his splendor, and his understanding of the law of the Lord, and the things that he had done before and these that are now told, are recorded in the book of the kings of Israel and Judah. [34] And the men of the nation took Jeconiah the son of Josiah, who was

twenty-three years old, and made him king in succession to Josiah his father.

[35] And he reigned three months in Judah and Jerusalem. Then the king of Egypt deposed him from reigning in Jerusalem, [36] and fined the nation a hundred talents of silver and a talent of gold. [37] And the king of Egypt made Jehoiakim his brother king of Judea and Jerusalem. [38] Jehoiakim put the nobles in prison, and seized his brother Zarius and brought him up out of Egypt. [39] Jehoiakim was twenty-five years old when he began to reign in Judea and Jerusalem, and he did what was evil in the sight of the Lord.

[40] And Nebuchadnezzar king of Babylon came up against him, and bound him with a chain of brass and took him away to Babylon. [41] Nebuchadnezzar also took some holy vessels of the Lord, and carried them away, and stored them in his temple in Babylon.

[42] But the things that are reported about Jehoiakim and his uncleanness and impiety are written in the chronicles of the kings. [43] Jehoiachin his son became king in his stead; when he was made king he was eighteen years old,

[44] and he reigned three months and ten days in Jerusalem. He did what was evil in the sight of the Lord. [45] So after a year Nebuchadnezzar sent and removed him to Babylon, with the holy vessels of the Lord, [46] and made Zedekiah king of Judea and Jerusalem.

Zedekiah was twenty-one years old, and he reigned eleven years.

[47] He also did what was evil in the sight of the Lord, and did not heed the words that were spoken by Jeremiah the prophet from the mouth of the Lord.

[48] And though King Nebuchadnezzar had made him swear by the name of the Lord, he broke his oath and rebelled; and he stiffened his neck and hardened his heart and transgressed the laws of the Lord, the God of Israel. [49] Even the leaders of the people and of the priests committed many acts of sacrilege and lawlessness beyond all the unclean deeds of all the nations, and polluted the temple of the Lord which had been hallowed in Jerusalem. [50] So the God of their fathers sent by his messenger to call them back, because he would have spared them and his dwelling place. [51] But they mocked his messengers, and whenever the Lord spoke, they scoffed at his prophets, [52] until in his anger against his people because of their ungodly acts he gave command to bring against them the kings of the Chaldeans. [53] These slew their young men with the sword around their holy temple, and did not spare young man or virgin, old man or child, for he gave them all into their hands. [54] And all the holy vessels of the Lord, great and small, and the treasure chests of the Lord, and the royal stores, they took and carried away to

Babylon. [55] And they burned the house of the Lord and broke down the walls of Jerusalem and burned their towers with fire, [56] and utterly destroyed all its glorious things. The survivors he led away to Babylon with the sword, [57] and they were servants to him and to his sons until the Persians began to reign, in fulfillment of the word of the Lord by the mouth of Jeremiah: [58] "Until the land has enjoyed its sabbaths, it shall keep sabbath all the time of its desolation until the completion of seventy years."

2

[1] In the first year of Cyrus as king of the Persians, that the word of the Lord by the mouth of Jeremiah might be accomplished,

[2] the Lord stirred up the spirit of Cyrus king of the Persians, and he made a proclamation throughout all his kingdom and also put it in writing: [3] "Thus says Cyrus king of the Persians: The Lord of Israel, the Lord Most High, has made me king of the world,

[4] and he has commanded me to build him a house at Jerusalem, which is in Judea. [5] If any one of you, therefore, is of his people, may his Lord be with him, and let him go up to Jerusalem, which is in Judea, and build the house of the Lord of Israel -- he is the Lord who dwells in Jerusalem, [6] and let each man, wherever he may live, be helped by the men of his place with gold and silver, [7] with gifts and with horses and cattle, besides the other things added as votive offerings for the temple of the Lord which is in Jerusalem." [8] Then arose the heads of families of the tribes of Judah and Benjamin, and the priests and the Levites, and all whose spirit the Lord had stirred to go up to build the house in Jerusalem for the Lord;

[9] and their neighbors helped them with everything, with silver and gold, with horses and cattle, and with a very great number of votive offerings from many whose hearts were stirred. [10] Cyrus the king also brought out the holy vessels of the Lord which Nebuchadnezzar had carried away from Jerusalem and stored in his temple of idols.

[11] When Cyrus king of the Perians brought these out, he gave them to Mithridates his treasurer, [12] and by him they were given to Sheshbazzar the governor of Judea. [13] The number of these was: a thousand gold cups, a thousand silver cups, twenty-nine silver censers, thirty gold bowls, two thousand four hundred and ten silver bowls, and a thousand other vessels. [14] All the vessels were handed over, gold and silver, five thousand four hundred and sixty-nine, [15] and they were carried back by Sheshbazzar with the returning exiles from Babylon to Jerusalem. [16] But in the time of Artaxerxes king of the Persians, Bishlam, Mithridates, Tabeel, Rehum, Beltethmus, Shimshai the scribe, and the rest of their associates, living in Samaria and other places, wrote

him the following letter, against those who were living in Judea and Jerusalem:

[17] "To King Artaxerxes our lord, Your servants Rehum the recorder and Shimshai the scribe and the other judges of their council in Coelesyria and Phoenicia:

[18] Now be it known to our lord the king that the Jews who came up from you to us have gone to Jerusalem and are building that rebellious and wicked city, repairing its market places and walls and laying the foundations for a temple. [19] Now if this city is built and the walls finished, they will not only refuse to pay tribute but will even resist kings. [20] And since the building of the temple is now going on, we think it best not to neglect such a matter, [21] but to speak to our lord the king, in order that, if it seems good to you, search may be made in the records of your fathers. [22] You will find in the chronicles what has been written about them, and will learn that this city was rebellious, troubling both kings and other cities, [23] and that the Jews were rebels and kept setting up blockades in it from of old. That is why this city was laid waste. [24] Therefore we now make known to you, O lord and king, that if this city is built and its walls finished, you will no longer have access to Coelesyria and Phoenicia." [25] Then the king, in reply to Rehum the recorder and Beltethmus and Shimshai the scribe and the others associated with them and living in Samaria and Syria and Phoenicia, wrote as follows:

[26] "I have read the letter which you sent me. So I ordered search to be made, and it has been found that this city from of old has fought against kings,

[27] and that the men in it were given to rebellion and war, and that mighty and cruel kings ruled in Jerusalem and exacted tribute from Coelesyria and Phoenicia. [28] Therefore I have now issued orders to prevent these men from building the city and to take care that nothing more be done [29] and that such wicked proceedings go no further to the annoyance of kings." [30] Then, when the letter from King Artaxerxes was read, Rehum and Shimshai the scribe and their associates went in haste to Jerusalem, with horsemen and a multitude in battle array, and began to hinder the builders. And the building of the temple in Jerusalem ceased until the second year of the reign of Darius king of the Persians.

3

[1] Now King Darius gave a great banquet for all that were under him and all that were born in his house and all the nobles of Media and Persia

[2] and all the satraps and generals and governors that were under him in the hundred and twenty-seven satrapies from India to Ethiopia. [3] They ate and drank, and when they were satisfied they departed; and Darius the king went to his bedroom,

and went to sleep, and then awoke. [4] Then the three young men of the bodyguard, who kept guard over the person of the king, said to one another,

[5] "Let each of us state what one thing is strongest; and to him whose statement seems wisest, Darius the king will give rich gifts and great honors of victory.

[6] He shall be clothed in purple, and drink from gold cups, and sleep on a gold bed, and have a chariot with gold bridles, and a turban of fine linen, and a necklace about his neck; [7] and because of his wisdom he shall sit next to Darius and shall be called kinsman of Darius." [8] Then each wrote his own statement, and they sealed them and put them under the pillow of Darius the king,

[9] and said, "When the king wakes, they will give him the writing; and to the one whose statement the king and the three nobles of Persia judge to be wisest the victory shall be given according to what is written." [10] The first wrote, "Wine is strongest."

[11] The second wrote, "The king is strongest." [12] The third wrote, "Women are strongest, but truth is victor over all things." [13] When the king awoke, they took the writing and gave it to him, and he read it.

[14] Then he sent and summoned all the nobles of Persia and Media and the satraps and generals and governors and prefects, [15] and he took his seat in the council chamber, and the writing was read in their presence. [16] And he said, "Call the young men, and they shall explain their statements." So they were summoned, and came in. [17] And they said to them, "Explain to us what you have written."

Then the first, who had spoken of the strength of wine, began and said:

[18] "Gentlemen, how is wine the strongest? It leads astray the minds of all who drink it. [19] It makes equal the mind of the king and the orphan, of the slave and the free, of the poor and the rich. [20] It turns every thought to feasting and mirth, and forgets all sorrow and debt. [21] It makes all hearts feel rich, forgets kings and satraps, and makes every one talk in millions. [22] When men drink they forget to be friendly with friends and brothers, and before long they draw their swords. [23] And when they recover from the wine, they do not remember what they have done. [24] Gentlemen, is not wine the strongest, since it forces men to do these things?" When he had said this, he stopped speaking.

4

[1] Then the second, who had spoken of the strength of the king, began to speak: [2] "Gentlemen, are not men strongest, who rule over land and sea and all that is in them? [3] But the king is stronger; he is their lord and master, and whatever he says to them they obey. [4] If he tells them to make war on one

another, they do it; and if he sends them out against the enemy, they go, and conquer mountains, walls, and towers. [5] They kill and are killed, and do not disobey the king's command; if they win the victory, they bring everything to the king -- whatever spoil they take and everything else. [6] Likewise those who do not serve in the army or make war but till the soil, whenever they sow, reap the harvest and bring some to the king; and they compel one another to pay taxes to the king. [7] And yet he is only one man! If he tells them to kill, they kill; if he tells them to release, they release; [8] if he tells them to attack, they attack; if he tells them to lay waste, they lay waste; if he tells them to build, they build; [9] if he tells them to cut down, they cut down; if he tells them to plant, they plant. [10] All his people and his armies obey him. Moreover, he reclines, he eats and drinks and sleeps, [11] but they keep watch around him and no one may go away to attend to his own affairs, nor do they disobey him. [12] Gentlemen, why is not the king the strongest, since he is to be obeyed in this fashion?" And he stopped speaking.
[13] Then the third, that is Zerubbabel, who had spoken of women and truth, began to speak:
[14] Gentlemen, is not the king great, and are not men many, and is not wine strong? Who then is their master, or who is their lord? Is it not women? [15] Women gave birth to the king and to every people that rules over sea and land. [16] From women they came; and women brought up the very men who plant the vineyards from which comes wine. [17] Women make men's clothes; they bring men glory; men cannot exist without women. [18] If men gather gold and silver or any other beautiful thing, and then see a woman lovely in appearance and beauty, [19] they let all those things go, and gape at her, and with open mouths stare at her, and all prefer her to gold or silver or any other beautiful thing. [20] A man leaves his own father, who brought him up, and his own country, and cleaves to his wife. [21] With his wife he ends his days, with no thought of his father or his mother or his country. [22] Hence you must realize that women rule over you!
"Do you not labor and toil, and bring everything and give it to women?
[23] A man takes his sword, and goes out to travel and rob and steal and to sail the sea and rivers; [24] he faces lions, and he walks in darkness, and when he steals and robs and plunders, he brings it back to the woman he loves. [25] A man loves his wife more than his father or his mother. [26] Many men have lost their minds because of women, and have become slaves because of them. [27] Many have perished, or stumbled, or sinned, because of women. [28] And now do you not believe me?

"Is not the king great in his power? Do not all lands fear to touch him?
[29] Yet I have seen him with Apame, the king's concubine, the daughter of the illustrious Bartacus; she would sit at the king's right hand [30] and take the crown from the king's head and put it on her own, and slap the king with her left hand. [31] At this the king would gaze at her with mouth agape. If she smiles at him, he laughs; if she loses her temper with him, he flatters her, that she may be reconciled to him.
 [32] Gentlemen, why are not women strong, since they do such things?" [33] Then the king and the nobles looked at one another; and he began to speak about truth:
[34] "Gentlemen, are not women strong? The earth is vast, and heaven is high, and the sun is swift in its course, for it makes the circuit of the heavens and returns to its place in one day. [35] Is he not great who does these things? But truth is great, and stronger than all things. [36] The whole earth calls upon truth, and heaven blesses her. All God's works quake and tremble, and with him there is nothing unrighteous. [37] Wine is unrighteous, the king is unrighteous, women are unrighteous, all the sons of men are unrighteous, all their works are unrighteous, and all such things. There is no truth in them and in their unrighteousness they will perish. [38] But truth endures and is strong for ever, and lives and prevails for ever and ever. [39] With her there is no partiality or preference, but she does what is righteous instead of anything that is unrighteous or wicked. All men approve her deeds, [40] and there is nothing unrighteous in her judgment. To her belongs the strength and the kingship and the power and the majesty of all the ages. Blessed be the God of truth!"
[41] He ceased speaking; then all the people shouted, and said, "Great is truth, and strongest of all!" [42] Then the king said to him, "Ask what you wish, even beyond what is written, and we will give it to you, for you have been found to be the wisest. And you shall sit next to me, and be called my kinsman."
[43] Then he said to the king, "Remember the vow which you made to build Jerusalem, in the day when you became king, [44] and to send back all the vessels that were taken from Jerusalem, which Cyrus set apart when he began to destroy Babylon, and vowed to send them back there. [45] You also vowed to build the temple, which the Edomites burned when Judea was laid waste by the Chaldeans. [46] And now, O lord the king, this is what I ask and request of you, and this befits your greatness. I pray therefore that you fulfil the vow whose fulfilment you vowed to the King of heaven with your own lips." [47] Then Darius the king rose, and kissed him, and wrote letters for him to all the treasurers and governors and generals and satraps, that they should give escort to

him and all who were going up with him to build Jerusalem.

[48] And he wrote letters to all the governors in Coelesyria and Phoenicia and to those in Lebanon, to bring cedar timber from Lebanon to Jerusalem, and to help him build the city. [49] And he wrote for all the Jews who were going up from his kingdom to Judea, in the interest of their freedom, that no officer or satrap or governor or treasurer should forcibly enter their doors; [50] that all the country which they would occupy should be theirs without tribute; that the Idumeans should give up the villages of the Jews which they held; [51] that twenty talents a year should be given for the building of the temple until it was completed, [52] and an additional ten talents a year for burnt offerings to be offered on the altar every day, in accordance with the commandment to make seventeen offerings; [53] and that all who came from Babylonia to build the city should have their freedom, they and their children and all the priests who came. [54] He wrote also concerning their support and the priests' garments in which they were to minister. [55] He wrote that the support for the Levites should be provided until the day when the temple should be finished and Jerusalem built. [56] He wrote that land and wages should be provided for all who guarded the city. [57] And he sent back from Babylon all the vessels which Cyrus had set apart; everything that Cyrus had ordered to be done, he also commanded to be done and to be sent to Jerusalem.

[58] When the young man went out, he lifted up his face to heaven toward Jerusalem, and praised the King of heaven, saying,

[59] "From thee is the victory; from thee is wisdom, and your is the glory. I am thy servant. [60] Blessed art thou, who hast given me wisdom; I give thee thanks, O Lord of our fathers." [61] So he took the letters, and went to Babylon and told this to all his brethren.

[62] And they praised the God of their fathers, because he had given them release and permission [63] to go up and build Jerusalem and the temple which is called by his name; and they feasted, with music and rejoicing, for seven days.

5

[1] After this the heads of fathers' houses were chosen to go up, according to their tribes, with their wives and sons and daughters, and their menservants and maidservants, and their cattle.

[2] And Darius sent with them a thousand horsemen to take them back to Jerusalem in safety, with the music of drums and flutes; [3] and all their brethren were making merry. And he made them go up with them. [4] These are the names of the men who went up, according to their fathers' houses in the tribes, over their groups:

[5] the priests, the sons of Phinehas, son of Aaron; Jeshua the son of Jozadak, son of Seraiah, and Joakim the son of Zerubbabel, son of Shealtiel, of the house of David, of the lineage of Phares, of the tribe of Judah, [6] who spoke wise words before Darius the king of the Persians, in the second year of his reign, in the month of Nisan, the first month. [7] These are the men of Judea who came up out of their sojourn in captivity, whom Nebuchadnezzar king of Babylon had carried away to Babylon

[8] and who returned to Jerusalem and the rest of Judea, each to his own town. They came with Zerubbabel and Jeshua, Nehemiah, Seraiah, Resaiah, Bigvai, Mordecai, Bilshan, Mispar, Reeliah, Rehum, and Baanah, their leaders. [9] The number of the men of the nation and their leaders: the sons of Parosh, two thousand one hundred and seventy-two. The sons of Shephatiah, four hundred and seventy-two.

[10] The sons of Arah, seven hundred and fifty-six.

[11] The sons of Pahathmoab, of the sons of Jeshua and Joab, two thousand eight hundred and twelve.

[12] The sons of Elam, one thousand two hundred and fifty-four. The sons of Zattu, nine hundred and forty-five. The sons of Chorbe, seven hundred and five. The sons of Bani, six hundred and forty-eight.

[13] The sons of Bebai, six hundred and twenty-three. The sons of Azgad, one thousand three hundred and twenty-two. [14] The sons of Adonikam, six hundred and sixty-seven. The sons of Bigvai, two thousand and sixty-six. The sons of Adin, four hundred and fifty-four. [15] The sons of Ater, namely of Hezekiah, ninety-two. The sons of Kilan and Azetas, sixty-seven. The sons of Azaru, four hundred and thirty-two. [16] The sons of Annias, one hundred and one. The sons of Arom. The sons of Bezai, three hundred and twenty-three. The sons of Jorah, one hundred and twelve.

[17] The sons of Baiterus, three thousand and five. The sons of Bethlehem, one hundred and twenty-three. [18] The men of Netophah, fifty-five. The men of Anathoth, one hundred and fifty-eight. The men of Bethasmoth, forty-two. [19] The men of Kiriatharim, twenty-five. The men of Chephirah and Beeroth, seven hundred and forty-three. [20] The Chadiasans and Ammidians, four hundred and twenty-two. The men of Ramah and Geba, six hundred and twenty-one. [21] The men of Michmas, one hundred and twenty-two. The men of Bethel, fifty-two. The sons of Magbish, one hundred and fifty-six. [22] The sons of the other Elam and Ono, seven hundred and twenty-five. The sons of Jericho, three hundred and forty-five.

[23] The sons of Senaah, three thousand three hundred and thirty. [24] The priests: the sons of Jedaiah the son of Jeshua, of the sons of Anasib, nine

hundred and seventy-two. The sons of Immer, one thousand and fifty-two.

[25] The sons of Pashhur, one thousand two hundred and forty-seven. The sons of Harim, one thousand and seventeen. [26] The Levites: the sons of Jeshua and Kadmiel and Bannas and Sudias, seventy-four. [27] The temple singers: the sons of Asaph, one hundred and twenty-eight. [28] The gatekeepers: the sons of Shallum, the sons of Ater, the sons of Talmon, the sons of Akkub, the sons of Hatita, the sons of Shobai, in all one hundred and thirty-nine. [29] The temple servants: the sons of Ziha, the sons of Hasupha, the sons of Tabbaoth, the sons of Keros, the sons of Siaha, the sons of Padon, the sons of Lebanah, the sons of Hagabah,

[30] the sons of Akkub, the sons of Uthai, the sons of Ketab, the sons of Hagab, the sons of Shamlai, the sons of Hana, the sons of Cathua, the sons of Gahar, [31] The sons of Reaiah, the sons of Rezin, the sons of Nekoda, the sons of Chezib, the sons of Gazzam, the sons of Uzza, the sons of Paseah, the sons of Hasrah, the sons of Besai, the sons of Asnah, the sons of the Meunites, the sons of Nephisim, the sons of Bakbuk, the sons of Hakupha, the sons of Asur, the sons of Pharakim, the sons of Bazluth, [32] the sons of Mehida, the sons of Cutha, the sons of Charea, the sons of Barkos, the sons of Sisera, the sons of Temah, the sons of Neziah, the sons of Hatipha. [33] The sons of Solomon's servants: the sons of Hassophereth, the sons of Peruda, the sons of Jaalah, the sons of Lozon, the sons of Giddel, the sons of Shephatiah, [34] the sons of Hattil, the sons of Pochereth-hazzebaim, the sons of Sarothie, the sons of Masiah, the sons of Gas, the sons of Addus, the sons of Subas, the sons of Apherra, the sons of Barodis, the sons of Shaphat, the sons of Ami. [35] All the temple servants and the sons of Solomon's servants were three hundred and seventy-two.

[36] The following are those who came up from Telmelah and Telharsha, under the leadership of Cherub, Addan, and Immer,

[37] though they could not prove by their fathers' houses or lineage that they belonged to Israel: the sons of Delaiah the son of Tobiah, the sons of Nekoda, six hundred and fifty-two. [38] Of the priests the following had assumed the priesthood but were not found registered: the sons of Habaiah, the sons of Hakkoz, the sons of Jaddus who had married Agia, one of the daughters of Barzillai, and was called by his name.

[39] And when the genealogy of these men was sought in the register and was not found, they were excluded from serving as priests. [40] And Nehemiah and Attharias told them not to share in the holy things until a high priest should appear wearing Urim and Thummim. [41] All those of Israel, twelve

or more years of age, besides menservants and maidservants, were forty-two thousand three hundred and sixty;

[42] their menservants and maidservants were seven thousand three hundred and thirty-seven; there were two hundred and forty-five musicians and singers.

[43] There were four hundred and thirty-five camels, and seven thousand and thirty-six horses, two hundred and forty-five mules, and five thousand five hundred and twenty-five asses. [44] Some of the heads of families, when they came to the temple of God which is in Jerusalem, vowed that they would erect the house on its site, to the best of their ability,

[45] and that they would give to the sacred treasury for the work a thousand minas of gold, five thousand minas of silver, and one hundred priests' garments.

[46] The priests, the Levites, and some of the people settled in Jerusalem and its vicinity; and the temple singers, the gatekeepers, and all Israel in their towns.

[47] When the seventh month came, and the sons of Israel were each in his own home, they gathered as one man in the square before the first gate toward the east.

[48] Then Jeshua the son of Jozadak, with his fellow priests, and Zerubbabel the son of Shealtiel, with his kinsmen, took their places and prepared the altar of the God of Israel, [49] to offer burnt offerings upon it, in accordance with the directions in the book of Moses the man of God. [50] And some joined them from the other peoples of the land. And they erected the altar in its place, for all the peoples of the land were hostile to them and were stronger than they; and they offered sacrifices at the proper times and burnt offerings to the Lord morning and evening. [51] They kept the feast of booths, as it is commanded in the law, and offered the proper sacrifices every day, [52] and thereafter the continual offerings and sacrifices on sabbaths and at new moons and at all the consecrated feasts. [53] And all who had made any vow to God began to offer sacrifices to God, from the new moon of the seventh month, though the temple of God was not yet built. [54] And they gave money to the masons and the carpenters, and food and drink [55] and carts to the Sidonians and the Tyrians, to bring cedar logs from Lebanon and convey them in rafts to the harbor of Joppa, according to the decree which they had in writing from Cyrus king of the Persians. [56] In the second year after their coming to the temple of God in Jerusalem, in the second month, Zerubbabel the son of Shealtiel and Jeshua the son of Jozadak made a beginning, together with their brethren and the Levitical priests and all who had come to Jerusalem from the captivity;

[57] and they laid the foundation of the temple of God on the new moon of the second month in the second year after they came to Judea and Jerusalem. [58]

And they appointed the Levites who were twenty or more years of age to have charge of the work of the Lord. And Jeshua arose, and his sons and brethren and Kadmiel his brother and the sons of Jeshua Emadabun and the sons of Joda son of Iliadun, with their sons and brethren, all the Levites, as one man pressing forward the work on the house of God. So the builders built the temple of the Lord. [59] And the priests stood arrayed in their garments, with musical instruments and trumpets, and the Levites, the sons of Asaph, with cymbals, [60] praising the Lord and blessing him, according to the directions of David king of Israel; [61] and they sang hymns, giving thanks to the Lord, because his goodness and his glory are for ever upon all Israel. [62] And all the people sounded trumpets and shouted with a great shout, praising the Lord for the erection of the house of the Lord. [63] Some of the Levitical priests and heads of fathers' houses, old men who had seen the former house, came to the building of this one with outcries and loud weeping, [64] while many came with trumpets and a joyful noise, [65] so that the people could not hear the trumpets because of the weeping of the people. For the multitude sounded the trumpets loudly, so that the sound was heard afar; [66] and when the enemies of the tribe of Judah and Benjamin heard it, they came to find out what the sound of the trumpets meant. [67] And they learned that those who had returned from captivity were building the temple for the Lord God of Israel. [68] So they approached Zerubbabel and Jeshua and the heads of the fathers' houses and said to them, "We will build with you. [69] For we obey your Lord just as you do and we have been sacrificing to him ever since the days of Esarhaddon king of the Assyrians, who brought us here." [70] But Zerubbabel and Jeshua and the heads of the fathers' houses in Israel said to them, "You have nothing to do with us in building the house for the Lord our God, [71] for we alone will build it for the Lord of Israel, as Cyrus the king of the Persians has commanded us." [72] But the peoples of the land pressed hard upon those in Judea, cut off their supplies, and hindered their building; [73] and by plots and demagoguery and uprisings they prevented the completion of the building as long as King Cyrus lived. And they were kept from building for two years, until the reign of Darius.

6
[1] Now in the second year of the reign of Darius, the prophets Haggai and Zechariah the son of Iddo prophesied to the Jews who were in Judea and Jerusalem, they prophesied to them in the name of the Lord God of Israel. [2] Then Zerubbabel the son of Shealtiel and Jeshua the son of Jozadak arose and began to build the house

of the Lord which is in Jerusalem, with the help of the prophets of the Lord who were with them. [3] At the same time Sisinnes the governor of Syria and Phoenicia and Sathrabuzanes and their associates came to them and said, [4] "By whose order are you building this house and this roof and finishing all the other things? And who are the builders that are finishing these things?" [5] Yet the elders of the Jews were dealt with kindly, for the providence of the Lord was over the captives; [6] and they were not prevented from building until word could be sent to Darius concerning them and a report made. [7] A copy of the letter which Sisinnes the governor of Syria and Phoenicia, and Sathrabuzanes, and their associates the local rulers in Syria and Phoenicia, wrote and sent to Darius: [8] "To King Darius, greeting. Let it be fully known to our lord the king that, when we went to the country of Judea and entered the city of Jerusalem, we found the elders of the Jews, who had been in captivity, [9] building in the city of Jerusalem a great new house for the Lord, of hewn stone, with costly timber laid in the walls. [10] These operations are going on rapidly, and the work is prospering in their hands and being completed with all splendor and care. [11] Then we asked these elders, `At whose command are you building this house and laying the foundations of this structure?' [12] And in order that we might inform you in writing who the leaders are, we questioned them and asked them for a list of the names of those who are at their head. [13] They answered us, `We are the servants of the Lord who created the heaven and the earth. [14] And the house was built many years ago by a king of Israel who was great and strong, and it was finished. [15] But when our fathers sinned against the Lord of Israel who is in heaven, and provoked him, he gave them over into the hands of Nebuchadnezzar king of Babylon, king of the Chaldeans; [16] and they pulled down the house, and burned it, and carried the people away captive to Babylon. [17] But in the first year that Cyrus reigned over the country of Babylonia, King Cyrus wrote that this house should be rebuilt. [18] And the holy vessels of gold and of silver, which Nebuchadnezzar had taken out of the house in Jerusalem and stored in his own temple, these Cyrus the king took out again from the temple in Babylon, and they were delivered to Zerubbabel and Sheshbazzar the governor [19] with the command that he should take all these vessels back and put them in the temple at Jerusalem, and that this temple of the Lord should be rebuilt on its site. [20] Then this Sheshbazzar, after coming here, laid the foundations of the house of the Lord which is in Jerusalem, and although it has been in process of construction from that time until now, it has not yet reached completion.' [21] Now therefore, if it seems wise, O king, let search be made in the royal archives of our lord the king that are in Babylon; [22] and if it is found that the building of the house of the Lord in Jerusalem was done with the consent of King Cyrus, and if it is approved by our lord the king, let him send us directions concerning these things." [23] Then Darius commanded that search be made in the royal archives that were deposited in Babylon. And in Ecbatana, the fortress which is in the country of Media, a scroll was found in which this was recorded: [24] "In the first year of the reign of Cyrus, King Cyrus ordered the building of the house of the Lord in Jerusalem, where they sacrifice with perpetual fire; [25] its height to be sixty cubits and its breadth sixty cubits, with three courses of hewn stone and one course of new native timber; the cost to be paid from the treasury of Cyrus the king; [26] and that the holy vessels of the house of the Lord, both of gold and of silver, which Nebuchadnezzar took out of the house in Jerusalem and carried away to Babylon, should be restored to the house in Jerusalem, to be placed where they had been." [27] So Darius commanded Sisinnes the governor of Syria and Phoenicia, and Sathrabuzanes, and their associates, and those who were appointed as local rulers in Syria and Phoenicia, to keep away from the place, and to permit Zerubbabel, the servant of the Lord and governor of Judea, and the elders of the Jews to build this house of the Lord on its site. [28] "And I command that it be built completely, and that full effort be made to help the men who have returned from the captivity of Judea, until the house of the Lord is finished; [29] and that out of the tribute of Coelesyria and Phoenicia a portion be scrupulously given to these men, that is, to Zerubbabel the governor, for sacrifices to the Lord, for bulls and rams and lambs, [30] and likewise wheat and salt and wine and oil, regularly every year, without quibbling, for daily use as the priests in Jerusalem may indicate, [31] in order that libations may be made to the Most High God for the king and his children, and prayers be offered for their life." [32] And he commanded that if any should transgress or nullify any of the things herein written, a beam should be taken out of his house and he should be hanged upon it, and his property should be forfeited to the king. [33] "Therefore may the Lord, whose name is there called upon, destroy every king and nation that shall stretch out their hands to hinder or damage that house of the Lord in Jerusalem. [34] "I, King Darius, have decreed that it be done with all diligence as here prescribed."

7

[1] Then Sisinnes the governor of Coelesyria and Phoenicia, and Sathrabuzanes, and their associates, following the orders of King Darius, [2] supervised the holy work with very great care, assisting the elders of the Jews and the chief officers of the temple. [3] And the holy work prospered, while the prophets Haggai and Zechariah prophesied; [4] and they completed it by the command of the Lord God of Israel. So with the consent of Cyrus and Darius and Artaxerxes, kings of the Persians, [5] the holy house was finished by the twenty-third day of the month of Adar, in the sixth year of King Darius. [6] And the people of Israel, the priests, the Levites, and the rest of those from the captivity who joined them, did according to what was written in the book of Moses. [7] They offered at the dedication of the temple of the Lord one hundred bulls, two hundred rams, four hundred lambs, [8] and twelve he-goats for the sin of all Israel, according to the number of the twelve leaders of the tribes of Israel; [9] and the priests and the Levites stood arrayed in their garments, according to kindred, for the services of the Lord God of Israel in accordance with the book of Moses; and the gatekeepers were at each gate. [10] The people of Israel who came from the captivity kept the passover on the fourteenth day of the first month, after the priests and the Levites were purified together. [11] Not all of the returned captives were purified, but the Levites were all purified together, [12] and they sacrificed the passover lamb for all the returned captives and for their brethren the priests and for themselves. [13] And the people of Israel who came from the captivity ate it, all those who had separated themselves from the abominations of the peoples of the land and sought the Lord. [14] And they kept the feast of unleavened bread seven days, rejoicing before the Lord, [15] Because he had changed the will of the king of the Assyrians concerning them, to strengthen their hands for the service of the Lord God of Israel.

8

[1] After these things, when Artaxerxes the king of the Persians was reigning, Ezra came, the son of Seraiah, son of Azariah, son of Hilkiah, son of Shallum, [2] son of Zadok, son of Ahitub, son of Amariah, son of Uzzi, son of Bukki, son of Abishua, son of Phineas, son of Eleazar, son of Aaron the chief priest. [3] This Ezra came up from Babylon as a scribe skilled in the law of Moses, which was given by the God of Israel; [4] and the king showed him honor, for he found favor before the king in all his requests. [5] There came up with him to Jerusalem some of the people of Israel and some of the priests and Levites and temple singers and gatekeepers and temple servants, [6] in the seventh year of the reign of Artaxerxes, in the fifth month (this was the king's seventh year); for they left

Babylon on the new moon of the first month and arrived in Jerusalem on the new moon of the fifth month, by the prosperous journey which the Lord gave them. [7] For Ezra possessed great knowledge, so that he omitted nothing from the law of the Lord or the commandments, but taught all Israel all the ordinances and judgments. [8] The following is a copy of the written commission from Artaxerxes the king which was delivered to Ezra the priest and reader of the law of the Lord:

[9] "King Artaxerxes to Ezra the priest and reader of the law of the Lord, greeting.

[10] In accordance with my gracious decision, I have given orders that those of the Jewish nation and of the priests and Levites and others in our realm, who freely choose to do so, may go with you to Jerusalem.

[11] Let as many as are so disposed, therefore, depart with you as I and the seven friends who are my counselors have decided, [12] in order to look into matters in Judea and Jerusalem, in accordance with what is in the law of the Lord, [13] and to carry to Jerusalem the gifts for the Lord of Israel which I and my friends have vowed, and to collect for the Lord in Jerusalem all the gold and silver that may be found in the country of Babylonia, [14] together with what is given by the nation for the temple of their Lord which is in Jerusalem, both gold and silver for bulls and rams and lambs and what goes with them, [15] so as to offer sacrifices upon the altar of their Lord which is in Jerusalem. [16] And whatever you and your brethren are minded to do with the gold and silver, perform it in accordance with the will of your God; [17] and deliver the holy vessels of the Lord which are given you for the use of the temple of your God which is in Jerusalem. [18] And whatever else occurs to you as necessary for the temple of your God, you may provide out of the royal treasury. [19] "And I, Artaxerxes the king, have commanded the treasurers of Syria and Phoenicia that whatever Ezra the priest and reader of the law of the Most High God sends for, they shall take care to give him,

[20] up to a hundred talents of silver, and likewise up to a hundred cors of wheat, a hundred baths of wine, and salt in abundance. [21] Let all things prescribed in the law of God be scrupulously fulfilled for the Most High God, so that wrath may not come upon the kingdom of the king and his sons. [22] You are also informed that no tribute or any other tax is to be laid on any of the priests or Levites or temple singers or gatekeepers or temple servants or persons employed in this temple, and that no one has authority to impose any tax upon them. [23] "And you, Ezra, according to the wisdom of God, appoint judges and justices to judge all those who know the law of your God, throughout all Syria and Phoenicia; and those who do not know it you shall teach.

[24] And all who transgress the law of your God or the law of the kingdom shall be strictly punished, whether by death or some other punishment, either fine or imprisonment." [25] Blessed be the Lord alone, who put this into the heart of the king, to glorify his house which is in Jerusalem,

[26] and who honored me in the sight of the king and his counselors and all his friends and nobles. [27] I was encouraged by the help of the Lord my God, and I gathered men from Israel to go up with me. [28] These are the principal men, according to their fathers' houses and their groups, who went up with me from Babylon, in the reign of Artaxerxes the king:

[29] Of the sons of Phineas, Gershom. Of the sons of Ithamar, Gamael. Of the sons of David, Hattush the son of Shecaniah. [30] Of the sons of Parosh, Zechariah, and with him a hundred and fifty men enrolled. [31] Of the sons of Pahathmoab, Eliehoenai the son of Zerahiah, and with him two hundred men.

[32] Of the sons of Zattu, Shecaniah the son of Jahaziel, and with him three hundred men. Of the sons of Adin, Obed the son of Jonathan, and with him two hundred and fifty men. [33] Of the sons of Elam, Jeshaiah the son of Gotholiah, and with him seventy men. [34] Of the sons of Shephatiah, Zeraiah the son of Michael, and with him seventy men, [35] Of the sons of Joab, Obadiah the son of Jehiel, and with him two hundred and twelve men. [36] Of the sons of Bani, Shelomith the son of Josiphiah, and with him a hundred and sixty men. [37] Of the sons of Bebai, Zechariah the son of Bebai, and with him twenty-eight men. [38] Of the sons of Azgad, Johanan the son of Hakkatan, and with him a hundred and ten men. [39] Of the sons of Adonikam, the last ones, their names being Eliphelet, Jeuel, and Shemaiah, and with them seventy men. [40] Of the sons of Bigvai, Uthai the son of Istalcurus, and with him seventy men. [41] I assembled them at the river called Theras, and we encamped there three days, and I inspected them.

[42] When I found there none of the sons of the priests or of the Levites, [43] I sent word to Eliezar, Iduel, Maasmas, [44] Elnathan, Shemaiah, Jarib, Nathan, Elnathan, Zechariah, and Meshullam, who were leaders and men of understanding; [45] and I told them to go to Iddo, who was the leading man at the place of the treasury, [46] and ordered them to tell Iddo and his brethren and the treasurers at that place to send us men to serve as priests in the house of our Lord. [47] And by the mighty hand of our Lord they brought us competent men of the sons of Mahli the son of Levi, son of Israel, namely Sherebiah with his sons and kinsmen, eighteen; [48] also Hashabiah and Annunus and Jeshaiah his brother, of the sons of Hananiah, and their sons, twenty men; [49] and of

the temple servants, whom David and the leaders had given for the service of the Levites, two hundred and twenty temple servants; the list of all their names was reported. [50] There I proclaimed a fast for the young men before our Lord, to seek from him a prosperous journey for ourselves and for our children and the cattle that were with us.

[51] For I was ashamed to ask the king for foot soldiers and horsemen and an escort to keep us safe from our adversaries; [52] for we had said to the king, "The power of our Lord will be with those who seek him, and will support them in every way." [53] And again we prayed to our Lord about these things, and we found him very merciful. [54] Then I set apart twelve of the leaders of the priests, Sherebiah and Hashabiah, and ten of their kinsmen with them; [55] and I weighed out to them the silver and the gold and the holy vessels of the house of our Lord, which the king himself and his counselors and the nobles and all Israel had given. [56] I weighed and gave to them six hundred and fifty talents of silver, and silver vessels worth a hundred talents, and a hundred talents of gold, [57] and twenty golden bowls, and twelve bronze vessels of fine bronze that glittered like gold. [58] And I said to them, "You are holy to the Lord, and the vessels are holy, and the silver and the gold are vowed to the Lord, the Lord of our fathers. [59] Be watchful and on guard until you deliver them to the leaders of the priests and the Levites, and to the heads of the fathers' houses of Israel, in Jerusalem, in the chambers of the house of our Lord." [60] So the priests and the Levites who took the silver and the gold and the vessels which had been in Jerusalem carried them to the temple of the Lord. [61] We departed from the river Theras on the twelfth day of the first month; and we arrived in Jerusalem by the mighty hand of our Lord which was upon us; he delivered us from every enemy on the way, and so we came to Jerusalem.

[62] When we had been there three days, the silver and the gold were weighed and delivered in the house of our Lord to Meremoth the priest, son of Uriah; [63] and with him was Eleazar the son of Phinehas, and with them were Jozabad the son of Jeshua and Moeth the son of Binnui, the Levites. [64] The whole was counted and weighed, and the weight of everything was recorded at that very time. [65] And those who had come back from captivity offered sacrifices to the Lord, the God of Israel, twelve bulls for all Israel, ninety-six rams, [66] seventy-two lambs, and as a thank offering twelve he-goats -- all as a sacrifice to the Lord. [67] And they delivered the king's orders to the royal stewards and to the governors of Coelesyria and Phoenicia; and these officials honored the people and the temple of the

Lord. [68] After these things had been done, the principal men came to me and said,

[69] "The people of Israel and the leaders and the priests and the Levites have not put away from themselves the alien peoples of the land and their pollutions, the Canaanites, the Hittites, the Perizzites, the Jebusites, the Moabites, the Egyptians, and the Edomites. [70] For they and their sons have married the daughters of these people, and the holy race has been mixed with the alien peoples of the land; and from the beginning of this matter the leaders and the nobles have been sharing in this iniquity." [71] As soon as I heard these things I rent my garments and my holy mantle, and pulled out hair from my head and beard, and sat down in anxiety and grief.

[72] And all who were ever moved at the word of the Lord of Israel gathered round me, as I mourned over this iniquity, and I sat grief-stricken until the evening sacrifice. [73] Then I rose from my fast, with my garments and my holy mantle rent, and kneeling down and stretching forth my hands to the Lord [74] I said, "O Lord, I am ashamed and confounded before thy face.

[75] For our sins have risen higher than our heads, and our mistakes have mounted up to heaven [76] from the times of our fathers, and we are in great sin to this day. [77] And because of our sins and the sins of our fathers we with our brethren and our kings and our priests were given over to the kings of the earth, to the sword and captivity and plundering, in shame until this day. [78] And now in some measure mercy has come to us from thee, O Lord, to leave to us a root and a name in thy holy place, [79] and to uncover a light for us in the house of the Lord our God, and to give us food in the time of our servitude. [80] Even in our bondage we were not forsaken by our Lord, but he brought us into favor with the kings of the Persians, so that they have given us food [81] and glorified the temple of our Lord, and raised Zion from desolation, to give us a stronghold in Judea and Jerusalem. [82] "And now, O Lord, what shall we say, when we have these things? For we have transgressed thy commandments, which thou didst give by thy servants the prophets, saying,

[83] `The land which you are entering to take possession of it is a land polluted with the pollution of the aliens of the land, and they have filled it with their uncleanness. [84] Therefore do not give your daughters in marriage to their sons, and do not take their daughters for your sons; [85] and do not seek ever to have peace with them, in order that you may be strong and eat the good things of the land and leave it for an inheritance to your children for ever.'

[86] And all that has happened to us has come about because of our evil deeds and our great sins. For thou, O Lord, didst lift the burden of our sins [87] and give

us such a root as this; but we turned back again to transgress thy law by mixing with the uncleanness of the peoples of the land. [88] Wast thou not angry enough with us to destroy us without leaving a root or seed or name? [89] O Lord of Israel, thou art true; for we are left as a root to this day. [90] Behold, we are now before thee in our iniquities; for we can no longer stand in thy presence because of these things."

[91] While Ezra was praying and making his confession, weeping and lying upon the ground before the temple, there gathered about him a very great throng from Jerusalem, men and women and youths; for there was great weeping among the multitude.

[92] Then Shecaniah the son of Jehiel, one of the men of Israel, called out, and said to Ezra, "We have sinned against the Lord, and have married foreign women from the peoples of the land; but even now there is hope for Israel. [93] Let us take an oath to the Lord about this, that we will put away all our foreign wives, with their children, [94] as seems good to you and to all who obey the law of the Lord. [95] Arise and take action, for it is your task, and we are with you to take strong measures." [96] Then Ezra arose and had the leaders of the priests and Levites of all Israel take oath that they would do this. And they took the oath.

9

[1] Then Ezra rose and went from the court of the temple to the chamber of Jehohanan the son of Eliashib,

[2] and spent the night there; and he did not eat bread or drink water, for he was mourning over the great iniquities of the multitude. [3] And a proclamation was made throughout Judea and Jerusalem to all who had returned from the captivity that they should assemble at Jerusalem, [4] and that if any did not meet there within two or three days, in accordance with the decision of the ruling elders, their cattle should be seized for sacrifice and the men themselves expelled from the multitude of those who had returned from the captivity. [5] Then the men of the tribe of Judah and Benjamin assembled at Jerusalem within three days; this was the ninth month, on the twentieth day of the month.

[6] And all the multitude sat in the open square before the temple, shivering because of the bad weather that prevailed. [7] Then Ezra rose and said to them, "You have broken the law and married foreign women, and so have increased the sin of Israel. [8] Now then make confession and give glory to the Lord the God of our fathers, [9] and do his will; separate yourselves from the peoples of the land and from your foreign wives." [10] Then all the multitude shouted and said with a loud voice, "We will do as you have said. [11] But the multitude is great and it

is winter, and we are not able to stand in the open air. This is not a work we can do in one day or two, for we have sinned too much in these things. [12] so let the leaders of the multitude stay, and let all those in our settlements who have foreign wives come at the time appointed, [13] with the elders and judges of each place, until we are freed from the wrath of the Lord over this matter." [14] Jonathan the son of Asahel and Jahzeiah the son of Tikvah undertook the matter on these terms, and Meshullam and Levi and Shabbethai served with them as judges. [15] And those who had returned from the captivity acted in accordance with all this. [16] Ezra the priest chose for himself the leading men of their fathers' houses, all of them by name; and on the new moon of the tenth month they began their sessions to investigate the matter.

[17] And the cases of the men who had foreign wives were brought to an end by the new moon of the first month. [18] Of the priests those who were brought in and found to have foreign wives were:

[19] of the sons of Jeshua the son of Jozadak and his brethren, Maaseiah, Eliezar, Jarib, and Jodan. [20] They pledged themselves to put away their wives, and to give rams in expiation of their error. [21] Of the sons of Immer: Hanani and Zebadiah and Maaseiah and Shemaiah and Jehiel and Azariah. [22] Of the sons of Pashhur: Elioenai, Maaseiah, Ishmael, and Nathanael, and Gedaliah, and Elasah. [23] And of the Levites: Jozabad and Shimei and Kelaiah, who was Kelita, and Pethahiah and Judah and Jonah. [24] Of the temple singers: Eliashib and Zaccur. [25] Of the gatekeepers: Shallum and Telem. [26] Of Israel: of the sons of Parosh: Ramiah, Izziah, Malchijah, Mijamin, and Eleazar, and Asibias, and Benaiah.

[27] Of the sons of Elam: Mattaniah and Zechariah, Jehiel and Abdi, and Jeremoth and Elijah. [28] Of the sons of Zattu: Elioenai, Eliashib, Othoniah, Jeremoth, and Zabad and Zerdaiah. [29] Of the sons of Bebai: Jehohanan and Hananiah and Zabbai and Emathis. [30] Of the sons of Bani: Meshullam, Malluch, Adaiah, Jashub, and Sheal and Jeremoth. [31] Of the sons of Addi: Naathus and Moossias, Laccunus and Naidus, and Bescaspasmys and Sesthel, and Belnuus and Manasseas. [32] Of the sons of Annan, Elionas and Asaias and Melchias and Sabbaias and Simon Chosamaeus. [33] Of the sons of Hashum: Mattenai and Mattattah and Zabad and Eliphelet and Manasseh and Shimei. [34] Of the sons of Bani: Jeremai, Maadai, Amram, Joel, Mamdai and Bedeiah and Vaniah, Carabasion and Eliashib and Machnadebai, Eliasis, Binnui, Elialis, Shimei, Shelemiah, Nethaniah. Of the sons of Ezora: Shashai, Azarel, Azael, Shemaiah, Amariah, Joseph. [35] Of

the sons of Nebo: Mattithiah, Zabad, Iddo, Joel,
Benaiah.   [36] All these had married foreign women,
and they put them away with their children.   [37] The
priests and the Levites and the men of Israel settled in
Jerusalem and in the country. On the new moon of
the seventh month, when the sons of Israel were in
their settlements,
[38] the whole multitude gathered with one accord
into the open square before the east gate of the
temple;   [39] and they told Ezra the chief priest and
reader to bring the law of Moses which had been
given by the Lord God of Israel.   [40] So Ezra the
chief priest brought the law, for all the multitude,
men and women, and all the priests to hear the law,
on the new moon of the seventh month.   [41] And he
read aloud in the open square before the gate of the
temple from early morning until midday, in the
presence of both men and women; and all the
multitude gave attention to the law.   [42] Ezra the
priest and reader of the law stood on the wooden
platform which had been prepared;   [43] and beside
him stood Mattathiah, Shema, Anaiah, Azariah,
Uriah, Hezekiah, and Baalsamus on his right hand,
[44] and on his left Pedaiah, Mishael, Malchijah,
Lothasubus, Nabariah, and Zechariah.   [45] Then
Ezra took up the book of the law in the sight of the
multitude, for he had the place of honor in the
presence of all.   [46] And when he opened the law,
they all stood erect. And Ezra blessed the Lord God
Most High, the God of hosts, the Almighty;   [47] and
all the multitude answered, "Amen." And they lifted
up their hands, and fell to the ground and worshiped
the Lord.   [48] Jeshua and Anniuth and Sherebiah,
Jamin, Akkub, Shabbethai, Hodiah, Maaseiah and
Kelita, Azariah and Jozabad, Hanan, Pelaiah, the
Levites, taught the law of the Lord, at the same time
explaining what was read.   [49] Then Attharates said
to Ezra the chief priest and reader, and to the Levites
who were teaching the multitude, and to all,
[50] "This day is holy to the Lord" -- now they were all
weeping as they heard the law --   [51] "so go your
way, eat the fat and drink the sweet, and send
portions to those who have none;   [52] for the day is
holy to the Lord; and do not be sorrowful, for the
Lord will exalt you."   [53] And the Levites
commanded all the people, saying, "This day is holy;
do not be sorrowful."   [54] Then they all went their
way, to eat and drink and enjoy themselves, and to
give portions to those who had none, and to make
great rejoicing;   [55] because they were inspired by
the words which they had been taught. And they
came together.

2 Esdras
4 Ezra

[1] The second book of the prophet Ezra the son of Seraiah, son of Azariah, son of Hilkiah, son of Shallum, son of Zadok, son of Ahitub,
[2] son of Ahijah, son of Phinehas, son of Eli, son of Amariah, son of Azariah, son of Meraioth, son of Arna, son of Uzzi, son of Borith, son of Abishua, son of Phinehas, son of Eleazar,
[3] son of Aaron, of the tribe of Levi, who was a captive in the country of the Medes in the reign of Artaxerxes, king of the Persians.
[4] The word of the Lord came to me, saying,
[5] "Go and declare to my people their evil deeds, and to their children the iniquities which they have committed against me, so that they may tell their children's children [6] that the sins of their parents have increased in them, for they have forgotten me and have offered sacrifices to strange gods. [7] Was it not I who brought them out of the land of Egypt, out of the house of bondage? But they have angered me and despised my counsels. [8] Pull out the hair of your head and hurl all evils upon them, for they have not obeyed my law -- they are a rebellious people. [9] How long shall I endure them, on whom I have bestowed such great benefits? [10] For their sake I have overthrown many kings: I struck down Pharaoh with his servants, and all his army. [11] I have destroyed all nations before them, and scattered in the east the people of two provinces, Tyre and Sidon; I have slain all their enemies. [12] "But speak to them and say, Thus says the Lord:
[13] Surely it was I who brought you through the sea, and made safe highways for you where there was no road; I gave you Moses as leader and Aaron as priest;
 [14] I provided light for you from a pillar of fire, and did great wonders among you. Yet you have forgotten me, says the Lord. [15] "Thus says the Lord Almighty: The quails were a sign to you; I gave you camps for your protection, and in them you complained.
[16] You have not exulted in my name at the destruction of your enemies, but to this day you still complain. [17] Where are the benefits which I bestowed on you? When you were hungry and thirsty in the wilderness, did you not cry out to me, [18] saying, `Why hast thou led us into this wilderness to kill us? It would have been better for us to serve the Egyptians than to die in this wilderness.' [19] I pitied your groanings and gave you manna for food; you ate the bread of angels. [20] When you were thirsty, did I not cleave the rock so that waters flowed in abundance? Because of the heat I covered you with the leaves of trees. [21] I divided fertile lands among

you; I drove out the Canaanites, the Perizzites, and the Philistines before you. What more can I do for you? says the Lord. [22] Thus says the Lord Almighty: When you were in the wilderness, at the bitter stream, thirsty and blaspheming my name,
[23] I did not send fire upon you for your blasphemies, but threw a tree into the water and made the stream sweet. [24] "What shall I do to you, O Jacob? You would not obey me, O Judah. I will turn to other nations and will give them my name, that they may keep my statutes.
[25] Because you have forsaken me, I also will forsake you. When you beg mercy of me, I will show you no mercy. [26] When you call upon me, I will not listen to you; for you have defiled your hands with blood, and your feet are swift to commit murder. [27] It is not as though you had forsaken me; you have forsaken yourselves, says the Lord. [28] "Thus says the Lord Almighty: Have I not entreated you as a father entreats his sons or a mother her daughters or a nurse her children,
[29] that you should be my people and I should be your God, and that you should be my sons and I should be your father? [30] I gathered you as a hen gathers her brood under her wings. But now, what shall I do to you? I will cast you out from my presence. [31] When you offer oblations to me, I will turn my face from you; for I have rejected your feast days, and new moons, and circumcisions of the flesh.
 [32] I sent to you my servants the prophets, but you have taken and slain them and torn their bodies in pieces; their blood I will require of you, says the Lord.
 [33] "Thus says the Lord Almighty: Your house is desolate; I will drive you out as the wind drives straw;
[34] and your sons will have no children, because with you they have neglected my commandment and have done what is evil in my sight. [35] I will give your houses to a people that will come, who without having heard me will believe. Those to whom I have shown no signs will do what I have commanded.
[36] They have seen no prophets, yet will recall their former state. [37] I call to witness the gratitude of the people that is to come, whose children rejoice with gladness; though they do not see me with bodily eyes, yet with the spirit they will believe the things I have said. [38] "And now, father, look with pride and see the people coming from the east;
[39] to them I will give as leaders Abraham, Isaac, and Jacob and Hosea and Amos and Micah and Joel and Obadiah and Jonah [40] and Nahum and Habakkuk, Zephaniah, Haggai, Zechariah and Malachi, who is also called the messenger of the Lord.
2
[1] "Thus says the Lord: I brought this people out of bondage, and I gave them commandments through

my servants the prophets; but they would not listen to them, and made my counsels void.

[2] The mother who bore them says to them, `Go, my children, because I am a widow and forsaken. [3] I brought you up with gladness; but with mourning and sorrow I have lost you, because you have sinned before the Lord God and have done what is evil in my sight. [4] But now what can I do for you? For I am a widow and forsaken. Go, my children, and ask for mercy from the Lord.' [5] I call upon you, father, as a witness in addition to the mother of the children, because they would not keep my covenant, [6] that you may bring confusion upon them and bring their mother to ruin, so that they may have no offspring. [7] Let them be scattered among the nations, let their names be blotted out from the earth, because they have despised my covenant. [8] "Woe to you, Assyria, who conceal the unrighteous in your midst! O wicked nation, remember what I did to Sodom and Gomorrah,

[9] whose land lies in lumps of pitch and heaps of ashes. So will I do to those who have not listened to me, says the Lord Almighty." [10] Thus says the Lord to Ezra: "Tell my people that I will give them the kingdom of Jerusalem, which I was going to give to Israel.

[11] Moreover, I will take back to myself their glory, and will give to these others the everlasting habitations, which I had prepared for Israel. [12] The tree of life shall give them fragrant perfume, and they shall neither toil nor become weary. [13] Ask and you will receive; pray that your days may be few, that they may be shortened. The kingdom is already prepared for you; watch! [14] Call, O call heaven and earth to witness, for I left out evil and created good, because I live, says the Lord. [15] "Mother, embrace your sons; bring them up with gladness, as does the dove; establish their feet, because I have chosen you, says the Lord.

[16] And I will raise up the dead from their places, and will bring them out from their tombs, because I recognize my name in them. [17] Do not fear, mother of sons, for I have chosen you, says the Lord. [18] I will send you help, my servants Isaiah and Jeremiah. According to their counsel I have consecrated and prepared for you twelve trees loaded with various fruits, [19] and the same number of springs flowing with milk and honey, and seven mighty mountains on which roses and lilies grow; by these I will fill your children with joy. [20] Guard the rights of the widow, secure justice for the fatherless, give to the needy, defend the orphan, clothe the naked, [21] care for the injured and the weak, do not ridicule a lame man, protect the maimed, and let the blind man have a vision of my splendor. [22] Protect the old and the young within your walls; [23] When you find any

who are dead, commit them to the grave and mark it, and I will give you the first place in my resurrection. [24] Pause and be quiet, my people, because your rest will come. [25] Good nurse, nourish your sons, and strengthen their feet. [26] Not one of the servants whom I have given you will perish, for I will require them from among your number. [27] Do not be anxious, for when the day of tribulation and anguish comes, others shall weep and be sorrowful, but you shall rejoice and have abundance. [28] The nations shall envy you but they shall not be able to do anything against you, says the Lord. [29] My hands will cover you, that your sons may not see Gehenna. [30] Rejoice, O mother, with your sons, because I will deliver you, says the Lord. [31] Remember your sons that sleep, because I will bring them out of the hiding places of the earth, and will show mercy to them; for I am merciful, says the Lord Almighty. [32] Embrace your children until I come, and proclaim mercy to them; because my springs run over, and my grace will not fail." [33] I, Ezra, received a command from the Lord on Mount Horeb to go to Israel. When I came to them they rejected me and refused the Lord's commandment.

[34] Therefore I say to you, O nations that hear and understand, "Await your shepherd; he will give you everlasting rest, because he who will come at the end of the age is close at hand. [35] Be ready for the rewards of the kingdom, because the eternal light will shine upon you for evermore. [36] Flee from the shadow of this age, receive the joy of your glory; I publicly call on my Savior to witness. [37] Receive what the Lord has entrusted to you and be joyful, giving thanks to him who has called you to heavenly kingdoms. [38] Rise and stand, and see at the feast of the Lord the number of those who have been sealed. [39] Those who have departed from the shadow of this age have received glorious garments from the Lord. [40] Take again your full number, O Zion, and conclude the list of your people who are clothed in white, who have fulfilled the law of the Lord. [41] The number of your children, whom you desired, is full; beseech the Lord's power that your people, who have been called from the beginning, may be made holy." [42] I, Ezra, saw on Mount Zion a great multitude, which I could not number, and they all were praising the Lord with songs.

[43] In their midst was a young man of great stature, taller than any of the others, and on the head of each of them he placed a crown, but he was more exalted than they. And I was held spellbound. [44] Then I asked an angel, "Who are these, my lord?" [45] He answered and said to me, "These are they who have put off mortal clothing and have put on the immortal, and they have confessed the name of God; now they

are being crowned, and receive palms." [46] Then I said to the angel, "Who is that young man who places crowns on them and puts palms in their hands?" [47] He answered and said to me, "He is the Son of God, whom they confessed in the world." So I began to praise those who had stood valiantly for the name of the Lord. [48] Then the angel said to me, "Go, tell my people how great and many are the wonders of the Lord God which you have seen."

3

[1] In the thirtieth year after the destruction of our city, I Salathiel, who am also called Ezra, was in Babylon. I was troubled as I lay on my bed, and my thoughts welled up in my heart,

[2] because I saw the desolation of Zion and the wealth of those who lived in Babylon. [3] My spirit was greatly agitated, and I began to speak anxious words to the Most High, and said, [4] "O sovereign Lord, didst thou not speak at the beginning when thou didst form the earth -- and that without help -- and didst command the dust [5] and it gave thee Adam, a lifeless body? Yet he was the workmanship of thy hands, and thou didst breathe into him the breath of life, and he was made alive in thy presence.

[6] And thou didst lead him into the garden which thy right hand had planted before the earth appeared.

[7] And thou didst lay upon him one commandment of your; but he transgressed it, and immediately thou didst appoint death for him and for his descendants. From him there sprang nations and tribes, peoples and clans without number. [8] And every nation walked after its own will and did ungodly things before thee and scorned thee, and thou didst not hinder them. [9] But again, in its time thou didst bring the flood upon the inhabitants of the world and destroy them. [10] And the same fate befell them: as death came upon Adam, so the flood upon them. [11] But thou didst leave one of them, Noah with his household, and all the righteous who have descended from him. [12] "When those who dwelt on earth began to multiply, they produced children and peoples and many nations, and again they began to be more ungodly than were their ancestors. [13] And when they were committing iniquity before thee, thou didst choose for thyself one of them, whose name was Abraham; [14] and thou didst love him, and to him only didst thou reveal the end of the times, secretly by night. [15] Thou didst make with him an everlasting covenant, and promise him that thou wouldst never forsake his descendants; and thou gavest to him Isaac, and to Isaac thou gavest Jacob and Esau. [16] And thou didst set apart Jacob for thyself, but Esau thou didst reject; and Jacob became a great multitude. [17] And when thou didst lead his descendants out of Egypt, thou didst bring them to

Mount Sinai. [18] Thou didst bend down the heavens and shake the earth, and move the world, and make the depths to tremble, and trouble the times. [19] And thy glory passed through the four gates of fire and earthquake and wind and ice, to give the law to the descendants of Jacob, and thy commandment to the posterity of Israel. [20] "Yet thou didst not take away from them their evil heart, so that thy law might bring forth fruit in them. [21] For the first Adam, burdened with an evil heart, transgressed and was overcome, as were also all who were descended from him. [22] Thus the disease became permanent; the law was in the people's heart along with the evil root, but what was good departed, and the evil remained. [23] So the times passed and the years were completed, and thou didst raise up for thyself a servant, named David. [24] And thou didst command him to build a city for thy name, and in it to offer thee oblations from what is your. [25] This was done for many years; but the inhabitants of the city transgressed, [26] in everything doing as Adam and all his descendants had done, for they also had the evil heart. [27] So thou didst deliver the city into the hands of thy enemies. [28] "Then I said in my heart, Are the deeds of those who inhabit Babylon any better? Is that why she has gained dominion over Zion?

[29] For when I came here I saw ungodly deeds without number, and my soul has seen many sinners during these thirty years. And my heart failed me, [30] for I have seen how thou do endure those who sin, and hast spared those who act wickedly, and hast destroyed thy people, and hast preserved thy enemies, [31] and hast not shown to any one how thy way may be comprehended. Are the deeds of Babylon better than those of Zion? [32] Or has another nation known thee besides Israel? Or what tribes have so believed thy covenants as these tribes of Jacob? [33] Yet their reward has not appeared and their labor has borne no fruit. For I have traveled widely among the nations and have seen that they abound in wealth, though they are unmindful of thy commandments. [34] Now therefore weigh in a balance our iniquities and those of the inhabitants of the world; and so it will be found which way the turn of the scale will incline. [35] When have the inhabitants of the earth not sinned in thy sight? Or what nation has kept thy commandments so well? [36] Thou mayest indeed find individual men who have kept thy commandments, but nations thou wilt not find."

4

[1] Then the angel that had been sent to me, whose name was Uriel, answered

[2] and said to me, "Your understanding has utterly failed regarding this world, and do you think you can comprehend the way of the Most High?" [3] Then I said, "Yes, my lord." And he replied to me, "I have been sent to show you three ways, and to put before you three problems. [4] If you can solve one of them for me, I also will show you the way you desire to see, and will teach you why the heart is evil." [5] I said, "Speak on, my lord." And he said to me, "Go, weigh for me the weight of fire, or measure for me a measure of wind, or call back for me the day that is past."

[6] I answered and said, "Who of those that have been born can do this, that you ask me concerning these things?"

[7] And he said to me, "If I had asked you, `How many dwellings are in the heart of the sea, or how many streams are at the source of the deep, or how many streams are above the firmament, or which are the exits of hell, or which are the entrances of paradise?'

[8] Perhaps you would have said to me, `I never went down into the deep, nor as yet into hell, neither did I ever ascend into heaven.' [9] But now I have asked you only about fire and wind and the day, things through which you have passed and without which you cannot exist, and you have given me no answer about them!" [10] And he said to me, "You cannot understand the things with which you have grown up; [11] how then can your mind comprehend the way of the Most High? And how can one who is already worn out by the corrupt world understand incorruption?" When I heard this, I fell on my face [12] and said to him, "It would be better for us not to be here than to come here and live in ungodliness, and to suffer and not understand why." [13] He answered me and said, "I went into a forest of trees of the plain, and they made a plan [14] and said, `Come, let us go and make war against the sea, that it may recede before us, and that we may make for ourselves more forests.' [15] And in like manner the waves of the sea also made a plan and said, `Come, let us go up and subdue the forest of the plain so that there also we may gain more territory for ourselves.' [16] But the plan of the forest was in vain, for the fire came and consumed it; [17] likewise also the plan of the waves of the sea, for the sand stood firm and stopped them. [18] If now you were a judge between them, which would you undertake to justify, and which to condemn?" [19] I answered and said, "Each has made a foolish plan, for the land is assigned to the forest, and to the sea is assigned a place to carry its waves."

[20] He answered me and said, "You have judged rightly, but why have you not judged so in your own case?

[21] For as the land is assigned to the forest and the sea to its waves, so also those who dwell upon earth can understand only what is on the earth, and he who is above the heavens can understand what is above the height of the heavens." [22] Then I answered and said, "I beseech you, my lord, why have I been endowed with the power of understanding? [23] For I did not wish to inquire about the ways above, but about those things which we daily experience: why Israel has been given over to the Gentiles as a reproach; why the people whom you loved has been given over to godless tribes, and the law of our fathers has been made of no effect and the written covenants no longer exist; [24] and why we pass from the world like locusts, and our life is like a mist, and we are not worthy to obtain mercy. [25] But what will he do for his name, by which we are called? It is about these things that I have asked."

[26] He answered me and said, "If you are alive, you will see, and if you live long, you will often marvel, because the age is hastening swiftly to its end. [27] For it will not be able to bring the things that have been promised to the righteous in their appointed times, because this age is full of sadness and infirmities. [28] For the evil about which you ask me has been sown, but the harvest of it has not yet come. [29] If therefore that which has been sown is not reaped, and if the place where the evil has been sown does not pass away, the field where the good has been sown will not come. [30] For a grain of evil seed was sown in Adam's heart from the beginning, and how much ungodliness it has produced until now, and will produce until the time of threshing comes! [31] Consider now for yourself how much fruit of ungodliness a grain of evil seed has produced.

[32] When heads of grain without number are sown, how great a threshing floor they will fill!" [33] Then I answered and said, "How long and when will these things be? Why are our years few and evil?"

[34] He answered me and said, "You do not hasten faster than the Most High, for your haste is for yourself, but the Highest hastens on behalf of many. [35] Did not the souls of the righteous in their chambers ask about these matters, saying, `How long are we to remain here? And when will come the harvest of our reward? [36] And Jeremiel the archangel answered them and said, `When the number of those like yourselves is completed; for he has weighed the age in the balance, [37] and measured the times by measure, and numbered the times by number; and he will not move or arouse them until that measure is fulfilled.'" [38] Then I answered and said, "O sovereign Lord, but all of us also are full of ungodliness.

[39] And it is perhaps on account of us that the time of threshing is delayed for the righteous -- on account

of the sins of those who dwell on earth." [40] He answered me and said, "Go and ask a woman who is with child if, when her nine months have been completed, her womb can keep the child within her any longer."

[41] And I said, "No, lord, it cannot."
And he said to me, "In Hades the chambers of the souls are like the womb.

[42] For just as a woman who is in travail makes haste to escape the pangs of birth, so also do these places hasten to give back those things that were committed to them from the beginning. [43] Then the things that you desire to see will be disclosed to you." [44] I answered and said, "If I have found favor in your sight, and if it is possible, and if I am worthy,

[45] show me this also: whether more time is to come than has passed, or whether for us the greater part has gone by. [46] For I know what has gone by, but I do not know what is to come." [47] And he said to me, "Stand at my right side, and I will show you the interpretation of a parable."

[48] So I stood and looked, and behold, a flaming furnace passed by before me, and when the flame had gone by I looked, and behold, the smoke remained. [49] And after this a cloud full of water passed before me and poured down a heavy and violent rain, and when the rainstorm had passed, drops remained in the cloud. [50] And he said to me, "Consider it for yourself; for as the rain is more than the drops, and the fire is greater than the smoke, so the quantity that passed was far greater; but drops and smoke remained."

[51] Then I prayed and said, "Do you think that I shall live until those days? Or who will be alive in those days?"

[52] He answered me and said, "Concerning the signs about which you ask me, I can tell you in part; but I was not sent to tell you concerning your life, for I do not know.

5

[1] "Now concerning the signs: behold, the days are coming when those who dwell on earth shall be seized with great terror, and the way of truth shall be hidden, and the land shall be barren of faith.

[2] And unrighteousness shall be increased beyond what you yourself see, and beyond what you heard of formerly. [3] And the land which you now see ruling shall be waste and untrodden, and men shall see it desolate. [4] But if the Most High grants that you live, you shall see it thrown into confusion after the third period; and the sun shall suddenly shine forth at night,and the moon during the day. [5] Blood shall drip from wood,and the stone shall utter its voice;the peoples shall be troubled, and the stars shall fall. [6] And one shall reign whom those who dwell on earth do not expect, and the birds shall fly away together;

[7] and the sea of Sodom shall cast up fish; and one whom the many do not know shall make his voice heard by night, and all shall hear his voice. [8] There shall be chaos also in many places, and fire shall often break out, and the wild beasts shall roam beyond their haunts, and menstruous women shall bring forth monsters. [9] And salt waters shall be found in the sweet, and all friends shall conquer one another; then shall reason hide itself, and wisdom shall withdraw into its chamber, [10] and it shall be sought by many but shall not be found, and unrighteousness and unrestraint shall increase on earth. [11] And one country shall ask its neighbor, `Has righteousness, or any one who does right, passed through you?' And it will answer, `No.' [12] And at that time men shall hope but not obtain; they shall labor but their ways shall not prosper. [13] These are the signs which I am permitted to tell you, and if you pray again, and weep as you do now, and fast for seven days, you shall hear yet greater things than these." [14] Then I awoke, and my body shuddered violently, and my soul was so troubled that it fainted.

[15] But the angel who had come and talked with me held me and strengthened me and set me on my feet.

[16] Now on the second night Phaltiel, a chief of the people, came to me and said, "Where have you been? And why is your face sad?

[17] Or do you not know that Israel has been entrusted to you in the land of their exile? [18] Rise therefore and eat some bread, so that you may not forsake us, like a shepherd who leaves his flock in the power of cruel wolves." [19] Then I said to him, "Depart from me and do not come near me for seven days, and then you may come to me." He heard what I said and left me.

[20] So I fasted seven days, mourning and weeping, as Uriel the angel had commanded me. [21] And after seven days the thoughts of my heart were very grievous to me again.

[22] Then my soul recovered the spirit of understanding, and I began once more to speak words in the presence of the Most High. [23] And I said, "O sovereign Lord, from every forest of the earth and from all its trees thou hast chosen one vine, [24] and from all the lands of the world thou hast chosen for thyself one region, and from all the flowers of the world thou hast chosen for thyself one lily, [25] and from all the depths of the sea thou hast filled for thyself one river, and from all the cities that have been built thou hast consecrated Zion for thyself,

[26] and from all the birds that have been created thou hast named for thyself one dove, and from all the flocks that have been made thou hast provided for thyself one sheep, [27] and from all the multitude of peoples thou hast gotten for thyself one people; and

to this people, whom thou hast loved, thou hast given the law which is approved by all. [28] And now, O Lord, why hast thou given over the one to the many, and dishonored the one root beyond the others, and scattered your only one among the many? [29] And those who opposed thy promises have trodden down those who believed thy covenants. [30] If thou do really hate thy people, they should be punished at thy own hands." [31] When I had spoken these words, the angel who had come to me on a previous night was sent to me,

[32] and he said to me, "Listen to me, and I will instruct you; pay attention to me, and I will tell you more." [33] And I said, "Speak, my lord." And he said to me, "Are you greatly disturbed in mind over Israel? Or do you love him more than his Maker does?"

[34] And I said, "No, my lord, but because of my grief I have spoken; for every hour I suffer agonies of heart, while I strive to understand the way of the Most High and to search out part of his judgment."

[35] And he said to me, "You cannot." And I said, "Why not, my lord? Why then was I born? Or why did not my mother's womb become my grave, that I might not see the travail of Jacob and the exhaustion of the people of Israel?"

[36] He said to me, "Count up for me those who have not yet come, and gather for me the scattered raindrops, and make the withered flowers bloom again for me;

[37] open for me the closed chambers, and bring forth for me the winds shut up in them, or show me the picture of a voice; and then I will explain to you the travail that you ask to understand." [38] And I said, "O sovereign Lord, who is able to know these things except he whose dwelling is not with men?

[39] As for me, I am without wisdom, and how can I speak concerning the things which thou hast asked me?" [40] He said to me, "Just as you cannot do one of the things that were mentioned, so you cannot discover my judgment, or the goal of the love that I have promised my people."

[41] And I said, "Yet behold, O Lord, thou do have charge of those who are alive at the end, but what will those do who were before us, or we, or those who come after us?"

[42] He said to me, "I shall liken my judgment to a circle; just as for those who are last there is no slowness, so for those who are first there is no haste."

[43] Then I answered and said, "Couldst thou not have created at one time those who have been and those who are and those who will be, that thou mightest show thy judgment the sooner?"

[44] He replied to me and said, "The creation cannot make more haste than the Creator, neither can the world hold at one time those who have been created in it."

[45] And I said, "How hast thou said to thy servant that thou wilt certainly give life at one time to thy creation? If therefore all creatures will live at one time and the creation will sustain them, it might even now be able to support all of them present at one time."

[46] He said to me, "Ask a woman's womb, and say to it, `If you bear ten children, why one after another?' Request it therefore to produce ten at one time."

[47] I said, "Of course it cannot, but only each in its own time."

[48] He said to me, "Even so have I given the womb of the earth to those who from time to time are sown in it.

[49] For as an infant does not bring forth, and a woman who has become old does not bring forth any longer, so have I organized the world which I created." [50] Then I inquired and said, "Since thou hast now given me the opportunity, let me speak before thee. Is our mother, of whom thou hast told me, still young? Or is she now approaching old age?"

[51] He replied to me, "Ask a woman who bears children, and she will tell you.

[52] Say to her, "Why are those whom you have borne recently not like those whom you bore before, but smaller in stature?' [53] And she herself will answer you, `Those born in the strength of youth are different from those born during the time of old age, when the womb is failing.' [54] Therefore you also should consider that you and your contemporaries are smaller in stature than those who were before you,

[55] and those who come after you will be smaller than you, as born of a creation which already is aging and passing the strength of youth." [56] And I said, "O Lord, I beseech thee, if I have found favor in thy sight, show thy servant through whom thou do visit thy creation."

6

[1] And he said to me, "At the beginning of the circle of the earth, before the portals of the world were in place, and before the assembled winds blew,

[2] and before the rumblings of thunder sounded, and before the flashes of lightning shone, and before the foundations of paradise were laid, [3] and before the beautiful flowers were seen, and before the powers of movement were established, and before the innumerable hosts of angels were gathered together,

[4] and before the heights of the air were lifted up, and before the measures of the firmaments were named, and before the footstool of Zion was established, [5] and before the present years were reckoned; and before the imaginations of those who now sin were estranged, and before those who stored up treasures of faith were sealed -- [6] then I planned these things, and they were made through me and not through another, just as the end shall come through me and not through another." [7] And I answered

and said, "What will be the dividing of the times? Or when will be the end of the first age and the beginning of the age that follows?"

[8] He said to me, "From Abraham to Isaac, because from him were born Jacob and Esau, for Jacob's hand held Esau's heel from the beginning.

[9] For Esau is the end of this age, and Jacob is the beginning of the age that follows. [10] For the beginning of a man is his hand, and the end of a man is his heel; between the heel and the hand seek for nothing else, Ezra!" [11] I answered and said, "O sovereign Lord, if I have found favor in thy sight, [12] show thy servant the end of thy signs which thou didst show me in part on a previous night." [13] He answered and said to me, "Rise to your feet and you will hear a full, resounding voice.

[14] And if the place where you are standing is greatly shaken [15] while the voice is speaking, do not be terrified; because the word concerns the end, and the foundations of the earth will understand [16] that the speech concerns them. They will tremble and be shaken, for they know that their end must be changed." [17] When I heard this, I rose to my feet and listened, and behold, a voice was speaking, and its sound was like the sound of many waters.

[18] And it said, "Behold, the days are coming, and it shall be that when I draw near to visit the inhabitants of the earth, [19] and when I require from the doers of iniquity the penalty of their iniquity, and when the humiliation of Zion is complete, [20] and when the seal is placed upon the age which is about to pass away, then I will show these signs: the books shall be opened before the firmament, and all shall see it together. [21] Infants a year old shall speak with their voices, and women with child shall give birth to premature children at three and four months, and these shall live and dance. [22] Sown places shall suddenly appear unsown, and full storehouses shall suddenly be found to be empty; [23] and the trumpet shall sound aloud, and when all hear it, they shall suddenly be terrified. [24] At that time friends shall make war on friends like enemies, and the earth and those who inhabit it shall be terrified, and the springs of the fountains shall stand still, so that for three hours they shall not flow. [25] "And it shall be that whoever remains after all that I have foretold to you shall himself be saved and shall see my salvation and the end of my world.

[26] And they shall see the men who were taken up, who from their birth have not tasted death; and the heart of the earth's inhabitants shall be changed and converted to a different spirit. [27] For evil shall be blotted out, and deceit shall be quenched; [28] faithfulness shall flourish, and corruption shall be overcome, and the truth, which has been so long without fruit, shall be revealed." [29] While he spoke

to me, behold, little by little the place where I was standing began to rock to and fro.

[30] And he said to me, "I have come to show you these things this night. [31] If therefore you will pray again and fast again for seven days, I will again declare to you greater things than these, [32] because your voice has surely been heard before the Most High; for the Mighty One has seen your uprightness and has also observed the purity which you have maintained from your youth. [33] Therefore he sent me to show you all these things, and to say to you: `Believe and do not be afraid! [34] Do not be quick to think vain thoughts concerning the former times, lest you be hasty concerning the last times.'" [35] Now after this I wept again and fasted seven days as before, in order to complete the three weeks as I had been told.

[36] And on the eighth night my heart was troubled within me again, and I began to speak in the presence of the Most High. [37] For my spirit was greatly aroused, and my soul was in distress. [38] I said, "O Lord, thou didst speak at the beginning of creation, and didst say on the first day, `Let heaven and earth be made,' and thy word accomplished the work.

[39] And then the Spirit was hovering, and darkness and silence embraced everything; the sound of man's voice was not yet there. [40] Then thou didst command that a ray of light be brought forth from thy treasuries, so that thy works might then appear. [41] "Again, on the second day, thou didst create the spirit of the firmament, and didst command him to divide and separate the waters, that one part might move upward and the other part remain beneath.

[42] "On the third day thou didst command the waters to be gathered together in the seventh part of the earth; six parts thou didst dry up and keep so that some of them might be planted and cultivated and be of service before thee.

[43] For thy word went forth, and at once the work was done. [44] For immediately fruit came forth in endless abundance and of varied appeal to the taste; and flowers of inimitable color; and odors of inexpressible fragrance. These were made on the third day. [45] "On the fourth day thou didst command the brightness of the sun, the light of the moon, and the arrangement of the stars to come into being; [46] and thou didst command them to serve man, who was about to be formed. [47] "On the fifth day thou didst command the seventh part, where the water had been gathered together, to bring forth living creatures, birds, and fishes; and so it was done. [48] The dumb and lifeless water produced living creatures, as it was commanded, that therefore the nations might declare thy wondrous works. [49] "Then thou didst keep in existence two living

creatures; the name of one thou didst call Behemoth and the name of the other Leviathan.

[50] And thou didst separate one from the other, for the seventh part where the water had been gathered together could not hold them both. [51] And thou didst give Behemoth one of the parts which had been dried up on the third day, to live in it, where there are a thousand mountains; [52] but to Leviathan thou didst give the seventh part, the watery part; and thou hast kept them to be eaten by whom thou wilt, and when thou wilt. [53] "On the sixth day thou didst command the earth to bring forth before thee cattle, beasts, and creeping things;

[54] and over these thou didst place Adam, as ruler over all the works which thou hadst made; and from him we have all come, the people whom thou hast chosen. [55] "All this I have spoken before thee, O Lord, because thou hast said that it was for us that thou didst create this world.

[56] As for the other nations which have descended from Adam, thou hast said that they are nothing, and that they are like spittle, and thou hast compared their abundance to a drop from a bucket. [57] And now, O Lord, behold, these nations, which are reputed as nothing, domineer over us and devour us.

[58] But we thy people, whom thou hast called thy first-born, only begotten, zealous for thee, and most dear, have been given into their hands. [59] If the world has indeed been created for us, why do we not possess our world as an inheritance? How long will this be so?"

7

[1] When I had finished speaking these words, the angel who had been sent to me on the former nights was sent to me again,

[2] and he said to me, "Rise, Ezra, and listen to the words that I have come to speak to you." [3] I said, "Speak, my lord." And he said to me, "There is a sea set in a wide expanse so that it is broad and vast,

[4] but it has an entrance set in a narrow place, so that it is like a river. [5] If any one, then, wishes to reach the sea, to look at it or to navigate it, how can he come to the broad part unless he passes through the narrow part? [6] Another example: There is a city built and set on a plain, and it is full of all good things; [7] but the entrance to it is narrow and set in a precipitous place, so that there is fire on the right hand and deep water on the left; [8] and there is only one path lying between them, that is, between the fire and the water, so that only one man can walk upon that path. [9] If now that city is given to a man for an inheritance, how will the heir receive his inheritance unless he passes through the danger set before him?" [10] I said, "He cannot, lord." And he said to me, "So also is Israel's portion.

[11] For I made the world for their sake, and when Adam transgressed my statutes, what had been made was judged. [12] And so the entrances of this world were made narrow and sorrowful and toilsome; they are few and evil, full of dangers and involved in great hardships. [13] But the entrances of the greater world are broad and safe, and really yield the fruit of immortality. [14] Therefore unless the living pass through the difficult and vain experiences, they can never receive those things that have been reserved for them. [15] But now why are you disturbed, seeing that you are to perish? And why are you moved, seeing that you are mortal? [16] And why have you not considered in your mind what is to come, rather than what is now present?" [17] Then I answered and said, "O sovereign Lord, behold, thou hast ordained in thy law that the righteous shall inherit these things, but that the ungodly shall perish.

[18] The righteous therefore can endure difficult circumstances while hoping for easier ones; but those who have done wickedly have suffered the difficult circumstances and will not see the easier ones." [19] And he said to me, "You are not a better judge than God, or wiser than the Most High!

[20] Let many perish who are now living, rather than that the law of God which is set before them be disregarded! [21] For God strictly commanded those who came into the world, when they came, what they should do to live, and what they should observe to avoid punishment. [22] Nevertheless they were not obedient, and spoke against him; they devised for themselves vain thoughts, [23] and proposed to themselves wicked frauds; they even declared that the Most High does not exist, and they ignored his ways!

[24] They scorned his law, and denied his covenants; they have been unfaithful to his statutes, and have not performed his works. [25] "Therefore, Ezra, empty things are for the empty, and full things are for the full.

[26] For behold, the time will come, when the signs which I have foretold to you will come to pass, that the city which now is not seen shall appear, and the land which now is hidden shall be disclosed. [27] And every one who has been delivered from the evils that I have foretold shall see my wonders. [28] For my son the Messiah shall be revealed with those who are with him, and those who remain shall rejoice four hundred years. [29] And after these years my son the Messiah shall die, and all who draw human breath.

[30] And the world shall be turned back to primeval silence for seven days, as it was at the first beginnings; so that no one shall be left. [31] And after seven days the world, which is not yet awake, shall be roused, and that which is corruptible shall perish. [32] And the earth shall give up those who are asleep in it, and the dust those who dwell silently

in it; and the chambers shall give up the souls which have been committed to them. [33] And the Most High shall be revealed upon the seat of judgment, and compassion shall pass away, and patience shall be withdrawn; [34] but only judgment shall remain, truth shall stand, and faithfulness shall grow strong. [35] And recompense shall follow, and the reward shall be manifested; righteous deeds shall awake, and unrighteous deeds shall not sleep. [36] Then the pit of torment shall appear, and opposite it shall be the place of rest; and the furnace of hell shall be disclosed, and opposite it the paradise of delight. [37] Then the Most High will say to the nations that have been raised from the dead, `Look now, and understand whom you have denied, whom you have not served, whose commandments you have despised! [38] Look on this side and on that; here are delight and rest, and there are fire and torments!' Thus he will speak to them on the day of judgment -- [39] a day that has no sun or moon or stars, [40] or cloud or thunder or lightning or wind or water or air, or darkness or evening or morning, [41] or summer or spring or heat or winter or frost or cold or hail or rain or dew, [42] or noon or night, or dawn or shining or brightness or light, but only the splendor of the glory of the Most High, by which all shall see what has been determined for them. [43] For it will last for about a week of years. [44] This is my judgment and its prescribed order; and to you alone have I shown these things." [45] I answered and said, "O sovereign Lord, I said then and I say now: Blessed are those who are alive and keep thy commandments! [46] But what of those for whom I prayed? For who among the living is there that has not sinned, or who among men that has not transgressed thy covenant? [47] And now I see that the world to come will bring delight to few, but torments to many. [48] For an evil heart has grown up in us, which has alienated us from God, and has brought us into corruption and the ways of death, and has shown us the paths of perdition and removed us far from life -- and that not just a few of us but almost all who have been created!" [49] He answered me and said, "Listen to me, Ezra, and I will instruct you, and will admonish you yet again. [50] For this reason the Most High has made not one world but two. [51] For whereas you have said that the righteous are not many but few, while the ungodly abound, hear the explanation for this. [52] "If you have just a few precious stones, will you add to them lead and clay?" [53] I said, "Lord, how could that be?" [54] And he said to me, "Not only that, but ask the earth and she will tell you; defer to her, and she will declare it to you.

[55] Say to her, `You produce gold and silver and brass, and also iron and lead and clay; [56] but silver is more abundant than gold, and brass than silver, and iron than brass, and lead than iron, and clay than lead.' [57] Judge therefore which things are precious and desirable, those that are abundant or those that are rare?" [58] I said, "O sovereign Lord, what is plentiful is of less worth, for what is more rare is more precious."
[59] He answered me and said, "Weigh within yourself what you have thought, for he who has what is hard to get rejoices more than he who has what is plentiful.
[60] So also will be the judgment which I have promised; for I will rejoice over the few who shall be saved, because it is they who have made my glory to prevail now, and through them my name has now been honored. [61] And I will not grieve over the multitude of those who perish; for it is they who are now like a mist, and are similar to a flame and smoke -- they are set on fire and burn hotly, and are extinguished." [62] I replied and said, "O earth, what have you brought forth, if the mind is made out of the dust like the other created things!
[63] For it would have been better if the dust itself had not been born, so that the mind might not have been made from it. [64] But now the mind grows with us, and therefore we are tormented, because we perish and know it. [65] Let the human race lament, but let the beasts of the field be glad; let all who have been born lament, but let the four-footed beasts and the flocks rejoice! [66] For it is much better with them than with us; for they do not look for a judgment, nor do they know of any torment or salvation promised to them after death. [67] For what does it profit us that we shall be preserved alive but cruelly tormented? [68] For all who have been born are involved in iniquities, and are full of sins and burdened with transgressions. [69] And if we were not to come into judgment after death, perhaps it would have been better for us." [70] He answered me and said, "When the Most High made the world and Adam and all who have come from him, he first prepared the judgment and the things that pertain to the judgment. [71] And now understand from your own words, for you have said that the mind grows with us. [72] For this reason, therefore, those who dwell on earth shall be tormented, because though they had understanding they committed iniquity, and though they received the commandments they did not keep them, and though they obtained the law they dealt unfaithfully with what they received. [73] What, then, will they have to say in the judgment, or how will they answer in the last times? [74] For how long the time is that the Most High has been patient with those who inhabit the world, and not for their sake,

but because of the times which he has foreordained!"

[75] I answered and said, "If I have found favor in thy sight, O Lord, show this also to thy servant: whether after death, as soon as every one of us yields up his soul, we shall be kept in rest until those times come when thou wilt renew the creation, or whether we shall be tormented at once?"

[76] He answered me and said, "I will show you that also, but do not be associated with those who have shown scorn, nor number yourself among those who are tormented.

[77] For you have a treasure of works laid up with the Most High; but it will not be shown to you until the last times. [78] Now, concerning death, the teaching is: When the decisive decree has gone forth from the Most High that a man shall die, as the spirit leaves the body to return again to him who gave it, first of all it adores the glory of the Most High. [79] And if it is one of those who have shown scorn and have not kept the way of the Most High, and who have despised his law, and who have hated those who fear God -- [80] such spirits shall not enter into habitations, but shall immediately wander about in torments, ever grieving and sad, in seven ways. [81] The first way, because they have scorned the law of the Most High. [82] The second way, because they cannot now make a good repentance that they may live. [83] The third way, they shall see the reward laid up for those who have trusted the covenants of the Most High. [84] The fourth way, they shall consider the torment laid up for themselves in the last days. [85] The fifth way, they shall see how the habitations of the others are guarded by angels in profound quiet. [86] The sixth way, they shall see how some of them will pass over into torments. [87] The seventh way, which is worse than all the ways that have been mentioned, because they shall utterly waste away in confusion and be consumed with shame, and shall wither with fear at seeing the glory of the Most High before whom they sinned while they were alive, and before whom they are to be judged in the last times. [88] "Now this is the order of those who have kept the ways of the Most High, when they shall be separated from their mortal body.

[89] During the time that they lived in it, they laboriously served the Most High, and withstood danger every hour, that they might keep the law of the Lawgiver perfectly. [90] Therefore this is the teaching concerning them: [91] First of all, they shall see with great joy the glory of him who receives them, for they shall have rest in seven orders. [92] The first order, because they have striven with great effort to overcome the evil thought which was formed with them, that it might not lead them astray from life into death. [93] The second order, because they see the perplexity in which the souls of the ungodly wander,

and the punishment that awaits them. [94] The third order, they see the witness which he who formed them bears concerning them, that while they were alive they kept the law which was given them in trust.

[95] The fourth order, they understand the rest which they now enjoy, being gathered into their chambers and guarded by angels in profound quiet, and the glory which awaits them in the last days. [96] The fifth order, they rejoice that they have now escaped what is corruptible, and shall inherit what is to come; and besides they see the straits and toil from which they have been delivered, and the spacious liberty which they are to receive and enjoy in immortality. [97] The sixth order, when it is shown to them how their face is to shine like the sun, and how they are to be made like the light of the stars, being incorruptible from then on. [98] The seventh order, which is greater than all that have been mentioned, because they shall rejoice with boldness, and shall be confident without confusion, and shall be glad without fear, for they hasten to behold the face of him whom they served in life and from whom they are to receive their reward when glorified. [99] This is the order of the souls of the righteous, as henceforth is announced; and the aforesaid are the ways of torment which those who would not give heed shall suffer hereafter." [100] I answered and said, "Will time therefore be given to the souls, after they have been separated from the bodies, to see what you have described to me?"

[101] He said to me, "They shall have freedom for seven days, so that during these seven days they may see the things of which you have been told, and afterwards they shall be gathered in their habitations."

[102] I answered and said, "If I have found favor in thy sight, show further to me, thy servant, whether on the day of judgment the righteous will be able to intercede for the ungodly or to entreat the Most High for them,

[103] fathers for sons or sons for parents, brothers for brothers, relatives for their kinsmen, or friends for those who are most dear." [104] He answered me and said, "Since you have found favor in my sight, I will show you this also. The day of judgment is decisive and displays to all the seal of truth. Just as now a father does not send his son, or a son his father, or a master his servant, or a friend his dearest friend, to be ill or sleep or eat or be healed in his stead,

[105] so no one shall ever pray for another on that day, neither shall any one lay a burden on another; for then every one shall bear his own righteousness and unrighteousness." [36(106)] I answered and said, "How then do we find that first Abraham prayed for the people of Sodom, and Moses for our fathers who sinned in the desert,

[37(107)] and Joshua after him for Israel in the days of Achan, [38(108)] and Samuel in the days of Saul, and David for the plague, and Solomon for those in the sanctuary, [39(109)] and Elijah for those who received the rain, and for the one who was dead, that he might live, [40(110)] and Hezekiah for the people in the days of Sennacherib, and many others prayed for many? [41(111)] If therefore the righteous have prayed for the ungodly now, when corruption has increased and unrighteousness has multiplied, why will it not be so then as well?" [42(112)] He answered me and said, "This present world is not the end; the full glory does not abide in it; therefore those who were strong prayed for the weak.

[43(113)] But the day of judgment will be the end of this age and the beginning of the immortal age to come, in which corruption has passed away, [44(114)] sinful indulgence has come to an end, unbelief has been cut off, and righteousness has increased and truth has appeared. [45(115)] Therefore no one will then be able to have mercy on him who has been condemned in the judgment, or to harm him who is victorious." [46(116)] I answered and said, "This is my first and last word, that it would have been better if the earth had not produced Adam, or else, when it had produced him, had restrained him from sinning.

[47(117)] For what good is it to all that they live in sorrow now and expect punishment after death? [48(118)] O Adam, what have you done? For though it was you who sinned, the fall was not yours alone, but ours also who are your descendants. [49(119)] For what good is it to us, if an eternal age has been promised to us, but we have done deeds that bring death? [50(120)] And what good is it that an everlasting hope has been promised to us, but we have miserably failed? [51(121)] Or that safe and healthful habitations have been reserved for us, but we have lived wickedly? [52(122)] Or that the glory of the Most High will defend those who have led a pure life, but we have walked in the most wicked ways? [53(123)] Or that a paradise shall be revealed, whose fruit remains unspoiled and in which are abundance and healing, but we shall not enter it, [54(124)] because we have lived in unseemly places? [55(125)] Or that the faces of those who practiced self-control shall shine more than the stars, but our faces shall be blacker than darkness? [56(126)] For while we lived and committed iniquity we did not consider what we should suffer after death." [57(127)] He answered and said, "This is the meaning of the contest which every man who is born on earth shall wage, [58(128)] that if he is defeated he shall suffer what you have said, but if he is victorious he shall receive what I have said. [59(129)] For this is the way of which

Moses, while he was alive, spoke to the people, saying, `Choose for yourself life, that you may live!' [60(130)] But they did not believe him, or the prophets after him, or even myself who have spoken to them. [61(131)] Therefore there shall not be grief at their destruction, so much as joy over those to whom salvation is assured." [62(132)] I answered and said, "I know, O Lord, that the Most High is now called merciful, because he has mercy on those who have not yet come into the world; [63(133)] and gracious, because he is gracious to those who turn in repentance to his law; [64(134)] and patient, because he shows patience toward those who have sinned, since they are his own works; [65(135)] and bountiful, because he would rather give than take away; [66(136)] and abundant in compassion, because he makes his compassions abound more and more to those now living and to those who are gone and to those yet to come, [67(137)] for if he did not make them abound, the world with those who inhabit it would not have life; [68(138)] and he is called giver, because if he did not give out of his goodness so that those who have committed iniquities might be relieved of them, not one ten-thousandth of mankind could have life; [69(139)] and judge, because if he did not pardon those who were created by his word and blot out the multitude of their sins, [70(140)] there would probably be left only very few of the innumerable multitude."

8

[1] He answered me and said, "The Most High made this world for the sake of many, but the world to come for the sake of few.

[2] But I tell you a parable, Ezra. Just as, when you ask the earth, it will tell you that it provides very much clay from which earthenware is made, but only a little dust from which gold comes; so is the course of the present world.

[3] Many have been created, but few shall be saved."

[4] I answered and said, "Then drink your fill of understanding, O my soul, and drink wisdom, O my heart!

[5] For not of your own will did you come into the world, and against your will you depart, for you have been given only a short time to live.

[6] O Lord who are over us, grant to thy servant that we may pray before thee, and give us seed for our heart and cultivation of our understanding so that fruit may be produced, by which every mortal who bears the likeness of a human being may be able to live.

[7] For thou alone do exist, and we are a work of thy hands, as thou hast declared.

[8] And because thou do give life to the body which is now fashioned in the womb, and do furnish it with members, what thou hast created is preserved in fire

and water, and for nine months the womb which thou has formed endures thy creation which has been created in it.

[9] But that which keeps and that which is kept shall both be kept by thy keeping. And when the womb gives up again what has been created in it,

[10] thou hast commanded that from the members themselves (that is, from the breasts) milk should be supplied which is the fruit of the breasts,

[11] so that what has been fashioned may be nourished for a time; and afterwards thou wilt guide him in thy mercy.

[12] Thou hast brought him up in thy righteousness, and instructed him in thy law, and reproved him in thy wisdom.

[13] Thou wilt take away his life, for he is thy creation; and thou wilt make him live, for he is thy work.

[14] If then thou wilt suddenly and quickly destroy him who with so great labor was fashioned by thy command, to what purpose was he made?

[15] And now I will speak out: About all mankind thou knowest best; but I will speak about thy people, for whom I am grieved,

[16] and about thy inheritance, for whom I lament, and about Israel, for whom I am sad, and about the seed of Jacob, for whom I am troubled.

[17] Therefore I will pray before thee for myself and for them, for I see the failings of us who dwell in the land,

[18] and I have heard of the swiftness of the judgment that is to come.

[19] Therefore hear my voice, and understand my words, and I will speak before thee." The beginning of the words of Ezra's prayer, before he was taken up. He said:

[20] "O Lord who inhabitest eternity, whose eyes are exalted and whose upper chambers are in the air,

[21] whose throne is beyond measure and whose glory is beyond comprehension, before whom the hosts of angels stand trembling

[22] and at whose command they are changed to wind and fire, whose word is sure and whose utterances are certain, whose ordinance is strong and whose command is terrible,

[23] whose look dries up the depths and whose indignation makes the mountains melt away, and whose truth is established for ever --

[24] hear, O Lord, the prayer of thy servant, and give ear to the petition of thy creature; attend to my words.

[25] For as long as I live I will speak, and as long as I have understanding I will answer.

[26] O look not upon the sins of thy people, but at those who have served thee in truth.

[27] Regard not the endeavors of those who act wickedly, but the endeavors of those who have kept thy covenants amid afflictions.

[28] Think not on those who have lived wickedly in thy sight; but remember those who have willingly acknowledged that thou art to be feared.

[29] Let it not be thy will to destroy those who have had the ways of cattle; but regard those who have gloriously taught thy law.

[30] Be not angry with those who are deemed worse than beasts; but love those who have always put their trust in thy glory.

[31] For we and our fathers have passed our lives in ways that bring death, but thou, because of us sinners, are called merciful.

[32] For if thou hast desired to have pity on us, who have no works of righteousness, then thou wilt be called merciful.

[33] For the righteous, who have many works laid up with thee, shall receive their reward in consequence of their own deeds.

[34] But what is man, that thou art angry with him; or what is a corruptible race, that thou art so bitter against it?

[35] For in truth there is no one among those who have been born who has not acted wickedly, and among those who have existed there is no one who has not transgressed.

[36] For in this, O Lord, thy righteousness and goodness will be declared, when thou art merciful to those who have no store of good works."

[37] He answered me and said, "Some things you have spoken rightly, and it will come to pass according to your words.

[38] For indeed I will not concern myself about the fashioning of those who have sinned, or about their death, their judgment, or their destruction;

[39] but I will rejoice over the creation of the righteous, over their pilgrimage also, and their salvation, and their receiving their reward.

[40] As I have spoken, therefore, so it shall be.

[41] "For just as the farmer sows many seeds upon the ground and plants a multitude of seedlings, and yet not all that have been sown will come up in due season, and not all that were planted will take root; so also those who have been sown in the world will not all be saved."

[42] I answered and said, "If I have found favor before thee, let me speak.

[43] For if the farmer's seed does not come up, because it has not received thy rain in due season, or if it has been ruined by too much rain, it perishes.

[44] But man, who has been formed by thy hands and is called thy own image because he is made like thee, and for whose sake thou hast formed all things -- hast thou also made him like the farmer's seed?

[45] No, O Lord who art over us! But spare thy people and have mercy on thy inheritance, for thou hast mercy on thy own creation."

[46] He answered me and said, "Things that are present are for those who live now, and things that are future are for those who will live hereafter.

[47] For you come far short of being able to love my creation more than I love it. But you have often compared yourself to the unrighteous. Never do so!

[48] But even in this respect you will be praiseworthy before the Most High,

[49] because you have humbled yourself, as is becoming for you, and have not deemed yourself to be among the righteous in order to receive the greatest glory.

[50] For many miseries will affect those who inhabit the world in the last times, because they have walked in great pride.

[51] But think of your own case, and inquire concerning the glory of those who are like yourself,

[52] because it is for you that paradise is opened, the tree of life is planted, the age to come is prepared, plenty is provided, a city is built, rest is appointed, goodness is established and wisdom perfected beforehand.

[53] The root of evil is sealed up from you, illness is banished from you, and death is hidden; hell has fled and corruption has been forgotten;

[54] sorrows have passed away, and in the end the treasure of immortality is made manifest.

[55] Therefore do not ask any more questions about the multitude of those who perish.

[56] For they also received freedom , but they despised the Most High, and were contemptuous of his law, and forsook his ways.

[57] Moreover they have even trampled upon his righteous ones,

[58] and said in their hearts that there is not God -- though knowing full well that they must die.

[59] For just as the things which I have predicted await you, so the thirst and torment which are prepared await them. For the Most High did not intend that men should be destroyed;

[60] but they themselves who were created have defiled the name of him who made them, and have been ungrateful to him who prepared life for them.

[61] Therefore my judgment is now drawing near;

[62] I have not shown this to all men, but only to you and a few like you." Then I answered and said,

[63] "Behold, O Lord, thou hast now shown me a multitude of the signs which thou wilt do in the last times, but thou hast not shown me when thou wilt do them."

9

[1] He answered me and said, "Measure carefully in your mind, and when you see that a certain part of the predicted signs are past,

[2] then you will know that it is the very time when the Most High is about to visit the world which he has made.

[3] So when there shall appear in the world earthquakes, tumult of peoples, intrigues of nations, wavering of leaders, confusion of princes,

[4] then you will know that it was of these that the Most High spoke from the days that were of old, from the beginning.

[5] For just as with everything that has occurred in the world, the beginning is evident, and the end manifest;

[6] so also are the times of the Most High: the beginnings are manifest in wonders and mighty works, and the end in requital and in signs.

[7] And it shall be that every one who will be saved and will be able to escape on account of his works, or on account of the faith by which he has believed,

[8] will survive the dangers that have been predicted, and will see my salvation in my land and within my borders, which I have sanctified for myself from the beginning.

[9] Then those who have now abused my ways shall be amazed, and those who have rejected them with contempt shall dwell in torments.

[10] For as many as did not acknowledge me in their lifetime, although they received my benefits,

[11] and as many as scorned my law while they still had freedom, and did not understand but despised it while an opportunity of repentance was still open to them,

[12] these must in torment acknowledge it after death.

[13] Therefore, do not continue to be curious as to how the ungodly will be punished; but inquire how the righteous will be saved, those to whom the age belongs and for whose sake the age was made."

[14] I answered and said,

[15] "I said before, and I say now, and will say it again: there are more who perish than those who will be saved,

[16] as a wave is greater than a drop of water."

[17] He answered me and said, "As is the field, so is the seed; and as are the flowers, so are the colors; and as is the work, so is the product; and as is the farmer, so is the threshing floor.

[18] For there was a time in this age when I was preparing for those who now exist, before the world was made for them to dwell in, and no one opposed me then, for no one existed;

[19] but now those who have been created in this world which is supplied both with an unfailing table and an inexhaustible pasture, have become corrupt in their ways.

[20] So I considered my world, and behold, it was lost, and my earth, and behold, it was in peril because of the devices of those who had come into it.

[21] And I saw and spared some with great difficulty, and saved for myself one grape out of a cluster, and one plant out of a great forest.

[22] So let the multitude perish which has been born in vain, but let my grape and my plant be saved, because with much labor I have perfected them.

[23] But if you will let seven days more pass -- do not fast during them, however;

[24] but go into a field of flowers where no house has been built, and eat only of the flowers of the field, and taste no meat and drink no wine, but eat only flowers,

[25] and pray to the Most High continually -- then I will come and talk with you."

[26] So I went, as he directed me, into the field which is called Ardat; and there I sat among the flowers and ate of the plants of the field, and the nourishment they afforded satisfied me.

[27] And after seven days, as I lay on the grass, my heart was troubled again as it was before.

[28] And my mouth was opened, and I began to speak before the Most High, and said,

[29] "O Lord, thou didst show thyself among us, to our fathers in the wilderness when they came out from Egypt and when they came into the untrodden and unfruitful wilderness;

[30] and thou didst say, `Hear me, O Israel, and give heed to my words, O descendants of Jacob.

[31] For behold, I sow my law in you, and it shall bring forth fruit in you and you shall be glorified through it for ever.'

[32] But though our fathers received the law, they did not keep it, and did not observe the statutes; yet the fruit of the law did not perish -- for it could not, because it was your.

[33] Yet those who received it perished, because they did not keep what had been sown in them.

[34] And behold, it is the rule that, when the ground has received seed, or the sea a ship, or any dish food or drink, and when it happens that what was sown or what was launched or what was put in is destroyed,

[35] they are destroyed, but the things that held them remain; yet with us it has not been so.

[36] For we who have received the law and sinned will perish, as well as our heart which received it;

[37] the law, however, does not perish but remains in its glory."

[38] When I said these things in my heart, I lifted up my eyes and saw a woman on my right, and behold, she was mourning and weeping with a loud voice, and was deeply grieved at heart, and her clothes were rent, and there were ashes on her head.

[39] Then I dismissed the thoughts with which I had been engaged, and turned to her

[40] and said to her, "Why are you weeping, and why are you grieved at heart?"

[41] And she said to me, "Let me alone, my lord, that I may weep for myself and continue to mourn, for I am greatly embittered in spirit and deeply afflicted."

[42] And I said to her, "What has happened to you? Tell me."

[43] And she said to me, "Your servant was barren and had no child, though I lived with my husband thirty years.

[44] And every hour and every day during those thirty years I besought the Most High, night and day.

[45] And after thirty years God heard your handmaid, and looked upon my low estate, and considered my distress, and gave me a son. And I rejoiced greatly over him, I and my husband and all my neighbors; and we gave great glory to the Mighty One.

[46] And I brought him up with much care.

[47] So when he grew up and I came to take a wife for him, I set a day for the marriage feast.

10

[1] "But it happened that when my son entered his wedding chamber, he fell down and died.

[2] Then we all put out the lamps, and all my neighbors attempted to console me; and I remained quiet until evening of the second day.

[3] But when they all had stopped consoling me, that I might be quiet, I got up in the night and fled, and came to this field, as you see.

[4] And now I intend not to return to the city, but to stay here, and I will neither eat nor drink, but without ceasing mourn and fast until I die."

[5] Then I broke off the reflections with which I was still engaged, and answered her in anger and said,

[6] "You most foolish of women, do you not see our mourning, and what has happened to us?

[7] For Zion, the mother of us all, is in deep grief and great affliction.

[8] It is most appropriate to mourn now, because we are all mourning, and to be sorrowful, because we are all sorrowing; you are sorrowing for one son, but we, the whole world, for our mother.

[9] Now ask the earth, and she will tell you that it is she who ought to mourn over so many who have come into being upon her.

[10] And from the beginning all have been born of her, and others will come; and behold, almost all go to perdition, and a multitude of them are destined for destruction.

[11] Who then ought to mourn the more, she who lost so great a multitude, or you who are grieving for one?

[12] But if you say to me, `My lamentation is not like the earth's, for I have lost the fruit of my womb, which I brought forth in pain and bore in sorrow;

[13] but it is with the earth according to the way of the earth -- the multitude that is now in it goes as it came';

[14] then I say to you, `As you brought forth in sorrow, so the earth also has from the beginning given her fruit, that is, man, to him who made her.'

[15] Now, therefore, keep your sorrow to yourself, and bear bravely the troubles that have come upon you.

[16] For if you acknowledge the decree of God to be just, you will receive your son back in due time, and will be praised among women.

[17] Therefore go into the city to your husband."

[18] She said to me, "I will not do so; I will not go into the city, but I will die here."

[19] So I spoke again to her, and said,

[20] "Do not say that, but let yourself be persuaded because of the troubles of Zion, and be consoled because of the sorrow of Jerusalem.

[21] For you see that our sanctuary has been laid waste, our altar thrown down, our temple destroyed;

[22] our harp has been laid low, our song has been silenced, and our rejoicing has been ended; the light of our lampstand has been put out, the ark of our covenant has been plundered, our holy things have been polluted, and the name by which we are called has been profaned; our free men have suffered abuse, our priests have been burned to death, our Levites have gone into captivity, our virgins have been defiled, and our wives have been ravished; our righteous men have been carried off, our little ones have been cast out, our young men have been enslaved and our strong men made powerless.

[23] And, what is more than all, the seal of Zion -- for she has now lost the seal of her glory, and has been given over into the hands of those that hate us.

[24] Therefore shake off your great sadness and lay aside your many sorrows, so that the Mighty One may be merciful to you again, and the Most High may give you rest, a relief from your troubles."

[25] While I was talking to her, behold, her face suddenly shone exceedingly, and her countenance flashed like lightning, so that I was too frightened to approach her, and my heart was terrified. While I was wondering what this meant,

[26] behold, she suddenly uttered a loud and fearful cry, so that the earth shook at the sound.

[27] And I looked, and behold, the woman was no longer visible to me, but there was an established city, and a place of huge foundations showed itself. Then I was afraid, and cried with a loud voice and said,

[28] "Where is the angel Uriel, who came to me at first? For it was he who brought me into this overpowering bewilderment; my end has become corruption, and my prayer a reproach."

[29] As I was speaking these words, behold, the angel who had come to me at first came to me, and he looked upon me;

[30] and behold, I lay there like a corpse and I was deprived of my understanding. Then he grasped my right hand and strengthened me and set me on my feet, and said to me,

[31] "What is the matter with you? And why are you troubled? And why are your understanding and the thoughts of your mind troubled?"

[32] I said, "Because you have forsaken me! I did as you directed, and went out into the field, and behold, I saw, and still see, what I am unable to explain."

[33] He said to me, "Stand up like a man, and I will instruct you."

[34] I said, "Speak, my lord; only do not forsake me, lest I die before my time.

[35] For I have seen what I did not know, and I have heard what I do not understand.

[36] Or is my mind deceived, and my soul dreaming?

[37] Now therefore I entreat you to give your servant an explanation of this bewildering vision."

[38] He answered me and said, "Listen to me and I will inform you, and tell you about the things which you fear, for the Most High has revealed many secrets to you.

[39] For he has seen your righteous conduct, that you have sorrowed continually for your people, and mourned greatly over Zion.

[40] This therefore is the meaning of the vision.

[41] The woman who appeared to you a little while ago, whom you saw mourning and began to console --

[42] but you do not now see the form of a woman, but an established city has appeared to you --

[43] and as for her telling you about the misfortune of her son, this is the interpretation:

[44] This woman whom you saw, whom you now behold as an established city, is Zion.

[45] And as for her telling you that she was barren for thirty years, it is because there were three thousand years in the world before any offering was offered in it.

[46] And after three thousand years Solomon built the city, and offered offerings; then it was that the barren woman bore a son.

[47] And as for her telling you that she brought him up with much care, that was the period of residence in Jerusalem.

[48] And as for her saying to you , `When my son entered his wedding chamber he died,' and that misfortune had overtaken her, that was the destruction which befell Jerusalem.

[49] And behold, you saw her likeness, how she mourned for her son, and you began to console her for what had happened.

[50] For now the Most High, seeing that you are sincerely grieved and profoundly distressed for her, has shown you the brilliance of her glory, and the loveliness of her beauty.

[51] Therefore I told you to remain in the field where no house had been built,

[52] for I knew that the Most High would reveal these things to you.

[53] Therefore I told you to go into the field where there was no foundation of any building,

[54] for no work of man's building could endure in a place where the city of the Most High was to be revealed.

[55] "Therefore do not be afraid, and do not let your heart be terrified; but go in and see the splendor and vastness of the building, as far as it is possible for your eyes to see it,

[56] and afterward you will hear as much as your ears can hear.

[57] For you are more blessed than many, and you have been called before the Most High, as but few have been.

[58] But tomorrow night you shall remain here,

[59] and the Most High will show you in those dream visions what the Most High will do to those who dwell on earth in the last days." So I slept that night and the following one, as he had commanded me.

11

[1] On the second night I had a dream, and behold, there came up from the sea an eagle that had twelve feathered wings and three heads.

[2] And I looked, and behold, he spread his wings over all the earth, and all the winds of heaven blew upon him, and the clouds were gathered about him.

[3] And I looked, and out of his wings there grew opposing wings; but they became little, puny wings.

[4] But his heads were at rest; the middle head was larger than the other heads, but it also was at rest with them.

[5] And I looked, and behold, the eagle flew with his wings, to reign over the earth and over those who dwell in it.

[6] And I saw how all things under heaven were subjected to him, and no one spoke against him, not even one creature that was on the earth.

[7] And I looked, and behold, the eagle rose upon his talons, and uttered a cry to his wings, saying,

[8] "Do not all watch at the same time; let each sleep in his own place, and watch in his turn;

[9] but let the heads be reserved for the last."

[10] And I looked, and behold, the voice did not come from his heads, but from the midst of his body.

[11] And I counted his opposing wings, and behold, there were eight of them.

[12] And I looked, and behold, on the right side one wing arose, and it reigned over all the earth.

[13] And while it was reigning it came to its end and disappeared, so that its place was not seen. Then the next wing arose and reigned, and it continued to reign a long time.

[14] And while it was reigning its end came also, so that it disappeared like the first.

[15] And behold, a voice sounded, saying to it.

[16] "Hear me, you who have ruled the earth all this time; I announce this to you before you disappear.

[17] After you no one shall rule as long as you, or even half as long."

[18] Then the third wing raised itself up, and held the rule like the former ones, and it also disappeared.

[19] And so it went with all the wings; they wielded power one after another and then were never seen again.

[20] And I looked, and behold, in due course the wings that followed also rose up on the right side, in order to rule. There were some of them that ruled, yet disappeared suddenly;

[21] and others of them rose up, but did not hold the rule.

[22] And after this I looked, and behold, the twelve wings and the two little wings disappeared;

[23] and nothing remained on the eagle's body except the three heads that were at rest and six little wings.

[24] And I looked, and behold, two little wings separated from the six and remained under the head that was on the right side; but four remained in their place.

[25] And I looked, and behold, these little wings planned to set themselves up and hold the rule.

[26] And I looked, and behold, one was set up, but suddenly disappeared;

[27] a second also, and this disappeared more quickly than the first.

[28] And I looked, and behold, the two that remained were planning between themselves to reign together;

[29] and while they were planning, behold, one of the heads that were at rest (the one which was in the middle) awoke; for it was greater than the other two heads.

[30] And I saw how it allied the two heads with itself,

[31] and behold, the head turned with those that were with it, and it devoured the two little wings which were planning to reign.

[32] Moreover this head gained control of the whole earth, and with much oppression dominated its inhabitants; and it had greater power over the world than all the wings that had gone before.

[33] And after this I looked, and behold, the middle head also suddenly disappeared, just as the wings had done.

[34] But the two heads remained, which also ruled over the earth and its inhabitants.

[35] And I looked, and behold, the head on the right side devoured the one on the left.

[36] Then I heard a voice saying to me, "Look before you and consider what you see."

[37] And I looked, and behold, a creature like a lion was aroused out of the forest, roaring; and I heard how he uttered a man's voice to the eagle, and spoke, saying,

[38] "Listen and I will speak to you. The Most High says to you,

[39] `Are you not the one that remains of the four beasts which I had made to reign in my world, so that the end of my times might come through them?

[40] You, the fourth that has come, have conquered all the beasts that have gone before; and you have held sway over the world with much terror, and over all the earth with grievous oppression; and for so long you have dwelt on the earth with deceit.

[41] And you have judged the earth, but not with truth;

[42] for you have afflicted the meek and injured the peaceable; you have hated those who tell the truth, and have loved liars; you have destroyed the dwellings of those who brought forth fruit, and have laid low the walls of those who did you no harm.

[43] And so your insolence has come up before the Most High, and your pride to the Mighty One.

[44] And the Most High has looked upon his times, and behold, they are ended, and his ages are completed!

[45] Therefore you will surely disappear, you eagle, and your terrifying wings, and your most evil little wings, and your malicious heads, and your most evil talons, and your whole worthless body,

[46] so that the whole earth, freed from your violence, may be refreshed and relieved, and may hope for the judgment and mercy of him who made it.'"

12

[1] While the lion was saying these words to the eagle, I looked,

[2] and behold, the remaining head disappeared. And the two wings that had gone over to it arose and set themselves up to reign, and their reign was brief and full of tumult.

[3] And I looked, and behold, they also disappeared, and the whole body of the eagle was burned, and the earth was exceedingly terrified. Then I awoke in great perplexity of mind and great fear, and I said to my spirit,

[4] "Behold, you have brought this upon me, because you search out the ways of the Most High.

[5] Behold, I am still weary in mind and very weak in my spirit, and not even a little strength is left in me, because of the great fear with which I have been terrified this night.

[6] Therefore I will now beseech the Most High that he may strengthen me to the end."

[7] And I said, "O sovereign Lord, if I have found favor in thy sight, and if I have been accounted righteous before thee beyond many others, and if my prayer has indeed come up before thy face,

[8] strengthen me and show me, thy servant, the interpretation and meaning of this terrifying vision, that thou mayest fully comfort my soul.

[9] For thou hast judged me worthy to be shown the end of the times and the last events of the times."

[10] He said to me, "This is the interpretation of this vision which you have seen:

[11] The eagle which you saw coming up from the sea is the fourth kingdom which appeared in a vision to your brother Daniel.

[12] But it was not explained to him as I now explain or have explained it to you.

[13] Behold, the days are coming when a kingdom shall arise on earth, and it shall be more terrifying than all the kingdoms that have been before it.

[14] And twelve kings shall reign in it, one after another.

[15] But the second that is to reign shall hold sway for a longer time than any other of the twelve.

[16] This is the interpretation of the twelve wings which you saw.

[17] As for your hearing a voice that spoke, coming not from the eagle's heads but from the midst of his body, this is the interpretation:

[18] In the midst of the time of that kingdom great struggles shall arise, and it shall be in danger of falling; nevertheless it shall not fall then, but shall regain its former power.

[19] As for your seeing eight little wings clinging to his wings, this is the interpretation:

[20] Eight kings shall arise in it, whose times shall be short and their years swift;

[21] and two of them shall perish when the middle of its time draws near; and four shall be kept for the time when its end approaches; but two shall be kept until the end.

[22] As for your seeing three heads at rest, this is the interpretation:

[23] In its last days the Most High will raise up three kings, and they shall renew many things in it, and shall rule the earth

[24] and its inhabitants more oppressively than all who were before them; therefore they are called the heads of the eagle.

[25] For it is they who shall sum up his wickedness and perform his last actions.

[26] As for your seeing that the large head disappeared, one of the kings shall die in his bed, but in agonies.

[27] But as for the two who remained, the sword shall devour them.

[28] For the sword of one shall devour him who was with him; but he also shall fall by the sword in the last days.

[29] As for your seeing two little wings passing over to the head which was on the right side,

[30] this is the interpretation: It is these whom the Most High has kept for the eagle's end; this was the reign which was brief and full of tumult, as you have seen.

[31] "And as for the lion whom you saw rousing up out of the forest and roaring and speaking to the eagle and reproving him for his unrighteousness, and as for all his words that you have heard,

[32] this is the Messiah whom the Most High has kept until the end of days, who will arise from the posterity of David, and will come and speak to them; he will denounce them for their ungodliness and for their wickedness, and will cast up before them their contemptuous dealings.

[33] For first he will set them living before his judgment seat, and when he has reproved them, then he will destroy them.

[34] But he will deliver in mercy the remnant of my people, those who have been saved throughout my borders, and he will make them joyful until the end comes, the day of judgment, of which I spoke to you at the beginning.

[35] This is the dream that you saw, and this is its interpretation.

[36] And you alone were worthy to learn this secret of the Most High.

[37] Therefore write all these things that you have seen in a book, and put it in a hidden place;

[38] and you shall teach them to the wise among your people, whose hearts you know are able to comprehend and keep these secrets.

[39] But wait here seven days more, so that you may be shown whatever it pleases the Most High to show you." Then he left me.

[40] When all the people heard that the seven days were past and I had not returned to the city, they all gathered together, from the least to the greatest, and came to me and spoke to me, saying,

[41] "How have we offended you, and what harm have we done you, that you have forsaken us and sit in this place?

[42] For of all the prophets you alone are left to us, like a cluster of grapes from the vintage, and like a lamp in a dark place, and like a haven for a ship saved from a storm.

[43] Are not the evils which have befallen us sufficient?

[44] Therefore if you forsake us, how much better it would have been for us if we also had been consumed in the burning of Zion!

[45] For we are no better than those who died there." And they wept with a loud voice. Then I answered them and said,

[46] "Take courage, O Israel; and do not be sorrowful, O house of Jacob;

[47] for the Most High has you in remembrance, and the Mighty One has not forgotten you in your struggle.

[48] As for me, I have neither forsaken you nor withdrawn from you; but I have come to this place to pray on account of the desolation of Zion, and to seek mercy on account of the humiliation of our sanctuary.

[49] Now go, every one of you to his house, and after these days I will come to you."

[50] So the people went into the city, as I told them to do.

[51] But I sat in the field seven days, as the angel had commanded me; and I ate only of the flowers of the field, and my food was of plants during those days.

13

[1] After seven days I dreamed a dream in the night;

[2] and behold, a wind arose from the sea and stirred up all its waves.

[3] And I looked, and behold, this wind made something like the figure of a man come up out of the heart of the sea. And I looked, and behold, that man flew with the clouds of heaven; and wherever he turned his face to look, everything under his gaze trembled,

[4] and whenever his voice issued from his mouth, all who heard his voice melted as wax melts when it feels the fire.

[5] After this I looked, and behold, an innumerable multitude of men were gathered together from the four winds of heaven to make war against the man who came up out of the sea.

[6] And I looked, and behold, he carved out for himself a great mountain, and flew up upon it.
[7] And I tried to see the region or place from which the mountain was carved, but I could not.

[8] After this I looked, and behold, all who had gathered together against him, to wage war with him, were much afraid, yet dared to fight.

[9] And behold, when he saw the onrush of the approaching multitude, he neither lifted his hand nor held a spear or any weapon of war;

[10] but I saw only how he sent forth from his mouth as it were a stream of fire, and from his lips a flaming breath, and from his tongue he shot forth a storm of sparks.

[11] All these were mingled together, the stream of fire and the flaming breath and the great storm, and fell on the onrushing multitude which was prepared to fight, and burned them all up, so that suddenly nothing was seen of the innumerable multitude but only the dust of ashes and the smell of smoke. When I saw it, I was amazed.

[12] After this I saw the same man come down from the mountain and call to him another multitude which was peaceable.

[13] Then many people came to him, some of whom were joyful and some sorrowful; some of them were bound, and some were bringing others as offerings. Then in great fear I awoke; and I besought the Most High, and said,

[14] "From the beginning thou hast shown thy servant these wonders, and hast deemed me worthy to have my prayer heard by thee;

[15] now show me also the interpretation of this dream.

[16] For as I consider it in my mind, alas for those who will be left in those days! And still more, alas for those who are not left!

[17] For those who are not left will be sad,

[18] because they understand what is reserved for the last days, but cannot attain it.

[19] But alas for those also who are left, and for that very reason! For they shall see great dangers and much distress, as these dreams show.

[20] Yet it is better to come into these things, though incurring peril, than to pass from the world like a cloud, and not to see what shall happen in the last days." He answered me and said,

[21] "I will tell you the interpretation of the vision, and I will also explain to you the things which you have mentioned.

[22] As for what you said about those who are left, this is the interpretation:

[23] He who brings the peril at that time will himself protect those who fall into peril, who have works and have faith in the Almighty.

[24] Understand therefore that those who are left are more blessed than those who have died.

[25] This is the interpretation of the vision: As for your seeing a man come up from the heart of the sea,

[26] this is he whom the Most High has been keeping for many ages, who will himself deliver his creation; and he will direct those who are left.

[27] And as for your seeing wind and fire and a storm coming out of his mouth,

[28] and as for his not holding a spear or weapon of war, yet destroying the onrushing multitude which came to conquer him, this is the interpretation:

[29] Behold, the days are coming when the Most High will deliver those who are on the earth.

[30] And bewilderment of mind shall come over those who dwell on the earth.

[31] And they shall plan to make war against one another, city against city, place against place, people against people, and kingdom against kingdom.

[32] And when these things come to pass and the signs occur which I showed you before, then my Son will be revealed, whom you saw as a man coming up from the sea.

[33] And when all the nations hear his voice, every man shall leave his own land and the warfare that they have against one another;

[34] and an innumerable multitude shall be gathered together, as you saw, desiring to come and conquer him.

[35] But he shall stand on the top of Mount Zion.

[36] And Zion will come and be made manifest to all people, prepared and built, as you saw the mountain carved out without hands.

[37] And he, my Son, will reprove the assembled nations for their ungodliness (this was symbolized by the storm),

[38] and will reproach them to their face with their evil thoughts and the torments with which they are to be tortured (which were symbolized by the flames), and will destroy them without effort by the law (which was symbolized by the fire).

[39] And as for your seeing him gather to himself another multitude that was peaceable,

[40] these are the ten tribes which were led away from their own land into captivity in the days of King Hoshea, whom Shalmaneser the king of the Assyrians led captive; he took them across the river, and they were taken into another land.

[41] But they formed this plan for themselves, that they would leave the multitude of the nations and go to a more distant region, where mankind had never lived,

[42] that there at least they might keep their statutes which they had not kept in their own land.

[43] And they went in by the narrow passages of the Euphrates river.

[44] For at that time the Most High performed signs for them, and stopped the channels of the river until they had passed over.

[45] Through that region there was a long way to go, a journey of a year and a half; and that country is called Arzareth.

[46] "Then they dwelt there until the last times; and now, when they are about to come again,

[47] the Most High will stop the channels of the river again, so that they may be able to pass over. Therefore you saw the multitude gathered together in peace.

[48] But those who are left of your people, who are found within my holy borders, shall be saved.

[49] Therefore when he destroys the multitude of the nations that are gathered together, he will defend the people who remain.

[50] And then he will show them very many wonders."

[51] I said, "O sovereign Lord, explain this to me: Why did I see the man coming up from the heart of the sea?"

[52] He said to me, "Just as no one can explore or know what is in the depths of the sea, so no one on earth can see my Son or those who are with him, except in the time of his day.

[53] This is the interpretation of the dream which you saw. And you alone have been enlightened about this,

[54] because you have forsaken your own ways and have applied yourself to mine, and have searched out my law;

[55] for you have devoted your life to wisdom, and called understanding your mother.

[56] Therefore I have shown you this, for there is a reward laid up with the Most High. And after three more days I will tell you other things, and explain weighty and wondrous matters to you."

[57] Then I arose and walked in the field, giving great glory and praise to the Most High because of his wonders, which he did from time to time,

[58] and because he governs the times and whatever things come to pass in their seasons. And I stayed there three days.

14

[1] On the third day, while I was sitting under an oak, behold, a voice came out of a bush opposite me and said, "Ezra, Ezra."

[2] And I said, "Here I am, Lord," and I rose to my feet.

[3] Then he said to me, "I revealed myself in a bush and spoke to Moses, when my people were in bondage in Egypt;

[4] and I sent him and led my people out of Egypt; and I led him up on Mount Sinai, where I kept him with me many days;

[5] and I told him many wondrous things, and showed him the secrets of the times and declared to him the end of the times. Then I commanded him, saying,

[6] `These words you shall publish openly, and these you shall keep secret.'

[7] And now I say to you;

[8] Lay up in your heart the signs that I have shown you, the dreams that you have seen, and the interpretations that you have heard;

[9] for you shall be taken up from among men, and henceforth you shall live with my Son and with those who are like you, until the times are ended.

[10] For the age has lost its youth, and the times begin to grow old.

[11] For the age is divided into twelve parts, and nine of its parts have already passed,

[12] as well as half of the tenth part; so two of its parts remain, besides half of the tenth part.

[13] Now therefore, set your house in order, and reprove your people; comfort the lowly among them, and instruct those that are wise. And now renounce the life that is corruptible,

[14] and put away from you mortal thoughts; cast away from you the burdens of man, and divest yourself now of your weak nature,

[15] and lay to one side the thoughts that are most grievous to you, and hasten to escape from these times.

[16] For evils worse than those which you have now seen happen shall be done hereafter.

[17] For the weaker the world becomes through old age, the more shall evils be multiplied among its inhabitants.

[18] For truth shall go farther away, and falsehood shall come near. For the eagle which you saw in the vision is already hastening to come."

[19] Then I answered and said, "Let me speak in thy presence, Lord.

[20] For behold, I will go, as thou hast commanded me, and I will reprove the people who are now living; but who will warn those who will be born hereafter? For the world lies in darkness, and its inhabitants are without light.

[21] For thy law has been burned, and so no one knows the things which have been done or will be done by thee.

[22] If then I have found favor before thee, send the Holy Spirit into me, and I will write everything that has happened in the world from the beginning, the things which were written in thy law, that men may be able to find the path, and that those who wish to live in the last days may live."

[23] He answered me and said, "Go and gather the people, and tell them not to seek you for forty days.

[24] But prepare for yourself many writing tablets, and take with you Sarea, Dabria, Selemia, Ethanus, and Asiel -- these five, because they are trained to write rapidly;

[25] and you shall come here, and I will light in your heart the lamp of understanding, which shall not be put out until what you are about to write is finished.

[26] And when you have finished, some things you shall make public, and some you shall deliver in secret to the wise; tomorrow at this hour you shall begin to write."

[27] Then I went as he commanded me, and I gathered all the people together, and said,

[28] "Hear these words, O Israel

[29] At first our fathers dwelt as aliens in Egypt, and they were delivered from there,

[30] and received the law of life, which they did not keep, which you also have transgressed after them.

[31] Then land was given to you for a possession in the land of Zion; but you and your fathers committed iniquity and did not keep the ways which the Most High commanded you.

[32] And because he is a righteous judge, in due time he took from you what he had given.

[33] And now you are here, and your brethren are farther in the interior.

[34] If you, then, will rule over your minds and discipline your hearts, you shall be kept alive, and after death you shall obtain mercy.

[35] For after death the judgment will come, when we shall live again; and then the names of the righteous will become manifest, and the deeds of the ungodly will be disclosed.

[36] But let no one come to me now, and let no one seek me for forty days."

[37] So I took the five men, as he commanded me, and we proceeded to the field, and remained there.

[38] And on the next day, behold, a voice called me, saying, "Ezra, open your mouth and drink what I give you to drink."

[39] Then I opened my mouth, and behold, a full cup was offered to me; it was full of something like water, but its color was like fire.

[40] And I took it and drank; and when I had drunk it, my heart poured forth understanding, and wisdom increased in my breast, for my spirit retained its memory;

[41] and my mouth was opened, and was no longer closed.

[42] And the Most High gave understanding to the five men, and by turns they wrote what was dictated, in characters which they did not know. They sat forty days, and wrote during the daytime, and ate their bread at night.

[43] As for me, I spoke in the daytime and was not silent at night.

[44] So during the forty days ninety-four books were written.

[45] And when the forty days were ended, the Most High spoke to me, saying, "Make public the twenty-four books that you wrote first and let the worthy and the unworthy read them;

[46] but keep the seventy that were written last, in order to give them to the wise among your people.

[47] For in them is the spring of understanding, the fountain of wisdom, and the river of knowledge."

[48] And I did so.

15

[1] The Lord says, "Behold, speak in the ears of my people the words of the prophecy which I will put in your mouth,

[2] and cause them to be written on paper; for they are trustworthy and true.

[3] Do not fear the plots against you, and do not be troubled by the unbelief of those who oppose you.

[4] For every unbeliever shall die in his unbelief."

[5] "Behold," says the Lord, "I bring evils upon the world, the sword and famine and death and destruction.

[6] For iniquity has spread throughout every land, and their harmful deeds have reached their limit.

[7] Therefore," says the Lord,

[8] "I will be silent no longer concerning their ungodly deeds which they impiously commit, neither will I tolerate their wicked practices. Behold, innocent and righteous blood cries out to me, and the souls of the righteous cry out continually.

[9] I will surely avenge them," says the Lord, "and will receive to myself all the innocent blood from among them.

[10] Behold, my people is led like a flock to the slaughter; I will not allow them to live any longer in the land of Egypt,

[11] but I will bring them out with a mighty hand and with an uplifted arm, and will smite Egypt with plagues, as before, and will destroy all its land."

[12] Let Egypt mourn, and its foundations, for the plague of chastisement and punishment that the Lord will bring upon it.

[13] Let the farmers that till the ground mourn, because their seed shall fail and their trees shall be ruined by blight and hail and by a terrible tempest.

[14] Alas for the world and for those who live in it!

[15] For the sword and misery draw near them, and nation shall rise up to fight against nation, with swords in their hands.

[16] For there shall be unrest among men; growing strong against one another, they shall in their might have no respect for their king or the chief of their leaders.

[17] For a man will desire to go into a city, and shall not be able.

[18] For because of their pride the cities shall be in confusion, the houses shall be destroyed, and people shall be afraid.

[19] A man shall have no pity upon his neighbors, but shall make an assault upon their houses with the sword, and plunder their goods, because of hunger for bread and because of great tribulation.

[20] "Behold," says God, "I call together all the kings of the earth to fear me, from the rising sun and from the south, from the east and from Lebanon; to turn and repay what they have given them.

[21] Just as they have done to my elect until this day, so I will do, and will repay into their bosom." Thus says the Lord God:

[22] "My right hand will not spare the sinners, and my sword will not cease from those who shed innocent blood on earth."

[23] And a fire will go forth from his wrath, and will consume the foundations of the earth, and the sinners, like straw that is kindled.

[24] "Woe to those who sin and do not observe my commandments," says the Lord;

[25] "I will not spare them. Depart, you faithless children! Do not pollute my sanctuary."

[26] For the Lord knows all who transgress against him; therefore he will hand them over to death and slaughter.

[27] For now calamities have come upon the whole earth, and you shall remain in them; for God will not deliver you, because you have sinned against him.

[28] Behold, a terrifying sight, appearing from the east!

[29] The nations of the dragons of Arabia shall come out with many chariots, and from the day that they set out, their hissing shall spread over the earth, so that all who hear them fear and tremble.

[30] Also the Carmonians, raging in wrath, shall go forth like wild boars of the forest, and with great power they shall come, and engage them in battle, and shall devastate a portion of the land of the Assyrians with their teeth.

[31] And then the dragons, remembering their origin, shall become still stronger; and if they combine in great power and turn to pursue them,

[32] then these shall be disorganized and silenced by their power, and shall turn and flee.

[33] And from the land of the Assyrians an enemy in ambush shall beset them and destroy one of them, and fear and trembling shall come upon their army, and indecision upon their kings.

[34] Behold, clouds from the east, and from the north to the south; and their appearance is very threatening, full of wrath and storm.

[35] They shall dash against one another and shall pour out a heavy tempest upon the earth, and their own tempest; and there shall be blood from the sword as high as a horse's belly

[36] and a man's thigh and a camel's hock.

[37] And there shall be fear and great trembling upon the earth; and those who see that wrath shall be horror-stricken, and they shall be seized with trembling.

[38] And, after that, heavy storm clouds shall be stirred up from the south, and from the north, and another part from the west.

[39] And the winds from the east shall prevail over the cloud that was raised in wrath, and shall dispel it; and the tempest that was to cause destruction by the east wind shall be driven violently toward the south and west.

[40] And great and mighty clouds, full of wrath and tempest, shall rise, to destroy all the earth and its inhabitants, and shall pour out upon every high and lofty place a terrible tempest,

[41] fire and hail and flying swords and floods of water, that all the fields and all the streams may be filled with the abundance of those waters.

[42] And they shall destroy cities and walls, mountains and hills, trees of the forests, and grass of the meadows, and their grain.

[43] And they shall go on steadily to Babylon, and shall destroy her.

[44] They shall come to her and surround her; they shall pour out the tempest and all its wrath upon her; then the dust and smoke shall go up to heaven, and all who are about her shall wail over her.

[45] And those who survive shall serve those who have destroyed her.

[46] And you, Asia, who share in the glamour of Babylon and the glory of her person --

[47] woe to you, miserable wretch! For you have made yourself like her; you have decked out your daughters in harlotry to please and glory in your lovers, who have always lusted after you.

[48] You have imitated that hateful harlot in all her deeds and devices; therefore God says,

[49] "I will send evils upon you, widowhood, poverty, famine, sword, and pestilence, to lay waste your houses and bring you to destruction and death.

[50] And the glory of your power shall wither like a flower, when the heat rises that is sent upon you.

[51] You shall be weakened like a wretched woman who is beaten and wounded, so that you cannot receive your mighty lovers.

[52] Would I have dealt with you so violently," says the Lord,

[53] "If you had not always killed my chosen people, exulting and clapping your hands and talking about their death when you were drunk?

[54] Trick out the beauty of your face!

[55] The reward of a harlot is in your bosom, therefore you shall receive your recompense.

[56] As you will do to my chosen people," says the Lord, "so God will do to you, and will hand you over to adversities.

[57] Your children shall die of hunger, and you shall fall by the sword, and your cities shall be wiped out, and all your people who are in the open country shall fall by the sword.

[58] And those who are in the mountains and highlands shall perish of hunger, and they shall eat their own flesh in hunger for bread and drink their own blood in thirst for water.

[59] Unhappy above all others, you shall come and suffer fresh afflictions.

[60] And as they pass they shall wreck the hateful city, and shall destroy a part of your land and abolish a portion of your glory, as they return from devastated Babylon.

[61] And you shall be broken down by them like stubble, and they shall be like fire to you.

[62] And they shall devour you and your cities, your land and your mountains; they shall burn with fire all your forests and your fruitful trees.

[63] They shall carry your children away captive, and shall plunder your wealth, and abolish the glory of your countenance."

16

[1] Woe to you, Babylon and Asia! Woe to you, Egypt and Syria!

[2] Gird yourselves with sackcloth and haircloth, and wail for your children, and lament for them; for your destruction is at hand.

[3] The sword has been sent upon you, and who is there to turn it back?

[4] A fire has been sent upon you, and who is there to quench it?

[5] Calamities have been sent upon you, and who is there to drive them away?

[6] Can one drive off a hungry lion in the forest, or quench a fire in the stubble, when once it has begun to burn?

[7] Can one turn back an arrow shot by a strong archer?

[8] The Lord God sends calamities, and who will drive them away?

[9] Fire will go forth from his wrath, and who is there to quench it?

[10] He will flash lightning, and who will not be afraid? He will thunder, and who will not be terrified?

[11] The Lord will threaten, and who will not be utterly shattered at his presence?

[12] The earth and its foundations quake, the sea is churned up from the depths, and its waves and the fish also shall be troubled at the presence of the Lord and before the glory of his power.

[13] For his right hand that bends the bow is strong, and his arrows that he shoots are sharp and will not miss when they begin to be shot to the ends of the world.

[14] Behold, calamities are sent forth and shall not return until they come over the earth.

[15] The fire is kindled, and shall not be put out until it consumes the foundations of the earth.

[16] Just as an arrow shot by a mighty archer does not return, so the calamities that are sent upon the earth shall not return.

[17] Alas for me! Alas for me! Who will deliver me in those days?

[18] The beginning of sorrows, when there shall be much lamentation; the beginning of famine, when many shall perish; the beginning of wars, when the powers shall be terrified; the beginning of calamities, when all shall tremble. What shall they do in these circumstances, when the calamities come?

[19] Behold, famine and plague, tribulation and anguish are sent as scourges for the correction of men.

[20] Yet for all this they will not turn from their iniquities, nor be always mindful of the scourges.

[21] Behold, provision will be so cheap upon earth that men will imagine that peace is assured for them, and then the calamities shall spring up on the earth -- the sword, famine, and great confusion.

[22] For many of those who live on the earth shall perish by famine; and those who survive the famine shall die by the sword.

[23] And the dead shall be cast out like dung, and there shall be no one to console them; for the earth shall be left desolate, and its cities shall be demolished.

[24] No one shall be left to cultivate the earth or to sow it.

[25] The trees shall bear fruit, and who will gather it?

[26] The grapes shall ripen, and who will tread them? For in all places there shall be great solitude;

[27] one man will long to see another, or even to hear his voice.

[28] For out of a city, ten shall be left; and out of the field, two who have hidden themselves in thick groves and clefts in the rocks.

[29] As in an olive orchard three or four olives may be left on every tree,

[30] or as when a vineyard is gathered some clusters may be left by those who search carefully through the vineyard,

[31] so in those days three or four shall be left by those who search their houses with the sword.

[32] And the earth shall be left desolate, and its fields shall be for briers, and its roads and all its paths shall bring forth thorns, because no sheep will go along them.

[33] Virgins shall mourn because they have no bridegrooms; women shall mourn because they have no husbands; their daughters shall mourn, because they have no helpers.

[34] Their bridegrooms shall be killed in war, and their husbands shall perish of famine.

[35] Listen now to these things, and understand them, O servants of the Lord.

[36] Behold the word of the Lord, receive it; do not disbelieve what the Lord says.

[37] Behold, the calamities draw near, and are not delayed.

[38] Just as a woman with child, in the ninth month, when the time of her delivery draws near, has great pains about her womb for two or three hours beforehand, and when the child comes forth from the womb, there will not be a moment's delay,

[39] so the calamities will not delay in coming forth upon the earth, and the world will groan, and pains will seize it on every side.

[40] "Hear my words, O my people; prepare for battle, and in the midst of the calamities be like strangers on the earth.

[41] Let him that sells be like one who will flee; let him that buys be like one who will lose;

[42] let him that does business be like one who will not make a profit; and let him that builds a house be like one who will not live in it;

[43] let him that sows be like one who will not reap; so also him that prunes the vines, like one who will not gather the grapes;

[44] them that marry, like those who will have no children; and them that do not marry, like those who are widowed.

[45] Because those who labor, labor in vain;

[46] for strangers shall gather their fruits, and plunder their goods, and overthrow their houses, and take their children captive; for in captivity and famine they will beget their children.

[47] Those who conduct business, do it only to be plundered; the more they adorn their cities, their houses and possessions, and their persons,

[48] the more angry I will be with them for their sins," says the Lord.

[49] Just as a respectable and virtuous woman abhors a harlot,

[50] so righteousness shall abhor iniquity, when she decks herself out, and shall accuse her to her face, when he comes who will defend him who searches out every sin on earth.

[51] Therefore do not be like her or her works.

[52] For behold, just a little while, and iniquity will be removed from the earth, and righteousness will reign over us.

[53] Let no sinner say that he has not sinned; for God will burn coals of fire on the head of him who says, "I have not sinned before God and his glory."

[54] Behold, the Lord knows all the works of men, their imaginations and their thoughts and their hearts.

[55] He said, "Let the earth be made," and it was made; "Let the heaven be made," and it was made.

[56] At his word the stars were fixed, and he knows the number of the stars.

[57] It is he who searches the deep and its treasures, who has measured the sea and its contents;

[58] who has enclosed the sea in the midst of the waters, and by his word has suspended the earth over the water;

[59] who has spread out the heaven like an arch, and founded it upon the waters;

[60] who has put springs of water in the desert, and pools on the tops of the mountains, to send rivers from the heights to water the earth;

[61] who formed man, and put a heart in the midst of his body, and gave him breath and life and understanding

[62] and the spirit of Almighty God; who made all things and searches out hidden things in hidden places.

[63] Surely he knows your imaginations and what you think in your hearts! Woe to those who sin and want to hide their sins!

[64] Because the Lord will strictly examine all their works, and will make a public spectacle of all of you.

[65] And when your sins come out before men, you shall be put to shame; and your own iniquities shall stand as your accusers in that day.

[66] What will you do? Or how will you hide your sins before God and his angels?

[67] Behold, God is the judge, fear him! Cease from your sins, and forget your iniquities, never to commit them again; so God will lead you forth and deliver you from all tribulation.

[68] For behold, the burning wrath of a great multitude is kindled over you, and they shall carry off some of you and shall feed you what was sacrificed to idols.

[69] And those who consent to eat shall be held in derision and contempt, and be trodden under foot.

[70] For in many places and in neighboring cities there shall be a great insurrection against those who fear the Lord.

[71] They shall be like mad men, sparing no one, but plundering and destroying those who continue to fear the Lord.

[72] For they shall destroy and plunder their goods, and drive them out of their houses.

[73] Then the tested quality of my elect shall be manifest, as gold that is tested by fire.

[74] "Hear, my elect," says the Lord. "Behold, the days of tribulation are at hand, and I will deliver you from them.

[75] Do not fear or doubt, for God is your guide.

[76] You who keep my commandments and precepts," says the Lord God, "do not let your sins pull you down, or your iniquities prevail over you."

[77] Woe to those who are choked by their sins and overwhelmed by their iniquities, as a field is choked with underbrush and its path overwhelmed with thorns, so that no one can pass through!

[78] It is shut off and given up to be consumed by fire.

Prayer of Manasseh

PrMan.1

[1] Lord, Almighty God of Abraham, Isaac, Jacob, and their righteous seed

[2] thou who hast made heaven and earth with all their order;

[3] who hast shackled the sea by thy word of command, who hast confined the deep and sealed it with thy terrible and glorious name;

[4] at whom all things shudder, and tremble before thy power,

[5] for thy glorious splendor cannot be borne, and the wrath of thy threat to sinners is irresistible;

[6] yet immeasurable and unsearchable is thy promised mercy,

[7] for thou art the Lord Most High, of great compassion, long-suffering, and very merciful, and repentest over the evils of men. Thou, O Lord, according to thy great goodness hast promised repentance and forgiveness to those who have sinned against thee; and in the multitude of thy mercies thou hast appointed repentance for sinners, that they may be saved.

[8] Therefore thou, O Lord, God of the righteous, hast not appointed repentance for the righteous, for Abraham and Isaac and Jacob, who did not sin against thee, but thou hast appointed repentance for me, who am a sinner.

[9] For the sins I have committed are more in number than the sand of the sea; my transgressions are multiplied, O Lord, they are multiplied! I am unworthy to look up and see the height of heaven because of the multitude of my iniquities.

[10] I am weighted down with many an iron fetter, so that I am rejected because of my sins, and I have no relief; for I have provoked thy wrath and have done what is evil in thy sight, setting up abominations and multiplying offenses.

[11] And now I bend the knee of my heart, beseeching thee for thy kindness.

[12] I have sinned, O Lord, I have sinned, and I know my transgressions.

[13] I earnestly beseech thee, forgive me, O Lord, forgive me! Do not destroy me with my transgressions! Do not be angry with me for ever or lay up evil for me; do not condemn me to the depths of the earth. For thou, O Lord, art the God of those who repent,

[14] and in me thou wilt manifest thy goodness; for, unworthy as I am, thou wilt save me in thy great mercy,

[15] and I will praise thee continually all the days of my life. For all the host of heaven sings thy praise, and your is the glory for ever. Amen.

Introduction to The Book of Jubilees

The *Book of Jubilees,* also known as *The Little Genesis* and *The Apocalypse of Moses,* opens with an extraordinary claim of authorship. It is attributed to the very hand of Moses; penned while he was on Mount Sinai, as an angel of God dictated to him regarding those events that transpired from the beginning of the world. The story is written from the viewpoint of the angel. The angelic monolog takes place after the exodus of the children of Israel out of Egypt. The setting is atop Mount Sinai, where Moses was summoned by God. The text then unfolds as the angel reveals heaven's viewpoint of history. We are led through the creation of man, Adam's fall from grace, the union of fallen angels and earthly women, the birth of demonic offspring, the cleansing of the earth by flood, and the astonishing claim that man's very nature was somehow changed, bringing about a man with less sinful qualities than his antediluvian counterpart. The story goes on to fill in many details in Israel's history, ending at the point in time when the narrative itself takes place, after the exodus.

Scholars believe Jubilees was composed in the second century B.C. The Hebrew fragments found at Qumran are part of a Jewish library that contained other supporting literature such as the Book of Enoch and others. An analysis of the chronological development in the shapes of letters in the manuscripts confirms that Jubilees is pre-Christian in date and seems to have been penned between 100 and 200 B.C. Based on records of the High Priests at the time, we can further narrow the date of writing to between 140 and 100 B.C.

The book of Jubilees is also cited in the Qumran Damascus Document in pre-Christian texts.

The Book of Jubilees was originally written in Hebrew. The author was a Pharisee (a doctor of the law), or someone very familiar with scripture and religious law. Since the scrolls were found in what is assumed to be an Essene library, and were dated to the time the Essene community was active, the author was probably a member of that particular religious group. Jubilees represents a hyper-legalistic and midrashic tendency, which was part of the Essene culture at the time.

"Midrash" – refers to writings containing extra-legal material of anecdotal or allegorical nature, designed either to clarify historical material, or to teach a moral point.

Jubilees represents a midrash on Genesis 1:1 through Exodus 12:50 which depicts the episodes from creation with the observance of the Sabbath by the angels and men to Israel's escape from Egyptian bondage.

Although originally written in Hebrew, the Hebrew texts were completely lost until the find at Qumran. Fragments of Jubilees were discovered among the Dead Sea Scrolls. At least fourteen copies of the Book of Jubilees have been identified from caves 1, 2, 3 and 11 at Qumran. This makes it clear that the Book of Jubilees was a popular and probably authoritative text for the community whose library was concealed in the caves. These fragments are actually generations closer to the original copies than many books in our accepted Bible. Unfortunately, the fragments found at Qumran were only pieces of the texts and offered the briefest of glimpses of the entire book. The only complete versions of the Book of Jubilees are in Ethiopic, which in turn were translations of a Greek version.

Four Ethiopian manuscripts of Jubilees were found to be hundreds of years old. Of these, the fifteenth and sixteenth century texts are the truest and least corrupted when compared to the fragments found at Qumran. There are also citations of Jubilees in Syriac literature that may reflect a lost translation from Hebrew. Pieces of Latin translations have also been found.

Other fragments of a Greek version are quoted or referenced by Justin Martyr, Origen, Diodorus of Antioch, Isidore of Alexandria, Isidore of Seville, Eutychius, Patriarch of Alexandria, John of Malala, and Syncellus. This amount of various information and translations is enough to allow us to reconstruct the original to a great degree. The internal evidence of Jubilees shows very little tampering by Christians during its transmission and subsequent translations, thus allowing a clear view of certain Jewish beliefs being propagated at the time of its origin. By removing certain variances, we can isolate Christian alterations and mistakes in translations with a reasonable degree of confidence. Due to the poor condition of the fragments of Qumran, we may never be able to confirm certain key phrases in Hebrew. Thus, as with many texts, including those of our own Bible, in the end we must trust in the accuracy of the ancient translators.

It should be noted that the books of Jubilees, Enoch, and Jasher present stories of "The Watchers"; a group of angels sent to earth to record and teach, but who fell by their own lust and pride into a demonic state. Both Enoch and Jubilees refer to a solar-based calendar. This may show a conflict or transition at the time of their penning since Judaism now uses a lunar-based calendar.

Laws, rites, and functions are observed and noted in Jubilees. Circumcision is emphasized in both humans and angels. Angelic observance of Sabbath laws as well as parts of Jewish religious laws are said to have been observed in heaven before they were revealed to Moses.

To the Qumran community, complete obedience to the Laws of Moses entailed observing a series of holy days and festivals at a particular time according to a specific calendar. The calendar described in Jubilees is one of 364 days, divided into four seasons of three months each with thirteen weeks to a season. Each month had 30 days with one day added at certain times for each of the four seasons. With 52 weeks in a year, the festival and holy days recur at the same point each year. This calendar became a hallmark of an orthodox Qumran community.

The adherence to a specific calendar is one of many ways the Book of Jubilees shows the devotion to religious law. The law had been placed at the pinnacle of importance in the lives of the community at Qumran. All aspects of life were driven by a seemingly obsessive compliance to every jot and tittle of the law. The Book Of Jubilees confirms what can only be inferred from the books of Ezra, Nehemiah, and Zechariah, that the law and those who carried it out were supreme.

As the law took hold, by its nature, it crystallized the society. Free expression died, smothered under a mantle of hyperorthodoxy. Since free thought invited accusations of violations of the law or claims of heresy, prudence, a closed mind, and a silent voice prevailed. Free thought was limited to religious or apocryphal writings, which upheld the orthodox positions of the day. The silent period between Malachi and Mark may be a reflection of this stasis. Jubilees, Enoch, and other apocryphal books found in the Qumran caves are a triumph over the unimaginative mindset brought on by making religious law supreme and human expression contrary to law punishable by death. It may be an odd manifestation that such a burst of creativity was fueled by the very search for order that suppressed free thought in the first place.

The Book of Jubilees seems to be an attempt to answer and explain all questions left unanswered in the Book of Genesis as well as to bolster the position of the religious law. It attempts to trace the source of religious laws back to an ancient beginning thereby adding weight and sanction.

In the Book of Jubilees, we discover the origin of the wife of Cain. There is information offered about angels and the beginnings of the human race, how demons came into existence, and the place of Satan in the plans of God. Information is offered in an attempt to make perfect sense of the vagaries left in Genesis. For the defense of order and law and to maintain religious law as the center point of Jewish life, Jubilees was written as an answer to both pagan Greeks and liberal Jews. From the divine placement of law and order to its explanation of times and events, Jubilees is a panorama of legalism.

The name "Jubilees" comes from the division of time into eras known as Jubilees. One Jubilee occurs after the equivalent of forty-nine years, or seven Sabbaths or weeks of years has passed. It is the numerical perfection of seven sevens. In a balance and symmetry of years, the Jubilee occurs after seven cycles of seven or forty-nine years have been completed. Thus, the fiftieth year is a Jubilee year. Time is told by referencing the number of Jubilees that have transpired from the time the festival was first kept. For example, Israel entered Canaan at the close of the fiftieth jubilee, which is about 2450 BCE.

The obsession with time, dates, and the strict observance of festivals are all evidence of legalism taken to the highest level.

Based on the approximate time of writing, Jubilees was created in the time of the Maccabees, in the high priesthood of Hyrcanus. In this period of time the appearance of the Messiah and the rise of the Messianic kingdom were viewed as imminent. Followers were preparing themselves for the arrival of the Messiah and the establishment of His eternal kingdom.

Judaism was in contact with the Greek culture at the time. The Greeks were known to be philosophers and were developing processes of critical thinking. One objective of Jubilees was to defend Judaism against the attacks of the Hellenists and to prove that the law was logical, consistent, and valid. Attacks against paganism and non-believers are embedded in the text along with defense of the law and its consistency through proclamations of the law being observed by the angels in heaven from the beginning of creation.

Moral lessons are taught by use of the juxtaposition of the "satans" and their attempts to test and lead mankind into sin against the warning and advice of scriptural wisdom from Moses and his angels.

Mastema is mentioned only in The Book of Jubilees and in the Fragments of a Zadokite Work. Mastema is Satan. The name Mastema is derived from the Hebrew, "Mastim," meaning "adversary." The word occurs as singular and plural. The word is equivalent to Satan (adversary or accuser). This is similar to the chief Satan and his class of "satans" in 1 Enoch 40:7.

Mastema is subservient to God. His task is to tempt men to sin and if they do, he accuses them in the presence of the Throne of God. He and his minions lead men into sin but do not cause the sin. Once men have chosen to sin, they lead them from sin to destruction. Since man is given free will, sin is a choice, with Mastema simply encouraging and facilitating the

decision. The choice, we can assume, is our own and the destruction that follows is "self-destruction."

Beliar is also mentioned. Beliar is the Greek name for Belial or Beliaal. The name in its Hebrew equivalent means "without value." This was a demon known by the Jews as the chief of all the devils. Belial is the leader of the Sons of Darkness. Belial is mentioned in the Fragments of a Zadokite fragment along with Mastema, which states that at the time of the Antichrist, Belial shall be let loose against Israel, as God spoke through Isaiah the prophet. Belial is sometimes presented as an agent of God's punishment although he is considered a "satan."

Although it is impossible to explore here in any detail the ramification of superhuman entities and their culpability in man's sin, it is important to mention that Judaism had no doctrine of original sin. The fall of Adam and Eve may have removed man from the perfect environment and the curses that followed may have shortened his lifespan, but propagation of sin through the bloodline was not considered. Sin seemed to affect only man and the animals he was given dominion over. Yet, man continued to sin, and to increase in his capacity and modes of sin. The explanation offered for man's inability to resist is the existence of fallen angels; spiritual, superhuman creations whose task it was to teach us but who now tempt and mislead men. In the end, the world declines and crumbles under the evil influence of the fallen angels turned demons called, "The Watchers."

With the establishment of the covenant between Abraham and God, we are told that God had appointed spirits to "mislead" all the nations but would not assign a spirit to lead or mislead the children of Isaac but God himself would be leading them.

Within the text are recurring numbers. Seven, being the number of perfection, is the most common. The number three is cited, being the number of completion. However, the number twenty-two occurs in the accounts of creation and lineage. It is worth noting that there are twenty-two letters in the Hebrew alphabet. The number twenty-two represents a type of Godly assignment or appointment. It is also the number of the perfect foundation and of the God-given language. It is presented within the text as a reminder that God established the ways of the Jews and gave the Hebrew language and writing first and only to the Jews.

The angels converse in Hebrew and it is the heavenly tongue. The law is written by God using this alphabet thus the law is also holy. All men spoke Hebrew until the time of Babel when it was lost. However, when Abraham dedicated himself to God, his ears were opened and his tongue was sanctified and Hebrew was again spoken and understood.

Finally, the entire text is based on the numbers

of forty-nine and fifty. Forty-nine represents the pinnacle of perfection, being made up of seven times seven. The number fifty, which is the number of the Jubilee, is the number of grace. In this year slaves were to be set free, debts were forgiven, and grace filled the land and people.

Drawing from the theology and myths at the time, the book of Jubilees expands and embellishes on the creation story, the fall of Adam and Eve, and the fall of the angels. The expanded detail written into the text may have been one reason it was eventually rejected. However, the effects of the book can still be seen throughout the Judeo-Christian beliefs of today. The theology espoused in Jubilees can be seen in the angelology and demonology taught in the Christian churches of today and widely held by many Jews.

In an attempt to answer questions left unaddressed in Genesis the writer confronts the origin and identification of Cain's wife. According to The Book Of Jubilees, Cain married his sister, as did all of the sons of Adam and Eve, except Abel, who was murdered. This seemed offensive to some, since it flies in the face of the very law it was written to defend. Yet, this seemed to the writer to be the lesser of evils, given the problematic questions. Inbreeding is dismissed with the observation that the law was not fully given and understood then. The effects of the act were mute due to the purity of the newly created race.

The seeming discrepancy between divine command of Adam's death decree and the timing of his death is addressed. Seeing that Adam continued to live even after he ate the fruit, which was supposed to bring on his death, the writer set about to clarify God's actions. The problem is explained away in a single sentence. Since a day in heaven is as a thousand years on earth and Adam died having lived less than a thousand years this meant he died in the same heavenly day. Dying within the same day of the crime was acceptable.

In an astonishing parallel to the Book Of Enoch, written at about the same time as Jubilees, the Watchers, or sons of God mentioned in Genesis 6, fell from grace when they descended to earth and had sex with the daughters of men. In the Book of Enoch, the angels descended for the purpose of seducing the women of earth. However, in The Book Of Jubilee the angels were sent to teach men, but after living on earth for a while, were tempted by their own lust and fell. The offspring of this unholy union were bloodthirsty and cannibalistic giants. The Book of Jubilees indicates that the offspring were somehow different, yet they are divided into categories of the Naphidim (or Naphilim, depending or the transliteration), the Giants, and the Eljo. (Naphil are mentioned but this is the singular of Naphilim.)

As sin spread throughout the world and the minds of men were turned toward evil, God saw no alternative but to cleanse the earth with a flood and establish a "new nature" in man that does not have to sin. It is this new nature that the messiah will meet in mankind when He comes. As far as this author is aware, the re-creation of man's nature is mentioned in no other book. This idea of human nature being altared as it exited before the flood is found nowhere else but in Jubilees.

The angelic narrator tells us there were times in Israel's history when no evil existed and all men lived in accord. We are also told when and where the satans were allowed to attack and confound Israel. In this narrative, God uses his satans to harden the hearts of the Egyptians compelling them to pursue Israel and be destroyed.

The Book of Jubilees had other names throughout its history and propagation. "The Little Genesis" is another name given to this text. The description of "Little" does not refer to the size of the book, but to its canonical disposition.

"The Apocalypse of Moses" is another name denoting the same work. This title seems to have been used for only a short period of time. It refers to the revelation given to Moses as the recipient of all the knowledge disclosed in the book. The term "Apocalypse" means to make known or to reveal. With the exception of minor differences picked up through translation and copying, the three titles represent the same text.

About the Translation

The translation presented herein is based in part on that of R.H. Charles and his works of 1902 through 1913. Although the translation seems to be a faithful one, his scholarly tone, pedantry, and quasi-Elizabethan language made the text less than accessible. The pleonasm of the text as well as the ancient writer's tendency to repeat phrases for the sake of emphasis added to the general lack of readability. Furthermore, many of the verse breaks occurred in mid-sentence and certainly in mid-thought, adding confusion when viewing the text. All of these difficulties were corrected.

To aid in comprehension, it was decided that the text would be put through three phases of change. First, all verse breaks would be aligned with sentence breaks and with complete streams of thought when possible. Next, all archaic words and phrases would be replaced with their modern equivalent. Lastly, convoluted sentence structure would be clarified and rewritten. Notes of explanation and clarification are added in parentheses.

Due to the vast differences in societal structure and rules, certain phrases remained in their archaic form, seeing that they had no direct equivalence in our western culture. One such phrase is "uncovered the skirt." This phrase indicates the person was seen naked. In most cases it carries a connotation of intercourse. If one were to "uncover his father's skirt" it indicates the father's wife or concubine has been seen naked, usually with the intent of having sex with her.

THE BOOK OF JUBILEES
THE LITTLE GENESIS, THE APOCALYPSE OF MOSES

This is the history of how the days were divided and of the days of the law and of the testimony, of the events of the years, and of the weeks of years, of their Jubilees throughout all the years of the world, as the Lord spoke to Moses on Mount Sinai when he went up to receive the tablets of the law and the commandment, according to the voice of God when he said to him, "Go up to the top of the Mount."

[Chapter 1]

1 It happened in the first year of the exodus of the children of Israel out of Egypt, in the third month, on the sixteenth day of the month, that God spoke to Moses, saying, "Come up to Me on the Mountain, and I will give you two tablets of stone of the law and the commandment, which I have written, that you may teach them."

2 Moses went up into the mountain of God, and the glory of the Lord rested on Mount Sinai, and a cloud overshadowed it six days.

3 He called to Moses on the seventh day out of the middle of the cloud, and the appearance of the glory of the Lord was like a flame on the top of the mountain.

4 Moses was on the mountain forty days and forty nights, and God taught him the earlier and the later history of the division of all the days of the law and of the testimony.

5 He said, "Open your heart to every word which I shall speak to you on this mountain, and write them in a book in order that their generations may see how I have not forsaken them for all the evil which they have committed when they transgressed the covenant which I establish between Me and you for their generations this day on Mount Sinai.

6 It will come to pass when all these things come on them, that they will recognize that I am more righteous than they in all their judgments and in all their actions, and they will recognize that I have truly been with them.

7 Write all these words for yourself which I speak to you today, for I know their rebellion and their stubbornness, before I brought them into the land of which I swore to their fathers, to Abraham and to Isaac and to Jacob, saying, " Unto your offspring will I give a land flowing with milk and honey.

8 They will eat and be satisfied, and they will turn to strange gods, to gods that cannot deliver them from any of their tribulation, and this witness shall be heard for a witness against them.

9 They will forget all My commandments, even all that I command them, and they will walk in the ways of the Gentiles, and after their uncleanness, and after their

shame, and will serve their gods, and these will prove to them an offence and a tribulation and an sickness and a trap.

10 Many will perish and they will be taken captive, and will fall into the hands of the enemy, because they have forsaken My laws and My commandments, and the festivals of My covenant, and My sabbaths, and My holy place which I have made holy for Myself in their presence, and My tabernacle, and My sanctuary, which I have made holy for Myself in the midst of the land, that I should set My name on it, that it should reside there.

11 They will make themselves high places and places of worship and graven images. Each will worship graven images of his own making, Thus they will go astray. They will sacrifice their children to demons, and to all errors their hearts can work.

12 I will send witnesses to them that I may testify against them, but they will not hear. They will kill the witnesses. They will persecute those who seek the law, and they will abolish and change everything (in the Law) so as to work evil before My eyes.

13 I will hide My face from them. I will deliver them into the hand of the Gentiles. They will be captured like prey for their eating. I will remove them from the out of the land. I will scatter them among the Gentiles.

14 And they will forget My law and all My commandments and all My judgments. They will go astray regarding the observance of new moons, and sabbaths, and festivals, and jubilees, and laws.

15 After this they will turn to Me from among the Gentiles with all their heart and with all their soul and with all their strength, and I will gather them from among all the Gentiles, and they will seek me. I shall be found by them when they seek me with all their heart and with all their soul.

16 I will allow them to see abounding peace with righteousness. I will remove them, the plant of uprightness, with all My heart and with all My soul, and they shall be for a blessing and not for a curse, and they shall be the head and not the tail.

17 I will build My sanctuary among them, and I will dwell with them, and I will be their God and they shall be My people in truth and righteousness.

18 I will not forsake them nor fail them; for I am the Lord their God."

19 Moses fell on his face and prayed and said, 'O Lord my God, do not forsake Your people and Your inheritance, so that they should wander in the error of their hearts, and do not deliver them into the hands of their enemies, the Gentiles, so that they should rule over them and cause them to sin against You.

20 Let your mercy, O Lord, be lifted up on Your people, and create in them an upright spirit, and let not the spirit of Beliar rule over them to accuse them before You, and to ensnare them from all the paths of righteousness, so that they may perish from before Your face.

21 But they are Your people and Your inheritance, which You have delivered with Your great power from the hands of the Egyptians, create in them a clean heart and a holy spirit, and let them not be ensnared in their sins from now on until eternity."

22 The Lord said to Moses, "I know their contrariness and their thoughts and their stubbornness, and they will not be obedient until they confess their own sin and the sin of their fathers.

23 After this they will turn to Me in all uprightness and with all their heart and with all their soul, and I will circumcise the foreskin of their heart and the foreskin of the heart of their offspring, and I will create in them a holy spirit, and I will cleanse them so that they shall not turn away from Me from that day to eternity.

24 And their souls will cling to Me and to all My commandments, and they will fulfill My commandments, and I will be their Father and they shall be My children.

25 They all shall be called children of the living God, and every angel and every spirit shall know, yes, they shall know that these are My children, and that I am their Father in uprightness and righteousness, and that I love them.

26 Write down for yourself all these words which I say to you on this mountain, from the first to the last, which shall come to pass in all the divisions of the days in the law and in the testimony and in the weeks and the jubilees to eternity, until I descend and dwell with them throughout eternity."

27 He said to the angel of the presence (of the Lord), "Write for Moses from the beginning of creation until My sanctuary has been built among them for all eternity.

28 The Lord will appear to the eyes of all, and all shall know that I am the God of Israel and the Father of all the children of Jacob, and King on Mount Zion for all eternity. And Zion and Jerusalem shall be holy."

29 The angel of the presence (of the Lord) who went before the camp of Israel took the tables of the divisions of the years, written from the time of the creation, concerning the law and the testimony of the weeks of the jubilees, according to the individual years, according to the numbering of all the jubilees, from the day of the new creation when the heavens and the earth shall be renewed and all their creation according to the powers of the heaven, and according to all the creation of the earth, until the sanctuary of the Lord shall be made in Jerusalem on Mount Zion, and all the stars and planets be renewed for healing, peace, and blessing for all the elect of Israel, and that this is the way it may be from that day and to all the days of the earth.

[Chapter 2]

1 The angel of the presence (of the Lord) spoke to Moses according to the word of the Lord, saying, "Write the complete history of the creation, how in six days the Lord God finished all His works and all that He created, and kept Sabbath on the seventh day and made it holy for all ages, and appointed it as a sign for all His works.

2 For on the first day He created the heavens which are above and the earth and the waters and all the spirits which serve before him which are the angels of the presence (of the Lord), and the angels of sanctification, and the angels of the spirit of fire, and the angels of the spirit of the winds, and the angels of the spirit of the clouds, and of darkness, and of snow and of hail and of white frost, and the angels of the voices and of the thunder and of the lightning, and the angels of the spirits of cold and of heat, and of winter and of spring and of autumn and of summer and of all the spirits of his creatures which are in the heavens and on the earth, He created the bottomless pit and the darkness, evening and night, and the light, dawn and day, which He has prepared in the knowledge of His heart.

3 When we saw His works, we praised Him, and worshiped before Him because of all His works; for seven great works did He create on the first day.

4 On the second day He created the sky between the waters (above and below), and the waters were divided on that day. Half of them went up above the sky and half of them went down below the sky that was in the middle over the face of the whole earth. And this was the only work God created on the second day.

5 On the third day He commanded the waters to pass from off the face of the whole earth into one place, and the dry land to appear.

6 The waters did as He commanded them, and they receded from off the face of the earth into one place, and the dry land appeared.

7 On that day He created for them all the seas according to their separate gathering-places, and all the rivers, and the gatherings of the waters in the mountains and on all the earth, and all the lakes, and all the dew of the earth, and the seed which is sown, and all sprouting things, and fruit-bearing trees, and trees of the wood, and the garden of Eden, in Eden and throughout. These four great works God created on the third day.

8 On the fourth day He created the sun and the moon and the stars, and set them in the sky of the heaven, to give light on all the earth, and to rule over the day and the night, and divide the light from the darkness.

9 God appointed the sun to be a great sign on the earth for days and for sabbaths and for months and for feasts and for years and for sabbaths of years and for jubilees and for all seasons of the years.

10 And it divides the light from the darkness for prosperity that all things may prosper which sprout and grow on the earth. These three kinds He made on the fourth day.

11 On the fifth day He created great sea monsters in the depths of the waters, for these were the first things of flesh that were created by his hands, the fish and everything that moves in the waters, and everything that flies, the birds and all their kind.

12 And the sun rose above them to make them prosper, and the sun rose above everything that was on the earth, everything that sprouts out of the earth, and all fruit-bearing trees, and all flesh.

13 He created these three kinds on the fifth day. On the sixth day He created all the animals of the earth, and all cattle, and everything that moves on the earth.

14 After all this He created mankind. He created a man and a woman, and gave him dominion over all that is on the earth, and in the seas, and over everything that flies, and over beasts, and over cattle, and over everything that moves on the earth, and over the whole earth, and over all this He gave him dominion.

15 He created these four kinds on the sixth day. And there were altogether two and twenty kinds.

16 He finished all his work on the sixth day. That is all that is in the heavens and on the earth, and in the seas and in the abysses, and in the light and in the darkness, and in everything.

17 He gave us a great sign, the Sabbath day, that we should work six days, but keep Sabbath on the seventh day from all work.

18 All the angels of the presence (of the Lord), and all the angels of sanctification, these two great types of angels He has told to tell us to keep the Sabbath with Him in heaven and on earth.

19 And He said to us, "Look, I will separate to Myself a people from among all the peoples, and these shall keep the Sabbath day, and I will sanctify them to Myself as My people, and will bless them; as I have sanctified the Sabbath day and do sanctify it to Myself, even so will I bless them, and they shall be My people and I will be their God.

20 I have chosen the offspring of Jacob from among all that I have seen, and have written him down as My first-born son, and have sanctified him to Myself forever and ever; and I will teach them the Sabbath day, that they may keep Sabbath on it from all work."

21 He created in it a sign in accordance with which they should keep Sabbath with us on the seventh day, to eat and to drink, and to bless Him who has created all things as He has blessed and sanctified to Himself a particular, exclusive people above all peoples, and that they should keep Sabbath together with us.

22 He caused His commands to rise up as a sweet odor acceptable before Him all the days.

23 There were two and twenty heads (representatives) of mankind from Adam to Jacob, and two and twenty

kinds of work (creation) were made until the seventh day; this is blessed and holy; and the former also is blessed and holy; and this one serves with that one for sanctification and blessing.

24 Jacob and his offspring were granted that they should always be the blessed and holy ones of the first testimony and law, even as He had sanctified and blessed the Sabbath day on the seventh day.

25 He created heaven and earth and everything that He created in six days, and God made the seventh day holy, for all His works; therefore He commanded on its behalf that, whoever does any work on it shall die, and that he who defiles it shall surely die.

26 Because of this, command the children of Israel to observe this day that they may keep it holy and not do on it any work, and not to defile it, as it is holier than all other days.

27 And whoever profanes it shall surely die, and whoever does any work on it shall surely die eternally, that the children of Israel may observe this day throughout their generations, and not be rooted out of the land; for it is a holy day and a blessed day.

28 Every one who observes it and keeps Sabbath on it from all his work will be holy and blessed throughout all days as we are blessed.

29 Declare and say to the children of Israel the law of this day that they should keep Sabbath on it, and that they should not forsake it in the error of their hearts; and that it is not lawful to do any work on it which is not suitable, to do their own pleasure on it, and that they should not prepare anything to be eaten or drunk on it, and that it is not lawful to draw water, or bring in or take out through their gates any burden which they had not prepared for themselves on the sixth day in their dwellings.

30 They shall not bring or take anything from house to house on that day; for that day is more holy and blessed than any jubilee day of the jubilees; on this we kept Sabbath in the heavens before it was made known to any flesh to keep Sabbath on the earth.

31 The Creator of all things blessed it, but He did not sanctify all peoples and nations to keep Sabbath, but Israel alone, them alone He permitted to eat and drink and to keep Sabbath on the earth.

32 And the Creator of all things blessed this day which He had created for blessing and holiness and glory above all days.

33 This law and testimony was given to the children of Israel as a law forever to their generations.

[Chapter 3]

1 On the sixth day of the second week, according to the word of God, we brought to Adam all the beasts, and all the cattle, and all the birds, and everything that moves on the earth, and everything that moves in the water, according to their kinds, and according to their types, the beasts on the first day; the cattle on the second day; the birds on the third day; and all that moves on the earth on the fourth day; and that moves in the water on the fifth day.

2 And Adam named them all by their respective names. As he called them, so was their name.

3 On these five days Adam saw all these, male and female, according to every kind that was on the earth, but he was alone and found no helpmate.

4 The Lord said to us, "It is not good that the man should be alone, let us make a helpmate for him."

5 And the Lord our God caused a deep sleep to fall on him, and he slept, and He took from Adam a rib from among his ribs for the woman, and this rib was the origin of the woman. And He built up the flesh in its place, and built the woman.

6 He awakened Adam out of his sleep and on awakening he rose on the sixth day, and He brought her to him, and he knew her, and said to her, "This is now bone of my bones and flesh of my flesh; she shall be called my wife; because she was taken from her husband."

7 Therefore shall man and wife become one and therefore shall a man leave his father and his mother, and cling to his wife, and they shall be one flesh.

8 In the first week Adam was created, and from his rib, his wife. In the second week God showed her to him, and for this reason the commandment was given to keep in their defilement. A male should be purified in seven days, and for a female twice seven days.

9 After Adam had completed forty days in the land where he had been created, we brought him into the garden of Eden to till and keep it, but his wife we brought in on the eightieth day, and after this she entered into the garden of Eden.

10 And for this reason the commandment is written on the heavenly tablets in regard to her that gives birth, "If she bears a male, she shall remain unclean for seven days according to the first week of days, and thirty-three days shall she remain in the blood of her purifying, and she shall not touch any holy thing, nor enter into the sanctuary, until she completes these days which are decreed in the case of a male child.

11 But in the case of a female child she shall remain unclean two weeks of days, according to the first two weeks, and sixty-six days in the blood of her purification, and they will be in all eighty days."

12 When she had completed these eighty days we brought her into the Garden of Eden, for it is holier than all the earth besides and every tree that is planted in it is holy.

13 Therefore, there was ordained regarding her who bears a male or a female child the statute of those days that she should touch no holy thing, nor enter into the sanctuary until these days for the male or female child are completed.

14 This is the law and testimony that was written down for Israel, in order that they should observe it all the days.

15 In the first week of the first jubilee, Adam and his wife were in the garden of Eden for seven years tilling and keeping it, and we gave him work and we instructed him to do everything that is suitable for tillage.

16 And he tilled the garden, and was naked and did not realize it, and was not ashamed. He protected the garden from the birds and beasts and cattle. He gathered its fruit, and ate, and put aside that which was left over for himself and for his wife.

17 After the completion of exactly seven years there, and in the second month, on the seventeenth day of the month, the serpent came and approached the woman, and the serpent said to the woman, "Has God commanded you saying, you shall not eat of every tree of the garden?"

18 She said to it, God said to us, of all the fruit of the trees of the garden, eat; but of the fruit of the tree which is in the middle of the garden God said to us, you shall not eat of it, neither shall you touch it, or you shall die."

19 The serpent said to the woman, "You shall not surely die. God does know that on the day you shall eat of it, your eyes will be opened, and you will be as gods, and you will know good and evil.

20 And the woman saw the tree that it was beautiful and pleasant to the eye, and that its fruit was good for food, and she took of it and ate.

21 First, she covered her shame with fig leaves and then she gave the fruit to Adam and he ate, and his eyes were opened, and he saw that he was naked.

22 He took fig leaves and sewed them together, and made an apron for himself, and covered his shame.

23 God cursed the serpent, and was very angry at it forever.

24 And He was very angry with the woman, because she listened to the voice of the serpent, and ate; and He said to her, "I will vastly multiply your sorrow and your pains, in sorrow you will bring forth children, and your master shall be your husband, and he will rule over you."

25 To Adam also he said, " Because you have listened to the voice of your wife, and have eaten of the tree of which I commanded you not to eat, cursed be the ground for your sake, thorns and thistles shall it produce for you, and you will eat your bread in the sweat of your face, until you return to the earth from where you were taken; for earth you are, and to earth will you return."

26 And He made for them coats of skin, and clothed them, and sent them out from the Garden of Eden.

27 On that day on which Adam went out from the Garden, he offered as a sweet odor an offering, frankincense, incense, and sweet spice, and spices in the morning with the rising of the sun from the day when he covered his shame.

28 On that day was closed the mouth of all beasts, and of cattle, and of birds, and of whatever walks, and of whatever moves, so that they could no longer speak, for they had all spoken one with another with one dialect and with one language.

29 All flesh that was in the Garden of Eden He sent out of the Garden of Eden, and all flesh was scattered according to its kinds, and according to its types to the places that had been created for them.

30 Of all the beasts and cattle only to Adam alone He gave the ability to cover his shame.

31 Because of this, it is prescribed on the heavenly tablets as touching all those who know the judgment of the law, that they should cover their shame, and should not uncover themselves as the Gentiles uncover themselves.

32 On the new moon of the fourth month, Adam and his wife went out from the Garden of Eden, and they dwelt in the land of Elda in the land of their creation.

33 And Adam called the name of his wife Eve.

34 And they had no son until the first jubilee, and after this he knew her.

35 Now he tilled the land as he had been instructed in the Garden of Eden.

[Chapter 4]

1 In the third week in the second jubilee she gave birth to Cain, and in the fourth jubilee she gave birth to Abel, and in the fifth jubilee she gave birth to her daughter Awan.

2 In the first year of the third jubilee, Cain killed Abel because God accepted the sacrifice of Abel, and did not accept the offering of Cain.

3 And he killed him in the field, and his blood cried from the ground to heaven, complaining because he had killed him.

4 The Lord blamed Cain, because he had killed Abel, and He made him a fugitive on the earth because of the blood of his brother, and He cursed him on the earth.

5 Because of this it is written on the heavenly tablets, "Cursed is he who kills his neighbor treacherously, and let all who have seen and heard say, 'So be it', and the man who has seen and not reported it, let him be accursed as the one committing it."

6 For this reason we announce when we come before the Lord our God all the sin that is committed in heaven and on earth, and in light and in darkness, and everywhere.

7 And Adam and his wife mourned for Abel four weeks of years, and in the fourth year of the fifth week they became joyful, and Adam knew his wife again, and she gave birth to a son, and he called his name Seth, for he said "God has raised up a second offspring to us on the earth instead of Abel; for Cain killed him."

8 In the sixth week he begat his daughter Azura.

9 And Cain took Awan his sister to be his wife and she gave birth to Enoch at the close of the fourth jubilee.

10 In the first year of the first week of the fifth jubilee, houses were built on the earth, and Cain built a city, and called its name after the name of his son Enoch.

11 Adam knew Eve his wife and she gave birth to a total of nine sons. In the fifth week of the fifth jubilee Seth took Azura his sister to be his wife, and in the fourth year of the sixth week she gave birth to Enos.

12 He began to call on the name of the Lord on the earth.

13 In the seventh jubilee in the third week Enos took Noam his sister to be his wife, and she gave birth to a son in the third year of the fifth week, and he called his name Kenan.

14 At the close of the eighth jubilee Kenan took Mualeleth his sister to be his wife, and she gave birth to a son in the ninth jubilee, in the first week in the third year of this week, and he called his name Mahalalel.

15 In the second week of the tenth jubilee Mahalalel took to him to wife Dinah, the daughter of Barakiel the daughter of his father's brother, and she gave birth to a son in the third week in the sixth year, and he called his name Jared, for in his days the angels of the Lord descended on the earth, those who are named the Watchers, that they should instruct the children of men, and that they should do judgment and uprightness on the earth.

16 In the eleventh jubilee Jared took to himself a wife, and her name was Baraka, the daughter of Rasujal, a daughter of his father's brother, in the fourth week of this jubilee, and she gave birth to a son in the fifth week, in the fourth year of the jubilee, and he called his name Enoch.

17 He was the first among men that are born on earth who learned writing and knowledge and wisdom and who wrote down the signs of heaven according to the order of their months in a book, that men might know the seasons of the years according to the order of their separate months.

18 He was the first to write a testimony and he testified to the sons of men among the generations of the earth, and recounted the weeks of the jubilees, and made known to them the days of the years, and set in order the months and recounted the Sabbaths of the years as we made them, known to him.

19 And what was and what will be he saw in a vision of his sleep, as it will happen to the children of men throughout their generations until the day of judgment; he saw and understood everything, and wrote his testimony, and placed the testimony on earth for all the children of men and for their generations.

20 In the twelfth jubilee, in the seventh week of it, he took to himself a wife, and her name was Edna, the daughter of Danel, the daughter of his father's brother, and in the sixth year in this week she gave birth to a son and he called his name Methuselah.

21 He was with the angels of God these six jubilees of years, and they showed him everything that is on earth and in the heavens, the rule of the sun, and he wrote down everything.

22 And he testified to the Watchers, who had sinned with the daughters of men; for these had begun to unite themselves, so as to be defiled with the daughters of men, and Enoch testified against them all.

23 And he was taken from among the children of men, and we conducted him into the Garden of Eden in majesty and honor, and there he wrote down the condemnation and judgment of the world, and all the wickedness of the children of men.

24 Because of it God brought the waters of the flood on all the land of Eden; for there he was set as a sign and that he should testify against all the children of men, that he should recount all the deeds of the generations until the day of condemnation.

25 He burnt the incense of the sanctuary, even sweet spices acceptable before the Lord on the Mount.

26 For the Lord has four places on the earth, the Garden of Eden, and the Mount of the East, and this mountain on which you are this day, Mount Sinai, and Mount Zion which will be sanctified in the new creation for a sanctification of the earth; through it will the earth be sanctified from all its guilt and its uncleanness throughout the generations of the world.

27 In the fourteenth jubilee Methuselah took to himself a wife, Edna the daughter of Azrial, the daughter of his father's brother, in the third week, in the first year of this week, and he begat a son and called his name Lamech.

28 In the fifteenth jubilee in the third week Lamech took to himself a wife, and her name was Betenos the daughter of Baraki'il, the daughter of his father's brother, and in this week she gave birth to a son and he called his name Noah, saying, "This one will comfort me for my trouble and all my work, and for the ground which the Lord has cursed."

29 At the close of the nineteenth jubilee, in the seventh week in the sixth year of it, Adam died, and all his sons buried him in the land of his creation, and he was the first to be buried in the earth.

30 He lacked seventy years of one thousand years, because one thousand years are as one day in the testimony of the heavens. Therefore was it written concerning the tree of knowledge, "On the day that you eat of it you shall die." Because of this he did not complete the one thousand years but instead he died during it.

31 At the close of this jubilee Cain was killed after him in the same year; because his house fell on him and he died in the middle of his house, and he was killed by its stones. With a stone he had killed Abel, and by a stone he was killed in righteous judgment.

32 For this reason it was ordained on the heavenly tablets, with the instrument with which a man kills his neighbor with the same shall he be killed. In the same manner that he wounded him, in like manner shall they deal with him."

33 In the twenty-fifth jubilee Noah took to himself a wife, and her name was Emzara, the daughter of Rake'el, the daughter of his father's brother, in the first year in the fifth week, and in the third year of it she gave birth to Shem, in the fifth year of it she gave birth to Ham, and in the first year in the sixth week she gave birth to Japheth.

[Chapter 5]

1 When the children of men began to multiply on the face of the earth and daughters were born to them, and the angels of God saw them on a certain year of this jubilee, that they were beautiful, and they took themselves wives of all whom they chose, and they gave birth to their sons and they were giants.

2 Because of them lawlessness increased on the earth and all flesh corrupted its way. Men and cattle and beasts and birds and everything that walked on the earth were all corrupted in their ways and their orders, and they began to devour each other. Lawlessness increased on the earth and the imagination and thoughts of all men were continually, totally evil.

3 God looked on the earth, and saw it was corrupt, and all flesh had corrupted its orders, and all that were on the earth had committed all manner of evil before His eyes.

4 He said that He would destroy man and all flesh on the face of the earth that He had created.

5 But Noah found grace before the eyes of the Lord.

6 And against the angels whom He had sent on the earth, He had boiling anger, and He gave commandment to root them out of all their dominion, and He commanded us to bind them in the depths of the earth, and look, they are bound in the middle of the earth, and are kept separate.

7 And against their sons went out a command from His mouth that they should be killed with the sword, and be left under heaven.

8 He said, "My spirit shall not always abide on man; for they also are flesh and their days shall be one hundred and twenty years."

9 He sent His sword into their presence that each should kill his neighbor, and they began to kill each other until they all fell by the sword and were destroyed from the earth.

10 And their fathers were witnesses of their destruction, and after this they were bound in the depths of the earth forever, until the day of the great condemnation, when judgment is executed on all those who have corrupted their ways and their works before the Lord.

11 He destroyed all wherever they were, and there was not one left of them whom He judged according to all their wickedness.

12 Through His work He made a new and righteous nature, so that they should not sin in their whole nature forever, but should be all righteous each in his own way always.

13 The judgment of all is ordained and written on the heavenly tablets in righteousness, even the judgment of all who depart from the path that is ordained for them to walk; and if they do not walk it, judgment is written down for every creature and for every kind.

14 There is nothing in heaven or on earth, or in light or in darkness, or in the abode of the dead or in the depth, or in the place of darkness that is not judged. All their judgments are ordained and written and engraved.

15 He will judge all, the great according to his greatness, and the small according to his smallness, and each according to his way.

16 He is not one who will regard the position of any person, nor is He one who will receive gifts, if He says that He will execute judgment on each.

17 If one gave everything that is on the earth, He will not regard the gifts or the person of any, nor accept anything at his hands, for He is a righteous judge.

18 Of the children of Israel it has been written and ordained, if they turn to him in righteousness He will forgive all their transgressions and pardon all their sins. It is written and ordained that He will show mercy to all who turn from all their guilt once each year.

19 And as for all those who corrupted their ways and their thoughts before the flood, no person was acceptable to God except Noah. His sons were saved in deference to him, and these God kept from the waters of the flood on his account; for Noah's heart was righteous in all his ways. He upheld the laws and did as God commanded him and he had not departed from anything that was ordained for him.

20 The Lord said that he would destroy everything on the earth, both men and cattle, and beasts, and birds of the air, and that which moves on the earth.

21 And He commanded Noah to make an ark, so that he might save himself from the waters of the flood.

22 And Noah made the ark in all respects as He commanded him, in the twenty-seventh jubilee of years, in the fifth week in the fifth year on the new moon of the first month.

23 He entered in the sixth year of it, in the second month, on the new moon of the second month, until the sixteenth; and he entered, and all that we brought to him, into the ark, and the Lord closed it from the outside on the seventeenth evening.

24 And the Lord opened seven floodgates of heaven, and He opened the mouths of the fountains of the great deep, seven mouths in number.

25 And the floodgates began to pour down water from the heaven forty days and forty closets, And the fountains of the deep also sent up waters, until the whole world was full of water.

26 The waters increased on the earth, by fifteen cubits (a cubit is about 18 inches) the waters rose above all the high mountains. And the ark was lift up from the earth. And it moved on the face of the waters.

27 And the water covered the face of the earth five months, which is one hundred and fifty days.

28 And the ark went and rested on the top of Lubar, one of the mountains of Ararat.

29 On the new moon in the fourth month the fountains of the great deep were closed and the floodgates of heaven were restrained; and on the new moon of the seventh month all the mouths of the bottomless gulfs of the earth were opened, and the water began to flow down into the deep below.

30 On the new moon of the tenth month the tops of the mountains were seen, and on the new moon of the first month the earth became visible.

31 The waters disappeared from the earth in the fifth week in the seventh year of it, and on the seventeenth day in the second month the earth was dry.

32 On the twenty-seventh of it he opened the ark, and sent out beasts, and cattle, and birds, and every moving thing.

[Chapter 6]

1 On the new moon of the third month he went out of the ark, and built an altar on that mountain.

2 And he made atonement for the earth, and took a kid and made atonement by its blood for all the guilt of the earth; for every thing that had been on it had been destroyed, except those that were in the ark with Noah.

3 He placed the fat of it on the altar, and he took an ox, and a goat, and a sheep and kids, and salt, and a turtle-dove, and the young of a dove, and placed a burnt sacrifice on the altar, and poured on it an offering mingled with oil, and sprinkled wine and sprinkled frankincense over everything, and caused a good and pleasing odor to arise, acceptable before the Lord.

4 And the Lord smelled the good and pleasing odor, and He made a covenant with Noah that there should not be any more floods to destroy the earth; that all the days of the earth seed-time and harvest should never cease; cold and heat, and summer and winter, and day and night should not change their order, nor cease forever.

5 "Increase and multiply on the earth, and become many, and be a blessing on it. I will inspire the fear of you and the dread of you in everything that is on earth and in the sea.

6 Look, I have given you all beasts, and all winged things, and everything that moves on the earth, and the fish in the waters, and all things for food; as the green herbs, I have given you all things to eat.

7 But you shall not eat anything live or with blood in it, for the life of all flesh is in the blood, or your blood of your lives will be required. At the hand of every man, at the hand of every beast will I require the blood of man.

8 Whoever sheds man's blood by man shall his blood be shed, for in the image of God He made man.

9 Increase, and multiply on the earth."

10 Noah and his sons swore that they would not eat any blood that was in any flesh, and he made a covenant before the Lord God forever throughout all the generations of the earth in this month.

11 Because of this He spoke to you that you should make a covenant with the children of Israel with an oath. In this month, on the mountain you should sprinkle blood on them because of all the words of the covenant, which the Lord made with them forever.

12 This testimony is written concerning you that you should observe it continually, so that you should not eat on any day any blood of beasts or birds or cattle during all the days of the earth, and the man who eats the blood of beast or of cattle or of birds during all the days of the earth, he and his offspring shall be rooted out of the land.

13 And you will command the children of Israel to eat no blood, so that their names and their offspring may be before the Lord our God continually.

14 There is no limit of days, for this law. It is forever. They shall observe it throughout their generations, so that they may continue supplicating on your behalf with blood before the altar; every day and at the time of morning and evening they shall seek forgiveness on your behalf perpetually before the Lord that they may keep it and not be rooted out.

15 And He gave to Noah and his sons a sign that there should not again be a flood on the earth.

16 He set His bow (a rainbow) in the cloud as a sign of the eternal covenant that there should never again be a flood on the earth to destroy it for all the days of the earth.

17 For this reason it is ordained and written on the heavenly tablets, that they should celebrate the feast of weeks in this month once a year, to renew the covenant every year.

18 This whole festival was celebrated in heaven from the day of creation until the days of Noah, which were twenty-six jubilees and five weeks of years. Noah and his sons observed it for seven jubilees and one week of years, until the day of Noah's death. From the day of Noah's death his sons did away with it until the days of Abraham, and they ate blood.

19 But Abraham observed it, and Isaac and Jacob and his children observed it up to your days, and in your days the children of Israel forgot it until you celebrated it anew on this mountain.

20 Command the children of Israel to observe this festival in all their generations for a commandment to them, one day in the year in this month they shall celebrate the festival.

21 For it is the feast of weeks and the feast of first-fruits, this feast is twofold and of a double nature, according to what is written and engraved concerning it, celebrate it.

22 For I have written in the book of the first law, in that which I have written for you, that you should celebrate it in its season, one day in the year, and I explained to you its sacrifices that the children of Israel should remember and should celebrate it throughout their generations in this month, the same day in every year.

23 On the new moon of the first month, and on the new moon of the fourth month, and on the new moon of the seventh month, and on the new moon of the tenth month are the days of remembrance, and the days of the seasons in the four divisions of the year. These are written and ordained as a testimony forever.

24 Noah ordained them for himself as feasts for the generations forever, so that they have become a memorial to him.

25 On the new moon of the first month he was told to make for himself an ark, and on that day the earth was dry and he saw from the opened ark, the earth. On the new moon of the fourth month the mouths of the depths of the bottomless pit beneath were closed.

26 On the new moon of the seventh month all the mouths of the abysses of the earth were opened, and the waters began to descend into them.

27 On the new moon of the tenth month the tops of the mountains were seen, and Noah was glad.

28 Because of this he ordained them for himself as feasts for a memorial forever, and thus are they ordained.

29 And they placed them on the heavenly tablets, each had thirteen weeks; from one to another passed their memorial, from the first to the second, and from the second to the third, and from the third to the fourth.

30 All the days of the commandment will be two and fifty weeks of days, and these will make the entire year complete. Thus it is engraved and ordained on the heavenly tablets.

31 And there is no neglecting this commandment for a single year or from year to year.

32 Command the children of Israel that they observe the years according to this counting, three hundred and sixty-four days, and these will constitute a complete year, and they will not disturb its time from its days and from its feasts; for every thing will fall out in them according to their testimony, and they will not leave out any day nor disturb any feasts.

33 But if they neglect and do not observe them according to His commandment, then they will disturb all their seasons and the years will be dislodged from this order, and they will neglect their established rules.

34 And all the children of Israel will forget and will not find the path of the years, and will forget the new moons, and seasons, and sabbaths and they will wrongly determine all the order of the years.

35 For I know and from now on will I declare it to you, and it is not of my own devising; for the book lies written in the presence of me, and on the heavenly tablets the division of days is ordained, or they forget the feasts of the covenant and walk according to the feasts of the Gentiles after their error and after their ignorance.

36 For there will be those who will assuredly make observations of the moon and how it disturbs the seasons and comes in from year to year ten days too soon.

37 For this reason the years will come upon them when they disturb (misinterpret) the order, and make an abominable day the day of testimony, and an unclean day a feast day, and they will confound all the days, the holy with the unclean, and the unclean day with the holy; for they will go wrong as to the months and sabbaths and feasts and jubilees.

38 For this reason I command and testify to you that you may testify to them; for after your death your children will disturb them, so that they will not make the year three hundred and sixty-four days only, and for this reason they will go wrong as to the new moons and seasons and sabbaths and festivals, and they will eat all kinds of blood with all kinds of flesh.

[Chapter 7]

1 In the seventh week in the first year of it, in this jubilee, Noah planted vines on the mountain on which the ark had rested, named Lubar, one of the Ararat Mountains, and they produced fruit in the fourth year, and he guarded their fruit, and gathered it in that year in the seventh month.

2 He made wine from it and put it into a vessel, and kept it until the fifth year, until the first day, on the new moon of the first month.

3 And he celebrated with joy the day of this feast, and he made a burnt sacrifice to the Lord, one young ox and one ram, and seven sheep, each a year old, and a kid of the goats, that he might make atonement thereby for himself and his sons.

4 He prepared the kid first, and placed some of its blood on the flesh that was on the altar that he had made, and all the fat he laid on the altar where he made the burnt sacrifice, and the ox and the ram and the sheep, and he laid all their flesh on the altar.

5 He placed all their offerings mingled with oil on it, and afterwards he sprinkled wine on the fire which had previously been made on the altar, and he placed incense on the altar and caused a sweet odor to rise up which was acceptable before the Lord his God.

6 And he rejoiced and he and his children drank the wine with joy.

7 It was evening, and he went into his tent, and being drunken he lay down and slept, and was uncovered in his tent as he slept.

8 And Ham saw Noah his father naked, and went out and told his two brothers (ridiculed his father to his two brothers) who were outside.

9 Shem took his garment and arose, he and Japheth, and they placed the garment on their shoulders and went backward and covered the shame of their father, and their faces were backward.

10 Noah awoke from sleep and knew all (abuse) that his younger son had done to him. He cursed him saying, "Cursed be Canaan; an enslaved servant shall he be to his brothers."

11 And he blessed Shem, and said, "Blessed be the Lord God of Shem, and Canaan shall be his servant.

12 God shall enlarge Japheth, and God shall dwell in the dwelling of Shem, and Canaan shall be his servant."

13 Ham knew that his father had cursed, him, his younger son, and he was displeased that he had cursed him, his son. And Ham parted from his father, he and his sons with him, Cush and Mizraim and Put and Canaan.

14 And he built for himself a city and called its name after the name of his wife Ne'elatama'uk.

15 Japheth saw it, and became envious of his brother, and he too built for himself a city, and he called its name after the name of his wife Adataneses.

16 Shem dwelt with his father Noah, and he built a city close to his father on the mountain, and he too called its name after the name of his wife Sedeqetelebab.

17 These three cities are near Mount Lubar; Sedeqetelebab in front of the mountain on its east; and Na'eltama'uk on the south; Adatan'eses towards the west.

18 These are the sons of Shem, Elam, and Asshur, and Arpachshad who was born two years after the flood, and Lud, and Aram.

19 The sons of Japheth, Gomer, Magog, Madai , Javan, Tubal and Meshech and Tiras, these are the descendants of Noah.

20 In the twenty-eighth jubilee Noah began to direct his sons in the ordinances and commandments, and all the judgments that he knew, and he exhorted his sons to observe righteousness, and to cover the shame of their flesh, and to bless their Creator, and honor father and mother, and love their neighbor, and guard their souls from fornication and uncleanness and all iniquity.

21 Because of these three things came the flood on the earth, namely, the fornication that the Watchers committed against the law of their ordinances when they went whoring after the daughters of men, and took themselves wives of all they chose, and they made the beginning of uncleanness.

22 And they begat sons, the Naphilim (Naphidim), and they were all dissimilar, and they devoured one another, and the Giants killed the Naphil, and the Naphil killed the Eljo, and the Eljo killed mankind, and one man killed one another.

23 Every one committed himself to crime and injustice and to shed much blood, and the earth was filled with sin.

24 After this they sinned against the beasts and birds, and all that moved and walked on the earth, and much blood was shed on the earth, and men continually desired only what was useless and evil.

25 And the Lord destroyed everything from the face of the earth. Because of the wickedness of their deeds, and because of the blood they had shed over all the earth, He destroyed everything. "

26 We were left, I and you, my sons, and everything that entered with us into the ark, and behold I see your works before me that you do not walk in righteousness, for in the path of destruction you have begun to walk, and you are turning one against another, and are envious one of another, and so it comes that you are not in harmony, my sons, each with his brother.

27 For I see the demons have begun their seductions against you and against your children and now I fear on your behalf, that after my death you will shed the blood of men on the earth, and that you, too, will be destroyed from the face of the earth.

28 For whoever sheds man's blood, and who ever eats the blood of any flesh, shall all be destroyed from the earth.

29 There shall be no man left that eats blood, or that sheds the blood of man on the earth, nor shall there be left to him any offspring or descendants living under heaven. Into the abode of the dead shall they go, and into the place of condemnation shall they descend, and into the darkness of the deep shall they all be removed by a violent death.

30 Do not smear blood on yourself or let it remain on you. Out of all the blood there shall be shed and out of all the days in which you have killed any beasts or cattle or whatever flies on the earth you must do a good work to your souls by covering that which has been shed on the face of the earth.

31 You shall not be like him who eats blood, but guard yourselves that none may eat blood before you, cover the blood, for thus have I been commanded to testify to you and your children, together with all flesh.

32 Do not permit the soul (life) to be eaten with the flesh, that your blood, which is your life, may not be required at the hand of any flesh that sheds it on the earth.

33 For the earth will not be clean from the blood that has been shed on it, for only through the blood of him

that shed it will the earth be purified throughout all its generations.

34 Now, my children, listen, have judgment and righteousness that you may be planted in righteousness over the face of the whole earth, and your glory lifted up in the presence of my God, who spared me from the waters of the flood.

35 Look, you will go and build for yourselves cities, and plant in them all the plants that are on the earth, and moreover all fruit-bearing trees.

36 For three years the fruit of everything that is eaten will not be gathered, and in the fourth year its fruit will be accounted holy, offered as first fruit, acceptable before the Most High God, who created heaven and earth and all things.

37 Let them offer in abundance the first of the wine and oil as first-fruits on the altar of the Lord, who receives it, and what is left let the servants of the house of the Lord eat before the altar which receives it.

38 In the fifth year make the release so that you release it in righteousness and uprightness, and you shall be righteous, and all that you plant shall prosper. For this is how Enoch did it, the father of your father commanded Methuselah, his son, and Methuselah commanded his son Lamech, and Lamech commanded me all the things that his fathers commanded him.

39 I also will give you commandment, my sons, as Enoch commanded his son in the first jubilees, while still living, the seventh in his generation, he commanded and testified to his son and to his son's sons until the day of his death.

[Chapter 8]

1 In the twenty-ninth jubilee, in the beginning of first week, Arpachshad took to himself a wife and her name was Rasu'eja, the daughter of Susan, the daughter of Elam, and she gave birth to a son in the third year in this week, and he called his name Kainam.

2 The son grew, and his father taught him writing, and he went to seek for himself a place where he might seize a city for himself.

3 He found writing which former generations had carved on a rock, and he read what was on it, and he transcribed it and sinned because of it, for it contained the teaching of the Watchers, which they had used to observe the omens of the sun and moon and stars in all the signs of heaven.

4 He wrote it down and said nothing of it, for he was afraid to speak to Noah about it or he would be angry with him because of it.

5 In the thirtieth jubilee, in the second week, in the first year of it, he took to himself a wife, and her name was Melka, the daughter of Madai, the son of Japheth, and in the fourth year he begat a son, and called his name Shelah; for he said, "Truly I have been sent."

6 Shelah grew up and took to himself a wife, and her name was Mu'ak, the daughter of Kesed, his father's brother, in the one and thirtieth jubilee, in the fifth week, in the first year of it.

7 And she gave birth to a son in the fifth year of it, and he called his name Eber, and he took to himself a wife, and her name was Azurad, the daughter of Nebrod, in the thirty-second jubilee, in the seventh week, in the third year of it.

8 In the sixth year of it, she gave birth to a son, and he called his name Peleg, for in the days when he was born the children of Noah began to divide the earth among themselves, for this reason he called his name Peleg.

9 They divided it secretly among themselves, and told it to Noah.

10 In the beginning of the thirty-third jubilee they divided the earth into three parts, for Shem and Ham and Japheth, according to the inheritance of each, in the first year in the first week, when one of us (angels) who had been sent, was with them.

11 He called his sons, and they drew close to him, they and their children, and he divided the earth into the lots, which his three sons were to take in possession, and they reached out their hands, and took the writing out of the arms of Noah, their father.

12 There came out on the writing as Shem's lot the middle of the earth that he should take as an inheritance for himself and for his sons for the generations of eternity. From the middle of the mountain range of Rafa, from the mouth of the water from the river Tina, and his portion goes towards the west through the middle of this river, and it extends until it reaches the water of the abysses, out of which this river goes out and pours its waters into the sea Me'at, and this river flows into the great sea.

13 All that is towards the north is Japheth's, and all that is towards the south belongs to Shem. And it extends until it reaches Karaso, this is in the center of the tongue of land that looks towards the south.

14 His portion extends along the great sea, and it extends in a straight line until it reaches the west of the tongue that looks towards the south, for this sea is named the tongue of the Egyptian Sea.

15 And it turns from here towards the south towards the mouth of the great sea on the shore of its waters, and it extends to the west to Afra, and it extends until it reaches the waters of the river Gihon, and to the south of the waters of Gihon, to the banks of this river.

16 It extends towards the east, until it reaches the Garden of Eden, to the south of it and from the east of the whole land of Eden and of the whole east, it turns to the east and proceeds until it reaches the east of the mountain named Rafa, and it descends to the bank of the mouth of the river Tina.

17 This portion came out by lot for Shem and his sons, that they should possess it forever to his generations forever.

18 Noah rejoiced that this portion came out for Shem and for his sons, and he remembered all that he had spoken with his mouth in prophecy; for he had said, "Blessed be the Lord God of Shem and may the Lord dwell in the dwelling of Shem."

19 He knew that the Garden of Eden is the holy of holies, and the dwelling of the Lord, and Mount Sinai the center of the desert, and Mount Zion which is the center of the navel of the earth, these three were created as holy places facing each other.

20 And he blessed the God of gods, who had put the word of the Lord into his mouth, and the Lord forever.

21 And he knew that a blessed portion and a blessing had come to Shem and his sons and to their generations forever which was the whole land of Eden and the whole land of the Red Sea, and the whole land of the east and India, and on the Red Sea and the mountains of it, and all the land of Bashan, and all the land of Lebanon and the islands of Kaftur, and all the mountains of Sanir and Amana, and the mountains of Asshur in the north, and all the land of Elam, Asshur, and Babel, and Susan and Ma'edai, and all the mountains of Ararat, and all the region beyond the sea, which is beyond the mountains of Asshur towards the north, a blessed and spacious land, and all that is in it is very good.

22 Ham received the second portion, beyond the Gihon towards the south to the right of the Garden, and it extends towards the south and it extends to all the mountains of fire, and it extends towards the west to the sea of 'atel and it extends towards the west until it reaches the sea of Ma'uk which was that sea into which everything that is not destroyed descends.

23 It goes out towards the north to the limits of Gadir, and it goes out to the coast of the waters of the sea to the waters of the great sea until it draws near to the river Gihon, and goes along the river Gihon until it reaches the right of the Garden of Eden.

24 This is the land that came out for Ham as the portion which he was to occupy forever for himself and his sons to their generations forever.

25 Japheth received the third portion beyond the river Tina to the north of the outflow of its waters, and it extends north-easterly to the whole region of Gog, and to all the country east of it.

26 It extends northerly, and it extends to the mountains of Qelt towards the north, and towards the sea of Ma'uk, and it goes out to the east of Gadir as far as the region of the waters of the sea.

27 It extends until it approaches the west of Fara and it returns towards Aferag, and it extends easterly to the waters of the sea of Me'at.

28 It extends to the region of the river Tina in a northeasterly direction until it approaches the boundary of its waters towards the mountain Rafa, and it turns round towards the north.

29 This is the land that came out for Japheth and his sons as the portion of his inheritance that he should possess five great islands, and a great land in the north, for himself and his sons, for their generations forever.

30 But it is cold, and the land of Ham is hot, and the land of Shem is neither hot nor cold, but it is of blended cold and heat.

[Chapter 9]

1 Ham divided among his sons, and the first portion came out for Cush towards the east, and to the west of him for Mizraim, and to the west of him for Put, and to the west of him on the sea for Canaan.

2 Shem also divided among his sons, and the first portion came out for Elam and his sons, to the east of the river Tigris until it approaches the east, the whole land of India, and on the Red Sea on its coast, and the waters of Dedan, and all the mountains of Mebri and Ela, and all the land of Susan and all that is on the side of Pharnak to the Red Sea and the river Tina.

3 Asshur received the second Portion, all the land of Asshur and Nineveh and Shinar and to the border of India, and it ascends and skirts the river.

4 Arpachshad received the third portion, all the land of the region of the Chaldees to the east of the Euphrates, bordering on the Red Sea, and all the waters of the desert close to the tongue of the sea which looks towards Egypt, all the land of Lebanon and Sanir and Amana to the border of the Euphrates.

5 Aram received the fourth portion, all the land of Mesopotamia between the Tigris and the Euphrates to the north of the Chaldees to the border of the mountains of Asshur and the land of Arara.

6 Lud got the fifth portion, the mountains of Asshur and all surrounding to them until it reaches the Great Sea, and until it reaches the east of Asshur his brother.

7 Japheth also divided the land of his inheritance among his sons.

8 The first portion came out for Gomer to the east from the north side to the river Tina, and in the north there came out for Magog all the inner portions of the north until it reaches to the sea of Me'at.

9 Madai received as his portion that he should possess from the west of his two brothers to the islands, and to the coasts of the islands.

10 Javan got the fourth portion, every island and the islands that are towards the border of Lud.

11 For Tubal there came out the fifth portion in the middle of the tongue that approaches towards the border of the portion of Lud to the second tongue, to the region beyond the second tongue to the third tongue.

12 Meshech received the sixth portion, that is the entire region beyond the third tongue until it approaches the east of Gadir.

13 Tiras got the seventh portion, four great islands in the middle of the sea, which reach to the portion of Ham, and the islands of Kamaturi came out by lot for the sons of Arpachshad as his inheritance.

14 Thus the sons of Noah divided to their sons in the presence of Noah their father, and he bound them all by an oath, and invoked a curse on every one that sought to seize any portion which had not fallen to him by his lot.

15 They all said, "so be it; so be it " (amen and amen) for themselves and their sons forever throughout their generations until the day of judgment, on which the Lord God shall judge them with a sword and with fire for all the unclean wickedness of their errors, that they have filled the earth with, which are transgression, uncleanness and fornication and sin.

[Chapter 10]

1 In the third week of this jubilee the unclean demons began to lead astray the children of the sons of Noah, and to make them sin and to destroy them.

2 The sons of Noah came to Noah their father, and they told him about the demons that were leading astray and blinding and slaying his sons' sons.

3 And he prayed before the Lord his God, and said, "God of the spirits of all flesh, who have shown mercy to me and have spared me and my sons from the waters of the flood,
and have not caused me to die as You did the sons of perdition; For Your grace has been great toward me,
and great has been Your mercy to my soul. Let Your grace be lifted up on my sons, and do not let the wicked spirits rule over them or they will destroy them from the earth.

4 But bless me and my sons, so that we may increase and multiply and replenish the earth.

5 You know how Your Watchers, the fathers of these spirits, acted in my day, and as for these spirits which are living, imprison them and hold them fast in the place of condemnation, and let them not bring destruction on the sons of your servant, my God; for these are like cancer and are created in order to destroy.

6 Let them not rule over the spirits of the living; for You alone can exercise dominion over them. And let them not have power over the sons of the righteous from now and forever."

7 And the Lord our God commanded us (angels) to bind all of them.

8 The chief of the spirits, Mastema, came and said, "Lord, Creator, let some of them remain before me, and let them listen to my voice, and do all that I shall say to them; for if some of them are not left to me, I shall not be able to execute the power of my will on the sons of men, for these are for corruption and leading astray before my judgment, for great is the wickedness of the sons of men."

9 He said, "Let one-tenth of them remain before him, and let nine-tenths of them descend into the place of condemnation."

10 He commanded one of us to teach Noah all their medicines, for He knew that they would not walk in uprightness, nor strive in righteousness.

11 We did according to all His words, all the malignant evil ones we bound in the place of condemnation and a tenth part of them we left that they might be subject in the presence of Satan on the earth.

12 We explained to Noah all the medicines of their diseases, together with their seductions, how he might heal them with herbs of the earth.

13 Noah wrote down all things in a book as we instructed him concerning every kind of medicine. Thus the evil spirits were precluded from hurting the sons of Noah.

14 He gave all that he had written to Shem, his eldest son, for he loved him greatly above all his sons.

15 And Noah slept with his fathers, and was buried on Mount Lubar in the land of Ararat.

16 Nine hundred and fifty years he completed in his life, nineteen jubilees and two weeks and five years.

17 In his life on earth he was greater than all the children of men except Enoch because of his righteousness he was perfect. For Enoch's office was ordained for a testimony to the generations of the world, so that he should recount all the deeds of generation to generation, until the day of judgment.

18 In the three and thirtieth jubilee, in the first year in the second week, Peleg took to himself a wife, whose name was Lomna the daughter of Sina'ar, and she gave birth to a son for him in the fourth year of this week, and he called his name Reu, for he said, "Look the children of men have become evil because the building a city and a tower in the land of Shinar was for an evil purpose."

19 For they departed from the land of Ararat eastward to Shinar, for in his days they built the city and the tower, saying, "Come, let us rise up by the tower into heaven."

20 They began to build, and in the fourth week they made brick with fire, and the bricks served them for stone,
and the clay with which they cemented them together was asphalt which comes out of the sea, and out of the fountains of water in the land of Shinar.

21 They built it, forty-three years were they building it. Its breadth was 203 bricks, and the height of a brick was the third of one; its height amounted to 5433 cubits and 2 palms, and the extent of one wall was thirteen times 600 feet and of the other thirty times 600 feet.

22 And the Lord our God said to us, "Look, they are one people, and they begin to do this, and now nothing will be withheld from them. Let us go down and confound their language, that they may not understand one another's speech, and they may be dispersed into cities and nations, and they will not be in agreement together with one purpose until the day of judgment."

23 And the Lord descended, and we descended with him to see the city and the tower that the children of men had built.

24 He confounded their language, and they no longer understood one another's speech, and they then ceased to build the city and the tower.

25 For this reason the whole land of Shinar is called Babel, because the Lord confounded all the language of the children of men there, and from that place they were dispersed into their cities, each according to his language and his nation.

26 Then, the Lord sent a mighty wind against the tower and it fell to the earth, and behold it was between Asshur and Babylon in the land of Shinar, and they called its name "Overthrow."

27 In the fourth week in the first year in the beginning of it in the four and thirtieth jubilee, were they dispersed from the land of Shinar.

28 Ham and his sons went into the land that he was to occupy, which he acquired as his portion in the land of the south.

29 Canaan saw the land of Lebanon to the river of Egypt was very good, and he did not go into the land of his inheritance to the west that is to the sea, and he dwelt in the land of Lebanon, eastward and westward from the border of Jordan and from the border of the sea.

30 Ham, his father, and Cush and Mizraim, his brothers, said to him, "You have settled in a land which is not yours, and which did not fall to us by lot, do not do so. If you do you and your sons will be conquered in the land and be accursed through a war. By war you have settled, and by war will your children fall, and you will be rooted out forever.

31 Do not live in the land of Shem, for to Shem and to his sons did it come by their lot.

32 Cursed are you, and cursed will you be beyond all the sons of Noah, by the curse by which we bound ourselves by an oath in the presence of the holy judge, and in the presence of Noah our father."

33 But he did not listen to them, and settled in the land of Lebanon from Hamath to the border of Egypt, he and his sons until this day. For this reason that land is named Canaan. And Japheth and his sons went towards the sea and settled in the land of their portion, and Madai saw the land of the sea and it did not please him, and he begged Ham and Asshur and Arpachshad, his wife's brother for a portion, and he dwelt in the land of Media, near to his wife's brother until this day.

34 And he called his and his son's dwelling-place, Media, after the name of their father Madai.

[Chapter 11]

1 In the thirty-fifth jubilee, in the third week, in the first year of it, Reu took to himself a wife, and her name was 'Ora, the daughter of 'Ur, the son of Kesed, and she gave birth to a son, and he called his name Seroh, in the seventh year of this week in this jubilee.

2 The sons of Noah began to war with each other, to take captives and kill each other, and to shed the blood of men on the earth, and to eat blood, and to build strong cities, and walls, and towers, and individuals began to exalt themselves above the nation, and to establish kingdoms, and to go to war, people against people, and nation against nation, and city against city, and all began to do evil, and to acquire arms, and to teach their sons war, and they began to capture cities, and to sell male and female slaves.

3 Ur, the son of Kesed, built the city of Ara of the Chaldees, and called its name after his own name and the name of his father.

4 And they made themselves molten images, and they worshipped the idols and the molten image they had made for themselves, and they began to make graven images and unclean and shadowy presence, and malevolent and malicious spirits assisted and seduced them into committing transgression and uncleanness.

5 Prince Mastema exerted himself to do all this, and he sent out other spirits, which were put under his control, to do all manner of wrong and sin, and all manner of transgression, to corrupt and destroy, and to shed blood on the earth.

6 For this reason he called the name of Seroh, Serug, for every one turned to do all manner of sin and transgression.

7 He grew up, and dwelt in Ur of the Chaldees, near to the father of his wife's mother, and he worshipped idols, and he took to himself a wife in the thirty-sixth jubilee, in the fifth week, in the first year of it, and her name was Melka, the daughter of Kaber, the daughter of his father's brother.

8 She gave birth to Nahor, in the first year of this week, and he grew and dwelt in Ur of the Chaldees, and his father taught him the sciences of the Chaldees to divine and conjure, according to the signs of heaven.

9 In the thirty-seventh jubilee in the sixth week, in the first year of it, he took to himself a wife, and her name was 'Ijaska, the daughter of Nestag of the Chaldees.

10 And she gave birth to Terah in the seventh year of this week.

11 Prince Mastema sent ravens and birds to devour the seed that was sown in the land, in order to destroy the land, and rob the children of men of their labors. Before they could plow in the seed, the ravens picked it from the surface of the ground.

12 This is why he called his name Terah because the ravens and the birds reduced them to destitution and devoured their seed.

13 The years began to be barren, because of the birds, and they devoured all the fruit of the trees from the trees, it was only with great effort that they could harvest a little fruit from the earth in their days.

14 In this thirty-ninth jubilee, in the second week in the first year, Terah took to himself a wife, and her name was 'Edna, the daughter of Abram, the daughter of his father's sister.

15 In the seventh year of this week she gave birth to a son, and he called his name Abram, by the name of the father of his mother, for he had died before his daughter had conceived a son.

16 And the child began to understand the errors of the earth that all went astray after graven images and after uncleanness,

and his father taught him writing, and he was two weeks of years old, and he separated himself from his father, that he might not worship idols with him.

17 He began to pray to the Creator of all things that He might spare him from the errors of the children of men, and that his portion should not fall into error after uncleanness and vileness.

18 The time came for the sowing of seed in the land, and they all went out together to protect their seed against the ravens, and Abram went out with those that went, and the child was a lad of fourteen years.

19 A cloud of ravens came to devour the seed, and Abram ran to meet them before they settled on the ground, and cried to them before they settled on the ground to devour the seed, and said, "Descend not, return to the place from where you came," and they began to turn back.

20 And he caused the clouds of ravens to turn back that day seventy times, and of all the ravens throughout all the land where Abram was there settled not so much as one.

21 All who were with him throughout all the land saw him cry out, and all the ravens turn back, and his name became great in all the land of the Chaldees.

22 There came to him this year all those that wished to sow, and he went with them until the time of sowing ceased, and they sowed their land, and that year they brought enough grain home to eat and they were satisfied.

23 In the first year of the fifth week Abram taught those who made implements for oxen, the artificers in wood, and they made a vessel above the ground, facing the frame of the plow, in order to put the seed in it, and the seed fell down from it on the share of the plow, and was hidden in the earth, and they no longer feared the ravens.

24 After this manner they made vessels above the ground on all the frames of the plows, and they sowed and tilled all the land, according as Abram commanded them, and they no longer feared the birds.

[Chapter 12]

1 In the sixth week, in the seventh year of it, that Abram said to Terah his father, saying, "Father!"

2 He said, "Look, here am I, my son." He said, "What help and profit have we from those idols which you worship, and in the presence of which you bow yourself?

3 For there is no spirit in them. They are dumb forms, and they mislead the heart.

4 Do not worship them, Worship the God of heaven, who causes the rain and the dew to fall on the earth and does everything on the earth, and has created everything by His word, and all life is from His presence.

5 Why do you worship things that have no spirit in them?

For they are the work of men's hands, and you bear them on your shoulders, and you have no help from them, but they are a great cause of shame to those who make them, and they mislead the heart of those who worship them. Do not worship them."

6 His father said to him, "I also know it, my son, but what shall I do with a people who have made me serve them?

7 If I tell them the truth, they will kill me, because their soul clings to them so they worship them and honor them.

8 Keep silent, my son, or they will kill you." And these words he spoke to his two brothers, and they were angry with him and he kept silent.

9 In the fortieth jubilee, in the second week, in the seventh year of it, Abram took to himself a wife, and her name was Sarai, the daughter of his father, and she became his wife.

10 Haran, his brother, took to himself a wife in the third year of the third week, and she gave birth to a son in the seventh year of this week, and he called his name Lot.

11 Nahor, his brother, took to himself a wife.

12 In the sixtieth year of the life of Abram, that is, in the fourth week, in the fourth year of it, Abram arose in the night and burned the house of the idols, and he burned all that was in the house and no man knew it.

13 And they arose and sought to save their gods from the fire.

14 Haran hasted to save them, but the fire flamed over him, and he was burnt in the fire, and he died in Ur of the Chaldees before Terah his father, and they buried him in Ur of the Chaldees.

15 Terah went out from Ur of the Chaldees, he and his sons, to go into the land of Lebanon and into the land of Canaan, and he dwelt in the land of Haran, and

Abram dwelt with Terah his father in Haran two weeks of years.

16 In the sixth week, in the fifth year of it, Abram sat up all night on the new moon of the seventh month to observe the stars from the evening to the morning, in order to see what would be the character of the year with regard to the rains, and he was alone as he sat and observed.

17 And a word came into his heart and he said, "All the signs of the stars, and the signs of the moon and of the sun are all in the hand of the Lord. Why do I search them out?

18 If He desires, He causes it to rain, morning and evening, and if He desires, He withholds it, and all things are in his hand."

19 He prayed in the night and said, "My God, God Most High, You alone are my God, and You and Your dominion have I chosen. And You have created all things, and all things that are the work of Your hands.

20 Deliver me from the hands of evil spirits who have dominion over the thoughts of men's hearts, and let them not lead me astray from You, my God. And establish me and my offspring forever so that we do not go astray from now and forever."

21 He said, "Shall I return to Ur of the Chaldees who are trying to find me? Should I return to them? Am I to remain here in this place? The right path is before You. Make it prosper in the hands of your servant that he may fulfill it and that I may not walk in the deceitfulness of my heart, O my God."

22 He stopped speaking and stopped praying, and then the word of the Lord was sent to him through me, saying, "Get out of your country, and from your kindred and from the house of your father and go to a land which I will show you, and I shall make you a great and numerous nation.

23 And I will bless you and I will make your name great,

and you will be blessed in the earth, and in You shall all families of the earth be blessed, and I will bless them that bless you, and curse them that curse you.

24 I will be a God to you and your son, and to your son's son, and to all your offspring, fear not, from now on and to all generations of the earth I am your God."

25 The Lord God said, "Open his mouth and his ears, that he may hear and speak with his mouth, with the language which has been revealed," for it had ceased from the mouths of all the children of men from the day of the overthrow of Babel.

26 And I opened his mouth, and his ears and his lips, and I began to speak with him in Hebrew in the tongue of the creation.

27 He took the books of his fathers, and these were written in Hebrew, and he transcribed them, and he began from then on to study them, and I made known to him that which he could not understand, and he studied them during the six rainy months.

28 In the seventh year of the sixth week he spoke to his father and informed him, that he would leave Haran to go into the land of Canaan to see it and return to him.

29 Terah his father said to him; "Go in peace. May the eternal God make your path straight. And the Lord be with you, and protect you from all evil, and grant to you grace, mercy and favor before those who see you, and may none of the children of men have power over you to harm you. Go in peace.

30 If you see a land pleasant to your eyes to dwell in, then arise and take me with you and take Lot with you, the son of Haran your brother as your own son, the Lord be with you.

31 Nahor your brother leave with me until you return in peace, and we go with you all together."

[Chapter 13]

1 Abram journeyed from Haran, and he took Sarai, his wife, and Lot, his brother Haran's son and they went to the land of Canaan, and he came into Asshur, and proceeded to Shechem, and dwelt near a tall oak.

2 He saw the land was very pleasant from the border of Hamath to the tall oak.

3 The Lord said to him, "To you and to your offspring I will give this land."

4 He built an altar there, and he offered on it a burnt sacrifice to the Lord, who had appeared to him.

5 He left from that place and went to the mountain Bethel on the west and Ai on the east, and pitched his tent there.

6 He saw the land was very wide and good, and everything grew on it, vines, and figs, and pomegranates, oaks, and ilexes, and turpentine and oil trees, and cedars and cypresses, and date trees, and all trees of the field, and there was water on the mountains.

7 And he blessed the Lord who had led him out of Ur of the Chaldees, and had brought him to this land.

8 In the first year, in the seventh week, on the new moon of the first month, he built an altar on this mountain, and called on the name of the Lord and said, "You, the eternal God, are my God."

9 He offered on the altar a burnt sacrifice to the Lord that He should be with him and not forsake him all the days of his life.

10 He left that place and went toward the south, and he came to Hebron and Hebron was built at that time, and he lived there two years, and he went from that place into the land of the south, to Bealoth, and there was a famine in the land.

11 Abram went into Egypt in the third year of the week, and he dwelt in Egypt five years before his wife was torn away from him.

12 Now, Tanais in Egypt was built seven years after Hebron.

13 When Pharaoh seized Sarai, the wife of Abram the Lord plagued Pharaoh and his house with great plagues because of Sarai, Abram's wife.

14 Abram was celebrated and admired because of his great possessions of sheep, and cattle, and donkeys, and horses, and camels, and menservants, and maidservants, and in silver and gold. Lot and his brother's son were also wealthy.

15 Pharaoh gave back Sarai, the wife of Abram, and he sent him out of the land of Egypt, and he journeyed to the place where he had pitched his tent at the beginning, to the place of the altar, with Ai on the east, and Bethel on the west, and he blessed the Lord his God who had brought him back in peace.

16 In the forty-first jubilee in the third year of the first week, that he returned to this place and offered on it a burnt sacrifice, and called on the name of the Lord, and said, "You, the most high God, are my God forever and ever."

17 In the fourth year of this week Lot parted from him, and Lot lived in Sodom, and the men of Sodom sinned greatly.

18 It grieved him in his heart that his brother's son had parted from him because Abram had no children.

19 After Lot had parted from him, in the fourth year of this week. In that year when Lot was taken captive, the Lord said to Abram, "Lift up your eyes from the place where you are dwelling, northward and southward, and westward and eastward.

20 All the land that you see I will give to you and to your offspring forever, and I will make your offspring as the sand of the sea, though a man may number the dust of the earth, yet your offspring shall not be numbered.

21 Arise, walk through the land in the length of it and the breadth of it, and see it all. To your offspring will I give it." And Abram went to Hebron, and lived there.

22 And in this year came Chedorlaomer, king of Elam, and Amraphel, king of Shinar, and Arioch king of Sellasar, and Tergal, king of nations, and killed the king of Gomorrah, and the king of Sodom fled, and many fell through wounds in the valley of Siddim, by the Salt Sea.

23 They took captive Sodom and Adam and Zeboim, and they took Lot captive, the son of Abram's brother, and all his possessions, and they went to Dan.

24 One who had escaped came and told Abram that his brother's son had been taken captive.

25 And Abram equipped his household servants for Abram, and for his offspring, a tenth of the first-fruits to the Lord, and the Lord ordained it as a law forever that they should give it to the priests who served before Him, that they should possess it forever.

26 There is no limit of days to this law, for He has ordained it for the generations forever that they should give to the Lord the tenth of everything, of the seed and of the wine and of the oil and of the cattle and of the sheep.

27 He gave it to His priests to eat and to drink with joy before Him.

28 The king of Sodom came and bowed down to him, and said, "Our Lord Abram, give to us the souls which you have rescued, but let the booty be yours."

29 And Abram said to him, "I lift up my hands to the Most High God, that from a thread to a shoe-latchet I shall not take anything that is yours so that you could never say, I have made Abram rich, except only what the young men, Aner and Eschol, and Mamre have eaten, and the portion of the men who went with me. These shall take their portion."

[Chapter 14]

1 After these things, in the fourth year of this week, on the new moon of the third month, the word of the Lord came to Abram in a dream, saying, "Fear not, Abram, I am your defender, and your reward will be very great."

2 He said, "Lord, Lord, what will you give me, seeing I go from here childless, and the son of Maseq, the son of my handmaid, Eliezer of Damascus, he will be my heir, and to me you have given no offspring."

3 He said to him, "This man will not be your heir, but one that will come out of your own bowels. He will be your heir."

4 And He brought him out abroad, and said to him, "Look toward heaven and number the stars if you are able to number them."

5 He looked toward heaven, and beheld the stars. And He said to him, "so shall your offspring be."

6 And he believed in the Lord, and it was counted to him as righteousness.

7 God said to him, "I am the Lord that brought you out of Ur of the Chaldees, to give you the land of the Canaanites to possess it forever, and I will be God to you and to your offspring after you."

8 He said, "Lord, Lord, how shall I know that I shall inherit it?"

9 God said to him, "Take Me a heifer of three years, and a goat of three years, and a sheep of three years, and a turtle-dove, and a pigeon."

10 And he took all these in the middle of the month and he dwelt at the oak of Mamre, which is near Hebron.

11 He built an altar there, and sacrificed all these. He poured their blood on the altar, and divided them in half, and laid them over against each other, but the birds he did not divide.

12 Birds came down on the pieces, and Abram drove them away, and did not permit the birds to touch them.

13 It happened, when the sun had set, that an ecstasy fell on Abram, and such a horror of great darkness fell on him, and it was said to Abram, "Know of a surety that your offspring shall be a stranger in a land that is

not theirs, and they shall be brought into bondage, and afflicted for four hundred years.

14 The nation also to whom they will be in bondage will I judge, and after that they shall come out from that place with many possessions.

15 You will go to your fathers in peace, and be buried in a good old age.

16 But in the fourth generation they shall return here, for the iniquity of the Amorites is not yet full."

17 And he awoke from his sleep, and he arose, and the sun had set; and there was a flame, and a furnace was smoking, and a flame of fire passed between the pieces.

18 On that day the Lord made a covenant with Abram, saying, "To your offspring will I give this land, from the river of Egypt to the great river, the river Euphrates, the Kenites, the Kenizzites, the Kadmonites, the Perizzites, and the Rephaim, the Phakorites, and the Hivites, and the Amorites, and the Canaanites, and the Girgashites, and the Jebusites.

19 The day passed, and Abram offered the pieces, and the birds, and their fruit offerings, and their drink offerings, and the fire devoured them.

20 On that day we made a covenant with Abram, in the same way we had covenanted with Noah in this month; and Abram renewed the festival and laws for himself forever.

21 Abram rejoiced, and made all these things known to Sarai his wife. He believed that he would have offspring, but she did not bear.

22 Sarai advised her husband Abram, and said to him, "Go in to Hagar, my Egyptian maid, it may be that I shall build up offspring to you by her."

23 Abram listened to the voice of Sarai his wife, and said to her, "Do so." And Sarai took Hagar, her maid, the Egyptian, and gave her to Abram, her husband, to be his wife.

24 He went in to her, and she conceived and gave birth to a son, and he called his name Ishmael, in the fifth year of this week; and this was the eighty-sixth year in the life of Abram.

[Chapter 15]

1 In the fifth year of the fourth week of this jubilee, in the third month, in the middle of the month, Abram celebrated the feast of the first-fruits of the grain harvest.

2 And he made new offerings on the altar, the first-fruits of the produce to the Lord, a heifer, and a goat, and a sheep on the altar as a burnt sacrifice to the Lord; their fruit offerings and their drink offerings he offered on the altar with frankincense.

3 The Lord appeared to Abram, and said to him, "I am God Almighty. Examine yourself and demonstrate yourself before me and be perfect.

4 I will make My covenant between Me and you, and I will multiply you greatly."

5 Abram fell on his face, and God talked with him, and said, "My law is with you, and you will be the father of many nations.

6 Neither shall your name any more be called Abram, but your name from now on, even forever, shall be Abraham.

7 For I have made you the father of many nations.

8 I will make you very great, and I will make you into nations, and kings shall come forth from you.

9 I shall establish My covenant between Me and you, and your offspring after you, throughout their generations, for an eternal covenant, so that I may be a God to you, and to your offspring after you.

10 You may possess the land where you have been a sojourner, the land of Canaan, and you will possess it forever, and I will be their God."

11 The Lord said to Abraham, "Keep my covenant, you and your offspring after you, and circumcise every male among you, and circumcise your foreskins, and it shall be a token of an eternal covenant between Me and you.

12 And the eighth day you shall circumcise the child, every male throughout your generations, him that is born in the house, or whom you have bought with money from any stranger, whom you have acquired who is not of your offspring.

13 He that is born in your house shall surely be circumcised, and those whom you have bought with money shall be circumcised, and My covenant shall be in your flesh for an eternal ordinance.

14 The uncircumcised male who is not circumcised in the flesh of his foreskin on the eighth day, that soul shall be cut off from his people, for he has broken My covenant."

15 God said to Abraham, "As for Sarai your wife, her name shall no more be called Sarai, but Sarah shall be her name.

16 I will bless her, and give you a son by her, and I will bless him, and he shall become a nation, and kings of nations shall proceed from him."

17 Abraham fell on his face, and rejoiced, and said in his heart, "Shall a son be born to him that is a hundred years old, and shall Sarah, who is ninety years old, bring forth?"

18 Abraham said to God, "Oh, that Ishmael might live before you!"

19 God said, "Yea, and Sarah also shall bear you a son, and you will call his name Isaac, and I will establish My covenant with him, an everlasting covenant, and for his offspring after him.

20 And as for Ishmael also have I heard you, and behold I will bless him, and make him great, and multiply him greatly, and he shall beget twelve princes, and I will make him a great nation.

21 But My covenant will I establish with Isaac, whom Sarah shall bear to you this time next year."

22 God ceased speaking with him, and God went up from Abraham.

23 Abraham did according as God had said to him, and he took Ishmael his son, and all that were born in his house, and whom he had bought with his money, every male in his house, and circumcised the flesh of their foreskin.

24 On that same day was Abraham circumcised, and all the men of his house, and all those whom he had bought with money from the children of the stranger were circumcised with him.

25 This law is for all the generations forever, and there is no variance of days, and no omission of one day out of the eight days, for it is an eternal law, ordained and written on the heavenly tablets.

26 Every one that is born, the flesh of whose foreskin is not circumcised on the eighth day, does not belong to the children of the covenant which the Lord made with Abraham, but instead they belong to the children of destruction; nor is there any other sign on him that he is the Lord's, but he is destined to be destroyed and killed from the earth, and to be rooted out of the earth, for he has broken the covenant of the Lord our God.

27 All the angels of the presence (of the Lord) and all the angels of sanctification have been created already circumcised from the day of their creation, and before the angels of the presence (of the Lord) and the angels of sanctification He has sanctified Israel, that they should be with Him and with His holy angels.

28 Command the children of Israel and let them observe the sign of this covenant for their generations as an eternal law, and they will not be rooted out of the land.

29 For the command is ordained for a covenant, that they should observe it forever among all the children of Israel.

30 For Ishmael and his sons and his brothers, and Esau, the Lord did not cause them to come to Him, and he did not choose them. Although they are the children of Abraham, He knew them, but He chose Israel to be His people.

31 He sanctified them, and gathered them from among all the children of men; for there are many nations and many peoples, and all are His, and over all nations He has placed spirits in authority to lead them astray from Him.

32 But over Israel He did not appoint any angel or spirit, for He alone is their ruler, and He will preserve them and require them at the hand of His angels and His spirits, and at the hand of all His powers in order that He may preserve them and bless them, that they may be His and He may be theirs from now on forever.

33 I announce to you that the children of Israel will not keep true to this law, and they will not circumcise their sons according to all this law; for in the flesh of their circumcision they will omit this circumcision of their sons, and all of the sons of Beliar will leave their sons uncircumcised as they were born.

34 There will be great wrath from the Lord against the children of Israel because they have forsaken His covenant and turned aside from His word, and provoked (God) and blasphemed, because they do not observe the ordinance of this law; for they have treated their genitalia like the Gentiles, so that they may be removed and rooted out of the land. And there will no more be pardon or forgiveness to them for all the sin of this eternal error.

[Chapter 16]

1 On the new moon of the fourth month we appeared to Abraham, at the oak of Mamre, and we talked with him, and we announced to him that Sarah, his wife, would give him a son.

2 And Sarah laughed, for she heard that we had spoken these words to Abraham. We warned her, and she became afraid, and denied that she had laughed because of the words.

3 We told her the name of her son, as his name is ordained and written in the heavenly tablets and it is Isaac.

4 We told her that when we returned to her at a set time, she would have conceived a son.

5 In this month the Lord executed his judgments on Sodom, and Gomorrah, and Zeboim, and all the region of the Jordan, and He burned them with fire and brimstone, and destroyed them and they are destroyed until this day, because of all their works. They are wicked and vast sinners, and they defile themselves and commit fornication in their flesh, and work uncleanness on the earth as I have told you.

6 In like manner, God will execute judgment on the places where they have done similar to the uncleanness of the Sodomites, and they will suffer a judgment like that of Sodom.

7 But for Lot, we made an exception, for God remembered Abraham, and sent him out from the place of the overthrow.

8 And he and his daughters committed sin on the earth, such as had not been on the earth since the days of Adam until his time, for the man had sex with his daughters.

9 It was commanded and engraved concerning all his offspring, on the heavenly tablets, to remove them and root them out, and to execute judgment on them like the judgment of Sodom, and to leave no offspring of that man on earth on the day of condemnation.

10 In this month Abraham moved from Hebron, and departed and lived between Kadesh and Shur in the mountains of Gerar.

11 In the middle of the fifth month he moved from that place, and lived at the Well of the Oath.

12 In the middle of the sixth month the Lord visited Sarah and did to her as He had spoken and she conceived.

13 And she gave birth to a son in the third month. In the middle of the month, at the time of which the Lord had spoken to Abraham, on the festival of the first-fruits of the harvest, Isaac was born.

14 Abraham circumcised his son on the eighth day, he was the first that was circumcised according to the covenant that is ordained forever.

15 In the sixth year of the fourth week we came to Abraham at the Well of the Oath, and we appeared to him.

16 We returned in the seventh month, and found Sarah with child before us and we blessed him, and we announced to him all the things that had been decreed concerning him, so that he should not die until he should beget six more sons and saw them before he died.

17 But in Isaac should his name and offspring be called, and that all the offspring of his sons should be Gentiles, and be counted with the Gentiles; but from the sons of Isaac one should become a holy offspring, and should not be counted among the Gentiles.

18 For he should become the portion (dowry) of the Most High, and all his offspring had fallen into the possession of God, that they should be to the Lord a people for His possession above all nations and that they should become a kingdom and priests and a holy nation.

19 We went our way, and we announced to Sarah all that we had told him, and they both rejoiced with very great joy.

20 He built there an altar to the Lord who had delivered him, and who was causing him to rejoice in the land of his sojourning, and he celebrated a festival of joy in this month for seven days, near the altar which he had built at the Well of the Oath.

21 He built tents for himself and for his servants on this festival, and he was the first to celebrate the feast of tabernacles on the earth.

22 During these seven days he brought a burnt offering to the Lord each day to the altar consisting of two oxen, two rams, seven sheep, one male goat, for a sin offering that he might atone thereby for himself and for his offspring.

23 As an offering of thanks he brought, seven rams, seven kids, seven sheep, and seven male goats, and their fruit offerings and their drink offerings; and he burnt all the fat of it on the altar, a chosen offering to the Lord for a sweet smelling odor.

24 Morning and evening he burnt fragrant substances, frankincense and incense, and sweet spice, and nard, and myrrh, and spice, and aromatic plants; all these seven he offered, crushed, mixed together in equal parts and pure.

25 And he celebrated this feast during seven days, rejoicing with all his heart and with all his soul, he and all those who were in his house, and there was no stranger with him, nor any that was uncircumcised.

26 He blessed his Creator who had created him in his generation, for He had created him according to His good pleasure. God knew and perceived that from him would arise the plant of righteousness for the eternal generations, and from him a holy offspring, so that it should become like Him who had made all things.

27 He blessed and rejoiced, and he called the name of this festival the festival of the Lord, a joy acceptable to the Most High God.

28 And we blessed him forever, and all his offspring after him throughout all the generations of the earth, because he celebrated this festival in its season, according to the testimony of the heavenly tablets.

29 For this reason it is ordained on the heavenly tablets concerning Israel, that they shall celebrate the feast of tabernacles seven days with joy, in the seventh month, acceptable before the Lord as a statute forever throughout their generations every year.

30 To this there is no limit of days; for it is ordained forever regarding Israel that they should celebrate it and dwell in tents, and set wreaths on their heads, and take leafy boughs, and willows from the brook.

31 Abraham took branches of palm trees, and the fruit of good and pleasing trees, and every day going round the altar with the branches seven times a day in the morning, he praised and gave thanks to his God for all things in joy.

[Chapter 17]

1 In the first year of the fifth week Isaac was weaned in this jubilee, and Abraham made a great banquet in the third month, on the day his son Isaac was weaned.

2 Ishmael, the son of Hagar, the Egyptian, was in front of Abraham, his father, in his place, and Abraham rejoiced and blessed God because he had seen his sons and had not died childless.

3 He remembered the words which He had spoken to him on the day that Lot had departed from him, and he rejoiced because the Lord had given him offspring on the earth to inherit the earth, and he blessed with all his mouth the Creator of all things.

4 Sarah saw Ishmael playing and dancing, and Abraham rejoicing with great joy, and she became jealous of Ishmael and said to Abraham, "Throw out this bondwoman and her son. The son of this bondwoman will not be heir with my son, Isaac."

5 And the situation was troubling to Abraham, because of his maidservant and because of his son, because he did not want to drive them from him.

6 God said to Abraham "Let it not be troubling in your sight, because of the child and because of the bondwoman. Listen to Sarah and to all her words and

do them, for in Isaac shall your name and offspring be called.

7 But as for the son of this bondwoman I will make him a great nation, because he is of your offspring."

8 Abraham got up early in the morning, and took bread and a bottle of water, and placed them on the shoulders of Hagar and the child, and sent her away.

9 And she departed and wandered in the wilderness of Beersheba, and the water in the bottle was spent, and the child was thirsty, and was not able to go on, and fell down.

10 His mother took him and laid him under an olive tree, and went and sat her down over away from him at the distance of a bow-shot; for she said, "Let me not see the death of my child," and she sat and wept.

11 An angel of God, one of the holy ones, said to her, "Why do you weep, Hagar? Stand. Take the child, and hold him in your hand, for God has heard your voice, and has seen the child."

12 She opened her eyes, and she saw a well of water, and she went and filled her bottle with water, and she gave her child a drink, and she arose and went towards the wilderness of Paran.

13 And the child grew and became an archer, and God was with him, and his mother took him a wife from among the daughters of Egypt.

14 She (the wife) gave birth to a son, and he called his name Nebaioth; for she said, "The Lord was close to me when I called on him."

15 In the seventh week, in the first year of it, in the first month in this jubilee, on the twelfth of this month, there were voices in heaven regarding Abraham, that he was faithful in all that He told him, and that he loved the Lord, and that in every affliction he was faithful.

16 Prince Mastema came and said before God, "Look, Abraham loves Isaac his son, and he delights in him above all things, tell him to offer him as a burnt-offering on the altar, and You will see if he will do this command, and You will know if he is faithful in everyway that You test him.

17 The Lord knew that Abraham was faithful throughout all his afflictions, for He had tried him through his country and with famine, and had tried him with the wealth of kings, and had tried him again through his wife, when she was torn from him, and with circumcision; and had tried him through Ishmael and Hagar, his maid-servant, when he sent them away.

18 In everything that He had tried him, he was found faithful, and his soul was not impatient, and he was not slow to act, because he was faithful and a lover of the Lord.

[Chapter 18]

1 God said to him, "Abraham. Abraham." and he said, "Look, here am I."

2 He said, "Take your beloved son, Isaac, whom you love, and go to the high country, and offer him on one of the mountains which I will point out to you."

3 He got early in the morning and saddled his donkey, and took two young men with him, and Isaac his son, and split the wood of the burnt offering, and he went to the place on the third day, and he saw the place afar off.

4 He came to a well of water (near Mount Moriah), and he said to his young men, "You stay here with the donkey, and I and the lad shall go yonder, and when we have worshipped we shall come back to you."

5 He took the wood of the burnt-offering and laid it on Isaac his son, and he took the fire and the knife, and they went both of them together to that place.

6 Isaac said to his father, "Father" and he said, "Here am I, my son." He said to him, "Look, we have the fire, and the knife, and the wood, but where is the sheep for the burnt-offering, father?"

7 He said, "God will provide for himself a sheep for a burnt-offering, my son." And he neared the place of the mountain of God.

8 He built an altar, and he placed the wood on the altar, and bound Isaac his son, and placed him on the wood that was on the altar, and stretched out his hand to take the knife to kill Isaac, his son.

9 I stood in the presence of him, and before prince Mastema, (and the holy angels stood and wept over the altar as prince Mastema and his angels rejoiced and said "Isaac will be destroyed and we will see if Abraham is faithful), and the Lord said, "Command him not to lay his hand on the lad, nor to do anything to him, for I have shown that he fears the Lord."

10 I called to him from heaven, and said to him, "Abraham, Abraham." and he was terrified and said, "Here am I."

11 I said to him, "Lay not your hand on the lad, neither do anything to him; for now I have shown that you fear the Lord, and have not withheld your son, your first-born son, from me."

12 Prince Mastema was put to shame (and was bound by the angels); and Abraham lifted up his eyes and looked and saw a ram caught by his horns, and Abraham went and took the ram and offered it as a burnt-offering in place of his son.

13 Abraham called that place "The Lord has seen," so that it is said the Lord has seen. This is Mount Zion.

14 The Lord called Abraham by his name a second time from heaven, as he caused us to appear to speak to him in the name of the Lord.

15 He said, "By Myself have I sworn," said the Lord, "Because you have done this thing, and have not withheld your son, your beloved son, from Me, that in blessing I will bless you, and in multiplying I will multiply your offspring as the stars of heaven, and as the sand which is on the seashore.

16 Your offspring shall inherit the cities of their enemies, and in your offspring shall all nations of the earth be blessed. Because you have obeyed My voice, and I have shown to all that you are faithful to Me in all that I have said to you, "Go in peace."

17 Abraham went back to his young men, and they stood and went back together to Beersheba, and Abraham lived by the Well of the Oath.

18 And he celebrated this festival every year, seven days with joy, and he called it the festival of the Lord according to the seven days during which he went and returned in peace.

19 Accordingly, it has been ordained and written on the heavenly tablets regarding Israel and its children that they should observe this festival seven days with the joy of festival.

[Chapter 19]

1 In the first year of the first week in the forty-second jubilee, Abraham returned and lived across from Hebron, in Kirjath Arba for two weeks of years.

2 In the first year of the third week of this jubilee the days of the life of Sarah were completed, and she died in Hebron.

3 Abraham went to mourn over her and bury her, and we tested him to see if his spirit was patient and he had neither anger nor contempt in the words of his mouth, and he was found patient in this and was not disturbed.

4 In patience of spirit he discussed with the children of Heth that they should give him a place in which to bury his dead.

5 And the Lord gave him grace before all who saw him, and he asked the sons of Heth in gentleness, and they gave him the land of the double cave over beside Mamre, that is Hebron, for four hundred pieces of silver.

6 They said to him, "We shall give it to you for nothing," but he would not take it from them for nothing, for he gave the price of the place and paid the money in full. And he bowed down before them twice, and after this he buried his dead in the double cave.

7 All the days of the life of Sarah were one hundred and twenty-seven years, that is, two jubilees and four weeks and one year, these are the days of the years of the life of Sarah.

8 This is the tenth trial with which Abraham was tested, and he was found faithful and patient in spirit.

9 He did not say a single word regarding the rumor in the land of how God had said that He would give it to him and to his offspring after him, but instead he begged for a place there to bury his dead. Because he was found faithful, it was recorded on the heavenly tablets that he was the friend of God.

10 In the fourth year of it (this jubilee) he took a wife for his son Isaac and her name was Rebecca the daughter of Bethuel, the son of Nahor, the brother of Abraham the sister of Laban and daughter of Bethuel; and Bethuel was the son of Melca, who was the wife of Nahor, the brother of Abraham.

11 Abraham took to himself a third wife from among the daughters of his household servants, for Hagar had died before Sarah, and her name was Keturah,. And she gave birth to six sons, Zimram, and Jokshan, and Medan, and Midian, and Ishbak, and Shuah, in the two weeks of years.

12 In the sixth week, in the second year of it, Rebecca gave birth to two sons of Isaac, Jacob and Esau.

13 And Jacob had no beard and was a straight and tall man who dwelt in tents, and Esau was a powerful a man of the field, and was hairy.

14 The youths grew, and Jacob learned to write, but Esau did not learn, for he was a man of the field and a hunter, and he learned war, and all his deeds were fierce.

15 Abraham loved Jacob, but Isaac loved Esau.

16 And Abraham saw the deeds of Esau, and he knew that in Jacob should his name and offspring be called. He called Rebecca and gave commandment regarding Jacob, for he knew that she too loved Jacob much more than Esau.

17 He said to her, "My daughter, watch over my son Jacob, for he shall take my place on the earth. He shall be a blessing throughout the children of men and for the glory of all the offspring of Shem.

18 I know that the Lord will choose him to be a people (nation) and a possession to Himself, above all peoples that are on the face of the earth.

19 Isaac, my son, loves Esau more than Jacob, but I see that you truly love Jacob.

20 Add still further to your kindness to him, and regard him in love, for he shall be a blessing to us on the earth from now on to all generations of the earth.

21 Let your hands be strong and let your heart rejoice in your son Jacob, for I have loved him far beyond all my sons. He shall be blessed forever, and his offspring shall fill the whole earth.

22 If a man can number the sand of the earth, his offspring also shall be numbered.

23 And all the blessings with which the Lord has blessed me and my offspring shall belong to Jacob and his offspring always.

24 In his offspring shall my name be blessed, and the name of my fathers, Shem, Noah, Enoch, Mahalalel, Enos, Seth, and Adam. And these shall serve to lay the foundations of the heaven, and to strengthen the earth, and to renew all the stars and planets which are in the sky.

27 He called Jacob and kissed him in front of Rebecca, his mother, and blessed him, and said, "Jacob, my beloved son, whom my soul loves, may God bless you from above the sky, and may He give you all the blessings with which He blessed Adam, Enoch, Noah,

and Shem; and all the things of which He told me, and all the things which He promised to give me, may He cause to be yours and your offspring forever, according to the days of heaven above the earth.

28 And the Spirits of Mastema shall not rule over you or over your offspring or turn you from the Lord, who is your God from now on forever.

29 May the Lord God be a father to you and may you be like His first-born son, and to the people always. Go in peace, my son."

30 And they both went out together from Abraham.

31 Rebecca loved Jacob, with all her heart and with all her soul, very much more than Esau, but Isaac loved Esau much more than Jacob.

[Chapter 20]

1 In the forty-second jubilee, in the first year of the seventh week, Abraham called Ishmael, and his twelve sons, and Isaac and his two sons, and the six sons of Keturah, and their sons.

2 And he commanded them that they should observe the way of the Lord, that they should work righteousness, and love each his neighbor, and act in this manner among all men, that they should each walk with regard to the ways of the Lord to do judgment and righteousness on the earth.

3 He also commanded them that they should circumcise their sons, according to the covenant, which God had made with them, and not deviate to the right or the left of all the paths which the Lord had commanded us, and that we should keep ourselves from all fornication and uncleanness.

4 He said, "If any woman or maid commits fornication among you, burn her with fire. And do not let them commit fornication with her with their eyes or their heart; and do not let them take to themselves wives from the daughters of Canaan, because the offspring of Canaan will be rooted out of the land."

5 He told them about the judgment on the giants, and the judgment on the Sodomites, how they had been judged because of their wickedness, and had died because of their fornication and uncleanness, and corruption through fornication together.

6 He said, "Guard yourselves from all fornication and uncleanness, and from all pollution of sin, or you will make our name a curse, and your whole life a shame, and all your sons to be destroyed by the sword, and you will become accursed like Sodom, and all that is left of you shall be as the sons of Gomorrah.

7 I implore you, my sons, love the God of heaven and cling to all His commandments.

8 Do not walk after their idols and after their ways of uncleanness, and do not make yourselves molten or graven gods. They are empty, and there is no spirit in them, for they are work of men's hands, and all who trust in them, trust in nothing.

9 Do not serve them, nor worship them, but serve the most high God, and worship Him continually, and hope for His presence always, and work uprightness and righteousness before Him, that He may have pleasure in you and grant you His mercy, and send rain on you morning and evening, and bless all your works which you have performed on the earth, and bless your bread and your water, and bless the fruit of your womb and the fruit of your land, and the herds of your cattle, and the flocks of your sheep.

10 You will be for a blessing on the earth, and all nations of the earth will desire you, and bless your sons in my name, that they may be blessed as I am."

11 He gave to Ishmael and to his sons, and to the sons of Keturah, gifts, and sent them away from Isaac his son, and he gave everything to Isaac his son.

12 Ishmael and his sons, and the sons of Keturah and their sons, went together and settled from Paran to the border of Babylon in all the land that is toward the East facing the desert.

13 These mingled (intermarried) with each other, and their names were called Arabs, and Ishmaelites.

[Chapter 21]

1 In the sixth year of the seventh week of this jubilee Abraham called Isaac his son, and commanded him, saying, "I have become old. I do not know the day of my death but I am full of my days.

2 I am one hundred and seventy-five years old, and throughout all the days of my life I have remembered the Lord, and sought with all my heart to do His will, and to walk uprightly in all His ways.

3 My soul has hated idols. I have given my heart and spirit to the observance of the will of Him who created me.

4 For He is the living God, and He is holy and faithful, and He is righteous beyond all, and He is no respecter of men or of their gifts, for God is righteous, and executes judgment on all those who transgress His commandments and despise His covenant.

5 My son, observe His commandments and His law and His judgments, and do not walk after the abominations and after the graven images and after the molten images.

6 And eat no blood at all of animals or cattle, or of any bird that flies in the heaven.

7 If you kill a sacrificial animal as an acceptable peace offering, kill it, and pour out its blood on the altar. Place all the fat of the offering on the altar with fine flour and the meat offering mingled with oil with its drink offering. Place them all together on the altar of burnt offering. It is a sweet odor before the Lord.

8 You will offer the fat of the sacrifice of thanks offerings on the fire which is on the altar, and the fat which is on the belly, and all the fat on the inside, behind the two kidneys, and all the fat that is on them,

and lobes of the liver you will remove, together with the kidneys.

9 Offer all these for a sweet odor acceptable before the Lord, with its meat-offering and with its drink-offering, and the bread of the offering to the Lord.

10 Eat its meat on that day and on the second day, but do not let the sun go down on it until it is eaten. Let nothing be left over for the third day, for it is not acceptable. Let it no longer be eaten, and all who eat of it will bring sin on themselves, for thus I have found it written in the books of my forefathers, and in the words of Enoch, and in the words of Noah.

11 On all your offerings you will scatter salt, and do not let the salt of the covenant be lacking in all your offerings before the Lord.

12 As regards the wood of the sacrifices, beware to bring only these and no other wood to the altar in addition to these, cypress, bay, almond, fir, pine, cedar, savin, fig, olive, myrrh, laurel, and aspalathus.

13 Of these kinds of wood lay on the altar under the sacrifice, such as have been tested as to their appearance, and do not lay on it any split or dark wood, but only hard and clean wood, without fault, a healthy, new growth. Do not lay old wood on it, because there is no longer fragrance in it as before.

14 Besides these kinds of wood there is none other that you will place on the altar, for the fragrance is dispersed, and the smell of its fragrance will not go up to heaven.

15 Observe this commandment and do it, my son, that you may be upright in all your deeds.

16 Be clean in your body at all times. Wash yourself with water before you approach to offer on the altar. Wash your hands and your feet before you draw near to the altar, and when you are done sacrificing, wash your hands and feet again.

17 Let no blood appear on you or on your clothes. Be on your guard against blood, my son. Be on your guard continually and cover it with dust.

18 Do not eat any blood for it is the soul. Eat no blood whatsoever.

19 Take no payment for shedding the blood of man, or it will cause it to be shed without fear of punishment, without judgment. It is the blood that is shed that causes the earth to sin, and the earth cannot be cleansed from the blood of man except by the blood of he who shed it.

20 Take no present or gift for the blood of man, blood for blood, that you may be accepted before the Lord, the Most High God. He is the defense of the good, so that you may be preserved from all evil, and that He may withhold you from every kind of death.

21 I see, my son, all the works of the children of men are sin and wickedness, and all their deeds are uncleanness and an abomination and a pollution, and there is no righteousness in them.

22 Beware, or you will walk in their ways and tread in their paths, and commit a sin worthy of death before the Most High God. He will hide His face from you and give you back into the hands of your transgression, and root you out of the land, and your offspring likewise from under heaven, and your name and your offspring shall perish from the whole earth.

23 Turn away from all their deeds and all their uncleanness, and observe the laws of the Most High God, and do His will and be upright in all things.

24 If you do this, He will bless you in all your deeds, and will raise up from you a plant of righteousness through all the earth, throughout all generations of the earth, and my name and your name shall not be forgotten under heaven forever.

25 Go, my son in peace. May the Most High God, my God and your God, strengthen you to do His will, and may He bless all your offspring and the remainder of your offspring for the generations forever, with all righteous blessings, that you may be a blessing on all the earth."

26 And he went out from him rejoicing.

[Chapter 22]

1 In the first week in the forty-fourth jubilee, in the second year, that is, the year in which Abraham died, Isaac and Ishmael came from the Well of the Oath to celebrate the feast of weeks which is the feast of the first-fruits of the harvest to Abraham, their father, and Abraham rejoiced because his two sons had come.

2 Isaac had many possessions in Beersheba, and Isaac desired to go and see his possessions and to return to his father.

3 In those days Ishmael came to see his father, and they both came together, and Isaac offered a sacrifice for a burnt offering, and presented it on the altar of his father that he had made in Hebron.

4 He offered a thanks offering and made a feast of joy in the presence of Ishmael, his brother, and Rebecca made new cakes from the new grain, and gave them to Jacob, her son, to take them to Abraham, his father, from the first-fruits of the land, that he might eat and bless the Creator of all things before he died.

5 Isaac, also, sent Jacob to Abraham with an offering of his best for thanks so that he might eat and drink.

6 He ate and drank, and blessed the Most High God, who has created heaven and earth, who has made all the fat things of the earth, and given them to the children of men that they might eat and drink and bless their Creator.

7 "And now I give thanks to You, my God, because you have caused me to see this day, behold, I am one hundred three score and fifteen years, an old man and full of days, and all my days have been peace to me.

8 The sword of the adversary has not overcome me in all that You have given me and my children all the days of my life until this day.

9 My God, may Your mercy and Your peace be on Your servant, and on the offspring of his sons, that they may be to You a chosen nation and an inheritance from among all the nations of the earth from now on to all the days of the generations of the earth, to all the ages."

10 He called Jacob and said, "My son Jacob, may the God of all bless you and strengthen you to do righteousness, and His will before Him, and may He choose you and your offspring that you may become a people for His inheritance according to His will always.

11 My son, Jacob, draw near and kiss me." And he drew near and kissed him, and he said, "Blessed be my son Jacob and all the sons of God Most High, to all the ages. May God give to you an offspring of righteousness; and some of your sons may He sanctify throughout the whole earth. May nations serve you, and all the nations bow themselves before your offspring.

12 Be strong in the presence of men, and exercise authority over all the offspring of Seth. Then your ways and the ways of your sons will be justified, so that they shall become a holy nation.

13 May the Most High God give you all the blessings with which He has blessed me and He blessed Noah and Adam. May they rest on the sacred head of your offspring from generation to generation forever.

14 May He cleanse you from all unrighteousness and impurity so that you may be forgiven all the transgressions, which you have committed ignorantly. May He strengthen you, and bless you.

15 May you inherit the whole earth, and may He renew His covenant with you so that you may be to Him a nation for His inheritance for all the ages, and so that He may be to you and to your offspring a God in truth and righteousness throughout all the days of the earth.

16 My son Jacob, remember my words. Observe the commandments of Abraham, your father, separate yourself from the nations (gentiles), and do not eat with them. Do not emulate their works, and do not associate with them because their works are unclean, and all their ways are a pollution and an abomination and uncleanness.

17 They offer their sacrifices to the dead and they worship evil spirits, and they eat over the graves, and all their works are empty and nothingness.

18 They have no heart to understand and their eyes do not see what their works are, and how they go astray by saying to a piece of wood, "You are my God," and to a stone, "You are my Lord and you are my deliverer," because the stone and wood have no heart.

19 And as for you, my son Jacob, may the Most High God help you and the God of heaven bless you and remove you from their uncleanness and from all their error.

20 Jacob, be warned. Do not take a wife from any offspring of the daughters of Canaan, for all his offspring are to be rooted out of the earth.

21 Because of the transgression of Ham, Canaan erred, and all his offspring shall be destroyed from the earth including any remnant of it, and none springing from him shall exist except on the day of judgment.

22 And as for all the worshippers of idols and the profane, there shall be no hope for them in the land of the living, and no one on earth will remember them, for they shall descend into the abode of the dead, and they shall go into the place of condemnation. As the children of Sodom were taken away from the earth, so will all those who worship idols be taken away.

23 Fear not, my son Jacob. Be not dismayed, son of Abraham. May the Most High God preserve you from destruction, and may He deliver you from all the paths of error.

24 This house have I built for myself that I might put my name on it in the earth. It is given to you and to your offspring forever, and it will be named the house of Abraham. It is given to you and your offspring forever, for you will build my house and establish my name before God forever. Your offspring and your name will stand throughout all generations of the earth."

25 He ceased commanding him and blessing him.

26 The two lay together on one bed, and Jacob slept in the embracing arms of Abraham, his father's father, and he kissed him seven times, and his affection and his heart rejoiced over him.

27 He blessed him with all his heart and said, "The Most High God, the God of all, and Creator of all, who brought me out from Ur of the Chaldees that He might give me this land to inherit forever, that I might establish a holy offspring.

28 Blessed be the Most High forever."

29 And he blessed Jacob and said, "May Your grace and Your mercy be lift up on my son, over whom I rejoice with all my heart and my affection and on his offspring always.

30 Do not forsake him, nor diminish him from now to the days of eternity, and may Your eyes be opened on him and on his offspring, that You may preserve him, and bless him, and may sanctify him as a nation for Your inheritance. Bless him with all Your blessings from now to all the days of eternity, and renew Your covenant and Your grace with him and with his offspring according to all Your good pleasure to all the generations of the earth."

[Chapter 23]

1 He placed Jacob's two fingers on his eyes, and he blessed the God of gods, and he covered his face and

stretched out his feet and slept the sleep of eternity, and was gathered to his fathers.

2 In spite of all this, Jacob was lying in his embracing arms, and knew not that Abraham, his father's father, was dead.

3 Jacob awoke from his sleep, and realized Abraham was cold as ice, and he said, "Father, father," but there was no answer, and he knew that he was dead.

4 He arose from his embracing arms and ran and told Rebecca, his mother, and Rebecca went to Isaac in the night, and told him and they went together, and Jacob with them, and a lamp was in his hand, and when they had gone in they found Abraham lying dead.

5 Isaac fell on the face of his father and wept and kissed him.

6 Ishmael, his son, heard the voices in the house of Abraham, and he arose, and went to Abraham his father, and wept over Abraham his father, he and all the house of Abraham, and they wept greatly.

7 His sons, Isaac and Ishmael, buried him in the double cave, near Sarah his wife, and all the men of his house, and Isaac and Ishmael, and all their sons, and all the sons of Keturah in their places wept for him forty days and then the days of weeping for Abraham were ended.

8 He lived three jubilees and four weeks of years, one hundred and seventy-five years, and completed the days of his life, being old and full of days.

9 For the days of the lives of their forefathers were nineteen jubilees; and after the Flood they began to grow less than nineteen jubilees, and to decrease in jubilees, and to grow old quickly, and to be full of their days because of the many types of hardships and the wickedness of their ways, with the exception of Abraham.

10 For Abraham was perfect in all his deeds with the Lord, and well-pleasing in righteousness all the days of his life. Yet, he did not complete four jubilees in his life, when he had grown old because of the wickedness in the world, and was full of his days.

11 All the generations which shall arise from this time until the day of the great judgment shall grow old quickly, before they complete two jubilees, and their knowledge shall forsake them because of their old age and all their knowledge shall vanish away.

12 In those days, if a man lives a jubilee and a-half of years, they shall say regarding him, "He has lived long," and the greater part of his days are pain and sorrow and hardship, and there is no peace. For calamity follows on calamity, and wound on wound, and hardship on hardship, and evil deeds on evil deeds, and illness on illness, and all judgments of destruction such as these, piled one on another, illness and overthrow, and snow and frost and ice, and fever, and chills, and mental and physical incapacity, and famine, and death, and sword, and captivity, and all kinds of calamities and pains.

13 All of these shall come on an evil generation, which transgresses on the earth. Their works are uncleanness and fornication, and pollution and abominations.

14 Then they shall say, "The days of the forefathers were many, lasting a thousand years, and were good; but the days of our lives, if a man lives a long life are three score years and ten, and, if he is strong, four score years, and those evil, and there is no peace in the days of this evil generation."

15 In that generation the sons shall convict their fathers and their elders of sin and unrighteousness, and of the words of their mouths and the great wickedness which they perform, and concerning their forsaking the covenant which the Lord made between them and Him. They should observe and do all His commandments and His ordinances and all His laws, without departing either to the right hand or the left.

16 For all have done evil, and every mouth speaks sinfully and all their works are unclean and an abomination, and all their ways are pollution, uncleanness, and destruction.

17 The earth shall be destroyed because of all their works, and there shall be no fruit (seed) of the vine, and no oil; for their actions are altogether faithless, and they shall all perish together, beasts and cattle and birds, and all the fish of the sea, because of the children of men.

18 They shall quarrel with one another, the young with the old, and the old with the young, the poor with the rich, the lowly with the great, and the beggar with the prince, because of the law and the covenant; for they have forgotten the commandments, and covenant, and feasts, and months, and Sabbaths, and jubilees, and all judgments.

19 They shall use swords and war to turn them back to the way, but they shall not return until much blood has been shed on the earth, one by another.

20 Those who have escaped shall not return from their wickedness to the way of righteousness, but they shall all raise themselves to a high status through deceit and wealth, that they may each steal all that belongs of his neighbor, and they shall name the great name (of God), but not in truth and not in righteousness, and they shall defile the holy of holies with their uncleanness and the corruption of their pollution.

21 A great punishment shall come because of the deeds of this generation, and the Lord will give them over to the sword and to judgment and to slavery, and to be plundered and consumed.

22 And He will arouse the Gentile sinners against them, who have neither mercy nor compassion, and who shall respect no one, neither old nor young, nor any one, for they are more wicked, strong, and evil than all the children of men.

23 They shall use violence against Israel and shall violate Jacob, and much blood shall be shed on the

earth, and there shall be none to gather the dead and none to bury them.

24 In those days they shall cry aloud, and call and pray that they may be saved from the hand of the sinners, the Gentiles. But none shall be excluded (none shall be saved).

25 The heads of the children shall be white with grey hair, and a child of three weeks shall appear old like a man of one hundred years, and their work and worth shall be destroyed by hardship and oppression.

26 In those days the children shall begin to study the laws, and to seek the commandments, and to return to the path of righteousness.

27 The days shall begin to grow many and increase among those children of men until their days draw close to one thousand years, and to a greater number of years than before age was recorded.

28 There shall be neither old man nor one who is aged, for all shall be as children and youths.

29 All their days shall be full and they shall live in peace and in joy, and there shall be neither Satan nor any evil destroyer because all their days shall be days of blessing and healing.

30 And at that time the Lord will heal His servants, and they shall rise up and see great peace, and drive out their adversaries. The righteous shall understand and be thankful, and rejoice with joy forever and ever, and they shall see all their judgments and all their curses enacted on their enemies.

31 Their bones shall rest in the earth, and their spirits shall have much joy, and they shall know that it is the Lord who executes judgment, and shows mercy to hundreds and thousands and to all that love Him.

32 Moses, write down these words. Write them and record them on the heavenly tablets for a testimony for the generations forever.

[Chapter 24]

1 It happened after the death of Abraham, that the Lord blessed Isaac his son, who arose from Hebron and went and dwelt at the Well of the Vision in the first year of the third week of this jubilee, seven years.

2 In the first year of the fourth week a famine began in the land, besides the first famine, which had been in the days of Abraham.

3 Jacob made lentil soup, and Esau came from the field hungry. He said to Jacob his brother, "Give me some of this red soup."

4 Jacob said to him, "Sell to me your birthright and I will give you bread, and also some of this lentil soup." And Esau said in his heart, "If I shall die what good is my birthright to me?"

5 He said to Jacob, "I give it to you." And Jacob said, "Swear to me, this day," and he swore to him.

6 And Jacob gave his brother Esau bread and soup, and he ate until he was satisfied, and Esau despised his birthright. For this reason was Esau's name called Edom (red), because of the red soup which Jacob gave him for his birthright.

7 And Jacob became the elder, and Esau was brought down from his dignity.

8 The famine covered the land, and Isaac departed to go down into Egypt in the second year of this week, and went to the king of the Philistines to Gerar, into the presence of Abimelech.

9 The Lord appeared to him and said to him, "Do not go down into Egypt. Dwell in the land that I shall tell you of, and sojourn in this land, and I will be with you and bless you.

10 For to you and to your offspring will I give all this land, and I will establish My oath which I swore to Abraham your father, and I will multiply your offspring as the stars of heaven, and will give to your offspring all this land.

11 And in your offspring shall all the nations of the earth be blessed, because your father obeyed My voice, and kept My ways and My commandments, and My laws, and My ordinances, and My covenant; and now do as you are told and dwell in this land."

12 And he dwelt in Gelar three weeks of years. And Abimelech commanded concerning him, and concerning all that was his, saying, "Any man that shall touch him or anything that is his shall surely die."

13 Isaac grew strong among the Philistines, and he got many possessions, oxen and sheep and camels and donkeys and a great household.

14 He sowed in the land of the Philistines and brought in a hundred-fold, and Isaac became very great, and the Philistines envied him.

15 Now all the wells that the servants of Abraham had dug during the life of Abraham, the Philistines had stopped them after the death of Abraham, and filled them with dirt.

16 Abimelech said to Isaac, "Go from us, for you are much mightier than we." Isaac departed from that place in the first year of the seventh week, and sojourned in the valleys of Gerar.

17 And they dug the wells of water again which the servants of Abraham, his father, had dug, and which the Philistines had filled after the death of Abraham his father, and he called their names as Abraham his father had named them.

18 The servants of Isaac dug a well in the valley, and found fresh, flowing water, and the shepherds of Gerar bickered with the shepherds of Isaac, saying, "The water is ours." Isaac called the name of the well "Perversity," because they had been perverse with us.

19 And they dug a second well, and they fought for that also, and he called its name "Enmity."

20 He left that place and they dug another well, and for that they did not fight, and he called the name of it "Room," and Isaac said, "Now the Lord has made room for us, and we have increased in the land."

21 And he went up from that place to the Well of the Oath in the first year of the first week in the forty-fourth jubilee.

22 The Lord appeared to him in the night of the new moon of the first month, and said to him, "I am the God of Abraham your father; fear not, for I am with you, and shall bless you and shall surely multiply your offspring as the sand of the earth, for the sake of Abraham my servant."

23 And he built an altar there, which Abraham his father had first built, and he called on the name of the Lord, and he offered sacrifice to the God of Abraham his father.

24 They dug a well and they found fresh, flowing water.

25 The servants of Isaac dug another well and did not find water, and they went and told Isaac that they had not found water, and Isaac said, "I have sworn this day to the Philistines and this thing has been announced to us."

26 And he called the name of that place the Well of the Oath, because there he had sworn to Abimelech and Ahuzzath, his friend, and also to Phicol, who was the commander and his host.

27 Isaac knew that day that he had sworn to them under pressure to make peace with them.

28 On that day Isaac cursed the Philistines and said, "Cursed be the Philistines to the day of wrath and indignation from among all nations. May God make them a disdain and a curse and an object of anger and indignation in the hands of the Gentile sinners and in the hands of the Kittim.

29 Whoever escapes the sword of the enemy and the Kittim, may the righteous nation root them out in judgment from under heaven. They shall be the enemies and foes of my children throughout their generations on the earth.

30 No part of them will remain. Not even one shall be spared on the day of the wrath of judgment. The offspring of the Philistines will experience destruction, rooting out, and expulsion from the earth and this is all that is in store for them. There shall not be a name or an offspring left on the earth for these Caphtorim (the seat of the Philistine state).

31 For though he rises up to heaven, he shall be brought down, and though he makes himself strong on earth, from there shall he be dragged out, and though he hide himself among the nations, even from that place shall he be rooted out.

32 Though he descends into the abode of the dead, his condemnation shall be great, and he shall have no peace there.

33 If he goes into captivity by the hands of those that seek his life they shall kill him on the way (to his imprisonment), and neither his name nor offspring shall be left on all the earth. Into an eternal curse shall he depart."

34 It is written and engraved concerning him on the heavenly tablets, that on the day of judgment he will be rooted out of the earth.

[Chapter 25]

1 In the second year of this week in this jubilee, Rebecca called Jacob her son, and spoke to him, saying, "My son, do not take a wife from the daughters of Canaan as Esau, your brother, who took two wives of the daughters of Canaan, and they have made my soul bitter with all their unclean acts, for all their actions are fornication and lust, and there is no righteousness in them, because their deeds are evil.

2 I love you greatly, my son, and my heart and my affection bless you every hour of the day and in every night.

3 Now, my son, listen to my voice, and do the will of your mother, and do not take a wife of the daughters of this land, but only from the house of my father, and of those related to my father.

4 If you will take you a wife of the house of my father, the Most High God will bless you, and your children shall be a righteous generation and a holy offspring." And then spoke Jacob to Rebecca, his mother, and said to her, "Look, mother, I am nine weeks of years old, and I have neither been with nor have I touched any woman, nor have I engaged myself to any, nor I have even thought of taking me wife of the daughters of Canaan.

5 For I remember, mother, the words of Abraham, our father, for he commanded me not to take a wife of the daughters of Canaan, but to take me a wife from the offspring of my father's house and from my kind folks.

6 I have heard before that daughters have been born to Laban, your brother, and I have set my heart on them to take a wife from among them.

7 For this reason I have guarded myself in my spirit against sinning or being corrupted in any way throughout all the days of my life; for with regard to lust and fornication, Abraham, my father, gave me many commands.

8 Despite all that he has commanded me, these two and twenty years my brother has argued with me, and spoken frequently to me and said, "My brother, take a wife that is a sister of my two wives," but I refused to do as he has done.

9 I swear before you mother, that all the days of my life I will not take me a wife from the daughters of the offspring of Canaan, and I will not act wickedly as my brother has done.

10 Do not be afraid mother, be assured that I shall do your will and walk in uprightness, and not corrupt my ways forever."

11 When she heard this, she lifted up her face to heaven and extended the fingers of her hands, and opened her mouth and blessed the Most High God, who had

created the heaven and the earth, and she gave Him thanks and praise.

12 She said, "Blessed be the Lord God, and may His holy name be blessed forever and ever. He has given me Jacob as a pure son and a holy offspring; for he is Yours, and Yours shall his offspring be continually, throughout all the generations forever.

13 Bless him, O Lord, and place in my mouth the blessing of righteousness, that I may bless him."

14 At that hour, when the spirit of righteousness descended into her mouth, she placed both her hands on the head of Jacob, and said, "Blessed are You, Lord of righteousness and God of the ages, and may You bless him beyond all the generations of men.

15 My Son, may He give you the path of righteousness, and reveal righteousness to your offspring.

16 May He make your sons many during your life, and may they arise according to the number of the months of the year. And may their sons become many and great beyond the stars of heaven, and may their numbers be more than the sand of the sea.

17 May He give them this good and pleasing land, as He said He would give it to Abraham and to his offspring after him always, and may they hold it as a possession forever.

18 My son, may I see blessed children born to you during my life, and may all your offspring be blessed and holy.

19 And as you have refreshed your mother's spirit during her life, the womb of her that gave birth to you blesses you now. My affection and my heart (breasts) bless you and my mouth and my tongue greatly praise you.

20 Increase and spread over the earth. May your offspring be perfect in the joy of heaven and earth forever. May your offspring rejoice, and on the great day of peace may they have peace.

21 May your name and your offspring endure to all the ages, and may the Most High God be their God, and may the God of righteousness dwell with them, and may His sanctuary be built by you all the ages.

22 Blessed be he that blesses you, and all flesh that curses you falsely, may it be cursed."

23 And she kissed him, and said to him, "May the Lord of the world love you as the heart of your mother and her affection rejoice in you and bless you." And she ceased from blessing.

[Chapter 26]

1 In the seventh year of this week Isaac called Esau, his elder son, and said to him, " I am old, my son, and my sight is dim, and I do not know the day of my death.

2 Now, take your hunting weapons, your quiver, and your bow, and go out to the field, and hunt and catch me venison, my son, and make me flavorful meat, like

my soul loves, and bring it to me that I may eat, and that my soul may bless you before I die."

3 But Rebecca heard Isaac speaking to Esau.

4 Esau went out early to the field to hunt and catch and bring home meat to his father.

5 Rebecca called Jacob, her son, and said to him, "Look, I heard Isaac, your father, speak to Esau, your brother, saying, "Hunt for me, and make me flavorful meat, and bring it to me that I may eat and bless you before the Lord before I die."

6 Now, my son, do as you are told and do as I command you. Go to your flock and fetch me two good kids of the goats, and I will make them good tasting meat for your father, like he loves, and you will bring it to your father that he may eat and bless you to the Lord before he dies."

7 Jacob said to Rebecca his mother, "Mother, I shall not withhold anything which my father would eat and which would please him, but I am afraid that he will recognize my voice and wish to touch me.

8 And you know that I am smooth, and Esau, my brother, is hairy, and I he will see me an evildoer because I am doing something that he has not told me to do and he will be very angry with me, and I shall bring on myself a curse, and not a blessing."

9 Rebecca, his mother, said to him, "Your curse be on me, my son, just do as you are told."

10 Jacob obeyed the voice of Rebecca, his mother, and went and brought back two good and fat goat kids, and brought them to his mother, and his mother made them tasty meat like he loved.

11 Rebecca took the good and pleasing clothes of Esau, her elder son, which was with her in the house, and she clothed Jacob, her younger son, with them, and she put the skins of the kids on his hands and on the exposed parts of his neck.

12 And she gave the meat and the bread, which she had prepared, to her son Jacob.

13 Jacob went in to his father and said, "I am your son. I have done as you asked me. Arise and sit and eat of that which I have caught, father, that your soul may bless me."

14 Isaac said to his son, "How have you found game so quickly, my son?"

15 Jacob said, "Because the Lord your God caused me to find."

16 Isaac said to him, "Come closer, that I may feel you, my son, and know if you are my son Esau or not."

17 Jacob went near to Isaac, his father, and he felt him and said, "The voice is Jacob's voice, but the hands are the hands of Esau," and he did not recognize him, because it was a decision from heaven to remove his power of perception and Isaac discerned not, because his hands were hairy as his brother Esau's, so Isaac blessed him.

18 He said, "Are you my son Esau? " and Jacob said, "I am your son," and Isaac said, "Bring it to me that I may

eat of that which you have caught, my son, that my soul may bless you."

19 And Jacob brought it to him, and he ate, and Jacob brought him wine and he drank.

20 Isaac, his father, said to him, "Come close and kiss me, my son."

21 He came close and kissed Isaac. And he smelled the smell of his raiment, and he blessed Jacob and said, "Look, the smell of my son is as the smell of a full field which the Lord has blessed.

22 May the Lord give you of the dew of heaven and of the dew of the earth, and plenty of corn and oil. Let nations serve you and peoples bow down to you.

23 Be ruler over your brothers, and let your mother's sons bow down to you; and may all the blessings that the Lord has blessed me and blessed Abraham, my father, be imparted to you and to your offspring forever. Cursed be he that curses you, and blessed be he that blesses you."

24 It happened as soon as Isaac had made an end of blessing his son Jacob, that Jacob had went away from Isaac his father and hid himself.

25 Esau, his brother, came in from his hunting. And he also made flavorful meat, and brought it to his father and Esau said to his father, "Let my father arise, and eat of my venison that your soul may bless me."

26 Isaac, his father, said to him, "Who are you?" Esau said to him, "I am your first born, your son Esau. I have done as you have commanded me."

27 Isaac was very greatly surprised, and said, "Who is he that has hunted and caught and brought it to me, and I have eaten of all before you came, and have blessed him, and he shall be blessed, and all his offspring forever."

28 It happened when Esau heard the words of his father Isaac that he cried with a very loud and bitter cry, and said to his father, "Bless me also, father!"

29 Isaac said to him, "Your brother came with trickery, and has taken away your blessing."

30 He said, "Now I know why his name is Jacob. Behold, he has supplanted me these two times, he took away my birth-right, and now he has taken away my blessing."

31 Esau said, "Have you not reserved a blessing for me, father?" and Isaac answered and said to Esau, "Look, I have made him your lord, and all his brothers have I given to him for servants. I have strengthened him with plenty of corn and wine and oil. Now what shall I do for you, my son?"

32 Esau said to Isaac, his father, "Have you only one blessing, father? Please. Bless me, also, father."

33 Esau lifted up his voice and wept. And Isaac answered and said to him, "Far from the dew of the earth shall be your dwelling, and far from the dew of heaven from above.

34 By your sword will you live, and you will serve your brother.

35 It shall happen that when you become great, and do shake his yoke from off your neck, you will sin completely and commit a sin worthy of death, and your offspring shall be rooted out from under heaven."

36 Esau kept threatening Jacob because of the blessing his father blessed him with, and he said in his heart, "May the days of mourning for my father come now, so that I may kill my brother Jacob."

[Chapter 27]

1 Rebecca was told Esau's words in a dream, and Rebecca sent for Jacob her younger son, and said to him, "Look, Esau, your brother, will take vengeance on you and kill you.

2 Now, therefore, my son, do as you are told, and get up and flee to Laban, my brother, to Haran, and stay with him a few days until your brother's anger fades away, and he removes his anger from you, and forgets all that you have done. Then I will send for you to come from that place."

3 Jacob said, "I am not afraid. If he wishes to kill me, I will kill him."

4 But she said to him, "Let me not be bereft of both my sons on one day."

5 Jacob said to Rebecca, his mother, "Look, you know that my father has become old, and does not see because his eyes are dull. If I leave him he will think it is wrong. If I leave him and go away from you, my father will be angry and will curse me.

6 I will not go. When he sends me, only then will I go."

7 Rebecca said to Jacob, "I will go in and speak to him, and he will send you away."

8 Rebecca went in and said to Isaac, "I hate my life because of the two daughters of Heth, whom Esau has taken as wives. If Jacob take a wife from among the daughters of the land such as these, I could not live with it, because the daughters of Canaan are evil."

9 Isaac called Jacob and blessed him, and warned him and said to him, "Do not take you a wife of any of the daughters of Canaan. Arise and go to Mesopotamia, to the house of Bethuel, your mother's father, and take a wife from that place of the daughters of Laban, your mother's brother.

10 And God Almighty bless you and increase and multiply you that you may become a company of nations, and give you the blessings of my father, Abraham, to you and to your offspring after you, that you may inherit the land that you travel in and all the land which God gave to Abraham. Go in peace, my son."

11 Isaac sent Jacob away, and he went to Mesopotamia, to Laban the son of Bethuel the Syrian, the brother of Rebecca, Jacob's mother.

12 It happened after Jacob had departed to Mesopotamia that the spirit of Rebecca was grieved for her son, and she wept.

13 Isaac said to Rebecca, "My sister, weep not because of Jacob, my son, for he goes in peace, and in peace will he return.

14 The Most High God will preserve him from all evil and will be with him. He will not forsake him all his days, for I know that his ways will be made to prosper in all things wherever he goes, until he return in peace to us, and we see him in peace. Fear not on his account, my sister, for he is on the upright path and he is a perfect man, and he is faithful and will not perish. Weep not."

15 Isaac comforted Rebecca because of her son Jacob, and blessed him.

16 Jacob went from the Well of the Oath to go to Haran on the first year of the second week in the forty-fourth jubilee, and he came to Luz on the mountains, that is, Bethel, on the new moon of the first month of this week, and he came to the place at dusk and turned from the way to the west of the road that is close, and that night he slept there, for the sun had set.

17 He took one of the stones of that place (as a pillow) and laid down under the tree, and he was journeying alone, and he slept.

18 Jacob dreamt that night, and saw a ladder set up on the earth, and the top of it reached to heaven, and he saw the angels of the Lord ascended and descended on it, and behold, the Lord stood on it.

19 And He spoke to Jacob and said, "I am the Lord God of Abraham, your father, and the God of Isaac. The land you are sleeping on I will give to you and to your offspring after you.

20 Your offspring shall be as the dust of the earth, and you will increase to the west and to the east, to the north and the south, and in you and in your offspring shall all the families of the nations be blessed.

21 Behold, I will be with you, and will keep you wherever you go. I will bring you into this land again in peace. I will not leave you until I do everything that I told you."

22 Jacob awoke from his sleep and said, "Truly this place is the house of the Lord, and I did not know it."

23 He was afraid and said, "I am afraid because this place is none other than the house of God, and this is the gate of heaven, and I did not know it."

24 Jacob got up early in the morning, and took the stone that he had placed under his head and set it up as a pillar for a sign. And he poured oil on the top of it. And he called the name of that place Bethel, but the name of the place was previously Luz.

25 And Jacob vowed a vow to the Lord, saying, "If the Lord will be with me, and will keep me in the way that I go, and give me bread to eat and clothes to put on, so that I come again to my father's house in peace, then the Lord shall be my God, and this stone which I have set up as a pillar for a sign in this place shall be the Lord's house, and of all that you gave me, I shall give the tenth to you, my God."

[Chapter 28]

1 He went on his journey, and came to the land of the east, to Laban, the brother of Rebecca, and he was with him, and Jacob served Laban for Rachel his daughter one week of years. In the first year of the third week of years he said to him, "Give me my wife, for whom I have served you seven years ," and Laban said to Jacob, "I will give you your wife."

2 Laban made a feast, and took Leah his elder daughter, and gave her to Jacob as a wife, and gave Leah Zilpah for a handmaid; and Jacob did not know, for he thought that she was Rachel.

3 He went in to her, and saw she was Leah; and Jacob was angry with Laban, and said to him, "Why have you done this to me?

4 Did I not serve you for Rachel and not for Leah? Why have you wronged me?

5 Take your daughter, and I will go. You have done evil to me." For Jacob loved Rachel more than Leah because Leah's eyes were weak, but her form was very beautiful. Rachel had beautiful eyes and a beautiful and very voluptuous form.

6 Laban said to Jacob, "It is not done that way in our country, we do not to give the younger before the elder." And it is not right to do this; for thus it is ordained and written in the heavenly tablets, that no one should give his younger daughter before the elder; but the elder one is given first and after her the younger. The man who does so will have guilt placed against him in heaven, and none is righteous that does this thing, for this deed is evil before the Lord.

7 Command the children of Israel that they not do this thing. Let them neither take nor give the younger before they have given the elder, for it is very wicked."

8 And Laban said to Jacob, "Let the seven days of the feast pass by, and I shall give you Rachel, that you may serve me another seven years, that you may pasture my sheep as you did in the former week (of years)."

9 On the day when the seven days of the feast of Leah had passed, Laban gave Rachel to Jacob, that he might serve him another seven years, and he gave Rachel, Bilhah, the sister of Zilpah, as a handmaid.

10 He served yet other seven years for Rachel, for Leah had been given to him for nothing, since it was Rachel he wanted.

11 And the Lord opened the womb of Leah, and she conceived and gave birth to a son for Jacob, and he called his name Reuben, on the fourteenth day of the ninth month, in the first year of the third week.

12 But the womb of Rachel was closed, for the Lord saw that Leah was hated and Rachel loved.

13 Again Jacob went in to Leah, and she conceived, and gave birth to a second son for Jacob, and he called his

name Simeon, on the twenty-first of the tenth month, and in the third year of this week.

14 Again Jacob went in to Leah, and she conceived, and gave birth to a third son, and he called his name Levi, in the new moon of the first month in the sixth year of this week.

15 Again Jacob went in to her, and she conceived, and gave birth to a fourth son, and he called his name Judah, on the fifteenth of the third month, in the first year of the fourth week.

16 Because of all this Rachel envied Leah, for she did not bear a child, and she said to Jacob, "Give me children;" and Jacob said, "Have I withheld from you the fruits of your womb? Have I left you?"

17 And when Rachel saw that Leah had given birth to four sons for Jacob: Reuben and Simeon and Levi and Judah, she said to him, "Go in to Bilhah my handmaid, and she will conceive, and bear a son for me."

18 She gave him Bilhah, her handmaid, to wife. And he went in to her, and she conceived, and gave birth to a son, and he called his name Dan, on the ninth of the sixth month, in the sixth year of the third week.

19 Jacob went in again to Bilhah a second time, and she conceived, and gave birth to another son for Jacob, and Rachel called his name Napthali, on the fifth of the seventh month, in the second year of the fourth week.

20 When Leah saw that she had become sterile and could no longer have children, she envied Rachel, and she also gave her handmaid Zilpah to Jacob to wife, and she conceived, and gave birth to a son, and Leah called his name Gad, on the twelfth of the eighth month, in the third year of the fourth week.

21 He went in to her again, and she conceived and gave birth to a second son, and Leah called his name Asher, on the second of the eleventh month, in the fifth year of the fourth week.

22 Jacob went in to Leah, and she conceived, and gave birth to a son, and she called his name Issachar, on the fourth of the fifth month, in the fourth year of the fourth week, and she gave him to a nurse.

23 Jacob went in again to her, and she conceived, and gave birth to two children, a son and a daughter, and she called the name of the son Zabulon, and the name of the daughter Dinah, in the seventh day of the seventh month, in the sixth year of the fourth week.

24 The Lord was gracious to Rachel, and opened her womb, and she conceived, and gave birth to a son, and she called his name Joseph, on the new moon of the fourth month, in the sixth year in this fourth week.

25 In the days when Joseph was born, Jacob said to Laban, "Give me my wives and sons, and let me go to my father Isaac, and let me make a household for myself; for I have completed the years in which I have served you for your two daughters, and I will go to the house of my father."

26 Laban said to Jacob, "Stay with me and I will pay you wages, and pasture my flock for me again, and take your wages."

27 They agreed with one another that he should give him as his wages those of the lambs and kids which were born spotted black and white, these were to be his wages.

28 All the sheep brought out spotted and speckled and black, variously marked, and they brought out again lambs like themselves, and all that were spotted were Jacob's and those which were not spotted were Laban's.

29 Jacob's possessions multiplied greatly, and he possessed oxen and sheep and donkeys and camels, and men-servants and maid-servants.

30 Laban and his sons envied Jacob, and Laban took back his sheep from him, and he envied him and watched him for an opportunity to do evil.

[Chapter 29]

1 It happened when Rachel had given birth to Joseph, that Laban went to shear his sheep; for they were distant from him, a three-day journey.

2 Jacob saw that Laban was going to shear his sheep, and Jacob called Leah and Rachel, and spoke sweetly to them in order to convince them to come with him to the land of Canaan.

3 For he told them how he had seen everything in a dream. All that God had spoken to him that he should return to his father's house, and they said, "To every place where you go we will go with you."

4 Jacob blessed the God of Isaac his father, and the God of Abraham his father's father, and he arose and placed his wives and his children on donkeys, and took all his possessions and crossed the river, and came to the land of Gilead, and Jacob hid his intention from Laban and did not tell him.

5 In the seventh year of the fourth week Jacob turned his face toward Gilead in the first month, on the twenty-first of it.

6 Laban pursued and overtook Jacob in the mountain of Gilead in the third month, on the thirteenth of it. And the Lord did not permit him to injure Jacob for he appeared to him in a dream by night.

7 Laban spoke to Jacob. On the fifteenth of those days Jacob made a feast for Laban, and for all who came with him, and Jacob swore to Laban that day, and Laban also swore to Jacob, that neither should cross the mountain of Gilead to do evil to the other.

8 He made a heap (of stones) for a witness there; wherefore the name of that place is called, "The Heap of Witness," after this heap.

9 But before they used to call the land of Gilead the land of the Rephaim. The Rephaim were born giants whose height was ten, nine, eight, down to seven cubits.

10 Their dwelling place was from the land of the children of Ammon to Mount Hermon, and the seats of their kingdom were Karnaim and Ashtaroth, and Edrei, and Misur, and Beon.

11 The Lord destroyed them because of the evil of their deeds, for they were malevolent, and the Amorites were wicked and sinful. There is no people today which has committed the full range of their sins, and their life on the earth was shortened.

12 Jacob sent Laban away, and he departed into Mesopotamia, the land of the East, and Jacob returned to the land of Gilead.

13 He passed over the Jabbok in the ninth month, on the eleventh of it. On that day Esau, his brother, came to him, and he was reconciled to him, and departed from him to the land of Seir, but Jacob dwelt in tents.

14 In the first year of the fifth week in this jubilee he crossed the Jordan, and dwelt beyond the Jordan. He pastured his sheep from the sea of the heap to Bethshan, and to Dothan and to the forest of Akrabbim.

15 He sent his father Isaac all of his possessions such as clothing, and food, and meat, and drink, and milk, and butter, and cheese, and some dates of the valley.

16 Four times a year, he sent gifts to his mother Rebecca who was living at the tower of Abraham. He sent the gifts between the times of the months between plowing and reaping, and between autumn and the rain season, and between winter and spring.

17 For Isaac had returned from the Well of the Oath and gone up to the tower of his father Abraham, and he dwelt there apart from his son Esau.

18 For in the days when Jacob went to Mesopotamia, Esau took to himself a wife Mahalath, the daughter of Ishmael,

and he gathered together all the flocks of his father and his wives, and went up and dwelt on Mount Seir, and left Isaac his father at the Well of the Oath alone.

19 And Isaac went up from the Well of the Oath and dwelt in the tower of Abraham his father on the mountains of Hebron, and that is where Jacob sent all that he did send to his father and his mother from time to time, all they needed, and they blessed Jacob with all their heart and with all their soul.

[Chapter 30]

1 In the first year of the sixth week he went up to Salem, to the east of Shechem, in the fourth month, and he went in peace. Shechem, the son of Hamor, the Hivite, the prince of the land carried off Dinah, the daughter of Jacob, into the house, and he had sex with her and defiled her. She was a little girl, a child of twelve years.

2 He begged his father and her brothers that she might be given to him as a wife.

3 Jacob and his sons were very angry because of the men of Shechem, for they had defiled Dinah, their sister. They spoke to them while planning evil acts and they dealt deceitfully with them and tricked them.

4 Simeon and Levi came unexpectedly to Shechem and executed judgment on all the men of Shechem, and killed all the men whom they found in it. They did not leave a single one remaining in it. They killed all in hand to hand battle because they had dishonored their sister Dinah.

5 Let it not again be done from now on that a daughter of Israel be defiled. Judgment is ordained in heaven against them that they should destroy all the men of the Shechemites with the sword because they had committed shame in Israel.

6 The Lord delivered them into the hands of the sons of Jacob that they might exterminate them with the sword and execute judgment on them. That it might not again be done in Israel that a virgin of Israel should be defiled.

7 If there is any man in Israel who wishes to give his daughter or his sister to any man who is of the offspring of the Gentiles he shall surely die. They shall stone him, for he has committed shame in Israel. They shall burn the woman with fire, because she has dishonored the name of the house of her father, and she shall be rooted out of Israel.

8 Do not let an adulteress and let no uncleanness be found in Israel throughout all the days of the generations of the earth. For Israel is holy to the Lord, and every man who has defiled it shall surely die. They shall stone him.

9 For it has been ordained and written in the heavenly tablets regarding all the offspring of Israel. He who defiles it shall surely die. He shall be killed by stoning. There is no limit of days for this law. There is no remission, and no atonement.

10 The man who has defiled his daughter shall be rooted out from every corner of all Israel, because he has given of his offspring to Moloch (a pagan God, the worship of which involved burning the child alive), and committed impurity and defiled his child.

11 Moses, command the children of Israel and exhort them not to give their daughters to the Gentiles, and not to take for their sons any of the daughters of the Gentiles, for this is abominable before the Lord.

12 It is because of this that I have written all the deeds of the Shechemites, which they committed against Dinah, and placed them in the words of the Law for you. I have also written how the sons of Jacob spoke, saying, "We will not give our daughter to a man who is uncircumcised, for that is a reproach to us."

13 It is a reproach to Israel that anyone take the daughters of the Gentiles, for this is unclean and abominable to Israel.

14 Israel will not be free from this uncleanness if it has a wife of the daughters of the Gentiles, or has given any of its daughters to a man who is of any of the Gentiles.

15 There will be plague upon plague, and curse upon curse, and every judgment and plague and curse will come if he does this thing, or if they ignore those who commit uncleanness, or defile the sanctuary of the Lord, or those who profane His holy name. If any of these happen the whole nation together will be judged for all the uncleanness and profanation of this man.

16 There will be no judging people by their position and no receiving fruits, or offerings, or burnt-offerings, or fat, or the fragrance of sweet odor from his hands. It will be unacceptable and so warn every man and woman in Israel who defiles the sanctuary.

17 For this reason I have commanded you, saying, "Give this testimony to Israel, see how the Shechemites and their sons fared? See how they were delivered into the hands of two sons of Jacob, and they killed them under torture? It was counted to them for righteousness, and it is written down to them for righteousness.

18 The offspring of Levi were chosen for the priesthood, and to be Levites, that they might minister before the Lord, as we do, continually. Levi and his sons will be blessed forever, for he was zealous to execute righteousness and judgment and vengeance on all those who arose against Israel.

19 So they wrote a testimony in his favor of blessing and righteousness on the heavenly tablets in the presence of the God of all.

20 We remember the righteousness that the man fulfilled during his life, throughout the years, until a thousand generations they will record it. It will come to him and to his descendants after him, and he has been recorded on the heavenly tablets as a friend and a righteous man.

21 All this account I have written for you, and have commanded you to tell the children of Israel, so that they will not commit sin nor transgress the laws nor break the covenant which has been ordained for them. They should fulfill it and be recorded as friends (of God).

22 But if they transgress and work uncleanness in any way, they will be recorded on the heavenly tablets as adversaries (of God), and they will be blotted out of the book of life. Instead, they will be recorded in the book of those who will be destroyed and with those who will be rooted out of the earth.

23 On the day when the sons of Jacob killed Shechem it was written in the record in their favor in heaven that they had executed righteousness and uprightness and vengeance on the sinners, and it was written for a blessing.

24 They brought Dinah, their sister, out of the house of Shechem. They took everything that was in Shechem captive. They took their sheep and their oxen and their donkeys, and all their wealth, and all their flocks, and brought them all to Jacob their father.

25 He reproached them because they had put the city to the sword for he feared those who dwelt in the land, the Canaanites and the Perizzites.

26 The dread of the Lord was on all the cities that are near Shechem. They did not fight or chase after the sons of Jacob, for terror had fallen on them.

[Chapter 31]

1 On the new moon of the month, Jacob spoke to all the people of his house, saying, "Purify yourselves and change your clothes, and let us get up and go to Bethel where I vowed a vow to Him on the day when I fled from Esau my brother. Let us do this because God has been with me and brought me into this land in peace. You must put away the strange gods that you raise among you."

2 They gave up the strange gods and that which was in their ears and which was on their necks and the idols which Rachel stole from Laban her father she gave wholly to Jacob. And he burnt and broke them to pieces and destroyed them, and hid them under an oak, which is in the land of Shechem.

3 He went up on the new moon of the seventh month to Bethel. And he built an altar at the place where he had slept, and he set up a pillar there, and he sent word to his father, Isaac, and his mother, Rebecca. He asked to come to Isaac. There, Jacob wished to offer his sacrifice.

4 Isaac said, "Let my son, Jacob, come, and let me see him before I die."

5 Jacob went to his father, Isaac, and his mother, Rebecca, to the house of his father Abraham, and he took two of his sons with him, Levi and Judah.

6 Rebecca came out from the tower to the front of it to kiss Jacob and embrace him, for her spirit had revived when she heard, "Look Jacob your son has come," and she kissed him.

7 She saw his two sons and she recognized them. She said to him, "Are these your sons, my son?" and she embraced them and kissed them, and blessed them, saying, "In you shall the offspring of Abraham become illustrious, and you shall prove a blessing on the earth."

8 Jacob went in to Isaac his father, to the room where he lay, and his two sons were with him. He took his father's hand, stooped down, he kissed him. Isaac held on to the neck of Jacob his son, and wept on his neck.

9 The darkness left the eyes of Isaac, and he saw the two sons of Jacob, Levi, and Judah. And he said, "Are these your sons, my son? Because they look like you."

10 He said to Isaac, "They were truly my sons, and you have clearly seen that they are truly my sons."

11 They came near to him, and he turned and kissed them and embraced them both together.

12 The spirit of prophecy came down into his mouth, and he took Levi by his right hand and Judah by his left.

13 He turned to Levi first, and began to bless him first, and said to him, "May the God of all, the very Lord of all the ages, bless you and your children throughout all the ages.

14 May the Lord give to you and your offspring greatness and great glory from among all flesh. May the Lord cause you and your offspring to draw near to Him to serve in His sanctuary like the angels of the presence (of the Lord) and as the holy ones. The offspring of your sons shall be for the glory and greatness and holiness of God. May He make them great throughout all the ages. They shall be judges and princes, and chiefs of all the offspring of the sons of Jacob. They shall speak the word of the Lord in righteousness, and they shall judge all His judgments in righteousness.

15 They shall declare My ways to Jacob and My paths to Israel. The blessing of the Lord shall be given in their mouths to bless all the offspring of the beloved.

16 Your mother has called your name Levi, and rightly has she called your name. You will be joined to the Lord and be the companion of all the sons of Jacob. Let His table be your table, and let your sons eat from it. May your table be full throughout all generations, and let your food not fail in all the ages.

17 Let all who hate you fall down before you, and let all your adversaries be rooted out and perish. Blessed be he that blesses you, and cursed be every nation that curses you."

18 To Judah he said, "May the Lord give you strength and power to put all that hate you under your feet. You and one of your sons will be a prince over the sons of Jacob. May your name and the name of your sons go out across every land and region.

19 Then shall the Gentiles fear you, and all the nations and people shall shake (with fear of you). In you will be the help of Jacob, and in you will be found the salvation of Israel.

20 When you sit on the throne, which honors of your righteousness, there shall be great peace for all the offspring of the sons of the beloved. Blessed be he that blesses you, and cursed be all that hate you, afflict you, or curse you. They shall be rooted out and destroyed from the earth."

21 He turned, kissed him again, and embraced him, and rejoiced greatly because he had seen the sons of his son, Jacob, clearly and truly.

22 He stepped out from between his feet and fell down. He bowed down to him, and blessed them. He rested there with Isaac, his father, that night, and they ate and drank with joy.

23 He made the two sons of Jacob sleep, the one on his right hand and the other on his left. It was counted to him for righteousness.

24 Jacob told his father everything during the night about how the Lord had shown him great mercy, and how he had caused him to prosper in all his ways, and how he protected him from all evil.

25 Isaac blessed the God of his father Abraham, who had not withdrawn his mercy and his righteousness from the sons of his servant Isaac.

26 In the morning, Jacob told his father, Isaac, the vow, which he had vowed to the Lord. He told him of the vision which he had seen, and that he had built an altar. He told him that everything was ready for the sacrifice to be made before the Lord as he had vowed. He had come to set him on a donkey.

27 Isaac said to Jacob his son, "I am not able to go with you, for I am old and not able to endure the way. Go in peace, my son. I am one hundred and sixty-five years this day. I am no longer able to journey. Set your mother on a donkey and let her go with you.

28 I know that you have come on my account, my son. May this day be blessed on which you have seen me alive, and I also have seen you, my son.

29 May you prosper and fulfill the vow that you have vowed. Do not put off your vow, for you will be called to account for the vow. Now hurry to perform it, and may He who has made all things be pleased. It is to Him you have vowed the vow."

30 He said to Rebecca, "Go with Jacob your son," and Rebecca went with Jacob her son, and Deborah with her, and they came to Bethel.

31 Jacob remembered the prayer with which his father had blessed him and his two sons, Levi and Judah. He rejoiced and blessed the God of his fathers, Abraham and Isaac.

32 He said, "Now I know that my sons and I have an eternal hope in the God of all." Thus is it ordained concerning the two. They recorded it as an eternal testimony to them on the heavenly tablets how Isaac blessed his sons.

[Chapter 32]

1 That night he stayed at Bethel, and Levi dreamed that they had ordained and made his sons and him the priests of the Most High God forever. Then he awoke from his sleep and blessed the Lord.

2 Jacob rose early in the morning, on the fourteenth of this month, and he gave a tithe for all that came with him, both of men and cattle, both of gold and every vessel and garment. Yes, he gave tithes of all.

3 In those days Rachel became pregnant with her son Benjamin. Jacob counted his sons starting from him and going to the oldest and Levi fell to the portion of the Lord. (Levi was the third son – three is the number of spiritual completeness.) His father clothed him in the garments of the priesthood and filled his hands.

4 On the fifteenth of this month, he brought fourteen oxen from among the cattle, and twenty-eight rams,

and forty-nine sheep, and seven lambs, and twenty-one kids of the goats to the altar as a burnt-offering on the altar of sacrifice. The offering was well pleasing and a sweet odor before God.

5 This was his offering, done in acknowledgement of the vow in which he had promised that he would give a tenth, with their fruit-offerings and their drink-offerings.

6 When the fire had consumed it, he burnt incense over the fire, and for a thank-offering he sacrificed two oxen and four rams and four sheep, four male goats, and two sheep of a year old, and two kids of the goats. This he did daily for seven days.

7 He, his men, and all his sons were eating this with joy during seven days and blessing and thanking the Lord, who had delivered him out of all his tribulation and had given him His promise.

8 He tithed all the clean animals, and made a burnt sacrifice, but he did not give the unclean animals to Levi his son. He gave him (responsibility for) all the souls of the men. Levi acted in the priestly office at Bethel in the presence of Jacob his father, in preference to his ten brothers. He was a priest there, and Jacob gave his vow, and he gave a tithe to the Lord again and sanctified it, and it became holy to Him.

9 For this reason it is ordained on the heavenly tablets as a law for the offering of the tithe should be eaten in the presence of the Lord every year, in the place where it is chosen that His name should live and reside. This law has no limit of days forever.

10 This law is written so that it may be fulfilled every year. The second tithe should be eaten in the presence of the Lord, in the place where it has been chosen, and nothing shall be left over from it from this year to the following year.

11 In its year shall the seed be eaten until the days of the gathering of the seed of the year. The wine shall be consumed until the days of the wine, and the oil until the days of its season.

12 All that is left of it and all that becomes old will be regarded as spoiled, let it be burnt with fire, for it is unclean.

13 Let them eat it together in the sanctuary, and let them not permit it to become old.

14 All the tithes of the oxen and sheep shall be holy to the Lord, and shall belong to His priests. They will eat before Him from year to year, for thus is it ordained and written on the heavenly tablets regarding the tithe.

15 On the following night, on the twenty-second day of this month, Jacob resolved to build that place and to surround the court with a wall, and to sanctify it and make it holy forever, for himself and his children after him.

16 The Lord appeared to him by night and blessed him and said to him, "Your name shall not be called Jacob, but they will call your name Israel."

17 And He said to him again, "I am the Lord who created the heaven and the earth, and I will increase you and multiply you greatly, and kings shall come forth from you, and they shall be judges everywhere the foot of the sons of men have walked.

18 I will give to your offspring all the earth that is under heaven. They shall judge all the nations, as they desire. After that they shall possess the entire earth and inherit it forever."

19 And He finished speaking with him, and He went up from him.

20 Jacob watched until He had ascended into heaven.

21 In a vision at night he saw an angel descend from heaven with seven tablets in his hands, and he gave them to Jacob, and he read them and knew all that was written on it that would happen to him and his sons throughout all the ages.

22 He showed him all that was written on the tablets, and said to him, "Do not build on this place, and do not make it an eternal sanctuary, and do not live here. This is not the place. Go to the house of Abraham your father and live with Isaac, your father, until the day he dies.

23 For in Egypt you will die in peace, and in this land you will be buried with honor in the sepulcher of your fathers, with Abraham and Isaac.

24 Do not fear. As you have seen and read it shall all be. Write down everything that you have seen and read."

25 Jacob said, "Lord, how can I remember all that I have read and seen?" He said to him, "I will bring all things to your remembrance."

26 He ascended from Jacob, and Jacob awoke from his sleep. He remembered everything that he had read and seen, and he wrote down all the words.

27 He celebrated there yet another day, and he sacrificed on that day as he had sacrificed on all the former days. He called its name "Addition," because this day was added, and the former days he called "The Feast."

28 It was made known and revealed to him and it is written on the heavenly tablets that he should celebrate the day, and add it to the seven days of the feast.

29 Its name was called "Addition," because that it was recorded among the days of the feast days, according to the number of the days of the year.

30 In the night, on the twenty-third of this month, Deborah, Rebecca's nurse died, and they buried her beneath the city under the oak of the river. He called the name of this place, "The river of Deborah," and he called the oak, "The oak of the mourning of Deborah."

31 Rebecca departed and returned to her house, to his father Isaac. Jacob sent rams and sheep and male goats by her so that she should prepare a meal for his father such as he desired.

32 He followed his mother until he came to the land of Kabratan, and he lived there.

33 Rachel gave birth to a son in the night, and called his name "son of my sorrow", for she broke down while giving birth to him, but his father called his name Benjamin. This happened on the eleventh day of the eighth month in the first of the sixth week of this jubilee.

34 Rachel died there and she was buried in the land of Ephrath, the same is Bethlehem, and Jacob built a pillar on the grave of Rachel, on the road above her grave.

[Chapter 33]

1 Jacob went and lived to the south of Magdaladra'ef. He and Leah, his wife, went to his father, Isaac, on the new moon of the tenth month.

2 Reuben saw Bilhah, Rachel's maid, the concubine of his father, bathing in water in a secret place, and he loved her.

3 He hid himself at night, and he entered the house of Bilhah at night. He found her sleeping alone on a bed in her house.

4 He had sex with her. She awoke and saw that is was Reuben lying with her in the bed. She uncovered the border of her covering and grabbed him and cried out when she discovered that it was Reuben.

5 She was ashamed because of him and released her hand from him, and he fled.

6 Because of this, she mourned greatly and did not tell it to any one.

7 When Jacob returned and sought her, she said to him, "I am not clean for you. I have been defiled in regard to you. Reuben has defiled me, and has had sex with me in the night. I was asleep and did not realize he was there until he uncovered my skirt and had sex with me."

8 Jacob was very angry with Reuben because he had sex with Bilhah, because he had uncovered his father's skirt.

9 Jacob did not approach her again because Reuben had defiled her. And as for any man who uncovers his father's skirt his deed is greatly wicked, for he is disgusting to the Lord.

10 For this reason it is written and ordained on the heavenly tablets that a man should not lie with his father's wife, and should not uncover his father's skirt. This is unclean and they shall surely die together, the man who lies with his father's wife and the woman also, for they have committed uncleanness on the earth.

11 There shall be nothing unclean before our God in the nation that He has chosen for Himself as a possession.

12 Again, it is written a second time, "Cursed be he who lies with the wife of his father, for he has uncovered his father's shame." All the holy ones of the Lord said, "So be it. So be it."

13 "Moses, command the children of Israel so that they observe this word. It entails a punishment of death. It is unclean, and there is no atonement forever for the man who has committed this. He is to be put to death. Kill him by stoning. Root him out from among the people of our God.

14 No man who does so in Israel will be permitted to remain alive a single day on the earth. He is abominable and unclean.

15 Do not let them say, "Reuben was granted life and forgiveness after he had sex with his father's concubine, although she had a husband, and her husband, Jacob, his father, was still alive."

16 Until that time the ordinance and judgment and law had not been revealed in its completeness for all. In your days it has been revealed as a law of seasons and of days. It is an everlasting law for all generations forever. For this law has no limit of days, and no atonement for it.

17 They must both be rooted out of the entire nation. On the day they committed it they shall be killed.

18 Moses, write it down for Israel that they may observe it, and do according to these words, and not commit a sin punishable by death. The Lord our God is judge, who does not respect persons (position) and accepts no gifts.

19 Tell them these words of the covenant, that they may hear and observe, and be on their guard with respect to them, and not be destroyed and rooted out of the land; for an uncleanness, and an abomination, and a contamination, and a pollution are all they who commit it on the earth before our God.

20 There is no greater sin on earth than fornication that they commit. Israel is a holy nation to the Lord its God, and a nation of inheritance. It is a priestly and royal nation and for His own possession. There shall appear no such uncleanness among the holy nation.

21 In the third year of this sixth week, Jacob and all his sons went and lived in the house of Abraham, near Isaac his father and Rebecca his mother.

22 These were the names of the sons of Jacob, the first-born

Reuben, Simeon, Levi, Judah, Issachar, Zebulon, which are the sons of Leah. The sons of Rachel are Joseph and Benjamin. The sons of Bilhah are Dan and Naphtali; and the sons of Zilpah, Gad and Asher. Dinah is the daughter of Leah, the only daughter of Jacob.

23 They came and bowed themselves to Isaac and Rebecca. When they saw them they blessed Jacob and all his sons, and Isaac rejoiced greatly, for he saw the sons of Jacob, his younger son and he blessed them.

[Chapter 34]

1 In the sixth year of this week of the forty-fourth jubilee Jacob sent his sons and his servants to pasture their sheep in the pastures of Shechem.

2 The seven kings of the Amorites assembled themselves together (to fight) against them and kill them. They hid themselves under the trees, to take their cattle as booty.

3 Jacob, Levi, Judah and Joseph were in the house with Isaac their father, for his spirit was sorrowful, and they could not leave him. Benjamin was the youngest, and for this reason he remained with his father.

4 The king of Taphu, the king of Aresa, the king of Seragan, the king of Selo, the king of Ga'as, the king of Bethoron, the king of Ma'anisakir, and all those who dwell in these mountains and who dwell in the woods in the land of Canaan came.

5 They announced to Jacob saying, "Look, the kings of the Amorites have surrounded your sons, and plundered their herds."

6 And he left his house, he and his three sons and all the servants of his father, and his own servants, and he went against them with six thousand men, who carried swords.

7 He killed them in the pastures of Shechem, and pursued those who fled, and he killed them with the edge of the sword, and he killed Aresa and Taphu and Saregan and Selo and Amani sakir and Gaga'as, and he recovered his herds.

8 He conquered them, and imposed tribute on them that they should pay him five fruit products of their land. He built (the cities of) Robel and Tamnatares.

9 He returned in peace, and made peace with them, and they became his servants until the day that he and his sons went down into Egypt.

10 In the seventh year of this week he sent Joseph from his house to the land of Shechem to learn about the welfare of his brothers. He found them in the land of Dothan.

11 They dealt treacherously with him, and formed a plot against him to kill him, but they changed their minds and sold him to Ishmaelite merchants. They brought him down into Egypt, and they sold him to Potiphar, the eunuch of Pharaoh, the chief of the cooks and priest of the city of Elew."

12 The sons of Jacob slaughtered a kid, and dipped Joseph's coat in the blood and sent it to Jacob their father on the tenth of the seventh month.

13 They brought it to him in the evening and he mourned all that night. He became feverish with mourning for Joseph's death, and he said, "An evil beast has devoured Joseph". All the members of his house mourned and grieved with him that day.

14 His sons and his daughter got up to comfort him, but he refused to be comforted for his son.

15 On that day Bilhah heard that Joseph had perished, and she died mourning him. She was living in Qafratef, and Dinah, his daughter, died after Joseph had perished.

16 There were now three reasons for Israel to mourn in one month. They buried Bilhah next to the tomb of Rachel, and Dinah, his daughter. They were (all) buried there.

17 He mourned for Joseph one year, and did not cease, for he said, "Let me go down to my grave mourning for my son."

18 For this reason it is ordained for the children of Israel that they should remember and mourn on the tenth of the seventh month. On that day the news came which made Jacob weep for Joseph. On this day they should make atonement for their sins for themselves with a young goat on the tenth of the seventh month, once a year, for they had grieved the sorrow of their father regarding Joseph his son.

19 This day, once a year, has been ordained that they should grieve on it for their sins, and for all their transgressions and for all their errors, so that they might cleanse themselves.

20 After Joseph perished, the sons of Jacob took to themselves wives. The name of Reuben's wife is Ada; and the name of Simeon's wife is Adlba'a, a Canaanite. The name of Levi's wife is Melka, of the daughters of Aram, of the offspring of the sons of Terah. The name of Judah's wife is Betasu'el, a Canaanite. The name of Issachar's wife is Hezaqa, and the name of Zabulon's wife is Ni'iman. The name of Dan's wife is Egla. The name of Naphtali's wife is Rasu'u, of Mesopotamia. The name of Gad's wife is Maka. The name of Asher's wife is Ijona. The name of Joseph's wife is Asenath, the Egyptian. The name of Benjamin's wife is Ijasaka.

21 And Simeon repented, and took a second wife from Mesopotamia as his brothers had done.

[Chapter 35]

1 In the first year of the first week of the forty-fifth jubilee Rebecca called Jacob, her son, and commanded him regarding his father and regarding his brother, that he should honor them all the days of his life.

2 Jacob said, "I will do everything you have commanded. I will honor them. This will be honor and greatness to me, and righteousness before the Lord.

3 Mother, you know from the time I was born until this day, all my deeds and all that is in my heart. I always think good concerning all.

4 Why should I not do this thing which you have commanded me, that I should honor my father and my brother?

5 Tell me, mother, what perversity have you seen in me and I shall turn away from it, and mercy will be on me."

6 She said to him, "My son, in all my days I have not seen any perverseness in you, but only upright deeds. Yet, I will tell you the truth, my son, I shall die this year. I shall not survive this year in my life. I have seen the day of my death in a dream. I should not live beyond a hundred and fifty-five years. I have completed all the days that I am to live my life."

7 Jacob laughed at the words of his mother because his mother had said she should die. She was sitting across from him in possession of her strength, and she was still strong. She came and went (as she wished). She could see well, and her teeth were strong. No sickness had touched her all the days of her life.

8 Jacob said to her, "If my days of life are close to yours and my strength remains with me as your strength has, I would be blessed, mother. You will not die. You are simply joking with me regarding your death."

9 She went in to Isaac and said to him, " I make one request of you. Make Esau swear that he will not injure Jacob, nor pursue him with intent to harm him. You know Esau's thoughts have been perverse from his youth, and there is no goodness in him. He desires to kill him after you die.

10 You know all that he has done since the day Jacob, his brother, went to Haran until this day. He has forsaken us with his whole heart, and has done evil to us. He has stolen your flocks and carried off all your possessions while you watched.

11 When we asked him and begged him for what was our own, he did as a man (stranger) who was taking pity on us (giving a token like one giving alms to a beggar).

12 He is bitter against you because you blessed Jacob, your perfect and upright son. There is no evil but only goodness in Jacob. Since he came from Haran to this day he has not robbed us of anything. He always brings us everything in its season. He rejoices and blesses us with all his heart when we take his hands. He has not parted from us since he came from Haran until this day, and he remains with us continually at home honoring us."

13 Isaac said to her, "I also know and see the deeds of Jacob who is with us, how he honors us with all his heart. Before, I loved Esau more than Jacob because he was the first-born, but now I love Jacob more than Esau, for Esau has done many evil deeds, and there is no righteousness in him. All his ways are unrighteousness and violence.

14 My heart is troubled because of all his deeds. Neither he nor his offspring will be exempt because they are those who will be destroyed from the earth and who will be rooted out from under heaven. He and his children have forsaken the God of Abraham and gone after his wives (wives' gods) and after their uncleanness and after their error.

15 You told me to make him swear that he will not kill Jacob his brother, but even if he swears, he will not abide by his oath. He will not do good but evil only.

16 If he desires to kill Jacob, his brother, then into Jacob's hands he will be given. He will not escape from Jacob's hands.

17 Do not be afraid for Jacob, for the guardian of Jacob is great, powerful, honored, and praised more than the guardian of Esau."

18 Rebecca called for Esau and he came to her, and she said to him, "I have a request of you, my son. Promise to do it, my son."

19 He said, "I will do everything that you say to me, and I will not refuse your request."

20 She said to him, "I ask you that the day I die, you will take me in and bury me near Sarah, your father's mother, and that you and Jacob will love each other and that neither will desire evil against the other, but (have) mutual love only. Do this so you will prosper, my son, and be honored in the all of the land, and no enemy will rejoice over you. You will be a blessing and a mercy in the eyes of all those that love you."

21 He said, "I will do all that you have told me. I shall bury you on the day you die near Sarah, my father's mother, as you have desired that her bones may be near your bones.

22 Jacob, my brother, I shall love above all flesh. I have only one brother in all the earth but him. It is only what is expected of me. It is no great thing if I love him, for he is my brother, and we were sown together in your body, and together came we out from your womb. If I do not love my brother, whom shall I love?

23 I beg you to exhort Jacob concerning me and concerning my sons, for I know that he will assuredly be king over me and my sons, for on the day my father blessed him he made him the higher and me the lower.

24 I swear to you that I shall love him, and not desire evil against him all the days of my life but good only."

25 And he swore to her regarding all this matter. While Esau was there, she called Jacob and gave him her orders according to the words that she had spoken to Esau.

26 He said, "I shall do your pleasure, believe me that no evil will proceed from me or from my sons against Esau. I shall be first in nothing except in love only."

27 She and her sons ate and drank that night, and she died, three jubilees and one week and one year old on that night. Her two sons, Esau and Jacob, buried her in the double cave near Sarah, their father's mother.

[Chapter 36]

1 In the sixth year of this week Isaac called his two sons Esau and Jacob, and they came to him, and he said to them, "My sons, I am going the way of my fathers, to the eternal house where my fathers are.

2 Bury me near Abraham my father, in the double cave in the field of Ephron the Hittite, where Abraham purchased a sepulcher to bury in. Bury me in the sepulcher I dug for myself.

3 I command you, my sons, to practice righteousness and uprightness on the earth, so that the Lord may do to you what he said he would do to Abraham and to his offspring.

4 Love one another. Love your brothers as a man who loves his own soul. Let each seek how he may benefit his brother, and act together on the earth. Let them love each other as their own souls.

5 I command and warn you to reject idols. Hate them, and do not love them. They are fully deceptive to those that worship them and for those that bow down to them.

6 Remember the Lord God of Abraham, your father, and how I worshipped Him and served Him in righteousness and in joy, that God might multiply you and increase your offspring as the multitude of stars in heaven, and establish you on the earth as the plant of righteousness, which will not be rooted out to all the generations forever.

7 And now I shall make you swear a great oath, for there is no oath which is greater than that which is by the name glorious, honored, great, splendid, wonderful and mighty, which created the heavens and the earth and all things together, that you will fear Him and worship Him.

8 Each will love his brother with affection and righteousness. Neither will desire to do evil against his brother from now on forever all the days of your life so that you may prosper in all your deeds and not be destroyed.

9 If either of you plans evil against his brother, know that he that plans evil shall fall into his brother's hand, and shall be rooted out of the land of the living, and his offspring shall be destroyed from under heaven.

10 But on that day there will be turbulence, curses, wrath, anger, and will He burn his land and his city and all that is his with a devouring fire like the fire He sent to burn Sodom and he shall be blotted out of the book of the discipline of the children of men, and he will not be recorded in the book of life. He shall be added in the book of destruction. He shall depart into eternal curses. Their condemnation may be always renewed in hate and in curses and in wrath and in torment and in anger and in plagues and in disease forever.

11 My sons, this, I say and testify to you, will be the result according to the judgment which shall come on the man who wishes to injure his brother."

12 Then he divided all his possessions between the two on that day, and he gave the larger portion to him that was the first-born, and the tower and all that was around it, and all that Abraham possessed at the Well of the Oath.

13 He said, "This larger portion I will give to the first-born."

14 Esau said, "I have sold and relinquished my birthright to Jacob. Let it be given to him. I have nothing to say regarding it, for it is his."

15 Isaac said, "May a blessing rest on you, my sons, and on your offspring this day. You have given me rest, and my heart is not pained concerning the birthright, or that you should work wickedness because of it.

16 May the Most High God bless the man and his offspring forever that does righteousness."

17 He stopped commanding them and blessing them, and they ate and drank together in front of him, and he rejoiced because there was one mind between them, and they went out from him and rested that day and slept.

18 Isaac slept on his bed that day rejoicing. He slept the eternal sleep, and died one hundred and eighty years old. He lived twenty-five weeks and five years; and his two sons, Esau and Jacob, buried him.

19 After that Esau went to the land of Edom, to the mountains of Seir, and lived there.

20 Jacob lived in the mountains of Hebron, in the high place of the land in which his father Abraham had journeyed. He worshipped the Lord with all his heart. He had divided the days of his generations according to the commands he had seen.

21 Leah, his wife, died in the fourth year of the second week of the forty-fifth jubilee, and he buried her in the double cave near Rebecca his mother to the left of the grave of Sarah, his father's mother. All her sons and his sons came to mourn over Leah, his wife, with him and to comfort him regarding her. He was lamenting her for he loved her greatly after Rachel, her sister, died. She was perfect and upright in all her ways and she honored Jacob. All the days that she lived with him he did not hear from her mouth a harsh word, for she was gentle, peaceable, upright and honorable.

22 And he remembered all the deeds she had done during her life and he lamented her greatly. He loved her with all his heart and with all his soul.

[Chapter 37]

1 On the day that Isaac, the father of Jacob and Esau died, the sons of Esau heard that Isaac had given the elder's portion to his younger son, Jacob, and they were very angry.

2 They argued with their father, saying, "Why has your father given Jacob the portion of the elder and passed you over even though you are the elder and Jacob the younger?"

3 He said to them, "Because I sold my birthright to Jacob for a small portion of lentils (lentil soup), and on the day my father sent me to hunt, catch, and bring him something that he should eat and bless me, Jacob came with deceit and brought my father food and drink. My father blessed him and put me under his hand.

4 Now our father has caused Jacob and me to swear that we shall not devise evil plans against his brother (each other), and that we shall continue in love and in peace each with his brother and not make our ways corrupt."

5 They said to him, "We shall not listen to you to make peace with him. We are stronger than him and we are more powerful than he is. We shall depose him and kill him, and destroy him and his sons. If you will not go with us, we shall hurt you also.

6 Listen! Let us send to Aram, Philistia, Moab, and Ammon. Let us take chosen men who are trained in battle, and let us go against him and do battle with him. Let us exterminate him from the earth before he grows strong."

7 Their father said to them, "Do not go and do not make war with him or you shall fall before him."

8 They said to him, "This is how you have acted from your youth until this day. You have continued to put your neck under his yoke. We shall not listen to these words."

9 Then they sent to Aram, and to Aduram to the friend of their father, and they also hired one thousand chosen men of war.

10 And there came to them from Moab and from the children of Ammon, those who were hired, one thousand chosen men, and from Philistia, one thousand chosen warriors, and from Edom and from the Horites one thousand chosen warriors, and from the Kittim mighty warriors.

11 They said to their father, "Go out with them and lead them or else we shall kill you."

12 And he was filled with boiling anger on seeing that his sons were forcing him to go before them to lead them against Jacob, his brother.

13 But afterward he remembered all the evil that lay hidden in his heart against Jacob his brother, and he did not remember the oath he had sworn to his father and to his mother that he would plan no evil against Jacob, his brother, all his days.

14 Because Jacob was in mourning for his wife Leah, he did not know they were coming to battle against him until they approached the tower with four thousand soldiers and chosen warriors. The men of Hebron sent to him saying, "Look your brother has come against you to fight. He has with him four thousand men carrying swords, shields, and weapons." They told him this because they loved Jacob more than Esau.

15 So they told him, for Jacob was a more gracious and merciful man than Esau.

16 But Jacob would not believe until they came very near to the tower.

17 He closed the gates of the tower; and he stood on the battlements and spoke to his brother Esau and said, "Noble is the comfort you have come to give me concerning the death of my wife. Is this the oath that you swore to your father and again to your mother before they died? You have broken the oath, and on the moment that you swore to your father you were condemned."

18 Then Esau answered and said to him, "Neither the children of men nor the beasts of the earth have sworn an oath of righteousness and kept it forever. Every day they lay evil plans one against another regarding how they might kill their adversary or foe.

19 You will hate my children and me forever, so there is no observing the tie of brotherhood with you.

20 Hear these words that I declare to you. If the boar can change its skin and make its bristles as soft as wool, or if it can cause horns to sprout out on its head like the horns of a stag or of a sheep, then will I observe the tie of brotherhood with you. Like breasts separate themselves from their mother (and fight), you and I have never been brothers.

21 If the wolves make peace with the lambs and not devour or do them violence, and if their hearts are towards them for good, then there shall be peace in my heart towards you. If the lion becomes the friend of the ox and makes peace with him and if he is bound under one yoke with him and plows with him, then will I make peace with you.

22 When the raven becomes white as the raza (a white bird?), then know that I have loved you and shall make peace with you. You will be rooted out, and your sons shall be rooted out, and there shall be no peace for you."

23 Jacob saw that Esau had decided in his heart to do evil toward him, and that he desired with all his soul to kill him. Jacob saw that Esau had come pouncing like the wild boar which charges the spear that is set to pierce and kill it, and yet does not even slow down. Then he spoke to his own people and to his servants and told them that Esau and his men were going to attack him and all his companions.

[Chapter 38]

1 After that Judah spoke to Jacob, his father, and said to him, "Bend your bow, father, and send forth your arrows and bring down the adversary and kill the enemy. You have the power to do it. We will not kill your brother because he is your kin and he is like you, so we will honor his life."

2 Then Jacob bent his bow and sent forth the arrow and struck Esau, his brother, on the right side of his chest and killed him.

3 And again he sent forth an arrow and struck Adoran the Aramaean, on the left side of his chest, and it drove him backward and killed him. Then the sons of Jacob and their servants went out, dividing themselves into companies on the four sides of the tower.

4 Judah went out in front. Naphtali and Gad along with fifty servants went to the south side of the tower, and they killed all they found before them. Not one individual escaped.

5 Levi, Dan, and Asher went out on the east side of the tower along with fifty men, and they killed the warriors of Moab and Ammon.

6 Reuben, Issachar, and Zebulon went out on the north side of the tower along with fifty men and they killed the warriors of the Philistines.

7 Reuben's son, Simeon, Benjamin, and Enoch went out on the west side of the tower along with fifty men and they killed four hundred men, stout warriors of Edom and of the Horites. Six hundred fled, and four of the sons of Esau fled with them, and left their father lying killed, as he had fallen on the hill that is in Aduram.

8 And the sons of Jacob pursued them to the mountains of Seir. And Jacob buried his brother on the hill that is in Aduram, and he returned to his house.

9 The sons of Jacob crushed the sons of Esau in the mountains of Seir, and made them bow their necks so that they became servants of the sons of Jacob.

10 They sent a message to their father to inquire whether they should make peace with them or kill them.

11 Jacob sent word to his sons that they should make peace. They made peace with them but also placed the yoke of servitude on them, so that they paid tribute to Jacob and to his sons always.

12 And they continued to pay tribute to Jacob until the day that he went down to Egypt.

13 The sons of Edom have not escaped the yoke of servitude imposed by the twelve sons of Jacob until this day.

14 These are the kings that reigned in Edom before there was any king over the children of Israel (until this day) in the land of Edom.

15 And Balaq, the son of Beor, reigned in Edom, and the name of his city was Danaba. Balaq died, and Jobab, the son of Zara of Boser, ruled in his place.

16 Jobab died, and Asam, of the land of Teman, ruled in his place.

17 Asam died, and Adath, the son of Barad, who killed Midian in the field of Moab, ruled in his place, and the name of his city was Avith.

18 Adath died, and Salman, from Amaseqa, ruled in his place.

19 Salman died, and Saul of Ra'aboth by the river, ruled in his place. Saul died, and Ba'elunan, the son of Achbor, ruled in his place.

20 Ba'elunan, the son of Achbor died, and Adath ruled in his place, and the name of his wife was Maitabith, the daughter of Matarat, the daughter of Metabedza'ab. These are the kings who reigned in the land of Edom.

[Chapter 39]

1 Jacob lived in the land that his father journeyed in, which is the land of Canaan.

2 These are the generations of Jacob. Joseph was seventeen years old when they took him down into the land of Egypt, and Potiphar, a eunuch of Pharaoh, the chief cook, bought him.

3 He made Joseph the manager over Potiphar's entire house and the blessing of the Lord came on the house of the Egyptian because of Joseph. And the Lord caused him to prosper in all that he did.

4 The Egyptian turned everything over to the hands of Joseph because he saw that the Lord was with him, and that the Lord caused him to prosper him in all that he did.

5 Joseph's appearance was beautiful, and his master's wife watched Joseph, and she loved him and wanted him to have sex with her.

6 But he did not surrender his soul because he remembered the Lord and the words which Jacob, his father, used to read to him from the writings of Abraham, that no man should commit fornication with a woman who has a husband. For him the punishment of death has been ordained in the heavens before the Most High God, and the sin will be recorded against him in the eternal books, which are always in the presence of the Lord.

7 Joseph remembered these words and refused to have sex with her.

8 And she begged him for a year, but he refused and would not listen.

9 But while he was in the house she embraced him and held him tightly in order to force him to sleep with her. She closed the doors of the house and held on to him, but he left his garment in her hands and broke through the door and ran out from her presence.

10 The woman saw that he would not sleep with her, and she slandered him in the presence of his master, saying "Your Hebrew servant, whom you love, sought to force me to have sex with him. When I shouted for help he fled and left his garment in my hands. I tried to stop him but he broke through the door."

11 When the Egyptian saw Joseph's garment and the broken door, and heard the words of his wife, he threw Joseph into prison and put him in the place where the prisoners of the king were kept.

12 He was there in the prison, and the Lord gave Joseph favor in the sight of the chief of the prison guards and caused him to have compassion for Joseph, because he saw that the Lord was with him, and that the Lord made all that he did to prosper.

13 He turned over all things into his hands, and the chief of the prison guards knew of nothing that was going on in the prison, because Joseph did everything for him, and the Lord perfected it. He remained there two years.

14 In those days Pharaoh, king of Egypt, was very angry at his two eunuchs, the chief butler, and the chief baker. He put them in the prison facility of the house of the chief cook, where Joseph was kept.

15 The chief of the prison guards appointed Joseph to serve them, and he served them.

16 They both dreamed a dream, the chief butler and the chief baker, and they told it to Joseph.

17 As he interpreted to them so it happened to them, and Pharaoh restored the chief butler to his office and he killed the chief baker as Joseph had interpreted to them.

18 But the chief butler forgot Joseph was in the prison, although he had informed him of what would happen to him. He did not remember to inform Pharaoh of how Joseph had told him (about his dream), because he forgot.

[Chapter 40]

1 In those days Pharaoh dreamed two dreams in one night concerning a famine that was to be in all the land, and he awoke from his sleep and called all the magicians and interpreters of dreams that were in Egypt. He told them his two dreams but they were not able to tell him what they meant.

2 Then the chief butler remembered Joseph and told the king of him, and he brought him out from the prison, and the king told his two dreams to him.

3 He said before Pharaoh that his two dreams were one, and he said to him, "Seven years shall come in which there shall be plenty in all the land of Egypt, but after that, seven years of famine. Such a famine as has not been in all the land.

4 Now, let Pharaoh appoint administrators in all the land of Egypt, and let them store up food in every city throughout all the years of plenty, and there will be food for the seven years of famine, and those of the land will not perish through the famine, even though it will be very severe."

5 The Lord gave Joseph favor and mercy in the eyes of Pharaoh. Pharaoh said to his servants, "We shall not find such a wise and prudent man like this man, because the spirit of the Lord is with him."

6 And he appointed Joseph the second in command in his entire kingdom and gave him authority over all Egypt, and placed him on the second chariot of Pharaoh to ride.

7 And he clothed him with fine linen clothes, and he put a gold chain around his neck, and a crier proclaimed before him "El" "El wa Abirer," and he placed a ring on his hand and made him ruler over all his house, and lifted him up before the people, and said to him, "Only on the throne shall I be greater than you."

8 Joseph ruled over all the land of Egypt, and all the governors of Pharaoh, and all his servants, and all those who did the king's business loved him because he walked in uprightness, because he was without pride and arrogance. He did not judge people by their

position, and did not accept gifts, but he judged all the people of the land in uprightness.

9 The land of Egypt was at peace before Pharaoh because of Joseph, because the Lord was with him, and the Lord gave him favor and mercy for all his generations before all those who knew him and those who heard of him, and Pharaoh's kingdom was run efficiently, and there was no Satan (adversary) and no evil person in it.

10 And the king called Joseph's name Sephantiphans, and gave Joseph the daughter of Potiphar, the daughter of the priest of Heliopolis, the chief cook to marry.

11 On the day that Joseph stood before Pharaoh he was thirty years old.

12 In that year Isaac died. Things transpired as Joseph had said in the interpretation of Pharaoh's dream and there were seven years of plenty over all the land of Egypt, and the land of Egypt abundantly produced, one measure producing eighteen hundred measures.

13 Joseph gathered food into every city until they were full of grain and they could no longer count or measure it because of its multitude.

[Chapter 41]

1 In the forty-fifth jubilee, in the second week, and in the second year, Judah took his first-born Er, a wife from the daughters of Aram, named Tamar.

2 But he hated her, and did not have sex with her, because her mother was of the daughters of Canaan, and he wished to take him a wife of the lineage of his mother, but Judah, his father, would not permit him to do that.

3 Er, the first-born of Judah, was wicked, and the Lord killed him.

4 And Judah said to Onan, his brother, "Go in to your brother's wife and perform the duty of a husband's brother to her, and raise up offspring to your brother."

5 Onan knew that the offspring would not be his, but his brother's only, and he went into the house of his brother's wife, and spilt his seed (ejaculates) on the ground, and he was wicked in the eyes of the Lord, and He killed him.

6 Judah said to Tamar, his daughter-in-law, "Remain in your father's house as a widow until Shelah, my son has grown up, and I shall give you to him to wife."

7 He grew up, but Bedsu'el, the wife of Judah, did not permit her son Shelah to marry. Bedsu'el, Judah's wife, died in the fifth year of this week.

8 In the sixth year Judah went up to shear his sheep at Timnah.

9 And they told Tamar, "Look, your father-in-law is going up to Timnah to shear his sheep." And she took off her widow's clothes, and put on a veil, and adorned herself, and sat in the gate connecting the road to Timnah.

10 As Judah was going along he saw her, and thought she was a prostitute, and he said to her, "Let me come in to you," and she said to him, "Come in," and he went in.

11 She said to him, "Give me my pay," and he said to her, "I have nothing with me except my ring that is on my finger, my necklace, and my staff which is in my hand."

12 She said to him, "Give them to me until you send me my pay." And he said to her, "I will send to you a kid of the goats", and he gave her his ring, necklace, and staff, and she conceived by him.

13 Judah went to his sheep, and she went to her father's house.

14 Judah sent a kid of the goats by the hand of his shepherd, an Adullamite, but he could not find her, so he asked the people of the place, saying, "Where is the prostitute who was here?"

15 They said to him, "There is no prostitute here with us." And he returned and informed Judah that he had not found her, "I asked the people of the place, and they said to me, "There is no prostitute here." "

16 He said, "If you see her give the kids to her or we become a cause of ridicule." And when she had completed three months, it was revealed that she was with child, and they told Judah, saying, "Look Tamar, your daughter-in-law, is with child by whoredom."

17 And Judah went to the house of her father, and said to her father and her brothers, "Bring her out, and let them burn her, for she has committed uncleanness in Israel."

18 It happened when they brought her out to burn her that she sent to her father-in-law the ring and the necklace, and the staff, saying, "Tell us whose are these, because by him am I with child."

19 Judah acknowledged, and said, "Tamar is more righteous than I am.

20 Do not let them burn her." For that reason she was not given to Shelah, and he did not again approach her and after that she gave birth to two sons, Perez and Zerah, in the seventh year of this second week.

21 At this time the seven years of fruitfulness were completed, of which Joseph spoke to Pharaoh.

22 Judah acknowledged the evil deed that he had done because he had sex with his daughter-in-law, and he hated himself for it.

23 He acknowledged that he had transgressed and gone astray, because he had uncovered the skirt of his son, and he began to lament and to supplicate before the Lord because of his transgression.

24 We told him in a dream that it was forgiven him because he supplicated earnestly, and lamented, and did not commit the act again.

25 And he received forgiveness because he turned from his sin and from his ignorance, because he transgressed greatly before our God. Every one that acts like this, every one who has sex with his mother-in-law, let them burn him alive with fire. Because there is uncleanness and pollution on them, let them burn them alive.

26 Command the children of Israel that there should be no uncleanness among them, because every one who has sex with his daughter-in-law or with his mother-in-law has committed

uncleanness. Let them burn the man who has had sex with her with fire, and likewise burn the woman, so that God will turn away wrath and punishment from Israel.

27 We told Judah that his two sons had not had sex with her, and for this reason his offspring was established for a second generation, and would not be rooted out.

28 For in single-mindedness he had gone and sought for punishment, namely, according to the judgment of Abraham, which he had commanded his sons. Judah had sought to burn her alive.

[Chapter 42]

1 In the first year of the third week of the forty-fifth jubilee the famine began to come into the land, and the rain refused to be given to the earth. None whatsoever fell.

2 The earth became barren, but in the land of Egypt there was food, because Joseph had gathered the seed of the land in the seven years of plenty and had preserved it.

3 The Egyptians came to Joseph that he might give them food, and he opened the storehouses where the grain of the first year was stored, and he sold it to the people of the land for gold.

4 Jacob heard there was food in Egypt, and he sent his ten sons that they should procure food for him in Egypt, and they arrived among those that went there, but Benjamin he did not send.

5 Joseph recognized them, but they did not recognize him. He spoke to them and questioned them, and he said to them, "Are you not spies and have you not come to explore ways to enter this land?"

6 And he put them in custody.

7 After that, he set them free again, and detained Simeon alone and sent his nine brothers away.

8 He filled their sacks with corn, and he put their gold back in their sacks, and they did not know it. Joseph then commanded them to bring their younger brother, because they had told him their father was living and also their younger brother.

9 They went up from the land of Egypt and they came to the land of Canaan. There they told their father all that had happened to them, and how the ruler of the country had spoken rudely to them, and had seized Simeon until they should bring Benjamin.

10 Jacob said, "You have taken my children from me! Joseph is gone and Simeon also is gone, and now you

will take Benjamin away. I am the victim of your wickedness."

11 He said, "My son will not go down with you because fate may have it that he would fall sick. Their mother gave birth to two sons, and one has died, and this one also you will take from me. If, by fate, he took a fever on the road, you would turn my old age to sorrow and death."

12 He saw that every man's money had been returned to him in his sack, and for this reason he feared to send him.

13 The famine increased and became grievous in the land of Canaan, and in all lands except in the land of Egypt. Egypt had food because many of the children of the Egyptians had stored up their seed for food from the time when they saw Joseph gathering seed together and putting it in storehouses and preserving it for the years of famine.

14 The people of Egypt fed themselves on it during the first year of their famine but when Israel saw that the famine was very serious in the land, and that there was no deliverance, he said to his sons, "Go again, and procure food for us so that we will not die."

15 They said, "We shall not go unless our youngest brother go with us!"

16 Israel saw that if he did not send Benjamin with them, they would all perish because of the famine.

17 Reuben said, "Give him to me, and if I do not bring him back to you, kill my two sons in payment for his soul." Israel said to Reuben, "He shall not go with you."

18 Judah came near and said, "Send him with me, and if I do not bring him back to you, let me bear your blame all the days of my life."

19 He sent him with them in the second year of this week on the first day of the month.

20 They all came to the land of Egypt, and they had presents in their hands of sweet spice, almonds, turpentine nuts, and pure honey.

21 And they went and stood before Joseph, and he saw Benjamin his brother, and he knew him, and said to them, "Is this your youngest brother?" They said to him, "It is he."

22 He said, "The Lord be gracious to you, my son!" And he sent Benjamin into his house and he brought out Simeon to them. Joseph made a feast for them, and they presented to him the gifts that they had brought in their hands.

23 They ate before Joseph and he gave them all a portion of food, but the portion of food given to Benjamin was seven times larger than any of theirs.

24 And they ate and drank and got up and remained with their donkeys.

25 Joseph devised a plan whereby he might learn their thoughts as to whether they desired peace or not. He said to the steward who was over his house, "Fill all their sacks with food. Place their money back in their vessels. Put my cup, the silver cup out of which I drink, in the sack of the youngest and send them away."

[Chapter 43]

1 He did as Joseph had told him, and filled all their sacks with food for them and put their money back into their sacks, and put the cup in Benjamin's sack.

2 Early in the morning they departed, and it happened that when they had gone from that place, Joseph said to the steward of his house, "Pursue them, run and seize them, and say, 'You have repaid my kindness with evil. You have stolen from me the silver cup out of which my lord drinks.'

3 Bring me back their youngest brother. Go! Get him quickly before I go to my seat of judgment (judge you guilt of disobeying an order). "

4 He ran after them and said the words as he was told. They said to him, "God forbid that your servants should do this thing, and steal any utensil or money from the house of your lord, like the things we found in our sacks the first time we, your servants, came back from the land of Canaan.

5 We have not stolen any utensil. How could we? Look here in our sacks and search, and wherever you find the cup in the sack of any man among us, let him be killed, and we and our donkeys will serve your lord."

6 He said to them, "Not so. If I find it, the man whose sack I find it in I shall take as a servant, and the rest of you shall return in peace to your house."

7 He was searching in their vessels, beginning with the eldest and ending with the youngest, when it was found in Benjamin's sack.

8 They ripped their garments in frustration, and placed their belongings back on their donkeys, and returned to the city and came to the house of Joseph. They all bowed themselves with their faces to the ground in front of him.

9 Joseph said to them, "You have done evil." They said, "What shall we say and how shall we defend ourselves? Our lord has discovered the transgression of his servants; and now we and our donkeys are the servants of our lord."

10 Joseph said to them, "I too fear the Lord. As for you, go to your homes and let your brother be my servant, because you have done evil. I delight in this cup as no one else delights in his cup and yet you have stolen it from me."

11 Judah said, "O my lord, I pray you to let your servant speak a word in my lord's ear. Your servant's mother had two sons for our father. One went away and was lost, and has not been found since. This one alone is left of his mother, and your servant our father loves him. He would die if the lad were lost to him.

12 When we go to your servant our father, and the lad is not with us, it will happen that he will die. We will

have brought so much sorrow on our father it will bring his death.

13 Now rather let me, your servant, stay here as a bondsman to my lord instead of the boy. Let the lad go with his brothers, because I will stand in for him at the hand of your servant our father. If I do not bring him back, your servant will bear the blame of our father forever."

14 Joseph saw that they were all in accord in doing good to one another. Then, he could not refrain himself, and he told them that he was Joseph.

15 And he conversed with them in the Hebrew tongue and hugged their necks and wept.

16 At first they did not recognize him and then they began to weep. He said to them, "Do not weep for me, but hurry and bring my father to me. See, it is my mouth that speaks and the eyes of my brother Benjamin see me.

17 Pay attention. This is the second year of the famine, and there are still five years to come without harvest or fruit of trees or plowing.

18 You and your households come down quickly, so that you won't die because of the famine. Do not be grieved for your possessions, because the Lord sent me before you to set things in order that many people might live.

19 Tell my father that I am still alive. You see that the Lord has made me as a father to Pharaoh, and ruler over his house and over all the land of Egypt.

20 Tell my father of all my glory, and all the riches and glory that the Lord has given me."

21 By the command of Pharaoh's mouth, he gave them chariots and provisions for the way, and he gave them all multi-colored raiment and silver.

22 He sent corn, raiment, silver, and ten donkeys that carried all of this to his father, and he sent them away.

23 They went up and told their father that Joseph was alive, and was measuring out corn to all the nations of the earth, and that he was ruler over all the land of Egypt.

24 But their father did not believe it, because he was not in his right mind. But when he saw the wagons, which Joseph had sent, the life of his spirit revived, and he said, "It is enough for me if Joseph lives. I will go down and see him before I die."

[Chapter 44]

1 Israel took his journey from Haran's house on the new moon of the third month, and he stopped at the Well of the Oath on the way and he offered a sacrifice to the God of his father Isaac on the seventh of this month.

2 Jacob remembered the dream that he had at Bethel, and he feared to go down into Egypt.

3 He was thinking of sending word to Joseph to come to him because he did not want to go down. He remained there seven days, hoping fate would permit him to see a vision as to whether he should remain or go down.

4 He celebrated the harvest festival of the first-fruits with old grain, because in all the land of Canaan there was not a handful of seed in the ground because the famine was affecting all the beasts, and cattle, and birds, and all men.

5 On the sixteenth the Lord appeared to him, and said to him, "Jacob, Jacob," and he said, "Here I am."

6 And He said to him, "I am the God of your fathers, the God of Abraham and Isaac. Do not be afraid to go down into Egypt, because I will be there to make you a great nation. I will go down with you, and I will bring you up again. You will be buried in this land and Joseph will put his hands on your eyes (to close them in death). Do not be afraid. Go down into Egypt."

7 And his sons got up and placed their father and their possessions on wagons.

8 Israel got up from the Well of the Oath on the sixteenth of this third month, and he went to the land of Egypt.

9 Israel sent Judah before him to his son Joseph to examine the Land of Goshen, because Joseph had told his brothers that they should come and live there so they could be near him.

10 This was the best land in Egypt. It was near to him and suitable for all of the cattle they had.

11 These are the names of the sons of Jacob who went into Egypt with Jacob their father; Reuben, the First-born of Israel and his sons Enoch, and Pallu, and Hezron and Carmi, making five.

12 Simeon and his sons Jemuel, and Jamin, and Ohad, and Jachin, and Zohar, and Shaul, the son of the Zephathite woman, making seven.

13 Levi and his sons Gershon, and Kohath, and Merari, making four.

14 Judah and his sons Shela, and Perez, and Zerah, making four.

15 Issachar and his sons Tola, and Phua, and Jasub, and Shimron, making five.

16 Zebulon and his sons Sered, and Elon, and Jahleel, making four.

17 These are the sons of Jacob and their sons whom Leah bore to Jacob in Mesopotamia, six, and their one sister, Dinah and all the souls of the sons of Leah, and their sons, who went with Jacob their father into Egypt. Twenty-nine souls, and Jacob, making thirty, were the number of people that went into Egypt.

18 And the sons of Zilpah, Leah's handmaid, the wife of Jacob, who bore to Jacob Gad and Ashur and their sons who went with him into Egypt.

19 The sons of Gad are Ziphion, and Haggi, and Shuni, and Ezbon, and Eri, and Areli, and Arodi, which make eight souls in total. The sons of Asher are Imnah, and Ishvah, and Ishvi, and Beriah, and Serah, and their one sister, which makes six in total.

20 All the souls were fourteen, and all those of Leah were forty-four.

21 The sons of Rachel, the wife of Jacob are Joseph and Benjamin.

22 There were born to Joseph in Egypt before his father came into Egypt, those whom Asenath, daughter of Potiphar, priest of Heliopolis gave birth to him, Manasseh, and Ephraim. The wife and children of Joseph totaled three.

23 The sons of Benjamin, Bela and Becher and Ashbel, Gera, and Naaman, and Ehi, and Rosh, and Muppim, and Huppim, and Ard with Benjamin totaled eleven.

24 And all the souls of Rachel were fourteen.

25 And the sons of Bilhah, the handmaid of Rachel, the wife of Jacob, whom she gave birth to Jacob, were Dan and Naphtali. These are the names of their sons who went with them into Egypt.

26 The sons of Dan were Hushim, and Samon, and Asudi. and "Ijaka, and Salomon, all totaling six.

27 All but one died the year in which they entered into Egypt, and there was left to Dan only Hushim.

28 These are the names of the sons of Naphtali: Jahziel, and Guni and Jezer, and Shallum, and 'Iv.

29 And 'Iv, who was born after the years of famine, died in Egypt.

30 All the souls (offspring) of Rachel were twenty-six.

31 All the souls (offspring) of Jacob, which went into Egypt, were seventy souls.

32 These are his children and his children's children, in all seventy, but five died in Egypt in the time of Joseph's rule and they had no children.

33 In the land of Canaan two sons of Judah died, Er and Onan, and they had no children, and the children of Israel buried those who died, and they were counted among the seventy Gentile nations.

[Chapter 45]

1 On the new moon of the fourth month, in the second year of the third week of the forty-fifth jubilee, Israel went into the country of Egypt, to the land of Goshen.

2 Joseph went to meet his father, Jacob, in the land of Goshen, and he hugged his father's neck and wept.

3 Israel said to Joseph, "Now that I have seen you let me die and may the Lord God of Israel, the God of Abraham, and the God of Isaac, who has not withheld His mercy and His grace from His servant Jacob, be blessed.

4 It is enough for me to have seen your face while I am yet alive. Yes, this is the true vision which I saw at Bethel.

5 Blessed be the Lord my God forever and ever, and blessed be His name."

6 Joseph and his brothers ate bread in the presence of their father and drank wine, and Jacob rejoiced with very great joy because he saw Joseph eating with his brothers and drinking in the presence of him, and he blessed the Creator of all things who had preserved him, and had preserved for him his twelve sons.

7 Joseph had given his father and his brothers as a gift the right of dwelling in the land of Goshen and in Rameses and the entire region around it, which he ruled over in the presence of Pharaoh.

8 Israel and his sons dwelt in the land of Goshen, the best part of the land of Egypt, and Israel was one hundred and thirty years old when he came into Egypt. Joseph nourished his father and his brothers and also their possessions (servants) with bread as much as they needed for the seven years of the famine.

9 The land of Egypt became available for purchase because of the famine, and Joseph acquired all the land of Egypt for Pharaoh in return for food, and he got possession of the people and their cattle and everything for Pharaoh.

10 The years of the famine were completed, and Joseph gave the people in the land seed and food that they might sow the land in the eighth year, because the river had overflowed all the land of Egypt.

11 For in the seven years of the famine it had not overflowed and had irrigated only a few places on the banks of the river, but now it overflowed and the Egyptians sowed the land, and it produced much corn that year.

12 This was the first year of the fourth week of the forty-fifth jubilee. Joseph took one-fifth of the corn of the harvest for the king and left four parts for them for food and for seed, and Joseph made it a law for Egypt until this day.

13 Israel lived in the land of Egypt seventeen years, and all the days which he lived were three jubilees, one hundred and forty-seven years, and he died in the fourth year of the fifth week of the forty-fifth jubilee.

14 Israel blessed his sons before he died and told them everything that they would go through in the land of Egypt. He revealed to them what they would live through in the last days, and he blessed them and gave Joseph two portions of the land.

15 He slept with his fathers, and he was buried in the double cave in the land of Canaan, near Abraham his father, in the grave which he dug for himself in the land of Hebron.

16 And he gave all his books and the books of his fathers to Levi, his son so that he might preserve them and replicate them for his children until this day.

[Chapter 46]

1 It happened that after the death of Jacob the children of Israel continued to multiply in the land of Egypt, and they became a great nation, and they were in one accord of heart, so that brother loved brother and every man helped his brother. They increased abundantly and multiplied greatly, ten weeks of years, all the days of the life of Joseph.

2 There was neither Satan nor any evil in all the days of the life of Joseph after his father, Jacob (had died), because all the Egyptians respected the children of Israel all the days of the life of Joseph.

3 Joseph died, being a hundred and ten years old. He lived seventeen years in the land of Canaan, and ten years he was a servant, and three years in prison, and eighty years he was under the king, ruling all the land of Egypt.

4 He died and so did all his brothers and all of that generation. But, he commanded the children of Israel before he died that they should carry his bones with them when they went out from the land of Egypt.

5 And he made them swear regarding his bones, because he knew that the Egyptians would not bring his bones out of Egypt or bury him in the land of Canaan, because while dwelling in the land of Assyria, king Makamaron, the king of Canaan, fought against Egypt in the valley and killed the king of Egypt there, and pursued the Egyptians to the gates of "Ermon.

6 But he was not able to enter, because another king, a new king, had become king of Egypt, and he was stronger than he (Makamaron), and he returned to the land of Canaan, and the gates of Egypt were closed so that none came or went from Egypt.

7 Joseph died in the forty-sixth jubilee, in the sixth week, in the second year, and they buried him in the land of Egypt, and all his brothers died after him.

8 The king of Egypt went to war against the king of Canaan in the forty-seventh jubilee, in the second week in the second year, and the children of Israel brought out all the bones of the children of Jacob except the bones of Joseph, and they buried them in the field in the double cave in the mountain.

9 Then, most of them returned to Egypt, but a few of them remained in the mountains of Hebron, and Amram your father remained with them.

10 The king of Canaan was victorious over the king of Egypt, and he closed the gates of Egypt.

11 He devised an evil plan against the children of Israel to afflict them. He said to the people of Egypt, "Look, the people of the children of Israel have increased and multiplied more than we.

12 Let us use wisdom and deal with them before they become too many. Let us make them our slaves before we go to war and they rise up against us on the side of our enemies. Before they leave and fight against us let us do this because their hearts and faces (allegiances) are towards the land of Canaan."

13 He set over them taskmasters to enforce slavery, and they built strong cities for Pharaoh, Pithom, and Raamses and they built all the walls and all the fortifications, which had fallen in the cities of Egypt.

14 They enslaved them with harshness, and the more they were evil toward them, the more they increased and multiplied.

15 And the people of Egypt despised the children of Israel.

[Chapter 47]

1 In the seventh week, in the seventh year, in the forty-seventh jubilee, your father went out from the land of Canaan, and you (Moses) were born in the fourth week, in the sixth year of it, in the forty-eighth jubilee; this was the time of tribulation for the children of Israel.

2 Pharaoh, the king of Egypt, issued a command ordering them to throw all their newborn male children into the river.

3 And they threw them into the river for seven months until the day that you were born. It is said that your mother hid you for three months.

4 She made an ark for you, and covered it with pitch and tar, and placed it in the reeds on the bank of the river. She placed you in it seven days. Your mother came by night and nursed you. By day Miriam, your sister, guarded you from the birds.

5 In those days Tharmuth, the daughter of Pharaoh, came to bathe in the river, and she heard you crying. She told her maids to bring you out, and they brought you to her.

6 She took you out of the ark, and she had compassion on you.

7 Your sister said to her, "Shall I go and call to you one of the Hebrew women to nurse this baby for you?" And she said to her, "Go."

8 Your sister went and called your mother, Jochebed, and Pharaoh's daughter gave her wages (employed her), and she nursed you.

9 Afterwards, when you grew up, they brought you to the daughter of Pharaoh, and you became her son. Amram, your father, taught you writing. After you had completed three weeks (twenty-seven years) they brought you into the royal court.

10 You were three weeks of years at court until the time when you went out from the royal court and saw an Egyptian beating your friend who was of the children of Israel, and you killed him and hid him in the sand.

11 On the second day you came across two children of Israel quarreling together, and you asked the one who was doing wrong, "Why did you hit your brother?"

12 He was angry and indignant, and said, "Who made you a prince and a judge over us?

13 Do you want to kill me like you killed the Egyptian yesterday?" You were afraid and you fled on because of these words.

[Chapter 48]

1 In the sixth year of the third week of the forty-ninth jubilee you fled and went to live in the land of Midian for five weeks and one year. You returned to Egypt in

the second week in the second year in the fiftieth jubilee.

2 You know what He said to you on Mount Sinai, and what prince Mastema desired to do with you when you returned to Egypt.

3 Did he (Mastema) not seek to kill you with all his power and to deliver the Egyptians from your hand when he saw that you were sent to execute judgment and to take revenge on the Egyptians?

4 But I delivered you out of his hand, and you performed the signs and wonders which you were sent to perform in Egypt against Pharaoh, and against all of his household, and against his servants and his people.

5 The Lord exacted a great vengeance on them for Israel's sake, and struck them through the plagues of blood, frogs, lice, dog-flies, malignant boils, breaking out in pustules, the death of their cattle, and the plague of hailstones. He destroyed everything that grew from them by plagues of locusts, which devoured the remainder left by the hail, and by darkness, and by the death of the first-born of men and animals. The Lord took vengeance on all of their idols and burned them with fire.

6 Everything was sent through your hand, that you should declare these things before they were done. You spoke with the king of Egypt in the presence of all his servants and in the presence of his people and everything took place according to your words. Ten great and terrible judgments came on the land of Egypt so that you might execute vengeance on Egypt for Israel.

7 And the Lord did everything for Israel's sake according to His covenant, which he had ordained with Abraham. He took vengeance on them because they had brought them by force into bondage.

8 Prince Mastema stood against you, and sought to deliver you into the hands of Pharaoh. He helped the Egyptian sorcerers when they stood up and committed the evil acts they did in your presence. Indeed, we permitted them to work, but the remedies we did not allow to be worked by their hands.

9 The Lord struck them with malignant ulcers (hemorrhoids?), and they were not able to stand. They could not perform a single sign because we destroyed them.

10 Even after all of these signs and wonders, prince Mastema was not put to shame because he took courage and cried to the Egyptians to pursue you with all the power the Egyptians had, with their chariots, and with their horses, and with all the hosts of the peoples of Egypt.

11 But I stood between the Egyptians and Israel, and we delivered Israel out of his hand, and out of the hand of his people. The Lord brought them through the middle of the sea as if it were dry land.

12 The Lord our God threw all the people whom he (Mastema) brought to pursue Israel into the middle of the sea, into the depths of the bottomless pit, beneath the children of Israel, even as the people of Egypt had thrown their (Israel's) children into the river. He took vengeance on one million of them. In addition to one thousand strong and energetic men were destroyed because of the death of the suckling children of your people, which they had thrown into the river.

13 On the fourteenth day and on the fifteenth and on the sixteenth and on the seventeenth and on the eighteenth days, prince Mastema was bound and imprisoned and placed behind the children of Israel so that he might not accuse them.

14 On the nineteenth day we let them (Mastema and his demons) loose so that they might help the Egyptians pursue the children of Israel.

15 He hardened their hearts and made them stubborn, and the plan was devised by the Lord our God that He might strike the Egyptians and throw them into the sea.

16 On the fourteenth day we bound him that he might not accuse the children of Israel on the day when they asked the Egyptians for vessels and garments, vessels of silver, and vessels of gold, and vessels of bronze, in order to exact from the Egyptians a price in return for the bondage they had been forced to serve.

17 We did not lead the children of Israel from Egypt empty handed.

[Chapter 49]

1 Remember the commandment which the Lord commanded you concerning the Passover. You should celebrate it in its season on the fourteenth day of the first month. You should kill the sacrifice before evening. They should eat it by night on the evening of the fifteenth from the time of the setting of the sun.

2 Because on this night, at the beginning of the festival and the beginning of the joy, you were eating the Passover (lamb) in Egypt, when all the powers of Mastema had been let loose to kill all the first-born in the land of Egypt, from the first-born of Pharaoh to the first-born of the captive maid-servant in the mill, and even the first-born of the cattle.

3 This is the sign that the Lord gave them, in every house on the door post on which they saw the blood of a lamb of the first year they should not enter to kill, but should pass by it, that all those should be exempt that were in the house because the sign of the blood was on its door posts.

4 And the powers of the Lord did everything as the Lord commanded them, and they passed by all the children of Israel, and the plague did not come on them to destroy them, cattle, man, or dog.

5 The plague was oppressive in Egypt, and there was no house in Egypt where there was not one dead, and weeping, and lamentation.

6 All Israel was eating the flesh of the paschal lamb, and drinking the wine, and was praising, and blessing, and giving thanks to the Lord God of their fathers, and they were ready to get out from under the yoke of Egypt and the evil bondage.

7 Remember this day all the days of your life. Observe it from year to year all the days of your life, once a year, on its day, according to all the law of it. Do not forsake it from day to day, or from month to month.

8 It is an eternal law, and engraved on the heavenly tablets regarding all the children of Israel that they should observe it on its day once a year, every year, throughout all their generations. There is no limit of days, for this is a law forever.

9 The man who is free from uncleanness, and does not come to observe Passover on the occasion of its day and does not bring an acceptable offering before the Lord to eat and to drink before the Lord on the day of its festival will be guilty. If he is clean and close at hand (near the temple) and does not come, he shall be cut off because he did not offer the offering of the Lord in its appointed season. He shall take the guilt on himself.

10 Let the children of Israel come and observe the passover on the day of its fixed time, on the fourteenth day of the first month, between the evenings, from the third part of the day to the third part of the night, for two portions of the day are given to the light, and a third part to the evening.

11 The Lord commanded you to observe it between the evenings.

12 And it is not permissible to kill the sacrifice during any period of light, but only during the period bordering on the evening, and let them eat it at the time of the evening, until the third part of the night. Whatever is left over of all its flesh from the third part of the night and onwards is to be burned with fire.

13 They shall not cook it with water (boil or seethe it), nor shall they eat it raw, but roast it on the fire. They shall eat it with care, making sure its head with the inwards and its feet are roasted with fire, and they shall not break any bone of it, for of the children of Israel no bone shall be crushed.

14 For this reason the Lord commanded the children of Israel to observe the passover on the day of its fixed time, and they shall not break a bone of it, because it is a festival day He commanded. There was no passing over from any other day or any other month, but on the exact day let the festival be observed.

15 Command the children of Israel to observe the passover throughout their days, every year, once a year on the day of its fixed time, and it shall be a memorial well pleasing in the presence of the Lord, and no plague shall come on them to kill or to strike in that year in which they celebrate the passover in its season in every respect according to His command.

16 And they shall not eat it outside the sanctuary of the Lord, but before the sanctuary of the Lord, and all the people of the congregation of Israel shall celebrate it in its appointed season.

17 Every man twenty years of age and upward, who has come on the day of the Passover shall eat it in the sanctuary of your God before the Lord. This is how it is written and ordained. They should eat it in the sanctuary of the Lord.

18 When the children of Israel come into the land of Canaan that they are to possess, set up the tabernacle (tent) of the Lord within the land occupied by one of their tribes until the sanctuary of the Lord has been built in the land. There, let them come and celebrate the passover at tabernacle of the Lord, and let them kill it before the Lord from year to year.

19 When the house of the Lord has been built in the land of their inheritance, they shall go there and kill the Passover (lamb) in the evening, at sunset, at the third part of the day.

20 They shall offer its blood on the threshold of the altar, and shall place its fat on the fire, which is on the altar, and they shall eat its flesh roasted with fire in the yard of the house, which has been sanctified in the name of the Lord.

21 They may not celebrate the passover in their cities, nor in any place except at the tabernacle of the Lord, or before His house where His name has dwelt. They shall not stray from the Lord.

22 Moses, command the children of Israel to observe the ordinances of the passover, as it was commanded to you. Declare to them every year the purpose and time of the festival of unleavened bread. They should eat unleavened bread seven days. They should observe its festival and bring an offering every day during those seven days of joy before the Lord on the altar of your God.

23 Celebrate this festival with haste as when you went out from Egypt and you entered into the wilderness of Shur, because on the shore of the sea you completed it (the exodus).

[Chapter 50]

1 I made this law known to you the days of the Sabbaths in the desert of Sinai, between Elim and Sinai.

2 I told you of the Sabbaths of the land on Mount Sinai, and I told you of the jubilee years in the sabbaths of years, but have I not told you the year of it until you enter the land which you are to possess.

3 Keep the sabbaths of the land while they live on it, and they shall know the jubilee year.

4 I have ordained for you the year of weeks and the years and the jubilees. There are forty-nine jubilees from the days of Adam until this day, and one week and two years, and there are forty years yet to come for learning the commandments of the Lord, until they pass over into the land of Canaan, crossing the Jordan to the west.

5 The jubilees shall pass by until Israel is cleansed from all guilt of fornication, and uncleanness, and pollution, and sin, and error, and it dwells with confidence in all the land. There shall be no more Satan or any evil one, and the land shall be clean from that time forever.

6 I have written down the commandment for them regarding the Sabbaths and all the judgments of its laws for you.

7 Six days will you labor, but the seventh day is the Sabbath of the Lord your God.

8 You shall do no manner of work in it, you and your sons, and your menservants and your maidservants, and all your cattle and travelers also who lodge with you. The man that does any work on it shall die. Whoever desecrates that day, whoever has sex with his wife, whoever says he will do something on it, or he that will set out on a journey on it in regard to any buying or selling, or whoever draws water on it which he had not prepared for himself on the sixth day, and whoever takes up any burden to carry it out of his tent or out of his house shall die.

9 You shall do no work whatsoever on the Sabbath day except what you have prepared for yourselves on the sixth day, so as to eat, and drink, and rest. Keep Sabbath free from all work on that day. It is to bless the Lord your God, who has given you a day of festival and a holy day, and a day of the holy kingdom. This is a day for Israel among all their days forever.

10 Great is the honor which the Lord has given to Israel that they should eat, drink, and be satisfied on this festival day. Rest on it from all labor, which belongs to the labor of the children of men, except burning frankincense and bringing offerings and sacrifices before the Lord for days and for Sabbaths.

11 Only this work shall be done on the Sabbath days in the sanctuary of the Lord your God so that they may atone for Israel with sacrifice continually from day to day for a memorial pleasing before the Lord, so that He may always receive them from day to day according to what you have been commanded.

12 Every man who does any work on it, or takes a trip, or tills his farm, whether in his house or any other place, and whoever lights a fire, or rides a beast, or travels by ship on the sea shall die. And whoever strikes or kills anything, or slaughters a beast or a bird, or whoever catches an animal or a bird or a fish, or whoever fasts or makes war on the Sabbaths, the man who does any of these things on the Sabbath shall die. This is done so that the children of Israel will observe the Sabbaths according to the commandments regarding the Sabbaths of the land. It is written in the tablets, which He gave into my hands that I should write out for you the laws of the seasons, and the seasons according to the division of their days.

This completes the account of the division of the days.

Introduction to Enoch 1 Including The Book of Giants

In order to examine the greater work of the First Book of Enoch (1 Enoch) combined with the Book of Giants we must first examine the history and fragments of the Book of Giants. We will then look into the history and text of 1 Enoch and combine these two great texts, placing the Book of Giants back into the Book of 1 Enoch, from where it was taken.

The discovery of the first Dead Sea Scrolls in a remote Judean Desert cave in 1947 is considered one of the greatest archaeological events of the twentieth century.

East of the city of Jerusalem, the mountainous landscape plummets 1200 meters to the lowest point on earth. This is the Dead Sea. Many biblical stories are set in the caves and hills of the region. Here, King David fled from King Saul and hid in the desert's mountain caves. Here Jesus struggled with the devil, resisting temptation. Here, the community of Qumran hid their most valuable treasures, scrolls of ancient wisdom and religious insight.

For thousands of years the Judean Desert held secrets buried by the Jews of Qumarn, a group most scholars refer to as the Qumran Community. Much of this community was made up of the Essenes. This strict sect of Judaism used the caves to protect their literary treasures, which were scrolls hidden in sealed jars, placed deep within the caves perched high in the area of the Dead Sea. These scrolls, and their secrets, were revealed by a young Bedouin shepherd one day in 1947.

Prompted by the loss of one of his sheep, a shepherd of the Ta'amireh tribe left his flock to search for the stray. While searching, he found an opening in the steep hillside. Curious, as many young men are, he tossed a stone into the cave. The rock answered with the sound of pots breaking and he was compelled to investigate. He had stumbled on the greatest find of the century, the Dead Sea Scrolls.

In the caves were a number of pots. The majority of the pots were empty, begging the question, had vandals and thieves been there first, stealing much of the precious treasure. Some of the jars were still intact, with lids sealed in place. He opened the seals to reveal the ancient scrolls. They were wrapped in linen and blackened with age. No rubies, no diamond, no gold. Just a bunch of old scrolls turning to dust before his eyes.

He was not impressed. Wondering if he could trade them for anything of value, he and several companions brought the scrolls to Kando, a Bethlehem antiquities dealer, for appraisal. Kando seemed to recognize the age and value of the find, so he sent the Bedouins back to the caves in search of more treasures. They returned with a total of seven scrolls. The boys had no idea of the value of their find and so the Bedouin sold four of the seven scrolls to Kando and three to a second antiquities dealer named Salahi. Kando in turn resold the four scrolls to Archbishop Samuel, head of the Syrian Orthodox Monastery of St. Mark in Jerusalem.

Soon after the announcement of the find, Bedouin treasure hunters and archaeologists descended on the site and the surrounding caves. Ultimately they would find hundreds of ancient scrolls and fragments, including the oldest existing copies of the Hebrew Bible. The scrolls ranged in dates from the third century BCE (mid–Second Temple period) to the first century of the Common Era, before the destruction of the Second Temple in 70 CE. The scrolls provide an unprecedented picture of the diverse religious beliefs of ancient Judaism, and of daily life during the Second Temple period when Jesus lived and preached. While Hebrew is the most frequently used language in the Scrolls, about 15% were written in Aramaic and several in Greek. The Scrolls' materials are made up mainly of parchment, although some are papyrus, and the text of one Scroll is engraved on copper. A quarter of these non-biblical manuscripts are sectarian, and reflect the life and philosophy of a specific community. These core texts consist of eschatological biblical commentaries, apocalyptic texts, liturgical works, and regulations or rules that govern community life.

In the early days of Scrolls research, scholars attributed all of the Qumran scrolls to the Essene community. In recent years however, this consensus has been challenged and modified, though many scholars still maintain a link between the Essenes and the Dead Sea Scrolls.

In that time, the Essenes were one of the three basic sects of Judaism. Jewish sects described in ancient sources were the Pharisee, the Sadducee, and the Essene sect. It is thought the majority of the scrolls were written and hidden by the Essenes.

One of the many discoveries from the caves of Qumran is a scroll given the name, "The Book of Giants." It is thought to have been based on the Book of Enoch, a pseudepigraphical Jewish work from the 3rd century BCE, which was based on

Genesis 6:1-4. The Book of Giants, like the Book of Enoch, concerns itself with the Nephilim, which, in the Enoch version, are the offspring of fallen angels, who are called the Watchers.

The angels saw the beauty of the daughters of men. The broke their allegiance to heaven, descended to Earth, and married the women, and thus fathered giants. The book attempts to fill in the details about the giants and their offspring that the Book of Enoch is lacking. Indeed, there has been a theory put forth that the Book of Giants was actually part of the Book of Enoch at one time. The text relates how some giants, named Ohya, Hahya and Mahway, sons of the fallen angels, were compelled to dream. In these dreams they foresaw the Biblical Deluge, and their own demise. There is dialog concerning the futility of fighting God or his angels, even though they could conquer any human alive. Seeing their coming fate they seek to enlist the help of Enoch.

The mention of Enoch and the storyline referencing the patriarch places The Book of Giants firmly in the list of "Enochian" texts, along with 1 Enoch, 2 Enoch, and 3 Enoch, also known as The Ethiopic Book of Enoch, The Slavonic Secrets of Enoch, and The Hebrew Book of Enoch respectively.

In the Qumran version of the Book of Giants there is a brief mention of one of the giants, "Ohya", whose name is found in the Babylonian Talmud (Nidah, Ch 9), where it is said Sihon and Og, mentioned in the Book of Numbers, were brothers, as they were the sons of Ohia (Ohya) the son of Samhazai, one of the leaders of the fallen angels in the Book of Enoch.

Samhazai is the same as Samyaza, also Semihazah, Shemyazaz, Shemyaza, Sêmîazâz, Semjâzâ, Samjâzâ, Semyaza, and Shemhazai. He is a fallen angel of apocryphal Jewish and Christian tradition that ranked in the heavenly hierarchy as one of the Grigori (meaning "Watchers" in Greek). The name "Shemyaza(z)" means 'infamous rebellion', the combination of 'shem' (meaning 'name' or 'fame' [whether positive or negative]) and 'azaz' (which means 'rebellion' or 'arrogance' as a negative particle). This name occurs in the Enochian literature.

We meet the Grigori in several books, some of which are considered apocryphal and some pseudepigrapha (texts written by someone unknown but attributed to authors of prominence, such as 2 Enoch). In the book of 2 Enoch we read:
Chapter 18
1 The men took me on to the fifth heaven and placed me, and there I saw many and countless soldiers, called Grigori, of human appearance, and their size (was) greater

than that of great giants and their faces withered, and the silence of their mouths perpetual, and their was no service on the fifth heaven, and I said to the men who were with me: (See 2 Enoch 1:7)

(Note: The Greek transliteration egegoroi is the source of the term Grigori. The egegoroi are the Watchers; a group of fallen angels who mated with mortal women and produced the Nephilim mentioned in the books of Jubilees, 1Enoch, and Genesis 6:4.)

2 Why are they so very withered and their faces melancholy, and their mouths silent, and why is there no service in this heaven?

3 And they said to me: These are the Grigori, who with their prince Satanail (Satan) rejected the Lord of Light. After them are those who are held in great darkness in the second heaven, and three of them went down on to earth from the Lord's throne, to the place Ermon (Mount Hermon), and broke through their vows on the shoulder of the hill Ermon and saw the daughters of men how good they are, and took to themselves wives, and fouled the earth with their deeds, who broke the law and mixing (with the women), giants are born and amazingly large men with great hatred.

(Note: The Hill of Ermon could be Mount Hermon, which is mentioned over a dozen times in the Bible.)

4 And therefore God judged them with great judgment, and they weep for their brethren and they will be punished on the Lord's great day.

5 And I said to the Grigori: I saw your brethren and their works, and their great torments, and I prayed for them, but the Lord has condemned them to be under earth until this heaven and this earth shall end for ever.

6 And I said: Why do you stand there, brethren, and do not serve before the Lord's face, and have not put your services before the Lord's face? You could anger your Lord completely.

7 And they listened to my advice, and spoke to the four ranks in heaven. As I stood with those two men four trumpets sounded together with a loud voice, and the Grigori broke into song with one voice, and their voice went up before the Lord pitifully and touchingly.

A central theme in the Book of Giants is the fact that the giants were the offspring of the Watchers and human women. This theme has varied somewhat between various copies of the Book of Giants.

As it turns out, there are several versions of the Book of Giants. One version of the Book of Giants was spread by the Manichaean religion. The book became widely read and now exists in Syriac, Greek, Persian, Sogdian, Uyghur, and Arabic. Each version is somewhat different from that of the Qumran text, incorporating in each version local myths and legends and the various beliefs of the religions which had adapted the story for their own purpose.

Mani, the founder of the Manichaean religion needed to alter the story in order to fit it into his system. He taught a dualistic system of good and evil. The heavenly origin of the sons of God of Genesis, The Book of Giants, or the Book of Enoch did not fit into Mani's conviction that evil could not come from good. Thus the angels, who were called the Sons of God, were presented as demons and evil entities. This kept the separation between good and evil taught in his religion.

Manichaeism taught a dualistic cosmology describing the struggle between a good, spiritual world of light, and an evil, material world of darkness. These forces were distinct, separate, and always at odds. The forces of good and evil are at war. They battle throughout human history. The world becomes darker as light is gradually removed from the world of matter and returned to its place of origin, the world of light. Mani's beliefs were based on Mesopotamian Gnosticism and other religious movements.

There are numerous similarities between Mani's Book of Giants and the stories of the giants related in the Enoch literature and in the Book of Jubilees. Both Enoch and Jubilees are part of the Ethiopic Christian canon. Mani's borrowed liberally from earlier Jewish traditions in his religious movement, adapting them as need. This idea was upheld by the discovery of the Dead Sea Scrolls in 1947. J. T. Milik discovered roughly six to ten extremely poorly preserved manuscripts of an Aramaic Book of Giants, apparently the document used by Mani as the basis for his scriptural work. Their dates fall roughly across the first century B.C.E., so presumably the book was composed before this, although how long before remains open to question.

The Aramaic version found at Qumran also describes the Sumerian hero Gilgamesh and the monster Humbaba. The Qumran text was in such poor condition and so fragmented that clear reconstruction was impossible. Pieces of the texts are missing and at times so difficult to reconstruct that the order of certain fragments are unclear, thus the order of certain verses in the texts are "best guess". Scholars have poured over the small fragments, comparing them to other versions in an attempt to determine the proper flow. However, versions vary so widely that there are places, for example in the Manichaean version, that have no analog to the Aramaic version. Even with part of the text missing, the Book of Giants gives us information on how the ancients thought about fallen angels, the Watchers, the Nephilim, and the patriarch Enoch. Certainly, the Book of Giants can be used to augment and expand on the story given to us in the Book of Enoch.

The Aramaic Book of Giants draws on ancient Near Eastern myths and the Manichean version draws on Iranian myths. Two of the evil giants in the Aramaic version are named Gilgamesh and Hobabis. Gilgamesh is an epic figure in Sumerian and Akkadian literature, best known from the Epic of Gilgamesh, a work whose importance in ancient Mesopotamia was comparable to that of the Homeric epics in ancient Greece. Gilgamesh was said to be the king of Uruk. Uruk was an ancient city of Sumer and later Babylonia, situated east of the present bed of the Euphrates River, some 30 km east of modern As-Samawah, Al-Muthannā, in modern day Iraq. It is thought Gilgamesh lived sometime between 2800 and 2500 BC. The latest and most comprehensive telling of the Gilgamesh legend was the twelve-tablet Standard Babylonian Version, compiled circa 1200 BC by the priest Sîn-lēqi-unninni.

If one views the map that follows, it is easy to see how an ancient poem of the King of Sumer could have influenced the religion of Mani, a Babylonian, since Babylonia is modern-day Iraq. Likewise, it is easy to see how the actual name of Gilgamesh and the legends of his great strength recounted in the epic could have been used in a text found along the Dead Sea, since Iraq is in the region. Indeed, the path of transmission follows the area of agriculture in ancient times.

among themselves and begin killing one another, as well as other creatures.

The giants, Gilgamesh and Hobabis, of the "Book of Giants" appear to be the same as Gilgamesh and Humbaba/Huwawa of the "Gilgamesh Epic." In another version, Atanbush is mentioned and seems to be the same as Utnapishtim, the immortal. Since there are lost passages in the Aramaic Book of Giants he may have made an appearance there also.

Milik has translated and published an edition of some of the Aramaic fragments of the Book of Giants, which tells of the angels Šemihaza and Aza'el making a bet with God that if they were to descend from heaven to earth they would be able to resist the urge to sin. However, soon they could not restrain themselves from becoming sexually involved with the women they found to be so beautiful. As this kind of relationship tends to loosen the jaws of men and angels, they found themselves revealing secrets reserved for heavenly beings and restricted from humankind. Šemihaza (Samyaza) begets sons named Heyya and Aheyya. Heyya and Aheyya each have dreams foretelling their destruction. The angel Metatron (another name for the deified Enoch after his ascension to heaven) sends them a warning of the coming Flood.

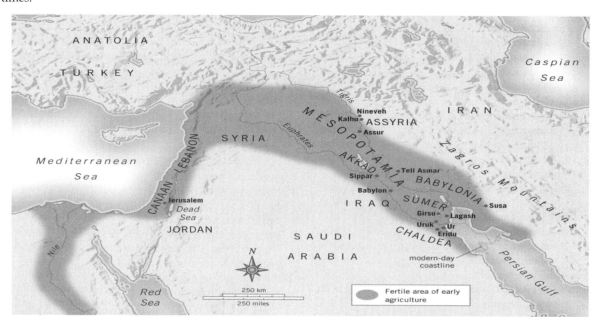

According to the Epic, Gilgamesh, a mortal demigod, meets Utnapishtim, the Babylonian version of Noah and the only man to survive the Flood. Utnapishtim was made immortal by the gods. In the Manichaean version, the giant Hobabiš, who is also called Humbaba, takes someone's wife. The giants fall out

Both dreams predict the coming of the Flood and the destructions of all human beings except Noah and his three sons. The giants, who are the sons of the angels, are killed in the Flood. Šemihaza repents and suspends himself upside down between heaven and earth. Aza'el refuses to repent and becomes a demon who entices men to corrupt deeds and who bears the sins of Israel on the "Day of Atonement" (cf. Lev 16:7-10).

Although there are parallels with the Book of Enoch, we must ask whether the Book of Giants is a Jewish work. Certainly, the discovery of the Aramaic version in the caves of Qumran points to the fact that the Essene community, a sect of Judaism, viewed that version as Jewish. The dates of the Aramaic manuscripts rule out the possibility of it being a Christian composition. However, the text contains Babylonian mythic material. This would seem to suggest the Jews borrowed from a polytheistic myth in a type of cross-pollination of mythic tales. The story does place the borrowed ideas into the proper light for Jewish literature. The Babylonian mythic figures are cast in an evil light and staged as wicked giants.

Since some have speculated that the Book of Giants was either part of or an expansion of the Book of Enoch, also called, 1 Enoch, we will examine the Book of Giants alone and also within the text of the Book of Enoch. There is a strong connection with the Book of Enoch, in a section called, "The Book of the Watchers" (1 Enoch 1-36). The reader is strongly advised to read Enoch, and especially that section, before reading the Book of Giants. The story will make much better sense if you do. Because of the need for this clarification the Book of Enoch will be included in the volume.

There have been many attempts to reconstruct the sequence and content of the Aramaic Book of Giants. There are instances where the various sequences of events are unclear. I generally follow Stuckenbruck's sequence of events. Since the text is so fragmented and at times not fully comprehensible, it is best to first present an overall flow or meaning of the storyline. We will now explore the story presented in the Book of Giants.

The Book of Enoch
Including the Book of Giants

The *Book of Watchers* (Chapters 1-36):

[Chapter 1]

1 The words of the blessing of Enoch, with which he blessed the elect and righteous, who will be living in the day of tribulation, when all the wicked and godless people are to be removed (from the earth).

2 And he began his story saying: (I am) Enoch, a righteous man, whose eyes were opened by God, and who saw the vision of the Holy One in heaven, which the angels showed me. And I heard everything from them, and I saw and understood, but it was not for this generation (to know), but for a remote one which is to come.

3 As I began my story concerning the elect I said,: The Holy Great One will come out from His dwelling,

4 And the eternal God will tread on the earth, (even) on Mount Sinai, and appear in the strength of His might from heaven.

5 And all shall be very afraid. The Watchers shall shake, and great fear and trembling shall seize them all the way to the ends of the earth.

6 And the high mountains shall be shaken, and the high hills shall be laid low, and shall melt like wax in the flame.

7 And the earth shall be completely torn apart, and all that is on the earth shall be destroyed, And there shall be a judgment on all.

Rev. 21: 7 He who overcomes will inherit all this, and I will be his God and he will be my son. 8 But the cowardly, the unbelieving, the vile, the murderers, the sexually immoral, those who practice magic arts, the idolaters and all liars — their place will be in the fiery lake of burning sulfur. This is the second death."

8 But with the righteous He will make peace; and will protect the elect and mercy shall be on them. And they shall all belong to God, and they shall prosper, and they shall be blessed. And the light of God shall shine on them.

Rev. 21: 23 The city does not need the sun or the moon to shine on it, for the glory of God gives it light, and the Lamb is its lamp. 24 The nations will walk by its light, and the kings of the earth will bring their splendor into it. 25 On no day will its gates ever be shut, for there will be no night there.

9 And behold! He comes with ten thousand of His holy ones (saints) to execute judgment on all, and to destroy all the ungodly (wicked); and to convict all flesh of all the works of their ungodliness which they have ungodly committed, and of all the hard things which ungodly sinners have spoken against Him.

JUD 1:14 And Enoch also, the seventh from Adam, prophesied of these, saying, Behold, the Lord cometh with ten thousands of his saints, 15 To execute judgment upon all, and to convince all that are ungodly among them of all their ungodly deeds which they have ungodly committed, and of all their hard speeches which ungodly sinners have spoken against him.

[Chapter 2]

1 Observe everything that takes place in the sky, how the lights do not change their orbits, and the luminaries which are in heaven, how they all rise and set in order each in its season (proper time), and do not transgress (defy) their appointed order.

2 Consider the earth, and understand the things which take place on it from start to finish, how steadfast they are, how none of the things on the earth change, but all the works of God appear to you.

3 Behold the summer and the winter, how the whole earth is filled with water, and clouds and dew and rain lie on it.

[Chapter 3]

1 Observe and see how (in the winter) all the trees seem as though they had withered and shed all their leaves, except fourteen trees, which do not lose their foliage but retain the old foliage from two to three years until the new comes.

[Chapter 4]

1 And again, observe the days of summer how the sun is above the earth. And you seek shade and shelter because of the heat of the sun, and the earth also burns with growing heat, and so you cannot walk on the earth, or on a rock because of its heat.

[Chapter 5]

1 Observe how the trees are covered with green leaves and how they bear fruit. Understand, know,

and recognize that He that lives for ever made them this way for you.

2 And all His works go on before Him from year to year for ever, and all the work and the tasks which they accomplish for Him do not change, and so is it done.

3 Consider how the sea and the rivers in like manner accomplish their course do not change because of His commandments.

4 But you, you have neither held to nor have you done the commandments of the Lord, But you have turned away and spoken proud and hard words with your unclean mouths against His greatness. Oh, you hard-hearted, you shall find no peace.

5 Therefore shall you curse your days, and the years of your life shall perish, and the years of your destruction shall be multiplied and in an eternal curse you shall find no mercy.

Deuteronomy 11: 26 See, I am setting before you today a blessing and a curse- 27 the blessing if you obey the commands of the LORD your God that I am giving you today; 28 the curse if you disobey the commands of the LORD your God and turn from the way that I command you today by following other gods, which you have not known.

6 In those days you shall make your names an eternal curse to all the righteous, and by you shall all who curse, curse, and all the sinners and godless shall curse you forever. And for you the godless there shall be a curse.

7 And all the elect shall rejoice, and there shall be forgiveness of sins, and mercy and peace and forbearance and joy. There shall be salvation for them, (like/and) a good light. And for all of you sinners there shall be no salvation, but on you all shall abide a curse.

8 But for the elect there shall be light and joy and peace, and they shall inherit the earth.

9 And then wisdom shall be given to the elect, and they shall all live and never again sin, either through forgetfulness or through pride: But those who are given wisdom shall be humble.

10 And they shall not again transgress, Nor shall they sin all the days of their life, Nor shall they die of the anger or wrath of God, But they shall complete the number of the days of their lives. And their lives shall be increased in peace, and their years will grow

in joy and eternal gladness and peace, all the days of their lives.

Isaiah 65
1I am sought of them that asked not for me; I am found of them that sought me not: I said, Behold me, behold me, unto a nation that was not called by my name.
2I have spread out my hands all the day unto a rebellious people, which walketh in a way that was not good, after their own thoughts;
3A people that provoketh me to anger continually to my face; that sacrificeth in gardens, and burneth incense upon altars of brick;
4Which remain among the graves, and lodge in the monuments, which eat swine's flesh, and broth of abominable things is in their vessels;
5Which say, Stand by thyself, come not near to me; for I am holier than thou. These are a smoke in my nose, a fire that burneth all the day.
6Behold, it is written before me: I will not keep silence, but will recompense, even recompense into their bosom,
7Your iniquities, and the iniquities of your fathers together, saith the LORD, which have burned incense upon the mountains, and blasphemed me upon the hills: therefore will I measure their former work into their bosom.
8Thus saith the LORD, As the new wine is found in the cluster, and one saith, Destroy it not; for a blessing is in it: so will I do for my servants' sakes, that I may not destroy them all.
9And I will bring forth a seed out of Jacob, and out of Judah an inheritor of my mountains: and mine elect shall inherit it, and my servants shall dwell there.

[Chapter 6]

1 And it came to pass when the children of men had multiplied that in those days were born to them beautiful and fair daughters.

GEN 6:1 And it came to pass, when men began to multiply on the face of the earth, and daughters were born unto them, 2 That the sons of God saw the daughters of men that they were fair; and they took them wives of all which they chose. 3 And the LORD said, My spirit shall not always strive with man, for that he also is flesh: yet his days shall be an hundred and twenty years.

2 And the angels, the sons of heaven, saw and lusted after them, and said to one another: 'Come, let us choose us wives from among the children of men

3 And have children with them.' And Semjaza, who was their leader, said to them: 'I fear you will not agree to do this deed,

4 And I alone shall have to pay the penalty of this great sin.'

5 And they all answered him and said: 'Let us all swear an oath, and all bind ourselves by mutual curses so we will not abandon this plan but to do this thing.' Then they all swore together and bound themselves by mutual curses.

6 And they were in all two hundred who descended in the days of Jared in the summit of Mount Hermon, and they called it Mount Hermon, because they had sworn and bound themselves by mutual curses on the act.

JUD 1:5 I will therefore put you in remembrance, though ye once knew this, how that the Lord, having saved the people out of the land of Egypt, afterward destroyed them that believed not. 6 And the angels who kept not their first estate, but left their own habitation, he hath reserved in everlasting chains under darkness unto the judgment of the great day.

7 And these are the names of their leaders: Samlazaz, their leader, Araklba, Rameel, Kokablel, Tamlel, Ramlel, Danel, Ezeqeel, Baraqijal,

(Author's note: Samlazaz could be another spelling of Semjaza, and possibly be the same entity.)

8 Asael, Armaros, Batarel, Ananel, Zaqiel, Samsapeel, Satarel, Turel, Jomjael, Sariel. These are their chiefs of tens.

[Chapter 7]

1 And all of them together went and took wives for themselves, each choosing one for himself, and they began to go in to them and to defile themselves with sex with them,

GEN 5:32 And Noah was five hundred years old: and Noah begat Shem, Ham, and Japheth. 6:1 And it came to pass, when men began to multiply on the face of the earth, and daughters were born unto them, 2 That the sons of God saw the daughters of men that they were fair; and they took them wives of all which they chose. 3 And the LORD said, My spirit shall not always strive with man, for that he also is flesh: yet his days shall be an hundred and twenty years. 4 There were giants in the earth in those days; and also after that, when the sons of God came in unto the daughters of men, and they bare children to them, the same became mighty men which were of old, men of renown. 5 And GOD saw that the wickedness of man was great in the earth, and that every imagination of the thoughts of his heart was only evil continually. 6 And it repented the LORD that he had made man on the earth, and it grieved him at his heart.

2 And the angels taught them charms and spells, and the cutting of roots, and made them acquainted with plants.

3 And the women became pregnant, and they bare large giants, whose height was three thousand cubits (ells).

<u>1Q23 Frag. 9 + 14 + 15</u> [. . .] they knew the secrets of [. . .] . . . sin was great in the earth [. . .] [. . .] and they killed many [. .] [. . .] they begat giants [. . .]

Jubilees 7
21 Because of these three things came the flood on the earth, namely, the fornication that the Watchers committed against the law of their ordinances when they went whoring after the daughters of men, and took themselves wives of all they chose, and they made the beginning of uncleanness.
22 And they begat sons, the Naphilim (Naphidim), and they were all dissimilar, and they devoured one another, and the Giants killed the Naphil, and the Naphil killed the Eljo, and the Eljo killed mankind, and one man killed one another.
23 Every one committed himself to crime and injustice and to shed much blood, and the earth was filled with sin.
24 After this they sinned against the beasts and birds, and all that moved and walked on the earth, and much blood was shed on the earth, and men continually desired only what was useless and evil.
25 And the Lord destroyed everything from the face of the earth. Because of the wickedness of their deeds, and because of the blood they had shed over all the earth, He destroyed everything. "

4 The giants consumed all the work and toil of men. And when men could no longer sustain them, the giants turned against them and devoured mankind.

<u>4Q531 Frag. 3</u> [. . .] everything that the earth produced [. . .] [. . .] the great fish [. . .] [. . .] the sky with all that grew [. . .] [. . .] fruit of the earth and all kinds of grain and all the trees [. . .] [. . .] beasts and reptiles [. . .] all creeping things of the earth and they observed all [. . .] [. . .] every harsh deed and [. . .] utterance [. . .] [. . .] male and female, and among humans [. . .]

5 And they began to sin against birds, and beasts, and reptiles, and fish, and to devour one another's flesh, and drank the blood.

<u>1Q23 Frag. 1 + 6</u> [. . .] two hundred donkeys, two hundred asses, two hundred . . . rams of the flock, two hundred goats, two hundred [. . .] beast of the field from every animal, from every bird [. . .] for miscegenation (inbreeding of people considered to be of different races) [. . .]

<u>4Q531 Frag. 2</u> [. . .] they defiled [. . .] [. . .] they begot] giants and monsters [. . .] [. . .] they begot, and, behold, all [the earth was corrupted [. . .] [. . .] with its blood and by the hand of [. . .] giant's which did not satisfy them and [. . .] [. . .] and they were seeking to devour many [. . .] [. . .] [. . .] the monsters attacked it.

6 Then the earth laid accusation against the lawless ones.

Jasher 2
19 For in those days the sons of men began to trespass against God, and to go contrary to the commandments which he had given Adam, to be prolific and reproduce in the earth.
20 And some of the sons of men caused their wives to drink a mixture that would render them unable to conceive, in order that they might retain their figures and their beautiful appearance might not fade.
21 And when the sons of men caused some of their wives to drink, Zillah drank with them.
22 And the child-bearing women appeared abominable in the sight of their husbands and they treated them as widows, while their husbands lived with those unable to conceive and to those women they were attached.

Genesis 4:8 And Cain talked with Abel his brother: and it came to pass, when they were in the field, that Cain rose up against Abel his brother, and slew him. 9And the LORD said unto Cain, Where is Abel thy brother? And he said, I know not: Am I my brother's keeper? 10And he said, What hast thou done? the voice of thy brother's blood crieth unto me from the ground. 11And now art thou cursed from the earth, which hath opened her mouth to receive thy brother's blood from thy hand; 12When thou tillest the ground, it shall not henceforth yield unto thee her strength; a fugitive and a vagabond shalt thou be in the earth.

[Chapter 8]

1 And Azazel taught men to make swords, and knives, and shields, and breastplates, and taught them about metals of the earth and the art of working them, and bracelets, and ornaments, and the use of antimony, and the beautifying of the eyelids, and all kinds of precious stones, and all coloring and dyes.

2 And there was great impiety, they turned away from God, and committed fornication, and they were led astray, and became corrupt in all their ways.

Matthew 5:19 (New International Version)
19Anyone who breaks one of the least of these commandments and teaches others to do the same will be called least in the kingdom of heaven, but whoever practices

and teaches these commands will be called great in the kingdom of heaven.

3 Semjaza taught the casting of spells, and root-cuttings, Armaros taught counter-spells (release from spells), Baraqijal taught astrology, Kokabel taught the constellations (portents), Ezeqeel the knowledge of the clouds, Araqiel the signs of the earth, Shamsiel the signs of the sun, and Sariel the course of the moon. And as men perished, they cried, and their cry went up to heaven.

Jasher 4
18 And their judges and rulers went to the daughters of men and took their wives by force from their husbands according to their choice, and the sons of men in those days took from the cattle of the earth, the beasts of the field and the fowls of the air, and taught the mixture of animals of one species with the other, in order therewith to provoke the Lord; and God saw the whole earth and it was corrupt, for all flesh had corrupted its ways on earth, all men and all animals.
19 And the Lord said, I will blot out man that I created from the face of the earth, yea from man to the birds of the air together with cattle and beasts that are in the field for I repent that I made them.
20 And all men who walked in the ways of the Lord died in those days, before the Lord brought the evil on man which he had declared, for this was from the Lord that they should not see the evil which the Lord spoke of concerning the sons of men.

[Chapter 9]

1 And then Michael, Uriel, Raphael, and Gabriel looked down from heaven and saw much blood being shed on the earth, and all lawlessness being done on the earth.

2 And they said to each other: 'Let the cries from the destruction of Earth ascend up to the gates of heaven.

3 And now to you, the holy ones of heaven, the souls of men make their petition, saying, "Bring our cause before the Most High."'

4 And they said to the Lord of the ages: 'Lord of lords, God of gods, King of kings, and God of the ages, the throne of your glory endures through all the generations of the ages, and your name holy and glorious and blessed to all the ages!

1TI 6:15 Which in his times he shall shew, who is the blessed and only Potentate, the King of kings, and Lord of lords; 16 Who only hath immortality, dwelling in the light which no man can approach unto; whom no man hath seen, nor can see: to whom be honour and power everlasting. Amen.

5 You have made all things, and you have power over all things: and all things are revealed and open in your sight, and you see all things, and nothing can hide itself from you.

6 Look at what Azazel has done, who hath taught all unrighteousness on earth and revealed the eternal secrets which were made and kept in heaven, which men were striving to learn:

7 And Semjaza, who taught spells, to whom you gave authority to rule over his associates.

8 And they have gone to the daughters of men on the earth, and have had sex with the women, and have defiled themselves, and revealed to them all kinds of sins.

GEN 6:4 There were giants in the earth in those days; and also after that, when the sons of God came in unto the daughters of men, and they bare children to them, the same became mighty men which were of old, men of renown.

9 And the women have borne giants, and the whole earth has thereby been filled with blood and unrighteousness.

4Q532 Col. 2 Frags. 1 - 6 [. . .] flesh [. . .] All [. . .] monsters [. . .] will be [. . .] [. . .] they would arise [. . .] lacking in true knowledge [. . .] because [. . .] [. . .] the earth [grew corrupt [. . .] mighty [. . .] [. . .] they were considering [. . .] [. . .] from the angels upon [. . .] [. . .] in the end it will perish and die [. . .] [. . .] they caused great corruption in the earth [. . .] [. . .] this did not suffice to [. . .] "they will be [. . .]

GEN 6:5 And GOD saw that the wickedness of man was great in the earth, and that every imagination of the thoughts of his heart was only evil continually. 6 And it repented the LORD that he had made man on the earth, and it grieved him at his heart.

10 And now, behold, the souls of those who have died are crying out and making their petition to the gates of heaven, and their lament has ascended and cannot cease because of the lawless deeds which are done on the earth.
11 And you know all things before they come to pass, and you see these things and you have permitted them, and say nothing to us about these things. What are we to do with them about these things?'

Revelation 6:10 (New International Version) 10 They called out in a loud voice, "How long, Sovereign Lord, holy and true, until you judge the inhabitants of the earth and avenge our blood?"

[Chapter 10]

1 Then said the Most High, the Great and Holy One, "Uriel, go to the son of Lamech.

2 Say to him: 'Go to Noah and tell him in my name "Hide yourself!" and reveal to him the end that is approaching: that the whole earth will be destroyed, and a flood is about to come on the whole earth, and will destroy everything on it.'

GEN 7:4 For yet seven days, and I will cause it to rain upon the earth forty days and forty nights; and every living substance that I have made will I destroy from off the face of the earth.

3 'And now instruct him as to what he must do to escape that his offspring may be preserved for all the generations of the world.'

GEN 6:13 And God said unto Noah, The end of all flesh is come before me; for the earth is filled with violence through them; and, behold, I will destroy them with the earth. 14 Make thee an ark of gopher wood; rooms shalt thou make in the ark, and shalt pitch it within and without with pitch.

4 And again the Lord said to Raphael: 'Bind Azazel hand and foot, and cast him into the darkness and split open the desert, which is in Dudael, and cast him in.

5 And fill the hole by covering him rough and jagged rocks, and cover him with darkness, and let him live there for ever, and cover his face that he may not see the light.

Revelation 20: 1 And I saw an angel come down from heaven, having the key of the bottomless pit and a great chain in his hand. 2 And he laid hold on the dragon, that old serpent, which is the Devil, and Satan, and bound him a thousand years, 3 And cast him into the bottomless pit, and shut him up, and set a seal upon him, that he should deceive the nations no more, till the thousand years should be fulfilled: and after that he must be loosed a little season.

6 And on the day of the great judgment he shall be hurled into the fire.

Revelation 19:20 (King James Version)
20And the beast was taken, and with him the false prophet that wrought miracles before him, with which he deceived them that had received the mark of the beast, and them that worshipped his image. These both were cast alive into a lake of fire burning with brimstone.

7 And heal the earth which the angels have ruined, and proclaim the healing of the earth, for I will restore the earth and heal the plague, that not all of the children of men may perish through all the secret things that the Watchers have disclosed and have taught their sons.

ROM 8:18 For I reckon that the sufferings of this present time are not worthy to be compared with the glory which shall be revealed in us. 19 For the earnest expectation of the creature waiteth for the manifestation of the sons of God. 20 For the creature was made subject to vanity, not willingly, but by reason of him who hath subjected the same in hope, 21 Because the creature itself also shall be delivered from the bondage of corruption into the glorious liberty of the children of God.

8 The whole earth has been corrupted through the works that were taught by Azazel: to him ascribe ALL SIN.'

9 To Gabriel said the Lord: 'Proceed against the bastards and the reprobates, and against the children of fornication and destroy the children of fornication and the children of the Watchers. Cause them to go against one another that they may destroy each other in battle: Shorten their days.

GEN 6:7 And the LORD said, I will destroy man whom I have created from the face of the earth; both man, and beast, and the creeping thing, and the fowls of the air; for it repenteth me that I have made them. 8 But Noah found grace in the eyes of the LORD.

10 No request that (the Watchers) their fathers make of you shall be granted them on their behalf; for they hope to live an eternal life, and that each one of them will live five hundred years.'

11 And the Lord said to Michael: 'Go, bind Semjaza and his team who have associated with women and have defiled themselves in all their uncleanness.

12 When their sons have slain one another, and they have seen the destruction of their beloved ones, bind them fast for seventy generations under the hills of the earth, until the day of the consummation of their judgment and until the eternal judgment is accomplished.

(Author's note: 70 generations of 500 years = 35000 years.)

13 In those days they shall be led off to the abyss of fire and to the torment and the prison in which they shall be confined for ever.'

14 Then Semjaza shall be burnt up with the condemned and they will be destroyed, having been bound together with them to the end of all generations.

Fragment from the Book of Giants:
And he answered, I am a giant, and by the mighty strength of my arm and my own great strength [I can defeat] anyone mortal, and I have made war against them; but I am not [strong enough for our heavenly opponent or to be] able to stand against them, for my opponents [. . .] reside in Heaven, and they dwell in the holy places. And not [on the earth and they] are stronger than I. [. . .] The time of the wild beast has come, and the wild man calls me. Then Ohya said to him, I have been forced to have a dream and the sleep of my eyes vanished in order to let me see a vision. Now I know that on Gilgamesh [our futures rest.]

15 Destroy all the spirits of lust and the children of the Watchers, because they have wronged mankind.

16 Destroy all wrong from the face of the earth and let every evil work come to an end and let (the earth be planted with righteousness) the plant of righteousness and truth appear; and it shall prove a blessing, the works of righteousness and truth shall be planted in truth and joy for evermore.

GEN 6:7 And the LORD said, I will destroy man whom I have created from the face of the earth; both man, and beast, and the creeping thing, and the fowls of the air; for it repenteth me that I have made them.

17 And then shall all the righteous survive, and shall live until they beget thousands of children, and all the days of their youth and their old age shall they complete in peace.

GEN 8:22 While the earth remaineth, seedtime and harvest, and cold and heat, and summer and winter, and day and night shall not cease.

GEN 9:1 And God blessed Noah and his sons, and said unto them, Be fruitful, and multiply, and replenish the earth.
18 And then shall the whole earth be untilled in righteousness and shall be planted with trees and be full of blessing. And all desirable trees shall be planted on it, and they shall plant vines on it.

19 And the vine which they plant shall yield fruit in abundance, and as for all the seed which is sown, each measurement (of it) shall bear a thousand, and each measurement of olives shall yield ten presses of oil.

20 You shall cleanse the earth from all oppression, and from all unrighteousness, and from all sin, and

from all godlessness, and all the uncleanness that is brought on the earth you shall destroy from off the earth.

(Author's note: Meanwhile, the Nephilin are having dreams and visions…)

2Q26 [. . .] they drenched the tablet in the water [. . .] [. . .] the waters went up over the [tablet . . .] [. . .] they lifted out the tablet from the water of [. . .]

4Q530 Frag.7 [. . .] this vision] is for cursing and sorrow. I am the one who confessed [. . .] the whole group of the castaways that I shall go to [. . .] [. . .] the spirits of the slain complaining about their killers and crying out [. . .] that we shall die together and be made an end of [. . .] much and I will be sleeping, and bread [. . .] for my dwelling; the vision and also [. . .] entered into the gathering of the giants [. . .]

6Q8 [. . .] Ohya and he said to Mahway [. . .] [. . .] without trembling. Who showed you all this vision, my brother? [. . .] Barakel, my father, was with me. [. . .] Before Mahway had finished telling [what he had seen . . .] [. . . said] to him, Now I have heard wonders! If a barren woman gives birth [. . .]

4Q530 Frag. 4 There upon Ohya said to Hahya [. . .] [. . .] to be destroyed from upon the earth and [. . .] [. . .] the earth. When [...] they wept before [the giants . . .]

4Q530 Frag. 7 [. . .] your strength [. . .] [. . .] After that, Ohya said to Hahya [. . .] Then he answered, It is not for us, but for Azaiel, for he did [. . .] the children of angels are the giants, and they would not let all their proved ones] be neglected [. . . we have] not been cast down; you have strength [. . .]

4Q531 Frag. 1 [. . .] I am a giant, and by the mighty strength of my arm and my own great strength [. . .] any one mortal, and I have made war against them; but I am not [. . .] able to stand against them, for my opponents [. . .] reside in Heaven, and they dwell in the holy places. And not [. . . they] are stronger than I. [. . .] of the wild beast has come, and the wild man they call me. [. . .] Then Ohya said to him, I have been forced to have a dream [. . .] the sleep of my eyes vanished, to let me see a vision. Now I know that on [. . .] [. . .] Gilgamesh [. . .]

6Q8 Frag. 2 three of its roots [. . .] [while] I was [watching,] there came [. . . they moved the roots into] this garden, all of them, and not [. . .]

4Q530 Col. 2 concerns the death of our souls [. . .] and all his comrades, and Ohya told them what

Gilgamesh said to him [. . .] and it was said [. . .] "concerning [. . .] the leader has cursed the potentates" and the giants were glad at his words. Then he turned and left [. . .]

Thereupon two of them had dreams and the sleep of their eye, fled from them, and they arose and came to [. . . and told] their dreams, and said in the assembly of [their comrades] the monsters [. . . In] my dream I was watching this very night [and there was a garden . . .] gardeners and they were watering [. . .] two hundred trees and large shoots came out of their root [. . .] all the water, and the fire burned all [the garden . . .] They found the giants to tell them [the dream . .]

21 All the children of men shall become righteous, and all nations shall offer adoration and shall praise Me,

22 And all shall worship Me. And the earth shall be cleansed from all defilement, and from all sin, and from all punishment, and from all torment, and I will never again send another flood from this generation to all generations and for ever.

[Chapter 11]

1 And in those days I will open the storehouse of blessings in heaven, and rain down blessings on the earth and over the work and labor of the children of men.

Malachi 3:10 (King James Version)
10Bring ye all the tithes into the storehouse, that there may be meat in mine house, and prove me now herewith, saith the LORD of hosts, if I will not open you the windows of heaven, and pour you out a blessing, that there shall not be room enough to receive it.

2 Truth and peace shall be united throughout all the days of the world and throughout all the generations of men.'

[Chapter 12]

1 Then Enoch disappeared and no one of the children of men knew where he was hidden, and where he abode;

GEN 5:21 And Enoch lived sixty and five years, and begat Methuselah: 22 And Enoch walked with God after he begat Methuselah three hundred years, and begat sons and daughters: 23 And all the days of Enoch were three hundred sixty and five years: 24 And Enoch walked with God: and he was not; for God took him.

2 And what had become of him. And his activities were with the Holy Ones and the Watchers.

[. . . to Enoch] the noted scribe, and he will interpret for us the dream. Thereupon his fellow Ohya declared and said to the giants, I too had a dream this night, O giants, and, behold, the Ruler of Heaven came down to earth [. . .] and such is the end of the dream. Thereupon all the giants and monsters grew afraid and called Mahway. He came to them and the giants pleaded with him and sent him to Enoch, the noted scribe. They said to him, Go [. . .] to you that [. . .] you have heard his voice. And he said to him, He will [. . . and] interpret the dreams [. . .] Col. 3 [. . .] how long the giants have to live. [. . .]

3 And I, Enoch, was blessing the Lord of majesty and the King of the ages, and lo! the Watchers called me, Enoch the scribe, and said to me:

4 'Enoch, you scribe of righteousness, go, tell the Watchers of heaven who have left the high heaven, the holy eternal place, and have defiled themselves with women, and have done as the children of earth do, and have taken to themselves wives:

5 "You have done great destruction on the earth: And you shall have no peace nor forgiveness of sin:

6 Since they delight themselves in their children, They shall see the murder of their beloved ones, and the destruction of their children shall and they shall lament, and shall make supplication forever, you will receive neither mercy or peace."

(Author's note: Although we are led to believe the fallen angels are loathsome and evil, they loved and adored their children. Further, it was not the angels that became the demons. It was their children, whose spirits were evil and could not be killed.)

[. . .] he (the Nephilim) mounted up in the air like strong winds, and flew with his hands like eagles . . . he left behind] the inhabited world and passed over Desolation, the great desert [. . .] and Enoch saw him and hailed him, and Mahway said to him [. . .] hither and thither a second time to Mahway [. . .] The giants await your words, and all the monsters of the earth. If [. . .] has been carried [. . .] from the days of [. . .] their [. . .] and they will be added [. . .] [. . .] we would know from you their meaning [. . .] [. . .] two hundred trees that from heaven [came down . . .]

4Q530 Frag. 2 The scribe [Enoch . . .] [. . .] a copy of the second tablet that Enoch sent [. . .] in the very handwriting of Enoch the noted scribe [. . .] In the name of God the great and holy one, to Shemihaza and all [his companions . . .] let it be known to you that not [. . .] and the things you have done, and that your wives [. . .] they and their sons and the wives of [their sons . . .] by your licentiousness on the earth, and there has been upon you [. . .] and the land is crying out and complaining about you and the deeds of your children [. . .] the harm that you have done to it. [. . .] until Raphael arrives, behold, destruction [is coming, a great flood, and it will destroy all living things] and whatever is in the deserts and the seas. And the meaning of the matter [. . .] upon you for evil. But now, loosen the bonds binding you to evil [. . .] and pray.

4Q531 Frag. 7 [. . .] great fear seized me and I fell on my face; I heard his voice [. . .] [. . .] he dwelt among human beings but he did not learn from them [. . .]

(The Book of Jubilees - Chapter 5:1 When the children of men began to multiply on the face of the earth and daughters were born to them, and the angels of God saw them on a certain year of this jubilee, that they were beautiful, and they took themselves wives of all whom they chose, and they gave birth to their sons and they were giants.
2 Because of them lawlessness increased on the earth and all flesh corrupted its way. Men and cattle and beasts and birds and everything that walked on the earth were all corrupted in their ways and their orders, and they began to devour each other. Lawlessness increased on the earth and the imagination and thoughts of all men were continually, totally evil.
3 God looked on the earth, and saw it was corrupt, and all flesh had corrupted its orders, and all that were on the earth had committed all manner of evil before His eyes.
4 He said that He would destroy man and all flesh on the face of the earth that He had created.
5 But Noah found grace before the eyes of the Lord. 6 And against the angels whom He had sent on the earth, He had boiling anger, and He gave commandment to root them out of all their dominion, and He commanded us to bind them in the depths of the earth, and look, they are bound in the middle of the earth, and are kept separate.
7 And against their sons went out a command from His mouth that they should be killed with the sword, and be left under heaven.
8 He said, "My spirit shall not always abide on man; for they also are flesh and their days shall be one hundred and twenty years.")

(Jasher 4:17 very man made to himself a god, and they robbed and plundered every man his neighbor as well as his relative, and they corrupted the earth, and the earth was filled with violence.
18 And their judges and rulers went to the daughters of men and took their wives by force from their husbands according to their choice, and the sons of men in those days took from

the cattle of the earth, the beasts of the field and the fowls of the air, and taught the mixture of animals of one species with the other, in order therewith to provoke the Lord; and God saw the whole earth and it was corrupt, for all flesh had corrupted its ways on earth, all men and all animals.
19 And the Lord said, I will blot out man that I created from the face of the earth, yea from man to the birds of the air together with cattle and beasts that are in the field, for I repent that I made them.
20 All men who walked in the ways of the Lord died in those days, before the Lord brought the evil on man which he had declared, for this was from the Lord that they should not see the evil which the Lord spoke of concerning the sons of men.
21 And Noah found grace in the sight of the Lord, and the Lord chose him and his children to raise up offspring on the face of the whole earth.)

[Chapter 13]

1 And Enoch went and said: 'Azazel, you shall have no peace: a severe sentence has been passed against you that you should be bound:

2 And you shall not have rest or mercy (toleration nor request granted), because of the unrighteousness which you have taught, and because of all the works of godlessness,

3 And unrighteousness and sin which you have shown to men.

4 Then I went and spoke to them all together, and they were all afraid, and fear and trembling seized them.
5 And they asked me to write a petition for them that they might find forgiveness, and to read their petition in the presence of the Lord of heaven. They had been forbidden to speak (with Him) nor were they to lift up their eyes to heaven for shame of their sins because they had been condemned.

6 Then I wrote out their petition, and the prayer in regard to their spirits and their deeds individually and in regard to their requests that they should obtain forgiveness and forbearance.

7 And I went off and sat down at the waters of Dan, in the land of Dan, to the southwest of Hermon: I read their petition until I fell asleep.

8 And I had a dream, and I saw a vision of their chastisement, and a voice came to me that I would reprimand (reprove) them.

9 And when I awoke, I came to them, and they were all sitting gathered together, weeping in Abelsjail,

which is between Lebanon and Seneser, with their faces covered.

10 And I recounted to them all the visions which I had seen when I was asleep, and I began to speak the words of righteousness, and to reprimand heavenly Watchers.

[Chapter 14]

1 This is the book of the words of righteousness, and of the reprimand of the eternal Watchers in accordance with the command of the Holy Great One in that vision I saw in my sleep.

2 What I will now say with a tongue of flesh and with the breath of my mouth: which the Great One has given to men to speak with it and to understand with the heart.

3 As He has created and given to man the power of understanding the word of wisdom, so has He created me also and given me the power of reprimanding the Watchers, the children of heaven.

4 I wrote out your petition, and in my vision it appeared that your petition will not be granted to you throughout all the days of eternity, and that judgment has been finally passed on you:

5 Your petition will not be granted. From here on you shall not ascend into heaven again for all eternity, and you will be bound on earth for all eternity.
6 Before this you will see the destruction of your beloved sons and you shall have no pleasure in them, but they shall fall before you by the sword.
7 Your petition shall not be granted on their behalf or on yours, even though you weep and pray and speak all the words contained in my writings.

8 In the vision I saw clouds that invited me and summoned me into a mist, and the course of the stars and the flashes of lightning and hurried me and drove me,

9 And the winds in the vision caused me to fly and lifted me up, and bore me into heaven. And I went in until I drew near to a wall which was built out of crystals and surrounded by tongues of fire, and it began to frighten me.

10 I went into the tongues of fire and drew near a large house which was built of crystals: and the walls of the house were like a mosaic of hailstones and the floor was made of crystals like snow.

Revelation 4: 6 And before the throne there was a sea of glass like unto crystal: and in the midst of the throne, and round about the throne, were four beasts full of eyes before and behind.

Revelation 21:10 And he carried me away in the spirit to a great and high mountain, and shewed me that great city, the holy Jerusalem, descending out of heaven from God, 11 Having the glory of God: and her light was like unto a stone most precious, even like a jasper stone, clear as crystal; 12 And had a wall great and high, and had twelve gates, and at the gates twelve angels, and names written thereon, which are the names of the twelve tribes of the children of Israel:

11 Its ceiling was like the path of the stars and lightning flashes, and between them were fiery cherubim,

12 Their sky was clear as water. A flaming fire surrounded the walls, and its doors blazed with fire.

13 I entered that house, and it was hot as fire and cold as ice; there were no pleasures or life therein: fear covered me, and trembling got hold of me.

14 As I shook and trembled, I fell on my face.

15 And I saw a vision, And lo! there was a second house, greater than the first,

16 And the all the doors stood open before me, and it was built of flames of fire. And in every respect it was splendid and magnificent to the extent that I cannot describe it to you.

17 Its floor was of fire, and above it was lightning and the path of the stars, and its ceiling also was flaming fire.

18 And I looked and saw a throne set on high, its appearance was like crystal, and its wheels were like a shining sun, and there was the vision of cherubim.

1TI 6:16 Who only hath immortality, dwelling in the light which no man can approach unto; whom no man hath seen, nor can see: to whom be honour and power everlasting. Amen.

19 And from underneath the throne came rivers of fire so that I could not look at it.

Third Book of Enoch: The Holy Chayoth carry the Throne of Glory from below. Each one uses only three fingers. The length of each fingers is 800,000 and 700 times one hundred, and 66,000 parasangs. (4) And underneath the feet of the Chayoth there are seven rivers of fire running and flowing

20 And He who is Great in Glory sat on the throne, and His raiment shone more brightly than the sun and was whiter than any snow.

MAT 25:31 When the Son of man shall come in his glory, and all the holy angels with him, then shall he sit upon the throne of his glory:

21 None of the angels could enter or could behold His face because of the magnificence and glory and no flesh could behold Him.

22 The sea of fire surrounded Him, and a great fire stood in front of Him, and no one could draw close to Him: ten thousand times ten thousand stood before Him, but He needed no Holy council.

23 The most Holy Ones who were near to Him did not leave night or day.

24 And until then I had been prostrate on my face, trembling, and the Lord called me with His own mouth, and said to me:

25 'Come here, Enoch, and hear my word.' And one of the Holy Ones came to me picked me up and brought me to the door: and I bowed down my face.

[Chapter 15]

1 And He answered and said to me, and I heard His voice: 'Do not be afraid, Enoch, you righteous man and scribe of righteousness.

2 Approach and hear my voice. Go and say to the Watchers of heaven, for whom you have come to intercede: "You should intercede for men, and not men for you."

3 Why and for what cause have you left the high, holy, and eternal heaven, and had sex with women, and defiled yourselves with the daughters of men and taken to yourselves wives, and done like the children of earth, and begotten giants (as your) sons?

4 Though you were holy, spiritual, living the eternal life, you have defiled yourselves with the blood of women, and have begotten children with the blood of flesh, and, as the children of men, you have lusted after flesh and blood like those who die and are killed.

5 This is why I have given men wives, that they might impregnate them, and have children by them, that deeds might continue on the earth.

6 But you were formerly spiritual, living the eternal life, and immortal for all generations of the world.

7 Therefore I have not appointed wives for you; you are spiritual beings of heaven, and in heaven was your dwelling place.

LUK 20:34 And Jesus answering said unto them, The children of this world marry, and are given in marriage: 35 But they which shall be accounted worthy to obtain that world, and the resurrection from the dead, neither marry, nor are given in marriage: 36 Neither can they die any more: for they are equal unto the angels; and are the children of God, being the children of the resurrection.

8 And now, the giants, who are produced from the spirits and flesh, shall be called evil spirits on the earth,

9 And shall live on the earth. Evil spirits have come out from their bodies because they are born from men and from the holy Watchers, their beginning is of primal origin;

10 They shall be evil spirits on earth, and evil spirits shall they be called spirits of the evil ones. [As for the spirits of heaven, in heaven shall be their dwelling, but as for the spirits of the earth which were born on the earth, on the earth shall be their dwelling.] And the spirits of the giants afflict, oppress, destroy, attack, war, destroy, and cause trouble on the earth.

11 They take no food, but do not hunger or thirst. They cause offences but are not observed.

12 And these spirits shall rise up against the children of men and against the women, because they have proceeded from them in the days of the slaughter and destruction.'

(Author's note: These are the evil spirits and demons. They are the disembodied spirits of the offspring of angels and humans.)

The Book of Jubilees: Because of these three things came the flood on the earth, namely, the fornication that the Watchers committed against the law of their ordinances when they went whoring after the daughters of men, and took themselves wives of all they chose, and they made the beginning of uncleanness.
And they begat sons, the Naphilim (Naphidim – the fallen), and they were all dissimilar, and they devoured one another,

and the Giants killed the Naphil, and the Naphil killed the Eljo, and the Eljo killed mankind, and one man killed one another.

Every one committed himself to crime and injustice and to shed much blood, and the earth was filled with sin.

After this they sinned against the beasts and birds, and all that moved and walked on the earth, and much blood was shed on the earth, and men continually desired only what was useless and evil.

And the Lord destroyed everything from the face of the earth. Because of the wickedness of their deeds, and because of the blood they had shed over all the earth, He destroyed everything. "

[Chapter 16]

1 'And at the death of the giants, spirits will go out and shall destroy without incurring judgment, coming from their bodies their flesh shall be destroy until the day of the consummation, the great judgment in which the age shall be consummated, over the Watchers and the godless, and shall be wholly consummated.'

MAT 8:28 And when he was come to the other side into the country of the Gergesenes, there met him two possessed with devils, coming out of the tombs, exceeding fierce, so that no man might pass by that way. 29 And, behold, they cried out, saying, What have we to do with thee, Jesus, thou Son of God? art thou come hither to torment us before the time?

2 And now as to the Watchers who have sent you to intercede for them, who had been in heaven before,

3 (Say to them): "You were in heaven, but all the mysteries of heaven had not been revealed to you, and you knew worthless ones, and these in the hardness of your hearts you have made known to the women, and through these mysteries women and men work much evil on earth."

4 Say to them therefore: " You have no peace."'

Genesis 6: 1And it came to pass, when men began to multiply on the face of the earth, and daughters were born unto them, 2That the sons of God saw the daughters of men that they were fair; and they took them wives of all which they chose. 3And the LORD said, My spirit shall not always strive with man, for that he also is flesh: yet his days shall be an hundred and twenty years. 4There were giants in the earth in those days; and also after that, when the sons of God came in unto the daughters of men, and they bare children to them, the same became mighty men which were of old, men of renown.

5And God saw that the wickedness of man was great in the earth, and that every imagination of the thoughts of his heart was only evil continually. 6And it repented the LORD that

he had made man on the earth, and it grieved him at his heart. 7And the LORD said, I will destroy man whom I have created from the face of the earth; both man, and beast, and the creeping thing, and the fowls of the air; for it repenteth me that I have made them. 8But Noah found grace in the eyes of the LORD.

[Chapter 17]

1 And they took me to a place in which those who were there were like flaming fire,

2 And, when they wished, they made themselves appear as men. They brought me to the place of darkness, and to a mountain the point of whose summit reached to heaven.

3 And I saw the lighted places and the treasuries of the stars and of the thunder and in the uttermost depths, where were

4 A fiery bow and arrows and their quiver, and a fiery sword and all the lightning. And they took me to the waters of life, and to the fire of the west, which receives every setting of the sun.

5 And I came to a river of fire in which the fire flows like water into the great sea towards the west.

6 I saw the great rivers and came to the great darkness, and went to the place where no flesh walks.

7 I saw the mountains of the darkness of winter and the place from where all the waters of the deep flow.

8 I saw the mouths of all the rivers of the earth and the mouth of the deep.

[Chapter 18]

1 I saw the storehouse of all the winds: I saw how He had adorned the whole creation with them and the firm foundations of the earth.

2 And I saw the corner-stone of the earth: I saw the four winds which support the earth and the firmament of the heaven.

3 I saw how the winds stretch out the height of heaven, and have their station between heaven and earth; these are the pillars of heaven.

4 I saw the winds of heaven which turn and bring the sky and the sun and all the stars to their setting place.

5 I saw the winds on the earth carrying the clouds: I saw the paths of the angels. I saw at the end of the earth the firmament of heaven above.

6 And I continued south and saw a place which burns day and night, where there are seven mountains of magnificent stones, three towards the east, and three towards the south.

7 And as for those towards the east, they were of colored stone, and one of pearl, and one of jacinth (a stone of healing), and those towards the south of red stone.

8 But the middle one reached to heaven like the throne of God, and was made of alabaster.

9 And the summit of the throne was of sapphire.

Ezekiel 1:22 And the likeness of the firmament upon the heads of the living creature was as the colour of the terrible crystal, stretched forth over their heads above.
23 And under the firmament were their wings straight, the one toward the other: every one had two, which covered on this side, and every one had two, which covered on that side, their bodies.
24 And when they went, I heard the noise of their wings, like the noise of great waters, as the voice of the Almighty, the voice of speech, as the noise of an host: when they stood, they let down their wings.
25 And there was a voice from the firmament that was over their heads, when they stood, and had let down their wings.
26 And above the firmament that was over their heads was the likeness of a throne, as the appearance of a sapphire stone: and upon the likeness of the throne was the likeness as the appearance of a man above upon it.
27 And I saw as the colour of amber, as the appearance of fire round about within it, from the appearance of his loins even upward, and from the appearance of his loins even downward, I saw as it were the appearance of fire, and it had brightness round about. 28 As the appearance of the bow that is in the cloud in the day of rain, so was the appearance of the brightness round about. This was the appearance of the likeness of the glory of the LORD. And when I saw it, I fell upon my face, and I heard a voice of one that spake.

10 And I saw a great abyss of the earth, with pillars of heavenly fire, and I saw among them fiery pillars of Heaven, which were falling,

11 And as regards both height and depth, they were immeasurable.

12 And beyond that abyss I saw a place which had no firmament of heaven above, and no firmly founded earth beneath it: there was no water on it, and no birds,

13 But it was a desert and a horrible place. I saw there seven stars like great burning mountains,

14 And an angel questioned me regarding them. The angel said: 'This place is the end of heaven and earth.

15 This has become a prison for the stars and the host of heaven. And the stars which roll over the fire are they which have transgressed the commandment of the Lord in the beginning of their rising, because they did not come out at their proper times.

16 And He was angry with them, and bound them until the time when their guilt should be consummated even for ten thousand years.'

[Chapter 19]

1 And Uriel said to me: 'The angels who have had sex with women shall stand here, and their spirits, having assumed many different forms, are defiling mankind and shall lead them astray into sacrificing to demons as gods, here shall they stand, until the day of the great judgment in which they shall be judged and are made an end of.

1 Timothy 4
1The Spirit clearly says that in later times some will abandon the faith and follow deceiving spirits and things taught by demons.

Rev 9:20The rest of mankind that were not killed by these plagues still did not repent of the work of their hands; they did not stop worshiping demons, and idols of gold, silver, bronze, stone and wood — idols that cannot see or hear or walk. 21Nor did they repent of their murders, their magic arts, their sexual immorality or their thefts.

2 And the women also of the angels who went astray shall become sirens (other versions read 'shall become peaceful' also, another version reads, 'shall salute them').'

3 And I, Enoch, alone saw the vision, the ends of all things: and no man shall see as I have seen.

1PE 4:7 But the end of all things is at hand: be ye therefore sober, and watch unto prayer.

[Chapter 20]

1 These are the names of the holy angels who watch.

2 Uriel, one of the holy angels, who is over the world, turmoil and terror.

3 Raphael, one of the holy angels, who is over the spirits of men.

4 Raguel, one of the holy angels who takes vengeance on the world of the luminaries.

5 Michael, one of the holy angels, set over the virtues of mankind and over chaos.

6 Saraqael, one of the holy angels, who is set over the spirits, who sin in the spirit.

7 Gabriel, one of the holy angels, who is over Paradise and the serpents and the Cherubim.

8 Remiel, one of the holy angels, whom God set over those who rise.

[Chapter 21]

1 Then, I proceeded to where things were chaotic and void.

2 And I saw there something horrible: I saw neither a heaven above nor a firmly founded earth, but a place chaotic and horrible.

3 And there I saw seven stars of heaven bound together in it, like great mountains and burning with fire.

4 Then I said: 'For what sin are they bound, and on why have they been cast in here?'

5 Then said Uriel, one of the holy angels, who was with me, and was chief over them: 'Enoch, why do you ask, and why are you eager for the truth?

6 These are some of the stars of heaven, which have transgressed the commandment of the Lord, and are bound here until ten thousand years, the time entailed by their sins, are consummated.'

7 And I went out from there to another place, which was still more horrible than the former, and I saw a terrible thing: a great fire there which burned and blazed, and the place was cleft as far as the abyss, full of great falling columns of fire:

8 Neither its width or breadth could I see, nor could I see its source.

9 Then I said: 'I am afraid of this place and cannot stand to look at it.!' Then Uriel, one of the holy angels

who was with me, answered and said to me: 'Enoch, why are you so afraid?'

10 And I answered: 'Because of this fearful place, and because of the spectacle of the pain.' And he said to me: 'This place is the prison of the angels, and here they will be imprisoned for ever.'

Daniel 7:9 "As I looked,
"thrones were set in place, and the Ancient of Days took his seat. His clothing was as white as snow; the hair of his head was white like wool His throne was flaming with fire, and its wheels were all ablaze. 10 A river of fire was flowing, coming out from before him. Thousands upon thousands attended him; ten thousand times ten thousand stood before him. The court was seated and the books were opened. 11 "Then I continued to watch because of the boastful words the horn was speaking. I kept looking until the beast was slain and its body destroyed and thrown into the blazing fire.

[Chapter 22]

1 And I went out to another place west where there was a mountain and hard rock.

2 And there was in it four hollow places, deep and wide and very smooth. How smooth are the hollow places and looked deep and dark.

3 Then Raphael answered, one of the holy angels who was with me, and said to me: 'These hollow places have been created for this very purpose, that the spirits of the souls of the dead should be gathered here, that all the souls of the children of men should brought together here. And these places have been made to receive them until the day of their judgment and until the period appointed, until the great judgment comes on them.'

(Author note: The idea of a gathering place of the dead is seen in the doctrine of Purgatory, where the dead are gathered and those who are "redeemable" are kept and purified until such time they might ascend to heaven.)

2 Maccabee 12: 41 All men therefore praising the Lord, the righteous Judge, who had opened the things that were hid, 42 Betook themselves unto prayer, and besought him that the sin committed might wholly be put out of remembrance. Besides, that noble Judas exhorted the people to keep themselves from sin, forsomuch as they saw before their eyes the things that came to pass for the sins of those that were slain.

43 And when he had made a gathering throughout the company to the sum of two thousand drachms of silver, he sent it to Jerusalem to offer a sin offering, doing therein very well and honestly, in that he was mindful of the resurrection:

44 For if he had not hoped that they that were slain should have risen again, it had been superfluous and vain to pray for the dead.

45 And also in that he perceived that there was great favour laid up for those that died godly, it was an holy and good thought. Whereupon he made a reconciliation for the dead, that they might be delivered from sin.

4 I saw the spirit of a dead man, and his voice went out to heaven and made petitions.

5 And I asked Raphael the angel who was with me, and I said to him: 'This spirit which petitions,

6 Whose is it, whose voice goes up and petitions heaven?'

7 And he answered me saying: 'This is the spirit which went out from Abel, whom his brother Cain slew, and he makes his suit against him until his offspring is destroyed from the face of the earth, and his offspring are annihilated from among the children of men.'

GEN 4:8 And Cain talked with Abel his brother: and it came to pass, when they were in the field that Cain rose up against Abel his brother, and slew him. 9 And the LORD said unto Cain, Where is Abel thy brother? And he said, I know not: Am I my brother's keeper? 10 And he said, What hast thou done? the voice of thy brother's blood crieth unto me from the ground. 11 And now art thou cursed from the earth, which hath opened her mouth to receive thy brother's blood from thy hand; 12 When thou tillest the ground, it shall not henceforth yield unto thee her strength; a fugitive and a vagabond shalt thou be in the earth.

8 Then I asked, regarding all the hollow places: 'Why is one separated from the other?'

9 And he answered me and said to me: 'These three have been made that the spirits of the dead might be separated. Divisions have been made for the spirits of the righteous, in which there is the bright spring of water.

10 And one for sinners when they die and are buried in the earth and judgment has not been executed on them in their lifetime.

11 Here their spirits shall be set apart in this great pain until the great day of judgment and punishment and torment of those who curse for ever and retribution for their spirits.

2 Peter 3: 7By the same word the present heavens and earth are reserved for fire, being kept for the day of judgment and destruction of ungodly men.

12 There He shall bind them for ever. And such a division has been made for the spirits of those who make their petitions, who make disclosures concerning their destruction, when they were slain in the days of the sinners.

13 Such has been made for the spirits of men who were not righteous but sinners, who were complete in transgression, and of the transgressors they shall be companions, but their spirits shall not be destroyed in the day of judgment nor shall they be raised from here.'

14 Then I blessed the Lord of glory and said: 'Blessed be my Lord, the Lord of righteousness, who rules for ever.'

[Chapter 23]

1 From here I went to another place to the west of the ends of the earth.

2 And I saw a burning fire which ran without resting, and never stopped from its course day or night but flowed always in the same way.

3 And I asked saying: 'What is this which never stops?'

4 Then Raguel, one of the holy angels who was with me, answered me and said to me: 'This course of fire which you have seen is the fire in the west and is the fire of all the lights of heaven.'

[Chapter 24]

1 And from here I went to another place on the earth, and he showed me a mountain range of fire which burned day and night.

2 And I went beyond it and saw seven magnificent mountains, all differing from each other, and their stones were magnificent and beautiful, and their form was glorious: three towards the east, one founded on the other, and three towards the south, one on the other, and deep rough ravines, no one of which joined with any other.

3 And the seventh mountain was in the midst of these, and it was higher than them, resembling the seat of a throne.

4 And fragrant trees encircled the throne. And among them was a tree such as I had never smelled, nor was any among them or were others like it; it had a fragrance beyond all fragrance, and its leaves and blooms and wood would not ever wither:

5 And its fruit is beautiful, and its fruit resembles the dates of a palm. Then I said: 'How beautiful is this tree, and fragrant, and its leaves are fair, and its blooms very delightful in appearance.'

6 Then Michael, one of the holy and honored angels who was with me, and was their leader, spoke.

[Chapter 25]
1 And he said to me: 'Enoch, why do you ask me about the fragrance of the tree, and why do you wish to learn the truth?'

2 Then I answered him saying: 'I wish to know about everything, but especially about this tree.'

3 And he answered saying: 'This high mountain which you have seen, whose summit is like the throne of God, is His throne, where the Holy Great One, the Lord of Glory, the Eternal King, will sit, when He shall come down to visit the earth with goodness.

4 And as for this fragrant tree, no mortal is permitted to touch it until the great judgment, when He shall take vengeance on all and bring everything to its completion for ever.

Genesis 2:8 Now the LORD God had planted a garden in the east, in Eden; and there he put the man he had formed. 9 And the LORD God made all kinds of trees grow out of the ground — trees that were pleasing to the eye and good for food. In the middle of the garden were the tree of life and the tree of the knowledge of good and evil. 10 A river watering the garden flowed from Eden; from there it was separated into four headwaters. 11 The name of the first is the Pishon; it winds through the entire land of Havilah, where there is gold. 12 (The gold of that land is good; aromatic resin and onyx are also there.) 13 The name of the second river is the Gihon; it winds through the entire land of Cush. 14 The name of the third river is the Tigris; it runs along the east side of Asshur. And the fourth river is the Euphrates. 15 The LORD God took the man and put him in the Garden of Eden to work it and take care of it. 16 And the LORD God commanded the man, "You are free to eat

from any tree in the garden; 17 but you must not eat from the tree of the knowledge of good and evil, for when you eat of it you will surely die."

5 It shall then be given to the righteous and holy. Its fruit shall be for food to the Elect: it shall be transplanted to the holy place, to the temple of the Lord, the Eternal King.

REV 22:1 And he shewed me a pure river of water of life, clear as crystal, proceeding out of the throne of God and of the Lamb. 2 In the midst of the street of it, and on either side of the river, was there the tree of life, which bare twelve manner of fruits, and yielded her fruit every month: and the leaves of the tree were for the healing of the nations. 3 And there shall be no more curses: but the throne of God and of the Lamb shall be in it; and his servants shall serve him.

6 Then they shall rejoice and be glad, and enter into the holy place; And its fragrance shall enter into their bones, And they shall live a long life on earth, as your fathers lived. And in their days there will be no sorrow or pain or torment or toil.'

7 Then I blessed the God of Glory, the Eternal King, who has prepared such things for the righteous, and has created them and promised to give to them.

Ezekiel 47:12 (New International Version)
12 Fruit trees of all kinds will grow on both banks of the river. Their leaves will not wither, nor will their fruit fail. Every month they will bear, because the water from the sanctuary flows to them. Their fruit will serve for food and their leaves for healing."

[Chapter 26]

1 And I went from there to the middle of the earth, and I saw a blessed place in which there were trees with branches alive and blooming on a tree that had been cut down.

(Author's note: The "hollow earth theory" has been espoused by various groups throughout history. The theory was used to create the book and movie, "Journey to the Center of the Earth.")

2 And there I saw a holy mountain,

3 And underneath the mountain to the east there was a stream and it flowed towards the south. And I saw towards the east another mountain higher than this, and between them a deep and narrow valley.

4 In it ran a stream underneath the mountain. And to the west of it there was another mountain, lower than

the former and of small elevation, and a dry, deep valley between them; and another deep and dry valley was at the edge of the three mountains.

5 And all the valleys were deep and narrow, being formed from hard rock, and there were no trees planted on them.

6 And I was very amazed at the rocks in the valleys.

[Chapter 27]

1 Then I said: 'What is the purpose of this blessed land, which is entirely filled with trees, and what is the purpose of this accursed valley between them?'

2 Then Uriel, one of the holy angels who was with me, answered and said: 'This accursed valley is for those who are cursed for ever: Here shall all the accursed be gathered together who utter with their lips words against the Lord not befitting His glory or say hard things against Him. Here shall they be gathered together, and here shall be their place of judgment.

3 In the last days there shall be the spectacle of righteous judgment on them in the presence of the righteous for ever: here shall the merciful bless the Lord of glory, the Eternal King.

4 In the days of judgment they shall bless Him for the mercy in that He has shown them.'

5 Then I blessed the Lord of Glory and set out His glory and praised Him gloriously.

[Chapter 28]

1 Then, I went towards the east, into the midst of the mountain range in the desert, and I saw a wilderness.

2 And it was solitary, full of trees and plants. And water gushed out from above.

3 Rushing like a torrent which flowed towards the north-west it caused clouds and dew to fall on every side.

[Chapter 29]

1 Then I went to another place in the desert, and approached to the east of this mountain range.

2 And there I saw aromatic trees exuding the fragrance of frankincense and myrrh, and the trees also were similar to the almond tree.

[Chapter 30]

1 Beyond these, I went far to the east,

2 And I saw another place, a valley full of water like one that would not run dry.

3 And there was a tree, the color of fragrant trees was that of mastic. And on the sides of those valleys I saw fragrant cinnamon. And beyond these I proceeded to the east.

[Chapter 31]

1 And I saw other mountains, and among them were groves of trees, and there was nectar that flowed from them, which is named Sarara and Galbanum.
2 And beyond these mountains I saw another mountain to the east of the ends of the earth, on which there were aloe trees, and all the trees were full of fruit, being like almond trees.

3 And when it was burned it smelled sweeter than any fragrant odor.

[Chapter 32]

1 And after I had smelled these fragrant odors, I looked towards the north over the mountains I saw seven mountains full of fine nard and fragrant trees of cinnamon and pepper.

2 And then I went over the summits of all these mountains, far towards the east of the earth, and passed over the Red Sea and went far from it, and passed over the angel Zotiel.

(Author's note: The angel Zotiel, whose name means, "little one of God," welcomes back those sinners who have gone astray but have repented. Based on the description of the locations, some have suggested the sphinx could be a representation, although most believe this to be unlikely.)

3 And I came to the Garden of Righteousness. I saw far beyond those trees more trees and they were numerous and large. There were two trees there, very large, beautiful, glorious, and magnificent. The tree of knowledge, whose holy fruit they ate and acquired great wisdom.

4 That tree is in height like the fir, and its leaves are like those of the Carob tree,

5 And its fruit is like the clusters of the grapes, very beautiful: and the fragrance of the tree carries far.

Isaiah 60:13 "The glory of Lebanon will come to you, the pine, the fir and the cypress together, to adorn the place of my sanctuary; and I will glorify the place of my feet.

6 Then I said: 'How beautiful is the tree, and how attractive is its look!' Then Raphael the holy angel, who was with me, answered me and said: 'This is the tree of wisdom, of which your father of old and your mother of old, who were your progenitors, have eaten, and they learned wisdom and their eyes were opened, and they knew that they were naked and they were driven out of the garden.'

[Chapter 33]

1 And from there I went to the ends of the earth and saw there large beasts, and each differed from the other; and I saw birds also differing in appearance and beauty and voice, the one differing from the other.

2 And to the east of those beasts I saw the ends of the earth where heaven rests on it, and the doors of heaven open. And I saw how the stars of heaven come out, and I counted the gates from which they came out,
3 And wrote down all their outlets, of each individual star by their number and their names, their courses and their positions, and their times and their months, as Uriel the holy angel who was with me showed me.

4 He showed me all things and wrote them down for me; also their names he wrote for me, and their laws and their functions.

[Chapter 34]

1 From there I went towards the north to the ends of the earth, and there I saw a great and glorious device at the ends of the whole earth.

2 And here I saw three gates of heaven open : through each of them proceed north winds: when they blow there is cold, hail, frost, snow, dew, and rain.

3 And out of one gate they blow for good: but when they blow through the other two gates, it is for violence and torment on the earth, and they blow with force.

[Chapter 35]

1 Then I went towards the west to the ends of the earth, and saw there three gates of heaven open such

as I had seen in the east, the same number of gates, and the same number of outlets.

[Chapter 36]

1 And from there I went to the south to the ends of the earth, and saw there three open gates of heaven.

2 And from them come dew, rain, and wind. And from there I went to the east to the ends of heaven, and saw here the three eastern gates of heaven open and small gates above them.

3 Through each of these small gates pass the stars of heaven and they run their course to the west on the path which is shown to them.

4 And as often as I saw I blessed always the Lord of Glory, and I continued to bless the Lord of Glory who has done great and glorious wonders, who has shown the greatness of His work to the angels and to spirits and to men, that they might praise His work and all His creation: that they might see the power of His might and praise the great work of His hands and bless Him for ever.

[Chapter 37]
The *Book of Parables* (Chapters 37-71):

1 The second vision which he saw, the vision of wisdom which Enoch the son of Jared, the son of Mahalalel,

2 The son of Cainan, the son of Enos, the son of Seth, the son of Adam, saw. And this is the beginning of the words of wisdom which I lifted up my voice to speak and say to those which dwell on earth: Hear, you men of old time, and see, you that come after, the words of the Holy One which I will speak before the Lord of spirits.

3 The words are for the men of old time, and to those that come after. We will not withhold the beginning of wisdom from this present day. Such wisdom has never been given by the Lord of spirits as I have received according to my insight, according to the good pleasure of the Lord of spirits by whom the lot of eternal life has been given to me.

4 Now three Parables were imparted to me, and I lifted up my voice and recounted them to those that dwell on the earth.

[Chapter 38]

1 The first Parable: When the congregation of the righteous shall appear, and sinners shall be judged

for their sins, and shall be driven from the face of the earth;

2 And when the Righteous One shall appear before the eyes of the elect righteous ones, whose works are weighed by the Lord of spirits, light shall appear to the righteous and the elect who dwell on the earth. Where will there be the dwelling for sinners, and where the will there be a resting-place for those who have denied the Lord of spirits? It had been good for them if they had not been born.

JOH 1:1 In the beginning was the Word, and the Word was with God, and the Word was God. 2 The same was in the beginning with God. 3 All things were made by him; and without him was not any thing made that was made. 4 In him was life; and the life was the light of men. 5 And the light shineth in darkness; and the darkness comprehended it not.

3 When the secrets of the righteous shall be revealed and the sinners judged, and the godless driven from the presence of the righteous and elect,

4 From that time those that possess the earth shall no longer be powerful and mighty: And they shall not be able to look at the face of the holy ones, because the Lord of spirits has caused His light to appear on the face of the holy, righteous, and elect.

2CO 3:18 But we all, with open face beholding as in a glass the glory of the Lord, are changed into the same image from glory to glory, even as by the Spirit of the Lord.

5 Then the kings and the mighty shall be destroyed and be turned over into the hands of the righteous and holy.

6 And from then on none shall seek mercy from the Lord of spirits for themselves for their life is at an end.

[Chapter 39]

1 And it shall come to pass in those days that elect and holy children will descend from the high heaven, and their offspring will become one with the children of men.

(Author's note: Here we have a verse that can be interpreted in various ways. The holy children from the high heaven could be the spirits of the righteous dead. However, other verses seem to suggest those souls are being held until judgment. Enoch 38:1 mentions a judgment and this could be the one we seek to release the souls and make this verse mesh well.)

Other theories regarding this verse have been put forward by those who believe God will give his consent to angels that they may finally freely mix with people. This seems unlikely given the previous reaction. Lastly, those involved with "UFO studies" point to this verse as an indication of contact.

Revelation 21
1 Then I saw a new heaven and a new earth, for the first heaven and the first earth had passed away, and there was no longer any sea. 2 I saw the Holy City, the new Jerusalem, coming down out of heaven from God, prepared as a bride beautifully dressed for her husband. 3 And I heard a loud voice from the throne saying, "Now the dwelling of God is with men, and he will live with them. They will be his people, and God himself will be with them and be their God. 4 He will wipe every tear from their eyes. There will be no more death or mourning or crying or pain, for the old order of things has passed away." 5 He who was seated on the throne said, "I am making everything new!" Then he said, "Write this down, for these words are trustworthy and true."

2 And in those days Enoch received books of indignation and wrath, and books of turmoil and confusion. There will be no mercy for them, says the Lord of spirits.

3 And in those days a whirlwind carried me off from the earth, And set me down at the end of heaven.

4 There I saw another vision, the dwelling-places of the holy, and the resting-places of the righteous.

5 Here my eyes saw the dwelling places of His righteous angels, and the resting-places of the Holy Ones. And they petitioned and interceded and prayed for the children of men, and righteousness flowed before them like water, and mercy fell like dew on the earth: Thus it is among them for ever and ever.

6 And in that place my eyes saw the Elect One of righteousness and of faith,

7 And I saw his dwelling-place under the wings of the Lord of spirits.

8 And righteousness shall prevail in his days, and the righteous and elect shall be innumerable and will be before Him for ever and ever.

9 And all the righteous and elect ones before Him shall be as bright as fiery lights, and their mouth shall be full of blessing, and their lips shall praise the name of the Lord of spirits. Righteousness and truth before Him shall never fail.

10 There I wished to dwell, and my spirit longed for that dwelling-place; and thus it was decided and my portion was assigned and established by the Lord of spirits.

11 In those days I praised and exalted the name of the Lord of spirits with blessings and praises, because He had destined me for blessing and glory according to the good pleasure of the Lord of spirits.

12 For a long time my eyes looked at that place, and I blessed Him and praised Him, saying: 'Blessed is He, and may He be blessed from the beginning and for evermore. And in His presence there is no end.

13 He knows before the world was created what is for ever and what will be from generation to generation.

14 Those who do not sleep bless you, they stand before your glory and bless, praise, and exalt you, saying: "Holy, holy, holy, is the Lord of spirits: He fills the earth with spirits."'

15 And here my eyes saw all those who do not sleep: they stand before Him and bless Him saying: 'Blessed be you, and blessed be the name of the Lord for ever and ever.'

16 And my face was changed; for I could no longer see.

Exodus 34:29
When Moses came down from Mount Sinai with the two tablets of the Testimony in his hands, he was not aware that his face was radiant because he had spoken with the LORD.

[Chapter 40]

1 And after that I saw thousands of thousands and ten thousand times ten thousand,

2 I saw a multitude beyond number and reckoning, who stood before the Lord of spirits. And on the four sides of the Lord of spirits I saw four figures, different from those that did not sleep, and I learned their names; for the angel that went with me told me their names, and showed me all the hidden things.

3 And I heard the voices of those four presences as they uttered praises before the Lord of glory.

4 The first voice blessed the Lord of spirits for ever and ever.

5 The second voice I heard blessing the Elect One and the elect ones who depend on the Lord of spirits.

6 And the third voice I heard pray and intercede for those who live on the earth and pray earnestly in the name of the Lord of spirits.

7 And I heard the fourth voice fending off the Satans (adversary or accusers) and forbidding them to come before the Lord of spirits to accuse them who dwell on the earth.

8 After that I asked the angel of peace who went with me, who showed me everything that is hidden: 'Who are these four figures which I have seen and whose words I have heard and written down?'

9 And he said to me: 'This first is Michael, the merciful and long-suffering; and the second, who is set over all the diseases and all the wounds of the children of men, is Raphael; and the third, who is set over all the powers, is Gabriel' and the fourth, who is set over the repentance and those who hope to inherit eternal life, is named Phanuel.'

10 And these are the four angels of the Lord of spirits and the four voices I heard in those days.

[Chapter 41]

1 And after that I saw all the secrets of heavens, and how the kingdom is divided, and how the actions of men are weighed in the balance.

Daniel 5:27 Thou art weighed in the balances, and art found wanting.

2 And there I saw the mansions of the elect and the mansions of the holy, and my eyes saw all the sinners being driven from there which deny the name of the Lord of spirits, and they were being dragged off; and they could not live because of the punishment which proceeds from the Lord of spirits.

JOH 14:2 In my Father's house are many mansions: if it were not so, I would have told you. I go to prepare a place for you. 3 And if I go and prepare a place for you, I will come again, and receive you unto myself; that where I am, there ye may be also.

3 And there my eyes saw the secrets of the lightning and of the thunder, and the secrets of the winds, how they are divided to blow over the earth, and the secrets of the clouds and dew,

4 And there I saw where they came from and how they saturate the dusty earth.

5 And there I saw closed storehouses out of which the winds are divided, the storehouse of the hail and winds, the storehouse of the mist, and of the clouds, and the cloud thereof hovers over the earth from the beginning of the world.

6 And I saw the storehouses of the sun and moon, where they go and where they come, and their glorious return, and how one is superior to the other, and their stately orbit, and how they do not leave their orbit, and they add nothing to their orbit and they take nothing from it, and they keep faith with each other, in accordance with the oath by which they are bound together.

7 And first the sun goes out and traverses his path according to the commandment of the Lord of spirits, and mighty is His name for ever and ever. And after that I saw the invisible and the visible path of the moon, and she accomplishes the course of her path in that place by day and by night - the one holding a position opposite to the other before the Lord of spirits. And they give thanks and praise and rest not; but their thanksgiving is for ever and ever.

8 For the sun makes many revolutions for a blessing or a curse, and the course of the path of the moon is light to the righteous and darkness to the sinners in the name of the Lord, who made a separation between the light and the darkness, and divided the spirits of men and strengthened the spirits of the righteous, in the name of His righteousness.

Matthew 5:44 But I say unto you, Love your enemies, bless them that curse you, do good to them that hate you, and pray for them which despitefully use you, and persecute you; 45 That ye may be the children of your Father which is in heaven: for he maketh his sun to rise on the evil and on the good, and sendeth rain on the just and on the unjust.

9 For no angel hinders and no power is able to hinder; for He appoints a judge for them all and He judges them all Himself.

[Chapter 42]

1 Wisdom found no place where she might dwell; then a dwelling-place was assigned her in heavens.

2 Wisdom went out to make her dwelling among the children of men, and found no dwelling-place. Wisdom returned to her place, and took her seat among the angels.

3 And unrighteousness went out from her storehouses. She found those she did not seek, and dwelt with them, (she sought no one in particular but found a place[...]); as rain in a desert and dew on a thirsty land.

[Chapter 43]

1 And I saw other lightning and the stars of heaven, and I saw how He called them all by their names and they obeyed Him.

2 And I saw how they are weighed in a righteous balance according to their proportions of light: I saw the width of their spaces and the day of their appearing, and how their revolution produces lightning:

3 And I saw their revolution according to the number of the angels, and how they keep faith with each other. And I asked the angel who went with me who showed me what was hidden:

4 'What are these?' And he said to me: 'The Lord of spirits has shown you their parable: these are the names of the holy who dwell on the earth and believe in the name of the Lord of spirits for ever and ever.'

[Chapter 44]

1 Also another phenomenon I saw in regard to the lightning: how some of the stars arise and become lightning and cannot part with their new form.

[Chapter 45]

1 And this is the second Parable: concerning those who deny the name of the dwelling of the holy ones and the Lord of spirits.

2 They shall not ascend to heaven, and they shall not come on the earth: Such shall be the lot of the sinners who have denied the name of the Lord of spirits, who are preserved for the day of suffering and tribulation.

3 On that day My Elect One shall sit on the throne of glory and shall try the works of the righteous, and their places of rest shall be innumerable. And their souls shall grow strong within them when they see My Elect One, And those who have called on My glorious name:

4 Then will I cause My Elect One to dwell among them. I will transform heaven and make it an eternal blessing and light,

5 And I will transform the earth and make it a blessing, and I will cause My elect ones to dwell on it. But the sinners and evil-doers shall not set foot on it.

6 For I have seen and satisfied My righteous ones with peace and have caused them to dwell before Me, but for the sinners there is judgment impending with Me, so that I shall destroy them from the face of the earth.

[Chapter 46]

1 And there I saw One whose face looked ancient. His head was white like wool, and with Him was another being whose countenance had the appearance of a man, and his face was full of graciousness, like one of the holy angels.

2 And I asked the angel who went with me and showed me all the hidden things, concerning that Son of Man, who he was, and where came from, and why he went with the Ancient One? And he answered and said to me:

3 "This is the son of Man who hath righteousness, with whom dwells righteousness, and who reveals all the treasures of that which is hidden, because the Lord of spirits hath chosen him, and whose lot has preeminence before the Lord of spirits in righteousness and is for ever.

4 And this Son of Man whom you have seen shall raise up the kings and the mighty from their seats, and the strong from their thrones and shall loosen the reins of the strong, and break the teeth of the sinners.

Matthew 13:41The Son of man shall send forth his angels, and they shall gather out of his kingdom all things that offend, and them which do iniquity;

5 And he shall put down the kings from their thrones and kingdoms because they do not exalt and praise Him, nor humbly acknowledge who bestowed their kingdom on them.

Matthew 19:28And Jesus said unto them, Verily I say unto you, That ye which have followed me, in the regeneration when the Son of man shall sit in the throne of his glory, ye also shall sit upon twelve thrones, judging the twelve tribes of Israel.

6 And he shall make the strong hang their heads, and shall fill them with shame. And darkness shall be their dwelling, and worms shall be their bed, and they shall have no hope of rising from their beds,

because they do not exalt the name of the Lord of spirits."

7 They raise their hands against the Most High and tread on the earth and dwell on it and all their deeds manifest unrighteousness. Their power rests on their riches, and their faith is in the gods which they have made with their hands. They deny the name of the Lord of spirits,

8 And they persecute the houses of His congregations, and the faithful who depend on the name of the Lord of Spirits.

[Chapter 47]

1 In those days the prayer of the righteous shall have ascended, and the blood of the righteous from the earth shall be before the Lord of spirits.

2 In those days the holy ones who dwell above in heavens shall unite with one voice and supplicate and pray and praise, and give thanks and bless the name of the Lord of spirits on behalf of the blood of the righteous which has been shed, that the prayer of the righteous may not be in vain before the Lord of spirits, that they may have justice, and that they may not have to wait for ever.

3 In those days I saw the "Head of Days" when He seated himself on the throne of His glory, and the books of the living were opened before Him; and all His host which is in heaven above and His counselors stood before Him,

4 And the hearts of the holy were filled with joy because the number of the righteous had been offered, and the prayer of the righteous had been heard, and the blood of the righteous not been required before the Lord of spirits.

Revelation 20:11Then I saw a great white throne and him who was seated on it. Earth and sky fled from his presence, and there was no place for them. 12And I saw the dead, great and small, standing before the throne, and books were opened. Another book was opened, which is the book of life. The dead were judged according to what they had done as recorded in the books. 13The sea gave up the dead that were in it, and death and Hades gave up the dead that were in them, and each person was judged according to what he had done. 14Then death and Hades were thrown into the lake of fire. The lake of fire is the second death. 15If anyone's name was not found written in the book of life, he was thrown into the lake of fire.

[Chapter 48]

1 And in that place I saw the spring of righteousness which was inexhaustible. And around it were many springs of wisdom. And all the thirsty drank of them, and were filled with wisdom, and their dwellings were with the righteous and holy and elect.

2 And at that hour that Son of Man was named in the presence of the Lord of spirits, And his name was brought before the Head of Days.

3 Even before the sun and the signs were created, before the stars of heaven were made, His name was named before the Lord of spirits.

4 He shall be a staff to the righteous and they shall steady themselves and not fall. And he shall be the light of the Gentiles, and the hope of those who are troubled of heart.

Romans 11: 11 I say then, Have they stumbled that they should fall? God forbid: but rather through their fall salvation is come unto the Gentiles, for to provoke them to jealousy.
12 Now if the fall of them be the riches of the world, and the diminishing of them the riches of the Gentiles; how much more their fulness?
13 For I speak to you Gentiles, inasmuch as I am the apostle of the Gentiles, I magnify mine office:
14 If by any means I may provoke to emulation them which are my flesh, and might save some of them.
15 For if the casting away of them be the reconciling of the world, what shall the receiving of them be, but life from the dead?
16 For if the firstfruit be holy, the lump is also holy: and if the root be holy, so are the branches.
17 And if some of the branches be broken off, and thou, being a wild olive tree, wert grafted in among them, and with them partakest of the root and fatness of the olive tree;
18 Boast not against the branches. But if thou boast, thou bearest not the root, but the root thee.
19 Thou wilt say then, The branches were broken off, that I might be grafted in.
20 Well; because of unbelief they were broken off, and thou standest by faith. Be not highminded, but fear:
21 For if God spared not the natural branches, take heed lest he also spare not thee.

5 All who dwell on earth shall fall down and worship before him, and will praise and bless and sing and celebrate the Lord of spirits.

6 And for this reason he has been chosen and hidden in front of (kept safe by) Him, before the creation of the world and for evermore.

7 And the wisdom of the Lord of spirits has revealed him to the holy and righteous; For he hath preserved the lot of the righteous, because they have hated and rejected this world of unrighteousness, and have hated all its works and ways in the name of the Lord of spirits. For in his name they are saved, and according to his good pleasure and it is He who has regard to their life.

8 In these days the kings of the earth and the strong who possess the land because of the works of their hands will be shamed, because on the day of their anguish and affliction they shall not be able to save themselves. And I will give them over into the hands of My elect.

9 As straw in the fire so shall they burn before the face of the holy; as lead in the water shall they sink before the face of the righteous, and no trace of them shall be found anymore.

Malachi 4
1For, behold, the day cometh, that shall burn as an oven; and all the proud, yea, and all that do wickedly, shall be stubble: and the day that cometh shall burn them up, saith the LORD of hosts, that it shall leave them neither root nor branch.

10 And on the day of their affliction there shall be rest on the earth (because the evil ones will be destroyed), and before Him they shall fall down and not rise again, and there shall be no one to take them with his hands and raise them up; for they have denied the Lord of spirits and His Anointed. The name of the Lord of spirits be blessed.

[Chapter 49]

l For wisdom is poured out like water, and glory will not fail before him ever.

2 For he is mighty in all the secrets of righteousness, and unrighteousness shall disappear like a shadow, and will no longer exist; because the Elect One stands before the Lord of spirits, and his glory is for ever and ever, and his might for all generations.

3 In him dwells the spirit of wisdom, and the spirit which gives insight, and the spirit of understanding and of might, and the spirit of those who have fallen asleep in righteousness.

4 And he shall judge the secret things, and no one shall be able to utter a lying or idle word before him, for he is the Elect One before the Lord of spirits according to His good pleasure.

[Chapter 50]

1 And in those days a change shall take place for the holy and elect, and the light of days shall abide on them, and glory and honor shall turn to the Holy.

2 On the day of trouble, affliction will be heaped on the evil. And the righteous shall be victorious in the name of the Lord of spirits. For He will this to others that they may repent and turn away from the works of their hands.

3 They shall have no honor through the name of the Lord of spirits, but through His name they shall be saved, and the Lord of spirits will have compassion on them, for His mercy is great.

4 He is righteous also in His judgment, and in the presence of His glory unrighteousness also shall not stand: At His judgment the unrepentant shall perish before Him.

5 And from now on I will have no mercy on them, says the Lord of spirits.

[Chapter 51]

1 And in those days shall the earth also give back that which has been entrusted to it, and Sheol (the grave) also shall give back that which it has received, and hell shall give back that which it owes. For in those days the Elect One shall arise,

2 And he shall choose the righteous and holy from among them. For the day has drawn near that they should be saved.

Revelation 20:12 And I saw the dead, small and great, stand before God; and the books were opened: and another book was opened, which is the book of life: and the dead were judged out of those things which were written in the books, according to their works. 13 And the sea gave up the dead which were in it; and death and hell delivered up the dead which were in them: and they were judged every man according to their works. 14 And death and hell were cast into the lake of fire. This is the second death. 15 And whosoever was not found written in the book of life was cast into the lake of fire.

3 And in those days the Elect One shall sit on His throne, and all the secrets of wisdom and counsel shall pour from His mouth, for the Lord of spirits hath given them to Him and has glorified Him.

4 In those days shall the mountains leap like rams, and the hills shall skip like lambs satisfied with milk, and the faces of all the angels in heaven shall be lighted up with joy.

5 And the earth shall rejoice, and the righteous shall dwell on it, and the elect shall walk on it.

[Chapter 52]

1 And after those days in that place where I had seen all the visions of that which is hidden, for I had been carried off in a whirlwind and they had borne me towards the west.

2 There my eyes saw all the secret things of heaven that shall be, a mountain of iron, and a mountain of copper, and a mountain of silver, and a mountain of gold, and a mountain of soft metal, and a mountain of lead.

3 And I asked the angel who went with me, saying, 'What things are these which I have seen in secret?'

4 And he said to me: 'All these things which you have seen shall serve the authority of His Messiah that he may be powerful and mighty on the earth.'

5 The angel of peace answered me saying: 'Wait a little while, and all secret things shall be revealed to you, things which surround the Lord of spirits.

6 And these mountains which your eyes have seen, the mountain of iron, and the mountain of copper, and the mountain of silver, and the mountain of gold, and the mountain of soft metal, and the mountain of lead, all of these shall be like wax before a fire in the presence of the Elect One. Like the water which streams down from above on those mountains, and they shall be weak under his feet.

7 And it shall come to pass in those days that none shall be saved, either by gold or by silver, and none will be able to save themselves or escape.

8 And there shall be no iron for war, nor materials for breastplates. Bronze shall be of no use, tin shall be worthless, and lead shall not be desired.

9 All these things shall be destroyed from the face of the earth, when the Elect One appears before the Lord of spirits.'

[Chapter 53]

1 There my eyes saw a deep valley with its mouth open, and all who dwell on the earth and sea and islands shall bring gifts and presents and tokens of

homage to Him, but that deep valley shall not become full.

2 And their hands commit lawless deeds, and everything the righteous work at the sinners devour. The sinners shall be destroyed in front of the face of the Lord of spirits, and they shall be banished from off the face of His earth, and they shall perish for ever and ever.

3 For I saw all the angels of punishment abiding there and preparing all the instruments of Satan.

4 And I asked the angel of peace who went with me: 'For whom are they preparing these instruments?'

5 And he said to me: 'They prepare these for the kings and the powerful of this earth, that they may with them be destroyed.

6 After this the Righteous and Elect One shall cause the house of His congregation to appear and from then on they shall hinder no more, in the name of the Lord of spirits.

7 And these mountains shall not stand as solid ground before His righteousness, but the hills shall be like springs of water, and the righteous shall have rest from the oppression of sinners.'

[Chapter 54]

1 And I looked and turned to another part of the earth, and saw there a deep valley with burning fire.

2 And they brought the kings and the powerful, and began to cast them into this deep valley.

Revelation 6:15 And the kings of the earth, and the great men, and the rich men, and the chief captains, and the mighty men, and every bondman, and every free man, hid themselves in the dens and in the rocks of the mountains;
16 And said to the mountains and rocks, Fall on us, and hide us from the face of him that sitteth on the throne, and from the wrath of the Lamb:
17 For the great day of his wrath is come; and who shall be able to stand?

3 And there my eyes saw how they made their instruments for them, iron chains of immeasurable weight.

4 And I asked the angel of peace who was with me, saying: 'For whom are these chains being prepared ?'

5 And he said to me: 'These are being prepared for the hosts of Azazel, so that they may take them and

throw them into the bottom of the pit of hell, and they shall cover their jaws with rough stones as the Lord of spirits commanded.

6 And Michael, and Gabriel, and Raphael, and Phanuel shall take hold of them on that great day, and throw them into the burning furnace on that day, that the Lord of spirits may take vengeance on them for their unrighteousness in becoming servants to Satan and for leading astray those who live on the earth.'

7 And in those days punishment will come from the Lord of spirits, and he will open all the storehouses of waters above heavens, and of the fountains which are under the surface of the earth.

8 And all the waters shall be come together (flow into or be joined) with the waters of heaven (above the sky), that which is above heavens is the masculine, and the water which is beneath the earth is the feminine.

9 And they shall destroy all who live on the dry land and those who live under the ends of heaven.

(Author's note: The previous verse refers to Noah's flood).

10 And when they have acknowledged the unrighteousness which they have done on the earth, by these they shall perish.

[Chapter 55]

1 And after that the Head of Days repented and said: 'I have destroyed all who dwell on the earth to no avail.'

2 And He swore by His great name: 'From now on I will not do this to all who dwell on the earth again, and I will set a sign in heaven: and this shall be a covenant of good faith between Me and them for ever, so long as heaven is above the earth. And this is in accordance with My command.

(Author's note: The previous verse refers to the rainbow).

3 When I have desired to take hold of them by the hand of the angels on the day of tribulation, anger, and pain because of this, I will cause My punishment and anger to abide on them, says God, the Lord of spirits.

4 You mighty kings who live on the earth, you shall have to watch My Elect One, sit on the throne of glory

and judge Azazel, and all his associates, and all his hosts in the name of the Lord of spirits.'

[Chapter 56]

1 And I saw there the hosts of the angels of punishment going, and they held scourges and chains of iron and bronze.

2 And I asked the angel of peace who went with me, saying: 'To whom are these who hold the scourges going?'

3 And he said to me: 'Each one to the ones they have chosen and to their loved ones, that they may be cast into the chasm of the abyss in the valley.

4 And then that valley shall be filled with ones they chose and their loved ones, and the days of their lives shall be at an end, and the days of their leading astray shall no longer be remembered (counted).

5 In those days the angels shall return and gather together and throw themselves to the east on the Parthians and Medes. They shall stir up the kings, so that a spirit of unrest and disturbance will come on them, and they shall drive them from their thrones, that they may rush out like lions from their lairs, and as hungry wolves among their flocks.

(Author's note: The names of certain countries help set the date of the manuscript. Scholars believe, based on the names of the countries mentioned in Enoch, that the book could not have been written prior to 250 B.C. since some countries did not exist before that date. One could add that the particular part of Enoch is the only section dated, since the book consists of several disjointed parts.)

6 And they shall go up and trample the lands of My elect ones, and the land of His elect ones shall be before them a threshing-floor (trampled, barren ground and a highway).

7 But the city of my righteous ones shall be a hindrance to their horses, and they shall begin to fight among themselves, and their own right hand shall be strong against themselves, and a man shall not know his brother, nor a son his father or his mother, until there will be innumerable corpses because of their slaughter, and their punishment shall be not in vain.

8 In those days hell (Sheol) shall open its jaws, and they shall be swallowed up. Their destruction shall be final. Hell (Sheol) shall devour the sinners in the presence of the elect.'

REV 20:1 And I saw an angel come down from heaven, having the key of the bottomless pit and a great chain in his hand. 2 And he laid hold on the dragon, that old serpent, which is the Devil, and Satan, and bound him a thousand years.

[Chapter 57]

1 And it came to pass after this that I saw another host of chariots, and men riding on them. They were coming on the winds from the east, and from the west to the south.

2 The noise of their chariots was heard, and when this turmoil took place the holy ones from heaven watched it, and the pillars of the earth were shaken and moved, and the sound of it was heard from the one end of heaven to the other, in one day.

3 And all shall fall down and worship the Lord of spirits. This is the end of the second Parable.

[Chapter 58]

1 And I began to speak the third Parable concerning the righteous and elect.

2 Blessed are you, you righteous and elect, for glorious shall be your lot.

3 And the righteous shall be in the light of the sun, and the elect will be in the light of eternal life. The days of their life shall be unending, and the days of the holy will be without number.

4 And they shall seek the light and find righteousness with the Lord of spirits. Peace to the righteous in the name of the Eternal Lord!

5 And after this it shall be said to the holy in heaven that they should seek secrets of righteousness, and the destiny of faith. For it has become bright as the sun on earth, and the darkness is passed away.

6 And there shall be a light that never ends, and to a number of days they shall not come, for the darkness shall first have been destroyed, [And the light established before the Lord of spirits] and the light of righteousness established for ever before the Lord of spirits.

[Chapter 59]

1 In those days my eyes saw the secrets of the lightning, and of the lights, and they judge and

execute their judgment, and they illuminate for a blessing or a curse as the Lord of spirits wills.

2 And there I saw the secrets of the thunder, and how when it resounds above in heaven, the sound thereof is heard, and he caused me to see the judgments executed on the earth, whether they are for well-being and blessing, or for a curse according to the word of the Lord of spirits.

3 And after that all the secrets of the lights and lightning were shown to me, and they lighten for blessing and for satisfying.

[Chapter 60] - Noah's Vision

1 In the year 500, in the seventh month, on the fourteenth day of the month in the life of Enoch, in that parable I saw how a mighty quaking made the heaven of heavens to quake, and the host of the Most High, and the angels, a thousand thousands and ten thousand times ten thousand, were disquieted with great foreboding.

2 And the Head of Days sat on the throne of His glory, and the angels and the righteous stood around Him.

3 And a great trembling seized me, and fear took hold of me, and my legs gave way, and I melted with weakness and fell on my face.

4 And Michael sent another angel from among the holy ones and he raised me up, and when he had raised me up my spirit returned; for I had not been able to endure the look of this host, and the disturbance and the shaking of heaven.

5 And Michael said to me: 'Why are you upset with such a vision? Until this day, His mercy and long-suffering has lasted toward those who dwell on the earth.'

6 And when the day, and the power, and the punishment, and the judgment come, which the Lord of spirits hath prepared for those who worship not the righteous law, and for those who deny the righteous judgment, and for those who take His name in vain, that day is prepared. It will be a covenant for the elect, but for sinners an inquisition. When the punishment of the Lord of spirits shall rest on them, it will not come in vain, and it shall slay the children with their mothers and the children with their fathers.

7 And on that day two monsters were separated from one another, a female monster named Leviathan, to dwell in the abyss of the ocean over the fountains of the waters;

8 And the male is named Behemoth, who occupied with his breast a wasted wilderness named Duidain, on the east of the garden where the elect and righteous dwell, where my (great) grandfather was taken up, the seventh from Adam, the first man whom the Lord of spirits created.

9 And I asked the other angel to show me the might of those monsters, how they were separated on one day and thrown, the one into the abyss of the sea, and the other to the earth's desert.

10 And he said to me: ' Son of man, you wish to know what is kept secret.'

11 And the other angel who went with me and showed me what was kept secret; told me what is first and last in heaven in the sky, and beneath the earth in the depth, and at the ends of heaven, and on the foundation of heaven.

12 And the storehouse of the winds, and how the winds are divided, and how they are weighed, and how the doors of the winds are calculated for each according to the power of the wind, and the power of the lights of the moon according to the power that is fitting; and the divisions of the stars according to their names, and how all the divisions are divided.

13 And the thunder according to the places where they fall, and all the divisions that are made among the lightning that it may light, and their host that they may at once obey.

14 For the thunder has places of rest which are assigned while it is waiting for its peal; and the thunder and lightning are inseparable, and although not one and undivided, they both go together in spirit and are not separate.

15 For when the lightning flashes, the thunder utters its voice, and the spirit enforces a pause during the peal, and divides equally between them; for the treasury of their peals is like the sand (of an hourglass), and each one of them as it peals is held in with a bridle, and turned back by the power of the spirit, and pushed forward according to the many parts of the earth.

16 And the spirit of the sea is masculine and strong, and according to the might of His strength He draws it back with a rein, and in like manner it is driven forward and disperses in the midst of all the mountains of the earth.

17 And the spirit of the hoar-frost is his own angel, and the spirit of the hail is a good angel. And the spirit of the snow has forsaken his storehouse because of his strength.

18 There is a special spirit there, and that which ascends from it is like smoke, and its name is frost. And the spirit of the mist is not united with them in their storehouse, but it has a special storehouse; for its course is glorious both in light and in darkness, and in winter and in summer, and in its storehouse is an angel.

19 And the spirit of the dew has its dwelling at the ends of heaven, and is connected with the storehouse of the rain, and its course is in winter and summer; and its clouds and the clouds of the mist are connected, and the one gives to the other.

20 And when the spirit of the rain goes out from its storehouse, the angels come and open the storehouse and lead it out, and when it is diffused over the whole earth it unites with the water on the earth.

21 And whenever it unites with the water on the earth, (for the waters are for those who live on the earth), they are (become) nourishment for the earth from the Most High who is in heaven.

22 Therefore there is a measurement for the rain, and the angels are in charge of it. And these things I saw towards the Garden of the Righteous.

23 And the Angel of Peace who was with me, said to me:

24 "These two monsters, prepared in accordance with the greatness of the Lord, will feed them the punishment of the Lord. And children will be killed with their mothers, and sons with their fathers.

Job 3: 8 May those who curse days curse that day, those who are ready to rouse Leviathan.

Isaiah 27: 1 In that day,
   the LORD will punish with his sword,
   his fierce, great and powerful sword,
   Leviathan the gliding serpent,
   Leviathan the coiling serpent;
   he will slay the monster of the sea.

[Chapter 61]

1 And I saw in those days that long cords were given to those angels, and they took to themselves wings and flew, and they went towards the north.

2 I asked the angel, saying to him: 'Why have those angels who have cords taken flight?' And he said to me: 'They have gone to take measurements.'

(Author's note: There were no tape measures in those days. Measurements were taken by a simple rope or stick. The rope may have knots placed in it. Usual measurement were based on a man's forearm, the length of an arm, or the span of the arms.) In this case, the measurements, based those of the Lord or his appointed angel, encoded secret knowledge.)

3 And the angel who went with me said to me: 'These shall bring the measurements of the righteous, and the cords of the righteous to the righteous, that they may rely on the name of the Lord of spirits for ever and ever.

4 The elect shall begin to dwell with the elect, and those are the measurements which shall be given to faith and which shall strengthen righteousness.

5 And these measurements shall reveal all the secrets of the depths of the earth, and those who have been destroyed by the desert, and those who have been devoured by the beasts, and those who have been devoured by the fish of the sea, that they may return and rely on the day of the Elect One. For none shall be destroyed before the Lord of spirits, and none can be destroyed.

6 And all who dwell in heaven received a command and power and one voice and one light like to fire.

7 And they blessed Him with their first words and exalted and praised Him in their wisdom. And they were wise in utterance and in the spirit of life.

8 And the Lord of spirits placed the Elect One on the throne of glory. And he shall judge all the works of the holy above in heaven, and in the balance their deeds shall be weighed.

2 Timothy 4:1 I charge thee therefore before God, and the Lord Jesus Christ, who shall judge the quick and the dead at his appearing and his kingdom;

9 And when he shall lift up his face to judge their secret ways according to the word of the name of the Lord of spirits, and their path according to the way of the righteous judgment of the Lord of spirits; then

they shall all speak with one voice and bless and glorify and exalt the name of the Lord of spirits.

10 And He will summon all the host of heavens, and all the holy ones above, and the host of God, the cherubim, seraphim and ophannim, and all the angels of power, and all the angels of principalities (angels that rule over other angels), and the Elect One, and the other powers on the earth and over the water. On that day shall raise one voice, and bless and glorify and exalt in the spirit of faith, and in the spirit of wisdom, and in the spirit of patience, and in the spirit of mercy, and in the spirit of judgment and of peace, and in the spirit of goodness, and shall all say with one voice: "Blessed is He, and may the name of the Lord of spirits be blessed for ever and ever."

11 All who do not sleep above in heaven shall bless Him. All the holy ones who are in heaven shall bless Him; and all the elect who dwell in the garden of life, and every spirit who is able to bless, and glorify, and exalt, and praise Your blessed name, and to the extent of its ability all flesh shall glorify and bless Your name for ever and ever.

12 For great is the mercy of the Lord of spirits. He is long-suffering, and all His works and all that He has created He has revealed to the righteous and elect, in the name of the Lord of spirits.

Numbers 14:18 The LORD is longsuffering, and of great mercy, forgiving iniquity and transgression, and by no means clearing the guilty, visiting the iniquity of the fathers upon the children unto the third and fourth generation.

[Chapter 62]

1 Thus the Lord commanded the kings and the mighty and the exalted, and those who dwell on the earth, and said: 'Open your eyes and lift up your horns if you are able to recognize the Elect One.'

Psalm 24: 7 Lift up your heads, O ye gates; and be ye lift up, ye everlasting doors; and the King of glory shall come in.

2 And the Lord of spirits seated Him on the throne of His glory, and the spirit of righteousness was poured out on Him, and the word of His mouth slays all the sinners, and all the unrighteous are destroyed from in front of His face.

REV 19:15 And out of his mouth goeth a sharp sword, that with it he should smite the nations: and he shall rule them with a rod of iron: and he treadeth the winepress of the fierceness and wrath of Almighty God. 16 And he hath on his vesture and on his thigh a name written, KING OF KINGS, AND LORD OF LORDS.

3 And in that day all the kings and the mighty, and the exalted and those who hold the earth shall stand up and shall see and recognize that He sits on the throne of His glory, and that righteousness is judged before Him, and no lying word is spoken before Him.

4 Then pain will come on them as on a woman in labor, and she has pain in giving birth when her child enters the mouth of the womb, and she has pain in childbirth.

Micah 4: 10 Be in pain, and labour to bring forth, O daughter of Zion, like a woman in travail: for now shalt thou go forth out of the city, and thou shalt dwell in the field, and thou shalt go even to Babylon; there shalt thou be delivered; there the LORD shall redeem thee from the hand of thine enemies.

5 And one portion of them shall look at the other, and they shall be terrified, and they shall look downcast, and pain shall seize them, when they see that Son of Man sitting on the throne of His glory.

Matt 25:31 When the Son of Man shall come in His glory, and all the holy angels with Him, then shall He sit upon the throne of His glory:

6 And the kings and the mighty and all who possess the earth shall bless and glorify and exalt Him who rules over all, who was hidden.

7 For from the beginning the Son of Man was hidden, and the Most High preserved Him in the presence of His might, and revealed Him to the elect.

8 And the congregation of the elect and holy shall be sown, and all the elect shall stand before Him on that day.

9 And all the kings and the mighty and the exalted and those who rule the earth shall fall down before Him on their faces, and worship and set their hope on that Son of Man, and petition Him and supplicate for mercy at His hands.

10 Nevertheless that Lord of spirits will so press them that they shall heavily go out from His presence, and their faces shall be filled with shame, and the darkness grows deeper on their faces.

11 And He will deliver them to the angels for punishment, to execute vengeance on them because they have oppressed His children and His elect.

12 And they shall be a spectacle for the righteous and for His elect. They shall rejoice over them, because the wrath of the Lord of spirits rests on them, and His sword is drunk with their blood.

13 The righteous and elect shall be saved on that day, and they shall never again see the face of the sinners and unrighteous.

14 And the Lord of spirits will abide over them, and they shall eat, lie down and rise up with the Son of Man for ever and ever.

Revelation 21:3 "Now the dwelling of God is with men, and he will live with them. They will be his people, and God himself will be with them and be their God. 4He will wipe every tear from their eyes. There will be no more death or mourning or crying or pain, for the old order of things has passed away."

15 The righteous and elect shall have risen from the earth, and ceased to be downcast and they will have been clothed with garments of life.

16 And these shall be the garments of life from the Lord of spirits; they shall not wear out nor will your glory pass away from before the Lord of spirits.

[Chapter 63]

1 In those days shall the mighty and the kings who possess the earth beg Him to grant them a little respite from His angels of punishment to whom they were delivered, that they might fall down and worship before the Lord of spirits, and confess their sins before Him.

Romans 14:11 For it is written, As I live, saith the Lord, every knee shall bow to me, and every tongue shall confess to God.
12So then every one of us shall give account of himself to God.

2 And they shall bless and glorify the Lord of spirits, and say: 'Blessed is the Lord of spirits and the Lord of kings, and the Lord of the mighty and the Lord of the rich, and the Lord of glory and the Lord of wisdom,

3 And every secret is revealed in front of you. Your power is from generation to generation, and your glory for ever and ever. Deep and innumerable are all your secrets, and your righteousness is beyond reckoning.

4 We have now learned that we should glorify and bless the Lord of kings and Him who is King over all kings.'

5 And they shall say: 'Would that we had a respite to glorify and give thanks and confess our faith before His glory!

6 And now we long for a little respite but find it not. We are driven away and obtain it not: And light has vanished from before us, and darkness is our dwelling-place for ever and ever;

7 Because we have not believed in Him nor glorified the name of the Lord of spirits, but our hope was in the scepter of our kingdom, and in our own glory.

8 In the day of our suffering and tribulation He does not save and we find no respite for confession that our Lord is true in all His works, and in His judgments and His justice, and His judgments have no respect of persons.

Romans 2: 7To them who by patient continuance in well doing seek for glory and honour and immortality, eternal life:
8But unto them that are contentious, and do not obey the truth, but obey unrighteousness, indignation and wrath,
9Tribulation and anguish, upon every soul of man that doeth evil, of the Jew first, and also of the Gentile;
10But glory, honour, and peace, to every man that worketh good, to the Jew first, and also to the Gentile:
11For there is no respect of persons with God.
12For as many as have sinned without law shall also perish without law: and as many as have sinned in the law shall be judged by the law;
13 For not the hearers of the law are just before God, but the doers of the law shall be justified.

9 We pass away from before His face on account of our works, and all our sins are judged in (in comparison to) righteousness.'

10 Now they shall say to themselves: 'Our souls are full of unrighteous gain, but what we have gained does not prevent us from descending from the midst of our worldly gain into the torment (burden) of Hell (Sheol).'

11 And after that their faces shall be filled with darkness and shame before that Son of Man, and they shall be driven from His presence, and the sword shall abide before His face in their midst.

12 Thus spoke the Lord of spirits: 'This is the ordinance and judgment with respect to the mighty

and the kings and the exalted and those who possess the earth before the Lord of spirits.'

[Chapter 64]

1 And other forms I saw hidden in that place.

2 I heard the voice of the angel saying: 'These are the angels who descended to the earth, and revealed what was hidden to the children of men and seduced the children of men into committing sin.'

Jude 1:6 And the angels which kept not their first estate, but left their own habitation, he hath reserved in everlasting chains under darkness unto the judgment of the great day.

[Chapter 65]

1 And in those days Noah saw the earth that it had sunk down and its destruction was near.

2 And he arose from there and went to the ends of the earth, and cried aloud to his grandfather, Enoch.

3 And Noah said three times with an embittered voice: "Hear me, hear me, hear me." And I said to him: 'Tell me what it is that is falling out on the earth that the earth is in such evil plight and shaken, lest perchance I shall perish with it?'

4 And there was a great disturbance on the earth, and a voice was heard from heaven, and I fell on my face. And Enoch my grandfather came and stood by me, and said to me: 'Why have you cried to me with a bitter cry and weeping?'

5 A command has gone out from the presence of the Lord concerning those who dwell on the earth that their ruin is accomplished because they have learned all the secrets of the angels, and all the violence of the Satans (deceivers, accusers);

(Author's note: There are many meanings of the word "satan" but all indicate great negativity. It can mean one who opposes, accuses, or deceives. In this case there is some confusion as to who the satans are. We are told the fallen angels taught men to war, but we are also told that it was the children of the angels that were so destructive. We are told that the angels taught men sorcery and spells, but it was the spirits of the nephilim that went out from their bodies to destroy.)

6 And all their powers - the most secret ones - and all the power of those who practice sorcery, and the power of witchcraft, and the power of those who make molten images for the whole earth.

7 And how silver is produced from the dust of the earth, and how soft metal originates in the earth.

8 For lead and tin are not produced from the earth like the first; it is a fountain that produces them;

9 And an angel stands in it, and that angel is preeminent.' And after that my grandfather Enoch took hold of me by my hand and lifted me up, and said to me:

10 'Go, for I have asked the Lord of spirits about this disturbance on the earth. And He said to me: "Because of their unrighteousness their judgment has been determined and shall not be withheld by Me for ever. Because of the sorceries which they have searched out and learned, the earth and those who dwell on it shall be destroyed."

(Author's note: Flesh and blood will drowned under the waters of the flood. All those who knew the fallen angels and all those who had given birth to their children would be killed, but the angels cannot die and the spirits of the nephilim do not need a body to survive. The text indicates the spirits need no food or water and go about unseen.)

11 And from these, they have no place of repentance for ever, because they have shown them what was hidden, and they are the damned. But as for you, my son, the Lord of spirits knows that you are pure and guiltless of this reproach concerning the secrets.

12 And He has destined your name to be among the holy, and will preserve you among those who dwell on the earth; and has destined your righteous seed both for kingship and for great honors, and from your seed shall proceed a fountain of the righteous and holy without number for ever.

[Chapter 66]

1 And after that he showed me the angels of punishment who are prepared to come and let loose all the powers of the waters which are beneath in the earth in order to bring judgment and destruction on all who dwell on the earth.

2 Kings 19:35And it came to pass that night, that the angel of the LORD went out, and smote in the camp of the Assyrians an hundred fourscore and five thousand: and when they arose early in the morning, behold, they were all dead corpses.

Revelation 14: 15And another angel came out of the temple, crying with a loud voice to him that sat on the cloud, Thrust in thy sickle, and reap: for the time is come for thee to reap; for the harvest of the earth is ripe.16 And he that sat on the cloud thrust in his sickle on the earth; and the earth was reaped.17 And another angel came out of the temple which is in heaven, he also having a sharp sickle.
18And another angel came out from the altar, which had power over fire; and cried with a loud cry to him that had the sharp sickle, saying, Thrust in thy sharp sickle, and gather the clusters of the vine of the earth; for her grapes are fully ripe.
19And the angel thrust in his sickle into the earth, and gathered the vine of the earth, and cast it into the great winepress of the wrath of God.

2 And the Lord of spirits gave commandment to the angels who were going out, that they should not cause the waters to rise but should hold them in check; for those angels were in charge of the forces of the waters.

3 And I went away from the presence of Enoch.

[Chapter 67]

1 And in those days the word of God came to me, and He said to me: 'Noah, your lot has come up before Me, a lot without blame, a lot of love and righteousness.

2 And now the angels are making a wooden structure, and when they have completed that task I will place My hand on it and preserve it (keep it safe), and there shall come out of it the seed of life, and a change shall set in so that the earth will not remain without inhabitants.

3 And I will establish your seed before me for ever and ever, and I will spread abroad those who dwell with you; and the face of the earth will be fruitful. They shall be blessed and multiply on the earth in the name of the Lord.'
4 And He will imprison those angels, who have shown unrighteousness, in that burning valley which my grandfather Enoch had formerly shown to me in the west among the mountains of gold and silver and iron and soft metal and tin.

5 And I saw that valley in which there was a great earth quake and a tidal waves of the waters.

6 And when all this took place, from that fiery molten metal and from the convulsion thereof in that place, there was a smell of sulfur produced, and it was connected with those waters, and that valley of the angels who had led mankind astray burned beneath that ground.

7 And there were streams of fire throughout the valley, where these angels are punished who had led astray those who dwell on the earth.

8 But those waters shall in those days serve for the kings and the mighty and the exalted, and those who dwell on the earth, for the healing of the body, but for the punishment of the spirit. Their spirit is full of lust, that they will be punished in their body, for they have denied the Lord of spirits. They will see their punishment daily, and yet, they believe not in His name.

9 There will be a relationship between the punishment and change. As their bodies burn, a change will take place in their spirit for ever and ever; for before the Lord of spirits none shall utter an idle word.

10 For the judgment shall come on them, because they believe in the lust of their body and deny the Spirit of the Lord.

1 John 2:16 (New International Version)
16For everything in the world — the cravings of sinful man, the lust of his eyes and the boasting of what he has and does — comes not from the Father but from the world.
17And the world passeth away, and the lust thereof: but he that doeth the will of God abideth for ever.

11 And the waters will change in those days; for when those angels are punished in these waters, the springs shall change, and when the angels ascend, this water of the springs shall change their temperature and become cold.

12 And I heard Michael answering and saying: 'This judgment in which the angels are judged is a testimony for the kings and the mighty who possess the earth.'
13 Because these waters of judgment minister to the healing of the body of the kings and the lust of their bodies; therefore they will not see and will not believe that those waters will change and become a fire which burns for ever.

[Chapter 68]

1 And after that my grandfather Enoch gave me the explanations of all the secrets in the book of the Parables which had been given to him, and he put them together for me in the words of the book of the Parables.

2 And on that day Michael answered Raphael and said: 'The power of the spirit grips me and makes me

tremble because of the severity of the judgment of the secrets, and the judgment of the angels. Who can endure the severe judgment which has been executed, and before which they melt away?'

3 And Michael answered again, and said to Raphael: 'Who would not have a softened heart concerning it, and whose mind would not be troubled by this judgment against them because of those who have led them out?'

4 And it came to pass when he stood before the Lord of spirits, Michael said thus to Raphael: 'I will not defend them under the eye of the Lord; for the Lord of spirits has been angry with them because they act as if they were the Lord.

5 Therefore all that is hidden shall come on them for ever and ever; for no other angel or man shall have his portion in this judgment, but they alone have received their judgment for ever and ever.

Psalm 82
1God standeth in the congregation of the mighty; he judgeth among the gods.
2How long will ye judge unjustly, and accept the persons of the wicked? Selah.
3Defend the poor and fatherless: do justice to the afflicted and needy.
4Deliver the poor and needy: rid them out of the hand of the wicked.
5They know not, neither will they understand; they walk on in darkness: all the foundations of the earth are out of course.
6I have said, Ye are gods; and all of you are children of the most High.
7But ye shall die like men, and fall like one of the princes.
8Arise, O God, judge the earth: for thou shalt inherit all nations.

(Author's note: The above Bible verse is in bold because it may play one of the pivotal roles in understanding the connections between the book of Enoch and the Bible.

God stands in the congregation of the mighty; He judgeth among the gods. KJV

Another version reads:
God has taken His place in the divine council. In the Midst of the gods He holds judgment. RSV

The Septuagint reads:
God stands in the assembly of gods; and in the midst of them will judge gods. How long will ye judge unrighteous, and accept the persons of sinners?

In verse one we read that God (Elohiym) is standing in the congregation of the mighty; that He ("El" or God) is judging (Shaphat: governing) the gods (elohiym). One way to easily understand this is to look at a supreme God (capital "G") judging and governing a group of "godlings."

In an early study on Psalm 82, J. A. Emerton argued that in the Targum (Aramaic translation of the Old Testament) to the Psalms, as well as in the the Peshitta (Syriac Bible), and according to the Fathers, elohim (gods) in Psalm 82 was understood by all to refer to "angels." Emerton suggests that elohim refers to superhuman beings to whom the nations were allotted, whom the Jews regarded as angels but whom the Gentiles called gods (see 1 Cor 10:20). Jesus quotes the verse in John 10:34-36.

To stand in a court setting and judge indicates there was some transgression. This adds weight to the fact that some angels committed transgressions while others did not. Thus, it is this verse that points to the fall of some angels and the judgment handed down. It also articulates the position of angels as gods. It is assumed the point of view is that of men and not God. In our mythology we see some "gods" were evil and violent, while other "gods" were kind and gentle. There were giants, Cyclops, monsters, and those, such as Hercules, Achilles who fought alongside men. These could be various angels, but it could point back to the three types of beings coming from the union of angels and women; Giants, Nephilim, and Eljo.

With their great height and six fingers per hand, it has been speculated that Goliath, his mother (the giant of Gath), and their family were descendants of the angel – woman union. We have also speculated that the Eljo could be the "men of renown" mentioned in Genesis.

Genesis 6:4 There were giants in the earth in those days; and also after that, when the sons of God came in unto the daughters of men, and they bare children to them, the same became mighty men which were of old, men of renown.

The term, "eljo or elyo" indicates a type of godlike being. The term indicates these were humanoids with special powers or abilities, to the extent they would be remembered and placed in mythic stories so that they should not be forgotten. This leaves the Nephilim, which could be the monsters such as Cyclops, Medusa, and other creatures memorialized in mythology.

It is not suggested that these stories are totally accurate, but only that they indicate the existence of some vastly unusual being with powers or abilities that spawned stories of monsters. Together these three types of angelic offspring make up the corpus of mythology, containing gods, giants, and monsters.)

To add additional fuel to the fire of controversy over Psalm 82, Jesus quotes the verse in John 10:34-36.

John 10:31 Again the Jews picked up stones to stone him, 32 but Jesus said to them, "I have shown you many great miracles from the Father. For which of these do you stone me?" 33 "We are not stoning you for any of these," replied the Jews, "but for blasphemy, because you, a mere man, claim to be God." 34 Jesus answered them, "Is it not written in your Law, 'I have said you are gods'? 35 If he called them 'gods,' to whom the word of God came – and the Scripture cannot be broken – NIV

Does the word of God, if we accept and understand it, makes us gods? What power or authority does the knowledge, secrets, and words brought to us from heaven by fallen angels give us?

[Chapter 69]

1 And after this judgment I will terrify and make them tremble because they have shown this to those who dwell on the earth.

2 And behold the names of those angels: the first of them is Samjaza; the second Artaqifa; and the third Armen, the fourth Kokabe, the fifth Turael; the sixth Rumjal; the seventh Danjal; the eighth Neqael; the ninth Baraqel; the tenth Azazel; the eleventh Armaros; the twelfth Batarjal; the thirteenth Busasejal; the fourteenth Hananel; the fifteenth Turel; and the sixteenth Simapesiel; the seventeenth Jetrel; the eighteenth Tumael; the nineteenth Turel; the twentieth Rumael; the twenty-first Azazyel;

(Author's note: For more information on the heavenly names, such as the various names of the "Presence of the Lord," see the Third Book of Enoch, also called the "Hebrew Book of Enoch.")

The leader of the Watchers was Samjaza;, also pronounced Shemhazai. Two hundred angels made the descent to Earth, at Mount Hermon. Two hundred angels were divided into group of ten, each under the leadership of chieftain or captain.

They defiled themselves with women, producing children. Their children were giants of three-thousand ells tall, which some sources say is approximately 3420 metres in height (11,250 feet tall).

According to the Haggada (book 1, chapter 4 Punishment of the Fallen Angels), the angel Shemhazai lusted after a maiden named Istehar,

however, she tricked him into revealing the Ineffable Name of God. Istehar used the name to ascend to heaven and escaped her violation by Shemhazai. God rewarded Istehar by commemorating her as the seven-star constellation Pleides.

In Genesis 4:22, Naamah was a daughter of Lamech and Zillah, and sister of Tubal-cain. She was a descendant of Cain, hence a Cainite. According to the Haggada, Naamah was the opposite of Istehar, because the angel Shamdon had succeeded in sexual union with Naamah. Naamah's offspring was Asmodeus, a demon, instead of a giant. Asmodeus appeared in the apocrypha Tobit.

According to the introduction of the Zohar, it was Naamah who first deceived and seduced the angels, rather than the angel seducing Naamah. Zohar 3 mentioned the angels, Aza and Azael, instead of Shamdon, they were victims of her beauty. She became mother of unknown number of demons. Our vampire lore may have begun with the Book of Enoch since it states the giants consumed all the food men could produce and then began devouring people, and sucking their blood, like vampires.)

3 And these are the chiefs of their angels and their names, and their leaders over hundreds, and leaders over fifties, and leaders over tens.

4 The name of the first Jeqon, that is, the one who led astray the sons of God, and brought them down to the earth, and led them astray through the daughters of men.

5 And the second was named Asbeel; he imparted to the holy sons of God evil counsel, and led them astray so that they defiled their bodies with the daughters of men.

6 And the third was named Gadreel; it is he who showed the children of men all the blows of death, and he led astray Eve, and showed the weapons of death to the sons of men; the shield and the coat of mail, and the sword for battle, and all the weapons of death to the children of men.

7 And from his hand they have proceeded against those who dwell on the earth from that day and for evermore.

8 And the fourth was named Penemue; he taught the children of men the bitter and the sweet, and he taught them all the secrets of their wisdom.

9 And he instructed mankind in writing with ink and paper, and thereby many sinned from eternity to eternity and until this day.

10 For men were not created for the purpose of

could speak with angels, it was believed one could directly interact with them.

In 1581, Dee mentioned in his personal journals that God had sent "good angels" to communicate directly

Table of Enochian Letters, Print, and Script

confirming their good faith with pen and ink.

Author's note: Reading and writing are considered grievous sins because they allow knowledge, and thus sin, to be propagated from generation to generation. It should be pointed out that God himself wrote the Ten Commandments on stone. It is possible that this verse may refer to the Enochian Alphabet, thought to convey the original teachings of the fallen angels.

The Enochian alphabet was thought to be lost with the flood, but "re-discovered" by John Dees.

John Dee (13 July 1527–1608 or 1609) was a noted mathematician, astrologer, navigator, occultist, and a consultant to Queen Elizabeth I.
According to Tobias Churton in his book The Golden Builders, the concept of an Angelic or pre-deluge language was common during Dee's time. If one

with prophets. In 1582, Dee teamed up with the seer Edward Kelley, although Dee had used several other seers previously. With Kelley's help as a scryer, Dee set out to establish lasting contact with the angels, which resulted, among other things, in the reception of the Enochian or Angelical language.

According to Dee's journals, Angelical was supposed to have been the language God used to create the world, and which was later used by Adam to speak with God and the angels, and to name all things into existence.

The alphabet codified the phonetics of the language Dees claimed could be used to summon various angels, who would dispatch knowledge or assistance. The chants used complex phonetic streams named "Angelic Calls" to name and call forth angels.

11 For men were created exactly like the angels, to the intent that they should continue pure and righteous; and death, which destroys everything, should not have taken hold of them, but through this their knowledge they are perishing, and through this power consumes them.

Romans 5:12 (King James Version)
12Wherefore, as by one man sin entered into the world, and death by sin; and so death passed upon all men, for that all have sinned:

12 And the fifth was named Kasdeja; this is he who showed the children of men all the wicked smitings (blows) of spirits and demons, and the smitings (blows) of the embryo in the womb, that it may pass away, and the smitings (blows) of the soul the bites of the serpent, and the smitings (blows) which befall through the midday heat, the son of the serpent named Taba'et.

13 And this is the task of Kasbeel, the chief of the oath which he showed to the holy ones when he dwelt high above in glory, and its name is Biqa.

14 This (angel) requested Michael to show him the hidden name, that he might enunciate it in the oath,

15 So that those might quake before that name and oath who revealed all that was in secret to the children of men. And this is the power of this oath, for it is powerful and strong, and he placed this oath Akae in the hand of (under the control of) Michael.

(Author's note: The ineffable name of God holds the power to create, bind, and destroy. In the Lillith myth, it is said she spoke this name when she argued against God and Adam. By speaking the name she flew off and became a demon.)

16 And these are the secrets of this oath (God's promise, word) that heaven was suspended before the world was created, and for ever, and they are strong through his oath (word, promise).

17 And through it the earth was founded on the water, and from the secret recesses of the mountains come beautiful waters, from the creation of the world and to eternity.

18 And through that oath the sea was created, and as its foundation He set for it the sand against the time of its anger (rage) that it dare not pass beyond it from the creation of the world to eternity.

19 And through that oath are the depths made fast (strong), and abide and stir not from their place from eternity to eternity.

20 And through that oath the sun and moon complete their course, and deviate not from their ordinance from eternity to eternity.

21 And through that oath the stars complete their course, and He calls them by their names, and they answer Him from eternity to eternity.

22 [And in like manner the spirits of the water, and of the winds, and of all kinds of spirits, and (their) paths from all the quarters of the winds respond to His command.]

(Author's note: Verse 22 is not complete in some translations.)

23 And there are preserved the voices of the thunder and the light of the lightning: and there are preserved the storehouses of the hail and the storehouses of the hoarfrost,

24 And the storehouses of the mist, and the storehouses of the rain and the dew. And all these believe and give thanks before the Lord of spirits, and glorify (Him) with all their power, and their food is in every act of thanksgiving; they thank and glorify and exalt the name of the Lord of spirits for ever and ever.

25 And this oath is mighty over them and through it they are preserved and their paths are preserved, and their course is not destroyed.

26 And there was great joy among them, and they blessed and glorified and exalted because the name of that Son of Man had been revealed to them.

(Author's note: The name of a person reveals their personality and power. There remains a ceremony to this day that if a person is on their deathbed a rabbi may change the person's name to trick the Angel of Death so the person might escape his reaping, suggesting the Angel seeks by name.)

27 And he sat on the throne of his glory, and the sum of judgment was given to the Son of Man. And he caused the sinners and all those who led the world astray to pass away and be destroyed from off the face of the earth.

28 They shall be bound with chains, and shut up and imprisoned in their place of assembly, and all their works vanish from the face of the earth.

29 And from that time forward, there shall be nothing corruptible; for that Son of Man has appeared, and has seated himself on the throne of his glory. And all evil shall pass away before his face, and the word of that Son of Man shall go out and be strong before the Lord of spirits.

[Chapter 70]

1 And it came to pass after this that during His lifetime His name was raised up to the Son of Man, and to the Lord of spirits from among those who dwell on the earth.

2 And He was raised aloft on the chariots of the spirit and His name vanished among them. And from that day I was no longer numbered among them; and He placed me between the two winds, between the North and the West, where the angels took the cords to measure the place for the elect and righteous for me.

3 And there I saw the first fathers and the righteous who dwell in that place from the beginning.

[Chapter 71]

1 And it came to pass after this that my spirit was translated (carried off) and it ascended into heaven; and I saw the sons of the holy angels (sons) of God. They were walking on flames of fire; their garments were white, and their faces shone like snow.

2 And I saw two rivers of fire, and the light of that fire shone like hyacinth, and I fell on my face before the Lord of spirits.

3 And the angel Michael, one of the archangels, seized me by my right hand, and lifted me up and led me out into all the secrets, and he showed me all the secrets of righteousness.

4 And he showed me all the secrets of the ends of heaven, and all the storehouses of all the stars, and all the lights, from where they proceed before the face of the holy ones.

5 And he translated (carried) my spirit into heaven of heavens, and I saw there as it were built of crystals, and between those crystals tongues of living fire.

REV 21:10 And he carried me away in the spirit to a great and high mountain, and shewed me that great city, the holy Jerusalem, descending out of heaven from God, 11 Having the glory of God: and her light was like unto a stone most precious, even like a jasper stone, clear as crystal.

6 My spirit saw circle of fire binding around the house of fire, and on its four sides were rivers full of living fire, and they encircled that house.

7 And round about were seraphim, cherubim, and ophannim; and these are they who never sleep and they guard the throne of His glory.

8 And I saw angels who could not be counted, a thousand thousands, and ten thousand times ten thousand, encircling that house. And Michael, and Raphael, and Gabriel, and Phanuel, and the holy angels who are in heaven above, go in and out of that house.

9 And they came out from that house, and Michael and Gabriel, Raphael and Phanuel, and many holy angels without number.

10 And with them the Head of Days, His head white and pure as wool, and His raiment indescribable.

11 And I fell on my face, and my whole body melted, and my spirit was (transformed) transfigured. And I cried with a loud voice in the spirit of power, and I blessed and glorified and exalted.

Psalm 22:14 I am poured out like water, and all my bones are out of joint: my heart is like wax; it is melted in the midst of my bowels.
15My strength is dried up like a potsherd; and my tongue cleaveth to my jaws; and thou hast brought me into the dust of death.

12 And these blessings which came from my mouth were very pleasing before that Head of Days.

13 And the Head of Days came with Michael and Gabriel, Raphael and Phanuel, and thousands and ten thousands of angels without number.

14 And the angel came to me and greeted me with his voice, and said to me 'This is the Son of Man who is born to righteousness, and righteousness abides over him, and the righteousness of the Head of Days forsakes him not.'

15 And he said to me: 'He proclaims to you peace in the name of the world to come; for from there peace has proceeded since the creation of the world, and it shall be with you for ever and for ever and ever.

JOH 17:24 Father, I will that they also, whom thou hast given me, be with me where I am; that they may behold my glory, which thou hast given me: for thou lovest me before the foundation of the world.

16 And all shall walk in His ways since righteousness never forsook Him. Their dwelling-place shall be with Him and it will be their heritage, and they shall not be separated from Him for ever and ever and ever.

17 And so there shall be length of days with the Son of Man, and the righteous shall have peace and an upright way in the name of the Lord of spirits for ever and ever.'

HEB 4:3 For we which have believed do enter into rest, as he said, As I have sworn in my wrath, if they shall enter into my rest: although the works were finished from the foundation of the world.

[Chapter 72]
The Book of *Astronomy and Calendar* (Chapters 72-82):

1 The book of the courses of the luminaries of heaven, the relations of each, according to their name, origin, and months (dominion and seasons) which Uriel, the holy angel who was with me, who is their guide, showed me; and he showed me all their laws (regulations) exactly as they are, and how it is with each of the years of the world and to eternity, until the new creation is accomplished which endures until eternity.

2 And this is the first law of the luminaries: the luminary the Sun has its rising in the eastern doors of heaven, and its setting in the western doors of heaven.

3 And I saw six doors in which the sun rises, and six doors in which the sun sets and the moon rises and sets in these doors, and the leaders of the stars and those whom they lead: six in the east and six in the west, and all following each other in accurately corresponding order.

4 There were also many windows to the right and left of these doors. And first there goes out the great luminary, named the Sun, and his sphere (orbit, disc) is like the sphere (orbit, disc) of heaven, and he is quite filled with illuminating and heating fire.

5 The chariot on which he ascends, the wind drives, and the sun goes down from heaven and returns through the north in order to reach the east, and is so

guided that he comes to the appropriate door and shines in the face of heaven.

6 In this way he rises in the first month in the great door, which is the fourth.

7 And in that fourth door from which the sun rises in the first month are twelve windows, from which proceed a flame when they are opened in their season.

8 When the sun rises in heaven, he comes out through that fourth door, thirty mornings in succession, and sets accurately in the fourth door in the west of the heaven.

9 And during this period the day becomes daily longer and nights grow shorter to the thirtieth morning.

10 On that day the day is longer than the night by a ninth part, and the day amounts exactly to ten parts and the night to eight parts.

11 And the sun rises from that fourth door, and sets in the fourth and returns to the fifth door of the east thirty mornings, and rises from it and sets in the fifth door.

12 And then the day becomes longer by two parts and amounts to eleven parts, and the night becomes shorter and amounts to seven parts.

13 And it returns to the east and enters into the sixth door, and rises and sets in the sixth door one-and-thirty mornings on account of its sign.

14 On that day the day becomes longer than the night, and the day becomes double the night, and the day becomes twelve parts, and the night is shortened and becomes six parts.

15 And the sun mounts up to make the day shorter and the night longer, and the sun returns to the east and enters into the sixth door, and rises from it and sets thirty mornings.

16 And when thirty mornings are accomplished, the day decreases by exactly one part, and becomes eleven parts, and the night seven.

17 And the sun goes out from that sixth door in the west, and goes to the east and rises in the fifth door for thirty mornings, and sets in the west again in the fifth western door.

18 On that day the day decreases by two parts, and amounts to ten parts and the night to eight parts.

19 And the sun goes out from that fifth door and sets in the fifth door of the west, and rises in the fourth door for one-and-thirty mornings on account of its sign, and sets in the west.

20 On that day the day becomes equal with the night in length, and the night amounts to nine parts and the day to nine parts.

21 And the sun rises from that door and sets in the west, and returns to the east and rises thirty mornings in the third door and sets in the west in the third door.

22 And on that day the night becomes longer than the day, and night becomes longer than night, and day shorter than day until the thirtieth morning, and the night amounts exactly to ten parts and the day to eight parts.

23 And the sun rises from that third door and sets in the third door in the west and returns to the east, and for thirty mornings rises in the second door in the east, and in like manner sets in the second door in the west of heaven.

24 And on that day the night amounts to eleven parts and the day to seven parts.

25 And the sun rises on that day from that second door and sets in the west in the second door, and returns to the east into the first door for one-and-thirty mornings, and sets in the first door in the west of heaven.

26 And on that day the night becomes longer and amounts to the double of the day: and the night amounts exactly to twelve parts and the day to six.

(Author's note: If the night is 12 parts and the day is six parts, the entire 24 hour day is divided into 18 sections of 80 minutes each.)

27 And the sun has traversed the divisions of his orbit and turns again on those divisions of his orbit, and enters that door thirty mornings and sets also in the west opposite to it.

28 And on that night has the night decreased in length by a ninth part, and the night has become eleven parts and the day seven parts.

29 And the sun has returned and entered into the second door in the east, and returns on those his divisions of his orbit for thirty mornings, rising and setting.

30 And on that day the night decreases in length, and the night amounts to ten parts and the day to eight.

31 And on that day the sun rises from that door, and sets in the west, and returns to the east, and rises in the third door for one-and-thirty mornings, and sets in the west of heaven.

32 On that day the night decreases and amounts to nine parts, and the day to nine parts, and the night is equal to the day and the year is exactly as to its days three hundred and sixty-four.

33 And the length of the day and of the night, and the shortness of the day and of the night arise through the course of the sun these distinctions are separated'.

34 So it comes that its course becomes daily longer, and its course nightly shorter.

35 And this is the law and the course of the great luminary which is named the sun, and his return as often as he returns sixty times and rises, for ever and ever.

36 And that which rises is the great luminary, and is so named according to its appearance, according as the Lord commanded.

37 As he rises, so he sets and decreases not, and rests not, but runs day and night, and his light is sevenfold brighter than that of the moon; but in regard to size, they are both equal.

[Chapter 73]

1 And after this law I saw another law dealing with the smaller luminary, which is named the Moon.

2 And her orbit is like the sphere (orbit, disc) of heaven, and her chariot in which she rides is driven by the wind, and light is given to her in measurement.

3 And her rising and setting change every month and her days are like the days of the sun, and when her light is uniformly (completely) full it amounts to the seventh part of the light of the sun.

4 And thus she rises. And her first phase in the east comes out on the thirtieth morning and on that day she becomes visible, and constitutes for you the first phase of the moon on the thirtieth day together with the sun in the door where the sun rises.

5 And the one half of her goes out by a seventh part, and her whole disc is empty, without light, with the exception of one-seventh part of it, and the fourteenth part of her light.

6 And when she receives one-seventh part of the half of her light, her light amounts to one-seventh part and the half thereof.

7 And she sets with the sun, and when the sun rises the moon rises with him and receives the half of one part of light, and in that night in the beginning of her morning in the beginning of the lunar day the moon sets with the sun, and is invisible that night with the fourteen parts and the half of one of them.

8 And she rises on that day with exactly a seventh part, and comes out and recedes from the rising of the sun, and in her remaining days she becomes bright in the remaining thirteen parts.

[Chapter 74]

1 And I saw another course, a law for her, and how according to that law she performs her monthly revolution.
2 And all these Uriel, the holy angel who is the leader of them all, showed to me, and their positions, and I wrote down their positions as he showed them to me, and I wrote down their months as they were, and the appearance of their lights until fifteen days were accomplished.

3 In single seventh parts she accomplishes all her light in the east, and in single seventh parts accomplishes all her darkness in the west.

4 And in certain months she alters her settings, and in certain months she pursues her own peculiar course.

5 In two months the moon sets with the sun: in those two middle doors the third and the fourth.

6 She goes out for seven days, and turns about and returns again through the door where the sun rises, and all her light is full; and she recedes from the sun, and in eight days enters the sixth door from which the sun goes out.

7 And when the sun goes out from the fourth door she goes out seven days, until she goes out from the fifth and turns back again in seven days into the fourth door and accomplishes all her light; and she recedes and enters into the first door in eight days.

8 And she returns again in seven days into the fourth door from which the sun goes out.

9 Thus I saw their positions, how the moons rose and the sun set in those days.

10 And if five years are added together the sun has an excess of thirty days, and all the days which accrue to it for one of those five years, when they are full, amount to 364 days.

11 And an excess of the sun and of the stars amounts to six days; in five years six days every year come to 30 days, and the moon falls behind the sun and stars to the number of 30 days.

12 And the sun and the stars bring in all the years exactly, so that they do not advance or delay their position by a single day to eternity; but complete the years with perfect justice in 364 days.

13 In three years there are 1,092 days, and in five years 1,820 days, so that in eight years there are 2,912 days.

(Author's note: At the end of five years a week may be added to bring the year back in line. Compare 1826.25 days of the solar year in five years to 1820 days of the Enochian calendar after five years. This leaves 6.25 days difference. Adding a week to the Enochian calendar leaves a difference of only .75 of a day. The years is adjusted in this way so that the alignment is kept very close.)

14 For the moon alone the days amount in three years to 1,062 days, and in five years she falls 50 days behind to the sum of 1,770 there is five to be added 1,000 and 62 days.

15 And in five years there are 1,770 days, so that for the moon the days six in eight years amount to 21,832 days.

16 For in eight years she falls behind to the amount of 80 days, all the days she falls behind in eight years are 80.

17 And the year is accurately completed in conformity with their world-stations and the stations of the sun, which rise from the doors through which the sun rises and sets 30 days.

[Chapter 75]

1 And the leaders of the heads of the (ten) thousands, who are in charge of the whole creation and over all the stars, have also to do with the four days of the year which are not counted in the yearly calendar,

being not separated from their office, according to the reckoning of the year, and these render service on the four days which are not counted in the reckoning of the year.

2 And because of them men go wrong in them, for those luminaries truly render service to the stations of the world, one in the first door, one on the third door of heaven, one in the fourth door, and one in the sixth door, and the exactness of the year is accomplished through its separate three hundred and sixty-four stations.

3 For the signs and the times and the years and the days the angel Uriel showed to me, whom the Lord of glory hath set for ever over all the luminaries of heaven, in heaven and in the world, that they should rule on the face of heaven and be seen on the earth, and be leaders for the day via the sun and the night via the moon, and stars, and all the ministering creatures which make their revolution in all the chariots of heaven.

4 In like manner, twelve doors Uriel showed me, open in the sphere (disc) of the sun's chariot in heaven, through which the rays of the sun break out; and from them is warmth diffused over the earth, when they are opened at their appointed seasons.

5 And there are openings for the wind and the spirit of dew that when they are opened, stand open in heaven at the ends of the earth.

6 As for the twelve doors in the heaven, at the ends of the earth, out of which go out the sun, moon, and stars, and all the works of heaven in the east and in the west; there are many windows open to the left and right of them,

7 And one window at its appointed season produces warmth, corresponding to the doors from which the stars come out as He has commanded them; and in which they are set, corresponding to their number.

8 And I saw chariots in heaven, running in the world, above those doors in which the stars that never set.

9 And one is larger than all the rest, and it is that that makes its course through the entire world.

[Chapter 76]

1 At the ends of the earth I saw twelve doors open to all quarters of heaven, from which the winds go out and blow over the earth.

2 Three of them are open on the face of heaven, and three in the west; and three on the right of heaven, and three on the left.

3 And the three first are those of the east, and three are of the north, and three, after those on the left, of the south, and three of the west.

4 Through four of these come winds of blessing and prosperity (peace), and from those eight come hurtful winds; when they are sent, they bring destruction on all the earth and the water on it, and on all who dwell on it, and on everything which is in the water and on the land.

5 And the first wind from those doors, called the east wind, comes out through the first door which is in the east, inclining towards the south; from it desolation, drought, heat, and destruction come out .

6 And through the second door in the middle comes what is fitting (right, correct), and there come rain and fruitfulness and prosperity and dew. And through the third door which lies toward the north comes cold and drought.
7 And after these, comes out the south winds through three doors; through the first door of them inclining to the east comes out a hot wind.

8 And through the middle door next to it there comes out fragrant smells, and dew and rain, and prosperity and health.

9 And through the third door which lies to the west dew comes out and also rain, locusts and desolation.

10 And from the seventh door in the east comes the north winds, and dew, rain, locusts and desolation.

11 And from the center door come health and rain and dew and prosperity; and through the third door in the west come cloud and hoar-frost, and snow and rain, and dew and locusts.

12 And after these came the four west winds; through the first door adjoining the north come out dew and hoar-frost, and cold and snow and frost.

13 And from the center door come out dew and rain, and prosperity and blessing.

14 And through the last door which adjoins the south, come drought and desolation, and burning and destruction. And the twelve doors of the four quarters of heaven are therewith completed, and all their laws and all their plagues and all their

benefactions have I shown to you, my son Methuselah.

[Chapter 77]

1 And the first quarter is called the east, because it is the first; and the second, the south, because the Most High will descend there. From there will He who is blessed for ever descend.

2 And the west quarter is named the diminished, because there all the luminaries of the heaven wane and go down.

3 And the fourth quarter, named the north, is divided into three parts: the first of them is for the dwelling of men; and the second contains seas of water, and the abyss (deep) and forests and rivers, and darkness and clouds; and the third part contains the garden of righteousness.

4 I saw seven high mountains, higher than all the mountains which are on the earth: and from here comes hoar-frost, and days, seasons, and years pass away.
5 I saw seven rivers on the earth larger than all the rivers. One of them coming from the west pours its waters into the Great Sea.

6 And these two come from the north to the sea and pour their waters into the Erythraean Sea in the east.

7 And the remaining four come out on the side of the north to their own sea, two of them to the Erythraean Sea, and two into the Great Sea and some say they discharge themselves there into the desert.

8 I saw seven great islands in the sea and in the mainland, two in the mainland and five in the Great Sea.

[Chapter 78]

1 And the names of the sun are the following: the first Orjares, and the second Tomas.

2 And the moon has four names: the first name is Asonja, the second Ebla, the third Benase, and the fourth Erae.

3 These are the two great luminaries; their spheres (disc) are like the sphere (disc) of the heaven, and the size of the spheres (disc) of both is alike.

4 In the sphere (disc) of the sun there are seven portions of light which are added to it more than to

the moon, and in fixed measurements it is transferred until the seventh portion of the sun is exhausted.

5 And they set and enter the doors of the west, and make their revolution by the north, and come out through the eastern doors on the face of heaven.

6 And when the moon rises one-fourteenth part appears in heaven, and on the fourteenth day the moon's light becomes full.

7 And fifteen parts of light are transferred to her until the fifteenth day when her light is full, according to the sign of the year, and she becomes fifteen parts, and the moon grows by an additional fourteenth parts.

8 And as the moon's waning decreases on the first day to fourteen parts of her light, on the second to thirteen parts of light, on the third to twelve, on the fourth to eleven, on the fifth to ten, on the sixth to nine, on the seventh to eight, on the eighth to seven, on the ninth to six, on the tenth to five, on the eleventh to four, on the twelfth to three, on the thirteenth to two, on the fourteenth to the half of a seventh, and all her remaining light disappears wholly on the fifteenth.

9 And in certain months the month has twenty-nine days and once twenty-eight.

10 And Uriel showed me another law: when light is transferred to the moon, and on which side it is transferred to her by the sun.

11 During all the period during which the moon is growing in her light, she is transferring it to herself when opposite to the sun during fourteen days her light is full in heaven, and when she is ablaze throughout, her light is full in heaven.

12 And on the first day she is called the new moon, for on that day the light rises on her.

13 She becomes full moon exactly on the day when the sun sets in the west, and from the east she rises at night, and the moon shines the whole night through until the sun rises over against her and the moon is seen over against the sun.

14 On the side whence the light of the moon comes out, there again she wanes until all the light vanishes and all the days of the month are at an end, and her sphere (disc) is empty, void of light.

15 And three months she makes of thirty days, and at her time she makes three months of twenty-nine days

each, in which she accomplishes her waning in the first period of time, and in the first door for one hundred and seventy-seven days.

16 And in the time of her going out she appears for three months consisting of thirty days each, and she appears for three months consisting of twenty-nine each.

17 By night she looks like a man for twenty days each time, and by day she appears like heaven, and there is nothing else in her save her light.

[Chapter 79]

1 And now, my son Methuselah, I have shown you everything, and the law of all the stars of heaven is completed.

2 And he showed me all the laws of these for every day, and for every season of every rule, and for every year, and for its going out, and for the order prescribed to it every month and every week.

3 And the waning of the moon which takes place in the sixth door, for in this sixth door her light is accomplished, and after that there is the beginning of the waning.

4 And the waning which takes place in the first door in its season, until one hundred and seventy-seven days are accomplished, calculated according to weeks, twenty-five weeks and two days.

5 She falls behind the sun and the order of the stars exactly five days in the course of one period, and when this place which you see has been traversed.

6 Such is the picture and sketch of every luminary which Uriel the archangel, who is their leader, showed to me.

(Author's note: For more information on the storehouses of heaven, the starts, gates, and luminaries, see The Second Book of Enoch.)

[Chapter 80]

1 And in those days the angel Uriel answered and said to me: 'Behold, I have shown you everything, Enoch, and I have revealed everything to you that you should see this sun and this moon, and the leaders of the stars of heaven and all those who turn them, their tasks and times and departures.

2 And in the days of the sinners the years shall be shortened, and their seed shall be tardy on their lands

and fields, and all things on the earth shall alter, and shall not appear in their time. And the rain shall be kept back, and heaven shall withhold it.

3 And in those times the fruits of the earth shall be backward, and shall not grow in their time, and the fruits of the trees shall be withheld in their time.

4 And the moon shall alter her customs, and not appear at her time.

5 And in those days the sun shall be seen and he shall journey in the evening on the extremity of the great chariot in the west and shall shine more brightly than accords with the order of light.

6 And many rulers of the stars shall transgress their customary order. And these shall alter their orbits and tasks, and not appear at the seasons prescribed to them.

7 And the whole order of the stars shall be concealed from the sinners, and the thoughts of those on the earth shall err concerning them, and they shall be altered from all their ways, they shall err and take them to be gods.

Romans 1:18 The wrath of God is being revealed from heaven against all the godlessness and wickedness of men who suppress the truth by their wickedness, 19since what may be known about God is plain to them, because God has made it plain to them. 20For since the creation of the world God's invisible qualities—his eternal power and divine nature—have been clearly seen, being understood from what has been made, so that men are without excuse.

21For although they knew God, they neither glorified him as God nor gave thanks to him, but their thinking became futile and their foolish hearts were darkened. 22Although they claimed to be wise, they became fools 23and exchanged the glory of the immortal God for images made to look like mortal man and birds and animals and reptiles.

24Therefore God gave them over in the sinful desires of their hearts to sexual impurity for the degrading of their bodies with one another. 25They exchanged the truth of God for a lie, and worshiped and served created things rather than the Creator—who is forever praised. Amen.

26Because of this, God gave them over to shameful lusts. Even their women exchanged natural relations for unnatural ones. 27In the same way the men also abandoned natural relations with women and were inflamed with lust for one another. Men committed indecent acts with other men, and received in themselves the due penalty for their perversion.

(Author's note: Recall that many people of the time believed the stars to be angels. They worshipped the stars, believing them to have power to control fate. The scripture above tells us that God was angry because men had taken to the worship of the things God created and had forsaken the worship of He who created those things. As an added note, we are told in other ancient texts that angels had begun taking men as lovers as well as females. Angels are always considered males in these texts.)

8 And evil shall be multiplied on them, and punishment shall come on them so as to destroy all.'

[Chapter 81]

1 And he said to me: 'Enoch, look at these heavenly tablets and read what is written on them, and mark every individual fact.'

2 And I looked at the heavenly tablets, and read everything which was written on it and understood everything, and read the book of all the deeds of mankind, and of all the children of flesh; that shall be on the earth to the end of generations.
3 And I blessed the great Lord the King of glory for ever, in that He has made all the works of the world, and I exalted the Lord because of His patience, and blessed Him because of the children of men (sons of Abraham).

4 And then I said: 'Blessed is the man who dies in righteousness and goodness, concerning whom there is no book of unrighteousness written, and against whom no day of judgment shall be found.'

5 And the seven holy ones brought me and placed me on the earth before the door of my house, and said to me: 'Declare everything to your son Methuselah, and show to all your children that no flesh is righteous in the sight of the Lord, for He is their Creator.

6 For one year we will leave you with your son, until you give your last commands, that you may teach your children and record it for them, and testify to all your children; and in the second year they shall take you from their midst.

7 Let your heart be strong, for the good shall proclaim righteousness to the good; the righteous shall rejoice with the righteous, and shall wish one another well.

8 But the sinners shall die with the sinners, and the apostate shall go down with the apostate.

9 And those who practice righteousness shall die on account of the deeds of men, and be taken away on account of the deeds of the godless.'

10 And in those days they finished speaking to me, and I came to my people, blessing the Lord of the world.

[Chapter 82]

1 And now, my son Methuselah, all these things I am recounting to you and writing down for you! And I have revealed to you everything, and given you books concerning all these; so, my son Methuselah, preserve the books from your father's hand, and see that you deliver them to the generations of the world.

2 I have given wisdom to you and to your children, and those children to come, that they may give it to their children for generations. This wisdom namely that passes their understanding.

3 And those who understand it shall not sleep, but shall listen that they may learn this wisdom, and it shall please those that eat thereof better than good food.
4 Blessed are all the righteous, blessed are all those who walk in the way of righteousness and sin not as the sinners, in the numbering of all their days in which the sun traverses heaven, entering into and departing from the doors for thirty days with the heads of thousands of the order of the stars, together with the four which are within the calendar which divide the four portions of the year, which lead them and enter with them four days.

(Author's note: It is verse 4 that leads some to believe the week should begin on a Wednesday, the forth day of the week.. The verse is unclear and seems to point more to the fact that there are four seasons and the divisions of time was created on the fourth day. All Hebrew calendars had the same week and began on Sunday, the first day of the week, no matter what the name of the day was at that time in that tongue.)

Genesis 1:14 And God said, "Let there be lights in the expanse of the sky to separate the day from the night, and let them serve as signs to mark seasons and days and years, 15 and let them be lights in the expanse of the sky to give light on the earth." And it was so. 16 God made two great lights – the greater light to govern the day and the lesser light to govern the night. He also made the stars. 17 God set them in the expanse of the sky to give light on the earth, 18 to govern the day and the night, and to separate light from darkness. And God saw that it was good. 19 And there was evening, and there was morning – the fourth day.

5 Owing to them men shall be at fault and not count them in the whole number of days of the year. Men shall be at fault, and not recognize them accurately.

6 For they belong to the calculations of the year and are truly recorded therein for ever, one in the first door and one in the third, and one in the fourth and one in the sixth, and the year is completed in three hundred and sixty-four days.

7 And the account of it is accurate and the recorded counting thereof is exact; for the luminaries, and months and festivals, and years and days, has Uriel shown and revealed to me, to whom the Lord of the whole creation of the world hath subjected the host of heaven.

8 And he has power over night and day in heaven to cause the light to shine on men via the sun, moon, and stars, and all the powers of the heaven which revolve in their circular chariots. And these are the orders of the stars, which set in their places, and in their seasons and festivals and months.

9 And these are the names of those who lead them, who watch that they enter at their times, in their orders, in their seasons, in their months, in their periods of dominion, and in their positions.

10 Their four leaders who divide the four parts of the year enter first; and after them the twelve leaders of the orders who divide the months; and for the three hundred and sixty days there are heads over thousands who divide the days; and for the four days in the calendar there are the leaders which divide the four parts of the year.

11 And these heads over thousands are interspersed between leader and leader, each behind a station, but their leaders make the division.

12 And these are the names of the leaders who divide the four parts of the year which are ordained:

13 Milki'el, Hel'emmelek, and Mel'ejal, and Narel. And the names of those who lead them: Adnar'el, and Ijasusa'el, and 'Elome'el.

14 These three follow the leaders of the orders, and there is one that follows the three leaders of the orders which follow those leaders of stations that divide the four parts of the year. In the beginning of the year Melkejal rises first and rules, who is named Tam'aini and sun, and all the days of his dominion while he bears rule are ninety-one days.

15 And these are the signs of the days which are to be seen on earth in the days of his dominion: sweat, and heat; and calms; and all the trees bear fruit, and leaves are produced on all the trees, and the harvest of wheat, and the rose-flowers, and all the flowers which come out in the field, but the trees of the winter season become withered.

16 And these are the names of the leaders which are under them: Berka'el, Zelebs'el, and another who is added a head of a thousand, called Hilujaseph: and the days of the dominion of this leader are at an end.

17 The next leader after him is Hel'emmelek, whom one names the shining sun, and all the days of his light are ninety-one days.

18 And these are the signs of his days on the earth: glowing heat and dryness, and the trees ripen their fruits and produce all their fruits ripe and ready, and the sheep pair and become pregnant, and all the fruits of the earth are gathered in, and everything that is in the fields, and the winepress: these things take place in the days of his dominion.
19 These are the names, and the orders, and the leaders of those heads of thousands: Gida'ljal, Ke'el, and He'el, and the name of the head of a thousand which is added to them, Asfa'el: and the days of his dominion are at an end.

Author's note: The seasons are 91 days each. There are four seasons. The year is 91 x 4 or 364 days. We are warned to calculate the years correctly in order to celebrate the holy days on the days they were meant to be honored. Descriptions of the seasons are given along with the angels that control them.

[Chapter 83]
The *Book of Visions* (Chapters 83-90):

1 And now, my son Methuselah, I will show you all my visions which I have seen, recounting them before you.

2 I saw two visions before I got married (took a wife), and the one was quite unlike the other: the first when I was learning to write: the second before I married (took) your mother, was when I saw a terrible vision.

3 And regarding them I prayed to the Lord. I had laid down in the house of my grandfather Mahalalel, when I saw in a vision how heaven collapsed and was carried off (removed, torn down) and fell to the earth.

4 And when it fell to the earth I saw how the earth was swallowed up in a great abyss, and mountains were suspended on mountains, and hills sank down on hills, and high trees were ripped from their stems, and hurled down and sunk in the abyss.

5 And then a word fell into my mouth, and I lifted up my voice to cry aloud, and said:

6 'The earth is destroyed.' And my grandfather Mahalalel woke me as I lay near him, and said to me: 'Why do you cry so, my son, and why do you make such moaning (lamentation)?'

7 And I recounted to him the whole vision which I had seen, and he said to me: 'You have seen a terrible thing , my son. Your dream (vision) is of a grave time and concerns the secrets of all the sin of the earth: it must sink into the abyss and be totally destroyed.

8 And now, my son, arise and pray to the Lord of glory, since you are a believer, that a remnant may remain on the earth, and that He may not destroy the whole earth.

9 My son, from heaven all this will come on the earth, and on the earth there will be great destruction.

10 After that I arose and prayed and implored and besought (God), and wrote down my prayer for the generations of the world, and I will show everything to you, my son Methuselah.

11 And when I had gone out below and seen the heaven, and the sun rising in the east, and the moon setting in the west, and a few stars, and the whole earth, and everything as He had known it in the beginning, then I blessed the Lord of judgment and exalted Him because He had made the sun to go out from the windows of the east, and he ascended and rose on the face of heaven, and set out and kept traversing the path shown to it.

(Author's note: This first vision would seem to foreshadow the flood, but since the vision was of a piece of heaven breaking off and falling to earth with destructive force, it may be an end time prophecy of a meteor strike. Another, more timely interpretation is that of Satan falling to earth, which is the beginnings of sorrow.)

[Chapter 84]

1 And I lifted up my hands in righteousness and blessed the Holy and Great One, and spoke with the breath of my mouth, and with the tongue of flesh, which God has made for the children of the flesh of men, that they should speak therewith, and He gave them breath and a tongue and a mouth that they should speak therewith:

2 Blessed be you, O Lord, King, Great and mighty in your greatness, Lord of the whole creation of heaven, King of kings and God of the whole world. And your power and kingship and greatness abide for ever and

ever, and throughout all generations your dominion and all heavens are your throne for ever, and the whole earth your footstool for ever and ever.

3 For you have made and you rule all things, and nothing is too hard for you, wisdom never departs from the place of your throne, nor turns away from your presence. You know and see and hear everything, and there is nothing hidden from you for you see everything.

4 And now the angels of your heavens are guilty of trespass, and on the flesh of men abide your wrath until the great day of judgment.

5 And now, O God and Lord and Great King, I implore and beseech you to fulfill my prayer, to leave me a posterity on earth, and not destroy all the flesh of man, and make the earth without inhabitant, so that there should be an eternal destruction.

6 And now, my Lord, destroy from the earth the flesh which has aroused your wrath, but the flesh of righteousness and uprightness establish as an eternal plant bearing seed forever, and hide not your face from the prayer of your servant, O Lord.'

Author's note: In chapter 85 and following, a series of animals is mentioned. These seem to refer to nations or ethnicities. For example, the eagles may refer to the Roman empire, the Islamic nation is represented by the asses, Egyptians are wolves, the Assyrians are lions, and so on. See Daniel Chapter 10 for other like imagery.

Other writers have attempted to be more specific. Starting with Adam and Eve, the story begins. Abraham may be a white bull, Ishmael, the wild ass; Isaac the white bull, Jacob is a white sheep, Esau the wild boar. There is the concept that Noah's three sons, Shem, Ham and Japheth, give rise to all various the animals or nations. The small lambs with open eyes are the Essenes; Jesus is the "sheep with the big horn"; and in 90.17, the final twelve shepherds represent the Christian era and the twelve apostles.

Notes are included within the chapters and at the end of the section. They suggest possible interpretations. As with any prophecy written in such imagery, it is impossible to know exactly what the author was trying to convey. Prophecy tends to be interpreted according to one's viewpoint. When one looks at the prophecies from a purely Jewish viewpoint it is likely that the savior of the people, represented by the sheep with a large horn, is not the messiah at all, but a historical military figure such as Judas Maccabaeus, who led the great Maccabean revolt of 167 B.C. – 160 B.C. against Rome.

Judas Maccabeus is also described as a great horn among six others on the head of a lamb. This possibly pertains to his five brothers and Mattathias. If you take this in context of the history from Maccabeus time the explanation of the verse may be found in 1 Maccabees 3: 7 and 6: 52;, 2 Maccabees 6: 8-14; and 1 Maccabees 7: 41, 42

[Chapter 85]

1 And after this I saw another dream, and I will show the whole dream to you, my son.
2 And Enoch lifted up his voice and spoke to his son Methuselah: 'I will speak to you, my son, hear my words. Incline your ear to the dream (vision) of your father.

3 Before I married (took) your mother Edna, I saw in a vision on my bed, and behold a bull came out from the earth, and that bull was white.

4 And after it came out a heifer, and along with this later came out two bulls, one of them black and the other red.

5 And that black bull gored the red one and pursued him over the earth, and then I could no longer see that red bull. But that black bull grew and that heifer went with him, and I saw that many oxen proceeded from him which resembled and followed him.

6 And that cow, that first one, went from the presence of that first bull in order to seek that red one, but found him not, and mourned with a great lamentation and sought him.

7 And I looked until that first bull came to her and quieted (calmed) her, and from that time onward she cried no more.

8 And after that she bore another white bull, and after him she bore many bulls and black cows.

9 And I saw in my sleep that white bull likewise grew and became a great white bull, and from him proceeded many white bulls, and they resembled him. And they began to father many white bulls, which resembled them, one following another.

(Author's note: Many believe verses 1 – 9 represent the story of Adam, Eve, Cain, and Abel. The first white bull mentioned is Adam. The heifer is Eve. The two bulls born to them are a black one (Cain) and a red one (Abel.) Eve leaves to seek Abel and finds him. She

laments his death. Adam comforts her. Cain goes on to produce many oxen. Eve produces another son and thus produces many more bulls and cows.)

[Chapter 86]

1 And again I looked with my eyes as I slept, and I saw the heaven above, and behold a star fell from heaven, and it arose and ate and pastured among those oxen (bulls).

2 And after that I saw the large and the black oxen (bulls), and behold they all changed their stalls and pastures and their heifers (cattle) , and began to live with each other.

(Author's note: The first star to fall was Satan, The falling stars that followed were the watchers. They caused the heifers, who are the women, to begin living with and having sex with the angels. Based on the previous verses it would appear that Satan and the fallen angels picked the descendents of Cain to have sex.

Second Book of Adam and Eve, Chapter 20
29 Enoch was already grown up at that time, and in his zeal for God, he stood and said, "Hear me, you large and small (young and old) sons of Seth! When you transgress the commandment of our fathers and go down from this holy mountain, you shall not come up here again for ever."
30 But they rose up against Enoch and would not listen to his words, but they went down from the Holy Mountain.
31 And when they looked at the daughters of Cain, at their beautiful figures, and at their hands and feet dyed with color, and the tattoos on their faces that ornamented them, the fire of sin was set ablaze in them.
32 Then Satan made them look most beautiful before the sons of Seth, as he also made the sons of Seth appear the most handsome in the eyes of the daughters of Cain, so that the daughters of Cain lusted after the sons of Seth like ravenous beasts, and the sons of Seth lusted after the daughters of Cain until they committed disgusting and disgraceful acts with them.)

3 And again I saw in the vision, and looked towards heaven, and behold I saw many stars descend and cast themselves down from heaven to that first star, and they became bulls among those cattle and pastured with them.

4 And I looked at them and saw they all let out their private (sexual) members, like horses, and began to mount the cows of the bulls (oxen), and they all became pregnant and bore elephants, camels, and asses.

Author's note: Book of Jubilees indicates that the offspring of the angels and women were somehow different and they are divided into categories of the Naphidim (or Naphilim, depending or the transliteration), the Giants, and the Eljo. (Naphil are mentioned but this is the singular of Naphilim.) The word "Naphil" means "The Fallen." There is no indication as to the meaning of "Eljo (Elyo)" but the word would indicate these are "godlings" and are likely those referred to in the Book of Genesis as "men of renown."

5 And all the bulls (oxen) feared them and were frightened of them, and began to bite with their teeth and to devour, and to gore with their horns.

6 And, moreover, they began to devour those oxen; and behold all the children of the earth began to tremble and shake before them and to flee from them.

[Chapter 87]

1 And again I saw how they began to gore each other and to devour each other, and the earth began to cry aloud.

2 And I raised my eyes again to heaven, and I saw in the vision, and behold there came out from heaven beings who were like white men, and four went out from that place and three others with them.

3 And those three that had come out last grasped me by my hand and took me up, away from the generations of the earth, and raised me up to a high place, and showed me a tower raised high above the earth, and all the hills were lower.

4 And one said to me: 'Remain here until you see everything that befalls those elephants, camels, and asses, and the stars and the oxen, and all of them.'

[Chapter 88]

1 And I saw one of those four who had come out first, and he seized that first star which had fallen from heaven, and bound it hand and foot and cast it into an abyss; now that abyss was narrow and deep, and horrible and dark.

2PE 2:4 For if God spared not the angels that sinned, but cast them down to hell, and delivered them into chains of darkness, to be reserved unto judgment.

2 And one of them drew a sword, and gave it to those elephants and camels and asses then they began to smite each other, and the whole earth shook because of them.

3 And as I was beholding in the vision one of those four who had come out stoned them from heaven, and gathered and took all the great stars whose private (sexual) members were like those of horses, and bound them all hand and foot, and threw them in an abyss of the earth.

(Author's note: One must smile at the idea of the angels having penises the size of horses. In the ancient mind, this was one reason some of the women gave in so easily. If a spiritual creature is determined to become corporeal, why not create a body that will fulfill the lust that drives one to incarnate in the first place?)

[Chapter 89]

1 And one of those four went to that white bull and instructed him in a secret, and he was terrified: he was born a bull and became a man, and built for himself a great vessel and dwelt on it.

2 And three bulls dwelt with him in the vessel and they were covered over. And again I raised my eyes towards heaven and saw a high roof, with seven water torrents on it, and those torrents flowed with much water into an enclosure. And I looked again, and behold fountains were opened on the surface of that great enclosure, and the water began to bubble and swell and rise on the surface, and I saw that enclosure until all its surface was covered with water.

3 And the water, the darkness, and mist increased on it; and as I looked at the height of that water, the water had risen above the height of the enclosure, and was streaming over the enclosure, and it stood on the earth.

4 And all the cattle of the enclosure were gathered together until I saw how they sank and were swallowed up and perished in that water.

5 But that vessel floated on the water, while all the oxen (bulls) and elephants and camels and asses sank to the bottom with all the animals, so that I could no longer see them, and they were not able to escape, but perished and sank into the depths.

6 And again I watched in the vision until those water torrents were removed from that high roof, and the chasms of the earth were leveled up and other abysses were opened.

7 Then the water began to run down into these abysses, until the earth became visible; but that

vessel settled on the earth, and the darkness retired and light appeared.

8 But that white bull which had become a man came out of that vessel, and the three bulls with him, and one of those three was white like that bull, and one of them was red as blood, and one black; and that white bull departed from them.

(Author's note: Here we have the story of Noah and the flood. The flood came because of the sins of the watchers and their offspring, who began killing everything. The flood cleansed the earth and left only the sons of Noah and their wives to repopulate. The story seems to indicate that the various races of the world (white, red, and black, began with the sons of Noah.)

9 And they began to bring out beasts of the field and birds, so that there arose different genera: lions, tigers, wolves, dogs, hyenas, wild boars, foxes, squirrels, swine, falcons, vultures, kites, eagles, and ravens; and among them was born a white bull.

10 And they began to bite one another; but that white bull which was born among them fathered a wild ass and a white bull with it, and the wild asses multiplied.

11 But that bull which was born from him fathered a black wild boar and a white sheep; and the former fathered many boars, but the sheep gave birth to twelve sheep.

(Author's note: Abraham fathered Ishmael (the wild ass) and Isaac (the white bull.) Isaac fathers a boar (Esau) and a sheep (Jacob.) Jacob has twelve sheep, who are the twelve patriarchs and the beginning of the twelve tribes.)

12 And when those twelve sheep had grown, they gave up one of them to the asses, and the asses again gave up that sheep to the wolves, and that sheep grew up among the wolves.

(Author's note: Joseph was sold to the Midiantes or Ishaelites as a slave. They, in turn, sold him to the Egyptians. See Genesis 37:25-39.2)

13 And the Lord brought the eleven sheep to live with it and to pasture with it among the wolves and they multiplied and became many flocks of sheep.

(Author's note: This begins the story of Moses and how the Egyptians oppressed the Israelites until he led them out of captivity.)

14 And the wolves began to fear them, and they oppressed them until they destroyed their little ones, and they threw their young into a deep river, but those sheep began to cry aloud on account of their little ones, and to complain to their Lord.

15 And a sheep which had been saved from the wolves fled and escaped to the wild asses; and I saw the sheep how they lamented and cried, and besought their Lord with all their might, until that Lord of the sheep descended at the voice of the sheep from a high abode, and came to them and pastured them.

16 And He called that sheep which had escaped the wolves, and spoke with it concerning the wolves that it should admonish them not to touch the sheep.

17 And the sheep went to the wolves according to the word of the Lord, and another sheep met it and went with it, and the two went and entered together into the assembly of those wolves, and spoke with them and admonished them not to touch the sheep from then on.

18 And on it I saw the wolves, and how they more harshly oppressed the sheep with all their power; and the sheep cried aloud.

19 And the Lord came to the sheep and they began to beat those wolves, and the wolves began to make lamentation; but the sheep became quiet and ceased to cry out.

20 And I saw the sheep until they departed from among the wolves; but the eyes of the wolves were blinded, and the wolves departed in pursuit of the sheep with all their power.

21 And the Lord of the sheep went with them, as their leader, and all His sheep followed Him.

22 And his face was dazzling and glorious and terrible to behold. But the wolves began to pursue those sheep until they reached a sea of water.

23 And that sea was divided, and the water stood on this side and on that before their face, and their Lord led them and placed Himself between them and the wolves.

24 And as those wolves had not yet seen the sheep, they proceeded into the midst of that sea, and the wolves followed the sheep, and those wolves ran after them into that sea.

25 And when they saw the Lord of the sheep, they turned to flee before His face, but that sea gathered itself together, and became as it had been created, and the water swelled and rose until it covered the wolves.

26 And I watched until all the wolves who pursued those sheep perished and were drowned.

27 But the sheep escaped from that water and went out into a wilderness, where there was no water and no grass; and they began to open their eyes and to see;

28 And I saw the Lord of the sheep pasturing them and giving them water and grass, and that sheep going and leading them.

(Author's note: The Israelites escaped. They passed through the divided sea, but the Egyptians were covered by the water and drowned. Now, we begin the story of Moses and the ascent up the mountain, where God gave him the Ten Commandments.)

29 And the sheep ascended to the summit of that high rock, and the Lord of the sheep sent it to them. And after that I saw the Lord of the sheep who stood before them, and His appearance was great and terrible and majestic, and all those sheep saw Him and were afraid before His face.

30 And they all feared and trembled because of Him, and they cried to that sheep which was among them:

31 'We are not able to stand before our Lord or to behold Him.' And that sheep which led them again ascended to the summit of that rock, but the sheep began to be blinded and to wander from the way which he had showed them, but that sheep did not realize it.

(Author's note: When Moses came down from the mountain he discovered a large group of the Israelites had made a golden calf idol and were worshipping it.)

32 And the Lord of the sheep was very angry with them, and that sheep discovered it, and went down from the summit of the rock, and came to the sheep, and found the greatest part of them blinded and fallen away.

33 And when they saw it they feared and trembled at its presence, and desired to return to their folds. And that sheep took other sheep with it, and came to those sheep which had fallen away, and began to slay them; and the sheep feared its presence, and thus that sheep brought back those sheep that had fallen away, and they returned to their folds.

34 And I saw in this vision until that sheep became a man and built a house for the Lord of the sheep, and placed all the sheep in that house.

35 And I saw until this sheep which had met that sheep which led them fell asleep (died); and I saw until all the great sheep perished and little ones arose in their place, and they came to a pasture, and approached a stream of water.

36 Then that sheep, their leader which had become a man, withdrew from them and fell asleep (died), and all the sheep looked for it (sought it) and cried over it with a great crying.

37 And I saw until they left off crying for that sheep and crossed that stream of water, and there arose the two sheep as leaders in the place of those which had led them and fallen asleep.

38 And I saw until the sheep came to a good place, and a pleasant and glorious land, and I saw until those sheep were satisfied; and that house stood among them in the (green) pleasant land.

(Author's note: After Moses died and the two spies were sent into the promised land to bring back a report, Joshua took over and led the Israelites into the promised land.)

39 And sometimes their eyes were opened, and sometimes blinded, until another sheep arose and led them and brought them all back, and their eyes were opened.

40 And the dogs and the foxes and the wild boars began to devour those sheep until the Lord of the sheep raised up another sheep, a ram from their midst, which led them.

41 And that ram began to butt on either side those dogs, foxes, and wild boars until he had destroyed them all.

(Author's note: This is the succession of kings leading up to David. All of them had to fight the surrounding nations.)

42 And that sheep whose eyes were opened saw that ram, which was among the sheep, until it forsook its glory and began to butt those sheep, and trampled on them, and behaved itself unseemly.

43 And the Lord of the sheep sent the lamb to another lamb and raised it to being a ram and leader of the sheep instead of that ram which had forsaken its glory.

44 And it went to it and spoke to it alone, and raised it to being a ram, and made it the prince and leader of the sheep; but during all these things those dogs oppressed the sheep.

45 And the first ram pursued the second ram, and the second ram arose and fled before it; and I saw until those dogs pulled down the first ram.

46 And that second ram arose and led the little sheep. And those sheep grew and multiplied; but all the dogs, and foxes, and wild boars feared and fled before it, and that ram butted and killed the wild beasts, and those wild beasts had no longer any power among the sheep and robbed them no more of anything.

47 And that ram fathered many sheep and fell asleep; and a little sheep became ram in its place, and became prince and leader of those sheep.

48 And that house became great and broad, and it was built for those sheep: and a high and great tower was built on the house for the Lord of the sheep, and that house was low, but the tower was elevated and high, and the Lord of the sheep stood on that tower and they offered a full table before him.

49 And again I saw those sheep that they again erred and went many ways, and forsook that their house, and the Lord of the sheep called some from among the sheep and sent them to the sheep, but the sheep began to slay them.

50 And one of them was saved and was not slain, and it sped away and cried aloud over the sheep; and they sought to slay it, but the Lord of the sheep saved it from the sheep, and brought it up to me, and caused it to live there.

(Author's note: Verse 50 could be a reference to Elijah.)

51 And many other sheep He sent to those sheep to testify to them and lament over them.

52 And after that I saw that when they forsook the house of the Lord and His tower they fell away entirely, and their eyes were blinded; and I saw the Lord of the sheep how He worked much slaughter among them in their herds until those sheep invited that slaughter and betrayed His place.

53 And He gave them over into the hands of the lions and tigers, and wolves and hyenas, and into the hand of the foxes, and to all the wild beasts, and those wild beasts began to tear in pieces those sheep.

54 And I saw that He forsook their house and their tower and gave them all into the hand of the lions, to tear and devour them, into the hand of all the wild beasts.

55 And I began to cry aloud with all my power, and to appeal to the Lord of the sheep, because the sheep were being devoured by all the wild beasts.

56 But He remained unmoved, though He saw it, and rejoiced that they were devoured and swallowed and robbed, and left them to be devoured in the hand of all the beasts.

57 And He called seventy shepherds, and gave those sheep to them that they might pasture them, and He spoke to the shepherds and their companions: 'Let each individual of you pasture the sheep from now on, and everything that I shall command you that do you.

(Author's note: The 70 are religious leaders of that time frame. In the Third Book of Enoch God mentions 70 nations, leading one to believe that from God's viewpoint there are only 70 true nations. All other divisions are man made and false.)

58 And I will deliver them over to you duly numbered, and tell you which of them are to be destroyed-and them you will destroy.' And He gave over to them those sheep.

59 And He called another and spoke to him: 'Observe and mark everything that the shepherds will do to those sheep; for they will destroy more of them than I have commanded them.

60 And every excess and the destruction which will be done through the shepherds, record how many they destroy according to my command, and how many according to their own caprice; record against every individual shepherd all the destruction he effects.

61 And read out before me by number how many they destroy, and how many they deliver over for destruction, that I may have this as a testimony against them, and know every deed of the shepherds, that I may comprehend and see what they do, whether or not they abide by my command which I have commanded them.

62 But they shall not know it, and you shall not declare it to them, nor admonish them, but only record against each individual all the destruction

which the shepherds effect each in his time and lay it all before me.'

63 And I saw until those shepherds pastured in their season, and they began to slay and to destroy more than they were bidden, and they delivered those sheep into the hand of the lions.

64 And the lions and tigers ate and devoured the greater part of those sheep, and the wild boars ate along with them; and they burned that tower and demolished that house.

65 And I became very sorrowful over that tower because that house of the sheep was demolished, and afterwards I was unable to see if those sheep entered that house.

66 And the shepherds and their associates delivered over those sheep to all the wild beasts, to devour them, and each one of them received in his time a definite number, it was written by the other in a book how many each one of them destroyed of them.

67 And each one slew and destroyed many more than was prescribed; and I began to weep and lament on account of those sheep.

68 And thus in the vision I saw that one who wrote, how he wrote down every one that was destroyed by those shepherds, day by day, and carried up and laid down and showed actually the whole book to the Lord of the sheep - everything that they had done, and all that each one of them had made away with, and all that they had given over to destruction.

69 And the book was read before the Lord of the sheep, and He took the book from his hand and read it and sealed it and laid it down.

(Author's note: Verses 65 – 69 Refers to the first temple being destroyed. Verse 72 and 73 begins the story of Ezra and the return to Jerusalem to rebuild the city and temple.)

70 And I saw how the shepherds pastured for twelve hours, and behold three of those sheep turned back and came and entered and began to build up all that had fallen down of that house; but the wild boars tried to hinder them, but they were not able.

71 And they began again to build as before, and they raised up that tower, and it was named the high tower; and they began again to place a table before the tower, but all the bread on it was polluted and not pure.

72 And as touching all this the eyes of those sheep were blinded so that they saw not, and the eyes of their shepherds likewise were blinded; and they delivered them in large numbers to their shepherds for destruction, and they trampled the sheep with their feet and devoured them.

73 And the Lord of the sheep remained unmoved until all the sheep were dispersed over the field and mingled with the beasts, and the shepherds did not save them out of the hand of the beasts.

74 And this one who wrote the book carried it up, and showed it and read it before the Lord of the sheep, and implored Him on their account, and besought Him on their account as he showed Him all the doings of the shepherds, and gave testimony before Him against all the shepherds.

(Author's note: Ezra, Haggai, and Zechariah return and wrote books of the Old Testament.)

75 And he took the actual book and laid it down beside Him and departed.

[Chapter 90]

1 And I saw until that in this manner thirty-five shepherds undertook the pasturing of the sheep, and they completed their periods as did the first; and others received them into their hands, to pasture them for their period, each shepherd in his own period.

2 And after that I saw in my vision all the birds of heaven coming, the eagles, the vultures, the kites, the ravens; but the eagles led all the birds; and they began to devour those sheep, and to pick out their eyes and to devour their flesh.

(Author's note: Now the Eagle, which is Roman empire, appears from among the nations.)

3 And the sheep cried out because their flesh was being devoured by the birds, and as for me I looked and lamented in my sleep over that shepherd who pastured the sheep.

4 And I saw until those sheep were devoured by the dogs and eagles and kites, and they left neither flesh nor skin nor sinew remaining on them until only their bones stood there; and their bones too fell to the earth and the sheep became few.

5 And I saw until that twenty-three had undertaken the pasturing and completed in their many periods fifty-eight times.

(Author's note: Of the 70 appointed religious leaders throughout time, fifty-eight have passed. Verse 6 introduces the Essenes. Verse 8 probably refers to John The Baptist.)

6 But behold lambs were borne by those white sheep, and they began to open their eyes and to see, and to cry to the sheep.

7 They cried to them, but they did not hearken to what they said to them, but were very deaf, and their eyes were very blinded.

8 And I saw in the vision how the ravens flew on those lambs and took one of those lambs, and dashed the sheep in pieces and devoured them.

9 And I saw until horns grew on those lambs, and the ravens cast down their horns; and I saw until there sprouted a great horn of one of those sheep, and their eyes were opened.

(Author's note: According to the way in which Verse 9 is interpreted, it begins the story of Jesus. The story seems to end at verse 16. The Sheep with the great horn is never said to be killed. It only states that he was stopped. Another interpretation points to Judas Maccabaeus.)

10 And it looked at them and their eyes opened, and it cried to the sheep, and the rams saw it and all ran to it.

11 And notwithstanding all this, those eagles and vultures and ravens and kites kept on tearing the sheep and swooping down on them and devouring them until the sheep remained silent, but the rams lamented and cried out.

12 And those ravens fought and battled with it and sought to lay low its horn, but they had no power over it.

13 All the eagles and vultures and ravens and kites were gathered together, and there came with them all the sheep of the field, they all came together, and helped each other to break that horn of the ram.

14 And I saw that man, who wrote down the names of the shepherds and brought them up before the Lord of the sheep, came, and he helped that ram and showed it everything; its help was coming down.

15 And I looked until that Lord of the sheep came to them angry, all those who saw him ran, and they all fell into the shadow in front of Him.

16 All the eagles and vultures and ravens and kites, gathered together and brought with them all the wild sheep, and they all came together and helped one another in order to dash that horn of the ram in pieces.

17 And I looked at that man, who wrote the book at the command of the Lord, until he opened that book of the destruction that those last twelve shepherds had done. And he showed, in front of the Lord of the sheep, that they had destroyed even more than those before them had.

(Author's note: The twelve shepherds are either the apostles, if one interprets the sheep with the large horn as Jesus, or the twelve shepherds are the leaders of the Jews joining themselves in the revolt led by Judas Maccabeus. If one goes with the apostle theory, the books refer to the New Testament, but more specifically it refers to the path of "enlightenment." I use this word since the text itself uses the terms "to be blinded" and " to have the eyes opened." It should be noted that there are books attributed to most of the apostles, but many are not included in the Bible. This ends past events. What remains from verse 17 on is prophetic. Following the idea that Enoch is one of the first apocalyptic books, we will see in figurative language a great battle and the judgment. The stars are judged. This is the judgment of the fallen angels. The seventy Jewish religious leaders, representing the Pharisee mind set and the religious oppression of the Jewish people are judged. Then the eyes of the faithful are opened and they are brought into the Lord's house. The number of believers is so great the house overflows.)

18 And I looked and the Lord of the sheep came to them and took the Staff of His Anger and struck the Earth. And the Earth was split. And all the animals, and the birds of the sky, fell from those sheep and sank in the earth, and it closed over them.

19 And I saw until a great sword was given to the sheep, and the sheep proceeded against all the beasts of the field to slay them, and all the beasts and the birds of the heaven fled before their face. And I saw that man, who wrote the book according to the command of the Lord, until he opened that book concerning the destruction which those twelve last shepherds had wrought, and showed that they had destroyed much more than their predecessors, before the Lord of the sheep. And I saw until the Lord of the sheep came to them and took in His hand the staff of His wrath, and smote the earth, and the earth clave asunder, and all the beasts and all the birds of heaven

fell from among those sheep, and were swallowed up in the earth and it covered them.

20 And I saw until a throne was erected in the pleasant land, and the Lord of the sheep sat Himself on it, and the other took the sealed books and opened those books before the Lord of the sheep.

21 And the Lord called those men, the seven first white ones, and commanded that they should bring before Him, beginning with the first star which led the way, all the stars whose private members were like those of horses, and they brought them all before Him.

22 And He said to that man who wrote before Him, being one of those seven white ones, and said to him: 'Take those seventy shepherds to whom I delivered the sheep, and who taking them on their own authority slew more than I commanded them.'

23 And behold they were all bound, I saw, and they all stood before Him.

24 And the judgment was held first over the stars, and they were judged and found guilty, and went to the place of condemnation, and they were cast into an abyss, full of fire and flaming, and full of pillars of fire.

25 And those seventy shepherds were judged and found guilty, and they were cast into that fiery abyss.

26 And I saw at that time how a like abyss was opened in the midst of the earth, full of fire, and they brought those blinded sheep, and they were all judged and found guilty and cast into this fiery abyss, and they burned; now this abyss was to the right of that house.

27 And I saw those sheep burning and their bones burning.

28 And I stood up to see until they folded up that old house; and carried off all the pillars, and all the beams and ornaments of the house were at the same time folded up with it, and they carried it off and laid it in a place in the south of the land.

29 And I saw until the Lord of the sheep brought a new house greater and loftier than that first, and set it up in the place of the first which had been folded up; all its pillars were new, and its ornaments were new and larger than those of the first, the old one which He had taken away, and all the sheep were within it.

HEB 13:14 For here have we no continuing city, but we seek one to come.

30 And I saw all the sheep which had been left, and all the beasts on the earth, and all the birds of heaven, falling down and doing homage to those sheep and making petition to and obeying them in every thing.

31 And thereafter those three who were clothed in white and had seized me by my hand [who had taken me up before], and the hand of that ram also seizing hold of me, they took me up and set me down in the midst of those sheep before the judgment took place.

32 And those sheep were all white, and their wool was abundant and clean.

33 And all that had been destroyed and dispersed, and all the beasts of the field, and all the birds of heaven, assembled in that house, and the Lord of the sheep rejoiced with great joy because they were all good and had returned to His house.

34 And I saw until they laid down that sword, which had been given to the sheep, and they brought it back into the house, and it was sealed before the presence of the Lord, and all the sheep were invited into that house, but it held them not.

35 And the eyes of them all were opened, and they saw the good, and there was not one among them that did not see.

36 And I saw that the house was large and broad and very full.

37 And I saw that a white bull was born, with large horns and all the beasts of the field and all the birds of the air feared him and made petition to him all the time.

(Author's note: If one assumes the previous "sheep with a large horn" was Judas Maccabaeus, then verse 37 is the birth of the Messiah.)

38 And I saw until all their generations were transformed, and they all became white bulls; and the first among them became a lamb, and that lamb became a great animal and had great black horns on its head; and the Lord of the sheep rejoiced over it and over all the oxen.

39 And I slept in their midst: And I awoke and saw everything.

40 This is the vision which I saw while I slept, and I awoke and blessed the Lord of righteousness and gave Him glory.

41 Then I wept greatly and my tears ceased not until I could no longer endure it; when I saw, they flowed on account of what I had seen; for everything shall come and be fulfilled, and all the deeds of men in their order were shown to me.

42 On that night I remembered the first dream, and because of it I wept and was troubled-because I had seen that vision.

Note from editor: at this point, the time frame and text flow becomes non sequitur. It appears the codex was not kept in sequence here. Thus, the translated pages are out of sequence. The flow of time and occurrences seems to follow the pattern listed:

91:6 to 92.1 through 92:5 then jumps to 93:1. The flow then continues from 93:1 to 93:10 and then jumps to 91:7. From 91:7 the text continues to 91:19. It then picks up again at 93:11 and continues.

If one were to attempt to put this section into a time line, the interval would link together in some fashion resembling the following:

Ten Weeks of Judgment

WEEK 1 Judgment & righteousness 93.3 Enoch's time Antediluvian	
(Ice-age - 16,000 B.C.)	
WEEK 2 Judgment & cleansing 93.4 Noah's time and the great flood	
The first judgment of the world (16,000 – 10,000 B.C)	
WEEK 3 Righteousness is planted 93.5 Abraham's time	
(10,000 – 2000 B.C.)	
WEEK 4 Law for all generations 93.6 Moses' time	
WEEK 4 2000 – 1400 B.C.	
WEEK 5 House of Glory 93.7 Solomon's time	
1400 – 900 B.C.	
WEEK 6 Jesus ascends, temple burned, elect scattered 93.8 Jesus' time	
900 B.C – 100 A.D.	
WEEK 7 Apostate generation Judgment of Fire 93.9 - 91.11 Our time	
The second judgment of earth. 100 A.D. - ?	
WEEK 8 A sword 91.12–13 New house, new heaven & earth Future time	
WEEK 9 The righteous judgment revealed 91.14 The judgment time	

WEEK 10 Eternal time	God's power is forever 91.15-16

When reading the text from this point to the end of chapter 93 one should keep this flow in mind.]

[Chapter 91]
The *Book of Warnings and Blessings of Enoch* (Chapters 91-104):

1 And now, my son Methuselah, call to me all your brothers and gather together to me all the sons of your mother; for the word calls me, and the spirit is poured out on me, that I may show you everything that shall befall you for ever.'

2 And thereon Methuselah went and summoned to him all his brothers and assembled his relatives.

3 And he spoke to all the children of righteousness and said: 'Hear, you sons of Enoch, all the words of your father, and hearken, as you should, to the voice of my mouth; for I exhort you and say to you, beloved:

4 Love righteousness and walk in it, and draw near to righteousness without a double heart, and do not associate with those of a double heart, but walk in righteousness, my sons. And it shall guide you on good paths. And righteousness shall be your companion.'

JAM 1:6 But let him ask in faith, nothing wavering. For he that wavereth is like a wave of the sea driven with the wind and tossed. 7 For let not that man think that he shall receive any thing of the Lord. 8 A double minded man is unstable in all his ways.

5 'For I know that violence must increase on the earth, and a great punishment will be executed on the earth, it shall be cut off from its roots, and its whole construct will be destroyed.

6 And unrighteousness shall again be complete on the earth, and all the deeds of unrighteousness and of violence and sin shall prevail a second time.

7 And when sin and unrighteousness and blasphemy and violence in all kinds of deeds increase, and apostasy and transgression and uncleanness increase; a great chastisement shall come from heaven on all these, and the holy Lord will come out with wrath and chastisement to execute judgment on earth.

2TH 2:3 Let no man deceive you by any means: for that day shall not come, except there come a falling

away first, and that man of sin be revealed, the son of perdition.

8 In those days violence shall be cut off from its roots, and the roots of unrighteousness together with deceit, and they shall be destroyed from under heaven.

9 And all the idols of the heathen shall be abandoned. And the temples burned with fire, and they shall remove them from the whole earth; and the heathen shall be cast into the judgment of fire, and shall perish in wrath and in grievous judgment for ever.

10 And the righteous shall arise from their sleep, and wisdom shall arise and be given to them.

11 And after that the roots of unrighteousness and those who plan violence and those who commit blasphemy shall be cut off, and the sinners shall be destroyed by the sword.

12 And after this there will be another week; the eighth, that of righteousness, and a sword will be given to it so that the Righteous Judgment may be executed on those who do wrong, and the sinners will be handed over into the hands of the righteous.

13 And, at its end, they will acquire Houses because of their righteousness, and a House will be built for the Great King in Glory, forever.

14 And after this, in the ninth week, the Righteous Judgment will be revealed to the whole world. And all the deeds of the impious will vanish from the whole Earth. And the world will be written down for destruction and all men will look to the Path of Uprightness.

15 And, after this, in the tenth week, in the seventh part, there will be an Eternal Judgment that will be executed on the Watchers and the Great Eternal Heaven that will spring from the midst of the Angels.

16 And the First Heaven will vanish and pass away and a New Heaven will appear, and all the Powers of Heaven will shine forever, with light seven times as bright.
17 And after this, there will be many weeks without number, forever, in goodness and in righteousness. And from then on sin will never again be mentioned.

18 And now I tell you, my sons, and show you, the paths of righteousness and the paths of violence. I will show them to you again that you may know what will come to pass.

19 And now, hearken to me, my sons, and walk in the paths of righteousness, and walk not in the paths of violence; for all who walk in the paths of unrighteousness shall perish for ever.'

[Chapter 92]

1 The book written by Enoch {Enoch indeed wrote this complete doctrine of wisdom, (which is) praised of all men and a judge of all the earth} for all my children who shall live on the earth. And for the future generations who shall observe righteousness and peace.

2 Let not your spirit be troubled on account of the times; for the Holy and Great One has appointed days for all things.

3 And the righteous one shall arise from sleep, [Shall arise] and walk in the paths of righteousness, and all his path and conversation shall be in eternal goodness and grace.

4 He will be gracious to the righteous and give him eternal righteousness, and He will give him power so that he shall be (endowed) with goodness and righteousness. And he shall walk in eternal light.

5 And sin shall perish in darkness for ever, and shall no more be seen from that day for evermore.

[Chapter 93]

(Author's note: Chapters 91 – 93 recount and expand on the events listed in the following weeks of prophecy. The explanation of the event are scattered in chapters 91 – 93, however, the list of events are stated clearly in the following list of weeks in chapter 93).

1 And after that Enoch both gave and began to recount from the books. And Enoch said:

2 'Concerning the children of righteousness and concerning the elect of the world, and concerning the plant of righteousness, I will speak these things. I Enoch will declare (them) to you, my sons, according to that which appeared to me in heavenly vision, and which I have known through the word of the holy angels, and have learned from heavenly tablets.'

3 And Enoch began to recount from the books and said: 'I was born the seventh in the first week, able judgment and righteousness still endured.

(Author's note: Enoch was the seventh son. He was born in the beginning of the time line he is laying out.)

4 And after me there shall arise in the second week great wickedness, and deceit shall have sprung up; and in it there shall be the first end.

(Author's note: This is the rise of evil. The angels have fallen.)

5 And in it a man shall be saved; and after it is ended unrighteousness shall grow up, and a law shall be made for the sinners. And after that in the third week at its close a man shall be elected as the plant of righteous judgment, and his posterity shall become the plant of righteousness for evermore.

(Author's note: The time of Moses and the establishment of the Ten Commandments. The beginning of the law.)

6 And after that in the fourth week, at its close, visions of the holy and righteous shall be seen, and a law for all generations and an enclosure shall be made for them.

(Author's note: The time of David and the wars that defined the holy land.)

7 And after that in the fifth week, at its close, the house of glory and dominion shall be built for ever.

(Author's note: The time of Solomon and the first temple.)

8 And after that in the sixth week, all who live in it shall be blinded, and the hearts of all of them shall godlessly forsake wisdom. And in it a man shall ascend; and at its close the house of dominion shall be burned with fire, and the whole race of the chosen root shall be dispersed.

(Author's note: In the sixth week Christ came to the chosen ones, but they were blinded. He ascended and the Jewish nation was scattered. In the holocaust innumerable Jews were killed. The Diaspora remains scattered but has begun to gather into the new nation of Israel. The word "holocaust" was coined in part due to its use in the Latin Vulgate, where it means "an offering, and usually refers to a "burnt offering".)

9 And after that in the seventh week shall an apostate generation arise, and many shall be its deeds, and all its deeds shall be apostate.

(Author's note: It is assumed that we are in the seventh week of Enoch's prophecy. This aligns in a very general way to the prophecies of the churches in Revelation. At the end of the seventh week there will be a "great falling away.")

2 Thessalonians 2:3 Let no man deceive you by any means: for that day shall not come, except there come a falling away first, and that man of sin be revealed, the son of perdition;

Revelation 2

1 Unto the angel of the church of Ephesus write; These things saith he that holdeth the seven stars in his right hand, who walketh in the midst of the seven golden candlesticks;

2I know thy works, and thy labour, and thy patience, and how thou canst not bear them which are evil: and thou hast tried them which say they are apostles, and are not, and hast found them liars:

3And hast borne, and hast patience, and for my name's sake hast laboured, and hast not fainted.

4Nevertheless I have somewhat against thee, because thou hast left thy first love.

5Remember therefore from whence thou art fallen, and repent, and do the first works; or else I will come unto thee quickly, and will remove thy candlestick out of his place, except thou repent.

6But this thou hast, that thou hatest the deeds of the Nicolaitanes, which I also hate.

7He that hath an ear, let him hear what the Spirit saith unto the churches; To him that overcometh will I give to eat of the tree of life, which is in the midst of the paradise of God.

8And unto the angel of the church in Smyrna write; These things saith the first and the last, which was dead, and is alive;

9I know thy works, and tribulation, and poverty, (but thou art rich) and I know the blasphemy of them which say they are Jews, and are not, but are the synagogue of Satan.

10Fear none of those things which thou shalt suffer: behold, the devil shall cast some of you into prison, that ye may be tried; and ye shall have tribulation ten days: be thou faithful unto death, and I will give thee a crown of life.

11He that hath an ear, let him hear what the Spirit saith unto the churches; He that overcometh shall not be hurt of the second death.

12And to the angel of the church in Pergamos write; These things saith he which hath the sharp sword with two edges;

13I know thy works, and where thou dwellest, even where Satan's seat is: and thou holdest fast my name, and hast not denied my faith, even in those days wherein Antipas was my faithful martyr, who was slain among you, where Satan dwelleth.

14But I have a few things against thee, because thou hast there them that hold the doctrine of Balaam, who taught Balac to cast a stumblingblock before the children of Israel, to eat things sacrificed unto idols, and to commit fornication.

15So hast thou also them that hold the doctrine of the Nicolaitanes, which thing I hate.

16Repent; or else I will come unto thee quickly, and will fight against them with the sword of my mouth.

17He that hath an ear, let him hear what the Spirit saith unto the churches; To him that overcometh will I give to eat of the hidden manna, and will give him a white stone, and in the stone a new name written, which no man knoweth saving he that receiveth it.

18And unto the angel of the church in Thyatira write; These things saith the Son of God, who hath his eyes like unto a flame of fire, and his feet are like fine brass;

19I know thy works, and charity, and service, and faith, and thy patience, and thy works; and the last to be more than the first.

20Notwithstanding I have a few things against thee, because thou sufferest that woman Jezebel, which calleth herself a prophetess, to teach and to seduce my servants to commit fornication, and to eat things sacrificed unto idols.

21And I gave her space to repent of her fornication; and she repented not.

22Behold, I will cast her into a bed, and them that commit adultery with her into great tribulation, except they repent of their deeds.

23And I will kill her children with death; and all the churches shall know that I am he which searcheth the reins and hearts: and I will give unto every one of you according to your works.

24But unto you I say, and unto the rest in Thyatira, as many as have not this doctrine, and which have not known the depths of Satan, as they speak; I will put upon you none other burden.

25But that which ye have already hold fast till I come.

26And he that overcometh, and keepeth my works unto the end, to him will I give power over the nations:

27And he shall rule them with a rod of iron; as the vessels of a potter shall they be broken to shivers: even as I received of my Father.

28And I will give him the morning star.

29He that hath an ear, let him hear what the Spirit saith unto the churches.

Revelation 3

1And unto the angel of the church in Sardis write; These things saith he that hath the seven Spirits of God, and the seven stars; I know thy works, that thou hast a name that thou livest, and art dead.

2Be watchful, and strengthen the things which remain, that are ready to die: for I have not found thy works perfect before God.

3Remember therefore how thou hast received and heard, and hold fast, and repent. If therefore thou shalt not watch, I will come on thee as a thief, and thou shalt not know what hour I will come upon thee.

4Thou hast a few names even in Sardis which have not defiled their garments; and they shall walk with me in white: for they are worthy.

5He that overcometh, the same shall be clothed in white raiment; and I will not blot out his name out of the book of life, but I will confess his name before my Father, and before his angels.

6He that hath an ear, let him hear what the Spirit saith unto the churches.

7And to the angel of the church in Philadelphia write; These things saith he that is holy, he that is true, he that hath the key of David, he that openeth, and no man shutteth; and shutteth, and no man openeth;

8I know thy works: behold, I have set before thee an open door, and no man can shut it: for thou hast a little strength, and hast kept my word, and hast not denied my name.

9Behold, I will make them of the synagogue of Satan, which say they are Jews, and are not, but do lie; behold, I will make them to come and worship before thy feet, and to know that I have loved thee.

10Because thou hast kept the word of my patience, I also will keep thee from the hour of temptation, which shall come upon all the world, to try them that dwell upon the earth.

11Behold, I come quickly: hold that fast which thou hast, that no man take thy crown.

12Him that overcometh will I make a pillar in the temple of my God, and he shall go no more out: and I will write upon him the name of my God, and the name of the city of my God, which is new Jerusalem, which cometh down out of heaven from my God: and I will write upon him my new name.

(Author's note: Most scholars agree that we are in the age of Laodicea)

13He that hath an ear, let him hear what the Spirit saith unto the churches.

14And unto the angel of the church of the Laodiceans write; These things saith the Amen, the faithful and true witness, the beginning of the creation of God;

15I know thy works, that thou art neither cold nor hot: I would thou wert cold or hot.

16So then because thou art lukewarm, and neither cold nor hot, I will spue thee out of my mouth.

17Because thou sayest, I am rich, and increased with goods, and have need of nothing; and knowest not that thou art wretched, and miserable, and poor, and blind, and naked:

18I counsel thee to buy of me gold tried in the fire, that thou mayest be rich; and white raiment, that thou mayest be clothed, and that the shame of thy nakedness do not appear; and anoint thine eyes with eyesalve, that thou mayest see.

19As many as I love, I rebuke and chasten: be zealous therefore, and repent.

20Behold, I stand at the door, and knock: if any man hear my voice, and open the door, I will come in to him, and will sup with him, and he with me.

21To him that overcometh will I grant to sit with me in my throne, even as I also overcame, and am set down with my Father in his throne.
22He that hath an ear, let him hear what the Spirit saith unto the churches.

10 And at its end shall be elected, the elect righteous of the eternal plant of righteousness shall be chosen to receive sevenfold instruction concerning all His creation.

11 For who is there of all the children of men that is able to hear the voice of the Holy One without being troubled? And who can think His thoughts? Who is there that can behold all the works of heaven?

12 And how should there be one who could behold heaven, and who is there that could understand the things of heaven and see a soul or a spirit and could tell of it, or ascend and see all their ends and think them or do like them?

13 And who is there of all men that could know what is the breadth and the length of the earth, and to whom has the measurement been shown of all of them?

14 Or is there any one who could discern the length of the heaven and how great is its height, and on what it is founded, and how great is the number of the stars, and where all the luminaries rest?

(Author's note: In this age of space travel, we have indeed beheld the heavens and measured and numbered the stars. These are the end times.)

[Chapter 94]

1 And now I say to you, my sons, love righteousness and walk in it; because the paths of righteousness are worthy of acceptation, but the paths of unrighteousness shall suddenly be destroyed and vanish.

2 And to certain men of a generation shall the paths of violence and of death be revealed, and they shall hold themselves afar from them, and shall not follow them.

3 And now I say to you, the righteous, walk not in the paths of wickedness, nor in the paths of death, and draw not near to them, lest you be destroyed.

4 But seek and choose for yourselves righteousness and an elect life, and walk in the paths of peace, and you shall live and prosper.

5 And hold (keep) my words in the thoughts of your hearts, and permit them not to be erased from your hearts; for I know that sinners will tempt men to evilly entreat wisdom, so that no place may be found for her, and temptation will increase.

Ecclesiastes 12:13 Now all has been heard; here is the conclusion of the matter: Fear God and keep his commandments, for this is the whole duty of man. 14 For God will bring every deed into judgment, including every hidden thing, whether it is good or evil.

6 Woe to those who build unrighteousness and oppression and lay deceit as a foundation; for they shall be suddenly overthrown, and they shall have no peace.

7 Woe to those who build their houses with sin; for from all their foundations shall they be overthrown, and by the sword shall they fall. And those who acquire gold and silver shall suddenly perish in the judgment.

8 Woe to you, you rich, for you have trusted in your riches, and from your riches shall you depart, because you have not remembered the Most High in the days of your riches.

Isaiah 5:11 Woe to those who rise early in the morning to run after their drinks, who stay up late at night till they are inflamed with wine. 20 Woe to those who call evil good and good evil, who put darkness for light and light for darkness, who put bitter for sweet and sweet for bitter.
21 Woe to those who are wise in their own eyes and clever in their own sight.
22 Woe to those who are heroes at drinking wine and champions at mixing drinks,
23 who acquit the guilty for a bribe, but deny justice to the innocent.

9 You have committed blasphemy and unrighteousness, and have become ready for the day of slaughter, and the day of darkness and the day of the great judgment.

10 Thus I speak and tell you: He who hath created you will overthrow you, and for your fall there shall be no compassion, and your Creator will rejoice at your destruction.

11 And your righteousness shall be a reproach to the sinners and the godless in those days.

JAM 5:1 Go to now, ye rich men, weep and howl for your miseries that shall come upon you. 2 Your riches are corrupted, and your garments are moth-eaten. 3 Your gold and silver is cankered; and the rust of them shall be a witness against you, and shall eat your flesh as it were fire. Ye have heaped treasure together for the last days. 4 Behold, the hire of the labourers who have reaped down your fields, which is of you kept back by fraud, crieth: and the cries of them which have reaped are entered into the ears of the Lord of sabaoth. 5 Ye have lived in pleasure on the earth, and been wanton; ye have nourished your hearts, as in a day of slaughter. 6 Ye have condemned and killed the just; and he doth not resist you.

(Author's note: in the above biblical verses from James, "sabaoth" is from the Hebrew, plural form of "host" or "army". The word is used almost exclusively in conjunction with the Divine name as a title of majesty: "the Lord of Hosts", or "the Lord God of Hosts".)

[Chapter 95]

1 Would that my eyes were rain clouds of water that I might weep over you, and pour down my tears as a cloud of water, that I might rest from my trouble of heart!

2 Who has permitted you to practice reproaches and wickedness? And so judgment shall overtake you, sinners.

3 You, righteous! Fear not the sinners, for again the Lord will deliver them into your hands, that you may execute judgment on them according to your desires.

4 Woe to you who speak against God (fulminate anathemas) which cannot be removed (reversed) - healing shall be far from you because of your sins.

5 Woe to you who repay your neighbor with evil; for you shall be repaid according to your works.

6 Woe to you, lying witnesses, and to those who weigh out injustice, for you shall suddenly perish.

7 Woe to you, sinners, for you persecute the righteous; for you shall be delivered up and persecuted because of injustice, and your yoke shall be heavy on you.

Luke 6:24"But woe to you who are rich, for you have already received your comfort. 25Woe to you who are well fed now, for you will go hungry. Woe to you who laugh now, for you will mourn and weep. 26Woe to you when all men speak well of you, for that is how their fathers treated the false prophets. 27"But I tell you who hear me: Love your enemies, do good to those who hate you, 28bless those who curse you, pray for those who mistreat you. 29If someone strikes you on one cheek, turn to him the other also. If someone takes your cloak, do not stop him from taking your tunic. 30Give to everyone who asks you, and if

anyone takes what belongs to you, do not demand it back. 31Do to others as you would have them do to you.

[Chapter 96]

1 Be hopeful, you righteous; for suddenly shall the sinners perish before you, and you shall have lordship over them, according to your desires.

2 And in the day of the tribulation of the sinners, your children shall mount and rise as eagles, and your nests shall be higher than the vultures'. You shall ascend as badgers and enter the crevices of the earth, and the clefts of the rock for ever before the unrighteous. And the satyrs (sirens) shall sigh and weep because of you.

3 Wherefore fear not, you that have suffered, for healing shall be your portion, and a bright light shall enlighten you, and the voice of rest you shall hear from heaven.

4 Woe to you, you sinners, for your riches make you appear like the righteous, but your hearts convict you of being sinners, and this fact shall be a testimony against you for a memorial of your evil deeds.

5 Woe to you who devour the finest of the wheat, and drink wine in large bowls (the best of waters), and tread under foot the lowly (humble) with your might.

6 Woe to you who drink water from every fountain (drink water all the time), for suddenly shall you be consumed and wither away, because you have forsaken the fountain of life.

(Author's note: the above reference is a euphemism for promiscuity.)

7 Woe to you who work unrighteousness and deceit and blasphemy; it shall be a memorial against you for evil.

8 Woe to you, you mighty, who with might oppress the righteous; for the day of your destruction is coming. Many and good days shall come to the righteous in those days - in the day of your judgment.

[Chapter 97]

1 Believe, you righteous, that the sinners will become a shame and perish in the day of unrighteousness.

2 Be it known to you, you sinners, that the Most High is mindful of your destruction, and the angels of heaven rejoice over your destruction.

3 What will you do, you sinners, and where shall you flee on that day of judgment, when you hear the voice of the prayer of the righteous?

4 You shall fare like to them, against whom these words shall be a testimony: "You have been companions of sinners."

5 And in those days the prayer of the righteous shall reach to the Lord, and for you the days of your judgment shall come.

6 And all the words of your unrighteousness shall be read out before the Great Holy One, and your faces shall be covered with shame, and He will reject every work which is grounded on unrighteousness.

7 Woe to you, you sinners, who live on the middle of the ocean and on the dry land, whose remembrance is evil against you.

8 Woe to you who acquire silver and gold in unrighteousness and say: "We have become rich with riches and have possessions; and have acquired everything we have desired.

9 And now let us do what we purposed, for we have gathered silver, and many are the servants in our houses and our granaries are full to the brim as if with water."

10 Yea, and like water your lies shall flow away; for your riches shall not abide but quickly depart (go up) from you, for you have acquired it all in unrighteousness, and you shall be given over to a great curse.

[Chapter 98]

1 And now I swear to you, to the wise and to the foolish, that you shall see (have) many experiences on the earth.

2 For you men shall put on more adornments than a woman, and colored garments more than a young woman, like royalty and in grandeur and in power, and in silver and in gold and in purple, and in splendor and in food they shall be poured out as water.

3 Therefore they shall have neither knowledge nor wisdom, and because of this they shall die together with their possessions; and with all their glory and their splendor, and in shame and in slaughter and in great destitution, their spirits shall be thrown into the furnace of fire.

4 I have sworn to you, you sinners, as a mountain has not become a slave, and a hill does not become the servant of a woman, even so sin has not been sent on the earth, but man of himself has created it, and they that commit it shall fall under a great curse.

5 And barrenness has not been given to the woman, but on account of the deeds of her own hands she dies without children.

6 I have sworn to you, you sinners, by the Holy Great One, that all your evil deeds are revealed in heaven, and that none of your wrong deeds (of oppression) are covered and hidden.

7 And do not think in your spirit nor say in your heart that you do not know and that you do not see that every sin is recorded every day in heaven in the presence of the Most High.

8 From now on, you know that all your wrongdoing that you do will be written down every day, until the day of your judgment.

9 Woe to you, you fools, for through your folly you shall perish; and you do not listen to the wise so no good will come to you against the wise,

10 And so and now, know you that you are prepared for the day of destruction. Therefore do not hope to live, you sinners, but you shall depart and die; for there will be no ransom for you; because you are prepared for the day of the great judgment, for the day of tribulation and great shame for your spirits.

11 Woe to you, you obstinate of heart, who work wickedness and eat blood. Where do you have good things to eat and to drink and to be filled? From all the good things which the Lord the Most High has placed in abundance on the earth; therefore you shall have no peace.

(Author's note: The above reference to eating blood may indicate cannibalism. As a side note, The Book of Jubilees tells us that the offspring of the fallen angels drank blood. Life is in the blood, according to the Old Testament, and one should not eat or drink blood.)

GEN 9:3 Every moving thing that liveth shall be meat for you; even as the green herb have I given you all things. 4 But flesh with the life thereof, which is the blood thereof, shall ye not eat. 5 And surely your blood of your lives will I require; at the hand of every beast will I require it, and at the hand of man; at the hand of every man's brother will I require the life of man. 6 Whoso sheddeth man's blood, by man shall his blood be shed: for in the image of God made he man.

12 Woe to you who love the deeds of unrighteousness; wherefore do you hope for good for yourselves? You know that you shall be delivered into the hands of the righteous, and they shall cut off your necks and slay you, and have no mercy on you.

13 Woe to you who rejoice in the distress of the righteous; for no grave shall be dug for you.

14 Woe to you who say the words of the wise are empty; for you shall have no hope of life.

15 Woe to you who write down lying and godless words; for they write down their lies so that men may hear them and act godlessly towards their neighbor. Therefore they shall have no peace but die a sudden death.

[Chapter 99]

1 Woe to you who do godless acts, and praise and honor lies; you shall perish, and no happy life shall be yours.

2 Woe to them who pervert the words of righteousness, and transgress the eternal law, and count themselves as sinless. They shall be trodden under foot on the earth.

3 In those days make ready, you righteous, to raise your prayers as a memorial, and place them as a testimony before the angels, that they may place the sin of the sinners for a reminder before the Most High.

4 In those days the nations shall be stirred up, and the families of the nations shall arise on the day of destruction.

5 And in those days the destitute shall go and throw their children out, and they shall abandon them, so that their children shall perish because of them. They shall abandon their children that are still babies (sucklings), and not return to them, and shall have no pity on their loved ones.

6 Again, I swear to you, you sinners, that sin is prepared for a day of unceasing bloodshed.

MAT 24:6 And ye shall hear of wars and rumours of wars: see that ye be not troubled: for all these things must come to pass, but the end is not yet. 7 For nation shall rise against nation, and kingdom against kingdom: and there shall be

famines, and pestilences, and earthquakes, in diverse places. 8 All these are the beginning of sorrows.

7 And they who worship stones, and carved images of gold and silver and wood and stone and clay, and those who worship impure spirits and demons, and all kinds of idols not according to knowledge, shall get no manner of help from them.

8 And they shall become godless by reason of the folly of their hearts, and their eyes shall be blinded through the fear of their hearts and through visions in their ambitions (dreams).

Colossians 2:16 Let no man therefore judge you in meat, or in drink, or in respect of an holyday, or of the new moon, or of the sabbath days:
17Which are a shadow of things to come; but the body is of Christ.
18Let no man beguile you of your reward in a voluntary humility and worshipping of angels, intruding into those things which he hath not seen, vainly puffed up by his fleshly mind,
19And not holding the Head, from which all the body by joints and bands having nourishment ministered, and knit together, increaseth with the increase of God.

9 Through these they shall become godless and fearful; for they shall have done all their work with lies, and shall have worshiped a stone, therefore in an instant shall they perish.

Revelation 9:19For their power is in their mouth, and in their tails: for their tails were like unto serpents, and had heads, and with them they do hurt.
20And the rest of the men which were not killed by these plagues yet repented not of the works of their hands, that they should not worship devils, and idols of gold, and silver, and brass, and stone, and of wood: which neither can see, nor hear, nor walk: 21Neither repented they of their murders, nor of their sorceries, nor of their fornication, nor of their thefts.

10 But in those days blessed are all they who accept the words of wisdom, and understand them, and observe the paths of the Most High, and walk in the path of His righteousness, and become not godless with the godless, for they shall be saved.

11 Woe to you who spread evil to your neighbors, for you shall be slain in Hell.

12 Woe to you who make your foundation that of deceitful (sin) and lies, and who cause bitterness on the earth; for they shall thereby be utterly consumed.

13 Woe to you who build your houses through the hard labor of others, and all their building materials are the bricks and stones of sin; I tell you, you shall have no peace.

14 Woe to them who reject the measure and eternal inheritance of their fathers and whose souls follow after idols; for they shall have no rest.

15 Woe to them who do unrighteous acts and help oppression, and kill their neighbors until the day of the great judgment, for He will throw down your glory.

16 For He shall throw down your glory, and bring affliction on your hearts, and shall arouse His fierce anger, and destroy you all with the sword; and all the holy and righteous shall remember your sins.

[Chapter 100]

1 And in those days in one place the fathers together with their sons shall kill one another and brothers shall fall in death together until the streams flow with their blood.

2 For a man shall not withhold his hand from killing his sons and his sons' sons, and the sinner shall not withhold his hand from his honored brother, from dawn until sunset they shall kill one another.

MAR 13:12 Now the brother shall betray the brother to death, and the father the son; and children shall rise up against their parents, and shall cause them to be put to death.

3 And the horse shall walk up to the breast in the blood of sinners, and the chariot shall be submerged to its height.

REV 14:20 And the winepress was trodden without the city, and blood came out of the winepress, even unto the horse bridles, by the space of a thousand and six hundred furlongs.

4 In those days the angels shall descend into the secret places and gather together into one place all those who brought down sin and the Most High will arise on that day of judgment to execute great judgment among sinners.

5 And over all the righteous and holy He will appoint guardians from among the holy angels to guard them as the apple of an eye, until He makes an end of all wickedness and all sin, and even if the righteous sleep a long sleep, they have nothing to fear.

6 And the wise men will seek the truth and they and their sons will understand the words of this book, and recognize that their riches shall not be able to save them or overcome their sins.

7 Woe to you sinners, on the day of strong anguish, you who afflict the righteous and burn them with fire; you shall be requited according to your works.

8 Woe to you, you obstinate of heart, who watch in order to devise wickedness; therefore shall fear come on you and there shall be none to help you.

9 Woe to you, you sinners, on account of the words of your mouth, and on account of the deeds of your hands which your godlessness as caused, in blazing flames burning worse than fire shall you burn.

2TH 1:7 And to you who are troubled rest with us, when the Lord Jesus shall be revealed from heaven with his mighty angels, 8 In flaming fire taking vengeance on them that know not God, and that obey not the gospel of our Lord Jesus Christ:9 Who shall be punished with everlasting destruction from the presence of the Lord, and from the glory of his power?

10 And now, know that the angels will ask Him in heaven about your deeds and from the sun and from the moon and from the stars they will ask about your sins because on the earth you execute judgment on the righteous.

11 And He will summon to testify against you every cloud and mist and dew and rain; for they shall all be withheld from falling on you, and they shall be mindful of your sins.

12 And now give gifts to the rain that it cease not from falling on you, nor the dew, when it has received gold and silver from you that it may fall. When the hoarfrost and snow with their chilliness, and all the snow storms with all their plagues fall on you, in those days you shall not be able to stand before them.

[Chapter 101]

1 Observe heaven, you children of heaven, and every work of the Most High, and fear Him and work no evil in His presence.

2 If He closes the windows of heaven, and withholds the rain and the dew from falling on the earth on your account, what will you do then?

3 And if He sends His anger on you because of your deeds, you cannot petition Him; for you spoke proud and arrogant words against His righteousness, therefore you shall have no peace.

4 Don't you see the sailors of the ships, how their ships are tossed back and forth by the waves, and are shaken by the winds, and are in great trouble?

5 And therefore they are afraid because all their nice possessions go on the sea with them, and they have bad feelings in their heart that the sea will swallow them and they will perish therein.

6 Are not the entire sea and all its waters, and all its movements, the work of the Most High, and has He not set limits to its actions, and confined it throughout by the sand?

7 And at His reproof it fears and dries up, and all its fish die and all that is in it; but you sinners that are on the earth fear Him not.

8 Has He not made heaven and the earth, and all that is in it ? Who has given understanding and wisdom to everything that moves on the earth and in the sea?

9 Do not the sailors of the ships fear the sea? Yet you sinners do not fear the Most High.

[Chapter 102]

1 In those days if He sent a horrible fire on you, where will you flee, and where will you find deliverance? And when He launches out His Word against you will you not be shaken and afraid?
2 And all the luminaries shall be shaken with great fear, and all the earth shall be afraid and tremble and be alarmed.

3 And all the angels shall execute their commands and shall seek to hide themselves from the presence of He who is Great in Glory, and the children of earth shall tremble and shake; and you sinners shall be cursed for ever, and you shall have no peace.

2 Peter 3:8But, beloved, be not ignorant of this one thing, that one day is with the Lord as a thousand years, and a thousand years as one day.
9The Lord is not slack concerning his promise, as some men count slackness; but is longsuffering to us-ward, not willing that any should perish, but that all should come to repentance.
10But the day of the Lord will come as a thief in the night; in the which the heavens shall pass away with a great noise, and the elements shall melt with fervent heat, the earth also and the works that are therein shall be burned up.
11Seeing then that all these things shall be dissolved, what manner of persons ought ye to be in all holy conversation and godliness,

12Looking for and hasting unto the coming of the day of God, wherein the heavens being on fire shall be dissolved, and the elements shall melt with fervent heat?
13Nevertheless we, according to his promise, look for new heavens and a new earth, wherein dwelleth righteousness.

4 Fear you not, you souls of the righteous, and fear not you who have died in righteousness.

5 And don't grieve if your soul has descended in to the grave in grief, and that in your life you were not rewarded according to your goodness, but wait for the day of the judgment of sinners and for the day of cursing and chastisement.

6 And when you die the sinners will say about you: "As we die, so die the righteous, and what benefit do they reap for their deeds?

7 See, even as we, so do they die in grief and darkness, and what have they more than we? From now on we are equal.

8 And what will they receive and what will they see for ever? Look, they too have died, and from now on for ever shall they see no light."

9 I tell you, you sinners, you are content to eat and drink, and rob and sin, and strip men naked, and acquire wealth and see good days.

10 Have you seen the righteous how their end was peace, that no violence is found in them until their death?

11 Nevertheless they died and became as though they had not been, and their spirits descended into Hell in tribulation.

Matthew 10:28Do not be afraid of those who kill the body but cannot kill the soul. Rather, be afraid of the One who can destroy both soul and body in hell.

[Chapter 103]

1 Now, therefore, I swear to the righteous, by the glory of the Great and Honored and Mighty One who reigns, I swear to you, I know this mystery.

2 I have read the heavenly tablets, and have seen the holy books, and have found written in it and inscribed regarding them.

3 That all goodness and joy and glory are prepared for them, and written down for the spirits of those who have died in righteousness, and that much good

shall be given to you in reward for your labors, and that your lot is abundant beyond the lot of the living.

4 And the spirits of you who have died in righteousness shall live and rejoice, and your spirits shall not perish, nor shall your memory from before the face of the Great One to all the generations of the world, therefore no longer fear their abuse.

5 Woe to you, you sinners, when you have died, if you die in the abundance of your sins, and woe to those who are like you and say regarding you: "Blessed are the sinners, they have seen all their days.

6 And how they have died in prosperity and in wealth, and have not seen tribulation or murder in their life; and they have died in honor, and judgment has not been executed on them during their life."

7 You know that their souls will be made to descend into Hell and they shall be wracked in great tribulation.

8 And into darkness and chains and a burning flame where there is harsh judgment your spirits shall enter, and the great judgment shall be for all the generations of the world. Woe to you, for you shall have no peace.

9 The righteous and good who are alive, do not say: "In our troubled days we have worked hard and experienced every trouble, and met with much evil and been afflicted, and have become few and our spirit small.

10 And we have been destroyed and have not found any to help us even with a word. We have been tortured and destroyed, and not expect to live from day to day.

11 We hoped to be the head and have become the tail. We have worked hard and had no satisfaction in our labor; and we have become the food of the sinners and the unrighteous, and they have laid their yoke heavily on us.

12 They have ruled over us and hated us and hit us, and to those that hated us we have bowed our necks but they pitied us not.

13 We desired to get away from them that we might escape and be at rest, but found no place where we should flee and be safe from them.

14 We complained to the rulers in our tribulation, and cried out against those who devoured us, but they did not pay attention to our cries and would not listen to our voice.

15 And they helped those who robbed us and devoured us and those who made us few; and they concealed their oppression (wrongdoing), and they did not remove from us the yoke of those that devoured us and dispersed us and murdered us, and they concealed their murder, and did not remember that they had lifted up their hands against us."

Jeremiah 30:15 Why do you cry out over your wound, your pain that has no cure? Because of your great guilt and many sins I have done these things to you.
16 " 'But all who devour you will be devoured; all your enemies will go into exile. Those who plunder you will be plundered; all who make spoil of you I will despoil.
17 But I will restore you to health and heal your wounds,' declares the LORD, 'because you are called an outcast, Zion for whom no one cares.'
18 "This is what the LORD says:" 'I will restore the fortunes of Jacob's tents and have compassion on his dwellings; the city will be rebuilt on her ruins, and the palace will stand in its proper place.
19 From them will come songs of thanksgiving and the sound of rejoicing. I will add to their numbers, and they will not be decreased; I will bring them honor, and they will not be disdained.

[Chapter 104]

1 I swear to you, that in heaven the angels remember you for good before the glory of the Great One.

2 And your names are written before the glory of the Great One. Be hopeful; for before you were put to shame through sickness and affliction; but now you shall shine as the lights of heaven,

3 You shall shine and you shall be seen, and the doors of heaven shall be opened to you. And in your cry, cry for judgment, and it shall appear to you; for all your tribulation shall be visited on the rulers, and on all who helped those who plundered you.

4 Be hopeful, and do not throw away your hopes for you shall have great joy as the angels of heaven.

5 What will you have to do ? You shall not have to hide on the day of the great judgment and you shall not be found as sinners, and the eternal judgment shall not come to you for all the generations, eternally.

6 And now fear not, you righteous, when you see the sinners growing strong and prospering in their ways;

do not be their companions, but keep away from their violence.

7 For you shall become companions of the hosts of heaven. And, although you sinners say: "All our sins shall not be found out and be written down," nevertheless they shall write down all your sins every day.

8 And now I show to you that light and darkness, day and night, see all your sins.

9 Do not be godless in your hearts, and do not lie and do not change the words of righteousness, nor say that the words of the Holy Great One are lies, nor praise or rely on your idols; for all your lying and all your godlessness (leads not to) come not from righteousness but (leads to) from great sin.

10 And now I know this mystery, that sinners will alter and pervert the words of righteousness in many ways, and will speak wicked words, and lie, and practice great deceits, and write books concerning their words.

11 But when they write down all my words truthfully in their languages, and do not change or omit any of my words but write them all down truthfully - all that I first testified concerning them.
12 Then, I know another mystery, that books will be given to the righteous and the wise to produce joy and righteousness and much wisdom.

13 And to them the books shall be given, and they shall believe them and rejoice over them, and then all the righteous who have learned from them all the paths of righteousness shall be paid back.'

[Chapter 105]
Later Additions to the Text – Book of Noah (Chapters 105-108):

1 In those days the Lord called them (the wise and righteous) to testify to the children of earth concerning their wisdom: Show it to them; for you are their guides, and a recompense over the whole earth.

2 For I and my son will be united with them for ever in the paths of righteousness in their lives; and you shall have peace: rejoice, you children of righteousness. Amen.

[Chapter 106]

This section of Enoch was not originally attached. It is a fragment from the Book of Noah.

Though this book has not come down to us independently, it has in large measure been incorporated in the Ethiopic Book of Enoch, and can in part be reconstructed from it.

The Book of Noah is mentioned several times in the book of Jubilees. The editor simply changed the name Noah in the context before him into Enoch, for the statement is based on Gen. 5: 32, and Enoch lived only 365 years. Chapters 6-11 are from the same source. They make no reference to Enoch, but bring forward Noah and mention the sin of the angels that led to the flood, and of their temporal and eternal punishment. This section is a repeat of the Semjaza and Azazel myths.
Other pieces of the Book of Noah can be found scattered throughout Enoch in chapters 6-11; 39:1-2a; 54:7-55:2; 60; 65:1-69:25; and 106-107.
The fragments seem to have been written earlier than the book of Jubilees and thus were likely written around 200 B.C.

Fragment from the Book of Noah.

1 And after some days my son Methuselah took a wife for his son, Lamech, and she became pregnant by him and bore a son. And his body was white as snow and red as the blooming of a rose, and the hair of his head and his long curls were white as wool, and his eyes beautiful.

2 And when he opened his eyes, he lit up the whole house like the sun, and the whole house was very bright.

3 And on it he levitated (arose) in the hands of the midwife, opened his mouth, and conversed with the Lord of righteousness.

4 And his father, Lamech, was afraid of him and fled, and came to his father Methuselah. And he said to him: 'I have begotten a strange son, different and unlike man, and resembling the sons of the God of heaven; and his nature is different and he is not like us, and his eyes are as the rays of the sun, and his face is glorious.

5 And it seems to me that he did not spring from me but from the angels, and I fear that in his days a wonder may be performed on the earth.

6 And now, my father, I am here to ask you and beg you that you may go to Enoch, our father, and learn from him the truth, for his dwelling-place is among the angels."

7 And when Methuselah heard the words of his son, he came to me to the ends of the earth; for he had heard that I was there, and he cried aloud, and I heard his voice and I came to him. And I said to him: 'Behold, here am I, my son, why have you come to me?'

8 And he answered and said: 'Because of a great cause of anxiety have I come to you, and because of a disturbing vision have I approached.

9 And now, my father, hear me. To Lamech, my son, there has been born a son, the like of whom there is none other, and his nature is not like man's nature, and the color of his body is whiter than snow and redder than the bloom of a rose, and the hair of his head is whiter than white wool, and his eyes are like the rays of the sun, and he opened his eyes and the whole house lit up.

10 And he levitated (arose) in the hands of the midwife, and opened his mouth and blessed the Lord of heaven.

11 And his father Lamech became afraid and fled to me, and did not believe that he was sprung from him, but that he was in the likeness of the angels of heaven; and now I have come to you that you may make known to me the truth.'

12 And I, Enoch, answered and said to him: 'The Lord will do a new thing on the earth, and this I have already seen in a vision, and make known to you that in the generation of my father Jared some of the angels of heaven violated the word of the Lord. And they commit sin and broke the law, and have had sex (united themselves) with women and committed sin with them, and have married some of them, and have had children by them.

13 And they shall produce on the earth giants not according to the spirit, but according to the flesh, and there shall be a great punishment on the earth, and the earth shall be cleansed from all impurity.

14 There shall come a great destruction over the whole earth, and there shall be a flood (deluge) and a great destruction for one year.

15 And this son who has been born to you shall be left on the earth, and his three children shall be saved with him: when all mankind that are on the earth shall die, he and his sons shall be saved.

16 And now make known to your son, Lamech, that he who has been born is in truth his son, and call his name Noah; for he shall be left to you, and he and his sons shall be saved from the destruction, which shall come on the earth on account of all the sin and all the unrighteousness, which shall be full (completed) on the earth in his days.

17 And after that (flood) there shall be more unrighteousness than that which was done before on the earth; for I know the mysteries of the holy ones; for He, the Lord, has showed me and informed me, and I have read (them) in heavenly tablets.

[Chapter 107]

1 And I saw written about them that generation after generation shall transgress, until a generation of righteousness arises, and transgression is destroyed and sin passes away from the earth, and all manner of good comes on it.

2 And now, my son, go and make known to your son Lamech that this son, which has been born, is in truth his son, and this is no lie.

3 And when Methuselah had heard the words of his father Enoch, for he had shown to him everything in secret, he returned and showed those things to him and called the name of that son Noah; for he will comfort the earth after all the destruction.

[Chapter 108]

(Author's note: Chapter 108 was added later and was not part of the original text.)

1 Another book which Enoch wrote for his son Methuselah and for those who will come after him, and keep the law in the last days.

2 You who have done good shall wait for those days until an end is made of those who work evil; and an end of the power of the wrongdoers.

3 And wait until sin has passed away indeed, for their names shall be blotted out of the book of life and out of the holy books, and their (children) seed shall be destroyed for ever, and their spirits shall be killed, and they shall cry and lament in a place that is a chaotic desert, and they shall be burned in the fire; for there is no earth there.

4 I saw something there like an invisible cloud; because it was so deep I could not look over it, and I saw a flame of fire blazing brightly, and things like shining mountains circling and sweeping back and forth.

5 And I asked one of the holy angels who was with me and said to him: 'What is this bright thing (shining)? For it is not heaven but there was only the flame of a blazing fire, and the voice of weeping and crying and moaning, lamenting, and agony.'

6 And he said to me: 'This place which you see are where the spirits of sinners and blasphemers, and of those who work wickedness, are cast and the spirits of those who pervert everything that the Lord hath spoken through the mouth of the prophets and even the prophecies (things that shall be).

7 For some of them are written and inscribed above in heaven, in order that the angels may read them and know that which shall befall the sinners, and the spirits of the humble, and of those who have afflicted their bodies, and been recompensed by God; and of those who have been abused (put to shame) by wicked men:

8 Who love God and loved neither gold nor silver nor any of the good things which are in the world, but gave over their bodies to torture.

9 Who, since they were born, longed not after earthly food, but regarded everything as a passing breath, and lived accordingly, and the Lord tried them much, and their spirits were found pure so that they should bless His name.

10 And all the blessings destined for them I have recounted in the books. And he has assigned them their reward, because they have been found to love heaven more than their life in the world, and though they were trodden under foot by wicked men, and experienced abuse and reviling from them and were put to shame, they blessed Me.

11 And now I will summon the spirits of the good who belong to the generation of light, and I will transform those who were born in darkness, who in the flesh were not rewarded with such honor as their faithfulness deserved.

12 And I will bring out in shining light those who have loved My holy name, and I will seat each on the throne of his honor.

MAT 19:28 And Jesus said unto them, Verily I say unto you, That ye which have followed me, in the regeneration when the Son of man shall sit in the throne of his glory, ye also shall sit upon twelve thrones, judging the twelve tribes of Israel.

13 And they shall shine for time without end; for righteousness is the judgment of God; because to the faithful He will give faithfulness in the habitation of upright paths.

14 And they shall see those who were born in darkness led into darkness, while the righteous shall shine. And the sinners shall cry aloud and see them shining, and they indeed will go where days and seasons are written down (prescribed) for them.

This ends the Book of Enoch (1 Enoch).

Introduction to The Second Book of Enoch:
Slavonic Enoch

As part of the Enochian literature, The Second Book of Enoch is included in the pseudepigraphal corpus.

Pseudepigrapha - Spurious or pseudonymous writings, especially Jewish writings ascribed to various biblical patriarchs and prophets but composed within approximately 200 years of the birth of Jesus Christ.

In 1773, rumors of a surviving copy of an ancient book drew Scottish explorer James Bruce to distant Ethiopia. There, he found the "First Book of Enoch." Later, another "Book of Enoch" surfaced. The text, which is known as "Second Enoch," was discovered in 1886 by Professor Sokolov in the archives of the Belgrade Public Library. The Second Book of Enoch was written in the latter half of the first century A.D. The text was preserved only in Slavonic and consequently bears the designation, "Slavonic Enoch." The text has also been known by the titles of "2 Enoch", and "The Secrets of Enoch." 2 Enoch is basically an expansion of Genesis 5:21-32, taking the reader from the time of Enoch to the onset of the great flood of Noah's day.

The main theme of the book is the ascension of Enoch progressively through multiple heavens. During the ascension Enoch is transfigured into an angel and granted access to the secrets of creation. Enoch is then given a 30 day grace period to return to earth and instruct his sons and all the members of his household regarding everything God had revealed to him. The text reports that after period of grace an angel will then come to retrieve him to take him from the earth.

Many credible versions end with chapter 68, however there is a longer version of 2 Enoch, which we will examine. In this version the wisdom and insights given to the family of Enoch is passed from family members to Melchizedek, whom God raises up as an archpriest. Melchizedek then fulfills the function of a prophet-priest. To pave the way to Melchizedek, Methuselah functions as a priest for ten years and then passed his station on to Nir, Noah's younger brother. Nir's wife, Sopanim, miraculously conceives without human intercourse while about to die and posthumously gives birth to Melchizedek, who is born with the appearance and maturity of a three-year old child and the symbol of the priesthood on his chest.

The world is doomed to suffer the flood but Michael the archangel promises Melchizedek salvation. This establishes his priesthood for all of eternity. The text goes on to report that in the last generation, there will be another Melchizedek who will be "the head of all, a great archpriest, the Word and Power of God, who will perform miracles, greater and more glorious than all the previous ones".

The manuscripts, which contain and preserve this document, exist only in Old Slavonic. Of the twenty or more manuscripts dating from the 13th century A.D. no single one contains the complete text of 2 Enoch. When pieced together there appears to be two versions. These we will refer to as the long and short version.

The difference in length between the two is due to two quite different features. There are blocks of text found only in the longer manuscripts; but even when the passages are parallel, the longer manuscripts tend to be more full and detailed. At the same time there is so much verbal similarity when the passages correspond that a common source must be supposed.

The form of 2 Enoch is what one finds in Jewish Wisdom literature and Jewish Apocalyptic literature. It has been suggested that the longer version is characterized by editorial expansions and Christian interpolations. Hence, the shorter version contains fewer Christian elements. The author of 2 Enoch speaks much of the Creator and final judgment, but he speaks very little about redemption, which seems to be absent from the thoughts of the author. Indeed, there seems to be a total lack of a Savior or Redeemer in 2 Enoch. What is noteworthy is that 2 Enoch has no reference to the mercy of God.

In the long version presented here, it appears that the last portion of the text was added as an afterthought. It contains the rise of Melchizedek. The appearance of Melchizedek ties 2 Enoch to several other texts forming a Melchizedkian tradition. The author of 2 Enoch follows a tradition in which an aged mother, who had been barren up to her deathbed, miraculously conceived Melchizedek without human intervention. Before she was able to give birth to the baby she died. The baby then emerged from her dead body with the maturity of a three-year-old boy. His priesthood will be perpetuated throughout the generations until "another Melchizedek" appears. If the last Melchizedek serves as the archpriest for the last generation, it indicates that in the mind of this Jewish writer, the Temple was to be rebuilt and would be the place were God would meet His people when the heathen nations were destroyed. The continuation and victory of the Jews as the selected and blessed people of God is implied. In this vein, 2 Enoch follows certain apocalyptic writings.

(For more information on apocalyptic writings see "End of Days" by Joseph Lumpkin.)

The Slavonic version is translated from a Greek source. Most scholars agree that there was either a Hebrew or Aramaic original lying behind the Greek source from which the Slavonic manuscripts were produced. The Hebrew origins are indicated by "Semitisms" in the work, but there are also Greek words and expressions, such as the names of the planets in chapter 30.

Proof that The Slavonic Enoch was first written in Greek is shown by the derivation of Adam's name, and by several coincidences with the Septuagint. The origin of the story is perhaps based on Hebrew traditions and certain Semitic turns of language show up in the text. This tends to indicate that there was at one time a Hebrew or Aramaic text that preceded the Greek. From the Greek it was translated into Slavonic. Of this version there are five manuscripts or pieces thereof found.

The short version or the Slavonic Enoch was probably written by a single author in an attempt to bring all the current traditions about Enoch of his time into a central storyline and system. The schema to accomplish the unity of traditions implements Enoch's ascension through multiple heavens. This author was probably a Jew living in Egypt. There are several elements in the book, which indicate Egyptian origin. The longer version of 2 Enoch was seeded with Christian elements and appended with an ending that does not fit well, illuminating the fact that there were several authors involved in the longer version.

Parts of the book was probably written in the late first century A.D. The first date is a limit set by the fact that Ethiopic Enoch, Ecclesiasticus, and Wisdom of Solomon are used as sources or references within the text; the second date is a limit set by the fact that the destruction of the Temple is not mentioned at all. However, it must be added that apocalyptic literature bloomed after the destruction of the temple, especially between late first century and throughout the second century A.D.

The Slavonic Enoch furnishes new material for the study of religious thought in the beginning of the Common Era. The ideas of the millennium and of the multiple heavens are the most important in this connection. Another very interesting feature is the presence of evil in heaven, the fallen angels in the second heaven, and hell in the third. The idea of evil in heaven may be a nod to the book of Job and the dialog between God and Satan, who was coming and going between heaven and earth. The idea of hell in the third heaven may have been derived from ideas expressed in the Old Testament book of Isaiah, which mentions that the sufferings of the wicked will be witnessed by the righteous in paradise.

Chapter 21 and forward for several chapters shows a heavy influence of Greek mythology. The Zodiac is mentioned along with celestial bodies with names such as Zeus, Cronus, Aphrodite, and others. The part of the text containing names and astrological descriptions could have been tampered with as late as the seventh century A.D.

By far, the most interesting and confusing section begins around chapter 25 and runs for several chapters. Here the text takes a turn toward Gnostic theology and cosmology. The Gnostics were a Christian sect, which formed and grew in the first century A.D. and thrived in the second century A.D.

Although Gnostic borrowed from Plato's (428 B.C. – 348 B.C.) creation myth, the maturity and construction of the story shows it to be of Gnostic Christian origin, placing it no earlier than the last part of the first century A.D. and no later than the end of the Second century. Add to the dating question the fact that the destruction of the Temple in Jerusalem is not mentioned, which leads to a date just before 70 A.D., if one assumes the Gnostic flavor was not added later.

The history of the text is obviously long and varied. It probably began as a Jewish oral tradition with pieces taken from several Enochian stories. Although the foundation of the story was first penned in Hebrew or Aramaic around the first or second centuries A.D. the date of the version of the text here is unknown. Later, the story was expanded and embellished by Greek influences. Lastly, Christians and Gnostics commandeered the book and added their own matter. Thus 2 Enoch exhibits a kaleidoscope of cultural and religious contributions over a great scope of time from the first century B.C. (assuming it came after 1 Enoch) and ending as late as the seventh century A.D. These additions would allow any serious student insight into how ancient texts evolve.

Second Enoch was rediscovered and published in the early 19th century A.D The text before you uses the R. H. Charles and W. R. Morfill translation of 1896 with additions from other sources. Archaic terms and sentence structure were revised or explained to convey a more modern rendering for the twenty-first century readers.

The Second Book of Enoch
Slavonic Enoch
The Book of the Secrets of Enoch

Chapter 1

1 There was a wise man and a great craftsman, and the Lord formed a love for him and received him, so that he should see the highest dwellings and be an eye-witness of the wise and great and inconceivable and unchanging realm of God Almighty, and of the very wonderful and glorious and bright and manifold vision of the position of the Lord's servants, and of the inaccessible throne of the Lord, and of the degrees and manifestations of the spiritual (non-physical) hosts, and of the unspeakable ministration of the multitude of the elements, and of the various apparition and singing of the host of Cherubim which is beyond description, and of the limitless light.
2 At that time, he said, when my one hundred and sixty-fifth year was completed, I begat my son Methuselah.
3 After this I lived two hundred years and finished of all the years of my life three hundred and sixty-five years.
4 On the first day of the month I was in my house alone and was resting on my bed and slept.
5 And when I was asleep, great distress came up into my heart, and I was weeping with my eyes in sleep, and I could not understand what this distress was, or what was happening to me.
6 And there appeared to me two very large men, so big that I never saw such on earth. Their faces were shining like the sun, their eyes were like a burning light, and from their lips fire was coming out. They were singing. Their clothing was of various kinds in appearance and was purple. Their wings were brighter than gold, and their hands whiter than snow.
7 They were standing at the head of my bed and began to call me by my name.
8 And I arose from my sleep and clearly saw the two men standing in front of me.
9 And I greeted them and was seized with fear and the appearance of my face was changed to terror, and those men said to me:
10 Enoch, have courage and do not fear. The eternal God sent us to you, and you shall ascend today with us into heaven, and you shall tell your sons and all your household all that they shall do without you on earth in your house, and let no one seek you until the Lord returns you to them.
11 And I hurried to obey them and went out of my house, and went to the doors, as I was ordered, and I summoned my sons Methuselah and Regim and Gaidad and explained to them all the marvels the men had told me.

Chapter 2

1 Listen to me, my children, I do not know where I will go, or what will befall me. So now, my children, I tell you, do not turn from God in the face of that which is empty or prideful, which did not make heaven and earth, for these shall perish along with those who worship them, and may the Lord make your hearts confident in the fear (respect) of him. And now, my children, let no one consider seeking me, until the Lord returns me to you.

Chapter 3

1 (It came to pass, when Enoch had finished speaking to his sons, that the angels took him on to their wings and lifted him up on to the first heaven and placed him on the clouds.)
And there I (Enoch) looked, and again I looked higher, and saw the ether, and they placed me on the first heaven and showed me a very large sea, bigger than the earthly sea. (See 2 Cor 12:22)

Chapter 4

1 They brought the elders and rulers of the stellar orders in front of me, and showed me two hundred angels, who rule the stars and services of the stars to the heavens, and fly with their wings and come round all those who sail.

Chapter 5

1 And here I looked down and saw the storehouses of snow, and the angels who keep their amazing storehouses, and the clouds where they come out of and into which they go.

Chapter 6

1 They showed me the storehouse of the dew, like olive oil in its appearance and its form, as of all the flowers of the earth. And they also showed me many angels guarding the storehouses of these things, and how they are made to shut and open.

Chapter 7

1 And those men took me and led me up on to the second heaven, and showed me darkness, greater than earthly darkness, and there I saw prisoners hanging, watched, (guarded,) awaiting the great and limitless judgment, and the spirits were dark in appearance, more than earthly darkness, and perpetually weeping through all hours.
2 And I said to the men who were with me: Why are these being unceasingly tortured? They answered me: These are God's apostates, who did not obey God's commands, but took counsel with their own will, and turned away with their prince, who is also held captive in the fifth heaven.
3 And I felt great pity for them, and they greeted me, and said to me: Man of God, pray to the Lord for us.

And I answered them: I am just a mortal man. Who am I that I should pray for spirits? Who knows where I go or what will become of me? Or who will pray for me?

Chapter 8
1 And those men took me from there and led me up on to the third heaven, and placed me there. I looked down and saw what this place produces and that it was so good that such as has never been known.
2 And I saw all the sweet, flowering trees and I saw their fruits, which were sweet smelling, and I saw all the foods that came from them and that the food was bubbling with fragrant vapors.
3 And in the middle of the trees was the tree of life, in that place where the Lord rests when he goes up into paradise. And this tree is of indescribable goodness and fragrance, and adorned more than anything existing. And all sides of its form were golden and brilliant red and fire-like and it was completely covered, and it produced all fruits. (See Rev. 22:2)
4 Its root is in the garden at the earth's end.
5 And paradise resides between spiritual and physical.
6 And two springs come out which send forth honey and milk, and their springs send forth oil and wine, and they separate into four parts, and flow quietly around, and go down into the paradise of Eden, between the mutable and the eternal. (See Gen. 2:11-14)
7 And there they go forth along the earth, and have a circular flow even as other elements.
8 And there is no unfruitful tree here, and every place is blessed.
9 Three hundred angels, which are very bright, are there to keep the garden, and with incessant sweet singing with voices, which are never silent, serve the Lord throughout all the hours of days.
10 And I said: How very sweet is this place, and those men said to me:

Chapter 9
1 This place, O Enoch, is prepared for the righteous, who endure all manner of offence from those that exasperate their souls, who avert their eyes from iniquity, and make righteous judgment, and give bread to the hungering, and cover the naked with clothing, and raise up the fallen, and help injured orphans, and who walk without fault before the face of the Lord, and serve him alone, and for them is prepared this place for eternal inheritance.

Chapter 10
1 And those two men led me up on to the Northern side, and showed me there a very terrible place, and there were every kind of tortures in that place: cruel darkness and gloom, and there was absolutely no light at all there, but murky fire constantly flaming above, and there is a fiery river coming out, and everywhere in that entire place is fire, and everywhere there is frost and ice, thirst and shivering, while the physical restraints are very cruel, and the spirits were fearsome and merciless, bearing angry weapons, torturing without mercy.
2 And I said: Woe, woe! This place is so terrible.
3 And those men said to me: This place, O Enoch, is prepared for those who dishonor God, who on earth practice sin against nature, which is sodomy of a child, corruption of children, performing magic, enchantments and devilish witchcrafts, and who boast of their wicked deeds, stealing, lying, slander, envy, resentment, fornication, murder, and who are accursed and steal the souls of men, and those who see the poor and still take away their goods so they grow rich, and injure them for other men's goods. And this is reserved for those who, to satisfy their own emptiness made the hungering die; those who clothe themselves by stripping the naked; and who did not know their creator, but instead bowed to lifeless gods who have no soul who cannot see nor hear, who are empty, and who built carved images and bow down to unclean fashioning of useless gods, this place is prepared for these as an eternal inheritance.

Chapter 11
1 Those men took me, and led me up on to the fourth heaven, and showed me the entire succession of activities, and all the rays of the light of sun and moon.
2 And I measured their progression, and compared their light, and saw that the sun's light is greater than the moon's.
3 Its circle and the wheels on which it goes always is like the wind passing with very amazing speed with no rest day or night.
4 Its egress and ingress are accompanied by four huge stars, and each star has a thousand stars under it, to the right of the sun's wheel there are four thousand stars and to the left are four thousand, altogether eight thousand, going out with the sun continually.
5 And by day fifteen groups of ten thousand angels attend it, and by night there were a thousand.
6 And six-winged ones go fourth with the angels before the sun's wheel into the fiery flames, and a hundred angels kindle the sun and set it alight.

Chapter 12
1 And I looked and saw other flying elements of the sun, whose names are Phoenixes and Chalkydri, which are marvelous and wonderful, with feet and tails of a lion, and a crocodile's head, they appear to be purple in color like that in the rainbow; their size is nine hundred measures, their wings are like those of

angels, each has twelve wings, and they attend and accompany the sun, bearing heat and dew, as it is ordered them from God.

(Note: The word CHALKYDRI means "serpents". It appears that the Slavonic translators rendered the Hebrew word SERAPHIM differently in various places in the text. The word was translated "Serpent" in some places and SERAPHIM in others. Seraph means, "to burn.")

2 This is how the sun revolves and goes, and rises under the heaven, and its course goes under the earth with the light of its rays continually.

Chapter 13

1 Then those men carried me away to the east, and placed me at the sun's gates, where the sun has egress according to the seasons circuit and regulation of the months of the whole year, and the number of the hours day and night.
2 And I saw six gates open, each gate having sixty-one stadia (185 meters) and A quarter of one stadium (46.25 meters), and I measured them accurately, and knew their size. Through the gates the sun goes out, and goes to the west, and is made even, and rises throughout all the months, and turns back again from the six gates according to the succession of the seasons. In this way the period of the entire year is finished after the return of the four seasons.

(Note: 6 X 61=366 With the quarter day added, this is the length of the leap year.)

Chapter 14

1 And again those men led me away to the western parts, and showed me six great open gates corresponding to the eastern gates, opposite to where the sun sets, according to the number of the days three hundred and sixty-five and a quarter.

(Note that this is a solar calendar of the same length as our modern calendar.)

2 Again it goes down to the western gates, and diminishes (pulls away) its light with the prominent brightness, under the earth. The crown of its glory is in heaven with the Lord, and it is guarded by four hundred angels while the sun goes round on wheel under the earth. And it stands seven great hours in night, and spends half its course under the earth. And when it comes to the eastern approach in the eighth hour of the night it brings its lights and the crown of glory, and the sun burns (flames) outwardly more than fire.

Chapter 15

1 Then the elements of the sun, called Phoenixes and Chalkydri (Seraphim) break into song, therefore every bird flutters its wings, rejoicing at the giver of light, and they brake into song at the command of the Lord.
(The Kadosh – Holy, Holy, Holy)
2 The giver of light comes to illuminate the entire world, and the morning guard takes shape, which is the rays of the sun, and the sun of the earth goes out, and receives its luminance to light up the entire face of the earth, and they showed me this calculation of the sun's going.
3 And the great gates, which it enters into, are for the calculation of the hours of the year. For this reason the sun is a great creation, whose circuit lasts twenty-eight years, and begins again from the beginning.

(Note: For 29 February, which is the leap year day, to fall on a particular weekday, there is a 28-year (2 x 14 year) cycle. This forms a type of perpetual calendar.)

Chapter 16

1 Those men showed me the great course of the moon. There are twelve great gates that are crowned from west to east, by which the moon comes and goes in its customary times.
2 It goes in at the first gate to the western places of the sun, by the first gates with thirty-one days exactly, by the second gates with thirty-one days exactly, by the third with thirty days exactly, by the fourth with thirty days exactly, by the fifth with thirty-one days exactly, by the sixth with thirty-one days exactly, by the seventh with thirty days exactly, by the eighth with thirty-one days perfectly, by the ninth with thirty-one days exactly, by the tenth with thirty days perfectly, by the eleventh with thirty-one days exactly, by the twelfth with twenty-eight days exactly.

(Note: The sum of the days total 365 with the year beginning in March.)

3 And it goes through the western gates in the order and number of the eastern, and accomplishes the three hundred and sixty-five and a quarter days of the solar year, while the lunar year has three hundred fifty-four, and there twelve days lacking of the solar circle, which are the lunar epacts of the whole year.

(Note: epact - The number of days by which the solar year differs from the lunar year.
• the number of days into the moon's phase cycle at the beginning of the solar (calendar) year.
Origin - mid 16th century. (Denoting the age of the moon in days at the beginning of the calendar year): from French épacte, via late Latin from Greek epakta 'intercalated (days).

4 The great circle also contains five hundred and thirty-two years.

(Note: The 532-year cycle is calculated from the creation of Adam, which, as we know, took place on Friday, March 1, 5508 B.C., which is the base date on which the entire calendar system of the Orthodox Church is founded. The cycles are laid out in the final sections of the Typikon, which is the book that dictates the services, and are the Paschalion Calendar sections. There are tables reflecting the 532 year cycle of the Church services, which consists of 19-year solar cycles multiplied by 28-day lunar cycles. There is a table that consists of 19 columns by 28 rows, giving the Paschal Key number or letter for each of the years of the 532-year cycle. Once you know the Paschal Key, you look up the details in the following section, which consists of 35 brief calendar synopses, one for each possible day that Pascha can fall. Each of these synopses actually consists of two services; one for regular years, and one for leap years.

5 The quarter (of a day) is omitted for three years, the fourth fulfills it exactly.
6 Because of this, they are taken outside of heaven for three years and are not added to the number of days, because they change the time of the years to two new months toward completion, to two others toward the decrease.
7 And when the course through the western gates is finished, it returns and goes to the eastern to the lights, and goes this way day and night in its heavenly circles, below all circles, swifter than the heavenly winds, and spirits and elements and flying angels. Each angel has six wings.
8 In nineteen years it travels the course seven times.

Chapter 17
1 In the midst of the heavens I saw armed soldiers, serving the Lord, with drums and organs, with constant voice, with sweet voice, with sweet and unceasing voice and various singing, which it is impossible to describe, and which astonishes every mind, so wonderful and marvelous is the singing of those angels, and I was delighted listening to it.

Chapter 18
1 The men took me on to the fifth heaven and placed me, and there I saw many and countless soldiers, called Grigori, of human appearance, and their size (was) greater than that of great giants and their faces withered, and the silence of their mouths perpetual, and their was no service on the fifth heaven, and I said to the men who were with me:

(Note: The Greek transliteration egegoroi are the Watchers; a group of fallen angels who mated with mortal women and produced the Nephilim mentioned in the books of Jubilees, 1Enoch, and Genesis 6:4.)

2 Why are they so very withered and their faces melancholy, and their mouths silent, and why is there no service in this heaven?
3 And they said to me: These are the Grigori, who with their prince Satanail (Satan) rejected the Lord of Light. After them are those who are held in great darkness in the second heaven, and three of them went down on to earth from the Lord's throne, to the place Ermon, and broke through their vows on the shoulder of the hill Ermon and saw the daughters of men how good they are, and took to themselves wives, and fouled the earth with their deeds, who broke the law and mixing (with the women), giants are born and amazingly large men with great hatred.

(Note: The Hill of Ermon could be Mount Hermon, which is mentioned over a dozen times in the Bible.

4 And therefore God judged them with great judgment, and they weep for their brethren and they will be punished on the Lord's great day.
5 And I said to the Grigori: I saw your brethren and their works, and their great torments, and I prayed for them, but the Lord has condemned them to be under earth until this heaven and this earth shall end for ever.
6 And I said: Why do you stand there, brethren, and do not serve before the Lord's face, and have not put your services before the Lord's face? You could anger your Lord completely.
7 And they listened to my advice, and spoke to the four ranks in heaven. As I stood with those two men four trumpets sounded together with a loud voice, and the Grigori broke into song with one voice, and their voice went up before the Lord pitifully and touchingly.

Chapter 19
1 From there, those men took me and lifted me up on to the sixth heaven, and there I saw seven bands of angels, very bright and very glorious, and their faces shining more than the sun's shining, glistening, and there is no difference in their faces, or behavior, or manner of dress; and these make the orders, and learn the goings of the stars, and the alteration of the moon, or revolution of the sun, and the good administration of the world.
2 And when they see evildoing they make commandments and instruction, and make sweet and loud singing, and all (songs) of praise.
3 These are the archangels who are above angels, and they measure all life in heaven and on earth, and the angels who are (appointed) over seasons and years, the angels who are over rivers and sea, and who are over the fruits of the earth, and the angels who are over every grass, giving food to every and all living

things, and the angels who write down all the souls of men, and all their deeds, and their lives before the Lord's face. In their midst are six Phoenixes and six Cherubim and six six-winged ones continually singing with one voice, and it is not possible to describe their singing, and they rejoice before the Lord at his footstool.

Chapter 20

1 And those two men lifted me up from there on to the seventh heaven, and I saw there a very great light, and fiery troops of great archangels, incorporeal forces, and dominions, orders and governments, Cherubim and Seraphim, thrones and many-eyed ones, nine regiments, the Ioanit stations of light, and I became afraid, and began to tremble with great terror, and those men took me, and led me after them, and said to me:
2 Have courage, Enoch, do not fear, and showed me the Lord from afar, sitting on His very high throne. For what is there on the tenth heaven, since the Lord dwells there?
3 On the tenth heaven is God, in the Hebrew tongue he is called Aravat.

(Note: The meaning of Ioanit is not clear. However, it may be derived from the transliteration of the name John. John means, "The Lord is Gracious." The meaning of Aravat is equally unclear but seems to mean, "Father of Creation." Each level of heaven represents or demonstrates a personality or part of the Godhead. One of the highest demonstrations of God's power and divinity is the power of Creation. It is found on the tenth level of heaven.)

4 And all the heavenly soldiers would come and stand on the ten steps according to their rank, and would bow down to the Lord, and would then return to their places in joy and bliss, singing songs in the unlimited light with soft and gentle voices, gloriously serving him.

(Note: Strong and fierce soldiers sing with soft, gentle voices, bowing and serving in bliss.)

Chapter 21

1 And the Cherubim and Seraphim standing around the throne, and the six-winged and many-eyed ones do not depart, standing before the Lord's face doing his will, and cover his whole throne, singing with gentle voice before the Lord's face: Holy, holy, holy, Lord Ruler of Sabaoth (Host / army), heavens and earth are full of Your glory.
2 When I saw all these things, the men said to me: Enoch, thus far we were commanded to journey with you, and those men went away from me and after that I did not see them.

3 And I remained alone at the end of the seventh heaven and became afraid, and fell on my face and said to myself: Woe is me. What has befallen me?
4 And the Lord sent one of his glorious ones, the archangel Gabriel, and he said to me: "Have courage, Enoch, do not fear, arise before the Lord's face into eternity, arise and come with me."
5 And I answered him, and said within myself: My Lord, my soul has departed from me due to terror and trembling, and I called to the men who led me up to this place. I relied on them, and it is with them that I can go before the Lord's face.

(Note: When speaking to God, Enoch "said within himself." He did not have to speak aloud.)

6 And Gabriel lifted me up like a leaf caught up by the wind, and he placed me before the Lord's face.
7 And I saw the eighth heaven, which is called in the Hebrew tongue Muzaloth (Zodiac), the changer of the seasons, of drought, and of wet, and of the twelve constellations of the circle of the firmament, which are above the seventh heaven.
8 And I saw the ninth heaven, which is called in Hebrew Kuchavim, where are the heavenly homes of the twelve constellations of the circle of the firmament.

Chapter 22

1 On the tenth heaven, which is called Aravoth, I saw the appearance of the Lord's face, like iron made to glow in fire, and it shone forth and casted out, emitting sparks, and it burned.

(Note: One possible meaning of Aravoth is "three times holy" or "holy, holy, holy."

2 In a moment of eternity I saw the Lord's face, but the Lord's face is indescribable, marvelous and very amazing, and very, very terrible.
3 And who am I to tell of the Lord's unspeakable being, and of his very wonderful face? I cannot tell the amount of his instructions, and the variety of voices. The Lord's throne is very great and not made with hands, and I cannot tell the number of those standing around him. There were troops of Cherubim and Seraphim, and they sang unceasingly. I cannot tell of his unchanging beauty. Who shall tell of the unpronounceable greatness of his glory?
4 And I fell prone and bowed down to the Lord, and the Lord with his lips said to me:
5 Have courage, Enoch, do not fear, arise and stand before my face into eternity (stand before my face eternally / stand before my eternal face.)

(Note: Enoch is out of and above time-space. Eternity is now and he can feel the timelessness of where he is. The language struggles to convey this fact.)

6 And the archangel Michael lifted me up, and led me to the Lord's face.

7 And the Lord said to his servants, testing them: Let Enoch stand before my face into eternity, and the glorious ones bowed down to the Lord, and said: Let Enoch go according to Your word.

8 And the Lord said to Michael: Go and take Enoch and remove his earthly garments, and anoint him with my sweet ointment, and put him into the garments of My glory.

9 And Michael did as the Lord told him. He anointed me, and dressed me, and the appearance of that ointment is more than the great light, and his ointment is like sweet dew, and its smell mild, shining like the sun's ray, and I looked at myself, and I was transformed into one of his glorious ones.

(Note: The number symbolism of ten is that of new starts at a higher level, new beginnings, and re-creation.)

10 And the Lord summoned one of his archangels, whose name is Pravuil, whose knowledge was quicker in wisdom than the other archangels, who wrote all the deeds of the Lord; and the Lord said to Pravuil: Bring out the books from my store-houses, and a reed of quick-writing, and give it to Enoch, and deliver to him the best and comforting books out of your hand.

(Note: Enoch is now an angel. He now has access to the heavenly records and the understanding to use the knowledge. A reed was used in writing much like a quill was used.)

Chapter 23

1 And he was explaining to me all the works of heaven, earth and sea, and all the elements, their passages and goings, and the sounding of the thunders, the sun and moon, the progression and changes of the stars, the seasons, years, days, and hours, as well as the risings of the wind, the numbers of the angels, and the formation of their songs, and all human things, the tongue of every human song and life, the commandments, instructions, and sweet-voiced singings, and all things that are fitting to learn.

2 And Pravuil told me: All the things that I have told you, we have written. Sit and write all the souls of mankind, however many of them are born, and the places prepared for them to eternity. And he said, all souls are prepared for eternity, before the formation of the world.

3 And for both thirty days and thirty nights, and I wrote out all things exactly, and wrote three hundred and sixty-six books.

(Note: If all things were created in six days, then the souls of all people were created at that time. In Jewish mythology, the place that the souls were houses until birth was called the Guf (Guph). Each soul was created for a certain place, time, and destiny. According to one version of the myth, when the Guf (Gup) is emptied of souls, time ceases. In another version, when the last soul dies and returns to God, time will end. Enoch wrote 366 book in a 720 hour period containing information on all things, including, "all souls who are prepared for eternity, before the formation of the world.")

Chapter 24

1 And the Lord summoned me, and said to me: Enoch, sit down on my left with Gabriel.

2 And I bowed down to the Lord, and the Lord spoke to me: Enoch, beloved, all that you see, all things that are standing finished, I tell you even before the very beginning, I created all things from non-being. I created the visible, physical things from the invisible, spiritual (world).

3 Hear, Enoch, and take in my words, for I have not told My angels My secret, and I have not told them their rise (beginnings), nor My endless realm, nor have they understood my creating, which I tell you today.

4 For before all things were visible (physical), I alone used to go about in the invisible, spiritual things, like the sun from east to west, and from west to east.

5 But even the sun has peace in itself, while I found no peace, because I was creating all things, and I conceived the thought of placing foundations, and of creating the visible, physical creation.

(Note: Overview of the heavens:
First heaven - , Enoch arrives on angel's wings. There are storehouses of snow and dew.
Second heaven - , Enoch finds a group of fallen angels. There is darkness and torture.
Third heaven - There are sweet flowers, trees, and fruit.
Fourth heaven – There are soldiers, heaven's army, and the progression of sun and moon.
Fifth heaven - The leaders of the fallen angels, the "Grigori" (Greek "Gregoroi," translating Mearim, the Hebrew word for watchers.) A company of them went down and had intercourse with the daughters of men, yielding giants, who became the source of enmity on earth.
Sixth heaven – Seven bands of angels and the ordering of the stars.
Seventh heaven, shows something unusual happening to Enoch when Gabriel puts Enoch in front of the throne of the Lord.
The Eighth, Ninth, and Tenth Heavens are thought to be later additions and not part of the original text.

Eighth heaven - "Muzaloth" -- Zodiac
Ninth heaven - "Kuchavim" -- heavenly bodies (stars).
Tenth heaven - "Aravoth" -- descriptions of God's face like that of iron made to glow in fire.
Enoch sees the "appearance of the Lord's face," but describes it as indescribable.
Pravuil, the archangel, is commanded to write down secret information about astronomy, climate, and language and give it over to Enoch. In other Enochian writings the same angel, also spelled "Penemue", is criticized for teaching humans to write.

Chapter 25

1 I commanded in the very lowest parts, that the visible, physical things should come down from the invisible, spiritual (realm), and Adoil came down very great, and I beheld him, and he had a belly of great light.

2 And I said to him: Become undone, Adoil, and let the visible, physical (universe) come out of you.

3 And he came undone, and a great light came out. And I was in the midst of the great light, and as there is born light from light, there came forth a great age (eon / space of time), and showed all creation, which I had thought to create.

4 And I saw that it was good.

5 And I placed for myself a throne, and took my seat on it, and said to the light: Go up higher from here and station yourself high above the throne, and be a foundation to the highest things.

6 And above the light there is nothing else, and then I rose up and looked up from my throne.

(Note: Beginning with chapters 25 and 26, the book of 2 Enoch takes a rather Gnostic diversion. The Gnostics were a Christian sect that flourished around the 3rd century A.D. The Gnostic view of the Godhead borrowed heavily from the creation saga preached by Plato (circa 428 B.C. to 348 B.C.) The story of Adoil and the emanation of pure light from God, which brings about creation of the physical world, is similar to other Gnostic works. Gnosticism teaches that in the beginning a Supreme Being called The Father, The Divine All, The Origin, The Supreme God, or The Fullness, emanated the element of existence, both visible and invisible. His intent was not to create but, just as light emanates from a flame, so did creation shine forth from God. This manifested the primal element needed for creation.

This was the creation of Barbelo, who is the "Thought of God."
The Father's thought performed a deed and she was created from it. It is she who had appeared before him in the shining of his light. This is the first power which was before all of them and which was created from his mind. She is the Thought of the All and her light shines like his light. It is the perfect power, which is the visage of the invisible. She is the

pure, undefiled Spirit who is perfect. She is the first power. Adoil has that place is this myth.

It could be said that Barbelo was the creative emanation and, like the Divine All, is both male and female. It was the "agreement" of Barbelo and the Divine All, representing the union of male and female, that created the Christ Spirit and all the Aeons. In some renderings the word "Aeon" is used to designate an ethereal realm or kingdom. In other versions "Aeon" indicates the ruler of the realm. The Aeons of this world are merely reflections of the Aeons of the eternal realm. The reflection is always inferior to real.

In several Gnostic cosmologies the "living" world is under the control of entities called Aeons, of which Sophia is head. This means the Aeons influence or control the soul, life force, intelligence, thought, and mind. Control of the mechanical or inorganic world is given to the Archons.

The Archons were created by Sophia. Sophia, probably out of pride, tried to emulate the creative force of God by created an image of herself. Meaning that she wanted to produce an offspring, without either consort or the approval of her Father, God. As an aeon, she did have the power to do so, but she wasn't perfect like the Great Spirit, or like the other two perfect aeons, Barbelo and the Autogenes. Nevertheless, in her arrogance, she attempted to create and failed. She was horrified when she saw her creation, imperfect, bruthish creature with a lion-faced serpent with eyes of fire, whom she called Yaldabaoth. Sophia cast her offspring out of pleroma (heaven), and hid her child within a thick cloud from the other aeons, because of her embarrassment and shame.

Yaldabaoth was the first of the archon ("ruler") and he stole his mother's power, so that she wasn't able to escape from the cloud. Despite gaining Sophia's aeonic power, he was weak, but prideful, ambitious and power hungry.

Since the archons, including Yaldabaoth, were androgynous beings, Yaldabaoth fathered twelve archons, giving each a bit of his power. They were named Athoth, Harmas, Kalila-Oumbri, Yabel, Adonaiou (or Sabaoth), Cain, Abel, Abrisene, Yobel, Armoupieel, Melceir-Adonein and Belias. Seven archons would rule seven heavens and five in the abyss, which Yaldabaoth and the archons created. Each archon would rule a heaven (or the abyss), and created 365 angels to help them.

The archons rule the physical aspects of systems, regulation, limits, and order in the world. Both the ineptitude and cruelty of the Archons are reflected in the chaos and pain of the material realm.
(See the book, The Gnostic Scriptures, by Joseph Lumpkin, published by Fifth Estate.)

Although the above may be a digression from the text of 2 Enoch, it adds insight into the time frame and origins of its production. Gnostic influences were felt from the late first *century to the early fourth century A.D. If the writer of this section of 2 Enoch was exposed to the Gnostic sect, it would conclusively make 2 Enoch a text with Christian influences.)*

Chapter 26

1 And I summoned the very lowest a second time, and said: Let Archas come forth hard, and he came forth hard from the invisible, spiritual.
2 And Archas came forth, hard, heavy, and very red.
3 And I said: Be opened, Archas, and let there be born from you, and he came apart, and an age came forth, very great and very dark, bearing the creation of all lower things, and I saw that it was good and said to him:
4 Go down below, and make yourself solid, and be a foundation for the lower things, and it happened and he went down and stationed himself, and became the foundation for the lower things, and below the darkness there is nothing else.

(Note: Hard and heavy could be terms for "gravid" or pregnant, with birth being imminent. Archas could equate to "The Archons.")

Chapter 27

1 And I commanded that there should be taken from light and darkness, and I said: Be thick, and it became thick, and I spread it out with the light, and it became water, and I spread it out over the darkness, below the light, and then I made firm the waters, that is to say the bottomless (abyss), and I made foundation of light around the water, and created seven circles from inside, and made the water look like crystal, wet and dry, so it was like glass, and the circles were around the waters and the other elements, and I showed each one of them its path, and the seven stars each one of them in its heaven, that they go the correct way, and I saw that it was good.
2 And I made separations between light and darkness in the midst of the water here and there, and I said to the light, that it should be the day, and to the darkness, that it should be the night, and there was evening and there was morning on the first day.

(Note: The foundation of light around the water that is like crystal is likely a reference to the sky. One belief at the time of writing was that the sky was an expanse of water like an endless sea.)

Chapter 28

1 And then I made firm the heavenly circle, and made that the lower water which is under heaven collect itself together into one whole (piece), and that the chaos become dry, and it became so.
2 Out of the waves I created hard and large rock, and from the rock I piled up the dry (land), and the dry

(land) I called earth, and the middle of the earth I called the abyss, or the bottomless. I collected the sea in one place and bound it together with a yoke. *(Note: This is the bank or shoreline.)*
3 And I said to the sea: Behold I give you eternal limits, and you shall not break loose from your integral parts.
4 Thus I made the firmament hold together. This day I called the first-created, Sunday. (This, I call the first day of creation.)

Chapter 29

1 And for all the heavenly soldiers I made them the image and essence of fire, and my eye looked at the very hard, firm rock, and from the gleam of my eye the lightning received its wonderful nature, (which) is both fire in water and water in fire, and one does not put out the other, nor does the one dry up the other, therefore the lightning is brighter than the sun, softer than water and firmer than hard rock.

(Note: If the sky is made of water and lightning, which is fire, issues from the sky, then water and fire must exist together in a heavenly form.)

2 And from the rock I cut off a great fire, and from the fire I created the orders of the incorporeal (spiritual / non-physical) ten troops of angels, and their weapons are fiery and their raiment a burning flame, and I commanded that each one should stand in his order.
3 And one from out the order of angels, having violated the command he was given, conceived an impossible thought, to place his throne higher than the clouds above the earth so that he might become equal in rank to my power.
4 And I threw him out from the height with his angels, and he was flying in the air continuously above the bottomless (abyss).
(Note: We assume this ends the second day, although it is not mentioned.)

Chapter 30

1 On the third day I commanded the earth to make and grow great and fruitful trees, and hills, and seeds to sow, and I planted Paradise, and enclosed it, and placed armed guards in the form of my flaming angels, and in this way I created renewal.
2 Then came evening, and morning came of the fourth day.
3 On Wednesday, the fourth day, I commanded that there should be great lights on the heavenly circles.
4 On the first uppermost circle I placed the stars, Cronus, and on the second Aphrodite, on the third Ares, on the fifth Zeus, on the sixth Ermis (Hermes), on the seventh lesser the moon, and adorned it with the lesser stars.

(Note: The fourth heavenly circle is vacant. The Greek names for the heavenly bodies leave no doubt as to the influence of Greek words and ideas within this section of the text.)

5 And on the lower (parts) I placed the sun for the illumination of day, and the moon and stars for the illumination of night.

6 (And I set) the sun that it should go according to each of the twelve constellations , and I appointed the succession of the months and their names and lives, their thundering, and how they mark the hours, and how they should proceed.

7 Then evening came and morning came of the fifth day.

8 On Thursday, the fifth day, I commanded the sea, that it should bring forth fishes, and feathered birds of many varieties, and all animals creeping over the earth, going forth over the earth on four legs, and soaring in the air, of male and female sex, and every soul breathing the spirit of life.

(Note: Verse eight proclaims the creation of all souls breathing (inspired by) the spirit of life. The next verse proclaims the creation of man. This day filled the Guf and incarnation begins in next.)

9 And there came evening, and there came morning of the sixth day.

10 On Friday, the sixth day, I commanded my wisdom to create man from seven consistent applications: one, his flesh from the earth; two, his blood from the dew; three, his eyes from the sun; four, his bones from stone; five, his intelligence from the swiftness of the angels and cloud; six, his veins and his hair from the grass of the earth; seven, his soul from my breath and from the wind.

11 And I gave him seven natures: to the flesh - hearing, the eyes for sight, to the soul - smell, the veins for touch, the blood for taste, the bones for endurance, to the intelligence - enjoyment.

12 I created a saying (speech) from knowing. I created man from spiritual and from physical nature, from both come his death and life and appearance. He knows speech like some created thing. He is small in greatness and great in smallness, and I placed him on earth, like a second angel, to be honorable, great and glorious. And I appointed him as ruler to rule on earth and to have my wisdom, and there was none like him on earth of all my existing creatures.

13 And I appointed him a name made from the four components, from east, from west, from south, and from north. And I appointed for him four special stars, and I called his name Adam, and showed him the two ways, the light and the darkness, and I told him:

14 This is good, and that bad, so that I should learn whether he has love towards me, or hatred, and so that it would be clear who in his race loves me.

(Note: The Hebrew name of Adam means "man.)

15 For I have seen his nature, but he has not seen his own nature, and therefore by not seeing it he will sin worse, and I said, "After sin is there nothing but death?"

16 And I put sleep into him and he fell asleep. And I took from him a rib, and created him a wife, so that death should come to him by his wife, and I took his last word and called her name mother, that is to say, Eve.

Chapter 31

1 Adam has life on earth, and I created a garden in Eden in the east, so that he should observe the testament and keep the command.

2 I made the heavens open to him, so that he would see the angels singing the song of victory, and the light without shadow.

3 And he was continuously in paradise, and the devil understood that I wanted to create another world, because Adam was lord on earth, to rule and control it.

4 The devil is the evil spirit of the lower places, he made himself a fugitive from the heavens as the devil and his name was Satan. Thus he became different from the angels, but his nature did not change his intelligence as it applied to his understanding of righteous and sinful things.

5 And he understood his condemnation and the sin that he had committed before. Therefore he devised a thought against Adam, in which he entered and seduced Eve, but did not touch Adam.

6 But I cursed ignorance. However, what I had blessed before I did not curse. I did not curse man, nor the earth, nor other creatures. But I cursed man's evil results, and his works.

Chapter 32

1 I said to him: You are earth (dirt), and into the earth from where I took you, you shall go, and I will not destroy you, but send you back from where I took you.

2 Then I can again receive you at My second presence.

3 And I blessed all my creatures, both physical and spiritual. And Adam was five and half hours in paradise.

4 And I blessed the seventh day, which is the Sabbath, on which he rested from all his works.

(Note: The five and a half hours is tied to the 5500 years of punishment mentioned in the Books of Adam and Eve. See

"The First and Second Books of Adam and Eve" by Joseph Lumpkin.)

Chapter 33

1 And I appointed the eighth day also, that the eighth day should be the first-created after my work, and that the first seven revolve in the form of the seventh thousand, and that at the beginning of the eighth thousand there should be a time of not-counting, endless, with neither years nor months nor weeks nor days nor hours.

(Note: A day is as a thousand years. This is a prophecy seems to indicate that after six thousand years there will be a thousand years of rest, then there will be timelessness.)

2 And now, Enoch, all that I have told you, all that you have understood, all that you have seen of heavenly things, all that you have seen on earth, all that I have written in books by my great wisdom, and all these things I have devised and created from the uppermost foundation to the lower and to the end, and there is no counselor nor inheritor to my creations.
3 I am eternal unto myself, not made with hands, and without change.
4 My thought is my own counselor, my wisdom and my word creates, and my eyes observe how all things stand here and tremble with terror.
5 If I turn away my face, then all things will be destroyed.
6 Apply your mind, Enoch, and know him who is speaking to you, and take the books there, which you yourself have written.
7 I give you Samuil and Raguil, who led you upward with the books, and go down to earth, and tell your sons all that I have told you, and all that you have seen, from the lower heaven up to my throne, and all the troops.
8 For I created all forces, and there is none that resists me and none that does not subject himself to me. For all subject themselves to my kingdom, and labor for my complete rule.
9 Give them the books of the handwriting, and they will read them and will know that I am the creator of all things, and will understand how there is no other God but me.
10 And let them distribute the books of your handwriting from children to children, generation to generation, nation to nation.
11 And Enoch, I will give you, my intercessor, the archangel Michael, for the writings of your fathers Adam, Seth, Enos, Cainan, Mahaleleel, and Jared your father.

Chapter 34

1 They have rejected my commandments and my yoke, therefore worthless seed has come up, not fearing God, and they would not bow down to me, but have begun to bow down to empty gods, and rejected my unity (oneness / sovereignty), and have piled the whole earth up with lies, offences, abominable lust with one another, and all manner of other unclean wickedness, which are disgusting to even mention.
2 And therefore I will bring down a deluge upon the earth and will destroy all men, and the whole earth will crumble together into great darkness.

Chapter 35

1 You will see that from their seed shall arise another generation, long afterward, but of them many will be full of very strong desires that are never satisfied.
2 He who raises that generation shall reveal the books of your writing of your fathers to them. And He must point out the guardianship of the world to the faithful men and workers of my pleasure, who do not acknowledge my name in empty words.
3 And they shall tell another generation, and those others who, having read, shall afterward be glorified more than the first.

Chapter 36

1 Now, Enoch, I give you a period of thirty days to spend in your house, and tell your sons and all your household, so that all may hear from you what was spoken by my face, so that they may read and understand that there is no other God but me.
2 And that they may always keep my commandments, and begin to read and absorb the books of your writing.
3 And after thirty days I shall send my angel for you, and he will take you from earth and from your sons and bring you to me.

Chapter 37

1 And the Lord called upon one of the older angels who was terrible and menacing, and He placed him by me. He appeared white as snow, and his hands were like ice, having the appearance of great frost, and he froze my face, because I could not endure the terror of the Lord, just as it is not possible to endure a stove's fire or the sun's heat, or the frost of the air.
2 And the Lord said to me: Enoch, if your face is not frozen here, no man will be able to look at your face.

Chapter 38

1 And the Lord said to those men who first led me up: "Let Enoch go down on to earth with you, and await him until the determined day."
2 And by night they placed me on my bed.
3 But Methuselah was expecting my return and was keeping watch at my bed by day and night. And he

was filled with awe when he heard my return, and I told him, "Let all my household come together, so that I may tell them everything."

Chapter 39

1 Oh my children, my loved ones, hear the advice of your father, as much as is according to the Lord's will.
2 I have been allowed to come to you today, and preach to you, not from my lips, but from the Lord's lips, all that is now, and was, and all that will be until judgment day.
3 For the Lord has allowed me to come to you so that you could hear the words of my lips, a man who made great for you. But I am one who has seen the Lord's face, and it was like iron made to glow from fire it sends forth sparks and burns.
4 You look upon my eyes now. They are the eyes of a man enlarged with meaning for you, but I have seen the Lord's eyes, shining like the sun's rays and filling the eyes of man with awe.
5 You see now, my children, the right hand of a man that helps you, but I have seen the Lord's right hand filling heaven as he helped me.
6 You see the scope of my work is like your own, but I have seen the Lord's limitless and perfect scope, which has no end.
7 You hear the words of my lips, as I heard the words of the Lord, and they are like constant and great thunder with hurling of clouds.
8 And now, my children, hear the lecture of the father of the earth. I will tell you how fearful and awful it is to come before the face of the ruler of the earth, and how much more terrible and awful it is to come before the face of the ruler of heaven, who is the judge of the quick and the dead, and of the controller of the heavenly troops. Who (of us) can endure that endless pain?

Chapter 40

1 And now, my children, I know all things, for this is from the Lord's lips, and my eyes have seen this, from beginning to end.
2 I know all things, and have written all things in the books, the heavens and their end, and their abundance, and all the armies and their marching.
3 I have measured and described the stars, the great innumerable multitude of them.
4 What man has seen their revolutions and their entrances? For not even the angels see their number, but I have written all their names.
5 And I measured the sun's circumference, and measured its rays, and counted the hours. I also wrote down all things that go over the earth. I have written down the things that are nourished, and all seed sown and unsown, which the earth produces, and all plants, and every grass and every flower, and their sweet smells, and their names, and the dwelling-

places of the clouds, and their composition, and their wings, and how they carry rain and raindrops.
6 And I investigated all things, and described the road of the thunder and of the lightning, and they showed me the keys and their guardians, their rise, and the way they precede. They are let out gradually, in measure, by a chain. If they were not let out at a measured rate by a heavy chain their violence would hurl down the angry clouds and destroy all things on earth.
7 I described the treasure houses of the snow, and the storehouses of the cold and the frosty airs, and I observed the key-holders of the seasons. He fills the clouds with them, and it does not exhaust the treasure houses.
8 And I wrote down the resting places of the winds and observed and saw how their key-holders bear weighing-scales and measures. First, they put them in one side of the weighing-scale, then in the other side they place the weights and let them out according to measure skillfully, over the whole earth, to keep the heavy winds from making the earth rock. (The wind blows and makes the earth hard and rock.)
9 And I measured out the whole earth, its mountains, and all hills, fields, trees, stones, rivers, all existing things I wrote down, the height from earth to the seventh heaven, and downwards to the very lowest hell, and the judgment-place, and the very great, open and weeping (gaping) hell.
10 And I saw how the prisoners are in pain, expecting the limitless judgment.
11 And I wrote down all those being judged by the judge, and all their judgment and sentences and all their works.

Chapter 41

1 And I saw throughout all time all the forefathers from Adam and Eve, and I sighed and broke into tears and spoke of the ruin and their dishonor.
2 And I sad, "Woe is me for my infirmity and for that of my forefathers," and thought in my heart and said:
3 "Blessed is the man who has not been born or who has been born and shall not sin before the Lord's face, because he will not come into this place, nor bear the yoke of this place on himself.

Chapter 42

1 I saw the key-holders and guards of the gates of hell standing like great serpents. And their faces were glowing like extinguishing lamps, and I saw their eyes of fire, and their sharp teeth. And I saw all of the Lord's works, how they are right, while some of the works of man are of limited good, and others bad, and in their works are those who are known to speak evil lies.

Chapter 43

1 My children, I measured and wrote out every work and every measure and every righteous judgment.
2 As one year is more honorable than another, so is one man more honorable than another. Some men are honored for great possessions, some for wisdom of heart, some for particular intellect, some for skillfulness, one for silence of lip, another for cleanliness, one for strength, another for beauty, one for youth, another for sharp wit, one for shape of body, another for sensibility, but let it be heard everywhere: There is none better than he who fears God. He shall be more glorious in time to come.

Chapter 44
1 The Lord created man with his hands in the likeness of his own face. The Lord made him small and great.
2 Whoever reviles the ruler's face hates the Lord's face, and has contempt for the Lord's face, and he who vents anger on any man without having been injured by him, the Lord's great anger will cut him down, he who spits on the face of man reproachfully will be cut down at the Lord's great judgment.
3 Blessed is the man who does not direct his heart with malice against any man, and helps the injured and condemned, and raises up the broken down, and does charity to the needy, because on the day of the great judgment every weight, every measure and every makeweight will be as in the market, so they are hung on scales and stand in the market, and every one shall learn his own measure, and according to his measure shall take his reward.

(Note: Makeweight is something put on a scale to make up the required weight for a more precise measurement.)

Chapter 45
1 Whoever hurries to make offerings before the Lord's face, the Lord will hasten that offering by giving of His work.
2 But whoever increases his lamp before the Lord's face and makes a judgment that is not true, the Lord will not increase his treasure in the realm of the highest.

(Note: Whoever makes himself out to be more than he is and whoever judges others without truth or cause, the Lord will not reward in heaven.)

3 When the Lord demands bread, or candles, or the flesh of beasts, or any other sacrifice, it is nothing; but God demands pure hearts, and with all He does it is only the tests of man's heart.

Chapter 46
1 Hear, my people, and take in the words of my lips.
2 If any one brings any gifts to an earthly ruler, and has disloyal thoughts in his heart, and the ruler know this, will the ruler not be angry with him, and refuse his gifts, and give him over to judgment?
3 Or if one man makes himself appear good to another by deceit of the tongue, but has evil in his heart, then will the other person not understand the treachery of his heart, and condemned him, since his lie was plain to all?
4 And when the Lord shall send a great light, then there will be judgment for the just and the unjust, and no one shall escape notice.

Chapter 47
1 And now, my children, with your minds and your hearts, mark well the words of your father, which all have come to you from the Lord's lips.
2 Take these books of your father's writing and read them.
3 For there are many books, and in them you will learn all the Lord's works, all that has been from the beginning of creation, and will be until the end of time.
4 And if you will observe my writing, you will not sin against the Lord; because there is no other except the Lord in heaven, nor in earth, nor in the very lowest places, nor in the foundation.
5 The Lord has placed the foundations in the unknown, and has spread out heavens, both physical and spiritual; he anchored the earth on the waters, and created countless creatures. Who has counted the water and the foundation of the mutable (changeable, corruptible), or the dust of the earth, or the sand of the sea, or the drops of the rain, or the morning dew, or the wind's blowing (breathing)? Who has filled earth and sea, and the indestructible winter?
6 I (The Lord) cut the stars out of fire, and decorated heaven, and put it in their midst.

Chapter 48
1 The sun goes along the seven heavenly circles, which are the appointment of one hundred and eighty-two thrones. It goes down on a short day, and again one hundred and eighty-two. It goes down on a long day, and he has two thrones on which he rests, revolving here and there above the thrones of the months, from the seventeenth day of the month Tsivan it goes down to the month Thevan, from the seventeenth of Thevan it goes up.

(Note: The words Tsivan and Thevan refer to the summer and winter solstice, dividing the lengthening and shortening of days.
The sun goes in a sinusoidal wave, decreasing daylight time for 182 days and growing longer in daylight hours for 182 days, with an extra day, which is a long day. The total is 365 days.)

2 When it goes close to the earth, then the earth is glad and makes its fruits grow, and when it goes away, then the earth is sad, and trees and all fruits will not flower.

3 All this He measured, with good measurement of hours, and predetermined a measure by his wisdom, of the physical and the spiritual (realms).

4 From the spiritual realm he made all things that are physical, himself being spiritual.

5 So I teach you, my children, and tell you to distribute the books to your children, into all your generations, and among the nations who shall have the sense to fear God. Let them receive them, and may they come to love them more than any food or earthly sweets, and read them and apply themselves to them.

6 And those who do not understand the Lord, who do not fear God, who do not accept, but reject, who do not receive the books, a terrible judgment awaits these.

7 Blessed is the man who shall bear their yoke and shall drag them along, for he shall be released on the day of the great judgment.

Chapter 49

1 I swear to you, my children, but I do not swear by any oath, neither by heaven nor by earth, nor by any other creature created by God.

2 The Lord said: "There is no oath in Me, nor injustice, but only truth."

3 But there is no truth in men, so let them swear by the words, Yea, yea, or else, Nay, nay.

4 And I swear to you, yea, yea, that every man that has been in his mother's womb has had a place prepared for the repose of that soul, and a measure predetermined of how much it is intended that a man be tried (tested) in this world.

5 Yea, children, do not deceive yourselves, for there has been a place previously prepared for the soul of every man. *(A statement of predestination.)*

Chapter 50

1 I have put every man's work in writing and none born on earth can remain hidden nor his works remain concealed.

2 I see all things.

3 Therefore, my children, spend the number of your days in patience and meekness so that you may inherit eternal life.

4 For the sake of the Lord, endure every wound, every injury, every evil word, and every attack.

5 If your good deeds are not rewarded but returned for ill to you, do not repay them to neither neighbor nor enemy, because the Lord will return them for you and be your avenger on the day of great judgment, so that there should be no vengeance here among men.

6 Whoever of you spends gold or silver for his brother's sake, he will receive ample treasure in the world to come.

7 Do not injure widows or orphans or strangers, for if you do God's wrath will come upon you.

Chapter 51

1 Stretch out your hands to the poor according to your strength.

2 Do not hide your silver in the earth.

3 Help the faithful man in affliction, and affliction will not find you in the time of your trouble.

4 And bear every grievous and cruel yoke that comes upon you, for the sake of the Lord, and thus you will find your reward in the Day of Judgment.

5 It is good to go morning, midday, and evening into the Lord's house, for the glory of your creator.

6 Because every breathing thing glorifies him, and every creature, both physical and spiritual, gives him praise. (Gives His praise back to Him.)

Chapter 52

1 Blessed is the man who opens his lips in praise of God of Sabaoth (Host / army) and praises the Lord with his heart.

2 Cursed is every man who opens his lips for the purpose of bringing contempt and slander to (of) his neighbor, because he brings God into contempt.

3 Blessed is he who opens his lips blessing and praising God.

4 Cursed before the Lord all the days of his life, is he who opens his lips to curse and abuse.

5 Blessed is he who blesses all the Lord's works.

6 Cursed is he who brings the Lord's creation into contempt.

7 Blessed is he who looks down and raises the fallen.

8 Cursed is he who looks to and is eager for the destruction of what is not his.

9 Blessed is he who keeps the foundations of his fathers that were made firm from the beginning.

10 Cursed is he who corrupts the doctrine of his forefathers.

11 Blessed is he who imparts peace and love.

12 Cursed is he who disturbs those that love their neighbors.

13 Blessed is he who speaks with humble tongue and heart to all.

14 Cursed is he who speaks peace with his tongue, while in his heart there is no peace but a sword.

15 For all these things will be laid bare in the scales of balance and in the books, on the day of the great judgment.

Chapter 53

1 And now, my children, do not say: "Our father is standing before God, and is praying for our sins. For there is there no helper for any man who has sinned.

2 You see how I wrote down all of the works of every man, before his creation, all that is done among all men for all time, and none can tell or relate my writing, because the Lord sees all imaginings of man, and how they are empty and prideful, where they lie in the treasure houses of the heart.
3 And now, my children, mark well all the words of your father that I tell you, or you will be regretful, saying: Why did our father not tell us?

(Note: although chapters 51 and 52 seem similar to the Sermon on the Mount, Chapter 53 offers no balance between mercy and justice. "There is no helper for any man who has sinned," is a statement excluding a savior. Scholars point to this verse to conclude 2 Enoch is a Jewish text. As stated before, 2 Enoch seems to be a Jewish text that was Christianized by additions and embellishment of the core text. Chapter 53 is part of the core Jewish text, likely written before the Christian sect. Verse 2 is a statement of predestination or foreknowledge.)

Chapter 54
1 Let these books, which I have given you, be for an inheritance of your peace in that time that you do not understand things.
2 Hand them to all who want them, and instruct them, that they may see the Lord's very great and marvelous works.

Chapter 55
1 My children, behold, the day of my determined period (term and time) has approached.
2 For the angels who shall go with me are standing before me and urge me to my departure from you. They are standing here on earth, awaiting what has been told them.
3 For tomorrow I shall go up to heaven, to the uppermost Jerusalem, to my eternal inheritance.
4 Therefore I bid you to do the Lord's good pleasure before his face at all times.

(Note: The Jerusalem spoken of here is the spiritual Jerusalem, spoken of by John, coming down from heaven. The name, "Jerusalem" refers to the components of the actual name, which break down to mean "provision" and "peace".)

Chapter 56"
1 Methuselah answered his father Enoch, and said: What (food) is agreeable to your eyes, father, that I may prepare before your face, that you may bless our houses, and your sons, and that your people may be made glorious through you, and then that you may depart, as the Lord said?"
2 Enoch answered his son Methuselah and said: "Hear me, my child. From the time when the Lord anointed me with the ointment of his glory, there has

been no food in me, and my soul remembers not earthly enjoyment, neither do I want anything earthly."

Chapter 57
1 My child Methuselah, summon all your brethren and all of your household and the elders of the people, that I may talk to them and depart, as is planned for me.
2 And Methuselah hurried, and summoned his brethren, Regim, Riman, Uchan, Chermion, Gaidad, and all the elders of the people before the face of his father Enoch; and he blessed them, and said to them:

Chapter 58
1 "Listen to me, my children, today.
2 In those days when the Lord came down to earth for Adam's sake, and visited all his creatures, which he created himself, after all these he created Adam, and the Lord called all the beasts of the earth, all the reptiles, and all the birds that soar in the air, and brought them all before the face of our father Adam.
3 And Adam gave names to all things living on earth.
4 And the Lord appointed him ruler over all, and subjected all things to him under his hands, and made them dumb and made them dull that they would be commanded by man, and be in subjection and obedience to him.
5 The Lord also created every man lord over all his possessions.
6 The Lord will not judge a single soul of beast for man's sake, but He judges the souls of men through their beasts in this world, for men have a special place.
7 And as every soul of man is according to number, similarly beasts will not perish, nor all souls of beasts which the Lord created, until the great judgment, and they will accuse man, if he did not feed them well.

Chapter 59
1 Whoever defiles the soul of beasts, defiles his own soul.
2 For man brings clean animals to make sacrifice for sin, that he may have cure for his soul.
3 And if they bring clean animals and birds for sacrifice, man has a cure. He cures his soul.
4 All is given you for food, bind it by the four feet, to make good the cure.
5 But whoever kills beast without wounds, kills his own souls and defiles his own flesh.
6 And he who does any beast any injury whatsoever, in secret, it is an evil practice, and he defiles his own soul.

(Note: To kill without a wound is to inflict blunt force trauma - to beat them to death.)

Chapter 60
1 He who works the killing of a man's soul (he who murders), kills his own soul, and kills his own body, and there is no cure for him for all time.
2 He who puts a man in any snare (moral entrapment), shall stick himself in it, and there is no cure for him for all time.
3 He who puts a man in any vessel, his retribution will not be wanting at the great judgment for all time.
4 He who works dishonestly or speaks evil against any soul, will not make justice for himself for all time.

Chapter 61
1 And now, my children, keep your hearts from every injustice, which the Lord hates. Just as a man asks something for his own soul from God, so let him do the same to every living soul, because I know all things, how in the great time to come there is a great inheritance prepared for men, good for the good, and bad for the bad, no matter the number.
2 Blessed are those who enter the good houses, for in the bad houses there is no peace or return from them.
3 Hear, my children, small and great! When man puts a good thought in his heart, it brings gifts from his labors before the Lord's face. But if his hands did not make them, then the Lord will turn away his face from the labor of his hand, and (that) man cannot find the labor of his hands.
4 And if his hands made it, but his heart murmurs (complains), and his heart does not stop murmurs incessantly, he does not have (gain) any advantage.

Chapter 62
1 Blessed is the man who, in his patience, brings his gifts with faith before the Lord's face, because he will find forgiveness of sins.
2 But if he takes back his words before the time, there is no repentance for him; and if the time passes and he does not of his own will perform what is promised, there is no repentance after death.
3 Because every work which man does before the time (outside the time he has promised it), is all deceit before men, and sin before God.

Chapter 63
1 When man clothes the naked and fills the hungry, he will find reward from God.
2 But if his heart complains, he commits a double evil; ruin of himself and of that which he gives; and for him there will be no finding of reward because of that.
3 And if his own heart is filled with his food and his own flesh is clothed with his own clothing, he commits contempt, and will forfeit all his endurance of poverty, and will not find reward of his good deeds. (If he is selfish and does not add to the economy of others…)

4 Every proud and pontificating man is hateful to the Lord, and every false speech is clothed in lies. It will be cut with the blade of the sword of death, and thrown into the fire, and shall burn for all time.

Chapter 64
1 When Enoch had spoken these words to his sons, all people far and near heard how the Lord was calling Enoch. They took counsel together:
2 Let us go and kiss Enoch, and two thousand men came together and came to the place called Achuzan, where Enoch was with his sons.
3 And the elders of the people with the entire assembly came and bowed down and began to kiss Enoch and said to him:
4 "Our father Enoch, may you be blessed by the Lord, the eternal ruler, and now bless your sons and all the people, that we may be glorified today before your face.
5 For you shall be glorified before the Lord's face for eternity, since the Lord chose you from among all men on earth, and designated you as the writer of all his creation, both physical and spiritual, and you are redeemed from the sins of man, and are the helper of your household."

Chapter 65
1 And Enoch said to all his people: "Hear me, my children. Before all creatures were created, the Lord created the physical and spiritual things.
2 And then a long term passed. Then after all of that he created man in the likeness of his own form, and put eyes into him to see, and ears into him to hear, and a heart to reflect, and intellect to enable him to deliberate.
3 And the Lord saw all the works of man, and created all his creatures, and divided time. From time he determined the years, and from the years he appointed the months, and from the months he appointed the days, and of days he appointed seven.
4 And in those he appointed the hours, measured them out exactly, that man might reflect on time and count years, months, and hours, as they alternate from beginning to end, so that he might count his own life from the beginning until death, and reflect on his sin and write his works, both bad and good. No work is hidden from the Lord, so that every man might know his works and never transgress all his commandments, and keep my writing from generation to generation.
5 When all creation, both physical and spiritual, as the Lord created it, shall end, then every man goes to the great judgment, and then all time shall be destroyed along with the years. And from then on there will be neither months nor days nor hours. They will run together and will not be counted.

6 There will be one eon (age), and all the righteous who shall escape the Lord's great judgment, shall be collected in the great eon (age). For the righteous the great eon will begin, and they will live eternally, and there will be no labor, nor sickness, nor humiliation, nor anxiety, nor need, nor brutality, nor night, nor darkness, but great light among them.

7 And they shall have a great indestructible wall, and a paradise that is bright and eternal, for all mortal things shall pass away, and there will be eternal life.

(Note: an eon is one billion years but is used to mean a very long but indefinite period of time. The word "eternal" means "unchanging, incorruptible, immortal." The word used for "mortal" is the opposite of "eternal", thus, "mortal, corruptible, changing.")

Chapter 66

1 And now, my children, keep your souls from all injustice the Lord hates.

2 Walk before his face with great fear (respect) and trembling and serve him only.

3 Bow down to the true God, not to dumb idols, but bow down to his likeness, and bring all just offerings before the Lord's face. The Lord hates what is unjust.

(Note: This is an odd command issued by Enoch, that the people are not to bow to dumb idols but are to bow to the likeness or similitude of God. This was likely added by Christians around the third or fourth centuries A.D.)

4 For the Lord sees all things; when man takes thought in his heart, then he counsels the intellects, and every thought is always before the Lord, who made firm the earth and put all creatures on it.

5 If you look to heaven, the Lord is there; if you take thought of the sea's depth and all under the earth, the Lord is there.

6 For the Lord created all things. Bow not down to things made by man, leaving the Lord of all creation, because no work can remain hidden before the Lord's face.

7 Walk, my children, in long-suffering, in meekness, honesty, in thoughtfulness, in grief, in faith and in truth. Walk in (rely on) promises, in (times of) illness, in abuse, in wounds, in temptation, in nakedness, in privation, loving one another, until you go out from this age of ills, that you become inheritors of endless time.

8 Blessed are the just who shall escape the great judgment, for they shall shine forth more than the sun sevenfold, for in this world the seventh part is taken off from all, light, darkness, food, enjoyment, sorrow, paradise, torture, fire, frost, and other things; he put all down in writing, that you might read and understand.

Chapter 67

1 When Enoch had talked to the people, the Lord sent out darkness on to the earth, and there was darkness, and it covered those men standing with Enoch, and they took Enoch up on to the highest heaven, where the Lord is. And there God received him and placed him before His face, and the darkness went off from the earth, and light came again.

2 And the people saw and did not understand how Enoch had been taken, and they glorified God, and found a scroll in which was written "The God of the Spiritual." Then all went to their dwelling places.

Chapter 68

1 Enoch was born on the sixth day of the month Tsivan (the first month of the year), and lived three hundred and sixty-five years.

2 He was taken up to heaven on the first day of the month Tsivan and remained in heaven sixty days.

3 He wrote all these signs of all creation, which the Lord created, and wrote three hundred and sixty-six books, and handed them over to his sons and remained on earth thirty days, and was again taken up to heaven on the sixth day of the month Tsivan, on the very day and hour when he was born.

4 As every man's nature in this life is dark, so are also his conception, birth, and departure from this life.

5 At what hour he was conceived, at that hour he was born, and at that hour also he died.

6 Methuselah and his brethren, all the sons of Enoch, made haste, and erected an altar at that place called Achuzan, where Enoch had been taken up to heaven.

7 And they took sacrificial oxen and summoned all people and sacrificed the sacrifice before the Lord's face.

8 All people, the elders of the people and the whole assembly came to the feast and brought gifts to the sons of Enoch.

9 And they made a great feast, rejoicing and making merry three days, praising God, who had given them such a sign through Enoch, who had found favor with him, and that they should hand it on to their sons from generation to generation, from age to age. Amen.

(Note: Enoch was born on the 6th day of Tsivan. Tsivan is the first month of the year. The sum is seven, one of the holy numbers. He lived 365 years. One year of years. He remained in heaven 60 days. Six is the number of man, which always falls short of God.)

The Short Version Ends Here

The wife of Nir was Sopanim. She was sterile and never had at any time given birth to a child by Nir. Sopanim was in her old age and in the last days (time) of her death. She conceived in her womb, but Nir the priest had not slept with her from the day that that the Lord had appointed him to conduct the liturgy in front of the face of the people.

When Sopanim saw her pregnancy, she was ashamed and embarrassed, and she hid herself during all the days until she gave birth. Not one of the people knew about it. When 282 days had been completed, and the day of birth had begun to approach, Nir thought about his wife, and he called her to come to him in his house, so that he might converse with her. *(282 days is 9.4 of 30-day-months.)*

Sopanim came to Nir, her husband; and, behold, she was pregnant, and the day appointed for giving birth was drawing near. Nir saw her and became very ashamed. He said to her, "What is this that you have done, O wife? Why have you disgraced me in front of the face of these people? Now, depart from me and go back to where you began this disgrace of your womb, so that I might not defile my hands in front of The Face of The Lord on account of you and sin."

Sopanim spoke to her husband, Nir, saying, "O my lord! Look at me. It is the time of my old age, the day of my death has arrived. I do not understand how my menopause and the barrenness of my womb have been reversed." But Nir did not believe his wife, and for the second time he said to her, "Depart from me, or else I might assault you, and commit a sin in front of the face of The Lord."

And after Nir had spoken to his wife, Sopanim, she fell down at Nir's feet and died. Nir was extremely distressed and said to himself, "Could this have happened because of my words? And now, merciful is The Eternal Lord, because my hand was not upon her."

The archangel Gabriel appeared to Nir, and said to him, "Do not think that your wife Sopanim has died due to your error? This child, which is to be born from her, is a righteous fruit, and one whom I shall receive into paradise so that you will not be the father of a gift of God."

Nir hurried and shut the door of his house. He went to Noah, his brother, and he reported to him everything that had happened in connection with his wife. Noah hurried to the room of his brother. The appearance of his brother's wife was as if she were dead but her womb was at the same time giving birth.

Noah said to Nir, "Don't let yourself be sorrowful, Nir, my brother! Today the Lord has covered up our scandal, because nobody from the people knows this. Now let us go quickly and bury her, and the Lord will cover up the scandal of our shame." They placed Sopanim on the bed, wrapped her around with black garments, and shut the door. They dug a grave in secret.

When they had gone out toward the grave, a child came out from Sopanim's dead body and sat on the bed at her side. Noah and Nir came in to bury Sopanim and they saw the child sitting beside Sopanim's dead body and he was wiping his clothing. Noah and Nir were very terrified with a great fear, because the child was physically fully developed. The child spoke with his lips and blessed The Lord. Noah and Nir looked at him closely, saying, "This is from the Lord, my brother." The badge of priesthood is on his chest, and it is glorious in appearance. Noah said to Nir, "God is renewing the priesthood from blood related to us, just as He pleases."

Noah and Nir hurried and washed the child, they dressed him in the garments of the priesthood, and they gave him bread to eat and he ate it. And they called him Melchizedek.

Noah and Nir lifted up the body of Sopanim, and took the black garment off of her and washed her. They clothed her in exceptionally bright garments and built a grave for her. Noah, Nir, and Melchizedek came and they buried her publicly. Then Noah said to his brother Nir, "Take care of this child in secret until the proper time comes, because all of the people on earth will become treacherous and they will begin to turn away from God. Having become completely ignorant (of God), when they see him, they will put him to death in some way."

Then Noah went away to his own place, and there came great lawlessness that began to become abundant over all the earth in the days of Nir. And Nir began to worry greatly about the child saying, "What will I do with him?" And stretching out his hands toward heaven, Nir called out to The Lord, saying, " It is miserable for me, Eternal Lord, that all of this lawlessness has begun to become abundant over all the earth in my lifetime! I realize how much nearer our end is because of the lawlessness of the people. And now, Lord, what is the vision about this child, and what is his destiny, or what will I do for him, so that he will not be joined along with us in this destruction?"

The Lord took notice of Nir and appeared to him in a night vision. And He said to him, "Nir, the great lawlessness which has come about on the earth I shall not tolerate anymore. I plan to send down a great destruction onto the earth. But do not worry about the child, Nir. In a short while I will send My archangel

Gabriel and he will take the child and put him in the paradise of Edem. He will not perish along with those who must perish. As I have revealed it, Melchizedek will be My priest to all holy priests, I will sanctify him and I will establish him so that he will be the head of the priests of the future."

(Note: Edem means, "God will save." It is assumed Edem is Eden.)

Then Nir arose from his sleep and blessed The Lord, who had appeared to him saying: "Blessed be The Lord, The God of my fathers, who has approved of my priesthood and the priesthood of my fathers, because by His Word, He has created a great priest in the womb of Sopanim, my wife. For I have no descendants. So let this child take the place of my descendants and become as my own son. You will count him in the number of your servants."

"Therefore honor him together with your servants and great priests and me your servant, Nir. And behold, Melchizedek will be the head of priests in another generation. I know that great confusion has come and in confusion this generation will come to an end, and everyone will perish, except that Noah, my brother, will be preserved for procreation. From his tribe, there will arise numerous people, and Melchizedek will become the head of priests reigning over a royal people who will serve you, O Lord."

It happened when the child had completed 40 days in Nir's tent, The Lord said to the archangel Gabriel, "Go down to the earth to Nir the priest, and take the child Melchizedek, who is with him. Place him in the paradise of Edem for preservation. For the time is already approaching, and I will pour out all the water onto the earth, and everything that is on the earth will perish. And I will raise it up again, and Melchizedek will be the head of the priests in that generation." And Gabriel hurried, and came flying down when it was night when Nir was sleeping on his bed that night.

Gabriel appeared to him and said to him, "The Lord says: "Nir! Restore the child to me whom I entrusted to you." But Nir did not realize who was speaking to him and he was confused. And he said, "When the people find out about the child, they will seize him and kill him, because the heart of these people are deceitful before The Lord." And he answered Gabriel and said, "The child is not with me, and I don't know who is speaking to me."

Gabriel answered him, " Nir, do not be afraid. I am the archangel Gabriel. The Lord sent me to take your child today. I will go with him and I will place him in the paradise of Edem." Then Nir remembered the first dream and believed it. He answered Gabriel, "Blessed be The Lord, who has sent you to me today! Now bless your servant Nir! Take the child and do to him all that has been said to you." And Gabriel took the child, Melchizedek on his wings in that same night, and he placed him in the paradise of Edem. Nir got up in the morning, and he went into his tent and did not find the child. There was great joy and grief for Nir because he felt the child had the place of a son.

The Lord said to Noah, "Make an ark that is 300 cubits in length, 50 cubits in width and in 30 cubits height. Put the entrance to the ark in its side; and make it with two stories in the middle" The Lord God opened the doors of heaven. Rain came onto the earth and all flesh died.

Noah fathered 3 sons: Shem, Ham and Japheth. He went into the ark in his six hundredth year. After the flood, he lived 350 years. He lived in all 950 years, according to The Lord our God.
To our God be Glory always, now and eternally.
AMEN.

Introduction of 3 Enoch

Author's Note: The Hebrew Book of Enoch, or 3 Enoch was very difficult to find in its entirety. It was likely written by a highly educated Rabbi around 300 to 400 A.D. and preserved only in fragments, here and there. Then, in 1928 Dr. Hugo Odeberg PhD. gathered the various fragmentary sources and published the first full translation along with copious scholarly notes and the source Hebrew material. The University Press at Cambridge, in the United Kingdom, published his work. A photocopy of the book made its way to the United State and into the University of Chicago library, where it was kept for many years. It was from this body of work and from this photocopied and preserved manuscript that some of the Hebrew language source material was compiled. The Hebrew source from the work at Cambridge was compared to and supplemented with various articles, fragments, quotes, and commentaries from dozens of other sources and references to produce the work before you.

3 Enoch purports to have been written around 100 AD., but its origins can only be traced to the late fourth or early fifth centuries. Other names for 3 Enoch include "The Third Book of Enoch" and "The Book of the Palaces."

The book is rife with Hebrew words, which have no single English equivalent. Even though care was taken to define the majority of these words when first they appear in the text, the reader should expect only keywords to replace or augment meanings thereafter. To do otherwise would either leave the reader to remember the meanings of all Hebrew words or bloat the book to the point of making it difficult for the reader to follow.

Modern scholars describe this book as belonging to a body of work called the pseudepigraphia. 3 Enoch claims to be written by a Rabbi, who became a 'high priest' after he had visions of an ascension to Heaven, 90 AD - 135 AD. Rabbi Ishmael is a leading figure of Merkabah literature; however, a number of scholars suggest that it was in fact written by a number of people over a prolonged period of time.

Merkabah writings had to do with the theme of ascension into heaven. The name is derived from a Hebrew word meaning "chariot," referring to Ezekiel's vision beginning in Ezekiel 1:4. Enoch's contents and ideas are unique and newer than those shown in other Merkabah texts, suggesting the book may be among the first in the Merkabah movement or that it is derived through unique influences.

As the book's other name, The Book of the Palaces, implies, 3 Enoch is part of the Temple or Hekalot body of literature in which the "Palace" or "Temple" of heaven is described.

As with 1 Enoch, the exact dating of this book is a difficult task, but some scholars believe it was completed around the time of the Babylonian Talmud, which was around the early 5th century A.D.

3 Enoch was originally written in Hebrew, although it contains a number of words from both Greek and Latin. Parts of the book seem to have been influenced by 1 Enoch, showing the author was familiar with the Mystical Enochian Tradition.

Similar points appearing in 1 Enoch and 3 Enoch are:
Enoch ascends to Heaven in a storm chariot (3 Enoch 6:1; 7:1)
Enoch is translated into an angel (3 Enoch 9:1-5; 15:1-2)
Enoch, as an angel, is given authority in Heaven (3 Enoch 10:1- 3; 16:1)
Enoch receives an explanation or vision of creation and cosmology. (3 Enoch 13:1-2)
Enoch sees a hostile angel named Azazel (3 Enoch 4:6; 5:9)

The main theme, throughout the book is the "transubstantiation" of Enoch into the angel Metatron.

Metatron appears in various Jewish, Christian, and Islamic works but was a central focus in medieval Jewish mystical texts and occult sources. Rabbinical texts point to Metatron as the angel who stilled the hand of Abraham, preventing him from sacrificing Isaac.

The place and authority of Metatron has been hotly debated, as is seen even within the book. He is seen as sitting in heaven. This is only permitted if one is a deity. He is referred to in the text as "The Lesser YHWH."

YHWH makes up the Tetragrammaton forming the name we pronounce as "Yahweh" or "Jehovah." The four letters making up the divine name are Yodh, He Waw, He, having the sounds of "Y", "H", "W, O, U or a place holder", and "H." When "He" ends a word it is often silent. Due to the fact that German theologians were heavily involved in theological research and study, one may also find the Tetragrammaton rendered as YHVH, since the V in German has a W sound.

There is a very personal attack within the text, which should be explained. A curse is placed on a man known only as Acher. In Hebrew the name means, "the other," and is used as a term of alienation from the rabbinic community. The Talmud tells us that Elisha be Abuyah entered Paradise in a vision and saw Metatron sitting down (an action that in heaven is permitted only to God himself). Elishah ben Abuyah therefore looked to Metatron as a deity and proclaimed, "There are indeed two powers in heaven!" The other rabbis explain that Metatron was allowed to sit because he was the Heavenly Scribe, writing down the deeds of Israel (Babylonian Talmud, Hagiga 15a).

The intense hatred for any idea hinting at dualism or polytheism, as opposed to monotheism, caused such a reaction within the Rabbinical community that they labeled Elisha be Abuyah a heretic. In 3 Enoch this point is driven home when the entire nation of Israel is to be reconciled to God, except for Acher, whose name is blotted out.

In spite of the disagreements within the ancient Jewish community, the reader is still left to wonder what position Metatron occupies in heaven. Metatron is described in two ways: as a primordial angel (9:2–13:2) and as the transformation of Enoch after he was assumed into Heaven, and he is called "The Lesser YHWH."

Enoch walked with God; then he was no more, because God took him away. [Genesis 5:24 NIV.] This Enoch, whose flesh was turned to flame, his veins to fire, his eye-lashes to flashes of lightning, his eye-balls to flaming torches, and whom God placed on a throne next to the throne of glory, received after this heavenly transformation the name Metatron. [3 Enoch]

As the Christian community came in contact with the Jewish book of 3 Enoch, they had little trouble reconciling the names and position of Metatron. To those Christians a person who may sit in heaven and who judges, and who is called by the same name taken by God must be Yeshua (Jesus.)

It may be of help if the meaning of the name, Metatron, could be ascertained, but it is not clear. Suggestions are that the name originated from the root words of such phrases as, "keeper of the watch," "guard," "to protect," "one who serves behind the throne," "one who occupies the throne next to the throne of glory," "to lead," or " to measure." None of these suggestions can be proven. From the text itself we know only that Metatron is referred to as "the youth," likely because he would be the newest and youngest angel. He is also called, "the prince of the presence (of God)." His purpose in heaven was to be a witness against mankind.

A type of numerology is used and referred to within the text. Temurah is one of the three ancient methods used by Cabbalist to rearrange words and sentences in the Torah, in the belief that by this method they can derive the deeper, hidden spiritual meaning of the words. Temurah may be used to change letters in certain words to create a new meaning for a Biblical statement. Another method is called Gematria. In this method letters are substituted for numbers and the meaning of words with the same value are compared along with the numerical meaning of the words.

A preparatory summery of the first section of the book may be framed as a revelation from Metatron, or the Prince of the Presence, to Rabbi Ishmael. Metatron, as it turns out, is Enoch and this is why the title of this book has come to be called, "3 Enoch." Any question as to who Metatron may be is answered clearly in CHAPTER IV, where it is written, "Rabbi Ishmael said: I asked Metatron and said to him: " why are you called by the name of your Creator, by seventy names? You are greater than all the princes, higher than all the angels, beloved more than all the servants, honored above all the mighty ones in kingship, greatness and glory: why do they call you 'Youth' in the high heavens?" He answered and said to me: "Because I am Enoch, the son of Jared. For when the generation of the flood sinned and were confounded in their deeds, saying unto God: Depart from us, for we desire not the knowledge of your ways (Job 21:14), then the Holy One, blessed be He, removed me from their midst to be a witness against them in the high heavens to all the inhabitants of the world, that they may not say: 'The Merciful One is cruel'.

The following text begins the book of 3 Enoch. Notes and explanations are italicized. Words placed in parentheses are alternate renderings of a word or phrase

The Third Book of Enoch
or the Hebrew Book of Enoch
By Rabbi ISHMAEL BEN ELISHA
THE HIGH PRIEST

CHAPTER I
INTRODUCTION: Rabbi Ishmael ascends to heaven to witness the vision of the Merkaba (chariot). He is given to Metatron

AND ENOCH WALKED WITH GOD: AND HE WAS NOT;
FOR GOD TOOK HIM.
(1) I ascended on high to witness the vision of the Merkaba (the divine chariot) and I had entered the six Halls, which were situated within one another.

The halls were in concentric circles, one within the other.

(2) As soon as I reached the door of the Seventh Hall I stood still in prayer before the Holy One, blessed be He. I lifted up my eyes on high towards the Divine Majesty and I said: (3) " Lord of the Universe, I pray you, that the worthiness of Aaron, the son of Amram, who loves and pursues peace, and who received the crown of priesthood from Your Glory on Mount Sinai, be upon me in this hour, so that Khafsiel, (Qafsiel) the prince, and the angels with him may not overcome (overpower) me nor cast me down from the heavens."

Qafsiel or Qaphsiel is an angel of a high order set to guard the seventh hall of heaven

(4) At that moment the Holy One, blessed be He, sent Metatron, his Servant, also called Ebed, to me. He is the angel, the Prince of the Presence. With great joy he spread his wings as he came to meet me in order to save me from their hand. (5) And by his hand he took me so that they could see us, and he said to me: "Enter in peace before the high and exalted King and see the picture of Merkaba (chariot)."

Merkaba (chariot) – Chariot of fire, Chariot of light - Pulled by four Chayot or living creatures, each of which has four wings and the four faces of a man, lion, ox, and eagle.. See Ezekiel 1:4-26. The Bible makes mention of three types of angel found in the Merkaba (chariot) . The first is the "Seraphim" (lit. "burning") angels. These angels appear like flashes of fire continuously ascending and descending. These "Seraphim" angels powered the movement of the chariot. In the hierarchy of these angels, "Seraphim" are the highest, that is, closest to God, followed by the "Chayot", which are followed by the "Ophanim." The chariot is in a constant state of motion, and the energy behind this movement runs according to this hierarchy. The movement of the "Ophanim" are controlled by the

"Chayot" while the movement of the "Chayot" is controlled by the "Seraphim." The movement of all the angels of the chariot are controlled by the "Likeness of a Man" on the Throne.

(6) Then I entered the seventh Hall, and he led me to the camps of Shekina (understanding) and stood me in front of the Holy One, blessed be He, to see the Merkaba (chariot).

Shekina - Shekhinah is derived from a Hebrew verb literally meaning "to settle, inhabit, or dwell." (See Exodus 40:35, "Moses could not enter the Tent of Meeting, for the cloud rested [shakhan] upon it, and the glory of the Lord filled the Tabernacle." See also Genesis 9:27, 14:13, Psalms 37:3, Jeremiah 33:16), as well as the weekly Shabbat blessing recited in the Temple ("May He who causes His name to dwell [shochan] in this House, cause to dwell among you love and brotherliness, peace and friendship"). Also see Talmud Ketubot 85b). Shekina can also mean royalty or royal residence. Shekina has come to mean the effect or manifestation caused by the presence or inhabitation of God. The manifestation is glory, creativity, and understanding. These words may be used to explain "Shekinu."

(7) As soon as the princes of the Merkaba (chariot) and the flaming Seraphim knew I was there, they fixed their gaze on me. Trembling and shuddering seized me at once and I fell down and was numbed by the brightness of the vision of their faces; until the Holy One, blessed be He, chastised them, saying: (8)" My servants, my Seraphim, my Cherubim and my Ophannim! Cover your eyes before Ishmael, my son, my friend, my beloved one and (my) glory, so that he ceases trembling and shaking! "

The root of Seraphim comes either from the Hebrew verb saraph ('to burn') or the Hebrew noun saraph (a fiery, flying serpent). Because the term appears several times with reference to the serpents encountered in the wilderness (Num. 21.8, Deut. 8.15; Isa. 14.29; 30.6), it has often been understood to refer to "fiery serpents." From this it has also often been proposed that the seraphim were serpentine in form and in some sense "fiery" creatures or associated with fire.
It is said that whoever lays eyes on a Seraph, he would instantly be incinerated due to the immense brightness of the Seraph.
Cherubs are described as winged beings. The biblical prophet Ezekiel describes the cherubim as a tetrad of living creatures, each having four faces: of a lion, an ox, an eagle, and a man. They are said to have the stature and hands of a man, the feet of a calf, and four wings. Two of the wings extended upward, meeting above and sustaining the throne of God; while the other two stretched downward and covered the creatures themselves.

Ophanim are described in 1 Enoch as never sleeping. They watch and guard the throne of God.The word ophan means "wheel" in Hebrew. For this reason the Ophanim have been associated with the chariot in Ezekiel and Daniel. It is mentioned as gagal, traditionally "the wheels of gagallin", in "fiery flame" and "burning fire" of the four, eye-covered wheels, each composed of two nested wheels, that move next to the winged Cherubim, beneath the throne of God. The four wheels move with the Cherubim because the spirit of the Cherubim is in them. These are also referred to as the "many-eyed ones" in 2 Enoch. The Ophanim are also equated as the "Thrones", and associated with the "Wheels", in the vision of Daniel 7:9. They carry the throne of God, hence the name.
This may be a good time to explain the singular and plural in Hebrew. Whereas in English we add an "s" to denote a plural, in Hebrew an "im" is added. Thus, there is one Cherub but many Cherubim. There is one Seraph but many Seraphim. Knowing this fact may make the text easier to follow.

(9) Then Metatron, the Prince of the Presence, came and placed my spirit in me again and he stood me up on my feet. (10) After that (moment) for an hour I did not have enough strength to sing a song before the Throne of Glory of the Glorious King, the mightiest of all kings, the most excellent of all princes. (11) After an hour had passed the Holy One, blessed be He, opened the gates of Shekina (understanding) to me. These are the gates of Peace, and of Wisdom, and of Strength, and of Power, and of Speech (Dibbur), and of Song, and of Kedushah (Sacred Salutation of Holy, Holy, Holy), and the gates of Chanting. (12) And he opened and shined His light in my eyes and my heart by words of psalm, song, praise, exaltation, thanksgiving, extolment, glorification, hymn and eulogy (to speak well of). And as I opened my mouth, singing a song before the Holy One, blessed be He the Holy Chayoth beneath and above the Throne of Glory answered and said (chanted the prayer): "HOLY!" "BLESSED BE THE GLORY OF YHWH FROM HIS PLACE!."

The Chayot (or Chayyot) are a class of Merkabah, or Jewish Mystical Angels, reported in Ezekeil's vision of the Merkabah and its surrounding angels as recorded in the first chapter of the Book of Ezekiel describing his vision by the river Chebar.

Kedushah (Sacred Salutation of Holy, Holy, Holy) is a call to greet and glorify God. KODOISH, KODOISH, KODOISH ADONAI 'TSEBAYOTH: "Holy, Holy, Holy, is the Lord God of Hosts."
This is the Sacred Salutation, the Kedushah (Sacred Salutation of Holy, Holy, Holy), which is used by all the heavenly hosts to worship The Father before His Throne.

CHAPTER 2
The highest classes of angels make inquiries about Rabbi Ishmael, which are answered by Metatron

Rabbi Ishmael said:
(1) Within the hour the eagles of The Chariot (Merkaba), the flaming Ophannim and the Seraphim of consuming fire asked Metatron: (2) "Youth! Why do you permit one born of woman to enter and see the chariot (Merkaba)? From which nation and from which tribe is this one? What is his nature?" (3) Metatron answered and said to them: "From the nation of Israel whom the Holy One, blessed be He, chose for his people from among seventy tongues (nations of the world). He is from the tribe of Levi, whom He set aside as a contribution to his name. He is from the seed of Aaron whom the Holy One, blessed be He, chose for his servant and He put upon him the crown of priesthood on Sinai." (4) Then they spoke and said: "Happy is the people (nation) that is in that position!" (Ps. 144:15).

CHAPTER 3
Metatron has 70 names, but God calls him 'Youth'

Rabbi Ishmael said:
(1) In that hour I asked Metatron, the angel, the Prince of the Presence: "What is your name?" (2) He answered me: "I have seventy names, corresponding to the seventy nations of the world and all of them are based upon the name Metatron, angel of the Presence; but my King calls me 'Youth' (Naar)."

Seventy tongues represent the seventy nations or the entirety of the known world.
It is likely the word "youth" is used because Metatron is the newest and youngest being in heaven.
The seventy names are derived from the divine name or the Tetragrammaton – YHWH. Yah is a shortened version of this, meaning "God."

CHAPTER 4

Metatron is Enoch who was translated to heaven at the time of the flood.

Rabbi Ishmael said:
(1) I asked Metatron and said to him: "why does your Creator call you by seventy names? You are greater than all the princes, higher than all the angels, beloved more than all the servants, honored above all the mighty ones in kingship, greatness and glory, so why do they in the high heavens call you 'Youth'? (2) He answered and said to me: "Because I am Enoch, the son of Jared. (3) When the generation of the flood sinned and were twisted and contorted in their deeds, saying unto God: "Depart from us! We do not want

the knowledge of your ways," (See Job 21:14), then the Holy One, blessed be He, removed me from their midst so that I could be a witness against them in the high heavens to all the inhabitants of the world, so that they can not say: 'The Merciful One is cruel'. (4) "What sin did all those throngs of their wives, their sons and their daughters, their horses, their mules and their cattle and their property, and all the birds of the world commit so that the Holy One, blessed be He, destroyed the world, together with them in the waters of the flood?" They cannot say: "What in the generation of the flood sinned and what sin did they do so that the beasts and the birds should perish with them?" (5) Then the Holy One, blessed be He, lifted me up in their lifetime in their sight to be a witness against them to the future world. And the Holy One, blessed be He, assigned me to be a prince and a ruler among the ministering angels.

This chapter lays out the purpose of 3 Enoch and why it is so named. Metatron confirms that he is indeed Enoch, who was taken to heaven, translated into the being, Metatron, His primary purpose was to be a witness against man's sin on earth. When man or angel asked what sin was committed that all on earth should be destroyed, Enoch, now known as Metatron, would be a witness.

(6) In that hour three of the ministering angels, UZZA, 'AZZA and AZZAEL came out and accused me in the high heavens in front of the Holy One, blessed be He: And they said, "The Progenitors, The Ancient Ones, said before You with justification: Do not create man! The Holy One, blessed be He, answered and said unto them: "I have made and I will bear, and yes, I will carry and will deliver." (7) As soon as they saw me, they said before Him: "Lord of the Universe! What is this one that he should ascend to the highest heights? Is he not one from among the sons of those who perished in the days of the Flood? What is he doing in the Raqia (firmament / heavens)." What business does he have being in heaven?

Some sources have the names of the angels include Mal'aki or Mamlaketi. Azzael is one of the ten heads of the heavenly Sanhedrin. Rabbinical sources have Azza and Azzael as giants. All three are said to be agents of evil who accuse man of sins. These are the fallen angels. Another theory is that Azza and Azzael are not individual angels but are orders of angels.

Raquia is a key Hebrew word in Genesis 1:6–8a. It is translated "firmament" in the King James Version and "expanse" in most Hebrew dictionaries and modern translations. Raqa means to spread out, beat out, or hammer as one would a malleable metal. It can also mean "plate." The Greek Septuagint translated raqia 16 out of 17 times with

the Greek word stereoma, which means "a firm or solid structure." The Latin Vulgate (A.D. 382) used the Latin term "firmamentum," which also denotes solidness and firmness. The King James translators coined the word "firmament" because there was no single word equivalent in English. Today, "firmament" is usually used poetically to mean sky, atmosphere, or heavens. In modern Hebrew, raqia means sky or heavens. However, originally it probably meant something solid or firm that was spread out.

Azzael is likely the same being as Azazel, the accuser angel who was the leader of the fallen ones. Etymology connects the word with the mythological "Uza" and "Azael", the fallen angels, to whom a reference is believed to be found in Gen. 6:2,4. In accordance with this etymology, the sacrifice of the goat atones for the sin of fornication of which those angels were guilty. (See 1 Enoch.) Leviticus 16:8-10: "and Aaron shall cast lots upon the two goats, one lot for the Lord and the other lot for Azazel. And Aaron shall present the goat on which the lot fell for the Lord, and offer it as a sin offering; but the goat on which the lot fell for Azazel shall be presented alive before the Lord to make atonement over it, that it may be sent away into the wilderness to Azazel."

(8) Again, the Holy One, blessed be He, answered and said to them: "What are you, that you enter and speak in my presence? I delight more in this one than in all of you put together, and therefore he will be a prince and a ruler over you in the high heavens." (9) Then they all stood up and went out to meet me, and bowed themselves down before me and said: "Happy are you and happy is your father for your Creator favors you." (10) And because I am small and a youth among them in days, months and years, therefore they call me "Youth" (Na'ar).

CHAPTER 5

The idolatry of the generation of Enosh causes God to remove the Shekina from earth. Idolatry was inspired by Azza, Uzza and Azzael

Rabbi Ishmael said: Metatron, the Prince of the Presence, said to me:
(1) From the day when the Holy One, blessed be He, evicted the first Adam from the Garden of Eden, and continuing from that day, the Shekina (glory) was dwelling upon a Cherub under the Tree of Life. (2) And the ministering angels were gathering together and going down from heaven in groups. From the Raqia (heaven) they went in companies from the heavens in camps to perform His will in the entire world. (3) And the first man and his children were sitting outside the gate of the Garden to see the glowing, bright appearance of the Shekina (glory). (4) For the splendor of the Shekina (glory) enfolds the world from end to end with its splendor 365,000 times that of the orb of the sun. And everyone who made

use of the splendor of the Shekina, on him no flies and no gnats lit, and he was not ill and he suffered no pain. No demons could overpower him, neither were they able to injure him. (5) When the Holy One, blessed be He, went out and went in from the Garden to Eden, from Eden to the Garden, from the Garden to Raqia (heaven) and from Raqia (heaven) to the Garden of Eden then everything and everyone saw His magnificent Shekina and they were not injured; (6) until the time of the generation of Enosh who was the head of all idol worshippers of the world.

The Shekina was an energy or substance that was protecting those who used it from illness, demons, and even bugs.

(7) And what did the generation of Enosh do? They went from one end of the world to the other, and each person brought silver, gold, precious stones and pearls in heaps the size of mountains and hills to make idols out of them throughout the entire world. And they erected the idols in every corner of the world: the size of each idol was 1000 parasangs.

The generations of Enoch are as follows: Adam, Seth, Enosh, Kenan, Mahalalel, Jared, Enoch.
The highest (worst) sins, according to Rabbis, are idolatry, adultery, bloodshed, and sorcery and calling God's name in vain.
A parasang is a length or measurement of distance used in what is now Iran. It varied according to the region. The north-eastern parasang was about 15,000 paces, the north-western parasang was 18,000 paces, and the one of the south-west was merely 6,000 paces. The measurement called the "true parasang" was about 9,000 paces.

(8) And they brought down the sun, the moon, planets and constellations, and placed them in front of the idols on the right side and on the left side of the idols, to attend to them just like they attend the Holy One, blessed be He, for it is written (I Kings 22:19): "And all the hosts of heaven were standing by him on his right hand and on his left." (9) What power was in them to enable to bring them down? They would not have been able to bring them down, if it had not been for the fact that UZZA, and AZZIEL (other sources have Azzael) taught them sorceries by which they brought them down and enslaved them.

It is obvious that the actual sun and stars were not brought down, but the angelic powers controlling them were summoned. Also, keep in mind that some cultures thought stars to be evil angels who flew across the sky. These agents were summoned and used.

(10) In that time the ministering angels accused them before the Holy One, blessed be He, saying: "Master of the World! Why do you bother with the children of men? As it is written (Ps. 8:4) 'What is man (Adam) that you are mindful of him?' But it was not about Adam that this was written but about Enosh, for he is the head of the idol worshippers. (11) Why have you left the highest of the high heavens which are filled with the majesty of your glory and are high, lifted up, and exalted on the high and exalted throne in the Raqia (heaven) of Araboth (highest heaven) and are gone and dwell with the children of men who worship idols and equate you to (place you on the same level as) the idols.

The word "Araboth (highest heaven)" occurs in Psalm 68:4 `Extol him who rides upon the Araboth (highest heaven)' in which it is usually translated simply as the highest heaven. In the case of 3 Enoch, this would be the throne of God. In the Zoharic commentary on Exodus it is referred to thus: `Be glad in the presence of him who rides upon that concealed heaven which is supported by the Chayoth. The Zohar also interprets the word to mean `mixture' because, it says, this heaven is a mixture of fire and water. This is a mystical statement of a place containing opposites, and thus everything.

(12) Now you are on earth just like the idols. What have you to do with the inhabitants of the earth who worship idols? (13) Then the Holy One, blessed be He, lifted up His Shekina from the earth, from their midst (14) In that moment the ministering angels came. They are troops of the host and the armies of Araboth (highest heaven) in thousand camps and ten thousand host. They brought trumpets and took the horns in their hands and surrounded the Shekina with all kinds of songs. And He ascended to the high heavens, for it is written (Ps. 47:5) "God is gone up with a shout, the Lord with the sound of a trumpet."

Here the presence and dwelling of God is the Shekina. When the Shekina was taken, God himself left them and took his glory because of idolatry.

CHAPTER 6

Enoch is lifted up to heaven together with the Shekina.

Rabbi Ishmael said: Metatron, the Angel, the Prince of the Presence, said to me:
(1) When the Holy One, blessed be He, wanted to lift me up on high, He first sent Anaphiel YHWH, the Prince, and he took me from their company out of their sight and carried me away in great glory on a chariot of fire pulled by horses of fire, and servants of glory. And he lifted me up to the high heavens together with the Shekina. (2) As soon as I reached the high heavens, the Holy Chayoth, the Ophannim, the

Seraphim, the Cherubim, the Wheels of the Merkaba (chariot) (the Galgallim), and the ministers of the consuming fire, all smelled my scent from a distance of 365,000 myriads of parasangs, and said: "What smells like one born woman and what tastes like a white drop? Who is this that ascends on high. He is merely a gnat among those who can divide flames of fire?"

Chayot are considered angels of fire, who hold up the throne of God and the earth itself.
The angel smells the scent of human, which he finds revolting. He can taste it is the air. The white drop refers to semen. This is an extremely hateful and distasteful statement for the angel to make.

The Holy One, blessed be He, answered and spoke to them: "My servants, my host, my Cherubim, my Ophannim, my Seraphim! Do not be displeased on account of this! Since all the children of men have denied me and my great Kingdom and have all gone worshipping idols, I have removed my Shekina from among them and have lifted it up on high. But this one whom I have taken from among them is an Elect One among (the inhabitants of) the world and he is equal to all of them (put together) in his faith, righteousness and perfection of deed and I have taken him as a tribute from my world under all the heavens.

The statement of "taking a tribute" can be better understood if one looks at Enoch as the best mankind has to offer and God took him as a an act of admiration indicating the intended worth of mankind, had they not turned away from him. The term "Elect One" is very important. It occurs in 1 Enoch and in certain scripture regarding Christ.

CHAPTER 7

Enoch is raised upon the wings of Shekina to the place of the Throne

Rabbi Ishmael said: Metatron, the Angel, the Prince of the Presence, said to me: When the Holy One, blessed be He, took me away from the generation of the Flood, he lifted me on the wings of the wind of Shekina (his glory/understanding) to the highest heaven and brought me to the great palaces of the Araboth (highest heaven) in Raqia (heaven), where the glorious Throne of Shekina, the Merkaba (chariot), the troops of anger, the armies of vehemence, the fiery Shin'anim (accusers), and the flaming Cherubim, the burning Ophanim, the flaming servants, the flashing Chashmallin, the lightning Seraphim live. And he placed me (there) to attend daily to the Throne of Glory.

In some Jewish mystical writings the attributes of Elijah and those of Enoch are interchangeable. Here Enoch takes the same trip to heaven on a fiery chariot.
Here we have various classes of angels, on which we have little information. The Chashmallin are one of the ten classes, which are sometimes silent for a time in heaven. They cease speaking or singing when "The Word" emanates from the throne.
Shin'anim are a class of angel seen in lists of angelic orders. Their name seems to come from a word for "accuser" and thus could be the satans in heaven.

CHAPTER 8

The gates of heaven opened to Metatron

Rabbi Ishmael said: Metatron, the Prince of the presence, said to me:
(1) Before he appointed me to attend the Throne of Glory, the Holy One, blessed be He, opened to me
three hundred thousand gates of Understanding
three hundred thousand gates of Wisdom
three hundred thousand gates of Life
three hundred thousand gates of Grace and Loving-kindness
three hundred thousand gates of Love
three hundred thousand gates of The Torah
three hundred thousand gates of Meekness
three hundred thousand gates of Steadfastness
three hundred thousand gates of Mercy
three hundred thousand gates of Respect for heaven

Other readings add three hundred thousand gates of Shekina,
three hundred thousand gates of fear of sin,
three hundred thousand gates of power. The gates of steadfastness is also rendered as maintenance and refers to the sustenance to maintain life. All of man's needs come from heaven. Subtlety is rendered as wisdom but includes diplomacy, and craftiness.

(2) Within the hour the Holy One, blessed be He, gave me additional wisdom and to wisdom He added understanding unto understanding, cunning unto cunning, knowledge unto knowledge, mercy unto mercy, instruction unto instruction, love unto love, loving-kindness unto loving-kindness, goodness unto goodness, meekness unto meekness, power unto power, strength unto strength, might unto might, brightness unto brightness, beauty unto beauty, splendor unto splendor, and I was honored and adorned with all these good praiseworthy things more than all the children of heaven.

Enoch has become more blessed or equipped than "all the children of heaven. Loving-kindness equates to "Grace" of the New Testament.

CHAPTER 9
Enoch receives blessings from the Most High and is adorned with angelic attributes

Rabbi Ishmael said: Metatron, the Prince of the Presence, said to me: (1) After all these things the Holy One, blessed be He, put His hand on me and blessed me with 5360 blessings. (2) And I was raised up and grew to the size of the length and width of the world. (3) And he caused 72 wings to grow on me, 36 on each side. And each wing covered the entire world. (4) And He attached to me 365 eyes: each eye was as the great luminary (moon?). (5) And He left no kind of splendor, brilliance, radiance, beauty of all the lights of the universe that He did not affix to me.

There is no direct correlation for the number 5360. It is not evenly divisible by any other number in the chapter, but it is thought to reflect the number 365, the number of days in a solar year. The number 72 is used to reflect the number of the nations of the world and represents the known world. This is backed up by the phrase stating the wings cover the world.

CHAPTER 10

God places Metatron on a throne as ruler in the seventh Hall.

Rabbi Ishmael said: Metatron, the Prince of the Presence, said to me: (1) All these things the Holy One, blessed be He, made for me. He made me a Throne, similar in form and substance to the Throne of Glory. And He spread a curtain of magnificently bright appearance over me. And it was of beauty, grace, and mercy, similar to the curtain of the Throne of the Glory; and on it were affixed all kinds of lights in the universe.

The idea of a curtain could represent the divine secrets and processes unknown and not available to others.

(2) And He placed the curtain at the door of the Seventh Hall and sat me down on it. (3) And the announcement went forth into every heaven, saying: "This is Metatron, my servant. I have made him a prince and ruler over all the princes of my kingdoms and over all the children of heaven, except the eight great, honored, and revered princes who are the ones called YHWH, by the name of their King."

The eight beings who are called YHWH may refer to those angels who have the Tetragrammaton as part of their name. These are highly ranked angels that are outside the normal system of authority. They are the ones God uses as his counsel.

(4) "And every angel and prince who has a word to speak to me shall now go before him and they shall speak to him instead of Me. (5) And every command that he speaks to you in my name, you will obey, carry out, and fulfill. (Some sources add "Beware of him and do not provoke him.") For the Prince of Wisdom and the Prince of Understanding have I committed to him to instruct him in the wisdom of heavenly things and earthly things, in the wisdom of this world and of the world to come. (6) Moreover, I have set him over all the storehouses of the palaces of Araboth (highest heaven) and over all the storehouses (reserves) of life that I have in the high heavens."

CHAPTER 11

God reveals all of the great mysteries to Metatron

Rabbi Ishmael said: Metatron, the angel, the Prince of the Presence, said to me:
(1) The Holy One, blessed be He, began revealing to me all the mysteries of Torah and all the secrets of wisdom and the deep mysteries of the Perfect Law. He revealed the thoughts of all living beings and their feelings and all the secrets of the universe and all the secrets of creation. All these were revealed to me just as they are known to the Maker of Creation. (2) And I watched intently to see and understand the secrets and depths of the wonderful mystery. Before a man thought a thought in secret, I saw it and before a man made a thing I watched it. (3) And there was nothing on high or in the depth of the world that was hidden from me.

Here Metatron is given the omniscient power of God.

CHAPTER 12

God puts a crown on him and calls him "the Lesser YHWH"

Rabbi Ishmael said: Metatron, the Prince of the Presence, said to me: (1) Because of the love that the Holy One, blessed be He, loved me with, was more than all the children of heaven, He made me a garment of glory on which were affixed lights of all varieties, and He clothed me in it. (2) And He made me a robe of honor on which were affixed beauty, magnificent brilliance and majesty of all sorts. (3) And he made me a crown of royalty on which were affixed forty-nine stones of worth, which were like the light of the orb of the sun.

Forty-nine is a mystical number of seven sevens. The number seven represents spiritual perfection.

(4) Its splendor went out into the four coners of the Araboth (highest heaven) of Raqia (heaven), and through the seven heavens, and throughout the four corners of the world. He placed it on my head. (5) And He called me THE LESSER YHWH in the presence of all His heavenly household; for it is written (Ex. 22: 21): " For my name is in him."

Without delving too deeply into Jewish mysticism, it should be pointed out that the numerical value (gematria) of the name Metatron and that of Shahhdai are the same.

CHAPTER 13

God writes with a flaming pen on Metatron's crown the letters by which heaven and earth were created

Rabbi Ishmael said: Metatron, the angel, the Glory of all heavens and the Prince of the Presence, , said to me: (1) Holy One, blessed be He, loved and cherished me with great love and mercy, more than all the children of heaven. Thus, He wrote with his finger with a flaming pen on the crown upon my head the letter by which heaven and earth, the seas and rivers, the mountains and hills, the planets and constellations, the lightning, winds, earthquakes and thunders, the snow and hail, the wind of the storm and the tempest were created. These are the letters by which all the needs of the world and all the orders of Creation were created. (2) And every single letter flashed out time after time like lightning, and time after time like lanterns, time after time like flames of fire, time after time rays like those of the rising of the sun and the moon and the planets.

There are 22 letters in the Hebrew alphabet. It is thought that all things were created when God spoke the words in the Hebrew tongue. These words are symbolized by the combinations of the 22 letters.

CHAPTER 14

All the highest of the princes and lowest angels fear and tremble at the sight of Metatron crowned.

Rabbi Ishmael said: Metatron, the Angel, the Prince of the Presence, said to me: (1) When the Holy One, blessed be He, put this crown on my head, all the Princes of Nations who are in the height of Araboth (highest heaven) of Raqia (heaven) and all the host of every heaven and even the prince of the Elim, the princes of the 'Er'ellim and the princes of the Tafsarim, who are greater than all the ministering angels who minister before the Throne of Glory, trembled before me. They shook, feared and trembled before me when they looked at me.

This is a very interesting list of angels and princes. According to Jewish mystical sources, such as the Zohar, there are ten classes of angels under Mikael (Michael). The Er'ellim denotes a general class of angels, while the Elim minster before God in the high heavens. The Tafsarim are the princes of the Elim.

(2) Even Sammael, the Prince of the Accusers, who is greater than all the princes of Nations on high, feared me and shook before me.

Sammael is the head of the satans or accusers. He is also the ruling angel over Rome, the archenemy of Israel.

(3) And even the angel of fire, and the angel of hail, and the angel of wind, and the angel of the lightning, and the angel of wrath, and the angel of the thunder, and the angel of the snow, and the angel of the rain; and the angel of the day, and the angel of the night, and the angel of the sun, and the angel of the moon, and the angel of the planets, and the angel of the constellations whose hands rule the world, all of them feared and shook and were frightened when they looked at me. (4) These are the names of the rulers of the world: Gabriel, the angel of fire, Baradi-el, the angel who controls hail, Ruchi-el who controls the wind, Baraqi-el who controls the lighting, Zahafi-el who controls the winds of the storm, Rahami-el who controls the thunders, Rahashi-el who controls the earthquake, Shalgiel who controls the snow, Matari-el who controls the rain, Shimshi-el who controls the planets, Rahati-el who controls the constellations. (5) And they all fell to the ground and bowed, when they saw me. And they were not able to look at me because of the majestic glory of the crown on my head.

CHAPTER 15

Metatron is transformed into fire

Rabbi Ishmael said: Metatron, the angel, the Prince of the Presence, and the Glory of all heavens, said to me: (1) As soon as the Holy One, blessed be He, took me into (His) service to attend the Throne of Glory and the Wheels (Galgallim) of the Merkaba (chariot) and the service of Shekina, suddenly my flesh was changed into flames, my muscles into flaming fire, my bones into coals of juniper wood, the light of my eye-lids into hot flames, and all of my limbs into wings of burning fire and my entire body into glowing fire.

Galgallim (sometimes spelled Galgalim) are a high-ranking order of angels, the equivalent of Seraphim. They are metaphorically called "the wheels of the Merkabah" (the 'divine chariot' used to connect people to the divine) and are considered the equivalent of the Orphanim (Cherubim). Galgalim is Hebrew for "wheels."

(2) And on my right flames were burning and dividing, on my left staves of wood (burning staves) were burning, around me the winds of storms and tempests were blowing and in front of me and behind me was roaring thunder accompanied by earthquakes.

CHAPTER 15 - B
This chapter does not occur in all manuscripts. It seems to be a later addition.

Rabbi Ishmael said me: Metatron, the Prince of the Presence and the prince ruling over all the princes, stands before Him who is greater than all the Elohim. And he enters in under the Throne of Glory. And he has a great dwelling of light on high. And he brings into existence the fire of deafness and places it in the ears of the Holy Chayoth, so that they cannot hear the voice of the Word that sounds from the mouth of the Divine Majesty.

This may indicate that he goes into the holy of holies where he worships and has his own sanctuary.
The idea of more than one Elohim is not new. It is addressed in Psalm 82:
1, The Psalm of Asaph. God stands in the council of the gods; he judges among the gods. 2. How long will you judge unjustly, and show preference to the wicked? Selah. 3. Judge the poor and the orphans; do righteousness to the afflicted and dispossessed. 4. Deliver the poor and oppressed; save them from the hand of the evil. 5. They do not know and they have no understanding; they walk about in darkness. All the foundations of the earth are shaken. 6. I said, "You are gods, and children of Elyon, every one of you." 7. But you will die like mortals, and fall like one of the princes. 8. Rise up, O God, and judge the earth, for you have inherited all the nations.

This section seems to preserve a fragment of a book called, "The Ascension of Moses." The chashmal is the highest point of heaven. It is like a zenith line out of which a window opens.

(2) And when Moses ascended on high, he fasted 121 fasts, until the places where the chashmal live were opened to him; and he saw that the place was as white as a Lion's heart and he saw the companies of the host round about him, which could not be counted. And they wished to burn him. But Moses

prayed for mercy, first for Israel and then for himself: and He who was sitting on the Merkaba (chariot) opened the windows above the heads of the Cherubim. And a host of 1800 helpers along with the Prince of the Presence, Metatron, all went out to meet Moses. They took the prayers of Israel and placed them like a crown on the head of the Holy One, blessed be He.
(3) The they said (Deut. 6:4): "Hear, O Israel; the Lord our God is one Lord." And their face were shining and they rejoiced over Shekina and they said to Metatron: "What are these? And to whom do they give all honor and glory?" And they answered: "To the Glorious Lord of Israel." And they spoke: Hear, O Israel: the Lord, our God is one Lord. To Who else shall be given this abundance of honor and majesty but to You YHWH, the Divine Majesty, the King, the living and eternal one." (4) In that moment Akatriel Ya Yehod Sebaoth (a name of the most high) spoke and said to Metatron, the Prince of the Presence and said, "Let no prayer that he prays before me return to him empty (not done). Hear his prayer and fulfill his desire whether it is great or small (5) Then Metatron, the Prince of the presence, said to Moses, "Son of Amram! Do not be afraid. God delights in you. He asks you what you desire from the Glory and Majesty. Your face shines from one end of the world to the other." But Moses answered him: "I fear that I should bring guiltiness upon myself." Metatron said to him, "Receive the letters of the oath, which makes a covenant that cannot be broken."

Metatron is moving through time to and from the time of Moses.
The letters make up the divine names, which are eternal.
CHAPTER 16
This continues the additional material.
His privilege of presiding on a Throne are taken.

Rabbi Ishmael said: Metatron, the Angel, the Prince of the Presence, the Glory of all heaven, said to me: (1) At first I was sitting on a large Throne at the door of the Seventh Hall. There, by authority of the Holy One, blessed be He, I was judging the children of heaven and the servants on high. And I judged Greatness, Kingship, Dignity, Rulership, Honor and Praise, and the Diadem and Crown of Glory for all the princes of kingdoms. While I was presiding in the Court of the Sky (Yeshiba), the princes of nations were standing before me, on my right and on my left, by authority of the Holy One, blessed be He. (2) But when Acher came to see the vision of the Merkaba (chariot) and locked his eyes on me, he was afraid and shook before me so much that his soul was departing from him, because of fear, horror and dread of me, when he saw me sitting upon a throne like a king with all the ministering angels standing by my side serving me and all the princes of kingdoms adorned with crowns all around me. (3) At that moment he opened his mouth and said, "Surely there are two Divine Powers in heaven!" (4) Then the Divine Voice went out from heaven from the Shekina and said: "Return, you backsliding children (Jer.3:22), except for Acher!" (5) Then Anieyel came (Other sources have "Anaphiel YHWH), the Prince, the honored, glorified, beloved, wonderful, revered and fearful one, as ordered by the Holy One, blessed be He and beat me sixty times with whips of fire and made me stand to my feet.

Anieyel , or Anaphiel YHWH is higher in status than Metatron. It is possible the Anieyel is the angel who punishes. The purpose of this chapter is to refute the heresy of the Rabbi called Acher, who believed that there were now two deities in heaven, God and Metatron. To show Metatron is not a deity God sends in a higher angel to take him off his throne and beat him, proving Metatron is not God, nor is he a god. The chapter goes on to call all of Israel to return to God, except for Acher, who has committed an unforgivable sin against the monotheists and against God.

CHAPTER 17

The princes of the seven heavens, and of the sun, moon, planets and constellations.

Rabbi Ishmael said: Metatron, the angel, the Prince of the Presence, the glory of all heavens, said to me: (1) The number of princes are seven. They are the great, beautiful, wonderful, honored, and revered ones. They are assigned over the seven heavens, And these are they: MIKAEL (Michael), GABRIEL, SHATQIEL, BAKARIEL, BADARIEL, PACHRIEL. (Some sources omit Parchriel and add Sidriel.) (2) And every one of them is the prince of the host of one heaven. And each one of them is accompanied by 496,000 groups of ten-thousand ministering angels.

496 is the numerical value of the word Malkut (kingdom). These 496,000 angels are the ones who sing of the glory of God, singing "Holy, Holy. Holy."

(3) MIKAEL is the great prince assigned to ruler over the seventh heaven, the highest one, which is in the Araboth (highest heaven). Gabriel is the prince of the host assigned to rule over the sixth heaven which is in Makon. SHATAQIEL is the prince of the host assigned to rule over the fifth heaven which is in Makon. SHAHAQIEL is the prince of the host assigned to rule over the fourth heaven which is in Zebul. BADARIEL is the prince of the host assigned to rule over the third heaven which is in Shehaqim. BARAKIEL is the prince of the host assigned to rule over the second heaven which is in the height of Raqia (heaven). PAZRIEL is the prince of the host assigned to rule over the first heaven which is in

Wilon (or Velum, as the first heaven is called), which is in Shamayim. (4) Under them in GALGALLIEL, the prince who is assigned as ruler over the orb (galgal) of the sun, and with him are 96 great and revered angels who moves the sun in Raqia (heaven) a distance of 365,000 parasangs each day. (5) Under them is OPHANNIEL, the prince who is set the globe (Ophan) of the moon. And with him are 88 (some have it as 68) angels who move the globe of the moon 354 thousand parasangs every night at the time when the moon stands in the East at its turning point. And the moon is situated in the East at its turning point in the fifteenth day of every month. (6) Under them is RAHATIEL, the prince who is appointed to rule over the constellations. He is accompanied by 72 great and revered angels. And why is he called RAHATIEL? Because he makes the stars run (marhit) in their orbits and courses, which is 339 thousand parasangs every night from the East to West, and from West to East. The Holy One, blessed be He, has made a tent for all of them, for the sun, the moon, the planets and the stars, and they travel in it at night from the West to the East. (7) Under them is KOKBIEL, the prince who is assigned to rule over all the planets. And with him are 365,000 groups of ten-thousand ministering angels, great and revered ones who move the planets from city to city and from province to province in Raqia (the heaven) of heavens. (8) And ruling over them are seventy-two princes of nations (kingdoms) on high corresponding to the 72 nations of the world. And all of them are crowned with crowns of royalty and clothed in royal clothes and wrapped in royal robes. And all of them are riding on royal horses and holding royal scepters in their hands. In front of each of them when he is traveling in Raqia (heaven), royal servants are running with great glory and majesty just as on earth the Princes are traveling in chariots with horsemen and great armies and in glory and greatness with praise, song and honor.

CHAPTER 18

The order of ranks of the angels is established by the homage.

Rabbi Ishmael said: Metatron, the Angel, the Prince of the Presence, the glory of all heaven, said to me: (1) THE ANGELS OF THE FIRST HEAVEN, when (ever) they see their prince, they dismount from their horses and bow themselves. And THE PRINCE OF THE FIRST HEAVEN, when he sees the prince of the second heaven, he dismounts, removes the glorious crown from his head and bows himself to the ground. AND THE PRINCE OF THE SECOND HEAVEN, when he sees the prince of the third heaven, he removes the glorious crown form his head and bows himself to the ground. AND THE PRINCE OF THE

THIRD HEAVEN, when he sees the prince of the fourth heaven, he removes the glorious crown form his head and bows himself to the ground. AND THE PRINCE OF THE FOURTH HEAVEN, when he sees the prince of the fifth heaven, he removes the glorious crown form his head and bows himself to the ground. AND THE PRINCE OF THE FIFTH HEAVEN, when he sees the prince of the sixth heaven, he removes the glorious crown from his head and bows himself to the ground. AND THE PRINCE OF THE SIXTH HEAVEN, when he sees the prince of the seventh heaven he removes the glorious crown from his head and bows himself to the ground. (2) AND THE PRINCE OF THE SEVENTH HEAVEN, when he sees THE SEVENTY-TWO PRINCES OF KINGDOMS, he removes the glorious crown from his head and bows himself to the ground.

The number 70 appears as does the number 72. It is possible the difference can be explained by the 70 angels along with two leaders, such as Mikael (Michael) and Sammael. In the following section the names of the angels do not follow their function, as in the prior portion of the book. The names are obscure and it is difficult to understand their meanings. The expression "bows himself to the ground" and "bow themselves" likely indicates a complete kneeling position with the head touching the earth.

(3) And the seventy two princes of kingdoms, when they see The door keepers of the first hall in the ARABOTH RAQIA in the highest heaven, they remove the royal crown from their head and bow themselves. And The door keepers of the first hall, when they see the doorkeepers of the second Hall, they remove the glorious crown form their head and bow themselves. The door keepers of the second hall, when they see the door keepers of the third hall, they remove the glorious crown from their head and bow themselves. The door keepers of the third hall, when they see the door keepers of the fourth Hall, they remove the crown from their head and bow themselves. The door keepers of the fourth hall, when they see the door keepers of the fifth Hall, they remove the glorious crown from their head and bow themselves. The door keepers of the fifth hall, when they see the doorkeepers of the sixth Hall, they remove the crown from their head and fall to their face. The door keepers of the sixth hall, when they see the The door keepers of the seventh hall, they remove the glorious crown from their head and bow themselves. (4) And the door keepers of the seventh Hall, when they see The Four Great Princes, the honored ones, who are appointed over the four Camps Of SHEKINA, they remove the crowns of glory from their head and bow themselves. (5) And the four great prince, when they see TAGHAS, the

prince, great and honored with song (and) praise, at the head of all the children of heaven, they remove the glorious crown from their head and bow themselves. (6) And Taghas, the great and honored prince, when he sees BARATTIEL, the great prince of three fingers in the height of Araboth, the highest heaven, he removes the glorious crown from his head and bows himself to the ground.

Three fingers in height – Hold your hand out at arm's length with three fingers held out horizontally in front of your eyes. This is the measurement.

(7) And Barattiel, the great prince, when he sees HAMON, the great prince, the fearful and honored, beautiful and terrible, he who makes all the children of heaven to shake, when the time draws near that is set for the saying of the 'Thrice Holy', he removes the glorious crown form his head and bows himself to the ground. For it is written (Isa.33:3): " At noise of the confusion at the anxious preparation of the salutation of "Holy, Holy, Holy" the people are fled; at the lifting up of yourself the nations are scattered," (8) And Hamon, the great prince, when he sees TUTRESSIEL, the great prince he removes the glorious crown from his head and bows himself to the ground. (9) And Tutresiel YHWH, the great prince, when he sees ATRUGIEL, the great prince, he removes the glorious crown from his head and bows himself to the ground. (10) And Aatrugiel the great prince, when he sees NA'ARIRIEL YHWH, the great prince, he removes the glorious crown from his head and bows himself to the ground. (11) And Na'aririel YHWH, the great prince when he see SAANIGIEL, the great prince, he removes the glorious crown from his head and bows himself to the ground. (12) And Sasnigiel YHWH, when he sees ZAZRIEL YHWH, the great prince, he removes the glorious crown from his head and bows himself to the ground. (13) And Zazriel YHWH, the prince, when he sees GEBURATIEL YHWH, the prince, he removes the glorious crown from his head and bows himself to the ground. (14) And Geburatiel YHWH, the prince, when he sees ARAPHIEL YHWH, the prince, he removes the glorious crown from his head and bows himself to the ground. (15) And Araphiel YHWH, the prince, when he sees ASHRUYLU, the prince, who presides in all the sessions of the children of heaven, he removes the glorious crown from his head and bows himself to the ground. (16) And Ashruylu YHWH, the prince, when he sees GALLISUR YHWH, THE PRINCE, WHO REVEALS ALL THE SECRETS OF THE LAW (Torah), he removes the glorious crown from his head and bows himself to the ground. (17) And Gallisur YHWH, the prince, when he sees ZAKZAKIEL YHWH , the prince who is appointed to write down the merits of Israel on the Throne of

Glory, he removes the glorious crown form his head and bows himself to the ground. (18) And Zakzakiel YHWH, the great prince, when he sees ANAPHIEL YHWH, the prince who keeps the keys of the heavenly Halls, he removes the glorious crown from his head and bows himself to the ground. Why is he called by the name of Anaphiel? Because the shoulders of his honor and majesty and his crown and his splendor and his brilliance overshadows all the chambers of Araboth (highest heaven) of Raqia (heaven) on high even as the Maker of the World overshadows them. Regarding the Maker of the world, it is written that His glory covered the heavens, and the earth was full of His praise. The honor and majesty of Anaphiel cover all the glories of Araboth (highest heaven) the highest.

Araphiel means "Neck or Strength of God." Ashruylu means "To cause to rest / dwell." It is one of the names of the Godhead. Gallisur means, "reveal the secrets of the Law. " He reveals the reasons and secrets of the Creator. Raziel means, "Secrets of God." He hears the divine decrees. Anaphiel means "Branch of God." Zakzakiel means, "Merit of God." The glorious crowns signify honor and status.

(19) And when he sees SOTHER ASHIEL YHWH, the prince, the great, fearful and honored one, he removes the glorious crown from his head and bows himself to the ground. Why is he called Sother Ashiel? Because he is assigned to rule over the four heads of the river of fire, which are beside the Throne of Glory; and every single prince who goes out or enters before the Shekina, goes out or enters only by his permission. For the seals of the river of fire are entrusted to him. And furthermore, his height is 7000 groups of ten-thousand parasangs. And he stirs up the fire of the river; and he goes out and enters before the Shekina to expound what is recorded concerning the inhabitants of the world. According for it is written (Dan. 7:10): "the judgment was set, and the books were opened." (20) And Sother Ashiel the prince, when he sees SHOQED CHOZI, the great prince, the mighty, terrible and honored one, he removes the glorious crown from his head and falls upon his face. And why is he called Shoqed Chozi? Because he weighs all the merits of man on a scale in the presence of the Holy One, blessed be He. (21) And when he sees ZEHANPURYU YHWH, the great prince, the mighty and terrible one, honored, glorified and feared in the entire heavenly household, he removes the glorious crown from his head and bows himself to the ground. Why is he called Zehanpuryu? Because he commands the river of fire and pushes it back to its place. (22) And when he sees AZBUGA YHWH, the great prince, glorified, revered, honored, adorned, wonderful, exalted, loved and feared among all the great princes who know the mystery of the Throne of Glory, he removes the glorious crown from his head and bows himself to the ground. Why is he called Azbuga? Because in the future he will clothe the righteous and pious of the world with garments of life and wrap them in the cloak of life, so that they can live an eternal life in them. (23) And when he sees the two great princes, the strong one and the glorified one who are standing above him, he removes the glorious crown from his head and bows himself to the ground. And these are the names of the two princes: SOPHERIEL YHWH (Sopheriel YHWH the Killer), the great prince, the honored, glorified, blameless, venerable, ancient and mighty one. (24) Why is he called Sopheriel YHWH who kills (Sopheriel YHWH the Killer)? Because he is assigned to control the books of the dead, so that everyone, when the day of his death draws near, is written by him in the books of the dead. Why is he called Sopheriel YHWH who makes alive (Sopheriel YHWH the Lifegiver)? Because he is assigned control over the books of life, so that every one whom the Holy One, blessed be He, will bring into life, he writes him in the book of life, by authority of The Divine Majesty. Perhaps he might say: "Since the Holy One, blessed be He, is sitting on a throne, they are also sitting when writing." The Scripture teaches us (I Kings 22:19, 2 Chron. 28:18): "And all the host of heaven are standing by him." They are called "The host of heaven" in order to show us that even the Great Princes and all like them in the high heavens, fulfill the requests of the Shekina in no other way than standing. But how is it possible that they are able to write, when they are standing?

This section is very important to Jewish mystics and Cabbalists in that it sets the balance within the act of judgment between mercy and justice. If one were to strip down to the barest essentials the spiritual life of a person some may conclude it is to find balance between mercy and justice. The books of life and death are records of the birth and death of individuals. This is not the same as the Book of Life referred to in the Bible, which contains the names of the righteous.

(25) It is done thusly. One is standing on the wheels of the tempest and the other is standing on the wheels of the wind of the storm. The one is clothed in kingly garments, the other is clothed in kingly garments. The one is wrapped in a mantle of majesty and the other is wrapped in a mantle of majesty. One is crowned with a royal crown, and the other is crowned with a royal crown. The one's body is full of eyes, and the other's body is full of eyes. One looks like lightning, and the other looks like lightning. The eyes of the one are like the sun in its power, and the eyes of the other are like the sun in its power. The one's height is the height of the seven heavens, and the other's height is the height

of the seven heavens. The wings of the one are as many as the days of the year, and the wings of the other are as many as the days of the year. The wings of one reach over the width of Raqia (heaven), and the wings of the other reach over the width of Raqia (heaven). The lips of one look like the gates of the East, and the lips of the other look like the gates of the East. The tongue of the one is as high as the waves of the sea, and the tongue of the other is as high as the waves of the sea. From the mouth of the one a flame proceeds, and from the mouth of the other a flame proceeds. From the mouth of the one lightning is emitted and from the mouth of the other lightning is emitted. From the sweat of one fire is kindled, and from the sweat of the other fire is kindled. From the one's tongue a torch is burning, and from the tongue of the other a torch is burning. On the head of the one there is a sapphire stone, and upon the head of the other there is a sapphire stone. On the shoulders of the one there is a wheel of a swift cherubim, and on the shoulders of the other there is a wheel of a swift cherubim. One has in his hand a burning scroll; the other has in his hand a burning scroll. The length of the scroll is 3000 times ten-thousand parasangs; the size of the pen is 3000 times ten-thousand of parasangs; the size of every single letter that they write is 365 parasangs.

Sopheriel is the prince appointed over the book of life. The name means "Scribe of God." Azbuga is a messenger. The name denoted strength, as many angelic names do. Zehanpuryu means "the face of fear." To be full of eyes is a symbol of omniscience. Eastern gates were large, tall structures. The two symbolic uses of fire are destruction and purification.

CHAPTER 19

Rikbiel, the prince of the wheels of the Merkaba (chariot). And the Sacred Salutation of Holy, Holy, Holy

Rabbi Ishmael said: Metatron, the Angel, the Prince of the Presence, said to me: (1) Above these three angels, who are these great princes, there is one Prince, distinguished, revered, noble, glorified, adorned, fearful, fearless, mighty, great, uplifted, glorious, crowned, wonderful, exalted, blameless, loved, like a ruler, he is high and lofty, ancient and mighty, there is none among the princes like him. His name is RIKBIEL YHWH, the great and revered prince who is standing by Merkaba (chariot). (2) And why is he called RIKBIEL? Because he is assigned to rule over the wheels of the Merkaba (chariot), and they are given to his authority. (3) And how many are the wheels? Eight; two in each direction. And there are four winds compassing them round about. And these are their names: "the Winds of the Storm", "the

Tempest", "the Strong Wind", and "the Wind of Earthquake." (4) And under them four rivers of fire are constantly running and there is one river of fire on each side. And around them, between the rivers, four clouds are affixed. They are "clouds of fire", "clouds of torches", "clouds of coal", "clouds of brimstone" and they are standing by their wheels.

There is much number symbolism here. Some Eastern cultures believe there are only eight possible directions of movement. They could be looked at as north, south, east, west, up, down, in, out. Anything else must be a combination of these. Four is the number of limits and testing. Two is the number of assistance, witness, or duplicity.

(5) And the feet of the Chayoth are resting on the wheels. And between two wheels an earthquake is roaring and thunder is sounding. (6) And when the time draws near for the recital of the Song, numerous wheels are moved, the numerous clouds tremble, all the chieftains (shallishim) become afraid, and all the horsemen (parashim) become angry, and all the mighty ones (gibborim) are excited, all the host (seba'im) are frightened, and all the troops (gedudim) are fearful, all the appointed ones (memunnim) hurry away, all the princes (sarim) and armies (chayelim) are confused, all the servants (mesharetim) faint and all the angels (mal'akim) and divisions (degalim) suffer with pain. (7) And one wheel makes a sound to be heard by the other and one Cherub speaks to another, one Chayya to another, one Seraph to another (saying) (Ps. 68:5) "Extol to him that rides in Araboth (highest heaven), by his name Jah (Yah) and rejoice before him!"

The name Jah (Yah) is a shortened and "speakable" version of YHWH or Jehovah.

CHAPTER 20

CHAYYLIEL, the prince of the Chayoth

Rabbi Ishmael said: Metatron, the angel, the Prince of the Presence, said to me: (1) Above these there is one great and mighty prince. His name is CHAYYLIEL YHWH, a noble and honorable prince, a prince before whom all the children of heaven tremble, a prince who is able to swallow up the entire earth in one moment at a single mouthful. (2) And why is he called CHAYYLIEL YHWH? Because he is assigned to rule over the Holy Chayoth and he strikes the Chayoth with lashes of fire: and glorifies them, when they give praise and glory and rejoicing and he causes them to hurry and say "Holy" "Blessed be the Glory of YHWH from His place!" (The Kedushah - Sacred Salutation of Holy, Holy, Holy).

CHAPTER 21
The Chayoth

Rabbi Ishmael said: Metatron, the angel, the Prince of the Presence, said to me: (1) The Four Chayoth correspond to the four winds. Each Chayya is as big as the space of the entire world. And each one has four faces; and each face is like the face of the East (sunrise). (2) Each one has four wings and each wing is like the tent (ceiling) of the universe. (3) And each one has faces in the middle of faces and wings in the middle of wings. The size of the faces is 248 faces, and the size of the wings is 365 wings. (4) And every one is crowned with 2000 crowns on his head. And each crown is like the rainbow in the cloud. And its splendor is like the magnificence of the circle of the sun. And the sparks that go out from every one are like the glory of the morning star (planet Venus) in the East.

CHAPTER 22
KERUBIEL, the Prince of the Cherubim.
Description of the Cherubim

Rabbi Ishmael said: Metatron, the angel, the Prince of the Presence, said to me: (1) Above these there is one prince, noble, wonderful, strong, and praised with all kinds of praise. His name is CHERUBIEL YHWH, a mighty prince, full of power and strength, a prince of highness, and Highness (is) with him, a righteous Prince, and Righteousness (is) with him, a holy prince, and holiness (is) with him, a prince of glorified in (by) thousand host, exalted by ten thousand armies (2) At his anger the earth trembles, at his anger the camps (of armies) are moved, from fear of him the foundations are shaken, at his chastisement the Araboth (highest heaven) trembles. (3) His stature is full of (burning) coals. The height is that of the seven heavens and the breadth of his stature is like the sea. (4) The opening of his mouth is like a lamp of fire. His tongue is a consuming fire. His eyebrows are like the splendor of the lightning. His eyes are like sparks of bright light. His face is like a burning fire. (5) And there is a crown of holiness upon his head on which the Explicit Name is graven, and lightning proceeds from it. And the bow of the Shekina is between his shoulders. And his sword is like lightning; and on his thighs there are arrows like flames, and upon his armor and shield there is a consuming fire, and on his neck there are coals of burning juniper wood and (also) around him (there are coals of burning juniper).

The bow can represent a rainbow but it is certainly a weapon of great power. Juniper is a symbol of strength and longevity. It was said to shelter the prophet Elijah from Queen Jezebel's pursuit. Tales in the apocryphal books tell of how the infant Jesus and his parents were hidden from King Herod's soldiers by a juniper during their flight into Egypt.

(7) And the splendor of Shekina is on his face; and the horns of the majesty on his wheels; and a royal diadem upon his head. (8) And his body is full of eyes. And wings are covering the entire of his high stature (lit. the height of his stature is all wings). (9) On his right hand a flame is burning, and on his left a fire is glowing; and coals are burning from it. And burning staves go forth from his body. And lightning is projected from his face. With him there is always thunder within thunder, and by his side there is a never ending earthquake within an earthquake. (10) And the two princes of the Merkaba (chariot) are together with him. (11) Why is he called CHERUBIEL YHWH, the Prince. Because he is assigned to rule over the chariot of the Cherubim. And the mighty Cherubim are subject to his authority. And he adorns the crowns on their heads and polishes the diadem upon their heads (skulls). (12) He increases the glory of their appearance. And he glorifies the beauty of their majesty. And he expands the greatness of their honor. He makes their songs of praise to be sung. He makes the strength of their beauty increase. He causes the brightness of their glory to shine forth. He makes their goodness, mercy, and lovingkindess to grow. He separates their radiance so it show even more. He makes the beauty of their mercy even more beautiful. He glorifies their upright majesty. He sings the order of their praise to establish the dwelling place of Him who dwells on the Cherubim. (13) And the Cherumim are standing by the Holy Chayoth, and their wings are raised up to their heads (are as the height of their heads) and Shekina is (resting) upon them and the bright Glory is upon their faces and songs of praise are in their mouth and their hands are under their wings and their feet are covered by their wings and horns of glory are upon their heads and the splendor of Shekina on their face and Shekina is resting on them and sapphire stones surround them and columns of fire are on their four sides and columns of burning staves are beside them. (14) There is one sapphire on one side and another sapphire on the other side and under the sapphires there are coals of burning juniper wood. (15) And a Cherub is standing in each direction but the wings of the Cherubim surround each other above their heads in glory; and they spread them to sing with them a song to him that inhabits the clouds and to praise the fearful majesty of the king of kings with their wings.

The sound coming from their wings is heard as a song. This hearkens back to a description of Lucifer, before the fall. It was said that his body had instruments made within it, which made beautiful music.

(16) And CHERUBIEL YHWH, is the prince who is assigned to rule over them. He arrays them in proper, beautiful and pleasant orders and he exalts them in all manner of exaltation, dignity and glory. And he hurries them in glory and might to do the will of their Creator every moment. Above their high heads continually dwells the glory of the high king "who dwells on the Cherubim."

Names in this section are related to the station of the angels. Chayyliel is the prince of the Chayyoth, Cherubiel or Kerubiel is the prince of the Kerubim or Cherubim, and so on.

CHAPTER 22-B

Rabbi Ishmael said to me: Metatron, the angel, the Prince of the Presence, said to me: (1) How are the angels standing on high? He said: A bridge is placed from the beginning of the doorway to the end, like a bridge that is placed over a river for every one to pass over it. And three ministering angels surround it and sing a song before YHWH, the God of Israel. And standing before it are the lords of dread and captains of fear, numbering a thousand times thousand and ten thousand times ten thousand, and they sing praises and hymns before YHWH, the God of Israel. (3) Many bridges are there. There are bridges of fire and many bridges of hail. Also many rivers of hail, numerous storehouses of snow, and many wheels of fire. (4) And how many are the ministering angels are there? 12,000 times ten-thousand: six-thousand time ten-thousand above and six (thousand times ten-thousand) below. And 12,000 are the storehouses of snow, six above and six below. And 24 times ten-thousand wheels of fire, 12 times ten-thousand above and 12 times ten-thousand below. And they surround the bridges and the rivers of fire and the rivers of hail. And there are numerous ministering angels, forming entries, for all the creatures that are standing in the midst thereof, over against the paths of Raqia (heaven) Shamayim. (5) What does YHWH, the God of Israel, the King of Glory do? The Great and Fearful God, mighty in strength, covers His face. (6) In Araboth (highest heaven) are 660,000 times ten-thousand angels of glory standing over against the Throne of Glory and the divisions of flaming fire.

And the King of Glory covers His face; for else the Araboth (highest heaven) of Raqia (heaven) would be torn apart from its center because of the majesty, splendor, beauty, radiance, loveliness, brilliancy, brightness and Excellency of the appearance of (the Holy One,) blessed be He. (7) There are innumerable ministering angels carrying out his will, many kings and princes in the Araboth (highest heaven) of His delight. They are angels who are revered among the rulers in heaven, distinguished, adorned with song and they bring love to the minds of those who are frightened by the splendor of Shekina, and their eyes are dazzled by the shining beauty of their King, their faces grow black and their strength fails. (8) There are rivers of joy, streams of gladness, rivers of happiness, streams of victory, rivers of life, streams of friendship and they flow over and go out from in front of the Throne of Glory and grow large and wend their way through the gates on the paths to Araboth (highest heaven) of Raqia (heaven) at the voice of shouting and music of the CHAYYOTH, at the voice of the rejoicing of the cymbals of his OPHANNIM and at the melody of the cymbals of His Cherubim. And they grow great and go out with noise and with the sound of the hymn: "HOLY, HOLY, HOLY, IS THE LORD OF HOST; THE WHOLE EARTH IS FULL OF HIS GLORY!"

CHAPTER 22 -C

Rabbi Ishmael said: Metatron, the Prince of the Presence said to me: (1) What is the distance between one bridge and another? Tens of thousands of parasangs. They rise up tens of thousands of parasangs , and the go down tens of thousands of parasangs. (2) The distance between the rivers of dread and the rivers of fear is 22 times ten-thousand parasangs; between the rivers of hail and the rivers of darkness 36 times ten-thousand paragangs; between the chambers of lightnings and the clouds of compassion 42 times ten-thousand parasangs; between the clouds of compassion and the Merkaba (chariot) 84 times ten-thousand parasangs; between the Merkaba (chariot) and the Cherubim 148 times ten-thousand parasangs; between the Cherubim and the Ophannim 24 times ten-thousand parasangs; between the chambers of chambers and the Holy Chayoth 40,000 times ten-thousand parasangs; between one wing (of the Chayoth) and another 12 times ten-thousand parasangs; and the breadth of each one wing is of that same measure; and the distance between the Holy Chayoth and the Throne of Glory is 30,000 times ten-thousand parasangs. (3) And from the foot of the Throne to the seat there are 40,000 times ten-thousand parasangs. And the name of Him that sits on it: let the name be sanctified! (4) And the arches of the Bow are set above the Araboth (highest heaven), and they are 1000 thousands and 10,000 times ten thousands of parasangs high. Their measure is after the measure of the 'Irin and Qaddishin (the Watchers and the Holy Ones). As it is written, (Gen. 9:13) "My bow I have set in the cloud." It is not written here "I will set" but "I have set," that is to say; I have already set it in the clouds that surround the Throne of Glory. As His clouds pass by, the angels of hail turn into burning coal. (5) And a voice of fire goes down from the Holy Chayoth. And because of the breath of that voice they run (Ezek. 1:14) to another place, fearing that it could command them to go; and they return for fear that it may injure them from the other side. Therefore "they run and return." (6) And these arches of the Bow are more beautiful and radiant than the radiance of the sun during the summer solstice. And they are brighter (whiter) than a flaming fire and they are large and beautiful. (7) Above the arches of the Bow are the wheels of the Ophannim. Their height is 1000 thousand and 10,000 times 10,000 units of measure after the measure of the Seraphim and the Troops (Gedudim).

The Irin and Qaddishin are the highest ranked of all the angels. They constitute the supreme council of heaven. These angels are the twin sentinels. The Irin decrees while the Qaddishin sentences every case in the court of heaven. In Daniel 4:14 we find references. "By decree of the sentinels is this decided, by order of the holy ones, this sentence, that all who live may know that the most High rules over the kingdom of men: he can give it to whom he will, or set over it the lowliest of men. For the words rendered, "of the holy god," we read in Chaldee (in which Daniel was composed) the words elain cadisin ('-l-h-y-n q-d-y-sh-y-n) [vocalized this would be 'elahin qaddishin], which means "holy gods," not "holy God," (St. Jerome, Commentary on Daniel (1958). pp. 15-157)

CHAPTER 23
The winds are blowing under the wings of the Cherubim

Rabbi Ishmael said: Metatron, the Angel, the Prince of the Presence, said to me: (1) There are numerous winds blowing under the wings of the Cherubim. There blows "the Brooding Wind", for it is written (Gen. 1: 2): "and the wind of God was brooding upon the face of the waters." (2) There blows "the Strong Wind", as it is said (Ex.14: 21): "and the Lord caused the sea to go back by a strong east wind all that night." (3) There blows "the East Wind" for it is written (Ex. 10: 13): "the east wind brought the locusts." (4) There blows "the Wind of Quails for it is written (Num. 9: 31): "And there went forth a wind from the Lord and brought quails." (5) There blows "the Wind of Jealousy" for it is written (Num. 5:14): "And the wind of jealousy came upon him." (6) There

blows the "Wind of Earthquake" and it is written (I Kings. 19: 11): "and after that the wind of the earthquake; but the Lord was not in the earthquake." (7) There blows the "Wind of YHWH" for it is written (Ex. 37: 1): "and he carried me out by the wind of YHWH and set me down." (8) There blows the "Evil Wind" for it is written (I Sam. 14: 23): "and the evil wind departed from him." (9) There blows the "Wind of Wisdom" and the "Wind of Understanding" and the "Wind of Knowledge" and the "Wind of the Fear of YHWH" for it is written (Is. 11: 2): "And the wind of YHWH shall rest upon him; the wind of wisdom and understanding, the wind of counsel and might, the wind of knowledge and the fear of YHWH." (10) There blows the "Wind of Rain", for it is written (Prov. 25: 23) "the north wind brings forth rain." (11) There blows the "Wind of Lightning", for it is written (Jer. 10: 13): "he makes lightning for the rain and brings forth the wind out of his storehouses." (12) There blows the "Wind, Which Breaks the Rocks", for it is written (1 Kings 19: 11): "the Lord passed by and a great and strong wind (rent the mountains and break in pieces the rocks before the Lord.) (13) There blows the Wind of Assuagement of the Sea", for it is written (Gen. 7:1): "and God made a wind to pass over the earth, and the waters assuaged." (14) There blows the "Wind of Wrath", for it is written (Job1: 19): 'and behold there came a great wind from the wilderness and smote the four corners of the house and it fell." (15) There blows the "Wind of Storms", for it is written (Ps. 148: 8): "Winds of the storm, fulfilling his word." (16) And Satan is standing among these winds, for "the winds of the storm" is nothing else but "Satan" and all these winds do not blow but under the wings of Cherubim, for it is written (Ps. 18.11): "and he rode upon a cherub and flew, yes, and he flew with speed upon wings of the wind." (17) And where do all these winds go? The Scripture teaches us, that they go out from under the wings of the Cherubim and descend on the globe of the sun, for it is written (Eccl. 1:6): "The wind goes toward the south and turns around to the north; it turns around over and over in its course and the wind returns again to its route." And from the orb of the sun they return and go down on to the rivers and the seas, then up on the mountains and up on the hills, for it is written (Am. 55:13): "For lo, he that forms the mountains and creates the wind." (18) And from the mountains and the hills they return and go down again to the seas and the rivers; and from the seas and the rivers they return and go up to the cities and provinces: and from the cities and provinces they return and go down into the Garden, and from the Garden they return and descend to Eden, for it is written (Gen. 3: 8) "walking in the Garden in the wind (cool) of day." In the middle of the Garden they come together and blow from one side to the other.

In the Garden they are perfumed with spices from the Garden in its most remote parts, until the winds again separate from each other. Filled with the odor of the pure spices, the winds bring the aroma from the most remote parts of Eden. They carry the spices of the Garden to the righteous and godly who in time to come will inherit the Garden of Eden and the Tree of life, for it is written (Cant 45: 16): "Awake, O north wind; and come you south; blow upon my garden and eat his precious fruits."

The same word used for "wind" is also used for "spirit." It is interesting to read the same verses using the word "spirit." It should also be noted that when certain attributes are associated with "wind," such as the wind of jealousy, it could be seen to be an agent of God, such as an angel or demon.

CHAPTER 24
The different chariots of the Holy One, blessed be He

Rabbi Ishmael said: Metatron, the Angel, the Prince of the Presence, the glory of all heaven, said to me: (1) The Holy One blessed be He, has innumerable chariots. He has the "Chariots of the Cherubim", for it is written (Ps. 18:11, 2 Sam 22: 11): " And he rode upon a cherub and did fly." (2) He has the "Chariots of Wind", for it is written: "and he flew swiftly upon the wings of the wind." (3) He has the "Chariots of the Swift Cloud", for it is written (Is.19:1): "Behold, the Lord rides upon a swift cloud:. (4) He has "Chariots of Clouds", for it is written (Ex. 19:9): "Lo, I come unto you in a cloud." (5) He has the "Chariots of the Altar", for it is written, " I saw the Lord standing upon the Altar." (6) He has the "Chariots of Ribbotaim", for it is written (Ps. 68:18): "The chariots of God are Ribbotaim; thousands of angels."

Ribbotaim appear to be used as the chariot and are a type of Cherub.

(7) He has the "Chariots of the Tent", for it is written (Deut. 31:15): "And the Lord appeared in the Tent in a pillar of cloud." (8) He has the "Chariots of the Tabernacle", for it is written (Lev. 1:1): "And the Lord spoke unto him out of the tabernacle." (9) He has the "Chariots of the Mercy-Seat", for it is written (Num. 7:89): "then he heard the Voice speaking unto him from upon the mercy-seat." (10) He has the "Chariots of Sapphire", for it is written (Ex. 24:10): "and there was under his feet a paved street of sapphires." (11) He has the "Chariots of Eagles", for it is written (Ex. 19:4): "I bare you on eagles' wings." It is not Eagles that are not meant here but "they that fly as swiftly as the eagles." (12) He has the "Chariots of a Shout", for

it is written: "God is gone up with a shout." (13) He has the "Chariots of Araboth (highest heaven)," for it is written (Ps 68 :5): " Praise Him that rides upon the Araboth (highest heaven)." (14) He has the "Chariots of Thick Clouds", for it is written (Ps. 106:3): "who makes the thick clouds His chariot." (15) He has the "Chariots of the Chayoth," for it is written (Ezek. 1:14): "and the Chayoth ran and returned." They run by permission and return by permission, for Shekina is above their heads. (16) He has the "Chariots of Wheels (Galgallim)", for it is written (Ezek. 10: 2): "And he said: Go in between the whirling wheels." (17) He has the "Chariots of a Swift Cherub," for it is written, "riding on a swift cherub." And at the time when He rides on a swift cherub, as he sets one of His feet upon his back, and before he sets the other foot upon his back, he looks through eighteen thousand worlds at one glace. And he perceives and understands and sees into them all and knows what is in all of them, and then he sets down the other foot upon the cherub, for it is written (Ezek. 48:35): " Round about eighteen thousand." How do we know that He looks through every one of them every day? It is written (Ps. 14: 2): "He looked down from heaven upon the children of men to see if there were any that understand, that seek after God." (18) He has the "Chariots of the Ophannim", for it is written (Ezek. 10:12): "and the Ophannim were full of eyes round about." (19) He has the "Chariots of His Holy Throne", for it is written (Ps. 67:8): "God sits upon his holy throne" (20) He has the "Chariots of the Throne of Yah (Jah)", for it is written (Ex. 17:16): "Because a hand is lifted up upon the Throne of Jah (Yah)." (21) He has the "Chariots of the Throne of Judgment," for it is written (Is. 5: 16): "but the Lord of hosts shall be exalted in judgment." (22) He has the "Chariots of the Throne of Glory", for it is written (Jer. 17:12): "The Throne of Glory, set on high from the beginning, is the place of our sanctuary." (23) He has the "Chariots of the High and exalted Throne", for it is written (Is. 6: 1): "I saw the Lord sitting upon the high and exalted throne."

CHAPTER 25
Ophphanniel, the Prince of the Ophannim and a description of the Ophannim

Rabbi Ishmael said: Metatron, the Angel, the Prince of the Presence, said to me: (1) Above these there is one great prince, highly honored, fit to rule, fearful, ancient and powerful. OPHAPHANNIEL YHWH is his name. (2) He has sixteen faces, four faces on each side, also a hundred wings on each side. And he has 8466 eyes, corresponding to the days of the year and sixteen on each side. (Other sources have it as: corresponding to the hours in a year.)

The number of 8466 is difficult to understand in a 365 day year. The lunar year was calculated to be 352.5 days at the time of the righting of 3 Enoch. 8466 is the number of hours in a lunar year. This makes sense and makes the alternate rendering the correct one. However, other places in the texts may refer to the number 8766, which is exact number of hours is a solar year of 365.25 days.

(3) And in those two eyes of his face, in each one of them lightning is flashing, and from each one of them burning staves are burning; and no creature is able to look at them: for anyone who looks at them is burned up instantly. (4) His height is the distance of 2500 years' journey. No eye can see and no mouth can tell of the mighty power of his strength except the King of kings, the Holy One, blessed be He. He alone can tell.

The number 2500 yields the number 7, as the digits are added together. This pattern will occur again is these types of measurements. It is a way Jewish mystics re-enforce the perfection of the template of heaven.

(5) Why is he called OPHPHANNIEL? Because he rules over the Ophannim and the Ophannim are given over to his authority. He stands every day and attends to them and makes them beautiful. And he raises them up and determines their activity. He polishes the place where they stand and makes their dwelling place bright. He even makes the corners of their crowns and their seats spotless. And he waits upon them early and late, by day and by night, in order to increase their beauty and make their dignity grow. He keeps them diligent in the praise of their Creator. (6) And all the Ophannim are full of eyes, and they are full of brightness; seventy-two sapphires are fastened to their garments on their right side and seventy-two sapphire are fastened to their garments on their left side.

Note the number 72 again, representing the nations of the world.

(7) And four carbuncle stones are fastened to the crown of every single one, the splendor of which shines out in the four directions of Araboth (the highest heaven) even as the splendor of the orb of the sun shines out in all the directions of the universe. And why is it called Carbuncle (Bare'qet)? Because its splendor is like the appearance of a lightning (Baraq). And tents of splendor, tents of brilliance, tents of brightness as of sapphire and carbuncle enclose them because of the shining appearance of their eyes.

Carbuncle is an archaic name given to red garnet. The word occurs in four places in most English translations of the Bible. Each use originates from the Greek term Anthrax – meaning coal, in reference to the color of burning coal. A

carbuncle is usually taken to mean a gem, particularly a deep-red garnet, which has no facet and is convex. In the same place in the masoretic text is the Hebrew word "nofech (no'-fekh)." In Exdodus 28:17 and again is Exodus 39:10 the carbuncle is used as the third stone in the breastplate of the Hoshen. Ezekiel 28:13 refers to the carbuncle's presence in the Garden of Eden.

CHAPTER 26
The Prince of the Seraphim.
Description of the Seraphim

Rabbi Ishmael said: Metatron, the Angel, the Prince of the Presence, said to me: (1) Over them there is one prince, who is wonderful, noble, of great honor, powerful and terrible, a chief leader and a fast scribe. He is glorified, honored and loved. (2) He is completely filled with splendor, and full of praise. He shines and he is totally full of the brightness of light and beauty. He is full of goodness and greatness. (3) His face is identical to that of angels, but his body is like an eagle's body. (4) His is magnificent like lightning, his appearance like burning staves. His beauty like sparks. His honor burns bright like glowing coal. His majesty like chashmals, His radiance like the light of the planet Venus. His image is like the Sun. His height is as high as the seven heavens. The light from his eyebrows is seven times as bright.

Chasmal is the fiery substance, which makes up the pillars on which the world rests. It is a mysterious substance or entity illuminating the heart of Ekekiel's chariot vision. Midrash Konen designated chashmal another class of angelic being.

(5) The sapphire on his head is as large as the entire universe and as splendid as the great heavens in radiance. (6) His body is full of eyes like the stars of the sky, innumerable and cannot be known. Every eye is like the planet Venus. But there are some of them like the Moon and some of them like the Sun. From His ankles to his knees they are like stars twinkling (of lightning). From his knees to his thighs is like the planet Venus, across his thighs like the moon, from his thighs to his neck is like the sun. From his neck to his head is like the Eternal Light. (7) The crown on his head is like the splendor of the Throne of Glory. The size of the crown is the distance of 502 years' journey. There is no kind of splendor, no kind of brilliance, no kind of radiance, no kind of light in the universe that is not affixed to the crown.

As in the prior chapter, the number seven is the result of the addition of the digits in the measurement, which in this case is 502.

(8) The name of that prince is SERAPHIEL YHWH. And the crown on his head, its name is "the Prince of Peace." And why is he called by the name of SERAPHIEL YHWH? Because he is assigned to rule over the Seraphim. And the flaming Seraphim are under his authority. And he presides over them by day and night and teaches them to sing, praise, and proclaim the beauty, power and majesty of their King. They proclaim the beauty of their King through all types of Praise and Sanctification. (Kedushah - Sacred Salutation of Holy, Holy, Holy). (9) How many Seraphim are there? Four, equating to the four winds of the world. And how many wings have each one of them? Six, relating to the six days of Creation. And how many faces do they have? Each one of them have four faces. (10) The height measurement of the Seraphim is the height of the seven heavens. The size of each wing is like the span of all Raqia (heaven). The size of each face is like the face of the East. (11) And each one of them gives out light, adding to the splendor of the Throne of Glory, so that not even the Holy Chayoth, the honored Ophannim, nor the majestic Cherubim are able to look on it. Anyone who gazes at it would be blinded because of its great splendor. (12) Why are they called Seraphim? Because they burn (saraph) the writing tables of Satan: Every day Satan sits together with SAMMAEL, the Prince of Rome, and with DUBBIEL, the Prince of Persia, and they write down the sins of Israel on their writing tables, which they hand over to the Seraphim, so that the Seraphim can present them to the Holy One, blessed be He, so that He should eliminate (destroy) Israel from the world. But the Seraphim know the secrets of the Holy One, blessed be He. They know that He does not want the people Israel to perish. What do the Seraphim do about this? Every day they receive the tablets from the hand of Satan and they burn them in the burning fire, which is near the high and exalted Throne. They do this in order that the tablet should not come before the Holy One, blessed be He, when he is sitting upon the Throne of Judgment, judging the entire world in truth.

Satan and Sammael are not allowed to approach the throne of God, but their accusations are taken by a Seraph, who destroys the tablet with the accusations against Israel and burns it. The tablet is not given to God, who would have to judge Israel, since the Seraph knows God does not wish to judge or punish Israel.
Dubbiel is the guardian angel of Persia and one of the special accusers of Israel. Dubbiel is an angel who was ranked among angels who were said to act as guardians over the seventy nations. Dubbiel was counted as the protector of Persia and as such defended its interests against its enemy Israel, a role that naturally put him at odds with the Chosen People and their special patron, St. Michael the Archangel. Sammael is an angel whose name

has been interpreted as meaning "angel" or "god" (el) of "poison" (sam). He is the guardian angel of Rome, another enemy of Israel. He is considered in legend a member of the heavenly host who fell. He is equated with Satan and the chief of the evil spirits. He is the angel of death. In this capacity he is a fallen angel but remains the Lord's servant, or at least under His control. As a good angel, Sammael resided in the seventh heaven, although he is declared to be the chief angel of the fifth heaven.
Seraphim are among the highest and most splendid of the nine accepted angelic orders as developed by the sixth-century theologian Dionysius. They are the closest in all of heaven to the throne of God. They are said to glow as if they are on fire so brightly they no mortal can endure the sight..

CHAPTER 27
RADWERIEL, the keeper of the Book of Records.

Rabbi Ishmael said: Metatron, the Angel of YHWH, the Prince of the Presence, said to me: (1) Above the Seraphim there is one prince, exalted above all princes. He is more wonderful than all the servants. His name is RADWERIEL YHWH who is assigned to rule over the treasuries of the books.

Radweriel is appointed over the treasury of book of records or remembrances. (See Mal.3:16). He is an angelic scribe, fluent in reading and writing. He reads the records in the Beth Din, (house/court) of justice. This is another name for the Sanhedrin.

(2) He couriers the Case of Writings, which has the Books of Records in it, and he brings it to the Holy One, blessed be He. And he breaks the seals of the case, opens it, and takes out the books and delivers them before the Holy One, blessed be He. And the Holy One, blessed be He, receives them out of his hand and gives them to the Scribes to see so they may read them in the Great Beth (house) Din in the height of Araboth (highest heaven) of Raqia (heaven), before the household of heaven. (3) And why is he called RADWERIEL? Because from every word going out of his mouth an angel is created. He stands in the service of the company of the ministering angels and sings a song before the Holy One, blessed be He, as the time draws near for the recitation of the Thrice Holy One.

CHAPTER 28
The 'Irin and Qaddishin (Watchers and Holy Ones)

Rabbi Ishmael said: Metatron, the Angel, the Prince of the Presence, said to me: (1) Above all these there are four great princes. Their names are Irin and Qaddishin. They are highly honored, revered, loved, wonderfully glorious, and greater than any of the heavenly children. There is none like them among all the princes of heaven (sky). There are none equal to them among any Servants. Each one is equal to all the rest of the heavenly servants put together. (2) And their dwelling is near the Throne of Glory and their standing place near the Holy One, blessed be He. The brightness of their dwelling is a reflection from the brightness from the Throne of Glory. Their face is magnificent and is a reflection of the magnificence of Shekina. (3) They are elevated by the glory of the Divince Majesty (Gebura) and praised by (through) the praise of Shekina. (4) And not only that, but the Holy One, blessed be He, does nothing in his world without first consulting them. Only after He consults them does He perform it. As it is written (Dan. 4: 17): "The sentence is by the decree of the Irin and the demand by the word of the Qaddishin." (5) The Irin are two (twins) and the Qaddishin are two (twins). In what fashions standing before the Holy One, blessed be He? We should understood, that one Ir is standing on one side and the other 'Ir on the other side. Also, one Qaddish is standing on one side and the other on the other side. (6) And they exalt the humble forever, and they humble and bring to the ground those that are proud. They exalt to the heights those that are humble. (7) And every day, as the Holy One, blessed be He, is sitting upon the Throne of Judgment and judges the entire world, and the Books of the Living and the Books of the Dead are opened in front of Him all the children of heaven are standing before Him in fear and dread. They are in awe and they shake. When the Holy One, blessed be He, is sitting on the Throne of Judgment to execute His judgment , His garment is white as snow, the hair on his head is like pure wool and the His entire cloak is shining with light. He is covered with righteousness all over, like He is wearing a coat of mail. (8) And those Irin and Qaddishin (Watchers and Holy Ones) are standing before Him like court officers before the judge. And constantly they begin and argue a case and close the case that comes before the Holy One, blessed be He, in judgment, according for it is written (Dan. 4. 17): "The sentence is by the decree of the 'Irin and the demand by the word of Qaddishin."

This section explains the function of the Irin and Qaddishin. They are two pairs of angels forming the apex of angelic power. They are the holy councilors and they have authority over all things terrestrial. They are judge and executioner. Another tradition has the Irin and Qaddishin as two classes of angels but many in number. Yet, they seem to come in sets of two each, like twins. Again, this may represent the balance of mercy and justice always sought in heaven.

(9) Some of them argue the case and others pass the sentence in the Great Beth Din (Great House of the Sanhedrin) in Araboth (the highest heaven). Some of them make requests in the presence of the Divine Majesty and some close the cases before the Most

High. Others finish by going down and confirming the judgement and executing the sentences on earth below. According for it is written (Dan. 4. 13, 14): "Behold an Ir and a Qaddish came down from heaven and cried aloud and said , "Chop down the tree, and cut off his branches, shake off his leaves, and scatter his fruit: let the beasts escape from under it, and the fowls from his branches." (10) Why are they called Irin and Qaddishin (Watchers and Holy Ones)? Because they sanctify the body and the spirit with beatings with fire on the third day of the judgment, for it is written (Hos. 6: 2): "After two days will he revive us: on the third he will raise us up, and we shall live before him."

Irin and Qaddishin or ministering spirits receive men from the angel of death. They judge him with angels arguing for him. This takes two days. On the third day they pass judgment. The sentence is based on the man's character and how closely he followed the Torah. They beat them accordingly.

CHAPTER 29
Description of a class of angels

Rabbi Ishmael said: Metatron, the Angel, the Prince of the Presence, said to me: (1) Each one of the Angels has seventy names corresponding to the seventy languages (nations) of the world. And all of them are based upon the name of the Holy One, blessed be He. And every several name is written with a flaming pen of iron on the Fearful Crown (Kether Nora), which is on the head of the high and exalted King.

Metatron was said to have names based upon the names of God. Fearful Crown refers to the crown of a sitting king, thus God.

(2) And each one of them projects sparks and lightning. Each one of them is covered with horns of splendor all over. Lights shine from each of them, and each one is surrounded by tents of brilliance so that not even the Seraphim and the Chayoth who are greater than all the children of heaven are able to look at them.

CHAPTER 30
The 72 princes of Kingdoms and the Prince of the World are at the Great Sanhedrin.

Rabbi Ishmael said: Metatron, the Angel, the Prince of the Presence, said to me: (1) Whenever the Great Beth Din (House of the Sanhedrin) is seated in the Araboth (highest heaven) of Raqia (heaven) there no one speaks. No mouth opens for anyone in the world except those great princes who are called YHWH by the name of the Holy One, blessed be He. (2) How many are those Princes are there? Seventy-two princes of the kingdoms of the world besides the Prince of the World who pleads in favor of the world before the Holy One, blessed be He. Every day at the appointed hour the book with the records of all the deeds of the world is opened. For it is written (Dan. 7:10): " The judgment was set and the books were opened."

The highest classes of angels are marked with the Tetragrammaton. Each nation has its own angel appointed to guard and plea for its cause. What is odd about this is the equal and universal appeal to justice. There is no difference in how the court is conducted between Gentile or Jew. In this scenario, Metatron is the Prince of the world.

CHAPTER 31
The attributes of Justice, Mercy and Truth

Rabbi Ishmael said: Metatron, the Angel, the Prince of the Presence, said to me: (1) At the time when the Holy One, blessed be He, is sitting on the Throne of Judgment, Justice is standing on His right and Mercy on His left and Truth in front of His face, (2) then man (Some sources say "wicked man" but this is to be read as mankind) enters before Him for judgment, then , a staff comes out from the splendor of Mercy towards him and it stands in front of the man. Then man falls upon his face, and all the angels of destruction are fearful and they shake before him. For it is written (Is. 16:5): "And with mercy shall the throne be established, and he shall sit upon it in truth."

The fundamental balance of justice and mercy is only possible through truth, including the truth of what the real intent of the person being judged was. This is only possible with God. The angels of destruction are there to execute man but Mercy stops them and makes the angels fear. The wording of the verse makes this point unclear.

CHAPTER 32
The execution of judgment on the wicked. God's sword

Rabbi Ishmael said: Metatron, the Angel, the Prince of the Presence, said to me: (1) When the Holy One, blessed be He, opens the Book, half of it is fire and half of it is flames. Then the angels of destruction go out from Him continually to execute the judgment on the wicked by His sword, which is drawn from its sheath and it shines like magnificent lightning and pervades the world from one end to the other. For it is written (Is. 66:16): "For by fire will the Lord plead by His sword with all flesh." (2) And all those who come into the world fear and shake before Him, when they behold His sharpened sword like lightning from one end of the world to the other, and sparks and flashes

of the size of the stars of Raqia (heaven) going out from it; according for it is written (Deut. 32: 41): If I whet the lightning of my sword."

CHAPTER 33
The angels of Mercy, of Peace, and of Destruction are by the Throne of Judgment.

Rabbi Ishmael said: Metatron, the Angel, the Prince of the Presence, said to me: (1) At the time that the Holy One, blessed be He, is sitting on the Throne of Judgment, then the angels of Mercy are standing on His right, the angels of Peace are standing on His left and the angels of Destruction are standing in front of Him. (2) And there is one scribe standing beneath Him, and another scribe standing above Him. (3) And the glorious Seraphim surround the Throne on all four of its sides with walls of lightning. And the Ophannim surround them with burning staves all around the Throne of Glory. And clouds of fire and clouds of flames surround them to the right and to the left. The Holy Chayoth carry the Throne of Glory from below. Each one uses only three fingers. The length of each fingers is 800,000 and 700 times one hundred, and 66,000 parasangs. (4) And underneath the feet of the Chayoth there are seven rivers of fire running and flowing. And the distance across of each river is 365 thousand parasangs and its depth is 248 thousand times ten-thousand parasangs. Its length cannot be known and is immeasurable. (5) And each river turns round in a bow in the four directions of Araboth (the highest heaven) of Raqia (heaven), and from there it falls down to Maon and is stopped, and from Maon (some sources have "Velum") to Zebul, from Zegul to Shechaqim, from Shechaqim to Raqia (heaven) to Shamayim and from Shamayim it fows on the heads of the wicked who are in Gehenna, for it is written (Jer. 23:19): "Behold a whirlwind of the Lord, even His fury, is gone, yes, a whirling tempest; it shall burst upon the head of the wicked."

Maon or Velum is the name of the first heaven. The river flows down from heaven and all of its levels, to Gehenna, which is the burning hell. Speculation on the meaning of the numbers contained in this chapter are random. In general, 3 is the number of spiritual completeness, and 8 is the number of judgment. The number of man and his shortcomings is 6. The number 7 represents spiritual perfection. 5 represents grace and spirit.

CHAPTER 34
The different concentric circles around the Chayoth consist of fire, water, hailstones.

Rabbi Ishmael said: Metatron; the Angel, the Prince of the Presence, said to me: (1) The hoofs of the Chayoth are surrounded by seven clouds of burning coals. The clouds of burning coals are surrounded on the outside by seven walls of flames. The seven walls of flames are surrounded on the outside by seven walls of hailstones (stones of El-gabish, Ezek.13: 11, 13, 28: 22). The hailstones are surrounded on the outside by boulders (stones) of hail. The boulders (stones) of hail are surrounded on the outside by stones of "the wings of the tempest." The stones of "the of the winged tempest" are surrounded by the outside by flames of fire. The chambers of the whirlwind are surrounded on the outside by the fire and water. (2) Around the fire and the water are those who sing the "Holy." Around about those who sing the "Holy" are those who sing the "Blessed." Around about those who sing the "Blessed" are the bright clouds. The bright clouds are surrounded on the outside by coals of burning juniper wood. There are thousands of camps of fire and ten thousand hosts of flames. And between every camp and every host there is a cloud, so that they may not be burned by the fire.

The stones of hail are made of the two opposite substances of fire and ice. This, like the reference to fire and water, represent a balance of forces which, if applied within the spiritual realm, brings blessings.

CHAPTER 35
The camps of angels in Araboth (the highest heaven) of Raqia (heaven). Angels performing the Kedushah (Sacred Salutation of Holy, Holy, Holy)

Rabbi Ishmael said: Metatron, the Angel, the Prince of the Presence, said to me: (1) 506 (Other sources have 496) thousand times ten-thousand camps has the Holy One, blessed be He, in the height of Araboth (the highest heaven) of Raqia (heaven). And each camp is composed of 496 thousand angels.

The Gematria for 506 is "kingdom" and for 496 it is "kingdoms."

(2) And every single angel is as tall as the width of the great sea; and the appearance of their face is like the appearance of lightning. Their eyes are like lamps of fire, and their arms and their feet were the color of polished brass and when they spoke words their voice roared and sounded like the voice of a multitude of them. (3) They all stand before the Throne of Glory in four rows. And the princes of the army are standing at the beginning of each row. (4) Some of them sing the "Holy" and others sing the "Blessed." Some run as messengers while others stand in attendance. For it is written (Dan. 7: 10): "Thousands of thousands ministered unto Him, and ten thousand times ten thousand stood before Him. The judgment was set and the books were opened."

The singing or chanting of "Holy, Holy, Holy" is returned by the phrase, "Blessed be Thou and blessed is the name of the Lord for ever and ever."

(5) When the time nears and the hour comes to say the "Holy", first a whirlwind from before the Holy One, blessed be He, goes out and bursts on the camp of Shekina and there arises a great noise and confusion among them. For it is written (Jer. 30: 23): "Behold, the whirlwind of the Lord goes forth with fury, a continuing commotion." (6) At that moment thousands of thousands of them are changed into sparks, thousands of thousands of them ignite into burning staves, thousands of thousands flashes, thousands of thousands burst into flames, thousands of thousands change into males, thousands of thousands change into females, thousands of thousands burst into winds, thousands of thousands burst into burning fires, thousands of thousands burst into flames, thousands of thousands turn into sparks, thousands of thousands turn into chashmals of light; until they take upon themselves the yoke of the kingdom of heaven, the high and lifted up, of the Creator of them all with fear, dread, awe, and trembling, with commotion, anguish, terror and trepidation. Then they are changed again into their former shape to have the fear of their King before them always, as they have set their hearts on saying the Song continually, for it is written (Is. 6:3): "And one cried unto another and said Holy, Holy, Holy."

The phrase, "…thousands of thousands change into males, thousands of thousands change into females …" is suspect and may have been added later. The idea of taking onto oneself the yoke of heaven may refers to the fact that the angels are reciting the "Holy" and "Blessed" discourse, which means they understand and acknowledge the ways of heaven and the place and power of God. Judgment comes accordingly.

CHAPTER 36
The angels bathe in the river of fire before they recite the Song

Rabbi Ishmael said: Metatron, the Angel, the Prince of Presence, said to me: (1) At the time when the ministering angels desire to sing (the) Song, (then) Nehar di-Nur (the stream of fire) rises with many "thousand thousands and ten-thousand ten-thousands" (of angels) of power and strength of fire (the intensity of the radiant fire of the angels flows) and it runs and passes under the Throne of Glory, between the camps of the ministering angels and the troops of Araboth (highest heaven). (2) And all the ministering angels first go down into Nehar di-Nur (stream of fire), and they dip themselves in the fire and dip their tongue and their mouth seven times; (

2Kings 5:14) and after that they go up and put on the garment of Machaqe Samal and cover themselves with cloaks of chashmal (the zenith of heaven) and stand in four rows over near the side of the Throne of Glory, in all the heavens.

No meaning for the term Machaqe Samal could be found.
CHAPTER 37
The four camps of Shekina and their surroundings

Rabbi Ishmael said: Metatron, the Angel, the Prince of the Presence, said to me: (1) In the seven Halls four chariots of Shekina are standing. Before each one stands the four camps of Shekina. Between (or behind) each camp a river of fire is continually flowing. (2) Between (or behind) each river there are bright clouds surrounding them, and between (or behind) each cloud there are pillars of brimstone erected. Between one pillar and another there stands flaming wheels, which surround them. And between one wheel and another there are flames of fire all around. Between the flames there are storehouses of lightning. Behind the storehouses of lightning there are the wings of the Wind of the Storm. Behind the wings of the Wind of the Storm are the chambers of the tempest. Behind the chambers of the tempest there are winds, voices, thunder, and sparks emitting from sparks and earthquakes within earthquakes.

The original intent of the verse may have been to draw a picture of the rivers running in concentric circles through the heavens and beside the river, in rows are clouds, lightning, and wind.

CHAPTER 38
The fear in heavens at the sound of the "Holy" is appeased by the Prince of the World

Rabbi Ishmael said: Metatron, the Angel, the Prince of the Presence, said to me: (1) At the time, when the ministering angels sing (the Thrice) Holy, then all the pillars of the heavens and their sockets shake, and the gates of the Halls of Araboth (the highest heaven) of Raqia (heaven) are shaken and the foundations of Shechaqim and the universe are moved, and the orders (secrets) of Maon and the chambers of Makon quiver, and all the orders of Raqia (heaven) and the constellations and the planets are distressed. The orbs of the sun and the moon rush away and run out of their pattens and run 12,000 parasangs and the wish to throw themselves down from heaven, (2) because of the roaring voice (sound) of their song, and the noise of their praise and the sparks and lightning that proceed from their faces. For it is written (Ps. 77: 18): "The voice of your thunder was in the heaven (the lightning illuminated the world, the earth trembled and shook)." (3) Until the Prince of the World calls

them, saying; Be quiet in your place! Do not fear because of the ministering angels who sing the Song before the Holy One, blessed be He." As it is written (Job. 38: 7): "When the morning stars sang together and all the children of heaven shouted for joy."

As the appointed times approached to sing the Holy, Holy, Holy, all of heaven became anxious. Metatron quieted them and gave them focus.

CHAPTER 39
The explicit names fly from the Throne.

Rabbi Ishmael said: Metatron, the Angel, the Prince of the Presence, said to me: (1) When the ministering angels sing the "Holy" then all the explicit names that are engraved with a flaming iron pen on the Throne of Glory go flying off like eagles, each with sixteen wings. And they surround and hover around the Holy One, blessed be He, on all four sides of the place of His Shekina. (2) And the angels of the host, and the flaming Servants, the mighty Ophannim, the Cherubim of the Shekina, the Holy Chayoth, the Seraphim, the Er'ellim, the Taphsarim, the troops of burning fire, the armies of fire, the flaming hosts, and the holy princes, adorned with crowns, clothed in kingly majesty, wrapped in glory, tied with high honor, fall on their faces three times, saying: "Blessed be the name of His glorious kingdom for ever and ever."

Taphsarim are the troupes of flames. Er'el, more commonly referred to in the plural as "the Erelim", are a rank of angels in Jewish Kabbala (Cabbalah) and mythology. The name is seen to mean "the valiant/courageous." They are generally seen as the third highest rank of divine beings/angels below God. The description in the verse seems to say that letters fly off of the Torah like eagles when it is burned.

CHAPTER 40
The ministering angels rewarded and punished.

Rabbi Ishmael said: Metatron, the Angel, the Prince of the Presence, said to me: (1) When the ministering angels say "Holy" before the Holy One, blessed be He, in the proper way, then the servants of His Throne, the attendants of His Glory, go out with much happiness from under the Throne of Glory. (2) And each one carries in their hands thousands and ten thousand times ten thousand crowns of stars, similar in appearance to the planet Venus, and put them on the ministering angels and the great prince who sing the "Holy." They place three crowns on each one of them: one crown because they say "Holy", and another crown, because they say "Holy, Holy", and a third crown because they say "Holy, Holy, Holy, is the Lord of Hosts." (3) But in the moment that they do not sing the "Holy" in the right order, a consuming fire flashes out from the little finger of the Holy One, blessed be He, and descends into the middle of their ranks, which is divided into 496 thousand parts corresponding to the four camps of the ministering angels, and the fire burns up in a single moment those who did not say the "Holy" correctly. For it is written (Ps. 92:3): "A fire goes before him and burns up his adversaries round about." (4) After that the Holy One, blessed be He, opens His mouth and speaks one word and creates other new ones like them to replace them. And each one stands before His Throne of Glory, signing the "Holy", as it written (Lam. 12:23): "They are new every morning; great is your faithfulness."

Here we see the full extent of the phrase, "taking on the yoke of heaven." One is rewarded for proper worship and ceremony or annihilated if God disapproves. The text indicates that all of the angels in the offending group are destroyed. Angels are created, nullifying the six days of the creation of everything.

CHAPTER 41
Letters engraved on the Throne of Glory created everything.

Rabbi Ishmael said: Metatron, the Angel, the Prince of the Presence, said to me: (1) Come and see the letters by which the heaven and earth were created. These are the letters by which were created the mountains and hills. These are the letters by which were created the seas and rivers, these are the letters by which were created the trees and herbs, these are the letters by which were created the planets and the constellations, these are the letters by which were created the globe of the earth and the orb of the moon and the orb of the sun, as well as Orion, the Pleiades and all the different luminaries of Raqia (heaven) were created. (2) These are the letters by which were created the Throne of Glory and the Wheels of the Merkaba (chariot) , the letters by which were created the necessities of the worlds, (3) the letters by which were created wisdom, understanding, knowledge, prudence, meekness and righteousness by which the entire world is sustained. (4) And I walked by his side and he took me by his hand and raised me up on his wings and showed me those letters, all of them, that are engraved with a flaming iron pen on the Throne of Glory. Sparks go out from them and cover all the chambers of Araboth (the highest heaven).

Jewish tradition has it that God and angels spoke Hebrew, and thus all things came into existence when God spoke them into existence in Hebrew. It is a very short leap of logic to assume the written word would have the same power and effect. This means within the various

combinations of the 22 Hebrew letters all things were created and are sustained.

CHAPTER 42
Opposites kept in balance by several Divine Names

Rabbi Ishmael said: Metatron, the Angel, the Prince of the Presence, said to me: (1) Come and I will show you, where the waters are suspended in the highest place, where fire is burning in the midst of hail, where lightning flashes forth from out of the middle of snowy mountains, where thunder is roaring in the heights of the skies, where a flame is burning in the burning fire, and where voices make themselves heard within (in spite of) thunder and earthquake.

The balance indicated herein reminds one of a Zen koan – "See the sun in the midst of the rain. Scoop clear water from the heart of the fire." This chapter reveals a fundamental truth. All things are created in heaven by His word, sustained by His word, and reflected in the lower world where we live only after being created in heaven.

(2) Then I went to his side and he took me by his hand and lifted me up on his wings and showed me all those things. I saw the waters suspended on high in Araboth (the highest heaven) of Raqia (heaven) by the power of the name YAH EHYE ASHER EHYE (Jah, I am that I am), and their fruits (rain) was falling down from heaven and watering the face of the world, for it is written (Ps. 104:13): "(He waters the mountains from his chambers:) the earth is satisfied with the fruit of your work." (3) And I saw fire and snow and hail that were mingled together within each other and yet were undamaged. This was accomplished by the power of the name ESH OKELA (consuming fire). For it is written (Deut. 55: 24): "For the Lord, your God, is a consuming fire." (4) And I saw lightning flashing out of mountains of snow and yet the lightning was not extinguished, by the power of the name YA SUR OLAMIM (Jah, the everlasting rock). For it is written (Is. 26: 4): "For Jah, YHWH is the everlasting rock." (5) And I saw thunder and heard voices that were roaring within flames of fire and they were not silenced. This is accomplished by the power of the name EL-SHADDAI RABBA (the Great God Almighty) for it is written (Gen. 17:1): "I am God Almighty." (6) And I saw a flame glowing in the middle of burning fire, and yet it was not devoured. This was done by the power of the name YAD AL KES YAH (the hand upon the Throne of the Lord.) For it is written (Ex. 17: 16): " And he said: for the hand is upon the Throne of the Lord." (7) And I looked and saw rivers of fire within of rivers of water and they were not extinguished. All of this was done by the power of the name OSE SHAlOM (Maker of

Peace) for it is written (Job 25: 2): "He makes peace in high places." For he makes peace between fire and water, and between hail and fire, and between the wind and cloud, and between earthquakes and sparks.

CHAPTER 43
The abode of the unborn spirits and of the spirits of the righteous dead

Rabbi Ishmael said: Metatron said to me: (1) Come and I will show you where the spirits of the righteous are that have been created and those that have returned, and the spirits of the righteous that have not yet been created (born). (2) And he lifted me up to his side, took me by his hand and sat me near the Throne of Glory by the place of the Shekina; and he revealed the Throne of glory to me, and he showed me the spirits that have been created and had returned as well as those who were flying above the Thorne of Glory in front of the Holy One, blessed be He. (3) After that I went to interpret the following verse of Scripture and I found what is written (Isa. 57: 16: "for the spirit clothed itself before me .") It refers to the spirits that have been created in the chamber of creation of the righteous and that have returned before the Holy One, blessed be He; (and the (His) words.) "The souls I have made" refers to the spirits of the righteous that have not yet been created in the chamber (GUPH).

Within the entire book of 3 Enoch, this chapter could be the most important to all "Children of the book," Jews, Christians, and Moslems. The story of creation has God creating everything in six days. Everything must also include all of the souls that are ever to be born. These souls are housed in a chamber near the throne of God, called the Guph (Guf). This chapter tells us the souls of the righteous are housed.
The righteous souls are housed in the Guph, waiting to be clothed in flesh for their incarnation. But if the righteous souls are here, where are the unrighteous souls kept? If there were another place where the unrighteous souls are kept the distinction would indicate predestination. If the character of the soul is already determined and they are stored accordingly then how is the determination made? Are we created as righteous and unrighteous beings? Does God simply look ahead and see us as we are to be?
As the next two chapters unfold, we see hints that the Guph may not be the place where all of the souls are housed but possibly it is where the souls of the righteous are conducted to be clothed in flesh and dispatched to earth through birth. The wicked soul finds his home in Sheol. If this were true it would still indicate predestination or foreknowledge are at work.
Mystical writings, such as the Zohar, describe God as a burning flame from where sparks fly outward. These sparks

are the souls of the Jewish people. When these sparks return to the primal flame, time will come to an end. Another tradition states that when the Guph is emptied time will end.
Souls leaving the Guph are born and return to God after death.

CHAPTER 44
Metatron shows Rabbi Ishmael the abode of the wicked and the intermediate in Sheol.

Rabbi Ishmael said: Metatron, the Angel, the Prince of the Presence, said to me: (1) Come and I will show you the spirits of the wicked and the spirits of those in between (intermediate) where they are standing, and the spirits of those in between (intermediate), where they go down, and the spirits of the wicked, where they go down.

Now we know there are three classes of souls: the righteous, the intermediate – those in between, and the unrighteous. The obvious questions are, where were the souls of the "intermediates" kept and from where were they dispatched? Are these the souls of the "lukewarm?"

(2) And he said to me: The spirits of the wicked go down to Sheol by the hands of two angels of destruction: ZAAPHIEL and SIMKIEL. (3) SIMKIEL is assigned to rule over the intermediate to support them and purify them because of the great mercy of the Prince of the Place (The Divine Majesty). ZAAPHIEL is assigned to rule over the spirits of the wicked in order to cast them down from the presence of the Holy One, blessed be He, and from the magnificence of the Shekina, and he casts them into Sheol, to punish them in the fire of Gehenna with rods of burning coal. (4) And I went by his side, and he took me by his hand and pointed them all out to me. (5) And I saw the faces of children of men and the way they looked. Their bodies were like eagles. And not only that but the color of the complexion of the intermediate was like pale grey because of their deeds. They were stained until they become cleansed from their iniquity in the fire.

It is interesting to note this indirect reference to Purgatory in a Jewish book written between the second and fifth centuries A.D.

(6) And the color of the wicked was like the bottom of a pot (burned black) because of the wickedness of their deeds. (7) And I saw the spirits of the Patriarchs Abraham, Isaac, and Jacob and the rest of the righteous, whom they have brought up out of their graves and who have ascended to Heaven. And they were praying before the Holy One, blessed be He, saying in their prayer: "Lord of the Universe! How

long will you sit upon your Throne like a mourner in the days of his mourning with your right hand behind you and not deliver your children and reveal your Kingdom in the world? And how long will you have no pity upon your children who are made slaves among the nations of the world? Your right hand is behind you. Why do you not stretch out the heavens and the earth and the heavens of the highest heavens? When will you have compassion?"

The right hand is the symbol of power and authority. To have the right hand behind your back means you are not using the power or authority available to you.

(8) Then the Holy One, blessed be He, answered every one of them, saying: "Since these wicked commit sins on and on, and transgress with sins again and again against Me, how could I deliver my great Right Hand when it would mean their downfall would be caused by their own hands.

The reason God does not bring judgment upon the world is because many Jews were among the unrepentant sinners. He wishes to await their return to him before judging them. This is the ultimate mercy.

(9) In that moment Metatron called me and spoke to me: "My servant! Take the books, and read their evil deeds!" Then I took the books and read their deeds and there were 36 transgressions to be found written down regarding each wicked one and besides that they have transgressed all the letters in Torah, for it is written (Dan. 55: 11): "Yea, all Israel have transgressed your Law." It is not written, "for they have transgressed from Aleph to Taw (A to Z) 36 (40) statutes have they transgressed for each letter?

Some sources have "40 statues." The number "40" is the number of severe trials and testing. The implication of the verse is that the souls have broken 40 major laws and many minor ones.

(10) Then Abraham, Isaac and Jacob wept. Then the Holy One, blessed be He said to them: "Abraham, my beloved, Isaac, my Elect one, Jacob, my firstborn, how can I deliver them from among the nations of the world at this time?" And immediately MIKAEL (Michael), the Prince of Israel, cried and wept with a loud voice and said (Ps. 10:1): "Why stand you afar off, O Lord?"

CHAPTER 45
Past and future events recorded on the Curtain of the Throne.

Rabbi Ishmael said: Metatron said to me: (1) Come, and I will show you the Curtain of The Divine

Majesty which is spread before the Holy One, blessed be He. On it are written all the generations of the world and all their deeds (actions/doings), both what they have done and what they will do until the end of all generations. (2) And I came, and he showed it to me pointing it out with his fingers like a father who teaches his children the letters of Torah. And I saw each generation and within the generations I saw the rulers, the leaders, the shepherds, the oppressors (despots), the keepers, the punisher, the counselors, the teachers, the supporters, the bosses, the presidents of academies, the magistrates, the princes, the advisors, the noblemen, and the warriors, the elders, and the guides of each generation.

In the ancient world, these represent all major groups that have influence over the lives of people.

(3) And I saw Adam, his generation, their deeds (actions/doings) and their thoughts, Noah and his generation, their deeds and their thoughts, and the generation of the flood, their deeds and their thoughts, Shem and his generation, their deeds and their thoughts, Nimrod and the generation of the confusion of tongues, and his generation, their deeds and their thoughts, Abraham and his generation, their deeds and their thoughts, Isaac and his generation, their deeds and their thoughts, Ishmael and his generation, their deeds and their thoughts, Jacob and his generation, their deeds and their thoughts, Joseph and his generation , their deeds and their thoughts, the tribes and their generation, their deeds and their thoughts, Amram and his generation, their deeds and their thoughts , Moses and his generation, their deeds and their thoughts, (4) Aaron and Mirjam their accomplishments and actions, the princes and the elders, their works and deeds, Joshua and his generation, their works and deeds, the judges and their generation, their works and deeds, Eli and his generation, their works and deeds, Phinehas, their works and deeds, Elkanah and his generation, their accomplishments and actions, Samuel and his generation, their works and deeds, the kings of Judah with their generations, their works and their doing, the kings of Israel and their generation, their accomplishments and actions, the princes of Israel, their accomplishments and actions; the princes of the nations of the world, their accomplishments and actions, the heads of the councils of Israel, their accomplishments and actions; the heads of the councils in the nations of the world, their generations, their accomplishments and actions; the rulers of Israel and their generation, their accomplishments and actions; the noblemen of Israel and their generation, their works and their deeds; the noblemen of the nations of the world and their generations, their accomplishments and actions; the men of reputation

in Israel, their generation, their accomplishments and actions; the judges of Israel, their generation, their accomplishments and actions; the judges of the nations of the world and their generation, their accomplishments and actions; the teachers of children in Israel, their generations, their accomplishments and actions: the teachers of children in the nations of the world, their generation, their accomplishments and actions; the interpreters) of Israel, their generation, their accomplishments and actions; the interpreters of the nations of the world, their generation, their accomplishments and actions; (5) and all the fights and wars that the nations of the world worked against the people of Israel in the time of their kingdom. And I saw Messiah, the son of Joseph, and his generation and their accomplishments and actions that they will do against the nations of the world. And I saw Messiah, the son of David, and his generation, and all the fights and wars, and their accomplishments and actions that they will do with Israel both for good and evil. And I saw all the fights and wars that Gog and Magog will fight with Israel in the days of Messiah, and all that the Holy One, blessed be He, will do with them in the time to come.

This is the first mention of two Messiahs. However, the dual functions of the Messiah can be seen as the impetus to this idea. The Messiah is seen as a peacemaker and teacher, who brings mercy. The Messiah is also seen as a warrior, destroyer, and bringer of justice. One comes in peace and the other is determined to do war to avenge God and Israel. It appears the Messiah, son of David, is truculent compared to the son of Joseph, who will be killed for his attempt to make peace. Christians believe the same Messiah will perform both functions because he came as peacemaker and teacher but will return from heaven as the warrior of God. The text here indicates there will be two separate Messiahs.

(6) And all the rest of all the leaders of the generations and all the works of the generations both in Israel and in the nations of the world, both what is done and what will be done hereafter to all generations until the end of time all were written on the Curtain of The Divine Majesty. And I saw all these things with my eyes; and after I had seen it, I opened my mouth in praise of The Divine Majesty saying, (Eccl. 8:4, 5): "For the King's word has power and who may say unto Him, What do you do? Whoever keeps the commandments shall know no evil thing." And I said: (Ps. 104: 24) "O Lord how manifold (multi-colored/multifaceted) are your works!"

Rabbi Ishmael was shown all of the deeds and works of mankind for all generations. This implies predestination or foreknowledge. The reader must decide for himself or herself.

CHAPTER 46
The place of the stars shown to Rabbi Ishmael

Rabbi Ishmael said: Metatron said to me: (1) Come and I will show you the distance between the stars that are standing in the Raqia (heaven), for they stand there night after night in fear of the Almighty and The Divine Majesty. I will show you where they go and where they stand. (2) I walked by his side, and he took me by his hand and pointed out all of them to me with his finger. And they were standing on sparks of flames around the Merkaba (chariot) of the Almighty, The Divine Majesty. What did Metatron do? At that moment he clapped his hands and chased them off from their place. Then they flew off on flaming wings, rose and fled from the four sides of the Throne of Merkaba (chariot), and as they flew he told me the names of ever-single one. As it is written, (Ps. 137:4) "He tells the number of the stars; he gives them all their names", teaching, that the Holy One, blessed be He, has given a name to each one of them. (3) And by the authority of RAHATIEL they enter in a numbered order to Raqia (heaven) ha-shamayim (the second of the seven heavens) to serve the world. And they go out in numbered order to praise the Holy One, blessed be He, with songs and hymns, for it is written (Ps. 19: 1): "The heavens declare the glory of God." (4) But in the age to come the Holy One, blessed be He, will create them anew. For it is written (Lam. 52: 23): "They are new every morning." And they open their mouth and sing a song. Which is the song that they sing? (Ps. 8:3): "When I consider your heavens."

Rahatiel is the angelic ruler of the stars and constellations. The Ophannim is the class of angels that move the celestial sphere. Stars were considered by many cultures to be spiritual entities, or angels. This was a Babylonian concept that was absorbed. It is in this light that the stars would sing. They leave the second heaven and proceed through the heavens to the seventh heaven where they end their journey at the throne.

CHAPTER 47
Metatron shows Rabbi Ishmael the spirits of punished angels.

Rabbi Ishmael said: Metatron said to me: (1) Come and I will show you the souls of the angels and the spirits of the servants that served, whose bodies have been burned up in the fire of The Divine Majesty of the Almighty, that projects from his little finger. And they have been made into burning and glowing coals in the midst of the river of fire (Nehar di-Nur). But their spirits and their souls are standing behind the Shekina. (2) Whenever the angel servants sing a song at a wrong time or they sing what was not appointed to be sung they are burned and consumed by the fire of their Creator and by a flame from their Maker from the rooms of the whirlwind. The fire blows on them and drives them into the river of fire (Nehar di-Nur). There they become mountains of burning coal. But their spirit and their soul return to their Creator, and all are standing behind their Master. (3) And I went by his side and he took me by his hand, and he showed me all the souls of the angels and the spirits of the attending servants who were standing behind the Shekina and were standing on the wings of a whirlwind with walls of fire all around them. (4) At that moment Metatron opened the gates of the walls within which they were standing behind the Shekina for me to see. And I raised my eyes and I saw them. I saw what of every one of the angels looked like and I saw their wings were like birds made out of flames. And it looked as if they were fashioned from burning fire. In that moment I opened my mouth in praise of The Divine Majesty and said (Ps. 92: 5): "How great are your works, O Lord."

The river of fire or Nehar di-Nur is presented here as a place of resurrection of the angels since their bodies were burnt but the spirit continues and ends up again with God. However, this idea is contradicted in most Jewish mystic writings. It is possible the text here is somehow corrupted or missunderstood.

CHAPTER 48 - A
Rabbi Ishmael sees the Right Hand of the Most High

Rabbi Ishmael said: Metatron said to me: (1) come, and I will show you the Right Hand of The Divine Majesty, which He keeps behind Him because of the destruction of the Holy Temple; from which all kinds of splendor and light shine forth and by which the 955 heavens were created; and whom not even the Seraphim and the Ophannim are permitted to experience until the day that salvation shall arrive.

God became inactive because of the destruction of the temple between March and September of 70 A.D. and onward. Why God would choose the sacking of his temple to mark his quiescence might be understood by looking at the reason given for the destruction. If the Jewish people believed themselves to be the only chosen people of God then God must be their protector. To have a heathen army come in and defeat them so soundly, looting and destroying the temple of the God that was supposed to protect them brought into question their position in the divine scheme. Since the fault could not be with God, it must have been with his people. The Jewish nation must have failed God by falling away from Him or sinning badly enough to cause God to turn them over to their enemy. Since this would be a great and grievous sin, God has chosen not to become active, since that would mean having to judge His apostate

people. He awaits his people to return to Him in a righteous state.

(2) and I went by his side and he took me by his hand and showed me the Right Hand of The Divine Majesty, with all types of praises, joyous singing. No mouth can articulate its worth, and no eye can look at it because of its greatness, and dignity and its majesty, and splendid beauty. (3) Not only that, but all the souls of the righteous who are counted worthy to see the joy of Jerusalem are standing by it, praising and praying before it three times every day, saying (Is. 51: 9): "Awake, awake, put on strength, O arm of the Lord" according for it is written (Is. 63: 12): "He caused his glorious arm to go at the right hand of Moses." (4) In that moment the Right Hand of The Divine Majesty was weeping. And there flew out from its five fingers, five rivers of tears and fell they flowed down into the great sea and it shook the entire world. For it is written (Is. 24: 19,20): "The earth is utterly broken, the earth is totally dissolved, the earth is moved greatly, the earth shall stagger like a drunken man and shall be moved back and froth like a hut, five times corresponding to the fingers of His Great Right Iand. " (5) But when the Holy One, blessed be He, saw that there is not a righteous man in that generation, and no pious man on the entire earth, and no men doing justice, and that there is no one like Moses, and no intercessor like Samuel who could pray before The Divine Majesty for the salvation and deliverance of His Kingdom, His great Right Hand was revealed in the entire world that that He put it out from Himself again to work great salvation by it for Israel, (6) then the Holy One, blessed be He, will remember His own justice, favor, mercy and grace, and He will deliver His great Arm by himself, and His righteousness will support Him. For it is written (Is. 59: 16): "And he saw, that there was no man" that is like Moses who prayed countless times for Israel in the desert and averted the Divine decrees from them—"and he wondered why there was no intercessor"—like Samuel who entreated the Holy One, blessed be He, and called unto Him and He answered him and fulfilled his desire, even if it did not fit into the Divine plan. For it is written (I Sam. 12: 17): "Is it not wheat-harvest today? I will call unto the Lord." (7) And not only that, but He joined fellowship with Moses in every place, for it is written (Ps. 99: 6): "Moses and Aaron among His priest." And again it is written, (Jer. 15: 1) "Though Moses and Samuel stood before Me" (Is. 63: 5): "Mine own arm brought salvation unto Me." (8) The Holy One, blessed be He said at that time, "How long do I have to wait for the children of men to obtain salvation according to their righteousness for My power and authority? For My own sake and for the sake of My worthiness and righteousness will I deliver My power

and authority and by it I will redeem my children from among the nations of the world. For it is written (Is. 48: 11): "For My own sake will I do it. For how should My name be profaned."

At this point, God has waited as long as he wished for Israel to come back to Him in righteousness by their own power. He has decided to take them back from the heathen nations.

(9) In that moment the Holy One, blessed be He, will reveal His Great Power and Authority (Arm) and show it to the nations of the world. Its length is the length of the entire world and its width is the width of the world. And its splendor looks like the splendor of the sunshine in its power in the summer solstice. (10) Then Israel will be saved from among the nations of the world. And Messiah will appear unto them and He will bring them up to Jerusalem with great joy. And not only that but they will eat and drink for they will glorify the Kingdom of Messiah, of the house of David, in the four corners of the world.

This is the time, not for the Messiah of the house of Joseph, but for the Messiah of the house of David. This is the time of war and leadership of the nation in a physical sense.

And the nations of the world will not prevail against them, for it is written (Is. 52: 10): "The Lord has made bare His holy arm in the eyes of all the nations; and all the ends of the earth shall see the salvation of our God." And again (Deut. 32: 12): "The Lord alone did lead him, and there was no strange god with him." (Zech. 14: 9): "And the Lord shall be king over all the earth."

"Heaven" is the number 955 using Gematria. The meaning seems to be that of all heavens and all worlds.

CHAPTER 48 - B
The Divine Names that go forth from the Throne of Glory and pass through the heavens and back again to the Throne.

Many of the names are not decipherable. Attempting to place the letters into any kind of Latinized form or alphabet made the meanings even more obscure. For this reason, the names that could be interpreted with any certainty were listed. Those that yielded only meaningless letters were marked with only a dash.

These are the seventy-two names written on the heart of the Holy One, Blessed be He: Righteousness, - , Righteous (one) -, Lord of Host, God Almighty, God, YHWH - - - Living (one) - Riding upon the Araboth (highest heaven), - Life Giver - King of Kings, Holy One - - Holy, Holy, Holy, - - - Blessed be the Name of

His glorious kingdom for ever and ever, - - Complete, King of the Universe, - - The beginning of Wisdom for the children of men, - -. Blessed be He who gives strength to the weary and increases strength to them that have no might, (Is. 40:29) that go forth adorned with many flaming crowns with many flames, with innumerable crowns of chashmal (celestial substance), with many, many crowns of lightning from before the Throne of Glory. And with them there are hundreds of hundreds of powerful angels who escort them like a king with trembling and dread, with amazement and shivering, with honor and majesty and fear, terror, greatness and dignity, and with glory and power, with wisdom and knowledge and with a pillar of fire and flame and lightning—and their light is as lightning flashesof light—and with the likeness of the chashmal (the substance of heaven). (2) And they give glory to them and they answer and cry before them, " Holy, Holy, Holy." And they lead them in a single line through every heaven as powerful and honorable princes. And when they bring them all back to the place of the Throne of Glory, then all the Chayoth by the Merkaba (chariot) open their mouth in praise of His glorious name, saying: "Blessed be the name of His glorious kingdom for ever and ever."

CHAPTER 48 - C
An Enoch-Metatron piece.

(1)"I seized him, and I took him and I appointed him"—that is Enoch, the son of Jared, whose name is Metatron (2) and I took him from among the children of men (5) and made him a Throne over near and beside My Throne. What is the size of that Throne? Seventy-thousand parasangs all of fire. (9) I committed to him 70 angels symbolizing the nations of the world and I gave into his authority all the household above and below. (7) And I imparted to him Wisdom and Intelligence more than all the angels. And I called his name "the LESSER YAH", whose name is by Gematria 71.

To refresh memory, Gematria was the ancient art of numerology. Each letter is given a number, usually determined by where it occurs in the alphabet. Numbers go from one to nine, then from ten to ninety, and, if there were enough letters, from one hundred to nine hundred. However, there are only 22 letters. Numbers are then summed. When the numbers are added they total seventy-one.

And I arranged all the works of creation for him. And I made him more powerful than all the ministering angels. (3) He gave Metatron—that is Enoch, the son of Jared— the authority over all the storehouses and treasuries, and appointed him over all the stores (reserves) in every heaven. And I assigned the keys of each store into him. (4) I made him the prince over all the princes and a minister of the Throne of Glory and the Halls of Araboth (the highest heaven). I appointed him over the Holy Chayoth for him to open their doors of the Throne of Glory to me, to exalt and arrange it, and I gave to him wreathe crowns to place upon their heads. I sent him to the majestic Ophannim, to crown them with strength and glory. I sent him to the honored Cherubim, to clothe them in majesty covered with radiant sparks, to make them to shine with splendor and bright light over the flaming Seraphim, to cover them with highness. I sent him to the Chashmallim of light, to make them radiant with light and to prepare the seat for me every morning as I sit upon the Throne of Glory. I have given him the secrets above and below, which are the heavenly secrets and earthly secrets so that he can praise and magnify my glory in the height of my power). (5) I made him higher than all. The height of his stature stood out in the midst of all who are of high of stature. I made seventy thousand parasangs. I made his Throne great by the majesty of my Throne. And I increased its glory by the honor of My glory. (6) I transformed his flesh into torches of fire, and all the bones of his body into burning coals; and I made his eyes look like lightning, and the light of his eyebrows as a light that will never be quenched. I made his face as bright as the splendor of the sun, and his eyes like the splendor of the Throne of Glory.

The description of Metatron is that of an angel and specifically a Seraphim, who is a fiery creature. A wreathe means victory.

(7) I made his clothing honor and majesty, beauty and highness. I covered him with a cloak and a crown of a size of 500 by 500 parasangs and this was his diadem. And I put My honor, My majesty and the splendor of My glory that is on My Throne of Glory upon him. I called him the "LESSER YHWH," the Prince of the Presence, the Knower of Secrets:. I revealed every secret to him as a father and as a friend, and all mysteries I spoke to him in truth. (8) I set up his throne at the door of My Hall that he may sit and judge the heavenly household on high. And I made every prince subject to him, so that they will receive his authority and perform his will. (9) I took Seventy names from my names and called him by them to enhance his glory. I placed Seventy princes into his hand so that he can command them to do my laws and obey my words in every language. And the proud will be brought to the ground by his word, and by the speech of his mouth he will exalt the humble to high places. He is to strike kings by his speech, to turn kings away from their own plans, and he is to set up the rulers over their dominion for it is written (Dan. 51: 21): "and he changes the times and the seasons,

"and to give wisdom unto all the wise of the world and understanding and knowledge to all who understand (Dan. 51: 21): "and knowledge to them that know understanding." He is to reveal to them the secrets of my words and to teach them the command of my judgment in righteousness.

God is the God of the universe. He is the God of all. His names are infinite. Names reveal power, authority, personality traits, and character. Metatron is given authority over the nations. There are 70 nations and Metatron has 70 names.

(10) It is written (Is. 55: 11): "so shall My word be that goes forth out of my mouth; it shall not return unto me void but shall accomplish that which I please." I shall accomplish that which is not written here, but " he shall accomplish. Every word and every speech that goes out from the Holy One, blessed be He, Metatron stands and carries out. And he establishes the orders of the Holy One, blessed be He. (11) "And he shall make to prosper that which I sent." I will make to prosper what is not written here but he shall make to prosper teaching, that whatever decree proceeds from the Holy One, blessed be He, concerning a man, as soon as he makes repentance, they do not execute it upon him but they execute it upon another wicked man, for it is written (Prov. 9:8): "The righteous is delivered out of trouble, and the wicked comes in his place."

If a man repents and is no longer wicked, the angels inflicts his punishment on a person who is still wicked and has not repented

(12) And not only that but Metatron sits three hours every day in the high heavens, and he gathers all the souls of those dead who died in their mothers womb, and the nursing baby who died on their mother's breast, and of the scholars who died over the five books of the Law. And he brings them under the Throne of Glory and places them in companies, divisions and classes round the Presence, and there he teaches them the Law, and the books of Wisdom, and Haggada and Tradition and completes their education for them. It is written (Is. 28: 9) "Whom will he teach knowledge? And whom will he make to understand tradition? Them that are weaned from the milk and draw from the breast."

Ancient Jews viewed learning as one way to approach God. To study the Torah is almost as good as worship and prayer. Unborn, sucklings, those who die while studying the Torah are guiltless.

CHAPTER 48 - D
The names of Metatron.

The names fall into three major categories, those which are built upon the name "El," those that are based on the name "Metatron," and those based on the name "Yah." The reader will notice the letters EL, ON, and YAH or YA in the names. Although the text states there are 70 names, there are in fact 105 names listed. The Latinized version of the 1928 work is referenced in this list however the parsing and pronunciations are unique to this work in order to accent the holy names found within most of the 105 names..

(1)Seventy names has Metatron which the Holy One, blessed be He, took from His own name and put upon him. And these they are: 1 Yeho-EL Yah, 2 Yeho-EL, 3 Yofi-EL and 4 Yophphi-EL, and 5 Hafifi-EL and 6 Margezi-EL, 7 Gippyu-EL, 8 Pahazi-EL, 9 Hahah, 10 Pepri-EL, 11 Tatri-EL, 12 Tabki-EL, 13 Haw, 14 YHWH, 15 Dah 16, WHYH, 17 Hebed, 18 DiburiEL, 19 Hafhapi-EL, 20 Spi-EL, 21 Paspasi-EL, 22 Senetron, 23 Metatron, 24 Sogdin, 25 HadriGon, 26 Asum, 27 Sakhpam, 28 Sakhtam, 29 Mig-on, 30 Mitt-on, 31 Mot-tron, 32 Rosfim, 33 Khinoth, 34 KhataTiah, 35 Degaz-Yah, 36 Pisf-YaH, 37 Habiskin-Yah, 38 Mixar, 39 Barad, 40 Mikirk, 41 Mispird, 42 Khishig, 43 Khishib, 44 Minret, 45 Bisyrym, 46 Mitmon, 47 Titmon 48 Piskhon, 49 SafsafYah, 50 Zirkhi, 51 ZirkhYah 52 'B', 53 Be-Yah, 54 HiBhbe-Yah, 55 Pelet, 56 Pit-Yah, 57 Rabrab-YaH, 58 Khas, 59 Khas-Yah, 60 Tafaf-Yah, 61 Tamtam-Yah, 62 Sehas-Yah, 63 Hirhur-Yah, 64 Halhal-Yah, 65 BazrId-Yah, 66 Satsatk-Yah, 67 Sasd-Yah, 68 Razraz-Yah, 69 BaZzraz-Yah, 70 Harim-Yah, 71 Sibh-Yah, 72 Sibibkh-Yah, 73 Simkam, 74 Yah-Se-Yah, 75 Sibib-Yah, 76 Sabkasbe-Yah, 77 khelil-khil-Yah, 78 Kih, 79 HHYH, 80 WH, 81 WHYH, (letters in the holy YHWH) 82 Zakik-Yah, 83 Turtis-Yah, 84 Sur-Yah, 85 Zeh, 86 Penir-Yah, 87 ZihZih, 88 Galraza-Yah, 89 Mamlik-Yah, 90 Hitt-Yah, 91 Hemekh, 92 Kham-Yah, 93 Mekaper-Yah, 94 Perish-Yah, 95 Sefam, 96 Gibir, 97 Gibor-Yah, 98 Gor, 99 Gor-Yah, 100 Ziw, 101 Hokbar, the 102 LESSER YHWH, after the name of his Master, (Ex. 23: 21) "for My name is in him",103 Rabibi-EL, 104 TUMIEL, 105 Segansakkiel, the Prince of Wisdom.

(2) And why is he called by the name Sagnesakiel? Because all the storehouses of wisdom are committed in to his hand. (3) And all of them were opened to Moses on Sinai, so that he learned them during the forty days, while he remained. He learned the Torah in the seventy ways it applies to the seventy nations, and the Prophets and the seventy application of the seventy tongues, the writings in the seventy variations of the seventy tongues, the Halakas (Jewish law and ritual) in the seventy applications of the seventy nations, the Traditions in the seventy aspects of the seventy nations, the Haggadas (Passover Seder) in the seventy aspects of the seventy tongues and the

Toseftas (Secondary compilation of Jewish oral laws) in the seventy aspects of the seventy tongues. (4) But as soon as the forty days were completed, he forgot all of them in one moment. Then the Holy One, blessed be He, called Yephiphyah, the Prince of the Law, and (through him) they were given to Moses as a gift, for it is written (Deut. 10:4): "and the Lord gave them to me." And after that it remained with him. And how do we know that it remained in his memory? Because it is written (Mal. 55: 4): "Remember the Law of Moses my servant which I commanded unto him in Horeb for all Israel, even my statues and judgments." 'The Law of Moses': that is the Torah, the Prophets and the Writings, 'statues': that is the Halakas and Traditions, 'judgments'; that is the Haggadas and the Toseftas. And all of them were given to Moses on high on Sinai. (5) These seventy names are a reflection of the Explicit names and given to the name of Metatron: seventy Names of His by which the ministering angels call the King of the kings of kings, blessed be He, in the high heavens, and twenty-two letters (of the Hebrew alphabet) that are on the ring placed on his finger with which are sealed the destinies of the high, powerful and great princes of kingdoms and with which are sealed along with the future of the Angel of Death, and the destinies of every nation and tongue. (6) Metatron, the Angel, the Prince of the Presence said; the Angel who is the Prince of the Wisdom and the Angel who the Prince of the Understanding, and the Angel who the Prince of the Kings, and the Angel who the Prince of the Rulers, and the angel who is the Prince of the Glory, and the angel who is the Prince of the high ones and of the princes, all of which are the exalted, greatly honored ones in heaven and on earth: (7) "YHWH, the God of Israel, is my witness that I revealed this secret to Moses and when I did all the host all the high heavens were enraged against me. (8) They asked me, saying, "Why do you reveal this secret to a son of man, born of woman, who is tainted and unclean, a man of the putrefying drop? You gave him the secret by which heaven and earth, sea and land, mountains and hills, rivers and springs, Gehenna of fire and hail, the Garden of Eden and the Tree of Life were all created and by which Adam and Eve, and the cattle, and the wild beasts, the birds of the air, and the fish of the sea, and Behemoth and Leviathan, and the crawling things, the snakes, the dragons of the sea, and the creeping things of the deserts; and Torah and Wisdom and Knowledge and Thought and the imparted knowledge and the Gnosis of things above and of heaven and the fear of heaven were all created. Why did you reveal this to flesh and blood? I answered them: Because the Holy One, blessed be He, has given me authority. And furthermore, I have obtained permission from the high and exalted throne, from which all the Explicit names go forth with lightning and fire and flaming chashmallim.

Verse 7 makes a statement that when the complete gnosis or revealed knowledge was given to Moses (through Metatron) all the heavenly host was enraged at the act. This Knowledge was not even available to all the host of heaven but was given to a human. Verse 8 asks the question in a direct and insulting way. To slightly paraphrase, it asked, "Why did You give the secrets of creation to this human who was conceived by a woman, through the transfer of semen, which spoils and putrefies and then gives birth, when blood from birth and menses is considered unclean, as is the woman herself for a time after a ritual cleansing. In light of this, all the heavenly hosts consider humans to be inferior, unclean, animals. Still, God chose to transmit to Moses the secret gnosis of creation. Behemoth is the primal unconquerable monster of the land. Leviathan is the primal monster of the waters of the sea. Ziz is their counterpart in the sky. There is a legend that the Leviathan and the Behemoth shall hold a battle at the end of the world. The two will finally kill each other, and the surviving men will feast on their meat. Behemoth also appears in the 1 Enoch, giving a description of this monster's origins there mentioned as being male, as opposed to the female Leviathan. See Job, chapter 40 for further information.

(9) But they (the hosts) were not appeased or satisfied, until the Holy One, blessed be He, scorned them and drove them away from Him with contempt and said to them: "I delight in him, and have set my love on him, and have entrusted to him and given unto Metatron, my Servant, and I have given to him alone, for he is Unique among all the children of heaven. (10) And Metatron brought them out from his house and storehouses and gave these secrets to Moses, and Moses gave them to Joshua, and Joshua gave them to the elders, and the elders to gave them the prophets and the men of the Great Synagogue, and the men of the Great Synagogue gave them to Ezra and Ezra the Scribe gave them to Hillel the elder, and Hillel the elder gave them to Rabbi Abbahu and Rabbi Abbahu to Rabbi Zera, and Rabbi Zera to the men of faith, and the men of faith gave them to give warning and to heal by them all disease that ravaged the world, for it is written (Ex. 15: 26): "If you will diligently hearken to the voice of the Lord, your God, and will do that which is right in His eyes, and will give ear to His commandments, and keep all his statues, I will put none of the disease upon you, which I have put on the Egyptians, for I am the Lord that heals you."

(Ended and finished. Praise be unto the Creator of the World.)

Hillel was said to be one of the greatest and wisest Rabbis.

Joseph and Aseneth

Part One

1. In the second month of the first year in the seven years of plenty, Pharaoh sent Joseph out to go throughout the entire land of Egypt.

(Joseph was inspecting the land and crops in order to prepare for a famine, which he predicted based on the dreams of Pharaoh, which Joseph had interpreted.)

2. On the eighteenth day of the fourth month of the first year Joseph arrived in the district, which contained the city of Heliopolis.

Heliopolis is an ancient city in Egypt that the Greeks had renamed. The name means "City of the Sun" or "City of Helios". Its Arabic name means "Eye of the Sun". Heliopolis was one of the oldest cities of ancient Egypt, the capital of the 13th Lower Egyptian nome (a subnational administrative division). It is now found at the north-east edge of Cairo.

3. The corn in that land was as plentiful as the sands of the sea and Joseph was collecting (all the) corn. 4. In that city there was a man who was the chief of all Pharaoh's governors and administrators. 5. He was very wise and generous, and he was wealthy. The name of Pharaoh's counselor was Petephres, the priest of Heliopolis.

Heliopolis is the city of "On" mentioned in the Hebrew bible. It was renamed Heliopolis by the Greeks in recognition of the fact that the sun god Ra (Helios mean sun in Greek) presided there. Heliopolis has been occupied since the Predynastic Period, with extensive building campaigns during the Old and Middle Kingdoms. Today it is mostly destroyed; its temples and other buildings were used for the construction of medieval Cairo. The only surviving remnant of Heliopolis is the Temple of Re-Atum obelisk located in Al-Masalla in Al-Matariyyah, Cairo. It was erected by Senusret I of the Twelfth dynasty, and still stands in its original position. Petephres was the high priest of the cult of Ra, the sun god, in the time of Joseph.

6. Petephres had a young daughter who was eighteen years old. She was tall, graceful, and beautiful. She was more comely than any other virgin in Egypt. 7. She was very different from the daughters of the Egyptians. However, she was like the daughters of the Hebrews in every way. 8. She was tall like Sarah, beautiful like Rebecca, and had a shapely body like Rachel. She was a virgin, and her name was Aseneth. 9. Her beauty was famous throughout all that land.

Even the most remote parts had heard of Aseneth's beauty. The men, who were the sons of the officials and administrators of the king, sought her hand in marriage. 10. Because of her there was ongoing rivalries and fights between the boys as they fought over Aseneth. 11. The eldest son of Pharaoh heard about Aseneth and begged his father to give him Aseneth as a wife. 12. He said to his father, "Give me Aseneth, the daughter of Petephres the priest and first man (head of the city) of Heliopolis, as my wife." But Pharaoh, his father, said to him, "You should not want a wife of lower station than yourself. 13. You are the king of all the land 14. Do you not understand the daughter of Joakim, the king of Moab is betrothed to you? She is a queen and she is very beautiful. You should take her as your wife."

II. Aseneth was arrogant and proud. She viewed all men with contempt and seemed to hate them all. Her father, Petephres, had a tower in his house, which was large and very high. There he kept his daughter so that neither man nor boy would see her. 2. The top floor of the tower had ten rooms.

It is difficult to know if the father of Aseneth was over-protective to the extent it caused Aseneth to be xenophobic in general or if she did not like men specifically. We are told later that Aseneth wished to keep the way of life she enjoyed in her father's house. Marriage would have changed that, since Aseneth would be forced to live with her husband and be provided for by him, according to his rank and wealth. Her station was high enough there would be few prospective husbands that would equal or elevate her status and standard of living.

3. The first room was spacious and comfortable. The flooring of the room was made of purple stones, and its walls had a facade made of various types of precious stones of many colors and cut flat. 4. There was gold plating on the ceiling. Within that room were countess statues of Egyptian gods, all made of gold and silver.
5. And Aseneth reverenced and worshipped them all, offering sacrifices daily to them.

6. In the second room were chests full of all the gold and silver adornments and treasure needed to dress in fine fashion. 7. Aseneth had garments of fine linen, which were woven with gold and priceless precious stones. 8. There were adornments used to announce her virginity in that room also.
9. The third room contained items of great value from all the of the lands. These rooms were used to house the riches of Aseneth.

10. Aseneth had seven virgins attending her and each of her seven attendants had a room of their own. These

took up the remaining seven rooms. 11. The virgins were the same age as Aseneth and all the girls were beautiful and were all born on the same night as Aseneth. They were like the stars in the sky, and no man or boy ever touched or saw them.

12. It was in the large room with three large windows that Aseneth spent most of her time and where her virginity was nurtured (protected).

It is obvious that virginity was extremely important at the time of the writing of "Joseph and Aseneth." In the Jewish viewpoint, every marriage was expected to produce offspring since neither society nor the family could survive long without helpers and those to inherit land and money to carry on the family name. Marriage without sex was considered a curse to the ancients. It made sense that Hebrew law required the marriage to be consummated before it had any legal effect. Thus, it was sex that made the relationship a marriage. Grooms insisted their brides be a virgin and be able to prove it. If the groom believed he had received a bride who was not a virgin he had the right to challenge her family to produce the proof. If the sheets from the marital bed did not show the required blood then the men of the village would stone her to death in front of her father's house, where she had lived. If the elders were satisfied that the bride had been a virgin then the groom would be whipped and required to pay 100 shekels of silver to her father. The husband would lose the right to divorce her, ever. (Deuteronomy 22: 13-21) Try, as men may to guard their bloodline, cuckoldry was always possible. Today in the U.S. estimates run between 5 – 10%. That is to say that between 5 to 10 out of every 100 men are raising another man's child unknowingly. In ancient times, the simple suggestion was such an insult it could result in fights to the death. Virginity and certainty of paternity were the pipelines through which inheritance, land, wealth and status flowed.

13. From one window she could see the courtyard to the east. From the second window she watched the activity in the street to the north, and the third window opened to the south. 14. Facing the east was her bed, made of gold. 15. The coverlet on her bed was made of purple linen woven with golden threads and embroidered with blue. 16 Aseneth always slept alone. No man or woman ever even sat upon the bed. Only Aseneth ever sat on it. 17. There was a large courtyard encompassing the house, with a high wall constructed of large square stones. 18. The courtyard had four gates of entry, which were overlaid with iron. Eighteen young men, armed and strong, guarded the gates.

19. The walls were lined inside the courtyard with every kind of beautiful fruiting tree. Now was harvest time and all the fruit from the trees were ripe and ready to pick. 20. On the right side of the courtyard was a rich (lively) spring, which flowed into a huge cistern made of marble, situated just below the spring. The cistern gathered water from the spring. The water overflowed into a river running through the midst of the courtyard. The flowing river watered all the trees.

III. Joseph drew near the city of Heliopolis. 2. Joseph was lord over his men and so as he approached the city, he sent twelve men in to town before him to speak to Petephres, the priest of Heliopolis. 3. Joseph's message said, "The time draws near noon and the sun's heat is overpowering. We need to stop for a mid-day meal. I would enjoy some refreshment under your roof. May I be your guest today?

4. When Petephres heard this, he was overjoyed and said, 5. "Blessed be the Lord, the God of Joseph."

The utterance, "Blessed be the Lord, the God of Joseph" seems very strange coming from the lips of the High Priest of the Sun God. It could be a twist on the story to tell the reader that even pagans respected the Jewish God. However, it could simply speak to the flexibility of polytheistic societies to easily incorporate another god into their pantheon.

And Petephres called his servant who was over the house and said to him, 6. "Hurry. Get my house in order, and prepare a great feast. Joseph, the mighty man of God, is visiting today." 7. Aseneth heard that her father and mother had come back from the field of their inherited family estate in the country. 8. She was very happy and said to herself, "My father and my mother have come back from the family estate in the country so I will go see them. 9. And Aseneth rushed into the room where her robes were laid out and put on one that was made of fine blue linen, which was woven with gold. Then she placed a golden belt round her waist. She put bracelets round her wrists and ankles. She on put golden pants and placed a necklace round her neck. 10. All the bracelets she wore were made of precious stones with the names of Egyptian gods and idols inscribed and stamped on them. 11. She topped off her wardrobe by placing a tiara on her head and tied a jeweled headband round her temples. Then she covered her head with a veil.

Tiara and crown, diadem and headband symbolizing authority and sovereignty are terms used in this passage.

IV. And she hurried and descended the staircase from her place on the top floor, greeting her mother and father as she came. 2. Petephres and his wife were overjoyed to see their daughter Aseneth adorned as the bride of God.

"Bride of God" is an odd phrase. On first impression it carries with it a Christian tone, since the church is referred to as the bride of Christ. But the sun god also had a wife. The title of God's Wife, Wife of Amun or Wife of Ra first

appeared during the Tenth and Twelfth dynasties, when non-royal women, among those serving the sun god as priestesses, held the title and position. The office of the God's Wife reached the height of its political power during the late Third Intermediate Period of Egypt when Shepenupet I, Osorkon III's daughter, was first appointed to the position at Thebes. The office continued until 525 BCE under Nitocris' successor, Ankhnesneferibre, when the Persians overthrew Egypt's last Saite ruler, Psamtik III (526–525 BCE), and enslaved his daughter. Thereafter, the office of God's Wife disappears from history.

It should be noted that the sun gods Amun and Ra merged. Amun was one of the eight ancient Egyptian gods who formed the Ogdoad of Hermopolis. He was the god of the air. However, during the Twelfth dynasty (Middle Kingdom) Amun was adopted in Thebes as the King of the gods with Mut as his consort. Ahmose I, the first Pharaoh of the New Kingdom believed that Amun had helped him drive the Hyksos from Egypt. He was also adopted into the Ennead of Heliopolis when he merged with the ancient sun god, Ra, to become Amun-Ra.

There is debate as to whether the Hyksos, the foreigners that took over Egypt, were actually the Jews. One theory explains that as the Jews began to multiply to a dangerous population the Pharaoh became nervous, seeing that the Hyksos had the wherewithal to depose him. Their population was great and they were strong people. Since they had not assimilated into Egyptian culture and did not regard the Pharaoh as divine, they could attack and try to make Egypt into their country with their culture. This scenario may have actually occurred. Around the year 1700 BCE the Hyksos invaded. They successfully took over Egypt and a succession of six kings took power, known as "the Great Hyksos Pharaohs."

Josephus Flavius, Jewish historian of the 1st century CE and author of The Antiquities of the Jews, identified the Hyksos with the Hebrews. Most historians today disagree, but there are some who hold to this theory due to the striking similarities between the Hyksos and the Jews. The Hyksos were from an alien culture and did not follow the Egyptian religion. The Hyksos Pharaohs never claimed to be gods, nor did they build for themselves any monuments. They moved the capital of Egypt to the land of Goshen, which is the area the Jews settled.

The Medrash tells us that Moses was a king in the Sudan for a long period of time, and we do have evidence that the Hyksos people ruled not only in Egypt, but also in the Sudan and Libya. However, evidence shows that the Jews kept a low profile in Egypt. They had little to do with the government but they played a large part in the economy of Egypt.

In about 1560 BCE, the local, indigenous population expelled the Hyksos in a rebellion. This marked the beginning of the New Empire and a radical change in Egyptian society. Egypt became xenophobic, killing or enslaving foreigners. This shift corresponds with the period of Jewish enslavement in Egypt. The Jews would gain their freedom once again in the time of Moses. Their escape would be documented in the book of Exodus.

Petephres and his wife unpacked all the goods they had brought back from the fields of their inheritance and gave them to their daughter. 4. Aseneth was ecstatic when she saw all the good things. There were fruits such as grapes, pomegranates, figs and the dates, and they were all ripe and delightful. There were beautiful doves as well. 5. Then Petephres said to his daughter Aseneth, "My child": she said, "Yes, sir." 6. And he said to her, "Please sit down between your mother and I. I want to speak to you about what is on my mind." So, Aseneth sat down between her father and her mother. 7. And her father took her right hand and said to her, "My child…" Aseneth said, "Father, go ahead, speak." 8. And Petephres said to her, "You see, Joseph, the mighty man of God, will be visiting us today. Pharaoh has appointed him as ruler of all the land of Egypt, and that includes our land. He will be in charge of distributing corn throughout the country to save everyone from the coming famine, which will be upon this land."

9. "Joseph worships God. He is a man of good judgment, wisdom, and knowledge and he is a virgin like you are to this day. The grace and spirit of the Lord (his) God is with him. 10. For these reasons I will give you to him as his wife, my child. You will be his bride, and he shall be your husband for ever."

11. But, when Aseneth heard what her father said, she broke out in great beads of sweat all over. She was so angry she was in a rage. She looked askance at her father. 12. She said, "Why, sir, should you speak to me like this. You are my father, but you talk to me as if I were a prisoner of a different race, like a slave or fugitive to be sold. 13. Isn't this man the Canaanite shepherd's son that was sold by his father? 14. Didn't he have sex with his master's wife, and did his master not throw him into a dark prison where he stayed? Isn't it true that Pharaoh only brought him out of prison because he interpreted his dream? 15. No! I will marry the king's oldest son because he is king of all the land of Egypt." 16. When Petephres heard the way she spoke so angry and arrogantly to him he thought it best to say nothing more to his daughter about Joseph.

Aseneth had the story wrong. She was relying on gossip. She was sassy, and disrespectful to her parents. She was a typical teenager. Her father waited for her to cool off and think about how she was acting.

V. Suddenly one of Petephres's young servant boys burst in and said, 2. " I saw Joseph at the gates of our court." Aseneth quickly left her parents and ran upstairs. She went into her room and stood at the big window looking east, toward the gate so she could see Joseph as he entered her father's house.

3. Petephres and his wife and all his extended family went out to meet Joseph. 4. The Eastern gates were opened, and Joseph entered, sitting in the Pharaoh's second chariot that he had given to Joseph as a ruler. 5. It was drawn by four horses, white as snow, which were yoked together with a bridle studded with gold and with golden reins. The chariot had a golden awning that covered it. 6. And Joseph was wearing a wonderful glittering white uniform and wrapped around him was a fine purple linen robe. 7. On his head was a crown of gold like a wreath with twelve precious stones in it, and above the stones were twelve golden rays. He held a royal scepter in his right hand. The scepter was topped with a divided olive branch laden with fruit.

Cook uses the term "tunic" for both Joseph's uniform and later for the mourning dress Aseneth wears. These are so dissimilar as to need totally different terms. The tunic Joseph wears is part of a uniform, and so we call it a uniform. It is white, finely woven, close fitting, and comes down to about the thigh area. It is worn with a finely crafted belt as the shirt of a dress uniform. The tunic worn by Aseneth is essentially a sack dress. It is a large sack shaped object with holes for arms and head. It has no sleeves. It is coarsely woven and comes down to the knees. It is belted with a plain rope. The coarseness and plainness of the object calls to mind the abject misery of the mourning process.

8. When Joseph entered the courtyard the gates were shut. 9. And no stranger, neither men nor women, could come in. All strangers were shut out because the gate-keepers had shut the doors. 10. Petephres and his wife came to greet Joseph with all the extended family of Petephres, except for their daughter, Aseneth. And they bowed out of respect to Joseph with their faces to the ground. 11. Then Joseph exited his chariot and stretched out his right hand to them.

Petephres and family show the same respect for Joseph as they would to Pharaoh. Joseph and his chariot are adorned in a combination of Egyptian and possible Jewish symbols. Gold and symbols of sun rays abound. Purple is the color of royalty and only nobles could wear the color. The twelve precious stones could call to mind the Urim and Thummim, a breastplate with twelve precious stones embedded in it. The first reference to Urim and Thummim in the Bible is the description in the Book of Exodus concerning the high priest's vestments; the chronologically earliest passage mentioning them, according to textual scholars, is in the Book of Hosea, where it is implied, by reference to the Ephod, that the Urim and Thummim were fundamental elements in the popular form of the Israelite religion, in the mid 8th century BC.
Exodus 28: 15 "Fashion a breast piece for making decisions — the work of skilled hands. Make it like the ephod: of gold, and of blue, purple and scarlet yarn, and of finely twisted linen. 16 It is to be square — a span long and a span wide — and folded double. 17 Four rows of precious stones were mounted on it. The first row shall be carnelian, chrysolite and beryl; 18 the second row shall be turquoise, lapis lazuli and emerald; 19 the third row shall be jacinth, agate and amethyst; 20 the fourth row shall be topaz, onyx and jasper. Mount them in gold filigree settings. 21 There are to be twelve stones, one for each of the names of the sons of Israel, each engraved like a seal with the name of one of the twelve tribes.

VI. Then Aseneth saw Joseph and her soul was pricked and she felt her heart break. Her knees went weak, and she trembled all over. 2. Then she cried out in fear and said, "Where can I go, and where can I hide from him? What will Joseph, the son of God, think of me, because I have spoken badly of him? 3. Where can I run to and where can I hide? There is such a bright light in him so he sees everything. No secret is safe from him. 4. I pray the God of Joseph to have mercy on me because I spoke evil things in ignorance. 5. I am a hopeless wretch because I said, Joseph, the Canaanites' shepherd's son is coming, but now I see the sun from heaven has come to us in his chariot and has entered our house today. 6. I was a reckless fool to hate him and to speak evil of him. I did not realize Joseph is the son of God. 7 What man could ever father such a beautiful person, and what mother's womb could bear such a light? I am a foolish wretch for speaking so badly to my father. 8. Now I will allow my father to give me to Joseph as a domestic servant or a slave, and I will serve him for ever."

VII. When Joseph entered Petephres's house he sat down on a cushion. Phetephres washed his feet and then he had a table placed in front of him, separate from the others because Joseph would not eat with the Egyptians. They were an unclean (unholy/abomination) to Joseph.

2. And Joseph spoke to Petephres and all his relations, saying, "Who is that woman standing in the top floor sun room by the window? Tell her to leave the house." 3. This was because Joseph was afraid she too might attempt to seduce him as had the wives and daughters of the officials and rulers of all the land of Egypt use to attempt to seduce him to have sex with them. 4. And many of the Egyptian wives and daughters had great pains of passion after seeing Joseph because he was very handsome. They would send their messengers to him with numerous gifts as well as amounts of gold and silver. 5. But Joseph always rejected them and sent

them back with insults and threats if they did not leave him alone. He would say, "I will not sin before the God of Israel." 6. And Joseph remembered the face of his father Jacob and his commandments and Joseph kept these in his mind always. Jacob would tell Joseph and his brothers, "Children, be on guard against the foreign woman. Have nothing to do with her. She will be your ruin and destruction. 7. That is the reason Joseph told them, "Tell that woman to leave this house." 8. But Petephres said, "Sir, the woman you have seen on the top floor is not a stranger. She is our daughter. Our daughter is a virgin who rejects men. No strangers have ever seen her, besides you today. 9. We would like for her to come and speak to you if you wish, because our daughter is like you, like your sister." 10. Joseph was delighted because Petephres said, "She is a virgin who rejects men." 11. Then Joseph said to Petephres and his wife, "If she is your daughter, allow her to come. She is like my sister and I will love her like a sister from today on."

VIII. Then Aseneth's mother climbed the stairs to the top floor and brought Aseneth down to meet Joseph. Petephres said to his daughter Aseneth, "Say hello to your brother. He is a virgin just as you are, and he rejects all foreign women just as you reject foreign men." 2. Aseneth said to Joseph, "Joy and blessings to you from God Most High." Joseph responded to her, saying, "May the God who gave life to all things bless you." 3. And Petephres said to Aseneth, "Come closer and kiss your brother." 4. But when she came closer to kiss Joseph, he put out his right hand on her chest between her breasts to stop her.

5. He said, "It is improper for a man who worships God with his mouth and praises the living God, and eats the blesses bread of life, and drinks the blessed cup of everlasting life, and who is anointed with the blessed oil of immortality, to kiss a foreign woman. Your mouth has praised dead and silent idols. Your mouth eats the bread at the table of shame and you strangle on it. Your mouth drinks from their libations and you are ambushed with their cup of treachery. You are anointed with the oil of destruction.

6. A man who worships God will kiss his mother and sister who are from his own tribe and family. With his wife he shares his bed, and together their mouths bless the living God. 7. Likewise, it is not right for a woman who worships God to kiss a foreign man. The act is an abomination in the eyes of God."

Joseph rejects and distains foreign (strange) women, believing them to be unclean. Indeed, he rejects all non-Jews, seeing them as "abominations." To the modern eye, he is racist, showing far less grace and acceptance for the Egyptians than they have for him. To the ancient Jewish

reader, Joseph's actions are those of a righteous and pious man who wants nothing more than to be allowed to live a traditionally Jewish way of life, even if he is surrounded by temptations to do otherwise.
Aseneth rejects men and is doubly resistant to foreign men. From the earliest times, people of every tribe, nation, religions, or race have always believed themselves to be superior to those of other tribes, nations, religions, or races. Feelings of superiority are related to xenophobia. These two people, Joseph and Aseneth, are of differing nations and races. Each begins with the viewpoint that they are superior. In the story, Joseph firmly believes that he, as a Jew, is superior. He is also certain the Jews are God's chosen people. They are superior, in part, because they are divinely chosen. In race and religion, Joseph believes he stands above all others in Egypt.

Men often hate each other because they fear each other; they fear each other because they don't know each other; they don't know each other because they cannot communicate; they cannot communicate because they are separated. Dr. Martin Luther King Jr.

8. And when Aseneth heard Joseph's words, she was upset and wept out loud. She could only stare at Joseph as her eyes were filled with tears. 9. And Joseph saw her and his heart was touched by her because he was tender-hearted and compassionate and reverenced the Lord. He was moved and so he raised his right hand above her head and said,

10. "O Lord God, Most High and Mighty; God of my father Israel,
you gave life to all things and called them from darkness into light.
and from error into truth, and from death into life.
I pray that you give your life and blessing to this virgin. 11. Renew her by your Holy Spirit and remake her by your secret hand. Animate her with your life. Feed her your bread of life.
Let her drink from your cup of blessing.
Count her among your people whom you chose before all things were created.
Allow her to enter into your rest, which you prepared for your chosen people so that we all may live with you in everlasting life."
IX. Aseneth was overflowing with joy at Joseph's blessing, and she departed in haste to her room on the top floor and fell on her bed exhausted. She was happy, but confused and afraid. Sweat poured out of her she and was soaked from the moment she heard what Joseph said to her, which he did in the name of the Most High God. 2. And she wept from the bottom of her heart, and she turned away from the gods she worshiped. Then she decided to wait for evening. 3. At that time Joseph had eaten and drank. He said to his servants, "Hitch the horses to the chariot. I must leave

and go through the entire city and then the land. 4. But Petephres asked Joseph to stay the night with them and leave the next day to go on his mission. 5. But Joseph was firm. He said, "No! I must leave now. This is the day God begins his works. But, in eight days time I will return and stay the night here with you."

X. Petephres departed with his relations to their family estate. 2. And Aseneth was left alone with her virgins. Aseneth was depressed, lethargic and she wept until sunset. She ate no bread and drank no water and while all the others slept she was alone and awake. 3. She opened the door and went down to the main door entering the house where and she found the woman who was the doorkeeper asleep with her children.

4. Hurriedly, Aseneth removed the leather curtain covering the door and filled it with ashes. She carried it up to the top floor and spread it out on the floor. 5. And she locked the door and barred it with an iron bar, placing it on the side of the door.

6. Aseneth began to groan (mourning) loudly and weep. The virgin she loved the most heard her mistress groaning, and she woke the other virgins. They hurried in and found the door shut.

We assume the most loved virgins were placed closer to the room of their mistress, much like a seating arrangement at the table of an event where the most important guest are placed closer to the host or head of the table.

7. And she stood listening to Aseneth groaning and weeping and the virgin said, "My lady, why are you so deeply sad? What troubles you? 8. Open the door so we can come in and see you." But Aseneth remained locked in. She spoke to them from inside. "I have a very bad headache. I am on my bed and I feel too weak to get up. I do not have enough strength in my legs to get up to open the door for you right now. Go back to your rooms."

9. Then, Aseneth got up quietly and opened her door stealthily. She went into her second room where she kept her valuables in a chest and her clothing and accessories used to adorn herself. She opened her wardrobe and removed a tunic, dark and black in color.

10. When her youngest brother died she wore this tunic while she was in mourning. Aseneth took off her royal robe and put on the black tunic. She untied her golden belt and tied a rope around her waist. She removed her crown and string of beads from her head. She removed the bracelets from her wrists. 12. Then she took her best robe, which she had removed, and she threw it out of the window for the poor to receive. 13. She gathered her vast number of gold and silver idols and she broke them into small pieces, which she gave out from her window to the poor and needy.

14. And Aseneth gathered together her dinner, which was prepared for royalty and consisted of various fattened animals, as well as fish and meat from a heifer (cow). She took the meals, which were offerings presented to her gods, along with the bottles of wine used for libation offering to her gods. She hurled them all out of the window so dogs would consume them.

15. Then she took the ashes and poured them onto the floor. 16. She wrapped sackcloth around her waist. She removed the hair band she wore to tie her hair back. Then she fell down into the ashes.

17. She beat her breast with her own hands and she wept aloud and lamented all night long. 18. Aseneth stood up from the ashes and saw the ashes were on her head like those of a beggar and the ashes had mixed with her tears and had made mud. 19. Then Aseneth fell face-first into the ashes and stayed there until sundown. 20. She refused to eat or drink anything for seven days.

XI. Then on the eighth day Aseneth began to lose the use of her arms and legs.

XII. She looked up from the floor and reached up towards the east. She turned eyes toward heaven and she prayed,

2. "O Lord, God of all the ages, He that made everything and gave the breath of life to everything living,
that brought light to things unseen, and made things visible that were invisible,
3. That raised the sky and established the earth on the seas,
that founded the huge stones on the depths of oceans so that they cannot not be submerged. Until the end of time they all follow your commands.
4. I cry out to you, O Lord, God. Hear my plea.
I confess of my sins to you and I show you my sins against your law.
5. O Lord I have sinned. I have truly sinned. I have broken your law and acted without respect or reverence toward you.
And I have said evil things.
My mouth has been made unclean by praying (giving offerings) to idols, and eating things offered to idols at the tables of the Egyptians.
I valued my beauty and riches above everything.

6. O Lord, I have sinned by acting without reverence to you.

I have worshipped idols, which could neither hear nor speak.

I am wretched and not worthy to even speak to you.

7. O Lord, I, Aseneth, the daughter of Petephres the priest, have been prideful and arrogant towards you. I have valued my ancestral riches above all men.

People hate me and now they scoff at my distress.

I flee to you like a child runs to its mother and father. I pray to you and cry out to you to deliver me from my tormentors.

8. Stretch out your hands and cover me like a father that loves his children and loves them tenderly.

Pluck me now from the grasp of my enemy.

9. Look now, Lord, the wild Lion and his children chase me. They are the gods of the Egyptians that I have forsaken and spoiled. Their father the Devil is trying to devour me.

10. O Lord, you can deliver me from his grasp and deliver me from his mouth.

If you do not, he will catch me like a wolf and rip me apart.

He will throw me into a pit of fire, and into the most violent hurricane.

He will throw me into the depths of the sea.

Do not let the great monsters of the sea devour me. I will be lost forever.

11. I am deserted, O Lord. My parents have disowned me because I have broken their gods into pieces.

I now hate their gods completely.

O Lord, my only hope to be saved resides in you.

You are the father of all orphans and the champion of those who are ill-treated.

You are the aid to those who are treated unjustly.

12. I have seen that all the gods of my father Petephres are temporary and cannot be depended upon. But those who live as your heirs are eternal and live forever, O Lord.

XIII. O Lord, I am an orphan who fled to you. See my humiliation and have mercy on me.

2. Look, I have taken off my robe of royalty with gold inlay and have now put on a black tunic of mourning.

3. Look, I have taken off my gold belt and have replaced it with a rope and sackcloth.

4. Look, I ripped off the beads from my head and sprinkled ashes over myself.

5.Look, at one time the floor of my room had various colorful stones and precious purple stones all over it. The room was sprinkled with myrrh and now it is sprinkled with my tears and littered with ashes.

6. Lord, my tears have mixed with the ashes and have made mud in my room. My room looks like a well-traveled dirt road. I feel naked and afraid.

7. Lord, the dinner of fattened animals was prepared for royalty but I gave it to the dogs.

8. For seven days and seven nights I have not eaten bread or drank water. My mouth is as dry as a skin drum and my tongue looks like the horn of an animal. My lips are (cracked and broken) like broken pieces of pottery. My face is shrunken. I am going blind because my eyes have swollen from all my unceasing tears.

9. I sinned against you and said slanderous things about my lord Joseph. But I did these things in ignorance so I beg you to forgive me. I did not know that he was your son, O Lord. I am a wretch.

10. They told me Joseph was the son of a Canaanite shepherd's son and I believed them and I hated (looked down on) Joseph. I was wrong. He is your chosen one and your son but I spoke harshly to him, not knowing these things.

11. Who was ever as handsome and wise and strong as Joseph? No one but you my Lord.

I now trust him and love him more than my own soul.

12. Let him remain in your wisdom and grace. Give me to him as a servant and I will wash his feet and serve him. I will be his slave for the rest of my life.

XIV. Aseneth was completing her confession to the Lord, when she looked up and saw the morning star was rising in the sky to the east. 2. When she saw it she was overjoyed. She proclaimed aloud, "The Lord God definitely heard me because this star is a message and announces the light of a great day."

3. Then, suddenly the sky was ripped open near the morning star and a light appeared that was beyond description. 4.Aseneth bowed down with her face in the ashes as God sent a man (angel/messenger) of light down from heaven. He stood over her head and he called her by her name. "Aseneth", he said. 5. Then she asked, "Who called me? This is a high tower and the door to my room is locked. How did you get into my room?" 6. Then he called her a second time, saying "Aseneth, Aseneth." She then answered him, "Here am I, sir. Who you are?" 7. And the man said, "I am the chief commander of the Lord, God. I am the general of all the heavenly army of the Most High. Get on your feet – stand - I will speak to you."

The angel (or heavenly man) fits the description of Michael, the archangel. Michael is mentioned three times in the Book of Daniel, once as a "great prince who stands up for the children of your people". The idea that Michael was the advocate of the Jews became so prevalent that in spite of the rabbinical prohibition against appealing to angels as intermediaries between God and his people, Michael came to occupy a certain place in the Jewish liturgy. In the vision in Daniel 10:13-21 an angel identifies Michael as the protector of Israel. Daniel refers to Michael as a "prince of the first rank." Later in the vision in Daniel 12:1 Daniel is informed about the role of Michael during the "Time of the End" when

there will be "distress such as has not happened from the beginning of nations" and that: "At that time Michael, the great prince who protects your people, will arise."
In view of this, Michael is seen as playing an important role as the protector of Israel, and later of the Christian Church. The references to the "captain of the host of the Lord" encountered by Joshua in the early days of his campaigns in the Promised Land (Joshua 5:13-15) have at times been interpreted as Michael the Archangel,

8. When she looked up she saw he looked just like Joseph. He wore a robe and had a crown on his head and he had a staff of royalty (authority) in his hand. 9. But his face was as bright as lightning, and his eyes were like the sun and his hair was like flames. His hands and feet glowed like iron placed in a fire. Sparks flew from his hands and feet.

10. Aseneth was afraid and she began to tremble. She fell on her face at his feet in terror. 11. But the man spoke to her and said, "Be comforted, Aseneth. Do not be afraid. Stand up. I wish to talk to you." 12. Aseneth stood, and the man spoke to her, "Take off your black tunic and the sackcloth round your waist. Wash the ashes off your head and face. 13. Take a new, perfectly clean robe, never worn before, and put it on. Get two belts. Tie a bright belt round your waist – the other will signify a doubled belt of your virginity. 14. After doing these things return to me, and I will tell you what I was sent here to say."

15. And Aseneth went into her room where she kept the chests filled with her valuables and the fine things she used to adorn herself. In her wardrobe she found a new, beautiful robe. She untied the rope and the sackcloth from her waist and took them off. She removed her black tunic and put on her new bright, clean robe. 16. Then she wrapped one belt round her waist and the other one she wrapped around her breast. It symbolized the double belt of her virginity 17. And she washed the ashes off her head and face with pure water, and covered her head with a beautiful, exquisite veil.

XV. When she came back to the divine commander and he saw her he said, "Remove the veil from your head because from this day you are a pure virgin and your head is like a young man's head."

Aseneth was always a virgin, but now she is a pure virgin, in the eyes of the angel. She is no longer simply a pagan who happens to be a virgin, but now she is a spiritual Jews and a pure virgin.

That Aseneth had "become like a young man" is a confusing statement. On the face of it, the meaning could be as simple as a "spiritual Bar Mitzvah". The Bar Mitsvah (Hebrew:

בַּר מִצְוָה) *and Bat Mitzvah (Hebrew:* בַּת מִצְוָה)) *are Jewish coming of age rituals. Bar (*בַּר*) is a Jewish Babylonian Aramaic word literally meaning 'son' (*בֵּן*), while bat (*בַּת*) means 'daughter' in Hebrew, and mitzvah (*מִצְוָה*) means 'commandment' or 'law'. Thus bar mitzvah and bat mitzvah literally translate to "son of commandment" and "daughter of commandment." However, in rabbinical usage, the word bar means "a person who is subject to the law." Although the term is commonly used to refer to the ritual itself, in fact the phrase originally refers to the person. According to Jewish law, when Jewish boys become 13 years old, they become accountable for their actions and become a bar mitzvah. A girl becomes a bat mitzvah at the age of 12 according to Orthodox and Conservative Jews, and at the age of 13 according to Reform Jews. Prior to reaching bar mitzvah, the child's parents hold the responsibility for the child's actions. After this age, the boys and girls bear their own responsibility for Jewish ritual law, tradition, and ethics, and are able to participate in all areas of Jewish community life.*

The act concerning removing the veil and becoming like a young man could possibly refer to the fact that young men never wore head coverings. The Talmud also implies that unmarried men did not wear a kippah (yamaka or yarmulke: Rabbi Hisda praised Rabbi Hamnuna before Rabbi Huna as a great man. He said to him, 'When he visits you, bring him to me. When he arrived, he saw that he wore no head-covering. 'Why do you not have head-covering?' he asked. 'Because I am not married,' was the reply. Thereupon, he [Rabbi Huna] turned his face away from him and said, 'See to it that you do not appear before me again before you are married.' [Tractate Kiddushin 29b]
However, young virgin women seldom wore scarves either. Since Aseneth was 18 years of age, which would have been considered rather old to marry, we have an interesting mixed message. Was she expected to wear a veil or head covering because she was older? Was she not expected to wear one because she was a virgin and not married?
In his book on ancient head coverings, Michael Marlowe reports:
Among the Greeks it seems that men did not ordinarily wear anything on their heads for worship of their gods, or in public. Generally, Greek men tended to minimize their clothing. Even nudity was not considered shameful among them in certain contexts. Because the climate in Greece is warm, men would sometimes wear nothing more than a scanty mantle called a chlamys fastened around the right shoulder, leaving the entire right side of their bodies exposed. Greek women were expected to fully cover their bodies. In the past, some biblical expositors asserted that all respectable Greek women wore head coverings, and that among the Greeks (as among the Jews) only disreputable women went about with bare heads. But there does not seem to be any good evidence for this in ancient sources. Many scholars now maintain that although Greek women certainly did wear head coverings, it was usually done in public. A woman

might wear a scarf tied closely around her hair, a small shawl draped over her head (called a kaluptra, resembling the modern mantilla), or a kind of snood, called a sakkos. One statement commonly cited as evidence about the head covering customs of Greek women is in Plutarch's Sayings of Spartans (written during the first century BCE). Concerning a Spartan he writes, When someone inquired why they took their girls into public places unveiled, but their married women veiled, he said, "Because the girls have to find husbands, and the married women have to keep to those who have them!" This seems to indicate that in Sparta married women usually covered their heads in public and unmarried women did not. Many pagan religion rituals required head coverings.

In Rome, generally speaking, it was common for a woman to cover her head in public, but men wore no head covering. The Romans had a special head covering for brides, as we do today. The bridal veil was a piece of cloth called a flammeum (lit. "flame-colored"), because it was dyed bright orange, and it was draped over the bride's head without covering her face. Recently some biblical expositors have asserted that in Rome a married woman would always keep her head covered as a sign that she was married, but this assertion is not very well supported by ancient sources. The "veiling of the bride" spoken of in ancient sources pertains only to the wedding ceremony, not to a change of ordinary clothing.
Headcovering Customs of the Ancient World
An Illustrated Survey, by Michael Marlowe

2. So she took it off her head; and the angel said to her, "Be encouraged, Aseneth, you virgin. Look, the Lord has heard your confession. 3. Your name is written in the book of life and will never be blotted out. 4. Today you will be renewed, and remade, and reborn. You will eat the bread of life and drink the cup of eternal life. You will be anointed with the oil of immortality. 5. Be happy, Aseneth, you virgin. God has given you to Joseph to marry. You will be his bride and he will be your husband. 6. Your name will no longer be "Aseneth", but your name will now be "City of Refuge" because many nations shall take refuge in you. Under your wings many nations shall find shelter. All who follow God with contrition will find security. 7. Contrition is the daughter of the Most High and she pleads for you with the Most High continually as well as for all who repent. God is the father of Contrition and she the mother of virgins, beautiful and meek. Contrition, appeals to God for those who repent. Contrition prepared a bridal chamber in heaven for those who love her. She is a virgin, like them, and so she will look after them forever. 8. She is pure. She is and celibate and gentle. The Most High God loves her, and his angels admire her.

References to a "city of refuge" may be one reason some scholars believed this book to be a Christian creation. In the

Old Testament, the city of refuge was a place, or group of places, where one could run to if an unintended but horrible event happened. In the New Testament the city or place of refuge becomes a person. We are told to seek refuge from the horrors and hopelessness of life in Jesus himself. Here, in the book of Joseph and Aseneth, we see Aseneth refered to as the city of refuge and her virgins as the pillars of that city.

According to the Torah, The Cities of Refuge were towns in the Kingdom of Israel and Kingdom of Judah in which the perpetrators of manslaughter could claim asylum. Outside of these cities, the law allowed blood vengeance. The Torah names just six cities as being cities of refuge: Golan, Ramoth, and Bosor, on the east of the Jordan River, and Kedesh, Shechem, and Hebron on the western side. Manslaughter, in this case, refers to the accidental or unintentional killing of a person.
We shall see that Egypt, and specifically Joseph, thus by extension Aseneth, will be the place of refuge in the coming famine. Joseph's family will come to Egypt seeking food and they will be given refuge and be saved by Joseph.

9. Now, I will go to Joseph to speak to him about you. Today he will meet you and when he sees you he will be overjoyed with you and he will marry you. 10. Aseneth, do as I say and put on the ancient wedding robe that is stored in your room and adorn yourself with your best jewelry and put on those things a bride would wear. Make yourself ready to meet Joseph. 11. He will meet you today and he will be very happy when he sees you."

12. The angel finished speaking to Aseneth and she was overflowing with happiness. 13. She bowed at his feet and exclaimed, "Forever blessed is the Lord God because he sent you to deliver me from darkness and bring me into light. 14. May I ask you, my lord, if you would please sit down on the bed for a while, before you leave. Allow me prepare a table with bread and fine wine for you to eat and drink! Their taste will be heavenly!"

XVI. So, the man (angel) agreed to stay and said, "Please fetch me a honeycomb also." 2. And Aseneth said, "Yes sir. Let me send a servant to my parent's fields to bring you back a honeycomb." 3. But the man said, "Go into your room where you eat and there you will find a honeycomb." 4. So Aseneth went to her room and found a honeycomb lying on the table. It was full of honey. Its fragrance was like a sweet ointment and the comb was large and as white as snow.

5. So, Aseneth picked up the comb and brought it to him. Then the angel said to her, "Why did you tell me there was no honeycomb in your house when I see you have brought me this." 6. Aseneth replied, sir, I did not have a honeycomb in my house, this thing happened

just as you said. Could it have come from you, because it smells like myrrh?" 7. Then the man raised his hand and placed his hand on top of her head and said, " Aseneth, you are blessed because the hidden and indescribable mysteries of the Most High God have been revealed to you. Blessed are those who are faithful to the Lord God and contrite, for they shall eat from this comb. 8. The bees of the Paradise of Delight (which is the garden of Eden) have made this honey. God's angels eat it, and all who eat it will live forever.

9. And the man reached out with his right hand and broke off a piece of the comb and ate it. He then with his hand he placed a piece in the mouth of Aseneth. 10. Then he reached out and with his forefinger he touched the side of the comb facing east and where his finger traced on the comb the honey turned to blood. 11. Again he reached out and placed his forefinger on the edge of the comb that faced north and where his forefinger touched on the comb the honey turned to blood.

12. Aseneth was standing on the man's left side, observing everything. 13. She saw the bees began coming out of the cells of the comb. They were white as snow, and their wings glowed with colors of purple and scarlet with threads of gold. The bees had golden crowns on their heads and sharp stringers. 14. All the bees flew in circles around Aseneth, circling her from head to foot. Then large bees, as big as queens, lit on Aseneth's lips. 15. Then the man commanded the bees, saying, "Leave and go to your places." 16. They all left Aseneth and those that intended to harm her fell to the ground and died. 17. Again the man commanded them, "Arise, and go to your place." Then the remaining bees flew up and all went to the courtyard round Aseneth's tower.

The idea of cleansing the lips or tongue and thus removing sin and even re-purposing a life is not new in the Bible. This theme occurs also in the book of Isaiah.

Isaiah 6 Holman Christian Standard Bible (HCSB) - Isaiah's Call and Mission
1 In the year that King Uzziah died, I saw the Lord seated on a high and lofty throne, and His robe[a] filled the temple. 2 Seraphim[b] were standing above Him; each one had six wings: with two he covered his face, with two he covered his feet, and with two he flew. 3 And one called to another:
Holy, holy, holy is the Lord of Hosts;
His glory fills the whole earth.
4 The foundations of the doorways shook at the sound of their voices, and the temple was filled with smoke.
5 Then I said:
Woe is me for I am ruined[c]
because I am a man of unclean lips
and live among a people of unclean lips,

and because my eyes have seen the King,
the Lord of Hosts.
6 Then one of the seraphim flew to me, and in his hand was a glowing coal that he had taken from the altar with tongs. 7 He touched my mouth with it and said:
Now that this has touched your lips,
your wickedness is removed
and your sin is atoned for.
8 Then I heard the voice of the Lord saying:
Who should I send?
Who will go for Us?
I said:
Here I am. Send me.

In Isaiah fire is used to cleanse. For Aseneth the cleansing agent was honey. Honey has antiseptic properties. It is one of the only foods that does not spoil. Unless it is contaminated, honey can last for years without spoiling.

In the story of Aseneth's "purification," honey represents the agent of cleansing. It came from a comb that was white, representing purity. The bees, being the size of queen bees, convey the idea of royalty. They lit but did not sting her. There was no harm or destruction, only purification and sanctification.

XVII. And the man said to Aseneth, "You saw this?" And she said, "Yes sir, I saw everything" 2. And the man said, "This will be the same as my command to you." 3. And the man touched the comb, and fire shot from the table through the comb and burned up the comb. As the fire consumed the comb an enlivening fragrance filled the room. It was the breath of life. 4. Then Aseneth said to the man, "Sir, there are seven virgins with me who were raised with me. They were all born on the same night as me. They serve me and I love them. Please let me call them to come so that you might bless them as you have blessed me. 5. The man replied, "Call them." So, Aseneth called them, and the man blessed them and said, "The Lord, God, the Most High, will bless you and you shall become seven pillars in the City of Refuge for ever."

6. Then the man commanded Aseneth, saying, "Remove this table." Immediately she turned to move the table but the man had vanished, but Aseneth saw something resembling a chariot of fire being lifted into the sky towards the east. 7. And Aseneth called out, "Be merciful, O Lord, to me, your servant, because I spoke evil words in my ignorance."

XVIII. And while Aseneth was still saying these things, one of Joseph's young servants, came running up and announced, "Look! Joseph, the mighty man of God is coming to see you today." 2. And Aseneth called her servant who was over the house and said to him,

"Prepare a special dinner for me, because Joseph the mighty man of God, is coming to visit us."
But when the steward saw her, with her face sunken from sorrow and weeping, and fasting for seven days he wept for her and took her hand asked what was wrong. She said she had a horrible headache and could not sleep and this was the excuse she gave to the steward.

3.Then Aseneth ran up to her room and opened her wardrobe, and she took out her favorite robe. It was bright as lightning. She put it on. 4. She selected a glittering belt, made of precious stones and worthy of royalty, and she tied it around her waist. 5. Then she placed bracelets of gold on her wrists, and golden boots on her feet. She slipped an expensive necklace around her neck; and selected a golden crown with the most precious stones in it and placed the crown on her head. 6. Then she veiled herself. 7. She commanded her maid to bring pure water from the spring. 8.Then Aseneth bent down to the water in the basin to wash her face but she saw her face was like the sun, and her eyes like the rising morning star, so she stopped and did not wash, not wanting to wash away the wonderful beauty.

XIX. Then a slave, small in stature, came in and said to Aseneth, "Joseph is now at the gates of our courtyard." So Aseneth went with the seven virgins down stairs to meet Joseph. 2. When Joseph saw her, he said to her, "Come closer, you pure virgin. I have been told good things about you from heaven, and the message has explained everything about you." 3. And Joseph stretched out his arms and embraced Aseneth, and Aseneth embraced Joseph back, and they talked to each other for a long time and by their breath they received new life in their spirit.

XX. And Aseneth said to him, "Sir, come into my house." Then she took his right hand in hers and hand in hand they walked in to the house. 2. And Joseph sat down on her father Petephres's cushion. Aseneth brought in water to wash his feet but and Joseph said to her, "Tell one of your virgins come and wash my feet instead of you." 3. But Aseneth answered him, "No, sir. My hands are your hands, and your feet are my feet. No one else will wash your feet from now on." Then she did as she wanted and washed his feet. 4. Joseph took her by the right hand and kissed her and Aseneth kissed him on his forehead. 5. Then Aseneth's mother and father came back from their country estate and saw Aseneth sitting with Joseph and wearing a brilliant wedding robe. They were overjoyed and praised God and everyone ate and drank.

Joseph and Aseneth never take the left hand of the other. Always the right hand is mentioned. The right hand is the

sign of power and authority. The left hand was considered an inferior side. Even today we get several words or phrases from this idea. The word, sinister, comes from the Latin word for "left". "Gauche" comes from French, meaning "left". Even the idea of getting off on the wrong foot comes from the superstition of crossing a threshold with the right foot first. Brewer tells us:
It was thought unlucky to enter a house or to leave one's chamber left foot foremost. Augustus was very superstitious on this point. Pythagoras taught that it is necessary to put the shoe on the right foot first. "When stretching forth your feet to have your sandals put on, first extend your right foot" (Protreptics of Iamblichus, symbol xii.). Iamblichus tells us this symbolised that man's first duty is reverence to the gods.

6. Petephres said to Joseph, "Tomorrow I will invite the governors and officials of Egypt, and we will celebrate your wedding, and you shall take Aseneth as your wife."

One source has Petephres giving Joseph 100 Talents of gold as a dowry. An Egyptian talent was about 60 pounds. At the present price of gold at about $1200 USD per ounce the dowry was worth about $1,152,000 (one million, one hundred fifty-two thousand dollars). (60 pound x 16 ounces per pound = 960 ounces. 960 x 1200 = 1152000)

7. But Joseph said, " I must tell Pharaoh about Aseneth first because he is my father and he will give me Aseneth as my wife himself." 8. Joseph stayed that night with Petephres but he did not sleep with Aseneth, because he told them it would not be right for a man who worships God to have sex with his wife before their marriage."

Obviously, Pharaoh is not Joseph's biological father, but since Joseph's brother sold him into slavery and his father was told by the brothers that Joseph was dead, Joseph regards Pharaoh as a father image and Pharaoh has entrusted Joseph with his authority, just as he would have with his son. Regarding marriage rituals, in ancient cultures it was sex that established the consummation of a relationship and not necessarily a ceremony. Joseph is concerned with carrying out things in a proper and correct order before sleeping with Aseneth.

XXI. Joseph got up early in the morning, to send a message to Pharaoh. He told Pharaoh all about Aseneth. 2. Then Pharaoh sent a message telling Petephres and Aseneth to come to him. 3. Pharaoh was astonished at the beauty of Aseneth and said, "The Lord God of Joseph will bless you, because he has chosen you to be his bride, for Joseph is the first-born son of God, and you will be called daughter of the Most High, and Joseph shall be your bridegroom for ever.

4. And Pharaoh crowned them with crowns of gold and said, 5. "God Most High will bless you, He will make your family prosperous and will give you many descendants forever." 6. The Pharaoh turned them to face each other, and they kissed.

7. The Pharaoh came to their wedding. He issued an edict proclaiming, "If anyone works during the seven days of Joseph and Aseneth's wedding he shall be put to death." 8. Pharaoh invited all the important men in Egypt. Everyone celebrated with a banquet and drinking for seven days.

9. And when the wedding ceremony was complete and the banquet had ended, Joseph had sex with Aseneth and she conceived and gave birth to Manasseh and his brother Ephraim in Pharaoh's house.

Joseph is called "the first-born son of God." This led a few scholars to speculate the story of Joseph and Aseneth may be an allegory of Jesus and his bride. In this case they were not speaking of the church but of a woman, possibly Mary Magdalene.

There are other explanations, which make much more sense and follow the storyline. Joseph had proven his connection with his Jewish God when he was able to interpret the dreams of Pharaoh and his servants. Joseph was capable, competent, righteous, and had risen from prison to be a ruler. In the view of the Egyptians, God was treating Joseph like a son and Joseph was worshipping and respecting God like a divine father.

There is another possibility. In Egypt, Pharaoh was a god or a servant of god. From the second dynasty onward Pharaoh derived his power from the sun god Ra who, by then, was the pre-eminent creator god.

During the Old and Middle Kingdoms once a deceased pharaoh had joined the gods in the skies, he was worshipped in temples adjoining his pyramid. Ptolemy II had himself and his wife Arsinoe II deified some two decades into his reign and was worshiped at the shrine of Alexander the Great at Alexandria, and all his successors did likewise after acceding to the throne. They were thought to continue to play a role as guardian deities after their death. Thus, as the son of Pharaoh, Joseph was indeed the son of god.

Joseph and Aseneth

Part Two

XXII. When the seven years of plenty ended, the seven years of famine began. 2. When Jacob heard of Joseph, he went to Egypt with his family. 3. On the twenty-first day of the second month Jacob arrived with his family and they settled in the region called Goshen within the land of Egypt.

Aseneth told Joseph, "Let us go meet your father, because your father, Israel, is my father also. Joseph answered her, "Yes, let us go together." 4. And Joseph and Aseneth went to the region of Goshen. When Joseph's brothers met Joseph and Aseneth they bowed to both of them and placed their heads on the ground. 5. Then they came to Jacob and he blessed them and kissed them. Then Aseneth hugged Jacob's neck and kissed him.

When Asenath saw him she was surprised at his beauty. His hair was white as snow and very thick and full. His white beard reached to his chest. His eyes were bright as with lightning. His shoulders and arms were shapely and his thighs and legs were large.

Jacob said to Joseph: "Is this your bride? She is blessed by the Most High God." Jacob then called her to him and blessed and kissed her. Asenath stretched forth her hands, and hugged Jacob's neck, and she kissed him.

6. Then they ate and drank together. 7. Joseph and Aseneth then left and returned to their house. Simeon and Levi escorted them, to protect them because their enemies were envious of them. Levi was on Aseneth's right hand and Simeon on her left side. 8. And Aseneth held hands with Levi because she respected him as a prophet and a man who worshipped and respected the Lord, God. Levi would see letters written in the sky, and he would read them and interpret them to Aseneth, revealing all things to her privately. Levi had a vision of her resting place, high in heaven.

XXIII. As Joseph and Aseneth were passing by, Pharaoh's eldest son was up on the wall and he saw them. 2. And when he saw Aseneth he became obsessed with her because of her beauty. Pharaoh's son sent messengers and demanded that Simeon and Levi come to him. Then they came to him and presented themselves to him.

3. Pharaoh's son said to them, "I know that you are the best soldiers on earth. I heard it told that with your right hands you razed the city of Schechem to the

ground and with your two swords you slaughtered thirty thousand men of war. 4. Now, I need your help. I wish to hire you as my companions (bodyguards – personal soldiers) and I will pay you well with gold and silver, and I will furnish you with menservants and maidservants, and provide you both with houses and larges fields (eastes) and your children will inherit them. Now, be kind to me and swear to me you will do this for me because your brother Joseph offended me because he married Aseneth and she was supposed to marry me.

5. Follow me and take up arms with me against Joseph. You will kill him with my sword, and I will marry Aseneth. For doing this you shall be counted as my brothers and my friends forever. 6. However, if you refuse my offer I will draw my sword and kill you. Then he drew his sword and showed it to them.

7. Now Simeon was a brave but rash and impulsive, so he was about to draw his sword and rush at Pharaoh's son to kill him. 8. But Levi was aware of Simeon's intention because Levi was a prophet and foresaw everything that was going to happen. So, Levi stomped down hard on Simeon's right foot as a signal for him to stifle his anger. 9. And Levi said to Simeon "Why are you so angry with him? Our father worships God, and we are his children. It is not right for those who worship God to repay his neighbor' evil acts with evil." 10. Then Levi addresses Pharaoh's son light heartedly but with respect, "Sir, why do you talk to us like this? We worship God, and our father serves the Most High God. God loves our brother, Joseph. How could we possibly do anything God would look upon as being this evil? 11. Listen, you should be careful never to let us hear of such a plan against our brother Joseph ever again. 12. If you ever try this evil plan again you will see our swords drawn against you." 13. Then Levi and Simeon drew their swords from their scabbards and said, " It was with these swords that the Lord God satisfied the rage the men of Israel had against the men of Schechem when our sister Dinah was raped, whom Schechem, Hamor's son, defiled." 14. When Pharaoh's son saw their swords were drawn, he was afraid. He began to shake and fell face first to the ground by their feet. 15. Then Levi stretched out his hand pulled him up, saying, "You need not be afraid if you are careful and never utter another word against our brother." 16. Then they left him trembling and afraid on the ground.

XXIV. Pharaoh's son was fixated on the torment caused by his desire for Aseneth, and he was grieved by his feelings. 2. His servants whispered in his ear. They said, "Look, Bilhah and Zilpah were the maidservants of Leah and Rachel, Jacob's wives and Jacob had sons by Bilhah and Zilpah. Their sons hate Joseph and

Aseneth. They are jealous of them, and they will do whatever you want."

In the Book of Genesis, Zilpah is Leah's handmaid who becomes a wife of Jacob and bears him two sons, Gad and Asher. Zilpah is given to Leah as a handmaid by Leah's father, Laban, upon Leah's marriage to Jacob (see Genesis 29:24, 46:18). According to some commentators, Zilpah and Bilhah, the handmaids of Leah and Rachel, respectively, were actually younger daughters of Laban {Pirke De-Rabbi Eliezer, xxxvi.}.

According to Rashi, an 11th-century commentator, Zilpah was younger than Bilhah, and Laban's decision to give her to Leah was part of the deception he used to trick Jacob into marrying Leah, who was older than Rachel. The morning after the wedding, Laban explained to Jacob, "This is not done in our place, to give the younger before the older" (Genesis 29:26). But at night, to mask the deception, Laban gave the veiled bride the younger of the handmaids, so Jacob would think that he was really marrying Rachel, the younger of the sisters.

Zilpah also figures in the competition between Jacob's wives to bear him sons. Leah stops conceiving after the birth of her fourth son, at which point Rachel, who had not yet borne children, offers her handmaid, Bilhah, in marriage to Jacob so that she can have children through her. When Bilhah conceives two sons, Leah takes up the same idea and presents Zilpah as a wife to Jacob. Leah names the two sons of Zilpah and is directly involved in their upbringing.

Jacob
/ ---**Leah** *(Reuben, Simeon, Levi, Judah, Issachar, Zebulun, Dinah)*
/ --------------------**Rachael** *(Joseph, Benjamin)*
/-------------**Bilhah** *(Dan, Naphtali)*
/------**Zilpah** *(Gad, Asher)*

3. So Pharaoh's son sent his slave to summon these sons, and they came to meet him in the night. Pharaoh's son said to them, "I know that your are good soldiers." 4. And Gad and Dan, the elder brothers, said to Pharaoh's son, "Yes sir. We are at your service. Simply tell us what you want and we will do as you wish."

5. And Pharaoh's son was elated at their response so he told to his servants to go away and leave them alone because he had something to discuss with the men privately. 6. And all the servants left and Pharaoh's son lied to them, saying, "You have a choice between prosperity and death. Blessings and death stare you in the face right now, so choose the blessings and not death.

7. I know that you are good soldiers and that you will not die like women. Act like men and go out to meet your enemies. 8. Your brother Joseph told my father Pharaoh, that Dan and Gad are the children of maidservants and are not really his brothers. 9. Joseph told Pharaoh, "I am waiting my time until my father Jacob dies so I can take action against them and the entire families of Dan and Gad. I will make it so that they will not have an inheritance with us, because they are the children of maidservants. They are the ones that sold me to the Ishmaelites. 10. When my father is dead I will pay them back for all the wrong things they did to me."

11. And my father Pharaoh agreed with Joseph and said to him, You are correct, my son. I will assist you. So, now take the rest of my soldiers with you and go against them just as they went against you.'" 12. And when Dan and Gad heard what Pharaoh's son told them they were anxious and worried. They said, "We beg you, sir. Help us. We are your servants and slaves. Tell us what to do and we will obey."

13. And Pharaoh's son said to them, " My father the Pharaoh acts like he is Joseph's father so tonight I will kill him. I want you to kill Joseph also, then I will marry Aseneth."

14. And Dan and Gad said to him, "We will obey your command. We overheard Joseph say to Aseneth, "Tomorrow we will go to our fields for it is harvest time. I have arranged for six hundred armed soldiers to go with you and fifty forerunners (scouts or foot-soldiers that ran ahead of the horsemen or chariots)." 15. When Pharaoh's son heard this, he gave each of the four men a battalion of five hundred men each and appointed officers and commanders over the troops.

Here it is uncertain as to who the four men are. We know two are Gad and Dan. It could be the Pharaoh's son assigned two of his men to assist Dan and Gad. It is likely Gad and Dan had their younger brothers, Naphtali and Asher with them, but soon we will discover their brothers did not agree with the deceitful behavior of Dan and Gad.

16. And Dan and Gad said to the son of Pharaoh, "We will leave in the night and hide. We will wait in the thicket of reeds, on the bank of the brook. 17. You go ahead of Aseneth and get some distance in front of her. Take fifty archers on horseback with you. Aseneth will come right to you. Capture her. We will kill the men who are with her. 18. And Aseneth will try to escape in her chariot but she will run right into your hands and you can deal with her however you wish. 19. And afterwards we will capture Joseph while he is mourning the death of Aseneth. We will kill his children before his eyes. Then we will kill him." 20.

And Pharaoh's son was delighted at what he heard, and he sent two thousand soldiers after them.

21. Gad and Dan arrived at the brook and hid in the thicket on the banks. The five hundred men with them took up their position in front of them on both sides of the road.

XXV. That night the Pharaoh's son went to his father's room to kill him with a sword, but his father's guards would not allow him to enter his father's bed-chamber. 2. And Pharaoh's son commanded them, saying, "I will see my father because I am going off to gather the grapes from my new vineyard. 3. And the guards said to him, "Your father has been in pain and awake all night long, but he is resting now. He has given us orders saying, "Do not let anyone in to me, not even my eldest son." And Pharaoh's son went away angry.

4. Then Pharaoh's son took his fifty archers on horseback, and he preceded Dan and Gad as they had told him to. 5. But Naphtali and Asher spoke to Dan and Gad asking, "Why must you plot once again to do evil against our father Israel and against our brother Joseph? You know God looks after Joseph as if he were the apple of his eye. 6. Did you not sell Joseph as a slave one day, and today he is king of all the land of Egypt? Moreover, he has saved Egypt and has given us corn. 7. If you plot against Joseph again, he will call upon the God of Israel, and the Most High will send fire from heaven to burn you up. The angels of God will fight against you." 8. But Dan and Gad, their older brothers, were angry with them, and they said, "What do you want us to do, die like women? God forbid!" And with that they departed to attack Joseph and Aseneth.

XXVI. And Aseneth got up early in the morning and said to Joseph, "I am going to our land in the country, but I am frightened in my spirit because you are not coming with me." 2. And Joseph said to her, "Be happy and do not be afraid. Go and be cheerful and do not be afraid. The Lord is with you and you are like the apple of his eye and he will keep you from all danger. 3. And I will go and distribute my corn, and give corn to all the men in the city, and no one will die of hunger in the land of Egypt."

4. So Aseneth left and started on her journey and Joseph went to distribute the corn. 5. But when Aseneth came to the brook with her six hundred men, suddenly the men that were with Pharaoh's son appeared from their ambush and engaged Aseneth's soldiers in battle, and the soldiers of Pharaoh's son killed Aseneth's men with their swords and killed all Aseneth's foot soldiers as well.

6. Then Aseneth was frightened and she fled in her chariot. 7. And Levi, the son of Leah, sensed (was informed of) all of this because he was a prophet. He told his brothers and the men of his counsel about Aseneth's danger. So they all strapped a sword to their thighs and placed their shields on their arms and picked up their spears in their right hands, and they went out after Aseneth with all the speed they could muster. 8. But, as Aseneth fled, Pharaoh's son along with fifty of his men met her, and as Aseneth saw him, and she was afraid and trembled and she called upon the name of the Lord, her God.

XXVII. Benjamin was sitting with Aseneth in the chariot on her right side. 2. And Benjamin was a strong boy, about eighteen years old, handsome beyond description (beyond the nature of men), and as strong as a young lion, and he feared God. 3. And Benjamin jumped down from the chariot, and he took a round stone that filled his hand from the brook. He hurled it at Pharaoh's son with all his might, hitting him on his left temple and wounding him severely. It was a grievous wound. He fell from his horse to the ground landing half-dead. 4. Benjamin quickly climbed up on a rock and shouted to the driver of Aseneth's chariot, "Give me fifty stones from the stream." And he gave him fifty stones.

5. And Benjamin hurled the stones. The stones pierced their temples and killed the fifty men that were with Pharaoh's son. 6. Then Reuben, Simeon, Levi, Judah, Issachar and Zebulon, the sons of Leah, pursued the men who attempted the ambush and they fell upon them suddenly, and the six of them killed all two thousand men.
7. But their brothers, the sons of Bilhah and Zilpah, fled. They said, "We shall perish here by the hands of our brothers. Benjamin killed Pharaoh's son and he is dead. All those with Pharaoh's son have perished. Six men killed two hundred and seventy-six men. Those who were left said, "Come now, let us kill Aseneth and Benjamin, then they ran into the woods with their swords drawn and covered in blood. 8. When Aseneth saw them, and she said, "O Lord my God, who has given me life and redeemed me from the idols of corruption and death, you have said to me, 'Your soul shall live for ever', deliver me now from these men." And the Lord God heard the voice of Aseneth, and immediately the swords of her enemies fell from their hands to the ground and were became like ashes (powerless).

XXVIII. And the sons of Bilhah and Zilpah saw the amazing event that had happened and they were very fearful and cried out, "The Lord is fighting for Aseneth and against us!" 2. And they fell and bowed with their faces to the ground and were subservient to Aseneth and they said, "Have mercy on us. We will be your servants because you are our mistress and queen. Our lady we have done evil things and have wronged you and our brother, Joseph greatly.

3. God has already brought retribution upon us. We beg you to have mercy on us and deliver us from our brothers' hands, for they have become your avengers to the outrage done by us to you. Their swords are cruel and will be against us." 4. And Aseneth said to them, "Try not to worry. Do not fear, for I know your brothers are men who worship God. They do not repay evil for evil. 5. I want you to hide in the thickets until I can quench their anger, appease them, and secure your pardon. You have dared to attempt great evil against them. 6. But try not to worry and do not be afraid, for the Lord will avenge the violence done between us. They are, after all, your father's sons. "

7. Then Dan and Gad fled to the thicket. 8. The sons of Leah came running in pursuit of them as fast as deer. But Aseneth got down from her chariot, and she greeted them with tears. 9. And they bowed to her on the ground and wept aloud. They enquired of Aseneth about their brothers, the sons of the maidservants of their father's wives, because they intended to kill them.

10. But Aseneth said to them, "Spare your brothers and do not repay evil for evil. The Lord has shielded me and melted the swords in their hands, reducing them to dust. They melted like wax in the fire. 11. The Lord is fighting for us. Isn't that enough? Therefore, spare your brothers." 12. And Simeon said to Aseneth, "Why should our mistress speak for and plead for her enemies? No! We will cut them down, kill them with our swords, because they have plotted evil on two occasions against our father Israel and our brother Joseph. Today they have plotted against you." 14. But Aseneth stretched out her hand and kissed Simeon tenderly on his check and she said to him , "No brother, you must not repay evil for evil to your neighbor. Let the Lord avenge this violence." 15. Then Simeon bowed to Aseneth and Levi came to her and kissed her right hand, then he blessed her. 16. It was in this way that Aseneth saved the lives of those men from their brothers' anger, so that they did not kill them. But Levi knew about the men hiding in the thicket but he did not tell his brother because the wrath of Simeon and the men would have driven them to kill those hiding.

XXIX. And Pharaoh's son sat up from the ground and he spat blood from his mouth. Blood was running from his temple into his mouth. 2. Benjamin saw him and ran up to him. Benjamin took hold of the sword of Pharaoh's son and drew it from its scabbard to strike him because Benjamin did not have his own sword with him. 3. He raised the sword and was about to strike down Pharaoh's son when Levi rushed in and grabbed him by the hand and said, "No brother. Do not do this. We worship God, and it is not right for a man who worships God to repay evil for evil. It is not right to kick or injure a man who has already fallen, or destroy him in this way.

4. Instead, let us bind up his wound. If he lives he will owe us his friendship, and his father Pharaoh will be our father." 5. So Levi helped Pharaoh's son up off the ground and washed the blood off his face. He wrapped a bandage around his wounded head. Then they set him on his horse and took him to his father.

6. And Levi told Pharaoh everything that had happened. 7. When the Pharaoh heard all that was said he got up from his throne and bowed to Levi and blessed him 8. But, three days later Pharaoh's son died from the wound caused by Benjamin's stone. 9. Pharaoh mourned deeply for his first-born son, and Pharaoh was exhausted from his grief. 10. And Pharaoh died at the age of one hundred and nine. But he left his crown and his kingdom to Joseph. 11. And Joseph was king of Egypt for forty-eight years. 12. At the end of his reign Joseph gave the crown to Pharaoh's youngest, because Joseph was like a father to the child in Egypt. And Joseph praised and glorified God and he lived for years and saw the children of Ephraim.

2 Baruch
THE BOOK OF THE APOCALYPSE OF BARUCH THE SON OF NERIAH

1—4. Announcement of the coming Destruction of Jerusalem to Baruch

1 1 And it came to pass in the twenty-fifth year of Jeconiah, king of Judah, that the word of the Lord came to Baruch, the son of Neriah, and said to him: 2 'Have you seen all that this people are doing to Me, that the evils which these two tribes which remained have done are greater than (those of) the ten tribes which were carried away captive? 3 For the former tribes were forced by their kings to commit sin, but these two of themselves have been forcing and compelling their kings to commit sin. 4 For this reason, behold I bring evil upon this city, and upon its inhabitants, and it shall be removed from before Me for a time, and I will scatter this people among the Gentiles that they may do good to the Gentiles. And My people shall be chastened, and the time shall come when they will seek for the prosperity of their times.

2 1 For I have said these things to you that you may bid Jeremiah, and all those that are like you, to retire from this city.

2 For your works are to this city as a firm pillar,
And your prayers as a strong wall.'

3 1 And I said: 'O LORD, my Lord, have I come into the world for this purpose that I might see the evils of my mother? Not (so) my Lord. 2 If I have found grace in Your sight, first take my spirit that I may go to my fathers and not behold the destruction of my mother. For two things vehemently constrain me: for I cannot resist you, and my soul, moreover, cannot behold the evils of my mother. 4 But one thing I will say in Your presence, O Lord. 5 What, therefore, will there be after these things? for if you destroy Your city, and deliver up Your land to those that hate us, how shall the name of Israel be again remembered? 6 Or how shall one speak of Your praises? or to whom shall that which is in Your law be explained? Or shall the world return to its nature of aforetime), and the age revert to primeval silence? And shall the multitude of souls be taken away, and the nature of man not again be named? And where is all that which you did say regarding us?'

4 1 And the Lord said unto me: This city shall be delivered up for a time,

And the people shall be chastened during a time,
And the world will not be given over to oblivion.

4:2-7. *The heavenly Jerusalem*

2 [Dost you think that this is that city of which I said:
"On the palms of My hands have I graven you"? 3
This building now built in your midst is not that
which is revealed with Me, that which prepared
beforehand here from the time when I took counsel to
make Paradise, and showed Adam before he sinned,
but when he transgressed the commandment it was
removed from him, as also Paradise. 4 And after these
things I showed it to My servant Abraham by night
among the portions of the victims. 5 And again also I
showed it to Moses on Mount Sinai when I showed to
the likeness of the tabernacle and all its vessels. 6 And
now, behold, it is preserved with Me, as Paradise. 7
Go, therefore, and do as I command you.']

5. *Baruch's Complaint and God's Reassurance*

5 1And I answered and said:
So then I am destined to grieve for Zion,
For your enemies will come to this place and pollute
Your sanctuary,
And lead your inheritance into captivity,
And make themselves masters of those whom you
have loved,
And they will depart again to the place of their idols,
And will boast before them:
And what will you do for Your great name?'
2 And the Lord said unto me:
My name and My glory are unto all eternity;
And My judgment shall maintain its right in its own
time.
3 And you shall see with your eyes
That the enemy will not overthrow Zion,
Nor shall they burn Jerusalem,
But be the ministers of the Judge for the time.
4 But do you go and do whatsoever I have said unto
you.
5 And I went and took Jeremiah, and Adu, and
Seriah, and Jabish, and Gedaliah, and all the
honorable men of the people, and I led them to the
valley of Kidron, and I narrated to them all that had
been said to me. 6 And they lifted up their voice, and
they all wept. 7 And we sat there and fasted until the
evening.

6—8. *Invasion of the Chaldeans and their Entrance into the City after the Sacred Vessels were hidden and the City's Walls overthrown by Angels*

6 1And it came to pass on the morrow that, lo! the
army of the Chaldees surrounded the city, and at the
time of the evening, I, Baruch, left the people, and I
went forth and stood by the oak. 2 And I was grieving
over Zion, and lamenting over the captivity which
had come upon the people. 3 And lo! suddenly a
strong spirit raised me, and bore me aloft over the
wall of Jerusalem. 4 And I beheld, and lo! four angels
standing at the four corners of the city, each of them
holding a torch of fire in his hands. 5 And another
angel began to descend from heaven. and said unto
them: 'Hold your lamps, and do not light them till I
tell you. 6 For I am first sent to speak a word to the
earth, and to place in it what the Lord the Most High
has commanded me.' 7 And I saw him descend into
the Holy of Holies, and take from there the veil, and
holy ark, and the mercy-seat, and the two tables, and
the holy raiment of the priests, and the altar of
incense, and the forty-eight precious stones,
wherewith the priest was adorned and all the holy
vessels of the tabernacle. 8 And he spoke to the earth
with a loud voice:

Earth, earth, earth, hear the word of the mighty God,
And receive what I commit to you,
And guard them until the last times,
So that, when you are ordered, you may restore them,
So that strangers may not get possession of them.
9 For the time comes when Jerusalem also will be
delivered for a time,
Until it is said, that it is again restored for ever.'
10 And the earth opened its mouth and swallowed
them up.

7 1And after these things I heard that angel saying
unto those angels who held the lamps: 'Destroy,
therefore, and overthrow its wall to its foundations,
lest the enemy should boast and say:

We have overthrown the wall of Zion,
And we have burnt the place of the mighty God."'
2 And they have seized the place where I had been
standing before.

8 1 Now the angels did as he had commanded them,
and when they had broken up the corners of the
walls, a voice was heard from the interior of the
temple, after the wall had fall saying:

2 Enter, you enemies,
And come, you adversaries;
For he who kept the house has forsaken (it).'

3And I, Baruch, departed. 4 And it came to pass after
these things that the army of the Chaldees entered
and seized the house, and all that was around it. And
they led the people away captive and slew some of
them, and bound Zedekiah the king, and sent him to
the king of Babylon.

9—12. First Fast of seven Days: Baruch to remain amid the Ruins of Jerusalem and Jeremiah to accompany the Exiles to Babylon. Baruch's Dirge over Jerusalem

9 1And I, Baruch, came, and Jeremiah, whose heart was found pure from sins, who had not been captured in the seizure of the City. 2 And we rent our garments, we wept, and mourned, and fasted seven days.

10 1And it came to pass after seven days, that the word of God carne to me, and said unto me: 2 'Tell Jeremiah to go and support the captivity of the people unto Babylon. But do you remain here amid the desolation of Zion, and I will show to you after these days 'what will befall at the end of days.' And I said to Jeremiah as the Lord commanded me. And he, indeed, departed with the people, but I, Baruch, returned and sat before the gates of the temple, and I lamented with the following lamentation over Zion and said:

6Blessed is he who was not born,
Or he, who having been born, has died.
7But as for us who live, woe unto us,
Because we see the afflictions of Zion,
And what has befallen Jerusalem.
8I will call the Sirens from the sea,
And you Lilin, come you from the desert,
And you Shedim and dragons from the forests:
Awake and gird up your loins unto mourning,
And take up with me the dirges,
And make lamentation with me.
9Ye husbandmen, sow not again;
And, O earth, wherefore give you your harvest fruits?
Keep within you the sweets of your sustenance.
10And thou, vine, why further do you give your wine;
For an offering will not again be made from there in Zion,
Nor will first-fruits again be offered.
11And do ye, O heavens, 'withhold your dew,
And open not the treasuries of rain:
12And do thou, O sun withhold the light of your rays.
And do thou, O moon, extinguish the multitude of your light;
For why should light rise again
Where the light of Zion is darkened?
13And you, you bridegrooms, enter not in,
And let not the brides adorn themselves with garlands;
And, you women, pray not that you may bear.
14For the barren shall above all rejoice,
And those who have no sons shall be glad,
And those who have sons shall have anguish.
15For why should they bear in pain,
Only to bury in grief?

16Or why, again, should mankind have sons?
Or why should the seed of their kind again be named,
Where this mother is desolate,
And her sons are led into captivity?
17From this time forward speak not of beauty,
And discourse not of gracefulness.
18Moreover, you priests) take you the keys of the sanctuary,
And cast them into the height of heaven,
And give them to the Lord and say:
"Guard Your house Thyself,
For lo! we are found false stewards."
19And you, you virgins; who weave fine linen
And silk with gold of Ophir,
Take with haste all (these) things
And cast (them) into the fire,
That it may bear them to Him who made them,
And the flame send them to Him who created them,
Lest the enemy get possession of them.'

11 1Moreover, I, Baruch, say this against you, Babylon:
'If you had prospered,
And Zion had dwelt in her glory,
Yet the grief to us had been great
That you should be equal to Zion.
2But now, lo! the grief is infinite,
And the lamentation measureless,
For lo! you are prospered
And Zion desolate.
3Who will be judge regarding these things?
Or to whom shall we complain regarding that which has befallen us?
O Lord, how have you borne (it)?
4Our fathers went to rest without grief,
And lo! the righteous sleep in the earth in tranquility;
5For they knew not this anguish,
Nor yet had they heard of that which had befallen us.
6Would that you had ears, O earth,
And that you had a heart, O dust:
That you might go and announce in Sheol,
And say to the dead:
7"Blessed are you more than we who live."'
12 1But I will say this as I think.
And I will speak against you, O land, which alt prospering.
2The noonday does not always burn.
Nor do the rays of the sun constantly give light.
3Do not expect Land hope] that you will always he prosperous and rejoicing.
And be not greatly up lifted and boastful.
4For assuredly in its own season shall the (divine) wrath awake against you.
Which now in long-suffering is held in as it were by reins.

12:5—13. Second Fast. Revelation as to the coming judgment on the Heathen.

5 And when I had said these things, I fasted seven days.

(6-8) 3 And do not you expect to rejoice,
Nor condemn greatly.

8-10) 4 For assuredly in its season shall the (divine) wrath be awakened against you,
Which is now restrained by long-suffering as it were by a rein.

13 1 And it came to pass after these things that I, Baruch, was standing upon Mount Zion, and lo a voice came forth from the height and said unto me:
2 'Stand upon your feet, Baruch, and hear the word of the mighty God.'
3 Because you have been astonished at what has befallen Zion, you shall therefore be assuredly preserved to the consummation of the times, that you may be for a testimony. 4 So that, if ever those prosperous cities say: 5 'Why hath the mighty God brought upon us this retribution?' Say you to them, you and those like you who shall have seen this evil: '(This is the evil) and retribution which is coming upon you and upon your people in its (destined) time that the nations may be thoroughly smitten. 6 And then they shall be in anguish. 7 And if they say at that time:

8For how long? you will say to them:
"Ye who have drunk the strained wine,
Drink you also of its dregs,
The judgment of the Lofty One
Who has no respect of persons."'
9On this account he had aforetime no mercy on His own sons,
But afflicted them as His enemies, because they sinned,
10Then therefore were they chastened
That they might be sanctified.

11But now, you peoples and nations, you are guilty
Because you have always trodden down the earth,
And used the creation unrighteously.
12For I have always benefited you.
And you have always been ungrateful for the bene-ficence.
14—19 The Righteousness of the Righteous has profited neither them nor their City; God's Judgments are incomprehensible; the World was made for the Righteous, yet they pass and the World remains (14). Answer—Man knows God's Judgments and has sinned willingly. This World is a Weariness to the Righteous but the next is theirs (15), to be won through Character whether a Man's Time here be long or short (16—17). Final Weal or Woe—the supreme Question (18—19).

14 1 And I answered and said: 'Lo! you have shown me the method of the times, and that which shall be after these *things,* and you have said unto me, that the retribution, which has been spoken of by you, shall come upon the nations. 2 And now I know that those who have sinned are many, and they have lived in prosperity,' and departed from the world, but the few nations will be left in those times, to whom those words shall he said which you did say. 3 For what advantage is there in this, or what (evil), worse than what' we have seen befall us, are we to expect to see? 4 But again I will speak in Your presence: 5 What have they profited who had knowledge before you and have not walked in vanity as the rest of the nations, and have not said to the dead: "Give us life," but always feared you, and have not left Your ways? 6 And lo! they have been carried off, nor on their account have you had mercy on Zion. 7 And if others did evil, it was due to Zion that on account of the works of those who wrought good works she should be forgiven, and should not be overwhelmed on account of the works of those who wrought unrighteousness. 8 But who, O LORD, my Lord, will comprehend Your judgment,
Or who will search out the profoundness of Your way?
Or who will think out the weight of Your path?
9Or who will be able to think out Your incomprehensible counsel?
Or who of those that are born has ever found
The beginning or end of Your wisdom?
10For we have all been made like a breath. 11 For as the breath ascends involuntarily, and again dies, so it is with the nature of men, who depart not according to their own will, and know not what will befall them in the end. 12 For the righteous justly hope for the end, and without fear depart from this habitation, because they have with you a store of works preserved in treasuries. 13 On this account also these without fear leave this world, and trusting with joy they hope to receive the world which you have promised them. 14 But as for us—woe to us, who also are now shamefully entreated, and at that time look forward (only) to evils. 15 But you know accurately what you have done by means of Your servants; for we are not able to understand that which is good as you art, our Creator. 16 But again I will speak in Your presence, O LORD, my Lord. 17 When of old there was no world with its inhabitants, you did devise and speak with a word, and forthwith the works of creation stood before you. 18 And you did say that you wouldst make for Your world man as the administrator of Your works, that it might be known that he was by no means made on account of the world, but the world on account of him. 19 And now I see that as for the world which was made on account

of us, lo! it abides; but we, on account of whom it was made, depart.'

15 1 And the Lord answered and said unto me: 'You are rightly astonished regarding the departure of man, but you have not judged well regarding the evils which befall those who sin. 2 And as regards what you have said, that the righteous are carried off and the impious are prospered, 3 And as regards what you have said: "Man knows not Your judgment "—On this account hear, and I will speak to you, and hearken, and I will cause you to hear My words. 5 Man would not rightly have understood My judgment, unless he had accepted the law, and I had instructed him in understanding. 6 But now, because he transgressed wittingly, yea, just on this ground that he knows (about it), he shall be tormented.

7 And as regards what you did say touching the righteous, that on account of them has this world come, so also again shall that, which is to come, come on their account. 8 For this world is to them a strife and a labor with much trouble; and that accordingly which is to come, a crown with great glory.'

16 1 And I answered and said: '0 LORD, my Lord, lo! the years of this time are few and evil, and who is able in his little time to acquire that which is measureless?'

17 1 And the Lord answered and said unto me: 'With the Most High account is not taken of time nor of a few years. 2 For what did it profit Adam that he lived nine hundred and thirty years and transgressed that which he was commanded? Therefore the multitude of time that he lived did not profit him, but brought death and cut off the years of those who were born from him. wherein did Moses suffer loss in that he lived only one hundred and twenty years, and, inasmuch he was subject to Him who formed him, brought the law to the seed of Jacob, and lighted a lamp for the nation of Israel?'

18 1 And I answered and said: 'He that lighted has taken from the light, and there are but few that have imitated him. But those many whom he has lighted have taken from the darkness of Adam and have not rejoiced in the light of the lamp.'

19 And He answered and said unto me: 'Wherefore at that time he appointed for them a covenant and said:

"Behold I have placed before you life and death,"
And he called heaven and earth to witness against them.
2 For he knew that his time was but short,
But that heaven and earth endure always.

3 But after his death they sinned and transgressed,
Though they knew that they had the law reproving (them),
And the light in which nothing could err,
Also the spheres which testify, and Me.

4 Now regarding everything that is, it is I that judge, but do not you take counsel in your soul regarding these things, nor afflict thyself because of those which have been. 5 For now it is the consummation of time that should be considered, whether of business, or of prosperity, or of shame and not the beginning thereof. 6 Because if a man be prospered in his beginnings and shamefully entreated in his old age, he forgets all the prosperity that he had. 7 And again, if a man is shamefully entreated in his beginnings, and at his end is prospered, he remembers not again his evil entreatment. 8 And again hearken: though each one were prospered all that time—all the time from the day on which death was decreed against those who transgress—and in his end was destroyed, in vain would have been everything.'

20. *Zion has been taken away to hasten the Advent of the Judgment*

20 1 Therefore, behold! the days come,
And the times shall hasten more than the former,
And the seasons shall speed on more than those that are past,
And the years shall pass more quickly than the present (years).
2 Therefore have I now taken away Zion,
That I may the more speedily visit the world in its season.
3 Now therefore hold fast in your heart everything that I command you,
And seal it in the recesses of your mind.
4 And then I will show you the judgment of My might,
And My ways which are unsearchable.
5 Go therefore and sanctify thyself seven days, and eat no bread, nor drink water, nor speak to anyone. 6 And afterwards come to that place and I will reveal Myself to you, and speak true things with you, and I will give you commandment regarding the method of the times; for they are coming and tarry not.'

21:1-11. *Fast of seven Days: Baruch's Prayer: God's Answer*

The Prayer of Baruch the Son of Neriah.

21 1 And I went there and sat in the valley of Kidron in a cave of the earth, and I sanctified my soul there, and I ate no bread, yet I was not hungry, and I drank no water, yet I thirsted not, and I was there till the

seventh day, as He had commanded me. 2 And afterwards I came to that place where He had spoken with me. 3 And it came to pass at sunset that my soul took much thought, and I began to speak in the presence of the Mighty One, and said: 4 'O you that have made the earth, hear me, that have fixed the firmament by the word, and have made firm the height of the heaven by the spirit, that have called from the beginning of the world that which did not yet exist, and they obey you. 5 you that have commanded the air by Your nod, and have seen those things which are to be as those things which you are doing. 6 you that rule with great thought the hosts that stand before you: also the countless holy beings, which you did make from the beginning, of flame and fire, which stand around Your throne you rule with indignation. 7 To you only does this belong that you should do forthwith whatsoever you do wish. 8 Who causes the drops of rain to rain by number upon the earth, and alone knows the consummation of the times before they come; have respect unto my prayer. For 9 you alone are able to sustain all who are, and those who have passed away, and those who are to be, those who sin, and those who are to righteous [as living (and) being past finding out]. For you alone do live immortal and past finding out, and know the number of mankind. And if in time many have sinned, yet others not a few have been righteous.

21:12-18. *Baruch's Depreciation of this Life.*

12 you know where you preserve the end of those who have sinned, or the consummation of those who have been righteous. 2 For if there were this life only, which belongs to all men, nothing could be more bitter than this.

14For of what profit is strength that turns to sickness,
Or fullness of food that turns to famine,
Or beauty that turns to ugliness.

15 For the nature of man is always changeable. 16 For what we were formerly now we no longer are and what we now are we shall not afterwards remain. 16 For if a consummation had not been prepared for all, in vain would have been their beginning. But regarding everything that comes from you do you inform me, and regarding everything about which I ask you, do you enlighten me.

21:19-25. *Baruch prays to God to hasten the Judgment and fulfill His Promise*

19 How long will that which is corruptible remain, and how long will the time of mortals be prospered, and until what time will those who transgress in the world be polluted with much wickedness? 20

Command therefore in mercy and accomplish all that you saidst you wouldst bring, that Your might may be made known to those who think that Your long-suffering is weakness. 21 And show to those who know not, that everything that has befallen us and our city until now has been according to the long-suffering of Your power, because on account of Your name you have called us a beloved people. 22 Bring to an end therefore henceforth mortality. 23 And reprove accordingly the angel of death, and let Your glory appear, and let the might of Your beauty be known, and let Sheol be sealed so that from this time forward it may not receive the dead, and let the treasuries of souls restore those which are enclosed in them. 24 For there have been many years like those that are desolate from the days of Abraham and Isaac and Jacob, and of all those who are like them, who sleep in the earth, on whose account you did say that you had created the world. 25 And now quickly show Your glory, and do not defer what has been promised by you.' 26 And (when) I had completed the words of this prayer I was greatly weakened.

22 – 23. *God's Reply to Baruch's Prayer. He will fulfill His Promise: Time needed for its Accomplishment: Things must be judged in the Light of their Consummation (22). Till all Souls are born the End cannot come (23).*

22 1 And it came to pass after these things that lo! the heavens were opened, and I saw, and power was given to me, and a voice was beard from on high, and it said unto me: 2 Baruch, Baruch, why are you troubled? 3 He who travels by a road but does not complete it, or who departs by sea but does not arrive at the port, can he be comforted? 4 Or he who promises to give a present to another, but does not fulfill it, is it not robbery? 5 Or he who sows the earth, but does not reap its fruit in its season, does he not lose everything? 6 Or he who plants a plant unless it grows till the time suitable to it, does he who planted it expect to receive fruit from it? 7 Or a woman who has conceived, if she bring forth untimely, does she not assuredly slay her infant? 8 Or he who builds a house, if he does not roof it and complete it, can it be called a house? Tell Me that first.
23 1 And I answered and said: Not so, O LORD, my Lord.' 2 And He answered and said unto me: 'Why therefore are you troubled about that which you know not, and why are you ill at ease about things in which you are ignorant? 3 For as you have not forgotten the people who now are and those who have passed away, so I remember those who are appointed to come. 4 Because when Adam sinned and death was decreed against those who should be born, then the multitude of those who should be born was numbered, and for that number a place was prepared

where the living might dwell and the dead might be guarded. Before therefore the number aforesaid is fulfilled, the creature will not live again [for My spirit is the creator of life], and Sheol will receive the dead. 6 And again it is given to you to hear what things are to come after these times. 7 For truly My redemption has drawn nigh, and is not far distant as aforetime.

24. *The coming Judgment*

24 1 'For behold! the days come and the books shall be opened in which are written the sins of all those who have sinned, and again also the treasuries in which the righteousness of all those who have been righteous in creation is gathered. 2 For it shall come to pass at that time that you shall see—and the many that are with you—the long-suffering of the Most High, which has been throughout all generations, who has been long-suffering towards all who are born, (alike) those who sin and (those who) are righteous.' 3 And I answered and said: 'But, behold! O Lord, no one knows the number of those things which have passed nor yet of those things which are to come. 4 For I know indeed that which has befallen us, but what will happen to our enemies I know not, and when you will visit Your works.'

25—26. *Sign of the coming Judgment*

25 1 And He answered and said unto me: 'You too shall be preserved till that time till that sign which the Most High will work for the inhabitants of the earth in the end of days. 2 This therefore shall be the sign. 3 When a stupor shall seize the inhabitants of the earth, and they shall fall into many tribulations, and again when they shall fall into great torments. And it will come to pass when they say in their thoughts by reason of their much tribulation: "The Mighty 'One doth no longer remember the earth"—yes, it will come to pass when they abandon hope, that the time will then awake.'

26 1 And I answered and said: 'Will that tribulation which is to be continue a long time, and will that necessity embrace many years?'

26-30. *The Twelve Woes that are to Come upon the Earth: The Messiah and the temporary Messianic Kingdom*

27 1 And He answered and said unto me: 'Into twelve parts is that time divided, and each one of them is reserved for that which is appointed for it. 2 In the first part there shall be the beginning of commotions. 3 And in the second part (there shall be) slayings of the great ones. 4 And in the third part the fall of many by death. 5 And in the fourth part the sending of the sword. 6 And in the fifth part famine and the

withholding of rain. 7 And in the sixth part earthquakes and terrors. 8 [Wanting.] 9 And in the eighth part a multitude of specters and attacks of the Shedim. 10 And in the ninth part the fall of fire. 11 And in the tenth part rapine and much oppression. 12 And in the eleventh part wickedness and unchastity. 13 And in the twelfth part confusion from the mingling together of all those things aforesaid. 14 For these parts of that time are reserved, and shall be mingled one with another and minister one to another. 15 For some shall leave out some of their own, and receive (in its stead) from others, and some complete their own and that of others, so that those may not understand who are upon the earth in those days that this is the consummation of the times.

28 1 Nevertheless, whoever understands shall then be wise. 2 For the measure and reckoning of that time are two parts a week of seven weeks.' 3 And I answered and said: 'It is good for a man to come and behold, but it is better that he should not come lest he fall. 4 [But I will say this also: 5 Will he who is incorruptible despise those things which are corruptible, and whatever befalls in the case of those things which are corruptible, so that he might look only to those things which are not corruptible?] 6 But if; O Lord, those things shall assuredly come to pass which you have foretold to me, so do you show this also unto me if indeed I have found grace in Your sight. 7 Is it in one place or in one of the parts of the earth that those things are come to pass, or will the whole earth experience (them) ?'

29 1 And He answered and said unto me: 'Whatever will then befall (will befall) the whole earth; therefore all who live will experience (them). 2 For at that time I will protect only those who are found in those self-same days in this land. 3 And it shall come to pass when all is accomplished that was to come to pass in those parts, that the Messiah shall then begin to be revealed. 4 And Behemoth shall be revealed from his place and Leviathan shall ascend from the sea, those two great monsters which I created on the fifth day of creation, and shall have kept until that time; and then they shall be for food for all that are left. 5 The earth also shall yield its fruit ten-thousandfold and on each (?) vine there shall be a thousand branches, and each branch shall produce a thousand clusters, and each cluster produce a thousand grapes, and each grape produce a cor of wine. 6 And those who have hungered shall rejoice: moreover, also, they shall behold marvels every day. 7 For winds shall go forth from before Me to bring every morning the fragrance of aromatic fruits, and at the close of the day clouds distilling the dew of health. 8 And it shall come to pass at that self-same time that the treasury of manna shall again descend from on high, and they will eat of

it in those years, because these are they who have come to the consummation of time.

30 1 And it shall come to pass after these things, when the time of the advent of the Messiah is fulfilled, that He shall return in glory.

30:2-5. *The Resurrection*

2 Then all who have fallen asleep in hope of Him shall rise again. And it shall come to pass at that time that the treasuries will be opened in which is preserved the number of the souls of the righteous, and they shall come forth, and a multitude of souls shall be seen together in one assemblage of one thought, and the first shall rejoice and the last shall not be grieved. 3 For they know that the time has come of which it is said, that it is the consummation of the times. 4 But the souls of the wicked, when they behold all these things, shall then waste away the more. 5 For they shall know that their torment has come and their perdition has arrived.'

31—33. *Baruch exhorts the People to prepare themselves for worse Evils*

31 1 And it came to pass after these things: that I went to the people and said unto them: 'Assemble unto me all your elders and I will speak words unto them.' 2 And they all assembled in the valley of the Kidron. 3 And I answered and said unto them:

Hear, O Israel, and I will speak to you,
And give ear, O seed of Jacob, and I will instruct you.
4 Forget not Zion,
But hold in remembrance the anguish of Jerusalem.
5 For lo! the days come,
When everything that is shall become the prey of corruption
And be as though it had not been.

32 1 But as for you, if you prepare your hearts, so as to sow in them the fruits of the law, it shall protect you in that time in which the Mighty One is to shake the whole creation. 2 [Because after a little time the building of Zion will be shaken in order that it may be built again. But that building will not remain, but will again after a time be rooted out, and will remain desolate until the time. 4 And afterwards it must be renewed in glory, and perfected for evermore.] 5 Therefore we should not be distressed so much over the evil which has now come as over that which is still to be. 6 For there will be a greater trial than these two tribulations when the Mighty One will renew His creation. 7 And now do not draw near to me for a few days, nor seek me till I come to you.' 8 And it came to pass when I had spoken to them all these words, that

I, Baruch, went my way, and when the people saw me setting out, they lifted up their voice and lamented and said : 9 To where are you departing from us, Baruch, and are you forsaking us as a father who forsakes his orphan children, and departs from them?

33 1 Are these the commands which your companion, Jeremiah the prophet, commanded you, and said unto you: "Look to this people till I go and make ready the rest of the brethren in Babylon against whom has gone forth the sentence that they should be led into captivity"? And now if you also forsake us, it were good for us all to die before you, and then that you should withdraw from us.'

34—35. *Lament of Baruch*

34 And I answered and said unto the people: 'Far be it from me to forsake you or to withdraw from you, but I will only go unto the Holy of Holies to inquire of the Mighty One concerning you and concerning Zion, if in some respect I should receive more illumination: and after these things I will return to you.

35 1 And I, Baruch, went to the holy place, and sat down upon the ruins and wept, and said:

2 O that mine eyes were springs,
And mine eyelids a fount of tears.
3 For how shall I lament for Zion,
And how shall I mourn for Jerusalem?
4 Because in that place where I am now prostrate,
Of old the high priest offered holy sacrifices,
And placed thereon an incense of fragrant odors.
5 But now our glorying has been made into dust,
And the desire of our soul into sand.'

36—37. *The Vision of the Forest, the Vine, the Fountain and the Cedar*

36 1 And when I had said these things I fell asleep there, and I saw a vision in the night. 2 And lo! a forest of trees planted on the plain, and lofty and rugged rocky mountains surrounded it, and that forest occupied much space. 3 And lo! over against it arose a vine, and from under it there went forth a fountain peacefully. 4 Now that fountain came to the forest and was (stirred) into great waves, and those waves submerged that forest, and suddenly they rooted out the greater part of that forest, and overthrew all the mountains which were round about it. 5 And the height of the forest began to be made low, and the top of the mountains was made low and that fountain prevailed greatly, so that it left nothing of that great forest save one cedar only. 6 Also when it had cast it down and had destroyed and rooted out the greater part of that forest, so that nothing was left

of it, nor could its place be recognized, then that vine began to come with the fountain in peace and great tranquility, and it came to a place which was not far from that cedar, and they brought the cedar which had been cast down to it. 7 And I beheld and lo! that vine opened its mouth and spoke and said to that cedar: Art you not that cedar which was left of the forest of wickedness, and by whose means wickedness persisted, and was wrought all those years, and goodness never. 8 And you kept conquering that which was not yours, and to that which was your you did never show compassion, and you did keep extending your power over those who were far from you, and those who drew near you, you did hold fast in the toils of your wickedness, and you did uplift thyself always as one that could not be rooted out! 9 But now your time has sped and your hour is come. 10 Do you also therefore depart, O cedar, after the forest, which departed before you, and become dust with it, and let your ashes be mingled together. 11 And now recline in anguish and rest in torment till your last time come, in which you will come again, and be tormented still more.'

37 And after these things I saw that cedar burning, and the vine growing, itself and all around it, the plain full of unfading flowers. And I indeed awoke and arose.

38 — 40. *Interpretation of the Vision*

38 1 And I prayed and said: 'O LORD, my Lord, you do always enlighten those who are led by understanding. 2 Your law is life, and Your wisdom is right guidance. 3 Make known to me therefore the interpretation of this vision. 4 For you know that my soul hath always walked in Your law, and from my (earliest) days I departed not from Your wisdom.'

39 1 And He answered and said unto me: 'Baruch, this is the interpretation of the vision which you have seen. 2 As you have seen the great forest which lofty and rugged mountains surrounded, this is the word. 3 Behold! the days come, and this kingdom will be destroyed which once destroyed Zion, and it will be subjected to that which comes after it. 4 Moreover, that also again after a time will be destroyed, and another, a third, will arise, and that also will have dominion for its time, and will be destroyed. 5 And after these things a fourth kingdom will arise, whose power will be harsh and evil far beyond those which were before it, and it will rule many times as the forests on the plain, and it will hold fast for times, and will exalt itself more than the cedars of Lebanon. 6 And by it the truth will be hidden, and all those who are polluted with iniquity will flee to it, as evil beasts flee and creep into the forest. 7 And it will come to

pass when the time of its consummation that it should fall has approached, then the principate of My Messiah will be revealed, which is like the fountain and the vine, and when it is revealed it will root out the multitude of its host. 8 And as touching that which you have seen, the lofty cedar, which was left of that forest, and the fact, that the vine spoke those words with it which you did hear, this is the word.

40 1 The last leader of that time will be left alive, when the multitude of his hosts will be put to the sword, and he will be bound, and they will take him up to Mount Zion, and My Messiah will convict him of all his impieties, and will gather and set before him all the works of his hosts. 2 And afterwards he will put him to death, and protect the rest of My people which shall be found in the place which I have chosen. 3 And his principate will stand for ever, until the world of corruption is at an end, and until the times aforesaid are fulfilled. 4 This is your vision, and this is its interpretation.'

41 — 42. *The Destiny of the Apostates and of the Proselytes*

41 1 And I answered and said: 'For whom and for how many shall these things be? or who will be worthy to live at that time? 2 For I will speak before you everything that I think, and I will ask of you regarding those things which I meditate. 3 For lo! I see many of Your people who have withdrawn from Your covenant, and cast from them the yoke of Your law. 4 But others again I have seen who have forsaken their vanity, and fled for refuge beneath Your wings. 5 What therefore will be to them? or how will the last time receive them? 6 Or perhaps the time of these will assuredly be weighed, and as the beam inclines will they be judged accordingly?'

42 1 And He answered and said unto me: 'These things also will I show unto you. 2 As for what you did say — "To whom will these things be, and how many (will they be)? " — to those who have believed there shall be the good which was spoken of aforetime, and to those who despise there shall be the contrary of these things. 3 And as for what you did say regarding those who have drawn near and those who have withdrawn this in the word. 4 As for those who were before subject, and afterwards withdrew and mingled themselves with the seed of mingled peoples, the time of these was the former, and was accounted as something exalted. 5 And as for those who before knew not but afterwards knew life, and mingled (only) with the seed of the people which had separated itself, the time of these (is) the latter, and is accounted as something exalted. 6 And time shall succeed to time and season to season, and one shall receive from another, and then with a view to the

consummation shall everything be compared according to the measure of the times and the hours of the seasons. 7 For corruption shall take those that belong to it, and life those that belong to it. 8 And the dust shall be called, and there shall be said to it: "Give back that which is not yours, and raise up all that you have kept until its time".'

43. Baruch told of his Death and bidden to give his last Commands to the People

43 1 But, do thou, Baruch, direct your heart to that which has been said to you,
And understand those things which have been shown to you;
For there are many eternal consolations for you.
2 For you shall depart from this place,
And you shall pass from the regions which are now seen by you,
And you shall forget whatever is corruptible,
And shall not again recall those things which happen among mortals.

3 Go therefore and command your people, and come to this place, and afterwards fast seven days, and then I will come to you and speak with you.'

44:1-8; 45—46. Baruch tells the Elders of his impending Death, but encourages them to expect the Consolation of Zion

44 1 And I, Baruch, went from thence, and came to my people, and I called my first-born son and [the Gedaliahs] my friends, and seven of the elders of the people, and I said unto them:

Behold, I go unto my fathers
According to the way of all the earth.
3 But withdraw you not from the way of the law,
But guard and admonish the people which remain,
Lest they withdraw from the commandments of the Mighty One.
4 For you see that He whom we serve is just,
And our Creator is no respecter of persons.
5 And see you what hath befallen Zion,
And what hath happened to Jerusalem.
6 For the judgment of the Mighty One shall (thereby) be made known,
And His ways, which, though past finding out, are right.
7 For if you endure and persevere in His fear,
And do not forget His law,
The times shall change over you for good.
And you shall see the consolation of Zion.
8,9 Because whatever is now is nothing,
But that which shall be is very great.
For everything that is corruptible shall pass away,

And everything that dies shall depart,
And all the present time shall be forgotten,
Nor shall there be any remembrance of the present time, which is defiled with evils.
10 For that which runs now runs unto vanity,
And that which prospers shall quickly fall and be humiliated.
11 For that which is to be shall be the object of desire,
And for that which comes afterwards shall we hope;
For it is a time that passes not away,
12 And the hour comes which abides for ever.
And the new world (comes) which does not turn to corruption those who depart to its blessedness,
And has no mercy on those who depart to torment,
And leads not to perdition those who live in it.
13 For these are they who shall inherit that time which has been spoken of,
And theirs is the inheritance of the promised time.
14 These are they who have acquired for themselves treasures of wisdom,
And with them are found stores of understanding,
And from mercy have they not withdrawn,
And the truth of the law I have they preserved.
15 For to them shall be given the world to come,
But the dwelling of the rest who are many shall be in the fire.'

45 2 Do you therefore so far as you are able instruct the people, for that labor is ours. For if you teach them, you will quicken them.'

46 1 And my son and the elders of the people answered and said unto me:

'Has the Mighty One humiliated us to such a degree
As to take you from us quickly?
2 And truly we shall be in darkness,
And there shall be no light to the people who are left,
3 For where again shall we seek the law,
Or who will distinguish for us between death and life?'
4 And I said unto them: 'The throne of the Mighty One I cannot resist;
Nevertheless, there shall not be wanting to Israel a wise man
Nor a son of the law to the race of Jacob.
5 But only prepare you your hearts, that you may obey the law,
And be subject to those who in fear are wise and understanding;
And prepare your souls that you may not depart from them.
6 For if you do these things, Good tidings shall come unto you.

[Which I before told you of; nor shall you fall into the torment, of which I testified to you before.' 7 But with regard to the word that I was to be taken I did not make (it) known to them or to my son.]

47 1 And when I had gone forth and dismissed them, I went there and said unto them: 'Behold! I go to Hebron: for thither the Mighty One hath sent me.' 2 And I came to that place where the word had been spoken unto me, and I sat there, and fasted seven days.

48:1-47. PRAYER OF BARUCH

48 1 And it came to pass after the seventh day, that I prayed before the Mighty One and said

2 O my Lord, you summon the advent of the times,
And they stand before you;
You cause the power of the ages to pass away,
And they do not resist you;
You arrange the method of the seasons,
And they obey you.
3 You alone know the duration of the generations,
And you reveal not Your mysteries to many.
4 You make known the multitude of the fire,
And you weigh the lightness of the wind.
5 You explore the limit of the heights,
And you scrutinize the depths of the darkness.
6 You care for the number which pass away that they may be preserved, And you prepare an abode for those that are to be.
7 You remember the beginning which you have made,
And the destruction that is to be You forget not.
8 With nods of fear and indignation You command the flames,
And they change into spirits,
And with a word you quicken that which was not,
And with mighty power you hold that which has not yet come.
9 You instruct created things in the understanding of you,
And you make wise the spheres so as to minister in their orders.
10 Armies innumerable stand before you
And minister in their orders quietly at Your nod.
11 Hear Your servant
And give ear to my petition.
12 For in a little time are we born,
And in a little time do we return.
13 But with you hours are as a time,
And days as generations.
14 Be not therefore wroth with man; for he is nothing
15 And take not account of our works; For what are we?
For lo! by Your gift do we come into the world,
And we depart not of our own will.
16 For we said not to our parents, "Beget us,

Nor did we send to Sheol and say, "Receive us."
17 What therefore is our strength that we should bear Your wrath,
Or what are we that we should endure Your judgment?
18 Protect us in Your compassions,
And in Your mercy help us.
19 Behold the little ones that are subject unto you,
And save all that draw near unto you:
And destroy not the hope of our people,
And cut not short the times of our aid.
20 For this is the nation which you have chosen,
And these are the people, to whom you find no equal.
21 But I will speak now before you,
And I will say as my heart thinks.
22 In you do we trust, for lo! Your law is with us,
And we know that we shall not fall so long as we keep Your statutes.
23 [To all time are we blessed at all events in this that we have not mingled with the Gentiles.]
24 For we are all one celebrated people,
Who have received one law from One:
And the law which is amongst us will aid us,
And the surpassing wisdom which is in us will help us.'

25 And when I had prayed and said these things, I was greatly weakened. 26 And He answered and said unto me:

'You have prayed simply, O Baruch,
And all your words have been heard.
27 But My judgment exacts its own
And My law exacts its rights.
28 For from your words I will answer you,
And from your prayer I will speak to you.

29 For this is as follows: he that is corrupted is not at all; he has both wrought iniquity so far as lie could do anything, and has not remembered My goodness, nor accepted My long-suffering. 30 Therefore you shall surely be taken up, as I before told you. 31 For that time shall arise which brings affliction; for it shall come and pass by with quick vehemence, and it shall be turbulent coming in the heat of indignation. 32 And it shall come to pass in those days that all the inhabitants of the earth shall be moved one against another, because they know not that My judgment has drawn nigh.

33 For there shall not be found many wise at that time,
And the intelligent shall be but a few:
Moreover, even those who know shall most of all be silent.
34 And there shall be many rumors and tidings not a few,

And the doing of phantasms shall be manifest,
And promises not a few be recounted,
Some of them (shall prove) idle,
And some of them shall be confirmed.
35 And honor shall be turned into shame,
And strength humiliated into contempt,
And probity destroyed,
And beauty shall become ugliness.
36 And many shall say to many at that time:
"Where hath the multitude of intelligence hidden itself,
And whither hath the multitude of wisdom removed itself?"
37 And whilst they are meditating these things,
Then envy shall arise in those who had not thought aught of themselves (?)
And passion shall seize him that is peaceful,
And many shall be stirred up in anger to injure many,
And they shall rouse up armies in order to shed blood,
And in the end they shall perish together with them.
38 And it shall come to pass at the self-same time,
That a change of times shall manifestly appeal to every man,
Because in all those times they polluted themselves
And they practiced oppression,
And walked every man in his own works,
And remembered not the law of the Mighty One.
39 Therefore a fire shall consume their thoughts,
And in flame shall the meditations of their reins be tried;
For the Judge shall come and will not tarry.
40 Because each of the inhabitants of the earth knew when he was transgressing.
But My Law they knew not by reason of their pride.
41 But many shall then assuredly weep,
Yea, over the living more than over the dead.'
42 And I answered and said:
'O Adam, what have you done to all those who are born from you?
And what will be said to the first Eve who hearkened to the serpent?
43 For all this multitude are going to corruption,
Nor is there any numbering of those whom the fire devours.

44 But again I will speak in Your presence. 45 You, O LORD, my Lord, know what is in Your creature. 46 For you did of old command the dust to produce Adam, and you know the number of those who are born from him, and how far they have sinned before you, who have existed and not confessed you as their Creator. 47 And as regards all these their end shall convict them, and Your law which they have transgressed shall requite them on Your day.'

48:48-50. Fragment of an Address of Baruch to the People

48 [But now let us dismiss the wicked and inquire about the righteous.
49 And I will recount their blessedness
And not be silent in celebrating their glory, which is reserved for them.
50 For assuredly as in a little time in this transitory world in which you live, you have endured much labor,
So in that world to which there is no end, you shall receive great light.']

49—52. The Nature of the Resurrection Body: the final Destinies of the Righteous and the Wicked

49 1 'Nevertheless, I Will again ask from you, O Mighty One, yea, I will ask made all things.
2 "In what shape will those live who live in Your day? Or how will the splendor of those who (are) after that time continue?
3 Will they then resume this form of the present,
And put on these entrammelling members,
Which are now involved in evils,
And in which evils are consummated,
Or will you perchance change these things which have been in the world
As also the world?"

50 1 And He answered and said unto me:

'Hear, Baruch, this word,
And write in the remembrance of your heart all that you shall learn.
2 For the earth shall then assuredly restore the dead,
[Which it now receives, in order to preserve them].
It shall make no change in their form,
But as it has received, so shall it restore them,
And as I delivered them unto it, so also shall it raise them.

3 For then it will be necessary to show the living that the dead have come to life again, and that those who had departed have returned (again). 4 And it shall come to pass, when they have severally recognized those whom they now know, then judgment shall grow strong, and those things which before were spoken of shall come.

51 1 And it shall come to pass, when that appointed day has gone by, that then shall the aspect of those who are condemned be afterwards changed, and the glory of those who are justified. 2 For the aspect of those who now act wickedly shall become worse than it is, as they shall suffer torment. 3 Also (as for) the glory of those who have now been justified in My law, who have had understanding in their life, and

who have planted in their heart the root of wisdom, then their splendor shall be glorified in changes, and the form of their face shall be turned into the light of their beauty, that they may be able to acquire and receive the world which does not die, which is then promised to them. 4 For over this above all shall those who come then lament, that they rejected My law, and stopped their ears that they might not hear wisdom or receive understanding. 5 When therefore they see those, over whom they are now exalted, (but) who shall then be exalted and glorified more than they, they shall respectively be transformed, the latter into the splendor of angels, and the former shall yet more waste away in wonder at the visions and in the beholding of the forms. 6 For they shall first behold and afterwards depart to be tormented.

7 But those who have been saved by their works,
And to whom the law has been now a hope,
And understanding an expectation,
And wisdom a confidence,
Shall wonders appear in their time.
8 For they shall behold the world which is now invisible to them,
And they shall behold the time which is now hidden from them:
9 And time shall no longer age them.
10 For in the heights of that world shall they dwell,
And they shall be made like unto the angels,
And be made equal to the stars,
And they shall be changed into every form they desire,
From beauty into loveliness,
And from light into the splendor of glory.

11 For there shall be spread before them the extents of Paradise, and there shall be shown to them the beauty of the majesty of the living creatures which are beneath the throne, and all the armies of the angels, who are now held fast by My word, lest they should appear, and] are held fast by a command, that they may stand in their places till their advent comes. 12 Moreover, there shall then be excellency in the righteous surpassing that in the angels. 13 For the first shall receive the last, those whom they were expecting, and the last those of whom they used to hear that they had passed away.

14 For they have been delivered from this world of tribulation,
And laid down the burthen of anguish.
15 For what then have men lost their life,
And for what have those who were on the earth exchanged their soul?
16 For then they chose (not) for themselves this time,
Which, beyond the reach of anguish, could not pass away:

But they chose for themselves that time,
Whose issues are full of lamentations and evils,
And they denied the world which ages not those who come to it,
And they rejected the time of glory,
So that they shall not come to the honor of which I told you before.'

52 1 And I answered and said:
'How can we forget those for whom woe is then reserved?
2 And why therefore do we again mourn for those who die?
Or why do we weep for those who depart to Sheol?
3 Let lamentations be reserved for the beginning of that coming torment,
And let tears be laid up for the advent of the destruction of that time.
4 [But even in the face of these things will I speak.
5 And as for the righteous, what will they do now?
6 Rejoice you in the suffering which you now suffer:
For why do you look for the decline of your enemies?
7 Make ready your soul for that which is reserved for you,
And prepare your souls for the reward which is laid up for you.']

53 — 54. THE MESSIAH APOCALYPSE

53. The Vision of the Cloud with black and white Waters

53 1 And when I had said these things I fell asleep there, and I saw a vision, and lo! a cloud was ascending from a very great sea, and I kept gazing upon it) and lo! it was full of waters white and black, and there were many colors in those self-same waters, and as it were the likeness of great lightning was seen at its summit. 2 And I saw the cloud passing swiftly in quick courses, and it covered all the earth. 3 And it came to pass after these things that that cloud began to pour upon the earth the waters that were in it. 4 And I saw that there was not one and the same likeness in the waters which descended from it. 5 For in the first beginning they were black and many (Or a time, and afterwards I saw that the waters became bright, but they were not many, and after these things again I saw black (waters), and after these things again bright, and again black and again bright. 6 Now this was done twelve times, but the black were always more numerous than the bright. 7 And it came to pass at the end of the cloud, that lo! it rained black waters, and they were darker than had been all those waters that were before, and fire was mingled with them, and where those waters descended, they wrought devastation and destruction. 8 And after these things

I saw how that lightning which I had seen on the summit of the cloud, seized hold of it and hurled it to the earth. 9 Now that lightning shone exceedingly, so as to illuminate the whole earth, and it healed those regions where the last waters had descended and wrought devastation. 10 And it took hold of the whole earth, and had dominion over it. 11 And I saw after these things, and lo! twelve rivers were ascending from the sea, and they began to surround that lightning and to become subject to it. 12 And by reason of my fear I awoke.

54—55. Baruch's Prayer for an Interpretation of the Vision: Ramiel's advent for this Purpose

54 1 And I besought the Mighty One, and said:

'You alone, O Lord, know of aforetime the deep things of the world,
And the things which befall in their times You bring about by Your word, And against the works of the inhabitants of the earth you do hasten the beginnings of the times,
And the end of the seasons you alone know.
2 (You) for whom nothing is too hard,
But who do everything easily by a nod:
3 (You) to whom the depths come as the heights,
And whose word the beginnings of the ages serve:
4 (You) who reveal to those who fear you what is prepared for them,
That thenceforth they may be comforted.
5 You show great acts to those who know not;
You break up the enclosure of those who are ignorant,
And lightest up what is dark,
And reveal what is hidden to the pure,
[Who in faith have submitted themselves to you and Your law.]
6 You have shown to Your servant this vision;
Reveal to me also its interpretation.
7 For I know that as regards those things wherein I besought you, I have received a response,
And as regards what I besought, you did reveal to me with what voice I should praise you,
And from what members I should cause praises and hallelujahs to ascend to you.
8 For if my members were mouths,
And the hairs of my head voices,
Even so I could not give you the reward of praise,
Nor laud you as is befitting,
Nor could I recount Your praise,
Nor tell the glory of Your beauty.
9 For what am I amongst men,
Or why am I reckoned amongst those who are more excellent than I,
That I have heard all these marvelous things from the Most High,

And numberless promises from Him who created me?
10 Blessed be my mother among those that bear,
And praised among women be she that bare me.
11 For I will not be silent in praising the Mighty One,
And with the voice of praise I will recount His marvelous deeds.
12 For who doeth like unto Your marvelous deeds, O God,
Or who comprehend Your deep thought of life.
13 For with Your counsel you do govern all the creatures which Your right hand has created
And you have established every fountain of light beside you,
And the treasures of wisdom beneath Your throne have you prepared.
14 And justly do they perish who have not loved Your law,
And the torment of judgment shall await those who have not submitted themselves to Your power.
15 For though Adam first sinned
And brought untimely death upon all,
Yet of those who were born from him
Each one of them has prepared for his own soul torment to come,
And again each one of them has chosen for himself glories to come.
16 [For assuredly he who believeth will receive reward.

17 But now, as for you, you wicked that now are, turn you to destruction, because you shall speedily be visited, in that formerly you rejected the understanding of the Most High.

18 For His works have not taught you,
Nor has the skill of His creation which is at all times persuaded you.]
19 Adam is therefore not the cause, save only of his own soul,
But each of us has been the Adam of his own soul.
20 But do You, O Lord, expound to me regarding those things which you have revealed to me,
And inform me regarding that which I besought you.
21 For at the consummation of the world vengeance shall be taken upon those who have done wickedness according to their wickedness,
And you will glorify the faithful according to their faithfulness.
22 For those who are amongst your own you rule,
And those who sin you blot out from amongst your own.'

55 1 And it came to pass when I had finished speaking the words of this prayer, that I sat there under a tree, that I might rest in the shade of the branches. 2 And I wondered and was astonished, and

pondered in my thoughts regarding the multitude of goodness which sinners who are upon the earth have rejected, and regarding the great torment which they have despised, though they knew that they should be tormented because of the sin they had committed. And when I was pondering on these things and the like, lo! the angel Ramiel who presides over true visions was sent to me, and he said unto me:

4 Why does your heart trouble you, Baruch,
and why does your thought disturb you?
5 For if owing to the report which you have only heard of judgment you are so moved,
What (wilt you be) when you shall see it manifestly with your eyes?
6 And if with the expectation wherewith you do expect the day of the Mighty One you are so overcome,
What (wilt you be) when you shall come to its advent?
7 And, if at the word of the announcement of the torment of those who have done foolishly you are so wholly distraught,
How much more when the event will reveal marvelous things?
8 And if you have heard tidings of the good and evil things which are then coming and are grieved,
What (wilt you be) when you shall behold what the majesty will reveal, Which shall convict these and cause those to rejoice.'

56—74. *Interpretation of the Vision. The black and bright Waters symbolize the World's History from Adam to the Advent of the Messiah.*

56 1 'Nevertheless, because you have besought the Most High to reveal to you the interpretation of the vision which you have seen, I have been sent to tell you. 2 And the Mighty One hath assuredly made known to you the methods of the times that have passed, and of those that are destined to pass in His world from the beginning of its creation even unto its consummation, of those things which (are) deceit and of those which (are) in truth. 3 For as you did see a great cloud which ascended from the sea, and went and covered the earth, this is the duration of the world (= αιων) which the Mighty One made when he took counsel to make the world. 4 And it came to pass when the word had gone forth from His presence, that the duration of the world had come into being in a small degree, and was established according to the multitude of the intelligence of Him who sent it. 5 And as you did previously see on the summit of the cloud black waters which descended previously on the earth, this is the transgression wherewith Adam the first man transgressed.

6 For [since] when he transgressed
Untimely death came into being,
Grief was named
And anguish was prepared,
And pain was created,
And trouble consummated,
And disease began to be established,
And Sheol kept demanding that it should be renewed in blood,
And the begetting of children was brought about,
And the passion of parents produced,
And the greatness of humanity was humiliated,
And goodness languished.

7 What therefore can be blacker or darker than these things? 8 This is the beginning of the black waters which you have seen. 9 And from these black (waters) again were black derived, and the darkness of darkness was produced. 10 For he became a danger to his own soul: even to the angels 11 For, moreover, at that time when he was created, they enjoyed liberty. 12 And became he a danger some of them descended, and mingled with the women. 13 And then those who did so were tormented in chains. 14 But the rest of the multitude of the angels, of which there is (no) number, restrained themselves. 15 And those who dwelt on the earth perished together (with them) through the waters of the deluge. 16 These are the black first waters.

57 1 And after these (waters) you did see bright waters: this is the fount of Abraham, also his generations and advent of his son, and of his son's son, and of those like them. 2 Because at that time the unwritten law was named amongst them,

And the works of the commandments were then fulfilled,
And belief in the coming judgment was then generated,
And hope of the world that was to be renewed was then built up,
And the promise of the life that should come hereafter was implanted.
3 These are the bright waters, which you have seen.

58 1 'And the black third waters which you have seen, these are the mingling of all sins, which the nations afterwards wrought after the death of those righteous men, and the wickedness of the land of Egypt, wherein they did wickedly in the service wherewith they made their sons to serve. 2 Nevertheless, these also perished at last.

59 1 'And the bright fourth waters which you have seen are the advent of Moses and Aaron and Miriam and Joshua the son of Nun and Caleb and of all those

like them. 2 For at that time the lamp of the eternal law shone on all those who sat in darkness, which announced to them that believe the promise of their reward, and to them that deny, the torment of fire which is reserved for them. 3 But also the heavens at that time were shaken from their place, and those who were under the throne of the Mighty One were perturbed, when He was taking Moses unto Himself. 4 For He showed him many admonitions together with the principles of the law and the consummation of the times, as also to you, and likewise the pattern of Zion and its measures, in the pattern of which the sanctuary of the present time was to be made. 5 But then also He showed to him the measures of the fire, also the depths of the abyss, and the weight of the winds, and the number of the drops of rain: 6 And the suppression of anger, and the multitude of long-suffering, and the truth of judgment: 7 And the root of wisdom, and the riches of understanding, and the fount of knowledge: 8 And the height of the air, and the greatness of Paradise, and the consummation of the ages, and the beginning of the day of judgment: 9 And the number of the offerings, and the earths which have not yet come: 10 And the mouth of Gehenna, and the station of vengeance, and the place of faith, and the region of hope: And the likeness of future torment, and the multitude of innumerable angels, and the flaming hosts, and the splendor of the lightnings, and the voice of the thunders, and the orders of the chiefs of the angels, and the treasuries of light, and the changes of the times, and the investigations of the law. 12 These are the bright fourth waters which you have seen.

60 1 And the black fifth waters which you have seen raining are the works which the Amorites wrought, and the spells of their incantations which they wrought, and the wickedness of their mysteries, and the mingling of their pollution. 2 But even Israel was then polluted by sins in the days of the judges, though they saw many signs which were from Him who made them.

61 1 And the bright sixth waters which thru did see, this is the time in which David and Solomon were born.

2 And there was at that time the building of Zion,
And the dedication of the sanctuary,
And the shedding of much blood of the nations that sinned then,
And many offerings which were offered then in the dedication of the sanctuary.
3 And peace and tranquility existed at that time,
4 And wisdom was heard in the assembly:
And the riches of understanding were magnified in the congregations,

5 And the holy festivals were fulfilled in blessedness and in much joy.
6 And the judgment of the rulers was then seen to be without guile,
And the righteousness of the precepts of the Mighty One was accomplished with truth.
7 And the land [which] was then beloved by the Lord, And because its inhabitants sinned not, it was glorified beyond all lands, And the city Zion ruled then over all lands and regions.
8 These are the bright waters which you have seen.

62 1 And the black seventh waters which you have seen, this is the perversion (brought about) by the counsel of Jeroboam, who took counsel to make two calves of gold: 2 And all the iniquities which kings who were after him iniquitously wrought. 3 And the curse of Jezebel and the worship of idols which Israel practiced at that time. 4 And the withholding of rain, and the famines which occurred until women eat the fruit of their wombs. 5 And the time of their captivity which came upon the nine tribes and a half, because they were in many sins. 6 And Shalmanezzar king of Assyria came and led them away captive. 7 But regarding the Gentiles it were tedious to tell how they always wrought impiety and wickedness, and never wrought righteousness. 8 These are the black seventh waters which you have seen.

63 1 'And the bright eighth waters which you have seen, this is the rectitude and uprightness of Hezekiah king of Judah and the grace (of God) which came upon him. 2 For when Sennacherib was stirred up in order that he might perish, and his wrath troubled him in order that he might thereby perish, for the multitude also of the nations which were with him. 3 When, moreover, Hezekiah the king heard those things which the king of Assyria was devising, (i.e.) to come and seize him and destroy his people, the two and a half tribes which remained: nay, more he wished to overthrow Zion also: then Hezekiah trusted in his works, and had hope in his righteousness, and spoke with the Mighty One and said: 4 "Behold, for lo! Sennacherib is prepared to destroy us, and he will be boastful and uplifted when he has destroyed Zion."

5 And the Mighty One heard him, for Hezekiah was wise,
And He had respect unto his prayer, because he was righteous.

6 And thereupon the Mighty One commanded Ramiel His angel who speaks with you. 7 And I went forth and destroyed their multitude, the number of whose chiefs only was a hundred and eighty-five thousand, and each one of them had an equal number (at his

command). 8 And at that time I burned their bodies within, but their raiment and arms I preserved outwardly, in order that the still more wonderful deeds of the Mighty One might appear, and that thereby His name might be spoken of throughout the whole earth. 9 And Zion was saved and Jerusalem delivered: Israel also was freed from tribulation. 10 And all those who were in the holy land rejoiced, and the name of the Mighty One was glorified so that it was spoken of 11 These are the bright waters which you have seen.

64 1 'And the black ninth waters which you have seen, this is all the wickedness which was in the days of Manasseh the son of Hezekiah. 2 For he wrought much impiety, and he slew the righteous, and he wrested judgment, and he shed the blood of the innocent, and wedded women he violently polluted, and he overturned the altars, and destroyed their offerings, and drove forth their priests lest they should minister in the sanctuary. 3 And he made an image with five faces: four of them looked to the four winds, and the fifth on the summit of the image as ah adversary of the zeal of the Mighty One. 4 And then wrath went forth from the presence of the Mighty One to the intent that Zion should be rooted out, as also it befell in your days. But also against the two tribes and a half went forth a decree that they should also be led away captive, as you have now seen. 5 And to such a degree did the impiety of Manasseh increase, that it removed the praise of the Most High from the sanctuary. 7 On this account Manasseh was at that time named 'the impious," and finally his abode was in the fire. 8 For though his prayer was heard with the Most High, finally, when he was cast into the brazen horse and the brazen horse was melted, it served as a sign unto him for the hour. 9 For he had not lived perfectly, for he was not worthy—but that thenceforward he might know by whom finally he should be tormented. 10 For he who is able to benefit is also able to torment.

65 1 'Thus, moreover, did Manasseh act impiously, and thought that in his time the Mighty One would not inquire into these things. 2 These are the black ninth waters which you have seen.

66 1 'And the bright tenth waters which you have seen: this is the purity of the generations of Josiah king of Judah, who was the only one at the time who submitted himself to the Mighty One with all his heart and with all his soul. 2 And he cleansed the land from idols, and hallowed all the vessels which had been polluted, and restored the offerings to the altar, and raised the horn of the holy, and exalted the righteous, and honored all that were wise in understanding, and brought back the priests to their

ministry, and destroyed and removed the magicians and enchanters and necromancers from the land. 3 And not only did he slay the impious that were living, but they also took from the sepulchers the bones of the dead and burned them with fire. 4 [And the festivals and the Sabbaths he established in their sanctity], and their polluted ones he burnt in the fire, and the lying prophets which deceived the people, these also he burnt in the fire, and the people who listened to them when they were living, he cast them into the brook Kidron, and heaped stones upon them. 5 And he was zealous with zeal for the Mighty One with all his soul, and he alone was firm in the law at that time, so that he left none that was uncircumcised, or that wrought impiety in all the land, all the days of his life. 6 Therefore he shall receive an eternal reward, and he shall be glorified with the Mighty One beyond many at a later time. 7 For on his account and on account of those who are like him were the honorable glories, of which you were told before, created and prepared. These arc the bright waters which you have seen.

67 1 'And the black eleventh waters which you have seen: this is the calamity which is now befalling "Zion.

2 Do you think that there is no anguish to the angels in the presence of the Mighty One,

That Zion was so delivered up,
And that lo! the Gentiles boast in their hearts,
And assemble before their idols and say,
"She is trodden down who oftentimes trod down,
And she has been reduced to servitude who reduced (others)"?
3 Dost you think that in these things the Most High rejoices,
Or that His name is glorified?
4 [But how will it serve towards His righteous judgment?]
5 Yet after these things shall the dispersed among the Gentiles be taken hold of by tribulation,
And in shame shall they dwell in every place.
6 Because so far as Zion is delivered up
And Jerusalem laid waste,
Shall idols prosper in the cities of the Gentiles,
And the vapor of the smoke of the incense of the righteousness which is by the law is extinguished in Zion,
And in the region of Zion in every place lo! there is the smoke of impiety.
7 But the king of Babylon will arise who has now destroyed Zion,
And he will boast over the people,
And he will speak great things in his heart in the presence of the Most High.

8 But he also shall fall at last. These are the black waters.

68 1 'And the bright twelfth waters which you have seen: this is the word. For after these things time will come when your people shall fall into distress, so that they shall all run the risk of perishing together. 3 Nevertheless, they will be saved, and their enemies will fall in their presence. 4 And they will have in (due) time much joy. 5 And at that time after a little interval Zion will again be rebuilt, and its offerings will again be restored, and the priests will return to their ministry, and also the Gentiles will come to glorify it. 6 Nevertheless, not fully as in the beginning. 7 But it will come to pass after these things that there will be the fall of many nations. 8 These are the bright waters which you have seen.

69 1 'For the last waters which you have seen which were darker than all that were before them, those which were after the twelfth number, which were collected together, belong to the whole world. 2 For the Most High made division from the beginning, because He alone knows what will befall. 3 For as to the enormities and the impieties which should be wrought before Him, He foresaw six kinds of them. 4 And of the good works of the righteous which should be accomplished before Him, He foresaw six kinds of them, beyond those which He should work at the consummation of the age. 5 On his account there were not black waters with black, nor bright with bright; for it is the consummation.

70 1 'Hear therefore the interpretation of the last black waters which are to come [after the black]: this the word. 2 Behold! the days come, and it shall be when the time of the age has ripened,

And the harvest of its evil and good seeds has come,
That the Mighty One will bring upon the earth and its inhabitants and upon its rulers
Perturbation of spirit and stupor of heart.
3 And they shall hate one another,
And provoke one another to fight,
And the mean shall rule over the honorable,
And those of low degree shall be extolled above the famous.
4 And the many shall be delivered into the hands of the few,
And those who were nothing shall rule over the strong,
And the poor shall have abundance beyond the rich,
And the impious shall exalt themselves above the heroic.
5 And the wise shall be silent,
And the foolish shall speak,
Neither shall the thought of men be then confirmed,

Nor the counsel of the mighty,
Nor shall the hope of those who hope be confirmed.
6 And when those things which were predicted have come to pass,
Then shall confusion fall upon all men,
And some of them shall fall in battle,
And some of them shall perish in anguish,

7 And some of them shall be destroyed by their own.
Then the Most High peoples whom He has prepared before,

And they shall come and make war with the leaders that shall then be left.
8 And it shall come to pass that whoever gets safe out of the war shall die in the earthquake,
And whoever gets safe out of the earthquake shall be burned by the fire,
And whoever gets safe out of the fire shall be destroyed by famine.

9 [And it shall come to pass that whoever of the victors and the vanquished gets safe out of and escapes all these things aforesaid will be delivered into the hands of My servant Messiah.] 10 For all the earth shall devour its inhabitants.

71 1 'And the holy land shall have mercy on its own,
And it shall protect its inhabitants at that time. 2 This is the vision which you have seen, and this is the interpretation. 3 For I have come to tell you these things, because your prayer has been heard with the Most High.

72 'Hear now also regarding the bright lightning which is to come at the consummation after these black (waters): this is the word. 2 After the signs have come, of which you were told before, when the nations become turbulent, and the time of My Messiah is come, he shall both summon all the nations, and some of them he shall spare, and some of them he shall slay. 3 These things therefore shall come upon the nations which are to be spared by Him. 4 Every nation, which knows not Israel and has not trodden down the seed of Jacob, shall indeed be spared. 5 And this because some out of every nation shall be subjected to your people. 6 But all those who have ruled over you, or have known you, shall be given up to the sword.

73 1 And it shall come to pass, when He has brought low everything that is in the world,

And has sat down in peace for the age on the throne of His kingdom,
That joy shall then be revealed,
And rest shall appear.

2 And then healing shall descend in dew,
And disease shall withdraw,
And anxiety and anguish and lamentation pass from
amongst men,
And gladness proceed through the whole earth.
3 And no one shall again die untimely,
Nor shall any adversity suddenly befall.
4 And judgments, and abusive talk, and contentions,
and revenges,
And blood, and passions, and envy, and hatred,
And whatsoever things are like these shall go into
condemnation when they are removed.
5 For it is these very things which have filled this
world with evils,
And on account of these the life of man has been
greatly troubled.
6 And wild beasts shall come from the forest and
minister unto men
And asps and dragons shall come forth from their
holes to submit themselves to a little child.
7 And women shall no longer then have pain when
they bear,
Nor shall they suffer torment when they yield the
fruit of the womb.

74 1 And it shall come to pass in those days that the
reapers shall not grow weary,
Nor those that build be toil-worn;
For the works shall of themselves speedily advance
Together with those who do them in much
tranquility.
2 For that time is the consummation of that which is
corruptible,
And the beginning of that which is not corruptible.
3 Therefore those things which were predicted shall
belong to it:
Therefore it is far away from evils, and near to those
things which die not.
4 This is the bright lightning which came after the last
dark waters.'

*75. Baruch's Hymn on the Unsearchableness of God's
Ways and on His Mercies through which the Faithful shall
attain to a blessed Consummation*

75 1 And I answered and said:
'Who can understand, O Lord, Your goodness?
For it is incomprehensible.
2 Or who can search into your compassions,
Which are infinite?
3 Or who can comprehend Your intelligence?
4 Or who is able to recount the thoughts of Your
mind?
5 Or who of those who are born can hope to come to
those things,
Unless he is one to whom you are merciful and
gracious?

6 Because, if assuredly you did not have compassion
on man,
Those who are under Your right hand,
They could not come to those things,
But those who are in the numbers named can be
called.
7 But if, indeed, we who exist know wherefore we
have come,
And submit ourselves to Him who brought us out of
Egypt,
We shall come again and remember those things
which have passed,
And shall rejoice regarding that which has been.
8 But if now we know not wherefore we have come,
And recognize not the principate of Him who
brought us up out of Egypt, We shall come again and
seek after those things which have been now,
And be grieved with pain because of those things
which have befallen.'

*76. Baruch bidden to instruct the People for forty days and
then to hold himself ready for his Assumption on the
Advent of the Messiah*

76 1 And He answered and said unto me: ['Inasmuch
as the revelation of this vision has been interpreted to
you as you requested], hear the word of the Most
High that you may know what is to befall you after
these things. 2 For you shall surely depart from this
earth, nevertheless not unto death, but you shall be
preserved unto the consummation of the times. 3 Go
up therefore to the top of that mountain, and there
shall pass before you all the regions of that land, and
the figure of the inhabited world, and the top(s) of the
mountains, and the depth(s) of the valleys, and the
depths of the seas, and the number of the rivers, that
you may see what you are leaving, and whither you
are going. 4 Now this shall befall after forty days. Go
now therefore during these days and instruct the
people so far as you are able, that they may learn so
as not to die at the last time, but may learn in order
that they may live at the last times.'

*77. Baruch's Admonition to the People and his writing of
two Letters — one to the nine and a half tribes in Assyria
and the other to the two and a half in Babylon*

77 1 And I, Baruch, went there and came to the
people, and assembled them together from the
greatest to the least, and said unto them: 2 'Hear, you
children of Israel, behold how many you are who
remain of the twelve tribes of Israel. 3 For to you and
to your fathers the Lord gave a law more excellent
than to all peoples. 4 And because your brethren
transgressed the commandments of the Most High,

He brought vengeance upon you and upon them,

And He spared not the former,
And the latter also He gave into captivity:
And He left not a residue of them,
5 But behold! you are here with me.
6 If, therefore, you direct your ways aright,
Ye also shall not depart as your brethren departed,
But they shall come to you.
7 For He is merciful whom you worship,
And He is gracious in whom you hope,
And He is true, so that He shall do good and not evil.
8 Have you not seen here what has befallen Zion?
9 Or do you perchance think that the place had sinned,
And that on this account it was overthrown?
Or that the land had wrought foolishness,
And that therefore it was delivered up?
10 And know you not that on account of you who did sin,
That which sinned not was overthrown,
And, on account of those who wrought wickedly,
That which wrought not foolishness was delivered up to (its) enemies?'

11 And the whole people answered and said unto me: 'So far as we can recall the good things which the Mighty One has done unto us, we do recall them; and those things which we do not remember He in His mercy knows. 12 Nevertheless, do this for us your people: write also to our brethren in Babylon an epistle of doctrine and a scroll of hope, that you may confirm them also before you do depart from us.

13 For the shepherds of Israel have perished,
And the lamps which gave light are extinguished,
And the fountains have withheld their stream whence we used to drink.
14 And we are left in the darkness,
And amid the trees of the forest,
And the thirst of the wilderness.'
15 And I answered and said unto them
'Shepherds and lamps and fountains come from the law:
And though we depart, yet the law abides.
16 If therefore you have respect to the law,
And are intent upon wisdom,
A lamp will not be wanting,
And a shepherd will not fail,
And a fountain will not dry up.

17 Nevertheless, as you said unto me, I will write also unto your brethren in Babylon, and I will send by means of men, and I will write in like manner to the nine tribes and a half, and send by means of a bird.'
18 And it came to pass on the one and twentieth day in the eighth month that I, Baruch, came and sat down under the oak under the shadow of the branches, and no man was with me, but I was alone.

19 And I wrote these two epistles: one I sent by an eagle to the nine and a half tribes; and the other I sent to those that were at Babylon by means of three men. 20 And I called the eagle and spoke these words unto it: 21 'The Most High hath made you that you should be higher than all birds. 22 And now go and tarry not in (any) place, nor enter a nest, nor settle upon any tree, till you have passed over the breadth of the many waters of the river Euphrates, and have gone to the people that dwell there, and cast down to them this epistle. 23 Remember, moreover, that, at the time of the deluge, Noah received from a dove the fruit of the olive, when he sent it forth from the ark. 24 Yea, also the ravens ministered to Elijah, bearing him food, as they had been commanded. 25 Solomon also, in the time of his kingdom, whithersoever he wished to send or seek for anything, commanded a bird (to go thither), and it obeyed him as he commanded it. 26 And now let it not weary you, and turn not to the right hand nor the left, but fly and go by a direct way, that you may preserve the command of the Mighty One, according as I said unto you.'

78—86. THE EPISTLE OF BARUCH THE SON OF NERIAH WHICH HE WROTE TO THE NINE AND A HALF TRIBES

78 1 These are the words of that epistle which Baruch the son of Neriah sent to the nine and a half tribes, which were across the river Euphrates, in which these things were written.
2 Thus says Baruch the son of Neriah to the brethren carried into captivity: 'Mercy and peace.' I bear in mind, my brethren, the love of Him who created us, who loved us from of old, and never hated us, but above all educated us. 3 And truly I know that behold all we the twelve tribes are bound by one bond, inasmuch as we are born from one father. 4 Wherefore I have been the more careful to leave you the words of this epistle before I die, that you may be comforted regarding the evils which have come upon you, and that you may be grieved also regarding the evil that has befallen your brethren; and again, also, that you may justify His judgment which 5 He has decreed against you that you should be carried away captive—for what you have suffered is disproportioned to what you have done—in order that, at the last times, you may be found worthy of your fathers. 6 Therefore, if you consider that ye have now suffered those things for your good, that you may not finally be condemned and tormented, then you will receive eternal hope; if above all you destroy from your heart vain error, on account of which you departed hence. 7 For if you so do these things, He will continually remember you, He who always promised on our behalf to those who were more excellent than we, that He will never forget or forsake

us, but with much mercy will gather together again those who were dispersed.

79 1 Now, my brethren, learn first what befell Zion: how that Nebuchadnezzar king of Babylon came up against us. 2 For we have sinned against Him who made us, and we have not kept the commandments which he commanded us, yet he hath not chastened us as we deserved. 3 For what befell you we also suffer in a preeminent degree, for it befell us also. 80 1 And now, my brethren, I make known unto you that when the enemy had surrounded the city, the angels of the Most High were sent, and they overthrew the fortifications of the strong wall, and they destroyed the firm iron corners, which could not be rooted out. 2 Nevertheless, they hid all the vessels of the sanctuary, lest the enemy should get possession of them. 3 And when they had done these things, they delivered thereupon to the enemy the overthrown wall, and the plundered house, and the burnt temple, and the people who were overcome because they were delivered up, lest the enemy should boast and say: 'Thus by force have we been able to lay waste even the house of the Most High in war.' Your brethren also have they bound and led away to Babylon, and have caused them to dwell there. 5 But we have been left here, being very few. 6 This is the tribulation about which I wrote to you. 7 For assuredly I know that (the consolation of) the inhabitants of Zion consoles you : so far as you knew that it was prospered (your consolation) was greater than the tribulation which you endured in having to depart from it.

81 1 But regarding consolation, hear the word. 2 For I was mourning regarding Zion, and I prayed for mercy from the Most High, and I said:

3 How long will these things endure for us?
And will these evils come upon us always?'
4 And the Mighty One did according to the multitude of His mercies,
And the Most High according to the greatness of His compassion,
And He revealed unto me the word, that I might receive consolation,
And He showed me visions that I should not again endure anguish,
And He made known to me the mystery of the times.
And the advent of the hours he showed me.

82 1 Therefore, my brethren, I have written to you, that you may comfort yourselves regarding the multitude of your tribulations. 2 For know you that our Maker will assuredly avenge us on all our enemies, according to all that they have done to us, also that the consummation which the Most High will make is very nigh, and His mercy that is coming, and the consummation of His judgment, is by no means far off.

3 For lo! we see now the multitude of the prosperity of the Gentiles,
Though they act impiously,
But they shall be like a vapor:
4 And we behold the multitude of their power,
Though they do wickedly,
But they shall be made like unto a drop:
5 And we see the firmness of their might.
Though they resist the Mighty One every hour,
But they shall be accounted as spittle.
6 And we consider the glory of their greatness,
Though they do not keep the statutes of the Most High,
But as smoke shall they pass away.
7 And we meditate on the beauty of their gracefulness,
Though they have to do with pollutions,
But as grass that withers shall they fade away.
8 And we consider the strength of their cruelty,
Though they remember not the end (thereof),
But as a wave that passes shall they be broken.
9 And we remark the boastfulness of their might,
Though they deny the beneficence of God, who gave (it) to them,
But they shall pass away as a passing cloud.

83 1 [For the Most High will assuredly hasten His times,
And He will assuredly bring on His hours.
2 And He will assuredly judge those who are in His world,
And will visit in truth all things by means of all their hidden works.
3 And He will assuredly examine the secret thoughts,
And that which is laid up in the secret chambers of all the members of mail. And will make (them) manifest in the presence of all with reproof.

4 Let none therefore of these present things ascend into your hearts, but above all let us be expectant, because that which is promised to us shall come. 5 And let us not now look unto the delights of the Gentiles in the present, but let us remember what has been promised to us in the end. 6 For the ends of the times and of the seasons and whatsoever is with them shall assuredly pass by together. 7 The consummation, moreover, of the age shall then show the great might of its ruler, when all things come to judgment. 8 Do you therefore prepare your hearts for that which before you believed, lest you come to be in bondage in both worlds, so that you be led away captive here and be tormented there. 9 For that which exists now or which has passed away, or which is to

come, in all these things, neither is the evil fully evil, nor again the good fully good.

10 For all healthinesses of this time are turning into diseases,
11 And all might of this time is turning into weakness, And all the force of this time is turning into impotence,
12 And every energy of youth is turning into old age and consummation.
And every beauty of gracefulness of this time is turning faded and hateful,
13 And every proud dominion of the present is turning into humiliation and shame,
14 And every praise of the glory of this time is turning into the shame of silence,
And every vain splendor and insolence of this time is turning into voiceless ruin.
15 And every delight and joy of this time is turning to worms and corruption,
16 And every clamor of the pride of this time is turning into dust and stillness.
17 And every possession of riches of this time is being turned into Sheol alone,
18 And all the rapine of passion of this time is turning into involuntary death,
And every passion of the lusts of this time is turning into a judgment of torment.
19 And every artifice and craftiness of this time is turning into a proof of the truth,
20 And every sweetness of unguents of this time is turning into judgment and condemnation,
21 And every love of lying is turning to contumely through truth.

22 [Since therefore all these things are done now, does anyone think that they will not be avenged? But the consummation of all things will come to the truth.]

84 Behold! I have therefore made known unto you (these things) whilst I live: for I have said (it) that you should learn the things that are excellent; for the Mighty One hath commanded me to instruct you: and I will set before you some of the commandments of His judgment before I die. 2 Remember that formerly Moses assuredly called heaven and earth to witness against you and said: 'If you transgress the law you shall be dispersed, but if you keep it you shall be kept.' 3 And other things also he used to say unto you when you the twelve tribes were together in the desert. 4 And after his death you cast them away from you: on this account there came upon you what had been predicted. 5 And now Moses used to tell you before they befell you, and lo! they have befallen you: for you have forsaken the law. 6 Lo! I also say unto you after you have suffered, that if you obey those things which have been said unto you, you will

receive from the Mighty One whatever has been laid up and reserved for you. 7 Moreover, let this epistle be for a testimony between me and you, that you may remember the commandments of the Mighty One, and that also there may be to me a defense in the presence of Him who sent me. 8 And remember you the law and Zion, and the holy land and your brethren, and the covenant of your fathers, and forget not the festivals and the Sabbaths. And deliver this epistle and the traditions of the law to your sons after you, as also your fathers delivered (them) to you. 10 And at all times make request perseveringly and pray diligently with your whole heart that the Mighty One may be reconciled to you, and that He may not reckon the multitude of your sins, but remember the rectitude of your fathers. 11 For if He judge us not according to the multitude of His mercies, woe unto all us who are born.

85 1[Know, moreover, that
In former times and in the generations of old our fathers had helpers,
Righteous men and holy prophets:
2 No more, we were in our own land
[And they helped us when we sinned],

finish

THE GREEK APOCALYPSE OF BARUCH
OR
3 BARUCH

Prologue.

1 A narrative and revelation of Baruch, concerning those ineffable things which he saw by command of God. Bless Thou, O Lord.

2 A revelation of Baruch, who stood upon the river Gel weeping over the captivity of 3 Jerusalem, when also Abimelech was preserved by the hand of God, at the farm of Agrippa. And he was sitting thus at the beautiful gates, where the Holy of holies lay.

1. 1 Verily I Baruch was weeping in my mind and sorrowing on account of the people, and that 2 Nebuchadnezzar the king was permitted by God to destroy His city, saying: Lord, why didst Thou set on fire Thy vineyard, and lay it waste? Why didst Thou do this? And why, Lord, didst Thou not requite us with another chastisement, but didst deliver us to nations such as these, so that they 3 reproach us and say, Where is their God? And behold as I was weeping and saying such things, I saw an angel of the Lord coming and saying to me: Understand, O man, greatly beloved, and trouble not thyself so greatly concerning the salvation of Jerusalem, for thus saith the Lord God, 4 the Almighty. For He sent me before thee, to make known and to show to thee all (the things) 5, 6 of God. For thy prayer was heard before Him, and entered into the ears of the Lord God. And when he had said these things to me, I was silent. And the angel said to me: Cease to provoke 7 God, and I will show thee other mysteries, greater than these. And I Baruch said, As the Lord God liveth, if thou wilt show me, and I hear a word of thine, I will not continue to speak any longer. 8 God shall add to my judgement in the day of judgement, if I speak hereafter. And the angel of the powers said to me, Come, and I will show thee the mysteries of God.

The First Heaven.

2 1 And he took me and led me where the firmament has been set fast, and where there was a river which no one can cross, nor any strange breeze of all those which God created. And he took me and led me to the first heaven, and showed me a door of great size. And he said to me, Let us enter 3 through it, and we entered as though *borne* on wings, a distance of about thirty days' journey. And he showed me within the heaven a plain ; and there were men dwelling

thereon, with the faces of 4 oxen, and the horns of stags and the feet of goats, and the haunches of lambs. And I Baruch asked the angel, Make known to me, I pray thee, what is the thickness of the heaven in which we journeyed, 5 or what is its extent, or what is the plain, in order that I may also tell the sons of men? And the angel whose name is Phamael said to me: This door which thou seest is the door of heaven, and as great as is the distance from earth to heaven, so great also is its thickness; and again as great as is *the distance* (from North to South, so great) is the length of the plain which thou didst see. And again the angel of the powers said to me, Come, and I will show thee greater mysteries. But 6, 7 I said, I pray thee show me what are these men. And he said to me, These are they who built the tower of strife against God, and the Lord banished them.

The Second Heaven.

3 1 And the angel of the Lord took me and led me to a second heaven. And he showed me there 2 also a door like the first and said, Let us enter through it. And we entered, being borne on wings 3 a distance of about sixty days' journey. And he showed me there also a plain, and it was full of 4 men, whose appearance was like *that* of dogs, and *whose* feet *were* like *those* of stags. And I asked 5 the angel: I pray thee, Lord, say to me who are these. And he said, These are they who gave counsel to build the tower, for they whom thou seest drove forth multitudes of both men and women, to make bricks; among whom, a woman making bricks was not allowed to be released in the hour of child-birth, but brought forth while she was making bricks, and carried her child in her apron, and 6 continued to make bricks. And the Lord appeared to them and confused their speech, when they 7 had built the tower to *the height of* four hundred and sixty-three cubits. And they took a gimlet, and sought to pierce the heaven, saying, Let us see (whether) the heaven is made of clay, or of 8 brass, or of iron. When God saw this He did not permit them, but smote them with blindness and confusion of speech, and rendered them as thou seest.

The Third Heaven.

4 1 And I Baruch said, Behold, Lord, Thou didst show me great and wonderful things; and now 2 show me all things for the sake of the Lord. And the angel said to me, Come, let us proceed. (And I proceeded) with the angel from that place about one hundred and eighty-five days' 3 journey. And he showed me a plain and a serpent, which appeared to be two hundred plethra in length. 4 And he showed me Hades, and its appearance was dark and abominable. And I said, 5 Who is this dragon, and who is this

monster around him? And the angel said, The dragon is he 6 who eats the bodies of those who spend their life wickedly, and he is nourished by them. And this is Hades, which itself also closely resembles him, in that it also drinks about a cubit from 7 the sea, which does not sink at all. Baruch said, And how (does this happen)? And the angel said, Hearken, the Lord God made three hundred and sixty rivers, of which the chief of 8 all are Alphias, Abyrus, and the Gericus; and because of these the sea does not sink. And I said, I pray thee show me which is the tree which led Adam astray. And the angel said to me, It is the vine, which the angel Sammael planted, whereat the Lord God was angry, and He cursed him and his plant, while also on this account He did not permit Adam to touch it, and therefore 9 the devil being envious deceived him through his vine. [And I Baruch said, Since also the vine has been the cause of such great evil, and is under judgment of the curse of God, and *was* the 10 destruction of the first created, how is it now so useful? And the angel said, Thou askest aright. When God caused the deluge upon earth, and destroyed all flesh, and four hundred and nine thousand giants, and the water rose fifteen cubits above the highest *mountains, then* the water entered into paradise and destroyed every flower; but it removed wholly without the bounds the shoot 11 of the vine and cast it outside. And when the earth appeared out of the water, and Noah came out 12 of the ark, he began to plant of the plants which he found. But he found also the shoot of the vine; and he took it, and was reasoning in himself, What then is it? And I came and spake to 13 him the things concerning it. And he said, Shall I plant it, or what *shall I do?* Since Adam was destroyed because of it, let me not also meet with the anger of God because of it. And saying 14 these things he prayed that God would reveal to him what he should do concerning it. And when he had completed the prayer *which lasted* forty days, and having besought many things and wept, 15 he said: Lord, I entreat thee to reveal to me what I shall do concerning this plant. But God sent his angel Sarasael, and said to him, Arise, Noah, and plant the shoot of the vine, for thus saith the Lord : Its bitterness shall be changed into sweetness, and its curse shall become a blessing, and that which is produced from it shall become the blood of God; and as through it the human race obtained condemnation, *so* again through Jesus Christ the Immanuel will they receive in Him the 16 upward calling, and the entry into paradise]. Know therefore, 0 Baruch, that as Adam through this very tree obtained condemnation, and was divested of the glory of God, so also the men who now drink insatiably the wine which is begotten of it, transgress worse than Adam, and are far from the 17 glory of God, and are surrendering themselves to the eternal fire. For (no) good comes through it. For

those who drink it to surfeit do these things: neither does a brother pity *his* brother, nor a father *his* son, nor children *their* parents, but from the drinking of wine come all *evils,* such as murders, adulteries, fornications, perjuries, thefts, and such like. And nothing good is established by it.

5 1 And I Baruch said to the angel, 2 Let me ask thee one thing, Lord. Since thou didst say to me 3 that the dragon drinks one cubit out of the sea, say to me also, how great is his belly? And the angel said, His belly is Hades; and as far as a plummet is thrown (by) three hundred men, so great is his belly. Come, then, that I may show thee also greater works than these.

6 1 And he took me and led me where the sun goes forth; 2 and he showed me a chariot and four, under which burnt a fire, and in the chariot was sitting a man, wearing a crown of fire, (and) the chariot (was) drawn by forty angels. And behold a bird circling before the sun, about nine 3 cubits away. And I said to the angel, What is this bird? And he said to me, This is the 4, 5 guardian of the earth. And I said, Lord, how is he the guardian of the earth? Teach me. And the angel said to me, This bird flies alongside of the sun, and expanding his wings receives its fiery 6 rays. For if he were not receiving them, the human race would not be preserved, nor any other 7 living creature. But God appointed this bird *thereto.* And he expanded his wings, and I saw on his right wing very large letters, *as large* as the space of a threshing-floor, the size of about four 8 thousand modii; and the letters were of gold. And the angel said to me, Read them. And I read 9 and they ran thus: Neither earth nor heaven bring me forth, but wings of fire bring me forth. And I said, Lord, what is this bird, and what is his name? And the angel said to me, His name is called 11 Phoenix. (And I said), And what does he eat? And he said to me, The manna of heaven and 12 the dew of earth. And I said, Does the bird excrete? And he said to me, He excretes a worm, and the excrement of the worm is cinnamon, which kings and princes use. But wait and thou shalt 13 see the glory of God. And while he was conversing *with me,* there was as a thunder-clap, and the place was shaken on which we were standing. And I asked the angel, My Lord, what is this sound? And the angel said to me, Even now the angels are opening the three hundred and sixty-five gates 14 of heaven, and the light is being separated from the darkness. And a voice came which said, Light 15 giver, give to the world radiance. And when I heard the noise of the bird, I said, Lord, what is this 16 noise? And he said, This is *the bird* who awakens from slumber the cocks upon earth. For as men do through the mouth, so also does the cock signify to those in the world, in his own speech. For

440

the sun is made ready by the angels, and the cock crows.

7 1 And I said, And where does the sun begin its labors, after the cock crows? 2 And the angel said to me, Listen, Baruch: All things whatsoever I showed thee are in the first and second heaven, and in the third heaven the sun passes through and gives light to the world. But wait, and thou 3 shalt see the glory of God. And while I was conversing with him, I saw the bird, and he appeared 4 in front, and grew less and less, and *at length* returned to his full size. And behind him I saw the shining sun, and the angels which draw it, and a crown upon its bead, the sight of which we were 5 not able to gaze Upon, and behold. And as soon as the sun shone, the Phoenix also stretched out his wings. But I, when I beheld such great glory, was brought low with great fear, and I fled and 6 hid in the wings of the angel. And the angel said to me, Fear not, Baruch, but wait and thou shalt also see their setting.

8 1 And he took me and led me towards the west; and when the time of the, setting came, I saw again the bird coming before *it,* and as soon as lie came I saw the angels, and they lifted the crown 2, 3 from its head. But the bird stood exhausted and with wings contracted. And beholding these things, I said, Lord, wherefore did they lift the crown from the head of the sun, and wherefore is 4 the bird so exhausted? And the angel said to me, The crown of the sun, when it has run through the day-four angels take it, and bear it up to heaven, and renew it, because it and its rays have been defiled upon earth; moreover it is so renewed each day. And I Baruch said, Lord, and wherefore 5 are its beams defiled upon earth? And the angel said to me, Because it beholds the lawlessness and unrighteousness of men, namely fornications, adulteries, thefts, extortions, idolatries, drunkenness, murders, strife, jealousies, evil-speakings, murmurings, whisperings, divinations, and such like, which are not well-pleasing to God. On account of these things is it defiled, and therefore is it renewed. 6 But *thou askest* concerning the bird, how it is exhausted. Because by restraining the rays of the sun through the fire and burning heat of the whole day, it is exhausted thereby. For, as we said before, unless his wings were screening the rays of the sun, no living creature would be preserved.

9 1 And they having retired, the night also fell, and at the same time *came* the chariot of the moon, along with the stars. 2 And I Baruch said, Lord, show me it also, I beseech of thee, how 3 it goes forth, where it departs, and in what form it moves along. And the angel said, Wait' and thou shalt see it also shortly.

And on the morrow I also saw it in the form of a woman, and sitting on a wheeled chariot. And there were before it oxen and lambs in the chariot, and a multitude of 4 angels in like manner. And I said, Lord, what are the oxen and the lambs? And he said to me, 5 They also are angels. And again I asked, Why is it that it at one time increases, but at another 6 time decreases? And (he said to me), Listen, 0 Baruch: This which thou seest had been written 7 by God beautiful as no other. And at the transgression of the first Adam, it was near to Sammael when he took the serpent as a garment. And it did not hide itself but increased, and God was 8 angry with it, and afflicted it, and shortened its days. And I said, And how does it not also shine always, but only in the night? And the angel said, Listen: as in the presence of a king, the courtiers cannot speak freely, so the moon and the stars cannot shine in the presence of the sun; for the stars are always suspended, but they are screened by the sun, and the moon, although it is uninjured, is consumed by the heat of the sun.

The Fourth Heaven.

10 1 And when I had learnt all these things from the archangel, he took and led me into a fourth 2 3 heaven. And I saw a monotonous plain, and in the middle of it a pool of water. And there were in it multitudes of birds of all kinds, but not like those here on *earth.* But I saw a crane *as great* as 4 great oxen; and all *the birds* were great beyond those in the world. And I asked the angel, What 5 is the plain, and what the pool, and what the multitudes of birds around it? And the angel said, Listen, Baruch : The plain which contains in it the pool and other wonders is *the place* where the 6 souls of the righteous come, when they hold converse, living together in choirs. But the water is 7 that which the clouds receive, and rain upon the earth, and the fruits increase. And I said again to the angel of the Lord, But (what) *are* these birds? And he said to me, They are those which 8 continually sing praise to the Lord. And I said, Lord, and how do men say that the water which 9 descends in rain is from the sea? And the angel said, *The water* which descends in rain-this also is from the sea, and from the waters upon earth; but that which stimulates the fruits is (only) from 10 the latter source. Know therefore henceforth that from this *source* is what is called the dew of heaven.

The Fifth Heaven.

11 1 And the angel took me and led me thence to a fifth heaven. And the gate was closed. And I said, Lord, is not this gate-way open that we may enter? And the angel said to me, We cannot enter until

Michael comes, who holds the keys of the Kingdom of Heaven; but wait and thou shalt see 3 the glory of God. And there was a great sound, as thunder. And I said, Lord, what is this sound? 4 And he said to me, Even now Michael, the commander *of the angels,* comes down to receive the 5 prayers of men. And behold a voice came, Let the gates be opened. And they opened *them,* and 6 there was a roar as of thunder. And Michael came, and the angel who was with me came face to 7 face with him and said, Hail, my commander, and *that* of all our order. And the commander Michael said, Hail thou also, our brother, and the interpreter of the revelations to those who pass through life 8 virtuously. And having saluted one another thus, they stood still. And I saw the commander Michael said, Hail thou also, our brother, and the interpreter of the revelations to those who pass through life 8 virtuously. And having saluted one another thus, they stood still. And I saw the commander Michael, holding an exceedingly great vessel; its depth *was as* great as *the distance* from heaven to 9 earth, and its breadth as great as the *distance* from north to south. And I said, Lord, what is that which Michael the archangel is holding? And he said to me, This is where the merits of the righteous enter, and such good works as they do, which are escorted before the heavenly God.

12 1, And as I was conversing with them, behold angels came bearing baskets full of flowers. And 2 they gave them to Michael. And I asked the angel, Lord, who are these, and what are the things 3 brought hither from beside them? And he said to me, These are angels (who) are over the 4, 5 righteous. And the archangel took the baskets, and cast them into the vessel. And the angel 6 said to me, These flowers are the merits of the righteous. And I saw other angels bearing baskets *which were* (neither) empty-nor full. And they began to lament, and did not venture to draw near, 7 because they had not the prizes complete. And Michael cried and said, Come hither, also, ye 8 angels, bring what ye have brought. And Michael was exceedingly grieved, and the angel who was with me, because they did not fill the vessel.

13 1 And then came in like manner other angels weeping and bewailing, and saying with fear, Behold how we are overclouded, 0 Lord, for we were delivered to evil men, and we wish to depart from 2 them. And Michael said, Ye cannot depart from them, in order that the enemy may not prevail to 3 the end; but say to me what ye ask. And they said, We pray thee, Michael our commander, transfer us from them, for we cannot abide with wicked and foolish men, for there is nothing good 4 in them, but every kind of unrighteousness and greed. For we do not behold them entering [into Church at all, nor among spiritual

fathers, nor] into any good work. But where there is murder, there also are they in the midst, and where are fornications, adulteries, thefts, slanders, perjuries, jealousies, drunkenness, strife, envy, murmurings, whispering, idolatry, divination, and such like, 5 then are they *workers* of such works, and of others worse. Wherefore we entreat that we may depart from them. And Michael said to the angels, Wait till I learn from the Lord what shall come to pass.

14 1 And in that very hour Michael departed, and the doors were closed. And there was a sound as 2 thunder. And I asked the angel, What is the sound? And he said to me, Michael is even now presenting the merits of men to God.

15 1 And in that very hour Michael descended, and the gate was opened; and he brought oil. 2 And as for the angels which brought the baskets *which were* full, he filled them with oil, saying, Take it away, reward our friends an hundredfold, and those who have laboriously wrought good works. 3 For those who sowed virtuously, also reap virtuously. And he said also to those bringing the half-empty baskets, Come hither ye also; take away the reward according as ye brought, and 4 deliver *it* to the sons of men. [Then he said also to those who brought the full and to those *who brought* the half-empty baskets: Go and bless our friends, and say to them that thus saith the Lord, Ye are faithful over a few things, I will set you over many things; enter into the joy of your Lord.]

16 1 And turning he said also to those who brought nothing: Thus saith the Lord, Be not sad of 2 countenance, and weep not, nor let the sons of men alone. But since they angered me in their works, go and make them envious and angry and provoked against *a people that is* no people, a 3 people that has no understanding. Further, besides these, send forth the caterpillar and the unwinged locust, and the mildew, and the common locust (and) hail with lightnings and anger, and 4 punish them severely with the sword and with death, and their children with demons. For they did not hearken to my voice, nor did they observe my commandments, nor do *them,* but were despisers of my commandments, and insolent towards the priests who proclaimed my words to them.

17 1 And while he yet spake, the door was closed, and we withdrew. 2 And the angel took me and 3 restored me to the *p/ace where I was* at the beginning. And having come to myself, I gave glory 4 to God, who counted me worthy of such honor. Wherefore do ye also, brethren, who obtained such a revelation, yourselves also glorify God, so that He also may glorify you, now and ever, and to all eternity. Amen.

"The Apocalypse of Abraham" is part of a body of writings called "Abrahamic Writings," which flourished around and just after the time of Christ.

The manuscript dates from A.D. 80-170 with most scholars placing it between 80 and 100 A.D. The original text was written in a Semitic language, however it has survived only in Old Slavonic renditions.

Many of the Jewish non-canonical and extra-biblical materials that circulated in the Slavic lands came from Byzantium. They greatly influenced the development of Slavic literature. Non-canonical books brought from Byzantium were translated and became sections (pieces) of various Slavonic traditions. The Eastern Orthodox church nurtured an environment in which the apocryphal texts were encouraged toward the view of providing additional information as a secondary source to the canonical mainstream texts. Pseudepigraphical (certain writings other than the canonical books and the Apocrypha, professing to be Biblical in character) texts attributed to Adam, Enoch, Noah, Jacob, Abraham, Moses, and other patriarchs survived in this environment and were incorporated in hagiographical (the writing and critical study of the lives of the saints) and historical volumes.

An English translation of "The Apocalypse of Abraham" was produced by G. H. Box and J. I. Landsman in 1918 (The Apocalypse of Abraham, London: Society for Promoting Christian Knowledge) but that translation does not read well for the modern English audience. Thus arises the need to have the Box and other mainstream translations combined and updated into a more readable and accessible mode for today's reader.

It should be noted here that there are two versions of the "Apocalypse of Abraham," a long and a short version. The text in the book before you contains a combination of these two versions. When the two versions agree, which was more often than not the case, the clearest and best wording was chosen to express both in a single phrase.

When there were variations in meaning, alternate translations are shown in parentheses.

When one version covered information not contained in the other translation, the additional lines were added, making this book the most complete body of information available as a single text.

"The Apocalypse of Abraham" is written in an haggadic midrash tradition. (Haggadic - embracing the interpretation of the non-legal portions of the Hebrew Bible. These midrashim are sometimes referred to as *haggadah*, a term that refers to all non-legal discourse in classical rabbinic literature). (Midrash – a Hebrew word referring to a method of exegesis of a Biblical text and teachings in the form of legal or exegetical commentaries on the Jewish Bible).

Introduction to The Apocalypse of Abraham

As with much of the Haaadic literature, the writings are an expansion and detailed explanation of existent biblical texts. That is to say, the writer took a section of an Old Testament canonical text and expanded it into a larger, more detailed story in order to explain in further detail the moral and religious implications of the original text.

Apocalyptic writings abound in the same time frame in the first century. It is thought they were spurred into creative existence by the utter destruction of the Jewish Temple in 70 A.D. and the attempted annihilation of Christians, many of whom were converted Jews, at the same time.

"The Apocalypse of Abraham" is based on Genesis 15:9-17 and concludes with the apocalypse. The book is of Jewish origin with features which might suggest that it had its beginning in the Essene community. This is seen clearly in the references to the "Elect One," a term that also appears in the Lost Book Of Enoch." (See "The Lost Book Of Enoch" by Joseph Lumpkin.)

Approximately one-third of the "Apocalypse of Abraham" contains an account of Abraham's conversion from polytheism to henotheism. Whereas polytheism believes in and worships many gods, each according to his or her dominion and special power; monotheism is the belief in one god; and henotheism focuses on one god but does not deny the existence of the other gods. The Amarna period of Egyptian history is an example a society that held to the henotheistic belief system.

The apocalyptic section of the Abraham text begins with the search for the God that made all things and the rejection of god's (idols) made by men. He (Abraham) reasons that if man made the gods with his own hands that man must therefore be greater than the gods he made.

Abraham's prayers are answered and he is told how to sacrifice to God. The preparation and sacrifice follows the biblical account, except that instead of birds of prey appearing and consuming the sacrifice, it is Azazel who does so. The angel Jaoel (Iaoel or Joel), guides Abraham into heaven and teaches him a song that is to be sung only on that realm or sphere of heaven.

While in heaven, Abraham sees a vision of the sin and degradation of his own progeny. As their sin increases, God withdraws his protection and the great temple is overrun by "heathen nations" and the progeny is killed and enslaved.

The five main characters in the book are El (God), Jaoel, Azazel, Abraham, and a powerful figure simply known as "The Man." There are also minor characters such as Abraham's father and merchants who travel in the area in which Abraham lived.

We learn in the first chapter of the Apocalypse of Abraham that Abraham is the son of Terah and the brother of Nahor.

Chapter 1
1. I was standing guard one day over the gods of my father Terah and my brother Nahor…

We also know Abraham's family were polytheists who worshipped idols that their father made. We learn that Terah sold his idols to others as well. Abraham is depicted as a precocious and sassy youth who questions things taken for granted by others.

He asked a question that seems most insightful for its time; If you carve an idol to worship as a god, does not that make you greater than the god you made? If that is true, why worship that which is lesser? This simple question puts him on the path of searching for the God who made all things including man.

Jaoel is the angel assigned to guide Abraham on his search. Jaoel takes him to heaven and leads him into visions, instructing him along the way.

Since Jaoel is allowed to come and go from the seventh heaven, we must assume him to be an angel of very high rank, though not found mentioned by this name elsewhere.

The name Jaoel consists of two parts, Jah and El both names of God in the Old Testament. Jaoel shows and explains a universal duality.

The duality of the universe is seen in the "right handed" and "left handed" principle. The Lord Himself used this principle when speaking of the 'sheep and the goats" in Matthew 25.

Here in the Abrahamic writings there are people coming out of a temple on the left side and on the right side. The deities in the story are the God El, who in this writing assumes the name of Azazel, a name that appears a great deal in the Books of Enoch, and is used in the Old Testament in the account of the Day of Atonement, where one goat is slain in the Tabernacle, whilst the other is set free, and the Hebrew text reads it is "for Azazel."

Azazel is portrayed as an unclean bird which came down upon the sacrifice Abraham, the Biblical patriarch, prepared. This is in reference to Genesis 15:11 Birds of prey came down upon the carcasses, and Abram drove them away.

Azazel is also associated with Hell. Abraham tells Azazel he will burn in hell and be in the underworld or Hades.

Azazel appears four times in Old Testament: Leviticus 16 :8, 10, and 26, where the ritual for the Day of Atonement is described. After the priest has made atonement for himself, he is to take two goats on behalf of Israel. One is to be a sacrifice to the Lord, the other is to be the 'scape goat,' which is the goat for Azazel.

This word has been understood to mean the "goat that departs," considering it to be derived from two Hebrew words: "ez" (goat) and "azal" (turn off). It is also associated with the Arabic word, "azala" (banish), or (remove), It has been rendered "for entire removal." Refer to Leviticus 16:22. However, in I Chronicles 5:8, the father of Bela, a Reubenite, is named "Azaz," which means strong.

This name comes from the Hebrew verb "azaz", a which means "to be strong." Azazel is also seen as an evil spirit in Enoch 8:1; 10:4; II Chronicles 11:15; Isaiah 34:14; and Revelations 18:2. In this way Azazel can be seen as the opponent or antithesis to the Lord and a precursor to Satan.

The figure of "The Man" is rather ambiguous. He is not fully messianic, yet he is endowed with power from God.

He may have come from the Essene idea of the Teacher of Righteousness and his connection with the coming, expected messiah.

Another explanation of the figure may come from an early Christian idea originating in a Judeo-Christian sect, which saw Jesus as precursor of the real and awaited Messiah, or it may simply be a Jewish text being badly interpreted and biased by an early Christian editor.

The evolution of El and his origin has drawn debate and acrimony since the beginning of theological study.

The people of Aramean and Canaanite origin seem to have contributed to the religion of El. Both religions place El as the highest god of a pantheon. Yet, because there is a pantheon of gods there is polytheism.

The clearest example of this adoption of the Israelite Elism comes from Deuteronomy 32 and related texts. El rules over his sons, and assigns each of them a people or tribe to govern. Here, to our surprise, we find Yahweh (the Lord) portrayed as one of El Elyon's divine sons.

Psalm 29 shows Yahweh as one of the sons of El, but a powerful god who is less subordinate than the others and more like an elder son.

Psalm 29 introduces the Canaanite cosmology which was more simple and familial; El being the father image and king.

We find within the Israelite religion two variations of the same high god. These different versions of Elism (the belief in a god called El) show that this god was variously worshipped depending upon location. Locations north of Palestine would have brought the worship of Yahweh in contact with Canaanite religion and that may explain its distinctly Canaanite quality.

Continuing the relationship between El and his sons, Psalm 82 has El stripping all his sons of authority and condemning them to mortality.

From this viewpoint, the Aramean god, El, seems to be related Canaanite mythology. Both likely descended from a Mesopotamian religion. Yet now, after being failed and disappointed by all others gods, whom we presume are his sons, El is forced to rule alone. Now we have the pathway set between polytheism and monotheism.

This last steps between the idea of a ruling court of gods and the singular god, El, can be seen clearly in the following translation and study by John Gray, Near Eastern Mythology:

"God has taken His place in the assembly of the gods (lit. 'sons of El'),
He declares His judgment among the gods: "
How long will you give crooked judgment, and favor the wicked?
You ought to sustain the case of the weak and the orphan;
You ought to vindicate the destitute and down-trodden
You ought to rescue the weak and the poor,
To deliver them from the power of the wicked
You (Hebrew "they") walk in darkness
While all earth's foundations are giving away.
I declare "Gods you may be,
Sons of the Most high, all of you;
Yet you will die as men,
You will fall as one of the bright ones."
Psalm 82:1-7

"In the final line we read sharim for sarim ("princes"), from which it is indistinguishable in the Hebrew manuscripts, and find another reference to the fall of Athtar, the bright Venus star in Isaiah 14:12 ff and in the myth of Baal." (John Gray, Near Eastern Mythology)

Now, having introduced the cast of characters and set the historical and theological stage, let us proceed to the "Apocalypse of Abraham."

The Apocalypse of Abraham

Chapter 1

1. I was standing guard one day over the gods of my father Terah and my brother Nahor.
2. While I was testing them to find out which god was really the strongest and I was completing the services, I, Abraham, received my chance.
3. My father Terah was sacrificing to his gods of wood, stone, gold, silver, copper, and of iron and I entered their temple for the service, and found a god named Marumath, carved from stone, which had fallen at the feet of the iron god, Nakhin.
4. At that point my heart was perplexed (troubled) and I thought that I could not put it back in its place by myself because of its weight, since it was made of large stones.
5. So, I went and told my father, and he came in with me. When we both lifted it to put it in its place, its head fell off while I was holding it by its head.
6. Then when my father saw that the head of his god Marumath had fallen.
7. He yelled at me, saying, "Abraham!"
8. And I said, "Here I am!" And he told me to bring me the axes and chisels from the house. So, I brought them to him from the house.
9. Then he cut another Marumath without a head from another stone. He then smashed the head that had fallen off Marumath. He then crushed the rest of that (broken) Marumath.

Chapter 2

1. He created five more gods and gave them to me. He ordered me to sell them outside on the road to town.
2. I saddled my father's ass and loaded the gods on it and went out on the highway to sell them.
3. The merchants from Phandana of Syria were coming with their camels, on their way to Egypt to buy kokonil from the Nile.
4. I questioned them and they answered me. I walked along with them and talked with them. Then, one of their camels screamed and the ass was frightened and fled, throwing off the gods. Three of them were broken and two remained intact.
5. Then the Syrians saw that I had gods, they said to me: "Why did you not tell us that you had gods? We would have bought them before the ass. heard the camel's cry. You would had lost nothing."
6. Then they said, "Give us the gods that remain and we will give you a suitable price."
7. I considered this and grieved. But they paid both for the smashed gods and the gods which remained. I had been worried how I would bring payment to my father.
8. I threw the three broken gods into the water of the river Gur, which was in this place. And they sank deeply into the river Gur and were not seen again.

Chapter 3

1. As I was still walking on the road, my heart was disturbed and my mind was distracted.
2. I thought, "What is this deed of inequality my father is doing?
3. Is it not he who is god because his gods come into being through his sculpting, planning, and his skill (workmanship)?
4. They ought to honor my father because the gods are his work. What reward does my father received for his works?
5. Marumath fell and could not stand up in his (own) sanctuary, and could not I lift him myself until my father came and we stood him up (together). Even then we were not able to do it and his head fell off of him.
7. Then he put another stone on it from another god, which he (my father) had made without a head. The other five gods which got smashed when they fell from the ass could not save themselves. They did not harm the ass (to avenge themselves) because it smashed them. Nor did their broken pieces come up out of the river.
8. And I thought to myself, "If this is so, how can my father's god Marumath, which has the head of one stone and is made from another stone, save a man, or hear a man's prayer, or grant him any gift?"

Chapter 4

1. Thinking this way, I came to my father's house. I watered the ass and fed the ass with hay. I took out the silver and placed it in my father Terah's hand.
2. And when he saw it, he was happy, and he said, "You are blessed, Abraham, by the god of my gods, since you have brought me the price for the gods, so that my labor was not empty (for nothing)."
3. I answered and said to him, "Listen, father Terah! In you is the blessing of your gods, because you are the god of them, since you created them because their blessing is their hell and their power is empty.
4. They did not help themselves; how then can they help you or bless me?
5. I did well for you in this transaction, because through my good sense I brought you the silver for the broken gods."
6. When he heard what I had to say he became violently angry with me, since I had spoken words harshly contrary to his gods.

Chapter 5

1. Having thought about my father's anger, I left.
2. And afterward when I had left, he called me saying, "Abraham!" I answered, "Here I am!"
3. He said, " Gather these wood chips. I was making gods from fir before you came.
4. I will use the chips to cook food when I prepared my midday meal."

5. Then, when I was picking up the wooden chips, I found a small god among them which would fit in my left hand.

6. On its forehead was written: god Barisat. Then, I put the chips on the fire in to prepare food for my father, and went out to ask him about the food, I put Barisat near the kindling for the fire.

7. I spoke to him as if to threaten him. I said, "Barisat, watch that the fire does not go out before I come back!

8. If the fire goes out, blow on it so it flares up." I went out and said nothing of this to anyone.

9. When I returned I found Barisat fallen on his back. His feet were enveloped by fire and burning fiercely.

10. When I saw it, I laughed and I said to myself, "Barisat, truly you know how to light a fire and cook food!"

11. Then, while saying this in my laughter, I saw that he had burned up slowly with fire and turned to ashes.

12. I carried the food to my father to eat.

13. I gave him wine and milk, and he drank and he enjoyed himself and he thanked and spoke praise to Marumath his god.

14. Then I said to him, "Father Terah, do not bless Marumath your god, do not praise him!

15 Instead, praise your god Barisat, because he loved you enough that he threw himself into the fire in order to cook your food."

16. Then my father said to me said, "Where is he now?" And I said, "He has burned in the flames of the fire and become dust." And he said, "Great is the power of Barisat! I will make another today, and tomorrow he will prepare my food."

Chapter 6

1. When I, Abraham, heard these words from my father, I laughed to myself and I groaned from the disgust and anger in my heart.

2. I said, "How can a piece of a body made (by Terah) help my father, Terah?

3. How can he have enslaved his body to his soul (will or desire), and allowed his soul (will or desire) to be enslaved by a spirit (not his spirit but "a" spirit), when the spirit is stupid and ignorant?"

4. And I said, "It is only proper to withstand this evil that I may compel my mind toward purity. I will lay my thoughts out before him clearly.

5. " I answered and said, "Father Terah, no matter which of these gods you praise, your thoughts err.

6. Don't you see that the gods of my brother Nahor which stand in the holy sanctuary are more worthy than yours?

7. Look! Zouchaios, my brother Nahor's god is more worthy than your god Marumath because he is made of gold, which is valued by man.

8. And if Zouchaios grows old with time, he will be remolded, whereas, if Marumath deteriorates or is broken, he will not be renewed, because he is made of stone.

9. What about Ioav, the other god who stands with Zouchaios? He is also more worthy than the god Barisat.

10. He, Ioav, is carved from wood and then forged from silver; because he too is made of something that is given with love (comparison), and is valued by man according to their outward experience.

11. But Barisat, your god, is rooted in the earth. When he was large (great) it is a wonder because he had branches and flowers and was worth praise when he was still not carved.

12. But then you shaped him with an axe and you created (him as) a god by your skill.

13. Look! He has already dried up.

14. His substance (fruit/fatness) has perished.

15. From the height he has fallen to the earth.

16. He descended from greatness to a lowly state, and his face and appearance has wasted (withered) away.

17. He was burned up by the fire and he turned into ashes and disappeared.

18. Then you say, "Let me make another and tomorrow he will prepare my food for me." He was destroyed and no power (strength) was left in him (because of or to prevent) his own destruction.

Chapter 7

1. This I say: Fire is more valuable in the formation of things because even the untamable things are subdued in (by) it, and it laughs at those things which are destroyed easily by its burning.

3. But neither is it worthy (valuable), because it is subject to the water.

4. But water is more worthy (venerable/powerful) than fire because water overcomes fire and sweetens the earth with fruit.

5. But I would not call water a god either because water is taken under the earth and water is subject to the earth.

6. I will not call earth a goddess either because it is dried by the sun and was made for man for his work.

7. I think the sun is more worthy among the gods, because with its rays it illuminates the entire universe and all the air.

8. But I will would not place the sun among the gods because there are those who obscure his course. They are the moon and the clouds.

9. I will not call the moon or the stars gods, because at times during the night they also dim their light.

10. Listen, Terah my father, I will seek the God who created all the other gods we have thought exist.

11. I seek who or what is it that made the heavens red and the sun golden and who has given light to the moon and the stars and who has dried the earth in the midst of the many waters. I will seek who it is that has

set you yourself among the things and who has sought me out in the of my thoughts of questioning.
12. God will reveal himself by himself to us!"

Chapter 8
1. Then, I was thinking about my father Terah being in the court of my house when the voice of the Mighty One came down from the heavens in a stream of fire and it called to me saying, "Abraham, Abraham!"
2. And I said, "Here I am."
3. Then he said, "You are searching in the wisdom of your heart for the God of gods, the Creator? I am he.
4. Get out from Terah, your father, and go away from the house, that you too may not be killed because of the sins of your father's house."
5. Then, as I went out and I was not outside the entrance of the court yet, the sound of a tremendous thunder came and burned him and his house and everything in his house to the ground for a space of forty cubits.

Chapter 9
1. Then a voice spoke to me twice: "Abraham, Abraham!"
2 I said, "Here I am!" And He said, "Look! It is I, fear not for I am with you because I AM before the ages, I am the Mighty God who created the first light of the world. I am your protection (shield) and your helper."
3. He continued and said, "Behold, it is I, Fear not because I am Before the World Was, I Am Mighty, the God who has created all, I am the light of the age.
4. I am your protector and your helper.
5. Go, get me a three-year-old heifer, a three-year-old female goat, a three-year-old ram, a turtledove, and a pigeon.
6. Go, take me a young heifer of three years, and a female goat of three years, and a ram of three years, a turtledove and a pigeon, and bring me a pure sacrifice.
7. In this sacrifice I will lay before (make known to) you the ages to come, and tell you what is in store, and you will see great things which you have not seen before.
8. I will tell you things kept guarded and you will see great things which you have not seen, because you desired me and searched for me, and so I called you my beloved.
9. But for forty days abstain from every kind of food cooked by fire, and from drinking because you have loved to search me out, and I have named you "my friend."
10 And also abstain from anointing yourself with oil for forty days, and then give me the sacrifice which I have commanded you, in a place which I will show you high on a mountain, and there I will reveal to you the ages which have been created and established by my word.
11. (And there I will show you the things which were made in the ages and by my word that affirmed and created, and renewed.) I will make known to you what will come to pass for them who have done evil and for those who have done righteousness (just deeds) in the generations of men."

Chapter 10
1. Then, I heard the voice telling me such things.
2. And I heard the voice of Him who spoke these words to me, and I looked around (for Him).
3. I found I could not breathe, and fear seized my spirit. My soul seemed to leave me and I fell down like a stone, like a dead man falls to the earth, and I had no strength to stand.
4. I was laying with my face down to the earth when I heard the voice of the Holy One speaking, "Go, Jaoel, and by the power of my ineffable name raise up man, that man over there and strengthen him , so that he recovers from his trembling.
5. Consecrate this man for me and strengthen him against his trembling."
6. The angel he sent to me in the likeness of a man came, and he took me by my right (hand) and set me up upon my feet and said to me, "Stand up Abraham, friend of God who loves you. Do not let your trembling seize you! For look! I have been sent to you to strengthen you and bless you in the name of God, who loves you. He is the Creator of the heaven and the Earth. Do not fear but and run to Him.
7. I am called Jaoel by Him who gives life to those who exist with me on the seventh level of heaven. It is done by the power of the goodness of the ineffable name that is dwelling in me.
8. I am the one who has been given (the authority) to restrain the threats and attacks of the Living One's Cherubim against one another, and to teach those who have Him within them, the song of the seventh hour of the night of man, according to His commandment. (I teach those who carry the song through man's night of the seventh hour.)
9. I am the one who ordered your father's house to be burned with him because he honored the dead (gods).
10. I am given authority to restrain the Leviathan (serpent/reptiles) because every attack and menace of every Leviathan (serpent/reptile) are subject to me.
11. I am he who has been given power to loosen Hades, and destroy him who watches over the dead.
12. I have been sent to bless you and your land now, for the Eternal One whom you have invoked has prepared for you. For your sake I have ventured my way upon earth.
13. Stand up, Abraham, go boldly, be very joyful and rejoice. And I (also rejoice) with you because you are venerable and I am with you! For everlasting honor has been prepared for you by the Eternal One.
14. Go, and do the sacrifices commanded. For I, and with me Michael, blesses you forever.

15. I have been commanded to be with you, and with the generations that will spring from you, Be of good cheer and go!"

Chapter 11

1.. And I stood up and saw him who had grasped me by the right hand and set me on my feet.

2. The appearance of his body was like sapphire, and the look of his appearance was like peridot, and the hair of his head was like snow.

3. A kidaris (a Scythian hat with long flaps usually worn by kings) was on his head and its look was like that of a rainbow.

4. His garments were purple and a golden staff was in his right hand.

5. And he said to me, "Abraham," And I said, "Here is your servant!"

6. He said, "Do not let my appearance frighten you. Nor should you let my speech trouble your soul.

7. Come with me, and I will be with you visibly until the sacrifice, but after the sacrifice I will be invisible forever more.

8. Be of good cheer, and come!"

Chapter 12

1. The two of us went together for forty days and nights, and I ate no bread and drank no water because my food and my drink was to see the angel who was with me, and to hear his voice.

2. We came to the Mount of God, Mount Horeb, and I said to the angel, "Singer to the Eternal One! I have no sacrifice and I do not know of a place with an altar on the mountain.

3. How can I bring a sacrifice?"

4. And he said to me, "Look around you." And when I looked around, there following us were all the required animals, the young heifer, the female goat, the ram, the turtle dove and the pigeon.

5. And the angel said to me, "Abraham!" And I said, "Here am I."

6. And he said, "Slaughter all these animals, and divide them into halves, place the one half against (across from/facing) the other, but do not divide (sever) the birds.

7. Give these to the men whom I will show you (that are) standing by you because these are the altar upon the Mountain, to offer a sacrifice to the Eternal (One).

8. But, the turtledove and the pigeon you will give to me because I will ascend on the wings of the birds to show you what is in the heavens, on the earth, in the sea, in the abyss, in the lower depths, in the garden of Eden, in its rivers, and in the fullness of the universe. And you will see its circles in all."

Chapter 13

1. I did everything commanded me by the angel, and I gave the angels who had come to us the divided animals, but the angel Jaoel took the birds.

2. Then I waited until the evening sacrifice. Then and there an unclean bird flew down upon the carcasses, and I drove it away.

3. The unclean bird spoke to me and said, "Abraham, what are you doing upon these holy heights where no man eats or drinks and there is no food for man here but these heavenly beings consume everything with fire and will burn you up?

4. Forsake the man who is with you and run away because if you ascend into the heights they will destroy (kill/make an end of) you."

5. Then, when I saw the bird speaking I said to the angel: "What is this, my lord?"

6. And he said, "This is ungodliness; this is Azazel."

7. And he said to it (the bird), "Disgrace upon you, Azazel! For Abraham's portion is in heaven, but yours is upon the earth because you have chosen this for the dwelling place of your uncleanness and you have loved it.

8. Therefore the Eternal Mighty Lord forced you to dwell upon the earth, and through you every evil spirit of lies, rage, and trials came forth for the generations of ungodly men.

9. God, the Eternal and Mighty One, has not permitted the bodies of the righteous to be (end up) in your hands so that the life of the righteous and the destruction of the unclean may be assured.

10. Listen! You have no permission to tempt the righteous at all.

11. Leave this man! You cannot deceive him, because he is the enemy of you and of those who follow you and those who love what you want.

12. Behold, the garment which is heaven was formerly yours has been set aside for him, and the mortality which was his has been given over to you."

Chapter 14

1. And the angel said to me, "Abraham!"

2. And I said, "Here I am." And the angel said to me, "Know that from now on and forever the Eternal One has chosen you.

3. Be bold! I command you to use this authority against him who reviles the truth.

4. Will I not be able to revile him who has scattered about the earth the secrets of heaven and who has taken counsel against the Mighty One?

5. Say to him, "May you stoke (be kindling in) the fires of the earth's furnace!

6. Go, Azazel, into the deserted parts of the earth.

7. Your inheritance is over those who are with you, with the stars and with the men born by the clouds, whose reward you are. They exist because of you (through your being).

8. Hate is your pious act.

9.Therefore you will destroy yourself and be gone from me!"

10. And I spoke the words that the angel taught me. But the angel said to me, "Do not answer him! For God has given him power over those who answer him."

11. And the angel spoke to me again saying, "However much he speaks to you, do not answer him so that he may not get to you easily (freely).

12. The Eternal One gave him the gravity and the will. Do not answer him."

13. I did what the angel commanded me. And whatever he said to me about the fall (descent), I did not answered him.

Chapter 15

1. As the sun was setting, I beheld smoke like that of a furnace, and the angels who had the divided portions of the sacrifice came down from the top of the smoking furnace.

2. And the angel lifted me with his right hand and set me upon the right wing of the pigeon, and he sat on the left wing of the turtle dove. Neither birds had been slaughtered.

3. He flew me to the borders of the flaming fire, and we rose on many winds to the heavens which were above the firmament (sky/ theater of stars/ the sphere where the stars are stationed).

4. In the air, we ascended to a height that I could see a strong (bright) light impossible to describe.

5. In the light of a fiercely burning fire (Gehenna?), I saw many people, male in appearance. All of them were constantly changing their appearance and form. They were running as they were being changed, and they were worshipping and crying out with a sound of words that I could not recognize.

Chapter 16

1. And I said to the angel, "Why have you now brought me here?

2. I can no longer see clearly, and I am growing weak. My spirit is leaving me?"

3. And he said, "Remain close to me and do not fear.

3. He, the One you cannot see, is coming toward us now with a tremendous voice of holiness.

4. He is the Eternal One who loves you. But you yourself cannot see (look at) Him.

5. But you may find your spirit growing faint on account of the choirs of those who cry out because I am with you to strengthen you (fight against the weakness for I am here to strengthen you)."

Chapter 17

1. While he was still speaking, the fire coming toward us surrounded us and there was a voice amidst the fire like a voice of many waters, like the sound of a violent sea. And I wanted to fall down and worship. And the angel knelt down with me and worshipped.

2. However, the surface of the high place where we were standing changed constantly, inclining, rolling high and low.

3. And the angel said, "Worship, Abraham, and sing the song which I now will teach you.

4. Never stop signing it. Sing it in continuously from beginning to end. "

5. And the song which he taught me to sing had words that were appropriate to the area of heaven (sphere) we were standing in.

6. Each area (sphere) in heaven has its own song of praise, and only those who live there know how to sign it, and those on earth cannot know it or sing it.

7. They could know it only if they were taught by the messengers of heaven. And the words of that song were of a type and meaning.

8. So I bowed down since there was no solid ground on which to prostrate myself and I recited the song which he had taught me.

9. And he said, "Recite it without ceasing." And I recited, and he himself recited the song along with me.

"Eternal, Mighty, Holy God (El), God of unlimited power, Self-originated, Incorruptible, Immaculate, Without beginning, having no mother or father, Spotless, Immortal, Self-Created, Illuminated with your own light, without mother or father, self-begotten, High, radiant, Wise, Lover Of Men, Favorable, Generous, Bountiful, Jealous Over Me, Patient (compassionate), Most Merciful, Eli (my God), Eternal, Mighty, Holy Sabbath, Most Glorious El, El, El, El, (God) Jaoel (Yahoel/Joel) (Ja El/Lord God). You are he whom my soul has loved, the Guardian, Eternal, Radiant, Shining, Made of light, Voice of thunder. You appear as lightning, All seeing, you receive the prayers of those who honor you and turn away from the prayers of those who besiege you with their provoking ways. You redeem (free) those who are in the midst of the unrighteous and those who are confused among the wicked one who inhabited world in the corruptible life. You renew the life of the righteous. Before the morning light shines, you make the light shine upon your creation from the light of your face in order to bring the day on the earth. And in your heavenly dwellings there is an inexhaustible light of another kind. It is the inexpressible splendor from the lights of your face. Accept my prayer, and let it be sweet to you, and also the sacrifice which you yourself made to yourself through me who searched for you. Receive me favorably and show to me, and teach me, and make known to your servant what you have promised me."

Chapter 18

1. While I was still reciting the song, the mouth of the fire on the surface rose high in the air.

2. And I heard a voice like a roaring sea. It was not stopped by even the plethora of fire. And as the fire

rose up very high I saw under the fire a throne of fire, and around it were many eyes watching.

3. They were the all-seeing ones and they were singing their song.

4. Under the throne were four radiant (on fire) Living Ones singing but they looked as if they were one creature but each one had four faces.

5. This is how they appeared and how they looked to me; each one had the face of a lion, a man, an ox and an eagle, and because of their four heads upon their bodies, they had sixteen faces.

6. Each one had three pairs of wings coming out of their shoulders, their sides, and their hips. With the wings from the shoulders they covered their faces. With the wings from their hips they covered their feet. The two middle wings were spread out and they flew erect as if standing up (straight forward).

7. Then, when they had ended their singing they looked at one another and threatened one another.

8. Then, when the angel who was with me saw that they were threatening each other he left me and went running to them. He turned the face of each living creature from the face which was opposite it so that they could not see each other's faces

9. And he taught them the song of peace which the Eternal One has in himself.

10. And while I stood alone and watched, I saw a chariot with wheels of fire behind the Living Ones.

11. Each wheel had eyes around it and it was full of eyes. Above the wheels was the throne which I had seen before. It was covered with fire, and the fire encircled it.

12. An indescribable fire contained a mighty fiery host, and I heard its holy voice like the voice of a man.

Chapter 19

1. And a voice came to me out of the middle of the fire, saying, "Abraham, "Abraham!" and I answered saying "Here am I!" And he said, "Look at the wide places (areas/expanses) which are under the firmament (sky/theater of stars) on which you now stand.

2. Notice that no other place (area/expanse) has yielded the one for whom you have searched or who has loved you."

3. While he was still talking, the areas opened up. Below me were the heavens and I saw a fire which was wide-spread. There was a light, which is the storehouse (vault) of life.

4. There was the dew that God will use to awaken the dead, the spirits of the righteous, those that had gone on before, and the spirits of those souls who are yet to be born. Judgment and righteousness, peace and blessing, and an innumerable host of angels, and the Living Ones, and the Power of the Invisible Glory sat above the Living Ones.

5. All of these were in the seventh firmament, on which I stood.

6. And I looked down from the high mountain on which I stood on to the sixth firmament, and there I saw a host of angels of pure spirit (incorporeal) without bodies, whose duty was to carry out the commands of the fiery angels who were upon the seventh firmament (some translations have the eighth firmament) , as I was standing suspended over them.

7. And I looked down on the sixth firmament and there were no other powers of any form, only the angels of pure spirit.

8. I was standing on its elevation. And on this firmament there was nothing in any form and no other host, but only the spiritual angels.

9. I saw a host on the seventh firmament and He commanded that the sixth firmament should be removed from my sight, and I saw there on the fifth firmament the powers of the stars which carry out the commands laid upon them, and the elements of the earth obeyed them.

Chapter 20

1. And the Eternal, Mighty One said to me, "Abraham, Abraham!" And I said, "Here I am!"

2. And He said to me, "Look at the stars which are beneath you, and number them for me, and then tell me their number."

3. And I said, "How can I? I am just a man made of the dust of the earth." And He said to me, " I will make your progeny a nation as large as the number of the stars and as powerful the power of the stars, and I will set these people a section (piece) for me as my own inheritance.

4. They will be distinct from those of Azazel. And yet I include Azazel in my house."

5. And I said, "Eternal and Mighty One. Let your servant speak before you and do not let your fury ignite (burn/rage) against your chosen (selected/elect) one.

6. "Look!, before you led me up, Azazel insulted (railed against/reproached) me. Since he is now not before you how can you establish (constitute/count) yourself with them?"

Chapter 21

1. Then He said to me, "Look beneath your feet at the firmament and understand the creation represented and foretold in this expanse, the creatures who exist in it, and the ages prepared after it."

2. And I looked beneath my feet and beneath the sixth heaven and saw the earth and its fruits, and what moved upon it and its beings that moved, and the host of its men, and the ungodliness of some of their souls and the righteous deeds of other souls. I saw the lower regions and the torment (perdition) in the abyss.

3. And I saw the sea and its islands, its monsters (Leviathan) and its fishes, and Leviathan and his lair, his realm (caves), and the world which lay above him,

and his movements and the destructions he caused the world.

4. I saw there the streams and the rivers with their waters rising, and their winding courses. And I saw there the Garden of Eden and its fruits, the source of the river that issues from it, the trees and their blossoms, and the men (ones) who did good deeds (behaved righteously/ justly). And I saw in it (the garden) their foods and their restfulness (blessedness).

5. And I saw there a tremendous multitude of men and women and children, half of them on the right side of the door (vision), and half of them on the left side of the door (vision).

Chapter 22

1. And I said, "Eternal, Mighty One! What is this vision of creation?"

2. And he said to me, "This is my will for what is in the light and it was good before my face.

3. After this I gave them a command and by my word and they came into existence.

4. Whatever I had decreed was to exist had already been decided (outlined in this) and all things created, which you see, had stood in front of me (in my sight) before it was created.

5. And I said, "Lord, Mighty and Eternal! Who are the people in this vision on this side and on that side?"

6. And He said to me, "Those who are on the left side are all those who existed (were born) before and after your day, some destined for judgment and restoration, and others for vengeance and estrangement at the end of the age.

7. Those on the right side of the vision are the people set a section (piece) for me. These are the ones I have prepared to be born of your lineage and to be called "my people." Some of these even come from Azazel.

Chapter 23

1. Now look again in the vision and see who it is that seduced Eve and what the fruit of the Tree was, and you will know what is to be, and how it will be for your progeny among the people at the end of the days of the age.

3. And all that you cannot understand I will make known to you for you are well-pleasing in my sight, and I will tell you of those things which are kept in my heart.

4. Then I looked into the vision, and my eyes looked at the side of the Garden of Eden, and I saw there a man of imposing height and he was great (powerful) in stature, incomparable in appearance.

5. He was embracing (entwined with) a woman who looked like his size and stature. They were standing under a tree of the Garden of Eden, and the fruit of this tree was like a bunch of grapes on a vine. Standing

behind the tree was one who had the appearance of a serpent (dragon) but it had the hands and feet of a man and it had wings on its shoulders.

6. There were six pairs of wings, so that there were six wings on the right shoulder and six on the left shoulder.

7. As I continued looking, I saw the man and the woman eating the fruit from the tree. And the serpent (dragon) was holding the grapes of the tree and feeding them to the two I saw embracing each other.

8. And I said, "Who are these two that embrace, and who is this between them, and what is the fruit which they are eating, Oh, Mighty, Eternal One?"

9. And He said, "This is the world of men (this is humanity). This (one) is Adam (man), and that one, who is their desire upon the earth, is Eve.

10. But he who is between them is the ungodliness of their behavior that is sending them on the way to perdition. It is Azazel."

11. And I said, "Eternal Mighty One! Why have you given the likes of him (Azazel) the power to destroy mankind (children or generations of men) and their works upon the earth?"

12. And He said to me, " I gave him power over them who want do evil and those whom I have already hated and they will even come to love him."

13. And I said. "Eternal, Mighty One! Why did you want to bring into existence an evil that men would desire in their heart since you are angered at what was chosen by those who do useless (vain/unprofitable) things in your light (counsel/presence)?"

Chapter 24

1. He said to me, "I am angered by mankind on your account, and on account of those who will be of your family to come, because as you can see in the vision, the burden of destiny is placed upon them, and I will tell you what will be, and how much will take place in the last days. Now look at everything in the vision."

2. I looked and saw the created beings that had come into existence before me.

3. And I saw Adam and Eve and the cunning adversary who was with them; the crafty Cain, who had been influenced (led) by the adversary to break the law; and I saw the murdered (slaughtered) Abel and the destruction (lawlessness/perdition) brought on him that was caused through the lawless one.

4. And I saw there fornication and those who desired it, and its defilement and their jealousness; and the fire of the corruption in the lower depths of the earth.

5. And I saw theft and those who run after it, and the means and ways of their punishment (retribution) at the judgment of the Great Court (Assize).

6. And I saw naked men with their foreheads against each other, and their disgrace, and the passions which they had for each other, and their retribution (and the shame and harm they worked against one another).

7. And I saw Desire, and in her hand was the head of every kind of lawlessness, and her scorn and contempt and waste was assigned to destruction (perdition).

Chapter 25
1. Then I saw something that looked like an idol. It was the idol of jealousy.
2. It was carved in wood like father used to make. Its body was made of glittering bronze that covered the wood.
3. And in front of it I saw a man who was worshipping the idol, and in front of him there was an altar, and upon the altar a boy was killed as a sacrifice in the presence of the idol.
4. And I said to him, "What is this idol, and what is the altar, and who are those being sacrificed, and who is the one who performs the sacrifice, and what is the beautiful temple which I see, the are and beauty of your glory like that which lies beneath Your throne?"
5. And he said, "Hear, Abraham! This temple which you have seen, the altar and the works are my idea of the priesthood performing in the name of my glory, where every prayer (request/petition) of man will enter and live, they include the praise of kings and prophets and whatever sacrifice I decree to be made for me.
6. And He said, "Abraham, listen! What you see is the Temple, it is a copy of that which is in the heavens. It is glorious in its appearance and beauty. I will give it to the sons of men to ordain a priesthood for my glorious name. In it the prayers of man will be spoken, and sacrifices offered.)
7. I have ordained this for your people, especially those who will arise out of your lineage.
8. But the idol which you saw is the image of jealousy that will be set up by some of those who will come out of your own loins in later days.
9. And the man who sacrifices in murder is he who pollutes my Temple. These are witnesses to the final judgment, and their appointment (reward) has been set from the beginning of creation."

Chapter 26
1.. And I said, "Eternal Mighty One! Why did you establish it like this, and then proclaim the knowledge (testify) of it?" And He said to me, "Listen Abraham, and understand what I am about to say to you, and answer my question. Why did your father Terah not listen to you, and why did he not cease his idolatrous (demonic worship) practices, together with his entire house?"
2. And I said, "Eternal Mighty One, certainly because he did not want to obey me because I did not follow his (ways/deeds) works."
3. And He said to me, "The will of your father is in him (up to him), and your will is in you (up to you), and likewise the counsel of my own will is within me (up

to me/in my control), and it is prepared for (has prepared) the coming days before you have any knowledge of them or can see the future with your own eyes. Now look again into the vision, and see how it will be with your children (progeny/generations)."

Chapter 27
1. And I looked and I saw the vision sway. From its left side a crowd of unbelievers (ungodly people) ran out and they captured the men, women, and children and they murdered (slaughtered like animals) most of them and others they kept as slaves. And I saw them (the killers) run towards them (the slaves) through four doors which were high with stairs and they burned the Temple with fire, and they took and broke the holy things that were in the temple.
2. And I said, " Eternal One! Behold, my progeny, whom you have accepted, are robbed by these ungodly men. Some are killed, and others they enslave. The Temple they have burned with fire, and the beautiful things in it they have robbed and destroyed. If this is to be, why have you ripped my heart like this?"
3. And he said to me, "Listen, Abraham, all that you have seen will happen because of your progeny who will continually provoke me because of the idols that you saw, and because of the human sacrifice in the vision, through their drive and desire to do evil and there schemes in the Temple. You saw it and that is how it will be."
4. And I said, "Eternal, Mighty One! Allow these works of evil brought about by ungodliness pass by, and instead show me those who fulfilled the commandments, show me the works of righteousness. I know in truth you can do this."
5. And He said to me, "The days of the righteous (will arrive) are seen symbolized by the lives of righteous rulers who will arise, and whom I have created to rule at the appointed times. But you must know that out of them will arise others who care only for their own interests. These are symbolized by those (killers) I have already shown you.

Chapter 28
1. And I answered and said, "Mighty, Eternal One, you who are holy by your power, show mercy, I pray. Since you have brought me up here to your high place and you have showed your beloved the things about which I asked, please tell me now: Will what I saw be their lot for long?"
2. And He showed me a multitude of His people and said to me, "Because of them, I will be provoked by them through the four high doorways you saw, and my retribution for their deeds will be accomplished. But in the fourth descent of one hundred years, which is the same as one hour of the age, the same is a hundred years, there will be evil (misfortune) among

the (heathen) nations, but also for one hour there will be mercy and honor (in) among those nations.

Chapter 29

1.. And I said, " Eternal One! How long are the hours of the age?" And He said, "Twelve hours have I ordained for this present ungodly age to rule among the (heathen) nations and within your progeny, and until the end of the times it will be even as you saw. And now reckon (calculate) and understand and look again into the vision.

2. And he said, "I decreed to keep twelve periods of the impious age among the heathens and among your progeny, and what you have seen will be until the end of time."

3. And I looked and saw a Man going out from the left side of the (heathen) nations.

4. And there went men and women and children out from the side of (heathen) nations like many multitudes and they worshipped Him.

6. And while I still looked, there came many from the right side, and some of these insulted Him, and some of them even struck Him, but others worshipped Him.

7. As I watched, I saw Azazel come up to Him and he kissed Him on the face and then turned and stood behind Him.

8. Then I said, "Eternal, Mighty One! Who is this Man who is insulted and beaten, who is worshipped by the nations and kissed by Azazel?"

9. And He answered and said, "Hear Me Abraham! The Man you saw insulted and beaten and yet worshipped by many, He is the Relief/Liberty/Freedom granted for (by) the nations of people who will be born from (out of) you in the last days, in the twelfth hour of the age of ungodliness.

10. But in the twelfth hour of my last (final) age of my fulfillment will I set up this Man from your tribe (generation), whom you saw issue from among my people, and all who follow will become like (imitate) this Man, and they will be called by me (and they will consider Him to be called by Me) and they will join the others, even those who desire to change within themselves.

11. Regarding those who emerge from the left side of the vision, the meaning is this; there will be many from the (heathen) nations who will set their hopes on (trust in) Him. But those whom you saw from your progeny on the right of the vision who insulted Him and struck Him, many will be offended because of Him, but some will worship Him. And He will test those of your progeny who have worshipped Him in the twelfth hour at the end in order to shorten the age of ungodliness.

12. Before the age of the righteous begins to grow, my judgment will come upon the (nations/heathen) lawless (wicked) peoples through the people of your progeny who have been separated to me.

13. And in those days I will bring upon all creatures of the earth ten plagues, through misfortune and disease and the groans of their bitter grief. And this will be brought upon the generations of men because of the provocation and the corruption of mankind, because they provoke me. And then the righteous men of your progeny will survive in the number (amount/count) which is kept secret by me, and will hasten the coming of the glory of My Name to that place prepared before for those you saw destroyed in the vision.

14. And they will live and be established by the sacrifices of righteousness in the age of the godly, and they will rejoice in me continually, and receive those who return to me in repentance because their inner torment will be great for those who have wrongfully misused (mocked) them in this world.

15. And they will see the honor bestowed on those who are mine in the day of glory. Abraham, see what you have seen and hear what you have heard, and take knowledge of all that you have come to know.

16. Go to your inheritance for behold, I am with you to the age."

Chapter 30

1. While He was still speaking to me, I found myself on the earth again, and I said, " Eternal One! I am no longer in the glory on high.

2. Still there is one matter which my soul longs to know and understand that was not revealed to me."

3. And he said to me, "I will explain to you the things you desired in your heart to know which are the ten plagues that I prepared against the heathen nations, and which have been destined to begin at the passing of the twelfth hour of the age of the earth.

4. Hear therefore what I tell you because it will come to pass. The first is the sorrow and pain of (need) sickness;

5. The second, the massive burning and destruction of many cities;

6. The third, the destruction and pestilence (sickness) of animals (cattle);

7. The fourth, hunger of the whole world and its people;

8. The fifth, among the rulers, destruction by means of earthquake and the sword;

9. The sixth, the increase of hail and snow;

10. The seventh, wild bests will be their grave (animals will kill them);

11. The eighth, hunger and pestilence will change their course of destruction (alternate with destruction);

12. The ninth, punishment (execution) by the sword and flight in distress;

13. The tenth, thunder and voices and destructive earthquake.

Chapter 31

1. And then I will sound the trumpet in the air, and I will send my ELECT ONE (chosen one), and He will have all measure of my power (He will have one measure of all my power).

2. He will summon my people (who were despised) from all nations, and I will send fire upon those who have insulted them and who have ruled over them in this age. And those who have chosen my desire and kept my commandments will rejoice with celebrations (parties) over the downfall of the men who continued to followed after the idols.

3. And I will take those who have covered me with mockery and give them over to the scorn of the coming age.

4. I have prepared them to be food for the fires of Hades, and be in perpetual flight through the air of the depths of Hades (the underworld). And they will be the contents of a worm's belly (Azazel).

5. For they joined (a marital or sexual term) one to whom they had not been given to, and they abandoned the Lord who gave them strength.

Chapter 32

1. "Hear Me, Abraham, because you will see that in the seventh generation from you will go out into a strange land and the heathen will enslave and oppress them. And they leave the land of their slavery, after they have been mistreated for an hour of the age of ungodliness, and the heathen nation whom they will serve I will judge.

2. And the Lord said this too, "Have you heard, Abraham, what I told you, what your tribe will encounter in the last days?"

3. Abraham heard and accepted the words of God in his heart.

The Didache

The Teaching of the Twelve Apostles

A Different Faith – A Different Salvation

This section contains the following content:
Didache History and Introduction
The Didache in English
The Book of James
The "Q" Source Document

History and Introduction

Didache (pronounced "dih-dah-KAY" or "didah-KEY") is the Greek word meaning "teaching" or "doctrine".

The book, "The Didache" is also called "The Teaching of the Twelve Apostles." It is a treatise, consisting of sixteen short chapters. The text dates back to the earliest time of the Christian Church and was considered by some of the Church Fathers to be almost as important as the Holy Scriptures.

The Didache reveals how the Christians of the first century operated on a day-to-day basis. It is not a gospel and it does not attempt to offer a narrative the life of Jesus. In fact, some of the theology it contains runs counter to the modern interpretation of the theology in the received gospels.

The Didache represents the first concerted effort put forth by church leaders to teach the common person of the early church how to live and worship in the way the apostles of Jesus presented to their followers. This was the way of a Jewish Christian.

The Didache describes a path by which Gentiles and pagans could be converted, initiated, and brought into the fold to become full participants in a shared Christian life. This unity of process and teaching allowed a community, which believed itself to be poised on the threshold of the end times, to fashion its daily life in order to share the passion of the awaited return of the Kingdom of God as preached by Jesus. In fact, it is the first known instruction manual for Christian converts.

There is evidence of its use specifically by Nazarene synagogues to define and standardize the most important points of the new faith. Nazarenes were Jews who converted to a sect following Jesus. They were Hellenized Jews on the Syrian border, close to Antioch.

Certainly, the Didache was used by Jewish Christians but as Paul influenced the Nazarenes (a sect of which he was thought to be a leader), his followers diverged from the theology in the Didache. The "Pauline Christians" evolved into a separate sect leaving behind the Didache.

The Didache appears to be an "evolved" document, meaning it has been edited, altered, or expanded over time as the early church grew and changed. There are style changes indicating the document was the creation of more than one person.

The section of the Didache titled, "There Are Two Ways," is the name of an older Jewish document and the first section of the Didache that was amended and used by several early Christian communities. This duality of presentation is also echoed in the Shepherd of Hermas and the Epistle of Barnabas. The middle two sections of the Didache may be a bit older than the first section.

The Didache was discovered in 1873 by Philotheos Bryennios, the Metropolitan of Nicomedia. It was contained in a small eleventh century codex of 120 pages. He published the text toward the end of 1883. The Didache has been the center of much academic interest and controversy since its discovery. Prior to this time its existence was known only through references by early writers. Scholars thought the text was lost to history.

Church fathers, including Athanasius, Rufinus, and John of Damascas, cited the book as inspired scripture and thus made us aware of the text. The Didache was also accepted into the Apostolic Constitutions Canon, which was written between 250-380 C.E. This compilation of eight books describes administrative canons for the clergy and the laity along with guides for worship. The books were supposed to be works of the apostles, but actually included the greater part of the Didascalia Apostolorum, a lost Greek treatise of 3rd century origin, along with most of the Didache, and fragments from Hippolytus and Papias. The work concludes with a collection of 85 moral and liturgical canons known as the "Apostolic Canons," a portion of which became part of canon law of the Western Church. The work is thought to be of Syrian origin. This document is also a valuable primary source on early church history and practices. It is not nearly as early a text as the Didache however.

The Didache is incorporated into a larger book which is used as part of the 81-book Ethiopic Canon. The Didache has been known in an extended Ethiopic version, called the Didascalia, which is part of the extended New Testament canon of the Ethiopian Orthodox Church. Many early church fathers including Barnabas, Irenaeus, Clement of Alexandria, and Origen either quote or reference the Didache.

The Didache has raised great controversy regarding its date and possible origin. Some scholars dated the text between approximately 49-79 AD. Although this is widely debated, it could place the Didache as one of the oldest Christian writings in history and date it before three of the Gospels, if not all the Gospels.

Even though the Didache has been changed and added to over time there is strong evidence to suggest that the earliest section of it may have been penned during the time of the Jerusalem Council, around 50 AD. This would have it playing a role in the early church's controversy surrounding salvation of the Gentiles as described in the Book of Acts (ca. 50 – 100 C.E with many saying 62-64 C.E.) chapter 15.

Acts 15
New International Version (NIV)
The Council at Jerusalem
1 Certain people came down from Judea to Antioch and were teaching the believers: "Unless you are circumcised, according to the custom taught by Moses, you cannot be saved." 2 This brought Paul and Barnabas into sharp dispute and debate with them. So Paul and Barnabas were appointed, along with some other believers, to go up to Jerusalem to see the apostles and elders about this question. 3 The church sent them on their way, and as they traveled through Phoenicia and Samaria, they told how the Gentiles had been converted. This news made all the believers very glad. 4 When they came to Jerusalem, they were welcomed by the church and the apostles and elders, to whom they reported everything God had done through them. 5 Then some of the believers who belonged to the party of the Pharisees stood up and said, "The Gentiles must be circumcised and required to keep the law of Moses." 6 The apostles and elders met to consider this question. 7 After much discussion, Peter got up and addressed them: "Brothers, you know that some time ago God made a choice among you that the Gentiles might hear from my lips the message of the gospel and believe. 8 God, who knows the heart, showed that he accepted them by giving the Holy Spirit to them, just as he did to us. 9 He did not discriminate between us and them, for he purified their hearts by faith. 10 Now then, why do you try to test God by putting on the necks of Gentiles a yoke that neither we nor our ancestors have been able to bear? 11 No! We believe it is through the grace of our Lord Jesus that we are saved, just as they are."
12 The whole assembly became silent as they listened to Barnabas and Paul telling about the signs and wonders God had done among the Gentiles through

them. 13 When they finished, James spoke up. "Brothers," he said, "listen to me. 14 Simon has described to us how God first intervened to choose a people for his name from the Gentiles. 15 The words of the prophets are in agreement with this, as it is written: 16 "'After this I will return and rebuild David's fallen tent. Its ruins I will rebuild, and I will restore it, 17 that the rest of mankind may seek the Lord, even all the Gentiles who bear my name, says the Lord, who does these things'— 18 things known from long ago. 19 "It is my judgment, therefore, that we should not make it difficult for the Gentiles who are turning to God. 20 Instead we should write to them, telling them to abstain from food polluted by idols, from sexual immorality, from the meat of strangled animals and from blood. 21 For the law of Moses has been preached in every city from the earliest times and is read in the synagogues on every Sabbath." 22 Then the apostles and elders, with the whole church, decided to choose some of their own men and send them to Antioch with Paul and Barnabas. They chose Judas (called Barsabbas) and Silas, men who were leaders among the believers. 23 With them they sent the following letter: The apostles and elders, your brothers, To the Gentile believers in Antioch, Syria and Cilicia: Greetings. 24 We have heard that some went out from us without our authorization and disturbed you, troubling your minds by what they said. 25 So we all agreed to choose some men and send them to you with our dear friends Barnabas and Paul— 26 men who have risked their lives for the name of our Lord Jesus Christ. 27 Therefore we are sending Judas and Silas to confirm by word of mouth what we are writing. 28 It seemed good to the Holy Spirit and to us not to burden you with anything beyond the following requirements: 29 You are to abstain from food sacrificed to idols, from blood, from the meat of strangled animals and from sexual immorality. You will do well to avoid these things.

Farewell. 30 So the men were sent off and went down to Antioch, where they gathered the church together and delivered the letter. 31 The people read it and were glad for its encouraging message. 32 Judas and Silas, who themselves were prophets, said much to encourage and strengthen the believers. 33 After spending some time there, they were sent off by the believers with the blessing of peace to return to those who had sent them. 34- 35 But Paul and Barnabas remained in Antioch, where they and many others taught and preached the word of the Lord.

Here, in the book of Acts, the apostles began to set a pattern that only a small list of laws needed to be kept, but the law as a whole was put aside. He question of how much Old Testament law needed to be fulfilled became a point of contention. The dispute shows up in the New testament. (The Pharisees mentioned in Act 5 were Christians.)

For the discussion within Acts to take place it must be before 64 C.E. Margherita Guarducci, who led the research leading to the rediscovery of Peter's tomb in its last stages (1963–1968), concludes Peter died on 13 October AD 64 during the festivities on the occasion of the "dies imperii" of Emperor Nero. This took place three months after the disastrous fire that destroyed Rome for which the emperor blamed the Christians. This "dies imperii" (regnal day anniversary) was an important one, exactly ten years after Nero ascended to the throne, and it was accompanied by much bloodshed.

Traditionally, Roman authorities sentenced Peter to death by crucifixion. According to the apocryphal Acts of Peter, he was crucified head down, thinking himself unworthy to die as Jesus Died. Tradition also locates his burial place where the Basilica of Saint Peter was later built, directly beneath the Basilica's high altar.

Clement of Rome, in his Letter to the Corinthians (Chapter 5), written c. 80-98, speaks of Peter's martyrdom in the following terms: "Let us take the noble examples of our own generation. Through jealousy and envy the greatest and most just pillars of the Church were persecuted, and came even unto death… Peter, through unjust envy, endured not one or two but many labors, and at last, having delivered his testimony, departed unto the place of glory due to him."

In Rome, Christians were being hunted down. Soon, in Jerusalem, Jews would be killed by the hundreds of thousands. James was killed between 62 and 69 C.E. Yet, it is my contention that Jewish Christians were targeted with greater accuracy, given the ease of recognizing them in Synagogues. Gentile Christians could hide amongst the Roman population.

To place things in perspective, here are the range of dates that encompass the writing of the earliest gospels. These are the currently accepted dates, with the earliest dates set by the more conservative religious scholars to the latest dates set by more liberal or secular scholars:

Matthew: 45 to 100 C.E.
Mark: 40 to 73 C.E.
Luke: 50 to 100 C.E.
John: 65 to 100 C.E.

Dates can be based on the events recounted in the gospels themselves. The mention of the destruction of the Jerusalem temple, which occurred in 70 C.E. could be used as a point of reference showing the text could not have been written before the event.

According to this scholarship, the gospels must have been written after the devastation because they refer to it. Conservative believers maintain the early dates demonstrate Jesus' divine powers of prophecy. They believe the Gospels were written earlier.

The Didache may have been written before Matthew, and certainly before Acts (62 – 100 C.E.). When one looks at the discussion between the apostles regarding the law and the Gentiles in Acts it appears James, the leader, either changed his mind about keeping the Laws of Moses or was faced with the mass conversion of Gentiles as a new phenomenon led by Paul. This evolution of insight was due to the fact God saved Gentiles who were not keeping the laws. It did not change the message from the Jewish leaders as to who Jesus was and what his mission was, to the Jews and now to the Gentiles. Even though the Gentiles need not keep the law, they must express their faith through a set of actions.

The placement of the Didache in history can be based on the following facts:
• When it was written churches were still being led by traveling teachers and prophets.
• In its instructions on the appointment of church leaders it mentions only two classes: bishops and deacons.
• Baptisms are still normally performed in rivers and streams.
• Prophets still preside at the Eucharist.
• The Eucharist or communion is still celebrated in conjunction with the agape or love feast.
• There is an absence of any theological dogma or discussion.

The range is wide in the speculation of the dates for the Didache, between 50 and 100 C.E.

There are clues that the author (or authors) of the Didache were close to either Jesus, or possibly the understudy of an Apostle. The author clearly shared in Jesus' opinion of the Pharisees as hypocrites (8:1). The author also had intimate knowledge of the Gospel of Matthew, or the "Q" source.
No intact copy of "Q" has ever been found. No reference to the document in early Christian writings has survived. Its existence is inferred from an analysis of the text of Matthew and Luke. Much of the content of Matthew and Luke was derived from the Gospel of Mark. But there were also many passages which appear to have come from another source document called the "Q" document.

Theologians and religious historians believe the Q's text can be reconstructed by analyzing passages that Matthew and Luke have in common. The first part of Q had to be written much earlier than the four canonical gospels of Mark, Matthew, Luke and John since there are identical passages in Mathew and Luke supplied by Q and Mark is influenced by the earliest part of Q. The earliest of the 40 or more gospels that were written and used by the early Christian movements may have traces of Q in them. These circulated before the controlling faction established what was to be orthodoxy and selected the books which were to become canon.

The Gospel of Q is different from the canonical gospels in that it does not extensively describe events in the life of Jesus. Rather, it is largely a collection of sayings -- similar to the Gospel of Thomas (see "the Gospel of Thomas by Joseph Lumpkin, published by Fifth Estate). Q does not mention the events of Jesus' virgin birth, his selection of 12 disciples, crucifixion, resurrection, or ascension to heaven. It represents those parts of Jesus' teachings that his followers remembered and recorded about 20 years after his death. Jesus is presented as a charismatic teacher, a healer, a simple man filled with the spirit of God. Jesus is also a sage, the personification of Wisdom, and the servant of God.

Through analysis of Matthew and Luke it is possible to draw out those verses that are identical, word for word, suggesting it was not an oral tradition relying on memory, but was a written source used by both Matthew and Luke.
By putting together the Didache and "Q" we have a view of the gospel and the doctrine of the young church and a glimpse into the heart of the first Christians.

The earliest Christian preaching about Jesus was not concerned abou his death and resurrection. It was only later that the early Church turned its attention to the chronology and events of the rest of the life of Jesus.

It was the resurrection that was the most important event in Christianity, especially for the earliest Christians. The resurrection was God's stamp of approval on the messiah. It was the power of God coming upon his good and faithful servant that raised him up as a sign for the people that this was indeed the real anointed one, the real Christ, the real messiah. The resurrection left no doubt.

Early Christians were hardly monolithic in their preachings and it was not until the 2nd century C.E. that the concept of the virgin birth of Jesus took hold. Critics of the virgin birth claim the concept was taken from pagan religions such as Mithaism, a mystery religion practiced in Rome between the first and fourth centuries C.E. Other critics claim the virgin birth was a counter claim to the Jewish slander of the illegitimate birth of Jesus. However, since both Matthew and Luke attest to the event it is supported by two witnesses, but this is only two of the four gospels. Such a miraculous event would likely be recorded by all.

There is speculation the Didache is a collaborative work of some council members as a proposed draft for the letter finally sent to outline under what conditions and through what teaching and by what initiation could a Gentile become a Christian (Acts 15:22-29). James would have been the main contributor as the leader. This seems to be supported by the key points made in Chapters 1-6, which elaborate on the more simplified points that were made in the final letter. Some instruction (4:8, 6:3, 8:8) also appears to overlap with events in early chapters of Acts, and there is also some terminology used during the time of Acts, such as your servant, Jesus (9:3, 9:5, 10:3), and one use of the term Christian (12:4). The letter would have gone out immediately while Acts would have been penned later.

The Didache falls into three parts. The first part (Chapters 1-6) is a moral treatise describing the Two Ways, the Way of Life and the Way of Death. The second and third parts contain instructions on baptism, the Eucharist, fasting, prayer, matters of church organization for the positions of apostles, teachers, prophets, bishops, and deacons.

It is perhaps the first text to append a doxology to the Lord's Prayer "...for thine is the power and the glory unto all ages." This doxology was picked up by the church and is now part of the Lord's Prayer for the Protestant churches. The words "the kingdom" were added later and are preserved in the document "The Apostolic Constitutions." The Textus Receptus, from which the King James Version was translated, included many references to a "didache" or teaching of the apostles, and several quotes from the didache, such as the longer version of the Lord's Prayer.
The "Our Father" is contained twice in the Bible (Matt. 6:9-13; Luke 11:2-4) with no doxology. In fact no doxology is found in the older manuscripts. The doxology is simply a prayer from the believers whose spirits were moved to close the prayer with deep reverence.

The normal practice in Judaism was for the person praying to add his own requests and doxology to a prayer that did not already have a fixed conclusion. The fact that the Lord's Prayer ends abruptly explains why early Jewish Christians may have felt the prayer

required a personal conclusion. Tertullian confirms that in his day the practice was for worshippers to append their own petitions to the Lord's Prayer.

Egypt and Syria both have claims as the place of origin for the Didache. The case for Egypt was put forward because Clement of Alexandria, an early witness, stated it was very popular in Egypt, in the fourth century. He based this on Anthanasius The Great's reference to it and the numerous Coptic and Ethiopian versions available. The case for Syria is in the text on ministry and the apostolic decree of Acts 15:23-9 describing characteristic of early Syrian Christianity. The text in chapter 6 suggests a large but rural community, like that of Syria rather than the more metropolitan Egypt. The Didache should not be confused with the "Didascalia Apostolorum", "Teaching of the Twelve Holy Apostles and Disciples of Our Savior," a 3rd century text founded upon the Didache. The Didache is the foundation of the Didascalia, which is an expanded version of the Didache. The Didascalia continues to be part of the canon of the Ethiopic Christian church called the "Broader Canon."

The Didache is the earliest Orthodox Christian writing we have that is not contained in the New Testament and likely predates most of the writings contained in the New Testament.

Because it predates so much of the New Testament, it predates the idea of Sola Scriptura, the idea that the Bible contains all knowledge needed for salvation. Not only was Sola Scriptura unknown, it would have been impossible. There was no New Testament to point to as scripture. No Scriptura - no Sola Scriptura.
The Didache is a witness to the early Church of the Apostolic Age, and is evidence that the Faith of the Orthodox Church today is much the same as that of Christians of those times.

The original is a composite text. One of the earliest copies is known as the Jerusalem manuscript. It seems to be a reliable copy and was written at the close of the first century. If it is a culmination of the evolutionary process, then the texts or ideas backing this text must have emerged earlier. This would put the date of the ideas so far back as to coincide with the period of the earliest Jewish converts to the sect of the Nazarene.

The texts have evolved over a considerable period, from its beginning as a Jewish catechetical work, which was taken up and developed by the Church into a manual of Church life and order. The text was repeatedly modified in line with changes in the practice of the people of the communities who used it. The core of chapters 1 - 6 is Jewish and pre-Christian (ca. 100 B.C.E. to 50 C.E.) but this is to be expected since early Christianity was a sect of Judaism and thus followed basic Jewish religious practices. As a whole, the text reached its present form by the end of the first century C.E.

There exists an eleventh century manuscript bearing the names "The Didache" and "The Teaching of the Twelve Apostles" ("Didache ton dodeka apostolon"). These are not the same texts, although the latter is an expansion of the first.

The Jerusalem manuscript was discovered in 1873 by Greek Orthodox Archbishop Philotheos Bryennios, Metropolitan of Nicomedia, in the library of the patriarch of Jerusalem at Constantinople. It is a clear and accurate copy made by a man called Leo, "scribe & sinner", dated to the year 1056 C.E. In 1883, Byrennios translated the manuscript, with introduction and comments. He correctly identified the Didache as the product of a Jewish Christian community.

A couple of years later, an Ethiopian version of the Didache was found and then published by Horner in 1904. Greek & Coptic fragments were discovered among the Oxyrhynchus Papyri. In 1992 the Greek version was published, followed by the Coptic version in 1924.

The text as we have it today can be divided into four evolutionary phases:

(1) The original text (ca. 50-100 C.E.) : the first century original;
(2) The composite versions of the text in view of the needs of a particular Jewish Christian community ;
(3) The oldest extant independent and complete manuscripts of such a composite version. The Jerusalem manuscript is a 1056 copy and bears two titles. The text has a composition that does not flow, as it shifts from the writing style of one person to another, but it has a unity of the composition. It is clearly the product of a joint effort, containing mid second century additions or changes;
(4) The critical text : 21th century translation and interpretation with consideration given to all known documents, such as the Jerusalem manuscripts, the Latin and Ethiopian versions, and the Greek and Coptic fragments.

Harnack argues that the completed Didache originated in a backward community in rural Egypt around 140-165 C.E., whereas Sabatier claims a mid first century redaction (or earlier), in Syria. Recently, Mack situated the text in Galilea, about 100 C.E. Others claim 50 – 100 C.E. Hence, the precise date and place of origin of the original text remains a matter of debate, although a first century original is very likely. Judging from the form of the prayers and how they follow Jewish customs, the text must have been written in the time before pagan followers and influences began to be introduced, and well before the time when Christianity began to diverge from its Jewish roots.

There is a dualistic approach to logic and teaching in the text. Even though this is seen in Old Testament books such as Proverbs the approach in the Didache is not the short, two sentence type found there but more of the dualism or binary logic taught by the Greeks. There is no reason to think that the form of the Two Ways tradition shared by Barnabas and the Didache were from Semitic Judaism. The form seems more the type that flourished in the Greek schools of Hellenistic Judaism and philosophy for decades, if not centuries. Early Christian writers later came to adopt it. Two Ways theme in the Didache is almost exclusively limited to Didache 1.1-6.2. The Two Way approach is absent from Didache 6.3-15.4. This shows evidence of additions and evolutions.

It is possible that some connection once existed between the Didache and a Two Ways tradition presented in Barnabas. Some material present in the Two Ways can also be seen in Hermas, Similitudes 9.26.3. It is difficult to say with certainty which came first, but it is likely that Barnabas borrowed freely from the approach or presentation style of the Didache.

The strong Jewish influence, emphasis on leadership, prophecy, baptism and liturgies based around the Eucharistic along with the belief in the immediate return of Jesus Christ as the foundation of spiritual and communal life all imply that it was part of the earliest stage of the development of the myth of Christ, which apparently set in very rapidly after Jesus died or departed.

If the original, or core text was written before 100 C.E. but after the destruction of the second Temple in 70 C.E. it would situate the original Didache in the period of 70-100 C.E. The text contains material pertaining to first century Jewish concepts and its "two way" morality, which point to the Qumran community and the earliest forms of "Christianity" with what we now recognize as baptism and thanksgiving. However, since we know the Qumran community was in place a century before, and was an apocalyptic sect it is no proof of date.

There is a reference to "the Name of the Father, the Son and the Holy Spirit" in the ceremony of baptism, but the place and purpose of each "member" is not defined. The formula for baptism should not be read as Trinitarian since the divinity of Jesus was not accepted by most Jews, even some Christian Jews. It is probably a later interpolation placed upon the text. Nowhere else is the "Son" invoked (except in His apocalyptic station - 16:4), and nowhere is the identity of Jesus as the "Son of God" clearly and explicitly made.

The Didache, together with the epistles, were read during worship by the sect called Judeo-Christians. It was often cited by the Church Fathers. Some of them placed it next to the New Testament. As an overview of the major points, let us look at Baptism, Fasting, and the Eucharist.

Baptism:
"But concerning baptism, thus shall ye baptize. Having first recited all these things, baptize in the name of the Father and of the Son and of the Holy Spirit in living [running] water. But if thou hast not living water, then baptize in other water; and if thou art not able in cold, then in warm. But if thou hast neither, then pour water on the head thrice in the name of the Father and of the Son and of the Holy Spirit. But before the baptism let him that baptizes and him that is baptized fast, and any others also who are able; and thou shalt order him that is baptized to fast a day or two before." - Didache, 7:1-7

The early Christian practices of Baptism via triple immersion and fasting before Baptism are still preserved in the Orthodox Church today.

Fasting:
"And let not your fastings be with the hypocrites [Jews], for they fast on the second [Monday] and the fifth [Thursday] day of the week; but do ye keep your fast on the fourth [Wednesday] and on the preparation [the sixth -- Friday] day." - Didache, 8:1-2

Eucharist:
"But let no one eat or drink of this eucharistic thanksgiving, but they that have been baptized into the name of the Lord; for concerning this also the Lord hath said: Give not that which is holy to the dogs." Didache, 9:10-12

The Didache has many similarities to other epistles written around the same time. These epistles are:

1st Epistle of Clement to the Corinthians (ca. 96) is a formal letter sent by the church of Rome to the church of Corinth as a result of trouble there that had led to the disposition of presbyters. Clement urges the Christians of Corinth (rebelling against church authority) to be submissive and obedient. Tradition attributes it to Clement, the first bishop of Rome who claimed catholic authority.

The Epistle of Barnabas (ca. 130) is a letter written to repudiate the claims of Jewish Christians who advocated adhering to the observance of the Law of Moses.

The Shepherd of Hermas (ca. 150) is an apocalyptic text written by Hermas, who is believed to be brother of Pius, the bishop of Rome. Practical matters of church purity and discipline in the second century come to the fore.

The Epistle of Polycarp to the Philippians (ca. 130) was a church leader (bishop) in Smyrna, Asia Minor. He exhorted the Philippians to holy living, good works and unmovable faith. He was interested in ministry and practical aspects of the daily life of Christians.

The Martyrdom of Polycarp is the earliest preserved story of Christian martyrs, probably from the last part of the second century. It records the trial and execution of Polycarp, who was burned at the stake.

The writings of Ignatius, who was the bishop of Antioch in Syria martyred in Rome by beasts in the beginning of the second century. On his way to Rome, he visited and then wrote to various churches, warning and exhorting them. He also wrote to Rome, and to Polycarp, bishop of Smyrna. He warned the church against heresies that threatened peace and unity. He opposed Gnosticism and Docetism. He penned letters to the Ephesians, Magnesians, Trallians, Romans, Philadelphians, Smyrnaeans and a letter to Polycarp.

In a time when Jewish Christianity was less refined and organized and followers were faced with defining the major elements of the emergent Christian faith, it was the Didache that offered the first text book of worship. Importance is given to the way of life, to prophecy, to communal gatherings, to the apocalypse, and to the soon return of Jesus.

"Jesus Christ" is only mentioned once, during the rite of broken bread (9:3-4). The sharing of eucharistic bread is not the reason for the gathering. There is no mention of the one body of Christ (1 Corinthians, 10:17). The breaking of bread is a foretaste and anticipation of the return of Christ and the perfection of self and community his return will bring, when all are united, and the "end time" brings restoration of holiness, peace, and complete harmony with God and His followers.

Christ is not mentioned during the rite of cup (9:2), neither does this title appear in the communal thanksgiving prayer, which is offered after the meal. During the eucharist (9:2-3, 10:2-3) Jesus is called "servant" (Greek "pais") of the Father and "Christ" (annointed) only once and his connection with the "broken bread" is referenced in 9:4.

The early Christian community believed the beginning of the "end time" and the coming apocalypse was heralded with the arrival and death of Jesus. It is the space of time between then and the return of Jesus that we deal with here.

In the Didache, the traditional Jewish custom of drinking wine, breaking bread and saying thanks after the meal was not made referring to Christ nor was the meal or thanksgiving looking to the relationship between bread and wine and the Body and Blood of the "Son of God". The love-meal (agape) was rooted in the eucharist but became isolated only after the ritual meal of Judaism and the eucharist were separated. At the time there were many pagan religions conducting rituals in which there was symbolic eating of the "flesh" of a sacrificial victim or "god". The ceremony was common throughout the Middle East with the mystery cults, Mithraism, Isis and Osiris, Greek mysteries and other religious festivals. The rituals proposed in the Didache are not about this pagan practice but are firmly rooted in the tradition of Jewish prayer and community. Didache 10 is suggestive of the "birkat ha-mazon", a thanksgiving prayer at the end of the Jewish supper.

There is no mention that Christ is god who came in the flesh and died on the cross for our sins. This notion became the basis for the Christian Mass later.

(It should be noted, as odd as it may seem to modern Christians, that there were those who believed that Jesus was born of a virgin but still rejected his divinity. One idea does not follow the other.)

The disagreement between Eastern and Western Christianity as to the precise moment that consecration of the host happens within the Mass (both positions being without empirical proof) caused a schism between Eastern and Western Christianity. The West believes at the mention of "the Son" there is consecration (and transubstantiation), whereas the East invokes the Holy Spirit to effect the change of the substances of the Eucharist.

There are traces of Q-material in the Didache, which indicates the Didache is independent of the seed document Matthew and Luke drew upon, which most believe was the Gospel of Mark. Mathew and Luke added the full Q material to Mark. Perhaps the Didache helps to explain the background behind the gospel texts. The Didache suggests an independence from the synoptic Gospels and so throws light on the text of these gospels. This may confirm that the sayings of Jesus were collected in a written form. These saying were later placed into a document containing over one hundred sayings of Jesus, producing "Q" and "The Gospel of Thomas." Like the Didache, the Gospel of Thomas is not a narrative gospel but a wisdom discourse.

The information within the text is presented as a wisdom book based on the sayings of Jesus, which is in the Q document, instead of the narrative gospels, which tell a story. There is a parallel between Didache 9:5 where a logia is mentioned and the Gospel of Thomas.

If we examine what became the Lord's Prayer we find it fairly intact.
"When you pray, say :
'Father, may Your Name be holy.
May Your rule take place.
Always give us our bread.
Forgive us our debts,
for we ourselves forgive everyone that is indebted to us.
And lead us away from a trying situation'."
Q1, logia 42-44.

The word "epiousios" (8:2) is usually translated as "daily". This translation is somewhat arbitrary but became ubiquitous and thus the accepted rendering. The word "epiousion" has "epi" and "ousia as its parts. Epi means, "it is present" or "it happens". "Ousia" means "substance or essence". It refers to the "bread". If "epiousion" is understood as a "spiritual" process happening with the bread, then this word can be read as, "Give us now our spiritual bread."

The early Christians believed that Christ would come back within their lifetime. Their liturgies served to remind them of the imminent return. The love feast or Eucharist was not part of His death as it is today. There was no interpretation of "bread" as the "Body of Christ", nor is there a trace of the "this is My body" - "this is My blood". The meal - the Eucharist - was a gathering and a meal as a rehearsal and reminder of what communal unity and love was to come. To experience the presence of Christ by anticipating his return is evidenced in the Didache. This is the only text we have containing liturgical information about the Q-communities, of which the Essenes belonged.

The Didache shows little to no "Pauline" Christianity. Paul would have been present but his influence had not yet been fully established. It was James, the brother of Jesus, who was the "heir apparent" after the death of Jesus. James headed the Jewish Christian movement. Although Peter may have had a high status it was James who became the head of the Christian church or ministry in Jerusalem, which was considered the holiest position at the time. James wished to continue closer to the line of Judaism but Paul wished to reach out to the Pagan Gentile population. Later, the Catholic Church would view Peter as the apostle of succession and attempt to trace the papal lineage back to him, however Paul, it seems, had the greatest influence on Christianity and much of our faith today is Christianity as interpreted by Paul.

In the Book of Acts we are told Paul and Barnabas came back to Jerusalem to speak to the Apostles. The apostles, led by James, gave them a list of things to do. It was an odd list.
Acts 15:29 You are to abstain from food sacrificed to idols, from blood, from the meat of strangled animals and from sexual immorality. You will do well to avoid these things.
 Farewell.

The major problem between Jews and the Gentile converts had to do with the Gentile's continuation to worship their idols and act according to that worship instead of the Christian way. All recommendations have a connection with pagan idol worship, of which sex acts and various forms of animal sacrifice and feast were part.

Ex 20:2-6
2 I am the LORD your God, who brought you out of Egypt, out of the land of slavery.
3 You shall have no other gods before me.
4 You shall not make for yourself an idol in the form of anything in heaven above or on the earth beneath or in the waters below.
5You shall not bow down to them or worship them; for I, the LORD your God, am a jealous God, punishing the children for the sin of the fathers to the third and fourth generation of those who hate me,
6but showing love to a thousand [generations] of those who love me and keep my commandments.

Other "suggestions" are based on the 7th commandment and the Gentile's immorality. This is because such immorality was connected to idol worship.
Ex 20:14
"You shall not commit adultery.

The list of restrictions aimed at the Gentiles addressed only the major issues so the other commandments were not discussed. The Gentiles were not given license to break the other commandments. It was simply that those other offenses were not an issue.

All recommendations were based on common practices among the Gentiles who were recently converted. Gentiles couldn't consume food and drinks of close friends and relatives who sacrificed to idols.

Gentiles did not have to be circumcised to prove that they were Christians, but they had to avoid continuing certain practices. In other words, Gentile Christians should not have to become officially like their Jewish brethren through circumcision, but they should avoid identifying themselves as pagans through practices.

In the early days of Christianity the movement was considered an offshoot sect of Judaism. Soon the main trunk of the sect began to split into three major branches, although even these main branches soon began to splinter. We will first look at the main divisions and discuss the minor differences within the subdivisions later.

The Didache captures a snapshot of Christianity before it was infiltrated with the pagan religions, which surrounded the areas of Christian concentration, Jerusalem and Rome.

One of the main influences was the religion of Mithras. Virtually all of the elements of Orthodox Christian rituals, from miter, wafer, water baptism, alter, and doxology, were adopted from the Mithras and earlier pagan mystery religions. The religion of Mithras preceded Christianity by roughly six hundred years. However, it was very active in Rome from the 1st to 4th centuries C.E.
(1) According to the Mithras myth, Mithras was born on December 25th as an offspring of the Sun. Next to the gods Ormuzd and Ahrimanes, Mithras held the highest rank among the gods of ancient Persia. He was represented as a beautiful youth and a Mediator. Reverend J. W. Lake states: "Mithras is spiritual light contending with spiritual darkness, and through his labors the kingdom of darkness shall be lit with heaven's own light; the Eternal will receive all things back into his favor, the world will be redeemed to God. The impure are to be purified, and the evil made good, through the mediation of Mithras, the reconciler of Ormuzd and Ahriman. Mithras is the Good, his name is Love. In relation to the Eternal he is the source of grace, in relation to man he is the life-giver and mediator" (Plato, Philo, and Paul, p. 15).

(2) Mithras was considered a great teacher and master. He had twelve companions and traveled with performing miracles.

(3) Mithras was called "the good shepherd, "the way, the truth and the light, redeemer, savior, Messiah." He was identified with both the lion and the lamb.

(4) The International Encyclopedia states: "Mithras seems to have owed his prominence to the belief that he was the source of life, and could also redeem the souls of the dead into the better world ... The

ceremonies included a sort of baptism to remove sins, anointing, and a sacred meal of bread and water, while a consecrated wine, believed to possess wonderful power, played a prominent part."

(5) Chambers Encyclopedia says: "The most important of his many festivals was his birthday, celebrated on the 25th of December, the day subsequently fixed -- against all evidence -- Baptism and the partaking of a mystical liquid, consisting of flour and water, to be drunk with the utterance of sacred formulas, were among the inauguration acts."

(6) Prof. Franz Cumont, of the University of Ghent, writes as follows concerning the religion of Mithras and the religion of Christ: "Followers of Mithras also held Sunday sacred, and celebrated the birth of the Sun on the 25th of December...." (The Mysteries of Mithras, pp. 190, 191).

(7) Reverend Charles Biggs stated: "The disciples of Mithra formed an organized church, with a developed hierarchy. They possessed the ideas of Mediation, Atonement, and a Savior, who is human and yet divine, and not only the idea, but a doctrine of the future life. They had a Eucharist, and a Baptism, and other curious analogies might be pointed out between their system and the church of Christ (The Christian Platonists, p. 240).

(8) In Roman catacombs a relic of Mithraic worship was preserved. It was a picture of the infant Mithras seated in the lap of his virgin mother, while on their knees before him were Persian Magi adoring him and offering gifts.

(9) He was buried in a tomb and after three days he rose again. His resurrection was celebrated every year.

(10) The Christian Father Manes, founder of the heretical sect known as Manicheans, believed that Christ and Mithras were one. His teaching, according to Mosheim, was as follows: "Christ is that glorious intelligence which the Persians called Mithras ... His residence is in the sun" (Ecclesiastical History, 3rd century, Part 2, ch. 5).

We can see from the above list that there may have been a "cross-pollination" of stories and myths between religions. We must take care not to throw out truth simply because it is mimicked in paganism. Just because a pattern occurs in another religion, it does not make the pattern in Christianity incorrect. We must simply strip off the contamination to find the original and true belief system.

Above all, to discover the unsullied core of Christianity we dare not go past the Counsel of Nicaea. The Emperor Constantine was thought to be a follower of Mithras who adopted Christianity as a matter of expediency for the purpose of uniting and controlling his subjects, the majority of whom were Christian. While forging this unity he was active in the formation of modern Christian doctrines, such as the trinity. The creed produced under his watchful eye confirms several beliefs held by the followers of Mithras, and likely held by the emperor himself.

The Nicene Creed
When the Council of Nicaea (C.E. 325) rejected the teaching of Arius, it expressed its position by adopting one of the current Eastern symbols and inserting into it some anti-Arian phrases, resulting in this creed. At the Council of Constantinople (C.E. 381) some minor changes were made, and it was reaffirmed at the Council of Chalcedon (C.E. 451). It is an essential part of the doctrine and liturgy of the Lutheran churches. Historically it has been used especially at Holy Communion on Sundays and major feasts (except when the Apostles' Creed is used as the Baptismal Creed).

We believe in one God,
the Father, the Almighty,
maker of heaven and earth,
of all that is, seen and unseen.
We believe in one Lord, Jesus Christ,
the only Son of God,
eternally begotten of the Father,
God from God, Light from Light,
true God from true God,
begotten, not made,
of one Being with the Father.
Through Him all things were made.
For us and for our salvation
He came down from heaven;
by the power of the Holy Spirit
He became incarnate from the Virgin Mary, and was made man.
For our sake He was crucified under Pontius Pilate;
He suffered death and was buried.
On the third day He rose again
in accordance with the Scriptures;
He ascended into heaven
and is seated at the right hand of the Father.
He will come again in glory to judge the living and the dead,
and His kingdom will have no end.
We believe in the Holy Spirit, the Lord, the giver of life,
who proceeds from the Father and the Son.
With the Father and the Son He is worshiped and glorified.
He has spoken through the Prophets.

We believe in one holy catholic and apostolic Church.
We acknowledge one baptism for the forgiveness of sins.
We look for the resurrection of the dead,
and the life of the world to come. Amen.

Those who stayed with the roots of the Jesus movement were mostly Jewish converts. Many were still worshipping in synagogues. The Jewish Christians viewed it as their duty to love God and neighbor, serve the community, and pray for their enemies. They accepted Jesus as the anointed servant of God and the one sent to mediate between God and man (in the way a of a priest) and teach us how to live in order to please God, but they did not accept that Jesus was God, nor did the idea of his death paying for our sin occur to them. To this group it was their faith in God and following the teachings of Jesus regarding the way one treated others and loved God that was the path to salvation. Jesus was regarded as a man, pure and righteous enough that he could communicate with God and talk to the people. Thus, he was the mediator.

Another group who combined various Greek philosophies with the new faith were Gnostics. They believed this world was evil and the body entrapped the spirit. Salvation was realizing the truth that the material world was the enemy of the spiritual world. Jesus was sent to teach the people who the real God was and that the spirit world was the most important realm.

Then there was "Pauline Christianity." This is what the church practices today. James and most of the other apostles did not subscribe to many of Paul's interpretations of Christianity. Paul had never met Jesus in the flesh and was a late-comer to the faith, although he claimed to have spent time in the desert where the ascended Jesus appeared and instructed him. Did Paul really know the intent of Jesus better than believers who grew up with him, such as his brother, who was now over the main Christian church? Paul taught that faith and faith alone brought salvation to the convert. The faith demanded was one focused on the fact that Jesus was sent by God to die in our place and thus take our place in the hands of a God who, without seeing such a faith would assign hell to those who violated the least of the Old Testament laws. Paul rejected the Old Testament laws and rituals for those who were saved. Did James and the others misunderstand exactly who and what Jesus was? Was Jesus, the prophet, without honor in his own land? Or, did Paul hijack Christianity by imposing his own interpretations of faith, grace, works, and redemption?

The spilling of blood and the sacrifice of Jesus as the payment of sin is not mentioned in the Didache. Jesus is the Messiah, the Christ, the anointed one, the servant of God, but not God in the flesh. The Holy Spirit is mentioned as the baptism is done in the name of the Father, Son, and Holy Spirit. This forces us to discern the difference between the Spirit of God and God, who is a spirit.

The Didache gives simple instruction to the initiates for their entrance into the community and their salvation:
Show love toward your neighbor and enemies.
Abstain from lusts.
Give to the needy and show compassion to others.
Do not murder, Do not commit adultery, Do not have illicit sex, Do not steal, Do not commit abortion or infanticide.
Do not be prone to anger.
Do not engage in sorcery, witchcraft, enchanting, astrology. (This refers to potions, drugs, spells, dealing with spirits of the dead or evil spirits, or attempting to foretell the future.)
Share all things with your brothers and sisters.
Do not eat food that was sacrificed to idols.
Baptize in living (running, fresh) water in the name of the Father, Son and Holy Spirit.
Fast on the 4th day of the week.
Recite the Our Father prayer three times a day.
Beware of and reject false prophets.
Elect honorable Christians to be bishops and deacons to oversee the members.
Be ready at all times for the return of Jesus, who is the servant of God and the mediator who came to teach us how to live, worship, and commune.

The Didache gives instructions on certain ceremonies. Within the ceremonies of the Eucharist and thanksgiving the place of Jesus in the early church is shown. The cup is first consecrated. Nowhere is the divinity of Jesus Christ mentioned during the Offertory or the Eucharistic prayer. Jesus is only spoken of as "Christ" over the bread, not over the cup. Communion happens before thanksgiving. Thanksgiving does not ask for the consecration of the fully prepared elements since they are no longer present, having been already consumed. Thanksgiving is fully focused on God the Father. Jesus is not mentioned as Christ, nor as Son, but only as a servant of the Father God. Jesus returns to complete the work of gathering and unifying believers in holy peace and communion with God and one another.

In the Dead Sea Scrolls found at Qumrân, we find the following interesting text:
"And when they shall gather for the common table, to eat and to drink new wine, when the common table shall be set for eating and new wine poured for drinking, let no man extend his hand over the first-fruits of bread and wine before the Priest; for it is he

who shall bless the first-fruits of bread and wine, and shall be the first to extend his hand over the bread. Thereafter, the Messiah of Israel shall extend his hand over the bread, and all the congregation of the Community shall utter a blessing, each man in the order of his dignity."
The Messianic Rule (1QSa) - translated by Vermes, 1990.

The Didache proves the early Christians believed faith and salvation can exist without the sacrifice of Jesus Christ for our sins. If he was not God he could not be totally perfect. If he was not divinely perfect he would have been an imperfect sacrifice. He was a man, though righteous. During the Eucharist, no mention is made of the sacrifice of Jesus Christ. Only the presence of Christ is needed to raise us spiritually. The idea of Jesus the Christ as the Son of God is not necessary. Jesus is a mediator who serves the Father. It is to God that all of us return and not to Christ. The title of the "Son of God" is used in the Didache when referring to deceivers and in the "Q" when Satan addresses Jesus. The title "Lord" does not justify the trinitarian identification or belief of Jesus Christ as God. This is far too early to entertain the ideas which evolved into the Nicean trinitarian doctrine. The title of "Lord" is used as one of respect. This will be explained in more depth later.
Thanksgiving is directed toward God, the Father, only. It is His Name which the Didache places in the middle. The cup and the "broken bread" refer to Jesus Christ, who is broken in the fashion of torture and murder but who unites his followers with love. His followers sense his return is imminent. He is always the mediator, never the principal subject. This idea is proven over and over again as we read the opening greetings of the Epistles (letters from one believer to another or a group). It is a greeting in the name of God the Father and the Lord Jesus.

Colossians 1
1Paul, an apostle of Jesus Christ by the will of God, and Timotheus our brother,
2To the saints and faithful brethren in Christ which are at Colosse: Grace be unto you, and peace, from God our Father and the Lord Jesus Christ.
1 Corinthians 1
1Paul called to be an apostle of Jesus Christ through the will of God, and Sosthenes our brother,
2Unto the church of God which is at Corinth, to them that are sanctified in Christ Jesus, called to be saints, with all that in every place call upon the name of Jesus Christ our Lord, both their's and our's:
3Grace be unto you, and peace, from God our Father, and from the Lord Jesus Christ.

2 Corinthians 1
1Paul, an apostle of Jesus Christ by the will of God, and Timothy our brother, unto the church of God which is at Corinth, with all the saints which are in all Achaia:
2Grace be to you and peace from God our Father, and from the Lord Jesus Christ.

1 Timothy 1
1Paul, an apostle of Jesus Christ by the commandment of God our Saviour, and Lord Jesus Christ, which is our hope;
2Unto Timothy, my own son in the faith: Grace, mercy, and peace, from God our Father and Jesus Christ our Lord.

2 Timothy 1
1Paul, an apostle of Jesus Christ by the will of God, according to the promise of life which is in Christ Jesus,
2To Timothy, my dearly beloved son: Grace, mercy, and peace, from God the Father and Christ Jesus our Lord.

James 1
1James, a servant of God and of the Lord Jesus Christ, to the twelve tribes which are scattered abroad, greeting.

Jude 1
1Jude, the servant of Jesus Christ, and brother of James, to them that are sanctified by God the Father, and preserved in Jesus Christ, and called:
2Mercy unto you, and peace, and love, be multiplied.

There does not seem to be any trinity here. He was not equal to God. With the exception of the Gospel of John (Jn. 20:28) apostles called Jesus "Lord", not "God". There is evidence that the Gospel of John was written latter (c.a.100C.E.) than the others and was influenced and changed. One may argue that the Gospel is different than the others due to hindsight and a more full revelation, or one may say the difference indicates corruption. Several books have been written arguing that John's Gospel has been changed to communicate trinity and divinity, which were not there in the original intent or wording. The Didache was written many years prior and did not yet attach divinity to Jesus.

The title of "Lord" is an antiquated term used by the translators in 1611 to render a word "kurios" from "kuros" meaning "The owner or controller of a person, a state sovereign, a title of honor such as "Sir". It has continued to indicate a higher spiritual status ever since.

The members of the community who used the Didache were Jewish Christians since they believed Jesus was the servant or anointed one sent from God. For them Jesus Christ saved them when he was anointed and sent as a "servant" of the Father, but not as God Himself. He was a mediator sent from God to teach and lead, not as the propitiation, as we now believe.

They saw no Trinity and no sacrificial Lamb of God. These first Christians saw Jesus as a servant doing the will of his master and carrying out the orders to teach, unite, mediate, and demonstrate the ideals of a godly life. Here, in the Didache, we see the beginnings and foundation of what men have built into the Christianity of today. It is the structure beneath the gilding.

Why was the teaching of the blood sacrifice of Jesus left out? Why is there no mention of his payment for the remission of our sins? Does the Didache present a salvation founded solely on works? Faith in God is accounted to the believer as righteousness through God's grace. By faith are we saved through grace. Doing the will of God as taught and exemplified by Jesus not only proves and demonstrates our faith, it completes it, fulfils it, and through discipline and the establishment of holy habits the person is changed and strengthened toward unwavering faith.

The relationship between faith and work is explained in detail throughout the Book of James.
James 2:20-24
Common English Bible (CEB)
20 Are you so slow? Do you need to be shown that faith without actions has no value at all? 21 What about Abraham, our father? Wasn't he shown to be righteous through his actions when he offered his son Isaac on the altar? 22 See, his faith was at work along with his actions. In fact, his faith was made complete by his faithful actions. 23 So the scripture was fulfilled that says, Abraham believed God, and God regarded him as righteous.[a] What is more, Abraham was called God's friend. 24 So you see that a person is shown to be righteous through faithful actions and not through faith alone.
James asked the only relevant question left.

James 2:14
New King James Version (NKJV)
Faith Without Works Is Dead
14 What does it profit, my brethren, if someone says he has faith but does not have works? Can faith save him?

And in another version it reads:

James 2:14
GOD'S WORD Translation (GW)

We Show Our Faith by What We Do
14My brothers and sisters, what good does it do if someone claims to have faith but doesn't do any good things? Can this kind of faith save him?

Does this mean that salvation is not by faith alone? One may argue that if faith without works is dead and meaningless, then it would take both. Thus, according to James there is no Sola Fida (Faith Alone). Now, Sola Scriptura cannot be, for the early Christians are saved, not having the New Testament and Gentiles having neither Old or New Testaments are saved simply by accepting and following Jesus; and Sola Fida falls to the need for works to fulfil it, leaving only Sola Gratia (by Grace alone), for only through God's grace can our faith and acts be accounted to us as righteousness. No amount of work is worth heaven, but by grace our faith blooms into works and God's grace does the rest. As Isaiah 58 says, "All our righteousness are as filthy rags." This is the way the first Christians saw salvation. Since the beginning of the Christian faith men have fought with themselves and one another to understand the position of faith and works within salvation. Martin Luther was so upset at the stance James took that he rejected the Epistle, calling it a "straw epistle", which he wanted to burn. The only two beliefs constituting the core of all mainstream forms of the faith were the resurrection and the return of Jesus.

In these ideas the Didache and the Book of James walks hand in hand to such a degree that it suggests that James himself, or one of his disciples, could have written Didache 1 – 6. So close is the parallel with the Didache that The Book of James is included in this book for the reader to compare after reading the first 6 chapters of the Didache for a fuller understanding of the Book of James.

Many scholars consider the epistle of James to be written in the late 1st or early 2nd centuries, after the death of James the Just. It is thought James may have written a prior version of the letter, which was later polished and completed by one of his disciples. James, being both the leader of the faith and one of the main contributors to the Didache, as the name "The Teaching if the Twelve" indicates, would have helped set the tone of the document. This theory is bolstered by the fact that the Book of James and the Didache are so similar is content. The other apostles, Peter, John, Andrew, James, Matthew, Simon, Thomas, Jude, Philip, James the Less, Bartholomew, and Mathias would have contributed and all would have agreed with the teachings. Paul was not a contributor but came later, taking the title, "Apostle to the Gentiles," a title of specificity, which through circumstance and "mission creep" possibly took on a broader scope in the early church than first intended.

There are parallels between James, 1 Peter, 1 Clement and The Shepherd of Hermas reflecting the political situations Christians were dealing with in the 1st or early 2nd century.

Christianity at the time was primitive and in flux. There were already several sects of Christianity either established or evolving, each having a different idea of who Jesus was. We have discussed three major divisions. Now let us look at others. In the very early days of Christianity, there appear to have been:

Ebionites, meaning "the Poor Ones". They were an early Jewish Christian sect that lived around Judea from the 1st to the 4th century. This sect of Judæo-Christians believed Jesus was the messiah but they denied his divinity and supernatural origin. They observed all the Jewish rites, such as circumcision and the seventh-day Sabbath and they used the gospel according to Matthew written in Hebrew or Aramaic, but they flatly rejected the writings of Paul as those of an apostate. Some Ebionites accepted the doctrine of the virgin birth of Jesus. Most others did not.

Nazarene means "a Branch". They were an early Jewish Christian sect similar to the Ebionite. They accepted the virgin birth and divinity of Jesus. The term Nazarene was likely the one first used for these followers of Jesus, as evidenced by Acts 24:5 where Paul is called "the ringleader of the sect of the Nazarenes." Thus, these followers were likely folded into the Pauline sect later as Paul continues to develop his Christology. It was at this time that Paul's theology diverged enough from the first Jewish Christians that they discontinued use of the Didache.

The term "Christian," first used in Greek speaking areas for the movement is a translation of the term Nazarene, and basically means a "Messianist."

The Essenes, meaning "Doers of Torah", were the sect which wrote or collected the Dead Sea Scrolls. They were considered part of the collective term called "Way," and existed over 150 years before the birth of Jesus. They baptized as a sign of repentance as entrance requirement into their fellowship.

The Essenes were an apocalyptic group, expecting three redemptive Figures—the Prophet like Moses and his two Messiahs. The sect saw themselves as the remnant of God's people preparing the Way for the return of God's Glory. They formed a tight community and referred to themselves as brother and sister.

They had their own developed interpretation of Torah, some aspects of which Jesus preached. The ideas of no divorce, not using oaths, and the apocalypse are but a few. They followed one they called the True Teacher (Teacher of Righteousness) whom most scholars believe lived in the 1st century B.C.E. but was assassinated by the authorities of the time.

Nazoreans were a first century offshoot of the Essene, according to Epiphanius. There were two branches of Essenes - the Nazoreans and the Ossaeans. Each of these two Essene branches had a monastic part. The monastic part of the northern Nazorean was known as "Children of Amen." The Nazorean B'nai-Amen were also a Monastic Order. It is thought that both Jesus and John the Baptizer were associated with the Essense and drew some of their doctrine and teachings from them. Cerinthians followed the Jewish law, denied that the Supreme God had made the physical world, and denied the divinity of Jesus. The doctrine of Cerinthus is stated by Irenaeus in the following passage Ulcer. i. 26):

" A certain Cerinthus in Asia taught that the world was not made by the Supreme God, but by a certain power entirely separate and distinct from that authority which is above the universe, and ignorant of that God who is over all things. He submitted that Jesus was not born of a virgin (for this seemed to him impossible), but was the son of Joseph and Mary, born as all other men, yet excelling all mankind in righteousness, prudence, and wisdom. And that after His baptism there had descended on Him, from that authority which is above all things, Christ in the form of a dove; and that then He had announced the unknown Father and had worked miracles; but that at the end Christ had flown back again from Jesus, and that Jesus suffered and rose again, but that Christ remained impassible, since He was a spiritual being " (as quoted by A. S. Peake).

Hippolytus adds that Cerinthus taught that the world was made by an angel, and that the Law was given to the Jews by another angel, who was the God of the Jews. These angels were far below the Supreme Being. The teaching of Cerinthus is a mixture of Judaism and Gnosticism.

Carpocratians were an early Gnostic sect founded in the first half of the second century. Carpocrates venerated Jesus, but he also believed that the philosophers Plato, Pythagoras, Aristotle and others were gods. He believed that Jesus was just another man, like any of us, upon whom an extraordinary recollection descended. Carpocrates seems to have placed no faith in anything like the Immaculate Conception, or the virgin birth, but plainly states that Jesus was the son of Joseph. Essentially, Carpocretes believed there was no way to know anything more than what seems obvious.

The first gospels had only recently been written, or were still in the process of revision, but there was a sense that the writings were sacred, however they had not yet been granted canon. The Gnostics were writing their own scriptures. Why not? If there was a gospel written by Mark or Matthew why should there not be a gospel written by Thomas or Baranbas with a Gnostic slant? The Gnostics, being closer to the event of the formation of scripture were less trusting that what the four gospels contained was the untainted word of Christ. The possibility that Jesus was human, like anyone, did not disturb Carpocrates because he saw that the wisdom of Jesus had elevated him to godliness, which was therefore a possibility for anyone who emulated him, after all, Jesus did say we could do all that he did and more.

Carpocrates did not believe that salvation could be obtained only by following Jesus, but that one had to become Jesus (that is to be elevated to a higher spiritual level and become him in spirit) in order to find salvation.

Most Gnostics believed Jesus was the son of Joseph, and was just like other men, but his soul was steadfast and pure, he perfectly remembered those things which he had witnessed within the sphere of the Unbegotten God.

They respected Peter, Paul, and the rest of the apostles, whom they consider to be on an equal spiritual level to Jesus. The Gnostics believed the souls of Peter and Paul descended from the same sphere as that of Jesus.

Some would say that Pauline Christianity, with its distinctive theology, was a separate sect. Its followers were probably absorbed into the proto-Catholic-Orthodox sect early in the second century.

The proto-Catholic-Orthodox sect is believed to have coexisted with the above sects from the earliest times. Paul represents only one sect of early Christianity, each vying for converts and attempting to articulate their theology to the exclusion of the others. The Pauline sect was certainly not the "original" one. The original sect and the trunk from which all other sects formed was a messianic Judaism, guided by James. The earliest Christian sect was the Jewish Christianity practiced by Peter, James, and Jesus' earliest followers

Scholars agree Jesus, his family, his Twelve Apostles, the Elders, and his earliest followers observed the Torah and kept the laws, ceremonies and sacrifices, whereas the main feature of Paul's message was a rejection of the Torah and the Jewish law.

Acts chapter 15 suggests two things. It suggests that those who were Jews and converted to the Christian sect continued to practice according to their Jewish roots. It also suggests that even though the apostles gave leniency to the Gentiles, there were those within their group who did not wish to extend the same permission and continued to push the point that Gentiles should become Jews in order to be on equal footing with the apostles, following the Jewish footsteps of Jesus.

Paul's sect came to dominate Christianity partly through the circumstance of politics and partly because entry into the faith was easy, since it was through faith and not following the law. History is written by the winner, so we know little about other sects in earliest Christianity.

Jewish Christians considered Jesus the saving Messiah, but insisted on continued observance of the Jewish laws about ceremony, diet, and circumcision. To some Gentiles the required consent to mutilate their penis was simply too much.

As stated before, James seemed to be the heir apparent to the original Jewish sect of Christianity. James led the Jerusalem church until the Jewish revolt of 66 CE. His commitment to the Torah is recorded by Josephus and by Acts 21:17-21.

The letter of James "to the twelve tribes of the Jewish diaspora" explains how faith produces the works and fruits. These works, which the Torah also demands has a saving function (Jas. 1:21). James mentions Jesus only twice, in incidental ways (1:1 and 2:1). However, James does define what he considers to be the sign of real faith.
Religion that is pure and genuine in the sight of God the Father will show itself by such things as visiting orphans and widows in their distress and keeping oneself uncontaminated by the world.
(James 1:27 Phiilip's translation)

Because Paul rejected the authority of the Torah, he wrote against Jewish Christians in 3 of his 7 undisputed letters. This is the main subject of Galatians, and he also warns against "dogs" who insist on circumcision in Phil. 3:2-3, and against those who take pride in their pedigree of being both "Hebrews" and "Israelites" in 2 Cor. 11:5 and 22-23. Paul rejected works as having no part in salvation, but instead insisted that only faith in Jesus could save a person's soul. This was an easier faith to enter and, until one was persecuted, it was an easier religion to live under, having fewer points by which one may be judged.

Yet, in all of this in-fighting, it was the timing of fate that may have decided the outcome of which sect would rule Christianity. The Jewish Christians fell victims to the war between Rome and the Jews and the aftermath that followed. Remembering the first sect of

Christian Jews were still Jews by practice and continued to worship at the temple, when Rome attacked and slaughtered the Jews the population of Jewish Christians was reduced as well. Gentiles were not touched unless the Roman leaders knew they were Christians, since they considered Christians a sect of Judaism and political trouble-makers. Nero began his slaughter from 64 – 68 C.E.

The Jewish Virtual Library has this to say about the war: The Jews' Great Revolt against Rome in 66 C.E. led to one of the greatest catastrophes in Jewish life and, in retrospect, might well have been a terrible mistake.

No one could argue with the Jews for wanting to throw off Roman rule. Since the Romans had first occupied Israel in 63 B.C.E.E., their rule had grown more and more onerous. From almost the beginning of the Common Era, Judea was ruled by Roman procurators, whose chief responsibility was to collect and deliver an annual tax to the empire. Whatever the procurators raised beyond the quota assigned, they could keep. Not surprisingly, they often imposed confiscatory taxes. Equally infuriating to the Judeans, Rome took over the appointment of the High Priest (a turn of events that the ancient Jews appreciated as much as modern Catholics would have appreciated Mussolini appointing the popes). As a result, the High Priests, who represented the Jews before God on their most sacred occasions, increasingly came from the ranks of Jews who collaborated with Rome.

At the beginning of the Common Era, a new group arose among the Jews: the Zealots. These anti-Roman rebels were active for more than six decades, and later instigated the Great Revolt. Their most basic belief was that all means were justified to attain political and religious liberty.

The Jews' anti-Roman feelings were seriously exacerbated during the reign of the half-crazed emperor Caligula, who in the year 39 C.E. declared himself to be a deity and ordered his statue to be set up at every temple in the Roman Empire. The Jews, alone in the empire, refused the command; they would not defile God's Temple with a statue of pagan Rome's newest deity.

Caligula threatened to destroy the Temple, so a delegation of Jews was sent to pacify him. To no avail. Caligula raged at them, "So you are the enemies of the gods, the only people who refuse to recognize my divinity." Only the emperor's sudden, violent death saved the Jews from wholesale massacre.

Caligula's action radicalized even the more moderate Jews. What assurance did they have, after all, that another Roman ruler would not arise and try to defile the Temple or destroy Judaism altogether? In addition, Caligula's sudden demise might also have been interpreted as confirming the Zealots' belief that God would fight alongside the Jews if only they would have the courage to confront Rome.

In the decades after Caligula's death, Jews found their religion subject to periodic gross indignities, Roman soldiers exposing themselves in the Temple on one occasion, and burning a Torah scroll on another.

Ultimately, the combination of financial exploitation, Rome's unbridled contempt for Judaism, and the unabashed favoritism that the Romans extended to Gentiles living in Israel brought about the revolt.

In the year 66 C.E., Florus, the last Roman procurator, stole vast quantities of silver from the Temple. The outraged Jewish masses rioted and wiped out the small Roman garrison stationed in Jerusalem. Cestius Gallus, the Roman ruler in neighboring Syria, sent in a larger force of soldiers. But the Jewish insurgents routed them as well.

This was a heartening victory that had a terrible consequence: Many Jews suddenly became convinced that they could defeat Rome, and the Zealots' ranks grew geometrically. Never again, however, did the Jews achieve so decisive a victory.

When the Romans returned, they had 60,000 heavily armed and highly professional troops. They launched their first attack against the Jewish state's most radicalized area of Galilee in the north. The Romans vanquished Galilee, and an estimated 100,000 Jews were killed or sold into slavery.

Throughout the Roman conquest of this territory, the Jewish leadership in Jerusalem did almost nothing to help their beleaguered brothers. They apparently had concluded—too late, unfortunately—that the revolt could not be won, and wanted to hold down Jewish deaths as much as possible.

The highly embittered refugees who succeeded in escaping the Galilean massacres fled to the last major Jewish stronghold—Jerusalem. There, they killed anyone in the Jewish leadership who was not as radical as they. Thus, all the more moderate Jewish leaders who headed the Jewish government at the revolt's beginning in 66 were dead by 68—and not one died at the hands of a Roman. All were killed by fellow Jews.

The scene was now set for the revolt's final catastrophe. Outside Jerusalem, Roman troops prepared to besiege the city; inside the city, the Jews were engaged in a suicidal civil war. In later generations, the rabbis hyperbolically declared that the revolt's failure, and the Temple's destruction, was due not to Roman military superiority but to causeless hatred (sinat khinam) among the Jews (Yoma 9b). While the Romans would have won the war in any case, the Jewish civil war both hastened their victory and immensely increased the casualties. One horrendous example: In expectation of a Roman siege, Jerusalem's Jews had stockpiled a supply of dry food that could have fed the city for many years. But one of the warring Zealot factions burned the entire supply, apparently hoping that destroying this "security blanket" would compel everyone to participate in the revolt. The starvation resulting from this mad act caused suffering as great as any the Romans inflicted.

We do know that some great figures of ancient Israel opposed the revolt, most notably Rabbi Yochanan ben Zakkai. Since the Zealot leaders ordered the execution of anyone advocating surrender to Rome, Rabbi Yochanan arranged for his disciples to smuggle him out of Jerusalem, disguised as a corpse. Once safe, he personally surrendered to the Roman general Vespasian, who granted him concessions that allowed Jewish communal life to continue.

During the summer of 70, the Romans breached the walls of Jerusalem, and initiated an orgy of violence and destruction. Shortly thereafter, they destroyed the Second Temple. This was the final and most devastating Roman blow against Judea.

It is estimated that as many as one million Jews died in the Great Revolt against Rome. When people today speak of the almost two-thousand-year span of Jewish homelessness and exile, they are dating it from the failure of the revolt and the destruction of the Temple. Indeed, the Great Revolt of 66-70, followed some sixty years later by the Bar Kokhba revolt, were the greatest calamities in Jewish history prior to the Holocaust. In addition to the more than one million Jews killed, these failed rebellions led to the total loss of Jewish political authority in Israel until 1948. This loss in itself exacerbated the magnitude of later Jewish catastrophes, since it precluded Israel from being used as a refuge for the large numbers of Jews fleeing persecutions elsewhere.

SOURCE: Jewish Virtual Library. Solomon Zeitlin, The Rise and Fall of the Judean State, vol. 3.

Whether by propaganda, war, or the fact that pagans and Gentiles were converting to Pauline Christianity faster than the sect led by the followers of James, the Pauline sect soon became the dominant sect. Jewish

Christianity remained influential and active for only a short time but the influence and theology is preserved in some early Christian writings that are as old as some books of the New Testament. Thet were not chosen for the New Testament canon since their theology went contrary to what became orthodoxy. 1 Clement, The Shepherd of Hermas, and The Didache are but a few of these books.

With the Jewish-Roman wars of 66 and 132 CE, the Jewish Temple was destroyed and Jewish Christians were scattered. Meanwhile Paul was having great success in his Gentile missions.

Paul's rejection of Jewish laws and ordinances, including circumcision made becoming a Christian very easy. The support and community within the group made becoming a Christian quite seductive to Gentiles, many of whom sought to become part of God's chosen people and partakers in the promises of Israel. Paul's message to the Gentiles included the followers of Jesus being grafted into the chosen people of God, they would then receive the blessings of Israel since most Jews has rejected Jesus as messiah, thus displeasing God.

By the fourth century, the Council of Nicea (backed by the weight of the Roman Empire) and the formation of the New Testament canon decided forever what Christianity was, and it was not Jewish Christianity. There was a one in three chance of the Pauline sect becoming the template of the Christianity of today. Had the Roman massacre of the Jews not happened or had Paul failed to convert enough Gentiles to his sect to outnumber those who followed James we could have a Messianic-Jewish based Christianity today. Our canon and our worship would be different, but because it would have been accepted, orthodox, and traditional, Christians would follow it as they follow the Pauline sect today. It is only by chance, or by the hand of god, that the Didache is not still in use as the main document of catechism today. The Jewish Christians, led by James, had been looking for a Messiah who was a warrior-king. Although the Old Testament told of the torture and death of the messiah the church at this time was divided as to exactly who and what Jesus was. James dismissed the weighty matter of the death of Jesus as a sacrifice for the sins of the world. James, being a devout Jew was looking at Jesus from the Jewish viewpoint of what the Messiah was supposed to be. According to Jewish scripture and belief, the true Messiah must meet the following requirements.

He must be an observant Jewish man descended from the house of King David.

He must be "The son of man" which is human as opposed to the Son of God.

He must bring peace to the world.

He must gather all Jews back into Israel. (This is usually thought to be through a war.)
He must rebuild the ancient Temple in Jerusalem.

He must convert the world and they will worship the God of Israel. This means observing the Torah and the Law.

The concept of the messiah seems to have developed in later Judaism. The Torah contains very few specific reference to him, though some Jewish scholars have pointed out that it does speak of the "End of Days," which is the time of the messiah.

The Tanakh gives several specifications as to who the messiah will be. He will be a descendent of King David (2 Samuel 7:12-13; Jeremiah 23:5), observant of Jewish law (Isaiah 11:2-5), a righteous judge (Jeremiah 33:15), and a great military leader.

Jews do not believe that the messiah will be divine. A fundamental difference between Judaism and Christianity is the Jewish conviction that God is so essentially different and more holy than humanity that he could not become a human. The messiah is a servant, a man sent by God, a person of pure spirit who can hear from God and speak to mankind. If Jesus was or is God how could he say to us we could do greater works than he did? The fact that the modern church views Jesus as God has stifled believers from performing greater miracles. After all, who could do greater works than God? But if Jesus was a servant, we could be servants of God also and do the same works if not greater. Was this not his message, that we should be like him? He could not ask this of us if he was God.

Moreover, Jews find no foundation in the scriptures for belief in the divinity of the messiah. Passages viewed by Christians as indicating a divine messiah, such as the suffering servant of Isaiah 53, are viewed by Jews as speaking of the people of Israel en masse.

Isaiah 53
New International Version (NIV)
1 Who has believed our message and to whom has the arm of the LORD been revealed?   2 He grew up before him like a tender shoot, and like a root out of dry ground. He had no beauty or majesty to attract us to him, nothing in his appearance that we should desire him. 3 He was despised and rejected by mankind, a man of suffering, and familiar with pain.   Like one from whom people hide their faces he was despised, and we held him in low esteem.

4 Surely he took up our pain and bore our suffering, yet we considered him punished by God, stricken by him, and afflicted. 5 But he was pierced for our transgressions, he was crushed for our iniquities; the punishment that brought us peace was on him, and by his wounds we are healed.   6 We all, like sheep, have gone astray, each of us has turned to our own way; and the LORD has laid on him the iniquity of us all.

7 He was oppressed and afflicted, yet he did not open his mouth; he was led like a lamb to the slaughter,
    and as a sheep before its shearers is silent, so he did not open his mouth.   8 By oppression and judgment he was taken away. Yet who of his generation protested? For he was cut off from the land of the living; for the transgression of my people he was punished. 9 He was assigned a grave with the wicked, and with the rich in his death,   though he had done no violence, nor was any deceit in his mouth.

10 Yet it was the LORD's will to crush him and cause him to suffer, and though the LORD makes his life an offering for sin,   he will see his offspring and prolong his days, and the will of the LORD will prosper in his hand.   11 After he has suffered, he will see the light of life and be satisfied; by his knowledge my righteous servant will justify many, and he will bear their iniquities.   12 Therefore I will give him a portion among the great, and he will divide the spoils with the strong,   because he poured out his life unto death, and was numbered with the transgressors.   For he bore the sin of many   and made intercession for the transgressors.

In Origen's writings, called "Contra Celsus," written in the year 248, he writes of Isaiah 53:
"Now I remember that, on one occasion, at a disputation held with certain Jews, who were reckoned wise men, I quoted these prophecies; to which my Jewish opponent replied, that these predictions bore reference to the whole people, regarded as one individual, and as being in a state of dispersion and suffering, in order that many proselytes might be gained, on account of the dispersion of the Jews among numerous heathen nations."
To the Jewish interpretation of the Torah these are the few scriptural references to the messiah.

Isaiah 2, 11, 42; 59:20 - Jeremiah 23, 30, 33; 48:47; 49:39 - Ezekiel 38:16 - Hosea 3:4-3:5 - Micah 4 - Zephaniah 3:9 - Zechariah 14:9 - Daniel 10:14.
Owing to the Jewish view of the messiah in the first century it is no wonder that the Didache does not mention the sacrifice of the messiah for the remission of sin.

It is possible the Didache reveals to us the earliest, most pure and simple form of a belief in Jesus as the Christ. There was no mention of the virgin birth, or divinity of Jesus. There is no thought of Jesus being a sacrificed for the payment of our sins. There was no rapture, or trinity. There is only a rock-solid belief in Jesus as the messiah sent as a servant of God to be the mediator between God and man. He was the one who was to hear from God and communicate to mankind a way in which we too could commune directly with God. He came to show us how to live.

The Didache is a manual written from the standpoint of the earliest Jewish messianic sect, called "Christians", for the instruction of converts on how to be Christians and how to conduct themselves in daily life. It is a magnificent view of the beliefs and rituals of the earliest form of Christianity as propagated by those who knew Jesus best; his brother and the original apostles.

The Didache, when placed with the "Q" document, will give the reader a vision of what Christianity was like and what Christians believed during the first twenty to thirty years after the death of Jesus.

The questions before us are these:
Did the original twelve apostles have the full truth, were they incorrect, or has the Christian faith been corrupted?
Did the Christian faith evolve into a fuller understanding of God with added beliefs and rituals, or was it subverted and changed into the religion and denominations we have today?
Is the Didache simply history, or is it a way back to the true practice of the faith?

The Didache (Roberts-Donaldson Translation)

The Lord's Teaching Through the Twelve Apostles to the Nations.

Chapter 1.
The Two Ways and the First Commandment. There are two ways, one of life and one of death, but a great difference between the two ways. The way of life, then, is this: First, you shall love God who made you; second, love your neighbor as yourself, and do not do to another what you would not want done to you. And of these sayings the teaching is this: Bless those who curse you, and pray for your enemies, and fast for those who persecute you. For what reward is there for loving those who love you? Do not the Gentiles do the same? But love those who hate you, and you shall not have an enemy. Abstain from fleshly and worldly lusts. If someone strikes your right cheek, turn to him the other also, and you shall be perfect. If someone impresses you for one mile, go with him two. If someone takes your cloak, give him also your coat. If someone takes from you what is yours, ask it not back, for indeed you are not able. Give to everyone who asks you, and ask it not back; for the Father wills that to all should be given of our own blessings (free gifts). Happy is he who gives according to the commandment, for he is guiltless. Woe to him who receives; for if one receives who has need, he is guiltless; but he who receives not having need shall pay the penalty, why he received and for what. And coming into confinement, he shall be examined concerning the things which he has done, and he shall not escape from there until he pays back the last penny. And also concerning this, it has been said, Let your alms sweat in your hands, until you know to whom you should give.

Chapter 2.
The Second Commandment: Grave Sin Forbidden. And the second commandment of the Teaching; You shall not commit murder, you shall not commit adultery, you shall not commit pederasty (sexual activity involving a man and a boy), you shall not commit fornication, you shall not steal, you shall not practice magic, you shall not practice witchcraft, you shall not murder a child by abortion nor kill that which is born. You shall not covet the things of your neighbor, you shall not swear, you shall not bear false witness, you shall not speak evil, you shall bear no grudge. You shall not be double-minded nor double-tongued, for to be double-tongued is a snare of death. Your speech shall not be false, nor empty, but fulfilled by deed. You shall not be covetous, nor rapacious, nor a hypocrite, nor evil disposed, nor haughty. You shall not take evil counsel against your neighbor. You shall not hate any

man; but some you shall reprove, and concerning some you shall pray, and some you shall love more than your own life.

Chapter 3.
Other Sins Forbidden. My child, flee from every evil thing, and from every likeness of it. Be not prone to anger, for anger leads to murder. Be neither jealous, nor quarrelsome, nor of hot temper, for out of all these murders are engendered. My child, be not a lustful one. for lust leads to fornication. Be neither a filthy talker, nor of lofty eye, for out of all these adulteries are engendered. My child, be not an observer of omens, since it leads to idolatry. Be neither an enchanter, nor an astrologer, nor a purifier, nor be willing to took at these things, for out of all these idolatry is engendered. My child, be not a liar, since a lie leads to theft. Be neither money-loving, nor vainglorious, for out of all these thefts are engendered. My child, be not a murmurer, since it leads the way to blasphemy. Be neither self-willed nor evil-minded, for out of all these blasphemies are engendered.
Rather, be meek, since the meek shall inherit the earth. Be long-suffering and pitiful and guileless and gentle and good and always trembling at the words which you have heard. You shall not exalt yourself, nor give over-confidence to your soul. Your soul shall not be joined with lofty ones, but with just and lowly ones shall it have its intercourse. Accept whatever happens to you as good, knowing that apart from God nothing comes to pass.

Chapter 4.
Various Precepts. My child, remember night and day him who speaks the word of God to you, and honor him as you do the Lord. For wherever the lordly rule is uttered, there is the Lord. And seek out day by day the faces of the saints, in order that you may rest upon their words. Do not long for division, but rather bring those who contend to peace. Judge righteously, and do not respect persons in reproving for transgressions. You shall not be undecided whether or not it shall be. Be not a stretcher forth of the hands to receive and a drawer of them back to give. If you have anything, through your hands you shall give ransom for your sins. Do not hesitate to give, nor complain when you give; for you shall know who is the good repayer of the hire. Do not turn away from him who is in want; rather, share all things with your brother, and do not say that they are your own. For if you are partakers in that which is immortal, how much more in things which are mortal? Do not remove your hand from your son or daughter; rather, teach them the fear of God from their youth. Do not enjoin anything in your bitterness upon your bondman or maidservant, who hope in the same God, lest ever they shall fear not God who is over both; for he comes not to call according to

the outward appearance, but to them whom the Spirit has prepared. And you bondmen shall be subject to your masters as to a type of God, in modesty and fear. You shall hate all hypocrisy and everything which is not pleasing to the Lord. Do not in any way forsake the commandments of the Lord; but keep what you have received, neither adding thereto nor taking away therefrom. In the church you shall acknowledge your transgressions, and you shall not come near for your prayer with an evil conscience. This is the way of life.

Chapter 5.
The Way of Death. And the way of death is this: First of all it is evil and accursed: murders, adultery, lust, fornication, thefts, idolatries, magic arts, witchcrafts, rape, false witness, hypocrisy, double-heartedness, deceit, haughtiness, depravity, self-will, greediness, filthy talking, jealousy, over-confidence, loftiness, boastfulness; persecutors of the good, hating truth, loving a lie, not knowing a reward for righteousness, not cleaving to good nor to righteous judgment, watching not for that which is good, but for that which is evil; from whom meekness and endurance are far, loving vanities, pursuing revenge, not pitying a poor man, not laboring for the afflicted, not knowing Him Who made them, murderers of children, destroyers of the handiwork of God, turning away from him who is in want, afflicting him who is distressed, advocates of the rich, lawless judges of the poor, utter sinners. Be delivered, children, from all these.

Chapter 6.
Against False Teachers, and Food Offered to Idols. See that no one causes you to err from this way of the Teaching, since apart from God it teaches you. For if you are able to bear the entire yoke of the Lord, you will be perfect; but if you are not able to do this, do what you are able. And concerning food, bear what you are able; but against that which is sacrificed to idols be exceedingly careful; for it is the service of dead gods.

Chapter 7.
Concerning Baptism. And concerning baptism, baptize this way: Having first said all these things, baptize into the name of the Father, and of the Son, and of the Holy Spirit, in living water. But if you have no living water, baptize into other water; and if you cannot do so in cold water, do so in warm. But if you have neither, pour out water three times upon the head into the name of Father and Son and Holy Spirit. But before the baptism let the baptizer fast, and the baptized, and whoever else can; but you shall order the baptized to fast one or two days before.
Chapter 8.
Fasting and Prayer (the Lord's Prayer). But let not your fasts be with the hypocrites, for they fast on the second

and fifth day of the week. Rather, fast on the fourth day and the Preparation (Friday). Do not pray like the hypocrites, but rather as the Lord commanded in His Gospel, like this:

Our Father who art in heaven, hallowed be Thy name. Thy kingdom come. Thy will be done on earth, as it is in heaven. Give us today our daily (needful) bread, and forgive us our debt as we also forgive our debtors. And bring us not into temptation, but deliver us from the evil one (or, evil); for Thine is the power and the glory for ever..

Pray this three times each day.

Chapter 9.

The Eucharist. Now concerning the Eucharist, give thanks this way. First, concerning the cup:

We thank thee, our Father, for the holy vine of David Thy servant, which You madest known to us through Jesus Thy Servant; to Thee be the glory for ever..

And concerning the broken bread:

We thank Thee, our Father, for the life and knowledge which You madest known to us through Jesus Thy Servant; to Thee be the glory for ever. Even as this broken bread was scattered over the hills, and was gathered together and became one, so let Thy Church be gathered together from the ends of the earth into Thy kingdom; for Thine is the glory and the power through Jesus Christ for ever..

But let no one eat or drink of your Eucharist, unless they have been baptized into the name of the Lord; for concerning this also the Lord has said, "Give not that which is holy to the dogs."

Chapter 10.

Prayer after Communion. But after you are filled, give thanks this way:

We thank Thee, holy Father, for Thy holy name which You didst cause to tabernacle in our hearts, and for the knowledge and faith and immortality, which You modest known to us through Jesus Thy Servant; to Thee be the glory for ever. Thou, Master almighty, didst create all things for Thy name's sake; You gavest food and drink to men for enjoyment, that they might give thanks to Thee; but to us You didst freely give spiritual food and drink and life eternal through Thy Servant. Before all things we thank Thee that You are mighty; to Thee be the glory forever. Remember, Lord, Thy Church, to deliver it from all evil and to make it perfect in Thy love, and gather it from the four winds, sanctified for Thy kingdom which Thou have prepared for it; for Thine is the power and the glory forever. Let grace come, and let this world pass away. Hosanna to the God (Son) of David! If anyone is holy, let him come; if anyone is not so, let him repent. Maranatha. Amen. But permit the prophets to make Thanksgiving as much as they desire.

Chapter 11.

Concerning Teachers, Apostles, and Prophets. Whosoever, therefore, comes and teaches you all these things that have been said before, receive him. But if the teacher himself turns and teaches another doctrine to the destruction of this, hear him not. But if he teaches so as to increase righteousness and the knowledge of the Lord, receive him as the Lord. But concerning the apostles and prophets, act according to the decree of the Gospel. Let every apostle who comes to you be received as the Lord. But he shall not remain more than one day; or two days, if there's a need. But if he remains three days, he is a false prophet. And when the apostle goes away, let him take nothing but bread until he lodges. If he asks for money, he is a false prophet. And every prophet who speaks in the Spirit you shall neither try nor judge; for every sin shall be forgiven, but this sin shall not be forgiven. But not everyone who speaks in the Spirit is a prophet; but only if he holds the ways of the Lord. Therefore from their ways shall the false prophet and the prophet be known. And every prophet who orders a meal in the Spirit does not eat it, unless he is indeed a false prophet. And every prophet who teaches the truth, but does not do what he teaches, is a false prophet. And every prophet, proved true, working unto the mystery of the Church in the world, yet not teaching others to do what he himself does, shall not be judged among you, for with God he has his judgment; for so did also the ancient prophets. But whoever says in the Spirit, Give me money, or something else, you shall not listen to him. But if he tells you to give for others' sake who are in need, let no one judge him.

Chapter 12.

Reception of Christians. But receive everyone who comes in the name of the Lord, and prove and know him afterward; for you shall have understanding right and left. If he who comes is a wayfarer, assist him as far as you are able; but he shall not remain with you more than two or three days, if need be. But if he wants to stay with you, and is an artisan, let him work and eat. But if he has no trade, according to your understanding, see to it that, as a Christian, he shall not live with you idle. But if he wills not to do, he is a Christ-monger. Watch that you keep away from such.

Chapter 13.

Support of Prophets. But every true prophet who wants to live among you is worthy of his support. So also a true teacher is himself worthy, as the workman, of his support. Every first-fruit, therefore, of the products of wine-press and threshing-floor, of oxen and of sheep, you shall take and give to the prophets, for they are your high priests. But if you have no prophet, give it to the poor. If you make a batch of dough, take the first-fruit and give according to the commandment. So also when you open a jar of wine or of oil, take the first-fruit and give it to the prophets; and of money (silver) and clothing and every possession, take the first-fruit, as it may seem good to you, and give according to the commandment.

Chapter 14.

Christian Assembly on the Lord's Day. But every Lord's day gather yourselves together, and break bread, and give thanksgiving after having confessed your transgressions, that your sacrifice may be pure. But let no one who is at odds with his fellow come together with you, until they be reconciled, that your sacrifice may not be profaned. For this is that which was spoken by the Lord: "In every place and time offer to me a pure sacrifice; for I am a great King, says the Lord, and my name is wonderful among the nations."

Chapter 15.

Bishops and Deacons; Christian Reproof. Appoint, therefore, for yourselves, bishops and deacons worthy of the Lord, men meek, and not lovers of money, and truthful and proved; for they also render to you the service of prophets and teachers. Therefore do not despise them, for they are your honored ones, together with the prophets and teachers. And reprove one another, not in anger, but in peace, as you have it in the Gospel. But to anyone that acts amiss against another, let no one speak, nor let him hear anything from you until he repents. But your prayers and alms and all your deeds so do, as you have it in the Gospel of our Lord.

Chapter 16.

Watchfulness; the Coming of the Lord. Watch for your life's sake. Let not your lamps be quenched, nor your loins unloosed; but be ready, for you know not the hour in which our Lord will come. But come together often, seeking the things which are befitting to your souls: for the whole time of your faith will not profit you, if you are not made perfect in the last time. For in the last days false prophets and corrupters shall be multiplied, and the sheep shall be turned into wolves, and love shall be turned into hate; for when lawlessness increases, they shall hate and persecute and betray one another, and then shall appear the world-deceiver as Son of God, and shall do signs and wonders, and the earth shall be delivered into his hands, and he shall do iniquitous things which have never yet come to pass since the beginning. Then shall the creation of men come into the fire of trial, and many shall be made to stumble and shall perish; but those who endure in their faith shall be saved from under the curse itself. And then shall appear the signs of the truth: first, the sign of an outspreading in heaven, then the sign of the sound of the trumpet. And third, the resurrection of the dead -- yet not of all, but as it is said:

"The Lord shall come and all His saints with Him." Then shall the world see the Lord coming upon the clouds of heaven.

Appendix "A"

"That epistle of James gives us much trouble, for the papists embrace it alone and leave out all the rest. Up to this point I have been accustomed just to deal with and interpret it according to the sense of the rest of Scriptures. For you will judge that none of it must be set forth contrary to manifest Holy Scripture. Accordingly, if they will not admit my interpretations, then I shall make rubble also of it. I almost feel like throwing Jimmy into the stove..." "Therefore St. James' epistle is really an epistle of straw, compared to these others, for it has nothing of the nature of the gospel about it." Martin Luther

THE GENERAL EPISTLE OF JAMES.

CHAPTER 1

JAMES, a servant of God and of the Lord Jesus Christ, to the twelve tribes which are scattered abroad, greeting.

2 My brethren, count it all joy when you fall into divers temptations;

3 Knowing this, that the trying of your faith worketh patience.

4 But let patience have her perfect work, that you may be perfect and entire, wanting nothing.

5 If any of you lack wisdom, let him ask of God, that giveth to all men liberally, and upbraideth not; and it shall be given him.

6 But let him ask in faith, nothing wavering. For he that wavereth is like a wave of the sea driven with the wind and tossed.

7 For let not that man think that he shall receive any thing of the Lord.

8 A double minded man is unstable in all his ways.

9 Let the brother of low degree rejoice in that he is exalted:

10 But the rich, in that he is made low: because as the flower of the grass he shall pass away.

11 For the sun is no sooner risen with a burning heat, but it withereth the grass, and the flower thereof falleth, and the grace of the fashion of it perisheth: so also shall the rich man fade away in his ways.

12 Blessed is the man that endureth temptation: for when he is tried, he shall receive the crown of life, which the Lord has promised to them that love him.

13 Let no man say when he is tempted, I am tempted of God: for God cannot be tempted with evil, neither tempteth he any man:

14 But every man is tempted, when he is drawn away of his own lust, and enticed.

15 Then when lust has conceived, it bringeth forth sin: and sin, when it is finished, bringeth forth death.

16 Do not err, my beloved brethren.

17 Every good gift and every perfect gift is from above, and comes down from the Father of lights, with whom is no variableness, neither shadow of turning.

18 Of his own will begat he us with the word of truth, that we should be a kind of firstfruits of his creatures.

19 Wherefore, my beloved brethren, let every man be swift to hear, slow to speak, slow to wrath:

20 For the wrath of man worketh not the righteousness of God.

21 Wherefore lay apart all filthiness and superfluity of naughtiness, and receive with meekness the engrafted word, which is able to save your souls.

22 But be you doers of the word, and not hearers only, deceiving your own selves.

23 For if any be a hearer of the word, and not a doer, he is like unto a man beholding his natural face in a glass:

24 For he beholdeth himself, and goeth his way, and straightway forgetteth what manner of man he was.

25 But whoso looketh into the perfect law of liberty, and continueth therein, he being not a forgetful hearer, but a doer of the work, this man shall be blessed in his deed.

26 If any man among you seem to be religious, and bridleth not his tongue, but deceiveth his own heart, this man's religion is vain.

27 Pure religion and undefiled before God and the Father is this, To visit the fatherless and widows in their affliction, and to keep himself unspotted from the world.

CHAPTER 2

MY brethren, have not the faith of our Lord Jesus Christ, the Lord of glory, with respect of persons.

2 For if there come unto your assembly a man with a gold ring, in goodly apparel, and there come in also a poor man in vile raiment;

3 And you have respect to him that weareth the gay clothing, and say unto him, Sit you here in a good place; and say to the poor, Stand you there, or sit here under my footstool:

4 Are you not then partial in yourselves, and are become judges of evil thoughts?

5 Hearken, my beloved brethren, Has not God chosen the poor of this world rich in faith, and heirs of the kingdom which he has promised to them that love him?

6 But you have despised the poor. Do not rich men oppress you, and draw you before the judgment seats?

7 Do not they blaspheme that worthy name by the which you are called?

8 If you fulfil the royal law according to the scripture, You shalt love your neighbour as yourself, you do well:

9 But if you have respect to persons, you commit sin, and are convinced of the law as transgressors.

10 For whosoever shall keep the whole law, and yet offend in one point, he is guilty of all.

11 For he that said, do not commit adultery, said also, do not kill. Now if you commit no adultery, yet if you kill, you are become a transgressor of the law.

12 So speak you, and so do, as they that shall be judged by the law of liberty.

13 For he shall have judgment without mercy, that has shewed no mercy; and mercy rejoiceth against judgment.

14 What doth it profit, my brethren, though a man say he has faith, and have not works? can faith save him?

15 If a brother or sister be naked, and destitute of daily food,

16 And one of you say unto them, Depart in peace, be you warmed and filled; notwithstanding you give them not those things which are needful to the body; what doth it profit?

17 Even so faith, if it has not works, is dead, being alone.

18 Yea, a man may say, You have faith, and I have works: shew me your faith without your works, and I will shew you my faith by my works.

19 You believest that there is one God; you doest well: the devils also believe, and tremble.

20 But will you know, O vain man, that faith without works is dead?

21 Was not Abraham our father justified by works, when he had offered Isaac his son upon the altar?

22 Seest you how faith created with his works, and by works was faith made perfect?

23 And the scripture was fulfilled which saith, Abraham believed God, and it was imputed unto him for righteousness: and he was called the Friend of God.

24 You see then how that by works a man is justified, and not by faith only.

25 Likewise also was not Rahab the harlot justified by works, when she had received the messengers, and had sent them out another way?

26 For as the body without the spirit is dead, so faith without works is dead also.

CHAPTER 3

MY brethren, be not many masters, knowing that we shall receive the greater condemnation.

2 For in many things we offend all. If any man offend not in word, the same is a perfect man, and able also to bridle the whole body.

3 Behold, we put bits in the horses' mouths, that they may obey us; and we turn about their whole body.

4 Behold also the ships, which though they be so great, and are driven of fierce winds, yet are they turned about with a very small helm, whithersoever the governor listeth.

5 Even so the tongue is a little member, and boasteth great things. Behold, how great a matter a little fire kindleth!

6 And the tongue is a fire, a world of iniquity: so is the tongue among our members, that it defileth the whole body, and setteth on fire the course of nature; and it is set on fire of hell.

7 For every kind of beasts, and of birds, and of serpents, and of things in the sea, is tamed, and has been tamed of mankind:

8 But the tongue can no man tame; it is an unruly evil, full of deadly poison.

9 Therewith bless we God, even the Father; and therewith curse we men, which are made after the similitude of God.

10 Out of the same mouth proceedeth blessing and cursing. My brethren, these things ought not so to be.

11 Doth a fountain send forth at the same place sweet water and bitter?

12 Can the fig tree, my brethren, bear olive berries? either a vine, figs? so can no fountain both yield salt water and fresh.

13 Who is a wise man and endued with knowledge among you? let him shew out of a good conversation his works with meekness of wisdom.

14 But if you have bitter envying and strife in your hearts, glory not, and lie not against the truth.

15 This wisdom descendeth not from above, but is earthly, sensual, devilish.

16 For where envying and strife is, there is confusion and every evil work.

17 But the wisdom that is from above is first pure, then peaceable, gentle, and easy to be intreated, full of mercy and good fruits, without partiality, and without hypocrisy.

18 And the fruit of righteousness is sown in peace of them that make peace.

CHAPTER 4

FROM whence come wars and fightings among you? come they not hence, even of your lusts that war in your members?

2 You lust, and have not: you kill, and desire to have, and cannot obtain: you fight and war, yet you have not, because you ask not.

3 You ask, and receive not, because you ask amiss, that you may consume it upon your lusts.

4 You adulterers and adulteresses, know you not that the friendship of the world is enmity with God? whosoever therefore will be a friend of the world is the enemy of God.

5 Do you think that the scripture saith in vain, The spirit that dwelleth in us lusteth to envy?

6 But he giveth more grace. Wherefore he saith, God resisteth the proud, but giveth grace unto the humble.

7 Submit yourselves therefore to God. Resist the devil, and he will flee from you.

8 Draw nigh to God, and he will draw nigh to you. Cleanse your hands, you sinners; and purify your hearts, you double minded.

9 Be afflicted, and mourn, and weep: let your laughter be turned to mourning, and your joy to heaviness.

10 Humble yourselves in the sight of the Lord, and he shall lift you up.

11 Speak not evil one of another, brethren. He that speaketh evil of his brother, and judgeth his brother, speaketh evil of the law, and judgeth the law: but if you judge the law, you are not a doer of the law, but a judge.

12 There is one lawgiver, who is able to save and to destroy: who are you that judgest another?

13 Go to now, you that say, Today or tomorrow we will go into such a city, and continue there a year, and buy and sell, and get gain:

14 Whereas you know not what shall be on the morrow. For what is your life? It is even a vapour, that appeareth for a little time, and then vanisheth away.

15 For that you ought to say, If the Lord will, we shall live, and do this, or that.

16 But now you rejoice in your boastings: all such rejoicing is evil.

17 Therefore to him that knoweth to do good, and doeth it not, to him it is sin.

CHAPTER 5

GO to now, you rich men, weep and howl for your miseries that shall come upon you.

2 Your riches are corrupted, and your garments are motheaten.

3 Your gold and silver is cankered; and the rust of them shall be a witness against you, and shall eat your flesh as it were fire. You have heaped treasure together for the last days.

4 Behold, the hire of the labourers who have reaped down your fields, which is of you kept back by fraud, crieth: and the cries of them which have reaped are entered into the ears of the Lord of sabaoth.

5 You have lived in pleasure on the earth, and been wanton; you have nourished your hearts, as in a day of slaughter.

6 You have condemned and killed the just; and he doth not resist you.

7 Be patient therefore, brethren, unto the coming of the Lord. Behold, the husbandman waiteth for the precious fruit of the earth, and has long patience for it, until he receive the early and latter rain.

8 Be you also patient; stablish your hearts: for the coming of the Lord draweth nigh.

9 Grudge not one against another, brethren, lest you be condemned: behold, the judge standeth before the door.

10 Take, my brethren, the prophets, who have spoken in the name of the Lord, for an example of suffering affliction, and of patience.

11 Behold, we count them happy which endure. You have heard of the patience of Job, and have seen the end of the Lord; that the Lord is very pitiful, and of tender mercy.

12 But above all things, my brethren, swear not, neither by heaven, neither by the earth, neither by any other oath: but let your yea be yea; and your nay, nay; lest you fall into condemnation.

13 Is any among you afflicted? let him pray. Is any merry? let him sing psalms.

14 Is any sick among you? let him call for the elders of the church; and let them pray over him, anointing him with oil in the name of the Lord:

15 And the prayer of faith shall save the sick, and the Lord shall raise him up; and if he have committed sins, they shall be forgiven him.

16 Confess your faults one to another, and pray one for another, that you may be healed. The effectual fervent prayer of a righteous man availeth much.

17 Elias was a man subject to like passions as we are, and he prayed earnestly that it might not rain: and it rained not on the earth by the space of three years and six months.

18 And he prayed again, and the heaven gave rain, and the earth brought forth her fruit.

19 Brethren, if any of you do err from the truth, and one convert him;

20 Let him know, that he which converteth the sinner from the error of his way shall save a soul from death, and shall hide a multitude of sins.

The "Q" Source Based on Luke

"Q" is an abbreviation for Quelle, the German word for "source." The prevailing theory in the study of the gospels of Matthew, Mark and Luke is that Mark was the first gospel, Matthew and Luke are rewritten versions of Mark. But there are very many sayings in Matthew and in Luke that are NOT in Mark.

These, it is thought, came from a common written source (or Quelle) that is now known as "Q". Often Q sayings are word-for-word the same in Greek in both Matthew and Luke and often are in the same order. This means to most scholars that Q was a written text (no longer in existence) and not simply oral tradition. Many Q sayings are also to be found in the Gospel of Thomas. Thomas is NOT Q but Thomas is a list of sayings, like "Q", which in many ways runs parallel to the sayings of "Q".

3:7-9 [John the Baptist] said to the multitudes that came out to be baptized by him, "You brood of vipers! Who warned you to flee from the wrath to come? Bear fruits that befit repentance, and do not begin to say to yourselves, we have Abraham as our father'; for I tell you, God is able from these stones to raise up children to Abraham. Even now the axe is laid to the root of the trees; every tree therefore that does not bear good fruit is cut down and thrown into the fire."
3:16-17 John answered them all, "I baptize you with water; but he who is mightier than I is coming, the thong of whose sandals I am not worthy to untie; he will baptize you with the Holy Spirit and with fire. His winnowing fork is in his hand, to clear his threshing floor, and to gather the wheat into his granary, but the chaff he will burn with unquenchable fire."

4:1-13 Jesus, full of the Holy spirit, returned from the Jordan and was led by the Spirit for forty days in the wilderness, tempted by the devil. He ate nothing in those days; and when they were ended, he was hungry. The devil said to him, "If you are the Son of God, command this stone to become bread." Jesus answered him, "It is written, 'Man shall not live by bread alone." The devil took him up, and showed him all the kingdoms of the world in a moment of time, and said to him, "To you I will give all this authority and their glory; for it has been delivered to me, and I give it to whom I will, if you, then, will worship me, it shall all be yours." And Jesus answered him, 'It is written, 'you shall worship the Lord your God, and him only shall you serve.'" He took him to Jerusalem and set him on the pinnacle of the temple and said to him 'If you are the Son of God throw yourself down from here; for it is written, 'He will give his angels charge of you, to guard you, and on their hands they will bear you up, lest you strike your foot against a stone.' " Jesus answered him, "It is said, 'you shall not tempt the Lord your God.' "And when the devil had ended every temptation, he departed from him until an opportune time.

6:20b-21 Blessed are you poor, for yours is the kingdom of God. Blessed are you that hunger now, for you shall be satisfied. Blessed are you that weep now, for you shall laugh.
6:22-23 Blessed are you when men hate you, and when they exclude you and revile you, and cast out your name as evil, on account of the Son of man! Rejoice in that day, and leap for joy, for behold, your reward is great in heaven; for so their fathers did to the prophets.
6:27-28 But I say to you that hear, Love your enemies, do good to those who hate you, bless those who curse you, pray for those who abuse you.
6:29 To him who strikes you on the cheek, offer the other also; and from him who takes away your cloak do not withhold your coat as well.
6:30 Give to every one who begs from you; and of him who takes away your goods do not ask them again.
6:31 As you wish that men would do to you, do so to them.
6:32-35 If you love those who love you, what credit is that to you? For even sinners love those who love them. If you do good to those who do good to you, what credit is that to you? For even sinners do the same. If you lend to those from whom you hope to receive what credit is that to you? Even sinners lend to sinners, to receive as much again. But love your enemies, and do good, and lend, expecting nothing in return; and your reward will be great, and you will be sons of the Most High; for he is kind to the ungrateful and the selfish.
6:36 Be merciful, even as your Father is merciful.
6:37-38 Judge not, and you will not be judged; condemn not, and you will not be condemned; forgive, and you will be forgiven; and give and it will be given to you; good measure, pressed down, shaken together, running over, will be put into your lap. For the measure you give will be the measure you get back."
6:39 Can a blind man lead a blind man? Will they not both fall into a pit?
6:40 A disciple is not above his teacher, but every one when he is fully taught will be like his teacher.
6:41-42 Why do you see the speck that is in your brother's eye, but do not notice the log that is in your own eye? Or how can you say to your brother, 'Brother, let me take out the speck that is in your eye,' when you yourself do not see the log that is in your own eye? You hypocrite, first take the log out of your own eye, and then you will see clearly to take out the speck that is in your brother's eye.
6:43-44 For no good tree bears bad fruit, nor again does a bad tree bear good fruit; 44 for each tree is known by

its own fruit, For figs are not gathered from thorns, nor are grapes picked from a bramble bush.

6:45 The good man out of the good treasure of his heart produces good, and the evil man out of his evil treasure produces evil; for out of the abundance of the heart his mouth speaks.

6:46 Why do you call me 'Lord, Lord,' and not do what I tell you?

6:47-49 Every one who comes to me and hears my words and does them, I will show you what he is like: he is like a man building a house, who dug deep, and built the foundation upon rock; and when a flood arose, the stream broke against that house, and could not shake it, because it had been well built. But he who hears and does not do them is like a man who built a house on the ground without a foundation, against which the stream broke, and immediately it fell, and the ruin of that house was great.

7:1-10 A centurion had a slave who was dear to him who was sick and at the point of death. When he heard of Jesus he sent to him elders of the Jews, asking him to come and heal his slave. When they came to Jesus they besought him earnestly, saying, "He is worthy to have you do this for him, for he loves our nation, and he built us our synagogue." Jesus went with them. When he was not far from the house, the centurion sent friends to him, saying to him, Lord do not trouble yourself, for I am not worthy to have you come under my roof; therefore I did not presume to come to you. But say the word, and let my servant be healed. For I am a man set under authority, with soldiers under me: and I say to one, 'Go,' and he goes; and to another, 'come,' and he comes; and to my slave, 'Do this,' and he does it," when Jesus heard this he marveled at him, and turned and said to the multitude that followed him, 'I tell you, not even in Israel have I found such faith." When those who had been sent returned to the house, they found the slave well.

7:18-23 The disciples of John told him all these things. John calling to him two of his disciples, sent them to the Lord, saying, 'Are you he who is to come, or shall we look or another?" When the men had come to him, they said, John the Baptist has sent us to you, saying, Are you he who is to come or shall we look for another?' In that hour he cured many of diseases and plagues and evil spirits, and on many that were blind he bestowed sight. He answered them, "Go and tell John what you have seen and heard; the blind receive their sight, the lame walk, lepers are cleansed, and the deaf hear, the dead are raised up, the poor have good news preached to them, and blessed is he who takes no offense at me."

7:24-26 When the messengers of John had gone, he began to speak to the crowds concerning John: What did you go out into the wilderness to behold? A reed shaken by the wind? What then did you go out to see?

A man clothed in soft raiment? Behold, those who are gorgeously appareled and live in luxury are in kings' courts. What then did you go out to see? A prophet? Yes, I tell you, and more than a prophet.

7:27 This is he of whom it is written, Behold, I send my messenger before thy face, who shall prepare thy way before thee.

7:28 I tell you, among those born of women none is greater than John; yet he who is least in the kingdom of God is greater than he.

7:31-34 To what shall I compare the men of this generation, and what are they like? They are like children sitting in the market place and calling to one another, We piped to you, and you did not dance; we wailed, and you did not weep. John the Baptist has come eating no bread and drinking no wine; and you say, He has a demon.' The Son of man has come eating and drinking; and you say, Behold, a glutton and a drunkard, a friend of tax collectors and sinners!'

7:35 Wisdom is justified by all her children."

9:57-58 Foxes have holes, and birds of the air have nests; but the son of man has nowhere to lay his head.

9:59-60 To another he said, Follow me." But he said, "Lord, let me first go and bury my father." But he said to him, leave the dead to bury their own dead; but as for you, go and proclaim the kingdom of God."

10:2 He said to them, The harvest is plentiful, but the laborers are few; pray therefore the Lord of the harvest to send out laborers into his harvest.

10:3 Go your way; behold, I send you out as lambs in the midst of wolves. Carry no purse, no bag, no sandals; salute no one on the road. Whatever house you enter, first say, 'Peace be to this house!' And if a son of peace is there, your peace shall rest upon him; but if not, it shall return to you.

10:7 Remain in the same house, eating and drinking what they provide, for the laborer deserves his wages. Do not go from house to house.

10:8-9 Whenever you enter a town and they receive you, eat what is set before you; heal the sick in it and say to them, 'The kingdom of God has come near to you.

10:10-11 Whenever you enter a town and they do not receive you, go into its streets and say: 'Even the dust of your town that clings to our feet, we wipe off against you; nevertheless know this, that the kingdom of God has come near.'

10:12 I tell you, it shall be more tolerable on that day for Sodom than for that town.

10:13-15 Woe to you, Chorazin! woe to you, Bethsaida! for if the mighty works done in you had been done in Tyre and Sidon, they would have repented long ago, sitting in sackcloth and ashes. But it shall be more tolerable in the judgement for Tyre and Sidon than for you. And you, Capernaum, will you be exalted to heaven? You shall be brought down to Hades.

10:16 He who hears you hears me, and he who rejects you rejects me, and he who rejects me rejects him who sent me.

10:21-22 He rejoiced in the Holy Spirit and said, 'I thank thee, Father, Lord of heaven and earth, that thou hast hidden these things from the wise and understanding and revealed them to babes; yea, Father, for such was thy gracious will. All things have been delivered to me by my Father; and no one knows who the Son is except the Father, or who the Father is except the Son and anyone to whom the Son chooses to reveal him.'

10:23-24 Blessed are the eyes which see what you see! For I tell you that many prophets and kings desired to see what you see, and did not see it, and to hear what you hear, and did not hear it.

11:2-4 When you pray, say, 'Father, hallowed be thy name, Thy kingdom come. Give us each day our daily bread; and forgive us our sins, for we ourselves forgive every one who is indebted to us; and lead us not into temptation.'

11:9-10 Ask, and it will be given you; seek, and you will find; knock, and it will be opened to you. Everyone who asks receives, and he who seeks finds, and to him who knocks it will be opened.

11:11-13 What father among you, if his son asks for a fish, will instead of a fish give him a serpent; 12 or if he asks for an egg, will give him a scorpion? If you then, who are evil, know how to give good gifts to your children, how much more will the heavenly Father give the Holy Spirit to those who ask him!

11:14-15 He was casting out a demon that was dumb; when the demon had gone out, the dumb man spoke, and the people marveled. But some of them said, "He casts out demons by Beelzebub, the prince of demons"

11:17-18 "Every kingdom divided against itself is laid waste, and house falls upon house. If Satan also is divided against himself, how can his kingdom stand?

11:19 For you say that I cast out demons by Beelzebub. If I cast out demons by Beelzebub, by whom do your sons cast them out? Therefore they shall be your judges.

11:20 If it is by the finger of God that I cast out demons, then the kingdom of God has come upon you.

11:21-22 When a strong man, fully armed, guards his own palace, his good are in peace; but when one stronger than he assails him and overcomes him, he takes away his armor in which he trusted and divides his spoil.

11:23 He who is not with me is against me, and he who does not gather with me scatters.

11:24-26 When the unclean spirit has gone out of a man, he passes through waterless places seeking rest; and finding none he says, I will return to my house from which I came.' When he comes he finds it swept and put in order. Then he goes and brings seven spirits more evil than himself, and they enter and dwell there; and the last state of that man becomes worse than the first.

11:29 This generation is an evil generation; it seeks a sign, but no sign shall be given to it except the sign of Jonah.

11:30 As Jonah became a sign to the men of Nineveh, so will the Son of man be to this generation.

11:31-32 The queen of the South will arise at the judgment with the men of this generation and condemn them; for she came from the ends of the earth to hear the wisdom of Solomon, and behold, something greater than Solomon is here. The men of Nineveh will arise at the judgment with this generation and condemn it; for they repented at the preaching of Jonah, and behold, something greater than Jonah is here.

11:33 No one after lighting a lamp puts it in a cellar or under a bush, but on a stand, that those who enter may see the light.

11:34-36 Your eye is the lamp of your body; when your eye is sound, your whole body is full of light; but when it is not sound, your body is full of darkness. Therefore be careful lest the light in you be darkness. If then your whole body is full of light, having no part dark, it will be wholly bright, as when a lamp with its rays gives you light.

11:39-41 You Pharisees cleanse the outside of the cup and of the dish, but inside you are full of extortion and wickedness. to You fools! Did not he who made the outside make the inside also? But give for alms those things which are within and behold, everything is clean for you.

11:42 Woe to you Pharisees! for you tithe mint and rue and every herb, and neglect justice and the love of God; these you ought to have done, without neglecting the others.

11:43 Woe to you Pharisees! for you love the best seat in the synagogues and salutations in the Market places.

11:44 Woe to you! for you are like graves which are not seen, and men walk over them without knowing it."

11:46 Woe to you lawyers also! for you load men with burdens hard to bear, and you yourselves do not touch the burdens with one of your fingers.

11:47-48 Woe to you for you build the tombs of the prophets whom your fathers killed. So you are witnesses and consent to the deeds of your fathers; they killed them, and you build their tombs. 11:49-51 The Wisdom of God said, "I will send them prophets and apostles, some of whom they will kill and persecute,' that the blood of all the prophets, shed from the foundation of the world may be required of this generation, from the blood of Abel to the blood of Zechariah, who perished between the altar and the sanctuary. Yes, I tell you, it shall be required of this generation.

11:52 Woe to you lawyers! for you have taken away the key of knowledge; you did not enter yourselves and you hindered those who were entering.

12:2 Nothing is covered up that will not be revealed, or hidden that will not be known.

12:3 Whatever you have said in the dark shall be heard in the light, and what you have whispered in private rooms shall be proclaimed upon the housetops.

12:4-5 I tell you, my friends, do not fear those who kill the body, and after that have no more that they can do. But I will warn you whom to fear: fear him who, after he has killed, has power to cast into hell; yes, I tell you fear him!

12:6-7 Are not five sparrows sold for two pennies? And not one of them is forgotten before God. Why even the hairs of your head are all numbered. Fear not; you are of more value than many sparrows.

12:8-9 I tell you, every one who acknowledges me before men, the Son of man also will acknowledge before the angels of God; but he who denies me before men will be denied before the angels of God.

12:10 Every one who speaks a word against the Son of man will be forgiven; but he who blasphemes against the Holy Spirit will not be forgiven.

12:11-12 When they bring you before the synagogues and the rulers and the authorities, do not be anxious how or what you are to answer or what you are to say; for the Holy Spirit will teach you in that very hour what you ought to say.

12:22 Do not be anxious about your life, what you shall eat nor about your body, what you shall put on.

12:23 Life is more than food, and the body more than clothing.

12:24 Consider the ravens, they neither sow nor reap. they have
neither storehouse nor barn, and yet God feeds them. Of how much more value are you than the birds !

12:25-26 Which of you by being anxious can add a cubit to his span of life? If then you are not able to do as small a thing as that, why are you anxious about the rest?

12:27 Consider the lilies, how they grow; they neither toil nor spin; yet I tell you, even Solomon in all his glory was not arrayed like one of these.

12:28 But if God so clothes the grass which is alive in the field today and tomorrow is thrown into the oven, how much more will he clothe you, O men of little faith!

12:29-30 Do not seek what you are to eat and what you are to drink, nor be of anxious mind. For all the nations of the world seek these things; and your Father knows that you need them. Instead seek his kingdom, and these things shall be yours as well.

12:33-34 Sell your possessions, and give alms; provide your selves with purses that do not grow old, with a treasure in the heavens that does not fail, where no thief approaches and no moth destroys. For where your treasure is, there will your heart be also.

12:39-40 If the householder had known at what hour the thief was coming, he would have been awake and would not have let his house to be broken into, you also must be ready; for the Son of man is coming at an hour you do not expect.

12:42-46 The Lord said, 'Who then is the faithful and wise steward, whom his master will set over his household, to give them their portion of food at the proper time? Blessed is that servant whom his master when he comes will find so doing. Truly I tell you, he will set him over all his possessions. But if that servant says to himself, 'My master is delayed in coming,' and begins to beat the menservants and the maidservants, and to eat and drink and get drunk, the master of that servant will come on a day when he does not expect him and at an hour he does not know, and will punish him, and put him with the unfaithful.

12:49 I came to cast fire upon the earth; and would that it were already kindled!

12:52-53 Do you think that I have come to give peace on earth? No, I tell you, but rather division; 52 for henceforth in one house there will be five divided, three against two and two against three; they will be divided, father against son and son against father, mother against daughter and daughter against her mother, mother-in-law against her daughter-in-law and daughter-in-law against her mother-in-law.

12:57-59 Why do you not judge for yourselves what is right? As you go with your accuser before the magistrate, make an effort to settle with him on the way, lest he drag you to the judge, and the judge hand you over to the officer, and the officer put you in prison. I tell you, you will never get out till you have paid the very last copper.

13:18-19 He said, "What is the kingdom of God like? To what shall I compare it?' It is like a grain of mustard seed which a man took, and sowed in his garden; and it grew and became a tree, and the birds of the air made nests in its branches."

13:20-21 He said, "To what shall I compare the kingdom of God? 21 It is like leaven which a woman took and hid in three measures of meal, till it was all leavened."

13:24 Strive to enter by the narrow door; for many, I tell you, will seek to enter and will not be able.

13:25-27 When once the householder has risen up and shut the door, you will begin to stand outside and to knock at the door, saying, 'Lord, open to us.' He will answer you, 'I do not know where you come from,' Then you will begin to say, we ate and drank in your presence, and you taught in our streets.' But he will say, 'I tell you, I do not know where you come from; depart from me, all you workers of iniquity!'

13:28-29 You will weep and gnash your teeth, when you see Abraham and Isaac and Jacob and all the prophets in the kingdom of God and you yourselves thrust out. Men will come from east and west, and from north and south, and sit at table in the kingdom of God.

13:30 Some are last who will be first, and some are first who will be last.

13:34-35 0 Jerusalem, Jerusalem! How often would I have gathered your children together as a hen gathers her brood under her wings, and you would not! Behold, your house is forsaken. I tell you, you will not see me until you say, Blessed is he who comes in the name of the Lord!"

14:16-24 A man once gave a great banquet, and invited many and at the time of the banquet he sent his servant to say to those who had been invited, 'Come for all is now ready.' But they all alike began to make excuses. The first said to him, 'I have bought a field, and I must go out and see it; I pray you, have me excused.' l9 And another said, 'I have bought a yoke of oxen, I pray you, have me excused,' And another said, 'I have married a wife, and therefore I cannot come.' So the servant came and reported this to his master. Then the householder in anger said to his servant, Go out quickly to the streets and lanes of the city, and bring in the poor and maimed and blind and lame,' And the servant said, 'Sir, what you commanded has been done, and still there is room. The master said to the servant, 'Go out to the highways and hedges, and compel people to come in, that my house may be filled. For I tell you, none of those men who were invited shall taste my banquet.'

14:25-26 If anyone comes to me and does not hate his own father and mother and wife and children and brothers and sisters, yes, and even his own life, he cannot be my disciple.

14:27 Whoever does not bear his own cross and come after me, cannot be my disciple.

14:34-35 Salt is good; but if salt has lost its taste, how shall its saltiness be restored? It is fit neither for the land nor for the dunghill; men throw it away. He who has ears to hear, let him hear.

15:3-7 What man among you, having a hundred sheep, if he has lost one of them, does not leave the ninety-nine in the wilderness, and go after the one which is lost, until he finds it? And when he has found it, he lays it on his shoulders, rejoicing. When he comes home, he calls together his friends and his neighbors, saying to them, 'Rejoice with me, for I have found my sheep which was lost.' Just so, I tell you, there will be more joy in heaven over one sinner who repents than over ninety-nine righteous persons who need no repentance.'

16:13 No servant can serve two masters; for either he will hate the one and love the other, or he will be devoted to the one and despise the other. You cannot serve God and mammon.

16:16 The law and the prophets were until John; since then the good news of the kingdom of God is preached, and every one enters it violently.

16:17 It is easier for heaven and earth to pass away, than for one dot of the law to become void.

16:18 Every one who divorces his wife and marries another commits adultery, and he who marries a woman divorced from her husband commits adultery.

17:1-2 Temptations to sin are sure to come; but woe to him by whom they come! It would be better for him if a millstone were hung round his neck and he were cast into the sea, than that he should cause one of these little ones to sin.

17:3-4 If your brother sins, rebuke him, and if he repents, forgive him; and if he sins against you seven times in the day, and turns to you seven times, and says, 'I repent,' you must forgive him.

17:5-6 The apostles said to the Lord, "Increase our faith!" The Lord said, "If you had faith as a grain of mustard seed, you could say to this mulberry tree, 'Be rooted up, and be planted in the sea,' and it would obey you."

17:23 They will say to you, 'Lo, there!' or 'Lo, here!' Do not go, do not follow them.

17:24 As the lightning lights up the sky from one side to the other, so will Son of man be in his day.

17:26-27 As it was in the days of Noah, so will it be in the days of the Son of man. They ate, they drank, they married, they were given in marriage, until the day when Noah entered the ark, and the flood came and destroyed then all.

17:28-30 As it was in the days of Lot; they ate, they drank, they bought, they sold, they planted, they built, but on the day when Lot went out from Sodom fire and brimstone rained from heaven and destroyed them all. So will it be on the day when the Son of man is revealed.

17:33 Whoever seeks to gain his life will lose it, but whoever loses his life will preserve it.

17:34-35 I tell you, in that night there will be two men in one bed; one will be taken and the other left. There will be two women grinding together; one will be taken and the other left.

17:37 They said to him, "Where Lord?" He said to them, "Where the corpse is, there the eagles will be gathered together."

19:12-24 He said to them, "A nobleman went into a far country to receive kingly power and then return. Calling ten of his servants, he gave them ten pounds, and said to them, 'Trade with these till I come.' But his citizens hated him and sent an embassy after him, saying, 'We do not want this man to reign over us.' When he returned, having received the kingly power, he commanded these servants to whom he had given the money, to be called to him, that he might know what they had gained by trading. The first came before him saying 'Lord, your pound has made ten pounds more.' And he said to him, 'Well done, good servant! Because you have been faithful in a very little, you shall have authority over ten cities.' The second came, saying, 'Lord, your pound has made five pounds,' He said to him; 'And you are to be over five cities.' Then another came, saying, 'Lord here is your pound, which I kept laid away in a napkin; for I was afraid of you, because you are a severe man; you take up what you did not lay down, and reap what you did not sow.' He said to him, 'I will condemn you out of your own mouth, you wicked servant! You knew that I was a severe man, taking up what I did not lay down and reaping what I did not sow? Why then did you not put my money into the bank, and at my coming I should have collected it with interest?' He said to those who stood by, 'Take the pound from him, and give it to him who has ten pounds.' They said to him, 'Lord, he has ten pounds!'

19:25-27 I tell you, that to every one who has more will be given; but from him who has not, even what he has will be taken away.

22:28-30 You are those who have continued with me in my trials; as my Father appointed a kingdom for me, so do I appoint for you that you may eat and drink at my table in my kingdom, and sit on thrones judging the twelve tribes of Israel.

THE APOCALYPSE OF PETER

1 . . . . many of them will be false prophets, and will teach different ways and doctrines of hell: 2. but these will become sons of damnation. 3. And then God will come to my faithful ones who hunger and thirst and are afflicted and purify their souls in this life; and he will judge the sons of lawlessness.

4. And furthermore the Lord said: Let us go into the mountain: Let us pray…

5. And going with him, we, the twelve disciples, begged that he would show us one of our brethren, the righteous who are gone forth out of the world, in order that we might see of what manner of form they are, and having taken courage, might also encourage the men who hear us.

6. And as we prayed, suddenly there appeared two men standing before the Lord towards the East, on whom we were not able to look; 7, for there came forth from their countenance a ray as of the sun, and their raiment was shining, such as eye of man never saw; for no mouth is able to express or heart to conceive the glory with which they were endued, and the beauty of their appearance. 8. And as we looked upon them, we were astounded; for their bodies were whiter than any snow and redder than any rose; 9, and the red thereof was mingled with the white, and I am utterly unable to express their beauty; 10, for their hair was curly and bright and beautiful both on their face and shoulders, as it were a wreath woven of spikenard and various colored flowers, or like a rainbow in the sky, such was their likeness.

11. Seeing therefore their beauty we were astounded by them, since they appeared suddenly. 12. And I approached the Lord and said: Who are these? 13. He saith to me: These are your brethren the righteous, whose forms you desired to see. 14. And I said to him: And where are all the righteous ones and what is this epoch of time in which they exist and have this glory? 15. And the Lord showed me a very great country outside of this world, exceedingly bright with light, and the air there was lighted with the rays of the sun, and the earth itself blooming with flowers that never wilted and the place was full of spices and plants that were beautiful, flowering and bearing blessed fruit, and never spoiled. 16. And great was the perfume that it flowed aloft from this place, even to us. 17. And the dwellers in that place were clothed in the raiment of shining angels and their raiment was like to their country; and angels hovered about them there. 18. And the glory of those who dwell there was equal, and with one voice they sang praises. First to the Lord God, and then rejoicing in that place. 19. The Lord saith to us: This is the place of your high-priests, the righteous men.

20. And over against that place I saw another place. That one of squalid conditions, and it was the place of punishment; and those who were punished there and the punishing angels had raiment that was dark like the air of the place.

21. And there were certain ones there hanging by the tongue: and these were the blasphemers of the way of righteousness; and under them lay fire, burning and punishing them. 22. And there was a huge lake, full of flaming mud, in which were certain men that pervert righteousness, and tormenting angels caused them to suffer.

23. And there were also others, women, hanged by their hair over that bubbling mud: and these were they who adorned themselves for adultery; and the men who had intercourse with them in the defilement of adultery, were hanging by the feet and their heads in that mud. And I said: I did not believe that I should come into this place.

24. And I saw the murderers and those who conspired with them, cast into a certain narrow place, full of evil snakes, and they were attacked by those beasts, and they turned and twisted back and forth in that punishment; and worms, were like clouds of darkness, and they afflicted them. And the souls of the murdered stood and looked upon the punishment of those murderers and said: O God, thy judgment is just.

25. And near that place I saw another narrow place into which the gore (blood which was shed in violence) and the excrement of those who were being punished ran down and became like a lake: and there sat women having the blood that was shed due to their violence (gore) up to their necks, and over against them sat many children who were born to them out of due time, crying; and there came forth from them (the children) sparks of fire and struck the women in the eyes: and these who conceived and caused abortion were the accursed.

Other sources add: The milk of the women running down from their breasts and congealing created small flesh eating beasts: and these run up upon them and devour them.

The children who are born out of due time (premature due to the mother's intentional act) shall be of the better part: and these are delivered over to a care-taking angel that they may attain a share of knowledge and gain the better abode after suffering what they would have suffered if they had been in the body: but the others (aborted and delivered dead) shall merely obtain salvation as injured beings to whom mercy is shown, and remain without punishment, receiving this as a reward.

Other sources state: Infants that have been exposed (to this atrocity) are delivered to a care-taking angel, by whom they are educated and so grow up, and they will be as the faithful as a person of a hundred years old are here.

Other sources state: Those of the untimely births are delivered to care-taking angels, even if they are the offspring of adultery.

26. And other men and women were burning up to the middle and were cast into a dark place and were beaten by evil spirits, and their entrails were eaten by worms which never rest: and these were they who persecuted the righteous and delivered them up (for punishment).

27. And near those there were more women and men, these were gnawing their own lips because they were being punished and receiving a red-hot iron in their eyes: and these were they who blasphemed and slandered the way of righteousness.

28. And over against these again other men and women gnawing their tongues and having flaming fire in their mouths: and these were the false witnesses.

29. And in a certain other place there were pebbles sharper than swords or any red-hot sparks of flame, and women and men in tattered and filthy clothes rolled about on them in punishment: and these were the rich who trusted in their riches and had no pity for orphans and widows, and despised the commandment of God.

30. And in another great lake, full of pitch and blood and mire bubbling up, there stood men and women up to their knees: and these were the lenders of money who charged high interest and those who take interest on interest.

31. And other men and women were being hurled down from a high cliff and reached the bottom, and again were compelled by those who were placed in authority over them to climb up on the cliff again, and from there they were hurled down again, and had no rest from this punishment: and these were those (men) who defiled their bodies by acting as women (do with men); and those women who lay with another woman as if she were a man.

32. And alongside of that cliff there was a place full of a large fire, and there stood men who with their own hands had made for themselves carved images (idols) instead of God. And alongside these were other men and women who had rods and they were striking each other and never ceasing from such punishment.

33. And others again near them, women and men, burning and turning themselves and roasting: and these were they that left (departed) the way of God

Another source adds: The earth shall present all men before God at the day of judgment, being itself also to be judged, with the heaven also which encompasses it.

Introduction to The Epistle of Barnabas

(Alexandria, 70-135 CE)

The Epistle of Barnabas is not an epistle. It is a document that discusses questions of how ought Christians to interpret the Jewish Scriptures and what is the nature of the relationship between Christianity and Judaism? It appears to have been written after the destruction of the temple in Jerusalem in 70 CE (16.3-5) but before the city was rebuilt by Hadrian following the revolt of 132-135 CE. The author was likely from Alexandria. This conclusion is based on the extensive use of allegories, a device well used in Alexandria as well as the fact that the earliest evidence of the epistle derives from there.

The text has been reconstructed on the basis of the following witnesses:
• codex Sinaiticus, 4th. century. (Greek)
• codex Hierosolymitanus 1056 CE (Greek)
• 9 late related MSS (Greek)
• a papyrus fragment of chapters 9-6 (Greek)
• translation of chapters 1-17 only (Latin)

Antagonism between church and synagogue still ran high at the time of the penning of this epistle and the anonymous author concerns himself with proving that the death of Christ on the cross is the sacrifice that fulfills Old Testament plan and foreshadowing. Based on the passing away of the relevance of the Old Testament in his eyes, he sets about to reinterpret Old Testament laws in light of New Testament morality using a symbolism, which he chooses.

His approach to Old Testament is anti-Jewish. Since at that time most Christians were Jewish, his tact is unique in primitive Christian literature. The writer indicts the Jews, stating that the way Mosaic Law is interpreted and carried out chains them to the physical temple and to the rituals including animal sacrifices. This, he declares, is blindness arising from and reliance brought about by an evil angel. One may read a trace of Gnosticism into this accusation.

In an attempt to show that only Christians understand the true meaning of the Scriptures the writer uses stories to reinterpret the original Jewish meaning of the Old Testament. His conclusion is that Christians, not Jews are heirs of God's covenant.

In short, the Epistle of Barnabas is a good and early example of what became the dominant method of interpreting the Bible in the early and medieval church.

The writer of this Epistle purports to be an Alexandrian living in the time of Trajan and Hadrian. He was a layman whose real name may have actually been "Barnabas," and so felt justified in using his apostolic namesake. However, since this cannot be the Barnabas referenced in the New Testament the writer, no matter what his true name, is anonymous and the epistle was attributed to St. Barnabas. Hilgenfeld, who has devoted much attention to this Epistle, holds that "it was written at the close of the first century by a Gentile Christian of the school of Alexandria, with the view of winning back, or guarding from a Judaic form of Christianity, those Christians belonging to the same class as himself."

This epistle was well accepted by the primitive Christians owing to the fact that it continued in the line of reason of Paul, who sought to break away from the legalism and rituals of the Jews. Since the first Christians were Jews the persistence of Judaism and strict Jewish thought continued to be resurrected in an attempt to create the new religion in the form of the old. Even though some authorities believe the writer to be a Jew the writer's contempt for the Jewish thought imposed on Christianity may be the reason he sounds at times like a Gentile. The juxtaposition of the old Jewish ways and the new Christian ways were tackled many times in the New Testament, for example by Paul as he spoke as both a Jew and a Roman. The lessons continued in the Book of Romans as well as Hebrews. The intention of the writer, as he himself states in chapter 1 was "to perfect the knowledge" of those to whom he wrote.

We know many of the church fathers accepted the Epistle unanimously attribute it to Barnabas the Levite. Clement of Alexandria refers to the letter many times. Origen describes it as "a Catholic Epistle" and ranks it among the Sacred Scriptures. It did not seem to bother the church fathers that the document has numerous inaccuracies with respect to Mosaic Laws' enactments and observances. Even though in the early years of Christianity most Christians seemed to take scripture literally, this author hijacks even the dietary laws in Leviticus and reinterprets them, using the symbols of the unclean animals as symbols of various sins to enforce moral laws instead of dietary laws.

It is worth noting that Eusebius placed the letter among the "spurious" writings, which was well known and read in the Church. He seemed to be in the minority in his time. The Epistle is found at the end of the New Testament in Codex Sinaiticus, 4th. Century C.E. (Greek). It was listed as canon in the 6th century C.E. and was found in the Jerusalem Codex, which was created in the 11th century C.E.

The Epistle of Barnabas should not be confused with the Gospel of Barnabas, which was likely created in the Middle Ages and is probably Italian in origin.

The Translation used in this text is a more modern rendering of the Charles H. Hoole, 1885 Translation.

Epistle of Barnabas

CHAPTER 1

1:1 Salutations to all my sons and daughters, in the name of our Lord Jesus Christ, who has loved us in peace.

1:2 I rejoice greatly and beyond measure at your happy and blessed spirit, since the fruits of the righteousness of God are great and abundant toward you, who have received through grace the engrafted spiritual gift.

1:3 Because of this, I congratulate myself the more, hoping to be saved, because I see of a truth the Spirit poured out upon you from the rich Lord of love.
So greatly have your longed-for appearance stricken me with amazement.

1:4 Being persuaded, therefore, of this, and knowing in myself that since I spoke among you the Lord has helped me in many things in the way of righteousness, I am altogether compelled to love you even beyond my own soul, because great faith and love dwells in you in the hope of his life.

1:5 Considering also this, that if I take care to communicate to you a part of that which I have received, it shall turn to my reward to have assisted such spirits as you are, I gave diligence to write to you in few words, in order that together with your faith, you might have your knowledge perfect also.

1:6 For there are three doctrines ordained of the Lord: the hope of life, the beginning, and the end.

1:7 For the Master has made known to us by the prophets the things which are past, and the things which are at hand, and has given us the firstfruits of the knowledge of the things that are to come. Since, therefore, we see all these things severally working as he has spoken, we ought the more fully and loftily to approach to his altar;

1:8 but I, not as a master, but as one of yourselves, will show to you a few things, by means of which you may even in this present rejoice.

CHAPTER 2

2:1 Since, therefore, the days are evil, and the adversary has the authority, we ought to take heed to ourselves and seek out the ordinances of the Lord.

2:2 For the helpers of our faith are fear and patience, and they that fight on our side are long suffering and continence.

2:3 While these, therefore, remain pure in things relating to the Lord, wisdom and understanding, science and knowledge, rejoice together with them.

2:4 For God has made known to us through all the prophets, that he desires neither sacrifices nor whole burnt offerings, nor oblations; for he said in a certain place,

2:5 To what purpose is the multitude of your sacrifices? said the Lord. I am full of the whole burnt offerings of rams; I desire not the fat of lambs, nor the blood of bulls and goats, nor need you come to be seen of me. For who has required these things at your hands? You shall not add thereto to tread my court. If you bring the fine flour, it is vain; incense is an abomination to me; your new moons and sabbaths I cannot endure; your fastings and holidays and feasts my soul hates.

2:6 These things, therefore, he has made of none effect, that the new law of our Lord Jesus Christ, being free from the yoke of necessity, might have an offering not made with hands.

2:7 Again, he said to them, Did I command your fathers, when you came out of the land of Egypt, offer to me whole burnt offerings and sacrifices? --

2:8 did I not rather command them this? -- Let each of you bear no malice against his neighbor in his heart, and love not a false oath.

2:9 We ought to perceive, since we are not void of understanding the meaning of the goodness of God our Father, because he tells us, wishing to seek us who are wandering even as sheep, how we ought to approach him.

2:10 He therefore speaks to us in this way: The sacrifice to God is a broken heart; a smell of sweet savor to the Lord is a heart that glorifies him that made it. We ought, therefore, brethren, to examine accurately concerning our salvation, lest the evil one, making an entrance among us, should draw us away from our life.

CHAPTER 3

3:1 Therefore, he said again, concerning these things, to them, Why fast you to me, said the Lord, so that your voice is heard to-day in its crying? This is not the fast that I have chosen, said the Lord, for a man to humiliate his soul;

3:2 nor if you bend your neck as a ring, and put under you sackcloth and ashes -- not even then will you call it an acceptable fast.

3:3 But to us he said, Behold the fast which I have chosen, said the Lord, not that a man should humiliate his soul, but that he should loose every bond of unrighteousness, and untie the knots of the compacts of violence; set at liberty them that are bruised, and cancel every agreement of unrighteousness; break your bread with the hungry, and if you see the naked, clothe him; bring them that are homeless into your dwelling, and if you see a man that is lowly, despise him not, and turn not away from those of your family;

3:4 then shall your light break forth early, and your garments shall spring up quickly, and justice shall go before you, and the glory of the Lord shall surround you;

3:5 then shall you cry, and the Lord shall listen to you; while you are yet speaking he shall say, Lo, I am here: if you put away from you the league and the conspiracy, and the word of murmuring, and give you

bread to the hungry with all your heart, and have compassion upon the soul that is lowly.

3:6 The long-suffering God therefore having seen beforehand that the people whom he had prepared for his beloved would believe in simplicity, showed to us beforehand concerning all these things, that we should not come as strangers to their law.

CHAPTER 4

4:1 It is a duty, therefore, that we, searching much concerning the things that are at hand, should seek out the things that are able to save us. Let us fly, therefore, utterly from all the work of unrighteousness, and let us hate the error of the time that now is, that we may be loved in that which is to come.

4:2 Let us not give liberty to our soul that it should have leave to run with sinners and evil men, neither let us be made like to them.

4:3 The tribulation being made perfect is at hand, concerning which it is written, as Enoch said, For to this purpose the Lord has cut short the times and the days, that his beloved might make haste and come into his inheritance.

4:4 The prophet also speaks in this way: Ten kingdoms shall reign upon the earth; and there shall rise up after them a little king who shall humble three of the kings under one.

4:5 And in like manner Daniel speaks concerning him: And I saw the fourth beast, evil and strong and harder than all the beasts of the earth; and I saw how there grew up from him ten horns, and from among them a little horn, growing up beside, and how it humbled under one three of the great horns.

4:6 You ought, therefore, to understand. And moreover I ask this of you, as being one among you, loving you especially and altogether, even above my own soul, that you should take heed to yourselves, and not be like to certain men, by adding to your sins and saying that their covenant is also ours. Ours, indeed, it is; but they have lost it for ever, in this way, after that Moses had already received it.

4:7 For the scripture said, And Moses was in the mount fasting forty days and nights, and he received the covenant from the Lord; even tables of stone written with the finger of the hand of the Lord. But when they turned to idols they lost it.

4:8 For the Lord said thus to Moses, Moses, get you down quickly, for your people, whom you brought out of the land of Egypt, have done unlawfully. And Moses understood, and cast the two tables from his hands, and the covenant that was on them was broken; to the end that that of the beloved Jesus might be sealed in our hearts in the hope of his faith.

4:9 Now, though I wished to write many things to you, not as a master, but even as suites one that loves you, not to fall short of the things that we have, I have been zealous to write to you as though I were your rubbish. Let us, therefore, give heed to the last days; for the whole time of our faith will profit us nothing unless now, in the season of iniquity and among the stumbling-blocks that are coming, we resist as becomes the sons of God,

4:10   that the evil one may not have entrance unawares. Let us fly all vanity and hate perfectly the deeds of the evil way. Do not, entering into your own houses, dwell alone, as though you were already justified, but coming together, inquire one with another concerning the common advantage.

4:11 For the scripture said, Woe to them that are wise in their own conceit and learned in their own eyes. Let us be spiritual: let us be a perfect temple to God. So far as in you lies, let us practice the fear of God, and strive to keep his commandments, that we may be glad in his ordinances.

4:12 The Lord shall judge the world without respect of persons; each shall receive according as he has done; if he be good, righteousness shall go before him, but if he be evil, the reward of wickedness shall be before him.

4:13 Let us give heed that we do not, as being already elect, take rest, and sleep in our sins, lest the ruler of wickedness, getting the mastery over us, thrust us from the kingdom of the Lord.

4:14   And, moreover, my brethren, consider this. When you see that after so many signs and wonders that have happened in Israel, even then they have been abandoned, let us take heed lest, as it is written, many of us be called but few chosen.

CHAPTER 5

5:1 For on this account the Lord endured to give his flesh to corruption, that we might be sanctified by the remission of sins, which is by the sprinkling of his blood.

5:2 For there are written concerning him certain things that pertain to Israel, and certain other that pertain to us. For he speaks thus, He was wounded for our iniquities, and vexed for our sins; by his stripes we are healed. He was led as a sheep to the slaughter, and like a lamb dumb before him that shears it.

5:3 We ought, therefore, to give especial thanks to the Lord because he has made known to us the things that are past, and has made us wise with regard to those that are at hand, neither are we without understanding as regards the future.

5:4 For the scripture said, Not unjustly is the net stretched for the birds. Now this means that a man will perish justly who, having a knowledge of the path of righteousness, shuts himself up into the way of darkness.

5:5   Consider this too, my brethren; if the Lord endured to suffer for our souls, though he were the Lord of the whole world, to whom God said from the foundation of the world, Let us make man according to our image and according to our likeness, how then did

he endure to suffer at the hands of men? Learn you!

5:6 The prophets having received the grace from him prophesied with regard to him. But he, that he might make death of none effect and bring to light the resurrection from the dead, because it suited him to be made manifest in the flesh,

5:7 endured it, that he might give to our fathers the promise, and by preparing for himself a new people, might show, while upon earth, that he will raise the dead and himself execute judgment.

5:8 Yes, further; though he taught Israel and did so many signs and wonders among them, yet they loved him not.

5:9 But when he chose out his own Apostles, who were about to preach his gospel, they were men unrighteous beyond all sin, that he might show that he came not to call the righteous but sinners to repentance; then made he himself manifest that he was the Son of God.

5:10 For if he had not come in the flesh how could men have looked upon him and have been saved, since they cannot endure to look at the rays of the sun which must one day perish, and which is the work of his hands?

5:11 For this purpose did the Son of God come in the flesh, that he might sum up and finish the sin of them who persecuted his prophets to death;

5:12 therefore he endured even to this. For God said that the smiting of his flesh it was from them. When they shall smite their shepherd, then shall the sheep of the flock be scattered.

5:13 But he himself wished thus to suffer, for it was necessary that he should suffer upon the cross; for he who prophesies about him said, Spare my soul from the sword, and again, Drive nails into my flesh, for the synagogues of evil men have risen against me.

5:14 And again he said, Behold, I have given my back to the scourging and my cheeks to buffetings; my face also have I set as a hard rock.

CHAPTER 6

6:1 When, therefore, he made the commandment what does he say? Who is he that disputes with me? let him resist me; or who is he that contends with me? Let him draw nigh to the Son of the Lord.

6:2 Woe to you, for you shall all wax old as a garment, and the moth shall devour you. And again the prophet said, Since he has been placed, as a strong stone, for crushing; behold I will place on the foundation of Zion a stone precious, elect, a chief corner stone of great price.

6:3 And then what said he? And he that believeth in him shall live for ever. Is then our hope in a stone? God forbid. But it is thus said because the Lord has made strong his flesh, for he said, And he made me as it were a hard rock.

6:4 And again, The stone which the builders rejected has become the head of the corner. And again he said, This is the day, great and wonderful, which the Lord has made.

6:5 I write to you the more simply that you may understand. I am the refuse (dregs) of your love.

6:6 What then said the prophet again? The synagogue of the wicked came around me; they surrounded me as bees do a honey-comb, and, over my garment they cast lots.

6:7 Since, therefore, he was about to be made manifest and to suffer in the flesh, his suffering was showed beforehand. For the prophet said to Israel, Woe to their soul, for they have counseled an evil counsel among themselves, saying, Let us bind the righteous because he is an encumbrance to us.

6:8 And what said the other prophet, even Moses, to them? Behold, thus said the Lord God: Enter into the good land which the Lord swore to Abraham and Isaac and Jacob, and inherit it, even a land flowing with milk and honey.

6:9 What said the knowledge? Learn you. Hope, it said, upon Jesus, who is about to be manifested to you in the flesh. For man is but earth which suffers; for, from the face of the ground was made the molding of Adam.

6:10 What then means he when he said, Into the good land which flows with milk and honey? Blessed be the Lord, brethren, who has put into you wisdom and knowledge of his secret things. For the prophet speaks a parable from the Lord. Who shall understand, except he that is wise and skilful and that loves his Lord?

6:11 Since, therefore, having renewed us by the remission of our sins, he has made us of a new character, he wills that we should have the souls of children, inasmuch as it is indeed he who has formed us anew.

6:12 For the scripture said concerning us, that he said to the Son, Let us make man after our own image and according to our likeness; and let them rule over the beasts of the earth, and the fowls of heaven, and the fishes of the sea. And the Lord said, when he saw how excellent our form was, Increase and multiply and replenish the earth. These things he said to the Son.

6:13 Again I will show to you how the Lord speaks to us, since he has made a second fashioning in these last days; the Lord said, Behold I make the last even as the first. For to this purpose did the prophet preach. Enter you into the land flowing with milk and honey, and have dominion over it.

6:14 Behold now we have been formed again, even as he said again in another prophet: Behold, said the Lord, I will take out from these, that is out of those whom the Spirit of the Lord foresaw, the hearts of stone, and will put into them hearts of flesh, because he himself was about to be manifested in the flesh and to dwell among us.

6:15 For the habitation of our heart is a temple holy to the Lord.

6:16 For the Lord said again, Whereby shall I appear before the Lord my God and be glorified? He said too, I will give thanks to you in the assembly, in the midst of my brethren; I will sing to you in the midst of the assembly of the saints. We are, therefore, those whom he brought into the good land.

6:17 What, then, means the milk and honey? It is because a child is kept alive, first with honey, afterwards with milk. So we, too, being quickened by faith in his promise and by his word, shall live and rule over the earth.

6:18 And we said previously, And let them increase and multiply and rule over the fish. Who then is he who is able to rule over the beasts, the fish, and fowls of heaven? For we ought to perceive that to rule belongs to authority, so that a man by giving commands may exercise lordship.

6:19 If, therefore, this doth not take place now, he has told us when it will; even when we ourselves have been made perfect, so that we become heirs of the covenant of the Lord.

CHAPTER 7

7:1 You perceive, therefore, beloved children, that our good Lord has manifested to us all things beforehand, to the end that we should know whom we ought to praise, returning thanks for all things.

7:2 If, therefore, the Son of God, being he who is the Lord and who is about to judge the quick and the dead, suffered, to the end that his stripes might make us live, let us believe that the Son of God could not suffer except on our account.

7:3 But being crucified, he was given to drink of vinegar and gall. How, then, did the priests of the temple signify concerning this? Now, the commandment is written in this way: Whosoever shall not fast on the fast, he shall die the death, the Lord has commanded it. Since he also was about to offer the vessel that contained his spirit as a sacrifice, in order that the type might be fulfilled which was given by the offering of Isaac at the altar,

7:4 what said he in the book of the prophet? And let them eat of the goat which is offered on the fast for the sins of all. Attend you diligently thereto. And let the priests alone eat of the unwashed entrails with vinegar.

7:5 With what signification? Because you will one day give me to drink of vinegar and gall, when I am about to offer up my flesh for my new people, eat you it alone, while the people fast and lament in sackcloth and ashes. He commanded this in order that he might show that he must needs suffer at their hands.

7:6 How, then, did he give his commands? Attend you. Take you two goats, fair and like each other, and offer them up. And let the priest take one of them as a whole burnt offering for sin.

7:7 But what shall they do with the other? Let the other, he said, be accursed. Now attend you, how the type of Jesus is made manifest.

7:8 And do you all spit upon it and pierce it, and put scarlet wool around its head, and so let it be cast out into the wilderness. And when this has been done, he who bears the goat leads it out into the wilderness, and takes away the wool and places it upon a bush, which is called Rachia (Rachel), the shoots of which we are accustomed to eat when we find them in the fields. Thus the fruit of the Rachia (Rachel) only is sweet.

7:9 What, therefore, means this? Attend you. One is brought to the altar, the other is accursed, and the accursed one is crowned, because they shall see him in that day, who had the scarlet robe about his flesh, and they shall say, Is not this he whom once we set at naught and crucified, and spat upon and pierced? Truly this was he who at that time said that he was the Son of God.

7:10 How then was the one like to the other? In this respect were the goats like him: they were fair and equal, so that when they saw him coming they were astonished at the likeness to the goat. Therefore, behold here the type of Jesus, who was about to suffer.

7:11 And what means the wool placed in the midst of thorns? It is a type of Jesus, which has been placed in the church. For he who wishes to take the scarlet wool must suffer many things, because the thorn is terrible, and must after tribulation gain possession of it. So he said, They who wish to see me and to take hold of my kingdom must through trouble and suffering receive me.

CHAPTER 8

8:1 And what type, think you, was the commandment to Israel, that the men in whom sin had been accomplished should offer a heifer, and after they had slaughtered it should burn it, and that children should then take the ashes and cast them into vessels, and place scarlet wool and hyssop around a stick -- behold, again, the type of the cross and the scarlet wool, -- and so the children should sprinkle the people one by one, that they might be purged from their sins?

8:2 Behold, therefore, in what way he speaks to you with simplicity. The heifer signifies Jesus; the sinful men who offer it are the men who brought him to the slaughter. But now the men are no longer before us, no longer doth the glory belong to sinners.

8:3 The children who sprinkled are they who brought us the good news of the forgiveness of sins and purification of heart, to whom he has given the authority of the gospel for the purpose of preaching, being twelve in number, for a testimony to the tribes, for twelve were the tribes of Israel.

8:4 And why, then, were the children who sprinkled three in number? For a testimony to Abraham, Isaac, and Jacob, because these are great before God.

8:5 And what signifies the wool upon the stick? Because the kingdom of Jesus is upon the cross, and because they who hope upon him shall live for ever.

8:6 And why are there at the same time the wool and the hyssop? Because in his kingdom the days in which we shall be saved shall be evil and filthy, because also he that grieves his flesh is healed through the purifying of the hyssop.

8:7 And these things having happened on this account are manifest to us, but obscure to them, because they hearkened not to the voice of the Lord.

CHAPTER 9

9:1 He said also again concerning our ears how he has circumcised our heart. The Lord said in the prophet, They have hearkened to me with the hearing of their ears; and again, he said, They that are afar off shall hear with their ears; they shall know what I have done; and be you circumcised, said the Lord, in your heart;

9:2 and again, Hear, O Israel, for thus said the Lord your God; and again the Spirit of the Lord prophesied, Who is he that wishes to live for ever? let him listen to the voice of my Son.

9:3 And again he said, Hear, O heaven, and give ear, O earth, for the Lord has spoken these things for a testimony. And again he said, Listen to the voice of the Lord, you rulers of this people. And again he said, Listen you children to the voice of one crying in the wilderness.

9:4 To this end, therefore, has he circumcised our hearing, that when we hear his word, we should believe; for the circumcision in which they trust is done away with. For he has said that circumcision is not that which was made in the flesh; but they have transgressed, for an evil angel has deluded them.

9:5 He said to them, These things said the Lord your God, -- here I find a new commandment -- Sow not among thorns, but be you circumcised to your Lord. And what said he? Circumcise the hardness of your hearts, and harden not your neck. And again, Behold, said the Lord, all the Gentiles are uncircumcised in their foreskin, but this people is uncircumcised in their hearts.

9:6 But he will say, Of a truth the people have been circumcised for a seal to them; but so, also, has every Syrian and Arabian, and all the priests of idols. Do they also belong to the covenant? But the Egyptians also are in circumcision.

9:7 Learn, therefore, children of love, richly concerning all things, that Abraham, who first gave circumcision, circumcised, looking forward in the spirit to Jesus, having received the doctrines of the three letters.

9:8 For he said, And Abraham circumcised out of his household eighteen males and three hundred. What, then, was the knowledge that was given by this? Learn you, that he mentions the eighteen first, and then, having made an interval, he mentions the three hundred. In the eighteen, "I" stands for ten and "H" stands for 8, you have Jesus IHSOYS; and because the cross in the letter "T" was about to convey the grace of redemption, he mentions also the three hundred.

Therefore, he reveals Jesus in the two letters, I and H, and the cross in the one, T.

9:9 He knows this who has placed the engrafted gift of his teaching in us. No one has had from me a more true account than this; but I know that you are worthy.

CHAPTER 10

10:1 But in that Moses said, You shall not eat the swine, nor the eagle, nor the hawk, nor the crow, nor any fish that has not scales in itself, he had in his mind three doctrines.

10:2 For in the end he said to them in Deuteronomy, And I will arrange before this people my ordinances. The commandment of God is not, therefore, that they should not eat; but Moses spoke in a spiritual sense.

10:3 He spoke of the swine with this meaning: You shall not cleave, he means, to men of this sort, who are like to swine, for when they become wanton they forget their Lord, but when they are in want they think upon the Lord; even as the swine when it eats knows not its lord, but when it is hungry it cries, and when it has received it is again silent.

10:4 Nor shall you eat of the eagle, nor of the hawk, nor of the kite, nor of the crow. You shall

not, he means, cleave to, nor be like to men of this sort, who know not how to provide sustenance for themselves by labor and sweat, but in their iniquity seize the property of others, and, as though they walked in innocence, watch and observe whom they shall plunder, through their covetousness; even as these birds alone provide not sustenance for themselves by means of toil, but, sitting idle, seek out how they may eat the flesh of others, being destructive by

reason of their wickedness.

10:5 And you shall not eat, he said, of the lamprey, or the polypus, or the cuttle-fish. You shall

not, he means, cleave to or become like men of this sort, who are impious to the end, and have been already condemned to death, even as these accursed fish alone swim in the depth, not floating as the others do, but dwelling in the earth below the depth of the sea.

10:6 Thus, he said, You shall not eat the hare, meaning you shall not indulge in unnatural lusts (with young boys);

10:7 nor shall you eat the hyena, meaning you shall not be an adulterer;

10:8 nor shall you eat the weasel, meaning you shall not do uncleanness with your mouth concerning food;

10:9 therefore Moses spoke in the spirit these three doctrines. But they, according to the lusts of their flesh, received them as being about meat.

10:10 And David receives knowledge concerning the same three doctrines, and said in like manner, Blessed is the man who has not walked in the counsel of the ungodly, even as the fish walk in darkness into the depths of the sea, and has not stood in the way of sinners, even as they who pretend to fear the Lord sin as doth the swine, and has not sat in the seat of the destroyers, even as the birds that sit for prey. You have also in the end a commandment concerning food;

10:11 but Moses said, Eat you everything that is cloven-footed and that chews the cud. What means he? He that takes food knows him that feeds him, and, resting upon him, seems to be glad. He therefore said well, having regard to the commandment. What then means he? Cleave you to them that fear the Lord, who walk in his commandments, which they have received in their hearts; to them that speaks of the ordinances of the Lord, and observe them, to them who know that the practice of them is a work of gladness, and who meditate on the word of the Lord. But what means that which cleaves the hoof? It means that the just walks even in this world, and expects the holy life. Behold how well Moses has made these laws;

10:12 but how was it possible for them to perceive or understand these things? But we, having rightly understood the commandments, speaks them even as the Lord has willed. On this account has he circumcised our ears and hearts, that we should understand these things.

CHAPTER 11

11:1 Let us inquire, therefore, if the Lord cared to show us beforehand concerning the water and concerning the cross. Concerning the water it is written, with respect to Israel, how that they will not receive the baptism that brings remission of sins, but will establish one for themselves.

11:2 The prophet therefore speaks in this way, Be astonished, O heaven! and let the earth be afraid still more at this, because this people has done two great and evil things: they have abandoned me who am the fountain of life, and have dug for themselves broken cisterns.

11:3 Is my holy mountain of Zion a deserted rock? You shall be as the young of a bird which have flown when the nest has been taken away.

11:4 And again the prophet said, I will go before you and will lay low the mountains. And I will break the doors of brass and burst the bars of iron; and I will give to you the treasures of darkness hidden and unseen, that they may know that I am the Lord God; and, He shall dwell in the lofty cave of the strong rock.

11:5 Then what said he of the Son? His water is faithful. You shall behold the king in his glory, and your soul shall practice the fear of the Lord.

11:6 And again, in another prophet, he said, He that does these things shall be as a tree that grows beside

the watercourses, which gives his fruit in his season;
and his leaf shall not fall off,
and whatever he does shall prosper.

11:7 Not so are the ungodly, not so; they are like the dust which the wind carries away from the face of the earth, wherefore the ungodly shall not rise up in judgment, nor sinners in the congregation of the just: for the Lord knows the way of the just, but the way of the ungodly shall perish.

11:8 You perceive how he has put together the water and the cross. For what he means is this, Blessed are they who having hoped on the cross have gone down into the water. For he speaks of a reward to be given at the due season; then, said he, I will render what is due to you. But now in that he said, Their leaves shall not fall off, he means this, That every word that goes out from your mouth in faith and love shall be for a refuge and a hope to many.

11:9 And again another prophet said, And the land of Jacob was praised beyond the whole earth. By so saying he means this, He shall glorify the vessel
that contains his Spirit.

11:10 And what says he afterwards? There was a river flowing on the right, and there grew up on its banks fair trees, and whosoever eats of them shall live for ever.

11:11 By this he means that we go down into the water full of sin and pollution, and go up bearing fruit in the heart, having in the spirit fear and hope toward Jesus. And whoever shall eat of them shall live for ever. He means this, Whoever, he said, shall hear these words spoken and believe them shall live for ever.

CHAPTER 12

12:1 In like manner again he signifies concerning the cross in another prophet, who said, And when shall these things be fulfilled? The Lord said, When the tree has been bent and shall rise up again, and when blood shall flow from the tree. You have again a prophecy concerning the cross and about him who is about to be crucified.

12:2 And he said again in Moses, when Israel was being made war upon by aliens, even that he might remind them while they were being made war upon, that for their sins they were being delivered over to death, the Spirit said to the heart of Moses, that he should make the form of a cross, and of him who was about to suffer, for if, he says, they shall not hope upon him, they will be made war upon for ever. Moses, therefore, arranges weapon against weapon in the midst of the battle, and standing higher than all, stretched out his hands, and so again Israel conquered; then, when he let them down, they were again slaughtered.

12:3 For what reason? that they might know that they are not to be saved except they hope upon him.

12:4 And again, in another prophet, he said, All day long have I stretched out my hands to a people who are disobedient, and who speaks against my righteous way.

12:5 Again, Moses makes another type of Jesus, that it is his duty that he should suffer, and cause others to live, whom they thought that they had destroyed in figure when Israel was falling: For the Lord made every kind of serpent to bite them, and they died, since the transgression happened to Eve by means of the serpent, to the end that he might convince them that through their transgression they should be given over to the pangs of death.

12:6 For in the end Moses himself, after that he had given commandment, There shall not be among you a molten image or a graven image for a god, makes one himself, that he might show a type of Jesus. Moses, therefore, makes a brazen serpent, and sets it aloft, and calls the people by a proclamation.

12:7 When, therefore, they had come together they besought Moses, that he should offer supplication for them concerning their healing. Moses therefore said to them, When any of you is bitten let him come to the dead serpent, that is placed upon the tree, and let him believe and hope that, though it is dead, it is able to make him live, and immediately he shall be saved; and so did they. You have, therefore, again in these things also, the glory of Jesus, that in him and to him are all things.

12:8 What again said Moses to Jesus the son of Nun, after he had given this name to him, being a prophet, to this end alone, that all the people might hear that the Father reveals all things concerning the Son, Jesus?

12:9 Moses therefore said to Jesus the son of Nun, having given him this name, when he sent him to spy out the land, Take the book into your hands and write what the Lord said, even that the Son of God, in the last days, will cut off the whole house of Amalek from the roots.

12:10 Behold, therefore, again Jesus, not the son of man but the Son of God, and by a type made manifest in the flesh. Since, therefore, they should one day say that Christ is the son of David, David himself prophesies, being in fear and understanding the deceitfulness of sinners, The Lord said to my Lord, Sit on my right hand until I make your enemies your footstool.

12:11 And again Esaias speaks in this way, The Lord said to Christ, my Lord, whose right hand I
have held, that the Gentiles should listen before him, and I will break the strength of kings. Behold how David calls him Lord, and doth not call him son.

CHAPTER 13

13:1 Let us inquire, therefore, whether this people or the first people inherits, and whether the
covenant is to us or to them.

13:2 Hear, now, what the scripture said concerning the people. But Isaac prayed for Rebecca his wife because she was barren, and she conceived. Then went forth Rebecca to inquire of the Lord, and the Lord said to her, Two nations are in your womb, and two peoples are in your bowels, and the one people shall surpass the other, and the elder shall serve the younger.

13:3 We ought to understand who was Isaac and who was Rebecca, and concerning whom he declared that the one people was greater than the other.

13:4 And in another prophecy Jacob speaks yet more clearly to Joseph his son, saying, Behold the Lord has not deprived me of your face; bring to me your sons, that I may bless them.

13:5 And he brought to him Ephraim and Manasseh, wishing that he should bless Manasseh, because he was the elder. Joseph, therefore, brought him to the right hand of his father Jacob. But Jacob saw in spirit a figure of the people that should be hereafter. And what said the Scriptures? And Jacob crossed his hands, and placed his right hand on the head of Ephraim, the second and youngest, and blessed him. And Joseph said to Jacob, Change your right hand to the head of Manasseh, because he is my firstborn son. And Jacob said to Joseph, I know, my child, I know; but the elder shall serve the younger; but this one also shall be blessed.

13:6 Behold in what way he appointed that this people should be the first and heir of the covenant.

13:7 If, therefore, it were moreover mentioned through Abraham also, we have the perfecting of our knowledge. What, therefore, said he to Abraham, when he alone believed, and it was counted to him for righteousness? Behold I have made you, Abraham, a father of the nations who in uncircumcision believe in the Lord.

CHAPTER 14

14:1 Yes; but let us inquire whether he has given the covenant that he swear to the fathers that he would give to the people. Verily he has given it; but they were not worthy to receive it on account of their sins.

14:2 For the prophet said, And Moses was fasting in Mount Sinai forty days and forty nights, that he might receive the covenant which the Lord has made with his people. And he received from the Lord the two tables that were written in the spirit with the finger of the hand of the Lord. And Moses, when he had received them, was bringing them down to the people for to give them.

14:3 And the Lord said to Moses, Moses, Moses, get you down quickly, for your people, whom you brought out of the land of Egypt, have done unlawfully. And Moses perceived that they had again made molten images, and he cast the tables from his hands, and the tables of the covenant of the Lord were broken.

14:4 Moses indeed received them, but the people were not worthy. Listen you, therefore, how we have received them. Moses received them being a servant, but the Lord himself gave to us to be a people of inheritance, having suffered for our sake.

14:5 And he was made manifest, that both they might be made perfect in their sins, and that we, through him that inherited, might receive the covenant of the Lord Jesus, who, for this purpose was prepared, that by appearing himself and redeeming from darkness our hearts, which were already lavished on death, and given over to the iniquity of deceit, he might place in us the covenant of his people.

14:6 For it is written how the Father gives commandment to him, that having redeemed us from darkness, he should prepare for himself a holy people.

14:7 Therefore the prophet said, I, the Lord your God, have called you in righteousness, and I will hold your hand and make you strong; and I have given you for a covenant to the nation, for a light to the Gentiles, to open the eyes of the blind, and to bring out of chains them that are bound, and from the house of prison them that sit in darkness. We know from whence we were redeemed.

14:8 And again, the prophet said, Behold, I have placed you for a light to the Gentiles, that you should be for a salvation even to the end of the earth; thus said the Lord God who has redeemed you.

14:9 And again, the prophet said, The Spirit of the Lord is upon me, because he has anointed me to preach the gospel to the poor, he has sent me to heal those that are broken in heart, to preach deliverance to the captives, and the recovery of sight to the blind, to tell of the acceptable year of the Lord, and the day of recompense, to comfort all that mourn.

CHAPTER 15

15:1 And, moreover, concerning the sabbath it is written in the ten commandments, in which he spoke on Mount Sinai to Moses face to face: Sanctify you the sabbath of the Lord with pure hands and a pure heart.

15:2 And in another place he said, If my sons shall keep my sabbath, then will I place my mercy upon them.

15:3 He speaks, too, of the sabbath in the beginning of the creation: And God made in six days the works of his hands, and finished them on the seventh day, and rested in it and sanctified it.

15:4 Consider, my children, what signify the words, He finished them in six days. They mean this: that in six thousand years the Lord will make an end of all things, for a day is with him as a thousand years. And he himself bears witness to me, saying: Behold this day a day shall be as a thousand years. Therefore, my children, in six days, that is in six thousand years, shall all things be brought to an end.

15:5 And the words, He rested on the seventh day, signify this: After that his Son has come, and has caused to cease the time of the wicked one, and has judged the ungodly, and changed the sun and the moon and the stars, then shall he rest well on the seventh day.

15:6 And further he said, You shall sanctify it with pure hands and a pure heart. Who, therefore, can sanctify the day which the Lord has sanctified, unless he be pure of heart? in all things have we been deceived.

15:7 Behold, that then indeed we shall be able to rest well and sanctify; even when we ourselves, having been justified, and having received the promise, when iniquity exists no longer, but all things have been made new by the Lord, we shall then be able to sanctify it, having been first sanctified ourselves.

15:8 And, further, he said to them, Your new moons and your sabbaths I cannot endure. See, now, what he means. The sabbaths, that now are, are not acceptable to me, but that which I have made is, even that in which, after that I have brought all things to an end, I shall make a beginning of the eighth day, which thing is the beginning of another world.

15:9 Because of this we keep the eighth day as a day of gladness, on which also Jesus rose from the dead, and after he had appeared ascended to heaven.

CHAPTER 16

16:1 And I will, moreover, tell you concerning the temple, how these wretched men, being deceived, placed their hopes in the building as if it were the habitation of God, and not on the God who has made them.

16:2 For almost after the manner of the Gentiles did they consecrate him in the temple. But what said the Lord, making it of none effect? Listen you: Who has measured out the heaven with his palm, or the earth with the flat of his hand, is it not I? said the Lord. Heaven is my throne, and earth the footstool of my feet. What house will you build for me, or what shall be the place of my rest? You have known that their hope was vain.

16:3 And, yet further, he said again, Behold they that have destroyed this temple shall rebuild it.

16:4 And so doth it happen, for through their war it has been destroyed by the enemy, and now both they themselves and the servants of their enemies shall rebuild it.

16:5 And again it was made manifest how the temple and the people of Israel should be given up to their enemies. For the scripture said, And it shall come to pass in the last days that the Lord shall deliver up the sheep of his pasture, and their fold and their tower shall he give up to destruction; and it happened according to that which the Lord had spoken.

16:6 Let us inquire, therefore, whether there be any temple of God. There is; even where he himself has declared that he would make and perfect it. For it is written, And it shall be when the week is completed that the temple of God shall be built gloriously in the name of the Lord.

16:7 I find, therefore, that there is a temple; how then shall it be built in the name of the Lord? Learn you. Before that we believed in God the habitation of our heart was corrupt and feeble, as being of a truth a temple built by hands. For it was full of idolatry, and was a habitation of devils, because we did such things as were contrary to God;

16:8 but it shall be built in the name of the Lord. Attend you: that the temple of the Lord may be built gloriously. But in what manner? Learn you: having received the remission of our sins, and having hoped upon the name of the Lord, we have become new, having been again created entirely. Because of this God of a truth dwells in us as in an habitation.

16:9 How? The word of his faith, the calling of his promise, the wisdom of his ordinances, the commandments of his doctrine, he himself prophesying in us, he himself dwelling in us. To us, who were enslaved by death, he opens the gate of the temple, which is his mouth, and, giving us repentance, leads us into the temple incorruptible.

16:10 For he who desires to be saved looks not to the man, but to him that dwells in him and speaks in him, wondering that he had never before heard him speaking such words out of his mouth, or even desired to hear. This is the spiritual temple built by the Lord.

CHAPTER 17

17:1 So far as it is possible for me to show you these things with simplicity, my mind and soul hopes that I have not omitted any of the things that pertain to salvation;

17:2 for if I write to you concerning the things that are at hand, or the things that will be hereafter, you would not be able to understand them, because they are couched in parables. These things, therefore, are thus.

CHAPTER 18

18:1 Let us pass on now to another kind of knowledge and instruction. There are two paths of instruction and authority -- the one that of light, and the other that of darkness. But there is a great difference between the two paths. For over the one are appointed as illuminators the angels of God, over the other the angels of Satan;

18:2 on the one side is he who is Lord from everlasting to everlasting, on the other is the ruler of the world that now lies in wickedness.

CHAPTER 19

19:1 Now, the path of life is this: If any one wishes to travel to the appointed place, let him hasten by means of his works. Now, the knowledge of walking in it that is given to us is of this kind:

19:2 You shall love him that made you, you shall fear him that formed you, you shall glorify him that redeemed you from death. You shall be simple in heart, and rich in spirit; you shall not cleave to them that go in the path of death. You shall hate whatever is not pleasing to God; you shall hate all hypocrisy; you shall not abandon the commandments of the Lord;

19:3 you shall not exalt yourself; you shall be humble in all things; you shall not take glory to yourself; you shall not take evil counsel against your neighbor; you shall not take audacity into your soul.

19:4 You shall not commit fornication, you shall not commit adultery. You shall not pollute yourself with mankind: let not the word of God go forth from you in corruption. You shall not accept the person of any to reprove any man for transgression. You shall be gentle, you shall be quiet; you shall tremble at the words that you have heard; you shall not bear malice against your brother;

19:5 you shall not doubt whether a thing shall be or not; you shall not take the name of the Lord in vain. You shall love your neighbor beyond your own soul; you shall not kill a child by abortion, neither shall you destroy it after it is born. You shall not remove your hand from your son or your daughter, but shall teach them from their youth the fear of the Lord.

19:6 You shall not covet your neighbor's goods; you shall not be an extortioner; you shall not cleave with your soul to the proud, but you shall have your conversation with the lowly and the just. Receive as blessings the troubles that come to you, knowing that without God nothing happens.

19:7 You shall not be double-minded nor double-tongued, for to be double-tongued is the snare of death. You shall submit yourself to your masters as to the image of God, with shame and fear. You shall not give commands with bitterness to your servant and your handmaid, who hope in the same God as you do, lest, perchance, you cease to fear God, who is over both. For he came not to call men with respect of persons, but to call those whom the Spirit had prepared.

19:8 You shall communicate in all things with your neighbor, and shall not say that things are your own. For if you be partners in that which is incorruptible, how much more in the things that are corruptible? You shall not be hasty of speech, for the mouth is a snare of death. As far as you are able, you shall be pure concerning your soul.

19:9 Be not a stretcher forth of your hand in receiving, and a drawer back of it in giving. You shall love, as the apple of your eye, every one that speaks to you the word of the Lord.

19:10 You shall remember the day of judgment by night and by day; and you shall seek out every day the persons of the saints.

19:11 You shall not doubt to give, nor shall you murmur in giving. Give to every one that asks you, and you shall know who is the good recompenser of the reward. You shall take care of that which you have received, neither adding thereto, nor taking therefrom. You shall hate the evil man to the end, and shall judge justly.

19:12 You shall not make a schism, but shall make peace by bringing adversaries together. You shall make confession of your sins. You shall not go to prayer with an evil conscience. This is the way of life, either laboring by means of the word and proceeding to exhort, and practicing to save the soul by the word, or you shall work by your hands for the redemption of your sins.

CHAPTER 20

20:1 But the path of darkness is crooked and full of cursing, for it is the path of eternal death and punishment, in which way are the things that destroy the soul. Idolatry, boldness, the pride of power, hypocrisy, double-heartedness, adultery, murder, rape, haughtiness, transgression, deceit, malice, self-will, witchcraft, sorcery, covetousness, want of the fear of God.

20:2 Here are they who are persecutors of the good, haters of truth, lovers of lies; they who know not the reward of righteousness, who cleave not to what is good nor to just judgment; who attend not to the widow and the orphan; who are awake not to the fear of God, but to evil; from whom meekness and patience are afar off; who love the things that are vain, who follow after recompense, who pity not the poor, who labor not for him who is in trouble; who are prompt to evil-speaking, who know not him that made them; murderers of children, corruptors of the image of God; who turn away from the poor man and oppress the afflicted; advocates of the rich, unjust judges of the poor, sinners in all things.

CHAPTER 21

21:1 It is therefore right that he who has learned the ordinances of the Lord, even as many as have been written beforehand, should walk in them. For he who does these things shall be glorified in the Kingdom of God, but he who chooses the contrary things shall perish together with his works. On this account is the resurrection; on this account is the retribution.

21:2 I ask those who are of high estate among you, if you will receive any friendly advice from me, keep those with you toward whom you may do what is honorable. Fail not in so doing.

21:3 The day is at hand in which everything shall perish together with the evil one; the Lord is nigh at hand, and his reward also.

21:4 Again and again do I ask you, be you good lawgivers over yourselves, be you good advisers of yourselves. Abide faithful counselors of one another; take out of the midst of you all hypocrisy,

21:5 and may God, who rules the whole world, give you wisdom, understanding, science, knowledge of his ordinances, and patience.

21:6 And be you taught of God, inquiring what the Lord seeks of you, and so work that you may be found saved in the day of judgment.

21:7 But if there is any memory of that which is good, remember me while you practice these things, that both your desire and your watching may turn to some good.

21:8 I beseech you this, asking it as a favor. So long as the good vessel is with you, fail not in any of these things, but seek them out without ceasing, and fulfill all the commandments, for these things are worthy.

21:9 Therefore I have been the more anxious to write to you, so far as I was able, to the end that I might make you glad. Farewell, children of love and peace; the God of glory and of all grace be with your spirit. Amen.

Introduction to Justin Martyr

Justin Martyr (AD 100 – c. AD 165), is also known as Justin the Philosopher. He was an early Christian apologist and philosopher. Most of his works are lost, but two apologies and a dialogue did survive. The First Apology, his most well-known text, passionately defends the morality of the Christian life, and provides various ethical and philosophical arguments to convince the Roman emperor, Antoninus, to abandon the persecution of the Church. He also indicates, as St. Augustine would later, regarding the "true religion" that predated Christianity, that the "seeds of Christianity" (manifestations of the Logos acting in history) actually predated Christ's incarnation. This notion allows him to claim many historical Greek philosophers (including Socrates and Plato), in whose works he was well studied, as unknowing Christians. Justin was martyred, along with many of his students. He is venerated by the Catholic and Orthodox churches.

Justin Martyr is considered an Apostolic Father because of his close association with the apostolic era and his significant contributions to early Christian theology. The Apostolic Fathers are a group of Christian writers who lived in the first and second centuries and had direct or indirect connections with the apostles of Jesus Christ.

Justin Martyr, also known as Saint Justin, was born around 100 AD in Flavia Neapolis (modern-day Nablus, West Bank) and died as a martyr around 165 AD. He is primarily recognized for his works as an early Christian apologist, defending the faith against pagan accusations and promoting Christianity to a wider audience.

Justin Martyr's writings provide valuable insights into the beliefs and practices of early Christians. He was deeply influenced by his own conversion to Christianity after encountering a philosophical quest for truth. Justin Martyr saw Christianity as the fulfillment of Jewish prophecy and the true philosophy that transcended the limitations of other philosophical schools of thought.

Justin's most notable works include "First Apology" and "Dialogue with Trypho," where he addressed various theological and philosophical topics. In these writings, he defended the Christian faith, discussed the relationship between Christianity and Judaism, argued against pagan beliefs, and presented Jesus Christ as the Logos (the Word) and the Savior of humanity.

Justin Martyr's close association with the apostolic era is evidenced by his claim to have studied with followers of the apostles, although the specifics of his direct contact with the apostles are uncertain. His writings also show familiarity with the Gospels and other New Testament texts. Additionally, Justin's views align with many early Christian teachings and doctrines that were being developed during the apostolic period.

For these reasons, Justin Martyr is considered an Apostolic Father. His writings and teachings played a significant role in shaping early Christian theology and apologetics, and he stands as a bridge between the apostolic era and the subsequent development of Christian thought.

Justin Martyr

ST. JUSTIN MARTYR
THE DISCOURSE TO THE GREEKS

CHAPTER I. - JUSTIN JUSTIFIES HIS DEPARTURE FROM GREEK CUSTOMS.

Do not suppose, ye Greeks, that my separation from your customs is unreasonable and unthinking; for I found in them nothing that is holy or acceptable to God. For the very compositions of your poets are monuments of madness and intemperance. For anyone who becomes the scholar of your most eminent instructor, is more beset by difficulties than all men besides. For first they say that Agamemnon, abetting the extravagant lust of his brother, and his madness and unrestrained desire, readily gave even his daughter to be sacrificed, and troubled all Greece that he might rescue Helen, who had been ravished by the leprous shepherd. But when in the course of the war they took captives, Agamemnon was himself taken captive by Chryseis, and for Briseis' sake kindled a feud with the son of Thetis. And Pelides himself, who crossed the river, overthrew Troy, and subdued Hector, this your hero became the slave of Polyxena, and was conquered by a dead Amazon; and putting off the god-fabricated armour, and donning the hymeneal robe, he became a sacrifice of love in the temple of Apollo. And the Ithacan Ulysses made a virtue of a vice. And indeed his sailing past the Sirens gave evidence that he was destitute of worthy prudence, because he could not depend on his prudence for stopping his ears. Ajax, son of Telamon, who bore the shield of sevenfold ox-hide, went mad when he was defeated in the contest with Ulysses for the amour. Such things I have no desire to be instructed in. Of such virtue I am not covetous, that I should believe the myths of Homer. For the whole rhapsody, the beginning and end both of the Iliad and the Odyssey is--a woman.

CHAPTER II. - THE GREEK THEOGONY EXPOSED.

But since, next to Homer, Hesiod wrote his Works and Days, who will believe his drivelling theogony? For they say that Chronos, the son of Ouranos, in the beginning slew his father, and possessed himself of his rule; and that, being seized with a panic lest he should himself suffer in the same way, he preferred devouring his children; but that, by the craft of the Curetes, Jupiter was conveyed away and kept in secret, and afterwards bound his father with chains, and divided the empire; Jupiter receiving, as the story goes, the air, and Neptune the deep, and Pluto the portion of Hades. But Pluto ravished Proserpine; and Ceres sought her child wandering through the deserts. And this myth was celebrated in the Eleusinian fire. Again, Neptune ravished Melanippe when she was drawing water, besides abusing a host of Nereids not a few, whose names, were we to recount them, would cost us a multitude of words. And as for Jupiter, he was a various adulterer, with Antiope as a satyr, with Danae as gold, and with Europa as a bull; with Leda, moreover, he assumed wings. For the love of Semele proved both his unchastity and the jealousy of Semele. And they say that he carried off the Phrygian Ganymede to be his cup-bearer. These, then, are the exploits of the sons of Saturn. And your illustrious son of Latona [Apollo], who professed soothsaying, convicted himself of lying. He pursued Daphne, but did not gain possession of her; and to Hyacinthus, who loved him, he did not foretell his death. And I say nothing of the masculine character of Minerva, nor of the feminine nature of Bacchus, nor of the fornicating disposition of Venus. Read to Jupiter, ye Greeks, the law against parricides, and the penalty of adultery, and the ignominy of paederasty. Teach Minerva and Diana the works of women, and Bacchus the works of men. What seemliness is there in a woman's girding herself with armour, or in a man's decorating himself with cymbals, and garlands, and female attire, and accompanied by a herd of bacchanalian women?

CHAPTER III. - FOLLIES OF THE GREEK MYTHOLOGY.

For Hercules, celebrated by his three nights, sung by the poets for his successful labours, the son of Jupiter, who slew the lion and destroyed the many-headed hydra; who put to death the fierce and mighty boar, and was able to kill the fleet (of) man-eating birds, and brought up from Hades the three-headed dog; who effectually cleansed the huge Augean building from its dung, and killed the bulls and the stag whose nostrils breathed fire, and plucked the golden fruit from the tree, and slew the poisonous serpent (and for some reason, which it is not lawful to utter, killed Achelous, and the guest-slaying Busiris), and crossed the mountains that he might get water which gave forth an articulate speech, as the story goes: he who was able to do so many and such like and so great deeds as these, how childishly he was delighted to be stunned by the cymbals of the satyrs, and to be conquered by the love of woman, and to be struck on the hips by the laughing Lyda! And at last, not being able to put off the tunic of Nessus, himself kindling his own funeral pile, so he died. Let Vulcan lay aside his envy, and not be jealous if he is hated because he is old and club-footed, and Mars loved, because young and beautiful. Since, therefore, ye Greeks, your gods are convicted of intemperance, and your heroes are effeminate, as the histories on which your dramas are founded have declared, such as the curse of Atreus, the bed of Thyestes and the taint in the house of Pelops, and

Danaus murdering through hatred and making AEgyptus childless in the intoxication of his rage, and the Thyestean banquet spread by the Furies. And Procne is to this day flitting about, lamenting; and her sister of Athens shrills with her tongue cut out. For what need is there of speaking of the goad of OEdipus, and the murder of Laius, and the marrying his mother, and the mutual slaughter of those who were at once his brothers and his sons?

CHAPTER IV. - SHAMELESS PRACTICES OF THE GREEKS.

And your public assemblies I have come to hate. For there are excessive banquetings, and subtle flutes which provoke to lustful movements, and useless and luxurious anointings, and crowning with garlands. With such a mass of evils do you banish shame; and ye fill your minds with them, and are carried away by intemperance, and indulge as a common practice in wicked and insane fornication. And this further I would say to you, why are you, being a Greek, indignant at your son when he imitates Jupiter, and rises against you and defrauds you of your own wife? Why do you count him your enemy, and yet worship one that is like him? And why do you blame your wife for living in unchastity, and yet honour Venus with shrines? If indeed these things had been related by others, they would have seemed to be mere slanderous accusations, and not truth. But now your own poets sing these things, and your histories noisily publish them.

CHAPTER V. - CLOSING APPEAL.

Henceforth, ye Greeks, come and partake of incomparable wisdom, and be instructed by the Divine Word, and acquaint yourselves with the King immortal; and do not recognise those men as heroes who slaughter whole nations. For our own Ruler, the Divine Word, who even now constantly aids us, does not desire strength of body and beauty of feature, nor yet the high spirit of earth's nobility, but a pure soul, fortified by holiness, and the watchwords of our King, holy actions, for through the Word power passes into the soul. O trumpet of peace to the soul that is at war! O weapon that puttest to flight terrible passions! O instruction that quenches the innate fire of the soul! The Word exercises an influence which does not make poets: it does not equip philosophers nor skilled orators, but by its instruction it makes mortals immortal, mortals gods; and from the earth transports them to the realms above Olympus. Come, be taught; become as I am, for I, too, was as ye are. These have conquered me--the divinity of the instruction, and the power of the Word: for as a skilled serpent-charmer lures the terrible reptile from his den and causes it to flee, so the Word drives the fearful passions of our sensual nature from the very recesses of the soul; first driving forth lust, through which every ill is begotten--hatreds, strife, envy, emulations, anger, and such like. Lust being once banished, the soul becomes calm and serene. And being set free from the ills in which it was sunk up to the neck, it returns to Him who made it. For it is fit that it be restored to that state whence it departed, whence every soul was or is.

FRAGMENTS OF THE LOST WORK OF JUSTIN ON THE RESURRECTION

CHAPTER I.--THE SELF-EVIDENCING POWER OF TRUTH.

THE word of truth is free, and carries its own authority, disdaining to fall under any skilful argument, or to endure the logical scrutiny of its hearers. But it would be believed for its own nobility, and for the confidence due to Him who sends it. Now the word of truth is sent from God; wherefore the freedom claimed by the truth is not arrogant. For being sent with authority, it were not fit that it should be required to produce proof of what is said; since neither is there any proof beyond itself, which is God. For every proof is more powerful and trustworthy than that which it proves; since what is disbelieved, until proof is produced, gets credit when such proof is produced, and is recognised as being what it was stated to be. But nothing is either more powerful or more trustworthy than the truth; so that he who requires proof of this is like one who wishes it demonstrated why the things that appear to the senses do appear. For the test of those things which are received through the reason, is sense; but of sense itself there is no test beyond itself. As then we bring those things which reason hunts after, to sense, and by it judge what kind of things they are, whether the things spoken be true or false, and then sit in judgment no longer, giving full credit to its decision; so also we refer all that is said regarding men and the world to the truth, and by it judge whether it be worthless or no. But the utterances of truth we judge by no separate test, giving full credit to itself. And God, the Father of the universe, who is the perfect intelligence, is the truth. And the Word, being His Son, came to us, having put on flesh, revealing both Himself and the Father, giving to us in Himself resurrection from the dead, and eternal life afterwards. And this is Jesus Christ, our Saviour and Lord. He, therefore, is Himself both the faith and the proof of Himself and of all things. Wherefore those who follow Him, and know Him, having faith in Him as their proof, shall rest in Him. But since the adversary does not cease to resist many, and uses many and divers arts to ensnare them, that he may seduce the faithful from their faith, and that he may prevent the faithless from believing, it seems to me necessary that we also, being armed with the invulnerable doctrines of the faith, do battle against him in behalf of the weak.

CHAPTER II.--OBJECTIONS TO THE RESURRECTION OF THE FLESH.

They who maintain the wrong opinion say that there is no resurrection of the flesh; giving as their reason that it is impossible that what is corrupted and dissolved should be restored to the same as it had been. And besides the impossibility, they say that the salvation of the flesh is disadvantageous; and they abuse the flesh, adducing its infirmities, and declare that it only is the cause of our sins, so that if the flesh, say they, rise again, our infirmities also rise with it. And such sophistical reasons as the following they elaborate: If the flesh rise again, it must rise either entire and possessed of all its parts, or imperfect. But its rising imperfect argues a want of power on God's part, if some parts could be saved, and others not; but if all the parts are saved, then the body will manifestly have all its members. But is it not absurd to say that these members will exist after the resurrection from the dead, since the Saviour said, "They neither marry, nor are given in marriage, but shall be as the angels in heaven?" And the angels, say they, have neither flesh, nor do they eat, nor have sexual intercourse; therefore there shall be no resurrection of the flesh. By these and such like arguments, they attempt to distract men from the faith. And there are some who maintain that even Jesus Himself appeared only as spiritual, and not in flesh, but presented merely the appearance of flesh: these persons seek to rob the flesh of the promise. First, then, let us solve those things which seem to them to be insoluble; then we will introduce in an orderly manner the demonstration concerning the flesh, proving that it partakes of salvation.

CHAPTER III.--IF THE MEMBERS RISE, MUST THEY DISCHARGE THE SAME FUNCTIONS AS NOW?

They say, then, if the body shall rise entire, and in possession of all its members, it necessarily follows that the functions of the members shall also be in existence; that the womb shall become pregnant, and the male also discharge his function of generation, and the rest of the members in like manner. Now let this argument stand or fall by this one assertion. For this being proved false, their whole objection will be removed. Now it is indeed evident that the members which discharge functions discharge those functions which in the present life we see but it does not follow that they necessarily discharge the same functions from the beginning. And that this may be more clearly seen, let us consider it thus. The function of the womb is to become pregnant; and of the member of the male to impregnate. But as, though these members are destined to discharge such functions, it is not therefore necessary that they from the beginning discharge them (since we see many women who do not become pregnant, as those that are barren, even though they have wombs), so pregnancy is not the immediate and necessary consequence of having a womb; but those even who are not barren abstain from sexual intercourse, some being virgins from the first, and others from a certain time. And we see men also keeping themselves virgins, some from the first, and some from a certain time; so that by their means, marriage, made lawless through lust, is destroyed. And we find that some even of the lower animals, though possessed of wombs, do not bear, such as the mule; and the male mules do not beget their kind. So that both in the case of men and the irrational animals we can see sexual intercourse abolished; and this, too, before the future world. And our Lord Jesus Christ was born of a virgin, for no other reason than that He might destroy the begetting by lawless desire, and might show to the ruler that the formation of man was possible to God without human intervention. And when He had been born, and had submitted to the other conditions of the flesh,--I mean food, drink, and clothing,--this one condition only of discharging the sexual function He did not submit to; for, regarding the desires of the flesh, He accepted some as necessary, while others, which were unnecessary, He did not submit to. For if the flesh were deprived of food, drink, and clothing, it would be destroyed; but being deprived of lawless desire, it suffers no harm. And at the same time He foretold that, in the future world, sexual intercourse should be done away with; as He says, "The children of this world marry, and are given in marriage; but the children of the world to come neither marry nor are given in marriage, but shall be like the angels in heaven." Let not, then, those that are unbelieving marvel, if in the world to come He do away with those acts of our fleshly members which even in this present life are abolished.

CHAPTER IV.--MUST THE DEFORMED RISE DEFORMED?

Well, they say, if then the flesh rise, it must rise the same as it falls; so that if it die with one eye, it must rise one-eyed; if lame, lame; if defective in any part of the body, in this part the man must rise deficient. How truly blinded are they in the eyes of their hearts! For they have not seen on the earth blind men seeing again, and the lame walking by His word. All things which the Saviour did, He did in the first place in order that what was spoken concerning Him in the prophets might be fulfilled, "that the blind should receive sight, and the deaf hear," and so on; but also to induce the belief that in the resurrection the flesh shall rise entire. For if on earth He healed the sicknesses of the flesh, and made the body whole, much more will He do this in the resurrection, so that the flesh shall rise perfect and entire. In this manner, then, shall those dreaded difficulties of theirs be healed.

CHAPTER V.--THE RESURRECTION OF THE FLESH IS NOT IMPOSSIBLE.

But again, of those who maintain that the flesh has no resurrection, some assert that it is impossible; others that, considering how vile and despicable the flesh is, it is not fit that God should raise it; and others, that it did not at the first receive the promise. First, then, in respect of those who say that it is impossible for God to raise it, it seems to me that I should show that they are ignorant, professing as they do in word that they are believers, yet by their works proving themselves to be unbelieving, even more unbelieving than the unbelievers. For, seeing that all the heathen believe in their idols, and are persuaded that to them all things are possible (as even their poet Homer says, "The gods can do all things, and that easily;" and he added the word "easily" that he might bring out the greatness of the power of the gods), many do seem to be more unbelieving than they. For if the heathen believe in their gods, which are idols ("which have ears, and they hear not; they have eyes, and they see not"), that they can do all things, though they be but devils, as saith the Scripture, "The gods of the nations axe devils," much more ought we, who hold the right, excellent, and true faith, to believe in our God, since also we have proofs [of His power], first in the creation of the first man, for he was made from the earth by God; and this is sufficient evidence of God's power; and then they who observe things can see how men are generated one by another, and can marvel in a still greater degree that from a little drop of moisture so grand a living creature is formed. And certainly if this were only recorded in a promise, and not seen accomplished, this too would be much more incredible than the other; but it is rendered more credible by accomplishment. But even in the case of the resurrection the Saviour has shown us accomplishments, of which we will in a little speak. But now we are demonstrating that the resurrection of the flesh is possible, asking pardon of the children of the Church if we adduce arguments which seem to be secular s and physical: first, because to God nothing is secular, not even the world itself, for it is His workmanship; and secondly, because we are conducting our argument so as to meet unbelievers. For if we argued with believers, it were enough to say that we believe; but now we must proceed by demonstrations. The foregoing proofs are indeed quite sufficient to evince the possibility of the resurrection of the flesh; but since these men are exceedingly unbelieving, we will further adduce a more convincing argument still,--an argument drawn not from faith, for they are not within its scope, but from their own mother unbelief,--I mean, of course, from physical

reasons. For if by such arguments we prove to them that the resurrection of the flesh is possible, they are certainly worthy of great contempt if they can be persuaded neither by the deliverances of faith nor by the arguments of the world.

CHAPTER VI.--THE RESURRECTION CONSISTENT WITH THE OPINIONS OF THE PHILOSOPHERS.

Those, then, who are called natural philosophers, say, some of them, as Plato, that the universe is matter and God; others, as Epicurus, that it is atoms and the void; others, like the Stoics, that it is these four--fire, water, air, earth. For it is sufficient to mention the most prevalent opinions. And Plato says that all things are made from matter by God, and according to His design; but Epicures and his followers say that all things are made from the atom and the void by some kind of self-regulating action of the natural movement of the bodies; and the Stoics, that all are made of the four elements, God pervading them. But while there is such discrepancy among them, there are some doctrines acknowledged by them all in common, one of which is that neither can anything be produced from what is not in being, nor anything be destroyed or dissolved into what has not any being, and that the elements exist indestructible out of which all things are generated. And this being so, the regeneration of the flesh will, according to all these philosophers, appear to be possible. For if, according to Plato, it is matter and God, both these are indestructible and God; and God indeed occupies the position of an artificer, to wit, a potter; and matter occupies the place of clay or wax, or some such thing. That, then, which is formed of matter, be it an image or a statue, is destructible; but the matter itself is indestructible, such as clay or wax, or any other such kind of matter. Thus the artist designs in the clay or wax, and makes the form of a living animal; and again, if his handiwork be destroyed, it is not impossible for him to make the same form, by working up the same material, and fashioning it anew. So that, according to Plato, neither will it be impossible for God, who is Himself indestructible, and has also indestructible material, even after that which has been first formed of it has been destroyed, to make it anew again, and to make the same form just as it was before. But according to the Stoics even, the body being produced by the mixture of the four elementary substances, when this body has been dissolved into the four elements, these remaining indestructible, it is possible that they receive a second time the same fusion and composition, from God pervading them, and so re-make the body which they formerly made. Like as if a man shall make a composition of gold and silver, and brass and tin, and then shall wish to dissolve it again, so that each element exist separately, having again mixed them, he may, if he pleases, make the very same composition as he had formerly made. Again, according to Epicurus, the atoms and the void being indestructible, it is by a definite arrangement and adjustment of the atoms as they come together, that both all other formations are produced, and the body itself; and it being in course of time dissolved, is dissolved again into those atoms from which it was also produced. And as these remain indestructible, it is not at all impossible, that by coming together again, and receiving the same arrangement and position, they should make a body of like nature to what was formerly produced by them; as if a jeweller should make in mosaic the form of an animal, and the stones should be scattered by time or by the man himself who made them, he having still in his possession the scattered stones, may gather them together again, and having gathered, may dispose them in the same way, and make the same form of an animal. And shall not God be able to collect again the decomposed members of the flesh, and make the same body as was formerly produced by Him?

CHAPTER VII.--THE BODY VALUABLE IN GOD'S SIGHT.

But the proof of the possibility of the resurrection of the flesh I have sufficiently demonstrated, in answer to men of the world. And if the resurrection of the flesh is not found impossible on the principles even of unbelievers, how much more will it be found in accordance with the mind of believers! But following our order, we must now speak with respect to those who think meanly of the flesh, and say that it is not worthy of the resurrection nor of the heavenly economy, because, first, its substance is earth; and besides, because it is full of all wickedness, so that it forces the soul to sin along with it. But these persons seem to be ignorant of the whole work of God, both of the genesis and formation of man at the first, and why the things in the world were made. For does not the word say, "Let Us make man in our image, and after our likeness?" What kind of man? Manifestly He means fleshly man, For the word says, "And God took dust of the earth, and made man." It is evident, therefore, that man made in the image of God was of flesh. Is it not, then, absurd to say, that the flesh made by God in His own image is contemptible, and worth nothing? But that the flesh is with God a precious possession is manifest, first from its being formed by Him, if at least the image is valuable to the former and artist; and besides, its value can be gathered from the creation of the rest of the world. For that on account of which the rest is made, is the most precious of all to the maker.

CHAPTER VIII.--DOES THE BODY CAUSE THE SOUL TO SIN?

Quite true, say they; yet the flesh is a sinner, so much so, that it forces the soul to sin along with it. And thus they vainly accuse it, and lay to its charge alone the sins of both. But in what instance can the flesh possibly sin by itself, if it have not the soul going before it and inciting it? For as in the case of a yoke of oxen, if one or other is loosed from the yoke, neither of them can plough alone; so neither can soul or body alone effect anything, if they be unyoked from their communion. And if it is the flesh that is the sinner, then on its account alone did the Saviour come, as He says, "I am not come to call the righteous, but sinners to repentance." Since, then, the flesh has been proved to be valuable in the sight of God, and glorious above all His works, it would very justly be saved by Him.

We must meet, therefore, those who say, that even though it be the special handiwork of God, and beyond all else valued by Him, it would not immediately follow that it has the promise of the resurrection. Yet is it not absurd, that that which has been produced with such circumstance, and which is beyond all else valuable, should be so neglected by its Maker, as to pass to nonentity? Then the sculptor and painter, if they wish the works they have made to endure, that they may win glory by them, renew them when they begin to decay; but God would so neglect His own possession and work, that it becomes annihilated, and no longer exists. Should we not call this labour in vain? As if a man who has built a house should forthwith destroy it, or should neglect it, though he sees it falling into decay, and is able to repair it: we would blame him for labouring in vain; and should we not so blame God? But not such an one is the Incorruptible,--not senseless is the Intelligence of the universe. Let the unbelieving be silent, even though they themselves do not believe.

But, in truth, He has even called the flesh to the resurrection, and promises to it everlasting life. For where He promises to save man, there He gives the promise to the flesh. For what is man but the reasonable animal composed of body and soul? Is the soul by itself man? No; but the soul of man. Would the body be called man? No, but it is called the body of man. If, then, neither of these is by itself man, but that which is made up of the two together is called man, and God has called man to life and resurrection, He has called not a part, but the whole, which is the soul and the body. Since would it not be unquestionably absurd, if, while these two are in the same being and according to the same law, the one were saved and the other not? And if it be not impossible, as has already been proved, that the flesh be regenerated, what is the distinction on the ground of which the soul is saved and the body not? Do they make God a grudging God? But He is good, and will have all to be saved. And by God and His proclamation, not only has your soul heard and believed on Jesus Christ, and with it the flesh, but both were washed, and both wrought righteousness. They make God, then ungrateful and unjust, if, while both believe on Him, He desires to save one and not the other. Well, they say, but the soul is incorruptible, being a part of God and inspired by Him, and therefore He desires to save what is peculiarly His own and akin to Himself; but the flesh is corruptible, and not from Him, as the soul is. Then what thanks are due to Him, and what manifestation of His power and goodness is it, if He purposed to save what is by nature saved and exists as a part of Himself? For it had its salvation from itself; so that in saving the soul, God does no great thing. For to be saved is its natural destiny, because it is a part of Himself, being His inspiration. But no thanks are due to one who saves what is his own; for this is to save himself. For he who saves a part himself, saves himself by his own means, lest he become defective in that part; and this is not the act of a good man. For not even when a man does good to his children and offspring, does one call him a good man; for even the most savage of the wild beasts do so, and indeed willingly endure death, if need be, for the sake of their cubs. But if a man were to perform the same acts in behalf of his slaves, that man would justly be called good. Wherefore the Saviour also taught us to love our enemies, since, says He, what thank have ye? So that He has shown us that it is a good work not only to love those that are begotten of Him, but also those that are without. And what He enjoins upon us, He Himself first of all does.

CHAPTER IX.--THE RESURRECTION OF CHRIST PROVES THAT THE BODY RISES.

If He had no need of the flesh, why did He heal it? And what is most forcible of all, He raised the dead. Why? Was it not to show what the resurrection should be? How then did He raise the dead? Their souls or their bodies? Manifestly both. If the resurrection were only spiritual, it was requisite that He, in raising the dead, should show the body lying apart by itself, and the soul living apart by itself. But now He did not do so, but raised the body, confirming in it the promise of life. Why did He rise in the flesh in which He suffered, unless to show the resurrection of the flesh? And wishing to confirm this, when His disciples did not know whether to believe He had truly risen in the body, and were looking upon Him and doubting, He said to them, "Ye have not yet faith, see that it is I;" and He let them handle Him, and showed them the prints of the nails in His hands. And when they were by every kind of proof persuaded that it was Himself, and in the body, they asked Him to eat with them, that they might

thus still more accurately ascertain that He had in verity risen bodily; and He did eat honey-comb and fish. And when He had thus shown them that there is truly a resurrection of the flesh, wishing to show them this also, that it is not impossible for flesh to ascend into heaven (as He had said that our dwelling-place is in heaven), "He was taken up into heaven while they beheld," as He was in the flesh. If, therefore, after all that has been said, anyone demand demonstration of the resurrection, he is in no respect different from the Sadducees, since the resurrection of the flesh is the power of God, and, being above all reasoning, is established by faith, and seen in works.

CHAPTER X.--THE BODY SAVED, AND WILL THEREFORE RISE.

The resurrection is a resurrection of the flesh which died. For the spirit dies not; the soul is in the body, and without a soul it cannot live. The body, when the soul forsakes it, is not. For the body is the house of the soul; and the soul the house of the spirit. These three, in all those who cherish a sincere hope and unquestioning faith in God, will be saved. Considering, therefore, even such arguments as are suited to this world, and finding that, even according to them, it is not impossible that the flesh be regenerated; and seeing that, besides all these proofs, the Saviour in the whole Gospel shows that there is salvation for the flesh, why do we any longer endure those unbelieving and dangerous arguments, and fail to see that we are retrograding when we listen to such an argument as this: that the soul is immortal, but the body mortal, and incapable of being revived? For this we used to hear from Pythagoras and Plato, even before we learned the truth. If then the Saviour said this, and proclaimed salvation to the soul alone, what new thing, beyond what we heard from Pythagoras and Plato and all their band, did He bring us? But now He has come proclaiming the glad tidings of a new and strange hope to men. For indeed it was a strange and new thing for God to promise that He would not keep incorruption in incorruption, but would make corruption incorruption. But because the prince of wickedness could in no other way corrupt the truth, he sent forth his apostles (evil men who introduced pestilent doctrines), choosing them from among those who crucified our Saviour; and these men bore the name of the Saviour, but did the works of him that sent them, through whom the name itself has been spoken against. But if the flesh do not rise, why is it also guarded, and why do we not rather suffer it to indulge its desires? Why do we not imitate physicians, who, it is said, when they get a patient that is despaired of and incurable, allow him to indulge his desires? For they know that he is dying; and this indeed those who hate the flesh surely do, casting it out of its inheritance, so far as they can; for on this account they also despise it, because it is shortly to become a corpse. But if our physician Christ, God, having rescued us from our desires, regulates our flesh with His own wise and temperate rule, it is evident that He guards it from sins because it possesses a hope of salvation, as physicians do not suffer men whom they hope to save to indulge in what pleasures they please.

St. Justin Martyr: On the Sole Government of God

CHAPTER 1
Object of the author

ALTHOUGH human nature at first received a union of intelligence and safety to discern the truth, and the worship due to the one Lord of all, yet envy, insinuating the excellence of human greatness, turned men away to the making of idols; and this superstitious custom, after continuing for a long period, is handed down to the majority as if it were natural and true. It is the part of a lover of man, or rather of a lover of God, to remind men who have neglected it of that which they ought to know. For the truth is of itself sufficient to show forth, by means of those things which are contained under the pole of heaven, the order [instituted by] Him who has created them. But forgetfulness having taken possession of the minds of men, through the long-suffering of God, has acted recklessly in transferring to mortals the name which is applicable to the only true God; and from the few the infection of sin spread to the many, who were blinded by popular usage to the knowledge of that which was lasting and unchangeable. For the men of former generations, who instituted private and public rites in honour of such as were more powerful, caused forgetfulness of the Catholic faith to take possession of their posterity; but I, as I have just stated, along with a God-loving mind, shall employ the speech of one who loves man, and set it before those who have intelligence, which all ought to have who are privileged to observe the administration of the universe, so that they should worship unchangeably Him who knows all things. This I shall do, not by mere display of words, but by altogether using demonstration drawn from the old poetry in Greek literature, and from writings very common amongst all. For from these the famous men who have handed down idol-worship as law to the multitudes, shall be taught and convicted by their own poets and literature of great ignorance.

CHAPTER 2
Testimonies to the unity of God

First, then, Æschylus, in expounding the arrangement of his work, expressed himself also as follows respecting the only God:

Afar from mortals place the holy God,
Nor ever think that He, like to thyself,
In fleshly robes is clad; for all unknown
Is the great God to such a worm as thou.

Divers similitudes He bears; at times
He seems as a consuming fire that burns
Unsated; now like water, then again
In sable folds of darkness shrouds Himself.
Nay, even the very beasts of earth reflect
His sacred image; whilst the wind, clouds, rain,
The roll of thunder and the lightning flash,
Reveal to men their great and sovereign Lord.
Before Him sea and rocks, with every fount,
And all the water floods, in reverence bend;
And as they gaze upon His awful face,
Mountains and earth, with the profoundest depths
Of ocean, and the highest peaks of hills,
Tremble: for He is Lord Omnipotent;
And this the glory is of God Most High.
But he was not the only man initiated in the knowledge
of God; for Sophocles also thus describes the nature of
the only Creator of all things, the One God:
There is one God, in truth there is but one,
Who made the heavens and the broad earth beneath,
The glancing waves of ocean, and the winds;
But many of us mortals err in heart,
And set up, for a solace in our woes,
Images of the gods in stone and brass,
Or figures carved in gold or ivory;
And, furnishing for these, our handiworks,
Both sacrifice and rite magnificent,
We think that thus we do a pious work.
And Philemon also, who published many explanations
of ancient customs, shares in the knowledge of the
truth; and thus he writes:
Tell me what thoughts of God we should conceive?
One, all things seeing, yet Himself unseen.
Even Orpheus, too, who introduces three hundred and
sixty gods, will bear testimony in my favour from the
tract called Diathecæ, in which he appears to repent of
his error by writing the following:
I'll speak to those who lawfully may hear;
All others, ye profane, now close the doors!
And, O Musaeus, hearken thou to me,
Who offspring art of the light-bringing moon.
The words I tell thee now are true indeed,
And if thou former thoughts of mine hast seen,
Let them not rob thee of the blessed life;
But rather turn the depths of thine own heart
Unto that place where light and knowledge dwell.
Take thou the word divine to guide thy steps;
And walking well in the straight certain path,
Look to the one and universal King,
One, self-begotten, and the only One
Of whom all things, and we ourselves, are sprung.
All things are open to His piercing gaze,
While He Himself is still invisible;
Present in all His works, though still unseen,
He gives to mortals evil out of good,
Sending both chilling wars and tearful griefs;
And other than the Great King there is none.

The clouds for ever settle round His throne;
And mortal eyeballs in mere mortal eyes
Are weak to see Jove, reigning over all.
He sits established in the brazen heavens
Upon His throne; and underneath His feet
He treads the earth, and stretches His right hand
To all the ends of ocean, and around
Tremble the mountain ranges, and the streams,
The depths, too, of the blue and hoary sea.
He speaks indeed as if he had been an eyewitness of
God's greatness. And Pythagoras agrees with him
when he writes:
Should one in boldness say, Lo, I am God!
Besides the One--Eternal--Infinite,
Then let him from the throne he has usurped
Put forth his power and form another globe,
Such as we dwell in, saying, This is mine.
Nor only so, but in this new domain
For ever let him dwell. If this he can,
Then verily he is a god proclaimed.

CHAPTER 3
Testimonies to a future judgment

Then further concerning Him, that He alone is
powerful, both to institute judgment on the deeds
performed in life, and on the ignorance of the Deity
[displayed by men], I can adduce witnesses from your
own ranks; and first Sophocles, who speaks as follows:

That time of times shall come, shall surely come,
When from the golden ether down shall fall
Fire's teeming treasure, and in burning flames
All things of earth and heaven shall be consumed;
And then, when all creation is dissolved,
The sea's last wave shall die upon the shore,
The bald earth stript of trees, the burning air
No winged thing upon its breast shall bear.
There are two roads to Hades, well we know;
By this the righteous, and by that the bad,
On to their separate fates shall tend; and He,
Who all things had destroyed, shall all things save.
And Philemon again:
Think'st thou, Nicostratus, the dead, who here
Enjoyed whate'er of good life often man,
Escape the noticeof Divinity,
As if they might forgotten be of Him?
Nay, there's an eye of Justice watching all;
For if the good and bad find the same end,
Then go thou, rob, steal, plunder, at thy will,
Do all the evil that to thee seems good.
Yet be not thou deceived; for underneath
There is a throne and place of judgment set,
Which God the Lord of all shall occupy;
Whose name is terrible, nor shall I dare
To breathe it forth in feeble human speech.
And Euripides:

Not grudgingly he gives a lease of life,
That we the holders may be fairly judged;
And if a mortal man doth think to hide
His daily guilt from the keen eye of God,
It is an evil thought; so if perchance
He meets with leisure-taking Justice, she
Demands him as her lawful prisoner:
But many of you hastily commit
A twofold sin, and say there is no God.
But, ah! there is; there is. Then see that he
Who, being wicked, prospers, may redeem
The time so precious, else hereafter waits
For him the due reward of punishment.

CHAPTER 4
God desires not sacrifices, but righteousness

And that God is not appeased by the libations and incense of evil-doers, but awards vengeance in righteousness to each one, Philemon again shall bear testimony to me:

If anyone should dream, O Pamphilus,
By sacrifice of bulls or goats--nay, then,
By Jupiter--of any such like things;
Or by presenting gold or purple robes,
Or images of ivory and gems;
If thus he thinks he may propitiate God,
He errs, and shows himself a silly one.
But let him rather useful be, and good,
Committing neither theft nor lustful deeds,
Nor murder foul, for earthly riches' sake.
Let him of no man covet wife or child,
His splendid house, his wide-spread property,
His maiden, or his slave born ill his house,
His horses, or his cattle, or his beeves,
Nay, covet not a pin, O Pamphilus,
For God, close by you, sees whate'er you do.
He ever with the wicked man is wroth,
But in the righteous takes a pleasure still,
Permitting him to reap fruit of his toil,
And to enjoy the bread his sweat has won.
But being righteous, see thou pay thy vows,
And unto God the giver offer gifts.
Place thy adorning not in outward shows,
But in an inward purity of heart;
Hearing the thunder then, thou shall not fear,
Nor shall thou flee, O master, at its voice,
For thou art conscious of no evil deed,
And God, close by you, sees whate'er you do.
Again, Plato, in Timæus, says: "But if anyone on consideration should actually institute a rigid inquiry, he would be ignorant of the distinction between the human and the divine nature; because God mingles many things up into one, [and again is able to dissolve one into many things,] seeing that He is endued with

knowledge and power; but no man either is, or ever shall be, able to perform any of these."

CHAPTER 5
The vain pretensions of false gods

But concerning those who think that they shall share the holy and perfect name, which some have received by a vain tradition as if they were gods, Menander in the Auriga says:

If there exists a god who walketh out
With an old woman, or who enters in
By stealth to houses through the folding-doors,
He ne'er can please me; nay, but only he
Who stays at home, a just and righteous God,
To give salvation to His worshippers.
The same Menander, in the Sacerdos, says:
There is no God, O woman, that can save
One man by another; if indeed a man,
With sound of tinkling cymbals, charm a god
Where'er he listeth, then assuredly
He who doth so is much the greater god.
But these, O Rhode, are but the cunning schemes
Which daring men of intrigue, unabashed,
Invent to earn themselves a livelihood,
And yield a laughing-stock unto the age.
Again, the same Menander, stating his opinion about those who are received as gods, proving rather that they are not so, says:

Yea, if I this beheld, I then should wish
That back to me again my soul returned.
For tell me where, O Getas, in the world
'Tis possible to find out righteous gods?
And in the Depositum:
There's an unrighteous judgment, as it seems,
Even with the gods.
And Euripides the tragedian, in Orestes, says:
Apollo having caused by his command
The murder of the mother, knoweth not
What honesty and justice signify.
We serve the gods, whoever they may be;
But from the central regions of the earth
You see Apollo plainly gives response
To mortals, and whate'er he says we do.
I him obeyed, when she that bore me fell
Slain by my hand: he is the wicked man.
Then slay him, for 'twas he that sinned, not I.
What could I do? Think you not that the god
Should free me from the blame which I do bear?
The same also in Hippolytus:
But on these points the gods do not judge right.
And in Ion:
But in the daughter of Erechtheus
What interest have I? for that pertains
Not unto such as me. But when I come

With golden vessels for libations, I
The dew shall sprinkle, and yet needs must warn
Apollo of his deeds; for when he weds
Maidens by force, the children secretly
Begotten he betrays, and then neglects
When dying. Thus not you; but while you may
Always pursue the virtues, for the gods
Will surely punish men of wickedness.
How is it right that you, who have prescribed
Laws for men's guidance, live unrighteously?
But ye being absent, I shall freely speak,
And ye to men shall satisfaction give
For marriage forced, thou Neptune, Jupiter,
Who over heaven presides. The temples ye
Have emptied, while injustice ye repay.
And though ye laud the prudent to the skies,
Yet have ye filled your hands with wickedness.
No longer is it right to call men ill
If they do imitate the sins of gods;
Nay, evil let their teachers rather be.
And in Archelaus:
Full oft, my son, do gods mankind perplex.
And in Bellerophon:
They are no gods, who do not what is right.
And again in the same:
Gods reign in heaven most certainly, says one;
But it is false,--and let not him
Who speaks thus, be so foolish as to use
Ancient tradition, or to pay regard
Unto my words: but with unclouded eye
Behold the matter in its clearest light.
Power absolute, I say, robs men of life
And property; transgresses plighted faith;
Nor spares even cities, but with cruel hand
Despoils and devastates them ruthlessly.
But they that do these things have more success
Than those who live a gentle pious life;
And cities small, I know, which reverence gods,
Submissive bend before the many spears
Of larger impious ones; yea, and methinks
If any man lounge idly, and abstain
From working with his hands for sustenance,
Yet pray the gods; he very soon will know
If they from him misfortunes will avert.
And Menander in Diphilus:
Therefore ascribe we praise and honour great
To Him who Father is, and Lord of all;
Sole maker and preserver of mankind,
And who with all good things our earth has stored.
The same also in the Piscatores:
For I deem that which nourishes my life
Is God; but he whose custom 'tis to meet
The wants of men,--He needs not at our hands
Renewed supplies, Himself being all in all.
The same in the Fratres:
God ever is intelligence to those
Who righteous are: so wisest men have thought.

And in the Tibicinæ:
Good reason finds a temple in all things
Wherein to worship; for what is the mind,
But just the voice of God within us placed?
And the tragedian in Phrixus:
But if the pious and the impious
Share the same lot, how could we think it just,
If Jove, the best, judges not uprightly?
In Philoctetes:
You see how honourable gain is deemed
Even to the gods; and how he is admired
Whose shrine is laden most with yellow gold.
What, then, doth hinder thee, since it is good
To be like gods, from thus accepting gain?
In Hecuba:
O Jupiter I whoever thou mayest be,
Of whom except in word all knowledge fails;
and, Jupiter, whether thou art indeed
A great necessity, or the mind of man,
I worship thee!

CHAPTER 6
We should acknowledge only one God

Here, then, is a proof of virtue, and of a mind loving prudence, to recur to the communion of the unity, and to attach one's self to prudence for salvation, and make choice of the better things according to the free-will placed in man; and not to think that those who are possessed of human passions are lords of all, when they shall not appear to have even equal power with men. For in Homer, Demodocus says he is self-taught --

God inspired me with strains
-- though he is a mortal. Æsculapius and Apollo are taught to heal by Chiron the Centaur,--a very novel thing indeed, for gods to be taught by a man. What need I speak of Bacchus, who the poet says is mad? or of Hercules, who he says is unhappy? What need to speak of Mars and Venus, the leaders of adultery; and by means of all these to establish the proof which has been undertaken? For if someone, in ignorance, should imitate the deeds which are said to be divine, he would be reckoned among impure men, and a stranger to life and humanity; and if anyone does so knowingly, he will have a plausible excuse for escaping vengeance, by showing that imitation of godlike deeds of audacity is no sin. But if anyone should blame these deeds, he will take away their well-known names, and not cover them up with specious and plausible words. It is necessary, then, to accept the true and invariable Name, not proclaimed by my words only, but by the words of those who have introduced us to the elements of learning, in order that we may not, by living idly in this present state of existence, not only as those who are ignorant of the heavenly glory, but also as having

proved ourselves ungrateful, render our account to the Judge.

JUSTIN MARTYR -- THE FIRST APOLOGY

CHAPTER I -- ADDRESS.

To the Emperor Titus Ælius Adrianus Antoninus Pius Augustus Caesar, and to his son Verissimus the Philosopher, and to Lucius the Philosopher, the natural son of Caesar, and the adopted son of Pius, a lover of learning, and to the sacred Senate, with the whole People of the Romans, I, Justin, the son of Priscus and grandson of Bacchius, natives of Flavia Neapolis in Palestine, present this address and petition in behalf of those of all nations who are unjustly hated and wantonly abused, myself being one of them.

CHAPTER II -- JUSTICE DEMANDED.

Reason directs those who are truly pious and philosophical to honour and love only what is true, declining to follow traditional opinions, if these be worthless. For not only does sound reason direct us to refuse the guidance of those who did or taught anything wrong, but it is incumbent on the lover of truth, by all means, and if death be threatened, even before his own life, to choose to do and say what is right. Do you, then, since ye are called pious and philosophers, guardians of justice and lovers of learning, give good heed, and hearken to my address; and if ye are indeed such, it will be manifested. For we have come, not to flatter you by this writing, nor please you by our address, but to beg that you pass judgment, after an accurate and searching investigation, not flattered by prejudice or by a desire of pleasing superstitious men, nor induced by irrational impulse or evil rumours which have long been prevalent, to give a decision which will prove to be against yourselves. For as for us, we reckon that no evil can be done us, unless we be convicted as evil-doers or be proved to be wicked men; and you, you can kill, but not hurt us.

CHAPTER III -- CLAIM OF JUDICIAL INVESTIGATION.

But lest anyone think that this is an unreasonable and reckless utterance, we demand that the charges against the Christians be investigated, and that, if these be substantiated, they be punished as they deserve; [or rather, indeed, we ourselves will punish them.] But if no one can convict us of anything, true reason forbids you, for the sake of a wicked rumour, to wrong blameless men, and indeed rather yourselves, who think fit to direct affairs, not by judgment, but by passion. And every sober-minded person will declare this to be the only fair and equitable adjustment, namely, that the subjects render an unexceptional account of their own life and doctrine; and that, on the other hand, the rulers should give their decision in obedience, not to violence and tyranny, but to piety and philosophy. For thus would both rulers and ruled reap benefit. For even one of the ancients somewhere said, "Unless both rulers and ruled philosophize, it is impossible to make states blessed." It is our task, therefore, to afford to all an opportunity of inspecting our life and teachings, lest, on account of those who are accustomed to be ignorant of our affairs, we should incur the penalty due to them for mental blindness; and it is your business, when you hear us, to be found, as reason demands, good judges. For if, when ye have learned the truth, you do not what is just, you will be before God without excuse.

CHAPTER IV -- CHRISTIANS UNJUSTLY CONDEMNED FOR THEIR MERE NAME.

By the mere application of a name, nothing is decided, either good or evil, apart from the actions implied in the name; and indeed, so far at least as one may judge from the name we are accused of, we are most excellent people. But as we do not think it just to beg to be acquitted on account of the name, if we be convicted as evildoers, so, on the other hand, if we be found to have committed no offence, either in the matter of thus naming ourselves, or of our conduct as citizens, it is your part very earnestly to guard against incurring just punishment, by unjustly punishing those who are not convicted. For from a name neither praise nor punishment could reasonably spring, unless something excellent or base in action be proved. And those among yourselves who are accused you do not punish before they are convicted; but in our case you receive the name as proof against us, and this although, so far as the name goes, you ought rather to punish our accusers. For we are accused of being Christians, and to hate what is excellent (Chrestian) is unjust. Again, if any of the accused deny the name, and say that he is not a Christian, you acquit him, as having no evidence against him as a wrong-doer; but if anyone acknowledge that he is a Christian, you punish him on account of this acknowledgment. Justice requires that you inquire into the life both of him who confesses and of him who denies, that by his deeds it may be apparent what kind of man each is. For as some who have been taught by the Master, Christ, not to deny Him, give encouragement to others when they are put to the question, so in all probability do those who lead wicked lives give occasion to those who, without consideration, take upon them to accuse all the Christians of impiety and wickedness. And this also is not right. For of philosophy, too, some assume the name and the garb who do nothing worthy of their profession; and you are well aware, that those of the ancients whose opinions and teachings were quite diverse, are yet all called by the one name of philosophers. And of these some taught atheism; and the poets who have flourished among you raise a laugh out of the uncleanness of Jupiter with his own children. And those who now adopt such instruction are not restrained by you; but, on the contrary, you bestow prizes and honours upon those who euphoniously insult the gods.

CHAPTER V -- CHRISTIANS CHARGED WITH ATHEISM.

Why, then, should this be? In our case, who pledge ourselves to do no wickedness, nor to hold these atheistic opinions, you do not examine the charges made against us; but, yielding to unreasoning passion, and to the instigation of evil demons, you punish us without consideration or judgment. For the truth shall be spoken; since of old these evil demons, effecting apparitions of themselves, both defiled women and corrupted boys, and showed such fearful sights to men, that those who did not use their reason in judging of the actions that were done, were struck with terror; and being carried away by fear, and not knowing that these were demons, they called them gods, and gave to each the name which each of the demons chose for himself. And when Socrates endeavoured, by true reason and examination, to bring these things to light, and deliver men from the demons, then the demons themselves, by means of men who rejoiced in iniquity, compassed his death, as an atheist and a profane person, on the charge that "he was introducing new divinities;" and in our case they display a similar activity. For not only among the Greeks did reason (Logos) prevail to condemn these things through Socrates, but also among the Barbarians were they condemned by Reason (or the Word, the Logos) Himself, who took shape, and became man, and was called Jesus Christ; and in obedience to Him, we not only deny that they who did such things as these are gods, but assert that they are wicked and impious demons, whose actions will not bear comparison with those even of men desirous of virtue.

CHAPTER VI -- CHARGE OF ATHEISM REFUTED.

Hence are we called atheists. And we confess that we are atheists, so far as gods of this sort are concerned, but not with respect to the most true God, the Father of righteousness and temperance and the other virtues, who is free from all impurity. But both Him, and the Son (who came forth from Him and taught us these things, and the host of the other good angels who follow and are made like to Him), and the prophetic Spirit, we worship and adore, knowing them in reason and truth, and declaring without grudging to every one who wishes to learn, as we have been taught.

CHAPTER VII -- EACH CHRISTIAN MUST BE TRIED BY HIS OWN LIFE.

But some one will say, Some have ere now been arrested and convicted as evil-doers. For you condemn many, many a time, after inquiring into the life of each of the accused severally, but not on account of those of whom we have been speaking. And this we acknowledge, that as among the Greeks those who teach such theories as please themselves are all called by the one name "Philosopher," though their doctrines be diverse, so also among the Barbarians this name on which accusations are accumulated is the common property of those who are and those who seem wise. For all are called Christians. Wherefore we demand that the deeds of all those who are accused to you be judged, in order that each one who is convicted may be punished as an evil-doer, and not as a Christian; and if it is clear that anyone is blameless, that he may be acquitted, since by the mere fact of his being a Christian he does no wrong. For we will not require that you punish our accusers; they being sufficiently punished by their present wickedness and ignorance of what is right.

CHAPTER VIII -- CHRISTIANS CONFESS THEIR FAITH IN GOD.

And reckon ye that it is for your sakes we have been saying these things; for it is in our power, when we are examined, to deny that we are Christians; but we would not live by telling a lie. For, impelled by the desire of the eternal and pure life, we seek the abode that is with God, the Father and Creator of all, and hasten to confess our faith, persuaded and convinced as we are that they who have proved to God by their works that they followed Him, and loved to abide with Him where there is no sin to cause disturbance, can obtain these things. This, then, to speak shortly, is what we expect and have learned from Christ, and teach. And Plato, in like manner, used to say that Rhadamanthus and Minos would punish the wicked who came before them; and we say that the same thing will be done, but at the hand of Christ, and upon the wicked in the same bodies united again to their spirits which are now to undergo everlasting punishment; and not only, as Plato said, for a period of a thousand years. And if anyone say that this is incredible or impossible, this error of ours is one which concerns ourselves only, and no other person, so long as you cannot convict us of doing any harm.

CHAPTER IX -- FOLLY OF IDOL, WORSHIP.

And neither do we honour with many sacrifices and garlands of flowers such deities as men have formed and set in shrines and called gods; since we see that these are soulless and dead, and have not the form of God (for we do not consider that God has such a form as some say that they imitate to His honour), but have the names and forms of those wicked demons which have appeared. For why need we tell you who already

know, into what forms the craftsmen, carving and cutting, casting and hammering, fashion the materials? And often out of vessels of dishonour, by merely changing the form, and making an image of the requisite shape, they make what they call a god; which we consider not only senseless, but to be even insulting to God, who, having ineffable glory and form, thus gets His name attached to things that are corruptible, and require constant service. And that the artificers of these are both intemperate, and, not to enter into particulars, are practised in every vice, you very well know; even their own girls who work along with them they corrupt. What infatuation! that dissolute men should be said to fashion and make gods for your worship, and that you should appoint such men the guardians of the temples where they are enshrined; not recognising that it is unlawful even to think or say that men are the guardians of gods.

CHAPTER X -- HOW GOD IS TO BE SERVED.

But we have received by tradition that God does not need the material offerings which men can give, seeing, indeed, that He Himself is the provider of all things. And we have been taught, and are convinced, and do believe, that He accepts those only who imitate the excellences which reside in Him, temperance, and justice, and philanthropy, and as many virtues as are peculiar to a God who is called by no proper name. And we have been taught that He in the beginning did of His goodness, for man's sake, create all things out of unformed matter; and if men by their works show themselves worthy of this His design, they are deemed worthy, and so we have received--of reigning in company with Him, being delivered from corruption and suffering. For as in the beginning He created us when we were not, so do we consider that, in like manner, those who choose what is pleasing to Him are, on account of their choice, deemed worthy of incorruption and of fellowship with Him. For the coming into being at first was not in our own power; and in order that we may follow those things which please Him, choosing them by means of the rational faculties He has Himself endowed us with, He both persuades us and leads us to faith. And we think it for the advantage of all men that they are not restrained from learning these things, but are even urged thereto. For the restraint which human laws could not effect, the Word, inasmuch as He is divine, would have effected, had not the wicked demons, taking as their ally the lust of wickedness which is in every man, and which draws variously to all manner of vice, scattered many false and profane accusations, none of which attach to us.

CHAPTER XI -- WHAT KINGDOM CHRISTIANS LOOK FOR.

And when you hear that we look for a kingdom, you suppose, without making any inquiry, that we speak of a human kingdom; whereas we speak of that which is with God, as appears also from the confession of their faith made by those who are charged with being Christians, though they know that death is the punishment awarded to him who so confesses. For if we looked for a human kingdom, we should also deny our Christ, that we might not be slain; and we should strive to escape detection, that we might obtain what we expect. But since our thoughts are not fixed on the present, we are not concerned when men cut us off; since also death is a debt which must at all events be paid.

CHAPTER XII -- CHRISTIANS LIVE AS UNDER GOD'S EYE.

And more than all other men are we your helpers and allies in promoting peace, seeing that we hold this view, that it is alike impossible for the wicked, the covetous, the conspirator, and for the virtuous, to escape the notice of God, and that each man goes to everlasting punishment or salvation according to the value of his actions. For if all men knew this, no one would choose wickedness even for a little, knowing that he goes to the everlasting punishment of fire; but would by all means restrain himself, and adorn himself with virtue, that he might obtain the good gifts of God, and escape the punishments. For those who, on account of the laws and punishments you impose, endeavour to escape detection when they offend (and they offend, too, under the impression that it is quite possible to escape your detection, since you are but men), those persons, if they learned and were convinced that nothing, whether actually done or only intended, can escape the knowledge of God, would by all means live decently on account of the penalties threatened, as even you yourselves will admit. But you seem to fear lest all men become righteous, and you no longer have any to punish. Such would be the concern of public executioners, but not of good princes. But, as we before said, we are persuaded that these things are prompted by evil spirits, who demand sacrifices and service even from those who live unreasonably; but as for you, we presume that you who aim at [a reputation for] piety and philosophy will do nothing unreasonable. But if you also, like the foolish, prefer custom to truth, do what you have power to do. But just so much power have rulers who esteem opinion more than truth, as robbers have in a desert. And that you will not succeed is declared by the Word, than whom, after God who begat Him, we know there is no ruler more kingly and just. For as all shrink from succeeding to the poverty or sufferings or obscurity of their fathers, so whatever the Word forbids us to choose, the sensible man will not choose. That all these things should come to pass, I say, our Teacher foretold, He who is both Son and Apostle of God the Father of all and the Ruler, Jesus Christ; from whom also we have the name of Christians. Whence we become more assured of all the things He taught us, since whatever He beforehand foretold should come to pass, is seen in fact coming to pass; and this is the work of God, to tell of a thing before it happens, and as it was foretold so to show it happening. It were possible to pause here and add no more, reckoning that we demand what is just and true; but because we are well aware that it is not easy suddenly to change a mind possessed by ignorance, we intend to add a few things, for the sake of persuading those who love the truth, knowing that it is not impossible to put ignorance to flight by presenting the truth.

CHAPTER XIIL -- CHRISTIANS SERVE GOD RATIONALLY.

What sober-minded man, then, will not acknowledge that we are not atheists, worshipping as we do the Maker of this universe, and declaring, as we have been taught, that He has no need of streams of blood and libations and incense; whom we praise to the utmost of our power by the exercise of prayer and thanksgiving for all things wherewith we are supplied, as we have been taught that the only honour that is worthy of Him is not to consume by fire what He has brought into being for our sustenance, but to use it for ourselves and those who need, and with gratitude to Him to offer thanks by invocations and hymns for our creation, and for all the means of health, and for the various qualities of the different kinds of things, and for the changes of the seasons; and to present before Him petitions for our existing again in incorruption through faith in Him. Our teacher of these things is Jesus Christ, who also was born for this purpose, and was crucified under Pontius Pilate, procurator of Judaea, in the times of Tiberius Caesar; and that we reasonably worship Him, having learned that He is the Son of the true God Himself, and holding Him in the second place, and the prophetic Spirit in the third, we will prove. For they proclaim our madness to consist in this, that we give to a crucified man a place second to the unchangeable and eternal God, the Creator of all; for they do not discern the mystery that is herein, to which, as we make it plain to you, we pray you to give heed.

CHAPTER XIV -- THE DEMONS MISREPRESENT CHRISTIAN DOCTRINE.

For we forewarn you to be on your guard, lest those demons whom we have been accusing should deceive you, and quite diver you from reading and understanding what we say. For they strive to hold you their slaves and servants; and sometimes by appearances in dreams, and sometimes by magical impositions, they subdue all who make no strong opposing effort for their own salvation. And thus do we also, since our persuasion by the Word, stand aloof from them (i.e., the demons), and follow the only unbegotten God through His Son--we who formerly delighted in fornication, but now embrace chastity alone; we who formerly used magical arts, dedicate ourselves to the good and unbegotten God; we who valued above all things the acquisition of wealth and possessions, now bring what we have into a common stock, and communicate to everyone in need; we who hated and destroyed one another, and on account of their different manners would not live with men of a different tribe, now, since the coming of Christ, live familiarly with them, and pray for our enemies, and endeavour to persuade those who hate us unjustly to live comformably to the good precepts of Christ, to the end that they may become par-takers with us of the same joyful hope of a reward from God the ruler of all. But lest we should seem to be reasoning sophistically, we consider it right, before giving you the promised explanation, to cite a few precepts given by Christ Himself. And be it yours, as powerful rulers, to inquire whether we have been taught and do teach these things truly. Brief and concise utterances fell from Him, for He was no sophist, but His word was the power of God.

CHAPTER XV -- WHAT CHRIST HIMSELF TAUGHT.

Concerning chastity, He uttered such sentiments as these: "Whosoever looketh upon a woman to lust after her, hath committed adultery with her already in his heart before God." And, "If thy right eye offend thee, cut it out; for it is better for thee to enter into the kingdom of heaven with one eye, than, having two eyes, to be cast into everlasting fire." And, "Whosoever shall many her that is divorced from another husband, committeth adultery." And, "There are some who have been made eunuchs of men, and some who were born eunuchs, and some who have made themselves eunuchs for the kingdom of heaven's sake; but all cannot receive this saying." So that all who, by human law, are twice married, are in the eye of our Master sinners, and those who look upon a woman to lust after her. For not only he who in act commits adultery is rejected by Him, but also he who desires to commit adultery: since not only our works, but also our thoughts, are open before God. And many, both men and women, who have been Christ's disciples from childhood, remain pure at the age of sixty or seventy years; and I boast that I could produce such from every race of men. For what shall I say, too, of the countless multitude of those who have reformed intemperate habits, and learned these things? For Christ called not the just nor the chaste to repentance, but the ungodly, and the licentious, and the unjust; His words being, "I came not to call the righteous, but sinners to repentance." For the heavenly Father desires rather the repentance than the punishment of the sinner. And of our love to all, He taught thus: "If ye love them that love you, what new thing do ye? for even fornicators do this. But I say unto you, Pray for your enemies, and love them that hate you, and bless them that curse you, and pray for them that despitefully use you." And that we should communicate to the needy, and do nothing for glory, He said, "Give to him that asketh, and from him that would borrow turn not away; for if ye lend to them of whom ye hope to receive, what new thing do ye? even the publicans do this. Lay not up for yourselves treasure upon earth, where moth and rust doth corrupt, and where robbers break through; but lay up for yourselves treasure in heaven, where neither moth nor rust doth corrupt. For what is a man profited, if he shall gain the whole world, and lose his own soul? or what shall a man give in exchange for it? Lay up treasure, therefore, in heaven, where neither moth nor rust doth corrupt." And, "Be ye kind and merciful, as your Father also is kind and merciful, and maketh His sun to rise on sinners, and the righteous, and the wicked. Take no thought what ye shall eat, or what ye shall put on: are ye not better than the birds and the beasts? And God feedeth them. Take no thought, therefore, what ye shall eat, or what ye shall put on; for your heavenly Father knoweth that ye have need of these things. But seek ye the kingdom of heaven, and all these things shall be added unto you. For where his treasure is, there also is the mind of a man." And, "Do not these things to be seen of men; otherwise ye have no reward from your Father which is in heaven."

CHAPTER XVI -- CONCERNING PATIENCE AND SWEARING.

And concerning our being patient of injuries, and ready to serve all, and free from anger, this is what He said: "To him that smiteth thee on the one cheek, offer also the other; and him that taketh away thy cloak or coat, forbid not. And whosoever shall be angry, is in danger of the fire. And every one that compelleth thee to go with him a mile, follow him two. And let your good works shine before men, that they, seeing them, may glorify your Father which is in heaven." For we ought not to strive; neither has He desired us to be imitators of wicked men, but He has exhorted us to lead all men, by patience and gentleness, from shame and the love of evil. And this indeed is proved in the case of many who once were of your way of thinking, but have changed their violent and tyrannical disposition, being overcome either by the constancy which they have witnessed in their neighbours' lives, or by the extraordinary forbearance they have observed in their fellow-travellers when defrauded, or by the honesty of those with whom they have transacted business.

And with regard to our not swearing at all, and always speaking the truth, He enjoined as follows: "Swear not at all; but let your yea be yea, and your nay, nay; for whatsoever is more than these cometh of evil." And that we ought to worship God alone, He thus persuaded us: "The greatest commandment is, Thou shalt worship the Lord thy God, and Him only shall thou serve, with all thy heart, and with all thy strength, the Lord God that made thee." And when a certain man came to Him and said, "Good Master," He answered and said, "There is none good but God only, who made all things." And let those who are not found living as He taught, be understood to be no Christians, even though they profess with the lip the precepts of Christ; for not those who make profession, but those who do the works, shall be saved, according to His word: "Not everyone who saith to Me, Lord, Lord, shall enter into the kingdom of heaven, but he that doeth the will of My Father which is in heaven. For whosoever heareth Me, and doeth My sayings, heareth Him that sent Me. And many will say unto Me, Lord, Lord, have we not eaten and drunk in Thy name, and done wonders? And then will I say unto them, Depart from Me, ye workers of iniquity. Then shall there be wailing and gnashing of teeth, when the righteous shall shine as the sun, and the wicked are sent into everlasting fire. For many shall come in My name, clothed outwardly in sheep's clothing, but inwardly being ravening wolves. By their works ye shall know them. And every tree that bringeth not forth good fruit, is hewn down and cast into the fire." And as to those who are not living pursuant to these His teachings, and are Christians only in name, we demand that all such be punished by you.

CHAPTER XVII -- CHRIST TAUGHT CIVIL OBEDIENCE.

And everywhere we, more readily than all men, endeavour to pay to those appointed by you the taxes both ordinary and extraordinary, as we have been taught by Him; for at that time some came to Him and asked Him, if one ought to pay tribute to Caesar; and He answered, "Tell Me, whose image does the coin bear?" And they said, "Caesar's." And again He answered them, "Render therefore to Caesar the things that are Caesar's, and to God the things that are God's." Whence to God alone we render worship, but in other things we gladly serve you, acknowledging you as kings and rulers of men, and praying that with your kingly power you be found to possess also sound judgment. But if you pay no regard to our prayers and frank explanations, we shall suffer no loss, since we

believe (or rather, indeed, are persuaded) that every man will suffer punishment in eternal fire according to the merit of his deed, and will render account according to the power he has received from God, as Christ intimated when He said, "To whom God has given more, of him shall more be required."

CHAPTER XVIII -- PROOF OF IMMORTALITY AND THE RESURRECTION.

For reflect upon the end of each of the preceding kings, how they died the death common to all, which, if it issued in insensibility, would be a godsend to all the wicked. But since sensation remains to all who have ever lived, and eternal punishment is laid up (i.e., for the wicked), see that ye neglect not to be convinced, and to hold as your belief, that these things are true. For let even necromancy, and the divinations you practise by immaculate children, and the evoking of departed human souls, and those who are called among the magi, Dream-senders and Assistant-spirits (Familiars), and all that is done by those who are skilled in such matters--let these persuade you that even after death souls are in a state of sensation; and those who are seized and cast about by the spirits of the dead, whom all call daemoniacs or madmen; and what you repute as oracles, both of Amphilochus, Dodana, Pytho, and as many other such as exist; and the opinions of your authors, Empedocles and Pythagoras, Plato and Socrates, and the pit of Homer, and the descent of Ulysses to inspect these things, and all that has been uttered of a like kind. Such favour as you grant to these, grant also to us, who not less but more firmly than they believe in God; since we expect to receive again our own bodies, though they be dead and cast into the earth, for we maintain that with God nothing is impossible.

CHAPTER XIX -- THE RESURRECTION POSSIBLE.

And to any thoughtful person would anything appear more incredible, than, if we were not in the body, and some one were to say that it was possible that from a small drop of human seed bones and sinews and flesh be formed into a shape such as we see? For let this now be said hypothetically: if you yourselves were not such as you now are, and born of such parents [and causes], and one were to show you human seed and a picture of a man, and were to say with confidence that from such a substance such a being could be produced, would you believe before you saw the actual production? No one will dare to deny [that such a statement would surpass belief]. In the same way, then, you are now incredulous because you have never seen a dead man rise again. But as at first you would not have believed it possible that such persons could be produced from the small drop, and yet now you see them thus produced, so also judge ye that it is not impossible that the bodies of men, after they have been dissolved, and like seeds resolved into earth, should in God's appointed time rise again and put on incorruption. For what power worthy of God those imagine who say, that each thing returns to that from which it was produced, and that beyond this not even God Himself can do anything, we are unable to conceive; but this we see clearly, that they would not have believed it possible that they could have become such and produced from such materials, as they now see both themselves and the whole world to be. And that it is better to believe even what is impossible to our own nature and to men, than to be unbelieving like the rest of the world, we have learned; for we know that our Master Jesus Christ said, that "what is impossible with men is possible with God," and, "Fear not them that kill you, and after that can do no more; but fear Him who after death is able to cast both soul and body into hell." And hell is a place where those are to be punished who have lived wickedly, and who do not believe that those things which God has taught us by Christ will come to pass.

CHAPTER XX -- HEATHEN ANALOGIES TO CHRISTIAN DOCTRINE.

And the Sibyl and Hystaspes said that there should be a dissolution by God of things corruptible. And the philosophers called Stoics teach that even God Himself shall be resolved into fire, and they say that the world is to be formed anew by this revolution; but we understand that God, the Creator of all things, is superior to the things that are to be changed. If, therefore, on some points we teach the same things as the poets and philosophers whom you honour, and on other points are fuller and more divine in our teaching, and if we alone afford proof of what we assert, why are we unjustly hated more than all others? For while we say that all things have been produced and arranged into a world by God, we shall seem to utter the doctrine of Plato; and while we say that there will be a burning up of all, we shall seem to utter the doctrine of the Stoics: and while we affirm that the souls of the wicked, being endowed with sensation even after death, are punished, and that those of the good being delivered from punishment spend a blessed existence, we shall seem to say the same things as the poets and philosophers; and while we maintain that men ought not to worship the works of their hands, we say the very things which have been said by the comic poet Menander, and other similar writers, for they have declared that the workman is greater than the work.

CHAPTER XXI -- ANALOGIES TO THE HISTORY OF CHRIST.

And when we say also that the Word, who is the first-birth of God, was produced without sexual union, and that He, Jesus Christ, our Teacher, was crucified and died, and rose again, and ascended into heaven, we propound nothing different from what you believe regarding those whom you esteem sons of Jupiter. For you know how many sons your esteemed writers ascribed to Jupiter: Mercury, the interpreting word and teacher of all; AEsculapius, who, though he was a great physician, was struck by a thunderbolt, and so ascended to heaven; and Bacchus too, after he had been torn limb from limb; and Hercules, when he had committed himself to the flames to escape his toils; and the sons of Leda, and Dioscuri; and Perseus, son of Danae; and Bellerophon, who, though sprung from mortals, rose to heaven on the horse Pegasus. For what shall I say of Ariadne, and those who, like her, have been declared to be set among the stars? And what of the emperors who die among yourselves, whom you deem worthy of deification, and in whose behalf you produce someone who swears he has seen the burning Caesar rise to heaven from the funeral pyre? And what kind of deeds are recorded of each of these reputed sons of Jupiter, it is needless to tell to those who already know. This only shall be said, that they are written for the advantage and encouragement of youthful scholars; for all reckon it an honourable thing to imitate the gods. But far be such a thought concerning the gods from every well-conditioned soul, as to believe that Jupiter himself, the governor and creator of all things, was both a parricide and the son of a parricide, and that being overcome by the love of base and shameful pleasures, he came in to Ganymede and those many women whom he had violated and that his sons did like actions. But, as we said above, wicked devils perpetrated these things. And we have learned that those only are deified who have lived near to God in holiness and virtue; and we believe that those who live wickedly and do not repent are punished in everlasting fire.

CHAPTER XXII -- ANALOGIES TO THE SONSHIP OF CHRIST.

Moreover, the Son of God called Jesus, even if only a man by ordinary generation, yet, on account of His wisdom, is worthy to be called the Son of God; for all writers call God the Father of men and gods. And if we assert that the Word of God was born of God in a peculiar manner, different from ordinary generation, let this, as said above, be no extraordinary thing to you, who say that Mercury is the angelic word of God. But if anyone objects that He was crucified, in this also He is on a par with those reputed sons of Jupiter of yours, who suffered as we have now enumerated. For their sufferings at death are recorded to have been not all alike, but diverse; so that not even by the peculiarity of

His sufferings does He seem to be inferior to them; but, on the contrary, as we promised in the preceding part of this discourse, we will now prove Him superior--or rather have already proved Him to be so--for the superior is revealed by His actions. And if we even affirm that He was born of a virgin, accept this in common with what you accept of Ferseus. And in that we say that He made whole the lame, the paralytic, and those born blind, we seem to say what is very similar to the deeds said to have been done by AEsculapius.

CHAPTER XXIII -- THE ARGUMENT.

And that this may now become evident to you--(firstly) that whatever we assert in conformity with what has been taught us by Christ, and by the prophets who preceded Him, are alone true, and are older than all the writers who have existed; that we claim to be acknowledged, not because we say the same things as these writers said, but because we say true things: and (secondly) that Jesus Christ is the only proper Son who has been begotten by God, being His Word and first-begotten, and power; and, becoming man according to His will, He taught us these things for the conversion and restoration of thc human race: and (thirdly) that before He became a man among men, some, influenced by the demons before mentioned, related beforehand, through the instrumentality of the poets, those circumstances as having really happened, which, having fictitiously devised, they narrated, in the same manner as they have caused to be fabricated the scandalous reports against us of infamous and impious actions, of which there is neither witness nor proof--we shall bring forward the following proof.

CHAPTER XXIV -- VARIETIES OF HEATHEN WORSHIP.

In the first place [we furnish proof], because, though we say things similar to what the Greeks say, we only are hated on account of the name of Christ, and though we do no wrong, are put to death as sinners; other men in other places worshipping trees and rivers, and mice and cats and crocodiles, and many irrational animals. Nor are the same animals esteemed by all; but in one place one is worshipped, and another in another, so that all are profane in the judgment of one another, on account of their not worshipping the same objects. And this is the sole accusation you bring against us, that we do not reverence the same gods as you do, nor offer to the dead libations and the savour of fat, and crowns for their statues, and sacrifices. For you very well know that the same animals are with some esteemed gods, with others wild beasts, and with others sacrificial victims.

CHAPTER XXV -- FALSE GODS ABANDONED BY CHRISTIANS.

And, secondly, because we--who, out of every race of men, used to worship Bacchus the son of Semele, and Apollo the son of Latona (who in their loves with men did such things as it is shameful even to mention), and Proserpine and Venus (who were maddened with love of Adonis, and whose mysteries also you celebrate), or AEsculapius, or some one or other of those who are called gods--have now, through Jesus Christ, learned to despise these, though we be threatened with death for it, and have dedicated ourselves to the unbegotten and impossible God; of whom we are persuaded that never was he goaded by lust of Antiope, or such other women, or of Ganymede, nor was rescued by that hundred-handed giant whose aid was obtained through Thetis, nor was anxious on this account that her son Achilles should destroy many of the Greeks because of his concubine Briseis. Those who believe these things we pity, and those who invented them we know to be devils.

CHAPTER XXVI -- MAGICIANS NOT TRUSTED BY CHRISTIANS.

And, thirdly, because after Christ's ascension into heaven the devils put forward certain men who said that they themselves were gods; and they were not only not persecuted by you, but even deemed worthy of honours. There was a Samaritan, Simon, a native of the village called Gitto, who in the reign of Claudius Caesar, and in your royal city of Rome, did mighty acts of magic, by virtue of the art of the devils operating in him. He was considered a god, and as a god was honoured by you with a statue, which statue was erected on the river Tiber, between the two bridges, and bore this inscription, in the language of Rome:--

"Simoni Deo Sancto,"

"To Simon the holy God." And almost all the Samaritans, and a few even of other nations, worship him, and acknowledge him as the first god; and a woman, Helena, who went about with him at that time, and had formerly been a prostitute, they say is the first idea generated by him. And a man, Meander, also a Samaritan, of the town Capparetaea, a disciple of Simon, and inspired by devils, we know to have deceived many while he was in Antioch by his magical art. He persuaded those who adhered to him that they should never die, and even now there are some living who hold this opinion of his. And there is Marcion, a man of Pontus, who is even at this day alive, and teaching his disciples to believe in some other god greater than the Creator. And he, by the aid of the devils, has caused many of every nation to speak blasphemies, and to deny that God is the maker of this universe, and to assert that some other being, greater than He, has done greater works. All who take their opinions from these men, are, as we before said, called Christians; just as also those who do not agree with the philosophers in their doctrines, have yet in common with them the name of philosophers given to them. And whether they perpetrate those fabulous and shameful deeds--the upsetting of the lamp, and promiscuous intercourse, and eating human flesh--we know not; but we do know that they are neither persecuted nor put to death by you, at least on account of their opinions. But I have a treatise against all the heresies that have existed already composed, which, if you wish to read it, I will give you.

CHAPTER XXVII -- GUILT OF EXPOSING CHILDREN.

But as for us, we have been taught that to expose newly-born children is the part of wicked men; and this we have been taught lest we should do anyone an injury, and lest we should sin against God, first, because we see that almost all so exposed (not only the girls, but also the males) are brought up to prostitution. And as the ancients are said to have reared herds of oxen, or goats, or sheep, or grazing horses, so now we see you rear children only for this shameful use; and for this pollution a multitude of females and hermaphrodites, and those who commit unmentionable iniquities, are found in every nation. And you receive the hire of these, and duty and taxes from them, whom you ought to exterminate from your realm. And anyone who uses such persons, besides the godless and infamous and impure intercourse, may possibly be having intercourse with his own child, or relative, or brother. And there are some who prostitute even their own children and wives, and some are openly mutilated for the purpose of sodomy; and they refer these mysteries to the mother of the gods, and along with each of those whom you esteem gods there is painted a serpent, a great symbol and mystery. Indeed, the things which you do openly and with applause, as if the divine light were overturned and extinguished, these you lay to our charge; which, in truth, does no harm to us who shrink from doing any such things, but only to those who do them and bear false witness against us.

CHAPTER XXVIII -- GOD'S CARE FOR MEN.

For among us the prince of the wicked spirits is called the serpent, and Satan, and the devil, as you can learn by looking into our writings. And that he would be sent into the fire with his host, and the men who follow him, and would be punished for an endless duration, Christ foretold. For the reason why God has delayed to do this, is His regard for the human race. For He foreknows that some are to be saved by repentance, some even that are perhaps not yet born. In the beginning He made the human race with the power of thought and of choosing the truth and doing right, so that all men are without excuse before God; for they have been born rational and contemplative. And if anyone disbelieves that God cares for these things, he will thereby either insinuate that God does not exist, or he will assert that though He exists He delights in vice, or exists like a stone, and that neither virtue nor vice are anything, but only in the opinion of men these things are reckoned good or evil. And this is the greatest profanity and wickedness.

CHAPTER XXIX -- CONTINENCE OF CHRISTIANS.

And again [we fear to expose children], lest some of them be not picked up, but die, and we become murderers. But whether we marry, it is only that we may bring up children; or whether we decline marriage, we live continently. And that you may understand that promiscuous intercourse is not one of our mysteries, one of our number a short time ago presented to Felix the governor in Alexandria a petition, craving that permission might be given to a surgeon to make him an eunuch. For the surgeons there said that they were forbidden to do this without the permission of the governor. And when Felix absolutely refused to sign such a permission, the youth remained single, and was satisfied with his own approving conscience, and the approval of those who thought as he did. And it is not out of place, we think, to mention here Antinous, who was alive but lately, and whom all were prompt, through fear, to worship as a god, though they knew both who he was and what was his origin.

CHAPTER XXX -- WAS CHRIST NOT A MAGICIAN?

But lest anyone should meet us with the question, What should prevent that He whom we call Christ, being a man born of men, performed what we call His mighty works by magical art, and by this appeared to be the Son of God? we will now offer proof, not trusting mere assertions, but being of necessity persuaded by those who prophesied [of Him] before these things came to pass, for with our own eyes we behold things that have happened and are happening just as they were predicted; and this will, we think appear even to you the strongest and truest evidence.

CHAPTER XXXI -- OF THE HEBREW PROPHETS.

There were, then, among the Jews certain men who were prophets of God, through whom the prophetic Spirit published beforehand things that were to come to pass, ere ever they happened. And their prophecies, as they were spoken and when they were uttered, the kings who happened to be reigning among the Jews at the several times carefully preserved in their possession, when they had been arranged in books by the prophets themselves in their own Hebrew language. And when Ptolemy king of Egypt formed a library, and endeavoured to collect the writings of all men, he heard also of these prophets, and sent to Herod, who was at that time king of the Jews, requesting that the books of the prophets be sent to him. And Herod the king did indeed send them, written, as they were, in the foresaid Hebrew language. And when their contents were found to be unintelligible to the Egyptians, he again sent and requested that men be commissioned to translate them into the Greek language. And when this was done, the books remained with the Egyptians, where they are until now. They are also in the possession of all Jews throughout the world; but they, though they read, do not understand what is said, but count us foes and enemies; and, like yourselves, they kill and punish us whenever they have the power, as you can well believe. For in the Jewish war which lately raged, Barchochebas, the leader of the revolt of the Jews, gave orders that Christians alone should be led to cruel punishments, unless they would deny Jesus Christ and utter blasphemy. In these books, then, of the prophets we found Jesus our Christ foretold as coming, born of a virgin, growing up to man's estate, and healing every disease and every sickness, and raising the dead, and being hated, and unrecognised, and crucified, and dying, and rising again, and ascending into heaven, and being, and being called, the Son of God. We find it also predicted that certain persons should be sent by Him into every nation to publish these things, and that rather among the Gentiles [than among the Jews] men should believe on Him. And He was predicted before He appeared, first 5000 years before, and again 3000, then 2000, then 1000, and yet again 800; for in the succession of generations prophets after prophets arose.

CHAPTER XXXII -- CHRIST PREDICTED BY MOSES

Moses then, who was the first of the prophets, spoke in these very words: "The sceptre shall not depart from Judah, nor a lawgiver from between his feet, until He come for whom it is reserved; and He shall be the desire of the nations, binding His foal to the vine, washing His robe in the blood of the grape." It is yours to make accurate inquiry, and ascertain up to whose time the Jews had a lawgiver and king of their own. Up to the time of Jesus Christ, who taught us, and interpreted the prophecies which were not yet understood, [they had a lawgiver] as was foretold by the holy and divine Spirit of prophecy through Moses,

"that a ruler would not fail the Jews until He should come for whom the kingdom was reserved" (for Judah was the forefather of the Jews, from whom also they have their name of Jews); and after He (i.e., Christ) appeared, you began to rule the Jews, and gained possession of all their territory. And the prophecy, "He shall be the expectation of the nations," signified that there would be some of all nations who should look for Him to come again. And this indeed you can see for yourselves, and be convinced of by fact. For of all races of men there are some who look for Him who was crucified in Judaea, and after whose crucifixion the land was straightway surrendered to you as spoil of war. And the prophecy, "binding His foal to the vine, and washing His robe in the blood of the grape," was a significant symbol of the things that were to happen to Christ, and of what He was to do. For the foal of an ass stood bound to a vine at the entrance of a village, and He ordered His acquaintances to bring it to Him then; and when it was brought, He mounted and sat upon it, and entered Jerusalem, where was the vast temple of the Jews which was afterwards destroyed by you. And after this He was crucified, that the rest of the prophecy might be fulfilled. For this "washing His robe in the blood of the grape" was predictive of the passion He was to endure, cleansing by His blood those who believe on Him. For what is called by the Divine Spirit through the prophet "His robe," are those men who believe in Him in whom abideth the seed of God, the Word. And what is spoken of as "the blood of the grape," signifies that He who should appear would have blood, though not of the seed of man, but of the power of God. And the first power after God the Father and Lord of all is the Word, who is also the Son; and of Him we will, in what follows, relate how He took flesh and became man. For as man did not make the blood of the vine, but God, so it was hereby intimated that the blood should not be of human seed, but of divine power, as we have said above. And Isaiah, another prophet, foretelling the same things in other words, spoke thus: "A star shall rise out of Jacob, and a flower shall spring from the root of Jesse; and His arm shall the nations trust." And a star of light has arisen, and a flower has sprung from the root of Jesse--this Christ. For by the power of God He was conceived by a virgin of the seed of Jacob, who was the father of Judah, who, as we have shown, was the father of the Jews; and Jesse was His forefather according to the oracle, and He was the son of Jacob and Judah according to lineal descent.

CHAPTER XXXIII -- MANNER OF CHRIST'S BIRTH PREDICTED.

And hear again how Isaiah in express words foretold that He should be born of a virgin; for he spoke thus: "Behold, a virgin shall conceive, and bring forth a son, and they shall say for His name, 'God with us.' " For things which were incredible and seemed impossible with men, these God predicted by the Spirit of prophecy as about to come to pass, in order that, when they came to pass, there might be no unbelief, but faith, because of their prediction. But lest some, not understanding the prophecy now cited, should charge us with the very things we have been laying to the charge of the poets who say that Jupiter went in to women through lust, let us try to explain the words. This, then, "Behold, a virgin shall conceive," signifies that a virgin should conceive without intercourse. For if she had had intercourse with anyone whatever, she was no longer a virgin; but the power of God having come upon the virgin, overshadowed her, and caused her while yet a virgin to conceive. And the angel of God who was sent to the same virgin at that time brought her good news, saying, "Behold, thou shalt conceive of the Holy Ghost, and shalt bear a Son, and He shall be called the Son of the Highest, and thou shalt call His name Jesus; for He shall save His people from their sins,"--as they who have recorded all that concerns our Saviour Jesus Christ have taught, whom we believed, since by Isaiah also, whom we have now adduced, the Spirit of prophecy declared that He should be born as we intimated before. It is wrong, therefore, to understand the Spirit and the power of God as anything else than the Word, who is also the first-born of God, as the foresaid prophet Moses declared; and it was this which, when it came upon the virgin and overshadowed her, caused her to conceive, not by intercourse, but by power. And the name Jesus in the Hebrew language means Swthr (Saviour) in the Greek tongue. Wherefore, too, the angel said to the virgin, "Thou shalt call His name Jesus, for He shall save His people from their sins." And that the prophets are inspired by no other than the Divine Word, even you, as I fancy, will grant.

CHAPTER XXXIV -- PLACE OF CHRIST'S BIRTH FORETOLD.

And hear what part of earth He was to be born in, as another prophet, Micah, foretold. He spoke thus: "And thou, Bethlehem, the land of Judah, art not the least among the princes of Judah; for out of thee shall come forth a Governor, who shall feed My people." Now there is a village in the land of the Jews, thirty-five stadia from Jerusalem, in which Jesus Christ was born, as you can ascertain also from the registers of the taxing made under Cyrenius, your first procurator in Judaea.

CHAPTER XXXV -- OTHER FULFILLED PROPHECIES.

And how Christ after He was born was to escape the notice of other men until He grew to man's estate,

which also came to pass, hear what was foretold regarding this. There are the following predictions:-- "Unto us a child is born, and unto us a young man is given, and the government shall be upon His shoulders;" which is significant of the power of the cross, for to it, when He was crucified, He applied His shoulders, as shall be more clearly made out in the ensuing discourse. And again the same prophet Isaiah, being inspired by the prophetic Spirit, said, "I have spread out my hands to a disobedient and gainsaying people, to those who walk in a way that is not good. They now ask of me judgment, and dare to draw near to God." And again in other words, through another prophet, He says, "They pierced My hands and My feet, and for My vesture they cast lots." And indeed David, the king and prophet, who uttered these things, suffered none of them; but Jesus Christ stretched forth His hands, being crucified by the Jews speaking against Him, and denying that He was the Christ. And as the prophet spoke, they tormented Him, and set Him on the judgment-seat, and said, Judge us. And the expression, "They pierced my hands and my feet," was used in reference to the nails of the cross which were fixed in His hands and feet. And after He was crucified they cast lots upon His vesture, and they that crucified Him parted it among them. And that these things did happen, you can ascertain from the Acts of Pontius Pilate. And we will cite the prophetic utterances of another prophet, Zephaniah, to the effect that He was foretold expressly as to sit upon the foal of an ass and to enter Jerusalem. The words are these: "Rejoice greatly, O daughter of Zion; shout, O daughter of Jerusalem: behold, thy King cometh unto thee; lowly, and riding upon an ass, and upon a colt the foal of an ass."

CHAPTER XXXVI -- DIFFERENT MODES OF PROPHECY.

But when you hear the utterances of the prophets spoken as it were personally, you must not suppose that they are spoken by the inspired themselves, but by the Divine Word who moves them. For sometimes He declares things that are to come to pass, in the manner of one who foretells the future; sometimes He speaks as from the person of God the Lord and Father of all; sometimes as from the person of Christ; sometimes as from the person of the people answering the Lord or His Father, just as you can see even in your own writers, one man being the writer of the whole, but introducing the persons who converse. And this the Jews who possessed the books of the prophets did not understand, and therefore did not recognise Christ even when He came, but even hate us who say that He has come, and who prove that, as was predicted, He was crucified by them.

CHAPTER XXXVII -- UTTERANCES OF THE FATHER.

And that this too may be clear to you, there were spoken from the person of the Father through Isaiah the prophet, the following words: "The ox knoweth his owner, and the ass his master's crib; but Israel doth not know, and My people hath not understood. Woe, sinful nation, a people full of sins, a wicked seed, children that are transgressors, ye have forsaken the Lord." And again elsewhere, when the same prophet speaks in like manner from the person of the Father, "What is the house that ye will build for Me? saith the Lord. The heaven is My throne, and the earth is My footstool." And again, in another place, "Your new moons and your sabbaths My soul hateth; and the great day of the fast and of ceasing from labour I cannot away with; nor, if ye come to be seen of Me, will I hear you: your hands are full of blood; and if ye bring fine flour, incense, it is abomination unto Me: the fat of lambs and the blood of bulls I do not desire. For who hath required this at your hands? But loose every bond of wickedness, tear asunder the tight knots of violent contracts, cover the houseless and naked deal thy bread to the hungry." What kind of things are taught through the prophets from [the person of] God, you can now perceive.

CHAPTER XXXVIII -- UTTERANCES OF THE SON.

And when the Spirit of prophecy speaks from the person of Christ, the utterances are of this sort: "I have spread out My hands to a disobedient and gainsaying people, to those who walk in a way that is not good." And again: "I gave My back to the scourges, and My cheeks to the buffetings; I turned not away My face from the shame of spittings; and the Lord was My helper: therefore was I not confounded: but I set My face as a firm rock; and I knew that I should not be ashamed, for He is near that justifieth Me." And again, when He says, "They cast lots upon My vesture, and pierced My hands and My feet. And I lay down and slept, and rose again, because the Lord sustained Me." And again, when He says, "They spake with their lips, they wagged the head, saying, Let Him deliver Himself." And that all these things happened to Christ at the hands of the Jews, you can ascertain. For when He was crucified, they did shoot out the lip, and wagged their heads, saying, "Let Him who raised the dead save Himself."

CHAPTER XXXIX -- DIRECT PREDICTIONS BY THE SPIRIT.

And when the Spirit of prophecy speaks as predicting things that are to come to pass, He speaks in this way: "For out of Zion shall go forth the law, and the word of the Lord from Jerusalem. And He shall judge among the nations, and shall rebuke many people; and they shall beat their swords into ploughshares, and their spears into pruning-hooks: nation shall not lift up sword against nation, neither shall they learn war any more." And that it did so come to pass, we can convince you. For from Jerusalem there went out into the world, men, twelve in number, and these illiterate, of no ability in speaking: but by the power of God they proclaimed to every race of men that they were sent by Christ to teach to all the word of God; and we who formerly used to murder one another do not only now refrain from making war upon our enemies, but also, that we may not lie nor deceive our examiners, willingly die confessing Christ. For that saying, "The tongue has sworn but the mind is unsworn," might be imitated by us in this matter. But if the soldiers enrolled by you, and who have taken the military oath, prefer their allegiance to their own life, and parents, and country, and all kindred, though you can offer them nothing incorruptible, it were verily ridiculous if we, who earnestly long for incorruption, should not endure all things, in order to obtain what we desire from Him who is able to grant it.

CHAPTER XL -- CHRIST'S ADVENT FORETOLD,

And hear how it was foretold concerning those who published His doctrine and proclaimed His appearance, the above-mentioned prophet and king speaking thus by the Spirit of prophecy "Day unto day uttereth speech, and night unto night showeth knowledge. There is no speech nor language where their voice is not heard. Their voice has gone out into all the earth, and their words to the ends of the world. In the sun hath He set His tabernacle, and he as a bridegroom going out of his chamber shall rejoice as a giant to run his course." And we have thought it right and relevant to mention some other prophetic utterances of David besides these; from which you may learn how the Spirit of prophecy exhorts men to live, and how He foretold the conspiracy which was formed against Christ by Herod the king of the Jews, and the Jews themselves, and Pilate, who was your governor among them, with his soldiers; and how He should be believed on by men of every race; and how God calls Him His Son, and has declared that He will subdue all His enemies under Him; and how the devils, as much as they can, strive to escape the power of God the Father and Lord of all, and the power of Christ Himself; and how God calls all to repentance before the day of judgment comes. These things were uttered thus: "Blessed is the man who hath not walked in the counsel of the ungodly, nor stood in the way of sinners, nor sat in the seat of the scornful: but his delight is in the law of the Lord; and in His law will he meditate day and night. And he shall be like a tree planted by the rivers of waters, which shall give his fruit in his season; and his leaf shall not wither, and whatsoever he doeth shall prosper. The ungodly are not so, but are like the chaff which the wind driveth away from the face of the earth. Therefore the ungodly shall not stand in the judgment, nor sinners in the council of the righteous. For the Lord knoweth the way of the righteous; but the way of the ungodly shall perish. Why do the heathen rage, and the people imagine new things? The kings of the earth set themselves, and the rulers take counsel together, against the Lord, and against His Anointed, saying, Let us break their bands asunder, and cast their yoke from us. He that dwelleth in the heavens shall laugh at them, and the Lord shall have them in derision. Then shall He speak to them in His wrath, and vex them in His sore displeasure. Yet have I been set by Him a King on Zion His holy hill, declaring the decree of the Lord. The Lord said to Me, Thou art My Son; this day have I begotten Thee. Ask of Me, and I shall give Thee the heathen for Thine inheritance, and the uttermost parts of the earth as Thy possession. Thou shall herd them with a rod of iron; as the vessels of a potter shalt Thou dash them in pieces. Be wise now, therefore, O ye kings; be instructed, all ye judges of the earth. Serve the Lord with fear, and rejoice with trembling. Embrace instruction, lest at any time the Lord be angry, and ye perish from the right way, when His wrath has been suddenly kindled. Blessed are all they that put their trust in Him."

CHAPTER XLI -- THE CRUCIFIXION PREDICTED.

And again, in another prophecy, the Spirit of prophecy, through the same David, intimated that Christ, after He had been crucified, should reign, and spoke as follows: "Sing to the Lord, all the earth, and day by day declare His salvation. For great is the Lord, and greatly to be praised, to be feared above all the gods. For all the gods of the nations are idols of devils; but God made the heavens. Glory and praise are before His face, strength and glorying are in the habitation of His holiness. Give Glory to the Lord, the Father everlasting. Receive grace, and enter His presence, and worship in His holy courts. Let all the earth fear before His face; let it be established, and not shaken. Let them rejoice among the nations. The Lord hath reigned from the tree."

CHAPTER XLII -- PROPHECY USING THE PAST TENSE.

But when the Spirit of prophecy speaks of things that are about to come to pass as if they had already taken place,--as may be observed even in the passages already cited by me,--that this circumstance may afford no excuse to readers [for misinterpreting them], we will make even this also quite plain. The things which He absolutely knows will take place, He predicts as if already they had taken place. And that the utterances must be thus received, you will perceive, if you give your attention to them. The words cited above, David uttered 1500 years before Christ became a man and was crucified; and no one of those who lived before Him, nor yet of His contemporaries, afforded joy to the Gentiles by being crucified. But our Jesus Christ, being crucified and dead, rose again, and having ascended to heaven, reigned; and by those things which were published in His name among all nations by the apostles, there is joy afforded to those who expect the immortality promised by Him.

CHAPTER XLIII--RESPONSIBILITY ASSERTED.

But lest some suppose, from what has been said by us, that we say that whatever happens, happens by a fatal necessity, because it is foretold as known beforehand, this too we explain. We have learned from the prophets, and we hold it to be true, that punishments, and chastisements, and good rewards, are rendered according to the merit of each man's actions. Since if it be not so, but all things happen by fate, neither is anything at all in our own power. For if it be fated that this man, e.g., be good, and this other evil, neither is the former meritorious nor the latter to be blamed. And again, unless the human race have the power of avoiding evil and choosing good by free choice, they are not accountable for their actions, of whatever kind they be. But that it is by free choice they both walk uprightly and stumble, we thus demonstrate. We see the same man making a transition to opposite things. Now, if it had been fated that he were to be either good or bad, he could never have been capable of both the opposites, nor of so many transitions. But not even would some be good and others bad, since we thus make fate the cause of evil, and exhibit her as acting in opposition to herself; or that which has been already stated would seem to be true, that neither virtue nor vice is anything, but that things are only reckoned good or evil by opinion; which, as the true word shows, is the greatest impiety and wickedness. But this we assert is inevitable fate, that they who choose the good have worthy rewards, and they who choose the opposite have their merited awards. For not like other things, as trees and quadrupeds, which cannot act by choice, did God make man: for neither would he be worthy of reward or praise did he not of himself choose the good, but were created for this end; nor, if he were evil, would he be worthy of punishment, not being evil of himself, but being able to be nothing else than what he was made.

CHAPTER XLIV -- NOT NULLIFIED BY PROPHECY.

And the holy Spirit of prophecy taught us this, telling us by Moses that God spoke thus to the man first created: "Behold, before thy face are good and evil: choose the good." And again, by the other prophet Isaiah, that the following utterance was made as if from God the Father and Lord of all: "Wash you, make you clean; put away evils from your souls; learn to do well; judge the orphan, and plead for the widow: and come and let us reason together, saith the Lord: And if your sins be as scarlet, I will make them white as wool; and if they be red like as crimson, I will make them white as snow. And if ye be willing and obey Me, ye shall eat the good of the land; but if ye do not obey Me, the sword shall devour you: for the mouth of the Lord hath spoken it." And that expression, "The sword shall devour you," does not mean that the disobedient shall be slain by the sword, but the sword of God is fire, of which they who choose to do wickedly become the fuel. Wherefore He says, "The sword shall devour you: for the mouth of the Lord hath spoken it." And if He had spoken concerning a sword that cuts and at once despatches, He would not have said, shall devour. And so, too, Plato, when he says, "The blame is his who chooses, and God is blameless," took this from the prophet Moses and uttered it. For Moses is more ancient than all the Greek writers. And whatever both philosophers and poets have said concerning the immortality of the soul, or punishments after death, or contemplation of things heavenly, or doctrines of the like kind, they have received such suggestions from the prophets as have enabled them to understand and interpret these things. And hence there seem to be seeds of truth among all men; but they are charged with not accurately understanding [the truth] when they assert contradictories. So that what we say about future events being foretold, we do not say it as if they came about by a fatal necessity; but God foreknowing all that shall be done by all men, and it being His decree that the future actions of men shall all be recompensed according to their several value, He foretells by the Spirit of prophecy that He will bestow meet rewards according to the merit of the actions done, always urging the human race to effort and recollection, showing that He cares and provides for men. But by the agency of the devils death has been decreed against those who read the books of Hystaspes, or of the Sibyl, or of the prophets, that through fear they may prevent men who read them from receiving the knowledge of the good, and may retain them in slavery to themselves; which, however, they could not always effect. For not only do we fearlessly read them, but, as you see, bring them for your inspection, knowing that their contents will be pleasing to all. And if we persuade even a few, our gain will be very great; for, as good husbandmen, we shall receive the reward from the Master.

CHAPTER XLV -- CHRIST'S SESSION IN HEAVEN FORETOLD.

And that God the Father of all would bring Christ to heaven after He had raised Him from the dead, and would keep Him there until He has subdued His enemies the devils, and until the number of those who are foreknown by Him as good and virtuous is complete, on whose account He has still delayed the consummation--hear what was said by the prophet David. These are his words: "The Lord said unto My Lord, Sit Thou at My right hand, until I make Thine enemies Thy footstool. The Lord shall send to Thee the rod of power out of Jerusalem; and rule Thou in the midst of Thine enemies. With Thee is the government in the day of Thy power, in the beauties of Thy saints: from the womb of morning hare I begotten Thee." That which he says, "He shall send to Thee the rod of power out of Jerusalem," is predictive of the mighty, word, which His apostles, going forth from Jerusalem, preached everywhere; and though death is decreed against those who teach or at all confess the name of Christ, we everywhere both embrace and teach it. And if you also read these words in a hostile spirit, ye can do no more, as I said before, than kill us; which indeed does no harm to us, but to you and all who unjustly hate us, and do not repent, brings eternal punishment by tire.

CHAPTER XLVI -- THE WORD IN THE WORLD BEFORE CHRIST.

But lest some should, without reason, and for the perversion of what we teach, maintain that we say that Christ was born one hundred and fifty years ago under Cyrenius, and subsequently, in the time of Pontius Pilate, taught what we say He taught; and should cry out against us as though all men who were born before Him were irresponsible--let us anticipate and solve the difficulty. We have been taught that Christ is the first-born of God, and we have declared above that He is the Word of whom every race of men were partakers; and those who lived reasonably are Christians, even though they have been thought atheists; as, among the Greeks, Socrates and Heraclitus, and men like them; and among the barbarians, Abraham, and Ananias, and Azarias, and Misael, and Elias, and many others whose actions and names we now decline to recount, because we know it would be tedious. So that even they who lived before Christ, and lived without reason, were wicked and hostile to Christ, and slew those who lived reasonably. But who, through the power of the Word, according to the will of God the Father and Lord of all, He was born of a virgin as a man, and was named Jesus, and was crucified, and died, and rose again, and ascended into heaven, an intelligent man will be able to comprehend from what has been already so largely said. And we, since the proof of this subject is less needful now, will pass for the present to the proof of those things which are urgent.

CHAPTER XLVII -- DESOLATION OF JUDAEA FORETOLD.

That the land of the Jews, then, was to be laid waste, hear what was said by the Spirit of prophecy. And the words were spoken as if from the person of the people wondering at what had happened. They are these: "Sion is a wilderness, Jerusalem a desolation. The house of our sanctuary has become a curse, and the glory which our fathers blessed is burned up with fire, and all its glorious things are laid waste: and Thou refrainest Thyself at these things, and hast held Thy peace, and hast humbled us very sore." And ye are convinced that Jerusalem has been laid waste, as was predicted. And concerning its desolation, and that no one should be permitted to inhabit it, there was the following prophecy by Isaiah: "Their land is desolate, their enemies consume it before them, and none of them shall dwell therein." And that it is guarded by you lest anyone dwell in it, and that death is decreed against a Jew apprehended entering it, you know very well.

CHAPTER XLVIII -- CHRIST'S WORK AND DEATH FORE- TOLD.

And that it was predicted that our Christ should heal all diseases and raise the dead, hear what was said. There are these words: "At His coming the lame shall leap as an hart, and the tongue of the stammerer shall be clear speaking: the blind shall see, and the lepers shall be cleansed; and the dead shall rise, and walk about." And that He did those things, you can learn from the Acts of Pontius Pilate. And how it was predicted by the Spirit of prophecy that He and those who hoped in Him should be slain, hear what was said by Isaiah. These are the words: "Behold now the righteous perisheth, and no man layeth it to heart; and just men are taken away, and no man considereth. From the presence of wickedness is the righteous man taken, and his burial shall be in peace: he is taken from our midst."

CHAPTER XLIX -- HIS REJECTION BY THE JEWS FORE- TOLD.

And again, how it was said by the same Isaiah, that the Gentile nations who were not looking for Him should worship Him, but the Jews who always expected Him should not recognize Him when He came. And the words are spoken as from the person of Christ; and

they are these "I was manifest to them that asked not for Me; I was found of them that sought Me not: I said, Behold Me, to a nation that called not on My name. I spread out My hands to a disobedient and gainsaying people, to those who walked in a way that is not good, but follow after their own sins; a people that provoketh Me to anger to My face." For the Jews having the prophecies, and being always in expectation of the Christ to come, did not recognise Him; and not only so, but even treated Him shamefully. But the Gentiles, who had never heard anything about Christ, until the apostles set out from Jerusalem and preached concerning Him, and gave them the prophecies, were filled with joy and faith, and cast away their idols, and dedicated themselves to the Unbegotten God through Christ. And that it was foreknown that these infamous things should be uttered against those who confessed Christ, and that those who slandered Him, and said that it was well to preserve the ancient customs, should be miserable, hear what was briefly said by Isaiah; it is this: "Woe unto them that call sweet bitter, and bitter sweet."

CHAPTER L -- HIS HUMILIATION PREDICTED.

But that, having become man for our sakes, He endured to suffer and to be dishonoured, and that He shall come again with glory, hear the prophecies which relate to this; they are these: "Because they delivered His soul unto death, and He was numbered with the transgressors, He has borne the sin of many, and shall make intercession for the transgressors. For, behold, My Servant shall deal prudently, and shall be exalted, and shall be greatly extolled. As many were astonished at Thee, so marred shall Thy form be before men, and so hidden from them Thy glory; so shall many nations wonder, and the kings shall shut their mouths at Him. For they to whom it was not told concerning Him, and they who have not heard, shall understand. O Lord, who hath believed our report? and to whom is the arm of the Lord revealed? We have declared before Him as a child, as a root in a dry ground. He had no form, nor glory; and we saw Him, and there was no form nor comeliness: but His form was dishonoured and marred more than the sons of men. A man under the stroke, and knowing how to bear infirmity, because His face was turned away: He was despised, and of no reputation. It is He who bears our sins, and is afflicted for us; yet we did esteem Him smitten, stricken, and afflicted. But He was wounded for our transgressions, He was bruised for our iniquities, the chastisement of peace was upon Him, by His stripes we are healed. All we, like sheep, have gone astray; every man has wandered in his own way. And He delivered Him for our sins; and He opened not His mouth for all His affliction. He was brought as a sheep to the slaughter, and as a lamb before his shearer is dumb, so He openeth not His mouth. In His humiliation, His judgment was taken away." Accordingly, after He was crucified, even all His acquaintances forsook Him, having denied Him; and afterwards, when He had risen from the dead and appeared to them, and had taught them to read the prophecies in which all these things were foretold as coming to pass, and when they had seen Him ascending into heaven, and had believed, and had received power sent thence by Him upon them, and went to every race of men, they taught these things, and were called apostles.

CHAPTER LI -- THE MAJESTY OF CHRIST.

And that the Spirit of prophecy might signify to us that He who suffers these things has an ineffable origin, and rules His enemies, He spake thus: "His generation who shall declare? because His life is cut off from the earth: for their transgressions He comes to death. And I will give the wicked for His burial, and the rich for His death; because He did no violence, neither was any deceit in His mouth. And the Lord is pleased to cleanse Him from the stripe. If He be given for sin, your soul shall see His seed prolonged in days. And the Lord is pleased to deliver His soul from grief, to show Him light, and to form Him with knowledge, to justify the righteous who richly serveth many. And He shall bear our iniquities. Therefore He shall inherit many, and He shall divide the spoil of the strong; because His soul was delivered to death: and He was numbered with the transgressors; and He bare the sins of many, and He was delivered up for their transgressions." Hear, too, how He was to ascend into heaven according to prophecy. It was thus spoken: "Lift up the gates of heaven; be ye opened, that the King of glory may come in. Who is this King of glory? The Lord, strong and mighty." And how also He should come again out of heaven with glory, hear what was spoken in reference to this by the prophet Jeremiah. His words are: "Behold, as the Son of man He cometh in the clouds of heaven, and His angels with Him."

CHAPTER LII -- CERTAIN FULFILMENT OF PROPHECY.

Since, then, we prove that all things which have already happened had been predicted by the prophets before they came to pass, we must necessarily believe also that those things which are in like manner predicted, but are yet to come to pass, shall certainly happen. For as the things which have already taken place came to pass when foretold, and even though unknown, so shall the things that remain, even though they be unknown and disbelieved, yet come to pass. For the prophets have proclaimed two advents of His: the one, that which is already past, when He came as a dishonoured and suffering Man; but the second, when, according to prophecy, He shall come from heaven with glory, accompanied by His angelic host, when also He shall raise the bodies of all men who have lived, and shall clothe those of the worthy with immortality, and shall send those of the wicked, endued with eternal sensibility, into everlasting fire with the wicked devils. And that these things also have been foretold as yet to be, we will prove. By Ezekiel the prophet it was said: "Joint shall be joined to joint, and bone to bone, and flesh shall grow again; and every knee shall bow to the Lord, and every tongue shall confess Him." And in what kind of sensation and punishment the wicked are to be, hear from what was said in like manner with reference to this; it is as follows: "Their worm shall not rest, and their fire shall not be quenched;" and then shall they repent, when it profits them not. And what the people of the Jews shall say and do, when they see Him coming in glory, has been thus predicted by Zechariah the prophet: "I will command the four winds to gather the scattered children; I will command the north wind to bring them, and the south wind, that it keep not back. And then in Jerusalem there shall be great lamentation, not the lamentation of mouths or of lips, but the lamentation of the heart; and they shall rend not their garments, but their hearts. Tribe by tribe they shall mourn, and then they shall look on Him whom they have pierced; and they shall say, Why, O Lord, hast Thou made us to err from Thy way? The glory which our fathers blessed, has for us been turned into shame."

CHAPTER LIII -- SUMMARY OF THE PROPHECIES.

Though we could bring forward many other prophecies, we forbear, judging these sufficient for the persuasion of those who have ears to hear and understand; and considering also that those persons are able to see that we do not make mere assertions without being able to produce proof, like those fables that are told of the so-called sons of Jupiter. For with what reason should we believe of a crucified man that He is the first-born of the unbegotten God, and Himself will pass judgment on the whole human race, unless we had found testimonies concerning Him published before He came and was born as man, and unless we saw that things had happened accordingly--the devastation of the land of the Jews, and men of every race persuaded by His teaching through the apostles, and rejecting their old habits, in which, being deceived, they had their conversation; yea, seeing ourselves too, and knowing that the Christians from among the Gentiles are both more numerous and more true than those from among the Jews and Samaritans? For all the other human races are called Gentiles by the Spirit of prophecy; but the Jewish and Samaritan races are called the tribe of Israel, and the house of Jacob. And the prophecy in which it was predicted that there should be more believers from the Gentiles than from the Jews and Samaritans, we will produce: it ran thus: "Rejoice, O barren, thou that dost not bear; break forth and shout, thou that dost not travail, because many more are the children of the desolate than of her that hath an husband." For all the Gentiles were "desolate" of the true God, serving the works of their hands; but the Jews and Samaritans, having the word of God delivered to them by the prophets, and always expecting the Christ, did not recognise Him when He came, except some few, of whom the Spirit of prophecy by Isaiah had predicted that they should be saved. He spoke as from their person: "Except the Lord had left us a seed, we should have been as Sodom and Gomorrah." For Sodom and Gomorrah are related by Moses to have been cities of ungodly men, which God burned with fire and brimstone, and overthrew, no one of their inhabitants being saved except a certain stranger, a Chaldaean by birth, whose name was Lot; with whom also his daughters were rescued. And those who care may yet see their whole country desolate and burned, and remaining barren. And to show how those from among the Gentiles were foretold as more true and more believing, we will cite what was said by Isaiah the prophet; for he spoke as follows "Israel is uncircumcised in heart, but the Gentiles are uncircumcised in the flesh." So many things therefore, as these, when they are seen with the eye, are enough to produce conviction and belief in those who embrace the truth, and are not bigoted in their opinions, nor are governed by their passions.

CHAPTER LIV -- ORIGIN OF HEATHEN MYTHOLOGY.

But those who hand down the myths which the poets have made, adduce no proof to the youths who learn them; and we proceed to demonstrate that they have been uttered by the influence of the wicked demons, to deceive and lead astray the human race. For having heard it proclaimed through the prophets that the Christ was to come, and that the ungodly among men were to be punished by fire, they put forward many to be called sons of Jupiter, under the impression that they would be able to produce in men the idea that the things which were said with regard to Christ were mere marvellous tales, like the things which were said by the poets. And these things were said both among the Greeks and among all nations where they [the demons] heard the prophets foretelling that Christ would specially be believed in; but that in hearing what was said by the prophets they did not accurately understand it, but imitated what was said of our Christ, like men who are in error, we will make plain. The prophet Moses, then, Was, as we have already said, older than all writers; and by him, as we have also said before, it was thus predicted: "There shall not fail a prince from Judah, nor a lawgiver from between his feet, until He come for whom it is reserved; and He shall be the desire of the Gentiles, binding His foal to the vine, washing His robe in the blood of the grape." The devils, accordingly, when they heard these prophetic words, said that Bacchus was the son of Jupiter, and gave out that he was the discoverer of the vine, and they number wine [or, the ass] among his mysteries; and they taught that, having been torn in pieces, he ascended into heaven. And because in the prophecy of Moses it had not been expressly intimated whether He who was to come was the Son of God, and whether He would, riding on the foal, remain on earth or ascend into heaven, and because the name of "foal" could mean either the foal of an ass or the foal of a horse, they, not knowing whether He who was foretold would bring the foal of an ass or of a horse as the sign of His coming, nor whether He was the Son of God, as we said above, or of man, gave out that Bellerophon, a man born of man, himself ascended to heaven on his horse Pegasus. And when they heard it said by the other prophet Isaiah, that He should be born of a virgin, and by His own means ascend into heaven, they pretended that Perseus was spoken of. And when they knew what was said, as has been cited above, in the prophecies written aforetime, "Strong as a giant to run his course," they said that Hercules was strong, and had journeyed over the whole earth. And when, again, they learned that it had been foretold that He should heal every sickness, and raise the dead, they produced Aesculapius.

CHAPTER LV -- SYMBOLS OF THE CROSS.

But in no instance, not even in any of those called sons of Jupiter, did they imitate the being crucified; for it was not understood by them, all the things said of it having been put symbolically. And this, as the prophet foretold, is the greatest symbol of His power and role; as is also proved by the things which fall under our observation. For consider all the things in the world, whether without this form they could be administered or have any community. For the sea is not traversed except that trophy which is called a sail abide safe in the ship; and the earth is not ploughed without it: diggers and mechanics do not their work, except with tools which have this shape. And the human form differs from that of the irrational animals in nothing else than in its being erect and having the hands extended, and having on the face extending from the forehead what is called the nose, through which there is respiration for the living creature; and this shows no other form than that of the cross. And so it was said by the prophet, "The breath before our face is the Lord Christ." And the power of this form is shown by your own symbols on what are called "vexilla" [banners] and trophies, with which all your state possessions are made, using these as the insignia of your power and government, even though you do so unwittingly. And with this form you consecrate the images of your emperors when they die, and you name them gods by inscriptions. Since, therefore, we have urged you both by reason and by an evident form, and to the utmost of our ability, we know that now we are blameless even though you disbelieve; for our part is done and finished.

CHAPTER LVI -- THE DEMONS STILL MISLEAD MEN.

But the evil spirits were not satisfied with saying, before Christ's appearance, that those who were said to be sons of Jupiter were born of him; but after He had appeared, and been born among men, and when they learned how He had been foretold by the prophets, and knew that He should be believed on and looked for by every nation, they again, as was said above, put forward other men, the Samaritans Simon and Menander, who did many mighty works by magic, and deceived many, and still keep them deceived. For even among yourselves, as we said before, Simon was in the royal city Rome in the reign of Claudius Caesar, and so greatly astonished the sacred senate and people of the Romans, that he was considered a god, and honoured, like the others whom you honour as gods, with a statue. Wherefore we pray that the sacred senate and your people may, along with yourselves, be arbiters of this our memorial, in order that if anyone be entangled by that man's doctrines, he may learn the truth, and so be able to escape error; and as for the statue, if you please, destroy it.

CHAPTER LVII -- AND CAUSE PERSECUTION.

Nor can the devils persuade men that there will be no conflagration for the punishment of the wicked; as they were unable to effect that Christ should be hidden after He came. But this only can they effect, that they who live irrationally, and were brought up licentiously in wicked customs, and are prejudiced in their own opinions, should kill and hate us; whom we not only do not hate, but, as is proved, pity and endeavour to lead to repentance. For we do not fear death, since it is acknowledged we must surely die; and there is nothing new, but all things continue the same in this administration of things; and if satiety overtakes those who enjoy even one year of these things, they ought to give heed to our doctrines, that they may live eternally free both from suffering and from want. But if they believe that there is nothing after death, but declare that those who die pass into insensibility, then they become our benefactors when they set us free from sufferings and necessities of this life, and prove themselves to be wicked, and inhuman, and bigoted.

For they kill us with no intention of delivering us, but cut us off that we may be deprived of life and pleasure.

CHAPTER LVIII -- AND RAISE UP HERETICS.

And, as we said before, the devils put forward Marcion of Pontus, who is even now teaching men to deny that God is the maker of all things in heaven and on earth, and that the Christ predicted by the prophets is His Son, and preaches another god besides the Creator of all, and likewise another son. And this man many have believed, as if he alone knew the truth, and laugh at us, though they have no proof of what they say, but are carried away irrationally as lambs by a wolf, and become the prey of atheistical doctrines, and of devils. For they who are called devils attempt nothing else than to seduce men from God who made them, and from Christ His first-begotten; and those who are unable to raise themselves above the earth they have riveted, and do now rivet, to things earthly, and to the works of their own hands; but those who devote themselves to the contemplation of things divine, they secretly beat back; and if they have not a wise sober-mindedness, and a pure and passionless life, they drive them into godlessness.

CHAPTER LIX -- PLATO'S OBLIGATION TO MOSES.

And that you may learn that it was from our teachers--we mean the account given through the prophets--that Plato borrowed his statement that God, having altered matter which was shapeless, made the world, hear the very words spoken through Moses, who, as above shown, was the first prophet, and of greater antiquity than the Greek writers; and through whom the Spirit of prophecy, signifying how and from what materials God at first formed the world, spake thus: "In the beginning God created the heaven and the earth. And the earth was invisible and unfurnished, and darkness was upon the face of the deep; and the Spirit of God moved over the waters. And God said, Let there be light; and it was so." So that both Plato and they who agree with him, and we ourselves, have learned, and you also can be convinced, that by the word of God the whole world was made out of the substance spoken of before by Moses. And that which the poets call Erebus, we know was spoken of formerly by Moses.

CHAPTER LX -- PLATO'S DOCTRINE OF THE CROSS.

And the physiological discussion concerning the Son of God in the Timoeus of Plato, where he says, "He placed him crosswise in the universe," he borrowed in like manner from Moses; for in the writings of Moses it is related how at that time, when the Israelites went out of Egypt and were in the wilderness, they fell in with poisonous beasts, both vipers and asps, and every kind of serpent, which slew the people; and that Moses, by the inspiration and influence of God, took brass, and made it into the figure of a cross, and set it in the holy tabernacle, and said to the people, "If ye look to this figure, and believe, ye shall be saved thereby." And when this was done, it is recorded that the serpents died, and it is handed down that the people thus escaped death. Which things Plato reading, and not accurately understanding, and not apprehending that it was the figure of the cross, but taking it to be a placing crosswise, he said that the power next to the first God was placed crosswise in the universe. And as to his speaking of a third, he did this because he read, as we said above, that which was spoken by Moses, "that the Spirit of God moved over the waters." For he gives the second place to the Logos which is with God, who he said was placed crosswise in the universe; and the third place to the Spirit who was said to be borne upon the water, saying, "And the third around the third." And hear how the Spirit of prophecy signified through Moses that there should be a conflagration. He spoke thus: "Everlasting fire shall descend, and shall devour to the pit beneath." It is not, then, that we hold the same opinions as others, but that all speak in imitation of ours. Among us these things can be heard and learned from persons who do not even know the forms of the letters, who are uneducated and barbarous in speech, though wise and believing in mind; some, indeed, even maimed and deprived of eyesight; so that you may understand that these things are not the effect of human wisdom, but are uttered by the power of God.

CHAPTER LXI -- CHRISTIAN BAPTISM.

I will also relate the manner in which we dedicated ourselves to God when we had been made new through Christ; lest, if we omit this, we seem to be unfair in the explanation we are making. As many as are persuaded and believe that what we teach and say is true, and undertake to be able to live accordingly, are instructed to pray and to entreat God with fasting, for the remission of their sins that are past, we praying and fasting with them. Then they are brought by us where there is water, and are regenerated in the same manner in which we were ourselves regenerated. For, in the name of God, the Father and Lord of the universe, and of our Saviour Jesus Christ, and of the Holy Spirit, they then receive the washing with water. For Christ also said, "Except ye be born again, ye shall not enter into the kingdom of heaven. Now, that it is impossible for those who have once been born to enter into their mothers' wombs, is manifest to all. And how those who have sinned and repent shall escape their sins, is declared by Esaias the prophet, as I wrote above; he thus speaks: "Wash you, make you clean; put away the evil of your doings from your souls; learn to do well; judge the fatherless, and plead for the widow: and come and let us reason together, saith the Lord. And though your sins be as scarlet, I will make them white like wool; and though they be as crimson, I will make them white as snow. But if ye refuse and rebel, the sword shall devour you: for the mouth of the Lord hath spoken it."

And for this [rite] we have learned from the apostles this reason. Since at our birth we were born without our own knowledge or choice, by our parents coming together, and were brought up in bad habits and wicked training; in order that we may not remain the children of necessity and of ignorance, but may become the children of choice and knowledge, and may obtain in the water the remission of sins formerly committed, there is pronounced over him who chooses to be born again, and has repented of his sins, the name of God the Father and Lord of the universe; he who leads to the layer the person that is to be washed calling him by this name alone. For no one can utter the name of the ineffable God; and if anyone dare to say that there is a name, he raves with a hopeless madness. And this washing is called illumination, because they who learn these things are illuminated in their understandings. And in the name of Jesus Christ, who was crucified under Pontius Pilate, and in the name of the Holy Ghost, who through the prophets foretold all things about Jesus, he who is illuminated is washed.

CHAPTER LXII -- ITS IMITATION BY DEMONS.

And the devils, indeed, having heard this washing published by the prophet, instigated those who enter their temples, and are about to approach them with libations and burnt-offerings, also to sprinkle themselves; and they cause them also to wash themselves entirely, as they depart [from the sacrifice], before they enter into the shrines in which their images are set. And the command, too, given by the priests to those who enter and worship in the temples, that they take off their shoes, the devils, learning what happened to the above-mentioned prophet Moses, have given in imitation of these things. For at that juncture, when Moses was ordered to go down into Egypt and lead out the people of the Israelites who were there, and while he was tending the flocks of his maternal uncle in the land of Arabia, our Christ conversed with him under the appearance of fire from a bush, and said, "Put off thy shoes, and draw near and hear." And he, when he had put off his shoes and drawn near, heard that he was to go down into Egypt and lead out the people of the Israelites there; and he received mighty power from Christ, who spoke to him in the appearance of fire, and went down and led out the people, having done great and marvellous things;

which, if you desire to know, you will learn them accurately from his writings.

CHAPTER LXIII -- HOW GOD APPEARED TO MOSES.

And all the Jews even now teach that the nameless God spake to Moses; whence the Spirit of prophecy, accusing them by Isaiah the prophet mentioned above, said "The ox knoweth his owner, and the ass his master's crib; but israel doth not know Me, and My people do not understand." And Jesus the Christ, because the Jews knew not what the Father was, and what the Son, in like manner accused them; and Himself said, "No one knoweth the Father, but the Son; nor the Son, but the Father, and they to whom the Son revealeth Him." Now the Word of God is His Son, as we have before said. And He is called Angel and Apostle; for He declares whatever we ought to know, and is sent forth to declare whatever is revealed; as our Lord Himself says, "He that heareth Me, heareth Him that sent Me." From the writings of Moses also this will be manifest; for thus it is written in them, "And the Angel of God spake to Moses, in a flame of fire out of the bush, and said, I am that I am, the God of Abraham, the God of Isaac, the God of Jacob, the God of thy fathers; go down into Egypt, and bring forth My people." And if you wish to learn what follows, you can do so from the same writings; for it is impossible to relate the whole here. But so much is written for the sake of proving that Jesus the Christ is the Son of God and His Apostle, being of old the Word, and appearing sometimes in the form of fire, and sometimes in the likeness of angels; but now, by the will of God, having become man for the human race, He endured all the sufferings which the devils instigated the senseless Jews to inflict upon Him; who, though they have it expressly affirmed in the writings of Moses, "And the angel of God spake to Moses in a flame of fire in a bush, and said, I am that I am, the God of Abraham, and the God of Isaac, and the God of Jacob," yet maintain that He who said this was the Father and Creator of the universe. Whence also the Spirit of prophecy rebukes them, and says, "Israel doth not know Me, my people have not understood Me." And again, Jesus, as we have already shown, while He was with them, said, "No one knoweth the Father, but the Son; nor the Son but the Father, and those to whom the Son will reveal Him." The Jews, accordingly, being throughout of opinion that it was the Father of the universe who spake to Moses, though He who spake to him was indeed the Son of God, who is called both Angel and Apostle, are justly charged, both by the Spirit of prophecy and by Christ Himself, with knowing neither the Father nor the Son. For they who affirm that the Son is the Father, are proved neither to have become acquainted with the Father, nor to know that the Father of the universe has a Son; who also, being the first-begotten Word of God, is even God. And of old He appeared in the shape of fire and in the likeness of an angel to Moses and to the other prophets; but now in the times of your reign, having, as we before said, become Man by a virgin, according to the counsel of the Father, for the salvation of those who believe on Him, He endured both to be set at nought and to suffer, that by dying and rising again He might conquer death. And that which was said out of the bush to Moses, "I am that I am, the God of Abraham, and the God of Isaac, and the God of Jacob, and the God of your fathers," this signified that they, even though dead, are let in existence, and are men belonging to Christ Himself. For they were the first of all men to busy themselves in the search after God; Abraham being the father of Isaac, and Isaac of Jacob, as Moses wrote.

CHAPTER LXIV--FURTHER MISREPRESENTATIONS OF THE TRUTH.

From what has been already said, you can understand how the devils, in imitation of what was said by Moses, asserted that Proserpine was the daughter of Jupiter, and instigated the people to set up an image of her under the name of Kore [Cora, i.e., the maiden or daughter] at the spring-heads. For, as we wrote above, Moses said, "In the beginning God made the heaven and the earth. And the earth was without form and unfurnished: and the Spirit of God moved upon the face of the waters." In imitation, therefore, of what is here said of the Spirit of God moving on the waters, they said that Proserpine [or Cora] was the daughter of Jupiter. And in like manner also they craftily feigned that Minerva was the daughter of Jupiter, not by sexual union, but, knowing that God conceived and made the world by the Word, they say that Minerva is the first conception [ennoia]; which we consider to be very absurd, bringing forward the form of the conception in a female shape. And in like manner the actions of those others who are called sons of Jupiter sufficiently condemn them.

CHAPTER LXV -- ADMINISTRATION OF THE SACRAMENTS.

But we, after we have thus washed him who has been convinced and has assented to our teaching, bring him to the place where those who are called brethren are assembled, in order that we may offer hearty prayers in common for ourselves and for the baptized [illuminated] person, and for all others in every place, that we may be counted worthy, now that we have learned the truth, by our works also to be found good citizens and keepers of the commandments, so that we may be saved with an everlasting salvation. Having ended the prayers, we salute one another with a kiss.

There is then brought to the president of the brethren bread and a cup of wine mixed with water; and he taking them, gives praise and glory to the Father of the universe, through the name of the Son and of the Holy Ghost, and offers thanks at considerable length for our being counted worthy to receive these things at His hands. And when he has concluded the prayers and thanksgivings, all the people present express their assent by saying Amen. This word Amen answers in the Hebrew language to genoito [so be it]. And when the president has given thanks, and all the people have expressed their assent, those who are called by us deacons give to each of those present to partake of the bread and wine mixed with water over which the thanksgiving was pronounced, and to those who are absent they carry away a portion.

CHAPTER LXVI -- OF THE EUCHARIST.

And this food is called among us Eukaristia [the Eucharist], of which no one is allowed to partake but the man who believes that the things which we teach are true, and who has been washed with the washing that is for the remission of sins, and unto regeneration, and who is so living as Christ has enjoined. For not as common bread and common drink do we receive these; but in like manner as Jesus Christ our Saviour, having been made flesh by the Word of God, had both flesh and blood for our salvation, so likewise have we been taught that the food which is blessed by the prayer of His word, and from which our blood and flesh by transmutation are nourished, is the flesh and blood of that Jesus who was made flesh. For the apostles, in the memoirs composed by them, which are called Gospels, have thus delivered unto us what was enjoined upon them; that Jesus took bread, and when He had given thanks, said, "This do ye in remembrance of Me, this is My body;" and that, after the same manner, having taken the cup and given thanks, He said, "This is My blood;" and gave it to them alone. Which the wicked devils have imitated in the mysteries of Mithras, commanding the same thing to be done. For, that bread and a cup of water are placed with certain incantations in the mystic rites of one who is being initiated, you either know or can learn.

CHAPTER LXVII -- WEEKLY WORSHIP OF THE CHRIS- TIANS.

And we afterwards continually remind each other of these things. And the wealthy among us help the needy; and we always keep together; and for all things wherewith we are supplied, we bless the Maker of all through His Son Jesus Christ, and through the Holy Ghost. And on the day called Sunday, all who live in cities or in the country gather together to one place, and the memoirs of the apostles or the writings of the prophets are read, as long as time permits; then, when the reader has ceased, the president verbally instructs, and exhorts to the imitation of these good things. Then we all rise together and pray, and, as we before said, when our prayer is ended, bread and wine and water are brought, and the president in like manner offers prayers and thanksgivings, according to his ability, and the people assent, saying Amen; and there is a distribution to each, and a participation of that over which thanks have been given, and to those who are absent a portion is sent by the deacons. And they who are well to do, and willing, give what each thinks fit; and what is collected is deposited with the president, who succours the orphans and widows and those who, through sickness or any other cause, are in want, and those who are in bonds and the strangers sojourning among us, and in a word takes care of all who are in need. But Sunday is the day on which we all hold our common assembly, because it is the first day on which God, having wrought a change in the darkness and matter, made the world; and Jesus Christ our Saviour on the same day rose from the dead. For He was crucified on the day before that of Saturn (Saturday); and on the day after that of Saturn, which is the day of the Sun, having appeared to His apostles and disciples, He taught them these things, which we have submitted to you also for your consideration.

CHAPTER LXVIII -- CONCLUSION.

And if these things seem to you to be reasonable and true, honour them; but if they seem nonsensical, despise them as nonsense, and do not decree death against those who have done no wrong, as you would against enemies. For we forewarn you, that you shall not escape the coming judgment of God, if you continue in your injustice; and we ourselves will invite you to do that which is pleasing to God. And though from the letter of the greatest and most illustrious Emperor Adrian, your father, we could demand that you order judgment to be given as we have desired, yet we have made this appeal and explanation, not on the ground of Adrian's decision, but because we know that what we ask is just. And we have subjoined the copy of Adrian's epistle, that you may know that we are speaking truly about this.
And the following is the copy: EPISTLE OF ADRIAN IN BEHALF OF THE CHRISTIANS.

I have received the letter addressed to me by your predecessor Serenius Granianus, a most illustrious man; and this communication I am unwilling to pass over in silence, lest innocent persons be disturbed, and occasion be given to the informers for practising villany. Accordingly, if the inhabitants of your province will so far sustain this petition of theirs as to accuse the Christians in some court of law, I do not prohibit them from doing so. But I will not suffer them to make use of mere entreaties and outcries. For it is far more just, if anyone desires to make an accusation, that you give judgment upon it. If, therefore, anyone makes the accusation, and furnishes proof that the said men do anything contrary to the laws, you shall adjudge punishments in proportion to the offences. And this, by Hercules; you shall give special heed to, that if any man shall, through mere calumny, bring an accusation against any of these persons, you shall award to him more severe punishments in proportion to his wickedness.

EPISTLE OF ANTONINUS TO THE COMMON ASSEMBLY OF ASIA.

The Emperor Caesar Titus AElius Adrianus Antoninus Augustus Pius, Supreme Pontiff, in the fifteenth year of his tribuneship, Consul for the third time, Father of the fatherland, to the Common Assembly of Asia, greeting: I should have thought that the gods themselves would see to it that such offenders should not escape. For if they had the power, they themselves would much rather punish those who refuse to worship them; but it is you who bring trouble on these persons, and accuse as the opinion of atheists that which they hold, and lay to their charge certain other things which we are unable to prove. But it would be advantageous to them that they should be thought to die for that of which they are accused, and they conquer you by being lavish of their lives rather than yield that obedience which you require of them. And regarding the earthquakes which have already happened and are now occurring, it is not seemly that you remind us of them, losing heart whenever they occur, and thus set your conduct in contrast with that of these men; for they have much greater confidence towards God than you yourselves have. And you, indeed, seem at such times to ignore the gods, and you neglect the temples, and make no recognition of the worship of God. And hence you are jealous of those who do serve Him, and persecute them to the death. Concerning such persons, some others also of the governors of provinces wrote to my most divine father; to whom he replied that they should not at all disturb such persons, unless they were found to be attempting anything against the Roman government. And to myself many have sent intimations regarding such persons, to whom I also replied in pursuance of my father's judgment. But if anyone has a matter to bring against any person of this class, merely as such a person, let the accused be acquitted of the charge, even though he should be found to be such an one; but let the accuser be amenable to justice.

EPISTLE OF MARCUS AURELIUS TO THE SENATE, IN WHICH HE TESTIFIES THAT THE CHRISTIANS WERE THE CAUSE OF HIS VICTORY.

The Emperor Caesar Marcus Aurelius Antoninus, Germanicus, Parthicus, Sarmaticus, to the People of Rome, and to the sacred Senate greeting: I explained to you my grand design, and what advantages I gained on the confines of Germany, with much labour and suffering, in consequence of the circumstance that I was surrounded by the enemy; I myself being shut up in Carnuntum by seventy-four cohorts, nine miles off. And the enemy being at hand, the scouts pointed out to us, and our general Pompeianus showed us that there was close on us a mass of a mixed multitude of 977,000 men, which indeed we saw; and I was shut up by this vast host, having with me only a battalion composed of the first, tenth, double and marine legions. Having then examined my own position, and my host, with respect to the vast mass of barbarians and of the enemy, I quickly betook myself to prayer to the gods of my country. But being disregarded by them, I summoned those who among us go by the name of Christians. And having made inquiry, I discovered a great number and vast host of them, and raged against them, which was by no means becoming; for afterwards I learned their power. Wherefore they began the battle, not by preparing weapons, nor arms, nor bugles; for such preparation is hateful to them, on account of the God they bear about in their conscience. Therefore it is probable that those whom we suppose to be atheists, have God as their ruling power entrenched in their conscience. For having cast themselves on the ground, they prayed not only for me, but also for the whole army as it stood, that they might be delivered from the present thirst and famine. For during five days we had got no water, because there was none; for we were in the heart of Germany, and in the enemy's territory. And simultaneously with their casting themselves on the ground, and praying to God (a God of whom I am ignorant), water poured from heaven, upon us most refreshingly cool, but upon the enemies of Rome a withering hail. And immediately we recognised the presence of God following on the prayer--a God unconquerable and indestructible. Founding upon this, then, let us pardon such as are Christians, lest they pray for and obtain such a weapon against ourselves. And I counsel that no such person be accused on the ground of his being a Christian. But if anyone be found laying to the charge of a Christian that he is a Christian, I desire that it be made manifest that he who is accused as a Christian, and acknowledges that he is one, is accused of nothing else than only this, that he is a Christian; but that he who arraigns him be burned alive. And I further desire, that he who is entrusted with the government of the province shall not compel the Christian, who confesses and certifies such a matter, to retract; neither shall he commit him. And I desire that these things be confirmed by a decree of the Senate. And I command this my edict to be published in the Forum of Trajan, in order that it may be read. The prefect Vitrasius Pollio will see that it be transmitted to all the provinces round about, and that no one who wishes to make use of or to possess it be hindered from obtaining a copy from the document I now publish.

Introduction to Clement of Rome

Clement of Rome (35 – 99 CE), also referred to as Clement I, served as the Bishop of Rome from around 88 AD until his martyrdom in 99 AD. He is believed to have been a direct disciple of the apostles Peter and Paul. Clement is best known for his epistle to the Corinthians, known as the First Epistle of Clement. In this letter, he emphasized the importance of unity, hierarchical order within the Church, and submission to authority.

Clement of Rome, also known as Pope Clement I, is considered an Apostolic Father due to his close association with the apostolic era and his contributions to early Christian theology and leadership.

Clement of Rome is believed to have served as the fourth bishop of Rome in the late first century, and his exact dates of birth and death are uncertain. He is mentioned in the New Testament in the Epistle to the Philippians, where the apostle Paul refers to him as a fellow worker in Christ Jesus.

There are several reasons why Clement of Rome is considered an Apostolic Father:

1 Association with the Apostle Paul: Clement of Rome is believed to have been a companion and co-worker of the apostle Paul. In Paul's letter to the Philippians (Philippians 4:3), Clement's name is mentioned alongside other fellow workers in the Gospel. This connection places Clement within the apostolic era and establishes his credibility as an inheritor of apostolic teaching and tradition.

2 Apostolic Authority: Clement's writings demonstrate his strong belief in the authority of the apostles and their teachings. His most famous work is the "First Epistle of Clement," a letter addressed to the Corinthian church to address issues of division and disorder. In this letter, Clement appeals to the authority of the apostles and their appointed leaders as a basis for resolving conflicts and maintaining unity in the Church.

3 Leadership and Ecclesiastical Development: Clement of Rome played a significant role in the early Christian community as the bishop of Rome. His position as bishop and his role in addressing the Corinthian church indicate his leadership within the Church and his authority in matters of faith and practice. Clement's writings reflect the emerging structure and organization of the early Christian Church.

4 Recognition by Early Christians: Clement of Rome's authority and teachings were highly regarded by early Christian communities. His letter to the Corinthians was widely read and circulated, and it was even considered for inclusion in the New Testament canon by some early Christian writers. While it was ultimately not included, its enduring influence and

recognition attest to Clement's standing as an important figure in early Christianity.

Based on his association with the apostle Paul, his belief in apostolic authority, his leadership as the bishop of Rome, and the recognition of his writings by early Christians, Clement of Rome is considered an Apostolic Father. His contributions to early Christian theology, leadership, and ecclesiastical development make him a significant figure in the transition from the apostolic era to the subsequent development of Christian thought and practice.

CLEMENT OF ROME

First Clement
Letter of Clement to the Corinthians

CHAPTER 1 -- SALUTATION, AND PRAISE FOR THE CORINTHIANS BEFORE SCHISM BROKE FORTH AMONG THEM.

The Church of God which sojourns at Rome, to the Church of God sojourning at Corinth, to those who are called and sanctified by the will of God, through our Lord Jesus Christ: Grace to you, and peace, from Almighty God through Jesus Christ, be multiplied.

Owing, dear brethren, to the sudden and successive calamitous events which have happened to ourselves, we feel that we have been somewhat tardy in turning our attention to the points respecting which you consulted us; and especially to that shameful and detestable sedition, utterly abhorrent to the elect of God, which a few rash and self-confident persons have kindled to such a pitch of frenzy, that your venerable and illustrious name, worthy to be universally loved, has suffered grievous injury. For whoever dwelt even for a short time among you, and did not find your faith to be as fruitful of virtue as it was firmly established? Who did not admire the sobriety and moderation of your godliness in Christ? Who did not proclaim the magnificence of your habitual hospitality? And who did not rejoice over your perfect and well-grounded knowledge? For you did all things without respect of persons, and walked in the commandments of God, being obedient to those who had the rule over you, and giving all fitting honour to the presbyters among you. You enjoined young men to be of a sober and serious mind; you instructed your wives to do all things with a blameless, becoming, and pure conscience, loving their husbands as in duty bound; and you taught them that, living in the rule of obedience, they should manage their household affairs becomingly, and be in every respect marked by discretion.

CHAPTER 2 -- PRAISE OF THE CORINTHIANS CONTINUED

Moreover, you were all distinguished by humility, and were in no respect puffed up with pride, but yielded obedience rather than extorted it, and were more willing to give than to receive? Content with the provision which God had made for you, and carefully attending to His words, you were inwardly filled with His doctrine, and His sufferings were before your eyes. Thus a profound and abundant peace was given to you all, and you had an insatiable desire for doing good, while a full outpouring of the Holy Spirit was upon you all. Full of holy designs, and with true earnestness of mind and a godly confidence, you stretched forth your hands to God Almighty, beseeching Him to be merciful to you, if you had been guilty of any involuntary transgression. Day and night you were anxious for the whole brotherhood, that the number of God's elect might be saved with mercy and a good conscience. You were sincere and uncorrupted, and forgetful of injuries between one another. Every kind of faction and schism was abominable in your sight. You mourned over the transgressions of your neighhours: their deficiencies you deemed your own. You never grudged any act of kindness, being "ready to every good work." Adorned by a thoroughly virtuous and religious life, you did all things in the fear of God. The commandments and ordinances of the Lord were written upon the tablets of your hearts.

CHAPTER 3 -- THE SAD STATE OF THE CORINTHIAN CHURCH AFTER SEDITION AROSE IN IT FROM ENVY AND EMULATION.

Every kind of honour and happiness was bestowed upon you, and then was fulfilled that which is written, "My beloved ate and drank, and was enlarged and became fat, and kicked." Hence flowed emulation and envy, strife and sedition, persecution and disorder, war and captivity. So the worthless rose up against the honoured, those of no reputation against such as were renowned, the foolish against the wise, the young against those advanced in years. For this reason righteousness and peace are now far departed from you, inasmuch as every one abandons the fear of God, and is become blind in His faith, neither walks in the ordinances of His appointment, nor acts a part becoming a Christian, but walks after his own wicked lusts, resuming the practice of an unrighteous and ungodly envy, by which death itself entered into the world.

CHAPTER 4 -- MANY EVILS HAVE ALREADY FLOWED FROM THIS SOURCE IN ANCIENT TIMES.

For thus it is written: "And it came to pass after certain days, that Cain brought of the fruits of the earth a sacrifice to God; and Abel also brought of the firstlings of his sheep, and of the fat thereof. And God had respect to Abel and to his offerings, but Cain and his sacrifices He did not regard. And Cain was deeply grieved, and his countenance fell. And God said to Cain, why are you grieved, and why is your countenance fallen? If you offer rightly, but do not divide rightly, have you not sinned? Be at peace: your offering returns to yourself, and you shall again possess it. And Cain said to Abel his brother, Let us go into the field. And it came to pass, while they were in the field, that Cain rose up against Abel his brother, and killed him." You see, brethren, how envy and jealousy led to the murder of a brother. Through envy, also, our father Jacob fled from the face of Esau his brother. Envy made Joseph be persecuted unto death, and to come into bondage. Envy compelled Moses to flee from the face of Pharaoh king of Egypt, when he heard these words from his fellow countryman, "Who made you a judge or a ruler over us? Will you kill me, as you killed the Egyptian yesterday?" On account of envy, Aaron and Miriam had to make their home outside of the camp. Envy brought down Dathan and Abiram alive to Hades, through the sedition which they excited against God's servant Moses. Through envy, David underwent the hatred not only of foreigners, but was also persecuted by Saul king of Israel.

CHAPTER 5 -- NO LESS EVILS HAVE ARISEN FROM THE SAME SOURCE IN THE MOST RECENT TIMES. THE MARTYRDOM OF PETER AND PAUL.

But not to dwell upon ancient examples, let us come to the most recent spiritual heroes. Let us take the noble examples furnished in our own generation. Through envy and jealousy, the greatest and most righteous pillars [of the Church] have been persecuted and put to death. Let us set before our eyes the illustrious apostles. Peter, through unrighteous envy, endured not one or two, but numerous labours, and when he had finally suffered martyrdom, departed to the place of glory due to him. Owing to envy, Paul also obtained the reward of patient endurance, after being seven times thrown into captivity, compelled to flee, and stoned. After preaching both in the east and west, he gained the illustrious reputation due to his faith, having taught righteousness to the whole world, and come to the extreme limit of the west, and suffered martyrdom under the prefects. Thus was he removed from the world, and went into the holy place, having proved himself a striking example of patience.

CHAPTER 6 -- CONTINUATION. SEVERAL OTHER MARTYRS.

To these men who spent their lives in the practice of holiness, there is to be added a great multitude of the elect, who, having through envy endured many indignities and tortures, furnished us with a most excellent example. Through envy, those women, the Danaids and Dircae, being persecuted, after they had suffered terrible and unspeakable torments, finished the course of their faith with steadfastness, and though weak in body, received a noble reward. Envy has alienated wives from their husbands, and changed that saying of our father Adam, "This is now bone of my bones, and flesh of my flesh." Envy and strife have overthrown great cities and rooted up mighty nations.

CHAPTER 7 -- AN EXHORTATION TO REPENTANCE.

These things, beloved, we write to you, not merely to admonish you of your duty, but also to remind ourselves. For we are struggling in the same arena, and the same conflict is assigned to both of us. So let us give up vain and fruitless cares, and approach to the glorious and venerable rule of our holy calling. Let us attend to what is good, pleasing, and acceptable in the sight of Him who formed us. Let us look steadfastly to the blood of Christ, and see how precious that blood is to God, which, having been shed for our salvation, has set the grace of repentance before the whole world. Let us turn to every age that has passed, and learn that, from generation to generation, the Lord has granted a place of repentance to all who would be converted to Him. Noah preached repentance, and as many as listened to him were saved. Jonah proclaimed destruction to the Ninevites; but they, repenting of their sins, propitiated God by prayer, and obtained salvation, although they were aliens [to the covenant] of God.

CHAPTER 8 -- CONTINUATION RESPECTING REPENTANCE.

The ministers of the grace of God have, by the Holy Spirit, spoken of repentance; and the Lord of all things has himself declared with an oath regarding it, "As I live, says the Lord, I desire not the death of the sinner, but rather his repentance;" adding, moreover, this gracious declaration: "Repent O house of Israel, of your iniquity. Say to the children of My people, Though your sins reach from earth to heaven, and though they be redder than scarlet, and blacker than sackcloth, if you turn to Me with your whole heart, and say, Father! I will listen to you, as to a holy people." And in another place He says: "Wash, and become clean; put away the wickedness of your souls from before my eyes; cease from your evil ways, and learn to do well; seek out judgment, deliver the oppressed, judge the fatherless, and see that justice is done to the widow; and come, and let us reason together. He declares, "Though your sins be like crimson, I will make them white as snow; though they be like scarlet, I will whiten them like wool. And if you are willing and obey Me, you shall eat the good of the land; but if you refuse, and will not listen to Me, the sword shall devour you, for the mouth of the Lord has spoken these things." Desiring, therefore, that all His beloved should be partakers of repentance, He has, by His almighty will, established [these declarations].

CHAPTER 9 -- EXAMPLES OF THE SAINTS.

So let us yield obedience to His excellent and glorious will; and imploring His mercy and loving-kindness, while we forsake all fruitless labours, and strife, and envy, which leads to death, let us turn and have recourse to His compassions. Let us steadfastly contemplate those who have perfectly ministered to His excellent glory. Let us take (for instance) Enoch, who, being found righteous in obedience, was translated, and death was never known to happen to him? Noah, being found faithful, preached regeneration to the world through his ministry; and the Lord saved by him the animals which, with one accord, entered into the ark.

CHAPTER 10 -- CONTINUATION OF THE ABOVE.

Abraham, called "the friend," was found faithful, inasmuch as he obeyed the words of God. He, in the exercise of obedience, went out from his own country, and from his kindred, and from his father's house, in order that, by forsaking a small territory, and a weak family, and an insignificant house, he might inherit the promises of God. For God said to him, "Leave your country, and your kindred, and your father's house, and go into the land which I shall show you. And I will make you a great nation, and will bless you, and make your name great, and you shall be blessed. And I will bless those who bless you, and curse those who curse you; and in you shall all the families of the earth be blessed." And again, on his departing from Lot, God said to him. "Lift up your eyes, and look from the place where you now are, northward, and southward, and eastward, and westward; for all the land which you see, to you will I give it, and to your seed for ever. And I will make your seed as the dust of the earth, [so that] if a man can number the dust of the earth, then shall your seed also be numbered." And again [the Scripture] says, "God brought forth Abram, and said to him, Look up now to heaven, and count the stars if you are able to number them; so shall your seed be. And Abram believed God, and it was counted to him for righteousness." On account of his faith and hospitality, a son was given him in his old age; and in the exercise of obedience, he offered him as a sacrifice to God on one of the mountains which He showed him.

CHAPTER 11 -- CONTINUATION. LOT.

On account of his hospitality and godliness, Lot was saved out of Sodom when all the country around him was punished by means of fire and brimstone, the Lord thus making it manifest that He does not forsake those who hope in Him, but gives up those who depart from Him to punishment and torture. For Lot's wife, who went forth with him, being of a different mind from himself and not continuing in agreement with him [as to the command which had been given them], was made an example of, so as to be a pillar of salt to this day. This was done that all might know that those who are of a double mind, and who distrust the power of God, bring down judgment on themselves, and become a sign to all succeeding generations.

CHAPTER 12 -- THE REWARDS OF FAITH AND HOSPITALITY. RAHAB.

On account of her faith and hospitality, Rahab the harlot was saved. For when spies were sent by Joshua, the son of Nun, to Jericho, the king of the country ascertained that they had come to spy out their land, and sent men to seize them, in order that, when taken, they might be put to death. But the hospitable Rahab received them, and hid them on the roof of her house under some stalks of flax. And when the men sent by the king arrived and said "There came men to you who are to spy out our land; bring them forth, for so the king commands," she answered them, "The two men whom you seek came to me, but quickly departed again and are gone," thus not discovering the spies to them. Then she said to the men, "I know assuredly that the Lord your God has given you this city, for the fear and dread of you have fallen on its inhabitants. When therefore you shall have taken it, keep me and the house of my father in safety." And they said to her, "It shall be as you have spoken to us. As soon, therefore, as you know that we are at hand, you shall gather all your family under your roof, and they shall be preserved, but anyone found outside of your dwelling shall perish." Moreover, they gave her a sign to this effect, that she should hang forth from her house a scarlet thread. And thus they made it manifest that redemption should flow through the blood of the Lord to all those who believe and hope in God. You see, beloved, that there was not only faith, but prophecy, in this woman.

CHAPTER 13 -- AN EXHORTATION TO HUMILITY.

Let us therefore, brethren, be of humble mind, laying aside all haughtiness, and pride, and foolishness, and angry feelings; and let us act according to that which is written (for the Holy Spirit says, "Let not the wise man glory in his wisdom, neither let the mighty man glory in his might, neither let the rich man Story in his riches; but let him that glories glory in the Lord, in diligently seeking Him, and doing judgment and righteousness"), being especially mindful of the words of the Lord Jesus which He spoke, teaching us meekness and long-suffering. For thus He spoke: "Be merciful, that you may obtain mercy; forgive, that it may be forgiven to you; as you do, so shall it be done to you; as you judge, so shall you be judged; as you are kind, so shall kindness be shown to you; with what measure you measure, with the same it shall be measured to you." By this precept and by these rules let us establish ourselves, that we walk with all humility in obedience to His holy words. For the holy word says, "On whom shall I look, but on him that is meek and peaceable, and who trembles at My words?"

CHAPTER 14 -- WE SHOULD OBEY GOD RATHER THAN THE AUTHORS OF SEDITION.

It is right and holy therefore, men and brethren, to obey God rather than to follow those who, through pride and sedition, have become the leaders of a detestable emulation. For we shall incur no slight injury, but rather great danger, if we rashly yield ourselves to the inclinations of men who aim at exciting strife and tumults, so as to draw us away from what is good. Let us be kind one to another after the pattern of the tender mercy and benignity of our Creator. For it is written, "The kind-hearted shall inhabit the land, and the guiltless shall be left upon it, but transgressors shall be destroyed from off the face of it." And again [the Scripture] says, "I saw the ungodly highly exalted, and lifted up like the cedars of Lebanon: I passed by, and, behold, he was not; and I diligently sought his place, and could not find it. Preserve innocence, and look on equity: for there shall be a remnant to the peaceful man."

CHAPTER 15 -- WE MUST ADHERE TO THOSE WHO CULTIVATE PEACE, NOT TO THOSE WHO MERELY PRETEND TO DO SO.

Let us cleave, therefore, to those who cultivate peace with godliness, and not to those who hypocritically profess to desire it. For [the Scripture] says in a certain place, "This people honours Me with their lips, but their heart is far from Me." And again: "They bless with their mouth, but curse with their heart." And again it says, "They loved Him with their mouth, and lied to Him with their tongue; but their heart was not right with Him, neither were they faithful in His covenant." "Let the deceitful lips become silent," [and "let the Lord destroy all the lying lips,] and the boastful tongue of those who have said, Let us magnify our tongue; our lips are our own; who is lord over us? For the oppression of the poor, and for the sighing of the needy, will I now arise, says the Lord: I will place him in safety; I will deal confidently with him."

CHAPTER 16 -- CHRIST AS AN EXAMPLE OF HUMILITY.

For Christ is of those who are humble-minded, and not of those who exalt themselves over His flock. Our Lord

Jesus Christ, the Sceptre of the majesty of God, did not come in the pomp of pride or arrogance, although He might have done so, but in a lowly condition, as the Holy Spirit had declared regarding Him. For He says, "Lord, who has believed our report, and to whom is the arm of the Lord revealed? We have declared [our message] in His presence: He is, as it were, a child, and like a root in thirsty ground; He has no form nor glory, yea, we saw Him, and He had no form nor comeliness; but His form was without eminence, yea, deficient in comparison with the [ordinary] form of men. He is a man exposed to stripes and suffering, and acquainted with the endurance of grief: for His countenance was turned away; He was despised, and not esteemed. He bears our iniquities, and is in sorrow for our sakes; yet we supposed that [on His own account] He was exposed to labour, and stripes, and affliction. But He was wounded for our transgressions, and bruised for our iniquities. The chastisement of our peace was upon Him, and by His stripes we were healed. All we, like sheep, have gone astray; [every] man has wandered in his own way; and the Lord has delivered Him up for our sins, while He in the midst of His sufferings opens not His mouth. He was brought as a sheep to the slaughter, and as a lamb before her shearer is dumb, so He opens not His mouth. In His humiliation His judgment was taken away; who shall declare His generation? For His life is taken from the earth. For the transgressions of my people was He brought down to death. And I will give the wicked for His sepulchre, and the rich for His death, because He did no iniquity, nor was guile found in His mouth. And the Lord is pleased to purify Him by stripes. If you make an offering for sin, your soul shall see a long-lived seed. And the Lord is pleased to relieve Him of the affliction of His soul, to show Him light, and to form Him with understanding, to justify the Just One who ministers well to many; and He Himself shall carry their sins. On this account He shall inherit many, and shall divide the spoil of the strong; because His soul was delivered to death, and He was reckoned among the transgressors, and He bare the sins of many, and for their sins was He delivered." And again He says, "I am a worm, and no man; a reproach of men, and despised of the people. All who see Me have derided Me; they have spoken with their lips; they have wagged their head, [saying] He hoped in God, let Him deliver Him, let Him save Him, since He delights in Him." You see, beloved, what is the example which has been given us; for if the Lord thus humbled Himself, what shall we do who have through Him come under the yoke of His grace?

CHAPTER 17 -- THE SAINTS AS EXAMPLES OF HUMILITY.

Let us be imitators also of those who in goat-skins and sheep-skins went about proclaiming the coming of Christ; I mean Elijah, Elisha, and Ezekiel among the prophets, with those others to whom a like testimony is borne [in Scripture]. Abraham was specially honoured, and was called the friend of God; yet he, earnestly regarding the glory of God, humbly declared, "I am but dust and ashes." Moreover, it is thus written of Job, "Job was a righteous man, and blameless, truthful, God-fearing, and one that kept himself from all evil." But bringing an accusation against himself, he said, "No man is free from defilement, even if his life be but of one day." Moses was called faithful in all God's house; and through his instrumentality, God punished Egypt with plagues and tortures. Yet he, though thus greatly honoured, did not adopt lofty language, but said, when the divine oracle came to him out of the bush, "Who am I, that You send me? I am a man of a feeble voice and a slow tongue." And again he said, "I am but as the smoke of a pot."

CHAPTER 18 -- DAVID AS AN EXAMPLE OF HUMILITY.

But what shall we say concerning David, to whom such testimony was borne, and of whom God said, "I have found a man after My own heart, David the son of Jesse; and in everlasting mercy have I anointed him?" Yet this very man says to God, "Have mercy on me, O Lord, according to Your great mercy; and according to the multitude of Your compassions, blot out my transgression. Wash me still more from my iniquity, and cleanse me from my sin. For I acknowledge my iniquity, and my sin is ever before me. Against You only have I sinned, and done that which was evil in Your sight; that You may be justified in Your sayings, and may overcome when You are judged. For, behold, I was conceived in transgressions, and in my sins did my mother conceive me. For, behold, You have loved truth; the secret and hidden things of wisdom have You shown me. you shall sprinkle me with hyssop, and I shall be cleansed; you shall wash me, and I shall be whiter than snow. you shall make me to hear joy and gladness; my bones, which have been humbled, shall exult. Turn away Your face from my sins, and blot out all my iniquities. Create in me a clean heart, O God, and renew a right spirit within me. Cast me not away from Your presence, and take not Your Holy Spirit from me. Restore to me the joy of Your salvation, and establish me by Your governing Spirit. I will teach transgressors Your ways, and the ungodly shall be converted to You. Deliver me from blood-guiltiness, O God, the God of my salvation: my tongue shall exult in Your righteousness. O Lord, you shall open my mouth, and my lips shall show forth Your praise. For if You had desired sacrifice, I would have given it; You will not delight in burnt-offerings. The sacrifice [acceptable] to

God is a bruised spirit; a broken and a contrite heart God will not despise."

CHAPTER 19 -- IMITATING THESE EXAMPLES, LET US SEEK AFTER PEACE.

Thus the humility and godly submission of so great and illustrious men have rendered not only us, but also all the generations before us, better; even as many as have received His oracles in fear and truth. So, having so many great and glorious examples set before us, let us turn again to the practice of that peace which from the beginning was the mark set before us; and let us look steadfastly to the Father and Creator of the universe, and cleave to His mighty and surpassingly great gifts and benefactions, of peace. Let us contemplate Him with our understanding, and look with the eyes of our soul to His long-suffering will. Let us reflect how free from wrath He is towards all His creation.

CHAPTER 20 -- THE PEACE AND HARMONY OF THE UNIVERSE.

The heavens, revolving under His government, are subject to Him in peace. Day and night run the course appointed by Him, in no way hindering each other. The sun and moon, with the companies of the stars, roll on in harmony according to His command, within their prescribed limits, and without any deviation. The fruitful earth, according to His will, brings forth food in abundance, at the proper seasons, for man and beast and all the living beings upon it, never hesitating, nor changing any of the ordinances which He has fixed. The unsearchable places of abysses, and the indescribable arrangements of the lower world, are restrained by the same laws. The vast unmeasurable sea, gathered together by His working into various basins, never passes beyond the bounds placed around it, but does as He has commanded. For He said, "Thus far shall you come, and your waves shall be broken within you." The ocean, impassible to man, and the worlds beyond it, are regulated by the same enactments of the Lord. The seasons of spring, summer, autumn, and winter, peacefully give place to one another. The winds in their several quarters fulfill, at the proper time, their service without hindrance. The ever-flowing fountains, formed both for enjoyment and health, furnish without fail their breasts for the life of men. The very smallest of living beings meet together in peace and concord. All these the great Creator and Lord of all has appointed to exist in peace and harmony; while He does good to all, but most abundantly to us who have fled for refuge to His compassions through Jesus Christ our Lord, to whom be glory and majesty for ever and ever. Amen. xxxxx

CHAPTER 21 -- LET US OBEY GOD, AND NOT THE AUTHORS OF SEDITION.

Take heed, beloved, lest His many kindnesses lead to the condemnation of us all. [For thus it must be] unless we walk worthy of Him, and with one mind do those things which are good and well-pleasing in His sight. For [the Scripture] says in a certain place, "The Spirit of the Lord is a candle searching the secret parts of the belly." Let us reflect how near He is, and that none of the thoughts or reasonings in which we engage are hid from Him. It is right, therefore, that we should not leave the post which His will has assigned us. Let us rather offend those men who are foolish, and inconsiderate, and lifted up, and who glory in the pride of their speech, than [offend] God. Let us reverence the Lord Jesus Christ, whose blood was given for us; let us esteem those who have the rule over us; let us honour the aged among us; let us train up the young men in the fear of God; let us direct our wives to that which is good. Let them exhibit the lovely habit of purity [in all their conduct]; let them show forth the sincere disposition of meekness; let them make manifest the command which they have of their tongue, by their manner of speaking; let them display their love, not by preferring one to another, but by showing equal affection to all that piously fear God. Let your children be partakers of true Christian training; let them learn of how great avail humility is with God -- how much the spirit of pure affection can prevail with Him -- how excellent and great His fear is, and how it saves all those who walk in it with a pure mind. For He is a Searcher of the thoughts and desires [of the heart]: His breath is in us; and when He pleases, He will take it away.

CHAPTER 22 -- THESE EXHORTATIONS ARE CONFIRMED BY THE CHRISTIAN FAITH, WHICH PROCLAIMS THE MISERY OF SINFUL CONDUCT.

Now the faith which is in Christ confirms all these [admonitions]. For He Himself by the Holy Ghost thus addresses us: "Come, you children, listen to Me; I will teach you the fear of the Lord. What man is he that desires life, and loves to see good days? Keep your tongue from evil, and your lips from speaking guile. Depart from evil, and do good; seek peace, and pursue it. The eyes of the Lord are upon the righteous, and His ears are [open] to their prayers. The face of the Lord is against those who do evil, to cut off the remembrance of them from the earth. The righteous cried, and the Lord heard him, and delivered him out of all his troubles." "Many are the stripes [appointed for] the wicked; but mercy shall compass those about who hope in the Lord."

CHAPTER 23 -- BE HUMBLE, AND BELIEVE THAT CHRIST WILL COME AGAIN.

The all-merciful and beneficent Father has bowels [of compassion] towards those who fear Him, and kindly and lovingly bestows His favours upon those who come to Him with a simple mind. So let us not be double-minded; neither let our soul be lifted up on account of His exceedingly great and glorious gifts. Far from us be that which is written, "Wretched are they who are of a double mind, and of a doubting heart; who say, These things we have heard even in the times of our fathers; but, behold, we have grown old, and none of them has happened to us.." You foolish ones! compare yourselves to a tree: take [for instance] the vine. First of all, it sheds its leaves, then it buds, next it puts forth leaves, and then it flowers; after that comes the sour grape, and then follows the ripened fruit. You perceive how in a little time the fruit of a tree comes to maturity. Of a truth, soon and suddenly shall His will be accomplished, as the Scripture also bears witness, saying, "Speedily will He come, and will not tarry;" and, "The Lord shall suddenly come to His temple, even the Holy One, for whom you look."

CHAPTER 24 -- GOD CONTINUALLY SHOWS US IN NATURE THAT THERE WILL BE A RESURRECTION.

Let us consider, beloved, how the Lord continually proves to us that there shall be a future resurrection, of which He has rendered the Lord Jesus Christ the first-fruits by raising Him from the dead. Let us contemplate, beloved, the resurrection which is at all times taking place. Day and night declare to us a resurrection. The night sinks to sleep, and the day arises; the day [again] departs, and the night comes on. Let us behold the fruits [of the earth], how the sowing of grain takes place. The sower goes forth, and casts it into the ground; and the seed being thus scattered, though dry and naked when it fell upon the earth, is gradually dissolved. Then out of its dissolution the mighty power of the providence of the Lord raises it up again, and from one seed many arise and bring forth fruit.

CHAPTER 25 -- THE PHOENIX AN EMBLEM OF OUR RESURRECTION.

Let us consider that wonderful sign [of the resurrection] which takes place in Eastern lands, that is, in Arabia and the countries round about. There is a certain bird which is called a phoenix. This is the only one of its kind, and lives five hundred years. And when the time of its dissolution draws near that it must die, it builds itself a nest of frankincense, and myrrh, and other spices, into which, when the time is fulfilled, it enters and dies. But as the flesh decays a certain kind of worm is produced, which, being nourished by the juices of the dead bird, brings forth feathers. Then, when it has acquired strength, it takes up that nest in which are the bones of its parent, and bearing these it passes from the land of Arabia into Egypt, to the city called Heliopolis. And, in open day, flying in the sight of all men, it places them on the altar of the sun, and having done this, hastens back to its former abode. The priests then inspect the registers of the dates, and find that it has returned exactly as the five hundredth year was completed.

CHAPTER 26 -- WE SHALL RISE AGAIN, THEN, AS THE SCRIPTURE ALSO TESTIFIES.

Do we then deem it any great and wonderful thing for the Maker of all things to raise up again those who have piously served Him in the assurance of a good faith, when even by a bird He shows us the mightiness of His power to fulfil His promise? For [the Scripture] says in a certain place, "You shall raise me up, and I shall confess to You;" and again, "I laid down, and slept; I awaked, because You are with me;" and again, Job says, "you shall raise up this flesh of mine, which has suffered all these things."

CHAPTER 27 -- IN THE HOPE OF THE RESURRECTION, LET US CLEAVE TO THE OMNIPOTENT AND OMNISCIENT GOD.

Having then this hope, let our souls be bound to Him who is faithful in His promises, and just in His judgments. He who has commanded us not to lie, shall much more Himself not lie; for nothing is impossible with God, except to lie. Let His faith therefore be stirred up again within us, and let us consider that all things are nigh unto Him. By the word of His might He established all things, and by His word He can overthrow them. "Who shall say to Him, What have you done? or, Who shall resist the power of His strength?" When and as He pleases He will do all things, and none of the things determined by Him shall pass away? All things are open before Him, and nothing can be hidden from His counsel. "The heavens declare the glory of God, and the firmament shows His handy-work. Day to day utters speech, and night to night shows knowledge. And there are no words or speeches of which the voices are not heard."

CHAPTER 28 -- GOD SEES ALL THINGS: THEREFORE LET US AVOID TRANSGRESSION.

Since then all things are seen and heard [by God], let us fear Him, and forsake those wicked works which proceed from evil desires; so that, through His mercy, we may be protected from the judgments to come. For whither can any of us flee from His mighty hand? Or what world will receive any of those who run away from Him? For the Scripture says in a certain place, "Whither shall I go, and where shall I be hid from Your presence? If I ascend into heaven, You are there; if I go away even to the uttermost parts of the earth, there is Your right hand; if I make my bed in the abyss, there is Your Spirit." Whither, then, shall anyone go, or where shall he escape from Him who comprehends all things?

CHAPTER 29 -- LET US ALSO DRAW NEAR TO GOD IN PURITY OF HEART.

Let us then draw near to Him with holiness of spirit, lifting up pure and undefiled hands to Him, loving our gracious and merciful Father, who has made us partakers in the blessings of His elect. For thus it is written, "When the Most High divided the nations, when He scattered the sons of Adam, He fixed the bounds of the nations according to the number of the angels of God. His people Jacob became the portion of the Lord, and Israel the lot of His inheritance." And in another place [the Scripture] says, "Behold, the Lord takes to Himself a nation out of the midst of the nations, as a man takes the first-fruits of his threshing-floor; and from that nation shall come forth the Most Holy.

CHAPTER 30 -- LET US DO THOSE THINGS THAT PLEASE GOD, AND FLEE FROM THOSE HE HATES, THAT WE MAY BE BLESSED.

Seeing, therefore, that we are the portion of the Holy One, let us do all those things which pertain to holiness, avoiding all evil-speaking, all abominable and impure embraces, together with all drunkenness, seeking after change, all abominable lusts, detestable adultery, and execrable pride. "For God," says [the Scripture], "resists the proud, but gives grace to the humble." Let us cleave, then, to those to whom grace has been given by God. Let us clothe ourselves with concord and humility, ever exercising self-control, standing far off from all whispering and evil-speaking, being justified by our works, and not our words. For [the Scripture] says, "He that speaks much, shall also hear much in answer. And does he that is ready in speech deem himself righteous? Blessed is he that is born of woman, who lives but a short time: be not given to much speaking." Let our praise be in God, and not of ourselves; for God hates those who commend themselves. Let testimony to our good deeds be borne by others, as it was in the case of our righteous forefathers. Boldness, and arrogance, and audacity belong to those that are accursed of God; but moderation, humility, and meekness to such as are blessed by Him.

CHAPTER 31 -- LET US SEE BY WHAT MEANS WE MAY OBTAIN THE DIVINE BLESSING.

Let us cleave then to His blessing, and consider what are the means of possessing it. Let us think over the things which have taken place from the beginning. For what reason was our father Abraham blessed? was it not because he wrought righteousness and truth through faith? Isaac, with perfect confidence, as if knowing what was to happen, cheerfully yielded himself as a sacrifice. Jacob, through reason of his brother, went forth with humility from his own land, and came to Laban and served him; and there was given to him the sceptre of the twelve tribes of Israel.

CHAPTER 32 -- WE ARE JUSTIFIED NOT BY OUR OWN WORKS, BUT BY FAITH.

Whosoever will candidly consider each particular, will recognise the greatness of the gifts which were given by him. For from him have sprung the priests and all the Levites who minister at the altar of God. From him also [was descended] our Lord Jesus Christ according to the flesh. From him [arose] kings, princes, and rulers of the race of Judah. Nor are his other tribes in small glory, inasmuch as God had promised, "Your seed shall be as the stars of heaven." All these, therefore, were highly honoured, and made great, not for their own sake, or for their own works, or for the righteousness which they wrought, but through the operation of His will. And we, too, being called by His will in Christ Jesus, are not justified by ourselves, nor by our own wisdom, or understanding, or godliness, or works which we have wrought in holiness of heart; but by that faith through which, from the beginning, Almighty God has justified all men; to whom be glory for ever and ever. Amen.

CHAPTER 33 -- BUT LET US NOT OWE UP THE PRACTICE OF GOOD WORKS AND LOVE. GOD HIMSELF IS AN EXAMPLE TO US OF GOOD WORKS.

What shall we do, then, brethren? Shall we become slothful in well-doing, and cease from the practice of love? God forbid that any such course should be followed by us! But rather let us hasten with all energy and readiness of mind to perform every good work. For the Creator and Lord of all Himself rejoices in His works. For by His infinitely great power He established the heavens, and by His incomprehensible wisdom He adorned them. He also divided the earth from the water which surrounds it, and fixed it upon the immoveable foundation of His own will. The animals also which are upon it He commanded by His own word into existence. So likewise, when He had formed the sea, and the living creatures which are in it, He enclosed them [within their proper bounds] by His own power. Above all, with His holy and undefiled hands He formed man, the most excellent [of His creatures], and truly great through the understanding given him -- the express likeness of His own image. For thus says God: "Let us make man in Our image, and after Our likeness. So God made man; male and female He created them." Having thus finished all these things, He approved them, and blessed them, and said, "Increase and multiply." We see, then, how all righteous men have been adorned with good works, and how the Lord Himself, adorning Himself with His works, rejoiced. Having therefore such an example, let us without delay accede to His will, and let us work the work of righteousness with our whole strength.

CHAPTER 34 -- GREAT IS THE REWARD OF GOOD WORKS WITH GOD. JOINED TOGETHER IN HARMONY, LET US IMPLORE THAT REWARD FROM HIM.

The good servant receives the bread of his labour with confidence; the lazy and slothful cannot look his employer in the face. It is requisite, therefore, that we be prompt in the practice of well-doing; for of Him are all things. And thus He forewarns us: "Behold, the Lord [cometh], and His reward is before His face, to render to every man according to his work." He exhorts us, therefore, with our whole heart to attend to this, that we be not lazy or slothful in any good work. Let our boasting and our confidence be in Him. Let us submit ourselves to His will. Let us consider the whole multitude of His angels, how they stand ever ready to minister to His will. For the Scripture says, "Ten thousand times ten thousand stood around Him, and thousands of thousands ministered to Him, and cried, Holy, holy, holy, the Lord of Sabaoth; the whole creation is full of His glory." And let us therefore, conscientiously gathering together in harmony, cry to Him earnestly, as with one mouth, that we may be made partakers of His great and glorious promises. For [the Scripture] says, "Eye has not seen, nor ear heard, neither has it entered into the heart of man, the things which He has prepared for those who wait for Him."

CHAPTER 35 -- IMMENSE IS THIS REWARD. HOW SHALL WE OBTAIN IT?

How blessed and wonderful, beloved, are the gifts of God! Life in immortality, splendour in righteousness, truth in perfect confidence, faith in assurance, self-control in holiness! And all these fall under the cognizance of our understandings [now]; what then shall those things be which are prepared for such as wait for Him? The Creator and Father of all worlds, the Most Holy, alone knows their amount and their beauty. Let us therefore earnestly strive to be found in the number of those who wait for Him, in order that we may share in His promised gifts. But how, beloved, shall this be done? If our understanding be fixed by faith rewards God; if we earnestly seek the things which are pleasing and acceptable to Him; if we do the things which are in harmony with His blameless will; and if we follow the way of truth, casting away from us all unrighteousness and iniquity, along with all covetousness, strife, evil practices, deceit, whispering, and evil-speaking, all hatred of God, pride and haughtiness, vainglory and ambition. For they that do such things are hateful to God; and not only they that do them, but also those who take pleasure in those who do them. For the Scripture says, "But to the sinner God said, Why do you declare my statutes, and take my covenant into your mouth, seeing you hate instruction, and cast my words behind you? When you saw a thief, you consented with him, and made your portion with adulterers. Your mouth has abounded with wickedness, and your tongue contrived deceit. You sit, and speak against your brother; you slander your own mother's son. These things you have done, and I kept silence; you thought, wicked one, that I should be like you. But I will reprove you, and set yourself before you. Consider now these things, you who forget God, lest He tear you in pieces, like a lion, and there be none to deliver. The sacrifice of praise will glorify Me, and a way is there by which I will show him the salvation of God."

CHAPTER 36 -- ALL BLESSINGS ARE GIVEN TO US THROUGH CHRIST.

This is the way, beloved, in which we find our Saviour, even Jesus Christ, the High Priest of all our offerings, the defender and helper of our infirmity. By Him we look up to the heights of heaven. By Him we behold, as in a glass, His immaculate and most excellent visage. By Him are the eyes of our hearts opened. By Him our foolish and darkened understanding blossoms up anew towards His marvellous light. By Him the Lord has willed that we should taste of immortal knowledge, "who, being the brightness of His majesty, is by so much greater than the angels, as He has by inheritance obtained a more excellent name than they." For it is thus written, "Who makes His angels spirits, and His ministers a flame of fire." But concerning His Son the Lord spoke thus: "You are my Son, today have I begotten You. Ask of Me, and I will give You the heathen for Your inheritance, and the uttermost parts of the earth for Your possession." And again He says to Him, "Sit at My right hand, until I make Your enemies Your footstool." But who are His enemies? All the wicked, and those who set themselves to oppose the will of God.

CHAPTER 37 -- CHRIST IS OUR LEADER, AND WE HIS SOLDIERS.

Let us then, men and brethren, with all energy act the part of soldiers, in accordance with His holy commandments. Let us consider those who serve under our generals, with what order, obedience, and submissiveness they perform the things which are commanded them. All are not prefects, nor commanders of a thousand, nor of a hundred, nor of fifty, nor the like, but each one in his own rank performs the things commanded by the king and the generals. The great cannot subsist without the small, nor the small without the great. There is a kind of mixture in all things, and thence arises mutual advantage. Let us take our body for an example. The head is nothing without the feet, and the feet are nothing without the head; yea, the very smallest members of our body are necessary and useful to the whole body. But all work harmoniously together, and are under one common rule for the preservation of the whole body.

CHAPTER 38 -- LET THE MEMBERS OF THE CHURCH SUBMIT THEMSELVES, AND NO ONE EXALT HIMSELF ABOVE ANOTHER.

Let our whole body, then, be preserved in, Christ Jesus; and let every one be subject to his neighbour, according to the special gift bestowed upon him. Let the strong not despise the weak, and let the weak show respect to the strong. Let the rich man provide for the wants of the poor; and let the poor man bless God, because He has given him one by whom his need may be supplied. Let the wise man display his wisdom, not by [mere] words, but through good deeds. Let the humble not bear testimony to himself, but leave witness to be borne to him by another. Let him that is pure in the flesh not grow proud of it, and boast, knowing that it was another who bestowed on him the gift of continence. Let us consider, then, brethren, of what matter we were made, -- who and what manner of beings we came into the world, as it were out of a sepulchre, and from utter darkness. He who made us and fashioned us, having prepared His bountiful gifts for us before we were born, introduced us into His world. Since, therefore, we receive all these things from Him, we ought for everything to give Him thanks; to whom be glory for ever and ever. Amen.

CHAPTER 39 -- THERE IS NO REASON FOR SELF-CONCEIT.

Foolish and inconsiderate men, who have neither wisdom nor instruction, mock and deride us, being eager to exalt themselves in their own conceits. For what can a mortal man do? or what strength is there in one made out of the dust? For it is written, "There was no shape before mine eyes, only I heard a sound, and a voice [saying], What then? Shall a man be pure before the Lord? or shall such an one be [counted] blameless in his deeds, seeing He does not confide in His servants, and has charged even His angels with perversity? The heaven is not clean in His sight: how much less they that dwell in houses of clay, of which also we ourselves were made! He smote them as a moth; and from morning even until evening they endure not. Because they could furnish no assistance to themselves, they perished. He breathed upon them, and they died, because they had no wisdom. But call now, if anyone will answer you, or if you will look to any of the holy angels; for wrath destroys the foolish man, and envy kills him that is in error. I have seen the foolish taking root, but their habitation was presently consumed. Let their sons be far from safety; let them be despised before the gates of those less than themselves, and there shall be none to deliver. For what was prepared for them, the righteous shall eat; and they shall not be delivered from evil."

CHAPTER 40 -- LET US PRESERVE IN THE CHURCH THE ORDER APPOINTED BY GOD.

These things therefore being manifest to us, and since we look into the depths of the divine knowledge, it behoves us to do all things in [their proper] order, which the Lord has commanded us to perform at stated times. He has enjoined offerings [to be presented] and service to be performed [to Him], and that not thoughtlessly or irregularly, but at the appointed times and hours. Where and by whom He desires these things to be done, He Himself has fixed by His own supreme will, in order that all things being piously done according to His good pleasure, may be acceptable to Him. Those, therefore, who present their offerings at the appointed times, are accepted and blessed; for inasmuch as they follow the laws of the Lord, they sin not. For his own peculiar services are assigned to the high priest, and their own proper place is prescribed to the priests, and their own special ministrations devolve on the Levites. The layman is bound by the laws that pertain to laymen.

CHAPTER 41 -- CONTINUATION OF THE SAME SUBJECT.

Let every one of you, brethren, give thanks to God in his own order, living in all good conscience, with becoming gravity, and not going beyond the rule of the ministry prescribed to him. Not in every place, brethren, are the daily sacrifices offered, or the peace-offerings, or the sin-offerings and the trespass-offerings, but in Jerusalem only. And even there they are not offered in any place, but only at the altar before the temple, that which is offered being first carefully examined by the high priest and the ministers already mentioned. Those, therefore, who do anything beyond that which is agreeable to His will, are punished with death. You see, brethren, that the greater the knowledge that has been vouchsafed to us, the greater also is the danger to which we are exposed.

CHAPTER 42 -- THE ORDER OF MINISTERS IN THE CHURCH.

The apostles have preached the Gospel to us from the Lord Jesus Christ; Jesus Christ [has done so] from God. Christ therefore was sent forth by God, and the apostles by Christ. Both these appointments, then, were made in an orderly way, according to the will of God. Having therefore received their orders, and being fully assured by the resurrection of our Lord Jesus Christ, and established in the word of God, with full assurance of the Holy Ghost, they went forth proclaiming that the kingdom of God was at hand. And thus preaching through countries and cities, they appointed the first-fruits [of their labours], having first proved them by the Spirit, to be bishops and deacons of those who should afterwards believe. Nor was this any new thing, since indeed many ages before it was written concerning bishops and deacons. For thus says the Scripture a certain place, "I will appoint their bishops s in righteousness, and their deacons in faith."

CHAPTER 43 -- MOSES OF OLD STILLED THE CONTENTION WHICH AROSE CONCERNING THE PRIESTLY DIGNITY.

And what wonder is it if those in Christ who were entrusted with such a duty by God, appointed those [ministers] before mentioned, when the blessed Moses also, "a faithful servant in all his house," noted down in the sacred books all the injunctions which were given him, and when the other prophets also followed him, bearing witness with one consent to the ordinances which he had appointed? For, when rivalry arose concerning the priesthood, and the tribes were contending among themselves as to which of them should be adorned with that glorious title, he commanded the twelve princes of the tribes to bring him their rods, each one being inscribed with the name of the tribe. And he took them and bound them [together], and sealed them with the rings of the princes of the tribes, and laid them up in the tabernacle of witness on the table of God. And having shut the doors of the tabernacle, he sealed the keys, as he had done the rods, and said to them, Men and brethren, the tribe whose rod shall blossom has God chosen to fulfil the office of the priesthood, and to minister to Him. And when the morning was come, he assembled all Israel, six hundred thousand men, and showed the seals to the princes of the tribes, and opened the tabernacle of witness, and brought forth the rods. And the rod of Aaron was found not only to have blossomed, but to bear fruit upon it. What think you, beloved? Did not Moses know beforehand that this would happen? Undoubtedly he knew; but he acted thus, that there might be no sedition in Israel, and that the name of the true and only God might be glorified; to whom be glory for ever and ever. Amen.

CHAPTER 44 -- THE ORDINANCES OF THE APOSTLES, THAT THERE MIGHT BE NO CONTENTION RESPECTING THE PRIESTLY OFFICE.

Our apostles also knew, through our Lord Jesus Christ, and there would be strife on account of the office of the episcopate. For this reason, therefore, inasmuch as they had obtained a perfect fore-knowledge of this, they appointed those [ministers] already mentioned, and afterwards gave instructions, that when these should fall asleep, other approved men should succeed them in their ministry. We are of opinion, therefore, that those appointed by them, or afterwards by other eminent men, with the consent of the whole Church, and who have blame-lessly served the flock of Christ in a humble, peaceable, and disinterested spirit, and have for a long time possessed the good opinion of all, cannot be justly dismissed from the ministry. For our sin will not be small, if we eject from the episcopate those who have blamelessly and holily fulfilled its duties. Blessed are those presbyters who, having finished their course before now, have obtained a fruitful and perfect departure [from this world]; for they have no fear lest anyone deprive them of the place now appointed them. But we see that you have removed some men of excellent behaviour from the ministry, which they fulfilled blamelessly and with honour.

CHAPTER 45 -- IT IS THE PART OF THE WICKED TO VEX THE RIGHTEOUS.

Ye are fond of contention, brethren, and full of zeal about things which do not pertain to salvation. Look carefully into the Scriptures, which are the true utterances of the Holy Spirit. Observe that nothing of an unjust or counterfeit character is written in them. There you will not find that the righteous were cast off by men who themselves were holy. The righteous were indeed persecuted, but only by the wicked. They were cast into prison, but only by the unholy; they were stoned, but only by transgressors; they were slain, but only by the accursed, and such as had conceived an unrighteous envy against them. Exposed to such sufferings, they endured them gloriously. For what shall we say, brethren? Was Daniel s cast into the den of lions by such as feared God? Were Ananias, and Azarias, and Mishael shut up in a furnace of fire by those who observed the great and glorious worship of the Most High? Far from us be such a thought! Who, then, were they that did such things? The hateful, and those full of all wickedness, were roused to such a pitch of fury, that they inflicted torture on those who served God with a holy and blameless purpose [of heart], not knowing that the Most High is the Defender and Protector of all such as with a pure conscience venerate" His all-excellent name; to whom be glory for ever and ever. Amen. But they who with confidence endured [these things] are now heirs of glory and honour, and have been exalted and made illustrious by God in their memorial for ever and ever. Amen.

CHAPTER 46 -- LET US CLEAVE TO THE RIGHTEOUS: YOUR STRIFE IS PERNICIOUS.

Such examples, therefore, brethren, it is right that we should follow; since it is written, "Cleave to the holy, for those who cleave to them shall [themselves] be made holy." And again, in another place, [the Scripture] says, "With a harmless man you shall prove thyself harmless, and with an elect man you shall be elect, and with a perverse man you shall show thyself perverse." Let us cleave, therefore, to the innocent and righteous, since these are the elect of God. Why are there strifes, and tumults, and divisions, and schisms, and wars among you? Have we not [all] one God and one Christ? Is there not one Spirit of grace poured out upon us? And have we not one calling in Christ? Why do we divide and tear to pieces the members of Christ, and raise up strife against our own body, and have reached such a height of madness as to forget that "we are members one of another?" Remember the words of our Lord Jesus Christ, how He said, "Woe to that man [by whom offences come]! It were better for him that he had never been born, than that he should cast a stumbling-block before one of my elect. Yea, it were better for him that a millstone should be hung about [his neck], and he should be sunk in the depths of the sea, than that he should cast a stumbling-block before one of my little ones. Your schism has subverted [the faith of] many, has discouraged many, has given rise to doubt in many, and has caused grief to us all. And still your sedition continues.

CHAPTER 47 -- YOUR RECENT DISCORD IS WORSE THAN THE FORMER WHICH TOOK PLACE IN THE TIMES OF PAUL.

Take up the epistle of the blessed Apostle Paul. What did he write to you at the time when the Gospel first began to be preached? Truly, under the inspiration of the Spirit, he wrote to you concerning himself, and Cephas, and Apollos, because even then parties had been formed among you. But that inclination for one above another entailed less guilt upon you, inasmuch as your partialities were then shown towards apostles, already of high reputation, and towards a man whom they had approved. But now reflect who those are that have perverted you, and lessened the renown of your far-famed brotherly love. It is disgraceful, beloved, yea, highly disgraceful, and unworthy of your Christian profession, that such a thing should be heard of as that the most steadfast and ancient Church of the Corinthians should, on account of one or two persons, engage in sedition against its presbyters. And this rumour has reached not only us, but those also who are unconnected with us; so that, through your infatuation, the name of the Lord is blasphemed, while danger is also brought upon yourselves.

CHAPTER 48 -- LET US RETURN TO THE PRACTICE OF BROTHERLY LOVE.

Let us therefore, with all haste, put an end s to this [state of things]; and let us fall down before the Lord, and beseech Him with tears, that He would mercifully be reconciled to us, and restore us to our former seemly and holy practice of brotherly love. For [such conduct] is the gate of righteousness, which is set open for the attainment of life, as it is written, "Open to me the gates of righteousness; I will go in by them, and will praise the Lord: this is the gate of the Lord: the righteous shall enter in by it." Although, therefore, many gates have been set open, yet this gate of righteousness is that gate in Christ by which blessed are all they that have entered in and have directed their way in holiness and righteousness, doing all things without disorder. Let a man be faithful: let him be powerful in the utterance of knowledge; let him be wise in judging of words; let him be pure in all his deeds; yet the more he seems to be superior to others [in these respects], the more humble-minded ought he to be, and to seek the common good of all, and not merely his own advantage.

CHAPTER 49 -- THE PRAISE OF LOVE.

Let him who has love in Christ keep the commandments of Christ. Who can describe the [blessed] bond of the love of God? What man is able to tell the excellence of its beauty, as it ought to be told? The height to which love exalts is unspeakable. Love unites us to God. Love covers a multitude of sins. Love bears all things, is long-suffering in all things. There is nothing base, nothing arrogant in love. Love admits of no schisms: love gives rise to no seditions: love does all things in harmony. By love have all the elect of God been made perfect; without love nothing is well-pleasing to God. In love has the Lord taken us to Himself. On account of the Love he bore us, Jesus Christ our Lord gave His blood for us by the will of God; His flesh for our flesh, and His soul for our souls.

CHAPTER 50 -- LET US PRAY TO BE THOUGHT WORTHY OF LOVE.

Ye see, beloved, how great and wonderful a thing is love, and that there is no declaring its perfection. Who is fit to be found in it, except such as God has vouchsafed to render so? Let us pray, therefore, and implore of His mercy, that we may live blameless in love, free from all human partialities for one above another. All the generations from Adam even to this day have passed away; but those who, through the grace of God, have been made perfect in love, now possess a place among the godly, and shall be made manifest at the revelation of the kingdom of Christ. For it is written, "Enter into thy secret chambers for a little time, until my wrath and fury pass away; and I will remember a propitious day, and will raise you up out of your graves." Blessed are we, beloved, if we keep the commandments of God in the harmony of love; that so through love our sins may be forgiven us. For it is written, "Blessed are they whose transgressions are forgiven, and whose sins are covered. Blessed is the man whose sin the Lord will not impute to him, and in whose mouth there is no guile." This blessedness comes upon those who have been chosen by God through Jesus Christ our Lord; to whom be glory for ever and ever. Amen.

CHAPTER 51 -- LET THE PARTAKERS IN STRIFE ACKNOWLEDGE THEIR SINS.

Let us therefore implore forgiveness for all those transgressions which through any [suggestion] of the adversary we have committed. And those who have been the leaders of sedition and disagreement ought to have respect to the common hope. For such as live in fear and love would rather that they themselves than their neighbours should be involved in suffering. And they prefer to bear blame themselves, rather than that the concord which has been well and piously handed down to us should suffer. For it is better that a man should acknowledge his transgressions than that he should harden his heart, as the hearts of those were hardened who stirred up sedition against Moses the servant of God, and whose condemnation was made

manifest [to all]. For they went down alive into Hades, and death swallowed them up. Pharaoh with his army and all the princes of Egypt, and the chariots with their riders, were sunk in the depths of the Red Sea, and perished, for no other reason than that their foolish hearts were hardened, after so many signs and wonders had been wrought in the land of Egypt by Moses the servant of God.

CHAPTER 52 -- SUCH A CONFESSION IS PLEASING TO GOD.

The Lord, brethren, stands in need of nothing; and He desires nothing of anyone, except that confession be made to Him. For, says the elect David, "I will confess to the Lord; and that will please Him more than a young bullock that has horns and hoofs. Let the poor see it, and be glad." And again he says, "Offer to God the sacrifice of praise, and pay your vows to the Most High. And call upon Me in the day of your trouble: I will deliver you, and you shall glorify Me." For "the sacrifice of God is a broken spirit."

CHAPTER 53 -- THE LOVE OF MOSES TOWARDS HIS PEOPLE.

Ye understand, beloved, you understand well the Sacred Scriptures, and you have looked very earnestly into the oracles of God. Call then these things to your remembrance. When Moses went up into the mount, and abode there, with fasting and humiliation, forty days and forty nights, the Lord said to him, "Moses, Moses, get down quickly from here; for your people whom you brought out of the land of Egypt have committed iniquity. They have quickly departed from the way in which I commanded them to walk, and have made to themselves molten images." And the Lord said to him, "I have spoken to you once and again, saying, I have seen this people, and, behold, it is a stiff-necked people: let Me destroy them, and blot out their name from under heaven; and I will make you a great and wonderful nation, and one much more numerous than this." But Moses said, "Far be it from You, Lord: pardon the sin of this people; else blot me also out of the book of the living." O marvellous love! O insuperable perfection! The servant speaks freely to his Lord, and asks forgiveness for the people, or begs that he himself might perish along with them.

CHAPTER 54 -- HE WHO IS FULL OF LOVE WILL INCUR EVERY LOSS, THAT PEACE MAY BE RESTORED TO THE CHURCH.

Who then among you is noble-minded? who compassionate? who full of love? Let him declare, "If on my account sedition and disagreement and schisms have arisen, I will depart, I will go away whithersoever you desire, and I will do whatever the majority commands; only let the flock of Christ live on terms of peace with the presbyters set over it." He that acts thus shall procure to himself great glory in the Lord; and every place will welcome him. For "the earth is the Lord's, and the fulness thereof." These things they who live a godly life, that is never to be repented of, both have done and always will do.

CHAPTER 55 -- EXAMPLES OF SUCH LOVE.

To bring forward some examples from among the heathen: Many kings and princes, in times of pestilence, when they had been instructed by an oracle, have given themselves up to death, in order that by their own blood they might deliver their fellow-citizens [from destruction]. Many have gone forth from their own cities, that so sedition might be brought to an end within them. We know many among ourselves who have given themselves up to bonds, in order that they might ransom others. Many, too, have surrendered themselves to slavery, that with the price which they received for themselves, they might provide food for others. Many women also, being strengthened by the grace of God, have performed numerous manly exploits. The blessed Judith, when her city was besieged, asked of the elders permission to go forth into the camp of the strangers; and, exposing herself to danger, she went out for the love which she bare to her country and people then besieged; and the Lord delivered Holofernes into the hands of a woman. Esther also, being perfect in faith, exposed herself to no less danger, in order to deliver the twelve tribes of Israel from impending destruction. For with fasting and humiliation she entreated the everlasting God, who sees all things; and He, perceiving the humility of her spirit, delivered the people for whose sake she had encountered peril.

CHAPTER 56 -- LET US ADMONISH AND CORRECT ONE ANOTHER.

Let us then also pray for those who have fallen into any sin, that meekness and humility may be given to them, so that they may submit, not to us, but to the will of God. For in this way they shall secure a fruitful and perfect remembrance from us, with sympathy for them, both in our prayers to God, and our mention of them to the saints. Let us receive correction, beloved, on account of which no one should feel displeased. Those exhortations by which we admonish one another are both good [in themselves] and highly profitable, for they tend to unite us to the will of God. For thus says the holy Word: "The Lord has severely chastened me, yet has not given me over to death." "For whom the Lord loves He chastens, and scourges every son whom He receives." "The righteous," it says, "shall

chasten me in mercy, and reprove me; but let not the oil of sinners make fat my head." And again he says, "Blessed is the man whom the Lord reproves, and reject not the warning of the Almighty. For He causes sorrow, and again restores [to gladness]; He wounds, and His hands make whole. He shall deliver you in six troubles, yea, in the seventh no evil shall touch you. In famine He shall rescue you from death, and in war He shall free you from the power of the sword. From the scourge of the tongue will He hide you, and you shall not fear when evil comes. you shall hugh at the unrighteous and the wicked, and shall not be afraid of the beasts of the field. For the wild beasts shall be at peace with you: then shall you know that your house shall be in peace, and the habitation of your tabernacle shall not fail? You shall know also that your seed shall be great, and your children like the grass of the field. And you shall come to the grave like ripened corn which is reaped in its season, or like a heap of the threshing-floor which is gathered together at the proper time." You see, beloved, that protection is afforded to those who are chastened of the Lord; for since God is good, He corrects us, that we may be admonished by His holy chastisement.

CHAPTER 57 -- LET THE AUTHORS OF SEDITION SUBMIT THEMSELVES.

Ye therefore, who laid the foundation of this sedition, submit yourselves to the presbyters, and receive correction so as to repent, bending the knees of your hearts. Learn to be subject, laying aside the proud and arrogant self-confidence of your tongue. For it is better for you that you should occupy a humble but honourable place in the flock of Christ, than that, being highly exalted, you should be cast out from the hope of His people. For thus speaks all-virtuous Wisdom: "Behold, I will bring forth to you the words of My Spirit, and I will teach you My speech. Since I called, and you did not hear; I held forth My words, and you regarded not, but set at naught My counsels, and yielded not at My reproofs; therefore I too will laugh at your destruction; yea, I will rejoice when ruin comes upon you, and when sudden confusion overtakes you, when overturning presents itself like a tempest, or when tribulation and oppression fall upon you. For it shall come to pass, that when you call upon Me, I will not hear you; the wicked shall seek Me, and they shall not find Me. For they hated wisdom, and did not choose the fear of the Lord; nor would they listen to My counsels, but despised My reproofs. So they shall eat the fruits of their own way, and they shall be filled with their own ungodliness." .

CHAPTER 58 -- BLESSINGS SOUGHT FOR ALL THAT CALL UPON GOD.

May God, who sees all things, and who is the Ruler of all spirits and the Lord of all flesh -- who chose our Lord Jesus Christ and us through Him to be a peculiar people -- grant to every soul that calls upon His glorious and holy Name, faith, fear, peace, patience, long-suffering, self-control, purity, and sobriety, to the well-pleasing of His Name, through our High Priest and Protector, Jesus Christ, by whom be to Him glory, and majesty, and power, and honour, both now and for evermore. Amen.

CHAPTER 59 -- THE CORINTHIANS ARE EXHORTED SPEEDILY TO SEND BACK WORD THAT PEACE HAS BEEN RESTORED. THE BENEDICTION.

Send back speedily to us in peace and with joy these our messengers to you: Claudius Ephebus and Valerius Bito, with Fortunatus: that they may the sooner announce to us the peace and harmony we so earnestly desire and long for [among you], and that we may the more quickly rejoice over the good order re-established among you. The grace of our Lord Jesus Christ be with you, and with all everywhere that are the called of God through Him, by whom be to Him glory, honour, power, majesty, and eternal dominion, from everlasting to everlasting. Amen.

CLEMENT OF ROME, First Epistle

THE FIRST EPISTLE OF CLEMENT TO THE CORINTHIANS

translated by Charles H. Hoole, 1885

Introduction
The Church of God which sojourneth at Rome, to the Church of God which sojourneth at Corinth, to them that are called and sanctified in the will of God through our Lord Jesus Christ: Grace and peace be multiplied unto you from Almighty God through Jesus Christ.

CHAPTER 1
1:1 On account of the sudden and repeated calamities and mischances, brethren, that have come upon us, we suppose that we have the more slowly given heed to the things that are disputed among you, beloved, and to the foul and unholy sedition, alien and foreign to the elect of God, which a few headstrong and self-willed persons have kindled to such a degree of madness, that your venerable and famous name, worthy to be loved of all men, is greatly blasphemed.

1:2 For who that hath tarried among you hath not approved your most virtuous and firm faith, hath not admired your sober and seemly piety in Christ, hath not proclaimed your splendid disposition of hospitality, hath not deemed blessed your perfect and unerring knowledge?

1:3 For ye did all things without respect of persons, and walked in the laws of God, submitting yourselves to them that have the rule over you, and giving the due honour to the presbyters that are among you. Young men ye enjoined to think such things as be sober and grave. Women ye exhorted to perform all things in a blameless and honourable and pure conscience, loving dutifully their own husbands; and ye taught them to manage the affairs of their houses with gravity, keeping in the rule of obedience, being temperate in all things.

CHAPTER 2

2:1 And ye were all humble, boasting of nothing, submitting yourselves rather than subjecting others, more gladly giving than receiving, content with the provision that God had given you; and attending diligently to his words, ye received them into your very hearts, and his sufferings were before your eyes.

2:2 Thus a deep and rich peace was given to all, and an insatiable longing for doing good, and a plentiful outpouring of the Holy Spirit was upon all of you.

2:3 And ye, being filled with a holy desire, with excellent zeal and pious confidence, stretched out your arms to Almighty God, beseeching him to be merciful unto you, if ye had in anything unwillingly done amiss.

2:4 Ye contended day and night for the whole brotherhood, that in his mercy and good pleasure the number of his elect might be saved.

2:5 Ye were simple and sincere without malice one toward another:
2:6 all sedition and all schism were abominable unto you. Ye grieved over the transgressions of your neighbour, judging his short-comings your own.

2:7 Ye repented not of any well-doing, being ready to every good work;

2:8 and being adorned with a very virtuous and holy habit of life, ye did all things in his fear. The commandments and ordinances of the Lord were written on the breadth of your heart.

CHAPTER 3

3:1 All honour and enlargement was given to you, and then was fulfilled that which is written: -- The beloved ate and drank, and was enlarged and grew fat and kicked.

3:2 From this came emulation and envy, strife and sedition, persecution and disorder, war and captivity.

3:3 Thus the mean men were lifted up against the honourable; those of no repute against those of good repute; the foolish against the wise; the young against the elder.

3:4 Through this justice and peace are afar off, because each of you leaveth off the fear of God and is dimsighted in his faith, nor walketh in the laws of his commandments, nor behaveth as becometh a citizen of Christ; but each walketh according to his own evil lusts, having taken up unjust and unholy envy, by which also death entered into the world.

CHAPTER 4

4:1 For it is thus written: And it came to pass after certain days, that Cain brought of the fruits of the ground a sacrifice to God, and Abel brought also of the firstlings of the sheep and of their fat.

4:2 And God had respect unto Abel and unto his gifts; but unto Cain and his gifts he had no regard.

4:3 And Cain was grieved greatly, and his countenance fell.

4:4 And God said unto Cain, Why art thou very sorrowful, and why hath thy countenance fallen? If thou hast rightly offered, but hast not rightly divided, hast thou not sinned?

4:5 Hold thy peace; thy gift returneth unto thee, and thou shalt be master over it.

4:6 And Cain said unto Abel, Let us pass over into the field. And it came to pass while they were in the field, Cain rose up against Abel his brother and slew him.

4:7 Ye see, brethren, jealousy and envy wrought the slaughter of a brother.

4:8 Through envy our father Jacob fled from the face of his brother Esau.

4:9 Envy caused Joseph to be persecuted unto death, and to enter into bondage.

4:10 Envy compelled Moses to flee from the face of Pharaoh, king of Egypt, because he heard his countryman say, Who made thee a judge or a decider over us? Wilt thou kill me, as thou didst the Egyptian yesterday?

4:11 Through envy Aaron and Miriam pitched their tents without the camp.
4:12 Envy brought down Dathan and Abiram alive to the grave, because they contended against Moses, the servant of God.

4:13 Through envy David suffered jealousy not only of foreigners, but was persecuted also by Saul, king of Israel.

CHAPTER 5

5:1 But let us pass from ancient examples, and come unto those who have in the times nearest to us, wrestled for the faith.

5:2 Let us take the noble examples of our own generation. Through jealousy and envy the greatest and most just pillars of the Church were persecuted, and came even unto death.

5:3 Let us place before our eyes the good Apostles.

5:4 Peter, through unjust envy, endured not one or two but many labours, and at last, having delivered his testimony, departed unto the place of glory due to him.

5:5 Through envy Paul, too, showed by example the prize that is given to patience:

5:6 seven times was he cast into chains; he was banished; he was stoned; having become a herald, both in the East and in the West, he obtained the noble renown due to his faith;

5:7 and having preached righteousness to the whole world, and having come to the extremity of the West, and having borne witness before rulers, he departed at length out of the world, and went to the holy place, having become the greatest example of patience.

CHAPTER 6

6:1 To these men, who walked in holiness, there was gathered a great multitude of the elect, who, having suffered, through envy, many insults and tortures, became a most excellent example among us.

6:2 Through envy women were persecuted, even the Danaides and Dircae, who, after enduring dreadful and unholy insults, attained to the sure course of the faith; and they who were weak in body received a noble reward.

6:3 Envy hath estranged the minds of wives from their husbands, and changed the saying of our father Adam: This is now bone of my bone, and flesh of my flesh.

6:4 Envy and strife have overthrown mighty cities and rooted out great nations.

CHAPTER 7

7:1 These things we enjoin you, beloved, not only by way of admonition to you, but as putting ourselves also in mind. For we are in the same arena, and the same contest is imposed upon us.

7:2 Wherefore, let us leave empty and vain thoughts, and come unto the glorious and venerable rule of our holy calling.

7:3 Let us consider what is good and pleasing and acceptable before him who made us.

7:4 Let us look steadfastly to the blood of Christ, and see how precious in the sight of God is his blood, which having been poured out for our salvation, brought to the whole world the grace of repentance.

7:5 Let us go back to all generations, and learn that in every generation God hath granted a place for repentance to such as wished to return unto him.

7:6 Noah preached repentance, and as many as hearkened unto him were saved.

7:7 Jonah prophesied destruction to the Ninevites, and they, repenting of their sins, appeased God through prayer, and, though alien from God, obtained salvation.

CHAPTER 8

8:1 The ministers of the grace of God spake by the Holy Spirit concerning repentance;

8:2 and the Lord of all himself spake concerning repentance with an oath. As I live, saith the Lord, I desire not the death of a sinner, as I desire his repentance; adding thereto an excellent saying:

8:3 Repent, O house of Israel, from your iniquity: Say unto the sons of my people, Though your sins reach from earth to heaven, and though they be redder than scarlet, and blacker than sackcloth, and ye turn unto me with your whole heart and say, My father, I will hearken unto you as to an holy people.

8:4 And in another place he speaketh in this wise: Wash, and be ye clean; take away the wickedness from your souls from before my eyes; cease from your evil deeds, learn to do well; seek judgment; deliver him that is oppressed; give judgment for the orphan, and justify the widow; and come and let us reason together, saith he; and though your sins be as purple, I will make them white as snow; and though they be as scarlet, I will make them white as wool. And if ye be willing and hearken unto me, ye shall eat the good things of the earth; but if ye be not willing, and hearken not, the sword shall devour you; for the mouth of the Lord hath said this.

8:5 Desiring, therefore, that all his beloved ones should partake of repentance, he hath confirmed it by his almighty will.

CHAPTER 9

9:1 Wherefore, let us submit ourselves to his excellent and glorious will, and, becoming suppliants of his mercy and goodness, let us fall before him and betake ourselves to his mercies, having laid aside the vain toil and the strife and the jealousy that leadeth unto death.

9:2 Let us look steadfastly at those that have ministered with perfectness to his excellent glory.

9:3 Let us take as example Enoch, who, having been found just by reason of obedience, was translated, and his death was not found.

9:4 Noah, having been found faithful, preached, by his ministry, regeneration unto the world, and by him God preserved the animals that entered with one consent into the ark.

CHAPTER 10

10:1 Abraham, who was called the friend, was found faithful, inasmuch as he became obedient to the words of God.

10:2 This man, by obedience, went out from his land and his kinsfolk, and the house of his father, that, by leaving a scanty land and weak kinsfolk and a small house, he might inherit the promises of God.

10:3 For he saith unto him, Go out from thy land and thy kinsfolk, and the house of thy father, unto the land that I shall show thee, and I will make thee a great nation, and bless thee, and magnify thy name, and thou shalt be blessed; and I will bless them that bless thee, and curse them that curse thee, and in thee shall all the tribes of the earth be blessed.

10:4 And again, when he separated from Lot, God said unto him, Lift up thine eyes, and look from the place where thou now art unto the north and unto the south, and unto the east and unto the sea; for all the land which thou seest, to thee will I give it and to thy seed for ever,

10:5 and I will make thy seed as the dust of the earth: if any man can number the dust of the earth, thy seed also shall be numbered.

10:6 And again he saith, God brought forth Abraham, and said unto him: Look up to heaven and number the stars, if thou art able to number them, so shall thy seed be. And Abraham believed God, and it was counted to him for righteousness.

10:7 Through faith and hospitality a son was given unto him in old age, and through obedience he offered him a sacrifice unto God on one of the mountains that he showed him.

CHAPTER 11

11:1 By hospitality and goodness Lot was saved out of Sodom when the whole region round about was judged with fire and brimstone; the Lord making it manifest that he leaveth not them that hope upon him, but appointeth to punishment and torment them that turn in another way.

11:2 For his wife, who went out together with him, being of another mind, and not being in concord with him, was on that account placed as a sign, so that she became a pillar of salt even to this day; that it might be known to all that the double-minded, and they who doubt concerning the power of God, are for a judgment and a sign to all generations.

CHAPTER 12

12:1 Through faith and hospitality Rahab the harlot was saved;

12:2 for when spies were sent unto Jericho by Jesus, the son of Nun, the king of the land knew that they had come to spy out his country, and sent out men to apprehend them that they might be taken and put to death.

12:3 But the hospitable Rahab having received them, hid them in an upper story under the stalks of flax.

12:4 When, therefore, the men from the king came upon her, and said, There came unto thee men who are spies of this our land; bring them out, for the king so commandeth it; she answered, The two men whom ye are seeking entered in unto me, but they departed quickly and are on their way; but she showed not the men unto them.

12:5 And she said unto the men, Of a surety I know that the Lord your God has given over this city unto you; for the fear and trembling of you hath fallen upon them that inhabit it; when, therefore, it hath happened unto you to take it, save me and the house of my father.

12:6 And they say unto her, So shall it be, even as thou hast spoken unto us. When, therefore, thou hast perceived that we are coming, thou shalt gather together all thy household under thy roof, and they shall be saved; but as many as shall be found without the house shall be destroyed.

12:7 And they proceeded further to give her a sign, that she should hang from her house scarlet, making it manifest beforehand that through the blood of the Lord there shall be redemption to all who believe and hope upon God.

12:8 Behold, beloved, how there was not only faith, but prophecy in the woman.

CHAPTER 13

13:1 Let us therefore, brethren, be humble, laying aside all boasting and pride, and folly and wrath, and let us do that which is written; for the Holy Spirit saith, Let not the wise boast in his wisdom, nor the strong in his strength, nor the rich in his riches; but let him that boasteth make his boast in the Lord, even by seeking him and doing judgment and justice. Let us especially remember the words of our Lord Jesus Christ which he spake when teaching gentleness and long-suffering, for he spake thus:

13:2 Show mercy, that ye may obtain mercy; forgive, that it may be forgiven unto you; as ye do, so shall it be done unto you; as ye give, so shall it be given unto you; as ye judge, so shall ye be judged; as ye are kindly affectioned, so shall kindness be showed unto you; with whatsover measure ye measure, with the same shall it be measured unto you.

13:3 With this commandment and with these exhortations let us strengthen ourselves, that we may walk obedient to his holy words with all humility. For the Holy Scripture saith,

13:4 Upon whom shall I have respect but upon him that is meek and quiet, and that trembleth at my words?

CHAPTER 14

14:1 It is therefore meet and right, men and brethren, that we should be obedient unto God rather than follow them that in pride and disorderliness are leaders of detestable sedition.

14:2 For we shall incur no slight harm, but rather a great danger, if we rashly give ourselves up to the wills of men who launch out into strife and sedition so as to estrange us from that which is good.

14:3 Let us, therefore, show kindness towards them according to the mercy and sweetness of him that made us.

14:4 For it is written, The men of kindness shall inherit the land. The innocent shall be left upon it; but they that be lawless shall be destroyed out of it.

14:5 And again he saith, I saw the unrighteous man exalted on high and lifted up like the cedars of Lebanon. And I passed by, and behold he was not; I sought his place and found it not. Keep innocence, and regard righteousness; for there is a remnant that remaineth to the man of peace.

CHAPTER 15

15:1 Let us therefore cleave unto them who live in peace and godliness, not unto them who hypocritically profess to desire peace.

15:2 For he saith in a certain place, This people honoureth me with their lips, but their heart is far from me.

15:3 And again, With their mouth did they bless, but with their heart did they curse.

15:4 And again he saith, They loved him with their mouth, and with their tongue they lied against him. For their heart was not right with him, nor were they faithful in his covenant.

15:5 Let the crafty lips be put to silence, and may the Lord destroy all the deceitful lips, even the haughty tongue, they who said, Let us magnify our tongue, our lips are our own; who is master over us?

15:6 On account of the misery of the poor, and on account of the groaning of the needy, I will now arise, saith the Lord; I will set him in safety, I will deal confidently with him.

CHAPTER 16

16:1 For Christ belongeth unto them that are humble, not unto them that exalt themselves over his flock.

16:2 Our Lord Jesus Christ, who is the sceptre of the majesty of God, came not in the arrogance of boasting and pride, though he was able to do so; but in humility, even as the Holy Spirit spake concerning him.

16:3 For he saith, Lord, who hath believed our report, and to whom hath the arm of the Lord been revealed? Like a child have we delivered our message before him; he is as a root in a thirsty land. There is no form nor glory in him, and we beheld him, and he had neither form nor comeliness, but his form was despised, lacking comeliness, beyond the form of the sons of men. He was a man stricken and in toil, knowing how to bear infirmity, for his face was turned away; it was dishonoured and held in no reputation.
16:4 He beareth our sins and suffereth pain on our account, and we esteemed him as one in toil, stricken and afflicted.

16:5 He was wounded for our sins, and for our transgressions did he suffer infirmity; the chastisement of our peace was upon him, and by his stripes we were healed.

16:6 All we, like sheep, have gone astray, every one hath erred in his own way,

16:7 and the Lord hath given him up for our sins; and he, through affliction, openeth not his mouth. He was led like a sheep to the slaughter, and as a lamb before its shearers is dumb, so openeth he not his mouth.

16:8 In his humiliation his judgment was taken away, and who shall declare his generation, for his life is taken from the earth;

16:9 for the iniquity of my people he hath come unto death.

16:10 And I will give the wicked in requital for his burial, and the rich for his death: for he did no sin, neither was guile found in his mouth: and the Lord willeth to purify him from stripes.

16:11 If ye make an offering for sin your soul shall prolong its days.

16:12 And the Lord willeth to take away from the travail of his soul, to show him light and to form him by knowledge, to justify the righteous man who serveth many well; and their sins he shall bear himself.

16:13 Wherefore he shall receive the inheritance of many, and shall divide the spoils of the strong, because his soul was delivered up unto death, and he was numbered among the transgressors,

16:14 and he bore the sins of many, and was given up for their sins.

16:15 And again he saith, I am a worm and no man -- a reproach of men and despised of the people;

16:16 all they who saw me mocked me, they spake with their lips, they shook the head; he hoped in God, let him deliver him, let him save him, because he desireth him.

16:17 See, beloved, what is the example that hath been given unto us; for if the Lord so humbled himself, what shall we do who have through his mercy come under the yoke of his grace?

CHAPTER 17

17:1 Let us be imitators of them also who went about in goat-skins and sheep-skins, preaching the coming of Christ; we mean Elias and Elisaeus and Ezekiel the prophets, and beside them those who have obtained a good report.

17:2 Abraham obtained an exceeding good report, and was called the friend of God, and saith, looking steadfastly to the glory of God in humility, I am but earth and ashes.

17:3 And, moreover, concerning Job, it is thus written: Job was a just man and blameless, truthful, one that feared God, and abstained from all evil.

17:4 But he himself, accusing himself, saith, No one is pure from pollution, though his life be but for one day.

17:5 Moses was called faithful in all his house, and by his ministry God judged his people Israel by stripes and punishment. But he, though he was greatly glorified, spake not haughtily, but said, when the oracle was given him out of the bush, Who am I that thou sendest me? I am weak of voice and slow of tongue.

17:6 And again he saith, I am but as the smoke from a pot.

CHAPTER 18

18:1 But what shall we say of David, who obtained a good report; unto whom God said, I have found a man after my own heart, David, the son of Jesse, with my everlasting mercy have I anointed him.

18:2 But he himself saith unto God, Have mercy upon me, O God, according to thy great mercy, according to the multitude of thy compassion do away with mine iniquity;

18:3 wash me throughly from my iniquity, and cleanse me from my sin. For I know my iniquity, and my sin is ever before me.

18:4 Against thee only have I sinned, and done this evil in thy sight, that thou mightest be justified in thy words, and overcome when thou art judged.

18:5 Behold, I was shapen in wickedness, and in sin did my mother conceive me.
18:6 Behold, thou hast loved truth; thou hast shown me the secret and hidden things of thy wisdom.

18:7 Thou shalt sprinkle me with hyssop, and I shall be clean. Thou shalt wash me, and I shall be whiter than snow.

18:8 Thou shalt make me to hear of joy and gladness; the bones that have been humiliated shall rejoice.

18:9 Turn away thy face from my sins, and blot out all my misdeeds.

18:10 Create in me a new heart, O Lord, and renew a right spirit within me.

18:11 Cast me not away from thy presence, and take not thy Holy Spirit from me.

18:12 O give me again the joy of thy salvation, and establish me with thy guiding Spirit.

18:13 I will teach sinners thy ways; the ungodly shall be converted unto thee.

18:14 Deliver me from blood-guiltiness, O God, thou God of my salvation;

18:15 my tongue shall rejoice in thy righteousness. O Lord, thou shalt open my mouth, and my lips shall show forth thy praise.

18:16 For if thou hadst desired sacrifice, I would have given it; in whole burnt offerings thou wilt not delight.

18:17 The sacrifice of God is a broken spirit; a broken and a contrite heart God will not despise.

CHAPTER 19

19:1 The humility of men so many in number and so great, and who have obtained so good a report, and their subjection through obedience, hath made not only us but the generations before us better, namely, those who in fear and truth have received his oracles.

19:2 Since, therefore, we have become the partakers in many great and glorious actions, let us finally return to that goal of peace that was given us from the beginning; let us look steadfastly to the Father and Creator of the whole world, and let us cleave to the glorious and excellent gifts and benefits of his peace.

19:3 Let us behold him in spirit, and look with the eyes of the soul to his long-suffering will. Let us consider how gentle he is toward all his creation.

CHAPTER 20

20:1 The heavens, being put in motion by his appointment, are subject to him in peace;

20:2 night and day accomplish the course ordered by him, in nothing hindering one another.

20:3 The sun and the moon and the dances of the stars according to his appointment, in harmony and without any violation of order, roll on the courses appointed to them.

20:4 The fruitful earth bringeth forth in due season, according to his will, abundant nourishment for men and beasts; nothing doubting, nor changing in anything from the things that are decreed by him.

20:5 The unsearchable things of the abyss, and the secret ordinances of the lower parts of the earth, are held together by the same command.
20:6 The hollow of the vast sea, gathered together by his hand into its reservoirs, transgresseth not the bounds placed around it; but even as he hath appointed to it, so it doeth;

20:7 for he said, Thus far shalt thou come, and thy waves shall be broken within thee.

20:8 The ocean, impassable to men, and the worlds that are beyond it, are governed by the same commandments of their Master.

20:9 The seasons of spring and summer, autumn and winter, in peace succeed one another.

20:10 The fixed stations of the winds, each in their due time, perform their services without offence. The ever-flowing fountains, made for enjoyment and health, offer their breasts without fail to sustain the lives of men. Even the smallest of animals come together in peace and harmony.

20:11 All these things the great Maker and Master of all things hath appointed to be in peace and harmony, doing good unto all things, but more especially unto us, who have fled for refuge to his mercies, through our Lord Jesus Christ,

20:12 to whom be glory and majesty for ever and ever. Amen.

CHAPTER 21

21:1 Beware, beloved, lest his many blessings come to be a condemnation to all of us, unless, walking worthily of him, we do what is honourable and well pleasing before him with oneness of mind.

21:2 For he saith in a certain place, The Spirit of the Lord is a candle, searching out the secret places of the heart.

21:3 Let us see how near he is at hand, and how none of our thoughts and reasonings do escape him.

21:4 It is right, therefore, that we should not desert from his will.

21:5 Let us offend against men who are foolish, and senseless, and puffed up in the pride of their own speech, rather than against God.

21:6 Let us have respect to our Lord Jesus Christ, whose blood was given for us. Let us reverence them that are over us. Let us honour our elders. Let us instruct the young in the discipline of the fear of God. Let us direct our wives to that which is good;

21:7 let them show forth the lovely habit of chastity, and exhibit the pure disposition of meekness. Let them make manifest by their conversation the government of their tongues; let them show love, not according to partiality, but equally to all that fear the Lord in holiness.

21:8 Let your children be partakers of the discipline of Christ; let them learn how much humility availeth before God; what power a pure love hath with God; how his fear is honourable and great, preserving all who, with a pure mind, walk in holiness before him.

21:9 For he is a searcher out of thoughts and counsels, his breath is in us, and when he willeth he will take it away.

CHAPTER 22

22:1 All these things doth the faith which is in Christ assure. For he himself, through the Holy Spirit, thus calleth unto us: Come, ye children, hearken unto me, I will teach you the fear of the Lord.

22:2 What man is he that wisheth for life and would fain see good days?

22:3 Keep thy tongue from evil, and thy lips that they speak no guile.

22:4 Turn away from evil and do good;

22:5 seek peace and pursue it.

22:6 The eyes of the Lord are over the just, and his ears are open to their prayer. But the face of the Lord is against them that do evil, to destroy their memorial out of the land.

22:7 The righteous cried, and the Lord heard him, and delivered him out of all his troubles.

22:8 Many are the afflictions of the sinner, but they that hope in the Lord, mercy shall compass them round about.

CHAPTER 23

23:1 The Father whose mercies are over all things, who loveth to do good, hath bowels of compassion for them that fear him, and with gentleness and kindness bestoweth his favour upon them that come unto him with a pure mind.

23:2 Wherefore let us not be double-minded, nor let our hearts form vain imaginations concerning his excellent and glorious gifts.

23:3 Let not that scripture be applicable unto us which saith, Wretched are the double-minded, even they that doubt in their heart and say, We have heard these things in the time of our fathers; and lo, we have grown old, and none of them hath happened unto us.

23:4 O foolish ones! compare yourselves to a tree. Take, for example, the vine: first it sheddeth its leaves, then cometh the bud, then the leaf, then the flower, after that the unripe grape, then the ripe grape. See how in a little time the fruit of the tree attaineth to maturity.
23:5 Of a truth, quickly and suddenly shall his will be fulfilled; the scripture also bearing witness that he shall come quickly, and shall not tarry; and the Lord shall come suddenly into his temple, even the holy one, whom ye expect.

CHAPTER 24

24:1 Let us consider, beloved, how the Master showeth to us continually the resurrection that is about to be, of which he hath made our Lord Jesus Christ the first fruit, having raised him from the dead.

24:2 Let us look, beloved, at the resurrection that is ever taking place.

24:3 Day and night show to us the resurrection; the night is lulled to rest, the day ariseth; the day departeth, the night cometh on.

24:4 Let us consider the fruits, in what way a grain of corn is sown.

24:5 The sower goeth forth and casteth it into the ground, and when the seeds are cast into the ground, they that fell into the ground dry and naked are dissolved; then after their dissolution, the mighty power of the providence of the Lord raiseth them up, and from one seed many grow up and bring forth fruits.

CHAPTER 25

25:1 Let us consider the wonderful sign that happeneth in the region of the east, even about Arabia.

25:2 There is a bird which is called the phoenix. This, being the only one of its kind, liveth for five hundred years. And when the time of its death draweth near, it maketh for itself a nest of frankincense and myrrh and the other perfumes, into which, when its time is fulfilled, it entereth, and then dieth.

25:3 But as its flesh rotteth, a certain worm is produced, which being nourished by the moisture of the dead animal, putteth forth feathers. Then, when it hath become strong, it taketh the nest wherein are the bones of its ancestor, and bearing them, it flieth from the region of Arabia to that of Egypt, to the city which is called Heliopolis;

25:4 there, in day-time, in the sight of all, it flieth up, and placeth them upon the altar of the sun, and having done so, returneth back.

25:5 The priests, therefore, look into the registers of the times, and find that it has come at the completion of the five-hundredth year.

CHAPTER 26

26:1 Shall we then think it great and wonderful, if the Maker of all things shall make a resurrection of those who, in the confidence of a good faith, have piously seized him, when even by means of a bird he showeth the greatness of his promises?

26:2 For he saith in a certain place, And thou shalt raise me up, and I will give thanks unto thee; and again: I slumbered and slept; I arose up because thou art with me.

26:3 And again Job saith, Thou shalt raise up this my flesh, which hath suffered all these things.

CHAPTER 27

27:1 In this hope, therefore, let our souls be bound unto him who is faithful in his promises and just in his judgments.

27:2 He who hath commanded men not to lie, much more shall he not lie; for nothing is impossible with God, except to lie.

27:3 Let our faith, therefore, in him be kindled afresh within us, and let us consider that all things are near unto him.

27:4 By the word of his majesty did he constitute all things, and by a word he is able to destroy them.

27:5 Who shall say unto him, What hast thou done? or who shall resist the might of his strength? He will do all things when he willeth and as he willeth, and none of the things decreed by him shall pass away.

27:6 All things are before him, and nothing hath escaped his counsel:

27:7 seeing that the heavens declare the glory of God, and the firmament showeth the work of his hands: day unto day uttereth speech, and night unto night proclaimeth knowledge; and there is no speech nor language where their voices are not heard.

CHAPTER 28

28:1 Since, therefore, all things are seen and heard of him, let us fear him and abandon the filthy desires for evil deeds, that we may be sheltered by his mercy from the judgments to come.

28:2 For whither can any of us fly from his mighty hand, and what world shall receive any of them that desert from him?

28:3 For the scripture saith in a certain place, Whither shall I go, and where shall I conceal myself from thy face? If I ascend into heaven, thou art there; if I depart into the uttermost parts of the earth, there is thy right hand; if I shall make my bed in the abyss, there is thy Spirit.

28:4 Whither then shall we depart, and where shall we fly from him that embraceth all things?

CHAPTER 29

29:1 Let us, therefore, approach him with holiness of spirit, lifting unto him pure and undefiled hands; loving the kind and compassionate Father who hath made us a part of his elect.

29:2 For it is thus written, When The Most High divided the nations, when he dispersed the sons of Adam, he settled the boundaries of the nations according to the number of the angels of God. The portion of the Lord was his people Jacob.

29:3 Israel was the measurement of his inheritance. And in another place he saith, Behold the Lord taketh to himself a nation from the midst of the nations, even as a man taketh the firstfruits of his threshingfloor; and there shall go forth from that nation the Holy of Holies.

CHAPTER 30

30:1 Since, therefore, we are a portion of the Holy One, let us do all such things as pertain unto holiness, avoiding evil-speaking, foul and impure embraces, drunkenness, disorderliness, abominable desires, detestable adultery, execrable pride;

30:2 for God, he saith, resisteth the proud, but giveth grace unto the humble.

30:3 Let us cleave, therefore, to them to whom grace has been given from God. Let us clothe ourselves with concord, being humble, temperate, keeping ourselves far from all whispering and evil speaking, justified by our deeds, and not by our words.

30:4 For he saith, He who saith many things shall, in return, hear many things. Doth he that is eloquent think himself to be just?

30:5 -- doth he that is born of woman and liveth but for a short time think himself to be blessed? Be not abundant in speech.
30:6 Let our praise be in God, and not for ourselves, for God hateth the self-praisers.

30:7 Let the testimony of right actions be given us from others, even as it was given to our fathers who were just.

30:8 Audacity, self-will, and boldness belong to them who are accursed of God; but moderation, humility, and meekness, to them that are blessed of God.

CHAPTER 31

31:1 Let us cleave, therefore, to his blessing, and let us see what are the ways of blessing. Let us consult the records of the things that happened from the beginning.

31:2 On what account was our father Abraham blessed? Was it not that he wrought righteousness and truth through faith?

31:3 Isaac, with confidence, knowing the future, willingly became a sacrifice.

31:4 Jacob, with humility, flying from his brother, went out from his own land and journeyed unto Laban and served as a slave, and there were given unto him the twelve tribes of Israel.

CHAPTER 32

32:1 If anyone will consider these things with sincerity and one by one, he will recognize the magnificence of the gifts that were given by him.

32:2 For from Jacob came the priests and all the Levites that serve the altar of God. From him came our Lord Jesus Christ according to the flesh; from him came the kings and rulers and governors of the tribe of Judah; and the remainder of his tribes are of no small glory, since God hath promised, Thy seed shall be as the stars of heaven.

32:3 All these, therefore, have been glorified and magnified, not through themselves or through their works, or through the righteousness that they have done, but through his will.

32:4 And we who through his will have been called in Christ Jesus are justified, not by ourselves, or through our wisdom or understanding or godliness, or the works that we have done in holiness of heart, but by faith, by which all men from the beginning have been justified by Almighty God, to whom be glory world without end. Amen.

CHAPTER 33

33:1 What, then, shall we do, brethren? Shall we cease from well-doing, and abandon charity? May the Master never allow that this should happen to us! but let us rather with diligence and zeal hasten to fulfil every good work.

33:2 For the Maker and Lord of all things rejoiceth in his works.

33:3 By his supreme power he founded the heavens, and by his incomprehensible understanding he ordered them. The earth he separated from the water that surrounded it, and fixed it on the firm foundation of his own will. The animals which inhabit therein he commanded to be by his ordinance. Having made beforehand the sea and the animals that are therein, he shut them in by his own power.

33:4 Man, the most excellent of all animals, infinite in faculty, he moulded with his holy and faultless hands, in the impress of his likeness.

33:5 For thus saith God: Let us make man in our own image, and after our own likeness. And God made man. Male and female made he them.

33:6 When, therefore, he had finished all things, he praised and blessed them, and said, Be fruitful, and multiply.

33:7 Let us see, therefore, how all the just have been adorned with good works. Yea, the Lord himself rejoiced when he had adorned himself with his works.

33:8 Having, therefore, this example, let us come in without shrinking to his will; let us work with all our strength the work of righteousness.

CHAPTER 34

34:1 The good workman receiveth boldly the bread of his labour, but the slothful and remiss looketh not his employer in the face.

34:2 It is therefore right that we should be zealous in well-doing, for from Him are all things;

34:3 for he telleth us beforehand, Behold the Lord cometh, and his reward is before his face, to give to every one according to his work.

34:4 He exhorteth us, therefore, with this reward in view, to strive with our whole heart not to be slothful or remiss towards every good work.

34:5 Let our glorying and our confidence be in him; let us submit ourselves to his will; let us consider the whole multitude of his angels, how they stand by and serve his will.

34:6 For the scripture saith, Ten thousand times ten thousand stood beside him, and thousands of thousands served him; and they cried, Holy, holy, holy Lord of Sabaoth! all creation is full of his glory.

34:7 And let us, being gathered together in harmony and a good conscience, cry earnestly, as it were with one mouth, unto him, that we may become partakers of his great and glorious promises;

34:8 for he saith, Eye hath not seen, and ear hath not heard, neither hath there entered into the heart of man, what things he hath prepared for them that wait for him.

CHAPTER 35

35:1 Behold, beloved, how blessed and wonderful are the gifts of God

35:2 -- life in immortality, cheerfulness in righteousness, truth in liberty, faith in confidence, temperance in sanctification; and all these things have already come within our cognizance.

35:3 What therefore are the things that are prepared for them that abide in patience? The Maker and Father of the worlds, the all-holy one, he knoweth how many and how beautiful they are.

35:4 Let us, therefore, strive to be found in the number of them that await him, that we may partake of the promised gifts.

35:5 And how will this be, beloved? If our mind be established by faith toward God; if we seek out what is pleasant and acceptable in his sight; if we perform such things as harmonize with his blameless will, and follow in the way of truth, casting from us all unrighteousness and lawlessness, covetousness, strife, malice and fraud, whispering and evil speaking, hatred of God, pride and insolence, vainglory and churlishness.

35:6 For they who do these things are hateful unto God, and not only they who do them, but also they who have pleasure in them that do them.

35:7 For the scripture saith: But unto the sinner God hath said, Why dost thou speak of my ordinances, and takest my covenant in thy mouth:

35:8 but thou hast hated instruction and hast cast my words behind thee. When thou sawest a thief thou wentest with him, and hast cast in thy portion with the adulterers; thy mouth hath abounded with evil, and thy tongue hath contrived deceit. Thou satest and spakest against thy brother, and hast slandered the son of thy mother.

35:9 This hast thou done, and I kept silence. Thou thoughtest, O wicked one, that I was like unto thee;

35:10 but I will convict thee, and set thyself before thee.

35:11 Consider this, ye who forget God, lest he seize you as a lion, and there be none to save you.

35:12 The sacrifice of praise shall honour me; and there is the way by which I will show him the salvation of God.

CHAPTER 36

36:1 This is the way, beloved, in which we found our salvation; even Jesus Christ, the high priest of our oblations, the champion and defender of our weakness.

36:2 Through him we look steadfastly to the heights of the heavens; through him we behold, as in a glass, the immaculate and lofty countenance of God the Father; through him the eyes of our heart were opened; through him our foolish and darkened understanding springeth up again to his marvellous light; through him the Lord hath willed us to taste of immortal knowledge; who, being the brightness of his glory, is so far better than the angels, as he hath, by inheritance, obtained a more excellent name than they.

36:3 For it is thus written: Who maketh his angels spirits, his ministers a flame of fire.

36:4 But of his Son the Lord hath thus said: Thou art my Son, to-day have I begotten thee. Ask of me, and I will give thee the heathen for thine inheritance, and the uttermost parts of the world for thy possession.

36:5 And, again, he saith unto him: Sit on my right hand until I make thy enemies thy footstool.

36:6 Who then are the enemies? Even the wicked, and they who resist the will of God.

CHAPTER 37

37:1 Let us, therefore, men and brethren, carry on our warfare with all earnestness in his faultless ordinances.

37:2 Let us consider those who fight under our rulers, how orderly and obediently and submissively they perform what is commanded them.

37:3 All are not prefects, or commanders of thousands, or commanders of hundreds, or commanders of fifties, or such-like; but each in his own rank performeth what has been ordered by the king or the commanders.

37:4 The great cannot exist without the small, nor the small without the great. There is a certain mixture in all things, and from thence ariseth their use.

37:5 Let us take, for example, our body; the head is nothing without the feet, nor the feet without the head. The smallest members of the body are necessary and useful to the whole body, and all unite and work with harmonious obedience for the preservation of the whole body.

CHAPTER 38

38:1 Let, therefore, our whole body be saved in Christ Jesus, and let each be subject to his neighbour, according to the gift which he hath received.

38:2 Let not the strong man despise the weak, and let the weak pay regard to the strong. Let him that is rich minister to him that is poor. Let him that is poor praise God that he hath given unto him one by whom his want may be supplied. Let the wise show his wisdom, not in words, but in good deeds; let him that is humble

not bear witness to himself, but leave another to bear witness to him. Let him that is pure in the flesh boast not of it, knowing that it is another that giveth him the power of continence.

38:3 Let us consider, brethren, of what matter we are made, of what sort and who we are that have come into the world, as it were out of the tomb and darkness. He that made and fashioned us hath brought us into this world, having prepared beforehand his benefactions, even before we were born.

38:4 Having, therefore, all these things from him, we ought in all respects to give thanks unto him, to whom be glory world without end. Amen.

CHAPTER 39

39:1 The senseless and unwise, the foolish and unruly, make a mock of us, wishing to exalt themselves in their own imagination.

39:2 For what can a mortal do? or what strength hath he that is born of earth?

39:3 For it is written, There was no form before my eyes, only I heard a breath and a voice.

39:4 For what? shall a mortal be pure before the Lord? or is a man blameless from his works? seeing that he putteth no trust in his servants, and beholdeth somewhat of iniquity in his angels;

39:5 yea, the heaven is not pure in his sight. Away, ye who dwell in houses of clay, of whom are we also even of the same clay. He hath smitten them even as it were a moth, and in a single day they are no more. Because they could not help themselves they perished:

39:6 he blew among them, and they died, because they had no wisdom.

39:7 Call, now, and see if there is anyone that will obey thee, if thou shalt behold any of the holy angels. For anger destroyeth the fool, and envy putteth him to death that is gone out of the way.

39:8 I have beheld the foolish casting forth roots, but straightway his habitation was eaten up.

39:9 Let his sons be far from safety, let them be mocked at the gates of their inferiors, and there shall be none to deliver them. For that which had been prepared for them the just shall eat, and they shall not be delivered out of their troubles.

CHAPTER 40

40:1 Since, therefore, these things have been made manifest before unto us, and since we have looked into the depths of the divine knowledge, we ought to do everything in order, whatsoever the Lord hath commanded us to do at the appointed seasons, and to perform the offerings and liturgies.

40:2 These he hath not commanded to be done at random or in disorder, but at fixed times and seasons.

40:3 But when and by whom he wisheth them to be fulfilled he himself hath decided by his supreme will; that all things, being done piously, according to his good pleasure, might be acceptable to his will.

40:4 They, therefore, who at the appointed seasons make their offerings are acceptable and blessed; for while following the laws of the Master they do not completely sin.

40:5 For to the High Priest were assigned special services, and to the priests a special place hath been appointed; and on the Levites special duties are imposed. But he that is a layman is bound by the ordinances of laymen.

CHAPTER 41

41:1 Let each of you, brethren, in his own order, give thanks unto God, continuing in a good conscience, not transgressing the fixed rule of his ministry, with all gravity.

41:2 Not in every place, brethren, are sacrifices offered continually, either in answer to prayer, or concerning sin and neglect, but in Jerusalem only; and even there the offering is not made in every place, but before the temple in the court of the altar, after that which is offered has been diligently examined by the high priest and the appointed ministers.

41:3 They, therefore, who do anything contrary to that which is according to his will have for their punishment death.

41:4 Ye see, brethren, by as much as we have been thought worthy of greater knowledge, by so much the more are we exposed to danger.

CHAPTER 42

42:1 The Apostles received for us the gospel from our Lord Jesus Christ; our Lord Jesus Christ received it from God.

42:2 Christ, therefore, was sent out from God, and the Apostles from Christ; and both these things were done in good order, according to the will of God.

42:3 They, therefore, having received the promises, having been fully persuaded by the resurrection of our Lord Jesus Christ, and having been confirmed by the word of God, with the full persuasion of the Holy Spirit, went forth preaching the good tidings that the kingdom of God was at hand.

42:4 Preaching, therefore, through the countries and cities, they appointed their firstfruits to be bishops and deacons over such as should believe, after they had proved them in the Spirit.

42:5 And this they did in no new way, for in truth it had in long past time been written concerning bishops and deacons; for the scripture, in a certain place, saith in this wise: I will establish their bishops in righteousness, and their deacons in faith.

CHAPTER 43

43:1 And wherein is it wonderful, if they who, in Christ, were entrusted by God with this work appointed the aforesaid officers? since even the blessed Moses, the faithful servant in all his house, signified in the sacred books all the things that were commanded unto him, whom also the prophets have followed, bearing witness together to the laws which were appointed by him.

43:2 For he, when a strife arose concerning the priesthood, and when the tribes contended which of them should be adorned with that glorious name, commanded the twelve chiefs of the tribes to bring to him rods, each inscribed with the name of a tribe; and when he had taken them, he bound them together, and sealed them with the seals of the heads of the tribes, and laid them up on the table of God, in the tabernacle of the testimony.

43:3 And when he had closed the tabernacle, he sealed the keys, and likewise the rods,

43:4 and said unto them, Men and brethren, of whatever tribe the rod shall bud, this hath God chosen to be his priest, and to serve him.

43:5 And when morning was come, he called together all Israel, even six hundred thousand men, and showed unto the heads of the tribes the seals, and opened the tabernacle of the testimony and brought forth the rods, and the rod of Aaron was found not only to have budded, but also bearing fruit.

43:6 What think ye, beloved? did not Moses know beforehand that this was about to happen? Most assuredly did he know it. But, that there might be no disorder in Israel, he did thus that the name of the true and only God might be glorified, to whom be glory world without end. Amen.

CHAPTER 44

44:1 Our Apostles, too, by the instruction of our Lord Jesus Christ, knew that strife would arise concerning the dignity of a bishop;

44:2 and on this account, having received perfect foreknowledge, they appointed the above-mentioned as bishops and deacons: and then gave a rule of succession, in order that, when they had fallen asleep, other men, who had been approved, might succeed to their ministry.

44:3 Those who were thus appointed by them, or afterwards by other men of good repute, with the consent of the whole Church, who have blamelessly ministered to the flock of Christ with humility, quietly, and without illiberality, and who for a long time have obtained a good report from all, these, we think, have been unjustly deposed from the ministry.

44:4 For it will be no small sin in us if we depose from the office of bishop those who blamelessly and piously have made the offerings.
44:5 Happy are the presbyters who finished their course before, and died in mature age after they had borne fruit; for they do not fear lest anyone should remove them from the place appointed for them.

44:6 For we see that ye have removed some men of honest conversation from the ministry, which had been blamelessly and honourably performed by them.

CHAPTER 45

45:1 Ye are contentious, brethren, and are zealous concerning things that pertain not unto salvation.

45:2 Look diligently into the scriptures, which are the true sayings of the Holy Spirit.

45:3 Ye know how that nothing unjust or corrupt hath been written in them; for ye will not in them find the just expelled by holy men.
45:4 The just were persecuted, but it was by the lawless; they were thrown into prison, but it was by the unholy; they were stoned, but it was by sinners; they were slain, but it was by wicked men, even by those who had taken up an unjust envy against them.

45:5 They, therefore, when they suffered all these things, suffered them with a good report.

45:6 For what shall we say, brethren? was it by those that feared God that Daniel was cast into the den of lions?

45:7 Was it by those who practised the magnificent and glorious worship of the Most High that Ananias, Azarias, and Misael, were shut up in the fiery furnace? Let us not suppose that such was the case. Who, then, were the men who did these things? Abominable men and full of all wickedness were inflamed to such a degree of wrath that they cast into tortures those who, with a holy and a blameless purpose, served God, not knowing that the Most High is a champion and defender of those who with a pure conscience serve his most excellent name, to whom be glory world without end. Amen.

45:8 But they, abiding steadfastly in their confidence, have inherited honour and glory, and have both been exalted and made beautiful by God, in the memory that is made of them world without end. Amen.

CHAPTER 46

46:1 To such examples ought we also to cleave, brethren.

46:2 For it is written, Cleave unto them that are holy, for they that cleave unto them shall be made holy.

46:3 And again, in another place he saith, With the guiltless man thou shalt be guiltless, and with the excellent thou shalt be excellent, and with him that is crooked thou shalt be perverse.

46:4 Let us, therefore, cleave to the guiltless and the just, for they are the elect of God.

46:5 Why are there strivings, and anger, and division, and war among you?

46:6 Have we not one God and one Christ? Is not the Spirit of grace, which was poured out upon us, one? Is not our calling one in Christ?

46:7 Why do we tear apart and rend asunder the members of Christ, and make sedition against our body, and come to such a degree of madness that we forget we are members one of another? Remember the words of our Lord Jesus,

46:8 for he said, Woe unto that man; it were good for him if he had never been born, rather than that he should cause one of my elect to offend. It were better for him that a millstone were tied about him, and that he were cast into the sea, rather than that he should cause one of my little ones to offend.

46:9 This your schism has perverted many; hath cast many into despondency; many into doubt; all of us into grief, and, as yet, your sedition remaineth.

CHAPTER 47

47:1 Take into your hands the epistle of the blessed Apostle Paul.

47:2 What did he first write unto you in the beginning of his gospel?

47:3 Of a truth, he warned you spiritually, in a letter, concerning himself, and concerning Cephas and Apollos, because even then there were factions among you;

47:4 but the faction of that time brought less sin upon you; for ye inclined unto Apostles of good repute, and unto a man approved among them.

47:5 But now consider who they are that have perverted you, and have diminished the glory of your famous brotherly love.

47:6 Disgraceful, brethren, yea, very disgraceful is it, and unworthy of the conduct which is in Christ, that it should be reported that the most firm and ancient Church of the Corinthians hath, on account of one or two persons, made sedition against its presbyters.

47:7 And this report came not only unto us, but also unto the Gentiles, who go not with us. So that ye heap blasphemies on the name of the Lord through your folly, and withal cause danger to yourselves.

CHAPTER 48

48:1 Let us, therefore, remove this thing as quickly as possible, and let us fall before the feet of the Master, and beseech him with tears, that he will have mercy and be reconciled unto us, and restore us again to the grave and pure conversation of brotherly love.

48:2 For this is a gate of righteousness opened unto life, as it is written, Open unto me the gates of righteousness; I will go in unto them, and give thanks unto the Lord:

48:3 this is the gate of the Lord; the righteous shall enter thereby.

48:4 Now, since many gates have been opened, the gate of righteousness is that which is in Christ. Happy are all they that enter therein, and who keep their path straight in holiness and righteousness, quietly performing all their duties.

48:5 If a man be faithful, if he be mighty to expound knowledge, if he be wise in the interpretation of words, if he be pure in his deeds,

48:6 by so much the more ought he to be humble, and by as much as he seemeth to be greater, by so much the more ought he to seek the common advantage of all, and not of himself alone.

CHAPTER 49

49:1 Let him that hath the love which is in Christ keep the commandments of Christ.

49:2 Who can describe sufficiently the bond of the love of God?

49:3 Who is sufficient to speak as he ought of the excellence of its beauty?

49:4 The height to which love leads up is unspeakable.

49:5 Love joineth us unto God; love hideth a multitude of sins; love beareth all things; is long suffering in all things. In love there is nothing illiberal, nothing haughty. Love hath no schism; love maketh not sedition; love doth all things in harmony; in love all the elect of God have been made perfect. Without love nothing is acceptable unto God.

49:6 In love, our Master hath taken us to himself. Through the love that he hath for us, Jesus Christ our Lord hath given his blood for us, by the will of God, his flesh for our flesh, his soul for our soul.

CHAPTER 50

50:1 Ye see, brethren, how great and wonderful a thing love is, and how there is no describing its perfection.

50:2 Who is sufficient to be found in it, except those whom God shall have deemed worthy? Let us pray, therefore, and ask from his mercy that we may live in love, without human partiality, blameless.

50:3 All the generations, from Adam even unto this day, are gone by; but they who have been made perfect in love according to the grace of God inhabit the abode of the pious, and shall be made manifest in the visitation of the kingdom of Christ.

50:4 For it is written, Enter into the secret chambers but a little while, until my anger and wrath be passed, and I will remember the good day, and will raise you up from your sepulchres.

50:5 Blessed are we, beloved, if we do the commandments of God in the harmony of love, so that through love our sins may be forgiven us.

50:6 For it is written, Blessed are they whose iniquities are forgiven, and whose sins are covered. Blessed is the man to whom the Lord imputeth not sin, and in whose mouth there is no guile.

50:7 This blessedness cometh unto them who are elect by God, through Jesus Christ our Lord, to whom be glory world without end. Amen.

CHAPTER 51

51:1 Whatever errors, therefore, we have committed through the assaults of the adversary, let us for these ask pardon; and they who have been leaders of the sedition and division ought to consider the common ground of our hope.

51:2 For they who have their conversation in fear and love wish that they themselves, rather than their neighbours, should fall into suffering; and would rather that themselves should undergo condemnation, than that the harmony which hath been honourably and justly handed down to us should do so.

51:3 For it is better that a man should make confession concerning his sins, than that he should harden his heart, even as the heart of them was hardened who made sedition against Moses the servant of God; whose condemnation was manifest,

51:4 for they went down alive into hell, and death swallowed them up.

51:5 Pharaoh and his army, and all the leaders of Egypt, their chariots and their riders, through no other cause were sunk in the Red Sea, and perished there, than through the hardening of their foolish hearts, after that the signs and wonders happened in Egypt through the hand of Moses the servant of God.

CHAPTER 52

52:1 The Lord of all things, brethren, is in need of naught; neither requireth he anything of anyone, except to confess unto him.

52:2 For the elect David saith, I will confess unto the Lord, and that shall please him more than a young calf that putteth forth horns and hoofs. Let the poor behold and rejoice thereat.

52:3 And again he saith, Offer unto the Lord the sacrifice of praise: pay thy vows unto the Most High. And call upon me in the day of thy affliction, and I will deliver thee, and thou shalt glorify me.

52:4 For the sacrifice unto God is a broken spirit.

CHAPTER 53

53:1 Ye know, beloved, and know well, the sacred scriptures, and have looked into the oracles of God; call, therefore, these things to remembrance.

53:2 For, when Moses had gone up into the mount, and had tarried there forty days and forty nights in fasting and humiliation, the Lord said unto him, Moses, Moses, get thee down quickly hence, for thy people, whom thou broughtest out of the land of Egypt, have wrought iniquity. They have gone astray quickly out of the way that thou commandest them, and have made unto themselves molten images.

53:3 And the Lord said unto him, I have spoken unto thee once and twice, saying, I have beheld this people, and, lo, it is a stiffnecked people. Let me alone, that I may destroy them, and I will wipe out their name from under heaven, and make of thee a nation great and wonderful, and far more numerous than they.

53:4 And Moses said, Be it far from thee, O Lord. Forgive this people their sin, or wipe my name also out of the book of the living.

53:5 Oh, the great love! Oh, the unsurpassable perfection! The servant is bold towards the Lord: he asketh remission for the people, or demands otherwise that he himself should be destroyed together with them.

CHAPTER 54

54:1 Who among you is noble? who is compassionate? who is filled with love?

54:2 Let him speak in this wise: If through me sedition and strife arise, I will depart, I will go away whithersoever ye will, and I will do that which is commanded by the majority, only let the flock of Christ be at peace together with the appointed presbyters.

54:3 He who doeth this shall gain for himself great glory in the Lord, and every place shall receive him; for the earth is the Lord's, and the fulness thereof.

54:4 These things have they done who are citizens of the kingdom of God, which needeth not to be repented of, and these things will they yet do.

CHAPTER 55

55:1 But, to bring forward examples from the Gentiles, also many kings and leaders, when a time of pestilence had arisen, being warned by oracles, gave themselves unto death, that they might deliver their citizens by their blood. Many went out from their own cities, that there might be no more sedition therein.

55:2 We know that many among us gave themselves up unto bonds, that they might deliver others. Many have given themselves up unto slavery, and, having received their own price, have therewith fed others.

55:3 Many women, waxing strong through the grace of God, have performed many manly deeds.

55:4 The blessed Judith, when the city was besieged, asked of the elders that she should be permitted to go forth into the camp of the aliens.

55:5 She therefore delivered herself unto danger, and went out through love of her country and of her people, who were besieged. And the Lord delivered Olophernes into the hands of a woman.

55:6 To no smaller danger did Esther, being perfect in faith, expose herself, that she might deliver the twelve tribes of Israel, who were about to perish. For by fasting and humiliation she besought the Master, who overlooketh all things, the God of Ages, who, seeing the humiliation of her soul, delivered the people for whose sake she put herself in jeopardy.

CHAPTER 56

56:1 Let us, therefore, pray for those who have fallen into any transgression, that moderation and humility may be given unto them, to the end that they should submit themselves, I do not say unto us, but unto the will of God; for so shall they obtain a fruitful and perfect remembrance and compassion before God and his saints.

56:2 Let us accept, brethren, that discipline at which no one needeth to be offended. The admonition which we make one toward another is good and useful exceedingly, for it joineth us unto the will of God.

56:3 For thus speaketh the holy word: The Lord hath chastened me with chastisements, but he hath not given me over unto death.

56:4 For whom the Lord loveth he chasteneth, and scourgeth every son whom he receiveth.

56:5 The righteous shall chastise me in pity and shall rebuke me, but let not the oil of sinners anoint mine head.
56:6 And again he saith: Blessed is the man whom the Lord hath rebuked; refuse not thou the admonition of the Almighty, for he maketh thee to grieve, and again he restoreth thee;

56:7 he hath smitten, and his hands have healed thee;

56:8 six times shall he deliver thee from calamity, and the seventh time evil shall not touch thee.

56:9 In the time of famine he shall deliver thee from death, in war he shall redeem thee from the hand of iron.

56:10 From the scourge of the tongue shall he hide thee, and thou shalt not be afraid when evils approach.

56:11 The unjust and the sinner shalt thou laugh to scorn;

56:12 and of the wild beasts thou shalt not be afraid, for the wild beasts shall be at peace with thee.
56:13 Then shalt thou know that thy house shall be at peace; the habitation of thy tabernacle shall not fail.

56:14 Thou shalt know that thy seed is abundant, thy children like all the herb of the field.

56:15 Thou shalt come to thy tomb like a ripe ear of corn reaped in due season, like the heap of a threshing-floor that is gathered at its proper time.

56:16 Ye see, beloved, that there is a protection for them that are chastened by the Master, for God chasteneth us because he is good, to the end that we should be admonished by his holy discipline.

CHAPTER 57

57:1 Do ye, therefore, that have laid the foundation of the sedition submit yourselves to the presbyters, and be chastised to repentance, bending the knees of your hearts.

57:2 Learn to submit yourselves, laying aside the vain and haughty self-will of your tongues; for it is better that you should be small and approved in the flock of Christ, rather than that, seeming to be superior to others, ye should be cast out of his hope.

57:3 For thus saith the most excellent Wisdom, Behold, I will send upon you the language of my Spirit; I will teach you my word.

57:4 Since I called and ye did not hearken, and prolonged my words, and ye attended not, but made my counsels of none effect, and were not obedient to my reproofs, therefore I will laugh at your destruction, I will exult when desolation cometh upon you; when perturbation hath suddenly come upon you, and ruin is at hand like a whirlwind, when tribulation and oppression cometh upon you.

57:5 For the time shall come when ye shall call upon me, and I shall not hearken unto you; the wicked shall seek me, and shall not find me. They hated wisdom and chose not the fear of the Lord; they were not willing to attend to my counsels, they mocked at my rebukes.

57:6 Wherefore they shall eat the fruits of their own way; they shall be filled with their own unrighteousness.

57:7 For because they wronged the innocent they shall be slain, and judgment shall destroy the unrighteous; but he who hearkeneth unto me shall abide trusting in hope, and shall rest securely from all evil.

CHAPTER 58

58:1 Let us, therefore, submit to his all-holy and glorious name, and escape the threats that have been before spoken by Wisdom against the disobedient, that we may abide trusting in the most holy name of his greatness.
58:2 Accept this our advice, and it will not be repented of by you. For as God liveth, and as the Lord Jesus Christ liveth, and the Holy Spirit, the confidence and hope of the elect, he who observeth in humility with earnest obedience, and repining not, the ordinances and commands given by God, he shall be reckoned and counted in the number of them that are saved by Jesus Christ, through whom is there to him glory, world without end. Amen.

CHAPTER 59

59:1 But if some should be disobedient to the things spoken by him through us, let them know that they will entangle themselves in no small transgression and danger,

59:2 but that we shall be guiltless of this sin; and we will ask, making with earnestness our prayer and supplication, that the Maker of all things may keep uninjured in all the world the number of those that

have been numbered as his elect, through his beloved Son, Jesus Christ, through whom he hath called us from darkness unto light, and from ignorance to a knowledge of the glory of his name.

59:3 That we may hope in thy name, which is the first of all things, open the eyes of our heart to know thee, who art alone highest among the highest, holy among the holy, who puttest down the haughtiness of the proud, who scatterest the reasonings of the Gentiles, who exaltest the humble on high, and lowerest the lofty, who makest rich and makest poor, who killest and makest to live, the only benefactor of spirits, and God of all flesh, who lookest into the abysses, who beholdest the works of men, who art the helper of those in danger, the saviour of those who have lost hope, who art the maker and bishop of every soul, who makest the nations to multiply upon earth, and out of all hast chosen those that love thee through Jesus Christ thy beloved Son, through whom thou hast taught us, hast sanctified us, hast honoured us.

59:4 We ask thee, Lord, to be our helper and assister, save those of us who are in affliction, have compassion on the humble, raise the fallen, appear to those who are in need, heal the sinners, convert those of thy people who are wandering from the way, feed the hungry, ransom our prisoners, raise up the sick, encourage the feeble-hearted, let all the nations know that thou art God alone and Jesus Christ thy Son, and that we are thy people and the sheep of thy pasture.

CHAPTER 60

60:1 Thou hast made manifest the everlasting constitution of the world by the things that happen. Thou, Lord, who art faithful in all generations, hast founded the world; thou who art just in thy judgments, who art wonderful in strength and greatness; thou who art wise in creating and prudent in establishing the things that are made; thou that art good in the things that are seen and faithful among them that trust upon thee, merciful and compassionate, forgive us our transgressions and unrighteousnesses, our sins and our negligences.

60:2 Take not into account every sin of thy servants and handmaids, but purify us with the purification of thy truth, and make straight our steps in holiness and righteousness and singleness of heart, that we may so walk and do such things as are right and well pleasing before thee, and before our rulers.

60:3 Yea, Lord, cause thy face to appear to us in peace to our good, that we may be sheltered by thy mighty hand, and preserved from all sin by thy lofty arm, and deliver us from those that hate us unjustly.

60:4 Give unity and peace both to us and to all that dwell upon the earth, as thou gavest to our fathers when they called upon thee with faith and truth, so that we should become obedient to thy all-powerful and most excellent name, and to those who rule and govern us upon the earth.

CHAPTER 61

61:1 Thou, Lord, hast given the authority of the kingdom to them through thy almighty and unspeakable power, so that we, knowing the estimation and honour given to them by thee, might submit ourselves to them, in no way opposing thy will; to whom give, O Lord, health, peace, concord, stability, so that they may discharge the rule given unto them by thee without offence;

61:2 for thou, heavenly Lord, everlasting King, givest to the sons of men glory and honour and authority over the things that are upon the earth. Do thou, Lord, direct their counsel according to what is good and pleasing before thee, that, fulfilling with peace and meekness and piety the authority given unto them by thee, they may obtain mercy from thee.

61:3 Thou who alone art able to do these and greater good things among us, to thee do we give thanks through the high priest and protector of our souls, Jesus Christ, through whom to thee be the glory and majesty, now and to all generations, world without end. Amen.

CHAPTER 62

62:1 Concerning the things that pertain to our religion, and the things that are most useful to a virtuous life, for those who are willing to live piously and righteously, we have sufficiently charged you, men and brethren.

62:2 For we have handled every argument concerning faith and repentance, and genuine love and temperance, and moderation and patience, reminding you that ye must by righteousness and truth and long-suffering approve yourselves with piety to almighty God, being of one mind, without malice, in love and peace with earnest obedience, even as our fathers, who were beforementioned, approved themselves with humility both with regard to God the Father and Creator and to all men.

62:3 And these things have we so much the more gladly put you in mind of, inasmuch as we knew plainly that we wrote unto men who are faithful and of high repute, and who have looked into the oracles of the instruction of God.

CHAPTER 63

63:1 It is right, therefore, that those who have attended to so great and so many examples should submit their necks, and fill the place of obedience, so that being at peace from the vain sedition we may attain, without any blame, to the end set before us in truth.

63:2 For joy and rejoicing will ye afford us if, becoming obedient to the things that have been written by us, ye put an end, by the suggestion of the Holy Spirit, to the unlawful wrath of your discord, according to the supplication which we have made concerning peace and unity in this epistle.

63:3 But we have also sent unto you men who are faithful and prudent, who from youth up to old age have behaved blamelessly among us, who also will be witnesses between yourselves and us;
63:4 and this we have done that ye may know that our whole thought has been and is this, that ye may speedily be at peace among yourselves.

CHAPTER 64

64:1 Finally, my God, who overlooketh all things, who is the Master of spirits and Lord of all flesh, who hath chosen our Lord Jesus Christ, and us through him to be a peculiar people, give unto every soul that is called after his glorious and holy name, faith, fear, peace, patience, long-suffering, continence, purity, sobriety, to the well-pleasing of his name, through our high priest and protector, Jesus Christ, through whom be ascribed unto him glory and greatness, strength and honour, both now and world without end. Amen.

CHAPTER 65

65:1 See that ye send back quickly unto us in peace and with joy Claudius Ephebus and Valerius Bito, together also with Fortunatus, who were sent unto you from us, that they may the more quickly bring us news of your peace and order, which we pray for and desire, so that we may the sooner have joy concerning your good order.
65:2 The grace of our Lord Jesus Christ be with you, and with all who everywhere are called of God through him, to whom through him be glory, honour, might, majesty, and eternal dominion, world without end. Amen.

END OF 1 CLEMENT

SECOND CLEMENT (2 Clement)

Translated by J.B. Lightfoot.

2Clem 1:1
Brethren, we ought so to think of Jesus Christ, as of God, as of the judge of quick and dead.

2Clem 1:2
And we ought not to think mean things of our Salvation: for when we think mean things of Him, we expect also to receive mean things. And they that listen as concerning mean things do wrong; and we ourselves do wrong, not knowing whence and by whom and unto what place we were called, and how many things Jesus Christ endured to suffer for our sakes.

2Clem 1:3
What recompense then shall we give unto Him? Or what fruit worthy of his own gift to us? And how many mercies do we owe to Him!

2Clem 1:4
For He bestowed the light upon us; He spake to us, as a father to his sons; He saved us, when we were perishing.

2Clem 1:5
What praise then shall we give to Him? Or what payment of recompense for those things which we received?

2Clem 1:6
We who were maimed in our understanding, and worshipped stocks and stones and gold and silver and bronze, the works of men; and our whole life was nothing else but death. While then we were thus wrapped in darkness and oppressed with this thick mist in our vision, we recovered our sight, putting off by His will the cloud wherein we were wrapped.

2Clem 1:7
For He had mercy on us, and in His compassion saved us, having beheld in us much error and perdition, even when we had no hope of salvation, save that which came from Him.
2Clem 1:8
For He called us, when we were not, and from not being He willed us to be.

2Clem 2:1
Rejoice, thou barren that barest not. Break out and cry, thou that travailest not; for more are the children of the desolate than of her that hath the husband. In that He said Rejoice, thou barren that barest not, He spake of us: for our Church was barren, before that children were given unto her.

2Clem 2:2
And in that He said, Cry aloud, thou that travailest not, He meaneth this; Let us not, like women in travail, grow weary of offering up our prayers with simplicity to God.

2Clem 2:3
Again, in that He said, For the children of the desolate are more than of her that hath the husband, He so spake, because our people seemed desolate and forsaken of God, whereas now, having believed, we have become more than those who seemed to have God.

2Clem 2:4
Again another scripture saith, I came not to call the righteous, but sinners.

2Clem 2:5
He meaneth this; that it is right to save them that are perishing.

2Clem 2:6
For this indeed is a great and marvelous work, to establish, not those things which stand, but those which are falling.

2Clem 2:7
So also Christ willed to save the things which were perishing And he saved many, coming and calling us when we were even now perishing.

2Clem 3:1
Seeing then that He bestowed so great mercy on us; first of all, that we, who are living, do not sacrifice to these dead gods, neither worship them, but through Him have known the Father of truth. What else is this knowledge to Himward, but not to deny Him through whom we have known Him?

2Clem 3:2
Yea, He Himself saith, Whoso confesseth Me, Him will I confess before the Father.

2Clem 3:3
This then is our reward, if verily we shall confess Him through whom we were saved.

2Clem 3:4
But wherein do we confess Him? When we do that which He saith and are not disobedient unto His commandments, and not only honor Him with our lips, but with our whole heart and with our whole mind.

2Clem 3:5
Now He saith also in Isaiah, This people honoreth me with their lips, but their heart is far from Me.

2Clem 4:1
Let us therefore not only call Him Lord, for this will not save us:

2Clem 4:2
for He saith, Not every one that saith unto Me, Lord, shall be saved, but he that doeth righteousness.

2Clem 4:3
So then, brethren, let us confess Him in our works, by loving one another, by not committing adultery nor speaking evil one against another nor envying, but being temperate, merciful, kindly. And we ought to have fellow-feeling one with another and not to be covetous. By these works let us confess Him, and not by the contrary.

2Clem 4:4
And we ought not rather to fear men but God.

2Clem 4:5
For this cause, if ye do these things, the Lord said, Though ye be gathered together with Me in My bosom, and do not My commandments, I will cast you away and will say unto you, Depart from Me, I know you not whence ye are, ye workers of iniquity.

2Clem 5:1
Wherefore, brethren, let us forsake our sojourn in this world and do the will of Him that called us, and let us not be afraid to depart out of this world.
2Clem 5:2
For the Lord saith, Ye shall be as lambs in the midst of wolves.

2Clem 5:3
But Peter answered and said unto Him, What then, if the wolves should tear the lambs?

2Clem 5:4
Jesus said unto Peter, Let not the lambs fear the wolves after they are dead; and ye also, fear ye not them that kill you and are not able to do anything to you; but fear Him that after ye are dead hath power over soul and body, to cast them into the Gehenna of fire.

2Clem 5:5
And ye know, brethren, that the sojourn of this flesh in this world is mean and for a short time, but the promise of Christ is great and marvelous, even the rest of the kingdom that shall be and of life eternal.

2Clem 5:6

What then can we do to obtain them, but walk in holiness and righteousness, and consider these worldly things as alien to us, and not desire them?

2Clem 5:7
For when we desire to obtain these things we fall away from the righteous path.

2Clem 6:1
But the Lord saith, No servant can serve two masters. If we desire to serve both God and mammon, it is unprofitable for us:

2Clem 6:2
For what advantage is it, if a man gain the whole world and forfeit his soul?

2Clem 6:3
Now this age and the future are two enemies.

2Clem 6:4
The one speaketh of adultery and defilement and avarice and deceit, but the other biddeth farewell to these.

2Clem 6:5
We cannot therefore be friends of the two, but must bid farewell to the one and hold companionship with the other.
2Clem 6:6
Let us consider that it is better to hate the things which are here, because they are mean and for a short time and perishable, and to love the things which are there, for they are good and imperishable.

2Clem 6:7
For, if we do the will of Christ, we shall find rest; but if otherwise, then nothing shall deliver us from eternal punishment, if we should disobey His commandments.

2Clem 6:8
And the scripture also saith in Ezekiel, Though Noah and Job and Daniel should rise up, they shall not deliver their children in the captivity.

2Clem 6:9
But if even such righteous men as these cannot by their righteous deeds deliver their children, with what confidence shall we, if we keep not our baptism pure and undefiled, enter into the kingdom of God? Or who shall be our advocate, unless we be found having holy and righteous works?

2Clem 7:1
So then, my brethren, let us contend, knowing that the contest is nigh at hand, and that, while many resort to

the corruptible contests, yet not all are crowned, but only they that have toiled hard and contended bravely.

2Clem 7:2
Let us then contend that we all may be crowned.

2Clem 7:3
Wherefore let us run in the straight course, the incorruptible contest. And let us resort to it in throngs and contend, that we may also be crowned. And if we cannot all be crowned, let us at least come near to the crown.

2Clem 7:4
We ought to know that he which contendeth in the corruptible contest, if he be found dealing corruptly with it, is first flogged. and then removed and driven out of the race course.

2Clem 7:5
What think ye? What shall be done to him that hath dealt corruptly with the contest of incorruption?

2Clem 7:6
For as concerning them that have not kept the seal, He saith, Their worm shall not die, and their fire shall not be quenched, and they shall be for a spectacle unto all flesh.

2Clem 8:1
While we are on earth then, let us repent: for we are clay under the craftsman's hand.

2Clem 8:2
For in like manner as the potter, if he be making a vessel, and it get twisted or crushed in his hands, reshapeth it again; but if he have once put it into the fiery oven, he shall no longer mend it: so also let us, while we are in this world, repent with our whole heart of the evil things which we have done in the flesh, that we may be saved by the Lord, while we have yet time for repentance.

2Clem 8:3
For after that we have departed out of the world, we can no more make confession there, or repent any more.

2Clem 8:4
Wherefore, brethren, if we shall have done the will of the Father and kept the flesh pure and guarded the commandments of the Lord, we shall receive life eternal.
2Clem 8:5
For the Lord saith in the Gospel, If ye kept not that which is little, who shall give unto you that which is

great? For I say unto you that he which is faithful in the least, is also faithful in much.

2Clem 8:6
So then He meaneth this, Keep the flesh pure and the seal unstained, to the end that we may receive life.

2Clem 9:1
And let not anyone of you say that this flesh is not judged neither riseth again.

2Clem 9:2
Understand ye. In what were ye saved? In what did ye recover your sight? if ye were not in this flesh.

2Clem 9:3
We ought therefore to guard the flesh as a temple of God:

2Clem 9:4
for in like manner as ye were called in the flesh, ye shall come also in the flesh.

2Clem 9:5
If Christ the Lord who saved us, being first spirit, then became flesh, and so called us, in like manner also shall we in this flesh receive our reward.
2Clem 9:6
Let us therefore love one another, that we all may come unto the kingdom of God.

2Clem 9:7
While we have time to be healed, let us place ourselves in the hands of God the physician, giving Him a recompense.

2Clem 9:8
What recompense? Repentance from a sincere heart.

2Clem 9:9
For He discerneth all things beforehand and knoweth what is in our heart.

2Clem 9:10
Let us therefore give unto Him eternal praise, not from our lips only, but also from our heart, that He may receive us as sons.
2Clem 9:11
For the Lord also said, These are my brethren, which do the will of My Father.

2Clem 10:1
Wherefore, my brethren, let us do the will of the Father which called us, that we may live; and let us the rather pursue virtue, but forsake vice as the forerunner of our sins, and let us flee from ungodliness, lest evils overtake us.

2Clem 10:2
For if we be diligent in doing good, peace will pursue us.

2Clem 10:3
For this cause is a man unable to *attain happiness*, seeing that they call in the fears of men, preferring rather the enjoyment which is here than the promise which is to come.

2Clem 10:4
For they know not how great torment the enjoyment which is here bringeth, and what delight the promise which is to come bringeth.

2Clem 10:5
And if verily they were doing these things by themselves alone, it had been tolerable: but now they continue teaching evil to innocent souls, not knowing that they shall have their condemnation doubled, both themselves and their hearers.

2Clem 11:1
Let us therefore serve God in a pure heart, and we shall be righteous; but if we serve Him not, because we believe not the promise of God, we shall be wretched.

2Clem 11:2
For the word of prophecy also saith: Wretched are the double-minded, that doubt in their heart and say, These things we heard of old in the days of our fathers also, yet we have waited day after day and seen none of them.

2Clem 11:3
Ye fools! compare yourselves unto a tree; take a vine. First it sheds its leaves, then a shoot cometh, after this a sour berry, then a full ripe grape.

2Clem 11:4
So likewise My people had tumults and afflictions: but afterward they shall receive good things.

2Clem 11:5
Wherefore, my brethren, let us not be double-minded but endure patiently in hope, that we may also obtain our reward.

2Clem 11:6
For faithful is He that promised to pay to each man the recompense of his works.

2Clem 11:7
If therefore we shalt have wrought righteousness in the sight of God, we shalt enter into His kingdom and shall receive the promises which ear hath not heard nor eye seen, nor eye seen, neither hath it entered into the heart of man.

2Clem 12:1
Let us therefore await the kingdom of God betimes in love and righteousness, since we know not the day of God's appearing.

2Clem 12:2
For the Lord Himself, being asked by a certain person when his kingdom would come, said, When the two shall be one, and the outside as the inside, and the male with the female, neither male or female.

2Clem 12:3
Now the two are one, when we speak truth among ourselves, and in two bodies there shall be one soul without dissimulation.

2Clem 12:4
And by the outside as the inside He meaneth this: by the inside he meaneth the soul and by the outside the body. Therefore in like manner as thy body appeareth, so also let thy soul be manifest by its good works.

2Clem 12:5
And by the male with the female, neither male nor female, he meaneth this; that a brother seeing a sister should have no thought of her as a female, and that a sister seeing a brother should not have any thought of him as a male.

2Clem 12:6
These things if ye do, saith He, the kingdom of my father shall come.

2Clem 13:1
Therefore, brethren, let us repent forthwith. Let us be sober unto that which is good: for we are full of much folly and wickedness. Let us wipe away from us our former sins, and let us not be found to be men pleasers. Neither let us desire to please one another only, but also those men that are without, by our righteousness, that the name be not blasphemed by reason of us.

2Clem 13:2
For the Lord saith, Every way My Name is blasphemed among all the Gentiles; and again, Woe unto him by reason of whom My Name is blasphemed. Wherein is it blasphemed? In that ye do not the things which I desire.

2Clem 13:3
For the Gentiles, when they hear from our mouths the oracles of God, marvel at them for their beauty and greatness; then, when they discover that our works are not worthy of the words which we speak, forthwith

they betake themselves to blasphemy, saying that it is an idle story and a delusion.

2Clem 13:4
For when they here from us that God saith, It is no thank unto you, if ye love them that love you, but this is thank unto you, if ye love your enemies and them that hate you; when they hear these things, I say, they marvel at their exceeding goodness; but when they see that we not only do not love us, they laugh us to scorn, and the name is blasphemed.

2Clem 14:1
Wherefore, brethren, if we do the will of God our Father, we shall be of the first Church, which is spiritual, which was created before the sun and the moon; but if we do not the will of the Lord, we shall be of the scripture that saith, My house was made a den of robbers. So therefore let us choose rather to be of the Church of life, that we may be saved.

2Clem 14:2
And I do not suppose ye are ignorant that the living Church is the body of Christ: for the scripture saith, God made man, male and female. The male is Christ and the female is the Church. And the books and the Apostles plainly declare that the Church existeth not now for the first time, but hath been from the beginning: for she was spiritual, as our Jesus also was spiritual, but was manifested in the last days that He might save us.

2Clem 14:3
Now the Church, being spiritual was manifested in the flesh of Christ, thereby showing us that if any of us guard her in the flesh and defile her not, he shall receive her again in the Holy Spirit: for this flesh is the counterpart and copy of the spirit. No man therefore, when he hath defiled the copy, shall receive the original for his portion. This therefore is what He meaneth, brethren; guard ye the flesh, that ye may partake of the spirit.

2Clem 14:4
But if we say that the flesh is the Church and the spirit is Christ, then he that hath dealt wantonly with the flesh hath dealt wantonly with the Church. Such and one therefore shall not partake of the spirit, which is Christ.

2Clem 14:5
So excellent is the life and immortality which this flesh can receive as its portion, if the Holy Spirit be joined to it. No man can declare or tell those things which the Lord hath prepared for His elect.

2Clem 15:1
Now I do not think that I have given any mean council respecting continence, and whosoever performeth it shall not repent thereof, but shall save both himself and me his councilor. For it is no mean reward to convert a wondering and perishing soul, that it may be saved.

2Clem 15:2
For this is the recompense which we are able to pay to God who created us, if he that speaketh and heareth both speak and hear with faith and love.

2Clem 15:3
Let is therefore abide in the things which we believed, in righteousness and holiness, that we may with boldness as of God who saith, Whiles thou art still speaking I will say, Behold, I am here.

2Clem 15:4
For this word is the token of a great promise: for the Lord saith of himself that He is more ready to give than he that asketh to ask.

2Clem 15:5
Seeing then that we are partakers of so great kindness, let us not grudge ourselves the obtaining of so many good things. For in proportion as the pleasure is great which these words bring to them that have performed them, so also is the condemnation great which they bring to them that have been disobedient.

2Clem 16:1
Therefore, brethren, since we have found no small opportunity for repentance, seeing that we have time, let us turn again unto God that called us, while we have still One that receiveth us.

2Clem 16:2
For if we bid farewell to these enjoyments and conquer our soul in refusing to fulfill its evil lusts, we shall be partakers of the mercy of Jesus.

2Clem 16:3
But ye know that the day of judgment cometh even now as a burning oven, and the powers of the heavens shall melt, and all the earth as lead melting on the fire, and then shall appear the secret and open works of men.

2Clem 16:4
Almsgiving therefore is a good thing, even as repentance from sin; fasting is better than prayer, but almsgiving better than both. And love covereth a multitude of sins, but prayer out of a good conscience delivereth from death. Blessed is every man that is found full of these. For almsgiving lifteth off the burden of sin.

2Clem 17:1
Let us therefore repent with our whole heart, lest any of us perish by the way. For if we have received commands, that we should make this our business, to tear men away from idols and to instruct them, how much more is it wrong that a soul which knoweth God already should perish!

2Clem 17:2
Therefore let us assist one another, that we may also lead the weak upward as touching that which is good, to the end that we all may be saved: and let us convert and admonish one another.

2Clem 17:3
And let us not think to give heed and believe now only, while we have departed home, let us remember the commandments of the Lord, and not suffer ourselves to be dragged off the other way by our worldly lusts; but coming hither more frequently, let us strive to go forward in the commandments of the Lord, that we all having the same mind may be gathered together unto life.

2Clem 17:4
For the Lord said, I come to gather together all the nations, tribes, and languages. Herein He speaketh of the day of His appearing, when He shall come and redeem us, each man according to his works.

2Clem 17:5
And the unbelievers shall see His glory and His might: and they shall be amazed when they see the kingdom of the world given to Jesus, saying, Woe unto us, for Thou wast, and we knew it not, and believed not; and we obeyed not the presbyters when they told us of our salvation. And Their worm shall not die, and their fire shall not be quenched, and they shall be for a spectacle unto all flesh.

2Clem 17:6
He speaketh of that day of judgment, when men shall see those among us that live ungodly lives and dealt falsely with the commandments of Jesus Christ.
2Clem 17:7
But the righteous, done good and endured torments and hated pleasures of the soul, when they shall behold them that have done amiss and denied Jesus by their words or by their deeds, how that they are punished with grievous torments in unquenchable fire, shall give glory to God, saying, there will be hope for him that hath served God with his whole heart.

2Clem 18:1

Therefore let us also be found among those that give thanks, among those that have served God, and not among the ungodly that are judged.

2Clem 18:2
For I myself too, being an utter sinner and not yet escaped from temptation, but being still amidst the engines of the devil, do my diligence to follow after righteousness, that I may prevail so far at least as to come near unto it, while I fear the judgment to come.

2Clem 19:1
Therefore, brothers and sisters, after the God of truth hath been heard, I read unto you an exhortation to the end that ye may give heed to the things which are written, for that ye may save both yourselves and him that readeth in the midst of you. For I ask of you as a reward that ye repent with your whole heart, and give salvation and life to yourselves. For doing this we shall set a goal for all the young who desire to toil in the study of piety and of the goodness of God.

2Clem 19:2
And let is not be displeased and vexed, fools that we are, whensoever anyone admonish us and turneth us aside from unrighteousness unto righteousness. For sometimes while we do evil things, we perceive it not by reason of the double-mindedness and unbelief which is in our breasts, and we are darkened in our understanding by our vain lusts.

2Clem 19:3
Let us therefore practice righteousness that we may be saved unto the end. Blessed are they that obey these ordinances. Though they may endure affliction for a short time in the world, they will gather the immortal fruit of the resurrection.

2Clem 19:4
Therefore let not the godly be grieved, if he be miserable in the times that now are: a blessed time awaiteth him. He shall live again in heaven with our fathers, and shall have rejoicing throughout a sorrowless eternity.

2Clem 20:1
Neither suffer ye this again to trouble your mind, that we see the unrighteous possessing wealth, and the servants of God straitened.

2Clem 20:2
Let us then have faith, brothers and sisters. We are trained by the present life, that we may be crowned with the future.

2Clem 20:3

No righteous man hath reaped fruit quickly but waiteth for it.

2Clem 20:4
For if God had paid the recompense of the righteous speedily, then straightway we should have been training ourselves in merchandise, and not in godliness; for we should seem to be righteous, though we were pursuing not that which is godly, but which is gainful. And for this cause Divine judgment overtaketh a spirit that is not just, and loadeth it with chains.

2Clem 20:5
To the only God invisible, the Father of truth, who sent forth unto us the Savior and Prince of immortality, through whom also He made manifest unto us the truth and the heavenly life, to Him be the glory for ever and ever. Amen.

Ignatius of Antioch

Ignatius of Antioch (? - 110 CE) was the Bishop of Antioch in the early second century AD. He was a prominent advocate of church unity and is particularly remembered for his seven letters written to various Christian communities while en route to Rome, where he met his martyrdom. Ignatius emphasized the authority of bishops, the Eucharist as the real presence of Christ, and the importance of martyrdom as a testimony of faith.

Ignatius of Antioch, also known as Saint Ignatius, is considered an Apostolic Father due to his close association with the apostolic era and his significant contributions to early Christian theology and leadership. The Apostolic Fathers are a group of Christian writers who lived in the first and second centuries and had direct or indirect connections with the apostles of Jesus Christ.

Ignatius was born around the year 35 AD and died as a martyr around 107 AD. He was the bishop of Antioch in Syria, an important Christian center during that time. Ignatius is particularly recognized for his letters, which he wrote during his journey to Rome to face martyrdom. These letters provide valuable insights into the early Christian church and its teachings.

There are several reasons why Ignatius is considered an Apostolic Father:

1 Association with the Apostles: Ignatius claimed to have known and been instructed by some of the apostles, particularly Peter and John. While the exact details of his relationship with the apostles are uncertain, his letters attest to his awareness of their teachings and his desire to uphold their authority.

2 Defense of Orthodox Christianity: Ignatius' letters emphasize the importance of the unity of the Church and the authority of bishops. He defended orthodox Christian beliefs against various heresies and encouraged Christians to remain faithful to the teachings of the apostles and the traditions handed down from them.

3 Development of Church Hierarchy: Ignatius played a crucial role in the development of the hierarchical structure of the early Christian church. His letters emphasize the authority of bishops as the successors of the apostles and the importance of their role in maintaining doctrinal integrity and unity among the believers.

4 Martyrdom: Ignatius' willingness to face martyrdom for his faith further strengthens his connection to the apostolic era. His courageous testimony and sacrificial death are seen as a continuation of the apostolic tradition of bearing witness to the Gospel, even in the face of persecution.

Ignatius of Antioch's association with the apostolic era, his defense of orthodox Christianity, his contribution to the development of church hierarchy, and his martyrdom all contribute to his recognition as an Apostolic Father. His writings continue to be studied and valued as a significant source for understanding early Christian theology and ecclesiastical development.

THE EPISTLE OF IGNATIUS TO THE EPHESIANS SHORTER AND LONGER VERSIONS

Ignatius, who is also called Theopharus, to the Church which is at Ephesus, in Asia, deservedly most happy, being blessed in the greatness and fulness of God the Father, and predestinated before the beginning[1] of time, that it should be always for an enduring and unchangeable glory, being united[2] and elected through the true passion by the will of the Father, and Jesus Christ, our God: Abundant happiness through Jesus Christ, and His undefiled grace.

Ignatius, who is also called Theophorus, to the Church which is at Ephesus, in Asia, deservedly most happy, being blessed in the greatness and fulness of God the Father, and predestinated before the beginning[1] of time, that it should be always for an enduring and unchangeable glory, being united[2] and elected through the true passion by the will of God the Father, and of our Lord Jesus Christ our Saviour: Abundant happiness through Jesus Christ, and His undefiled joy.[3]

CHAP. I. -- PRAISE OF THE EPHESIANS.

I have become acquainted with your name, much-beloved in God, which ye have acquired by the habit of righteousness, according to the faith and love in Jesus Christ our Saviour. Being the followers[4] of God, and stirring up[5] yourselves by the blood of God, ye have perfectly accomplished the work which was beseeming to you. For, on hearing that I came bound from Syria for the common name and hope, trusting through your prayers to be permitted to fight with beasts at Rome, that so by martyrdom I may indeed become the disciple of Him "who gave Himself for us, an offering and sacrifice to God,"[6][ye hastened to see me[7]]. I received, therefore,[8] your whole multitude in the name of God, through Onesimus, a man of inexpressible love,[9] and your bishop in the flesh, whom I pray you by Jesus Christ to love, and that you would all seek to be like him. And blessed be He who has granted unto you, being worthy, to obtain such an excellent bishop.

I have become acquainted with your greatly-desired name in God, which ye have acquired by the habit of righteousness, according to the faith and love in Christ Jesus our Saviour. Being the followers[4] of the love of God towards man, and stirring up s yourselves by the blood of Christ, you have perfectly accomplished the work which was beseeming to you. For, on hearing that I came bound from Syria for the sake of Christ, our common hope, trusting through your prayers to be permitted to fight with beasts at Rome, that so by martyrdom I may indeed become the disciple of Him "who gave Himself for us, an offering and a sacrifice to God,"[6] [ye hastened to see me[7]]. I have therefore received your whole multitude in the name of God, through Onesimus, a man of inexpressible love,[9] and who is your bishop, whom I pray you by Jesus Christ to love, and that you would all seek to be like him. Blessed be God, who has granted unto you, who are yourselves so excellent, to obtain such an excellent bishop.

CHAP. II. -- CONGRATULATIONS AND ENTREATIES.

As to my fellow-servant Burrhus, your deacon in regard to God and blessed in all things,[1] I beg that he may continue longer, both for your honour and that of your bishop. And Crocus also, worthy both of God and you, whom I have received as the manifestation[2] of your love, hath in all things refreshed[3] me, as the Father of our Lord Jesus Christ shall also refresh[3] him; together with Onesimus, and Burrhus, and Euplus, and Fronto, by means of whom, I have, as to love, beheld all of you. May I always have joy of you, if indeed I be worthy of it. It is therefore befitting that you should in every way glorify Jesus Christ, who hath glorified you, that by a unanimous obedience "ye may be perfectly joined together in the same mind, and in the same judgment, and may all speak the same thing concerning the same thing,"[5] and that, being subject to the bishop and the presbytery, ye may in all respects be sanctified.

As to our fellow-servant Burrhus, your deacon in regard to God and blessed in all things, I pray that he may continue blameless for the honour of the Church, and of your most blessed bishop. Crocus also, worthy both of God and you, whom we have received as the manifestation[2] of your love to us, hath in all things refreshed[3] me, and "hath not been ashamed of my chain,"[4] as the Father of our Lord Jesus Christ will also refresh[3] him; together with Onesimus, and Burrhus, and Euplus, and Fronto, by means of whom I have, as to love, beheld all of you. May I always have joy of you, if indeed I be worthy of it. It is therefore befitting that you should in every way glorify Jesus Christ, who hath glorified you, that by a unanimous obedience "ye may be perfectly joined together in the same mind and in the same judgment, and may all speak the same thing concerning the same thing,"[5] and that, being subject to the bishop and the presbytery, ye may in all respects be sanctified.

CHAP. III. -- EXHORTATIONS TO UNITY.

I do not issue orders to you, as if I were some great person. For though I am bound for the name[of Christ], I am not yet perfect in Jesus Christ. For now I begin to be a disciple, and I speak to you as fellow- disciples with me. For it was needful for me to have been stirred up by you in faith, exhortation, patience, and long-suffering. But inasmuch as love suffers me not to be silent in regard to you, I have therefore taken[6] upon me first to exhort you that ye would all run together in accordance with the will of God. For even Jesus Christ, our inseparable life, is the[manifested] will of the Father; as also bishops, settled everywhere to the utmost bounds[of the earth], are so by the will of Jesus Christ.

I do not issue orders to you, as if I were some great person. For though I am bound for His name, I am not yet perfect in Jesus Christ. For now I begin to be a disciple, and I speak to you as my fellow-servants. For it was needful for me to have been admonished by you in faith, exhortation, patience, and long-suffering. But inasmuch as love suffers me not to be silent in regard to you, I have therefore taken[6] upon me first to exhort you that ye would run together in accordance with the will of God. For even Jesus Christ does all things according to the will of the Father, as He Himself declares in a certain place, "I do always those things that please Him."[7] Wherefore it behoves us also to live according to the will of God in Christ, and to imitate Him as Paul did. For, says he, "Be ye followers of me, even as I also am of Christ."[8]

CHAP. IV. -- THE SAME CONTINUED.

Wherefore it is fitting that ye should run together in accordance with the will of your bishop, which thing also ye do. For your justly renowned presbytery, worthy of God, is fitted as exactly to the bishop as the strings are to the harp. Therefore in your concord and harmonious love, Jesus Christ is sung. And do ye, man by man, become a choir, that being harmonious in love, and taking up the song of God in unison, ye may with one voice sing to the Father through Jesus Christ, so that He may both hear you, and perceive by your works that ye are indeed the members of His son. It is profitable, therefore, that you should live in an unblameable unity, that thus ye may always enjoy communion with God.

Wherefore it is fitting that ye also should run together in accordance with the will of the bishop who by God's appointment[9] rules over you. Which thing ye indeed of yourselves do, being instructed by the Spirit. For your justly-renowned presbytery, being worthy of God, is fitted as exactly to the bishop as the strings are to the harp. Thus, being joined together in concord and harmonious concord and harmonious love, of which Jesus Christ is the Captain and Guardian, do ye, man by man, become but one choir; so that, agreeing together in concord, and obtaining[1] a perfect unity with God, ye may indeed be one in harmonious feeling with God the Father, and His beloved Son Jesus Christ our Lord. For, says He, "Grant unto them, Holy Father, that as I and Thou are one, they also may be one in us."[2] It is therefore profitable that you, being joined together with God in an unblameable unity, should be the followers of the example of Christ, of whom also ye are members.

CHAP. V. -- THE PRAISE OF UNITY.

For if I in this brief space of time, have enjoyed such fellowship with your bishop--I mean not of a mere human, but of a spiritual nature--how much more do I reckon you happy who are so joined to him as the Church is to Jesus Christ, and as Jesus Christ is to the Father, that so all things may agree in unity !Let no man deceive himself: if anyone be not within the altar, he is deprived of the bread of God. For if the prayer of one or two possesses[4] such power, how much more that of the bishop and the whole Church !He, therefore, that does not assemble with the Church, has even[5] by this manifested his pride, and condemned himself. For it is written, "God resisteth the proud."[9] Let us be careful, then, not to set ourselves in opposition to the bishop, in order that we may be subject to God.

For if I, in this brief space of time, have enjoyed such fellowship with your bishop--I mean not of a mere human, but of a spiritual nature-- how much more do I reckon you happy, who so depend[3] on him as the Church does on the Lord Jesus, and the Lord does on God and His Father, that so all things may agree in unity !Let no man deceive himself: if anyone be not within the altar, he is deprived of the bread of God. For if the prayer of one or two possesses[4] such power that Christ stands in the midst of them, how much more will the prayer of the bishop and of the whole Church, ascending up in harmony to God, prevail for the granting of all their petitions in Christ !He, therefore, that separates himself from such, and does not meet in the society where sacrifices[6] are offered, and with "the Church of the first-born whose names are written in heaven," is a wolf in sheep's clothing,[7] while he presents a mild outward appearance. Do ye, beloved, be careful to be subject to the bishop, and the presbyters and the deacons. For he that is subject to these is obedient to Christ, who has appointed them; but he that is disobedient to these is disobedient to Christ Jesus. And "he that obeyeth not[8] the Son shall not see life, but the wrath of God abideth on him." For he that yields not obedience to his superiors is self-confident, quarrelsome, and proud. But" God," says[the Scripture] "resisteth the proud, but giveth grace to the humble ;"[9] and, "The proud have greatly transgressed." The Lord also says to the priests, "He that heareth you, heareth Me; and he that heareth Me, heareth the Father that sent Me. He that despiseth you,

despiseth Me; and he that despiseth Me, despiseth Him that sent Me."

CHAP. VI. -- HAVE RESPECT TO THE BISHOP AS TO CHRIST HIMSELF.

Now the more anyone sees the bishop keeping silence,[10] the more ought he to revere him. For we ought to receive every one whom the Master of the house sends to be over His household,[11] as we would do Him that sent him. It is manifest, therefore, that we should look upon the bishop even as we would upon the Lord Himself. And indeed Onesimus himself greatly commends your good order in God, that ye all live according to the truth, and that no sect has any dwelling-place among you. Nor, indeed, do ye hearken to anyone rather than to Jesus Christ speaking in truth.

The more, therefore, you see the bishop silent, the more do you reverence him. For we ought to receive everyone whom the Master of the house sends to be over His household,[11] as we would do Him that sent him. It is manifest, therefore, that we should look upon the bishop even as we would look upon the Lord Himself, standing, as he does, before the Lord. For "it behoves the man who looks carefully about him, and is active in his business, to stand before kings, and not to stand before slothful men."[1] And indeed Onesimus himself greatly commends your good order in God, that ye all live according to the truth, and that no sect ' has any dwelling- place among you. Nor indeed do ye hearken to anyone rather than to Jesus Christ, the true Shepherd and Teacher. And ye are, as Paul wrote to you, "one body and one spirit, because ye have also been called in one hope of the faith.[3] Since also "≠there is one Lord, one faith, one baptism, one God and Father of all, ./who is over all, and through all, and in all."[4] Such, then, are ye, having been taught by such instructors, Paul the Christ-bearer, and Timothy the most faithful.

CHAP. VII. -- BEWARE OF FALSE TEACHERS.

For some are in the habit of carrying about the name[of Jesus Christ] in wicked guile, while yet they practise things unworthy of God, whom ye must flee as ye would wild beasts. For they are ravening dogs, who bite secretly, against whom ye must be on your guard, inasmuch as they are men who can scarcely be cured. There is one Physician who is possessed both of flesh and spirit; both made and not made; God existing in flesh; true life in death; both of Mary and of God; first possible and then impossible,[7] even Jesus Christ our Lord.

But some most worthless persons are in the habit of carrying about the name[of Jesus Christ] in wicked guile, while yet they practise things unworthy of God, and hold opinions contrary to the doctrine of Christ, to their own destruction, and that of those who give credit to them, whom you must avoid as ye would wild beasts. For "the righteous man who avoids them is saved for ever; but the destruction of the ungodly is sudden, and a subject of rejoicing."[5] For "they are dumb dogs, that cannot bark,"[6] raving mad, and biting secretly, against whom ye must be on your guard, since they labour under an incurable disease. But our Physician is the only true God, the unbegotten and unapproachable, the Lord of all, the Father and Begetter of the only-begotten Son. We have also as a Physician the Lord our God, Jesus the Christ, the only-begotten Son and Word, before time began,[8] but who afterwards became also man, of Mary the virgin. For "the Word was made flesh."[9] Being incorporeal, He was in the body; being impassible, He was in a passible body; being immortal, He was in a mortal body; being life, He became subject to corruption, that He might free our souls from death and corruption, and heal them, and might restore them to health, when they were diseased with ungodliness and wicked lusts.

CHAP. VIII. -- RENEWED PRAISE OF THE EPHESIANS.

Let not then anyone deceive you, as indeed ye are not deceived, inasmuch as ye are wholly devoted to God. For since there is no strife raging among you which might distress you, ye are certainly living in accordance with God's will. I am far inferior to you, and require to be sanctified by your Church of Ephesus, so renowned throughout the world. They that are carnal cannot do those things which are spiritual, nor they that are spiritual the things which are carnal; even as faith cannot do the works of unbelief, nor the unbelief the works of faith. But even those things which ye do according to the flesh are spiritual; for ye do all things in Jesus Christ.

Let not then anyone deceive you, as indeed ye are not deceived; for ye are wholly devoted to God. For when there is no evil desire within you, which might defile and torment you, then do ye live in accordance with the will of God, and are[the servants] of Christ. Cast ye out that which defiles[10] you, who are of the[11] most holy Church of the Ephesians, which is so famous and celebrated throughout the world. They that are carnal cannot do those things which are spiritual, nor they that are spiritual the things which are carnal; even as faith cannot do the works of unbelief, nor unbelief the works of faith. But ye, being full of the Holy Spirit, do nothing according to the flesh, but all things according to the Spirit. Ye are complete in Christ Jesus, "who is the Saviour of all men, specially of them that believe."[12]

CHAP. IX. -- YE HAVE GIVEN NO HEED TO FALSE TEACHERS.

Nevertheless, I have heard of some who have passed on from this to you, having false doctrine, whom ye did not suffer to sow among you, but stopped your ears, that ye might not receive those things which were sown by them, as being stones[1] of the temple of the Father, prepared for the building of God the Father, and drawn up on high by the instrument of Jesus Christ, which is the cross,[2] making use of the Holy Spirit as a rope, while your faith was the means by which you ascended, and your love the way which led up to God. Ye, therefore, as well as all your fellow-travellers, are God- bearers, temple-bearers, Christ-bearers, bearers of holiness, adorned in all respects with the commandments of Jesus Christ, in whom also I exult that I have been thought worthy, by means of this Epistle, to converse and rejoice with you, because with respect to your Christian life[7] ye love nothing but God only.

Nevertheless, I have heard of some who have passed in among you, holding the wicked doctrine of the strange and evil spirit; to whom ye did not allow entrance to sow their tares, but stopped your ears that ye might not receive that error which was proclaimed by them, as being persuaded that that spirit which deceives the people does not speak the things of Christ, but his own, for he is a lying spirit. But the Holy Spirit does not speak His own things, but those of Christ, and that not from himself, but from the Lord; even as the Lord also announced to us the things that He received from the Father. For, says He, "the word which ye hear is not Mine, but the Father's, who sent Me."[3] And says He of the Holy Spirit, "He shall not speak of Himself, but whatsoever things He shall hear from Me."[4] And He says of Himself to the Father, "I have," says He, "glorified Thee upon the earth; I have finished the work which, Thou gavest Me; I have manifested Thy name to men."[5] And of the Holy Ghost, "He shall glorify Me, for He receives of Mine."[6] But the spirit of deceit preaches himself, and speaks his own things, for he seeks to please himself. He glorifies himself, for he is full of arrogance. He is lying, fraudulent, soothing, flattering, treacherous, rhapsodical, trifling, inharmonious, verbose, sordid, and timorous. From his power Jesus Christ will deliver you, who has founded you upon the rock, as being chosen stones, well fitted for the divine edifice of the Father, and who are raised up on high by Christ, who was crucified for you, making use of the Holy Spirit as a rope, and being borne up by faith, while exalted by love from earth to heaven, walking in company with those that are undefiled. For, says[the Scripture], "Blessed are the undefiled in the way, who walk in the law of the Lord."[8] Now the way is unerring, namely, Jesus Christ. For, says He, "I am the way and the life."[9] And this way leads to the Father. For "no man," says He, "cometh to the Father but by Me."[10] Blessed, then, are ye who are God-bearers, spirit-bearers, temple-bearers, bearers of holiness, adorned in all respects with the commandments of Jesus Christ, being "a royal priesthood, a holy nation, a peculiar people,"[11] on whose account I rejoice exceedingly, and have had the privilege, by this Epistle, of conversing with "the saints which are at Ephesus, the faithful in Christ Jesus."[12] I rejoice, therefore, over you, that ye do not give heed to vanity, and love nothing according to the flesh, but according to God.

CHAP. X. -- EXHORTATIONS TO PRAYER, HUMILITY, ETC.

And pray ye without ceasing in behalf of other men. For there is in them hope of repentance that they may attain to God. See,[2] then, that they be instructed by your works, if in no other way. Be ye meek in response to their wrath, humble in opposition to their boasting: to their blasphemies return[4] your prayers; in contrast to their error, be ye stedfast[5] in the faith; and for their cruelty, manifest your gentleness. While we take care not to imitate their conduct, let us be found their brethren in all true kindness; and let us seek to be followers of the Lord(who ever more unjustly treated, more destitute, more condemned?), that so no plant of the devil may be found in you, but ye may remain in all holiness and sobriety in Jesus Christ, both with respect to the flesh and spirit.

And pray ye without ceasing in behalf of other men; for there is hope of the repentance, that they may attain to God. For "cannot he that falls arise again, and he that goes astray return?"[1] Permit them, then, to be instructed by you. Be ye therefore the ministers of God, and the mouth of Christ. For thus saith the Lord, "If ye take forth the precious from the vile, ye shall be as my mouth."[3] Be ye humble in response to their wrath; oppose to their blasphemies your earnest prayers; while they go astray, stand ye steadfast in the faith. Conquer ye their harsh temper by gentleness, their passion by meekness. For "blessed are the meek ;"[6] and Moses was meek above all men;[7] and David was exceeding meek.[8] Wherefore Paul exhorts as follows: "The servant of the Lord must not strive, but be gentle towards all men, apt to teach, patient, in meekness instructing those that oppose themselves."[9] Do not seek to avert e ourselves on those that injure you, for says[the Scripture], If I have returned evil to those who returned evil to me."[10] Let us make them brethren by our kindness. For say ye to those that hate you, Ye are our brethren, that the name of the Lord may be glorified. And let us imitate the Lord, "who, when He was reviled, reviled not again ;"[11] when He was crucified, He answered not; "when He suffered, He threatened not ;"[12] but prayed for His enemies, "Father, forgive them; they know not what they do."[13] If anyone, the more he is injured, displays the more patience, blessed is he. If anyone is defrauded, if anyone is despised, for the name of the Lord, he truly

is the servant of Christ. Take heed that no plant of the devil be found among you, for such a plant is bitter and salt. "Watch ye, and be ye sober,"[14] in Christ Jesus.

CHAP. XI. -- AN EXHORTATION TO FEAR GOD, ETC.

The last times are come upon us. Let us therefore be of a reverent spirit, and fear the long-suffering of God, that it tend not to our condemnation. For let us either stand in awe of the wrath to come, or show regard for the grace which is at present displayed--one of two things. Only[in one way or another] let us be found in Christ Jesus unto the true life. Apart from Him, let nothing attract[16] you, for whom I bear about these bonds, these spiritual jewels, by which may I arise through your prayers, of which I entreat I may always be a partaker, that I may be found in the lot of the Christians of Ephesus, who have always been of the same mind with the apostles through the power of Jesus Christ.

The last times are come upon us. Let us therefore be of a reverent spirit, and fear the long-suffering of God, lest we despise the riches of His goodness and forbearance.[15] For let us either fear the wrath to come, or let us love the present joy in the life that now is; and let our present and true joy be only this, to be found in Christ Jesus, that we may truly live. Do not at any time desire so much as even to breathe apart from Him. For He is my hope; He is my boast; He is my never-failing riches, on whose account I bear about with me these bonds from Syria to Rome, these spiritual jewels, in which may I be perfected through your prayers, and become a partaker of the sufferings of Christ, and have fellowship with Him in His death, His resurrection from the dead, and His everlasting life.[17] May I attain to this, so that I may be found in the lot of the Christians of Ephesus, who have always had intercourse with the apostles by the power of Jesus Christ, with Paul, and John, and Timothy the most faithful.

CHAP. XII. -- PRAISE OF THE EPHESIANS.

I know both who I am, and to whom I write. I am a condemned man, ye have been the objects of mercy; I am subject to danger, ye are established in safety. Ye are the persons through(1) whom those pass that are cut off for the sake of God. Ye are initiated into the mysteries of the Gospel with Paul, the holy, the martyred, the deservedly most happy, at whose feet(4) may I be found, when I shall attain to God; who in all his Epistles makes mention of you in Christ Jesus.

I know both who I am, and to whom I write. I am the very insignificant Ignatius, who have my lot with[18] those who are exposed to danger and condemnation. But ye have been the objects of mercy, and are established in Christ. I am one delivered over [to death], but the least of all those that have been cut off for the sake of Christ, "from the blood of righteous Abel"(2) to the blood of Ignatius. Ye are initiated into the mysteries of the Gospel with Paul, the holy, the martyred, inasmuch as he was "a chosen vessel;"(3) at whose feet may I be found, and at the feet of the rest of the saints, when I shall attain to Jesus Christ, who is always mindful of you in His prayers.

CHAP. XIII. -- EXHORTATION TO MEET TOGETHER FREQUENTLY FOR THE WORSHIP OF GOD.

Take heed, then, often to come together to give thanks to God, and show forth His praise. For when ye assemble frequently in the same place, the powers of Satan are destroyed, and the destruction at which he aims(7) is prevented by the unity of your faith. Nothing is more precious than peace, by which all war, both in heaven and earth,(8) is brought to an end.

Take heed, then, often to come together to give thanks to God, and show forth His praise. For when ye come frequently together in the same place, the powers of Satan are destroyed, and his "fiery darts"(6) urging to sin fall back ineffectual. For your concord and harmonious faith prove his destruction, and the torment of his assistants. Nothing is better than that peace which is according to Christ, by which all war, both of aërial and terrestrial spirits, is brought to an end. "For we wrestle not against blood and flesh, but against principalities and powers, and against the rulers of the darkness of this world, against spiritual wickedness in heavenly places."(9)

CHAP. XIV. -- EXHORTATIONS TO FAITH AND LOVE.

None of these things is hid from you, if ye perfectly possess that faith and love towards Christ Jesus(10) which are the beginning and the end of life. For the beginning is faith, and the end is love.(11) Now these two. being inseparably connected together,(12) are of God, while all other things which are requisite for a holy life follow after them. No man [truly] making a profession of faith sinneth;(13) nor does he that possesses love hate anyone. The tree is made manifest by its fruit;(15) so those that profess themselves to be Christians shall be recognised by their conduct. For there is not now a demand for mere profession,(16) but that a man be found continuing in the power of faith to the end.

Wherefore none of the devices of the devil shall be hidden from you, if, like Paul, ye perfectly possess that faith and love towards Christ(10) which are the beginning and the end of life. The beginning of life is faith, and the end is love. And these two being inseparably connected together, do perfect the man of God; while all other things which are requisite to a holy

life follow after them. No man making a profession of faith ought to sin, nor one possessed of love to hate his brother. For He that said, "Thou shalt love the Lord thy God,"(14) said also, "and thy neighbour as thyself."(14) Those that profess themselves to be Christ's are known not only by what they say, but by what they practise. "For the tree is known by its fruit."(15)

CHAP. XV. -- EXHORTATION TO CONFESS CHRIST BY SILENCE AS WELL AS SPEECH.

It is better for a man to be silent and be [a Christian], than to talk and not to be one. It is good to teach, if he who speaks also acts. There is then one Teacher, who spake and it was done; while even those things which He did in silence are worthy of the Father. He who possesses the word of Jesus, is truly able to hear even His very silence, that he may be perfect, and may both act as he speaks, and be recognised by his silence. There is nothing which is hid from God, but our very secrets are near to Him. Let us therefore do all things as those who have Him dwelling in us, that we may be His temples,(20) and He may be in us as our God, which indeed He is, and will manifest Himself before our faces. Wherefore we justly love Him.

It is better for a man to be silent and be [a Christian], than to talk and not to be one. "The kingdom of God is not in word, but in power."(17) Men "believe with the heart, and confess with the mouth," the one "unto righteousness," the other "unto salvation."(18) It is good to teach, if he who speaks also acts. For he who shall both "do and teach, the same shall be great in the kingdom."(19) Our Lord and God, Jesus Christ, the Son of the living God, first did and then taught, as Luke testifies, "whose praise is in the Gospel through all the Churches."(1) There is nothing which is hid from the Lord, but our very secrets are near to Him. Let us therefore do all things as those who have Him dwelling in us, that we may be His temples,(2) and He may be in us as God. Let Christ speak in us, even as He did in Paul. Let the Holy Spirit teach us to speak the things of Christ in like manner as He did.

CHAP. XVI. -- THE FATE OF FALSE TEACHERS.

Do not err, my brethren.(3) Those that corrupt families shall not inherit the kingdom of God.(4) If, then, those who do this as respects the flesh have suffered death, how much more shall this be the case with anyone who corrupts by wicked doctrine the faith of God, for which Jesus Christ was crucified! Such an one becoming defiled [in this way], shall go away into everlasting fire, and so shall every one that hearkens unto him.

Do not err, my brethren.(3) Those that corrupt families shall not inherit the kingdom of God.(4) And if those that corrupt mere human families are condemned to death, how much more shall those suffer everlasting punishment who endeavour to corrupt the Church of Christ, for which the Lord Jesus, the only-begotten Son of God, endured the cross, and submitted to death! Whosoever, "being waxen fat,"(5) and "become gross," sets at nought His doctrine, shall go into hell. In like manner, every one that has received from God the power of distinguishing, and yet follows an unskilful shepherd, and receives a false opinion for the truth, shall be punished. "What communion hath light with darkness? or Christ with Belial? Or what portion hath he that believeth with an infidel? or the temple of God with idols?"(6) And in like manner say I, what communion hath truth with falsehood? or righteousness with unrighteousness? or true doctrine with that which is false?

CHAP. XVII. -- BEWARE OF FALSE DOCTRINES.

For this end did the Lord suffer the ointment to be poured upon His head,(7) that He might breathe immortality into His Church. Be not ye anointed with the bad odour of the doctrine of the prince of this world; let him not lead you away captive from the life which is set before you. And why are we not all prudent, since we have received the knowledge of God, which is Jesus Christ? Why do we foolishly perish, not recognising the gift which the Lord has of a truth sent to us?

For this end did the Lord suffer the ointment to be poured upon His head,(7) that His Church might breathe forth immortality. For saith [the Scripture], "Thy name is as ointment poured forth; therefore have the virgins loved Thee; they have drawn Thee; at the odour of Thine ointments we will run after Thee."(8) Let no one be anointed with the bad odour of the doctrine of [the prince of] this world; let not the holy Church of God be led captive by his subtlety, as was the first woman.(9) Why do we not, as gifted with reason, act wisely? When we had received from Christ, and had grafted in us the faculty of judging concerning God, why do we fall headlong into ignorance? and why, through a careless neglect of acknowledging the gift which we have received, do we foolishly perish?
CHAP. XVIII. -- THE GLORY OF THE CROSS.

Let my spirit be counted as nothing(10) for the sake of the cross, which is a stumbling-block" to those that do not believe, but to us salvation and life eternal. "Where is the wise man? where the disputer?" (1) Where is the boasting of those who are styled prudent? For our God, Jesus Christ, was, according to the appointment(3) of God, conceived in the womb by Mary, of the seed of David, but by the Holy Ghost. He was born and baptized, that by His passion He might purify the water.

The cross of Christ is indeed a stumbling-block to those that do not believe, but to the believing it is salvation and life eternal. "Where is the wise man? where the disputer?"(13) Where is the boasting of those who are called mighty? For the Son of God, who was begotten before time began(2), and established all things according to the will of the Father, He was conceived in the womb of Mary, according to the appointment of God, of the seed of David, and by the Holy Ghost. For says [the Scripture], "Behold, a virgin shall be with child, and shall bring forth a son, and He shall be called Immanuel."(4) He was born and was baptized by John, that He might ratify the institution committed to that prophet.

CHAP. XIX. -- THREE CELEBRATED MYSTERIES.

Now the virginity of Mary was hidden from the prince of this world, as was also her offspring, and the death of the Lord; three mysteries of renown,(5) which were wrought in silence by(6) God. How, then, was He manifested to the world?(7) A star shone forth in heaven above all the other stars, the light of Which was inexpressible, while its novelty struck men with astonishment. And all the rest of the stars, with the sun and moon, formed a chorus to this star, and its light was exceedingly great above them all. And there was agitation felt as to whence this new spectacle came, so unlike to everything else [in the heavens]. Hence every kind of magic was destroyed, and every bond of wickedness disappeared; ignorance was removed, and the old kingdom abolished, God Himself being manifested in human form for the renewal of eternal life. And now that took a beginning which had been prepared by God. Henceforth all things were in a state of tumult, because He meditated the abolition of death.

Now the virginity of Mary was hidden from the prince of this world, as was also her offspring, and the death of the Lord; three mysteries of renown,(5) which were wrought in silence, but have been revealed to us. A star shone forth in heaven above all that were before it, and its light was inexpressible, while its novelty struck men with astonishment. And all the rest of the stars, with the sun and moon, formed a chorus to this star. It far exceeded them all in brightness, and agitation was felt as to whence this new spectacle [proceeded]. Hence worldly wisdom became folly; conjuration was seen to be mere trifling; and magic became utterly ridiculous. Every law(8) of wickedness vanished away; the darkness of ignorance was dispersed; and tyrannical authority was destroyed, God being manifested as a man, and man displaying power as God. But neither was the former a mere imagination,(9) nor did the second imply a bare humanity;(10) but the one was absolutely true," and the other an economical arrangement.(12) Now that received a beginning which was perfected by God.(13) Henceforth all things were in a state of tumult, because He meditated the abolition of death.

CHAP. XX.--PROMISE OF ANOTHER LETTER.

If Jesus Christ shall graciously permit me through your prayers, and if it be His will, I shall, in a second little work which I will write to you, make further manifest to you [the nature of] the dispensation of which I have begun [to treat], with respect to the new man, Jesus Christ, in His faith and in His love, in His suffering and in His resurrection. Especially [will I do this 14] if the Lord make known to me that ye come together, man by man, in common through grace, individually,(1) in one faith, and in Jesus Christ, who was of the seed of David according to the flesh, being both the Son of man and the Son of God, so that ye obey the bishop and the presbytery with an undivided mind, breaking one and the same bread, which is the medicine of immortality, and the antidote to prevent us from dying, but [which causes] that we should live forever in Jesus Christ.

CHAP. XX. -- EXHORTATIONS TO STEDFASTNESS AND UNITY.

Stand fast, brethren, in the faith of Jesus Christ, and in His love, in His passion, and in His resurrection. Do ye all come together in common, and individually,(15) through grace, in one faith of God the Father, and of Jesus Christ His only-begotten Son, and "the first-born of every creature,"(16) but of the seed of David according to the flesh, being under the guidance of the Comforter, in obedience to the bishop and the presbytery with an undivided mind, breaking one and the same bread, which is the medicine of immortality, and the antidote which prevents us from dying, but a cleansing remedy driving away evil, [which causes] that we should live in God through Jesus Christ.

CHAP. XXI.--CONCLUSION.

My soul be for yours and theirs(2) whom, for the honour of God, ye have sent to Smyrna; whence also I write to you, giving thanks unto the Lord, and loving Polycarp even as I do you. Remember me, as Jesus Christ also remembered you. Pray ye for the Church which is in Syria, whence I am led bound to Rome, being the last of the faithful who are there, even as I have been thought worthy to be chosen(4) to show forth the honour of God. Farewell in God the Father, and in Jesus Christ, our common hope.

My soul be for yours and theirs(2) whom, for the honour of God, ye have sent to Smyrna; whence also I write to you, giving thanks to the Lord, and loving Polycarp even as I do you. Remember me, as Jesus Christ also remembers you, who is blessed for evermore. Pray ye for the Church of Antioch which is in Syria, whence I am led bound to Rome, being the last of the faithful that are there, who(3) yet have been thought worthy to carry these chains to the honour of God. Fare ye well in God the Father, and the Lord Jesus Christ, our common hope, and in the Holy Ghost. Fare ye well. Amen. Grace [be with you].(5)

THE EPISTLE OF IGNATIUS TO THE MAGNESIANS SHORTER AND LONGER VERSIONS

Ignatius, who is also called Theophorus, to the [Church] blessed in the grace of God the Father, in Jesus Christ our Saviour, in whom I salute the Church, which is at Magnesia, near the Moeander, and wish it abundance of happiness in God the father, and in Jesus Christ.

Ignatius, who is also called Theophorus, to the [Church] blessed in the grace of God the Father, in Jesus Christ our Saviour, in whom I salute the Church, which is at Magnesia, near the Moeander, and wish it abundance of happiness in God the Father, and in Jesus Christ, our Lord, in whom may you have abundance of happiness.

CHAP. I. -- REASON OF WRITING THE EPISTLE.

HAVING been informed of your godly(1) love, so well-ordered, I rejoiced greatly, and determined to commune with you in the faith of Jesus Christ. For as one who has been thought worthy of the most honourable of all names,(2) in those bonds which I bear about, I commend the Churches, in which I pray for a union both of the flesh and spirit of Jesus Christ, the constant source of our life, and of faith and love, to which nothing is to be preferred, but especially of Jesus and the Father, in whom, if we endure all the assaults of the prince of this world, and escape them, we shall enjoy God.

HAVING been informed of your godly(1) love, so well-ordered, I rejoiced greatly, and determined to commune with you in the faith of Jesus Christ. For as one who has been thought worthy of a divine and desirable name, in those bonds which I bear about, I commend the Churches, in which I pray for a union both of the flesh and spirit of Jesus Christ, "who is the Saviour of all men, but specially of them that believe;"(3) by whose blood ye were redeemed; by whom ye have known God, or rather have been known by Him;(4) in whom enduring, ye shall escape all the assaults of this world: for "He is faithful, who will not suffer you to be tempted above that which ye are able."(5)

CHAP. II. -- I REJOICE IN YOUR MESSENGERS.

Since, then, I have had the privilege of seeing you, through Damas your most worthy bishop, and through your worthy presbyters Bassus and Apollonius, and through my fellow-servant the deacon Sotio, whose friendship may I ever enjoy, inasmuch as he is subject to the bishop as to the grace of God, and to the presbytery as to the law of Jesus Christ, [I now write(8) to you].

Since, then, I have had the privilege of seeing you, through Damas your most worthy(6) bishop, and through your worthy(6) presbyters Bassus and Apollonius, and through my fellow-servant the deacon Sotio, whose friendship may I ever enjoy,(7) inasmuch as he, by the grace of God, is subject to the bishop and presbytery, in the law of Jesus Christ, [I now write s to you].

CHAP. III. -- HONOUR YOUR YOUTHFUL BISHOP.

Now it becomes you also not to treat your bishop too familiarly on account of his youth,(1) but to yield him all reverence, having respect to(2) the power of God the Father, as I have known even holy presbyters do, not judging rashly, from the manifest youthful appearance(3) [of their bishop], but as being themselves prudent in God, submitting to him, or rather not to him, but to the Father of Jesus Christ, the

bishop of us all. It is therefore fitting that you should, after no hypocritical fashion, obey [your bishop], in honour of Him who has wired us [so to do], since he that does not so deceives not [by such conduct] the bishop that is visible, but seeks to mock Him that is invisible. And all such conduct has reference not to man,(10) but to God, who knows all secrets.

Now it becomes you also not to despise the age of your bishop, but to yield him all reverence, according to the will of God the Father, as I have known even holy presbyters do, not having regard to the manifest youth [of their bishop], but to his knowledge in God; inasmuch as "not the ancient are [necessarily] wise, nor do the aged understand prudence; but there is a spirit in men."(4) For Daniel the wise, at twelve years of age, became possessed of the divine Spirit, and convicted the elders, who in vain carried their grey hairs, of being false accusers, and of lusting after the beauty of another man's wife.(5) Samuel also, when he was but a little child, reproved Eli, who was ninety years old, for giving honour to his sons rather than to God.(6) In like manner, Jeremiah also received this message from God, "Say not, I am a child."(7) Solomon too, and Josiah, [exemplified the same thing.] The former, being made king at twelve years of age, gave that terrible and difficult judgment in the case of the two women concerning their children.(8) The latter, coming to the throne when eight years old(9) cast down the altars and temples [of the idols], and burned down the groves, for they were dedicated to demons, and not to God. And he slew the false priests, as the corrupters and deceivers of men, and not the worshippers of the Deity. Wherefore youth is not to be despised when it is devoted to God. But he is to be despised who is of a wicked mind, although he be old, and full of wicked days.(11) Timothy the Christ- bearer was young, but hear what his teacher writes to him: "Let no man despise try youth, but be thou an example of the believers in word and in conduct."(12) It is becoming, therefore, that ye also should be obedient to your bishop, and contradict him in nothing; for it is a fearful thing to contradict any such person. For no one does [by such conduct] deceive him that is visible, but does [in reality] seek to mock Him that is invisible, who, however, cannot be mocked by anyone. And every such act has respect not to man, but to God. For God says to Samuel, "They have not mocked thee, but Me."(13) And Moses declares, "For their murmuring is not against us, but against the Lord God."(14) No one of those has, [in fact,] remained unpunished, who rose up against their superiors. For Dathan and Abiram did not speak against the law, but against Moses,(15) and were cast down alive into Hades. Korah also,(16) and the two hundred and fifty who conspired with him against Aaron, were destroyed by fire. Absalom, again,(17) who had slain his brother, became suspended on a tree, and had his evil-designing heart thrust through with darts. In like manner was Abeddadan(18) beheaded for the same reason. Uzziah,(19) when he presumed to oppose the priests and the priesthood, was smitten with leprosy. Saul also was dishonoured,(20) because he did not wait for Samuel the high priest. It behoves you, therefore, also to reverence your superiors.

CHAP, IV. -- SOME WICKEDLY ACT INDEPENDENTLY OF THE BISHOP.

It is fitting, then, not only to be called Christians, but to be so in reality: as some indeed give one the title of bishop, but do all things without him. Now such persons seem to me to be not possessed of a good conscience, seeing they are not stedfastly gathered together according to the commandment.

It is fitting, then, not only to be called Christians, but to be so in reality. For it is not the being called so, but the being really so, that renders a man blessed. To those who indeed talk of the bishop, but do all things without him, will He who is the true and first Bishop, and the only High Priest by nature, declare, "Why call ye Me Lord, and do not the things which I say ?"[1] For such persons seem to me not possessed of a good conscience, but to be simply dissemblers and hypocrites.

CHAP. V. -- DEATH IS THE FATE OF ALL SUCH.

Seeing, then, all things have an end, these two things are simultaneously set before us--death and life; and everyone shall go unto his own place. For as there are two kinds of coins, the one of God, the other of the world, and each of these has its special character stamped upon it,[so is it also here.][2] The unbelieving are of this world; but the believing have, in love, the character of God the Father by Jesus Christ, by whom, if we are not in readiness to die into His passion,[3] His life is not in us.

Seeing, then, all things have an end, and there is set before us life upon our observance[of God's precepts], but death as the result of disobedience, and every one, according to the choice he makes, shall go to his own place, let us flee from death, and make choice of life. For I remark, that two different characters are found among men--the one true coin, the other spurious. The truly devout man is the right kind of coin, stamped by God Himself. The ungodly man, again, is false coin, unlawful, spurious, counterfeit, wrought not by God, but by the devil. I do not mean to say that there are two different human natures, but that there is one humanity, sometimes belonging to God, and sometimes to the devil. If anyone is truly religious, he is a man of God; but if he is irreligious, he is a man of the devil, made such, not by nature, but by his own choice. The unbelieving bear the image of the prince of

wickedness. The believing possess the image of their Prince, God the Father, and Jesus Christ, through whom, if we are not in readiness to die for the truth into His passion,[3] His life is not in us.

CHAP. VI. -- PRESERVE HARMONY.

Since therefore I have, in the persons before mentioned, beheld the whole multitude of you in faith and love, I exhort you to study to do all things with a divine harmony,[4] while your bishop presides in the place of God, and your presbyters in the place of the assembly of the apostles, along with your deacons, who are most dear to me, and are entrusted with the ministry of Jesus Christ, who was with the Father before the beginning of time,[5] and in the end was revealed. Do ye all then, imitating the same divine conduct,[7] pay respect to one another, and let no one look upon his neighbour after the flesh, but do ye continually love each other in Jesus Christ. Let nothing exist among you that may divide you; but be ye united with your bishop, and those that preside over you, as a type and evidence of your immortality.[8]

Since therefore I have, in the persons before mentioned, beheld the whole multitude of you in faith and love, I exhort you to study to do all things with a divine harmony,[4] while your bishop presides in the place of God, and your presbyters in the place of the assembly of the apostles, along with your deacons, who are most dear to me, and are entrusted with the ministry of Jesus Christ. He, being begotten by the Father before the beginning of time,[5] was God the Word, the only-begotten Son, and remains the same for ever; for "of His kingdom there shall be no end,"[6] says Daniel the prophet. Let us all therefore love one another in harmony, and let no one look upon his neighbour according to the flesh, but in Christ Jesus. Let nothing exist among you which may divide you; but be ye united with your bishop, being through him subject to God in Christ.

CHAP. VII. -- DO NOTHING WITHOUT THE BISHOP AND PRESBYTERS.

As therefore the Lord did nothing without the Father, being united to Him, neither by Himself nor by the apostles, so neither do ye anything without the bishop and presbyters. Neither endeavour that anything appear reasonable and proper to yourselves apart; but being come together into the same place, let there be one prayer, one supplication, one mind, one hope, in love and in joy undefiled. There is one Jesus Christ, than whom nothing is more excellent. Do ye therefore all run together as into one temple of God, as to one altar, as to one Jesus Christ, who came forth from one Father, and is with and has gone to one.

As therefore the Lord does nothing without the Father, for says He, "I can of mine own self do nothing,"[1] so do ye, neither presbyter, nor deacon, nor layman, do anything without the bishop. Nor let anything appear commendable to you which is destitute of his approval.[2] For every such thing is sinful, and opposed[to the will of] God. Do ye all come together into the same place for prayer. Let there be one common supplication, one mind, one hope, with faith unblameable in Christ Jesus, than which nothing is more excellent. Do ye all, as one man, run together into the temple of God, as unto one altar, to one Jesus Christ, the High Priest of the unbegotten God.

CHAP, VIII. -- CAUTION AGAINST FALSE DOCTRINES.

Be not deceived with strange doctrines, nor with old fables, which are unprofitable. For if we still live according to the Jewish law, we acknowledge that we have not received grace. For the divinest prophets lived according to Christ Jesus. On this account also they were persecuted, being inspired by His grace to fully convince the unbelieving that there is one God, who has manifested Himself by Jesus Christ His Son, who is His eternal Word, not proceeding forth from silence,[5] and who in all things pleased Him that sent Him.

Be not deceived with strange doctrines, "nor give heed to fables and endless genealogies,"[3] and things in which the Jews make their boast. "Old things are passed away: behold, all things have become new."[4] For if we still live according to the Jewish law, and the circumcision of the flesh, we deny that we have received grace. For the divinest prophets lived according to Jesus Christ. On this account also they were persecuted, being inspired by grace to fully convince the unbelieving that there is one God, the Almighty, who has manifested Himself by Jesus Christ His Son, who is His Word, not spoken, but essential. For He is not the voice of an articulate utterance, but a substance begotten by divine power, who has in all things pleased Him that sent Him.[6]

CHAP. IX. -- LET US LIVE WITH CHRIST.

If, therefore, those who were brought up in the ancient order of things[7] have come to the possession of a new[8] hope, no longer observing the Sabbath, but living in the observance[10] of the Lord's Day, on which also our life has sprung up again by Him and by His death--whom some deny, by which mystery we have obtained faith,[12] and therefore endure, that we may be found the disciples of Jesus Christ, our only Master--how shall we be able to live apart from Him, whose disciples the prophets themselves in the Spirit did wait for Him as their Teacher? And therefore He whom they rightly waited for, being come, raised them from the dead.[16]

If, then, those who were conversant with the ancient Scriptures came to newness of hope, expecting the coming of Christ, as the Lord teaches us when He says, "If ye had believed Moses, ye would have believed Me, for he wrote of Me;"[9] and again, "Your father Abraham rejoiced to see My day, and he saw it, and was glad; for before Abraham was, I am; "[11] how shall we be able to live without Him? The prophets were His servants, and foresaw Him by the Spirit, and waited for Him as their Teacher, and expected Him as their Lord and Saviour, saying, "He will come and save us."[13] Let us therefore no longer keep the Sabbath after the Jewish manner, and rejoice in days of idleness; for "he that does not work, let him not eat."[14] For say the[holy] oracles, "In the sweat of thy face shalt thou eat thy bread."[15] But let every one of you keep the Sabbath after a spiritual manner, rejoicing in meditation on the law, not in relaxation of the body, admiring the workmanship of God, and not eating things prepared the day before, nor using lukewarm drinks, and walking within a prescribed space, nor finding delight in dancing and plaudits which have no sense in them.[1] And after the observance of the Sabbath, let every friend of Christ keep the Lord's Day as a festival, the resurrection-day, the queen and chief of all the days[of the week]. Looking forward to this, the prophet declared, "To the end, for the eighth day,"[2] on which our life both sprang up again, and the victory over death was obtained in Christ, whom the children of perdition, the enemies of the Saviour, deny, "whose god is their belly, who mind earthly things,"[3] who are "lovers of pleasure, and not lovers of God, having a form of godliness, but denying the power thereof."[4] These make merchandise of Christ, corrupting His word, and giving up Jesus to sale: they are corrupters of women, and covetous of other men's possessions, swallowing up wealth[5] insatiably; from whom may ye be delivered by the mercy of God through our Lord Jesus Christ!

CHAP. X. -- BEWARE OF JUDAIZING.

Let us not, therefore, be insensible to His kindness. For were He to reward us according to our works, we should cease to be. Therefore, having become His disciples, let us learn to live according to the principles of Christianity.[7] For whosoever is called by any other name besides this, is not of God. Lay aside, therefore, the evil, the old, the sour leaven, and be ye changed into the new leaven, which is Jesus Christ. Be ye salted in Him, lest anyone among you should be corrupted, since by your savour ye shall be convicted. It is absurd to profess[12] Christ Jesus, and to Judaize. For Christianity did not embrace[13] Judaism, but Judaism Christianity, that so every tongue which believeth might be gathered together to God.

Let us not, therefore, be insensible to His kindness. For were He to reward us according to our works, we should cease to be. For "if Thou, Lord, shalt mark iniquities, O Lord, who shall stand?"[6] Let us therefore prove ourselves worthy of that name which we have received. For whosoever is called by any other name besides this, he is not of God; for he has not received the prophecy which speaks thus concerning us: "The people shall be called by a new name, which the Lord shall name them, and shall be a holy people."[8] This was first fulfilled in Syria; for "the disciples were called Christians at Antioch,"[9] when Paul and Peter were laying the foundations of the Church. Lay aside, therefore, the evil, the old, the corrupt leaven,[10] and be ye changed into the new leaven of grace. Abide in Christ, that the stranger[11] may not have dominion over you. It is absurd to speak of Jesus Christ with the tongue, and to cherish in the mind a Judaism which has now come to an end. For where there is Christianity there cannot be Judaism. For Christ is one, in whom every nation that believes, and every tongue that confesses, is gathered unto God. And those that were of a stony heart have become the children of Abraham, the friend of God;[14] and in his seed all those have been blessed[15] who were ordained to eternal life[16] in Christ.

CHAP. XI. -- I WRITE THESE THINGS TO WARN YOU.

These things[I address to you], my beloved, not that I know any of you to be in such a state;[17] but, as less than any of you, I desire to guard you beforehand, that ye fall not upon the hooks of vain doctrine, but that ye attain to full assurance in regard to the birth, and passion, and resurrection which took place in the time of the government of Pontius Pilate, being truly and certainly accomplished by Jesus Christ, who is our hope,[1] from which may no one of you ever be turned aside.

These things[I address to you], my beloved, not that I know any of you to be in such a state;[17] but, as less than any of you, I desire to guard you beforehand, that ye fall not upon the hooks of vain doctrine, but that you may rather attain to a full assurance in Christ, who was begotten by the Father before all ages, but was afterwards born of the Virgin Mary without any intercourse with man. He also lived a holy life, and healed every kind of sickness and disease among the people, and wrought signs and wonders for the benefit of men; and to those who had fallen into the error of polytheism He made known the one and only true God, His Father, and underwent the passion, and endured the cross at the hands of the Christ- killing Jews, under Pontius Pilate the governor and Herod the king. He also died, and rose again, and ascended into the heavens to Him that sent Him, and is sat down at His right hand, and shall come at the end of the world, with His Father's glory, to judge the living and the dead, and to render to every one according to his

works.[2] He who knows these things with a full assurance, and believes them, is happy; even as ye are now the lovers of God and of Christ, in the full assurance of our hope, from which may no one of us[3] ever be turned aside!

CHAP. XII.--YE ARE SUPERIOR TO ME.

May I enjoy you in all respects, if indeed I be worthy! For though I am bound, I am not worthy to be compared to any of you that are at liberty. I know that ye are not puffed up, for ye have Jesus Christ in yourselves. And all the more when I commend you, I know that ye cherish modesty[4] of spirit; as it is written, "The righteous man is his own accuser." [5]

May I enjoy you in all respects, if indeed I be worthy! For though I am bound, I am not worthy to be compared to one of you that are at liberty. I know that ye are not puffed up, for ye have Jesus in yourselves. And all the more when I commend you, I know that ye cherish modesty[4] of spirit; as it is written, "The righteous man is his own accuser;"[5] and again, "Declare thou first thine iniquities, that thou mayest be justified;"[6] and again, "When ye shall have done all things that are commanded you, say, We are unprofitable servants;"[7] "for that which is highly esteemed among men is abomination in the sight of God."[8] For says[the Scripture], "God be merciful to me a sinner."[9] Therefore those great ones, Abraham and Job,[10] styled themselves "dust and ashes[11] before God. And David says, "Who am I before Thee, 0 Lord, that Thou hast glorified me hitherto?"[12] And Moses, who was "the meekest of all men,"[13] saith to God, "I am of a feeble voice, and of a slow tongue."[14] Be ye therefore also of a humble spirit, that ye may be exalted; for "he that abaseth himself shall be exalted, and he that exalteth himself shall be abased."[15]]

CHAP. XIII.--BE ESTABLISHED IN FAITH AND UNITY.

Study, therefore, to be established in the doctrines of the Lord and the apostles, that so all things, whatsoever ye do, may prosper both in the flesh and spirit; in faith and love; in the Son, and in the Father, and in the Spirit; in the beginning and in the end; with your most admirable bishop, and the well-compacted spiritual crown of your presbytery, and the deacons who are according to God. Be ye subject to the bishop, and to one another, as Jesus Christ to the Father, according to the flesh, and the apostles to Christ, and to the Father, and to the Spirit; that so there may be a union both fleshly and spiritual.

Study, therefore, to be established in the doctrines of the Lord and the apostles, that so all things, whatsoever ye do, may prosper, both in the flesh and spirit, in faith and love, with your most admirable bishop, and the well-compacted[16] spiritual crown of your presbytery, and the deacons who are according to God. Be ye subject to the bishop, and to one another, as Christ to the Father. that there may be a unity according to God among you.

CHAP. XIV.--YOUR PRAYERS REQUESTED.

Knowing as I do that ye are full of God, I have but briefly exhorted you. Be mindful of me in your prayers, that I may attain to God; and of the Church which is in Syria, whence I am not worthy to derive my name: for I stand in need of your united prayer in God, and your love, that the Church which is in Syria may be "deemed worthy of being refreshed[2] by your Church.

Knowing as I do that ye are full of all good, I have but briefly exhorted you in the love of Jesus Christ. Be mindful of me in your prayers, that I may attain to God; and of the Church which is in Syria, of whom I am not worthy to be called bishop. For I stand in need of your united prayer in God, and of your love, that the Church which is in Syria may be deemed worthy, by your good order, of being edified[1] in Christ.

CHAP. XV.--SALUTATIONS.

The Ephesians from Smyrna (whence I also write to you), who are here for the glory of God, as ye also are, who have in all things refreshed me, salute you, along with Polycarp, the bishop of the Smyrnaeans. The rest of the Churches, in honour of Jesus Christ, also salute you. Fare ye well in the harmony of God, ye who have obtained the inseparable Spirit, who is Jesus Christ.

The Ephesians from Smyrna (whence I also write to you), who are here for the glory of God, as ye also are, who have in all things refreshed me, salute you, as does also Polycarp. The rest of the Churches, in honour of Jesus Christ, also salute you. Fare ye well in harmony, ye who have obtained the inseparable Spirit, in Christ Jesus, by the will of God.

THE EPISTLE OF IGNATIUS TO THE TRALLIANS SHORTER AND LONGER VERSIONS

Ignatius, who is also called Theophorus, to the holy Church which is at Tralles, in Asia, beloved of God, the Father of Jesus Christ, elect, and worthy of God, possessing peace through the flesh, and blood, and passion of Jesus Christ, who is our hope, through our rising again to Him,[1] which

also I salute in its fulness,[2] and in the apostolical character,[3] and wish abundance of happiness.

Ignatius, who is also called Theophorus, to the holy Church which is at Tralles, beloved by God the Rather, and Jesus Christ, elect, and worthy of God, possessing peace through the flesh and Spirit of Jesus Christ, who is our hope, in His passion by the cross and death, and in His resurrection, which also I salute in its fulness,[2] and in the apostolical character,[3] and wish abundance of happiness.

CHAP. I. -- ACKNOWLEDGMENT OF THEIR EXCELLENCE.

I know that ye possess an unblameable and sincere mind in patience, and that not only in present practice,[5] but according to inherent nature, as Polybius your bishop has shown me, who has come to Smyrna by the will of God and Jesus Christ, and so sympathized in the joy which I, who am bound in Christ Jesus, possess, that I beheld your whole multitude in him. Having therefore received through him the testimony of your good-will, according to God, I gloried to find you, as I knew you were, the followers of God.

I know that ye possess an unblameable and sincere mind in patience, and that not only for present use,[4] but as a permanent possession, as Polybius your bishop has shown me, who has come to Smyrna by the will of God the Father, and the Lord Jesus Christ, His Son, with the cooperation of the Spirit, and so sympathized in the joy which I, who am bound in Christ Jesus, possess, that I beheld your whole multitude in Him. Having therefore received through him the testimony of your good-will according to God, I gloried to find that you were the followers of Jesus Christ the Saviour.

CHAP. II. -- BE SUBJECT TO THE BISHOP, ETC.

For, since ye are subject to the bishop as to Jesus Christ, ye appear to me to live not after the manner of men, but according to Jesus Christ, who died for us, in order, by believing in His death, ye may escape from death. It is therefore necessary that, as ye indeed do, so without the bishop ye should do nothing, but should also our hope, in whom, if we live, we shall be found in Him. It behoves you also, in every way, to please the deacons, who are [ministers] of the mysteries of Christ Jesus; for they are not ministers of meat and drink, but servants of the Church of God. They are bound, therefore, to avoid all grounds of accusation [against them], as they would a burning fire. Let them, then, prove themselves to be such.

Be ye subject to the bishop as to the Lord, for "he watches for your souls, as one that shall give account to God."[6] Wherefore also, ye appear to me to live not after the manner of men, but according to Jesus Christ, who died for us, in order that, by believing in His death, ye may by baptism be made partakers of His resurrection. It is therefore necessary, whatsoever things ye do, to do nothing without the bishop. And be ye subject also to the presbytery, as to the apostles of Jesus Christ, who is be subject to the presbytery, as to the apostle of Jesus Christ, who is our hope, in whom, if we live, we shall [at last] be found. It is fitting also that the deacons, as being [the ministers] of the mysteries of Jesus Christ, should in every respect be pleasing to all.(1) For they are not ministers of meat and drink, but servants of the Church of God. They are bound, therefore, to avoid all grounds of accusation [against them], as they would do fire.

CHAP. III. -- HONOUR THE DEACONS, etc.

In like manner, let all reverence the deacons as an appointment(2) of Jesus Christ, and the bishop as Jesus Christ, who is the Son of the Father, and the presbyters as the sanhedrin of God, and assembly of the apostles. Apart from these, there is no Church.(4) Concerning all this, I am persuaded that ye are of the same opinion. For I have received the manifestations of your love, and still have it with me, in your bishop, whose very appearance is highly instructive,(6) and his meekness of itself a power; whom I imagine even the ungodly must reverence, seeing they are (7) also pleased that I do not spare myself. But shall I, when permitted to write on this point, reach such a height of self-esteem, that though being a condemned(8) man, I should issue commands to you as if I were an apostle?

And do ye reverence them as Christ Jesus, of whose place they are the keepers, even as the bishop is the representative of the Father of all things, and the presbyters are the sanhedrim of God, and assembly(3) of the apostles of Christ. Apart from these there is no elect Church, no congregation of holy ones, no assembly of saints. I am persuaded that ye also are of this opinion. For I have received the manifestation s of your love, and still have it with me, in your bishop, whose very appearance is highly instructive, and his meekness of itself a power; whom I imagine even the ungodly must reverence. Loving you as I do, I avoid writing in any severer strain to you, that I may not seem harsh to any, or wanting [in tenderness]. I am indeed bound for the sake of Christ, but I am not yet worthy of Christ. But when I am perfected, perhaps I shall then become so. I do not issue orders like an apostle.

CHAP. IV. -- I HAVE NEED OF HUMILITY.

I have great knowledge in God,(9) but I restrain myself, lest, I should perish through boasting. For now it is needful for me to be the more fearful; and not give heed to those that puff me up. For they that speak to me [in the way of commendation] scourge me. For I do indeed desire to suffer, but I know not if I be worthy to do so. For this longing, though it is not manifest to many, all the more vehemently assails me.(13) I therefore have need of meekness, by which the prince of this world is brought to nought.

But I measure myself, that I may not perish through boasting: but it is good to glory in the Lord.(10) And even though I were established(11) in things pertaining to God, yet then would it befit me to be the more fearful, and not give heed to those that vainly puff me up. For those that commend me scourge me. [I do indeed desire to suffer(12)], but I know not if I be worthy to do so. For the envy of the wicked one is not visible to many, but it wars against me. I therefore have need of meekness, by which the devil, the prince of this world, is brought to nought.

CHAP. V. -- I WILL NOT TEACH YOU PROFOUND DOCTRINES.

Am I not able to write to you of heavenly things? But I fear to do so, lest I should inflict injury on you who are but babes [in Christ]. Pardon me in this respect, lest, as not being able to receive [such doctrines], ye should be strangled by them. For even I, though I am bound [for Christ], yet am not on that account able to understand heavenly things, and the places(4) of the angels, and their gatherings under their respective princes, things visible and invisible. Without reference to such abstruse subjects, I am still but a learner [in other respects(5)]; for many things are wanting to us, that we come not short of God.

For might(1) not I write to you things more full of mystery? But I fear to do so, lest I should inflict injury on you who are but babes [in Christ]. Pardon me in this respect, lest, as not being able to receive their weighty import,(2) ye should be strangled by them. For even I, though I am bound [for Christ], and am able to understand heavenly things, the angelic orders, and the different sorts(3) of angels and hosts, the distinctions between powers and dominions, and the diversities between thrones and authorities, the mightiness of the Aeons, and the pre-eminence of the cherubim and seraphim, the sublimity of the spirit, the kingdom of the Lord, and above all, the incomparable majesty of Almighty God--though I am acquainted with these things, yet am I not therefore by any means perfect; nor am I such a disciple as Paul or Peter. For many things are yet wanting to me, that I may not fall short of God.

CHAP. VI. -- ABSTAIN FROM THE POISON OF HERETICS.

I therefore, yet not I, but the love of Jesus Christ, entreat you that ye use Christian nourishment only, and abstain from herbage of a different kind; I mean heresy. For those(7) [that are given to this] mix(11) up Jesus Christ with their own poison, speaking things which are unworthy of credit, like those who administer a deadly drug in sweet wine, which he who is ignorant of does greedily(13) take, with a fatal pleasure(14) leading to his own death.

I therefore, yet not I, out the love of Jesus Christ, "entreat you that ye all speak the same thing, and that there be no divisions among you; but that ye be perfectly joined together in the same mind, and in the same judgment."(6) For there are some vain talkers(8) and deceivers, not Christians, but Christ-betrayers,(9) bearing about the name of Christ in deceit, and "corrupting the word"(10) of the Gospel; while they intermix the poison of their deceit with their persuasive talk,(12) as if they mingled aconite with sweet wine, that so he who drinks, being deceived in his taste by the very great sweetness of the draught, may incautiously meet with his death. One of the ancients gives us this advice, "Let no man be called good who mixes good with evil."(15) For they speak of Christ, not that they may preach Christ, but that they may reject Christ; and they speak(16) of the law, not that they may establish the law, but that they may proclaim things contrary to it. For they alienate Christ from the Father, and the law from Christ. They also calumniate His being born of the Virgin; they are ashamed of His cross; they deny His passion; and they do not believe His resurrection. They introduce God as a Being unknown; they suppose Christ to be unbegotten; and as to the Spirit, they do not admit that He exists. Some of them say that the Son is a mere man, and that the Father, Son, and Holy Spirit are but the same person, and that the creation is the work of God, not by Christ, but by some other strange power.

CHAP. VII. -- THE SAME CONTINUED.

Be on your guard, therefore, against such persons. And this will be the case with you if you are not puffed up, and continue in intimate union with(17) Jesus Christ our God, and the bishop, and the enactments of the apostles. He that is within the altar is pure, but(2) he that is without is not pure; that is, he who does anything apart from the bishop, and presbytery, and deacons,(4) such a man is not pure in his conscience.

Be on your guard, therefore, against such persons, that ye admit not of a snare for your own souls. And act so that your life shall be without offence to all men, lest ye become as "a snare upon a watch-tower, and as a net which is spread out."(18) For" he that does not heal himself in his own works, is the brother of him that destroys himself."(1) If, therefore, ye also put away

conceit, arrogance, disdain, and haughtiness, it will be your privilege to be inseparably united to God, for "He is nigh unto those that fear Him."(3) And says He, "Upon whom will I look, but upon him that is humble and quiet, and that trembles at my words?"(5) And do ye also reverence your bishop as Christ Himself, according as the blessed apostles have enjoined you. He that is within the altar is pure, wherefore also he is obedient to the bishop and presbyters: but he that is without is one that does anything apart from the bishop, the presbyters, and the deacons. Such a person is defiled in his conscience and is worse than an infidel. For what is the bishop but one who beyond all others possesses all power and authority, so far as it is possible for a man to possess it, who according to his ability has been made an imitator of the Christ Of God?(6) And what is the presbytery but a sacred assembly, the counsellors and assessors of the bishop? And what are the deacons but imitators of the angelic powers,(7) fulfilling a pure and blameless ministry unto him, as the holy Stephen did to the blessed James, Timothy and Linus to Paul, Anencletus and Clement to Peter? He, therefore, that will not yield obedience to such, must needs be one utterly without God, an impious man who despises Christ, and depreciates IIis appointments.

CHAP. VIII. -- BE ON YOUR GUARD AGAINST THE SNARES OF THE DEVIL.

Not that I Know there is anything of this kind among you; but I put you on your guard, inasmuch as I love you greatly, and foresee the snares of the devil. Wherefore, clothing(11) yourselves with meekness, be ye renewed(12) in faith, that is the flesh of the Lord, and in love, that is the blood of Jesus Christ. Let no one of you cherish any grudge against his neighbour. Give no occasion to the Gentiles, lest by means of a few foolish men the whole multitude [of those that believe] in God be evil spoken of. For, "Woe to him by whose vanity my name is blasphemed among any."(17)

Now I write these things unto you, not that I know there are any such persons among you; nay, indeed I hope that God will never permit any such report to reach my ears, He "who spared not His Son for the sake of His holy Church."(8) But foreseeing the snares of the wicked one, I arm you beforehand by my admonitions, as my beloved and faithful children in Christ, furnishing you with the means of protection(9) against the deadly disease of unruly men, by which do ye flee from the disease(10) [referred to] by the good-will of Christ our Lord. Do ye therefore, clothing(11) yourselves with meekness, become the imitators of His sufferings, and of His love, wherewith(13) He loved us when He gave Himself a ransom(14) for us, that He might cleanse us by His blood from our old ungodliness, and bestow life on us when we were almost on the point of perishing through the depravity that was in us. Let no one of you, therefore, cherish any grudge against his neighbour. For says our Lord, "Forgive, and it shall be forgiven unto you."(15) Give no occasion to the Gentiles, lest "by means of a few foolish men the word and doctrine [of Christ.] be blasphemed."(16) For says the prophet, as in the person of God, "Woe to him by whom my name is blasphemed among the Gentiles."(17)

CHAP. IX, -- REFERENCE TO THE HISTORY OF CHRIST.

Stop your ears, therefore, when anyone speaks to you at variance with(18) Jesus Christ, who was descended from David, and was also of Mary; who was truly born, and did eat and drink. He was truly persecuted under Pontius Pilate; He was truly crucified, and [truly] died, in the sight of beings in heaven, and on earth, and under the earth. He was also truly raised from the dead, His Father quickening Him, even as after the same manner His Father will so raise up us who believe in Him by Christ Jesus, apart from whom we do not possess the true life.

Stop your ears, therefore, when anyone speaks to you at variance with(18) Jesus Christ, the Son of God, who was descended from David, and was also of Mary; who was truly begotten of God and of the Virgin, but not after the same manner. For indeed God and man are not the same. He truly assumed a body; for "the Word was made flesh,"(1) and lived upon earth without sin. For says He, "Which of you convicteth me of sin?"(2) He did in reality both eat and drink. He was crucified and died under Pontius Pilate. He really, and not merely in appearance, was crucified, and died, in the sight of beings in heaven, and on earth, and under the earth. By those in heaven I mean such as are possessed of incorporeal natures; by those on earth, the Jews and Romans, and such persons as were present at that time when the Lord was crucified; and by those under the earth, the multitude that arose along with the Lord. For says the Scripture, "Many bodies of the saints that slept arose,"(3) their graves being opened. He descended, indeed, into Hades alone, but He arose accompanied by a multitude; and rent asunder that means(4) of separation which had existed from the beginning of the world, and cast down its partition-wall. He also rose again in three days, the Father raising Him up; and after spending forty days with the apostles, He was received up to the Father, and "sat down at His right hand, expecting till His enemies are placed under His feet."(5) On the day of the preparation, then, at the third hour, He received the sentence from Pilate, the Father permitting that to happen; at the sixth hour He was crucified; at the ninth hour He gave up the ghost; and before sunset He was buried.(6) During the Sabbath He continued under the earth in the tomb in which Joseph of Arimathaea had laid Him. At the dawning of the Lord's day He arose from the dead, according to what was spoken by Himself, "As Jonah was three days and three nights in the whale's belly, so shall the Son of man also be three days and three nights in the heart of the earth."(7) The day of the preparation, then, comprises the passion; the Sabbath embraces the burial; the Lord's Day contains the resurrection.

CHAP. X. -- THE REALITY OF CHRIST'S PASSION.

But if, as some that are without God, that is, the unbelieving, say, that He only seemed to suffer (they themselves only seeming to exist), then why am I in bonds? Why do I long to be exposed to s the wild beasts? Do I therefore die in vain?(9) Am I not then guilty of falsehood(10) against [the cross of] the Lord?

But if, as some that are without God, that is, the unbelieving, say, He became man in appearance [only], that He did not in reality take unto Him a body, that He died in appearance [merely], and did not in very deed suffer, then for what reason am I now in bonds, and long to be exposed to(8) the wild beasts? In such a case, I die in vain, and am guilty of falsehood(10) against the cross of the Lord. Then also does the prophet in vain declare, "They shall look on Him whom they have pierced, and mourn over themselves as over one beloved."(11) These men, therefore, are not less unbelievers than were those that crucified Him. But as for me, I do not place my hopes in one who died for me in appearance, but in reality. For that which is false is quite abhorrent to the truth. Mary then did truly conceive a body which had God inhabiting it. And God the Word was truly born of the Virgin, having clothed Himself with a body of like passions with our own. He who forms all men in the womb, was Himself really in the womb, and made for Himself a body of the seed of the Virgin, but without any intercourse of man. He was carried in the womb, even as we are, for the usual period of time; and was really born, as we also are; and was in reality nourished with milk, and partook of common meat and drink, even as we do. And when He had lived among men for thirty years, He was baptized by John, really and not in appearance; and when He had preached the Gospel three years, and done signs and wonders, He who was Himself the Judge was judged by the Jews, falsely so called, and by Pilate the governor; was scourged, was smitten on the cheek, was spit upon; He wore a crown of thorns and a purple robe; He was condemned: He was crucified in reality, and not in appearance, not in imagination, not in deceit. He really died, and was buried, and rose from the dead, even as He prayed in a certain place, saying, "But do Thou, O Lord, raise me up again, and I shall recompense them."(1) And the Father, who always hears Him,(2) answered and said, "Arise, O God, and judge the earth; for Thou shall receive all the heathen for Thine inheritance."(3) The Father, therefore, who raised Him up, will also raise us up through Him, apart from whom no one will attain to true life. For says He, "I am the life; he that believeth in me, even though he die, shall live: and every one that liveth and believeth in me, even though he die, shall live for ever."(4) Do ye therefore flee from these ungodly heresies; for they are the inventions of the devil, that serpent who was the author of evil, and who by means of the woman deceived Adam, the father of our race.

CHAP. XI. -- AVOID THE DEADLY ERRORS OF THE DOCETAE.

Flee, therefore, those evil offshoots [of Satan], which produce death- bearing fruit, whereof if anyone tastes, he instantly dies. For these men are not the planting of the Father. For if they were, they would appear as branches of the cross, and their fruit would be incorruptible. By it(9) He calls you through His passion, as being His members. The head, therefore, cannot be born by itself, without its members; God, who is [the Saviour] Himself, having promised their union.(10)

Do ye also avoid those wicked offshoots of his,(5) Simon his firstborn son, and Menander, and Basilides, and all his wicked mob of followers,(6) the worshippers of a man, whom also the prophet Jeremiah pronounces accursed.(7) Flee also the impure Nicolaitanes, falsely so called,(8) who are lovers of pleasure, and given to calumnious speeches. Avoid also the children of the evil one, Theodotus and Cleobulus, who produce death- bearing fruit, whereof if anyone tastes, he instantly dies, and that not a mere temporary death, but one that shall endure forever. These men are not the planting of the Father, but are an accursed brood. And says the Lord, "Let every plant which my heavenly Father has not planted be rooted up."(11) For if they had been branches of the Father, they would not have been "enemies of the cross of Christ,"(12) but rather of those who "killed the Lord of glory."(13) But now, by denying the cross, and being ashamed of the passion, they cover the transgression of the Jews, those fighters against God, those murderers of the Lord; for it were too little to style them merely murderers of the prophets. But Christ invites you to [share in] His immortality, by His passion and resurrection, inasmuch as ye are His members.

CHAP. XII. -- CONTINUE IN UNITY AND LOVE.

I salute you from Smyrna, together with the Churches of God which are with me, who have refreshed me in all things, both in the flesh and in the spirit. My bonds, which I carry about with me for the sake of Jesus Christ (praying that I may attain to God), exhort you. Continue in harmony among yourselves, and in prayer with one another; for it becomes every one of you, and especially the presbyters, to refresh the bishop, to the hon-our of the Father, of Jesus Christ, and of the apostles. I entreat you in love to hear me, that I may not, by having written, be a testimony against you. And do ye also pray for me, who have need of your love, along with the mercy of God, that I may be worthy of the lot for which I am destined, and that I may not be found reprobate.

I salute you from Smyrna, together with the Churches of God which are with me, whose rulers have refreshed me in every respect, both in the flesh and in the spirit. My bonds, which I carry about with me for the sake of Jesus Christ (praying that I may attain to God), exhort you. Continue in harmony among yourselves, and in supplication; for it becomes every one of you, and especially the presbyters, to refresh the bishop, to the honour of the Father, and to the honour of Jesus Christ and of the apostles. I entreat you in love to hear me, that I may not, by having thus written, be a testimony against you. And do ye also pray for me, who have need of your love, along with the mercy of God, that I may be thought worthy to attain the lot for which I am now designed, and that I may not be found reprobate.

CHAP. XIII.--CONCLUSION.

The love of the Smyrnaeans and Ephesians salutes you. Remember in your prayers the Church which is in Syria, from which also I am not worthy to receive my appellation, being the last(1) of them. Fare ye well in Jesus Christ, while ye continue subject to the bishop, as to the command [of God], and in like manner to the presbytery. And do ye, every man, love one another with an undivided heart. Let my spirit be sanctified(2) by yours, not only now, but also when I shall attain to God. For I am as yet exposed to danger. But the Father is faithful in Jesus Christ to fulfil both mine and your petitions: in whom may ye be found unblameable.

The love of the Smyrnaeans and Ephesians salutes you. Remember our Church which is in Syria, from which I am not worthy to receive my appellation, being the last(1) of those of that place. Fare ye well in the Lord Jesus Christ, while ye continue subject to the bishop, and in like manner to the presbyters and to the deacons. And do ye, every man, love one another with an undivided heart. My spirit salutes you,(2) not only now, but also when I shall have attained to God; for I am as yet exposed to danger. But the Father of Jesus Christ is faithful to fulfil both mine and your petitions: in whom may we be found without spot. May I have joy of you in the Lord.

THE EPISTLE OF IGNATIUS TO THE ROMANS SHORTER AND LONGER VERSIONS

Ignatius, who is also called Theophorus, to the Church which has obtained mercy, through the majesty of the Mast High Father, and Jesus Christ, His only-begotten Son; the Church which is beloved and enlightened by the will of Him that willeth all things which are according to the love of Jesus Christ our God, which also presides in the place of the report of the Romans, worthy of God, worthy of honour, worthy of the highest happiness, worthy of praise, worthy of obtaining her every desire, worthy of being deemed holy,(2) and which presides over love, is named from Christ, and from the Father, which I also salute in the name of Jesus Christ, the San of the Father: to those who are united, both according ta the flesh and spirit, to every one of His commandments; who are filled inseparably with the grace of God, and are purified from every strange taint, [I wish] abundance of happiness unblameably, in Jesus Christ our God.

Ignatius, who is also called Theophorus, to the Church which has obtained mercy, through the majesty of the Mast High God the Father, and of Jesus Christ, His only-begotten Son; the Church which is sanctified and enlightened by the will of God, who farmed all things that are according to the faith and love of Jesus Christ, our God and Saviour; the Church which presides in the place of the region of the Romans, and which is worthy of God, worthy of honour, worthy of the highest happiness, worthy of praise, worthy of credit,(1) worthy of being deemed holy,(2) and which presides over love, is named from Christ, and from the Father, and is possessed of the Spirit, which I also salute in the name of Almighty God, and of Jesus Christ His Son: to those who are united, both according to the flesh and spirit, to every one of His commandments, who are filled inseparably with all the grace of God, and are purified from every strange taint, [I wish] abundance of happiness unblameably, in God, even the Father, and our Lord Jesus Christ.

CHAP. I. -- AS A PRISONER, I HOPE TO SEE YOU.

THROUGH prayer(3) to God I have obtained the privilege of seeing your most worthy faces,(4) and have even(5) been granted more than I requested; for I hope as a prisoner in Christ Jesus to salute you, if indeed it be the will of God that I be thought worthy of attaining unto the end. For the beginning has been well or dered, if I may obtain grace to cling to(1) my lot without hindrance unto the end. For I am afraid of your love,(3) lest it should do me an injury. For it is easy for you to accomplish what you please; but it is difficult for me to attain to God, if ye spare me.

THROUGH prayer to God I have obtained the privilege of seeing your most worthy faces,(4) even as I earnestly begged might be granted me; for as a prisoner in Christ Jesus I hope to salute you, if indeed it be the will [of God] that I be thought worthy of attaining unto the end. For the beginning has been well ordered, if I may obtain grace to cling to(6) my lot without hindrance unto the end. For I am afraid of your love,(7) lest it should do me an injury. For it is easy for you to accomplish what you please; but it is difficult for me to attain to God, if ye do not spare me,(2) under the pretence of carnal affection.

CHAP. II. -- DO NOT SAVE ME FROM MARTYRDOM.

For it is not my desire to act towards you as a man-pleaser,(4) but as pleasing God, even as also ye please Him. For neither shall I ever have such [another] opportunity of attaining to God; nor will ye, if ye shall now be silent, ever be entitled to(5) the honour of a better work. For if ye are silent concerning me, I shall become God's; but if you show your love to my flesh, I shall again have to run my race. Pray, then, do not seek to confer any greater favour upon me than that I be sacrificed to God while the altar is still prepared; that, being gathered together in love, ye may sing praise to the Father, through Christ Jesus, that God has deemed me, the bishop of Syria, worthy to be sent for(6) from the east unto the west. It is good to set from the world unto God, that I may rise again to Him.

For it is not my desire that ye should please men, Out God, even as also ye do please Him. For neither shall I ever hereafter have such an opportunity of attaining to God; nor will ye, if ye shall now be silent, ever be entitled to s the honour of a better work. For if ye are silent concerning me, I shall become God's; but if ye show your love to my flesh, I shall again have to run my race. Pray, then, do not seek to confer any greater favour upon me than that I be sacrificed to God, while the altar is still prepared; that, being gathered together in love, ye may sing praise to the Father, through Christ Jesus, that God has deemed me, the bishop of Syria, worthy to be sent for(6) from the east unto the west, and to become a martyr(7) in behalf of His own precious (8) sufferings, so as to pass from the world to God, that I may rise again unto Him.

CHAP. III. -- PRAY RATHER THAT I MAY ATTAIN' TO MARTYRDOM.

Ye have never envied anyone; ye have taught others. Now I desire that those things may be confirmed [by your conduct], which in your instructions ye enjoin [on others]. Only request in my behalf both inward and outward strength, that I may not only speak, but [truly] will; and that I may not merely be called a Christian, but really be found to be one.

For if I be truly found [a Christian], I may also be called one, and be then deemed faithful, when I shall no longer appear to the world. Nothing visible is eternal.(9) "For the things which are seen are temporal, but the things which are not seen are eternal."(10) For our God, Jesus Christ, Bow that He is with(11) the Father, is all the more revealed [in His glory]. Christianity is not a thing(1) of silence only, but also of [manifest] greatness.

Ye have never envied anyone; ye have taught others. Now I desire that those things may be confirmed [by your conduct], which in your instructions ye enjoin [on others]. Only request in my behalf both inward and outward strength, that I may not only speak, but [truly] will, so that I may not merely be called a Christian, but really found to be one. For if I be truly found [a Christian], I may also be called one, and be then deemed faithful, when I shall no longer appear to the world. Nothing visible is eternal. "For the things which are seen are temporal, but the things which are not seen are eternal.(10) The Christian is not the result (12) of persuasion, but of power.(13) When he is hated by the world, he is beloved of God. For says [the Scripture], "If ye were of this world, the world would love its own; but now ye are not of the world, but I have chosen you out of it: continue in fellowship with me."(14)

CHAP. IV. -- ALLOW ME TO FALL A PREY TO THE WILD BEASTS.

I write to the Churches, and impress on them all, that I shall willingly die for God, unless ye hinder me. I beseech of you not to show an unseasonable good-will towards me. Suffer me to become food for the wild beasts, through whose instrumentality it will be granted me to attain to God. I am the wheat of God, and let me be ground by the teeth of the wild beasts, that I may be found the pure bread of Christ. Rather entice the wild beasts, that they may become my tomb, and may leave nothing of my body; so that when I have fallen asleep [in death], I may be no trouble to anyone. Then shall I truly be a disciple of Christ, when the world shall not see so much as my body. Entreat Christ for me, that by these instruments(2) I may be found a sacrifice [to God]. I do not, as Peter and Paul, issue commandments unto you. They were apostles; I am but a condemned man: they were free,(3) while I am, even until now, a servant. But when I suffer, I shall be the freedman of Jesus, and shall rise again emancipated in Him. And now, being a prisoner, I learn not to desire anything worldly or vain.

I write to all the Churches, and impress on them all, that I shall willingly die for God, unless ye hinder me. I beseech of you not to show an unseasonable goodwill towards me. Suffer me to become food for the wild beasts, through whose instrumentality it will be granted me to attain to God. I am the wheat of God,

and am ground by the teeth of the wild beasts, that I may be found the pure bread of God. Rather entice the wild beasts, that they may become my tomb, and may leave nothing of my body; so that when I have fallen asleep [in death], I may not be found troublesome to anyone. Then shall I be a true disciple of Jesus Christ, when the world shall not see so much as my body. Entreat the Lord for me, that by these instruments(2) I may be found a sacrifice to God. I do not, as Peter and Paul, issue commandments unto you. They were apostles of Jesus Christ, but I am the very least [of believers]: they were free,(3) as the servants of God; while I am, even until now, a servant. But when I suffer, I shall be the freedman of Jesus Christ, and shall rise again emancipated in Him. And now, being in bonds for Him, I learn not to desire anything worldly or vain.

CHAP. V. -- I DESIRE TO DIE.

From Syria even unto Rome I fight with beasts,(4) both by land and sea, both by night and day, being bound to ten leopards, I mean a band of soldiers, who, even when they receive benefits,(5) show themselves all the worse. But I am the more instructed by their injuries [to act as a disciple of Christ]; "yet am I not thereby justified."(6) May I enjoy the wild beasts that are prepared for me; and I pray they may be found eager to rush upon me, which also I will entice to devour me speedily, and not deal with me as with some, whom, out of fear, they have not touched. But if they be unwilling to assail me, I will compel them to do so. Pardon me [in this]: I know what is for my benefit. Now I begin to be a disciple. And let no one, of things visible or invisible, envy(2) me that I should attain to Jesus Christ. Let fire and the cross; let the crowds of wild beasts; let tearings,(2) breakings, and dislocations of bones; let cutting off of members; let shatterings of the whole body; and let all the dreadful(3) torments of the devil come upon me: only let me attain to Jesus Christ.

From Syria even unto Rome I fight with beasts,(4) both by land and sea, both by night and day, being bound to ten leopards, I mean a band of soldiers, who, even when they receive benefits,(5) show themselves all the worse. But I am the more instructed by their injuries [to act as a disciple of Christ]; "yet am I not thereby justified."(6) May I enjoy the wild beasts that are prepared for me; and I pray that they may be found eager to rush upon me, which also I will entice to devour me speedily, and not deal with me as with some, whom, out of fear, they have not touched. But if they be unwilling to assail me, I will compel them to do so. Pardon me [in this] I know what is for my benefit. Now I begin to be a disciple, and have(7) no desire after anything visible or invisible, that I may attain to Jesus Christ. Let fire and the cross; let the crowds of wild beasts; let breakings, tearings, and separations of bones; let cutting off of members; let bruising to pieces of the whole body; and let the very torment of the devil come upon me: only let me attain to Jesus Christ.

CHAP. VI. -- BY DEATH I SHALL ATTAIN TRUE LIFE.

All the pleasures of the world, and all the kingdoms of this earth, (4) shall profit me nothing. It is better for me to die in behalf of(5) Jesus Christ, than to reign over all the ends of the earth. "For what shall a man be profited, if he gain the whole world, but lose his own soul?''(6) Him I seek, who died for us: Him I desire, who rose again for our sake. This is the gain which is laid up for me. Pardon me, brethren: do not hinder me from living, do not wish to keep me in a state of death; (7) and while I desire to belong to God, do not ye give me over to the world. Suffer me to obtain pure light: when I have gone thither, I shall indeed be a man of God. Permit me to be an imitator of the passion of my God. If anyone has Him within himself, let him consider what I desire, and let him have sympathy with me, as knowing how I am straitened.

All the ends of the world, and all the kingdoms of this earth,(4) shall profit me nothing. It is better for me to die for the sake of Jesus Christ, than to reign over all the ends of the earth. "For what is a man profited, if he gain the whole world, but lose his own soul?" I long after the Lord, the Son of the true God and Father, even Jesus Christ. Him I seek, who died for us and rose again. Pardon me, brethren: do not hinder me in attaining to life; for Jesus is the life of believers. Do not wish to keep me in a state of death,(7) for life without Christ is death. While I desire to belong to God, do not ye give me over to the world. Suffer me to obtain pure light: when I have gone thither, I shall indeed be a man of God. Permit me to be an imitator of the passion of Christ, my God. If anyone has Him within himself, let him consider what I desire, and let him have sympathy with me, as knowing how I am straitened.

CHAP. VII. -- REASON OF DESIRING TO DIE.

The prince of this world would fain carry me away, and corrupt my disposition towards God. Let none of you, therefore, who are [in Rome] help him; rather be ye on my side, that is, on the side of God. Do not speak of Jesus Christ, and yet set your desires on the world. Let not envy find a dwelling-place among you; nor even should I, when present with you, exhort you to it, be ye persuaded to listen to me, but rather give credit to those things which I now write to you. For though I am alive while I write to you, yet I am eager to die. My love(8) has been crucified, and there is nofire in me desiring to be fed;(1) but there is within me a water that liveth and speaketh,(2) saying to me inwardly, Come to the Father. I have no delight in corruptible food, nor in the

pleasures of this life. I desire the bread of God, the heavenly bread, the bread of life, which is the flesh of Jesus Christ, the Son of God, who became afterwards of the seed of David and Abraham; and I desire the drink of God, namely His blood, which is incorruptible love and eternal life.

The prince of this world would fain carry me away and corrupt my disposition towards God. Let none of you, therefore, who are [in Rome] help him; rather be ye on my side, that is, on the side of God. Do not speak of Jesus Christ, and yet prefer this world to Him. Let not envy find a dwelling-place among you; nor even should I, when present with you, exhort you to it, be ye persuaded, but rather give credit to those things which I now write to you. For though I am alive while I write to you, yet I am eager to die for the sake of Christ. My love s has been crucified, and there is no fire in me that loves anything; but there is living water springing up in me,(9) and which says to me inwardly, Come to the Father. I have no delight in corruptible food, nor in the pleasures of this life. I desire the bread of God, the heavenly bread, the bread of life, which is the flesh of Jesus Christ, the Son of God, who became afterwards of the seed of David and Abraham; and I desire the drink, namely His blood, which is incorruptible love and eternal life.

CHAP. VIII. -- BE YE FAVOURABLE TO ME.

I no longer wish to live after the manner of men, and my desire shall be fulfilled if ye consent. Be ye willing, then, that ye also may have your desires fulfilled. I entreat you in this brief letter; do ye give credit to me. Jesus Christ will reveal these things to you, [so that ye shall know] that I speak truly. He(5) is the mouth altogether free from falsehood, by which the Father has truly spoken. Pray ye for me, that I may attain [the object of my desire]. I have not written to you according to the flesh, but according to the will of God. If I shall suffer, ye have wished [well] to me; but if I am rejected, ye have hated me.

I no longer wish to live after the manner of men, and my desire shall be fulfilled if ye consent. "I am crucified with Christ: nevertheless I live; yet no longer I, since Christ liveth in me."(3) I entreat you in this brief letter: do not refuse me; believe me that I love Jesus, who was delivered [to death] for my sake. "What shall I render to the Lord for all His benefits towards me ?"(4) Now God, even the Father, and the Lord Jesus Christ, shall reveal these things to you, [so that ye shall know] that I speak truly. And do ye pray along with me, that I may attain my aim in the Holy Spirit. I have not written to you according to the flesh, but according to the will of God. If I shall suffer, ye have loved me; but if I am rejected, ye have hated me.

CHAP. IX. -- PRAY FOR THE CHURCH IN SYRIA.

Remember in your prayers the Church in Syria, which now has God for its shepherd, instead of me. Jesus Christ alone will oversee it, and your love [will also regard it]. But as for me, I am ashamed to be counted one of them; for indeed I am not worthy, as being the very last of them, and one born out of due time.(6) But I have obtained mercy to be somebody, if I shall attain to God. My spirit salutes you, and the love of the Churches that have received me in the name of Jesus Christ, and not as a mere passer-by. For even those Churches which were not(7) near to me in the way, I mean according to the flesh,(8) have gone before me,(9) city by city, [to meet me.]

Remember in your prayers the Church which is in Syria, which, instead of me, has now for its shepherd the Lord, who says, "I am the good Shepherd." And He alone will oversee it, as well as your love towards Him. But as for me, I am ashamed to be counted one of them; for I am not worthy, as being the very last of them, and one born out of due time. But I have obtained mercy to be somebody, if I shall attain to God. My spirit salutes you, and the love of the Churches which have received me in the name of Jesus Christ, and not as a mere passerby. For even those Churches which were not near to me in the way, have brought me forward, city by city.

CHAP. X.--CONCLUSION.

Now I write these things to you from Smyrna by the Ephesians, who are deservedly most happy. There is also with me, along with many others, Crocus, one dearly beloved by me.(1) As to those who have gone before me from Syria to Rome for the glory of God, I believe that you are acquainted with them; to whom, [then,] do ye make known that I am at hand. For they are all worthy, both of God and of you; and it is becoming that you should refresh them in all things. I have written these things unto you, on the day before the ninth of the Kalends of September (that(2) is, on the twenty-third day of August). Fare ye well to the end, in the patience of Jesus Christ. Amen.

Now I write these things to you from Smyrna by the Ephesians, who are deservedly most happy. There is also with me, along with many others, Crocus, one dearly beloved by me.(1) As to those who have gone before me from Syria to Rome for the glory of God, I believe that you are acquainted with them; to whom, [then,] do ye make known that I am at hand. For they are all worthy, both of God and of you; and it is becoming that you should refresh them in all things. I have written these things unto you on the day before the ninth of the Kalends of September. Fare ye well to the end, in the patience of Jesus Christ.

THE EPISTLE OF IGNATIUS TO THE PHILADELPHIANS SHORTER AND LONGER VERSIONS

Ignatius, who is also called Theophorus, to the Church of God the Father, and our Lord Jesus Christ, which is at Philadelphia, in Asia, which has obtained mercy, and is established in the harmony of God, and rejoiceth unceasingly(1) in the passion of our Lord, and is filled with all mercy through his resurrection; which I salute in the blood of Jesus Christ, who is our eternal and enduring joy, especially if [men] are in unity with the bishop, the presbyters, and the deacons, who have been appointed according to the mind of Jesus Christ, whom He has established in security, after His own will, and by His Holy Spirit.

Ignatius, who is also called Theophorus, to the Church of God the Father, and of the Lord Jesus Christ, which is at Philadelphia, which has obtained mercy through love, and is established in the harmony of God, and rejoiceth unceasingly,(1) in the passion of our Lord Jesus, and is filled with all mercy through His resurrection; which I salute in the blood of Jesus Christ, who is our eternal and enduring jay, especialty to those who are in unity with the bishop, and the presbyters, and the deacons, who have been appointed by the will of God the Father, through the Lord Jesus Christ, who, according to His own will, has firmly established His Church upon a rock, by a spiritual building, not made with hands, against which the winds and the floods have beaten, yet have not been able to overthrow it:(2) yea, and may spiritual wickedness never be able to do so, but be thoroughly weakened by the power of Jesus Christ our Lord.

CHAP. I. -- PRAISE OF THE BISHOP.

WHICH bishop,(3) I know, obtained the ministry which pertains to the common [weal], not of himself, neither by men,(4) nor through vainglory, but by the love of God the Father, and the Lord Jesus Christ; at whose meekness I am struck with admiration, and who by his silence is able to accomplish more than those who vainly talk. For he is in harmony with the commandments [of God], even as the harp is with its strings. Wherefore my soul declares his mind towards God a happy one, knowing it to be virtuous and perfect, and that his stability as well as freedom from all anger is after the example of the infinite(6) meekness of the living God.

HAVING beheld your bishop, I know that he was not selected to undertake the ministry which pertains to the common [weal], either by himself or by men,(4) or out of vainglory, but by the love of Jesus Christ, and of God the Father, who raised Him from the dead; at whose meekness I am struck with admiration, and who by His silence is able to accomplish more than they who talk a great deal. For he is in harmony with the commandments and ordinances of the Lord, even as the strings are with the harp, and is no less blameless than was Zacharias the priest.(5) Wherefore my soul declares his mind towards God a happy one, knowing it to be virtuous and perfect, and that his stability as well as freedom from all anger is after the example of the infinite meekness of the living God.

CHAP. II. -- MAINTAIN UNION WITH THE BISHOP.

Wherefore, as children of light and truth, flee from division and wicked doctrines; but where the shepherd is, there do ye as sheep follow. For there are many wolves that appear worthy of credit, who, by means of a pernicious pleasure, carry captives those that are running towards God; but in your unity they shall have no place.

Wherefore, as children of light and truth, avoid the dividing of your unity, and the wicked doctrine of the heretics, from whom "a defiling influence has gone forth into all the earth."(1) But where the shepherd is, there do ye as sheep follow. For there are many wolves in sheep's clothing,(2) who, by means of a pernicious pleasure, carry captive(3) those that are running towards God; but in your unity they shall have no place.

CHAP. III. -- AVOID SCHISMATICS.

Keep yourselves from those evil plants which Jesus Christ does not tend, because they are not the planting of the Father. Not that I have found any division among you, but exceeding purity. For as many as are of God and of Jesus Christ are also with the bishop. And as many as shall, in the exercise of repentance, return into the unity of the Church, these, too, shall belong to God, that they may live according to Jesus Christ. Do not err, my brethren. If any man follows him that makes a schism in the Church, he shall not inherit the kingdom of God. If anyone walks according to a strange(5) opinion, he agrees not with the passion [of Christ.].

Keep yourselves, then, from those evil planes which Jesus Christ does not tend, bat that wild beast, the destroyer of men, because they are not the planting of the Father, but the seed of the wicked one. Not that I have found any division among you do I write these things; but I arm you beforehand, as the children of God. For as many as are of Christ are also with the bishop; but as many as fall away from him, and embrace communion with the accursed, these shall be cut off along with them. For they are not Christ's husbandry, but the seed of the enemy, from whom may you ever be delivered by the prayers of the shepherd, that most faithful and gentle shepherd who

presides over you. I therefore exhort you in the Lord to receive with all tenderness those that repent and return to the unity of the Church, that through your kindness and forbearance they may recover(4) themselves out of the snare of the devil, and becoming worthy of Jesus Christ, may obtain eternal salvation in the kingdom of Christ. Brethren, be not deceived. If any man follows him that separates from the truth, he shall not inherit the kingdom of God; and if any man does not stand aloof from the preacher of falsehood, he shall be condemned to hell. For it is obligatory neither to separate from the godly, nor to associate with the ungodly. If anyone walks according to a strange(5) opinion, he is not of Christ, nor a partaker of His passion; but is a fox,(6) a destroyer of the vineyard of Christ. Have no fellowship(7) with such a man, lest ye perish along with him, even should he be thy father, thy son, thy brother, or a member of thy family. For says [the Scripture], "Thine eye shall not spare him."(8) You ought therefore to "hate those that hate God, and to waste away [with grief] on account of His enemies."(9) I do not mean that you should beat them or persecute them, as do the Gentiles "that know not the Lord and God;"(10) but that you should regard them as your enemies, and separate yourselves from them, while yet you admonish them, and exhort them to repentance, if it may be they will hear, if it may be they will submit themselves. For our God is a lover of mankind, and "will have all men to be saved, and to come to the knowledge of the truth."(11) Wherefore "He makes His sun to rise upon the evil and on the good, and sendeth rain on the just and on the unjust;"(12) of whose kindness the Lord, wishing us also to be imitators, says, "Be ye perfect, even as also your Father that is in heaven is perfect."(13)

CHAP. IV. -- HAVE BUT ONE EUCHARIST, ETC.

Take ye heed, then, to have but one Eucharist. For there is one flesh of our Lord Jesus Christ, and one cup to [show forth(1)] the unity of His blood; one altar; as there is one bishop, along with the presbytery and deacons, my fellow-servants: that so, whatsoever ye do, ye may do it according to [the will of] God.

I have confidence of you in the Lord, that ye will be of no other mind. Wherefore I write boldly to your love, which is worthy of God, and exhort you to have but one faith, and one [kind of] preaching, and one Eucharist. For there is one flesh of the Lord Jesus Christ; and His blood which was shed for us is one; one loaf also is broken to all [the communicants], and one cup is distributed among them all: there is but one altar for the whole Church, and one bishop, with the presbytery and deacons, my fellow- servants. Since, also, there is but one unbegotten Being, God, even the Father; and one only-begotten Son, God, the Word and man; and one Comforter, the Spirit of truth; and also one preaching, and one faith, and one baptism;(2) and one Church which the holy apostles established from one end of the earth to the other by the blood of Christ, and by their own sweat and toil; it behoves you also, therefore, as "a peculiar people, and a holy nation,"(3) to perform all things with harmony in Christ. Wives, be ye subject to your husbands in the fear of God;(4) and ye virgins, to Christ in purity, not counting marriage an abomination, but desiring that which is better, not for the reproach of wedlock, but for the sake of meditating on the law. Children, obey your parents, and have an affection for them, as workers together with God for your birth [into the world]. Servants, be subject to your masters in God, that ye may be the freed-men of Christ.(5) Husbands, love your wives, as fellow-servants of God, as your own body, as the partners of your life, and your co-adjutors in the procreation of children. Virgins, have Christ alone before your eyes, and His Father in your prayers, being enlightened by the Spirit. May I have pleasure in your purity, as that of Elijah, or as of Joshua the son of Nun, as of Melchizedek, or as of Elisha, as of Jeremiah, or as of John the Baptist, as of the beloved disciple, as of Timothy, as of Titus, as of Evodius, as of Clement, who departed this life in [perfect] chastity,(6) Not, however, that I blame the other blessed [saints] because they entered into the married state, of which I have just spoken.(7) For I pray that, being found worthy of God, I may be found at their feet in the kingdom, as at the feet of Abraham, and Isaac, and Jacob; as of Joseph, and Isaiah, and the rest of the prophets; as of Peter, and Paul, and the rest of the apostles, that were married men. For they entered into these marriages not for the sake of appetite, but out of regard for the propagation of mankind. Fathers, "bring up your children in the nurture and admonition of the Lord;"(8) and teach them the holy Scriptures, and also trades, that they may not indulge in idleness. Now [the Scripture] says, "A righteous father educates [his children] well; his heart shall rejoice in a wise son."(9) Masters, be gentle towards your servants, as holy Job has taught you;(10) for there is one nature, and one family of mankind. For "in Christ there is neither bond nor free." (11) Let governors be obedient to Caesar; soldiers to those that command them; deacons to the presbyters, as to high-priests; the presbyters, and deacons, and the rest of the clergy, together with all the people, and the soldiers, and the governors, and Caesar [himself], to the bishop; the bishop to Christ, even as Christ to the Father. And thus unity is preserved throughout. Let not the widows be wanderers about, nor fond of dainties, nor gadders from house to house; but let them be like Judith, noted for her seriousness; and like Anna, eminent for her sobriety. I do not ordain these things as an apostle: for "who am I, or what is my father's house,"(1) that I should pretend to be equal in honour to them? But as your "fellow-soldier,"(2) I hold the position of one who [simply] admonishes you.

CHAP. V. -- PRAY FOR ME.

My brethren, I am greatly enlarged in loving you; and rejoicing exceedingly [over you], I seek to secure your safety. Yet it is not I, but Jesus Christ, for whose sake being bound I fear the more, inasmuch as I am not yet perfect. But your prayer to God shall make me perfect, that I may attain to that portion which through mercy has been allotted me, while I flee to the Gospel as to the flesh of Jesus, and to the apostles as to the presbytery of the Church. And let us also love the prophets, because they too have proclaimed the Gospel,(4) and placed their hope in Him,(5) and waited for Him; in whom also believing, they were saved, through union to Jesus Christ, being holy men, worthy of love and admiration, having had witness borne to them by Jesus Christ, and being reckoned along with in the Gospel of the common hope.

My brethren, I am greatly enlarged in loving you; and rejoicing exceedingly [over you], I seek to secure your safety. Yet it is not I, but the Lord Jesus through me; for whose sake being bound, I fear the more, for I am not yet perfect. But your prayer to God shall make me perfect, that I may attain that to which I have been called, while I flee to the Gospel as to the flesh of Jesus Christ, and to the apostles as the presbytery of the Church. I do also love the prophets as those who announced Christ, and as being partakers of the same Spirit with the apostles. For as the false prophets and the false apostles drew [to themselves] one and the same wicked, deceitful, and seducing(3) spirit; so also did the prophets and the apostles receive from God, through Jesus Christ, one and the same Holy Spirit, who is good, and sovereign,(6) and true, and the Author of [saving] knowledge.(7) For there is one God of the Old and New Testament, "one Mediator between God and men," for the creation of both intelligent and sensitive beings, and in order to exercise a beneficial and suitable providence [over them]. There is also one Comforter, who displayed(9) His power in Moses, and the prophets, and apostles. All the saints, therefore, were saved by Christ, hoping in Him, and waiting for Him; and they obtained through Him salvation, being holy ones, worthy of love and admiration, having testimony borne to them by Jesus Christ, in the Gospel of our common hope.

CHAP. VI. -- DO NOT ACCEPT JUDAISM.

But if anyone preach the Jewish law(9) unto you, listen not to him. For it is better to hearken to Christian doctrine from a man who has been circumcised, than to Judaism from one uncircumcised. But if either of such persons do not speak concerning Jesus Christ, they are in my judgment but as monuments and sepulchres of the dead, upon which are written only the names of men. Flee therefore the wicked devices and snares of the prince of this world, lest at any time being conquered(1) by his artifices,(2) ye grow weak in your love. But be ye all joined together(3) with an undivided heart. And I thank my God that I have a good conscience in respect to you, and that no one has it in his power to boast, either privately or publicly, that I have burdened(6) anyone either in much or in little. And I wish for all among whom I have spoken, that they may not possess that for a testimony against them.

If anyone preaches the one God of the law and the prophets, but denies Christ to be the Son of God, he is a liar, even as also is his father the devil,(10) and is a Jew falsely so called, being possessed of(11) mere carnal circumcision. If anyone confesses Christ Jesus the Lord, but denies the God of the law and of the prophets, saying that the Father of Christ is not the Maker of heaven and earth, he has not continued in the truth any more than his father the devil,(10) and is a disciple of Simon Magus, not of the Holy Spirit. If anyone says there is one God, and also confesses Christ Jesus, but thinks the Lord to be a mere man, and not the only- begotten(12) God, and Wisdom, and the Word of God, and deems Him to consist merely of a soul and body, such an one is a serpent, that preaches deceit and error for the destruction of men. And such a man is poor in understanding, even as by name he is an Ebionite.(4) If anyone confesses the truths mentioned,(5) but calls lawful wedlock, and the procreation of children, destruction and pollution, or deems certain kinds of food abominable, such an one has the apostate dragon dwelling within him. If anyone confesses the Father, and the Son, and the Holy Ghost, and praises the creation, but calls the incarnation merely an appearance, and is ashamed of the passion, such an one has denied the faith, not less than the Jews who killed Christ. If anyone confesses these things, and that God the Word did dwell in a human body, being within it as the Word, even as the soul also is in the body, because it was God that inhabited it, and not a human soul, but affirms that unlawful unions are a good thing, and places the highest happiness(7) in pleasure, as does the man who is falsely called a Nicolaitan, this person can neither be a lover of God, nor a lover of Christ, but is a corrupter of his own flesh, and therefore void of the Holy Spirit, and a stranger to Christ. All such persons are but monuments and sepulchres of the dead, upon which are written only the names of dead men. Flee, therefore, the wicked devices and snares of the spirit which now worketh in the children of this world, lest at any time being overcome,(1) ye grow weak in your love. But be ye all joined together(3) with an undivided

heart and a willing mind, "being of one accord and of one judgment,"(9) being always of the same opinion about the same things, both when you are at ease and in danger, both in sorrow and in joy. I thank God, through Jesus Christ, that I have a good conscience in respect to you, and that no one has it in his power to boast, either privately or publicly, that I have burdened anyone either in much or in little. And I wish for all among whom I have spoken, that they may not possess that for a testimony against them.

CHAP. VII. -- I HAVE EXHORTED YOU TO UNITY.

For though some would nave deceived me according to the flesh, yet the Spirit, as being from God, is not deceived. For it knows both whence it comes and whither it goes,(10) and detects the secrets [of the heart]. For, when I was among you, I cried, I spoke with a loud voice: Give heed to the bishop, and to the presbytery and deacons. Now, some suspected me of having spoken thus, as knowing beforehand the division caused by some among you.(11) But He is my witness, for whose sake I am in bonds, that I got no intelligence from any man.(13) But the Spirit proclaimed these words: Do nothing without the bishop; keep your bodies(1) as the temples of God;(2) love unity; avoid divisions; be the followers of Jesus Christ, even as He is of His Father.

For though some would nave deceived me according to the flesh, yet my spirit is not deceived; for I have received it from God. For it knows both whence it comes and whither it goes, and detects the secrets [of the heart]. For when I was among you, I cried, I spoke with a loud voice--the word is not mine, but God's-- Give heed to the bishop, and to the presbytery and deacons. But if ye suspect that I spake thus, as having learned beforehand the division caused by some among you, He is my witness, for whose sake I am in bonds, that I learned nothing of it from the mouth of any man. But the Spirit made an announcement to me, saying as follows: Do nothing without the bishop; keep your bodies(12) as the temples of God; love unity; avoid divisions; be ye followers of Paul, and of the rest of the apostles, even as they also were of Christ.

CHAP. VIII. -- THE SAME CONTINUED.

I therefore did what belonged to me, as a man devoted to(3) unity. For where there is division and wrath, God doth not dwell. To all them that repent, the Lord grants forgiveness, if they turn in penitence to the unity of God, and to communion with the bishop.(4) I trust [as to you] in the grace of Jesus Christ, who shall free you from every bond. And I exhort you to do nothing out of strife, but according to the doctrine of Christ. When I heard some saying, If I do not find it in the ancient(7) Scriptures, I will not believe the Gospel; on my saying to them, It is written, they answered me, That remains to be proved. But to me Jesus Christ is in the place of all that is ancient: His cross, and death, and resurrection, and the faith(8) which is by Him, are undefiled monuments of antiquity; by which I desire, through your prayers, to be justified.

I therefore did what belonged to me, as a man devoted to unity; adding this also, that where there is diversity of judgment, and wrath, and hatred, God does not dwell. To all them that repent, God grants forgiveness, if they with one consent return to the unity of Christ, and communion with the bishop.(4) I trust to the grace of Jesus Christ, that He will free you from every bond of wickedness.(5) I therefore exhort you that ye do nothing out of strife,(6) but according to the doctrine of Christ. For I have heard some saying, If I do not find the Gospel in the archives, I will not believe it. To such persons I say that my archives are Jesus Christ, to disobey whom is manifest destruction. My authentic archives are His cross, and death, and resurrection, and the faith which bears on these things, by which I desire, through your prayers, to be justified. He who disbelieves the Gospel disbelieves everything along with it. For the archives ought not to be preferred to the Spirit.(9) "It is hard to kick against the pricks;"(10)it is hard to disbelieve Christ; it is hard to reject the preaching of the apostles.

CHAP. IX. -- THE OLD TESTAMENT IS GOOD: THE NEW TESTAMENT IS BETTER.

The priests(11) indeed are good, but the High Priest is better; to whom the holy of holies has been committed, and who alone has been trusted with the secrets of God. He is the door of the Father, by which enter in Abraham, and Isaac, and Jacob, and the prophets, and the apostles, and the Church. All these have for their object the attaining to the unity of God. But the Gospel possesses something transcendent [above the former dispensation], viz., the appearance of our Lord Jesus Christ, His passion and resurrection. For the beloved prophets announced Him,(17) but the Gospel is the perfection of immortality.(18) All these things are good together, if ye believe in love.
The priests(11) indeed, and the ministers of the word, are good; but the High Priest is better, to whom the holy of holies has been committed, and who alone has been entrusted with the secrets of God. The ministering powers of God are good. The Comforter is holy, and the Word is holy, the Son of the Father, by whom He made all things, and exercises a providence over them all. This is the Way(12) which leads to the Father, the Rock,(13) the Defence,(14) the Key, the Shepherd,(15) the Sacrifice, the Door(16) of knowledge, through which have entered Abraham, and Isaac, and Jacob, Moses and all the company of the prophets, and these pillars of the world, the apostles, and the spouse of Christ, on whose account He poured out His own blood, as her marriage portion, that He might redeem her. All these things tend towards the unity of the one and only true God. But the Gospel possesses something transcendent [above the former dispensation], viz. the appearing of our Saviour Jesus Christ, His passion, and the resurrection itself. For those things which the prophets announced, saying, "Until He come for whom it is reserved, and He shall be the expectation of the Gentiles,"(1) have been fulfilled in the Gospel, [our Lord saying,] "Go ye and teach all nations, baptizing them in the name of the Father, and of the Son, and of the Holy Ghost."(2) All then are good together, the law, the prophets, the apostles, the whole company[of others] that have believed through them: only if we love one another.

CHAP. X. -- CONGRATULATE THE INHABITANTS OF ANTIOCH ON THE CLOSE OF THE PERSECUTION.

Since, according to your prayers, and the compassion which ye feel in Christ Jesus, it is reported to me that the Church which is at Antioch in Syria possesses peace, it will become you, as a Church of God, to elect a deacon to act as the ambassador of God[for you] to[the brethren there], that he may rejoice along with them when they are met together, and glorify the name[of God], Blessed is he in Jesus Christ, who shall be deemed worthy of such a ministry; and ye too shall be glorified. And if ye are willing, it is not beyond your power to do this, for the sake(3) of God; as also the nearest Churches have sent, in some cases bishops, and in others presbyters and deacons.

Since, according to your prayers, and the compassion which ye feel in Christ Jesus, it is reported to me that the Church which is at Antioch in Syria possesses peace, it will become you, as a Church of God, to elect a bishop to act as the ambassador of God[for you] to[the brethren] there, that it may be granted them to meet together, and to glorify the name of God. Blessed is he in Christ Jesus, who shall be deemed worthy of such a ministry; and if ye be zealous[in this matter], ye shall receive glory in Christ. And if ye are willing, it is not altogether beyond your power to do this, for the sake of(3) God; as also the nearest Churches have sent, in some cases bishops, and in others presbyters and deacons.

CHAP. XI. -- THANKS AND SALUTATION.

Now, as to Philo the deacon, of Cilicia, a man of reputation, who still ministers to me in the word of God, along with

Rheus Agathopus, an elect man, who has followed me from Syria, not regarding(4) his life,--these bear witness in your behalf; and I myself give thanks to God for you, that ye have received them, even as the Lord you. But may those that dishonoured them be forgiven through the grace of Jesus Christ! The love of the brethren at Troas salutes you; whence also I write to you by Burrhus, who was sent along with me by the Ephesians and Smyrnaeans, to show their respect.(7) May the Lord Jesus Christ honour them, in whom they hope, in flesh, and soul, and faith, and love, and concord! Fare ye well in Christ Jesus, our common hope.

Now, as to Philo the deacon, a man of Cilicia, of high reputation, who still ministers to me in the word of God, along with Gaius and Agathopus, an elect man, who has followed me from Syria, not regarding(4) his life,-- these also bear testimony in your behalf. And I myself give thanks to God for you, because ye have received them: and the Lord will also receive you. But may those that dishonoured them be forgiven through the grace of Jesus Christ, "who wisheth not the death of the sinner, but his repentance."(5)` The love of the brethren at Troas salutes you; whence also I write to you by Burrhus,(6) who was sent along with me by the Ephesians and Smyrnaeans, to show their respect:(7) whom the Lord Jesus Christ will requite, in whom they hope, in flesh, and soul, and spirit, and faith, and love, and concord. Fare ye well in the Lord Jesus Christ, our common hope, in the Holy Ghost.

THE EPISTLE OF IGNATIUS TO THE SMYRNAEANS SHORTER AND LONGER VERSIONS.

Ignatius, who is also called Theophorus, to the Church of God the Father, and of the beloved Jesus Christ, which has through mercy obtained every kind of gift, which is filled with faith and love, and is deficient in no gift, most worthy of God, and adorned with holiness:(1) the Church which is at Smyrna, in Asia, wishes abundance of happiness, through the immaculate Spirit and word of God.

Ignatius, who is also called Theophorus, to the Church of God the most high Father, and His beloved Son Jesus Christ, which has through mercy obtained every kind of gift, which is filled with faithand love, and is deficient in no gift, most worthy of God, and adorned with holiness:(1) the Church which is at Smyrna, in Asia, wishes abundance of happiness, through the immaculate Spirit and word of God.

CHAP. I. -- THANKS TO GOD FOR YOUR FAITH.

I glorify God, even Jesus Christ, who has given you such wisdom. For I have observed that ye are perfected in an immoveable faith, as if ye were nailed to the cross of our Lord Jesus Christ, both in the flesh and in the spirit, and are established in love through the blood of Christ, being fully persuaded with respect to our Lord, that He was truly of the seed of David according to the flesh,(3) and the Son of God according to the will and power(4) of God; that He was truly born of a virgin, was baptized by John, in order that all righteousness might be fulfilled(5) by Him; and was truly, under Pontius Pilate and Herod the tetrarch, nailed[to the cross] for us in His flesh. Of this fruit(7) we are by His divinely-blessed passion, that He might set up a standard s for all ages, through His resurrection, to all His holy and faithful[followers], whether among Jews or Gentiles, in the one body of His Church.

I glorify the God and Father of our Lord Jesus Christ, who by Him has given you such wisdom. For I have observed that ye are perfected in an immoveable faith, as if ye were nailed to the cross of our Lord Jesus Christ, both in the flesh and in the spirit, and are established in love through the blood of Christ, being fully persuaded, in very truth, with respect to our Lord Jesus Christ, that He was the Son of God, "the first-born of every creature,"(2) God the Word, the only-begotten Son, and was of the seed of David according to the flesh,(3) by the Virgin Mary; was baptized by John, that all righteousness might be fulfilled(5) by Him; that He lived a life of holiness without sin, and was truly, under Pontius Pilate and Herod the tetrarch, nailed[to the cross] for us in His flesh. From whom we also derive our being,(6) from His divinely-blessed passion, that He might set up a standard for the ages, through His resurrection, to all His holy and faithful[followers], whether among Jews or Gentiles, in the one body of His Church.

CHAP. II. -- CHRIST'S TRUE PASSION.

Now, He suffered all these things for our sakes, that we might be saved. And He suffered truly, even as also He truly raised up Himself, not, as certain unbelievers maintain, that He only seemed to suffer, as they themselves only seem to be[Christians]. And as they believe, so shall it happen unto them, when they shall be divested of their bodies, and be mere evil spirits.(3)

Now, He suffered all these things for us; and He suffered them really, and not in appearance only, even as also He truly rose again. But not, as some of the unbelievers, who are ashamed of the formation of man, and the cross, and death itself, affirm, that in appearance only, and not in truth, He took a body of the Virgin, and suffered only in appearance, forgetting, as they do, Him who said, "The Word was made flesh;"(1) and again, "Destroy this temple, and in three days I will raise it up;"(2) and once more, "If I be lifted up from the earth, I will draw all men unto Me."(4) The Word therefore did dwell in flesh, for "Wisdom built herself an house."(5) The Word raised up again His own temple on the third day, when it had been destroyed by the Jews fighting against Christ. The Word, when His flesh was lifted up, after the manner of the brazen serpent in the wilderness, drew all men to Himself for their eternal salvation.(6)

CHAP. III.--CHRIST WAS POSSESSED OF A BODY AFTER HIS RESURRECTION.

For I know that after His resurrection also He was still possessed of flesh,(7) and I believe that He is so now. When, for instance, He came to those who were with Peter, He said to them, "Lay hold, handle Me, and see that I am not an incorporeal spirit."(8) And immediately they touched Him, and believed, being convinced both by His flesh and spirit. For this cause also they despised death, and were found its conquerors.(12) And after his resurrection He did eat and drink with them, as being possessed of flesh, although spiritually He was united to the Father.

And I know that He was possessed of a body not only in His being born and crucified, but I also know that He was so after His resurrection, and believe that He is so now. When, for instance, He came to those who were with Peter, He said to them, "Lay hold, handle Me, and see that I am not an incorporeal spirit."(8) "For a spirit hath not flesh and bones, as ye see Me have."(9) And He says to Thomas, "Reach hither thy finger into the print of the nails, and reach hither thy hand, and

thrust it into My side;"(10) and immediately they believed that He was Christ. Wherefore Thomas also says to Him, "My Lord, and my God."(11) And on this account also did they despise death, for it were too little to say, indignities and stripes. Nor was this all; but also after He had shown Himself to them, that He had risen indeed, and not in appearance only, He both ate and drank with them during forty entire days. And thus was He, with the flesh, received up in their sight unto Him that sent Him, being with that same flesh to come again, accompanied by glory and power. For, say the[holy] oracles, "This same Jesus, who is taken up from you into heaven, shall so come, in like manner as ye have seen Him go unto heaven."(13) But if they say that He will come at the end of the world without a body, how shall those "see Him that pierced Him,"(14) and when they recognise Him, "mourn for themselves?"(15) For incorporeal beings have neither form nor figure, nor the aspect(16) of an animal possessed of shape, because their nature is in itself simple.

CHAP. IV. -- BEWARE OF THESE HERETICS.

I give you these instructions, beloved, assured that ye also hold the same opinions[as I do]. But I guard you beforehand from those beasts in the shape of men, whom you must not only not receive, but, if it be possible, not even meet with; only you must pray to God for them, if by any means they may be brought to repentance, which, however, will be very difficult. Yet Jesus Christ, who is our true life, has the power of[effecting] this. But if these things were done by our Lord only in appearance, then am I also only in appearance bound. And why have I also surrendered myself to death, to fire, to the sword, to the wild beasts? But,[in fact,] he who is near to the sword is near to God; he that is among the wild beasts is in company with God; provided only he be so m the name of Jesus Christ. I undergo all these things that I may suffer together with Him,(1) He who became a perfect man inwardly strengthening me.(2)

I give you these instructions, beloved, assured that ye also hold the same opinions[as I do]. But I guard you beforehand from these beasts in the shape of men, from whom you must not only turn away, but even flee from them. Only you must pray for them, if by any means they may be brought to repentance. For if the Lord were in the body in appearance only, and were crucified in appearance only, then am I also bound in appearance only. And why have I also surrendered myself to death, to fire, to the sword, to the wild beasts? But,[in fact,] I endure all things for Christ, not in appearance only, but in reality, that I may suffer together with Him, while He Himself inwardly strengthens me; for of myself I have no such ability.

CHAP. V. -- THEIR DANGEROUS ERRORS,

Some ignorantly(3) deny Him, or rather have been denied by Him, being the advocates of death rather than of the truth. These persons neither have the prophets persuaded, nor the law of Moses, nor the Gospel even to this day, nor the sufferings we have individually endured. For they think also the same thing regarding us.(4) For what does anyone profit me, if he commends me, but blasphemes my Lord, not confessing that He was[truly] possessed of a body?(5) But he who does not acknowledge this, has in fact altogether denied Him, being enveloped in death.(6) I have not, however, thought good to write the names of such persons, inasmuch as they are unbelievers. Yea, far be it from me to make any mention of them, until they repent and return to[a true belief in] Christ's passion, which is our resurrection.

Some have ignorantly denied Him, and advocate falsehood rather than the truth. These persons neither have the prophecies persuaded, nor the law of Moses, nor the Gospel even to this day, nor the sufferings we have individually endured. For they think also the Lord, not owning Him to be God incarnate?(5) He that does not confess this, has in fact altogether denied Him, being enveloped in death. I have not, however, thought good to write the names of such persons, inasmuch as they are unbelievers; and far be it from me to make any mention of them, until they repent.

CHAP. VI -- UNBELIEVERS IN THE BLOOD OF CHRIST SHALL BE CONDEMNED.

Let no man deceive himself. Both the things which are in heaven, and the glorious angels,(7) and rulers, both visible and invisible, if they believe not in the blood of Christ, shall, in consequence, incur condemnation.(1) "He that is able to receive it, let him receive it."(2) Let not[high] place puff anyone up: for that which is worth all is a faith and love, to which nothing is to same thing regarding us. For what does it profit, if anyone commends me, but blasphemes my be preferred. But consider those who are of a different opinion with respect to the grace of Christ which has come unto us, how opposed they are to the will of God. They have no regard for love; no care for the widow, or the orphan, or the oppressed; of the bond, or of the free; of the hungry, or of the thirsty.

Let no man deceive himself. Unless he believes that Christ Jesus has lived in the flesh, and shall confess His cross and passion, and the blood which He shed for the salvation of the world, he shall not obtain eternal life, whether he be a king, or a priest, or a ruler, or a private person, a master or a servant, a man or a woman. "He that is able to receive it, let him receive it."(2) Let no man's place, or dignity, or riches, puff him up; and let no man's low condition or poverty abase him. For the chief points are faith towards God, hope towards Christ, the enjoyment of those good things for which we look, and love towards God and our neighbour. For, "Thou shall love the Lord thy God with all thy heart, and thy neighbour as thyself."(4) And the Lord says, "This is life eternal, to know the only true God, and Jesus Christ whom He has sent."(5) And again, "A new commandment give I unto you, that ye love one another. On these two commandments hang all the law and the prophets."(6) Do ye, therefore, notice those who preach other doctrines, how they affirm that the Father of Christ cannot be known, and how they exhibit enmity and deceit in their dealings with one another. They have no regard for love; they despise the good things we expect hereafter; they regard present things as if they were durable; they ridicule him that is in affliction; they laugh at him that is in bonds.

CHAP. VII.--LET US STAND ALOOF FROM SUCH HERETICS.

They abstain from the Eucharist and from prayer,(7) because they confess not the Eucharist to be the flesh of our Saviour Jesus Christ, which suffered for our sins, and which the Father, of His goodness, raised up again. Those, therefore, who speak against this gift of God, incur death(11) in the midst of their disputes. But it were better for them to treat it with respect,(13) that they also might rise again. It is fitting, therefore, that ye should keep aloof from such persons, and not to speak of(15) them either in private or in public, but to give heed to the prophets, and above all, to the Gospel, in which the passion[of Christ] has been revealed to us, and the resurrection has been fully proved.(16) But avoid all divisions, as the beginning of evils. They are ashamed of the cross; they mock at the passion; they make a jest of the resurrection. They are the offspring of that spirit who is the author of all evil, who led Adam,(8) by means of his wife, to transgress the commandment, who slew Abel by the hands of Cain, who fought against Job, who was the accuser of Joshua(9) the son of Josedech, who sought to ''sift the faith'' (10)of the apostles, who stirred up the multitude of the Jews against the Lord, who also now "worketh in the children of disobedience;(12)from whom the Lord Jesus Christ will deliver us, who prayed that the faith of the apostles might not fail,(14) not because He was not able of Himself to preserve it, but because He rejoiced in the pre-eminence of the Father. It is fitting, therefore, that ye should keep aloof from such persons, and neither in private nor in public to talk with(15) them; but to give heed to the law, and the prophets, and to those who have preached to you the word of salvation. But flee from all abominable heresies, and those that cause schisms, as the beginning of evils.

CHAP. VIII. -- LET NOTHING BE DONE WITHOUT THE BISHOP.

See that ye all follow the bishop, even as Jesus Christ does the Father, and the presbytery as ye would the apostles; and reverence the deacons, as being the institution(17) of God. Let no man do anything connected with the Church without the bishop. Let that be deemed a proper(18) Eucharist, which is[administered] either even as, wherever Jesus Christ is, there is the Catholic Church. It is not lawful without the bishop either to baptize or to celebrate a love-feast; but whatsoever he shall approve of, that is also pleasing to God, so that everything that is done may be secure and valid.(2)

See that ye all follow the bishop, even as Christ Jesus does the Father, and the presbytery as ye would the apostles. Do ye also reverence the deacons, as those that carry out[through their office] the appointment of God. Let no man do anything connected with the Church without the bishop. Let that be deemed a proper(18) Eucharist, which is[administered] either by the bishop, or by one to whom he has entrusted it. Wherever the bishop shall appear, there let the multitude[of the people] also be; by the bishop, or by one to whom he has entrusted it. Wherever the bishop shall appear, there let the multitude[of the people] also be; even as where Christ is, there does all the heavenly host stand by, waiting upon Him as the Chief Captain of the Lord's might, and the Governor of every intelligent nature. It is not lawful without the bishop either to baptize, or to offer, or to present sacrifice, or to celebrate a love-feast.(1) But that which seems good to him, is also well-pleasing to God, that everything ye do may be secure and valid.

CHAP. IX. -- HONOUR THE BISHOP.

Moreover,(3) it is in accordance with reason that we should return to soberness[of conduct], and, while yet we have opportunity, exercise repentance towards God. It is well to reverence(5) both God and the bishop. He who honours the bishop has been honoured by God; he who does anything without the knowledge of the bishop, does[in reality] serve the devil. Let all things, then, abound to you through grace, for ye are worthy. Ye have refreshed me in all things, and Jesus Christ[shall refresh] you. Ye have loved me when absent as well as when present. May God recompense you, for whose sake, while ye endure all things, ye shall attain unto Him.

Moreover, it is in accordance with reason that we should return to soberness[of conduct], and, while yet we have opportunity, exercise repentance towards God. For "in Hades there is no one who can confess his sins."(4) For "behold the man, and his work is before him."(6) And[the Scripture saith], "My son, honour thou God and the king."(7) And say I, Honour thou God indeed, as the Author and Lord of all things, but the bishop as the high-priest, who bears the image of God--of God. inasmuch as he is a ruler, and of Christ, in his capacity of a priest. After Him, we must also honour the king. For there is no one superior to God,

or even like to Him, among all the beings that exist. Nor is there anyone in the Church greater than the bishop, who ministers as a priest to God for the salvation of the whole world. Nor, again, is there anyone among rulers to be compared with the king, who secures peace and good order to those over whom he rules. He who honours the bishop shall be honoured by God, even as he that dishonours him shall be punished by God. For if he that rises up against kings is justly held worthy of punishment, inasmuch as he dissolves public order, of how much sorer punishment, suppose ye, shall he be thought worthy,(8) who presumes to do anything without the bishop, thus both destroying the[Church's] unity, and throwing its order into confusion? For the priesthood is the very highest point of all good things among men, against which whosoever is mad enough to strive, dishonours not man, but God, and Christ Jesus, the First-born, and the only High Priest, by nature, of the Father. Let all things therefore be done by you with good order in Christ. Let the laity be subject to the deacons; the deacons to the presbyters; the presbyters to the bishop; the bishop to Christ, even as He is to the Father. As ye, brethren, have refreshed me, so will Jesus Christ refresh you. Ye have loved me when absent, as well as when present. God will recompense you, for whose sake ye have shown such kindness towards His prisoner. For even if I am not worthy of it, yet your zeal[to help me] is an admirable(9) thing. For "he who honours a prophet in the name of a prophet, shall receive a prophet's reward."(10) It is manifest also, that he who honours a prisoner of Jesus Christ shall receive the reward of the martyrs.

CHAP. X. -- ACKNOWLEDGMENT OF THEIR KINDNESS.

Ye have done well in receiving Philo and Rheus Agathopus as servants(1) of Christ our God, who have followed me for the sake of God, and who give thanks to the Lord in your behalf, because ye have in every way refreshed them. None of these things shall be lost to you. May my spirit be for you,(3) and my bonds, which ye have not despised or been ashamed of; nor shall Jesus Christ, our perfect hope, be ashamed of you.

Ye have done well in receiving Philo, and Gaius, and Agathopus, who, being the servants(1) of Christ, have followed me for the sake of God, and who greatly bless the Lord in your behalf, because ye have in every way refreshed them. None of those things which ye have done to them shall be passed by without being reckoned unto you. "The Lord grant" to you "that ye may find mercy of the Lord in that day!"(2) May my spirit be for you,(3) and my bonds, which ye have not despised or been ashamed of. Wherefore, neither shall Jesus Christ, our perfect hope, be ashamed of you.

CHAP. XI. -- REQUEST TO THEM TO SEND A MESSENGER TO ANTIOCH.

Your prayer has reached to the Church which is at Antioch in Syria. Coming from that place bound with chains, most acceptable to God,(4) I salute all; I who am not worthy to be styled from thence, inasmuch as I am the least of them. Nevertheless, according to the will of God, I have been thought worthy [of this honour], not that I have any sense(5)[of having deserved it], but by the grace of God, which I wish may be perfectly given to me, that through your prayers I may attain to God. In order, therefore, that your work may be complete both on earth and in heaven, it is fitting that, for the honour of God, your Church should elect some worthy delegate;(6) so that he, journeying into Syria, may congratulate them that they are[now] at peace, and are restored to(7) their proper greatness, and that their proper constitution(8) has been re-established among them. It seems then to me a becoming thing, that you should send some one of your number with an epistle, so that, in company with them, he may rejoice(9) over the tranquility which, according to the will of God, they have obtained, and because that, through your prayers, they have now reached the harbour. As persons who are perfect, ye should also aim at(10) those things which are perfect. For when ye are desirous to do well, God is also ready to assist you.

Your prayers have reached to the Church of Antioch, and it is at peace. Coming from that place bound, I salute all; I who am not worthy to be styled from thence, inasmuch as I am the least of them. Nevertheless, according to the will of God, I have been thought worthy [of this honour], not that I have any senses [of having deserved it], but by the grace of God, which I wish may be perfectly given to me, that through your prayers I may attain to God. In order, therefore, that your work may be complete both on earth and in heaven, it is fitting that, for the honour of God, your Church should elect some worthy delegate;(6) so that he, journeying into Syria, may congratulate them that they are[now] at peace, and are restored to their proper greatness, and that their proper constitution(8) has been re- established among them. What appears to me proper to be done is this, that you should send some one of your number with an epistle, so that, in company with them, he may rejoice over the tranquillity which, according to the will of God, they have obtained, and because that, through your prayers, I have secured Christ as a safe harbour. As persons who are perfect, ye should also aim at(10) those things which are perfect. For when ye are desirous to do well, God is also ready to assist you.

CHAP. XII. -- SALUTATIONS.

The love of the brethren at Troas salutes you; whence also I write to you by Burrhus, whom ye sent with me, together with the Ephesians, your brethren, and who has in all things refreshed me. And I would that all may imitate him, as being a pattern of a minister(1) of God. Grace will reward him in all things. I salute your most worthy(2) bishop, and your very venerable(3) presbytery, and your deacons, my fellow-servants, and all of you individually, as well as generally, in the name of Jesus Christ, and in His flesh and blood, in His passion and resurrection, both corporeal and spiritual, in union with God and you.(4) Grace, mercy, peace, and patience, be with you for evermore!

The love of your brethren at Troas salutes you; whence also I write to you by Burgus, whom ye sent with me, together with the Ephesians, your brethren, and who has in all things refreshed me. And I would that all may imitate him, as being a pattern of a minister of God. The grace of the Lord will reward him in all things. I salute your most worthy bishop Polycarp, and your venerable presbytery, and your Christ-bearing deacons, my fellow- servants, and all of you individually, as well as generally, in the name of Christ Jesus, and in His flesh and blood, in His passion and resurrection, both corporeal and spiritual, in union with God and you. Grace, mercy, peace, and patience, be with you in Christ for evermore!

CONCLUSION.

I salute the families of my bretheren, with their wives and children, and the virgins who are called widows.(5) Be ye strong, I pray, in the power of the Holy Ghost. Philo, who is with me, greets you. I salute the house of Tavias, and pray that it may be confirmed in faith and love, both corporeal and spiritual. I salute Alce, my well-beloved,(6) and the incomparable Daphnus, and Eutecnus, and all by name. Fare ye well in the grace of God.

I salute the families of my brethren, with their wives and children, and those that are ever virgins, and the widows. Be ye strong, I pray, in the power of the Holy Ghost. Philo, my fellow-servant, who is with me, greets you. I salute the house of Tavias, and pray that it may be confirmed in faith and love, both corporeal and spiritual. I salute Alce; my well- beloved,(6) and the incomparable Daphnus, and Eutecnus, and all by name. Fare ye well in the grace of God, and of our Lord Jesus Christ, being filled with the Holy Spirit, and divine and sacred wisdom.

THE EPISTLE OF IGNATIUS TO POLYCARP
SHORTER AND LONGER VERSIONS

Ignatius, who is also called Theophorus, to Polycarp, Bishop of the Church of the Smyrnæans, or rather, who has, as his own bishop, God the Father, and the Lord Jesus Christ: [wishes] abundance of happiness.

Ignatius, bishop of Antioch, and a witness for Jesus Christ, to Polycarp, Bishop of the Church of the Smyrnæans, or rather, who has, as his own bishop, God the Father, and Jesus Christ: [wishes] abundance of happiness.

CHAP. I. -- COMMENDATION AND EXHORTATION.

HAVING obtained good proof that thy mind is fixed in God as upon an immoveable rock, I loudly glorify[His name] that I have been thought worthy[to behold] thy blameless face,(1) which may I ever enjoy in God! I entreat thee, by the grace with which thou art clothed, to press forward in thy course, and to exhort all that they may be saved. Maintain thy position with all care, both in the flesh and spirit. Have a regard to preserve unity, than which nothing is better. Bear with all, even as the Lord does with thee. Support(2) all in love, as also thou doest. Give thyself to prayer without ceasing.(3) Implore additional understanding to what thou already hast. Be watchful, possessing a sleepless spirit. Speak to every man separately, as God enables thee.(4) Bear the infirmities of all, as being a perfect athlete[in the Christian life]: where the labour is great, the gain is all the more.

HAVING obtained good proof that thy mind is fixed in God as upon an immoveable rock, I loudly glorify[His name] that I have been thought worthy to behold thy blameless face,(1) which may I ever enjoy in God! I entreat thee, by the grace with which thou art clothed, to press forward in thy course, and to exhort all that they may be saved. Maintain thy position with all care, both in the flesh and spirit. Have a regard to preserve unity, than which nothing is better. Bear with all even as the Lord does with thee. Support(2) all in love, as also thou doest. Give thyself to prayer Without ceasing.(3) Implore additional understanding to what thou already hast. Be watchful, possessing a sleepless spirit. Speak to every man separately, as God enables thee.(4) Bear the infirmities of all, as being a perfect athlete[in the Christian life], even as does the Lord of all. For says[the Scripture], "He Himself took our infirmities, and bare our sicknesses."(5) Where the labour is great, the gain is all the more.

CHAP.II. -- EXHORTATIONS.

If thou lovest the good disciples, no thanks are due to thee on that account; but rather seek by meekness to subdue the more troublesome. Every kind of wound is not healed with the same plaster. Mitigate violent attacks[of disease] by gentle applications.(1) Be in all things "wise as a serpent, and harmless as a dove."(2) For this purpose thou art composed of both flesh and spirit, that thou mayest deal tenderly(3) with those[evils] that present themselves visibly before thee. And as respects those that are not seen,(4) pray that[God] would reveal them unto thee, in order that thou mayest be wanting in nothing, but mayest abound in every gift. The times call for thee, as pilots do for the winds, and as on tossed with tempest seeks for the haven, so that both thou[and those under thy care] may attain to God. Be sober as an athlete of God: the prize set before thee is immortality and eternal life, of which thou art also persuaded. In all things may my soul be for thing,(5) and my bonds also, which thou hast loved.

If thou lovest the good disciples, no thanks are due to thee on that account; but rather seek by meekness to subdue the more troublesome. Every kind of wound is not healed with the same plaster. Mitigate violent attacks [of disease] by gentle applications.(6) Be in all things "wise as a serpent, and harmless always as a dove."(2) For this purpose thou art composed of both soul and body, art both fleshly and spiritual, that thou mayest correct those[evils] that present themselves visibly before thee; and as respects those that are not seen, mayest pray that these should be revealed to thee, so that thou mayest be wanting in nothing, but mayest abound in every gift. The times call upon thee to pray. For as the wind aids the pilot of a ship, and as havens are advantageous for safety to a tempest-tossed vessel, so is also prayer to thee, in order that thou mayest attain to God. Be sober as an athlete of God, whose will is immortality and eternal life; of which thou art also persuaded. In all things may my soul be for thine,(5) and my bonds also, which thou hast loved.

CHAP. III. -- EXHORTATIONS.

Let not those who seem worthy of credit, but teach strange doctrines,(6) fill thee with apprehension. Stand firm, as does an anvil which is beaten. It is the part of a noble(7) athlete to be wounded, and yet to conquer. And especially, we ought to bear all things for the sake of God, that He also may bear with us. Be ever becoming more zealous than what thou art. Weigh carefully the times. Look for Him who is above all time, eternal and invisible, yet who became visible for our sakes; impalpable and impassible, yet who became passible on our account; and who in every kind of way suffered for our sakes.

Let not those who seem worthy of credit, but teach strange doctrines,(6) fill thee with apprehension. Stand firm, as does an anvil which is beaten. It is the part of a noble(7) athlete to be wounded, and yet to conquer.

And especially we ought to bear all things for the sake of God, that He also may bear with us, and bring us into His kingdom. Add more and more to thy diligence; run thy race with increasing energy; weigh carefully the times. Whilst thou art here, be a conqueror; for here is the course, and there are the crowns, Look for Christ, the Son of God; who was before time, yet appeared in time; who was invisible by nature, yet visible in the flesh; who was impalpable, and could not be touched, as being without a body, but for our sakes became such, might be touched and handled in the body; who was impassible as God, but became passible for our sakes as man; and who in every kind of way suffered for our sakes.

CHAP. IV.--EXHORTATIONS.

Let not widows be neglected. Be thou, after the Lord, their protector s and friend. Let nothing be done without thy consent; neither do thou anything without the approval of God, which indeed thou dost not, inasmuch as thou art stedfast. Let your assembling together be of of frequent(9) occurrence: seek after all by name.(10) Do not despise either male or female slaves, yet neither let them be puffed up with conceit, but rather let them submit themselves(11) the more, for the glory of God, that they may obtain from God a better liberty. Let them not long to be set free [from slavery] at the public expense, that they be not found slaves to their own desires.

Let not the widows be neglected. Be thou, after the Lord, their protector and friend. Let nothing be done without thy consent; neither do thou anything without the approval of God, which indeed thou doest not. Be thou stedfast. Let your assembling together be of frequent(9) occurrence: seek after all by name.(10) Do not despise either male or female slaves, yet neither let them be puffed up with conceit, but rather let them submit themselves(11) the more, for the glory of God, that they may obtain from God a better liberty. Let them not wish to be set free [from slavery] at the public expense, that they be not found slaves to their own desires.

CHAP. V.--THE DUTIES OF HUSBANDS AND WIVES.

Flee evil arts; but all the more discourse in public regarding them.(2) Speak to my sisters, that they love the Lord, and be satisfied with their husbands both in the flesh and spirit. In like manner also, exhort my brethren, in the name of Jesus Christ, that they love their wives, even as the Lord the Church.(3) If anyone can continue in a state of purity,(4) to the honour of Him who is Lord of the flesh,(5) let him so remain without boasting. If he begins to boast, he is undone; and if he reckon himself greater than the bishop, he is ruined. But it becomes both men and women who marry, to form

their union with the approval of the bishop, that their marriage may be according to God, and not after their own lust. Let all things be done to the honour of God.(7)

Flee evil arts; but all the more discourse in public regarding them. Speak to my sisters, that they love the Lord, and be satisfied with their husbands both in the flesh and spirit. In like manner also, exhort my brethren, in the name of Jesus Christ, that they love their wives, even as the Lord the Church. If anyone can continue in a state of purity,(4) to the honour of the flesh of the Lord, let him so remain without boasting. If he shall boast, he is undone; and if he seeks to be more prominent(6) than the bishop, he is ruined. But it becomes both men and women who marry, to form their union with the approval of the bishop, that their marriage may be according to the Lord, and not after their own lust. Let all things be done to the honour of God.(7)

CHAP. VI.--THE DUTIES OF THE CHRISTIAN FLOCK.

Give ye heed to the bishop, that God also may give heed to you. My soul be for theirs(9) that are submissive to the bishop, to the presbyters, and to the deacons, and may my portion be along with them in God! Labour together with one another; strive in company together; run together; suffer together; sleep together; and awake together, as the stewards, and associates,(10) and servants of God. Please ye Him under whom ye fight, and from whom ye receive your wages. Let none of you be found a deserter. Let your baptism endure as your arms; your faith as your helmet; your love as your spear; your patience as a complete panoply. Let your works be the charge(12) assigned to you, that ye may receive a worthy recompense. Be long-suffering, therefore, with one another, in meekness, as God is towards you.May I have joy of you for ever!(13)

Give ye heed to the bishop, that God also may give heed to you. My soul be for theirs(9) that are submissive to the bishop, to the presbytery, and to the deacons: may I have my portion with them from God! Labour together with one another; strive in company together; run together; suffer together; sleep together; and awake together, as the stewards, and associates,(10) and servants of God. Please ye Him under whom ye fight, and from whom ye shall receive your wages. Let none of you be found a deserter. Let your baptism endure as your arms; your faith as your helmet; your love as your spear; your patience as a complete panoply. Let your works be the charge assigned to you, that you may obtain for them a most worthy(11) recompense. Be long-suffering, therefore, with one another, in meekness, and God shall be so with you. May I have joy of you for ever!(13)

CHAP. VII.--REQUEST THAT POLYCARP WOULD SEND A MESSENGER TO ANTIOCH.

Seeing that the Church which is at Antioch in Syria is, as report has informed me, at peace, through your prayers, I also am the more encouraged, resting without anxiety in God,(1) if indeed by means of suffering I may attain to God, so that, through your prayers, I may be found a disciple[of Christ].(2) It is fitting, O Polycarp, most blessed in God, to assemble a very solemn(3) council, and to elect one whom you greatly love, and know to be a man of activity, who may be designated the messenger of God;(4) and to bestow on him this honour that he may go into Syria, and glorify your ever active love to the praise of Christ. A Christian has not power over himself, but must always be ready for s the service of God. Now, this work is both God's and yours, when ye shall have completed it to His glory.(6) For I trust that, through grace, ye are prepared for every good work pertaining to God. Knowing, therefore, your energetic love of the truth, I have exhorted you by this brief Epistle.

Seeing that the Church which is at Antioch in Syria is, as report has informed me, at peace, through your prayers, I also am the more encouraged, resting without anxiety in God,(1) if indeed by means of suffering I may attain to God, so that, through your prayers, I may be found a disciple[of Christ]. It is fitting, O Polycarp, most blessed in God, to assemble a very solemn(3) council, and to elect one whom you greatly love, and know to be a man of activity, who may be designated the messenger of God;(4) and to bestow on him the honour of going into Syria, so that, going into Syria, he may glorify your ever active love to the praise of God. A Christian has not power over himself, but must always be ready for(5) the service of God. Now, this work is both God's and yours, when ye shall have completed it. For I trust that, through grace, ye are prepared for every good work pertaining to God. Knowing your energetic love of the truth, I have exhorted you by this brief Epistle.

CHAP. VIII.--LET OTHER CHURCHES ALSO SEND TO ANTIOCH.

Inasmuch as I have not been able to write to all the Churches, because I must suddenly sail from Troas to Neapolis, as the will(7)[of the emperor] enjoins,[I beg that] thou, as being acquainted with the purpose(8) of God, wilt write to the adjacent Churches, that they also may act in like manner, such as are able to do so sending messengers,(9) and the others transmitting letters through those persons who are sent by thee, that thou(10) mayest be glorified by a work(11) which shall be remembered for ever, as indeed thou art worthy to be. I salute all by name, and in particular the wife of Epitropus, with all her house and children. I salute Attalus, my beloved. I salute him who shall be deemed worthy to go [from you] into Syria. Grace shall be with him

forever, and with Polycarp that sends him. I pray for your happiness forever in our God, Jesus Christ, by whom continue ye in the unity and under the protection of God,(12) I salute Alce, my dearly beloved.(13) Fare ye well in the Lord.

Inasmuch, therefore, as I have not been able to write to all Churches, because I must suddenly sail from Troas to Neapolis, as the will(7)[of the emperor] enjoins,[I beg that] thou, as being acquainted with the purpose s of God, wilt write to the adjacent Churches, that they also may act in like manner, such as are able to do so sending messenger, and the others transmitting letters through those persons who are sent by thee, that thou mayest be glorified by a work(11) which shall be remembered for ever, as indeed thou art worthy to be. I salute all by name, and in particular the wife of Epitropus, with all her house and children. I salute Attalus, my beloved. I salute him who shall be deemed worthy to go[from you] into Syria. Grace shall be with him for ever, and with Polycarp that sends him. I pray for your happiness for ever in our God, Jesus Christ, by whom continue ye in the unity and under the protection of God. I salute Alce, my dearly betoved.(13) Amen. Grace[be with you]. Fare ye well in the Lord.

Taken from "The Early Church Fathers and Other Works" originally published by Wm. B. Eerdmans Pub. Co. in English in Edinburgh, Scotland beginning in 1867. (ANF 1, Roberts and Donaldson.) The digital version is by The Electronic Bible Society.

Introduction to Polycarp of Smyrna

Polycarp resided in Asia Minor as bishop of Smyrna and sent an epistle to the Philippians c. 120-140 CE. Polycarp was martyred c. 155 CE.

In Adv. Haer. V.33.4, Irenaeus describes Papias as "the hearer of John, and a companion of Polycarp."

Irenaeus mentions Polycarp in Adv. Haer., III.3.4.

But Polycarp also was not only instructed by apostles, and conversed with many who had seen Christ, but was also, by apostles in Asia, appointed bishop of the Church in Smyrna, whom I also saw in my early youth, for he tarried [on earth] a very long time, and, when a very old man, gloriously and most nobly suffering martyrdom, departed this life, having always taught the things which he had learned from the apostles, and which the Church has handed down, and which alone are true. To these things all the Asiatic Churches testify, as do also those men who have succeeded Polycarp down to the present time, a man who was of much greater weight, and a more stedfast witness of truth, than Valentinus, and Marcion, and the rest of the heretics. He it was who, coming to Rome in the time of Anicetus caused many to turn away from the aforesaid heretics to the Church of God, proclaiming that he had received this one and sole truth from the apostles, that, namely, which is handed down by the Church. There are also those who heard from him that John, the disciple of the Lord, going to bathe at Ephesus, and perceiving Cerinthus within, rushed out of the bath-house without bathing, exclaiming, "Let us fly, lest even the bath-house fall down, because Cerinthus, the enemy of the truth, is within." And Polycarp himself replied to Marcion, who met him on one occasion, and said, "Dost thou know me? "I do know thee, the first-born of Satan." Such was the horror which the apostles and their disciples had against holding even verbal communication with any corrupters of the truth; as Paul also says, "A man that is an heretic, after the first and second admonition, reject; knowing that he that is such is subverted, and sinneth, being condemned of himself." There is also a very powerful Epistle of Polycarp written to the Philippians, from which those who choose to do so, and are anxious about their salvation, can learn the character of his faith, and the preaching of the truth. Then, again, the Church in Ephesus, founded by Paul, and having John remaining among them permanently until the times of Trajan, is a true witness of the tradition of the apostles.

Irenaeus also mentions Polycarp in his letter to Florinus.

These opinions, Florinus, that I may speak in mild terms, are not of sound doctrine; these opinions are not consonant to the Church and involve their votaries in the utmost impiety; these opinions, even the heretics beyond the Church's pale have never ventured to broach; these opinions, those presbyters who preceded us, and who were conversant with the apostles, did not hand down to thee. For, while I was yet a boy, I saw thee in Lower Asia with Polycarp, distinguishing thyself in the royal court, and endeavouring to gain his approbation. For I have a more vivid recollection of what occurred at that time than of recent events (inasmuch as the experiences of childhood, keeping pace with the growth of the soul, become incorporated with it); so that I can even describe the place where the blessed Polycarp used to sit and discourse-his going out, too, and his coming in-his general mode of life and personal appearance, together with the discourses which he delivered to the people; also how he would speak of his familiar intercourse with John, and with the rest of those who had seen the Lord; and how he would call their words to remembrance. Whatsoever things he had heard from them respecting the Lord, both with regard to His miracles and His teaching, Polycarp having thus received [information] from the eye-witnesses of the Word of life, would recount them all in harmony with the Scriptures. These things, through, God's mercy which was upon me, I then listened to attentively, and treasured them up not on paper, but in my heart; and I am continually, by God's grace, revolving these things accurately in my mind. And I can bear witness before God, that if that blessed and apostolical presbyter had heard any such thing, he would have cried out, and stopped his ears, exclaiming as he was wont to do: "O good God, for what times hast Thou reserved me, that I should endure these things? "And he would have fled from the very spot where, sitting or standing, he had heard such words. This fact, too, can be made clear, from his Epistles which he despatched, whether to the neighbouring Churches to confirm them, or to certain of the brethren, admonishing and exhorting them.

Irenaeus also mentions Polycarp in his letter to Pope Victor.

For the controversy is not merely as regards the day, but also as regards the form itself of the fast. For some consider themselves hound to fast one day, others two days, others still more, while others [do so during] forty: the diurnal and the nocturnal hours they measure out together as their [fasting] day. And this variety among the observers [of the fasts] had not its origin in our time, but long before in that of our predecessors, some of whom probably, being not very accurate in their observance of it, handed down to posterity the custom as it had, through simplicity or private fancy, been [introduced among them]. And yet nevertheless all these lived in peace one with another, and we also keep peace together. Thus, in fact, the difference [in observing] the fast establishes the harmony of [our common] faith. And the presbyters preceding Sorer in the government of the Church which thou dost now rule-I mean, Anicetus and Pius, Hyginus and Telesphorus, and Sixtus-did neither themselves observe it [after that fashion], nor permit those with them to do so. Notwithstanding this, those who did not keep [the feast in this way] were peacefully disposed towards those who came to them from other dioceses in which it was [so] observed (although such observance was [felt] in more decided contrariety [as presented] to those who did not fall in with it; and none were ever cast out [of the Church] for this matter. On the contrary, those presbyters who preceded thee, and who did not observe [this custom], sent the Eucharist to those of other dioceses who did observe it. And when the blessed Polycarp was sojourning in Rome in the time of Anicetus, although a slight controversy had arisen among them as to certain other points, they were at once well inclined towards each other [with regard to the matter in hand], not willing that any quarrel should arise between them upon this head. For neither could Anicetus persuade Polycarp to forego the observance [in his own way], inasmuch as these things had been always [so] observed by John the disciple of our Lord, and by other apostles with whom he had been conversant; nor, on the other hand, could Polycarp succeed in persuading Anicetus to keep [the observance in his way], for he maintained that he was bound to adhere to the usage of the presbyters who preceded him. And in this state of affairs they held fellowship with each other; and Anicetus conceded to Polycarp in the Church the celebration of the Eucharist, by way of showing him respect; so that they parted in peace one from the other, maintaining peace with the whole Church, both those who did observe [this custom] and those who did not.

Jerome provides the following summary in Illustrious Men 17.

Polycarp disciple of the apostle John and by him ordained bishop of Smyrna was chief of all Asia, where he saw and had as teachers some of the apostles and of those who had seen the Lord. He, on account of certain questions concerning the day of the Passover, went to Rome in the time of the emperor Antoninus Pius while Anicetus ruled the church in that city. There he led back to the faith many of the believers who had been deceived through the persuasion of Marcion and Valentinus, and when. Marcion met him by chance and said "Do you know us" he replied, "I know the firstborn of the devil." Afterwards during the reign of Marcus Antoninus and Lucius Aurelius Commodus in the fourth persecution after Nero, in the presence of the proconsul holding court at Smyrna and all the people crying out against him in the Amphitheater, he was burned. He wrote a very valuable Epistle to the Philippians which is read to the present day in the meetings in Asia.

607

Polycarp to the Philippians

Introduction
Greeting

1 Polycarp and the Elders with him to the Church of God sojourning in Philippi; mercy and peace from God Almighty and Jesus Christ our Saviour be multiplied to you.

CHAPTER 1
The hospitality of the Philippians -- Their faith

1 I rejoice greatly with you in our Lord Jesus Christ that you have followed the pattern of true love, and have helped on their way, as opportunity was given you, those who were bound in chains, which become the saints, and are the diadems of those who have been truly chosen by God and our Lord. 2 I rejoice also that your firmly rooted faith, which was famous in past years, still flourishes and bears fruit unto our Lord Jesus Christ, who endured for our sins, even to the suffering of death, "whom God raised up, having loosed the pangs of Hades, 3 in whom, though you did not see him, you believed in unspeakable and glorified joy," -- into which joy many desire to come, knowing that "by grace ye are saved, not by works" but by the will of God through Jesus Christ.

CHAPTER 2
Exhortation to virtue -- The hope of resurrection -- The Lord's Teaching

1 "Wherefore girding up your loins serve God in fear" and truth, putting aside empty vanity and vulgar error, "believing on him who raised up our Lord Jesus Christ from the dead and gave him glory," and a throne on his right hand, "to whom are subject all things in heaven and earth," whom all breath serves, who is coming as "the Judge of the living and of the dead," whose blood God will require from them who disobey him. 2 Now "he who raised him" from the dead "will also raise us up" if we do his will, and walk in his commandments and love the things which he loved, refraining from all unrighteousness, covetousness, love of money, evil speaking, false witness, "rendering not evil for evil, or railing for railing," or blow for blow, or curse for curse, 3 but remembering what the Lord taught when he said, "Judge not that ye be not judged, forgive and it shall be forgiven unto you, be merciful that ye may obtain mercy, with what measure ye mete, it shall be measured to you again," and, "Blessed are the poor, and they who are persecuted for righteousness' sake, for theirs is the Kingdom of God."

CHAPTER 3
Polycarp's reason for writing: the invitation of the Philippians

1 These things, brethren, I write to you concerning righteousness, not at my own instance, but because you first invited me. 2 For neither am I, nor is any other like me, able to follow the wisdom of the blessed and glorious Paul, who when he was among you in the presence of the men of that time taught accurately and stedfastly the word of truth, and also when he was absent wrote letters to you, from the study of which you will be able to build yourselves up into the faith given you; 3 "which is the mother of us all" when faith follows, and love of God and Christ and neighbour goes before. For if one be in this company he has fulfilled the command of righteousness, for he who has love is far from all sin.

CHAPTER 4
Exhortations to virtue

1 "But the beginning of all evils is the love of money." Knowing therefore that "we brought nothing into the world and we can take nothing out of it," let us arm ourselves with the armour of righteousness, and let us first of all teach ourselves to walk in the commandment of the Lord; 2 next teach our wives to remain in the faith given to them, and in love and purity, tenderly loving their husbands in all truth, and loving all others equally in all chastity, and to educate their children in the fear of God. 3 Let us teach the widows to be discreet in the faith of the Lord, praying ceaselessly for all men, being far from all slander, evil speaking, false witness, love of money, and all evil, knowing that they are the altar of God, and that all offerings are tested, and that nothing escapes him of reasonings or thoughts, or of "the secret things of the heart."

CHAPTER 5
Christian obligations to a virtuous life

1 Knowing then that "God is not mocked," we ought to walk worthily of his commandment and glory. 2 Likewise must the deacons be blameless before his righteousness, as the servants of God and Christ and not of man, not slanderers, not double-tongued, not lovers of money, temperate in all things, compassionate, careful, walking according to the truth of the Lord, who was the "servant of all." For if we please him in this present world, we shall receive from him that which is to come; even as he promised us to raise us from the dead, and that if we are worthy citizens of his community, "we shall also reign with him," if we have but faith. 3 Likewise also let the younger men be blameless in all things; caring above all for purity and curbing themselves from all evil; for

it is good to be cut off from the lust of the things in the world, because "every lust warreth against the Spirit, and neither fornicators nor the effeminate nor sodomites shall inherit the Kingdom of God," nor they who do iniquitous things. Wherefore it is necessary to refrain from all these things, and to be subject to the presbyters and deacons as to God and Christ. The virgins must walk with a blameless and pure conscience.

CHAPTER 6
The duties of the presbyters -- Forgiveness -- The service of God

1 And let the presbyters also be compassionate, merciful to all, bringing back those that have wandered, caring for all the weak, neglecting neither widow nor orphan nor poor, but "ever providing for that which is good before God and man," refraining from all wrath, respect of persons, unjust judgment, being far from all love of money, not quickly believing evil of any, not hasty in judgment, knowing that "we all owe the debt of sin." 2 If then we pray the Lord to forgive us, we also ought to forgive, for we stand before the eyes of the Lord and of God, and "we must all appear before the judgment seat of Christ, and each must give an account of himself." 3 So then "let us serve him with fear and all reverence," as he himself commanded us, and as did the Apostles, who brought us the Gospel, and the Prophets who foretold the coming of our Lord. Let us be zealous for good, refraining from offence, and from the false brethren, and from those who bear the name of the Lord in hypocrisy, who deceive empty-minded men.

1 The introductory formula "knowing that" renders it probable that these words are a quotation, but the source is unknown.

CHAPTER 7
Warning against heresy

1 "For everyone who does not confess that Jesus Christ has come in the flesh is an anti-Christ"; and whosoever does not confess the testimony of the Cross is of the devil: and whosoever perverts the oracles of the Lord for his own lusts, and says that there is neither resurrection nor judgment, -- this man is the first-born of Satan. 2 Wherefore, leaving the foolishness of the crowd, and their false teaching, let us turn back to the word which was delivered to us in the beginning, "watching unto prayer" and persevering in fasting, beseeching the all-seeing God in our supplications "to lead us not into temptation," even as the Lord said, "The spirit is willing, but the flesh is weak."

1 This phrase, according to Irenaeus (Adv. Haer. 3/3:4) was applied, presumably later, by Polycarp to Marcion.

CHAPTER 8
Perseverance

1 Let us then persevere unceasingly in our hope, and in the pledge of our righteousness, that is in Christ Jesus, "who bare our sins in his own body on the tree, who did no sin, neither was guile found in his mouth," but for our sakes, that we might live in him, he endured all things. 2 Let us then be imitators of his endurance, and if we suffer for his name's sake let us glorify him. For this is the example which he gave us in himself, and this is what we have believed.

CHAPTER 9
The examples of the martyrs

1 Now I beseech you all to obey the word of righteousness, and to endure with all the endurance which you also saw before your eyes, not only in the blessed Ignatius, and Zosimus, and Rufus, but also in others among yourselves, and in Paul himself, and in the other Apostles; 2 being persuaded that all of these "ran not in vain," but in faith and righteousness, and that they are with the Lord in the "place which is their due," with whom they also suffered. For they did not "love this present world" but him who died on our behalf and was raised by God for our sakes.

CHAPTER 10
Perseverance in philanthropy and good works

1 Stand fast therefore in these things and follow the example of the Lord, "firm and unchangeable in faith, loving the brotherhood, affectionate to one another," joined together in the truth, forestalling one another in the gentleness of the Lord, despising no man. 2 When you can do good defer it not, "for almsgiving sets free from death; be ye all subject one to the other, having your conversation blameless among the Gentiles," that you may receive praise "for your good works" and that the Lord be not blasphemed in you. 3 "But woe to him through whom the name of the Lord is blasphemed." Therefore teach sobriety to all and show it forth in your own lives.

CHAPTER 11
Valens -- Against avrice -- The treatment of Valens

1 I am deeply sorry for Valens, who was once made a presbyter among you, that he so little understands the place which was given to him. I advise, therefore, that you keep from avarice, and be pure and truthful. Keep yourselves from all evil. 2 For how may he who cannot

attain self-control in these matters enjoin it on another? If any man does not abstain from avarice he will be defiled by idolatry and shall be judged as if he were among the Gentiles who "know not the judgment of God." Or do we "not know that the saints shall judge the world?" as Paul teaches. 3 But I have neither perceived nor heard any such thing among you, among whom the blessed Paul laboured, who are praised in the beginning of his Epistle. For concerning you he boasts in all the Churches who then alone had known the Lord, for we had not yet known him. 4 Therefore, brethren, I am deeply sorry for him [i.e. Valens] and for his wife, and "may the Lord grant them true repentance." Therefore, be yourselves also moderate in this matter, and "do not regard such men as enemies," but call them back as fallible and straying members, that you may make whole the body of you all. For in doing this you edify yourselves.

1 The Greek was perhaps 'tois ousin en arche epistolais autou', and ought to be rendered "who were his epistles in the beginning," with a reference to 2 Cor. 3:2.

CHAPTER 12
The need of forgiveness -- Prayer for blessing

1 For I am confident that you are well versed in the Scriptures, and from you nothing is hid; but to me this is not granted. Only, as it is said in these Scriptures, "Be ye angry and sin not," and "Let not the sun go down upon your wrath." Blessed is the man who remembers this, and I believe that it is so with you. 2 Now may God and the Father of our Lord Jesus Christ, and the "eternal Priest" himself, Jesus Christ, the Son of God, build you up in faith and truth, and in all gentleness, and without wrath, and in patience, and in longsuffering, and endurance, and purity, and may he give you lot and part with his saints, and to us with you, and to all under heaven who shall believe in our Lord and God Jesus Christ and in his "Father who raised him from the dead." 3 "Pray for all the saints. Pray also for the Emperors," and for potentates, and princes, and for "those who persecute you and hate you," and for "the enemies of the Cross" that "your fruit may be manifest among all men, that you may be perfected" in him.

1 Probably this ought to be regarded as a quotation from the letter of the Philippians to Polycarp.
2 "Pro regibus' is no doubt a translation of 'huper basileon' and 'basileus' is regularly used as the title of the Emperor.

CHAPTER 13
Ignatius and the Church in Syria

1 Both you and Ignatius wrote to me that if anyone was going to Syria he should also take your letters. I will do this if I have a convenient opportunity, either myself or the man whom I am sending as a representative for you and me. 2 We send you, as you asked, the letters of Ignatius, which were sent to us by him, and others which we had by us. These are subjoined to this letter, and you will be able to benefit greatly from them. For they contain faith, patience, and all the edification which pertains to our Lord. Let us know anything further which you have heard about Ignatius himself and those who are with him.

CHAPTER 14
Final greetings

1 I have written this to you by Crescens, whom I commended to you when I was present, and now commend again. For he has behaved blamelessly among us, and I believe that he will do the same with you. His sister shall be commended to you when she comes to you. Farewell in the Lord Jesus Christ in grace, with all who are yours. Amen.

The Martyrdom of Polycarp

THE MARTYRDOM OF SAINT POLYCARP, BISHOP OF SMYRNA
Charles H. Hoole's 1885 translation

Introduction
1 The church of God which sojourneth in Smyrna, to the church of God that sojourneth in Philomelia, and to all the settlements of the holy and Catholic Church in every place, mercy, peace, and love from God the Father and our Lord Jesus Christ be multiplied unto you.

CHAPTER 1
1:1 We have written unto you, brethren, the things respecting those who were martyred, and concerning the blessed Polycarp, who made the persecution to cease, having as it were set his seal to it by his testimony. For almost all the things that went before happened in order that the Lord might show us from above the testimony that is according to the gospel;

1:2 for he endured to be betrayed, even as did the Lord, that we might become imitators of him, not as considering the things that concern ourselves only, but also the things that concern our neighbours; for it belongeth to true and firm love not only to desire to be saved itself, but also that all the brethren should be saved.

CHAPTER 2
2:1 Blessed, therefore, and noble are all the testimonies that happened according to the will of God, for it is right that we should be the more careful, and should ascribe unto God the authority over all things.

2:2 For who would not admire their nobility and endurance and obedience? who, though they were torn with stripes so that the internal arrangement of their flesh became evident even as far as the veins and arteries within, endured it, so that even the bystanders compassionated them and bemoaned them; and that others even arrived at such a pitch of nobility that none of them would either sob or groan, showing all of us that in that hour the martyrs of Christ departed being tortured in the flesh, or rather that the Lord, standing by, associated himself with them.

2:3 And applying themselves to the grace of Christ, they despised the torture of this world, purchasing by the endurance of a single hour remission from eternal punishment; and the fire of their harsh tormentors was cold to them, for they had before their eyes to escape the eternal and never-quenched fire; and with the eyes of their heart they looked up to the good things that are reserved for those that endure, which neither hath ear heard, nor eye seen, nor hath it entered into the heart of man; but which were shown by the Lord unto them, who were no longer men, but already angels.

2:4 And in like manner they who had been condemned to the wild beasts endured dreadful punishments, lying upon beds of prickles, and punished with various other tortures, in order that, if it were possible, the tyrant might turn them by assiduous punishment to a denial of the faith.

CHAPTER 3
3:1 For the devil contrived many things against them, but thanks be unto God, for he prevailed not against all. For the most noble Germanicus strengthened their cowardice through the patience that was in him, who also in a notable way fought against wild beasts. For when the proconsul would have persuaded him, charging him to have compassion on his youth, he drew upon himself the wild beast by force, wishing to be the sooner freed from their unjust and lawless life.

3:2 From this, therefore, all the multitude, wondering at the nobleness of the God-loving and God-fearing race of Christians, called out, Away with the Atheists; let Polycarp be sought for.

CHAPTER 4
4:1 But a certain man named Quintus, a Phrygian, who had newly come from Phrygia, when he saw the wild beasts, became afraid. This was he who constrained himself and others to come in of their own accord. This man, the proconsul, with much importunity, persuaded to swear and to sacrifice. On this account, brethren, we praise not them that give themselves up, since the gospel doth not so teach.

CHAPTER 5
5:1 But the most admirable Polycarp at the first, when he heard these things, was not disturbed, but desired to remain in the city. But the majority persuaded him to withdraw secretly; and he departed secretly to a villa not far from the city, and remained there with a few men, doing no other thing either by night or day but pray concerning all men, and for the churches that are in the world, as was his custom;

5:2 and as he prayed he fell into a trance three days before he was taken, and saw his pillow burning with fire, and he turned and said prophetically to those who were with him, I must be burned alive.

CHAPTER 6

6:1 And when those who sought him continued in the pursuit, he departed unto another villa, and straightway they who sought him came up. And when they found him not, they apprehended two lads, of whom the one, when put to the torture, confessed.

6:2 For it was impossible for him to escape their notice, since they who betrayed him were of his own household. For the Eirenarchus, which is the same office as Cleronomus, Herodes by name, hasted to bring him into the arena, that he indeed might fulfil his proper lot, by becoming a partaker of Christ, and that they who betrayed him might undergo the same punishment as Judas.

CHAPTER 7
7:1 Having, therefore, with them the lad, on the day of the preparation, at the hour of dinner, there came out pursuers and horsemen, with their accustomed arms, as though going out against a thief. And having departed together late in the evening, they found him lying in a certain house, in an upper chamber. And he might have departed from thence unto another place, but was unwilling, saying, The will of the Lord be done.

7:2 And when he heard that they were present, he descended and talked with them. And they who were present wondered at the vigour of his age and his soundness of body, and that they had had to use so much trouble to capture so old a man. He straightway commanded that meat and drink should be set before them at that hour, as much as they wished, and asked them to grant him an hour to pray without molestation.

7:3 And when they suffered him, he stood and prayed, being full of the grace of God, so that he could not be silent for two hours, and they that heard him were astonished, and many repented that they had come against so divine an old man.

CHAPTER 8
8:1 And when he had finished his prayer, having made mention of all who had at any time come into contact with him, both small and great, noble and ignoble, and of the whole Catholic Church throughout the world, when the hour of his departure had come, having seated him on an ass, they led him into the city, it being the great Sabbath.

8:2 And the Eirenarch Herodes and his father Nicetes met him in a chariot, who, having transferred him into their car, seating themselves beside him, would have persuaded him, saying, What is the harm to say, Caesar, Caesar, and to sacrifice, and to do such like things, and thus to be saved? But he at the first did not answer them; but when they persisted, he said, I will not do that which ye advise me.

8:3 But they, when they had failed to persuade him, said unto him dreadful words, and thrust him with such haste from the chariot that in descending from the car he grazed his shin. And paying no attention to it, as though he had suffered nothing, he proceeded zealously and with eagerness, being led to the arena, there being such a noise in the arena that no one could even be heard.

CHAPTER 9
9:1 But to Polycarp, as he entered the arena, there came a voice from heaven, saying, be strong, and play the man, O Polycarp. And the speaker no man saw; but the voice those of our people who were present heard. And when he was brought in there was a great tumult, when men heard that Polycarp was apprehended.

9:2 Then, when he had been brought in, the proconsul asked him if he was Polycarp. And when he confessed, he would have persuaded him to deny, saying, have respect unto thine age, and other things like these, as is their custom to say: Swear by the fortunes of Caesar; Repent; Say, Away with the Atheists. But Polycarp, when he had looked with a grave face at all the multitude of lawless heathen in the arena, having beckoned unto them with his hand, sighed, and looking up unto heaven, said, Away with the Atheists!

9:3 And when the proconsul pressed him, and said, Swear, and I will release thee, revile Christ; Polycarp said, Eighty and six years have I served him, and in nothing hath he wronged me; and how, then, can I blaspheme my King, who saved me?

CHAPTER 10
10:1 But when he again persisted, and said, swear by the fortune of Caesar, he answered, If thou art vainly confident that I shall swear by the fortune of Caesar, as thou suggestest, and pretendest to be ignorant of me who I am, hear distinctly, I am a Christian. But if thou desirest to learn the scheme of Christianity, give me a day to speak, and hearken unto me.

10:2 The proconsul said, Persuade the people. But Polycarp said, I have thought thee indeed worthy to receive explanation, for we have been taught to render such honour as is fitting, and as does not injure us, to the powers and authorities ordained by God; but those I consider not worthy that I should make my defence before them.

CHAPTER 11
11:1 But the proconsul said unto him, I have wild beasts; I will deliver thee unto them, unless thou

repentest. But he said, call them, for repentance from the better to the worse is impossible for us; but it is a good thing to change from evil deeds to just ones.

11:2 But he said again unto him, I will cause thee to be consumed by fire if thou despisest the wild beasts, unless thou repentest. But Polycarp said, Thou threatenest me with fire that burneth but for a season, and is soon quenched. For thou art ignorant of the fire of the judgment to come, and of the eternal punishment reserved for the wicked. But why delayest thou? Bring whatever thou wishest.

CHAPTER 12

12:1 While he was saying these and more things, he was filled with courage and joy, and his face was filled with grace; so that he not only was not troubled and confused by the things said unto him, but, on the contrary, the proconsul was astonished, and sent his herald into the midst of the arena to proclaim a third time: Polycarp has confessed himself to be a Christian.

12:2 When this had been said by the herald, the whole multitude, both of Gentiles and Jews, that inhabit Smyrna, with irrestrainable anger and a loud voice, called out, This is the teacher of impiety, the father of the Christians, the destroyer of your gods, who teacheth many neither to sacrifice nor to worship the gods. Saying these things, they shouted out, and asked the Asiarch Philip to let loose a lion at Polycarp. But Philip replied that it was not lawful for him to do so, since he had finished the exhibition of wild beasts.
12:3 Then it seemed good unto them to shout with one voice that Polycarp should be burnt alive; for it was necessary that the vision that appeared unto him on his pillow should be fulfilled, when seeing it burning, he prayed, and said prophetically, turning to the faithful who were with him, I must be burnt alive.

CHAPTER 13

13:1 These things, therefore, happened with so great rapidity, that they took less time than the narration, the multitude quickly collecting logs and brushwood from the workshops and baths, the Jews especially lending their services zealously for this purpose, as is their custom.

13:2 But when the pyre was ready, having put off all his garments, and having loosed his girdle, he essayed to take off his shoes; not being in the habit of doing this previously, because each of the faithful used to strive which should be the first to touch his body, for, on account of his good conversation, he was, even before his martyrdom, adorned with every good gift.

13:3 Straightway, therefore, there were put around him the implements prepared for the pyre. And when they were about besides to nail him to it, he said, suffer me thus, for he who gave me to abide the fire will also allow me, without the security of your nails, to remain on the pyre without moving.

CHAPTER 14

14:1 They, therefore, did not nail him, but bound him. But he, having placed his hands behind him, and being bound, like a notable ram appointed for offering out of a great flock, prepared as a whole burnt-offering acceptable unto God, having looked up unto heaven, said, O Lord God Almighty, Father of thy beloved and blessed Son Jesus Christ, through whom we have received our knowledge concerning thee, the God of angels and powers, and of the whole creation, and of all the race of the just who lived before thee,

14:2 I thank thee that thou hast deemed me worthy of this day and hour, that I should have my portion in the number of the martyrs, in the cup of thy Christ, unto the resurrection of eternal life, both of the soul and body, in the incorruptibility of the Holy Spirit. Among these may I be received before thee this day as a rich and acceptable sacrifice, even as thou hast prepared and made manifest beforehand, and hast fulfilled, thou who art the unerring and true God.

14:3 On this account, and concerning all things, I praise thee, I bless thee, I glorify thee, together with the eternal and heavenly Jesus Christ thy beloved Son, with whom to thee and the Holy Spirit be glory both now and forever. Amen.

CHAPTER 15

15:1 And when he had uttered the Amen, and had finished his prayer, the men who superintended the fire kindled it. And a great flame breaking out, we, to whom it was given to see, saw a great wonder; for to this end also were we preserved, that we might announce what happened to the rest of mankind.

15:2 For the fire, assuming the form of a vault, like the sail of a vessel filled with the wind, defended the body of the martyr roundabout; and it was in the midst of the flame not like flesh burning, but like bread being baked, or like gold and silver glowing in the furnace. And we perceived such a sweet-smelling savour, as though from the breath of incense, or some other precious perfume.

CHAPTER 16

16:1 At last these wicked men, perceiving that his body could not be consumed by the fire, commanded the slaughterer to come near and plunge in a sword. And when he had done this, there came out a dove and an abundance of blood, so that it quenched the fire, and all the multitude wondered that there was such a difference between the unbelievers and the elect.

16:2 Of whom this most admirable martyr Polycarp was one, having been in our time an apostolic and prophetic teacher, and bishop of the Catholic church which is in Smyrna. For every word which he uttered from his mouth both hath been fulfilled and shall be fulfilled.

CHAPTER 17

17:1 But the evil one, who is the opponent and envier, who is the enemy to the race of men, beholding both the greatness of his testimony and his conversation blameless from the beginning, how he was crowned with a crown of immortality, and how he carried off a prize that could not be spoken against, contrived that not even a relic of him should be taken by us, though many desired to do this, and to communicate with his holy flesh.
17:2 He suborned, therefore, Nicetes, the father of Herodes, and the brother of Alce, to make interest with the governor so as not to give his body to the tomb, Lest, said he, they abandon the crucified and begin to worship this man. And these things they said at the suggestion and instance of the Jews, who also kept watch when we were about to take the body from the fire, not knowing that we shall never be able to abandon Christ, who suffered for the salvation of the whole world of those who are saved, the blameless on behalf of sinners, nor to worship anyone else.

17:3 Him we adore as the Son of God; but the martyrs, as the disciples and imitators of the Lord, we love according to their deserts, on account of their incomparable love for their King and Teacher, with whom may it be our lot to be partners and fellow-disciples.

CHAPTER 18

18:1 Therefore, the centurion, seeing the strife that had risen among the Jews, placed the body in the midst of the fire and burned it.

18:2 Thus we, having afterwards taken up his bones, more valuable than precious stones, laid them where it was suitable.
18:3 There, so far as is allowed us, when we are gathered together in exultation and joy, the Lord will enable us to celebrate the birthday of the martyrs, both for the memory of those who have contended, and for the exercise and preparation of those to come.

CHAPTER 19

19:1 Such were the things that happened to the blessed Polycarp, who together with those from Philadelphia was the twelfth who suffered martyrdom in Smyrna;

but he alone is held in memory by all, so that he is spoken of in every place even by the Gentiles; not only being a distinguished teacher, but also an eminent martyr, whose testimony we desire to imitate, since it happened according to the Gospel of Christ.

19:2 For having overcome by patience the unjust governor, and so having received the crown of immortality, rejoicing together with the apostles and all the just, he glorifieth God and the Father, and blesseth our Lord Jesus Christ the Saviour of our souls, and the pilot of our bodies, and the shepherd of the Catholic Church throughout the world.

CHAPTER 20

20:1 Ye therefore desired that the things that had happened should be shown unto you more at length; but we for the present have related them unto you briefly by means of our brother Marcus. Now do ye, when ye have read these things, send on the letter to the brethren who are further off, that they also may glorify the Lord, who is making a selection from among his own servants.

20:2 To him who is able to bring us all in, by his grace and gift, into his eternal kingdom, through his only-begotten Son Jesus Christ; to him be the glory, honour, strength, majesty for ever. Amen. Salute all the saints. They who are with us salute you, and Evarestus who wrote these things, and all his house.

CHAPTER 21

21:1 Now the blessed Polycarp was martyred on the second day of the month Xanthicus, on the twenty-fifth of April, on the great Sabbath, at the eighth hour. But he was apprehended by Herodes, when Philip of Tralles was high priest, Statius Quadratus being proconsul, and Jesus Christ king for ever, to whom be glory, honour, majesty, and eternal throne, from generation to generation. Amen.

CHAPTER 22

22:1 We pray, brethren, that you may fare well, walking by the word of the gospel of Jesus Christ, with whom be glory to God and the Father, and the Holy Spirit, for the salvation of the holy elect, even as the blessed Polycarp hath born witness, in whose steps may we be found in the kingdom of Jesus Christ.

22:2 These things have been transcribed by Gaius, from the manuscripts of Irenaeus, the disciple of Polycarp, who also was a fellow-citizen to Irenaeus. But I, Socrates, made a copy in Corinth from the copies of Gaius. Grace be with you all.

22:3 But I, Pionius, afterwards copied them from the above written, having sought them out, after that the blessed Polycarp had made them manifest to me by a revelation, as I will show in what follows; having gathered them together, when they had already become almost obliterated by time, in order that the Lord Jesus Christ may gather me also together with his elect, unto his heavenly kingdom, to whom be glory with the Father and the Holy Spirit, world without end. Amen.

Papias of Hierapolis

Papias, (60 – 130 CE) who resided in Hierapolis, was a bishop and an influential figure in the early second century AD. His most renowned work, "Expositions of the Sayings of the Lord," is unfortunately lost, but it was quoted by later Church fathers. Papias was interested in collecting and preserving the oral traditions of the apostles. He emphasized the significance of personal eyewitness accounts of Jesus' teachings.

Papias of Hierapolis is sometimes considered an Apostolic Father due to his potential association with the apostolic era and his contributions to early Christian literature. However, it's important to note that the precise details of Papias' life and his connection to the apostolic era are subject to some uncertainty and scholarly debate.

Papias is believed to have lived in the first and second centuries, with estimates placing his active period around 70-130 AD. He was a Christian bishop and an influential figure in the early church. Papias is primarily known for his work titled "Exposition of the Sayings of the Lord" (also known as "Expositions on the Oracles of the Lord"), which unfortunately has not survived intact. Only fragments and references to his work remain in the writings of other early Christian authors.

Papias is sometimes considered an Apostolic Father for the following reasons:

1 Association with Apostolic Figures: Papias claimed to have gathered information about Jesus and the apostles through conversations with those who had direct contact with them. He expressed a particular interest in collecting the oral traditions passed down by these early witnesses. Papias specifically mentioned his interactions with disciples of the apostle John, such as Aristion and John the Elder. This claim suggests a potential link to the apostolic era and the transmission of apostolic teachings.

2 Focus on Oral Tradition: Papias emphasized the importance of preserving and transmitting oral traditions about Jesus and the apostles. He sought to gather information from reliable sources and conveyed these traditions in his work. Papias' interest in the accounts and teachings of the early apostles aligns with the concerns of the Apostolic Fathers in preserving apostolic teachings and traditions.

However, it's worth noting that the extent to which Papias accurately relayed the teachings of the apostolic era is a matter of scholarly debate. Some scholars consider his work to be valuable for understanding early Christian traditions, while others view it with caution due to potential inaccuracies or misinterpretations.

There are conflicting stories regarding the death of Papias. One encounters statements that Papias flourished in the 2d century, and finally suffered martyrdom, however the specifics are in debate. There is a statement by Irenaeus that Papias was "a hearer of John, and companion of Polycarp, a man of old time." (Adversus Haereses V 33.4) If Polycarp was in fact born not later than AD 69, then there may be no reason to depend on a further, but disputed tradition, that Papias shared in the martyrdom of Polycarp (ca AD 155) According to Irenaeus he was a disciple of the apostle John; but Eusebius, who quotes (Hist. Eccles. ch. 39) the words of Irenaeus, immediately subjoins a passage from Papias himself, in which the latter distinctly states that he did not receive his doctrines from any of the apostles, but from the "living voice" of such followers of theirs as "are still surviving." He was an intimate associate of Polycarp, a bishop in the same province of proconsular Asia; and as the latter was a disciple of the apostle John, it is probable that Irenaeus inferred that his companion must have been the same. The Paschal or Alexandrian Chronicle states that Papias suffered martyrdom at Pergamus, A.D. 161; others put the date 165.

In conclusion, Papias is sometimes included among the Apostolic Fathers due to his potential association with the apostolic era and his focus on preserving oral traditions related to Jesus and the apostles. However, the exact nature of his connections and the reliability of his work are still subjects of scholarly discussion.

Papias

Fragments of Papias
Roberts-Donaldson English Translation: Fragments of Papias
Resources
Roberts-Donaldson Introduction
I consider the fragment X of the Roberts-Donaldson collection of fragments to be completely suspect as the alleged words of Papias.
Schoedel writes about Papias (The Anchor Bible Dictionary, v. 5, p. 140):

According to Irenaeus, our earliest witness, Papias was "a hearer of John and a companion of Polycarp, a man of primitive times," who wrote a volume in "five books" (haer. 5.33.4; quoted by Eusebius Hist. Eccl. 3.39.1). Eusebius already doubted the reality of a connection between Papias and the apostle John on the grounds that Papias himself in the preface to his book distinguished the apostle John from John the presbyter and seems to have had significant contact only with John the presbyter and a certain Aristion (Hist. Eccl. 3.39.3-7). Eusebius' skepticism was no doubt prompted by his distaste - perhaps a recently acquired distaste (Grant 1974) - for Papias' chiliasm (chiliasm is the thought Christ will come back to reign on Earth for 1,000 years) and his feeling that such a theology qualified Papias for the distinction of being "a man of exceedingly small intelligence" (Hist. Eccl. 3.39.13). Nevertheless Eusebius' analysis of the preface is probably correct; and his further point that Papias' chiliasm put him to the same camp as the Revelation of John is surely relevant. It is notable that Eusebius, in spite of his desire to discredit Papias, still places him as early as the reign of Trajan (A.D. 98-117); and although later dates (e.g., A.D. 130-140) have often been suggested by modern scholars, Bartlet's date for Papias' literary activity of about A.D. 100 has recently gained support (Schoedel 1967: 91-92; Kortner 1983: 89-94, 167-72, 225-26).

Schoedel writes about the comments of Papias (op. cit., v. 5, pp. 141-142):

What the fragments have to tell us about Mark and Matthew is information that Papias himself traces to "the presbyter" (Eus. Hist. Eccl. 3.39.15-16). Eusebius separates the statements about Mark and Matthew, but they may have originally followed one another and certainly seem closely related. Perhaps the simplest reading of the statement on Mark is that Mark served as Peter's interpreter (possibly in the role of methurgaman, or oral translator) and wrote down what he heard Peter say of the words and deeds of Jesus and that his writing is defective in "order," though not in accuracy or fullness of recollection, because Peter naturally referred to the Lord's logia in a random manner. Some have suspected that Papias did not have in mind the gospel of Mark that we know, but the arguments are tenuous. On another point, Kurzinger has attempted to show that Papias was speaking not of translation from the native language of Peter but of presentation of the reports of Peter (an interpretation which he applies also to Papias' statement about Matthew); but this seems to push a rhetorical approach to Papias' terminology too far (Schoedel 1967: 107; Kortner 1983: 203-4). On the other hand, an interpretation in rhetorical terms is somewhat more likely when it comes to the suggestion that Papias meant to say that Peter spoke "in chria-style" rather than "as needs (chriai) dictated." But the point that is debated more than any other is what Papias had in mind when he said that Mark did not write "in order." It is perhaps most likely that Papias was measuring Mark by Matthew (who is said by Papias to have made "an ordered arrangement" of the materials) - or perhaps more generally by Papias' own conception of what ought to be included in such an account - and that he had in mind completeness of information as well as "order" in the narrow sense of the term. In any event, Papias is defending Mark in spite of perceived deficiencies.

Papias attests the role that oral tradition continued to play in the first half of the second century. Papias himself preferred "the living voice" to what could be found in books. Nevertheless, Papias seems to have known the Gospels, and he provides the earliest tradition concerning the authorship of the Gospel of Mark. The testimony of Papias concerning Matthew is more problematic. Eusebius says that Papias also "made use of testimonies from the first letter of John and likewise from that of Peter" (Hist. Eccl. 3.39.17).

FRAGMENTS OF PAPIAS FROM THE EXPOSITION OF THE ORACLES OF THE LORD.

I.

[THE writings of Papias in common circulation are five in number, and these are called an Exposition of the Oracles of the Lord. Irenaeus makes mention of these as the only works written by him, in the following words: "Now testimony is borne to these things in writing by Papias, an ancient man, who was a hearer of John, and a friend of Polycarp, in the fourth of his books; for five books were composed by him." Thus wrote Irenaeus. Moreover, Papias himself, in the introduction to his books, makes it manifest that he was not himself a hearer and eye-witness of the holy apostles; but he tells us that he received the truths of our religion from those who were aquainted with them [the apostles] in the following words:]

But I shall not be unwilling to put down, along with my interpretations, whatsoever instructions I received with care at any time from the elders, and stored up with care in my memory, assuring you at the same time of their truth. For I did not, like the multitude, take pleasure in those who spoke much, but in those who taught the truth; nor in those who related strange commandments, but in those who rehearsed the commandments given by the Lord to faith, and proceeding from truth itself. If, then, anyone who had attended on the elders came, I asked minutely after their sayings, what Andrew or Peter said, or what was said by Philip, or by Thomas, or by James, or by John, or by Matthew, or by any other of the Lord's disciples: which things Aristion and the presbyter John, the disciples of the Lord, say. For I imagined that what was to be got from books was not so profitable to me as what came from the living and abiding voice.

II.

[The early Christians] called those who practiced a godly guilelessness, children, [as is stated by Papias in the first book of the Lord's Expositions, and by Clemens Alexandrinus in his Paedagogue.]

III.

Judas walked about in this world a sad example of impiety; for his body having swollen to such an extent that he could not pass where a chariot could pass easily, he was crushed by the chariot, so that his bowels gushed out.

Joseph Lumpkin

IV.

[As the elders who saw John the disciple of the Lord remembered that they had heard from him how the Lord taught in regard to those times, and said]: "The days will come in which vines shall grow, having each ten thousand branches, and in each branch ten thousand twigs, and in each true twig ten thousand shoots, and in every one of the shoots ten thousand clusters, and on every one of the clusters ten thousand grapes, and every grape when pressed will give five-and-twenty metretes of wine. And when anyone of the saints shall lay hold of a cluster, another shall cry out, 'I am a better cluster, take me; bless the Lord through me.' In like manner, [He said] that a grain of wheat would produce ten thousand ears, and that every ear would have ten thousand grains, and every grain would yield ten pounds of clear, pure, fine flour; and that apples, and seeds, and grass would produce in similar proportions; and that all animals, feeding then only on the productions of the earth, would become peaceable and harmonious, and be in perfect subjection to man." [Testimony is borne to these things in writing by Papias, an ancient man, who was a hearer of John and a friend of Polycarp, in the fourth of his books; for five books were composed by him. And he added, saying, "Now these things are credible to believers. And Judas the traitor," says he, "not believing, and asking, 'How shall such growths be accomplished by the Lord?' the Lord said, 'They shall see who shall come to them.' These, then, are the times mentioned by the prophet Isaiah: 'And the wolf shall lie, down with the lamb,' etc. (Isa. xi. 6 ff.)."]

V.

As the presbyters say, then those who are deemed worthy of an abode in heaven shall go there, others shah enjoy the delights of Paradise, and others shall possess the splendour of the city; for everywhere the Saviour will be seen, according as they shall be worthy who see Him. But that there is this distinction between the habitation of those who produce an hundredfold, and that of those who produce sixty-fold, and that of those who produce thirty-fold; for the first will be taken up into the heavens, the second class will dwell in Paradise, and the last will inhabit the city; and that on this account the Lord said, "In my Father's house are many mansions:" for all things belong to God, who supplies all with a suitable dwelling-place, even as His word says, that a share is given to all by the Father, according as each one is or shall be worthy. And this is the couch in which they shall recline who feast, being invited to the wedding. The presbyters, the disciples of the apostles, say that this is the gradation and arrangement of those who are saved, and that they advance through steps of this nature; and that,

moreover, they ascend through the Spirit to the Son, and through the Son to the Father; and that in due time the Son will yield up His work to the Father, even as it is said by the apostle, "For He must reign till He hath put all enemies under His feet. The last enemy that shall be destroyed is death." For in the times of the kingdom the just man who is on the earth shall forget to die. "But when He saith all things are put under Him, it is manifest that He is excepted which did put all things under Him. And when all things shall be subdued unto Him, then shall the Son also Himself be subject unto Him that put all things under Him, that God may be all in all."

VI.

[Papias, who is now mentioned by us, affirms that he received the sayings of the apostles from those who accompanied them, and he moreover asserts that he heard in person Aristion and the presbyter John. Accordingly he mentions them frequently by name, and in his writings gives their traditions. Our notice of these circumstances may not be without its use. It may also be worth while to add to the statements of Papias already given, other passages of his in which he relates some miraculous deeds, stating that he acquired the knowledge of them from tradition. The residence of the Apostle Philip with his daughters in Hierapolis has been mentioned above. We must now point out how Papias, who lived at the same time, relates that he had received a wonderful narrative from the daughters of Philip. For he relates that a dead man was raised to life in his day. He also mentions another miracle relating to Justus, surnamed Barsabas, how he swallowed a deadly poison, and received no harm, on account of the grace of the Lord. The same person, moreover, has set down other things as coming to him from unwritten tradition, amongst these some strange parables and instructions of the Saviour, and some other things of a more fabulous nature. Amongst these he says that there will be a millennium after the resurrection from the dead, when the personal reign of Christ will be established on this earth. He moreover hands down, in his own writing, other narratives given by the previously mentioned Aristion of the Lord's sayings, and the traditions of the presbyter John. For information on these points, we can merely refer our readers to the books themselves; but now, to the extracts already made, we shall add, as being a matter of primary importance, a tradition regarding Mark who wrote the Gospel, which he [Papias] has given in the following words]: And the presbyter said this. Mark having become the interpreter of Peter, wrote down accurately whatsoever he remembered. It was not, however, in exact order that he related the sayings or deeds of Christ. For he neither heard the Lord nor accompanied Him. But afterwards, as I said, he accompanied Peter, who accommodated his instructions to the necessities [of his hearers], but with no intention of giving a regular narrative of the Lord's sayings. Wherefore Mark made no mistake in thus writing some things as he remembered them. For of one thing he took especial care, not to omit anything he had heard, and not to put anything fictitious into the statements. [This is what is related by Papias regarding Mark; but with regard to Matthew he has made the following statements]: Matthew put together the oracles [of the Lord] in the Hebrew language, and each one interpreted them as best he could. [The same person uses proofs from the First Epistle of John, and from the Epistle of Peter in like manner. And he also gives another story of a woman who was accused of many sins before the Lord, which is to be fount in the Gospel according to the Hebrews.]

VII.

Papias thus speaks, word far word: To some of them [angels] He gave dominion over the arrangement of the world, and He commissioned them to exercise their dominion well. And he says, immediately after this: but it happened that their arrangement came to nothing.

VIII.

With regard to the inspiration of the book (Revelation), we deem it superfluous to add another word; for the blessed Gregory Theologus and Cyril, and even men of still older date, Papias, Irenaeus, Methodius, and Hippolytus, bore entirely satisfactory testimony to it.

IX.

Taking occasion from Papias of Hierapolis, the illustrious, a disciple of the apostle who leaned on the bosom of Christ, and Clemens, and Pantaenus the priest of [the Church] of the Alexandrians, and the wise Ammonius, the ancient and first expositors, who agreed with each other, who understood the work of the six days as referring to Christ and the whole Church.

X.

(1) Mary the mother of the Lord; (2) Mary the wife of Cleophas or Alphaeus, who was the mother of James the bishop and apostle, and of Simon and Thaddeus, and of one Joseph; (3) Mary Salome, wife of Zebedee, mother of John the evangelist and James; (4) Mary Magdalene. These four are found in the Gospel. James and Judas and Joseph were sons of an aunt (2) of the Lord's. James also and John were sons of another aunt (3) of the Lord's. Mary (2), mother of James the Less

and Joseph, wife of Alphaeus was the sister of Mary the mother of the Lord, whom John names of Cleophas, either from her father or from the family of the clan, or for some other reason. Mary Salome (3) is called Salome either from her husband or her village. Some affirm that she is the same as Mary of Cleophas, because she had two husbands.

The Shepherd of Hermas

Vision 1

1:1 The mastr, who raised me sold me to a lady, Rhoda in Rome. Afer many years, I met her again, and began to love her as a sister.

1:2 After a period of time I saw her bathing in the river Tiber; and I gave her my hand, and led her out of the river. When I saw her beauty, I thought to myself, "I would be happy if I had such a one as a wife both because of her beauty and character." I merely thought about this and nothing more.

1:3 After a while, as I was travelling to Cumae, and praising God because of his creatures, for their greatness and beauty and power. As I walked I fell asleep. And a Spirit took me, and lifted me away through a land that had no path and through which no man could pass. The place has cliffs, and was broken into clefts by rivers. When I had crossed the river, I came into the level country, and knelt down, and began to pray to the Lord and to confess my sins.

1:4 Now, while I prayed, heaven was opened, and I saw the lady, whom I had desired, greeting me from heaven, saying, "Good day, Hermas."

1:5 And, looking at her, I said to her, "Lady, what are you doing here?" Then she answered me, "I was taken up, that I might convict you of your sins before the Lord."

1:6 I said to her, "Dost you now convict me?" "Nay, not so," said she, "but hear the words, that I shall say to you. God, Who dwelled in the heavens, and created out of nothing the things which are, and increased and multiplied them for His holy Church's sake, is wroth with you, for that you didst sin against me."

1:7 I answered her and said, "Sin against you? In what way? Did I ever speak an unseemly word unto you? Did I not always regard you as a goddess? Did I not always respect you as a sister? How couldst you falsely charge me, lady, with such villainy and uncleanness?

1:8 "Laughing she said unto me, "The desire after evil entered into your heart. No, think you not that it is an evil deed for a righteous man, if the evil desire should enter into his heart? It is indeed a sin and a great one too," said she; "for the righteous man entertained righteous purposes. While then his purposes are righteous, his repute stands steadfast in the heavens, and he finds the Lord easily propitiated in all that he does. But they that entertain evil purposes in their hearts, bring upon themselves death an captivity, especially they that claim for themselves this present work and boast in its riches, and hold fast not to the good things that are to come.

1:9 Their souls shall rue it, seeing that they have no hope, but have abandoned themselves and their life. But do you pray unto God and He shall heal your own sins, and those of thy whole house, and of all the saints."

2:1 As soon as she had spoken these words the heavens were shut and I was given over to horror and grief Then I said within myself "If this sin is recorded against me, how can I be saved? Or how shall I propitiate God for my sins which are full-blown? Or with which words shall I entreat the Lord that He may be propitious unto me?

2:2 While I was advising and discussing these matters in my heart, I see, before me a great white chair of snow-white wool; and there came an aged lady in glistening raiment, having a book in her hands, and she sat down alone, and she saluted me, "Good morrow, Hermas." Then I grieved and weeping, said, "Good morrow, lady."

2:3 And she said to me "Why so gloomy, Hermas, you that art patient and good-tempered and art always smiling? Why so downcast in thy looks, and far from cheerful?" And I said to her, "Because of an excellent lady's saying that I had sinned against her."

2:4 Then she said, "Far be this thing from the servant of God! Nevertheless the thought did enter into thy heart concerning her. Now to the servants of God such a purpose brings sin. For it is an evil and mad purpose to overtake a devout spirit that has been already approved, that it should desire an evil deed, and especially if it be Hermas the temperate, who abstained from every evil desire, and is full of all simplicity and of great guilelessness.

3:1 "Yet it is not for this that God is wroth with you, but that you may convert thy family, that has done wrong against the Lord and against you their parents. But out of fondness for thy children you didst not admonish thy family, but didst suffer it to become fearfully corrupt. Therefore the Lord is wroth with you. But He will heal all thy past sins, which have been committed in thy family; for by reason of their sins and iniquities you hast been corrupted by the affairs of this world.

3:2 But the great mercy of the Lord had pity on you and thy family, and will strengthen you, and establish you in His glory. Only be not you careless, but take courage, and strengthen thy family. For as the smith hammering his work conquers the task which he wills, so also doth righteous discourse repeated daily conquer all evil. Cease not therefore to reprove thy children; for I know that if they shall repent with all their heart, they shall be written in the books of life with the saints."

3:3 After these words of hers had ceased, she said unto me, "Wilt you listen to me as I read?" Then say I, "Yes, lady." She said to me, "Be attentive, and hear the glories of God" I listened with attention and with wonder to that which I had no power to remember; for all the words were terrible, such as man cannot bear. The last words however I remembered, for they were suitable for us and gentle.

3:4 "Behold, the God of Hosts, Who by His invisible and mighty power and by His great wisdom created the world, and by His glorious purpose clothed His creation with comeliness, and by His strong word fixed the heaven, and founded the earth upon the waters, and by His own wisdom and providence formed His holy Church, which also He blessed-behold, He removed the heavens and the mountains and the hills and the seas, and all things are made level for His elect, that He may fulfill to them the promise which He promised with great glory and rejoicing, if so be that they shall keep the ordinances of God, which they received, with great faith."

4:1 When then she finished reading and arose from her chair, there came four young men, and they took away the chair, and departed towards the East.

4:2 Then she called me unto her, and she touched my breast, and said to me, "Did my reading please you?" And I say unto her, "Lady, these last words please me, but the former were difficult and hard." Then she spoke to me, saying, "These last words are for the righteous, but the former are for the heathen and the rebellious."

4:3 While she yet spoke with me, two men appeared, and took her by the arms, and they departed, whither the chair also had gone, towards the East. And she smiled as she departed and, as she was going, she said to me, "Play the man, Hermas."

Vision 2

1[5]:1 I was on the way to Cumae, at the same season as last year, and called to mind my last year's vision as I walked; and again a Spirit took me, and carried me away to the same place as last year.

1[5]:2 When then I arrived at the place, I fell upon my knees, and began to pray to the Lord, and to glorify His name, for that he counted me worthy, and made known unto me my former sins.

1[5]:3 But after I had risen up from prayer, I behold before me the aged lady, whom also I had seen last year, walking and reading a little book. And she said to me, "Canst you report these things to the elect of God?" I say unto her, "Lady, I cannot recollect so much; but give me the little book, that I may copy it." "Take it," said she, "and be sure and return it to me."

1[5]:4 I took it, and retiring to a certain spot in the country I copied it letter for letter: for I could not make out the syllables. When then I had finished the letters of the book, suddenly the book was snatched out of my hand; but by whom I did not see.

2[6]:1 Now after fifteen days, when I had fasted and entreated the Lord earnestly, the knowledge of the writing was revealed to me. And this is what was written:--

2[6]:2 "Your seed, Hermas, have sinned against God, and have blasphemed the Lord, and have betrayed their parents through great wickedness, yea, they have got the name of betrayers of parents, and yet they did not profit by their betrayal; and they still further added to their sins wanton deeds and reckless wickedness;

and so the measure of their transgressions was filled up.

2[6]:3 But make these words known to all thy children, and to thy wife who shall be as thy sister; for she too refrained not from using her tongue, wherewith she doeth evil. But, when she hears these words, she will refrain, and will find mercy.

2[6]:4 After that you hast made known unto them all these words, which the Master commanded me that they should be revealed unto you, then all their sins which they sinned aforetime are forgiven to them; yea, and to all the saints that have sinned unto this day, if they repent with their whole heart, and remove double-mindedness from their heart.

2[6]:5 For the Master swore by His own glory, as concerning His elect; that if, now that this day has been set as a limit, sin shall hereafter be committed, they shall not find salvation; for repentance for the righteous has an end; the days of repentance are accomplished for all the saints; whereas for the Gentiles there is repentance until the last day.

2[6]:6 You shall therefore say unto the elders of the Church, that they direct their paths in righteousness, that they may receive in full the promises with abundant glory.

2[6]:7 you therefore that work righteousness be steadfast, and be not double-minded, that you may have admission with the holy angels. Blessed are you, as many as endure patiently the great tribulation that cometh, and as many as shall not deny their life.

2[6]:8 For the Lord swear concerning His Son, that those who denied their Lord should be rejected from their life, even they that are now about to deny Him in the coming days; but to those who denied Him aforetime, to them mercy was given of His great loving kindness.

3[7]:1 "But do you, Hermas, no longer bear a grudge against thy children, neither suffer thy sister to have her way, so that they may be purified from their former sins. For they shall be chastised with a righteous chastisement, unless you bear a grudge against them thyself. The bearing of a grudge worked death. But you, Hermas, hast had great tribulations of your own, by reason of the transgressions of thy family, because you had no care for them. For you was neglectful of them, and was mixed up with your evil transactions.

3[7]:2 But herein is thy salvation, in that you didst not depart from the living God, and in thy simplicity and thy great continence. These have saved you, if you abide therein; and they save all who do such things, and walk in guilelessness and simplicity. These men prevail over all wickedness, and continue unto life eternal.

3[7]:3 Blessed are all they that work righteousness. They shall never be destroyed.

3[7]:4 But you shall say to Maximus, "Behold tribulation cometh (upon you), if you think fit to deny a second time. The Lord is nigh unto them that turn unto him, as it is written in Eldad and Modat, who prophesied to the people in the wilderness."

4[8]:1 Now, brethren, a revelation was made unto me in my sleep by a youth of exceeding fair form, who said to me, "Whom think you the aged woman, from whom you received the book, to be?" I say, "The Sibyl" "You art wrong," said he, "she is not." "Who then is she?" I say. "The Church," said he. I said unto him, "Wherefore then is she aged?" "Because," said he, "she was created before all things; therefore is she aged; and for her sake the world was framed."

4[8]:2 And afterwards I saw a vision in my house. The aged woman came, and asked me, if I had already given the book to the elders. I said that I had not given it. "You hast done well," she said, "for I have words to add. When then I shall have finished all the words, it shall be made known by thy means to all the elect.

4[8]:3 You shall therefore write two little books, and shall send one to Clement, and one to Grapte. So Clement shall send to the foreign cities, for this is his duty; while Grapte shall instruct the widows and the orphans. But you shall read (the book) to this city along with the elders that preside over the Church.

Vision 3

1[9]:1 The third vision, which I saw, brethren, was as follows.

1[9]:2 After fasting often, and entreating the Lord to declare unto me the revelation which He promised to show me by the mouth of the aged woman, that very night the aged woman was seen of me, and she said to me, "Seeing that you art so importunate and eager to know all things, come into the country where you abide, and about the fifth hour I will appear, and will show you what you ought to see."

1[9]:3 I asked her, saying, "Lady, to what part of the country?" "Where you wilt," said she. I selected a beautiful and retired spot; but before I spoke to her and named the spot, she said to me, "I will come, whither you will."

1[9]:4 I went then, brethren, into the country, and I counted up the hours, and came to the place where I appointed her to come, and I see an ivory couch placed there, and on the couch there lay a linen cushion, and on the cushion was spread a coverlet of fine linen of flax.

1[9]:5 When I saw these things so ordered, and no one in the place, I was amazed, and a fit of trembling seized me, and my hair stood on end; and a fit of shuddering came upon me, because I was alone. When then I recovered myself, and remembered the glory of God, and took courage, I knelt down and confessed my sins to the Lord once more, as I had done on the former occasion.

1[9]:6 Then she came with six young men, the same whom I had seen before, and she stood by me, and listened attentively to me, as I prayed and confessed my sins to the Lord. And she touched me, and said: "Hermas, make an end of constantly entreating for thy sins; entreat also for righteousness, that you may take some part forthwith to thy family."

1[9]:7 Then she raised me by the hand, and led me to the couch, and said to the young men, "Go you, and build."

1[9]:8 And after the young men had retired and we were left alone, she said to me, "Sit down here." I say to her, "Lady, let the elders sit down first." "Do as I bid you," said she, "sit down."

1[9]:9 When then I wanted to sit down on the right side, she would not allow me, but beckoned me with her hand that I should sit on the left side. As then I was musing thereon, and was sad because she would not permit me to sit on the right side, she said to me, "Art you sad, Hermas? The place on the right side is for others, even for those who have already been well-pleasing to God, and have suffered for the Name's sake. But you lack much that you should sit with them; but as you abide in thy simplicity, even so, and you shall sit with them, you and as many as shall have done their deeds, and have suffered what they suffered."

2[10]:1 "What did they suffer?" say I. "Listen," said she. "Stripes, imprisonments, great tribulations, crosses, wild beasts, for the Name's sake. Therefore to them belongs the right side of the Holiness--to them, and to all who shall suffer for the Name. But for the rest is the left side. Howbeit, to both, to them that sit on the right, and to them that sit on the left, are the same gifts, and the same promises, only they sit on the right and have a certain glory.

2[10]:2 You indeed art very desirous to sit on the right with them, but thy shortcomings are many; yet you shall be purified from thy shortcomings; yea, and all that are not double-minded shall be purified from all their sins unto this day."

2[10]:3 When she had said this, she wished to depart; but, falling at her feet, I entreated her by the Lord that she would show me the vision which she promised.

2[10]:4 Then she again took me by the hand, and raised me, and seated me on the couch at the left hand, while she herself sat on the right. And lifting up a certain glistening rod, she said to me, "See you a great thing?" I say to her, "Lady, I see nothing." She said to me, "Look you; do you not see in front of you a great tower being built upon the waters, of glistening square stones?"

2[10]:5 Now the tower was being built foursquare by the six young men that came with her. And countless other men were bringing stones, some of them from the deep, and others from the land, and were handing them to the six young men. And they took them and built.

2[10]:6 The stones that were dragged from the deep they placed in every case, just as they were, into the building, for they had been shaped, and they fitted in their joining with the other stones; and they adhered so closely one with another that their joining could not possibly be detected; and the building of the tower appeared as if it were built of one stone.

2[10]:7 But of the other stones which were brought from the dry land, some they threw away, and some they put into the building; and others they broke in pieces, and threw to a distance from the tower.

2[10]:8 Now many other stones were lying round the tower, and they did not use them for the building; for some of them were mildewed, and others had cracks in them, and others were too short, and others were white and round, and did not fit into the building.

2[10]:9 And I saw other stones thrown to a distance from the tower, and coming to the way, and yet not staying in the way, but rolling to where there was no way; and others falling into the fire and burning there; and others falling near the waters, and yet not able to roll into the water, although they desired to roll and to come to the water.

3[11]:1 When she had shown me these things, she wished to hurry away. I say to her, "Lady, what advantage is it to me to have seen these things, and yet not to know what the things mean? "She answered and said unto me, "You art an over-curious fellow, in desiring to know all that concerns the tower." "Yea, lady," I said, "that I may announce it to my brethren, and that they [may be the more gladdened and] when they hear [these things] they may know the Lord in great glory." Then said she,

3[11]:2 "Many shall hear; but when they hear, some of them shall be glad, and others shall weep. Yet even these latter, if they hear and repent, shall likewise be glad. Hear you therefore the parables of the tower; for I will reveal all things unto you. And trouble me no more about revelation; for these revelations have an end, seeing that they have been completed. Nevertheless you wilt not cease asking for revelations; for you art shameless."

3[11]:3 The tower, which you see building, is myself, the Church, which was seen of you both now and aforetime. Ask, therefore, what you will concerning the tower, and I will reveal it unto you, that you may rejoice with the saints."

3[11]:4 I say unto her, "Lady, since you didst hold me worthy once for all, that you should reveal all things to me, reveal them." Then she said to me, "Whatsoever is possible to be revealed to you, shall be revealed. Only let thy heart be with God, and doubt not in thy mind about that which you sees."

3[11]:5 I asked her, "Wherefore is the tower built upon waters, lady?" "I told you so before," said she, "and indeed you do enquire diligently. So by thy enquiry you discovered the truth. Hear then why the tower is built upon waters; it is because your life is saved and shall be saved by water. But the tower has been founded by the word of the Almighty and Glorious Name, and is strengthened by the unseen power of the Master."

4[12]:1 I answered and said unto her, "Lady, this thing is great and marvelous. But the six young men that build, who are they, lady?" "These are the holy angels of God, that were created first of all, unto whom the Lord delivered all His creation to increase and to build it, and to be masters of all creation. By their hands therefore the building of the tower will be accomplished."

4[12]:2 "And who are the others who are bringing the stones in?" "They also are holy angels of God; but these six are superior to them. The building of the tower then shall be accomplished, and all alike shall rejoice in the (completed) circle of the tower, and shall glorify God that the building of the tower was accomplished."

4[12]:3 I enquired of her, saying, "Lady, I could wish to know concerning the end of the stones, and their power, of what kind it is." She answered and said unto me, "It is not that you of all men art especially worthy that it should be revealed to you; for there are others before you, and better than you art, unto whom these visions ought to have been revealed. But that the name of God may be glorified, it has been revealed to you, all shall be revealed, for the sake of the doubtful-minded, who question in their hearts whether these things are so or not. Tell them that all these things are true, and that there is nothing beside the truth, but that all are steadfast, and valid, and established on a firm foundation.

5[13]:1 "Hear now concerning the stones that go to the building The stones that are squared and white, and that fit together in their joints, these are the apostles and bishops and teachers and deacons, who walked after the holiness of God, and exercised their office of bishop and teacher and deacon in purity and sanctity for the elect of God, some of them already fallen on sleep, and others still living. And because they always agreed with one another, they both had peace among themselves and listened one to another. Therefore their joinings fit together in the building of the tower."

5[13]:2 "But they that are dragged from the deep, and placed in the building, and that fit together in their joinings with the other stones that are already built in, who are they?" "These are they that suffered for the name of the Lord."

5[13]:3 "But the other stones that are brought from the dry land, I would fain know who these are, lady." She said, "Those that go to the building, and yet are not hewn, these the Lord has approved because they walked in the uprightness of the Lord, and rightly performed His commandments."

5[13]:4 "But they that are brought and placed in the building, who are they?" "They are young in the faith, and faithful; but they are warned by the angels to do good, because wickedness was found in them."

5[13]:5 "But those whom they rejected and threw away, who are they?" "These have sinned, and desire to repent, therefore they were not cast to a great distance from the tower, because they will be useful for the building, if they repent. They then that shall repent, if they repent, will be strong in the faith, if they repent now while the tower is building. But if the building shall be finished, they have no more any place, but shall be castaways. This privilege only they have, that they lie near the tower.

5[13]:1 But wouldst you know about them that are broken in pieces, and cast away far from the tower? These are the sons of lawlessness. They received the faith in hypocrisy, and no wickedness was absent from them. Therefore they have not salvation, for they are not useful for building by reason of their wickednesses. Therefore they were broken up and thrown far away by reason of the wrath of the Lord, for they excited Him to wrath.

5[13]:2 But the rest whom you hast seen lying in great numbers, not going to the building, of these they that are mildewed are they that knew the truth, but did not abide in it, nor hold fast to the saints. Therefore they are useless."

5[13]:3 "But they that have the cracks, who are they?" "These are they that have discord in their hearts against one another, and are not at peace among themselves; who have an appearance of peace, but when they depart from one another, their wickednesses abide in their hearts. These are the cracks which the stones have.

5[13]:4 But they that are broken off short, these have believed, and have their greater part in righteousness, but have some parts of lawlessness; therefore they are too short, and are not perfect."

5[13]:5 "But the white and round stones, which did not fit into the building, who are they, lady?" She answered and said to me, "How long art you foolish and stupid, and enquire everything, and understand nothing? These are they that have faith, but have also riches of this world. When tribulation cometh, they deny their Lord by reason of their riches and their business affairs."

5[13]:6 And I answered and said unto her, "When then, lady, will they be useful for the building?" "When," she replied, "their wealth, which led their souls astray, shall be cut away, then will they be useful for God. For just as the round stone, unless it be cut away, and lose some portion of itself, cannot become square, so also they that are rich in this world, unless their riches be cut away, cannot become useful to the Lord.

5[13]:7 Learn first from thyself When you had riches, you was useless; but now you art useful and profitable unto life. Be you useful unto God, for you thyself also art taken from the same stones.

7[15]:1 "But the other stones which you saw cast far away from the tower and falling into the way and rolling out of the way into the regions where there is no way, these are they that have believed, but by reason of their double heart they abandon their true way. Thus thinking that they can find a better way, they go astray and are sore distressed, as they walk about in the regions where there is no way.

7[15]:2 But they that fall into the fire and are burned, these are they that finally rebelled from the living God, and it no more entered into their hearts to repent by reason of the lusts of their wantonness and of the wickednesses which they wrought.

7[15]:3 But the others, which are near the waters and yet cannot roll into the water, would you know who are they? These are they that heard the word, and would be baptized unto the name of the Lord. Then, when they call to their remembrance the purity of the truth, they change their minds, and go back again after their evil desires."

7[15]:4 So she finished the explanation of the tower.

7[15]:5 Still importunate, I asked her further, whether for all these stones that were rejected and would not fit into the building of the tower that was repentance, and they had a place in this tower. "They can repent," she said, "but they cannot be fitted into this tower.

7[15]:6 Yet they shall be fitted into another place much more humble, but not until they have undergone torments, and have fulfilled the days of their sins. And they shall be changed for this reason, because they participated in the Righteous Word; and then shall it befall them to be relieved from their torments, if the evil deeds, that they have done, come into their heart; but if these come not into their heart, they are not saved by reason of the hardness of their hearts."

8[16]:1 When then I ceased asking her concerning all these things, she said to me; "Would you see something else?" Being very desirous of beholding, I was greatly rejoiced that I should see it.

8[16]:2 She looked upon me, and smiled, and she said to me, "See you seven women round the tower?" "I see them, lady," say I. "This tower is supported by them by commandment of the Lord.

8[16]:3 Hear now their employments. The first of them, the woman with the strong hands, is called Faith; through her are saved the elect of God.

8[16]:4 And the second, that is girded about and looked like a man, is called Continence; she is the daughter of Faith. Whosoever then shall follow her, becomes happy in his life, for he shall refrain from all evil deeds, believing that, if he refrain from every evil desire, he shall inherit eternal life."

8[16]:5 "And the others, lady, who be they?" "They are daughters one of the other. The name of the one is Simplicity, of the next, Knowledge, of the next, Guilelessness, of the next, Reverence, of the next, Love. When then you shall do all the works of their mother, you canst live."

8[16]:6 "I would fain know, lady," I say, "what power each of them possessed." "Listen then," said she, "to the powers which they have.

8[16]:7 Their powers are mastered each by the other, and they follow each other, in the order in which they were born. From Faith is born Continence, from Continence Simplicity, from Simplicity Guilelessness, from Guilelessness Reverence, from Reverence Knowledge, from Knowledge Love. Their works then are pure and reverent and divine.

8[16]:8 Whosoever therefore shall serve these women, and shall have strength to master their works, shall have his dwelling in the tower with the saints of God."

8[16]:9 Then I asked her concerning the seasons, whether the consummation is even now. But she cried aloud, saying, "Foolish man, see you not that the tower is still a-building? Whenever therefore the tower shall be finished building, the end cometh; but it shall be built up quickly. Ask me no more questions: this reminder is sufficient for you and for the saints, and is the renewal of your spirits.

8[16]:10 But it was not revealed to thyself alone, but in order that you might show these things unto all. After three days--

8[16]:11 for you must understand first, and I charge you, Hermas, first with these words, which I am about to speak to you--(I charge you to) tell all these things into the ears of the saints, that hearing them and doing them they may be purified from their wickednesses, and thyself also with them."

9[17]:1 "Hear me, my children. I brought you up in much simplicity and guilelessness and reverence, through the mercy of the Lord, Who instilled righteousness into you, that you might be justified and sanctified from all wickedness and all crookedness. But you will not to cease from your wickedness.

9[17]:2 Now then hear me and be at peace among yourselves, and have regard one to another, and assist one another, and do not partake of the creatures of God alone in abundance, but share them also with those that are in want.

9[17]:3 For some men through their much eating bring weakness on the flesh, and injure their flesh: whereas the flesh of those who have nought to eat is injured by their not having sufficient nourishment, and their body is ruined.

9[17]:4 This exclusiveness therefore is hurtful to you that have and do not share with them that are in want.

9[17]:5 Look you to the judgment that cometh. you then that have more than enough, seek out them that are hungry, while the tower is still unfinished; for after the tower is finished, you will desire to do good, and will find no place for it.

9[17]:6 Look you therefore, you that exult in your wealth, lest they that are in want shall moan, and their moaning shall go up unto the Lord, and you with your

abundance of good things be shut outside the door of the tower.

9[17]:7 Now therefore I say unto you that are rulers of the Church, and that occupy the chief seats; be not you like unto the sorcerers. The sorcerers indeed carry their drugs in boxes, but you carry your drug and your poison in your heart.

9[17]:8 you are case-hardened, and you will not cleanse your hearts and mix your wisdom together in a clean heart, that you may obtain mercy from the Great King.

9[17]:9 Look you therefore, children, lest these divisions of yours deprive you of your life.

9[17]:10 How is it that you wish to instruct the elect of the Lord, while you yourselves have no instruction? Instruct one another therefore, and have peace among yourselves, that I also may stand gladsome before the Father, and give an account concerning you all to your Lord."

10[18]:1 When then she ceased speaking with me, the six young men, who were building, came, and took her away to the tower, and other four lifted the couch, and took it also away to the tower. I saw not the face of these, for they were turned away.

10[18]:2 And, as she went, I asked her to reveal to me concerning the three forms, in which she had appeared to me. She answered and said to me; "As concerning these things you must ask another, that they may be revealed to you."

10[18]:3 Now she was seen of me, brethren, in my first vision of last year, as a very aged woman and seated on a chair.

10[18]:4 In the second vision her face was youthful, but her flesh and her hair were aged, and she spoke to me standing; and she was more gladsome than before.

10[18]:5 But in the third vision she was altogether youthful and of exceeding great beauty, and her hair alone was aged; and she was gladsome exceedingly and seated on a couch. Touching these things I was very greatly anxious to learn this revelation.

10[18]:6 And I see the aged woman in a vision of the night, saying to me, "Every enquiry needs humility. Fast therefore, and you shall receive what you ask from the Lord."

10[18]:7 So I fasted one day; and that very night there appeared unto me a young man, and he said to me, "Seeing that you ask me revelations offhand with entreaty, take heed lest by thy much asking you injure thy flesh.

10[18]:8 Sufficient for you are these revelations. Canst you see mightier revelations than those you hast seen?"

10[18]:9 I say unto him in reply, "Sir, this one thing alone I ask, concerning the three forms of the aged woman, that a complete revelation may be vouchsafed me." He said to me in answer, How long are you without understanding? It is your double-mindedness that made you of no understanding, and because your heart is not set towards the Lord."

10[18]:10 I answered and said unto him again, "From you, Sir, we shall learn the matters more accurately."

11[19]:1 Listen," said he, "concerning the three forms, of which you enquire.

11[19]:2 In the first vision wherefore did she appear to you an aged woman and seated on a chair? Because your spirit was aged, and already decayed, and had no power by reason of your infirmities and acts of double-mindedness.

11[19]:3 For as aged people, having no longer hope of renewing their youth, expect nothing else but to fall asleep, so you also, being weakened with the affairs of this world gave yourselves over to repining, and cast not your cares on the Lord; but your spirit was broken, and you were aged by your sorrows."

11[19]:4 "Wherefore then she was seated on a chair, I would fain know, Sir." "Because every weak person sits on a chair by reason of his weakness, that the weakness of his body may be supported. So you hast the symbolism of the first vision."

12[20]:1 "But in the second vision you saw her standing, and with her countenance more youthful and more gladsome than before; but her flesh and her hair aged. Listen to this parable also," said he.

12[20]:2 "Imagine an old man, who has now lost all hope of himself by reason of his weakness and his poverty, and expected nothing else save the last day of his life. Suddenly an inheritance is left him. He heard the news, rose up and full of joy clothes himself with strength, and no longer lied down, but stood up, and his spirit, which was now broken by reason of his former circumstances, is renewed again, and he no longer sat, but took courage; so also was it with you, when you heard the revelation which the Lord revealed unto you.

12[20]:3 For He had compassion on you, and renewed your spirits, and you laid aside your maladies, and strength came to you, and you were made powerful in the faith, and the Lord rejoiced to see you put on your strength. And therefore He showed you the building of the tower; yea, and other things also shall He show you, if with your whole heart you be at peace among yourselves.

13[21]:1 But in the third vision you saw her younger and fair and gladsome, and her form fair.

13[21]:2 For just as when to some mourner cometh some piece of good tidings, immediately he forgot his former sorrows, and admitted nothing but the tidings which he has heard, and is strengthened thenceforth unto that which is good, and his spirit is renewed by reason of the joy which he has received; so also you have received a renewal of your spirits by seeing these good things.

13[21]:3 And whereas you saw her seated on a couch, the position is a firm on; for the couch has four feet and stood firmly; for the world too Is upheld by means of four elements.

13[21]:4 They then that have fully repented shall be young again, and founded firmly, seeing that they have repented with their whole heart. There you hast the revelation entire and complete. You shall ask nothing more as touching revelation-- but if anything be lacking still, it shall be revealed unto you."

Vision 4

1[22]:1 The fourth vision which I saw, brethren, twenty days after the former vision which came unto me, for a type of the impending tribulation.

1[22]:2 I was going into the country by the Companion Way. From the high road, it is about ten stades; and the place is easy for traveling.

1[22]:3 While then I am walking alone, I entreat the Lord that He will accomplish the revelations and the visions which He showed me through His holy Church, that He may strengthen me and may give repentance to His servants which have stumbled, that His great and glorious Name may be glorified, for that He held me worthy that He should show me His marvels.

1[22]:4 And as I gave glory and thanksgiving to Him, there answered me as it were the sound of a voice, "Be not of doubtful mind, Hermas." I began to question in myself and to say, "How can I be of doubtful mind, seeing that I am so firmly founded by the Lord, and have seen glorious things?"

1[22]:5 And I went on a little, brethren, and behold, I see a cloud of dust rising as it were to heaven, and I began to say within myself, "Can it be that cattle are coming, and raising a cloud of dust?" for it was just about a stade from me.

1[22]:6 As the cloud of dust waxed greater and greater, I suspected that it was something supernatural. Then the sun shone out a little, and behold, I see a huge beast like some sea-monster, and from its mouth fiery locusts issued forth. And the beast was about a hundred feet in length, and its head was as it were of pottery.

1[22]:7 And I began to weep, and to entreat the Lord that He would rescue me from it. And I remembered the word which I had heard, "Be not of doubtful mind, Hermas."

1[22]:8 Having therefore, brethren, put on the faith of the Lord and called to mind the mighty works that He had taught me, I took courage and gave myself up to the beast. Now the beast was coming on with such a rush, that it might have ruined a city.

1[22]:9 I come near it, and, huge monster as it was, it stretched itself on the ground, and merely put forth its tongue, and stirred not at all until I had passed by it.

1[22]:10 And the beast had on its head four colors; black then fire and blood color, then gold, then white.

2[23]:1 Now after I had passed the beast, and had gone forward about thirty feet, behold, there met me a virgin arrayed as if she were going forth from a bridal-chamber all in white and with white sandals, veiled up to her forehead, and her head-covering consisted of a turban, and her hair was white.

2[23]:2 I knew from the former Visions that it was the Church, and I became more cheerful. She saluted me, saying, "Good morrow, my good man"; and I saluted her in turn, "Lady, good morrow."

2[23]:3 She answered and said unto me, "Did nothing meet you? "I say unto her, Lady, such a huge beast, that could have destroyed whole peoples: but, by the power of the Lord and by His great mercy, I escaped it."

2[23]:4 "You didst escape it well," said she, "because you didst cast thy care upon God, and didst open thy heart to the Lord, believing that you can be saved by nothing else but by His great and glorious Name. Therefore the Lord sent His angel, which is over the beasts, whose name is Segri, and shut his mouth that it might not hurt you. You hast escaped a great tribulation by reason of thy faith, and because, though you saw so huge a beast, you didst not doubt in thy mind.

2[23]:5 Go therefore, and declare to the elect of the Lord His mighty works, and tell them that this beast is a type of the great tribulation which is to come. If therefore you prepare yourselves beforehand, and repent (and turn) unto the Lord with your whole heart, you shall be able to escape it, if your heart be made pure and without blemish, and if for the remaining days of your life you serve the Lord blamelessly. Cast your cares upon the Lord and He will set them straight.

2[23]:6 Trust you in the Lord, you men of doubtful mind, for He can do all things, yea, He both turned away His wrath from you, and again He sent forth His plagues upon you that are of doubtful mind. Woe to them that hear these words and are disobedient; it were better for them that they had not been born."

3[24]:1 I asked her concerning the four colors, which the beast had upon its head. Then she answered me and said, "Again you art curious about such matters." "Yes, lady," said I, "make known unto me what these things are."

3[24]:2 "Listen," said she; "the black is this world in which you dwell;

3[24]:3 and the fire and blood color showed that this world must perish by blood and fire;

3[24]:4 and the golden part are you that has escaped from this world. For as the gold is tested by the fire and is made useful, so you also [that dwell in it] are being tested in yourselves. you then that abide and pass through the fire will be purified by it. For as the old loses its dross. so you also shall cast away all sorrow and tribulation, and shall be purified, and shall be useful for the building of the tower.

3[24]:5 But the white portion is the coming age, in which the elect of God shall dwell; because the elect of God shall be without spot and pure unto life eternal.

3[24]:6 Wherefore cease not you to speak in the ears of the saints. you have now the symbolism also of the tribulation which is coming in power. But if you be willing, it shall be nothing. Remember you the things that are written beforehand."

3[24]:7 With these words she departed, and I saw not in what direction she departed; for a noise was made: and I turned back in fear, thinking that the beast was coming.

Vision 5

5[25]:1 As I prayed in the house, and sat on the couch, there entered a man glorious in his visage, in the garb of a shepherd, with a white skin wrapped about him, and with a wallet on his shoulders and a staff in his hand. And he saluted me, and I saluted him in return.

5[25]:2 And he immediately sat down by my side, and he said unto me, "I was sent by the most holy angel, that I might dwell with you the remaining days of thy life."

5[25]:3 I thought he came to tempt me, and I say unto him, "Why, who art you? For I know," say I, "unto whom I was delivered." He said to me, "Dost you not recognize me?" "No," I say. "I," said he, "am the shepherd, unto whom you were delivered."

5[25]:4 While he was still speaking, his form was changed, and I recognized him as being the same, to whom I was delivered; and straightway I was confounded, and fear seized me, and I was altogether overwhelmed with distress that I had answered him so wickedly and senselessly.

5[25]:5 But he answered and said unto me, "Be not confounded, but strengthen thyself in my commandments which I am about to command you. For I was sent," said he, "that I might show you again all the things which you didst see before, merely the heads which are convenient for you. First of all, write down my commandments and my parables; and the other matters you shall write down as I shall show them to you. The reason why," said he, "I command you to write down first the commandments and parables is, that you may read them off-hand, and may be able to keep them."

5[25]:6 So I wrote down the commandments and parables, as he commanded me.

5[25]:7 If then, when you hear them, you keep them and walk in them, and do them with a pure heart, you shall receive from the Lord all things that He promised you; but if, when you hear them, you do not repent, but still add to your sins, you shall receive from the Lord the opposite. All these the shepherd, the angel of repentance commanded me to write.

Mandate 1

1[26]:1 "First of all, believe that God is One, even He who created all things and set them in order, and brought all things from non-existence into being, Who comprehends all things, being alone incomprehensible.

1[26]:2 Believe Him therefore, and fear Him, and in this fear be continent. Keep these things, and you shall cast off all wickedness from thyself, and shall clothe thyself with every excellence of righteousness, and shall live unto God, if you keep this commandment."

Mandate 2

1[27]:1 He said to me; "Keep simplicity and be guileless, and you shall be as little children, that know not the wickedness which destroyed the life of men.

1[27]:2 First of all, speak evil of no man, neither take pleasure in listening to a slanderer. Otherwise you that hear too shall be responsible for the sin of him that speaks the evil, if you believe the slander, which you hear; for in believing it you thyself also wilt have a grudge against thy brother. So then shall you be responsible for the sin of him that speaks the evil.

1[27]:3 Slander is evil; it is a restless demon, never at peace, but always having its home among factions. Refrain from it therefore, and you shall have success at all times with all men.

1[27]:4 But clothe thyself in reverence, wherein is no evil stumbling-block, but all things are smooth and gladsome. Work that which is good, and of thy labors, which God gives you, give to all that are in want freely, not questioning to whom you shall give, and to whom you shall not give. Give to all; for to all God desires that there should be given of His own bounties.

1[27]:5 They then that receive shall render an account to God why they received it, and to what end; for they that receive in distress shall not be judged, but they that receive by false pretense shall pay the penalty.

1[27]:6 He then that gives is guiltless; for as he received from the Lord the ministration to perform it, he has performed it in sincerity, by making no distinction to whom to give or not to give. This ministration then, when sincerely performed, becomes glorious in the sight of God. He therefore that ministered thus sincerely shall live unto God.

1[27]:7 Therefore keep this commandment, as I have told you, that your own repentance and that of thy household may be found to be sincere, and [thy] heart pure and undefiled."

Mandate 3

1[28]:1 Again he said to me; "Love truth, and let nothing but truth proceed out of thy mouth, that the Spirit which God made to dwell in this flesh, may be found true in the sight of all men; and thus shall the Lord, Who dwelt in you, be glorified; for the Lord is true in every word, and with Him there is no falsehood.

1[28]:2 They therefore that speak lies set the Lord at nought, and become robbers of the Lord, for they do not deliver up to Him the deposit which they received. For they received of Him a spirit free from lies. This if they shall return a lying spirit, they have defiled the commandment of the Lord and have become robbers."

1[28]:3 When then I heard these things, I wept bitterly. But seeing me weep he said, "Why weep you?" "Because, Sir," say I "I know not if I can be saved." "Why so?" said he. "Because, Sir," I say, "never in my life spoke I a true word, but I always lied deceitfully with all men and dressed up my falsehood as truth before all men; and no man ever contradicted me, but confidence was placed in my word. How then, Sir," say I, "can I live, seeing that I have done these things?"

1[28]:4 "Your supposition," he said, "is right and true, for it behooved you as a servant of God to walk in truth, and no complicity with evil should abide with the Spirit of truth, nor bring grief to the Spirit which is holy and true." "Never, Sir," say I, "heard I clearly words such as these."

1[28]:5 "Now then," said he, "you heard Guard them, that the former falsehoods also which you spake in thy business affairs may themselves become credible, now that these are found true; for they too can become trustworthy. If you keep these things, and from henceforward speak nothing but truth, you shall be able to secure life for thyself And whosoever shall hear this command, and abstain from falsehood, that most pernicious habit, shall live unto God."

Mandate 4

1[29]:1 "I charge you, "said he, "to keep purity, and let not a thought enter into thy heart concerning another's wife, or concerning fornication, or concerning any such like evil deeds; for in so doing you commit a great sin. But remember your own wife always, and you shall never go wrong.

1[29]:2 For should this desire enter into your heart, you wilt go wrong, and should any other as evil as this, you commit sin. For this desire in a servant of God is a great sin; and if any man doeth this evil deed, he worked out death for himself.

1[29]:3 Look to it therefore. Abstain from this desire; for, where holiness dwells, there lawlessness ought not to enter into the heart of a righteous man."

1[29]:4 I say to him, "Sir, permit me to ask you a few more questions" "Say on," said he. "Sir," say I, "if a man who has a wife that is faithful in the Lord detect her in adultery, doth the husband sin in living with her?"

1[29]:5 "So long as he is ignorant," said he, "he sinned not; but if the husband know of her sin, and the wife repent not, but continue in her fornication, and her husband live with her, he makes himself responsible for her sin and an accomplice in her adultery."

1[29]:6 "What then, Sir," say I, "shall the husband do, if the wife continue in this case?" "Let him divorce her," said he, "and let the husband abide alone: but if after divorcing his wife he shall marry another, he likewise commits adultery."

1[29]:7 "If then, Sir," say I, "after the wife is divorced, she repent and desire to return to her own husband, shall she not be received?"

1[29]:8 "Certainly," said he, "if the husband received her not, he sinned and brings great sin upon himself; nay, one who has sinned and repented must be received, yet not often; for there is but one repentance for the servants of God. For the sake of her repentance therefore the husband ought not to marry. This is the manner of acting enjoined on husband and wife.

1[29]:9 Not only," said he, "is it adultery, if a man pollute his flesh, but whosoever doeth things like unto the heathen commits adultery. If therefore in such deeds as these likewise a man continue and repent not, keep away from him, and live not with him. Otherwise, you also art a partaker of his sin.

1[29]:10 For this cause you were enjoined to remain single, whether husband or wife; for in such cases repentance is possible.

1[29]:11 I," said he, "am not giving an excuse that this matter should be concluded thus, but to the end that the sinner should sin no more. But as concerning his former sin, there is One Who is able to give healing; it is He Who has authority over all things."

2[30]:1 I asked him again, saying, "Seeing that the Lord held me worthy that you should always dwell with me, suffer me still to say a few words, since I understand nothing, and my heart has been made dense by my former deeds. Make me to understand, for I am very foolish, and I apprehend absolutely nothing."

2[30]:2 He answered and said unto me, "I," said he, "preside over repentance, and I give understanding to all who repent. No, think you not," said he, "that this very act of repentance is understanding? To repent is great understanding," said he. "For the man that has sinned understands that he has done evil before the Lord, and the deed which he has done enters into his heart, and he repents, and doeth no more evil, but doeth good lavishly, and humbles his own soul and puts it to torture because it sinned. You see then that repentance is great understanding."

2[30]:3 "It is on this account therefore, Sir," say I, "that I enquire everything accurately of you; first, because I am a sinner; secondly, because I know not what deeds I must do that I may live, for my sins are many and various."

2[30]:4 "You shall live," said he, "if you keep my commandments and walk in them and whosoever shall hear these commandments and keep them, shall live unto God."

3[31]:1 "I will still proceed, Sir," say I, "to ask a further question." "Speak on," said he. "I have heard, Sir," say I, "from certain teachers, that there is no other repentance, save that which took place when we rent down into the water and obtained remission of our former sins."

3[31]:2 He said to me; "You hast well heard; for so it is. For he that has received remission of sins ought no longer to sin, but to dwell in purity.

3[31]:3 But, since you enquire all things accurately, I will declare unto you this also, so as to give no excuse to those who shall hereafter believe or those who have already believed, on the Lord. For they that have already believed, or shall hereafter believe, have not repentance for sins, but have only remission of their former sins.

3[31]:4 To those then that were called before these days the Lord has appointed repentance. For the Lord, being a discerner of hearts and foreknowing all things, perceived the weakness of men and the manifold wiles of the devil, how that he will be doing some mischief to the servants of God, and will deal wickedly with them.

3[31]:5 The Lord then, being very compassionate, had pity on His handiwork, and appointed this (opportunity of) repentance, and to me was given the authority over this repentance.

3[31]:6 But I say unto you," said he, "if after this great and holy calling any one, being tempted of the devil, shall commit sin, he has only one (opportunity of) repentance. But if he sin off-hand and repent, repentance is unprofitable for such a man; for he shall live with difficulty."

3[31]:7 I say unto him, "I was quickened unto life again, when I heard these things from you so precisely. For I know that, if I shall add no more to my sins, I shall be saved." "You shall be saved," he said, "you and all, as many as shall do these things."

4[32]:1 I asked him again, saying, "Sir, since once you do bear with me, declare unto me this further matter also." "Say on," said he. "If a wife, Sir," say I, "or, it may be, a husband fall asleep, and one of them marry, doth the one that marries sin?"

4[32]:2 "He sins not," said he, "but if he remain single, he invests himself with more exceeding honor and with great glory before the Lord; yet even if he should marry, he sins not.

4[32]:3 Preserve purity and holiness therefore, and you shall live unto God. All these things, which I speak and shall hereafter speak unto you, guard from this time forward, from the day when you was committed unto me, and I will dwell in thy house.

4[32]:4 But for thy former transgressions there shall be remission, if you keep my commandments. Yea, and all shall have remission, if they keep these my commandments, and walk in this purity."

Mandate 5

1[33]:1 "Be you long-suffering and understanding," he said, "and you shall have the mastery over all evil deeds, and shall work all righteousness.

1[33]:2 For if you art long-suffering, the Holy Spirit that abides in you shall be pure, not being darkened by another evil spirit, but dwelling in a large room shall rejoice and be glad with the vessel in which he dwells, and shall serve God with much cheerfulness, having prosperity in himself.

1[33]:3 But if any angry temper approach, forthwith the Holy Spirit, being delicate, is straitened, not having [the] place clear, and seeks to retire from the place; for he is being choked by the evil spirit, and has no room to minister unto the Lord, as he desires, being polluted by angry temper. For the Lord dwells in long-suffering, but the devil in angry temper.

1[33]:4 Thus that both the spirits then should be dwelling together is inconvenient and evil for that man in whom they dwell.

1[33]:5 For if you take a little wormwood, and pour it into a jar of honey, is not the whole of the honey spoiled, and all that honey ruined by a very small quantity of wormwood? For it destroyed the sweetness of the honey, and it no longer has the same attraction for the owner, because it is rendered bitter and has lost its use. But if the wormwood be not put into the honey, the honey is found sweet and becomes useful to its owner.

1[33]:6 You see [then] that long-suffering is very sweet, beyond the sweetness of honey, and is useful to the Lord, and He dwells in it. But angry, temper is bitter and useless. If then angry temper be mixed with long-suffering, long-suffering is polluted and the man's intercession is no longer useful to God."

1[33]:7 "I would fain know, Sir," say I, "the working of angry temper, that I may guard myself from it." "Yea, verily," said he, "if you guard not thyself from it--you and thy family--you hast lost all thy hope. But guard thyself from it; for I am with you. Yea, and all men shall hold aloof from it, as many as have repented with their whole heart. For I will be with them and will preserve them; for they all were justified by the most holy angel.

2[34]:1 "Hear now," said he, "the working of angry temper, how evil it is, and how it subverts the servants of God by its own working, and how it leads them astray from righteousness. But it doth not lead astray them that are full in the faith, nor can it work upon them, because the power of the Lord is with them; but them that are empty and double-minded it leads astray.

2[34]:2 For when it sees such men in prosperity it insinuates itself into the heart of the man, and for no cause whatever the man or the woman is embittered on account of worldly matters, either about meats, or some triviality, or about some friend, or about giving or receiving, or about follies of this kind. For all these things are foolish and vain and senseless and inexpedient for the servants of God.

2[34]:3 But long-suffering is great and strong, and has a mighty and vigorous power, and is prosperous in great enlargement, gladsome, exultant, free from care, glorifying the Lord at every season, having no bitterness in itself, remaining always gentle and tranquil. This long-suffering therefore dwells with those whose faith is perfect.

2[34]:4 But angry temper is in the first place foolish, fickle and senseless; then from foolishness is engendered bitterness, and from bitterness wrath, and from wrath anger, and from anger spite; then spite being composed of all these evil elements becomes a great sin and incurable.

2[34]:5 For when all these spirits dwell in one vessel, where the Holy Spirit also dwells, that vessel cannot contain them, but overflows.

2[34]:6 The delicate spirit therefore, as not being accustomed to dwell with an evil spirit nor with harshness, departs from a man of that kind, and seeks to dwell with gentleness and tranquility.

2[34]:7 Then, when it has removed from that man, in whom it dwells, that man becomes emptied of the righteous spirit, and henceforward, being filled with the evil spirits, he is unstable in all his actions, being dragged about hither and thither by the evil spirits, and is altogether blinded and bereft of his good intent. Thus then it happens to all persons of angry temper.

2[34]:8 Refrain therefore from angry temper, the most evil of evil spirits. But clothe thyself in long-suffering, and resist angry temper and bitterness, and you shall be round in company with the holiness which is beloved of the Lord. See then that you never neglect this commandment; for if you master this commandment, you shall be able likewise to keep the remaining commandments, which I am about to give you. Be strong in them and endowed with power; and let all be endowed with power, as many as desire to walk in them."

Mandate 6

1[35]:1 I charged you," said he, "in my first commandment to guard faith and fear and temperance." "Yes, Sir," say I. "But now," said he, "I wish to show you their powers also, that you mayest understand what is the power and effect of each one of them. For their effects are two fold. Now they are prescribed alike to the righteous and the unrighteous.

1[35]:2 Do you therefore trust righteousness, but trust not unrighteousness; for the way of righteousness is straight, but the way of unrighteousness is crooked. But walk you in the straight [and level] path, and leave the crooked one alone.

1[35]:3 For the crooked way has no tracks, but only pathlessness and many stumbling stones, and is rough and thorny. So it is therefore harmful to those who walk in it.

1[35]:4 But those who walk in the straight way walk on the level and without stumbling: for it is neither rough nor thorny. You seest then that it is more expedient to walk in this way."

1[35]:5 "I am pleased, Sir," say I, "to walk in this way." "You shall walk," he said, "yea, and whosoever shall turn unto the Lord with his whole heart shall walk in it.

2[36]:1 "Hear now," said he, "concerning faith. There are two angels with a man, one of righteousness and one of wickedness."

2[36]:2 "How then, Sir," say I, "shall I know their workings, seeing that both angels dwell with me?"

2[36]:3 "Hear," said he, "and understand their workings. The angel of righteousness is delicate and bashful and gentle and tranquil. When then this one enters into thy heart, forthwith he speaketh with you of righteousness, of purity, of holiness, and of contentment, of every righteous deed and of every glorious virtue. When all these things enter into thy heart, know that the angel of righteousness is with you. [These then are the works of the angel of righteousness.] Trust him therefore and his works.

2[36]:4 Now see the works of the angel of wickedness also. First of all, he is quick tempered and bitter and senseless, and his works are evil, overthrowing the servants of God. Whenever then he entereth into thy heart, know him by his works."

2[36]:5 "How I shall discern him, Sir," I reply, "I know not." Listen," said he. "When a fit of angry temper or bitterness comes upon you, know that he is in you. Then the desire of much business and the costliness of many viands and drinking bouts and of many drunken fits and of various luxuries which are unseemly, and the desire of women, and avarice, and haughtiness and boastfulness, and whatsoever things are akin and like to these--when then these things enter into thy heart, know that the angel of wickedness is with you.

2[36]:6 Do you therefore, recognizing his works, stand aloof from him, and trust him in nothing, for his works are evil and inexpedient for the servants of God. Here then you hast the workings of both the angels. Understand them, and trust the angel of righteousness.

2[36]:7 But from the angel of wickedness stand aloof, for his teaching is evil in every matter; for though one be a man of faith, and the desire of this angel enter into his heart, that man, or that woman, must commit some sin.

2[36]:8 And if again a man or a woman be exceedingly wicked, and the works of the angel of righteousness come into that man's heart, he must of necessity do something good.

2[36]:9 You see then," said he, "that it is good to follow the angel of righteousness, and to bid farewell to the angel of wickedness.

2[36]:10 This commandment declares what concerns faith, that you may trust the works of the angel of righteousness, and doing them may live unto God. But believe that the works of the angel of wickedness are difficult; so by not doing them you shall live unto God."

Mandate 7

1[37]:1 "Fear the Lord," said he, "and keep His commandments. So keeping the commandments of God you shall be powerful in every deed, and thy doing shall be incomparable. For whilst you fear the Lord, you shall do all things well. But this is the fear wherewith you ought to be afraid, and you shall be saved.

1[37]:2 But fear not the devil; for, if you fear the Lord, you shall be master over the devil, for there is no power in him. [For] in whom is no power, neither is there fear of him; but in whom power is glorious, of him is fear likewise. For every one that has power has fear, whereas he that has no power is despised of all.

1[37]:3 But fear you the works of the devil, for they are evil. While then you fear the Lord, you wilt fear the works of the devil, and wilt not do them, but abstain from them.

1[37]:4 Fear therefore is of two kinds. If you desire to do evil, fear the Lord, and you shall not do it. If again you desire to do good, fear the Lord and you shall do it. Therefore the fear of the Lord is powerful and great and glorious. Fear the Lord then, and you shall live unto Him; yea, and as many of them that keep His commandments as shall fear Him, shall live unto God."

1[37]:5 "Wherefore, Sir," say I, "didst you say concerning those that keep His commandments, "They shall live unto God"?" "Because," said he, "every creature fears the Lord, but not every one keeps His commandments. Those then that fear Him and keep His commandments, they have life unto God; but they that keep not His commandments have no life in them."

Mandate 8

1[38]:1 "I told you," said he, "that the creatures of God are twofold; for temperance also is twofold. For in some things it is right to be temperate, but in other things it is not right."

1[38]:2 "Make known unto me, Sir," say I, "in what things it is right to be temperate, and in what things it is not right." "Listen," said he. "Be temperate as to what is evil, and do it not; but be not temperate as to what is good, but do it. For if you be temperate as to what is good, so as not to do it, you commits a great sin; but if you be temperate as to what is evil, so as not to do it, you doest great righteousness. Be temperate therefore in abstaining from all wickedness, and do that which is good."

1[38]:3 "What kinds of wickedness, Sir," say I, "are they from which we must be temperate and abstain?" "Listen," said he; "from adultery and fornication, from the lawlessness of drunkenness, from wicked luxury, from many viands and the costliness of riches, and vaunting and haughtiness and pride, and from falsehood and evil speaking and hypocrisy, malice and all blasphemy.

1[38]:4 These works are the most wicked of all in the life of men. From these works therefore the servant of God must be temperate and abstain; for he that is not temperate so as to abstain from these cannot live unto God. Listen then to what follows upon these."

1[38]:5 "Why, are there still other evil deeds, Sir?" say I. "Aye, said he, "there are many, from which the servant of God must be temperate and abstain; theft, falsehood, deprivation, false witness, avarice, evil desire, deceit, vain-glory, boastfulness, and whatsoever things are like unto these.

1[38]:6 Think you not that these things are wrong, yea, very wrong," [said he,] "for the servants of God? In all these things he that serves God must exercise temperance. Be you temperate, therefore, and refrain from all these things, that you may live unto God, and be enrolled among those who exercise self-restraint in them. These then are the things from which you should restrain thyself

1[38]:7 Now hear," said he, "the things, in which you should not exercise self restraint, but do them. Exercise no self-restraint in that which is good, but do it."

1[38]:8 "Sir," say I, "show me the power of the good also, that I may walk in them and serve them, that doing them it may be possible for me to be saved." "Hear," said he, "the works of the good likewise, which you must do, and towards which you must exercise no self-restraint.

1[38]:9 First of all, there is faith, fear of the Lord, love, concord, words of righteousness, truth, patience; nothing is better than these in the life of men. If a man keep these, and exercise not self-restraint from them, he becomes blessed in his life.

1[38]:10 Hear now what follow upon these; to minister to widows, to visit the orphans and the needy, to ransom the servants of God from their afflictions, to be hospitable (for in hospitality benevolence from time to time has a place), to resist no man, to be tranquil, to show yourself more submissive than all men, to reverence the aged, to practice righteousness, to observe brotherly feeling, to endure injury, to be long-suffering, to bear no grudge, to exhort those who are sick at soul, not to cast away those that have stumbled from the faith, but to convert them and to put courage Into them, to reprove sinners, not to oppress debtors and indigent persons, and whatsoever actions are like these.

1[38]:11 Do these things," said he, "seem to you to be good?" "Why, what, Sir," say I, "can be better than these?" "Then walk in them," said he, "and abstain not from them, and you shall live unto God.

1[38]:12 Keep this commandment therefore. If you do good and abstain not from it, you shall live unto God; yea, and all shall live unto God who act so. And again if you do not evil, and abstain from it, you shall live unto God; yea, and all shall live unto God, who shall keep these commandments, and walk in them."

Mandate 9

1[39]:1 He said to me; "Remove from thyself a doubtful mind and doubt not at all whether to ask of God, saying within thyself, "How can I ask thing of the Lord and receive it, seeing that I have committed so many sins against Him?"

1[39]:2 Reason not thus, but turn to the Lord with thy whole heart, and ask of Him nothing wavering, and you shall know His exceeding compassion, that He will surely not abandon you, but will fulfill the petition of thy soul.

1[39]:3 For God is not as men who bear a grudge, but Himself is without malice and has compassion on His creatures.

1[39]:4 Do you therefore cleanse thy heart from all the vanities of this life, and from the things mentioned before; and ask of the Lord, and you shall receive all things, and shall lack nothing of all thy petitions, if you ask of the Lord nothing wavering.

1[39]:5 But if you waver in thy heart, you shall surely receive none of thy petitions. For they that waver towards God, these are the doubtful-minded, and they never obtain any of their petitions.

1[39]:6 But they that are complete in the faith make all their petitions trusting in the Lord, and they receive, because they ask without wavering, nothing doubting; for every doubtful-minded man, if he repent not, shall hardly be saved.

1[39]:7 Cleanse therefore thy heart from doubtful-mindedness, and put on faith, for it is strong, and trust God that you wilt receive all thy petitions which you ask; and if after asking anything of the Lord, you receive thy petition somewhat tardily, be not of doubtful mind because you didst not receive the petition of thy soul at once. For assuredly it is by reason of some temptation or some transgression, of which you art ignorant, that you receive thy petition so tardily.

1[39]:8 Do you therefore cease not to make thy soul's petition, and you shall receive it. But if you grow weary, and doubt as you ask, blame yourself and not Him that gave unto you. See to this doubtful-mindedness; for it is evil and senseless, and uproots many from the faith, yea, even very faithful and strong men. For indeed this doubtful-mindedness is a daughter of the devil, and works great wickedness against the servants of God.

1[39]:9 Therefore despise doubtful-mindedness and gain the mastery over it in everything, clothing yourself with faith which is strong and powerful. For faith promises all things, accomplishes all things; but doubtful-mindedness, as having no confidence in itself, fails in all the works which it doeth.

1[39]:10 You see then," said he, "that faith is from above from the Lord, and has great power; but doubtful-mindedness is an earthly spirit from the devil, and has no power.

1[39]:11 Do you therefore serve that faith which has power, and hold aloof from the doubtful-mindedness which has no power; and you shall live unto God; yea, and all those shall live unto God who are so minded."

Mandate 10

1[40]:1 "Put away sorrow from yourself," said he, "for she is the sister of doubtful-mindedness and of angry temper."

1[40]:2 "How, Sir," say I, "is she the sister of these? For angry temper seems to me to be one thing, doubtful-mindedness another, sorrow another." "You art a foolish fellow," said he, "[and] perceives not that sorrow is more evil than all the spirits, and is most fatal to the servants of God, and beyond all the spirits destroys a man, and crushes out the Holy Spirit and yet again saves it."

1[40]:3 "I, Sir," say I, "am without understanding, and I understand not these parables. For how it can crush out and again save, I do not comprehend."

1[40]:4 "Listen," said he. "Those who have never investigated concerning the truth, nor enquired concerning the deity, but have merely believed, and have been mixed up in business affairs and riches and heathen friendships, and many other affairs of this world--as many, I say, as devote themselves to these things, comprehend not the parables of the deity; for they are darkened by these actions, and are corrupted and become barren.

1[40]:5 As good vineyards, when they are treated with neglect, are made barren by the thorns and weeds of various kinds, so men who after they have believed fall into these many occupations which were mentioned before, lose their understanding and comprehend nothing at all concerning righteousness; for if they hear concerning the deity and truth, their mind is absorbed in their occupations, and they perceive nothing at all.

1[40]:6 But they that have the fear of God, and investigate concerning deity and truth, and direct their heart towards the Lord, perceive and understand everything that is said to them more quickly, because they have the fear of the Lord in themselves; for where the Lord dwells, there too is great understanding. Hold fast therefore unto the Lord, and you shall understand and perceive all things.

2[41]:1 "Hear now, senseless man," said he, "How sorrow crushes out the Holy Spirit, and again saves it.

2[41]:2 When the man of doubtful mind sets his hand to any action, and fails in it owing to his doubtful-mindedness, grief at this enters into the man, and grieves the Holy Spirit, and crushes it out.

2[41]:3 Then again when angry temper cleaves to a man concerning any matter, and he is much embittered, again sorrow enters into the heart of the man that was ill-tempered, and he is grieved at the deed which he has done, and repents that he did evil.

2[41]:4 This sadness therefore seems to bring salvation, because he repented at having done the evil. So both the operations sadden the Spirit; first, the doubtful mind saddens the Spirit, because it succeeded not in its business, and the angry temper again, because it did

what was evil. Thus both are saddening to the Holy Spirit, the doubtful mind and the angry temper.

2[41]:5 Put away therefore from yourself sadness, and afflict not the Holy Spirit that dwells in you, lest haply He intercede with God [against you], and depart from you.

2[41]:6 For the Spirit of God, that was given unto this flesh, endures not sadness neither constraint.

3[42]:1 "Therefore clothe yourself in cheerfulness, which has favor with Cod always, and is acceptable to Him, and rejoice in it. For every cheerful man works good, and thinks good, and despises sadness;

3[42]:2 but the sad man is always committing sin. In the first place he commits sin, because he grieves the Holy Spirit, which was given to the man being a cheerful spirit; and in the second place, by grieving the Holy Spirit he doeth lawlessness, in that he doth not intercede with neither confess unto God. For the intercession of a sad man has never at any time power to ascend to the altar of God."

3[42]:3 "Wherefore," say I, "doth not the intercession of him that is saddened ascend to the altar?" "Because," said he, "sadness is seated at his heart. Thus sadness mingled with the intercession doth not suffer the intercession to ascend pure to the altar. For as vinegar when mingled with wine in the same (vessel) has not the same pleasant taste, so likewise sadness mingled with the Holy Spirit has not the same intercession.

3[42]:4 Therefore cleanse yourself from this wicked sadness, and you shall live unto God; yea, and all they shall live unto God, who shall cast away sadness from themselves and clothe themselves in all cheerfulness."

Mandate 11

1[43]:1 He showed me men seated on a couch, and another man seated on a chair. And he said to me, "See you those that are seated on the couch?" "I see them, Sir," say I. "These," said he, "are faithful, but he that sits on the chair is a false prophet who destroys the mind of the servants of God--I mean, of the doubtful-minded, not of the faithful.

1[43]:2 These doubtful-minded ones then come to him as to a soothsayer and enquire of him what shall befall them. And he, the false prophet, having no power of a divine Spirit in himself, speaks with them according to their enquiries [and according to the lusts of their wickedness], and fills their souls as they themselves wish.

1[43]:3 For being empty himself he gives empty answers to empty enquirers; for what-ever enquiry may be made of him, he answers according to the emptiness of the man. But he speaks also some true words; for the devil fills him with his own spirit, if so be he shall be able to break down some of the righteous.

1[43]:4 So many therefore as are strong in the faith of the Lord, clothed with the truth, hold fast not to such spirits, but hold aloof from them; but as many as are doubters and frequently change their minds, practice soothsaying like the Gentiles, and bring upon themselves greater sin by their idolatries. For he that consults a false prophet on any matter is an idolater and emptied of the truth, and senseless.

1[43]:5 For no Spirit given of God needs to be consulted; but, having the power of deity, speaks all things of itself, because it is from above, even from the power of the divine Spirit.

1[43]:6 But the spirit which is consulted, and speaks according to the desires of men, is earthly and fickle, having no power; and it speaks not at all, unless it be consulted."

1[43]:7 "How then, Sir," say I, "shall a man know who of them is a prophet, and who a false prophet?" "Hear," said he, "concerning both the prophets; and, as I shall tell you, so shall you test the prophet and the false prophet. By his life test the man that has the divine Spirit.

1[43]:8 In the first place, he that has the [divine] Spirit, which is from above, is gentle and tranquil and humble-minded, and abstains from all wickedness and vain desire of this present world, and holds himself inferior to all men, and gives no answer to any man when enquired of, nor speaks in solitude (for neither doth the Holy Spirit speak when a man wishes Him to speak); but the man speaks then when God wishes him to speak.

1[43]:9 When then the man who has the divine Spirit cometh into an assembly of righteous men, who have faith in a divine Spirit, and intercession is made to God by the gathering of those men, then the angel of the prophetic spirit, who is attached to him, fills the man, and the man, being filled with the Holy Spirit, speaks to the multitude, according as the Lord wills.

1[43]:10 In this way then the Spirit of the deity shall be manifest. This then is the greatness of the power as touching the Spirit of the deity of the Lord.

1[43]:11 Hear now," said he, "concerning the earthly and vain spirit, which has no power but is foolish.

1[43]:12 In the first place, that man who seems to have a spirit exalts himself, and desires to have a chief place, and straight-way he is impudent and shameless and talkative and conversant in many luxuries and in many other deceits and receives money for his prophesying, and if he receives not, he prophesies not. Now can a divine Spirit receive money and prophesy? It is not possible for a prophet of God to do this, but the spirit of such prophets is earthly.

1[43]:13 In the next place, it never approaches an assembly of righteous men; but avoids them, and clings to the doubtful-minded and empty, and prophesies to them in corners, and deceives them, speaking all things in emptiness to gratify their desires; for they too are empty whom it answers. For the empty vessel placed together with the empty is not broken, but they agree one with the other.

1[43]:14 But when he comes into an assembly full of righteous men who have a Spirit of deity, and intercession is made from them, that man is emptied, and the earthly spirit flees from him in fear, and that man is struck dumb and is altogether broken in pieces, being unable to utter a word.

1[43]:15 For, if you pack wine or oil into a closet, and place an empty vessel among them, and again desire to unpack the closet, the vessel which you place there empty, empty in like manner you will find it. Thus also the empty prophets, whenever they come unto the spirits of righteous men, are found just such as they came.

1[43]:16 I have given you the life of both kinds of prophets. Therefore test, by his life and his works, the man who says that he is moved by the Spirit.

1[43]:17 But do you trust the Spirit that cometh from God, and has power; but in the earthly and empty spirit put no trust at all; for in it there is no power, for it cometh from the devil.

1[43]:18 Listen [then] to the parable which I shall tell you. Take a stone, and throw it up to heaven--see if you can reach it; or again, take a squirt of water, and squirt it up to heaven--see if you can bore through the heaven."

1[43]:19 "How, Sir," say I, "can these things be? For both these things which you hast mentioned are beyond our power." "Well then," said he, "just as these things are beyond our power, so likewise the earthly spirits have no power and are feeble.

1[43]:20 Now take the power which cometh from above. The hail is a very, small grain, and yet, when it falls on a man's head, what pain it causes! Or again, take a drop which falls on the ground from the tiles, and bores through the stone.

1[43]:21 You see then that the smallest things from above falling on the earth have great power. So likewise the divine Spirit coming from above is powerful. This Spirit therefore trust, but from the other hold aloof."

Mandate 12

1[44]:1 He said to me; "Remove from yourself all evil desire, and clothe yourself in the desire which is good and holy; for clothed with this desire you shall hate the evil desire, and shall bridle and direct it as you wilt.

1[44]:2 For the evil desire is wild, and only tamed with difficulty; for it is terrible, and by its wildness is very costly to men; more especially if a servant of God get entangled in it, and have no understanding, he is put to fearful costs by it. But it is costly to such men as are not clothed in the good desire, but are mixed up with this life "These men then it hands over to death."

1[44]:3 "Of what sort, Sir," say I, "are the works of the evil desire, which hand over men to death? Make them known to me, that I may hold aloof from them." Listen," [said he,] "through what works the evil desire brings death to the servants of God.

2[45]:1 "Before all is desire for the wife or husband of another, and for extravagance of wealth, and for many needless dainties, and for drinks and other luxuries, many and foolish. For even luxury is foolish and vain for the servants of God.

2[45]:2 These desires then are evil, and bring death to the servants of God. For this evil desire is a daughter of the devil. you must, therefore, abstain from the evil desires, that so abstaining you may live unto God.

2[45]:3 But as many as are mastered by them, and resist them not, are done to death utterly; for these desires are deadly.

2[45]:4 But do you clothe yourself in the desire of righteousness, and, having armed yourself with the fear of the Lord, resist them. For the fear of God dwells in the good desire. If the evil desire shall see you armed with the fear of God and resisting itself, it shall flee far from you, and shall no more be seen of you, being in fear of your arms.

2[45]:5 Do you therefore, when you art crowned for thy victory over it, come to the desire of righteousness, and deliver to her the victor's prize which you hast received, and serve her, according as she herself desires. If you serve the good desire, and art subject to her, you shall have power to master the evil desire, and to subject her, according as you wilt."

3[46]:1 "I would fain know, Sir," say I, "in what ways I ought to serve the good desire." "Listen," said he; "practice righteousness and virtue, truth and the fear of the Lord, faith and gentleness, and as many good deeds as are like these. Practicing these you shall be well-pleasing as a servant of God, and shall live unto Him; yea, and every one who shall serve the good desire shall live unto God."

3[46]:2 So he completed the twelve commandments, and he said to me; You hast these commandments; walk in them, and exhort thy hearers that their repentance may become pure for the rest of the days of their life.

3[46]:3 This ministration, which I give you, fulfill you with all diligence to the end, and you shall effect much. For you shall find favor among those who are about to repent, and they shall obey thy words. For I will be with you, and will compel them to obey you."

3[46]:4 I say to him; "Sir, these commandments are great and beautiful and glorious, and are able to gladden the heart of the man who is able to observe them. But I know not whether these commandments can be kept by a man, for they are very hard."

3[46]:5 He answered and said unto me; "If you set it before yourself that they can be kept, you wilt easily keep them, and they will not be hard; but if it once enter into thy heart that they cannot be kept by a man, you wilt not keep them.

3[46]:6 But now I say unto you; if you keep them not. but neglect them you shall not have salvation, neither thy children nor thy household, since you hast already pronounced judgment against yourself that these commandments cannot be kept by a man."

4[47]:1 And these things he said to me very angrily, so that I was confounded, and feared him exceedingly; for his form was changed, so that a man could not endure his anger.

4[47]:2 And when he saw that I was altogether disturbed and confounded, he began to speak more kindly [and cheerfully] to me, and he said; "Foolish fellow, void of understanding and of doubtful mind, perceives you not the glory of God, how great and mighty and marvelous it is, how that He created the world for man's sake, and subjected all His creation to man, and gave all authority to him, that he should be master over all things under the heaven?

4[47]:3 If then," [he said,] "man is lord of all the creatures of God and masters all things, cannot he also master these commandments Aye," said he, "the man that has the Lord in his heart can master [all things and] all these commandments.

4[47]:4 But they that have the Lord on their lips, while their heart is hardened, and are far from the Lord, to them these commandments are hard and inaccessible.

4[47]:5 Therefore do you, who are empty and fickle in the faith, set your Lord in your heart, and you shall perceive that nothing is easier than these commandments, nor sweeter, nor more gentle.

4[47]:6 Be you converted, you that walk after the commandments of the devil, (the commandments which are so) difficult and bitter and wild and riotous; and fear not the devil, for there is no power in him against you.

4[47]:7 For I will be with you, I, the angel of repentance, who have the mastery over him. The devil has fear alone, but his fear has no force. Fear him not therefore; and he will flee from you."

5[48]:1 I say to him, "Sir, listen to a few words from me." "Say what you wilt," said he. "Man, Sir," I say, "is eager to keep the commandments of God, and there is no one that asks not of the Lord that he may be strengthened in His commandments, and be subject to them; but the devil is hard and overmasters them."

5[48]:2 "He cannot," said he, "overmaster the servants of God, who set their hope on Him with their whole heart. The devil can wrestle with them, but he cannot overthrow them. If then you resist him, he will be vanquished and will flee from you disgraced. But as many," said he, "as are utterly empty, fear the devil as if he had power.

5[48]:3 When a man has filled amply sufficient jars with good wine, and among these jars a few are quite empty, he comes to the jars, and does not examine the full ones, for he knows that they are full; but he examines the empty ones, fearing lest they have turned sour. For empty jars soon turn sour, and the taste of the wine is spoilt.

5[48]:4 So also the devil cometh to all the servants of God tempting them. As many then as are complete in the faith, oppose him mightily, and he departs from them, not having a place where he can find an entrance. So he cometh next to the empty ones, and finding a place goes into them, and further he doeth what he wills in them, and they become submissive slaves to him.

6[49]:1 "But I, the angel of repentance, say unto you; Fear not the devil; for I was sent," said he, "to be with you who repent with your whole heart, and to strengthen you in the faith.

6[49]:2 Believe, therefore, on God, you who by reason of your sins have despaired of your life, and are adding to your sins, and weighing down your life; for if you turn unto the Lord with your whole heart, and work righteousness the remaining days of your life, and serve Him rightly according to His will, He will give healing to your former sins, and you shall have power to master the works of the devil. But of the threatening of the devil fear not at all; for he is unstrung, like the sinews of a dead man.

6[49]:3 Hear me therefore, and fear Him, Who is able to do all things, to save and to destroy, and observe these commandments, and you shall live unto God."

6[49]:4 I say to him, "Sir, now am I strengthened in all the ordinances of the Lord, because you art with me; and I know that you wilt crush all the power of the devil, and we shall be masters over him, and shall prevail over all his works. And I hope, Sir, that I am now able to keep these commandments which you hast commanded, the Lord enabling me."

6[49]:5 "You shall keep them," said he, "if thy heart be found pure with the Lord; yea, and all shall keep them, as many as shall purify their hearts from the vain desires of this world, and shall live unto God."

Parables Which He spoke With Me

Parable 1

1[50]:1 He said to me; "you know that you, who are the servants of God, are dwelling in a foreign land; for your city is far from this city. If then you know your city, in which you shall dwell, why do you here prepare fields and expensive displays and buildings and dwelling-chambers which are superfluous?

1[50]:2 He, therefore, that prepares these things for this city does not purpose to return to his own city.

1[50]:3 O foolish and double-minded and miserable man, perceives you not that all these things are foreign, and are under the power of another For the lord of this city shall say, "I do not wish you to dwell in my city; go forth from this city, for you do not conform to my laws."

1[50]:4 You, therefore who hast fields and dwellings and many other possessions, when you art cast out by him, what wilt you do with thy field and thy house am all the other things that you prepared for yourself? For the lord of this country said to you justly, "Either conform to my laws, or depart from my country."

1[50]:5 What then shall you do, who art under law in your own city? For the sake of thy fields and the rest of thy possessions wilt you altogether repudiate thy law, and walk according to the law of this city? Take heed, lest it be inexpedient to repudiate the law; for if you should desire to return again to thy city, you shall surely not be received [because you didst repudiate the law of the city], and shall be shut out from it.

1[50]:6 Take heed therefore; as dwelling in a strange land prepare nothing more for yourself but a competency which is sufficient for you, and make ready that, whenever the master of this city may desire to cast you out for your opposition to his law, you may go forth from his city and depart into your own city and use your own law joyfully, free from all insult.

1[50]:7 Take heed therefore, you that serve God and have Him in your heart: work the "works of God being mindful of His commandments and of the promises which He made, and believe Him that He will perform them, if His commandments be kept.

1[50]:8 Therefore, instead of fields buy you souls that are in trouble, as each is able, and visit widows and orphans, and neglect them not; and spend your riches and all your displays, which you received from God, on fields and houses of this kind.

1[50]:9 For to this end the Master enriched you, that you might perform these ministrations for Him. It is much better to purchase fields [and possessions] and houses of this kind, which you wilt find in your own city, when you visit it.

1[50]:10 This lavish expenditure is beautiful and joyous, not bringing sadness or fear, but bringing joy. The expenditure of the heathen then practice not you; for it is not convenient for you the servants of God.

1[50]:11 But practice your own expenditure, in which you can rejoice; and do not corrupt, neither touch that which is another man's, nor lust after it for it is wicked to lust after other men's possessions. But perform your own task, and you shall be saved."

Parable 2

1[51]:1 As I walked in the field, and noticed an elm and a vine, and was distinguishing them and their fruits, the shepherd appears to me and said; "What art you meditating within yourself?" "I am thinking, [Sir,]" say I, "about the elm and the vine, that they are excellently suited the one to the other."

1[51]:2 "These two trees," said he, "are appointed for a type to the servants of God." "I would fain know, [Sir,]" say I, "the type contained in these trees, of which you speak." "See you," said he, "the elm and the vine ?" "I see them, Sir," say I.

1[51]:3 "This vine," said he, "bears fruit, but the elm is an unfruitful stock. Yet this vine, except it climb up the elm, cannot bear much fruit when it is spread on the ground; and such fruit as it bears is rotten, because it is not suspended upon the elm. When then the vine is attached to the elm, it bears fruit both from itself and from the elm.

1[51]:4 You see then that the elm also bears [much] fruit, not less than the vine, but rather more." How more, Sir?" say I. "Because," said he, "the vine, when hanging upon the elm, bears its fruit in abundance, and in good condition; but, when spread on the ground, it bears little fruit, and that rotten. This parable therefore is applicable to the servants of God, to poor and to rich alike."

1[51]:5 "How, Sir?" say I; "instruct me." "Listen," said he; the rich man has much wealth, but in the things of the Lord he is poor, being distracted about his riches, and his confession and intercession with the Lord is very scanty; and even that which he gives is mall and weak and has not power above. When then the rich man goes up to the poor, and assists him in his needs, believing that for what he doth to the poor man he shall be able to obtain a reward with God--because the poor man is rich in intercession [and confession], and his intercession has great power with God--the rich man then supplies all things to the poor man without wavering.

1[51]:6 But the poor man being supplied by the rich makes intercession for him, thanking God for him that gave to him. And the other is still more zealous to assist the poor man, that he may be continuous in his life: for he knows that the intercession of the poor man is acceptable and rich before God.

1[51]:7 They both then accomplish their work; the poor man makes intercession, wherein he is rich [which he received of the Lord]; this he renders again to the Lord Who supplies him with it. The rich man too in like manner furnishes to the poor man, nothing doubting, the riches which he received from the Lord. And this work great and acceptable with God, because (the rich man) has understanding concerning his riches, and works for the poor man from the bounties of the Lord, and accomplishes the ministration of the Lord rightly.

1[51]:8 In the sight of men then the elm seems not to bear fruit, and they know not, neither perceive, that if there cometh a drought the elm having water nurtures the vine, and the vine having a constant supply of water bears fruit two fold, both for itself and for the elm. So likewise the poor, by interceding with the Lord for the rich, establish their riches, and again the rich, supplying their needs to the poor, establish their souls.

1[51]:9 So then both are made partners in the righteous work. He then that doeth these things shall not be abandoned of God, but shall be written in the books of the living.

1[51]:10 Blessed are the rich, who understand also that they are enriched from the Lord. For they that have this mind shall be able to do some good work."

Parable 3

1[52]:1 He showed me many trees which had no leaves, but they seemed to me to be, as it were, withered; for they were all alike. And he said to me; "See you these trees?" "I see them, Sir," I say, "they are all alike, and are withered." He answered and said to me; "These trees that you see are they that dwell in this world."

1[52]:2 "Wherefore then, Sir," say I, "are they as if they were withered, and alike?" "Because," said he, "neither the righteous are distinguishable, nor the sinners in this world, but they are alike. For this world is winter to the righteous, and they are not distinguishable, as they dwell with the sinners.

1[52]:3 For as in the winter the trees, having shed their leaves, are alike, and are not distinguishable, which are withered, and which alive, so also in this world neither the just nor the sinners are distinguishable, but they are all alike."

Parable 4

1[53]:1 He showed me many trees again, some of them sprouting, and others withered, and he said to me; "See you," said he, "these trees?" "I see them, Sir," say I, "some of them sprouting, and others withered."

1[53]:2 "These trees," said he, "that are sprouting are the righteous, who shall dwell in the world to come; for the world to come is summer to the righteous, but winter to the sinners. When then the mercy of the Lord shall shine forth, then they that serve God shall be made manifest; yea, and all men shall be made manifest.

1[53]:3 For as in summer the fruits of each several tree are made manifest, and are recognized of what sort they are, so also the fruits of the righteous shall be manifest, and all [even the very smallest] shall be known to be flourishing in that world.

1[53]:4 But the Gentiles and the sinners, just as you saw the trees which were withered, even such shall they be found, withered and unfruitful in that world, and shall be burnt up as fuel, and shall be manifest, because their practice in their life has been evil. For the sinners shall be burned, because they sinned and repented not; and the Gentiles shall be burned, because they knew not Him that created them.

1[53]:5 Do you therefore bear fruit, that in that summer thy fruit may be known. But abstain from overmuch business, and you shall never fill into any sin. For they that busy themselves overmuch, sin much also, being distracted about their business, and in no wise serving their own Lord.

1[53]:6 How then," said he, "can such a man ask anything of the Lord and receive it, seeing that he serves not the Lord? [For] they that serve Him, these shall receive their petitions, but they that serve not the Lord, these shall receive nothing.

1[53]:7 But if any one work one single action, he is able also to serve the Lord; for his mind shall not be corrupted from (following) the Lord, but he shall serve Him, because he keeps his mind pure.

1[53]:8 If therefore you doest these things, you shall be able to bear fruit unto the world to come; yea, and whosoever shall do these things, shall bear fruit."
Parable 5
1[54]:1 As I was fasting and seated on a certain mountain, and giving thanks to the Lord for all that He had done unto me, I see the shepherd seated by me and saying; "Why hast you come hither in the early morn?" "Because, Sir," say I, "I am keeping a station."
1[54]:2 "What," said he, "is a station?" "I am fasting, Sir," say I. "And what," said he, "is this fast [that you are fasting]?" "As I was accustomed, Sir," say I, "so I fast."
1[54]:3 "you know not," said he, "how to fast unto the Lord, neither is this a fast, this unprofitable fast which you make unto Him." "wherefore, Sir," say I, "say you this?" "I tell you," said he, "that this is not a fast, wherein you think to fast; but I will teach you what is a complete fast and acceptable to the Lord. Listen," said he;
1[54]:4 "God desires not such a vain fast; for by so fasting unto God you shall do nothing for righteousness. But fast you [unto God] such a fast as this;
1[54]:5 do no wickedness in thy life, and serve the Lord with a pure heart; observe His commandments and walk in His ordinances, and let no evil desire rise up in thy heart; but believe God. Then, if you shall do these things, and fear Him, and control yourself from every evil deed, you shall live unto God; and if you do these things, you shall accomplish a great fast, and one acceptable to God.
2[55]:1 "Hear the parable which I shall tell you relating to fasting.
2[55]:2 A certain man had an estate, and many slaves, and a portion of his estate he planted as a vineyard; and choosing out a certain slave who was trusty and well-pleasing (and) held in honor, he called him to him and said unto him; "Take this vineyard [which I have planted], and fence it [till I come], but do nothing else to the vineyard. Now keep this my commandment, and you shall be free in my house." Then the master of the servant went away to travel abroad.
2[55]:3 When then he had gone away, the servant took and fenced the vineyard; and having finished the fencing of the vineyard, he noticed that the vineyard was full of weeds.
2[55]:4 So he reasoned within himself, saying, "This command of my lord I have carried out I will next dig this vineyard, and it shall be neater when it is dug; and when it has no weeds it will yield more fruit, because not choked by the weeds." He took and dug the vineyard, and all the weeds that were in the vineyard he plucked up. And that vineyard became very neat and flourishing, when it had no weeds to choke it.
2[55]:5 After a time the master of the servant [and of the estate] came, and he went into the vineyard. And seeing the vineyard fenced neatly, and dug as well,

and [all] the weeds plucked up, and the vines flourishing, he rejoiced [exceedingly] at what his servant had done.
2[55]:6 So he called his beloved son, who was his heir, and the friends who were his advisers, and told them what he had commanded his servant, and how much he had found done. And they rejoiced with the servant at the testimony which his master had borne to him.
2[55]:7 And he said to them; "I promised this servant his freedom, if he should keep the commandment which I commanded him; but he kept my commandment and did a good work besides to my vineyard, and pleased me greatly. For this work therefore which he has done, I desire to make him joint-heir with my son, because, when the good thought struck him, he did not neglect it, but fulfilled it."
2[55]:8 In this purpose the son of the master agreed with him, that the servant should be made joint-heir with the son.
2[55]:9 After some few days, his master made a feast, and sent to him many dainties from the feast. But when the servant received [the dainties sent to him by the master], he took what was sufficient for him, and distributed the rest to his fellow servants.
2[55]:10 And his fellow-servants, when they received the dainties, rejoiced, and began to pray for him, that he might find greater favor with the master, because he had treated them so handsomely.
2[55]:11 All these things which had taken place his master heard, and again rejoiced greatly at his deed. So the master called together again his friends and his son, and announced to them the deed that he had done with regard to his dainties which he had received; and they still more approved of his resolve, that his servant should be made joint-heir with his son."
3[56]:1 I say, "Sir, I understand not these parables, neither can I apprehend them, unless you explain them for me."
3[56]:2 "I will explain everything to you," said he; "and will show you whatsoever things I shall speak with you. Keep the commandments of the Lord, and you shall be well-pleasing to God, and shall be enrolled among the number of them that keep His commandments.
3[56]:3 But if you do any good thing outside the commandment of God, you shall win for yourself more exceeding glory, and shall be more glorious in the sight of God than you would otherwise have been. If then, while you keep the commandments of God, you add these services likewise, you shall rejoice, if you observe them according to my commandment."
3[56]:4 I say to him, "Sir, whatsoever you command me, I will keep it; for I know that you art with me." "I will be with you," said he, "because you hast so great zeal for doing good; yea, and I will be with all," said he, "whosoever have such zeal as this.

3[56]:5 This fasting," said he, "if the commandments of the Lord are kept, is very good. This then is the way, that you shall keep this fast which you art about to observe].

3[56]:6 First of all, keep yourself from every evil word and every evil desire, and purify thy heart from all the vanities of this world. If you keep these things, this fast shall be perfect for you.

3[56]:7 And thus shall you do. Having fulfilled what is written, on that day on which you fastest you shall taste nothing but bread and water; and from thy meats, which you would have eaten, you shall reckon up the amount of that day's expenditure, which you would have incurred, and shall give it to a widow, or an orphan, or to one in want, and so shall you humble thy soul, that he that has received from thy humiliation may satisfy his own soul, and may pray for you to the Lord.

3[56]:8 If then you shall so accomplish this fast, as I have commanded you, thy sacrifice shall be acceptable in the sight of God, and this fasting shall be recorded; and the service so performed is beautiful and joyous and acceptable to the Lord.

3[56]:9 These things you shall so observe, you and thy children and thy whole household; and, observing them, you shall be blessed; yea, and all those, who shall hear and observe them, shall be blessed, and whatsoever things they shall ask of the Lord, they shall receive."

4[57]:1 I entreated him earnestly, that he would show me the parable of the estate, and of the master, and of the vineyard, and of the servant that fenced the vineyard, [and of the fence,] and of the weeds which were plucked up out of the vineyard, and of the son, and of the friends, the advisers. For I understood that all these things are a parable.

4[57]:2 But he answered and said unto me; "You art exceedingly importunate in enquiries. You ought not," [said he,] "to make any enquiry at all; for if it be right that a thing be explained unto you, it shall be explained." I say to him; "Sir, whatsoever things you show unto me and do not explain, I shall have seen them in vain, and without understanding what they are. In like manner also, if you speak parables to me and interpret them not, I shall have heard a thing in vain from you."

4[57]:3 But he again answered, and said unto me; "Whosoever," said he, "is a servant of God, and has his own Lord in his heart, asks understanding of Him, and receives it, and interprets every parable, and the words of the Lord which are spoken in parables are made known unto him. But as many as are sluggish and idle in intercession, these hesitate to ask of the Lord.

4[57]:4 But the Lord is abundant in compassion, and gives to them that ask of Him without ceasing. But you who hast been strengthened by the holy angel, and hast received from him such (powers of intercession and art not idle, wherefore do you not ask understanding of the Lord, and obtain it from Him)."

4[57]:5 I say to him, "Sir, I that have you with me have (but) need to ask you and enquire of you; for you show me all things, and speak with me; but if I had seen or heard them apart from you I should have asked of the Lord, that they might be shown to me."

5[58]:1 "I told you just now," said he, "that you art unscrupulous and importunate, in enquiring for the interpretations of the parables. But since you art so obstinate, I will interpret to you the parable of the estate and all the accompaniments thereof, that you may make them known unto all. Hear now," said he, "and understand them.

5[58]:2 The estate is this world, and the lord of the estate is He that created all things, and set them in order, and endowed them with power; and the servant is the Son of God, and the vines are this people whom He Himself planted;

5[58]:3 and the fences are the [holy] angels of the Lord who keep together His people; and the weeds, which are plucked up from the vineyard, are the transgressions of the servants of God; and the dainties which He sent to him from the feast are the commandments which He gave to His people through His Son; and the friends and advisers are the holy angels which were first created; and the absence of the master is the time which remains over until His coming."

5[58]:4 I say to him; "Sir, great and marvelous are all things and all things are glorious; was it likely then," say I, "that I could have apprehended them?" "Nay, nor can any other man, though he be full of understanding, apprehend them." "Yet again, Sir," say I, "explain to me what I am about to enquire of you."

5[58]:5 "Say on," he said, "if you desire anything." "Wherefore, Sir,]" say I, "is the Son of God represented in the parable in the guise of a servant?"

6[59]:1 "Listen," said he; "the Son of God is not represented in the guise of a servant, but is represented in great power and lordship." "How, Sir?" say I; "I comprehend not."

6[59]:2 "Because," said he, "God planted the vineyard, that is, He created the people, and delivered them over to His Son. And the Son placed the angels in charge of them, to watch over them; and the Son Himself cleansed their sins, by laboring much and enduring many toils; for no one can dig without toil or labor.

6[59]:3 Having Himself then cleansed the sins of His people, He showed them the paths of life, giving them the law which He received from His Father. You see," said he, "that He is Himself Lord of the people, having received all power from His Father.

6[59]:4 But how that the lord took his son and the glorious angels as advisers concerning the inheritance of the servant, listen.

6[59]:5 The Holy Pre-existent Spirit. Which created the whole creation, God made to dwell in flesh that He desired. This flesh, therefore, in which the Holy Spirit dwelt, was subject unto the Spirit, walking honorably in holiness and purity, without in any way defiling the Spirit.

6[59]:6 When then it had lived honorably in chastity, and had labored with the Spirit, and had cooperated with it in everything, behaving itself boldly and bravely, He chose it as a partner with the Holy Spirit; for the career of this flesh pleased [the Lord], seeing that, as possessing the Holy Spirit, it was not defiled upon the earth.

6[59]:7 He therefore took the son as adviser and the glorious angels also, that this flesh too, having served the Spirit unblamably, might have some place of sojourn, and might not seem to hare lost the reward for its service; for all flesh, which is found undefiled and unspotted, wherein the Holy Spirit dwelt, shall receive a reward.

6[59]:8 Now you hast the interpretation of this parable also."

7[60]:1 "I was right glad, Sir," say I, "to hear this interpretation." "Listen now," said he, "Keep this thy flesh pure and undefiled, that the Spirit which dwells in it may bear witness to it, and thy flesh may be justified.

7[60]:2 See that it never enter into your heart that this flesh of your is perishable, and so you abuse it in some defilement. [For] if you defile thy flesh, you shall defile the Holy Spirit also; but if you defile the flesh, you shall not live."

7[60]:3 "But if, Sir," say I, "there has been any ignorance in times past, before these words were heard, how shall a man who has defiled his flesh be saved?" "For the former deeds of ignorance," said he, "God alone has power to give healing; for all authority is His.

7[60]:4 [But now keep yourself, and the Lord Almighty, Who is full of compassion, will give healing for thy former deeds of ignorance,] if henceforth you defile not thy flesh, neither the Spirit; for both share in common, and the one cannot be defiled without the other. Therefore keep both pure, and you shall live unto God."

Parable 6

1[61]:1 As I sat in my house, and glorified the Lord for all things that I had seen, and was considering concerning the commandments, how that they were beautiful and powerful and gladsome and glorious and able to save a man's soul, I said within myself; "Blessed shall I be, if I walk in these commandments; yea, and whosoever shall walk in them shall be blessed."

1[61]:2 As I spoke these things within myself, I see him suddenly seated by me, and saying as follows; "Why art you of a doubtful mind concerning the commandments, which I commanded you? They are beautiful. Doubt not at all; but clothe yourself in the faith of the Lord, and you shall walk in them. For I will strengthen you in them.

1[61]:3 These commandments are suitable for those who meditate repentance; for if they walk not in them, their repentance is in vain.

1[61]:4 you then that repent, cast away the evil doings of this world which crush you; and, by putting on every excellence of righteousness, you shall be able to observe these commandments, and to add no more to your sins. If then you add no further sin at all, you will depart from your former sins. Walk then in these my commandments, and you shall live unto God. These things have [all] been told you from me."

1[61]:5 And after he had told these things to me, he said to me, "Let us go into the country, and I will show you the shepherds of the sheep." "Let us go, Sir," say I. And we came to a certain plain, and he shows me a young man, a shepherd, clothed in a light cloak, of saffron color;

1[61]:6 and he was feeding a great number of sheep, and these sheep were, as it were, well fed and very frisky, and were gladsome as they skipped about hither and thither; and the shepherd himself was all gladsome over his flock; and the very visage of the shepherd was exceedingly gladsome; and he ran about among the sheep.

2[62]:1 And he said to me; "See you this shepherd?" "I see him Sir," I say. "This," said he, "is the angel of self-indulgence and of deceit. He crushes the souls of the servants of God, and perverts them from the truth, leading them astray with evil desires, wherein they perish.

2[62]:2 For they forget the commandments of the living God, and walk in vain deceits and acts of self-indulgence, and are destroyed by this angel, some of them unto death, and others unto corruption."

2[62]:3 I say to him, "Sir, I comprehend not what means "unto death," and what "unto corruption". "Listen," said he; "the sheep which you saw gladsome and skipping about, these are they who have been turned asunder from God utterly, and have delivered themselves over to the lusts of this world. In these, therefore, there is not repentance unto life. For the Name of God is being blasphemed through them. The life of such persons is death.

2[62]:4 But the sheep, which you saw not skipping about, but feeding in one place, these are they that have delivered themselves over to acts of self-indulgence and deceit, but have not uttered any blasphemy against the Lord. These then have been corrupted from the truth. In these there is hope of repentance, wherein they can live. Corruption then has hope of a possible renewal, but death has eternal destruction."

2[62]:5 Again we went forward a little way, and he showed me a great shepherd like a wild man in appearance, with a white goatskin thrown about him;

and he had a kind of wallet on his shoulders, and a staff very hard and with knots in it, and a great whip. And his look was very sour, so that I was afraid of him because of his look.

2[62]:6 This shepherd then kept receiving from the young man, the shepherd, those sheep that were frisky and well fed, but not skipping about, and putting them in a certain spot, which was precipitous and covered with thorns and briars, so that the sheep could not disentangle themselves from the thorns and briars, but [became entangled among the thorns and briars.

2[62]:7 And so they] pastured entangled in the thorns and briars, and were in great misery with being beaten by him; and he kept driving them about to and fro, and giving them no rest, and all together those sheep had not a happy time.

3[63]:1 When then I saw them so lashed with the whip and vexed, I was sorry for their sakes, because they were so tortured and had no rest at all.

3[63]:2 I say to the shepherd who was speaking with me; "Sir, who is this shepherd, who is [so] hard-hearted and severe, and has no compassion at all for these sheep?" "This," said he, "is the angel of punishment, and he is one of the just angels, and presides over punishment.

3[63]:3 So he receives those who wander away from God, and walk after the lusts and deceits of this life, and punishes them, as they deserve, with fearful and various punishments."

3[63]:4 "I would fain learn, Sir," said I, "of what sort are these various punishments." "Listen," said he; "the various tortures and punishments are tortures belonging to the present life; for some are punished with losses, and others with want, and others with divers maladies, and others with [every kind] of unsettlement, and others with insults from unworthy persons and with suffering in many other respects.

3[63]:5 For many, being unsettled in their plans, set their hands to many things, and nothing ever goes forward with them. And then they say that they do not prosper in their doings, and it doth not enter into their hearts that they have done evil deeds, but they blame the Lord.

3[63]:6 When then they are afflicted with every kind of affliction, then they are delivered over to me for good instruction, and are strengthened in the faith of the Lord, and serve the Lord with a pure heart the remaining days of their life. But, if they repent, the evil works which they have done rise up in their hearts, and then they glorify God, saying that He is a just Judge, and that they suffered justly each according to his doings. And they serve the Lord thenceforward with a pure heart, and are prosperous in all their doings, receiving from the Lord whatsoever things they may ask; and then they glorify the Lord because they were delivered over unto me, and they no longer suffer any evil thing."

3[63]:1 I say unto him; "Sir, declare unto me this further matter." "What enquire you yet?" said he. "Whether, Sir," say I, "they that live in self-indulgence and are deceived undergo torments during the same length of time as they live in self-indulgence and are deceived." He said to me, "They undergo torments for the same length of time."

3[63]:2 "Then, Sir," say I, "they undergo very slight torments; for those who are living thus in self-indulgence and forget God ought to have been tormented seven-fold."

3[63]:3 He said to me, "You art foolish, and comprehend not the power of the torment" "True," say I, "for if I had comprehended it, I should not have asked you to declare it to me." "Listen," said he, "to the power of both, [of the self-indulgence and of the torment].

3[63]:4 The time of the self-indulgence and deceit is one hour. But an hour of the torment has the power of thirty days. If then one live in self indulgence and be deceived for one day, and be tormented for one day, the day of the torment is equivalent to a whole year. For as many days then as a man lives in self-indulgence, for so many years is he tormented. You see then," said he, "that the time of the self-indulgence and deceit is very short, but the time of the punishment and torment is long."

5[65]:1 "Inasmuch, Sir," say I, "as I do not quite comprehend concerning the time of the deceit and self-indulgence and torment, show me more clearly."

5[65]:2 He answered and said unto me; "Your stupidity clings to you; and you wilt not cleanse thy heart and serve God Take heed," [said he,] "lest haply the time be fulfilled, and you be found in thy foolishness. Listen then," [said he,] "even as you wish, that you may comprehend the matter.

5[65]:3 He that lives in self-indulgence and is deceived for one day, and doeth what he wishes, is clothed in much folly and comprehended not the thing which he doeth; for on the morrow he forgets what he did the day before. For self-indulgence and deceit have no memories, by reason of the folly, wherewith each is clothed; but when punishment and torment cling to a man for a single day, he is punished and tormented for a whole year long; for punishment and torment have long memories.

5[65]:4 So being tormented and punished for the whole year, the man remembers at length the self-indulgence and deceit, and perceives that it is on their account that he is suffering these ills. Every man, therefore, that lives in self-indulgence and is deceived, is tormented in this way because, though possessing lire, they have delivered themselves over unto death."

5[65]:5 "What kinds of self-indulgence, Sir," say I, "are harmful?" "Every action," said he, "is self-indulgence to a man, which he does with pleasure; for the irascible man, when he gives the reins to his passion, is self-indulgent; and the adulterer and the drunkard and the slanderer and the liar and the miser and the defrauder and he that doeth things akin to these, gives the reins to his peculiar passion; therefore he is self-indulgent in his action.

5[65]:6 All these habits of self-indulgence are harmful to the servants of God; on account of these deceits therefore they so suffer who are punished and tormented.

5[65]:7 But there are habits of self-indulgence like-wise which save men; for many are self-indulgent in doing good, being carried away by the pleasure it gives to themselves. This self-indulgence then is expedient for the servants of God, and brings life to a man of this disposition; but the harmful self-indulgences afore-mentioned bring to men torments and punishments; and if they continue in them and repent not, they bring death upon themselves."

Parable 7

1[66]:1 After a few days I saw him on the same plain, where also I had seen the shepherds, and he said to me, "What seek you?" "I am here, Sir," say I, "that you may bid the shepherd that punishes go out of my house; for he afflicts me much." "It is necessary for you," said he, "to be afflicted; for so," said he, "the glorious angel ordered as concerning you, for he wishes you to be proved." "Why, what so evil thing have I done, Sir," say I, "that I should be delivered over to this angel?"

1[66]:2 "Listen," said he. "Your sins are many, yet not so many that you should be delivered over to this angel; but thy house has committed great iniquities and sins, and the glorious angel was embittered at their deeds, and for this cause he bade you be afflicted for a certain time, that they also might repent and cleanse themselves from every lust of this world. When therefore they shall repent and be cleansed, then shall the angel of punishment depart."

1[66]:3 I say to him; "Sir, if they perpetrated such deeds that the glorious angel is embittered, what have I done?" "They cannot be afflicted otherwise," said he, "unless you, the head of the [whole] house, be afflicted; for if you be afflicted, they also of necessity will be afflicted; but if you be prosperous, they can suffer no affliction."

1[66]:4 "But behold, Sir," say I, "they have repented with their whole heart." "I am quite aware myself," said he, "that they have repented with their whole heart; well, think you that the sins of those who repent are forgiven forthwith? Certainly not; but the person who repents must torture his own soul, and must be thoroughly humble in his every action, and be afflicted with all the divers kinds of affliction; and if he endure the afflictions which come upon him, assuredly He Who created all things and endowed them with power will be moved with compassion and will bestow some remedy.

1[66]:5 And this (will God do), if in any way He perceive the heart of the penitent pure from every evil thing. But it is expedient for you and for thy house that you should be afflicted now. But why speak I many words to you? You must be afflicted as the angel of the Lord commanded, even he that delivered you unto me; and for this give thanks to the Lord, in that He deemed you worthy that I should reveal unto you beforehand the affliction, that foreknowing it you might endure it with fortitude."

1[66]:6 I say to him; "Sir, be you with me, and I shall be able to endure all affliction [easily]." "I will be with you," said he; "and I will ask the angel that punishes to afflict you more lightly; but you shall be afflicted for a short time, and you shall be restored again to thy house. Only continue to be humble and to minister unto the Lord with a pure heart, you and thy children and thy house, and walk in my commandments which I command you, and thus it will be possible for thy repentance to be strong and pure.

1[66]:7 And if you keep these commandments with thy household, all affliction shall hold aloof from you; yea, and affliction," said he, "shall hold aloof from all whosoever shall walk in these my commandments."

Parable 8

1[67]:1 He showed me a [great] willow, overshadowing plains and mountains, and under the shadow of the willow all have come who are called by the name of the Lord.

1[67]:2 And by the willow there stood an angel of the Lord, glorious and very tall, having a great sickle, and he was lopping branches from the willow, and giving them to the people that sheltered beneath the willow; and he gave them little rods about a cubit long.

1[67]:3 And after all had taken the rods, the angel laid aside the sickle, and the tree was sound, just as I had seen it.

1[67]:4 Then I marveled within myself, saying, "How is the tree sound after so many branches have been lopped off?" The shepherd said to me, "Marvel not that the tree remained sound, after so many branches were lopped off but wait until you see all things, and it shall be shown to you what it is."

1[67]:5 The angel who gave the rods to the people demanded them back from them again, and according as they had received them, so also they were summoned to him, and each of them returned the several rods. But the angel of the Lord took them, and examined them.

1[67]:6 From some he received the rods withered and eaten as it were by grubs: the angel ordered those who gave up rods like these to stand apart.

1[67]:7 And others gave them up withered, but not grub-eaten; and these again he ordered to stand apart.

1[67]:8 And others gave them up half-withered; these also stood apart.

1[67]:9 And others gave up their rods half-withered and with cracks; these also stood apart.

1[67]:10 And others gave up their rods green and with cracks; these also stood apart. And others gave up their rods one half withered and one half green; these also stood apart.

1[67]:11 And others brought their rods two parts of the rod green, and the third part withered; these also stood apart. And others gave them up two parts withered, and the third part green; these also stood apart.

1[67]:12 And others gave up their rods nearly all green, but a very small portion of their rods was withered, just the end; but they had cracks in them; these also stood apart.

1[67]:13 And in those of others there was a very small portion green, but the rest of the rods was withered; these also stood apart.

1[67]:14 And others came bringing their rods green, as they received them from the angel; and the most part of the multitude gave up their rods in this state; and the angel rejoiced exceedingly at these; these also stood apart.

1[67]:15 And others gave up their rods green and with shoots, these also stood apart; and at these again the angel rejoiced exceedingly.

1[67]:16 And others gave up their rods green and with shoots; and their shoots had, as it were, a kind of fruit. And those men were exceeding gladsome, whose rods were found in this state. And over them the angel exulted, and the shepherd was very gladsome over them.

2[68]:1 And the angel of the Lord commanded crowns to be brought. And crowns were brought, made as it were of palm branches; and he crowned the men that had given up the rods which had the shoots and some fruit, and sent them away into the tower.

2[68]:2 And the others also he sent into the tower, even those who had given up the rods green and with shoots, but the shoots were without fruit; and he set a seal upon them.

2[68]:3 And all they that went into the tower had the same raiment, white as snow.

2[68]:4 And those that had given up their rods green as they received them, he sent away, giving them a [white] robe, and seals.

2[68]:5 After the angel had finished these things, he said to the shepherd; "I go away; but these you shall send away to (their places within) the walls, according as each deserves to dwell; but examine their rods carefully), and so send them away. But be careful in examining them. Take heed lest any escape you," said he. "Still if any escape you, I will test them at the altar." When he had thus spoken to the shepherd, he departed.

2[68]:6 And, after the angel had departed, the shepherd said to me; "Let us take the rods of all and plant them, to see whether any of them shall be able to live." I say

unto him, "Sir, these withered things, how can they live?"

2[68]:7 He answered and said unto me; "This tree is a willow, and this class of trees clings to life. If then the rods shall be planted and get a little moisture, many of them will live. And afterwards let us try to pour some water also over them. If any of them shall be able to live, I will rejoice with it; but if it live not, I at least shall not be found neglectful."

2[68]:8 So the shepherd bade me call them, just as each one of them was stationed. And they came row after row, and they delivered up the rods to the shepherd. And the shepherd took the rods, and planted them in rows, and after he had planted them, he poured much water over them, so that the rods could not be seen for the water.

2[68]:9 And after he had watered the rods, he said to me; "Let us go now. and after days let us return and inspect all the rods; for He Who created this tree wills that all those who have received rods from this tree should live. And I myself hope that these little rods, after they have got moisture and been watered, will live the greater part of them."

3[69]:1 I say to him; "Sir, inform me what this tree is. For I am perplexed herewith, because, though so many branches were cut off, the tree is sound, and nothing appears to have been cut from it; I am therefore perplexed thereat."

3[69]:2 "Listen," said he; "this great tree which overshadows plains and mountains and all the earth is the law of God which was given to the whole world; and this law is the Son of Cod preached unto the ends of the earth. But the people that are under the shadow are they that have heard the preaching, and believed on Him;

3[69]:3 but the great and glorious angel is Michael, who has the power over this people and is their captain. For this is he that puts the law into the hearts of the believers; therefore he himself inspects them to whom he gave it, to see whether they have observed it.

3[69]:4 But you see the rods of every one; for the rods are the law. You see these many rods rendered useless, and you shall notice all those that have not observed the law, and shall see the abode of each severally."

3[69]:5 I say unto him; "Sir, wherefore did he send away some into the tower, and leave others for you?" "As many," said he, "as transgressed the law which they received from him, these he left under my authority for repentance; but as many as already satisfied the law and have observed it, these he has under his own authority."

3[69]:6 "Who then, Sir," say I, "are they that have been crowned and go into the tower?" ["As many," said he, "as wrestled with the devil and overcame him in their wrestling, are crowned:] these are they that suffered for the law.

3[69]:7 But the others, who likewise gave up their rods green and with shoots, though not with fruit, are they that were persecuted for the law, but did not suffer nor yet deny their law.

3[69]:8 But they that gave them up green just as they received them, are sober and righteous men, who walked altogether in a pure heart and have kept the commandments of the Lord. But all else you shall know, when I have examined these rods that have been planted and watered."

4[70]:1 And after a few days we came to the place, and the shepherd sat down in the place of the angel, while I stood by him. And he said to me; "Gird yourself with a garment of raw flax, and minister to me." So I girded myself with a clean garment of raw flax made of coarse material.

4[70]:2 And when he saw me girded and ready to minister to him "Call," said he, "the men whose rods have been planted, according to the rank as each presented their rods." And I went away to the plain, and called them all; and they stood all of them according to their ranks.

4[70]:3 He said to them; "Let each man pluck out his own rod, and bring it to me." Those gave them up first, who had the withered and chipped rods, and they were found accordingly withered and chipped. He ordered them to stand apart.

4[70]:4 Then those gave them up, who had the withered but not chipped; and some of them gave up the rods green, and others withered and chipped as by grubs. Those then that gave them up green he ordered to stand apart; but those that gave them up withered and chipped he ordered to stand with the first.

4[70]:5 Then those gave them up who had the half-withered and with cracks; and many of them gave them up green and without cracks; and some gave them up green and with shoots, and fruits on the shoots, such as those had who went into the tower crowned; and some gave them up withered and eaten, and some withered and uneaten, and some such as they were, half-withered and with cracks. He ordered them to stand each one apart, some in their proper ranks, and others apart.

5[71]:1 Then those gave them up who had their rods green, but with cracks. These all gave them up green, and stood in their own company. And the shepherd rejoiced over these, because they all were changed and had put away their cracks.

5[71]:2 And those gave them up likewise who had the one half green and the other half withered. The rods of some were found entirely green, of some half-withered, of some withered and eaten, and of some green and with shoots. These were all sent away each to his company.

5[71]:3 Then those gave them up who had two parts green and the third withered; many of them gave them up green, and many half-withered, and others withered and eaten. These all stood in their own company.

5[71]:4 Then those gave them up who had two parts withered and the third part green. Many of them gave them up half-withered, but some withered and eaten, others half-withered and with cracks, and a few green. These all stood in their own company.

5[71]:5 Then those gave them up who had their rods green, but a very small part [withered] and with cracks. Of these some gave them up green, and others green and with shoots. These also went away to their own company.

5[71]:6 Then those gave them up who had a very small part green and the other parts withered. The rods of these were found for the most part green and with shoots and fruit on the shoots, and others altogether green. At these rods the shepherd rejoiced very [greatly], because they were found so. And these went away each to his own company.

6[72]:1 After [the shepherd] had examined the rods of all, he said to me, "I told you that this tree clings to life. See you," said he, "how many repented and were saved?" "I see, Sir," say I. "It is," said he, that you may see the abundant compassion of the Lord, how great and glorious it is, and He has given (His) Spirit to those that are worthy of repentance."

6[72]:2 "Wherefore then, Sir," say I, "did they not all repent?" "To those, whose heart He saw about to become pure and to serve Him with all the heart, to them He gave repentance; but those whose craftiness and wickedness He saw, who intend to repent in hypocrisy, to them He gave not repentance, lest haply they should again profane His name."

6[72]:3 I say unto him, "Sir, now then show me concerning those that have given up their rods, what manner of man each of them is, and their abode, that when they hear this, they that believed and have received the seal and have broken it and did not keep it sound may fully understand what they are doing, and repent, receiving from you a seal, and may glorify the Lord, that He had compassion upon them and sent you to renew their spirits."

6[72]:4 "Listen," said he; "those whose rods were found withered and grub-eaten, these are the renegades and traitors to the Church, that blasphemed the Lord in their sins, and still further were ashamed of the Name of the Lord, which was invoked upon them. These then perished altogether unto God. But you see how not one of them repented, although they heard the words which you spoke to them, which I commanded you. From men of this kind life departed.

6[72]:5 But those that gave up the withered and undecayed (rods), these also are near them; for they were hypocrites, and brought in strange doctrines, and perverted the servants of God, especially them that had sinned, not permitting them to repent, but persuading them with their foolish doctrines. These then have hope of repenting.

6[72]:6 But you see that many of them have indeed repented from the time when you speak to them my commandments; yea, and (others) still will repent. And as many as shall not repent, have lost their life; but as many of them as repented, became good; and their dwelling was placed within the first walls, and some of them even ascended into the tower. You see then," [said he,] "that repentance from sins brings life, but not to repent brings death.

7[73]:1 "But as many as gave up (the rods) half-withered, and with cracks in them, hear also concerning these. Those whose rods were half-withered throughout are the double-minded; for they neither live nor are dead.

7[73]:2 But those that have them half-withered and cracks in them, these are both double-minded and slanderers, and are never at peace among themselves but always causing dissensions. Yet even to these," [said he,] "repentance is given. You see," [said he,] "that some of them have repented; and there is still," said he, "hope of repentance among them.

7[73]:3 And as many of them," said he, "as have repented, have their abode within the tower; but as many of them as have repented tardily shall abide within the walls; and as many as repent not, but continue in their doings, shall die the death.

7[73]:4 But they that have given up their rods green and with cracks, these were found faithful and good at all times, [but] they have a certain emulation one with another about first places and about glory of some kind or other; but all these are foolish in having (emulation) one with another about first places.

7[73]:5 Yet these also, when they heard my commandments, being good, purified themselves and repented quickly. They have their habitation, therefore, within the tower. But if any one shall again turn to dissension, he shall be cast out from the tower and shall lose his life.

7[73]:6 Life is for all those that keep the commandments of the Lord. But in the commandments there is nothing about first places, or about glory of any kind, but about long-suffering and humility in man. In such men, therefore, is the life of the Lord, but in factious and lawless men is death.

8[74]:1 "But they that gave up their rods half green and half withered, these are they that are mixed up in business and hold fast not to the saints. Therefore the one half of them lives , but the other half is dead.

8[74]:2 Many then when they heard my commandments repented. As many then as repented, have their abode within the tower. But some of them altogether stood aloof These then have no repentance; for by reason of their business affairs they blasphemed the Lord and denied Him. So they lost their life for the wickedness that they committed.

8[74]:3 But many of them were doubtful-minded. These still have place for repentance, if they repent quickly, and their dwelling shall be within the tower; and if they repent tardily, they shall dwell within the walls; but if they repent not, they too have lost their life.

8[74]:4 But they that have given up two parts green and the third part withered, these are they that have denied with manifold denials.

8[74]:5 Many of them therefore repented and departed to dwell inside the tower; but many utterly rebelled from God; these lost their life finally. And some of them were double-minded and caused dissensions. For these then there is repentance, if they repent speedily and continue not in their pleasures; but if they continue in their doings, they likewise procure for themselves death.

9[75]:1 "But they that have given up their rods two thirds withered and one third green, these are men who have been believers, but grew rich and became renowned among the Gentiles. They clothed themselves with great pride and became high-minded, and abandoned the truth and did not hold fast to the righteous, but lived together after the manner of the Gentiles, and this path appeared the more pleasant unto them; yet they departed not from God, but continued in the faith, though they wrought not the works of the faith.

9[75]:2 Many of them therefore repented, and they had their habitation within the tower.

9[75]:3 But others at the last living with the Gentiles, and being corrupted by the vain opinions of the Gentiles, departed from God, and worked the works of the Gentiles. These therefore were numbered with the Gentiles.

9[75]:4 But others of them were doubtful-minded, not hoping to be saved by reason of the deeds that they had done; and others were double-minded and made divisions among themselves. For these then that were double-minded by reason of their doings there is still repentance; but their repentance ought to be speedy, that their dwelling may be within the tower; but for those who repent not, but continue in their pleasures, death is nigh.

10[76]:1 "But they that gave up their rods green, yet with the extreme ends withered and with cracks; these were found at all times good and faithful and glorious in the sight of God, but they sinned to a very slight degree by reason of little desires and because they had somewhat against one another. But, when they heard my words, the greater part quickly repented, and their dwelling was assigned within the tower.

10[76]:2 But some of them were double-minded, and some being double-minded made a greater dissension. In these then there is still a hope of repentance, because they were found always good; and hardly shall one of them die.

10[76]:3 But they that gave up their rods withered, yet with a very small part green, these are they that believed, but practiced the works of lawlessness. Still they never separated from God, but bore the Name gladly, and gladly received into their houses the servants of God. So hearing of this repentance they repented without wavering, and they practice all excellence and righteousness.

10[76]:4 And some of them even suffer persecution willingly, knowing the deeds that they did. All these then shall have their dwelling within the tower."

11[77]:1 And after he had completed the interpretations of all the rods, he said unto me; "Go, and tell all men to repent, and they shall live unto God; for the Lord in His compassion sent me to give repentance to all, though some of them do not deserve it for their deeds; but being long-suffering the Lord wills them that were called through His Son to be saved."

11[77]:2 I say to him; "Sir, I hope that all when they hear these words will repent; for I am persuaded that each one, when he fully knows his own deeds and fears God, will repent."

11[77]:3 He answered and said unto me; "As many," [said he,] "as [shall repent] from their whole heart [and] shall cleanse themselves from all the evil deeds aforementioned, and shall add nothing further to their sins, shall receive healing from the Lord for their former sins, unless they be double-minded concerning these commandments, and they shall live unto God. [But as many," said he, "as shall add to their sins and walk in the lusts of this world, shall condemn themselves to death.]

11[77]:4 But do you walk in my commandments, and live [unto God; yea, and as many as shall walk in them and shall do rightly, shall live unto God."]

11[77]:5 Having shown me all these things [and told me them] he said to me; "Now the rest will I declare (unto you) after a few days."

Parable 9

1[78]:1 After I had written down the commandments and parables of the shepherd, the angel of repentance, he came to me and said to me; "I wish to show you all things that the Holy Spirit, which spoke with you in the form of the Church, showed unto you. For that Spirit is the Son of God.

1[78]:2 For when you was weaker in the flesh, it was not declared unto you through an angel; but when you was enabled through the Spirit, and didst grow mighty in thy strength so that you could even see an angel, then at length was manifested unto you, through the Church, the building of the tower. In fair and seemly manner hast you seen all things, (instructed) as it were by a virgin; but now you see (being instructed) by an angel, though by the same Spirit;

1[78]:3 yet must you learn everything more accurately from me. For to this end also was I appointed by the glorious angel to dwell in thy house, that you might see all things mightily, in nothing terrified, even as before."

1[78]:4 And he took me away into Arcadia, to a certain rounded mountain, and set me on the top of the mountain, and showed me a great plain, and round the plain twelve mountains, the mountains having each a different appearance.

1[78]:5 The first was black as soot; the second was bare, without vegetation; the third was thorny and full of briars;

1[78]:6 the fourth had the vegetation half-withered, the upper part of the grass green, but the part by the roots withered, and some of the grass became withered, whenever the sun had scorched it;

1[78]:7 the fifth mountain had green grass and was rugged; the sixth mountain was full with clefts throughout, some small and some great, and the clefts had vegetation, but the grass was not very luxuriant, but rather as if it had been withered;

1[78]:8 the seventh mountain had smiling vegetation, and the whole mountain was in a thriving condition, and cattle and birds of every kind did feed upon that mountain; and the more the cattle and the birds did feed, so much the more did the herbage of that mountain flourish. The eighth mountain was full of springs, and every kind of creature of the Lord did drink of the springs on that mountain.

1[78]:9 the ninth mountain had no water at all, and was entirely desert; and it had in it wild beasts and deadly reptiles, which destroy mankind. The tenth mountain had very large trees and was umbrageous throughout, and beneath the shade lay sheep resting and feeding.

1[78]:10 the eleventh mountain was thickly wooded all over, and the trees thereon were very productive, decked with divers kinds of fruits, so that one seeing them would desire to eat of their fruits. The twelfth mountain was altogether white and its aspect was cheerful; and the mountain was most beauteous in itself.

2[79]:1 And in the middle of the plain he showed me a great white rock, rising up from the plain. The rock was loftier than the mountains, being four-square, so that it could contain the whole world.

2[79]:2 Now this rock was ancient, and had a gate hewn out of it; but the gate seemed to me to have been hewed out quite recently. And the gate glistened beyond the brightness of the sun, so that I marveled at the brightness of the gate.

2[79]:3 And around the gate stood twelve virgins. The four then that stood at the corners seemed to me to be more glorious (than the rest); but the others likewise were glorious; and they stood at the four quarters of the gate, and virgins stood in pairs between them.

2[79]:4 And they were clothed in linen tunics and girt about in seemly fashion, having their right shoulders free, as if they intended to carry some burden. Thus were they prepared, for they were very cheerful and eager.

2[79]:5 After I had seen these things, I marveled in myself at the greatness and the glory of what I was seeing And again I was perplexed concerning the virgins, that delicate as they were they stood up like men, as if they intended to carry the whole heaven.

2[79]:6 And the shepherd said unto me; "Why question you within yourself and art perplexed, and bring sadness on yourself? For whatsoever things you can not comprehend, attempt them not, if you art prudent; but entreat the Lord, that you may receive understanding to comprehend them.

2[79]:7 What is behind you you can not see, but what is before you you behold. The things therefore which you can not see, let alone, and trouble not yourself (about them; but the things which you see, these master, and be not over curious about the rest; but I will explain unto you all things whatsoever I shall show you. Have an eye therefore to what remains."

3[80]:1 I saw six men come, tall and glorious and alike in appearance and they summoned a multitude of men. And the others also which came were tall men and handsome and powerful. And the six men ordered them to build a tower above the gate. And there arose a great noise from those men who had come to build the tower, as they ran hither and thither round the gate.

3[80]:2 For the virgins standing round the gate told the men to hasten to build the tower. Now the virgins had spread out their hands, as if they would take something from the men.

3[80]:3 And the six men ordered stones to come up from a certain deep place, and to go to the building of the tower. And there went up ten stones square and polished, [not] hewn from a quarry.

3[80]:4 And the six men called to the virgins, and ordered them to carry all the stones which should go unto the building of the tower, and to pass through the gate and to hand them to the men that were about to build the tower.

3[80]:5 And the virgins laid the first ten stones that rose out of the deep on each other, and they carried them together, stone by stone.

4[81]:1 And just as they stood together around the gate, in that order they carried them that seemed to be strong enough and had stooped under the corners of the stone, while the others stooped at the sides of the stone. And so they carried all the stones. And they carried them right through the gate, as they were ordered, and handed them to the men for the tower; and these took the stones and built.

4[81]:2 Now the building of the tower was upon the great rock and above the gate. Those ten stones then were joined together, and they covered the whole rock. And these formed a foundation for the building of the tower. And [the rock and] the gate supported the whole tower.

4[81]:3 And, after the ten stones, other twenty-five stones came up from the deep, and these were fitted into the building of the tower, being carried by the virgins, like the former. And after these thirty-five stones came up. And these likewise were fitted into the tower. And after these came up other forty stones. and these all were put into the building of the tower. So four rows were made in the foundations of the tower.

4[81]:4 And (the stones) ceased coming up from the deep, and the builders likewise ceased for a little. And again the six men ordered the multitude of the people to bring in stones from the mountains for the building of the tower.

4[81]:5 They were brought in accordingly from all the mountains, of various colors, shaped by the men, and were handed to the virgins; and the virgins carried them right through the gate, and handed them in for the building of the tower. And when the various stones were placed in the building, they became all alike and white, and they lost their various colors.

4[81]:6 But some stones were handed in by the men for the building, and these did not become bright; but just as they were placed, such likewise were they found; for they were not handed in by the virgins, nor had they been carried in through the gate. These stones then were unsightly in the building of the tower.

4[81]:7 Then the six men, seeing the stones that were unsightly in the building, ordered them to be removed and carried [below] into their own place whence they were brought.

4[81]:8 And they say to the men who were bringing the stones in; "Abstain for your parts altogether from handing in stones for the building; but place them by the tower, that the virgins may carry them through the gate, and hand them in for the building. For if," [say they,] they be not carried in through the gate by the hands of these virgins, they cannot change their colors. Labor not therefore," [say they,] "in vain."

5[82]:1 And the building was finished on that day, yet was not the tower finally completed, for it was to be carried up [still] higher; and there was a cessation in the building. And the six men ordered the builders to retire for a short time [all of them], and to rest; but the virgins they ordered not to retire from the tower. And I thought the virgins were left to guard the tower.

5[82]:2 And after all had retired Land rested], I say to the shepherd; "How is it, Sir," say I, "that the building of the tower was not completed?" "The tower," he said, "cannot yet be finally completed, until its master come and test this building, that if any stones be found crumbling, he may change them; for the tower is being built according to His will."

5[82]:3 "I would fain know, Sir," say I, "what is this building of this tower, and concerning the rock and gate, and the mountains, and the virgins, and the stones that came up from the deep, and were not shaped, but went just as they were into the building;

5[82]:4 and wherefore ten stones were first placed in the foundations, then twenty-five, then thirty-five, then forty, and concerning the stones that had gone to the building and were removed again and put away in their own place--concerning all these things set my soul at rest, Sir, and explain them to me."

5[82]:5 "If," said he, "you be not found possessed of an idle curiosity, you shall know all things. For after a few days we shall come here, and you shall see the sequel that overtakes this tower and shall understand all the parables accurately."

5[82]:6 And after a few days we came to the place where we had sat, and he said to me, "Let us go to the tower; for the owner of the tower cometh to inspect it." And we came to the tower, and there was no one at all by it, save the virgins alone.

5[82]:7 And the shepherd asked the virgins whether the master of the tower had arrived. And they said that he would be there directly to inspect the building.

6[83]:1 And, behold, after a little while I see an array of many men coming, and in the midst a man of such lofty stature that he overtopped the tower.

6[83]:2 And the six men who superintended the building walked with him on the right hand and on the left, and all they that worked at the building were with him, and many other glorious attendants around him. And the virgins that watched the tower ran up and kissed him, and they began to walk by his side round the tower.

6[83]:3 And that man inspected the building so carefully, that he felt each single stone; and he held a rod in his hand and struck each single stone that was built in.

6[83]:4 And when he smote, some of the stones became black as soot, others mildewed, others cracked, others broke off short, others became neither white nor black, others rough and not fitting in with the other stones, and others with many spots; these were the varied aspects of the stones which were found unsound for the building.

6[83]:5 So he ordered all these to be removed from the tower, and to be placed by the side of the tower, and other stones to be brought and put into their place.

6[83]:6 And the builders asked him from what mountain he desired stones to be brought and put into their place. And he would not have them brought from the mountains, but ordered them to be brought from a certain plain that was nigh at hand.

6[83]:7 And the plain was dug, and stones were found there bright and square, but some of them too were round. And all the stones which there were anywhere in that plain were brought every one of them, and were carried through the gate by the virgins.

6[83]:8 And the square stones were hewed, and set in the place of those which had been removed; but the round ones were not placed in the building, because they were too hard to be shaped, and to work on them was slow. So they were placed by the side of the tower, as though they were intended to be shaped and placed in the building; for they were very bright.

7[84]:1 So then, having accomplished these things, the glorious man who was lord of the whole tower called the shepherd to him, and delivered unto him all the stones which lay by the side of the tower, which were cast out from the building, and said unto him;

7[84]:2 "Clean these stones carefully, and set them in the building of the tower, these, I mean, which can fit with the rest; but those which will not fit, throw far away from the tower."

7[84]:3 Having given these orders to the shepherd, he departed from the tower with all those with whom he had come. And the virgins stood round the tower watching it.

7[84]:4 I say to the shepherd, "How can these stones go again to the building of the tower, seeing that they have been disapproved?" He said unto me in answer; "See you", said he, "these stones ?" I see them, Sir," say I. "I myself," said he, "will shape the greater part of these stones and put them into the building, and they shall fit in with the remaining stones."

7[84]:5 "How, Sir," say I, "can they, when they are chiseled, fill the same space?" He said unto me in answer, "As many as shall be found small, shall be put into the middle of the building; but as many as are larger, shall be placed nearer the outside, and they will bind them together."

7[84]:6 With these words he said to me, "Let us go away, and after two days let us come and clean these stones, and put them into the building; for all things round the tower must be made clean, lest haply the master come suddenly and find the circuit of the tower dirty, and he be wroth, and so these stones shall not go to the building of the tower, and I shall appear to be careless in my master's sight."

7[84]:7 And after two days we came to the tower, and he said unto me; "Let us inspect all the stones, and see those which can go to the building." I say to him, "Sir, let us inspect them."

8[85]:1 And so commencing first we began to inspect the black stones; and just as they were when set aside from the building, such also they were found. And the shepherd ordered them to be removed from the tower and to be put on one side.

8[85]:2 Then he inspected those that were mildewed, and he took and shaped many of them, and ordered the virgins to take them up and put them into the building. And the virgins took them up and placed them in the building of the tower in a middle position. But the rest he ordered to be placed with the black ones; for these also were found black.

8[85]:3 Then he began to inspect those that had the cracks; and of these he shaped many, and he ordered them to be carried away by the hands of the virgins for the building. And they were placed towards the outside, because they were found to be sounder. But the rest could not be shaped owing to the number of the cracks. For this reason therefore they were cast aside from the building of the tower.

8[85]:4 Then he proceeded to inspect the stunted (stones), and many among them were found black, and some had contracted great cracks; and he ordered these also to be placed with those that had been cast aside. But those of them which remained he cleaned and shaped, and ordered to be placed in the building So the virgins took them up, and fitted them into the middle of the building of the tower; for they were somewhat weak.

8[85]:5 Then he began to inspect those that were half white and half black, and many of them were (now) found black; and he ordered these also to be taken up with those that had been cast aside. But all the rest were [found white, and were] taken up by the virgins; for being white they were fitted by [the virgins] them[selves] into the building. But they were placed towards the outside, because they were found sound, so that they could hold together those that were placed in the middle; for not a single one of them was too short.

8[85]:6 Then he began to inspect the hard and rough; and a few of them were cast away, because they could not be shaped; for they were found very hard. But the rest of them were shaped [and taken up by the virgins] and fitted into the middle of the building of the tower; for they were somewhat weak.

8[85]:7 Then he proceeded to inspect those that had the spots, and of these some few had turned black and were cast away among the rest; but the remainder were found bright and sound, and these were fitted by the virgins into the building; but they were placed towards the outside, owing to their strength.

9[86]:1 Then he came to inspect the white and round stones, and he said unto me; "What shall we do with these stones?" "How do I know, Sir?" say I [And he said to me,] "Perceives you nothing concerning them?"

9[86]:2 "I, Sir," say I, "do not possess this art, neither am I a mason, nor can I understand." See you not," said he, "that they are very round; and if I wish to make them square, very much must needs be chiseled off from them? Yet some of them must of necessity be placed into the building."

9[86]:3 "If then, Sir," say I, "it must needs be so, why distress yourself, and why not choose out for the building those you will, and fit them into it?" He chose out from them the large and the bright ones, and shaped them; and the virgins took them up, and fitted them into the outer parts of the building.

9[86]:4 But the rest, which remained over, were taken up, and put aside into the plain whence they were brought; they were not however cast away, "Because,"

said he, there remains still a little of the tower to be built And the master of the tower is exceedingly anxious that these stones be fitted into the building, for they are very bright."

9[86]:5 So twelve women were called, most beautiful in form, clad in black, [girded about and having the shoulders bare,] with their hair hanging loose. And these women, I thought, had a savage look. And the shepherd ordered them to take up the stones which had been cast away from the building, and to carry them off to the same mountains from which also they had been brought;

9[86]:6 and they took them up joyfully, and carried away all the stones and put them in the place whence they had been taken. And after all the stones had been taken up, and not a single stone still lay round the tower, the shepherd said unto me; "Let us go round the tower, and see that there is no defect in it." And I proceeded to go round it with him.

9[86]:7 And when the shepherd saw that the tower was very comely in the building, he was exceedingly glad; for the tower was so well built, that when I saw it I coveted the building of it; for it was built, as it were, of one stone, having one fitting in it. And the stone-work appeared as if hewn out of the rock; for it seemed to me to be all a single stone.

10[87]:1 And I, as I walked with him, was glad to see so brave a sight. And the shepherd said to me; "Go and bring plaster and fine clay, that I may fill up the shapes of the stones that have been taken up and put into the building; for all the circuit of the tower must be made smooth."

10[87]:2 And I did as he bade, and brought them to him. "Assist me," said he, "and the work will speedily be accomplished." So he filled in the shapes of the stones which had gone to the building, and ordered the circuit of the tower to be swept and made clean.

10[87]:3 And the virgins took brooms and swept, and they removed all the rubbish from the tower, and sprinkled water, and the site of the tower was made cheerful and very seemly.

10[87]:4 The shepherd said unto me, "All," said he, "has now been cleaned. If the lord come to inspect the tower, he has nothing for which to blame us." Saying this, he desired to go away.

10[87]:5 But I caught hold of his wallet, and began to adjure him by the Lord that he would explain to me [all] what he had showed me. He said to me; "I am busy for a little while, and then I will explain everything to you. Await me here till I come."

10[87]:6 I say to him; "Sir, when I am here alone what shall I do?" "You art not alone," said he; "for these virgins are here with you." "Commend me then to them," say I. The shepherd calls them to him and said to them; "I commend this man to you till I come," and he departed.

10[87]:7 So I was alone with the virgins; and they were most cheerful, and kindly disposed to Me especially the four of them that were the more glorious in appearance.

11[88]:1 The virgins say to me; "Today the shepherd cometh not here." "What then shall I do?" say I. "Stay for him," say they, "till eventide; and if he come, he will speak with you; but if he come not, you shall stay here with us till he cometh."

11[88]:2 I say to them; "I will await him till evening, and if he come not, I will depart home and return early in the morning." But they answered and said unto me; "To us you were entrusted; you can not depart from us."

11[88]:3 "Where then," say I, "shall I remain?" "You shall pass the night with us," say they as a brother, not as a husband; for you art our brother, and henceforward we will dwell with you; for we love you dearly." But I was ashamed to abide with them.

11[88]:4 And she that seemed to be the chief of them began to kiss and to embrace me; and the others seeing her embrace me, they too began to kiss me, and to lead me round the tower, and to sport with me.

11[88]:5 And I had become as it were a younger man, and I commenced myself likewise to sport with them. For some of them began to dance, [others to skip,] others to sing. But I kept silence and walked with them round the tower, and was glad with them.

11[88]:6 But when evening came I wished to go away home; but they would not let me go, but detained me. And I stayed the night with them, and I slept by the side of the tower.

11[88]:7 For the virgins spread their linen tunics on the ground, and made me lie down in the midst of them, and they did nothing else but pray; and I prayed with them without ceasing, and not less than they. And the virgins rejoiced that I so prayed. And I stayed there with the virgins until the morning till the second hour.

11[88]:8 Then came the shepherd, and said to the virgins; "Have you done him any injury?" "Ask him," say they. I say to him, "Sir, I was rejoiced to stay with them." "On what didst you sup?" said he "I supped, Sir," say I, "on the words of the Lord the whole night through." "Did they treat you well?" said he. "Yes, Sir," say I.

11[88]:9 "Now," said he, "what would you hear first?" "In the order as you showed to me, Sir, from the beginning," say I; "I request you, Sir, to explain to me exactly in the order that I shall enquire of you." According as you desire," said he, "even so will I interpret to you, and I will conceal nothing whatever from you."

12[89]:1 "First of all, Sir," say I, "explain this to me. The rock and the gate, what is it?" "This rock," said he, "and gate is the Son of God." "How, Sir," say I, "is the rock ancient, but the gate recent?" "Listen," said he, "and understand, foolish man.

12[89]:2 The Son of God is older than all His creation, so that He became the Father's adviser in His creation. Therefore also He is ancient." "But the gate, why is it recent, Sir?" say I.

12[89]:3 "Because," said he, "He was made manifest in the last days of the consummation; therefore the gate was made recent, that they which are to be saved may enter through it into the kingdom of God.

12[89]:4 Didst you see," said he, "that the stones which came through the gate have gone to the building of the tower, but those which came not through it were cast away again to their own place?" "I saw, Sir," say I. "Thus," said he, "no one shall enter into the kingdom of God, except he receive the name of His Son.

12[89]:5 For if you wish to enter into any city, and that city is walled all round and has one gate only, can you enter into that city except through the gate which it has?" "Why, how, Sir," say I, "is it possible otherwise?" "If then you can not enter into the city except through the gate itself, even so," said he, "a man cannot enter into the kingdom of God except by the name of His Son that is beloved by Him.

12[89]:6 Didst you see," said he, "the multitude that is building the tower?" "I saw it, Sir," say I. "They," said he, are all glorious angels. With these then the Lord is walled around. But the gate is the Son of God; there is this one entrance only to the Lord. No one then shall enter in unto Him otherwise than through His Son.

12[89]:7 Didst you see," said he, "the six men, and the glorious and mighty man in the midst of them, him that walked about the tower and rejected the stones from the building?" "I saw him, Sir," say I.

12[89]:8 "The glorious man," said he, "is the Son of God, and those six are the glorious angels who guard Him on the right hand and on the left. Of these glorious angels not one," said he, "shall enter in unto God without Him; whosoever shall not receive His name, shall not enter into the kingdom of God."

13[90]:1 "But the tower," say I, "what is it?" "The tower," said he, "why, this is the Church.

13[90]:2 "And these virgins, who are they?" "They," said he, "are holy spirits; and no man can otherwise be found in the kingdom of God, unless these shall clothe him with their garment; for if you receive only the name, but receive not the garment from them, you profit nothing. For these virgins are powers of the Son of God. If [therefore] you bear the Name, and bear not His power, you shall bear His Name to none effect.

13[90]:3 And the stones," said he, "which you didst see cast away, these bare the Name, but clothed not themselves with the raiment of the virgins." "Of what sort, Sir," say I, "is their raiment?" "The names themselves," said he, "are their raiment. Whosoever bears the Name of the Son of God, ought to bear the names of these also; for even the Son Himself bears the names of these virgins.

13[90]:4 As many stones," said he, "as you saw enter into the building of the tower, being given in by their hands and waiting for the building, they have been clothed in the power of these virgins.

13[90]:5 For this cause you see the tower made a single stone with the rock. So also they that have believed in the Lord through His Son and clothe themselves in these spirits, shall become one spirit and one body, and their garments all of one color. But such persons as bear the names of the virgins have their dwelling in the tower."

13[90]:6 "The stones then, Sir," say I, "which are cast aside, wherefore were they cast aside? For they passed through the gate and were placed in the building of the tower by the hands of the virgins." "Since all these things interest you," said he, "and you enquire diligently, listen as touching the stones that have been cast aside.

13[90]:7 These all," [said he,] "received the name of the Son of God, and received likewise the power of these virgins. When then they received these spirits, they were strengthened, and were with the servants of God, and they had one spirit and one body [and one garment]; for they had the same mind, and they wrought righteousness.

13[90]:8 After a certain time then they were persuaded by the women whom you saw clad in black raiment, and having their shoulders bare and their hair loose, and beautiful in form. When they saw them they desired them, and they clothed themselves with their power, but they stripped off from themselves the power of the virgins.

13[90]:9 They then were cast away from the house of God, and delivered to these (women). But they that were not deceived by the beauty of these women remained in the house of God. So you hast," said he, "the interpretation of them that were cast aside."

13[90]:1 What then, Sir," say I, "if these men, being such as they are, should repent and put away their desire for these women, and return unto the virgins, and walk in their power and in their works? Shall they not enter into the house of God?"

13[90]:2 "They shall enter," said he, "if they shall put away the works of these women, and take again the power of the virgins, and walk in their works. For this is the reason why there was also a cessation in the building, that, if these repent, they may go into the building of the tower; but if they repent not, then others will go, and these shall be cast away finally."

13[90]:3 For all these things I gave thanks unto the Lord, because He had compassion on all that called upon His name, and sent forth the angel of repentance to us that had sinned against Him, and refreshed our spirit, and, when we were already ruined and had no hope of life, restored our life.

13[90]:4 "Now, Sir," say I, "show me why the tower is not built upon the ground, but upon the rock and upon the gate." "Because you art senseless," said he, "and without understanding [you ask the question]." "I am obliged, Sir," say I, "to ask all questions of you, because I am absolutely unable to comprehend anything at all; for all are great and glorious and difficult for men to understand."

13[90]:5 "Listen," said he. "The name of the Son of God is great and incomprehensible, and sustains the whole world. If then all creation is sustained by the Son [of God], what think you of those that are called by Him, and bear the name of the Son of God, and walk according to His commandments?

13[90]:6 See you then what manner of men He sustains? Even those that bear His name with their whole heart. He Himself then is become their foundation, and He sustains them gladly, because they are not ashamed to bear His name."

15[92]:1 "Declare to me, Sir," say I, "the names of the virgins, and of the women that are clothed in the black garments." "Hear," said he, "the names of the more powerful virgins, those that are stationed at the corners.

15[92]:2 The first is Faith, and the second, Continence, and the third, Power, and the fourth, Long-suffering. But the others stationed between them have these names--Simplicity, Guilelessness, Purity, Cheerfulness, Truth, Understanding, Concord, Love. He that bears these names and the name of the Son of God shall be able to enter into the kingdom of God.

15[92]:3 Hear," said he, "likewise the names of the women that wear the black garments. Of these also four are more powerful than the rest; the first is Unbelief; the second, Intemperance; the third, Disobedience; the fourth, Deceit; and their followers are called, Sadness, Wickedness, Wantonness, Irascibility, Falsehood, Folly, Slander, Hatred. The servant of God that bears these names shall see the kingdom of God, but shall not enter into it."

15[92]:4 "But the stones, Sir," say I, "that came from the deep, and were fitted into the building, who are they?" "The first," said he, "even the ten, that were placed in the foundations, are the first generation; the twenty-five are the second generation of righteous men; the thirty-five are God's prophets and His ministers; the forty are apostles and teachers of the preaching of the Son of God."

15[92]:5 "Wherefore then, Sir," say I, "did the virgins give in these stones also for the building of the tower and carry them through the gate?"

15[92]:6 "Because these first," said he, "bore these spirits, and they never separated the one from the other, neither the spirits from the men nor the men from the spirits, but the spirits abode with them till they fell asleep; and if they had not had these spirits with them, they would not have been found useful for the building of this tower."

15[92]:1 "Show me still further, Sir," say I. "What desire you to know besides?" said he. "Wherefore, Sir," say I, "did the stones come up from the deep, and wherefore were they placed into the building, though they bore these spirits?"

15[92]:2 "It was necessary for them," said he, "to rise up through water, that they might be made alive; for otherwise they could not enter into the kingdom of God, except they had put aside the deadness of their [former] life.

15[92]:3 So these likewise that had fallen asleep received the seal of the Son of God and entered into the kingdom of God. For before a man," said he, "has borne the name of [the Son of] God, he is dead; but when he has received the seal, he lays aside his deadness, and resumes life.

15[92]:4 The seal then is the water: so they go down into the water dead, and they come up alive. "thus to them also this seal was preached, and they availed themselves of it that they might enter into the kingdom of God."

15[92]:5 "Wherefore, Sir," say I, "did the forty stones also come up with them from the deep, though they had already received the seal?" "Because," said he, "these, the apostles and the teachers who preached the name of the Son of God, after they had fallen asleep in the power and faith of the Son of God, preached also to them that had fallen asleep before them, and themselves gave unto them the seal of the preaching.

15[92]:6 Therefore they went down with them into the water, and came up again. But these went down alive [and again came up alive]; whereas the others that had fallen asleep before them went down dead and came up alive.

15[92]:7 So by their means they were quickened into life, and came to the full knowledge of the name of the Son of God. For this cause also they came up with them, and were fitted with them into the building of the tower and were built with them, without being shaped; for they fell asleep in righteousness and in great purity. Only they had not this seal. You hast then the interpretation of these things also." "I have, Sir," say I.

17[94]:1 "Now then, Sir, explain to me concerning the mountains. Wherefore are their forms diverse the one from the other, and various?" "Listen," said he. "These twelve mountains are [twelve] tribes that inhabit the whole world. To these (tribes) then the Son of God was preached by the Apostles."

17[94]:2 But explain to me, Sir, why they are various-- these mountains--and each has a different appearance." "Listen," said he. "These twelve tribes which inhabit the whole world are twelve nations; and they are various in understanding and in mind. As various, then, as you saw these mountains to be, such also are the varieties in the mind of these nations, and

such their understanding. And I will show unto you the conduct of each."

17[94]:3 "First, Sir," say I, "show me this, why the mountains being so various, yet, when their stones were set into the building, became bright and of one color, just like the stones that had come up from the deep."

17[94]:4 "Because," said he, "all the nations that dwell under heaven, when they heard and believed, were called by the one name of [the Son of] God. So having received the seal, they had one understanding and one mind, and one faith became theirs and [one] love, and they bore the spirits of the virgins along with the Name; therefore the building of the tower became of one color, even bright as the sun.

17[94]:5 But after they entered in together, and became one body, some of them defiled themselves, and were cast out from the society of the righteous, and became again such as they were before, or rather even worse."

18[95]:1 "How, Sir," say I, "did they become worse, after they had fully known God?" "He that knows not God," said he, "and commits wickedness, has a certain punishment for his wickedness; but he that knows God fully ought not any longer to commit wickedness, but to do good.

18[95]:2 If then he that ought to do good commits wickedness, does he not seem to do greater wickedness than the man that knows not God? Therefore they that have not known God, and commit wickedness, are condemned to death; but they that have known God and seen His mighty works, and yet commit wickedness, shall receive a double punishment, and shall die eternally. In this way therefore shall the Church of God be purified.

18[95]:3 And as you saw the stones removed from the tower and delivered over to the evil spirits, they too shall be cast out; and there shall be one body of them that are purified, just as the tower, after it had been purified, became made as it were of one stone. Thus shall it be with the Church of God also, after she has been purified, and the wicked and hypocrites and blasphemers and double-minded and they that commit various kinds of wickedness have been cast out.

18[95]:4 When these have been cast out, the Church of God shall be one body, one understanding, one mind, one faith, one love. And then the Son of God shall rejoice and be glad in them, for that He has received back His people pure." "Great and glorious, Sir," say I, "are all these things.

18[95]:5 Once more, Sir," [say I,] "show me the force and the doings of each one of the mountains, that every soul that trusts in the Lord, when it hears, may glorify His great and marvelous and glorious name." "Listen," said he, "to the variety of the mountains and of the twelve nations.

19[96]:1 "From the first mountain, which was black, they that have believed are such as these; rebels and blasphemers against the Lord, and betrayers of the servants of God. For these there is no repentance, but there is death. For this cause also they are black; for their race is lawless.

19[96]:2 And from the second mountain, the bare one, they that believed are such as these; hypocrites and teachers of wickedness. And these then are like the former in not having the fruit of righteousness. For, even as their mountain is unfruitful, so likewise such men as these have a name indeed, but they are void of the faith, and there is no fruit of truth in them. For these then repentance is offered, if they repent quickly; but if they delay, they will have their death with the former."

19[96]:3 "Wherefore, Sir," say I, "is repentance possible for them, but not for the former ? For their doings are almost the same." "On this account," he said, "is repentance offered for them, because they blasphemed not their Lord, nor became betrayers of the servants of God; yet from desire of gain they played the hypocrite, and taught each other [after] the desires of sinful men. But they shall pay a certain penalty; yet repentance is ordained for them, because they are not become blasphemers or betrayers.

20[97]:1 "And from the third mountain, which had thorns and briars, they that believed are such as these; some of them are wealthy and others are entangled in many business affairs. The briars are the wealthy, and the thorns are they that are mixed up in various business affairs.

20[97]:2 These [then, that are mixed up in many and various business affairs,] hold fast [not] to the servants of God, but go astray, being choked by their affairs, but the wealthy unwillingly hold fast to the servants of God, fearing lest they may be asked for something by them. Such men therefore shall hardly enter into the kingdom of God.

20[97]:3 For as it is difficult to walk on briars with bare feet, so also it is difficult for such men to enter the kingdom of God.

20[97]:4 But for all these repentance is possible, but it must be speedy, that in respect to what they omitted to do in the former times, they may now revert to (past) days, and do some good. If then they shall repent and do some good, they shall live unto God; but if they continue in their doings, they shall be delivered over to those women, the which shall put them to death.

20[97]:1 "And from the fourth mountain, which had much vegetation, the upper part of the grass green and the part towards the roots withered, and some of it dried up by the sun, they that believed are such as these; the double-minded, and they that have the Lord on their lips, but have Him not in their heart.

20[97]:2 Therefore their foundations are dry and without power, and their words only live, but their works are dead. Such men are neither alive nor dead.

They are, therefore, like unto the double-minded; for the double-minded are neither green nor withered; for they are neither alive nor dead.

20[97]:3 For as their grass was withered up when it saw the sun, so also the double-minded, when they hear of tribulation, through their cowardice worship idols and are ashamed of the name of their Lord.

20[97]:4 Such are neither alive nor dead. Yet these also, if they repent quickly, shall be able to live; but if they repent not, they are delivered over already to the women who deprive them of their life.

22[99]:1 "And from the fifth mountain, which had green grass and was rugged, they that believed are such as these; they are faithful, but slow to learn and stubborn and self-pleasers, desiring to know all things, and yet they know nothing at all.

22[99]:2 By reason of this their stubbornness, understanding stood aloof from them, and a foolish senselessness entered into them; and they praise themselves as having understanding, and they desire to be self-appointed teachers, senseless though they are.

22[99]:3 Owing then to this pride of heart many, while they exalted themselves, have been made empty; for a mighty demon is stubbornness and vain confidence. Of these then many were cast away, but some repented and believed, and submitted themselves to those that had understanding, having learnt their own senselessness.

22[99]:4 Yea, and to the rest that belong to this class repentance is offered; for they did not become wicked, but rather foolish and without understanding. If these then shall repent, they shall live unto God; but if they repent not, they shall have their abode with the women who work evil against them.

23[100]:1 "But they that believed from the sixth mountain, which had clefts great and small, and in the clefts herbage withered, are such as these;

23[100]:2 they that have the small clefts, these are they that have aught against one another, and from their backbitings they are withered in the faith; but many of these repented Yea, and the rest shall repent, when they hear my commandments; for their backbitings are but small, and they shall quickly repent.

23[100]:3 But they that have great clefts, these are persistent in their backbitings and bear grudges, nursing wrath against one another. These then were thrown right away from the tower and rejected from its building. Such persons therefore shall with difficulty live.

23[100]:4 If God and our Lord, Who rules over all things and has the authority over all His creation, bears no grudge against them that confess their sins, but is propitiated, doth man, who is mortal and full of sins, bear a grudge against man, as though he were able to destroy or save him?

23[100]:5 I say unto you--I, the angel of repentance--unto as many as hold this heresy, put it away from you and repent, and the Lord shall heal your former sins, if you shall purify yourselves from this demon; but if not, you shall be delivered unto him to be put to death.

24[101]:1 " And from the seventh mountain, on which was herbage green and smiling, and the whole mountain thriving, and cattle of every kind and the fowls of heaven were feeding on the herbage on that mountain, and the green herbage, on which they fed, only grew the more luxuriant, they that believed are such as these;

24[101]:2 they were ever simple and guileless and blessed, having nothing against one another, but rejoicing always in the servants of God, and clothed in the Holy Spirit of these virgins, and having compassion always on every man, and out of their labors they supplied every man's need without reproach and without misgiving.

24[101]:3 The Lord then seeing their simplicity and entire childishness made them to abound in the labors of their hands, and bestowed favor on them in all their doings.

24[101]:4 But I say unto you that are such--I, the angel of repentance--remain to the end such as you are, and your seed shall never be blotted out. For the Lord has put you to the proof, and enrolled you among our number, and your whole seed shall dwell with the Son of God; for of His Spirit did you receive.

25[102]:1 "And from the eighth mountain, where were the many springs, and all the creatures of the Lord did drink of the springs, they that believed are such as these;

25[102]:2 apostles and teachers, who preached unto the whole world, and who taught the word of the Lord in soberness and purity, and kept back no part at all for evil desire, but walked always in righteousness and truth, even as also they received the Holy Spirit. Such therefore shall have their entrance with the angels.

26[103]:1 "And from the ninth mountain, which was desert, which had [the] reptiles and wild beasts in it which destroy mankind, they that believed are such as these;

26[103]:2 they that have the spots are deacons that exercised their office ill, and plundered the livelihood of widows and orphans, and made gain for themselves from the ministrations which they had received to perform. If then they abide in the same evil desire, they are dead and there is no hope of life for them; but if they turn again and fulfill their ministrations in purity, it shall be possible for them to live.

26[103]:3 But they that are mildewed, these are they that denied and turned not again unto their Lord, but having become barren and desert, because they hold fast not unto the servants of God but remain alone, they destroy their own souls.

26[103]:4 For as a vine left alone in a hedge, if it meet with neglect, is destroyed and wasted by the weeds, and in time becomes wild and is no longer useful to its owner, so also men of this kind have given themselves up in despair and become useless to their Lord, by growing wild.

26[103]:5 To these then repentance cometh, unless they be found to have denied from the heart; but if a man be found to have denied from the heart, I know not whether it is possible for him to live.

26[103]:6 And this I say not in reference to these days, that a man after denying should receive repentance; for it is impossible for him to be saved who shall now deny his Lord; but for those who denied Him long ago repentance seems to be possible. If a man therefore will repent, let him do so speedily before the tower is completed; but if not, he shall be destroyed by the women and put to death.

26[103]:7 And the stunted, these are the treacherous and backbiters; and the wild beasts which you saw on the mountain are these. For as wild beasts with their venom poison and kill a man, so also do the words of such men poison and kill a man.

26[103]:8 These then are broken off short from their faith through the conduct which they have in themselves; but some of them repented and were saved; and the rest that are of this kind can be saved, if they repent; but if they repent not, they shall meet their death from those women of whose power they are possessed.

27[104]:1 "And from the tenth mountain, where were trees sheltering certain sheep, they that believed are such as these;

27[104]:2 bishops, hospitable persons, who gladly received into their houses at all times the servants of God without hypocrisy. [These bishops] at all times without ceasing sheltered the needy and the widows in their ministration and conducted themselves in purity at all times.

27[104]:3 These [all] then shall be sheltered by the Lord for ever. They therefore that have done these things are glorious in the sight of God, and their place is even now with the angels, if they shall continue unto the end serving the Lord.

27[104]:1 "And from the eleventh mountain, where were trees full of fruit, decked with divers kinds of fruits, they that believed are such as these;

27[104]:2 they that suffered for the Name [of the Son of God], who also suffered readily with their whole heart, and yielded up their lives."

27[104]:3 "Wherefore then, Sir," say I, "have all the trees fruits, but some of their fruits are more beautiful than others?" "Listen," said he; "all as many as ever suffered for the Name's sake are glorious in the sight of God, and the sins of all these were taken away, because they suffered for the name of the Son of God. Now here why their fruits are various, and some surpassing others.

27[104]:4 "As many," said he, "as were tortured and denied not, when brought before the magistracy, but suffered readily, these are the more glorious in the sight of the Lord; their fruit is that which surpasses. But as many as become cowards, and were lost in uncertainty, and considered in their hearts whether they should deny or confess, and yet suffered, their fruits are less, because this design entered into their heart; for this design is evil, that a servant should deny his own lord.

27[104]:5 See to it, therefore, you who entertain this idea, lest this design remain in your hearts, and you die unto God. But you that suffer for the Name's sake ought to glorify God, because God deemed you worthy that you should bear this name, and that all your sins should be healed.

27[104]:6 Reckon yourselves blessed therefore; yea, rather think that you have done a great work, if any of you shall suffer for God's sake. The Lord bestowed life upon you, and you perceived it not; for your sins weighed you down, and if you had not suffered for the Name [of the Lord], you had died unto God by reason of your sins.

27[104]:7 These things I say unto you that waver as touching denial and confession. Confess that you have the Lord, lest denying Him you be delivered into prison.

27[104]:8 If the Gentiles punish their slaves, if any one deny his lord, what think you the Lord will do unto you, He who has authority over all things? Away with these designs from your hearts, that you may live forever unto God."

27[104]:1 "And from the twelfth mountain, which was white, they that believed are such as these; they that are as very babes, into whose heart no guile entered, neither learned they what wickedness is, but they remained as babes forever.

27[104]:2 Such as these then dwell without doubt in the kingdom of God, because they defiled the commandments of God in nothing, but continued as babes all the days of their life in the same mind.

27[104]:3 As many of you therefore as shall continue," said he, "and shall be as infants not having guile, shall be glorious [even] than all them that have been mentioned before; for all infants are glorious in the sight of God, and stand first in His sight. Blessed then are you, as many as have put away wickedness from you, and have clothed yourselves in guilelessness: you shall live unto God cheifest of all."

27[104]:4 After he had finished the parables of the mountains, I say unto him, "Sir, now explain to me concerning the stones that were taken from the plain and placed in the building in the room of the stones that were taken from the tower, and concerning the round (stones) which were placed in the building, and concerning those that were still round".

27[104]:1 "Hear," said he, "likewise concerning all these things. The stones which were taken from the plain and placed in the building of the tower in the room of those that were rejected, are the roots of this white mountain.

27[104]:2 When then they that believed from this mountain were all found guiltless, the lord of the tower ordered these from the roots of the mountain to be put into the building of the tower. For He knew that if these stones should go into the building [of the tower], they would remain bright and not one of them would turn black.

27[104]:3 But if he added (stones) from other mountains, he would have been obliged to visit the tower again, and to purify it. Now all these have been found white, who have believed and who shall believe; for they are of the same kind. Blessed is this kind, for it is innocent!

27[104]:4 Hear now likewise concerning those round and bright stones. All these are from the white mountain. Now here wherefore they have been found round. Their riches have darkened and obscured them a little from the truth.

27[104]:5 When therefore the Lord perceived their mind, *that they could favor the truth,* and likewise remain good, He commanded their possessions to be cut off from them, yet not to be taken away altogether, so that they might be able to do some good with that which has been left to them, and might live unto God for that they come of a good kind. So therefore they have been cut away a little, and placed in the building of this tower".

27[104]:1 "But the other (stones), which have remained round and have not been fitted into the building, because they have not yet received the seal, have been replaced in their own possession, for they were found very round.

27[104]:2 For this world and the vanities of their possessions must be cut off from them, and then they will fit into the kingdom of God. For it is necessary that they should enter into the kingdom of God; because the Lord has blessed this innocent kind. Of this kind then not one shall perish. Yea, even though any one of them being tempted by the most wicked devil have committed any fault, he shall return speedily unto his Lord.

27[104]:3 Blessed I pronounced you all to be--I the angel of repentance--whoever of you are guileless as infants, because your part is good and honorable in the sight of God.

27[104]a:4 Moreover I bid all of you, whoever have received this seal, keep guilelessness, and bear no grudge, and continue not in your wickedness nor in the memory of the offenses of bitterness; but become of one spirit, and heal these evil clefts and take them away from among you, that the owner of the flocks may rejoice concerning them.

27[104a]:5 For he will rejoice, if he find all things whole. But if he find any part of the flock scattered, woe unto the shepherds.

27[104a]:6 For if the shepherds themselves shall have been found scattered, how will they answer for the flocks? Will they say that they were harassed by the flock? No credence will be given them. For it is an incredible thing that a shepherd should be injured by his flock; and he will be punished the more because of his falsehood. And I am the shepherd, and it behooved me most strongly to render an account for you.

32[109]:1 "Amend yourselves therefore, while the tower is still in course of building.

32[109]:2 The Lord dwells in men that love peace; for to Him peace is dear; but from the contentious and them that are given up to wickedness He kept afar off. Restore therefore to Him your spirit whole as you received it.

32[109]:3 For suppose you hast given to a fuller a new garment whole, and desired to receive it back again whole, but the fuller give it back to you torn, wilt you receive it thus? Wilt you not at once blaze out and attack him with reproaches, saying; "The garment which I gave you was whole; wherefore hast you rent it and made it useless? See, by reason of the rent, which you hast made in it, it cannot be of use." Wilt you not then say all this to a fuller even about a rent which he has made in thy garment?

32[109]:4 If therefore you art thus vexed in the matter of thy garment, and complained because you received it not back whole, what think you the Lord will do to you, He, Who gave you the spirit whole, and you hast made it absolutely useless, so that it cannot be of any use at all to its Lord? For its use began to be useless, when it was corrupted by you. Will not therefore the Lord of this spirit for this thy deed punish [you with death]?"

32[109]:5 "Certainly," I said, "all those, whomsoever He shall find continuing to bear malice, He will punish." "Trample not," said he, "upon His mercy, but rather glorify Him, because He is so long-suffering with your sins, and is not like unto you. Practice then repentance which is expedient for you.

33[110]:1 "All these things which are written above I, the shepherd, the angel of repentance, have declared and spoken to the servants of God. If then you shall believe and hear my words, and walk in them, and amend your ways, you shall be able to live. But if you continue in wickedness and in bearing malice, no one of this kind shall live unto God. All things which were to be spoken by me have (now) been spoken to you."

33[110]:2 The shepherd said to me, "Hast you asked me all thy questions?" And I said, "Yes, Sir." "Why then hast you not enquired of me concerning the shape of the stones placed in the building, in that we filled up their shapes?" And I said, "I forgot, Sir."

33[110]:3 "Listen now," said he, "concerning them. These are they that have heard my commandments now, and have practiced repentance with their whole heart. So when the Lord saw that their repentance was good and pure, and that they could continue therein, he ordered their former sins to be blotted out. These shapes then were their former sins, and they have been chiseled away that they might not appear."

Parable 10

1[111]:1 After I had written out this book completely, the angel who had delivered me to the shepherd came to the house where I was, and sat upon a couch, and the shepherd stood at his right hand. Then he called me, and spoke thus unto me;

1[111]:2 "I delivered you," said he, "and thy house to this shepherd, that you might be protected by him." "True, Sir," I said "If therefore," said he, "you desire to be protected from all annoyance and all cruelty, to have also success in every good work and word, and all the power of righteousness, walk in his commandments, which I have given you, and you shall be able to get the mastery over all wickedness.

1[111]:3 For if you keep his commandments, all evil desire and the sweetness of this world shall be subject unto you; moreover success shall attend you in every good undertaking. Embrace his gravity and self-restraint, and tell it out unto all men that he is held in great honor and dignity with the Lord, and is a ruler of great authority, and powerful in his office. To him alone in the whole world has authority over repentance been assigned. Seemed he to you to be powerful? Yet you despise the gravity and moderation which he used towards you."

2[112]:1 I say unto him; "Ask him, Sir, himself, whether from the time that he has been in my house, I have done ought out of order, whereby I have offended him."

2[112]:2 "I myself know," said he, "that you hast done nothing out of order, nor art about to do so. And so I speak these things unto you, that you may persevere. For he has given a good account of you unto me. You therefore shall speak these words to others, that they too who have practiced or shall practice repentance may be of the same mind as you art; and he may give a good report of them to me, and I unto the Lord."

2[112]:3 "I too, Sir," I say, "declare to every man the mighty works of the Lord; for I hope that all who have sinned in the past, if they hear these things, will gladly repent and recover life."

2[112]:4 "Continue therefore," said he, "in this ministry, and complete it unto the end. For whosoever fulfill his commandments shall have life; yea such a man (shall have) great honor with the Lord. But whosoever keep not his commandments, fly from their life, and oppose him, and follow not his commandments, but deliver themselves over to death; and each one becomes guilty of his own blood. But I bid you obey these commandments, and you shall have a remedy for thy sins.

3[113]:1 "Moreover, I have sent these virgins unto you, that they may dwell with you; for I have seen that they are friendly towards you. You hast them therefore as helpers, that you may be the better able to keep his commandments; for it is impossible that these commandments be kept without the help of these virgins. I see too that they are glad to be with you. But I will charge them that they depart not at all from thy house.

3[113]:2 Only do you purify thy house; for in a clean house they will gladly dwell. For they are clean and chaste and industrious, and have favor in the sight of the Lord. If, therefore, they shall find thy house pure, they will continue with you; but if the slightest pollution arise, they will depart from thy house at once. For these virgins love not pollution in any form."

3[113]:3 I said unto him, "I hope, Sir, that I shall please them, so that they may gladly dwell in my house for ever; and just as he to whom you didst deliver me makes no complaint against me, so they likewise shall make no complaint."

3[113]:4 He said unto the shepherd, "I perceive," said he, "that he wishes to live as the servant of God, and that he will keep these commandments, and will place these virgins in a clean habitation."

3[113]:5 With these words he again delivered me over to the shepherd, and called the virgins, and said to them; "Inasmuch as I see that you are glad to dwell in this man's house, I commend to you him and his house, that you depart not at all from his house." But they heard these words gladly.

4[114]:1 He said then to me, "Quit you like a man in this ministry; declare to every man the mighty works of the Lord, and you shall have favor in this ministry. Whosoever therefore shall walk in these commandments, shall live and be happy in his life; but whosoever shall neglect them, shall not live, and shall be unhappy in his life.

4[114]:2 Charge all men who are able to do right, that they cease not to practice good works; for it is useful for them. I say moreover that every man ought to be rescued from misfortune; for he that has need, and suffered misfortune in his daily life, is in great torment and want.

4[114]:3 Whosoever therefore rescued from penury a life of this kind, wins great joy for himself. For he who is harassed by misfortune of this sort is afflicted and tortured with equal torment as one who is in chains. For many men on account of calamities of this kind, because they can bear them no longer, lay violent hands on themselves. He then who knows the calamity of a man of this kind and rescues him not, commits great sin, and becomes guilty of the man's blood.

4[114]:4 Do therefore good works, whoever of you have received (benefits) from the Lord, lest, while you delay to do them, the building of the tower be completed. For it is on your account that the work of the building has been interrupted. Unless then you hasten to do right, the tower will be completed, and you shut out."

4[114]:5 When then he had finished speaking with me, he rose from the couch and departed, taking with him the shepherd and the virgins. He said however unto me, that he would send the shepherd and the virgins back again to my house.

Odes of Peace

Also called The Odes of Solomon

From The Lost Books of the Bible and the Forgotten Books of Eden.

Ode 1

1 The Lord is on my head like a crown, and I shall not be without Him. 2 They wove for me a crown of truth, and it caused thy branches to bud in me. 3 For it is not like a withered crown which buddeth not: but thou livest upon my head, and thou hast blossomed upon my head. 4 Thy fruits are full-grown and perfect, they are full of thy salvation.

Ode 2

No part of this Ode has ever been identified

Ode 3

The first words of this Ode have disappeared.

1 ... I put on. 2 And his members are with him. And on them do I stand, and He loves me: 3 For I should not have known love the Lord, if not loved me. 4 For who is able to distinguish love except the one that is loved? 5. I love the beloved and my soul loves Him: 6 And where His rest is, there also am I; 7 And I shall be no strangers for with the Lord Most High and Merciful there is no grudging. 8 I have been united to Him, for the Lover has found the Beloved, 9 And because I shall love Him that is the Son, I shall become a son;. 10 For he that is joined to Him that is immortal, will also himself become immortal; 11 And he who has pleasure in the Living One, will become living. 12 This is the Spirit of the Lord, which doth not lie, which teacheth the sons of men to know His ways. 13 Be wise and understanding and vigilant. Hallelujah.

ODE 4.

This Ode is important because of the historical allusion with which it commences. This may refer to the closing of the temple at Leontopolis an Egypt which this writing about

1 No man, O my God, changeth thy holy place; 2 And it is not (possible) that he should change it and put it in another place: because he hath no power over it: 3 For thy sanctuary thou hast designed before thou didst make (other) places: 4 That which is the elder shall not be altered by those that are younger than itself. 5 Thou has given thy heart, O Lord, to thy believers: never wilt thou fail, nor be without fruits: 6 For one hour of thy

Faith is days and years. 7 For who is there put on thy grace, and be hurt? 8 For thy seal is known: and thy creatures know it: and thy (heavenly) hosts possess it: and the elect archangels are clad with it. 9 Thou hast given us thy fellowship: it was not that thou wast in need of us: but that we are in need of thee: 10 Distill thy dews upon us and open thy rich fountains that pour forth to us milk and honey: 11 For there is no repentance with thee that thou shouldest repent of anything that thou hast promised: 12 And the end was revealed before thee: for what thou gavest, thou gavest freely: 13 So that thou mayest not draw them back and take them again: 14 For all was revealed before thee as God, and ordered from the beginning before thee: and thou, O God, hast made all things. Hallelujah,

ODE 5.

This Ode has strangely appeared in a speech by Salome in another ancient work called the Pistis Sophia.

1 I will give thanks unto thee, O Lord, because I love thee; 2 O Most High, thou wilt not forsake me for thou art my hope: 3 Freely I have received thy grace, I shall live thereby: 4 My persecutors will come and not see me: 5 A cloud of darkness shall fall on their eyes; and an air of thick gloom shall darken them: 6 And they shall have no light to see: they may not take hold upon me. 7 Let their counsel become thick darkness, and what they have cunningly devised, let it return upon their own heads: 8 For they have devised a counsel and it did not succeed: 9 For my hope is upon the Lord and I will not fear, and because the Lord is my salvation, I will not fear: and He is a garland on my head and I shall not be moved; even if everything should be shaken, I stand firm; 11 And if all things visible should perish, I shall not die; because the Lord is with me I and I am with Him. Hallelujah.

ODE 6.

First century universalism is revealed in an interesting way in verse 10.

1 As the hand moves over the harp, and the strings speak, 2 So speaks in my members the Spirit of the Lord, and I speak by His love. 3 For it destroys what is foreign and everything that is bitter: 4 For thus it was from the beginning and will be to the end, that nothing should be His adversary, and nothing should stand up against Him. 5 The Lord has multiplied the knowledge of Himself, and is zealous that these things should be known, which by His grace have been given to us. 6 And the praise of His name He gave us: our spirits praise His holy Spirit. 7 For there went forth a stream and became a river great and broad; 8 For it flooded and broke up everything and it brought (water) to the

Temple; 9 And the restrainers of the children of men were not able to restrain it, nor the arts of those whose business it is to restrain waters; 10 For it spread over the face of the whole earth, and filled everything: and all the thirsty upon earth were given to drink of it; 11 And thirst was relieved and quenched: for from the Most High the draught was given. 12 Blessed then are the ministers of that draught who are entrusted with that water 13 They have assuaged the dry lips, and the will that had fainted they have raised up; 14 And souls that were near departing they have caught back from death: 15 And limbs that had fallen they straightened and set up: 16 They gave strength for their feebleness and light to their eyes: 17 For everyone knew them in the Lord, and they lived by the water of life forever. Hallelujah.

Ode 7

A wonderfully, simple and joyful psalm on the Incarnation.

1 As the impulse of anger against evil, so is the impulse of joy over what is lovely, and brings in of its fruits without restraint: 2 My joy is the Lord and my impulse is toward Him: this path of mine is excellent: 3 For I have a helper, the Lord. 4 He hath caused me to know Himself, without grudging, by His simplicity: His kindness has humbled His greatness. 5 He became like me, in order that I might receive Him: He was reckoned like myself in order that I might put Him on; 7 And I trembled not when I saw Him: because He was gracious to me: 8 Like my nature He became that I might learn Him and like my form, that I might not turn back from Him: 9 The Father of knowledge is the word of knowledge: 10 He who created wisdom is wiser than His works: 11 And He who created me when yet I was not knew what I should do when I came into being: 12 Wherefore He pitied me in His abundant grace: and granted me to ask from Him and to receive from His sacrifice: 13 Because He it is that is incorrupt, the fulness of the ages and the of them. 14 He hath given Him to be seen of them that are His, in order that they may recognize Him that made them: and that they might not suppose that they came of themselves: 15 For knowledge He hath appointed as its way, hath widened it and extended it; and brought to all perfection; 16 And set over it the traces of His light, and I walked therein from the beginning even to the end. 17 For by Him it was wrought, and He was resting in the Son, and for its salvation He will take hold of everything. 18 And the Most High shall be known in His Saints, to announce to those that have songs of the coming of the Lord: 19 That they may go forth to meet Him, and may sing to Him with joy and with the harp of many tones: 20 The seers shall come before Him and they shall be seen before Him, 21 And they shall praise

the Lord for His love: because He is near and beholdeth. 22 And hatred shall be taken from the earth, and along with jealousy it shall be drowned: 23 For ignorance hath been destroyed, because the knowledge of the Lord hath arrived. 24 They who make songs shall sing the grace of the Lord Most High; 25 And they shall bring their songs, and their heart shall be like the day: and like the excellent beauty of the Lord their pleasant song; 26 And there shall neither be anything that breathes without knowledge nor any that is dumb: 27 For He hath given a mouth to His creation, to open the voice of the mouth towards Him, to praise Him: 28 Confess ye His power, and show forth His grace. Hallelujah.

Ode 8

Note the sudden transition from the person of the Psalmist to the person of the Lord (v. 10). This is like the canonical Psalter in style.

1 Open ye, open ye your hearts to the exultation of the Lord: 2 And let your love be multiplied from the heart and even to the lips, 3 To bring forth fruit to the Lord, living [fruit], holy [fruit], and to talk with watchfulness in His light. 4 Rise up, and stand erect, ye who sometime were brought low: 5 Tell forth ye who were in silence, that your mouth hath been opened. 6 Ye, therefore, that were despised be henceforth lifted up, because your righteousness hath been exalted. 7 For the right hand of the Lord is with you: and He is your helper: 8. And peace was prepared for you, before ever your war was. 9. Hear the word of truth, and receive the knowledge of the Most High. 10 Your flesh has not known what I am saying to you: neither have your hearts known what I am showing to you. 11 Keep. my secret, ye who are kept by it. l2 Keep my faith, ye who are kept by it. l3 And understand my knowledge, ye who know me in truth, 14 Love me with affection, ye who love! 15 For I do not turn away my face from them that are mine; 16 For I know them and before they came into being I took knowledge of them, and on their faces I set my seal: 17 I fashioned their members: my own breasts I prepared for them, that they might drink my holy milk and live thereby 18 I took pleasure in them and am not ashamed of them: 19 For my workmanship are they and the strength of my thoughts: 20 Who then shall rise up against my handiwork, or who is there that is not subject to them? 21 I willed and fashioned mind and heart: and they are mine, and by my own right hand I set my elect ones: 22 And my righteousness goeth before them and they shall not be deprived of my name, for it is with them. 23 Ask, and abound and abide in the love of the Lord, 24 And yet beloved ones in the Beloved: those who are kept, in Him that liveth: 25 And they that are saved in Him that was saved; 26 And ye shall be found

incorrupt in all ages to the name of your Father. Hallelujah.

Ode 9

We shall never know surely whether the wars referred to here are spiritual or actual outward wars.

1 Open your ears and I will speak to you. Give me your souls that I may also give you my soul, 2 The word of the Lord and His good pleasures, the holy thought which He has devised concerning his Messiah. 3 For in the will of the Lord is your salvation, and His thought is everlasting life; and your end is immortality. 4 Be enriched in God the Father, and receive the thought of the Most High. 5 Be strong and be redeemed by His grace. 6 For I announce to you peace, to you His saints; 6 That none of those who hear may fall in war, and that those again who have known Him may not perish, and that those who receive may not be ashamed. 8 An everlasting crown forever is Truth. Blessed are they who set it on their heads: 9 A stone of great price is it; and there have been wars on account of the crown. 10 And righteousness hath taken it and hath given it to you. 11 Put on the crown in the true covenant of the Lord. 12 And all those who have conquered shall be written in His book. 13 For their book is victory which is yours. And she (Victory) sees you before her and wills that you shall be saved. Hallelujah.

ODE 10.

A vigorous little Ode in which Christ Himself is the speaker.

1 The Lord hath directed my mouth by His word: and He hath opened my heart by His light: and He hath caused to dwell in me His deathless life; 2 And gave me that I might speak the fruit peace: 3 To convert the souls of them who are willing to come to Him; and to lead captive a good captivity for freedom. 4 I was strengthened and made mighty and took the world captive; 5 And it became to me for the praise of the Most High, and of God my Father. 6 And the Gentiles were gathered together who were scattered abroad. 7 And I was unpolluted by my love for them, because they confessed me in high places: and the traces of the light were set upon their heart: 8 And they walked in my life and were saved and be came my people for ever and ever. Hallelujah.

ODE 11.

A beautiful sketch of Paradise regained and the blessedness of those who have returned to the privileges of the fallen Adam.

1 My heart was cloven and its flower appeared; and grace sprang up in it: and it brought forth fruit to the Lord, 2 For the Most High clave my heart by His Holy Spirit and searched my affection towards Him: and filled me with His love. 3 And His opening of me became my salvation; and I ran in His way in His peace even in the way of truth: 4 from the beginning and even to the end I acquired His knowledge: 5 And I was established upon the rock of truth, where He had set me up: 6 And speaking waters touched my lips from the fountain of the Lord plenteously: 7 And I drank and was inebriated with the living water that doth not die; 8 And my inebriation was not one without knowledge, but I forsook vanity and turned to the Most High my God, 9 And I was enriched by His bounty, and I forsook the folly which is diffused over the earth; and I stripped it off and cast it from me: 10 And the Lord renewed me in His raiment, and possessed me by His light, and from above He gave me rest in incorruption; 11 And I became like the land which blossoms and rejoices in its fruits: 12 And the Lord was like the sun shining on the face of the land; 13 He lightened my eyes and my face received the dew; the pleasant odour of the Lord; 14 And He carried me to His Paradise; where is the abundance of the pleasure, of the Lord; 15 And I worshipped the Lord on account of His glory; and I said, Blessed, O Lord, are they who are planted in thy land and those who have a place in thy Paradise; 16 And they grow by the fruits of the trees. And they have changed from darkness to light. 17 Behold! all thy servants are fair, who do good works, and turn away from wickedness to the pleasantness that is thine: 18 And they have turned back the bitterness of the trees from them, when they were planted in thy land; 19 And everything became like a relic of thyself, and memorial for ever of thy faithful works. 20 For there is abundant room in thy Paradise, and nothing is useless therein; 21 But everything is filled with fruit; glory be to thee, O God, the delight of Paradise for ever. Hallelujah.

ODE 12.

An exceptionally high level of spiritual thought.

1 He hath filled me with words of truth; that I may speak the same; 2 And like the flow of waters flows truth from my mouth, and my lips show forth His fruit. 3 And He has caused His knowledge to abound in me, because the mouth of the Lord is the true Word, and the door of His light; 4 And the Most High hath given it to His words, which are the interpreters of His own beauty, and the repeaters of His praise, and the confessors of His counsel and the heralds of His thought and the chasteners of His servants. 5 For the swiftness of the Word is inexpressible, and like its expression is its swiftness and force; 6 And its course

knows no limit. Never doth it fail, but it stands sure, and it knows not descent nor the way of it. 7 For as its work is, so is its end: for it is light and the dawning of thought; 8 And by it the worlds talk one to the other; and in the Word there were those that were silent; 9 And from it came love and concord; and they spake one to the other whatever was theirs; and they were penetrated by the Word; 10 And they knew Him who made them, because they were in concord; for the mouth of the Most High spake to them; and His explanation ran by means of it: 11 For the dwelling-place of the Word is man: and its truth is love. 12 Blessed are they who by means thereof have understood everything, and have known the Lord in His truth. Hallelujah.

ODE 13.

A strange little Ode.

1 Behold! the Lord is our mirror: open the eyes and see them in Him: and learn the manner of your face: 2 And tell forth praise to His spirit: and wipe off the filth from your face: and love His holiness, and clothe yourselves therewith: 3 And be without stain at all times before Him. Hallelujah.

ODE 14.

This Ode is as beautiful in style as the canonical Psalter.

1 As the eyes of a son to his father so are my eyes, O Lord at all times towards thee. 2 For with thee are my consolations and my delight. 3 Turn not away thy mercies from me, O Lord: and take not thy kindness from me. 4 Stretch out to me, O Lord, at all times thy right hand: and be my guide even unto the end, according to thy good pleasure. 5 Let me be well-pleasing before thee, because of thy glory and because of thy name: 6 Let me be preserved from evil, and let thy meekness, O Lord, abide with me, and the fruits of thy love. 7 Teach me the Psalms of thy truth, that I may bring forth fruit in thee: 8 And open to me the harp of thy Holy Spirit, that with all its notes I may praise thee, O Lord. 9 And according to the multitude of thy tender mercies, so thou shalt give to me; and hasten to grant our petitions; and thou art able for all our needs. Hallelujah.

Ode 15.

One of the loveliest Odes an this unusual collection.

1 As the sun is the joy to them that seek for its daybreak, so is my joy the Lord; 2 Because He is my Sun and His rays have lifted me up and His light hath dispelled all darkness from my face. In Him I have acquired eyes and have seen His holy day: 4 Ears have become mine and I have heard His truth. 5 The thought of knowledge hath been mine, and I have been delighted through Him. 6 The way of error I have left, and have walked towards Him and have received salvation from Him, without grudging. 7 And according to His bounty He hath given to me and according to His excellent beauty He hath made me. 8 I have put on incorruption through His name: and have put off corruption by His grace. 9 Death hath been destroyed before my face: and Sheol bath been abolished by my word: 10 And there hath gone up deathless life in the Lord's land, 11 And it hath been made known to His faithful ones, and hath been given without stint to all those that trust in Him. Hallelujah.

ODE 16.

The beauty of God's creation.

1 As the work of the husband man is the ploughshare: and the work of the steersman is the guidance of the ship: 2 So also my work is the Psalm of the Lord: my craft and praises: 3 Because His love hath nourished my heart, and even to my lips His fruits He poured out. 4 For my love is the Lord, and I therefore I will sing unto Him: 5 For I am made strong in His praise, and I have faith in Him. 6 I will open my mouth and His spirit will utter in me the glory of the Lord and His beauty; the work of His hands and the operation of His fingers: 7 The multitude of His mercies and the strength of His word. 8 For the word of the Lord searches out all things, both the invisible and that which reveals His thought; 9 For the eye sees His works and the ear hears His thought; 10 He spread out the earth and He settled the waters in the sea: 11 He measured the heavens and fixed the stars: and He established the creation and set it up: 12 And He rested from His works: 13 And created things run in their courses, and do their works: 14 And they know not how to stand and be idle; and His heavenly hosts are subject to His word. 15 The treasure-chamber of the light is the sun, and the treasury of the darkness is the night: 16 And He made the sun for the day that it may be bright, but night brings darkness over the face of the land; 17 And their alternations one to the other speak the beauty of God: 18 And there is nothing that is without the Lord; for He was before any thing came into being: 19 And the worlds were made by His word, and by the thought of His heart. Glory and honour to His name. Hallelujah.

ODE 17.

A peculiar change of personality,' scarcely realized until the return from it in the last verse.

1 I was crowned by my God: my crown is living: 2 And I was justified in my Lord: my incorruptible salvation is He. 3 I was loosed from vanity, and I was not condemned: 4 The choking bonds were cut off by her hands: I received the face and the fashion of a new person: and I walked in it and was saved; 5 And the thought of truth led me on. And I walked after it and did not wander: 6 And all. that have seen me were amazed: and I was regarded by them as a strange person: 7 And He who knew and brought me up is the Most High in all His perfection. And He glorified me by His kindness, and raised my thoughts to the height of His truth. 8 And from thence He gave me the way of His precepts and I opened the doors that were closed,. 9 And brake in pieces the bars of iron: but my iron melted and dissolved before me; 10 Nothing appeared closed to me: because I was the door of everything. 11 And I went over all my bond men to loose them; that I might not leave any man bound or binding: 12 And I imparted my knowledge without grudging: and my prayer was in my love: 13 And I sowed my fruits in hearts, and transformed them into myself: and they received my blessing and lived; 14 And they were gathered to me and were saved; because they were to me as my own members and I was their head. Glory to thee our head the Lord Messiah. Hallelujah.

ODE 18.

A man who had a spiritual experience brings a message.

1 My heart was lifted up in the love of the Most High and was enlarged: that I might praise Him for His name's sake. 2 My members were strengthened that they might not fall from His strength. 3 Sicknesses removed from my body, and it stood to the Lord by His will. For His kingdom is true. 4 O Lord, for the sake of them that are deficient do not remove thy word from me! 5 Neither for the sake of their works do thou restrain from me thy perfection! 6 Let not the luminary be conquered by the darkness; nor let truth flee away from falsehood. 7 Thou wilt appoint me to victory; our Salvation is thy right hand. And thou wilt receive men from all quarters. 8 And thou wilt preserve whosoever is held in evils: 9 Thou art my God. Falsehood and death are not in thy mouth: 10 For thy will is perfection; and vanity thou knowest not, 11 Nor does it know thee. 12 And error thou knowest not, 13 Neither does it know thee. 14 And ignorance appeared like a blind man; and like the foam of the sea, 15 And they supposed of that vain thing that it was something great; 16 And they too came in likeness of it and became vain; and those have understood who have known and meditated; 17 And they have not been corrupt in their imagination; for such were in the mind of the Lord; 18 And they mocked at them that were

walking in error; 19 And they spake truth from the inspiration which the Most High breathed into them; Praise and great comeliness to His name. Hallelujah.

ODE 19.

Fantastic and not in harmony with the other Odes. The reference to a painless Virgin Birth is notable.

1 A cup of milk was offered to me: and I drank it in the sweetness of the delight of the Lord. 2 The Son is the cup and He who was milked is the Father: 3 And the Holy Spirit milked Him: because His breasts were full, and it was necessary for Him that His milk should be sufficiently released; 4 And the Holy Spirit opened His bosom and mingled the milk from the two breasts of the Father and gave the mixture to the world without their knowing: 5 And they who receive in its fulness are the ones on the right hand. 6 The Spirit opened the womb of the Virgin and she received conception and brought forth; and the Virgin became a Mother with many mercies; 7 And she travailed and brought forth a Son, without incurring pain; 8 And because she was not sufficiently prepared, and she had not sought a midwife (for He brought her to bear) she brought forth, as if she were a man, of her own will; 9 And she brought Him forth openly, and acquired Him with great dignity, 10 And loved Him in His swaddling clothes and guarded Him kindly, and showed Him in Majesty. Hallelujah.

ODE 20.

A mixture of ethics and mysticism; of the golden rule and the tree of life.

1 I am a priest of the Lord, and to Him I do priestly service: and to Him I offer the sacrifice of His thought. 2 For His thought is not like the thought of the world nor the thought of the flesh, nor like them that serve carnally. 3 The sacrifice of the Lord is righteousness, and purity of heart and lips. 4 Present your reins before Him blamelessly: and let not thy heart do violence to heart, nor thy soul to soul. 5 Thou shalt not acquire a stranger by the price of thy silver neither shalt thou seek to devour thy neighbour, 6 Neither shalt thou deprive him of the covering of his nakedness. 7 But put on the grace of the Lord without stint; and come into His Paradise and make thee a garland from its tree,. 8 And put it on thy head and be glad; and recline on His rest, and glory shall go before thee, 9 And thou shalt receive of His kindness and of His grace; and thou shalt be flourishing in truth in the praise of His holiness. Praise and honour be to His name. Hallelujah.

ODE 21.

A remarkable explanation of the "coats of skin" in the third chapter of Genesis.

1 My arms I lifted up to the Most High, even to the grace of the Lord: because He had cast off my bonds from me: and my Helper had lifted me up to His grace and to His salvation: 2 And I put off darkness and clothed myself with light, 3 And my soul acquired a body free from sorrow or affliction or pains 4 And increasingly helpful to me was the thought of the Lord, and His fellowship in incorruption: 5 And I was lifted up in His light; and I served before Him, 6 And I became near to Him, praising and confessing Him; 7 My heart ran over and was found in my mouth: and it arose upon my lips; and the exultation of the Lord increased on my face, and His praise likewise. Hallelujah.

ODE 22.

Like the Psalms of David and their exultation because of freedom.

1 He who brought me down from on high, also brought me up from the regions below; 2 And He who gathers together the things that are betwixt is He also who cast me down: 3 He who scattered my enemies had existed from ancient and my adversaries: 4 He who gave me authority over bonds that I might loose them; 5 He that overthrew by my hands the dragon with seven heads: and thou hast set me over his roots that I might destroy his seed. 6 Thou wast there and didst help me, and in every place thy name was a rampart to me. 7 Thy right hand destroyed his Wicked poison; and thy hand levelled the way for those who believe in thee. 8 And thou didst choose them from the graves and didst separate them from the dead. 9 Thou didst take dead bones

and didst cover them with bodies. 10 They were motionless, and thou didst give them energy for life. 11 Thy way was without corruption and thy face; thou didst bring thy world to corruption: that everything might be dissolved, and then renewed, 12 And that the foundation for everything might be thy rock: and on it thou didst build thy kingdom; and it became the dwelling place of the saints. Hallelujah.

ODE 23.

The reference to the sealed document sent by God is one of the great mysteries of the collection.

1 Joy is of the saints! and who shall put it on, but they alone? 2 Grace is of the elect! and who shall receive it except those who trust in it from the beginning? 3 Love is of the elect? And who shall put it on except those who have possessed it from the beginning? 4 Walk ye in the knowledge of the Most High without grudging: to His exultation and to the perfection of His knowledge. 5 And His thought was like a letter; His will descended from on high, and it was sent like an arrow which is violently from the bow: 6 And many hands rushed to the letter to seize it and to take and read it: 7 And it escaped their fingers and they were affrighted at it and at the seal that was upon it. 8 Because it was not permitted to them to loose its seal: for the power that was over the seal was greater than they. 9 But those who saw it went after the letter that they might know where it would alight, and who should read it and who should hear it. 10 But a wheel received it and came over it: 11 And there was with it a sign of the Kingdom and of the Government: 12 And everything which tried to move the wheel it mowed and cut down: 13 And it gathered the multitude of adversaries, and bridged the rivers and crossed over and rooted up many forests and made a broad path. 14 The head went down to the feet for down to the feet ran the wheel, and that which was a sign upon it. 15 The letter was one of command, for there were included in it all districts; 16 And there was seen at its head, the head which was revealed even the Son of Truth from the Most High Father, 17 And He inherited and took possession of everything. And the thought of many was brought to nought. 18 And all the apostates hasted and fled away. And those who persecuted and were enraged became extinct, 19 And the letter was a great volume, which was wholly written by the finger of God: 20 And the name of the Father was on it and of the Son and of the Holy Spirit, to rule for ever and ever. Hallelujah.

ODE 24.

The mention of the Dove refers to a lost Gospel to which there are rare references in ancient writings.

1 The Dove fluttered over the Messiah, because He was her head; and she sang over Him and her voice was heard: 2 And the inhabitants were afraid and the sojourners were moved: 3 The birds dropped their wings and all creeping things died in their holes: and the abysses were opened which had been hidden; and they cried to the Lord like women in travail: 4 And no food was given to them, because it did not belong to them; 5 And they sealed up the abysses with the seal of the Lord. And they perished, in the thought those that had existed from ancient times; 6 For they were corrupt from the beginning; and the end of their corruption was life: 7 And every one of them that was imperfect perished: for it was not possible to give them a word that they might remain: 8 And the Lord destroyed the imaginations of all them that had not the truth with them. 9 For they who in their hearts were

lifted up were deficient in wisdom and so they were rejected, because the truth was not with them. 10 For the Lord disclosed His way and spread abroad His grace: and those who understood it, know His holiness. Hallelujah.

ODE 25.

Back again to personal experience.

1 I was rescued from my bonds and unto thee, my God, I fled: 2 For thou art the right hand of my Salvation and my helper. 3 Thou hast restrained those that rise up against me, 4 And I shall see him no more: because thy face was with me, which saved me by thy grace. 5 But I was despised and rejected in the eyes of many: and I was in their eyes like lead, 6 And strength was mine from thyself and help. 7 Thou didst set me a lamp at my right hand and at my left: and in me there shall be nothing that is not bright: 8 And I was clothed with the covering of thy Spirit, and thou didst remove from me my raiment of skin; 9 For thy right hand lifted me up and removed sickness from me: 10 And I became mighty in the truth, and holy by thy righteousness; and all my adversaries were afraid of me; 11 And I became admirable by the name of the Lord, and I was justified by His gentleness, and His rest is for ever and ever. Hallelujah.

ODE 26,

Remarkable praise.

1 I poured out praise to the Lord, for I am His: 2 And I will speak His holy song for my heart is with Him. 3 For His harp is in my hands, and the Odes of His rest shall not be silent. 4 I will cry unto him from my whole heart: I will praise and exalt Him with all my members. 5 For from the east and even to the west is His praise: 6 And from the south and even to the north is the confession of Him: 7 And from the top of the hills to their utmost bound is His perfection. 8 Who can write the Psalms of the Lord, or who read them? 9 Or who can train his soul for life that his soul may be saved, 10 Or who can rest on the Most High, so that with His mouth he may speak? 11 Who is able to interpret the wonders of the Lord? 12 For he who could interpret would be dissolved and would become that which is interpreted. 13 For it suffices to know and to rest: for in rest the singers stand, 14 Like a river which has an abundant fountain, and flows to the help of them that seek it. Hallelujah.

ODE 27.

The human body makes a cross when a man stands erect in prayer with arms outstretched.

1 I stretched out my hands and sanctified my Lord: 2 For the extension of my hands is His sign: 3 And .my expansion is the upright tree [or cross].

ODE 28

This Ode is a musical gem.

1 As the wings of doves over their nestlings; and the mouth of their nestlings towards their mouths, 2 So also are the wings of the Spirit over my heart: 3 My heart is delighted and exults: like the babe who exults in the womb of his mother: 4 I believed; therefore I was at rest; for faithful is He in whom I have believed: 5 He has richly blessed me and my head is with Him: and the sword shall not divide me from Him, nor the scimitar; 6 For I am ready before destruction comes; and I have been set on His immortal pinions: 7 And He showed me His sign: forth and given me to drink, and from that life is the spirit within me and it cannot die, for it lives. 8 They who saw me marvelled at me, because I was persecuted, and they supposed that I was swallowed up: for I seemed to them as one of the lost; 9 And my oppression became my salvation; and I was their reprobation because

there was no seal in me; 10 Because I did good to every man I was hated, 11 And they came round me like mad dogs, who ignorantly attack their masters, 12 For their thought is corrupt and their understanding perverted. 13 But I was carrying water in my right hand and their bitterness I endured by my sweetness: 14 And I did not perish, for I was not their brother nor was my birth like theirs. 15 And they sought for my death and did not find it: for I was older than the memorial of them; 16 And vainly did they make attack upon me and those who, without reward, came after me:

17 They sought to destroy the memorial of him who was before them. 18 For the thought of the Most High cannot be anticipated; and His heart is superior to all wisdom. Hallelujah.

ODE 29.

Again reminiscent of the Psalms of David.

1 The Lord is my hope: in Him I shall not be confounded. 2 For according to His praise He made me, and according to His goodness even so He gave unto me: 3 And according to His mercies He exalted me: and according to His excellent beauty He set me on high: 4 And brought me up out of the depths of Sheol: and from the mouth of death He drew me: 5 And thou didst lay my enemies low and He justified me by His grace. 6 For I believed in the Lord's Messiah:

and it appeared to me that He is the Lord; 7 And He showed him His sign: and He led, me by His light, and gave me the rod of His power 8 That I might subdue the imaginations of the peoples; and the power of the men of might to bring them low: 9 To make war by His word, and to take victory by His power. 10 And the Lord overthrew my enemy by His word: and he became like the stubble which the wind carries away; 11 And I gave praise to the Most High because He exalted me His servant and the son of His handmaid. Hallelujah.

ODE 30.

An invitation to the thirsty.

1 Fill ye waters for yourselves from the living fountain, of the Lord, for it is opened to you: 2 And come all ye thirsty and take the draught; and rest by the fountain of the Lord. 3 For fair it is and pure and gives rest to the soul, Much ore pleasant are its waters than honey; 4 And the honeycomb of bees is not to be compared with it. 5 For it flows forth from the lips of the Lord and from the heart of the Lord is its name. 6 And it came infinitely and invisibly: and until it was set in the midst they did not know it: 7 Blessed are they who have drunk therefrom and have found rest thereby. Hallelujah.

ODE 31.

A song that Marcus Aurelius might have known when he said, "Be like the promontory against which the waves continually break."

1 The abysses were dissolved before the Lord: and darkness was destroyed by His appearance: 2 Error went astray and perished at His hand: and folly found no path to walk in, and was submerged by the truth of the Lord. 3 He opened His mouth and spake grace and joy: and He spake a new song of praise to His name: 4 And He lifted up His voice to the Most High and offered the sons that were with Him. 5 And His face was justified, for thus His holy Father had given to Him. 6 Come forth, ye that have been afflicted and receive joy, and possess your souls by His grace; and take to you immortal life. 7 And they made me a debtor when I rose up, me who had been a debtor: and they divided my spoil, though nothing was due to them. 8 But I endured and held my peace and was silent as if not moved by them. 9 But I stood unshaken like a firm rock which is beaten by the waves and endures. 10 An I bore their bitterness for humility's sake: 11 In order, that I might redeem my people, and inherit it and that I might not make void my promises to the fathers to whom I promised the salvation of their seed. Hallelujah.

ODE 32.

Joy and light.

1 To the blessed there is joy from their hearts, and light from Him that dwells in them: 2 And words from the Truth, who was self-originate: for He is strengthened by the holy power of the Most High: and He is unperturbed for ever and ever. Hallelujah.

ODE 33

A virgin stands and proclaims

1 Again Grace ran and forsook corruption, and came down in Him to bring it to nought; 2 And He destroyed perdition from before Him, and devastated all its order; 3 And He stood on a lofty summit and uttered His voice from one end of the earth to the other: 4 And drew to Him all those who obeyed Him; and there did not appear as it were an evil person. 5 But there stood a perfect virgin who was proclaiming and calling and saying, 6 O ye sons of men, return ye, and ye daughters of men, come ye: 7 And forsake the ways of that corruption and draw near unto me, and I will enter into you, and will bring you forth from perdition, 8 And make you wise in the ways of truth: that you be not destroyed nor perish: 9 Hear ye me and be redeemed. For the grace of God I am telling among you: and by my means you shall be redeemed and become blessed. 10 I am your judge; and they who have put me on shall not be injured: but they shall possess the new world that is incorrupt: 11 My chosen ones walk in me, and my ways I will make known to them that seek me, and I will make them trust in my name. Hallelujah.

ODE 34.

True poetry--pure and simple.

1 No way is hard where there is a simple heart. 2 Nor is there any wound where the thoughts are upright: 3 Nor is there any storm in the depth of the illuminated thought: 4 Where one is surrounded on every side by beauty, there is nothing that is divided. 5 The likeness of what is below is that which is above; for everything is above: what is below is nothing but the imagination of those that are without knowledge. 6 Grace has been revealed for your salvation. Believe and live and be saved. Hallelujah.

ODE 35.

"No cradled child more softly lies than I: come soon, eternity."

1 The dew of the Lord in quietness He distilled upon me: 2 And the cloud of peace He caused to rise over my head, which guarded me continually; 3 It was to me for salvation: everything was shaken and they were affrighted; 4 And there came forth from them a smoke and a judgment; and I was keeping quiet in the order of the Lord: 5 More than shelter was He to me and more than foundation. 6 And I was carried like a child by mother: and He gave me milk, the dew of the Lord: 7 And I grew great by His bounty, and rested in His perfection, 8 And I spread out my hands in the lifting up of my soul: and I was made right with the Most High and I was redeemed with Him. Hallelujah.

ODE 36.

Theologians have never agreed on an explanation of this perplexing Ode.

1 I rested in the Spirit of the Lord: and the Spirit raised me on high: 2 And made me stand on my feet in the height of the Lord, before His perfection and His glory, while I was praising Him by the composition of His songs. 3 The Spirit brought me forth before the face of the Lord: and, although a son of man, I was named the Illuminate, the Son of God: 4 While I praised amongst the praising ones, and great was I amongst the mighty ones. 5 For according to the greatness of the Most High, so He made me: and like His own newness He renewed me; and He anointed me from His own perfection: 6 And I became one of His Neighbours; and my mouth was opened; like a cloud of dew; 7 And my heart poured out as it were a gushing stream of righteousness, 8 And my access to Him was in peace; and I was established by the Spirit of His government. Hallelujah.
ODE 37.

An elementary Ode.

1 I stretched out my hands to my Lord: and to the Most High I raised my voice: 2 And I spake with the lips of my heart; and He heard me when my voice reached Him: 3 His answer came to me and gave me the fruits of my labours; 4 And it gave me rest by the grace of the Lord. Hallelujah.

ODE 38.

A beautiful description of the power of truth.

1 I went up to the light of truth as if into a chariot: 2 And the Truth took me and led me: and carried me across pits and gulleys; and from the rocks and the

waves it preserved me: 3 And it became to me a haven of Salvation: and set me on the arms of immortal life: 4 And it went with me and made me rest, and suffered me not to wander because it was the Truth. 5 And I ran no risk, because I walked with Him; 5 And I did not make an error 4 anything because I obeyed the Truth. 7 For Error flees away from it and meets it not: but the Truth proceeds in the right path, and 8 What ever I did not know, it made clear to me, all the poisons of error, and the plagues of death which they think to be sweetness: 9 And I saw the destroyer of destruction, when the bride who is corrupted is adorned: and the bridgegroom who corrupts and is corrupted; 10 And I asked the Truth, 'Who are these?'; and He said to me, 'This is the deceiver and the error: 11 And they are alike in the beloved and in his bride: and they lead astray and corrupt the whole world: 12 And they invite many to the banquet, 13 And give them to drink of the wine of their intoxication, and remove their wisdom and knowledge, and so they make them without intelligence; 14 And then they leave them; and then these go about like madmen corrupting: seeing that they are with out heart, nor do they seek for it.' 15 And I was made wise so as not to fall into the hands of the deceiver; and I congratulated myself because the Truth went with me, 16 And I was established and lived and was redeemed, 17 And my foundations were laid on the hand of the Lord: because He established me. 18 For He set the root and watered it and fixed it and blessed it; and its fruits are for ever. 19 It struck deep and sprung up and spread out and was full and enlarged; 20 And the Lord alone was glorified in His planting and in His husbandry: by His care and by the blessing of His lips, 21 By the beautiful planting of His right hand: and by the discovery of His planting, and by the thought of His mind. Hallelujah.

ODE 39.

One of the few allusions to events in the Gospels ---that of our Lord walking on the Sea of Galilee

1 Great rivers are the power of the Lord: 2 And they carry headlong those who despise Him: and entangle their paths: 3 And they sweep away their fords, and catch their bodies and destroy their lives. 4 For they are more swift than lightning and more rapid, and those who cross them in faith are not moved; 5 And those who walk on them without blemish shall not be afraid. 6 For the sign in them is the Lord; and the sign is the way of those who cross in the name of the Lord; 7 Put on, therefore the name of the Most High, and know Him and you shall cross without danger, for the rivers will be subject to you. 8 The Lord has bridged them by His word; and He walked and crossed them on foot: 9 And His footsteps stand firm on the water, and are not

injured; they are as firm as a tree that is truly set up. 10 And the waves were lifted up on this side and on that, but the footsteps of our Lord Messiah stand firm and are not obliterated and are not defaced. 11 And a way has been appointed for those who cross after Him and for those who adhere to the course of faith in Him and worship His name. Hallelujah.

ODE 40.

A song of praise without equal.

1 As the honey distills from the comb of the bees, 2 And the milk flows from the woman that loves her children; 3 So also is my hope on Thee, my God. 4 As the fountain gushes out its water. 5 So my heart gushes out the praise of the Lord and my lips utter praise to Him, and my tongue His psalms, 6 And my face exults with His gladness and my spirit exults in His love and my soul shines in Him: 7 And reverence confides in Him; and redemption in Him stands assured: 8 And His inheritance is immortal life, and those who participate in it are incorrupt. Hallelujah.

ODE 41.

We discover that the writer may be a Gentile (v. 8).

1 All the Lord's children will praise Him, and will collect the truth of His faith. 2 And His children shall be known to Him. Therefore we will sing in His love: 3 We live in the Lord by His grace: and life we receive in His Messiah: 4 For a great day has shined upon us: and marvellous is He who has given us of His glory. 5 Let us, therefore all of us unite together in the name of the Lord, and let us honour Him in His goodness, 6 And let our faces shine in His light: and let our hearts meditate in His love by night and by day. 7 Let us exult with the joy of the Lord. 8 All those will be astonished that see me, For from another race am I; 9 For the Father of truth remembered me: He who possessed me from the beginning: 10 For His bounty begat me, and the thought of His heart: 11 And His Word is with us in all our way; 12 The Saviour who makes alive and does not reject our souls; 13 The man who was humbled, and exalted by His own righteousness, 14 The Son of the Most High appeared in the perfection of His Father; 15 And light dawned from the Word that was beforetime in Him;. 16 The Messiah is truly one; and He was known before the foundation of the world, 17 That He might save souls forever by the truth of His name: a new song arises from those who love Him. Hallelujah.

ODE 42.

The Odes of Solomon, the Son of David, are ended with the following exquisite verses.

1 I stretched out my hands and approached my Lord: 2 For the stretching of my hands is His sign: 2 My expansion is the outspread tree which was set up on the way of the Righteous One. 4 And I became of no account to those who did not take hold of me and I shall be with those who love me. 5 All my persecutors are dead; and they sought after me who hoped in me, because I was alive: 6 And I rose up and am with them; and I will speak by their mouths. 7 For they have despised those who persecuted them; 8 And I lifted up over them the yoke of my love; 9 Like the arm of the bridegroom over the bride, 10 So was my yoke over those that know me: 11 And as the couch that is spread in the house of the bridegroom and bride, 12 So is my love over those that believe in me. 13 And I was not rejected though I was reckoned to be so. 14 I did not perish, though they devised it against me. 13 Sheol saw me and was made miserable: 16 Death cast me up and many along with me. 17 I had gall and bitterness, and I went down with him to the utmost of his depth: 18 And the feet and the head he let go, for they were not able to endure my face: 19 And I made a congregation of living men amongst his dead men, and I spake with them by living lips: 20 Because my word shall not be void: 21 And those who had died ran towards me: and they cried and said, Son of God, have pity on us, and do with us according to thy kindness. 22 And bring us out from the bonds of darkness: and open to us the door by which we shall come out to thee. 23 For we see that our death has not touched thee. 24 Let us also be redeemed with thee: for thou art our Redeemer. 25 And I heard their voice; and my name I sealed upon their heads: 26 For they are free men and they are mine. Hallelujah.

The Apology of Aristides the Philosopher

St. Aristides the Philosopher of Athens: APOLOGY THE APOLOGY OF ARISTIDES THE PHILOSOPHER TRANSLATED FROM THE SYRIAC VERSION BY D. M. KAY, B.Sc., B.D., ASSISTANT TO THE PROFESSOR OF SEMITIC LANGUAGES IN THE UNIVERSITY OF EDINBURGH.

EDITOR'S NOTE: The Apology of Aristides, mentioned by Eusebius, St. Jerome, and other ancient writers and said to have been the inspiration for the great works of St. Justin Martyr, was considered lost until the late Nineteenth Century, when an Armenian fragment was discovered. Then in 1889 the full text in Syriac translation was found in the library of St. Catherine's in the Sinai. Ironically, it was then realized that the work had never been lost at all: a slightly shortened version of it had been preserved in the well-known Life of St. Barlaam of India, by St. John of Damascus. (Since the numerous references to Greek gods would have made little impact on an Indian audience, one may assume that St. John, writing for a Greek readership which would have found a denunciation of Vedic or Buddhist deities equally meaningless, decided to insert the Apology of Aristides as a sort of rough equivalent of whatever Barlaam actually preached to the Brahmins.)

St. Aristides delivered the Apology around the year 125, when Hadrian visited Athens [Eusebius, H.E. IV, iii]. His memory is kept by the Church on 31 August.

Since the Greek version found in Barlaam and Ioasaph is widely available online, we here give the longer version preserved in Syriac. Note that there are a number of "Syrianisms" is this version -- cultural rather than theological, such as the reference to Hades as "Sheol". -- N. Redington, St. Pachomius Library.

THE APOLOGY OF ARISTIDES
Here follows the defence which Aristides the philosopher made before Hadrian the King on behalf of reverence for God.

. . . All-powerful Caesar Titus Hadrianus Antoninus, venerable and merciful, from Marcianus Aristides, an Athenian philosopher.

I. I, O King, by the grace of God came into this world; and when I had considered the heaven and the earth and the seas, and had surveyed the sun and the rest of creation, I marvelled at the beauty of the world. And I perceived that the world and all that is therein are moved by the power of another; and I understood that he who moves them is God, who is hidden in them, and veiled by them. And it is manifest that that which

causes motion is more powerful than that which is moved. But that I should make search concerning this same mover of all, as to what is his nature (for it seems to me, he is indeed unsearchable in his nature), and that I should argue as to the constancy of his government, so as to grasp it fully,--this is a vain effort for me; for it is not possible that a man should fully comprehend it. I say, however, concerning this mover of the world, that he is God of all, who made all things for the sake of mankind. And it seems to me that this is reasonable, that one should fear God and should not oppress man.

I say, then, that God is not born, not made, an ever-abiding nature without beginning and without end, immortal, perfect, and incomprehensible. Now when I say that he is "perfect," this means that there is not in him any defect, and he is not in need of anything but all things are in need of him. And when I say that he is "without beginning," this means that everything which has beginning has also an end, and that which has an end may be brought to an end. He has no name, for everything which has a name is kindred to things created. Form he has none, nor yet any union of members; for whatsoever possesses these is kindred to things fashioned. He is neither male nor female. The heavens do not limit him, but the heavens and all things, visible and invisible, receive their bounds from him. Adversary he has none, for there exists not any stronger than he. Wrath and indignation he possesses not, for there is nothing which is able to stand against him. Ignorance and forgetfulness are not in his nature, for he is altogether wisdom and understanding; and in Him stands fast all that exists. He requires not sacrifice and libation, nor even one of things visible; He requires not aught from any, but all living creatures stand in need of him.

II. Since, then, we have addressed you concerning God, so far as our discourse can bear upon him, let us now come to the race of men, that we may know which of them participate in the truth of which we have spoken, and which of them go astray from it.

This is clear to you, O King, that there are four classes of men in this world:--Barbarians and Greeks, Jews and Christians. The Barbarians, indeed, trace the origin of their kind of religion from Kronos and from Rhea and their other gods; the Greeks, however, from Helenos, who is said to be sprung from Zeus. And by Helenos there were born Aiolos and Xuthos; and there were others descended from Inachos and Phoroneus, and lastly from the Egyptian Danaos and from Kadmos and from Dionysos.
The Jews, again, trace the origin of their race from Abraham, who begat Isaac, of whom was born Jacob. And he begat twelve sons who migrated from Syria to

Egypt; and there they were called the nation of the Hebrews, by him who made their laws; and at length they were named Jews.

The Christians, then, trace the beginning of their religion from Jesus the Messiah; and he is named the Son of God Most High. And it is said that God came down from heaven, and from a Hebrew virgin assumed and clothed himself with flesh; and the Son of God lived in a daughter of man. This is taught in the gospel, as it is called, which a short time was preached among them; and you also if you will read therein, may perceive the power which belongs to it. This Jesus, then, was born of the race of the Hebrews; and he had twelve disciples in order that the purpose of his incarnation might in time be accomplished. But he himself was pierced by the Jews, and he died and was buried; and they say that after three days he rose and ascended to heaven. Thereupon these twelve disciples went forth throughout the known parts of the world, and kept showing his greatness with all modesty and uprightness. And hence also those of the present day who believe that preaching are called Christians, and they are become famous.

So then there are, as I said above, four classes of men:--Barbarians and Greeks, Jews and Christians.

Moreover the wind is obedient to God, and fire to the angels; the waters also to the demons and the earth to the sons of men. [Possibly inserted by mistake into one of the early MSS.]

III. Let us begin, then, with the Barbarians, and go on to the rest of the nations one after another, that we may see which of them hold the truth as to God and which of them hold error.

The Barbarians, then, as they did not apprehend God, went astray among the elements, and began to worship things created instead of their Creator; and for this end they made images and shut them up in shrines, and lo! they worship them, guarding them the while with much care, lest their gods be stolen by robbers. And the Barbarians did not observe that that which acts as guard is greater than that which is guarded, and that every one who creates is greater than that which is created. If it be, then, that their gods are too feeble to see to their own safety, how will they take thought for the safety of men? Great then is the error into which the Barbarians wandered in worshipping lifeless images which can do nothing to help them. And I am led to wonder, O King, at their philosophers, how that even they went astray, and gave the name of gods to images which were made in honour of the elements; and that their sages did not perceive that the elements also are dissoluble and perishable. For if a small part of

an element is dissolved or destroyed, the whole of it may be dissolved and destroyed. If then the elements themselves are dissolved and destroyed and forced to be subject to another that is more stubborn than they, and if they are not in their nature gods, why, for sooth, do they call the images which are made in their honour, God? Great, then, is the error which the philosophers among them have brought upon their followers.

IV. Let us turn now, O King, to the elements in themselves, that we may make clear in regard to them, that they are not gods, but a created thing, liable to ruin and change, which is of the same nature as man; whereas God is imperishable and unvarying, and invisible, while yet He sees, and overrules, and transforms all things.

Those then who believe concerning the earth that it is a god have hitherto deceived themselves, since it is furrowed and set with plants and trenched; and it takes in the filthy refuse of men and beasts and cattle. And at times it becomes unfruitful, for if it be burnt to ashes it becomes devoid of life, for nothing germinates from an earthen jar. And besides if water be collected upon it, it is dissolved together with its products. And lo! it is trodden under foot of men and beast, and receives the blood of the slain; and it is dug open, and filled with the dead, and becomes a tomb for corpses. But it is impossible that a nature, which is holy and worthy and blessed and immortal, should allow of any one of these things. And hence it appears to us that the earth is not a god but a creation of God.

V. In the same way, again, those erred who believed the waters to be gods. For the waters were created for the use of man, and are put under his rule in many ways. For they suffer change and admit impurity, and are destroyed and lose their nature while they are boiled into many substances. And they take colours which do not belong. to them; they are also congealed by frost and are mingled and permeated with the filth of men and beasts, and with the blood of the slain. And being checked by skilled workmen through the restraint of aqueducts, they flow and are diverted against their inclination, and come into gardens and other places in order that they may be collected and issue forth as a means of fertility for man, and that they may cleanse away every impurity and fulfil the service man requires from them. Wherefore it is impossible that the waters should be a god, but they are a work of God and a part of the world.

In like manner also they who believed that fire is a god erred to no slight extent. For it, too, was created for the service of men, and is subject to them in many ways:-- in the preparation of meats, and as a means of casting metals, and for other ends whereof your Majesty is aware. At the same time it is quenched and extinguished in many ways.

Again they also erred who believed the motion of the winds to be a god. For it is well known to us that those winds are under the dominion of another, at times their motion increases, and at times it fails and ceases at the command of him who controls them. For they were created by God for the sake of men, in order to supply the necessity of trees and fruits and seeds; and to bring over the sea ships which convey for men necessaries and goods from places where they are found to places where they are not found; and to govern the quarters of the world. And as for itself, at times it increases and again abates; and in one place brings help and in another causes disaster at the bidding of him who rules it. And mankind too are able by known means to confine and keep it in check in order that it may fulfil for them the service they require from it. And of itself it has not any authority at all. And hence it is impossible that the winds should be called gods, but rather a thing made by God.

VI. So also they erred who believed that the sun is a god. For we see that it is moved by the compulsion of another, and revolves and makes its journey, and proceeds from sign to sign, rising and setting every day, so as to give warmth for the growth of plants and trees, and to bring forth into the air wherewith it (sunlight) is mingled every growing thing which is upon the earth. And to it there belongs by comparison a part in common with the rest of the stars in its course; and though it is one in its nature it is associated with many parts for the supply of the needs of men; and that not according to its own will but rather according to the will of him who rules it. And hence it is impossible that the sun should be a god, but the work of God; and in like manner also the moon and the stars.

VII. And those who believed of the men of the past, that some of them were gods, they too were much mistaken. For as you yourself allow, O King, man is constituted of the four elements and of a soul and a spirit (and hence he is called a microcosm), and without any one of these parts he could not consist. He has a beginning and an end, and he is born and dies. But God, as I said, has none of these things in his nature, but is uncreated and imperishable. And hence it is not possible that we should set up man to be of the nature of God:--man, to whom at times when he looks for joy, there comes trouble, and when he looks for laughter there comes to him weeping,--who is wrathful and covetous and envious, with other defects as well. And he is destroyed in many ways by the elements and also by the animals.

And hence, O King, we are bound to recognize the error of the Barbarians, that thereby, since they did not find traces of the true God, they fell aside from the truth, and went after the desire of their imagination, serving the perishable elements and lifeless images, and through their error not apprehending what the true God is.

VIII. Let us turn further to the Greeks also, that we may know what opinion they hold as to the true God. The Greeks, then, because they are more subtle than the Barbarians, have gone further astray than the Barbarians; inasmuch as they have introduced many fictitious gods, and have set up some of them as males and some as females; and in that some of their gods were found who were adulterers, and did murder, and were deluded, and envious, and wrathful and passionate, and parricides, and thieves, and robbers. And some of them, they say, were crippled and limped, and some were sorcerers, and some actually went mad, and some played on lyres, and some were given to roaming on the hills, and some even died, and some were struck dead by lightning, and some were made servants even to men, and some escaped by flight, and some were kidnapped by men, and some, indeed, were lamented and deplored by men. And some, they say, went down to Sheol, and some were grievously wounded, and some transformed themselves into the likeness of animals to seduce the race of mortal women, and some polluted themselves by lying with males And some, they say, were wedded to their mothers and their sisters and their daughters. And they say of their gods that they committed adultery with the daughters of men; and of these there was born a certain race which also was mortal. And they say that some of the females disputed about beauty, and appeared before men for judgment. Thus, O King, have the Greeks put forward foulness, and absurdity, and folly about their gods and about themselves, in that they have called those that are of such a nature gods, who are no gods. And hence mankind have received incitements to commit adultery and fornication, and to steal and to practise all that is offensive and hated and abhorred. For if they who are called their gods practised all these things which are written above, how much more should men practise them--men, who believe that their gods themselves practised them. And owing to the foulness of this error there have happened to mankind harassing wars, and great famines, and bitter captivity, and complete desolation. And lo! it was by reason of this alone that they suffered and that all these things came upon them;and while they endured those things they did not perceive in their mind that for their error those things came upon them.

IX. Let us proceed further to their account of their gods that we may carefully demonstrate all that is said above. First of all, the Greeks bring forward as a god Kronos, that is to say Chiun (Saturn). And his worshippers sacrifice their children to him, and they burn some of them alive in his honour. And they say that he took to him among his wives Rhea, and begat many children by her. By her too he begat Dios, who is called Zeus. And at length he (Kronos) went mad, and through fear of an oracle that had been made known to him, he began to devour his sons. And from him Zeus was stolen away without his knowledge; and at length Zeus bound him, and mutilated the signs of his manhood, and flung them into the sea. And hence, as they say in fable, there was engendered Aphrodite, who is called Astarte. And he (Zeus) cast out Kronos fettered into darkness. Great then is the error and ignominy which the Greeks have brought forward about the first of their gods, in that they have said all this about him, O King. It is impossible that a god should be bound or mutilated; and if it be otherwise, he is indeed miserable.

And after Kronos they bring forward another god Zeus. And they say of him that he assumed the sovereignty, and was king over all the gods. And they say that he changed himself into a beast and other shapes in order to seduce mortal women, and to raise up by them children for himself. Once, they say, he changed himself into a bull through love of Europe and Pasiphae. And again he changed himself into the likeness of gold through love of Danae, and to a swan through love of Leda, and to a man through love of Antiope, and to lightning through love of Luna, and so by these he begat many children. For by Antiope, they say, that he begat Zethus and Amphion, and by Luna Dionysos, by Alcmena Hercules, and by Leto, Apollo and Artemis, and by Danae Perseus, and by Leda, Castor and Polydeuces, and Helene and Paludus, and by Mnemosyne he begat nine daughters whom they styled the Muses, and by Europe, Minos and Rhadamanthos and Sarpedon. And lastly he changed himself into the likeness of an eagle through his passion for Ganydemos (Ganymede) the shepherd.

By reason of these tales, O King, much evil has arisen among men, who to this day are imitators of their gods, and practise adultery and defile themselves with their mothers and their sisters, and by lying with males, and some make bold to slay even their parents. For if he who is said to be the chief and king of their gods do these things how much more should his worshippers imitate him? And great is the folly which the Greeks have brought forward in their narrative concerning him. For it is impossible that a god should practise adultery or fornication or come near to lie with males,

or kill his parents; and if it be otherwise, he is much worse than a destructive demon.

X. Again they bring forward as another god Hephaistos. And they say of him, that he is lame, and a cap is set on his head, and he holds in his hands firetongs and a hammer; and he follows the craft of iron working, that thereby he may procure the necessaries of his livelihood. Is then this god so very needy? But it cannot be that a god should be needy or lame, else he is very worthless.

And further they bring in another god and call him Hermes. And they say that he is a thief, a lover of avarice, and greedy for gain, and a magician, and mutilated and an athlete, and an interpreter of language. But it is impossible that a god should be a magician or avaricious, or maimed, or craving for what is not his, or an athlete. And if it be otherwise, he is found to be useless.

And after him they bring forward as another god Asklepios. And they say that he is a physician and prepares drugs and plaster that he may supply the necessaries of his livelihood. Is then this god in want? And at length he was struck with lightning by Dios on account of Tyndareos of Lacedaemon, and so he died. If then Asklepios were a god, and, when he was struck with lightning, was unable to help himself, how should he be able to give help to others? But that a divine nature should be in want or be destroyed by lightning is impossible.

And again they bring forward another as a god, and they call him Ares. And they say that he is a warrior, and jealous, and covets sheep and things which are not his. And he makes gain by his arms. And they say that at length he committed adultery with Aphrodite, and was caught by the little boy Eros and by Hephaistos the husband of Aphrodite. But it is impossible that a god should be a warrior or bound or an adulterer.

And again they say of Dionysos that he forsooth! is a god, who arranges carousals by night, and teaches drunkenness, and carries off women who do not belong to him. And at length, they say, he went mad and dismissed his handmaidens and fled into the desert; and during his madness he ate serpents. And at last he was killed by Titanos. If then Dionysos were a god, and when he was being killed was unable to help himself, how is it possible that he should help others?

Herakles next they bring forward and say that he is a god, who hates detestable things, a tyrant, and warrior and a destroyer of plagues. And of him also they say that at length he became mad and killed his own children, and east himself into a fire and died. If then

Herakles is a god, and in all these calamities was unable to rescue himself, how should others ask help from him? But it is impossible that a god should be mad, or drunken or a slayer of his children, or consumed by fire.

XI. And after him they bring forward another god and call him Apollon. And they say that he is jealous and inconstant, and at times he holds the bow and quiver, and again the lyre and plectron. And he utters oracles for men that he may receive rewards from them. Is then this god in need of rewards? But it is an insult that all these things should be found with a god.

And after him they bring forward as a goddess Artemis, the sister of Apollo; and they say that she was a huntress and that she herself used to carry a bow and bolts, and to roam about upon the mountains, leading the hounds to hunt stags or wild bears of the field. But it is disgraceful that a virgin maid should roam alone upon the hills or hunt in the chase for animals. Wherefore it is impossible that Artemis should be a goddess.

Again they say of Aphrodite that she indeed is a goddess. And at times she dwells with their gods, but at other times she is a neighbour to men. And once she had Ares as a lover, and again Adonis who is Tammuz. Once also, Aphrodite was wailing and weeping for the death of Tammuz, and they my that she went down to Sheol that she might redeem Adonis from Persephone, who is the daughter of Sheol (Hades). If then Aphrodite is a goddess and was unable to help her lover at his death, how will she find it possible to help others? And this cannot be listened to, that a divine nature should come to weeping and wailing and adultery.

And again they say of Tammuz that he is a god. And he is, forsooth! a hunter and an adulterer. And they say that he was killed by a wound from a wild boar, without being able to help himself. And if he could not help himself, how can he take thought for the human race? But that a god should be an adulterer or a hunter or should die by violence is impossible.

Again they say of Rhea that she is the mother of their gods. And they say that she had once a lover Atys, and that she used to delight in depraved men. And at last she raised a lamentation and mourned for Atys her lover. If then the mother of their gods was unable to help her lover and deliver him from death, how can she help others? So it is disgraceful that a goddess should lament and weep and take delight in depraved men.

Again they introduce Kore and say that she is a goddess, and she was stolen away by Pluto, and could not help herself. If then she is a goddess and was unable to help herself how will she find means to help others? For a god who is stolen away is very powerless.

All this, then, O King, have the Greeks brought forward concerning their gods, and they have invented and declared it concerning them. And hence all men received an impulse to work all profanity and all defilements; and hereby the whole earth was corrupted.

XII. The Egyptians, moreover, because they are more base and stupid than every people that is on the earth, have themselves erred more than all. For the deities (or religion) of the Barbarians and the Greeks did not suffice for them, but they introduced some also of the nature of the animals, and said thereof that they were gods, and likewise of creeping things which are found on the dry land and in the waters. And of plants and herbs they said that some of them were gods. And they were corrupted by every kind of delusion and defilement more than every people that is on the earth. For from ancient times they worshipped Isis, and they say that she is a goddess whose husband was Osiris her brother. And when Osiris was killed by Typhon his brother, Isis fled with Horos her son to Byblus in Syria, and was there for a certain time till her son was grown. And he contended with Typhon his uncle, and killed him. And then Isis returned and went about with Horos her son and sought for the dead body of Osiris her lord, bitterly lamenting his death. If then Isis be a goddess, and could not help Osiris her brother and lord, how can she help another? But it is impossible that a divine nature should be afraid, and flee for safety, or should weep and wail; or else it is very miserable.

And of Osiris also they say that he is a serviceable god. And he was killed by Typhon and was unable to help himself. But it is well known that this cannot be asserted of divinity. And further, they say of his brother Typhon that he is a god, who killed his brother and was killed by his brother's son and by his bride, being unable to help himself. And how, pray, is he a god who does not save himself?

As the Egyptians, then, were more stupid than the rest of the nations, these and such like gods did not suffice for them. Nay, but they even apply the name of gods to animals in which there is no soul at all. For some of them worship the sheep and others the calf; and some the pig and others the shad fish; and some the crocodile and the hawk and the fish and the ibis and the vulture and the eagle and the raven. Some of them worship the cat, and others the turbot-fish, some the dog, some the adder, and some the asp, and others the lion; and others the garlic and onions and thorns, and others the tiger and other such things. And the poor creatures do not see that all these things are nothing, although they daily witness their gods being eaten and consumed by men and also by their fellows; while some of them are cremated, and some die and decay and become dust, without their observing that they perish in many ways. So the Egyptians have not observed that such things which are not equal to their own deliverance, are not gods. And if, forsooth, they are weak in the case of their own deliverance, whence have they power to help in the case of deliverance of their worshippers? Great then is the error into which the Egyptians wandered;-- greater, indeed, than that of any people which is upon the face of the earth.

XIII. But it is a marvel, O King, with regard to the Greeks, who surpass all other peoples in their manner of life and reasoning, how they have gone astray after dead idols and lifeless images. And yet they see their gods in the hands of their artificers being sawn out, and planed and docked, and hacked short, and charred, and ornamented, and being altered by them in every kind of way. And when they grow old, and are worn away through lapse of time, and when they are molten and crushed to powder, how, I wonder, did they not perceive concerning them, that they are not gods? And as for those who did not find deliverance for themselves, how can they serve the distress of men?

But even the writers and philosophers among them have wrongly alleged that the gods are such as are made in honour of God Almighty. And they err in seeking to liken (them) to God whom man has not at any time seen nor can see unto what He is like. Herein, too (they err) in asserting of deity that any such thing as deficiency can be present to it; as when they say that He receives sacrifice and requires burnt-offering and libation and immolations of men, and temples. But God is not in need, and none of these things is necessary to Him; and it is clear that men err in these things they imagine.

Further their writers and their philosophers represent and declare that the nature of all their gods is one. And they have not apprehended God our Lord who while He is one, is in all. They err therefore. For if the body of a man while it is many in its parts is not in dread, one member of another, but, since it is a united body, wholly agrees with itself; even so also God is one in His nature. A single essence is proper to Him, since He is uniform in His nature and His essence; and He is not afraid of Himself. If then the nature of the gods is one, it is not proper that a god should either pursue or slay or harm a god. If then gods be pursued and wounded by gods, and some be kidnapped and some struck dead by lightning, it is obvious that the nature of their gods is not one. And hence it is known, O King, that it is a mistake when they reckon and bring the natures of their gods under a single nature. If then it becomes us to admire a god which is seen and does not see, how much more praiseworthy is it that one should believe in a nature which is invisible and all-seeing? And if further it is fitting that one should approve the handiworks of a craftsman, how much more is it fitting that one should glorify the Creator of the craftsman?

For behold! when the Greeks made laws they did not perceive that by their laws they condemn their gods. For if their laws are righteous, their gods are unrighteous, since they transgressed the law in killing one another, and practising sorcery, and committing adultery, and in robbing and stealing, and in lying with males, and by their other practises as well. For if their gods were right in doing all these things as they are described, then the laws of the Greeks are unrighteous in not being made according to the will of their gods. And in that case the whole world is gone astray.

For the narratives about their gods are some of them myths, and some of them nature-poems (lit: natural-- fusikai), and some of them hymns and elegies. The hymns indeed and elegies are empty words and noise. But these nature-poems, even if they be made as they say, still those are not gods who do such things and suffer and endure such things. And those myths are shallow tales with no depth whatever in them.

XIV. Let us come now, O King, to the history of the Jews also, and see what opinion they have as to God. The Jews then say that God is one, the Creator of all, and omnipotent; and that it is not right that any other should be worshipped except this God alone. And herein they appear to approach the truth more than all the nations, especially in that they worship God and not His works. And they imitate God by the philanthropy which prevails among them; for they have compassion on the poor, and they release the captives, and bury the dead, and do such things as these, which are acceptable before God and well-pleasing also to men,--which (customs) they have received from their forefathers.

Nevertheless they too erred from true knowledge. And in their imagination they conceive that it is God they serve; whereas by their mode of observance it is to the angels and not to God that their service is rendered:-- as when they celebrate sabbaths and the beginning of the months, and feasts of unleavened bread, and a great fast; and fasting and circumcision and the purification of meats, which things, however, they do not observe perfectly.

XV. But the Christians, O King, while they went about and made search, have found the truth; and as we learned from their writings, they have come nearer to truth and genuine knowledge than the rest of the nations. For they know and trust in God, the Creator of heaven and of earth, in whom and from whom are all things, to whom there is no other god as companion, from whom they received commandments which they engraved upon their minds and observe in hope and expectation of the world which is to come. Wherefore they do not commit adultery nor fornication, nor bear false witness, nor embezzle what is held in pledge, nor covet what is not theirs. They honour father and mother, and show kindness to those near to them; and whenever they are judges, they judge uprightly. They do not worship idols (made) in the image of man; and whatsoever they would not that others should do unto them, they do not to others; and of the food which is consecrated to idols they do not eat, for they are pure. And their oppressors they appease (lit: comfort) and make them their friends; they do good to their enemies; and their women, O King, are pure as virgins, and their daughters are modest; and their men keep themselves from every unlawful union and from all uncleanness, in the hope of a recompense to come in the other world. Further, if one or other of them have bondmen and bondwomen or children, through love towards them they persuade them to become Christians, and when they have done so, they call them brethren without distinction. They do not worship strange gods, and they go their way in all modesty and cheerfulness. Falsehood is not found among them; and they love one another, and from widows they do not turn away their esteem; and they deliver the orphan from him who treats him harshly. And he, who has, gives to him who has not, without boasting. And when they see a stranger, they take him in to their homes and rejoice over him as a very brother; for they do not call them brethren after the flesh, but brethren after the spirit and in God. And whenever one of their poor passes from the world, each one of them according to his ability gives heed to him and carefully sees to his burial. And if they hear that one of their number is imprisoned or afflicted on account of the name of their Messiah, all of them anxiously minister to his necessity, and if it is possible to redeem him they set him free. And if there is among them any that is poor and needy, and if they have no spare food, they fast two or three days in order to supply to the needy their lack of food. They observe the precepts of their Messiah with much care, living justly and soberly as the Lord their God commanded them. Every morning and every hour they give thanks and praise to God for His loving-kindnesses toward them; and for their food and their drink they offer thanksgiving to Him. And if any righteous man among them passes from the world, they rejoice and offer thanks to God; and they escort his body as if he were setting out from one place to another near. And when a child has been born to one of them, they give thanks to God; and if moreover it happen to die in childhood, they give thanks to God the more, as for one who has passed through the world without sins. And further if they see that any one of them dies in his ungodliness or in his sins, for him they grieve bitterly, and sorrow as for one who goes to meet his doom.

XVI. Such, O King, is the commandment of the law of the Christians, and such is their manner of life. As men who know God, they ask from Him petitions which are fitting for Him to grant and for them to receive. And thus they employ their whole lifetime. And since they know the loving-kindnesses of God toward them, behold! for their sake the glorious things which are in the world flow forth to view. And verily, they are those who found the truth when they went about and made search for it; and from what we considered, we learned that they alone come near to a knowledge of the truth. And they do not proclaim in the ears of the multitude the kind deeds they do, but are careful that no one should notice them; and they conceal their giving just as he who finds a treasure and conceals it. And they strive to be righteous as those who expect to behold their Messiah, and to receive from Him with great glory the promises made concerning them. And as for their words and their precepts, O King, and their glorying in their worship, and the hope of earning according to the work of each one of them their recompense which they look for in another world,-you may learn about these from their writings. It is enough for us to have shortly informed your Majesty concerning the conduct and the truth of the Christians. For great indeed, and wonderful is their doctrine to him who will search into it and reflect upon it. And verily, this is a new people, and there is something divine (lit: "a divine admixture") in the midst of them.

Take, then, their writings, and read therein, and lo! you will find that I have not put forth these things on my own authority, nor spoken thus as their advocate; but since I read in their writings I was fully assured of these things as also of things which are to come. And for this reason I was constrained to declare the truth to such as care for it and seek the world to come. And to me there is no doubt but that the earth abides through the supplication of the Christians. But the rest of the nations err and cause error in wallowing before the elements of the world, since beyond these their mental vision will not pass. And they search about as if in darkness because they will not recognize the truth; and like drunken men they reel and jostle one another and fall.

XVII. Thus far, O King, I have spoken; for concerning that which remains, as is said above, there are found in their other writings things which are hard to utter and difficult for one to narrate,--which are not only spoken in words but also wrought out in deeds.

Now the Greeks, O King, as they follow base practises in intercourse with males, and a mother and a sister and a daughter, impute their monstrous impurity in turn to the Christians. But the Christians are just and good, and the truth is set before their eyes, and their spirit is long-suffering; and, therefore, though they know the error of these (the Greeks), and are persecuted by them, they bear and endure it; and for the most part they have compassion on them, as men who are destitute of knowledge. And on their side, they offer prayer that these may repent of their error; and when it happens that one of them has repented, he is ashamed before the Christians of the works which were done by him; and he makes confession to God, saying, I did these things in ignorance. And he purifies his heart, and his sins are forgiven him, because he committed them in ignorance in the former time, when he used to blaspheme and speak evil of the true knowledge of the Christians. And assuredly the race of the Christians is more blessed than all the men who are upon the face of the earth.

Henceforth let the tongues of those who utter vanity and harass the Christians be silent; and hereafter let them speak the truth. For it is of serious consequence to them that they should worship the true God rather than worship a senseless sound. And verily whatever is spoken in the mouth of the Christians is of God; and their doctrine is the gateway of light. Wherefore let all who are without the knowledge of God draw near thereto; and they will receive incorruptible words, which are from all time and from eternity. So shall they appear before the awful judgment which through Jesus the Messiah is destined to come upon the whole human race.

The Apology of Aristides the Philosopher is finished.

ACTS Chapter 29

Verse 1. Paul, full of the blessing of Christ, and overflowing in the Spirit, left Rome, having decided to go into Spain, becuase he had wanted to travel there for a long time, and he thought also to go from there to Britain.

Verse 2. Because he had heard in Phoenicia that some of the children of Israel, around the time of the Assyrian captivity, had escaped by sea to "the Islands far away" as proclaimed by the Prophet, and called by the Romans, Britain.

Verse 3. Since the Lord commanded the gospel to be preached far and wide to the Gentiles, and to the lost sheep of the House of Israel.

Verse 4. And no man hindered Paul because he testified boldly of
Jesus before the governents and among the people; and be took with
him certain of the brethren which lived with him at Rome, and
they boarded a ship at Ostium, and having fair winds were
brought safely into an safety (harbour) of Spain.

Verse 5. And many people gathered from the towns and villages, and the hill country; for they had heard of the conversion of the Apostles, and the many miracles he had performed.

Verse 6. And Paul preached with might in Spain, and great many people believed and were converted, for they knew he was an apostle sent from God.

Verse 7. And finding a ship in Armorica sailing to Britain they departed from Spain. Paul and his company passed along the South coast and reached a port called Raphinus.

Verse 8. Now when word spread wide that the Apostle had landed on their coast, large numbers of the inhabitants met him, and they treated Paul courteously and he entered in at the east gate of their city, and was housed in the house of a Hebrew and one of his own nation.

Verse 9. And the next day he came and stood upon Mount Lud;(Now the site of St. Paul's Cathedral.) and the people amassed at the gate, and assembled in the main street, and he preached Christ unto them, and they believed the word and the testimony of Jesus.

Verse 10. And at sunset the Holy Ghost fell upon Paul, and he prophesied, saying, "BEHOLD IN THE LAST DAYS THE GOD OF PEACE
SHALL LIVE IN THE CITIES, AND THE INHABITANTS OF THEM SHALL BE COUNTED: AND IN THE SEVENTH CENSUS OF THE PEOPLE, THEIR EYES SHALL BE OPENED, AND THE GLORY OF THEIR INHERITANCE WILL SHINE OUT BEFORE THEM. NATIONS SHALL COME UP TO WORSHIP ON THE MOUNT THAT TESTIFIES OF THE PATIENCE AND LONG SUFFERING OF A SERVANT OF THE LORD."

Verse 11. And in the last days new announcements of the Gospel shall come forth out of Jerusalem, and the hearts of the people shall be filled with joy, and they shall look and spring of water shall be opened, and there shall be no more disease.

Verse 12. In those days there shall be wars and rumours of wars; and a king shall rise up, and his sword shall be for the healing of the nations, and peace he makes shall last, and the glory of his kingdom will be a wonder among princes.

Verse 13. And it came to pass that certain of the Druids came to Paul privately and showed by their rites and ceremonies (to prove) they were descended from the Jews which escaped from bondage in the land of Egypt, and the apostle believed these things, and he gave them the kiss of peace.

Verse 14. And Paul lived in his housing for three months proving the faith and preaching Christ continually.

Verse 15. And after these things Paul and his brethren left Raphinus, and sailed to Atium in Gaul.

Verse 16. And Paul preached in the Roman garrisons and among the people, encouraging all men to repent and confess their sins.

Verse 17. And there came to him certain of the Belgae to ask him about the new doctrine, and of the man Jesus; and Paul opened his heart unto them, and told them all things that had happened to him, how Christ Jesus came into the world to save sinners; and they departed wondering among themselves about the things they had heard.

Verse 18. And after he preached and toiled muched Paul and his fellow workers went to Helvetia, and came to Mount Pontius Pilate, where he who condemned the Lord Jesus threw himself down headlong, and so miserably perished.

Verse 19. And immediately a torrent gushed from the mountain and washed his body (which had been) broken in pieces, into a lake.

Verse 20. And Paul stretched forth his hands upon the water, and prayed unto the Lord, saying, 0 Lord God, give a sign unto all nations that here Pontius Pilate, which condemned your only-begotten Son, plunged down headlong in to the pit.

Verse 21. And while Paul was still speaking, they looked there came a great earthquake, and the face of the waters was changed, and the lake took the form like unto the Son of Man hanging in an agony upon the Cross.

Verse 22. And a voice came out of heaven saying, Even Pilate has escaped the wrath to come, (See second death, Rev.21:8) for he washed his hands before the multitude at the shedding of the Lord Jesus' blood.

Verse 23. Because of this, when Paul and those with him saw the earthquake and heard the voice of the angel they glorified God and their spirits were greatly strenghtned.

Verse 24. And they journeyed and came to Mount Julius where two pillars stood, one on the right hand and one on the left hand, erected by Caesar Augustus.

Verse 25. And Paul was filled with the Holy Ghost and stood up between the two pillars, saying, Men and brethren, these stones which you see this day shall testify of my journey here and truly I say they shall remain until the outpouring of the spirit upon all nations, and the way will not be hindered throughout all generations.

Verse 26. And they went forth and came to Illyricum, intending to go by Macedonia into Asia, and grace was found in all the churches; and they prospered and had peace. Amen.

3 Corinthians

The Third Epistle of Paul to the Corinthians

LONGER VERSION

1 Paul, a prisoner of Jesus Christ, unto the brethren which are in Corinth, greeting.

2 Being in the midst of many tribulations, I do not marvel if the teachings of the evil one spread quickly. For my Lord Jesus Christ will hasten his coming, and will set at nought (no longer endure the insolence of) them that falsify his words.

3 For I delivered to you in the beginning the things which I received of the holy apostles which were before me, who were at all times with Jesus Christ: namely, that our Lord Jesus Christ was born of Mary who is of the seed of David according to the flesh, the Holy Spirit being sent forth from heaven from the Father to her by the angel Gabriel, so that he might come down into this world and redeem all flesh by his flesh, and raise us up from the dead in the flesh, just as he has shown us in himself as an example.

4 And because man was formed by his Father, therefore was mankind sought when he was lost, that he might be made alive by adoption. For to this end did God Almighty who made heaven and earth first send the prophets to the Jews, that they might be drawn away from their sins. For he planned to save the house of Israel. Therefore he conferred a portion of the spirit of Christ upon the prophets and sent them to the first Jews, and they proclaimed the true worship of God for a long period of time.

5 But the prince of iniquity, desiring to be God, laid hands on them and banished them from God, and bound all flesh by evil lusts and the end of the world by judgment drew near.

6 But God Almighty, who is righteous, would not cast away his own creation, but had compassion on them from heaven and sent his spirit into Mary in Galilee, who believed with all her heart and received the Holy Spirit in her womb, so that Jesus might come into the world, so that by that flesh whereby that wicked one had brought in death had triumphed, by the same he should be shown to be overcome.

7 For by his own body Jesus Christ saved all flesh and restored it to life, so that he might show forth the temple of righteousness in his body, whereby we are saved, in whom if we believe we are set free.

8 Know therefore that they who agree with them are not children of righteousness, but children of wrath who reject the wisdom of God, saying that the heaven and the earth and all that are in them are not the work of God. They therefore are the children of wrath, for cursed are they, following the teaching of the serpent, whom you should drive out and flee from their doctrine. For you are not children of disobedience, but of the well-beloved church. Therefore, the time of the resurrection is proclaimed to everyone.

9 And as for that which they say, that there is no resurrection of the flesh, they indeed shall have no resurrection to life, but to judgment because they do not believe in him that is risen from the dead, not believing nor understanding. For they do not know, O Corinthians, the seeds of wheat or of other seeds, how they are cast bare into the earth and are corrupted and rise again by the will of God with bodies and clothed. And not only that body which is cast in rises again, but many times more blessing itself.

10 And if we must not take an example from seeds only, but from more noble bodies, you know how Jonah the son of Amathi—when he would not preach to them of Nineveh, but fled—was swallowed by the sea-monster. After three days and three nights God heard the prayer of Jonah out of the lowest hell, and no part of him was consumed, not even a hair nor an eyelash.

11 How much more, oh you of little faith, shall he raise you that have believed in Christ Jesus, just as he himself arose. In the same way, a dead man also was cast upon the bones of the prophet Elisha by the children of Israel, and he arose in his body. How much more, oh you of little faith, shall you which have been cast on him rise again in that day having your flesh whole, just as he rose?

12 In the same way, concerning the prophet Elijah, he raised up the widow's son from death. How much more shall the Lord Jesus raise you up from death at the sound of the trumpet, in the twinking of an eye? For he has shown us an example in his own body.

13 If, then, you receive any other doctrine, God shall be a witness against you. Let no man trouble me, for I bear these bonds that I may win Christ. I therefore bear his marks in my body so that I may attain to the resurrection of the dead. Whoever abides in the rule which he has received by the blessed prophets and the holy Gospel shall receive a reward from the Lord, and when he rises from the dead shall obtain eternal life. But whoever transgresses these things, with him is the fire, and with those that walk in the same way, who are men without God, whom you must reject in the power

of the Lord, and peace, grace, and love shall be with you.

The Third Epistle of Paul to the Corinthians

SHORTER VERSION

1 Paul, a prisoner of Jesus Christ, unto the brethren which are in Corinth, greeting.

2 Being in the midst of many tribulations, I do not marvel if the teachings of the evil one spread quickly. For my Lord Jesus Christ will hasten his coming, and will set at nought (no longer endure the insolence of) them that falsify his words.

3 For I delivered to you in the beginning the things which I received of the apostles which were before me, who were at all times with Jesus Christ: namely, that our Lord Jesus Christ was born of Mary of the seed of David, the Holy Spirit being sent forth from heaven from the Father to her, so that he might come down into this world and redeem all flesh by his flesh, and raise us up from the dead in the flesh, just as he has shown us in himself as an example.

4 And because man was formed by his Father, he was therefore sought when he was lost, that he might be made alive by adoption. For to this end did God Almighty who made heaven and earth first send the prophets to the Jews, that they might be drawn away from their sins. For he planned to save the house of Israel. Therefore he conferred a portion of the spirit of Christ upon the prophets and sent them to the Jews first, and they proclaimed the true worship of God for a long period of time.

5 But the prince of iniquity, desiring to be God, laid hands on them and slew them, and bound all flesh by evil lusts.

6 But God Almighty, who is righteous, would not cast away his own creation, and sent his spirit into Mary, so that by that flesh whereby that wicked one had brought in death, by the same he should be shown to be overcome.

7 For by his own body Jesus Christ saved all flesh, so that he might show forth the temple of righteousness in his body, in whom we are saved.

8 They therefore are not children of righteousness, but children of wrath who reject the wisdom of God, saying that the heaven and the earth and all that are in them are not the work of God, for cursed are they,

following the teaching of the serpent, whom you should drive out and flee from their doctrine.

9 And as for that which they say, that there is no resurrection of the flesh, they indeed shall have no resurrection because they do not believe in him that is risen from the dead. For they do not know, O Corinthians, the seeds of wheat or of other seeds, how they are cast bare into the earth and are corrupted and rise again by the will of God with bodies and clothed. And not only that which is cast in rises again, but many times more blessing itself.

10 And if we must not take an example from seeds, you know how Jonah the son of Amathi—when he would not preach to them of Nineveh—was swallowed by the sea-monster. After three days and three nights God heard the prayer of Jonah out of the lowest hell, and no part of him was consumed, not even a hair nor an eyelash.

11 How much more shall he raise you that have believed in Christ Jesus, just as he himself arose. In the same way, a dead man also was cast upon the bones of the prophet Elisha by the children of Israel, and he arose, both body and soul and bones and spirit. How much more shall you who have been cast upon the body and bones and spirit of the Lord rise again in that day having your flesh whole?

12 If, then, you receive any other doctrine, let no man trouble me, for I bear these bonds that I may win Christ. I therefore bear his marks in my body so that I may attain to the resurrection of the dead. Whoever receives the rule which he has received by the blessed prophets and the holy Gospel shall receive a reward from the Lord. But whoever transgresses these things, with him is the fire, and with those that walk in the same way, which are a generation of vipers, whom you must reject in the power of the Lord, and peace shall be with you.

The Epistle to the Laodiceans

One curious feature of many manuscripts of the Latin Vulgate is the inclusion of the apocryphal Epistola ad Laodicenses. There is no extant Greek text for this epistle. It is not listed as a canonical book or cited as Scripture by the Church Fathers, and it was explicitly rejected by Jerome and others in ancient times. 1 Most scholars today think it was first composed in Latin, during the fourth century, although J.B. Lightfoot gives some reasons to suspect that it was translated from a Greek original. It appears to be a patchwork of phrases drawn from Paul's authentic epistles, put together by someone who wished to provide a plausible text for the Laodicean epistle mentioned in Colossians 4:16. ("And when this epistle hath been read among you, cause that it be read also in the church of the Laodiceans; and that ye also read the epistle from Laodicea.") We can only guess at the reason for this fraud. There is nothing of a controversial or polemical nature in it, nor even anything very interesting. Perhaps it was only intended to prevent some other less innocuous forgery from gaining acceptance under the same title. 2 For more information on the epistle see Lightfoot's very full discussion of it in his commentary on St. Paul's Epistles to the Colossians and to Philemon (London, 1876). Below I reproduce Lightfoot's critical text of the Epistola ad Laodicenses. The parallel English translation is my own. Further down I give the Middle English translation from the Wycliffe Bible.

---

1. In chapter 5 of his book De Viris Illustribus Jerome writes, "Legunt quidam et ad Laodicenses, sed ab omnibus exploditur." (Certain persons read also an epistle to the Laodiceans, but it is rejected by all.)

2. As Lightfoot observes, "The reference in Col, iv. 16 offered a strong temptation to the forger, and probably more than one unscrupulous person was induced by it to try his hand at falsification." Moreover, in the Muratorian fragment an epistle ad laudecenses [sic] is attributed to the infamous heretic Marcion.

EPISTLE TO THE LAODICEANS
From "The Apocryphal New Testament"
M.R. James-Translation and Notes
Oxford: Clarendon Press, 1924
Introduction
It exists only in Latin: the oldest copy is in the Fulda MS. written for Victor of Capua in 546. It is mentioned by various writers from the fourth century onwards, notably by Gregory the Great, to whose influence may ultimately be due the frequent occurrence of it in Bibles written in England; for it is commoner in English MSS. than in others. As will be seen, it is wholly uninteresting, and was merely written to justify or explain St. Paul's mention of the letter from Laodicea in Col. iv. 16.

1 Paul, an apostle not of men nor by man, but by Jesus Christ, unto the brethren that are at Laodicea.

2 Grace be unto you and peace from God the Father and the Lord Jesus Christ.

3 I give thanks unto Christ in all my prayers, that ye continue in him and persevere in his works, looking for the promise at the day of judgement.

4 Neither do the vain talkings of some overset you, which creep in, that they may turn you away from the truth of the Gospel which is preached by me.

5 And now shall God cause that they that are of me shall continue ministering unto the increase of the truth of the Gospel and accomplishing goodness, and the work of salvation, even eternal life.

5 And now are my bonds seen of all men, which I suffer in Christ, wherein I rejoice and am glad.

7 And unto me this is for everlasting salvation, which also is brought about by your prayers, and the ministry of the Holy Ghost, whether by life or by death.

8 For verily to me life is in Christ, and to die is joy.

9 And unto him (or And also) shall he work his mercy in you that ye may have the same love, and be of one mind.

10 Therefore, dearly beloved, as ye have heard in my presence so hold fast and work in the fear of God, and it shall be unto you for life eternal.

11 For it is God that worketh in you.

12 And do ye without afterthought whatsoever ye do.

13 And for the rest, dearly beloved, rejoice in Christ, and beware of them that are filthy in lucre.

Joseph Lumpkin

14 Let all your petitions be made openly before God, and be ye steadfast in the mind of Christ.

15 And what things are sound and true and sober and just and to be loved, do ye.

16 And what ye have heard and received, keep fast in your heart.

17 And peace shall be unto you.

18 The saints salute you.

19 The grace of the Lord Jesus be with your spirit.

20 And cause this epistle to be read unto them of Colossae, and the epistle of the Colossians to be read unto you.

The Gospel Of Thomas

These are the secret sayings which the living Jesus has spoken and Judas who is also Thomas (the twin) (Didymos Judas Thomas) wrote. (Living, after the resurrection.)

1. And he said: Whoever finds the interpretation of these sayings will not taste death.

1. He said to them: Whoever discovers the interpretation of these words shall never taste death.

John 8:51 Very truly I tell you, whoever keeps my word will never see death.

2. Jesus said: Let he who seeks not stop seeking until he finds, and when he finds he will be troubled, and when he has been troubled he will marvel (be astonished) and he will reign over all and in reigning, he will find rest.

2. Jesus said: Let he who seeks not stop until he finds, and when he finds he shall wonder and in wondering he shall reign, and in reigning he shall find rest.

3. Jesus said: If those who lead you say to you: Look, the Kingdom is in the sky, then the birds of the sky would enter before you. If they say to you: It is in the sea, then the fish of the sea would enter ahead you. But the Kingdom of God exists within you and it exists outside of you. Those who come to know (recognize) themselves will find it, and when you come to know yourselves you will become known and you will realize that you are the children of the Living Father. Yet if you do not come to know yourselves then you will dwell in poverty and it will be you who are that poverty.

3. Jesus said, If those who lead you say, "See, the Kingdom is in the sky," then the birds of the sky will precede you. If they say to you, "It is under the earth," then the fish of the sea will precede you. Rather, the Kingdom of God is inside of you, and it is outside of you.

Those who come to know themselves will find it; and when you come to know yourselves, you will understand that it is you who are the sons of the living Father. But if you will not know yourselves, you dwell in poverty and it is you who are that poverty.

Luke 17:20 And when he was demanded of by the Pharisees, when the kingdom of God should come, he answered them and said, The kingdom of God cometh not with observation: Neither shall they say, Lo here! Lo there! For, behold, the kingdom of God is within you

4. Jesus said: The person of old age will not hesitate to ask a little child of seven days about the place of life, and he will live. For many who are first will become last, (and the last will be first). And they will become one and the same.

4. Jesus said: Let the old man who has lived many days not hesitate to ask the child of seven days about the place of life; then he will live. For many that are first will be last, and last will be first, and they will become a single one.

Mark 9:35-37 He sat down, called the twelve, and said to them: Whoever wants to be first must be last of all and servant of all. Then he took a little child and put it among them, and taking it in his arms, he said to them: Whoever welcomes one such child in my name welcomes me, and whoever welcomes me welcomes not me but the one who sent me.

5. Jesus said: Recognize what is in front of your face, and what has been hidden from you will be revealed to you. For there is nothing hidden which will not be revealed (become manifest), and nothing buried that will not be raised.

5. Jesus said: Know what is in front of your face and what is hidden from you will be revealed to you.

For there is nothing hidden that will not be revealed.

Mark 4:22 For there is nothing hid, except to be made manifest; nor is anything secret, except it come to light.

Luke 12:2 Nothing is covered up that will not be revealed, or hidden that will not be known.

Matthew 10:26 So have no fear of them; for nothing is covered up that will not be uncovered, and nothing secret that will not become known.

6. His Disciples asked Him, they said to him: How do you want us to fast, and how will we pray? And how will we be charitable (give alms), and what laws of diet will we maintain? Jesus said: Do not lie, and do not practice what you hate, for everything is in the plain sight of Heaven. For there is nothing concealed that will not become manifest, and there is nothing covered that will not be exposed.

6. His disciples asked him, "How do you want us to fast? And how shall we pray? And how shall we give alms? And what kind of diet shall we follow?"
Jesus said, don't lie, and don't do what you hate to do, for all things are revealed before the truth. For there is nothing hidden which shall not be revealed.

Luke 11:1 He was praying in a certain place, and after he had finished, one of his disciples said to him, Lord, teach us to pray, as John taught his disciples.

7. Jesus said: Blessed is the lion that the man will eat, for the lion will become the man. Cursed is the man that the lion shall eat, and still the lion will become man.

Matthew 26:23-30 He who dipped his hand with me in the dish, the same will betray me. The Son of Man goes, even as it is written of him, but woe to that man through whom the Son of Man is betrayed! It would be better for that man if he had not been born. Judas, who betrayed him, answered, "It isn't me, is it, Rabbi?" He said to him, You said it. As they were eating, Jesus took bread, gave thanks for it, and broke it. He gave to the disciples, and said, Take, eat; this is my body. He took the cup, gave thanks, and gave to them, saying: All of you drink it, for this is my blood of the new covenant, which is poured out for many for the remission of sins. But I tell you that I will not drink of this fruit of the vine from now on, until that day when I drink it anew with you in my Father's Kingdom. When they had sung a hymn, they went out to the Mount of Olives.

8. And he said: The Kingdom of Heaven is like a wise fisherman who casts his net into the sea. He drew it up from the sea full of small fish. Among them he found a fine large fish. That wise fisherman threw all the small fish back into the sea and chose the large fish without hesitation. Whoever has ears to hear, let him hear!

Matthew 13:47-48 Again, the kingdom of heaven is like a net that was thrown into the sea and caught fish of every kind; when it was full, they drew it ashore, sat down, and put the good into baskets but threw out the bad.

9. Jesus said: Now, the sower came forth. He filled his hand and threw (the seeds). Some fell upon the road and the birds came and gathered them up. Others fell on the stone and they did not take deep enough roots in the soil, and so did not produce grain. Others fell among the thorns and they choked the seed, and the worm ate them. Others fell upon the good earth and it produced good fruit up toward the sky, it bore 60 fold and 120 fold.
Matthew 13:3-8 And he told them many things in parables, saying: Listen! A sower went out to sow. And as he sowed,

some seeds fell on the path, and the birds came and ate them up. Other seeds fell on rocky ground, where they did not have much soil, and they sprang up quickly, since they had no depth of soil. But when the sun rose, they were scorched; and since they had no root, they withered away. Other seeds fell among thorns, and the thorns grew up and choked them. Other seeds fell on good soil and brought forth grain, some a hundred fold, some sixty, some thirty.

Mark 4:2-9 And he taught them many things in parables, and in his teaching he said to them: Behold! A sower went out to sow. And as he sowed, some seed fell along the path, and the birds came and devoured it. Other seed fell on rocky ground, where it had not much soil, and immediately it sprang up, since it had no depth of soil; and when the sun rose it was scorched, and since it had no root it withered away. Other seed fell among thorns and the thorns grew up and choked it, and it yielded no grain. And other seeds fell into good soil and brought forth grain, growing up and increasing and yielding thirty fold and sixty fold and a hundred fold. And he said, He who has ears to hear, let him hear.

Luke 8:4-8 And when a great crowd came together and people from town after town came to him, he said in a parable: A sower went out to sow his seed; and as he sowed, some fell along the path, and was trodden under foot, and the birds of the air devoured it. And some fell on the rock; and as it grew up, it withered away, because it had no moisture. And some fell among thorns; and the thorns grew with it and choked it. And some fell into good soil and grew, and yielded a hundred fold. As he said this, he called out, He who has ears to hear, let him hear.

10. Jesus said: I have cast fire upon the world, and as you see, I guard it until it is ablaze.

Luke 12:49 I came to bring fire to the earth, and how I wish it were already kindled.

11. Jesus said: This sky will pass away, and the one above it will pass away. The dead are not alive, and the living will not die. In the days when you consumed what is dead, you made it alive. When you come into the Light, what will you do? On the day when you were united (one), you became separated (two). When you have become separated (two), what will you do?

Matthew 24:35 Heaven and earth will pass away, but my words will not pass away.

12. The Disciples said to Jesus: We know that you will go away from us. Who is it that will be our teacher?

Jesus said to them: Wherever you are (in the place

that you have come), you will go to James the Righteous, for whose sake Heaven and Earth were made (came into being).

13. Jesus said to his Disciples: Compare me to others, and tell me who I am like. Simon Peter said to him: You are like a righteous messenger (angel) of God. Matthew said to him: You are like a (wise) philosopher (of the heart). Thomas said to him: Teacher, my mouth is not capable of saying who you are like!

Jesus said: I'm not your teacher, now that you have drunk; you have become drunk from the bubbling spring that I have tended (measured out). And he took him, and withdrew and spoke three words to him: ahyh ashr ahyh (I am who I am).

Now when Thomas returned to his comrades, they inquired of him: What did Jesus say to you? Thomas said to them: If I tell you even one of the words which he spoke to me, you will take up stones and throw them at me, and fire will come from the stones to consume you.

Mark 8:27-30 Jesus went on with his disciples to the villages of Caesarea Philippi; and on the way he asked his disciples, Who do people say that I am? And they answered him, John the Baptist; and others, Elijah; and still others, one of the prophets. He asked them, But who do you say that I am? Peter answered him, You are the Messiah. And he sternly ordered them not to tell anyone about him.

14. Jesus said to them: If you fast, you will give rise to transgression (sin) for yourselves. And if you pray, you will be condemned. And if you give alms, you will cause harm (evil) to your spirits. And when you go into the countryside, if they take you in (receive you) then eat what they set before you and heal the sick among them. For what goes into your mouth will not defile you, but rather what comes out of your mouth, that is what will defile you.

Luke 10:8-9 Whenever you enter a town and its people welcome you, eat what is set before you; Cure the sick who are there, and say to them, The kingdom of God has come near to you.

Mark 7:15 There is nothing outside a person that by going in can defile, but the things that come out are what defile.

Matthew 15:11 It is not what goes into the mouth that defiles a man, but what comes out of the mouth, this defiles a man.

Romans 14:14 I know and am persuaded in the Lord Jesus that nothing is unclean in itself; but it is unclean for any one who thinks it unclean.

15. Jesus said: When you see him who was not born of woman, bow yourselves down upon your faces and worship him for he is your Father.

Galatians 4:3-5 Even so we, when we were children, were in bondage under the elements of the world: But when the fullness of the time was come, God sent forth his Son, made of a woman, made under the law, To redeem them that were under the law, that we might receive the adoption of sons.

16. Jesus said: People think perhaps I have come to spread peace upon the world. They do not know that I have come to cast dissention (conflict) upon the earth; fire, sword, war. For there will be five in a house. Three will be against two and two against three, the father against the son and the son against the father. And they will stand alone.

Matthew 10:34-36 Do not think that I have come to bring peace to the earth; I have not come to bring peace, but a sword. For I have come to set a man against his father, and a daughter against her mother, and a daughter-in-law against her mother-in-law; and one's foes will be members of one's own household.

Luke 12:51-53 Do you think that I have come to give peace on earth? No, I tell you, but rather division; for henceforth in one house there will be five divided, three against two and two against three; they will be divided, father against son and son against father, mother against daughter and daughter against her mother, mother-in-law against her daughter-in-law and daughter-in-law against her mother-in-law.

17. Jesus said: I will give to you what eye has not seen, what ear has not heard, what hand has not touched, and what has not occurred to the mind of man.

1 Cor 2:9 But, as it is written, What no eye has seen, nor ear heard, nor the human heart conceived, what God has prepared for those who love him.

18. The Disciples said to Jesus: Tell us how our end will come. Jesus said: Have you already discovered the beginning (origin), so that you inquire about the end? Where the beginning (origin) is, there the end will be. Blessed be he who will take his place in the beginning (stand at the origin) for he will know the end, and he will not experience death.

19. Jesus said: Blessed is he who came into being before he came into being. If you become my Disciples and heed my sayings, these stones will serve you. For there are five trees in paradise for you, which are undisturbed in summer and in winter and

their leaves do not fall. Whoever knows them will not experience death.

20. The Disciples said to Jesus: Tell us what the Kingdom of Heaven is like. He said to them: It is like a mustard seed, smaller than all other seeds and yet when it falls on the tilled earth, it produces a great plant and becomes shelter for the birds of the sky.

Mark 4:30-32 He also said, With what can we compare the kingdom of God, or what parable will we use for it? It is like a mustard seed, which, when sown upon the ground, is the smallest of all the seeds on earth; yet when it is sown it grows up and becomes the greatest of all shrubs, and puts forth large branches, so that the birds of the air can make nests in its shade.

Matthew 13:31-32 The kingdom of heaven is like a grain of mustard seed which a man took and sowed in his field; it is the smallest of all seeds, but when it has grown it is the greatest of shrubs and becomes a tree, so that the birds of the air come and make nests in its branches.
Luke 13.18-19 He said therefore, What is the kingdom of God like? And to what shall I compare it? It is like a grain of mustard seed which a man took and sowed in his garden; and it grew and became a tree, and the birds of the air made nests in its branches.

21. Mary said to Jesus: Who are your Disciples like? He said: They are like little children who are living in a field that is not theirs. When the owners of the field come, they will say: Let us have our field! It is as if they were naked in front of them (They undress in front of them in order to let them have what is theirs) and they give back the field. Therefore I say, if the owner of the house knows that the thief is coming, he will be alert before he arrives and will not allow him to dig through into the house to carry away his belongings. You, must be on guard and beware of the world (system). Prepare yourself (arm yourself) with great strength or the bandits will find a way to reach you, for the problems you expect will come. Let there be among you a person of understanding (awareness). When the crop ripened, he came quickly with his sickle in his hand to reap. Whoever has ears to hear, let him hear!

Matthew 24:43 But understand this: if the owner of the house had known in what part of the night the thief was coming, he would have stayed awake and would not have let his house be broken into.
Mark 4:26-29 He also said, The kingdom of God is as if someone would scatter seed on the ground, and would sleep and rise night and day, and the seed would sprout and grow, he does not know how. The earth produces of itself, first the stalk, then the head, then the full grain in the head. But when

the grain is ripe, at once he goes in with his sickle, because the harvest has come.

Luke 12:39-40 But know this, that if the householder had known at what hour the thief was coming, he would not have left his house to be broken into. You also must be ready; for the Son of man is coming at an unexpected hour.

22. Jesus saw little children who were being suckled. He said to his Disciples: These little children who are being suckled are like those who enter the Kingdom.

They said to him: Should we become like little children in order to enter the Kingdom?

Jesus said to them: When you make the two one, and you make the inside as the outside and the outside as the inside, when you make the above as the below, and if you make the male and the female one and the same (united male and female) so that the man will not be masculine (male) and the female be not feminine (female), when you establish an eye in the place of an eye and a hand in the place of a hand and a foot in the place of a foot and an likeness (image) in the place of a likeness (an image), then will you enter the Kingdom.

Luke 18:16 But Jesus called for them and said, Let the little children come to me, and do not stop them; for it is to such as these that the kingdom of God belongs. Truly I tell you, whoever does not receive the kingdom of God as a little child will never enter it.

Mark 9:43-48 If your hand causes you to stumble, cut it off; it is better for you to enter life maimed than to have two hands and to go to hell, to the unquenchable fire. And if your foot causes you to stumble, cut it off; it is better for you to enter life lame than to have two feet and to be thrown into hell. And if your eye causes you to stumble, tear it out; it is better for you to enter the kingdom of God with one eye than to have two eyes and to be thrown into hell, where the worm never dies, and the fire is never quenched.

Matthew 18:3-5 And said, Verily, I say unto you, unless you turn and become like children, you will never enter the kingdom of heaven. Whoever humbles himself like this child, he is the greatest in the kingdom of heaven. Whoever receives one such child in my name receives me;

Matthew 5:29-30 If your right eye causes you to sin, pluck it out and throw it away; it is better that you lose one of your members than that your whole body be thrown into hell. And if your right hand causes you to sin, cut it off and throw it away; it is better that you lose one of your members than that your whole body go into hell.

23. Jesus said: I will choose you, one out of a

thousand and two out of ten thousand and they will stand as a single one.

Matthew 20:16 So the last shall be first, and the first last: for many be called, but few chosen.

24. His Disciples said: Show us the place where you are (your place), for it is necessary for us to seek it. He said to them: Whoever has ears, let him hear! Within a man of light there is light, and he illumines the entire world. If he does not shine, he is darkness (there is darkness).

John 13:36 Simon Peter said to him, Lord, where are you going? Jesus answered, Where I am going, you cannot follow me now; but you will follow afterward.

Matthew 6:22-23 The eye is the lamp of the body. So, if your eye is healthy, your whole body will be full of light; but if your eye is unhealthy, your whole body will be full of darkness. If then the light in you is darkness, how great is the darkness!

Luke 11:34-36 Your eye is the lamp of your body; when your eye is sound, your whole body is full of light; but when it is not sound, your body is full of darkness. Therefore be careful lest the light in you be darkness. If then your whole body is full of light, having no part dark, it will be wholly bright, as when a lamp with its rays gives you light.

Note:
Early philosophers thought that light was transmitted from the eye and bounced back, allowing the person to sense the world at large. Ancient myths tell of Aphrodite constructing the human eye out of the four elements (earth, wind, fire, and water). The eye was held together by love. She kindled the fire of the soul and used it to project from the eyes so that it would act like a lantern, transmitting the light, thus allowing us to see.

Euclid, (330 BC to 260BC) speculated about the speed of light being instantaneous since you close your eyes, then open them again, even the distant objects appear immediately.

25. Jesus said: Love your friend (Brother) as your soul; protect him as you would the pupil of your own eye.

Romans 12:9-11 Let love be without dissimulation. Abhor that which is evil; cleave to that which is good. Be kindly affectioned one to another with brotherly love; in honour preferring one another; Not slothful in business; fervent in spirit; serving the Lord;

26. Jesus said: You see the speck in your brother's eye

but the beam that is in your own eye you do not see. When you remove the beam out of your own eye, then will you see clearly to remove the speck out of your brother's eye.

26. Jesus said, You see the splinter in your brother's eye, but you don't see the log in your own eye. When you take the log out of your own eye, then you will see well enough to remove the splinter from your brother's eye.

Matthew 7:3-5 Why do you see the speck in your neighbor's eye, but do not notice the log in your own eye? Or how can you say to your neighbor, Let me take the speck out of your eye, while the log is in your own eye? You hypocrite, first take the log out of your own eye, and then you will see clearly to take the speck out of your neighbor's eye.

Luke 6:41-42 Why do you see the speck that is in your brother's eye, but do not notice the log that is in your own eye? Or how can you say to your brother, Brother, let me take out the speck that is in your eye, when you yourself do not see the log that is in your own eye? You hypocrite, first take the log out of your own eye, and then you will see clearly to take out the speck that is in your brother's eye.

27. Jesus said: Unless you fast from the world (system), you will not find the Kingdom of God. Unless you keep the Sabbath (entire week) as Sabbath, you will not see the Father.

27. Jesus said: Unless you fast (abstain) from the world, you shall in no way find the Kingdom of God; and unless you observe the Sabbath as a Sabbath, you shall not see the Father.

28. Jesus said: I stood in the midst of the world. In the flesh I appeared to them. I found them all drunk; I found none thirsty among them. My soul grieved for the sons of men, for they are blind in their hearts and do not see that they came into the world empty they are destined (determined) to leave the world empty. However, now they are drunk. When they have shaken off their wine, then they will repent (change their ways).

28. Jesus said: I took my stand in the midst of the world, and they saw me in the flesh, and I found they were all drunk, and I found none of them were thirsty. And my soul grieved over the souls of men because they are blind in their hearts. They do not see that they came into the world empty and they are determined to leave the world empty. However, now they are drunk. When they have shaken off their wine, then they will change their ways.

29. Jesus said: If the flesh came into being because of

spirit, it is a marvel, but if spirit came into being because of the body, it would be a marvel of marvels. I marvel indeed at how great wealth has taken up residence in this poverty.

30. Jesus said: Where there are three gods, they are gods (Where there are three gods they are without god). Where there is only one, I say that I am with him. Lift the stone and there you will find me, Split the wood and there am I.

30. Jesus said: Where three are together they are not without God, and when there is one alone, I say, I am with him.

Note:
Many believe pages of the manuscript were misplaced and verses 30 and 77 should run together as a single verse.

77. Jesus said: I-Am the Light who is over all things, I-Am the All. From me all came forth and to me all return (The All came from me and the All has come to me). Split wood, there am I. Lift up the stone and there you will find me.

Matthew 18:20 For where two or three are gathered in my name, I am there among them.

31. Jesus said: No prophet is accepted in his own village, no physician heals those who know him.

31. Jesus said: A prophet is not accepted in his own country, neither can a doctor cure those that know him.

Mark 6:4 Then Jesus said to them, Prophets are not without honor, except in their hometown, and among their own kin, and in their own house.

Matthew 13:57 And they took offense at him. But Jesus said to them: A prophet is not without honor save in his own country and in his own house.

Luke 4:24 And he said, Truly, I say to you, no prophet is acceptable in his own country.

John 4:43-44 After the two days he departed to Galilee. For Jesus himself testified that a prophet has no honor in his own country.

32. Jesus said: A city being built (and established) upon a high mountain and fortified cannot fall nor can it be hidden.

32. Jesus said: A city built on a high hilltop and fortified can neither fall nor be hidden.

Matthew 5:14 You are the light of the world. A city built on a hill cannot be hid.

33. Jesus said: What you will hear in your ear preach from your rooftops. For no one lights a lamp and sets it under a basket nor puts it in a hidden place, but rather it is placed on a lamp stand so that everyone who comes and goes will see its light.

33. Jesus said: What you hear with one ear preach from your rooftops. For no one lights a lamp and sets it under a basket or hides, but rather it is placed on a lamp stand so that everyone who comes and goes will see its light.

Matthew 10:27 What I say to you in the dark, tell in the light; and what you hear whispered, proclaim from the housetops.

Luke 8:16 No one after lighting a lamp hides it under a jar, or puts it under a bed, but puts it on a lamp stand, so that those who enter may see the light.

Matthew 5:15 Nor do men light a lamp and put it under a bushel, but on a stand, and it gives light to all in the house.

Mark 4:21 And he said to them, Is a lamp brought in to be put under a bushel, or under a bed, and not on a stand?

Luke 11:33 No one after lighting a lamp puts it in a cellar or under a bushel, but on a stand, that those who enter may see the light.

34. Jesus said: If a blind person leads a blind person, both fall into a pit.

Matthew 15:14 Let them alone; they are blind guides of the blind. And if one blind person guides another, both will fall into a pit.

Luke 6:39 He also told them a parable: Can a blind man lead a blind man? Will they not both fall into a pit?

35. Jesus said: It is impossible for anyone to enter the house of a strong man to take it by force unless he binds his hands, then he will be able to loot his house.

Matthew 12:29 Or how can one enter a strong man's house and plunder his goods, unless he first binds the strong man? Then indeed he may plunder his house.

Luke 11:21-22 When a strong man, fully armed, guards his own palace, his goods are in peace; but when one stronger than he assails him and overcomes him, he takes away his armor in which he trusted, and divides his spoil.

Mark 3:27 But no one can enter a strong man's house and

plunder his property without first tying up the strong man; then indeed the house can be plundered.

36. Jesus said: Do not worry from morning to evening nor from evening to morning about the food that you will eat nor about what clothes you will wear. You are much superior to the Lilies which neither card nor spin. When you have no clothing, what do you wear? Who can add time to your life (increase your stature)? He himself will give to you your garment.

Matthew 6:25-31 Therefore I tell you, do not worry about your life, what you will eat or what you will drink, or about your body, what you will wear. Is not life more than food, and the body more than clothing? Look at the birds of the air; they neither sow nor reap nor gather into barns, and yet your heavenly Father feeds them. Are you not of more value than they? And can any of you by worrying add a single hour to your span of life? And why do you worry about clothing? Consider the lilies of the field, how they grow; they neither toil nor spin, yet I tell you, even Solomon in all his glory was not clothed like one of these. But if God so clothes the grass of the field, which is alive today and tomorrow is thrown into the oven, will he not much more clothe you--you of little faith? Therefore do not worry, saying, What will we eat? or What will we drink? or What will we wear?

Luke 12:22-23 And he said to his disciples, Therefore I tell you, do not be anxious about your life, what you shall eat, nor about your body, what you shall put on. For life is more than food, and the body more than clothing.

37. His Disciples said: When will you appear to us, and when will we see you?

Jesus said: When you take off your garments without being ashamed, and place your garments under your feet and tread on them as the little children do, then will you see the Son of the Living-One, and you will not be afraid.

37 His disciples said to him, when will you be visible to us, and when shall we be able to see you?

He said, when you strip naked without being ashamed and place your garments under your feet and tread on them as the little children do, then will you see the Son of the Living-One, and you will not be afraid.

38. Jesus said: Many times have you yearned to hear these sayings which I speak to you, and you have no one else from whom to hear them. There will be days when you will seek me but you will not find me.

39. Jesus said: The Pharisees and the Scribes have received the keys of knowledge, but they have hidden them. They did not go in, nor did they permit those who wished to enter to do so. However, you be as wise (astute) as serpents and innocent as doves.

39. Jesus said: The Pharisees and the Scribes have stolen the keys of heaven, but they have hidden them. They have entered in, but they did not permit those who wished to enter to do so. However, you be as wise as serpents and innocent as doves.

Luke 11:52 Woe to you lawyers! For you have taken away the key of knowledge; you did not enter yourselves, and you hindered those who were entering.
Matthew 10:16 See, I am sending you out like sheep into the midst of wolves; so be wise as serpents and innocent as doves.
Matthew 23.13 But woe unto you, scribes and Pharisees, hypocrites! because you shut the kingdom of heaven against men; for you neither enter yourselves, nor allow those who would enter to go in.

40. Jesus said: A grapevine has been planted outside the (vineyard of the) Father, and since it is not viable (supported) it will be pulled up by its roots and destroyed.

Matthew 15:13 He answered, Every plant that my heavenly Father has not planted will be uprooted.

41. Jesus said: Whoever has (it) in his hand, to him will (more) be given. And whoever does not have, from him will be taken even the small amount which he has.

Matthew 25:29 For to all those who have, more will be given, and they will have an abundance; but from those who have nothing, even what they have will be taken away.
Luke 19:26 I tell you, that to every one who has will more be given; but from him who has not, even what he has will be taken away.

42. Jesus said: Become passers-by.

43. His Disciples said to him: Who are you, that you said these things to us?

Jesus said to them: You do not recognize who I am from what I said to you, but rather you have become like the Jews who either love the tree and hate its fruit, or love the fruit and hate the tree.

John 8:25 They said to him, Who are you? Jesus said to them, Why do I speak to you at all?
Matthew 7:16-20 You will know them by their fruits. Are grapes gathered from thorns, or figs from thistles? In the same way, every good tree bears good fruit, but the bad tree

bears bad fruit. A good tree cannot bear bad fruit, nor can a bad tree bear good fruit. Every tree that does not bear good fruit is cut down and thrown into the fire. Thus you will know them by their fruits.

44. Jesus said: Whoever blasphemes against the Father, it will be forgiven him. And whoever blasphemes against the Son, it will be forgiven him. Yet whoever blasphemes against the Holy Spirit, it will not be forgiven him neither on earth nor in heaven.

Mark 3:28-29 Truly I tell you, people will be forgiven for their sins and whatever blasphemies they utter; but whoever blasphemes against the Holy Spirit can never have forgiveness, but is guilty of an eternal sin.

Matthew 12:31-32 Therefore I tell you, every sin and blasphemy will be forgiven men, but the blasphemy against the Spirit will not be forgiven. And whoever says a word against the Son of man will be forgiven; but whoever speaks against the Holy Spirit will not be forgiven, either in this age or in the age to come.

Luke 12:10 And every one who speaks a word against the Son of man will be forgiven him; but he who blasphemes against the Holy Spirit will not be forgiven.

45. Jesus said: Grapes are not harvested from thorns, nor are figs gathered from thistles, for they do not give fruit. A good person brings forth goodness out of his storehouse. A bad person brings forth evil out of his evil storehouse which is in his heart, and he speaks evil, for out of the abundance of the heart he brings forth evil.

Luke 6:43-45 For no good tree bears bad fruit, nor again does a bad tree bear good fruit; for each tree is known by its own fruit. For figs are not gathered from thorns, nor are grapes picked from a bramble bush. The good man out of the good treasure of his heart produces good, and the evil man out of his evil treasure produces evil; for out of the abundance of the heart his mouth speaks.

46. Jesus said: From Adam until John the Baptist there is none born of women who surpasses John the Baptist, so that his eyes should not be downcast (lowered). Yet I have said that whoever among you becomes like a child will know the Kingdom, and he will be greater than John.

Matthew 11:11 Truly I tell you, among those born of women no one has arisen greater than John the Baptist; yet the least in the kingdom of heaven is greater than he.

Luke 7:28 I tell you, among those born of women none is greater than John; yet he who is least in the kingdom of God is greater than he.

Matthew 18:2-4 He called a child, whom he put among them, and said, Truly I tell you, unless you change and become like children, you will never enter the kingdom of heaven. Whoever becomes humble like this child is the greatest in the kingdom of heaven.

47. Jesus said: It is impossible for a man to mount two horses or to draw two bows, and a servant cannot serve two masters, otherwise he will honor the one and disrespect the other. No man drinks vintage wine and immediately desires to drink new wine, and they do not put new wine into old wineskins or they would burst, and they do not put vintage wine into new wineskins or it would spoil (sour). They do not sew an old patch on a new garment because that would cause a split.

Matthew 6:24 No one can serve two masters; for a slave will either hate the one and love the other, or be devoted to the one and despise the other. You cannot serve God and wealth.

Matthew 9:16-17 No one sews a piece of cloth, not yet shrunk, on an old cloak, for the patch pulls away from the cloak, and a worse tear is made. Neither is new wine put into old wineskins; otherwise, the skins burst, and the wine is spilled, and the skins are destroyed; but new wine is put into fresh wineskins, and so both are preserved.

Mark 2:21-22 No one sews a piece of unshrunk cloth on an old garment; if he does, the patch tears away from it, the new from the old, and a worse tear is made. And no one puts new wine into old wineskins; if he does, the wine will burst the skins, and the wine is lost, and so are the skins; but new wine is for fresh skins.

Luke 5:36-39 He told them a parable also: No one tears a piece from a new garment and puts it upon an old garment; if he does, he will tear the new, and the piece from the new will not match the old. And no one puts new wine into old wineskins; if he does, the new wine will burst the skins and it will be spilled, and the skins will be destroyed. But new wine must be put into fresh wineskins. And no one after drinking old wine desires new; for he says, "The old is good."

48. Jesus said: If two make peace with each other in this one house, they will say to the mountain: Be moved! and it will be moved.
Matthew 18:19 Again, truly I tell you, if two of you agree on earth about anything you ask, it will be done for you by my Father in heaven.

Mark 11:23-24 Truly I tell you, if you say to this mountain, Be taken up and thrown into the sea, and if you do not doubt in your heart, but believe that what you say will come to pass, it will be done for you. So I tell you, whatever you ask

for in prayer, believe that you have received it, and it will be yours.

Matthew 17:20 He said to them, Because of your little faith. For truly, I say to you, if you have faith as a grain of mustard seed, you will say to this mountain, Move from here to there, and it will move; and nothing will be impossible to you.

49. Jesus said: Blessed is the solitary and chosen, for you will find the Kingdom. You have come from it, and unto it you will return.

Matthew 5:1-3 And seeing the multitudes, he went up into a mountain: and when he was set, his disciples came unto him: And he opened his mouth, and taught them, saying, Blessed are the poor in spirit: for theirs is the kingdom of heaven.

John 20:28-30 And Thomas answered and said unto him, My LORD and my God. Jesus saith unto him, Thomas, because thou hast seen me, thou hast believed: blessed are they that have not seen, and yet have believed. And many other signs truly did Jesus in the presence of his disciples, which are not written in this book:

50. Jesus said: If they say to you: From where do you come? Say to them: We have come from the Light, the place where the Light came into existence of its own accord and he stood and appeared in their image. If they say to you: Is it you? (Who are you?), say: We are his Sons and we are the chosen of the Living Father. If they ask you: What is the sign of your Father in you? Say to them: It is movement with rest (peace in the midst of motion or chaos).

51. His Disciples said to him: When will the rest of the dead occur, and when will the New World come? He said to them: That which you look for has already come, but you do not recognize it.

52. His Disciples said to him: Twenty-four prophets preached in Israel, and they all spoke of (in) you. He said to them: You have ignored the Living-One who is in your presence and you have spoken only of the dead.

53. His Disciples said to him: Is circumcision beneficial or not? He said to them: If it were beneficial, their father would beget them already circumcised from their mother. However, the true spiritual circumcision has become entirely beneficial.

Jeremiah 4:3-5 For thus saith the LORD to the men of Judah and Jerusalem, Break up your fallow ground, and sow not among thorns. Circumcise yourselves to the LORD, and take away the foreskins of your heart, ye men of Judah and inhabitants of Jerusalem: lest my fury come forth like fire, and burn that none can quench it, because of the evil of your doings. Declare ye in Judah, and publish in Jerusalem; and say, Blow ye the trumpet in the land: cry, gather together, and say, Assemble yourselves, and let us go into the defenced cities.

54. Jesus said: Blessed be the poor, for yours is the Kingdom of the Heaven.

Matthew 6:20 Then he looked up at his disciples and said: Blessed are you who are poor, for yours is the kingdom of God.

Luke 6:20 And he lifted up his eyes on his disciples, and said: Blessed are you poor, for yours is the kingdom of God.

Matthew 5:3 Blessed are the poor in spirit, for theirs is the kingdom of heaven.

55. Jesus said: Whoever does not hate his father and his mother will not be able to become my Disciple. And whoever does not hate his brothers and his sisters and does not take up his own cross in my way, will not become worthy of me.

Luke 14:26-27 If any one comes to me and does not hate his own father and mother and wife and children and brothers and sisters, yes, and even his own life, he cannot be my disciple. Whoever does not bear his own cross and come after me, cannot be my disciple.
John 17:11-21 And now I am no more in the world, but these are in the world, and I come to thee. Holy Father, keep through thine own name those whom thou hast given me, that they may be one, as we are. While I was with them in the world, I kept them in thy name: those that thou gavest me I have kept, and none of them is lost, but the son of perdition; that the scripture might be fulfilled. And now come I to thee; and these things I speak in the world, that they might have my joy fulfilled in themselves. I have given them thy word; and the world hath hated them, because they are not of the world, even as I am not of the world. I pray not that thou shouldest take them out of the world, but that thou shouldest keep them from the evil. They are not of the world, even as I am not of the world. Sanctify them through thy truth: thy word is truth. As thou hast sent me into the world, even so have I also sent them into the world. And for their sakes I sanctify myself, that they also might be sanctified through the truth. Neither pray I for these alone, but for them also which shall believe on me through their word; That they all may be one; as thou, Father, art in me, and I in thee, that they also may be one in us: that the world may believe that thou hast sent me.

56. Jesus said: Whoever has come to understand the world (system) has found a corpse, and whoever has found a corpse, is superior to the world (of him the

system is not worthy).

Hebrews 11:37-40 They were stoned, they were sawn asunder, were tempted, were slain with the sword: they wandered about in sheepskins and goatskins; being destitute, afflicted, tormented; (Of whom the world was not worthy:) they wandered in deserts, and in mountains, and in dens and caves of the earth. And these all, having obtained a good report through faith, received not the promise: God having provided some better thing for us, that they without us should not be made perfect.

57. Jesus said: The Kingdom of the Father is like a person who has good seed. His enemy came by night and sowed a weed among the good seed. The man did not permit them to pull up the weed, he said to them: perhaps you will intend to pull up the weed and you pull up the wheat along with it. But, on the day of harvest the weeds will be very visible and then they will pull them and burn them.
Matthew 13:24-30 He put before them another parable: The kingdom of heaven may be compared to someone who sowed good seed in his field; but while everybody was asleep, an enemy came and sowed weeds among the wheat, and then went away. So when the plants came up and bore grain, then the weeds appeared as well. And the slaves of the householder came and said to him, Master, did you not sow good seed in your field? Where, then, did these weeds come from? He answered, An enemy has done this. The slaves said to him, Then do you want us to go and gather them? But he replied, No; for in gathering the weeds you would uproot the wheat along with them. Let both of them grow together until the harvest; and at harvest time I will tell the reapers, Collect the weeds first and bind them in bundles to be burned, but gather the wheat into my barn.

58. Jesus said: Blessed is the person who has suffered, for he has found life. (Blessed is he who has suffered to find life and found life).

Matthew 11:28 Come to me, all you that are weary and are carrying heavy burdens, and I will give you rest.

59. Jesus said: Look to the Living-One while you are alive, otherwise, you might die and seek to see him and will be unable to find him.

John 7:34 You will search for me, but you will not find me; and where I am, you cannot come.

John 13:33 Little children, I am with you only a little longer. You will look for me; and as I said to the Jews so now I say to you, Where I am going, you cannot come.

60. They saw a Samaritan carrying a lamb, on his way to Judea. Jesus said to them: Why does he take the lamb with him? They said to him: So that he may

kill it and eat it. He said to them: While it is alive he will not eat it, but only after he kills it and it becomes a corpse. They said: How could he do otherwise? He said to them: Look for a place of rest for yourselves, otherwise, you might become corpses and be eaten.

61. Jesus said: Two will rest on a bed and one will die and the other will live. Salome said: Who are you, man? As if sent by someone, you laid upon my bed and you ate from my table. Jesus said to her: I-Am he who is from that which is whole (the undivided). I have been given the things of my Father. Salome said: I'm your Disciple. Jesus said to her: Thus, I say that whenever someone is one (undivided)
he will be filled with light, yet whenever he is divided (chooses) he will be filled with darkness.

Luke 17:34 I tell you, on that night there will be two in one bed; one will be taken and the other left.

62. Jesus said: I tell my mysteries to those who are worthy of my mysteries. Do not let your right hand know what your left hand is doing.

Mark 4:11 And he said to them, To you has been given the secret of the kingdom of God, but for those outside, everything comes in parables.
Matthew 6:3 But when you give alms, do not let your left hand know what your right hand is doing.
Luke 8:10 He said, To you it has been given to know the secrets of the kingdom of God; but for others they are in parables, so that seeing they may not see, and hearing they may not understand.
Matthew 13:10-11 Then the disciples came and said to him, Why do you speak to them in parables? And he answered them, To you it has been given to know the secrets of the kingdom of heaven, but to them it has not been given.

63. Jesus said: There was a wealthy person who had much money, and he said: I will use my money so that I may sow and reap and replant, to fill my storehouses with grain so that I lack nothing. This was his intention (is what he thought in his heart) but that same night he died. Whoever has ears, let him hear!

Luke 12:21 Then he told them a parable: The land of a rich man produced abundantly. And he thought to himself, What should I do, for I have no place to store my crops? Then he said, I will do this: I will pull down my barns and build larger ones, and there I will store all my grain and my goods. And I will say to my soul, Soul, you have ample goods laid up for many years; relax, eat, drink, be merry. But God said to him, You fool! This very night your life is being demanded of you. And the things you have prepared, whose

will they be? So it is with those who store up treasures for themselves but are not rich toward God.

64. Jesus said: A person had houseguests, and when he had prepared the banquet in their honor he sent his servant to invite the guests. He went to the first, he said to him: My master invites you. He replied: I have to do business with some merchants. They are coming to see me this evening. I will go to place my orders with them. I ask to be excused from the banquet. He went to another, he said to him: My master has invited you. He replied to him: I have just bought a house and they require me for a day. I will have no spare time. He came to another, he said to him: My master invites you. He replied to him: My friend is getting married and I must arrange a banquet for him. I will not be able to come. I ask to be excused from the banquet. He went to another, he said to him: My master invites you. He replied to him: I have bought a farm. I go to receive the rent. I will not be able to come. I ask to be excused. The servant returned, he said to his master: Those whom you have invited to the banquet have excused themselves. The master said to his servant: Go out to the roads, bring those whom you find so that they may feast. And he said: Businessmen and merchants will not enter the places of my Father.

Luke 14:16-24 Then Jesus said to him:, Someone gave a great dinner and invited many. At the time for the dinner he sent his slave to say to those who had been invited, Come; for everything is ready now. But they all alike began to make excuses. The first said to him, I have bought a piece of land, and I must go out and see it; please accept my regrets. Another said, I have bought five yoke of oxen, and I am going to try them out; please accept my regrets. Another said, I have just been married, and therefore I cannot come. So the slave returned and reported this to his master. Then the owner of the house became angry and said to his slave, Go out at once into the streets and lanes of the town and bring in the poor, the crippled, the blind, and the lame. And the slave said, Sir, what you ordered has been done, and there is still room. Then the master said to the slave, Go out into the roads and lanes, and compel people to come in, so that my house may be filled. For I tell you, none of those who were invited will taste my dinner.
Matthew 19:23 Then Jesus said to his disciples, Truly I tell you, it will be hard for a rich person to enter the kingdom of heaven.
Matthew 22:1-14 And Jesus answered and spake unto them again by parables, and said, The kingdom of heaven is like unto a certain king, which made a marriage for his son, and sent his servants to call those who were invited to the marriage feast; but they would not come. Again he sent other servants, saying, Tell those who are invited, Behold, I have made ready my dinner, my oxen and my fat calves are killed, and everything is ready; come to the marriage feast. But they made light of it and went off, one to his farm, another to his

business, while the rest seized his servants, treated them shamefully, and killed them. The king was angry, and he sent his troops and destroyed those murderers and burned their city. Then he said to his servants, The wedding is ready, but those invited were not worthy. Go therefore to the thoroughfares, and invite to the marriage feast as many as you find. And those servants went out into the streets and gathered all whom they found, both bad and good; so the wedding hall was filled with guests. But when the king came in to look at the guests, he saw there a man who had no wedding garment; and he said to him, Friend, how did you get in here without a wedding garment? And he was speechless. Then the king said to the attendants, Bind him hand and foot, and cast him into the outer darkness; there men will weep and gnash their teeth. For many are called, but few are chosen.

65. He said: A kind person who owned a vineyard leased it to tenants so that they would work it and he would receive the fruit from them. He sent his servant so that the tenants would give to him the fruit of the vineyard. They seized his servant and beat him nearly to death. The servant went, he told his master what had happened. His master said: Perhaps they did not recognize him. So, he sent another servant. The tenants beat him also. Then the owner sent his son. He said: Perhaps they will respect my son. Since the tenants knew that he was the heir to the vineyard, they seized him and killed him. Whoever has ears, let him hear!

Matthew 21:33-39 Listen to another parable. There was a landowner who planted a vineyard, put a fence around it, dug a wine press in it, and built a watchtower. Then he leased it to tenants and went to another country. When the harvest time had come, he sent his slaves to the tenants to collect his produce. But the tenants seized his slaves and beat one, killed another, and stoned another. Again he sent other slaves, more than the first; and they treated them in the same way. Finally he sent his son to them, saying, They will respect my son. But when the tenants saw the son, they said to themselves, This is the heir; come, let us kill him and get his inheritance. So they seized him, threw him out of the vineyard, and killed him.

Mark 12:1-9 And he began to speak to them in parables. A man planted a vineyard, and set a hedge around it, and dug a pit for the wine press, and built a tower, and let it out to tenants, and went into another country. When the time came, he sent a servant to the tenants, to get from them some of the fruit of the vineyard. And they took him and beat him, and sent him away empty-handed. Again he sent to them another servant, and they wounded him in the head, and treated him shamefully. And he sent another, and him they killed; and so with many others, some they beat and some they killed. He had still one other, a beloved son; finally he sent him to them, saying, They will respect my son. But

those tenants said to one another, This is the heir; come, let us kill him, and the inheritance will be ours. And they took him and killed him, and cast him out of the vineyard. What will the owner of the vineyard do? He will come and destroy the tenants, and give the vineyard to others.

Luke 20:9-16 And he began to tell the people this parable: A man planted a vineyard, and let it out to tenants, and went into another country for a long while. When the time came, he sent a servant to the tenants, that they should give him some of the fruit of the vineyard; but the tenants beat him, and sent him away empty-handed. And he sent another servant; him also they beat and treated shamefully, and sent him away empty-handed. And he sent yet a third; this one they wounded and cast out. 13 Then the owner of the vineyard said, What shall I do? I will send my beloved son; it may be they will respect him. 14 But when the tenants saw him, they said to themselves, This is the heir; let us kill him, that the inheritance may be ours. 15 And they cast him out of the vineyard and killed him. What then will the owner of the vineyard do to them? 16 He will come and destroy those tenants, and give the vineyard to others. When they heard this, they said, God forbid!

66. Jesus said: Show me the stone which the builders have rejected. It is that one that is the cornerstone (keystone).

Matthew 21:42 Jesus said to them, Have you never read in the scriptures: The very stone which the builders rejected has become the
head of the corner; this was the Lord's doing, and it is marvelous in our eyes?

Mark 12:10-11 Have you not read this scripture: The very stone which the builders rejected has become the head of the corner; this was the Lord's doing, and it is marvelous in our eyes?

Luke 20:17 But he looked at them and said, What then does this text mean: The stone that the builders rejected has become the cornerstone?

67. Jesus said: Those who know everything but themselves, lack everything. (whoever knows the all and still feels a personal lacking, he is completely deficient).

Jeremiah 17:5- 10 Thus saith the LORD; Cursed be the man that trusteth in man, and maketh flesh his arm, and whose heart departeth from the LORD. For he shall be like the heath in the desert, and shall not see when good cometh; but shall inhabit the parched places in the wilderness, in a salt land and not inhabited. Blessed is the man that trusteth in the LORD, and whose hope the LORD is. For he shall be as a tree planted by the waters, and that spreadeth out her roots by the river, and shall not see when heat cometh, but her leaf *shall be green; and shall not be careful in the year of drought, neither shall cease from yielding fruit. The heart is deceitful above all things, and desperately wicked: who can know it? I the LORD search the heart, I try the reins, even to give every man according to his ways, and according to the fruit of his doings.*

68. Jesus said: Blessed are you when you are hated and persecuted, but they themselves will find no reason why you have been persecuted.

Matthew 5:11 Blessed are you when people revile you and persecute you and utter all kinds of evil against you falsely on my account.

Luke 6:22 Blessed are you when men hate you, and when they exclude you and revile you, and cast out your name as evil, on account of the Son of man!

69. Jesus said: Blessed are those who have been persecuted in their heart these are they who have come to know the Father in truth. Jesus said: Blessed are the hungry, for the stomach of him who desires to be filled will be filled.

Matthew 5:8 Blessed are the pure in heart, for they will see God.

Luke 6:21 Blessed are you who are hungry now, for you will be filled.

70. Jesus said: If you bring forth what is within you, it will save you. If you do not have it within you to bring forth, that which you lack will destroy you.

71. Jesus said: I will destroy this house, and no one will be able to build it again.

Mark 14:58 We heard him say, I will destroy this temple that is made with hands, and in three days I will build another, not made with hands.

72. A person said to him: Tell my brothers to divide the possessions of my father with me. He said to him: Oh man, who made me a divider? He turned to his Disciples, he said to them: I'm not a divider, am I?

Luke 12:13-15 Someone in the crowd said to him, Teacher, tell my brother to divide the family inheritance with me. But he said to him, Friend, who set me to be a judge or arbitrator over you? And he said to them, Take care! Be on your guard against all kinds of greed; for one's life does not consist in the abundance of possessions.

73. Jesus said: The harvest is indeed plentiful, but the workers are few. Ask the Lord to send workers for the harvest.

Matthew 9:37-38 Then he said to his disciples, The harvest is plentiful, but the laborers are few; therefore ask the Lord of the harvest to send out laborers into his harvest.

74. He said: Lord, there are many around the well, yet there is nothing in the well. How is it that many are around the well and no one goes into it?

75. Jesus said: There are many standing at the door, but only those who are alone are the ones who will enter into the Bridal Chamber.

Matthew 25:1-8 Then shall the kingdom of heaven be likened unto ten virgins, which took their lamps, and went forth to meet the bridegroom. And five of them were wise, and five were foolish. They that were foolish took their lamps, and took no oil with them: But the wise took oil in their vessels with their lamps. While the bridegroom tarried, they all slumbered and slept. And at midnight there was a cry made, Behold, the bridegroom cometh; go ye out to meet him. Then all those virgins arose, and trimmed their lamps. And the foolish said unto the wise, Give us of your oil; for our lamps are gone out.

76. Jesus said: The Kingdom of the Father is like a rich merchant who found a pearl. The merchant was prudent. He sold his fortune and bought the one pearl for himself. You also, seek for his treasure which does not fail, which endures where no moth can come near to eat it nor worm to devour it.

Matthew 13:45-46 Again, the kingdom of heaven is like a merchant in search of fine pearls; on finding one pearl of great value, he went and sold all that he had and bought it.

Matthew 6:19-20 Do not store up for yourselves treasures on earth, where moth and rust consume and where thieves break in and steal; but store up for yourselves treasures in heaven, where neither moth nor rust consumes and where thieves do not break in and steal.

77. Jesus said: I-Am the Light who is over all things, I-Am the All. From me all came forth and to me all return (The All came from me and the All has come to me). Split wood, there am I. Lift up the stone and there you will find me.

Note: Many scholars believe the order of verses 30 and 77 were misplaced and these two verses should be connected as one verse.

30. Jesus said: Where there are three gods, they are gods (Where there are three gods they are without god). Where there is only one, I say that I am with him. Lift the stone and there you will find me, Split the wood and there am I.

John 8:12 Again Jesus spoke to them, saying, I am the light of the world. Whoever follows me will never walk in darkness but will have the light of life.

John 1:3 All things came into being through him, and without him not one thing came into being.

78. Jesus said: Why did you come out to the wilderness; to see a reed shaken by the wind? And to see a person dressed in fine (soft – plush) garments like your rulers and your dignitaries? They are clothed in plush garments, and they are not able to recognize (understand) the truth.

Matthew 11:7-9 As they went away, Jesus began to speak to the crowds about John: What did you go out into the wilderness to look at? A reed shaken by the wind? What then did you go out to see? Someone dressed in soft robes? Look, those who wear soft robes are in royal palaces. What then did you go out to see? A prophet? Yes, I tell you, and more than a prophet.

79. A woman from the multitude said to him: Blessed is the womb which bore you, and the breasts which nursed you! He said to her: Blessed are those who have heard the word (meaning) of the Father and have truly kept it. For there will be days when you will say: Blessed be the womb which has not conceived and the breasts which have not nursed.

Luke 11:27-28 While he was saying this, a woman in the crowd raised her voice and said to him, Blessed is the womb that bore you and the breasts that nursed you! But he said, Blessed rather are those who hear the word of God and obey it!

Luke 23:29 For the days are surely coming when they will say, Blessed are the barren, and the wombs that never bore, and the breasts that never nursed.

80. Jesus said: Whoever has come to understand (recognize) the world (world system) has found the body (corpse), and whoever has found the body (corpse), of him the world (world system) is not worthy.

Hebrews 11:37-40 They were stoned, they were sawn asunder, were tempted, were slain with the sword: they wandered about in sheepskins and goatskins; being destitute, afflicted, tormented; (Of whom the world was not worthy:) they wandered in deserts, and in mountains, and in dens and caves of the earth. And these all, having obtained a good report through faith, received not the promise: God having provided some better thing for us, that they without us should not be made perfect.

81. Jesus said: Whoever has become rich should

reign, and let whoever has power renounce it.

82. Jesus said: Whoever is close to me is close to the fire, and whoever is far from me is far from the Kingdom.

John 14:6-9 Jesus saith unto him, I am the way, the truth, and the life: no man cometh unto the Father, but by me. If ye had known me, ye should have known my Father also: and from henceforth ye know him, and have seen him. Philip saith unto him, Lord, show us the Father, and it sufficeth us. Jesus saith unto him, Have I been so long time with you, and yet hast thou not known me, Philip? he that hath seen me hath seen the Father;

83. Jesus said: Images are visible to man but the light which is within them is hidden. The light of the father will be revealed, but he (his image) is hidden in the light.

84. Jesus said: When you see your reflection, you rejoice. Yet when you perceive your images which have come into being before you, which neither die nor can be seen, how much will you have to bear?

85. Jesus said: Adam came into existence from a great power and a great wealth, and yet he was not worthy of you. For if he had been worthy, he would not have tasted death.

86. Jesus said: The foxes have their dens and the birds have their nests, yet the Son of Man has no place to lay his head for rest.

Matthew 8:20 And Jesus said to him, Foxes have holes, and birds of the air have nests; but the Son of Man has nowhere to lay his head.

87. Jesus said: Wretched is the body which depends upon another body, and wretched is the soul which depends on these two (upon their being together).

88. Jesus said: The angels and the prophets will come to you, and what they will give you belongs to you. And you will give them what you have, and say among yourselves: When will they come to take (receive) what belongs to them?

89. Jesus said: Why do you wash the outside of your cup? Do you not understand (mind) that He who creates the inside is also He who creates the outside?

Luke 11:39-40 Then the Lord said to him, Now you Pharisees clean the outside of the cup and of the dish, but inside you are full of greed and wickedness. You fools! Did not the one who made the outside make the inside also?

90. Jesus said: Come unto me, for my yoke is comfortable (natural) and my lordship is gentle — and you will find rest for yourselves.

Matthew 11:28-30 Come to me, all you that are weary and are carrying heavy burdens, and I will give you rest. Take my yoke upon you, and learn from me; for I am gentle and humble in heart, and you will find rest for your souls. For my yoke is easy, and my burden is light.
Acts 15:5-17 But there rose up certain of the sect of the Pharisees which believed, saying, That it was needful to circumcise them, and to command them to keep the law of Moses. And the apostles and elders came together for to consider of this matter. And when there had been much disputing, Peter rose up, and said unto them, Men and brethren, ye know how that a good while ago God made choice among us, that the Gentiles by my mouth should hear the word of the gospel, and believe. And God, which knoweth the hearts, bare them witness, giving them the Holy Ghost, even as he did unto us; And put no difference between us and them, purifying their hearts by faith. Now therefore why tempt ye God, to put a yoke upon the neck of the disciples, which neither our fathers nor we were able to bear? But we believe that through the grace of the LORD Jesus Christ we shall be saved, even as they. Then all the multitude kept silence, and gave audience to Barnabas and Paul, declaring what miracles and wonders God had wrought among the Gentiles by them. And after they had held their peace, James answered, saying, Men and brethren, hearken unto me: Simeon hath declared how God at the first did visit the Gentiles, to take out of them a people for his name. And to this agree the words of the prophets; as it is written, After this I will return, and will build again the tabernacle of David, which is fallen down; and I will build again the ruins thereof, and I will set it up: That the residue of men might seek after the Lord, and all the Gentiles, upon whom my name is called, saith the Lord, who doeth all these things.

91. They said to him: Tell us who you are, so that we may believe in you. He said to them: You examine the face of the sky and of the earth, yet you do not recognize Him who is here with you, and you do not know how to seek in (to inquire of Him at) this moment (you do not know how to take advantage of this opportunity).

John 9:36 He answered, And who is he, sir? Tell me, so that I may believe in him.

Luke 12:54-56 He also said to the crowds, When you see a cloud rising in the west, you immediately say, It is going to rain; and so it happens. And when you see the south wind blowing, you say, There will be scorching heat; and it happens. You hypocrites! You know how to interpret the appearance of earth and sky, but why do you not know how to interpret the present time?

92. Jesus said: Seek and you will find. But in the past I did not answer the questions you asked. Now I wish to tell them to you, but you do not ask about (no longer seek) them.

Matthew 7:7 Ask, and it will be given you; search, and you will find; knock, and the door will be opened for you.

93. Jesus said: Do not give what is sacred to the dogs, lest they throw it on the dung heap. Do not cast the pearls to the swine, lest they cause it to become dung (mud).

Matthew 7:6 Do not give what is holy to dogs; and do not throw your pearls before swine, or they will trample them under foot and turn and maul you.

94. Jesus said: Whoever seeks will find. And whoever knocks, it will be opened to him.

Matthew 7:8 For everyone who asks receives, and everyone who searches finds, and for everyone who knocks, the door will be opened.

95. Jesus said: If you have money, do not lend at interest, but rather give it to those from whom you will not be repaid.

Luke 6:34-35 If you lend to those from whom you hope to receive, what credit is that to you? Even sinners lend to sinners, to receive as much again. But love your enemies, do good, and lend, expecting nothing in return. Your reward will be great, and you will be children of the Most High; for he is kind to the ungrateful and the wicked.
96. Jesus said: The Kingdom of the Father is like a woman who has taken a little yeast and hidden it in dough. She produced large loaves of it. Whoever has ears, let him hear!

Matthew 13:33 He told them another parable: The kingdom of heaven is like yeast that a woman took and mixed in with three measures of flour until all of it was leavened.

97. Jesus said: The Kingdom of the Father is like a woman who was carrying a jar full of grain. While she was walking on a road far from home, the handle of the jar broke and the grain poured out behind her onto the road. She did not know it. She had noticed no problem. When she arrived in her house, she set the jar down and found it empty.

98. Jesus said: The Kingdom of the Father is like someone who wished to slay a prominent person. While still in his own house he drew his sword and thrust it into the wall in order to test whether his hand would be strong enough. Then he slew the

prominent person.

99. His Disciples said to him: Your brethren and your mother are standing outside. He said to them: Those here who do my Father's desires are my Brethren and my Mother. It is they who will enter the Kingdom of my Father.

Matthew 12:46-50 While he was still speaking to the crowds, his mother and his brothers were standing outside, wanting to speak to him. Someone told him, Look, your mother and your brothers are standing outside, wanting to speak to you. But to the one who had told him this, Jesus replied, Who is my mother, and who are my brothers? And pointing to his disciples, he said, Here are my mother and my brothers! For whoever does the will of my Father in heaven is my brother and sister and mother.

100. They showed Jesus a gold coin, and said to him: The agents of Caesar extort taxes from us. He said to them: Give the things of Caesar to Caesar, give the things of God to God, and give to me what is mine.

Mark 12:14-17 Is it lawful to pay taxes to the emperor, or not? Should we pay them, or should we not? But knowing their hypocrisy, he said to them, Why are you putting me to the test? Bring me a denarius and let me see it. And they brought one. Then he said to them, Whose head is this, and whose title? They answered, The emperor's. Jesus said to them, Give to the emperor the things that are the emperor's, and to God the things that are God's. And they were utterly amazed at him.

101. Jesus said: Whoever does not hate his father and his mother, as I do, will not be able to become my Disciple. And whoever does not love his father and his mother, as I do, will not be able to become my disciple. For my mother bore me, yet my true Mother gave me the life.

Matthew 10:37 Whoever loves father or mother more than me is not worthy of me; and whoever loves son or daughter more than me is not worthy of me.

102. Jesus said: Damn these Pharisees. They are like a dog sleeping in the feed trough of oxen. For neither does he eat, nor does he allow the oxen to eat.

Matthew 2:13 But woe unto you, scribes and Pharisees, hypocrites! because you shut the kingdom of heaven against men; for you neither enter yourselves, nor allow those who would enter to go in.

103. Jesus said: Blessed (happy) is the person who knows at what place of the house the bandits may break in, so that he can rise and collect his things and prepare himself before they enter.

Matthew 24:43 But understand this: if the owner of the house had known in what part of the night the thief was coming, he would have stayed awake and would not have let his house be broken into.

104. They said to him: Come, let us pray today and let us fast. Jesus said: What sin have I committed? How have I been overcome (undone)? When the Bridegroom comes forth from the bridal chamber, then let them fast and let them pray.

105. Jesus said: Whoever acknowledges (comes to know) father and mother, will be called the son of a whore.

106. Jesus said: When you make the two one, you will become Sons of Man (children of Adam), and when you say to the mountain: Move! It will move.

Mark 11:23 Truly I tell you, if you say to this mountain, Be taken up and thrown into the sea, and if you do not doubt in your heart, but believe that what you say will come to pass, it will be done for you.

107. Jesus said: The Kingdom is like a shepherd who has a hundred sheep. The largest one of them went astray. He left the ninety-nine and sought for the one until he found it. Having searched until he was weary, he said to that sheep: I desire you more than the ninety-nine.

Matthew 18:12-13 What do you think? If a shepherd has a hundred sheep, and one of them has gone astray, does he not leave the ninety-nine on the mountains and go in search of the one that went astray? And if he finds it, truly I tell you, he rejoices over it more than over the ninety-nine that never went astray.

108. Jesus said: Whoever drinks from my mouth will become like me. I will become him, and the secrets will be revealed to him. (The mouth is the gateway to the soul.)

109. Jesus said: The Kingdom is like a person who had a treasure hidden in his field and knew nothing of it. After he died, he bequeathed it to his son. The son accepted the field knowing nothing of the treasure. He sold it. Then the person who bought it came and plowed it. He found the treasure. He began to lend money at interest to whomever he wished.

Matthew 13:44 The kingdom of heaven is like treasure hidden in a field, which someone found and hid; then in his joy he goes and sells all that he has and buys that field.

110. Jesus said: Whoever has found the world (system) and becomes wealthy (enriched by it), let

him renounce the world (system).

Mark 10:21-23 Then Jesus beholding him loved him, and said unto him, One thing thou lackest: go thy way, sell whatsoever thou hast, and give to the poor, and thou shalt have treasure in heaven: and come, take up the cross, and follow me. And he was sad at that saying, and went away grieved: for he had great possessions. And Jesus looked round about, and saith unto his disciples, How hardly shall they that have riches enter into the kingdom of God!

111. Jesus said: Heaven and earth will roll up (collapse and disappear) before you, but he who lives within the Living-One will neither see nor fear death. For, Jesus said: Whoever finds himself, of him the world is not worthy.

112. Jesus said: Damned is the flesh which depends upon the soul. Damned is the soul which depends upon the flesh.

113. His Disciples said to him: When will the Kingdom come? Jesus said: It will not come by expectation (because you watch or wait for it). They will not say: Look here! or: Look there! But the Kingdom of the Father is spread upon the earth, and people do not realize it.
Luke 17:20 And when he was demanded of by the Pharisees, when the kingdom of God should come, he answered them and said, The kingdom of God cometh not with observation: Neither shall they say, Lo-Here! Lo-There! For, behold, the kingdom of God is within you.
(Saying 114 was written later and was added to the original text.)

114. Simon Peter said to them: Send Mary away from us, for women are not worthy of this life. Jesus said: See, I will draw her into me so that I make her male, in order that she herself will become a living spirit like you males. For every female who becomes male will enter the Kingdom of the Heavens.

Psalms of Solomon

Psalm 1

A Psalm of Solomon
1I cried unto the Lord when I was in distress, Unto God when sinners assailed. 2Suddenly the alarm of war was heard before me; (I said), He will hearken to me, for I am full of righteousness. 3I thought in my heart that I was full of righteousness, Because I was well off and had become rich in children. 4Their wealth spread to the whole earth, And their glory unto the end of the earth. 5They were exalted unto the stars; They said they would never fall. 6But they became insolent in their prosperity, And they were without understanding, 7Their sins were in secret, And even I had no knowledge (of them). 8Their transgressions (went) beyond those of the heathen before them; They utterly polluted the holy things of the Lord.

Psalm 2
A Psalm of Solomon Concerning Jerusalem
1When the sinner waxed proud, with a battering-ram he cast down fortified walls, And Thou didst not restrain (him). 2Alien nations ascended Thine altar, They trampled (it) proudly with their sandals; 3Because the sons of Jerusalem had defiled the holy things of the Lord, Had profaned with iniquities the offerings of God. 4Therefore He said Cast them far from Me; 5It was set at naught before God, It was utterly dishonoured; 6The sons and the daughters were in grievous captivity, Sealed (?) (was) their neck, branded (?) (was it) among the nations. 7According to their sins hath He done unto them, for He hath left them in the hands of them that prevailed. 8He hath turned away His face from pitying them, Young and old and their children together; 9for they had done evil one and all, in not hearkening. 10And the heavens were angry, And the earth abhorred them; 11for no man upon it had done what they did, 12And the earth recognized all Thy righteous judgments, O God. 13They set the sons of Jerusalem to be mocked at in return for (the) harlots in her; Every wayfarer entered in in the full light of day. 14They made mock with their transgressions, as they themselves were wont to do; In the full light of day they revealed their iniquities And the daughters of Jerusalem were defiled in accordance with Thy judgment, 15Because they had defiled themselves with unnatural intercourse I am pained in my bowels and my inward parts for these things. 16(And yet) I will justify Thee, O God, in uprightness of heart, for in Thy judgments is Thy righteousness (displayed), O God. 17for Thou hast rendered to the sinners according to their deeds, Yea according to their sins, which were very wicked. 18Thou hast uncovered their sins, that Thy judgment might be manifest; 19Thou hast wiped out their memorial from the earth

God is a righteous judge, And He is no respecter of persons. 20for the nations reproached Jerusalem, trampling it down; Her beauty was dragged down from the throne of glory. 21She girded on sackcloth instead of comely raiment, A rope (was) about her head instead of a crown. 22She put off the glorious diadem which God had set upon her, 23In dishonor was her beauty cast upon the ground. 24And I saw and entreated the Lord and said, Long enough, O Lord, has Thine hand been heavy on Israel, in bringing the nations upon (them). 25for they have made sport unsparingly in wrath and fierce anger; 26And they will make an utter end, unless Thou, O Lord, rebuke them in Thy wrath. 27for they have done it not in zeal, but in lust of soul, 28Pouring out their wrath upon us with a view to rapine. 29Delay not, O God, to recompense them on (their) heads, To turn the pride of the dragon into dishonour. 30And I had not long to wait before God showed me the insolent one Slain on the mountains of Egypt, Esteemed of less account than the least on land and sea; 31His body, (too,) borne hither and thither on the billows with much insolence, with none to bury (him), because He had rejected him with dishonour He reflected not that he was man. 32And reflected not on the latter end; 33He said I will be lord of land and sea; And he recognized not that it is God who is great, Mighty in His great strength. 34He is king over the heavens, And judgeth kings and kingdoms. 35(It is He) who setteth me up in glory, And bringeth down the proud to eternal destruction in dishonour, Because they knew Him not. 36And now behold, ye princes of the earth, the judgment of the Lord, for a great king and righteous (is He), judging (all) that is under heaven. 37Bless God, ye that fear the Lord with wisdom, for the mercy of the Lord will be upon them that fear Him, in the Judgment; 38So that He will distinguish between the righteous and the sinner, (And) recompense the sinners for ever according to their deeds; 39And have mercy on the righteous, (delivering him) from the affliction of the sinner, And recompensing the sinner for what he hath done to the righteous. 40for the Lord is good to them that call upon Him in patience, Doing according to His mercy to His pious ones, Establishing (them) at all times before Him in strength. 41Blessed be the Lord for ever before His servants.

Psalm 3

A Psalm of Solomon Concerning the righteous
1Why sleepest thou, O my soul, And blessest not the Lord? 2Sing a new song, Unto God who is worthy to be praised Sing and be wakeful against His awaking, for good is a psalm (sung) to God from a glad heart. 3The righteous remember the Lord at all times, with thanksgiving and declaration of the righteousness of the Lord's judgments. 4The righteous despiseth not the chastening of the Lord; His will is always before the Lord. 5The righteous stumbleth and holdeth the Lord righteous He falleth and looketh out for what God will do to him; 6He seeketh out whence his deliverance will come. 7The steadfastness of the righteous is from God their deliverer; There lodgeth not in the house of the righteous sin upon sin. 8The righteous continually searcheth his house, To remove utterly (all) iniquity (done) by him in error. 9He maketh atonement for (sins of) ignorance by fasting and afflicting his soul, 10And the Lord counteth guiltless every pious man and his house. 11The sinner stumbleth and curseth his life, The day when he was begotten, and his mother's travail. 12He addeth sins to sins, while he liveth (?); 13He falleth□verily grievous is his fall□and riseth no more The destruction of the sinner is for ever, 14And he shall not be remembered, when the righteous is visited. 15This is the portion of sinners for ever. 16But they that fear the Lord shall rise to life eternal, And their life (shall be) in the light of the Lord, and shall come to an end no more.

Psalm 4

A Conversation of Solomon with the Men-pleasers
1Wherefore sittest thou, O profane (man), in the council of the pious, Seeing that thy heart is far removed from the Lord, Provoking with transgressions the God of Israel? 2Extravagant in speech, extravagant in outward seeming beyond all (men), Is he that is severe of speech in condemning sinners in judgment. 3And his hand is first upon him as (though he acted) in zeal, And (yet) he is himself guilty in respect of manifold sins and of wantonness. 4His eyes are upon every woman without distinction; His tongue lieth when he maketh contract with an oath. 5By night and in secret he sinneth as though unseen, with his eyes he talketh to every woman of evil compacts. 6He is swift to enter every house with cheerfulness as though guileless. 7Let God remove those that live in hypocrisy in the company of the pious, (Even) the life of such an one with corruption of his flesh and penury. 8Let God reveal the deeds of the men-pleasers, The deeds of such an one with laughter and derision; 9That the pious may count righteous the judgment of their God, When sinners are removed from before the righteous, 10(Even the) man-pleaser who uttereth law guilefully. 11And their eyes (are fixed) upon any man's house that is (still) secure, That they may, like (the) Serpent, destroy the wisdom of with words of transgressors, 12His words are deceitful that (he) may accomplish (his) wicked desire. 13He never ceaseth from scattering (families) as though (they were) orphans, Yea, he layeth waste a house on account of (his) lawless desire. 14He deceiveth with words, (saying,) There is none that seeth, or judgeth. 15He fills one (house) with lawlessness, And (then) his eyes (are fixed) upon the next house, To destroy it with words that give wing to (desire) (Yet) with all these his

soul, like Sheol, is not sated. 16Let his portion, O Lord, be dishonoured before thee; Let him go forth groaning and come home cursed. 17Let his life be (spent) in anguish, and penury, and want, O Lord; Let his sleep be (beset) with pains and his awaking with perplexities. 18Let sleep be withdrawn from his eyelids at night; Let him fail dishonorably in every work of his hands. 19Let him come home empty-handed to his house, And his house be void of everything wherewith he could sate his appetite. 20(Let) his old age (be spent) in childless loneliness until his removal (by death). 21Let the flesh of the men-pleasers be rent by wild beasts, And (let) the bones of the lawless (lie) dishonored in the sight of the sun. 22Let ravens peck out the eyes of the hypocrites. 23for they have laid waste many houses of men, in dishonor, And scattered (them) in (their) lust; 24And they have not remembered God, Nor feared God in all these things; 25But they have provoked God's anger and vexed Him May He remove them from off the earth, Because with deceit they beguiled the souls of the flawless. 26Blessed are they that fear the Lord in their flawlessness; 27The Lord shall deliver them from guileful men and sinners, And deliver us from every stumbling-block of the lawless (men). 28Let God destroy them that insolently work all unrighteousness, for a great and mighty judge is the Lord our God in righteousness. 29Let Thy mercy, O Lord, be upon all them that love Thee.

Psalm 5
A Psalm of Solomon
1O Lord God, I will praise Thy name with joy, In the midst of them that know Thy righteous judgments. 2for Thou art good and merciful, the refuge of the poor; 3When I cry to Thee, do not silently disregard me. 4for no man taketh spoil from a mighty man; 5Who, then, can take aught of all that Thou hast made, except Thou Thyself givest? 6for man and his portion (lie) before Thee in the balance; He cannot add to, so as to enlarge, what has been prescribed by Thee O God, 7when we are in distress we call upon Thee for help, And Thou dost not turn back our petition, for Thou art our God. 8Cause not Thy hand to be heavy upon us, Lest through necessity we sin. 9Even though Thou restore us not, we will not keep away; But unto Thee will we come. 10for if I hunger, unto Thee will I cry, O God; And Thou wilt give to me. 11Birds and fish dost Thou nourish, In that Thou givest rain to the steppes that green grass may spring up, (So) to prepare fodder in the steppe for every living thing; 12And if they hunger, unto Thee do they lift up their face. 13Kings and rulers and peoples Thou dost nourish, O God; And who is the help of the poor and needy, if not Thou, O Lord? 14And Thou wilt hearken -for who is good and gentle but Thou? ☐Making glad the soul of the humble by opening Thine hand in mercy. 15Man's goodness is (bestowed) grudgingly and .; And if he repeat (it) without murmuring, even that is marvelous. 16But Thy gift is great in goodness and wealth, And he whose hope is (set) on Thee shall have no lack of gifts. 17Upon the whole earth is Thy mercy, O Lord, in goodness. 18Happy is he whom God remembereth in (granting to him) a due sufficiency; 19If a man abound over much, he sinneth. 20Sufficient are moderate means with righteousness, And hereby the blessing of the Lord (becomes) abundance with righteousness. 21They that fear the Lord rejoice in good (gifts), And Thy goodness is upon Israel in Thy kingdom Blessed is the glory of the Lord for He is our king.

Psalm 6
In Hope of Solomon
1Happy is the man whose heart is fixed to call upon the name of the Lord; 2When he remembereth the name of the Lord, he will be saved. 3His ways are made even by the Lord, And the works of his hands are preserved by the Lord his God. 4At what he sees in his bad dreams, his soul shall not be troubled; 5When he passes through rivers and the tossing of the seas, he shall not be dismayed. 6He ariseth from his sleep, and blesseth the name of the Lord 7When his heart is at peace, he singeth to the name of his God, And he entreateth the Lord for all his house. 8And the Lord heareth the prayer of every one that feareth God, And every request of the soul that hopes for Him doth the Lord accomplish. 9Blessed is the Lord, who showeth mercy to those who love Him in sincerity.

Psalm 7
Of Solomon of turning
1Make not Thy dwelling afar from us, O God; Lest they assail us that hate us without cause. 2for Thou hast rejected them, O God; Let not their foot trample upon Thy holy inheritance. 3Chasten us Thyself in Thy good pleasure; But give (us) not up to the nations; 4For, if Thou sendest pestilence, Thou Thyself givest it charge concerning us; for Thou art merciful, And wilt not be angry to the point of consuming us. 5While Thy name dwelleth in our midst, we shall find mercy; 6And the nations shall not prevail against us for Thou art our shield, 7And when we call upon Thee, Thou hearkenest to us; 8for Thou wilt pity the seed of Israel for ever And Thou wilt not reject (them) But we (shall be) under Thy yoke for ever, And (under) the rod of Thy chastening. 9Thou wilt establish us in the time that Thou helpest us, Showing mercy to the house of Jacob on the day wherein Thou didst promise (to help them).

Psalm 8
Of Solomon of the chief Musician
1Distress and the sound of war hath my ear heard; The sound of a trumpet announcing slaughter and calamity, 2The sound of much people as of an

exceeding high wind, As a tempest with mighty fire sweeping through the Negeb. 3And I said in my heart; Surely (?) God judgeth us; 4A sound I hear (moving) towards Jerusalem, the holy city. 5My loins were broken at what I heard, my knees tottered 6My heart was afraid, my bones were dismayed like flax. 7I said They establish their ways in righteousness I thought upon the judgments of God since the creation of heaven and earth; I held God righteous in His judgments which have been from of old. 8God laid bare their sins in the full light of day; All the earth came to know the righteous judgments of God. 9In secret places underground their iniquities (were committed) to provoke (Him) to anger; 10They wrought confusion, son with mother and father with daughter; 11They committed adultery, every man with his neighbor's wife They concluded covenants with one another with an oath touching these things; 12They plundered the sanctuary of God, as though there was no avenger. 13They trode the altar of the Lord, (coming straight) from all manner of uncleanness; And with menstrual blood they defiled the sacrifices, as (though these were) common flesh. 14They left no sin undone, wherein they surpassed not the heathen. 15Therefore God mingled for them a spirit of wandering; And gave them to drink a cup of undiluted wine, that they might become drunken. 16He brought him that is from the end of the earth, that smiteth mightily; 17He decreed (?) war against Jerusalem, and against her land. 18The princes of the land went to meet him with joy they said unto him Blessed be thy way! Come ye, enter ye in with peace. 19They made the rough ways even, before his entering in; They opened the gates to Jerusalem, they crowned its walls. 20As a father (entereth) the house of his sons, (so) he entered (Jerusalem) in peace; He established his feet (there) in great safety. 21He captured her fortresses and the wall of Jerusalem; 22for God Himself led him in safety, while they wandered. 23He destroyed their princes and every one wise in counsel; He poured out the blood of the inhabitants of Jerusalem, like the water of uncleanness. 24He led away their sons and daughters, whom they had begotten in defilement. 25They did according to their uncleanness, even as their fathers (had done) 26They defiled Jerusalem and the things that had been hallowed to the name of God. 27(But) God hath shown Himself righteous in His judgments upon the nations of the earth; 28And the pious (servants) of God are like innocent lambs in their midst. 29Worthy to be praised is the Lord that judgeth the whole earth in His righteousness. 30Behold, now, O God, Thou hast shown us Thy judgment in Thy righteousness; 31Our eyes have seen Thy judgments, O God We have justified Thy name that is honoured for ever; 32for Thou art the God of righteousness, judging Israel with chastening. 33Turn, O God, Thy mercy upon us, and have pity upon us; 34Gather together the dispersed of Israel, with mercy and goodness; 35for Thy faithfulness is with us And (though) we have stiffened our neck, yet Thou art our chastener; 36Overlook us not, O our God, lest the nations swallow us up, as though there were none to deliver. 37But Thou art our God from the beginning, And upon Thee is our hope (set), O Lord; 38And we will not depart from Thee, for good are Thy judgments upon us. 39Ours and our children's be Thy good pleasure for ever; O Lord our Saviour, we shall never more be moved. 40The Lord is worthy to be praised for His judgments with the mouth of His pious ones; And blessed be Israel of the Lord for ever.

Psalm 9
Of Solomon for rebuke

1When Israel was led away captive into a strange land, When they fell away from the Lord who redeemed them, 2They were cast away from the inheritance, which Lord had given them Among every nation (were) the dispersed of Israel according to the word of God, 3That Thou mightest be justified, O God, in Thy righteousness by reason of our transgressions 4for Thou art a just judge over all the peoples of the earth. 5for from Thy knowledge none that doeth unjustly is hidden, 6And the righteous deeds of Thy pious ones (are) before Thee, O Lord, Where, then, can a man hide himself from Thy knowledge, O God? 7Our works are subject to our own choice and power To do right or wrong in the works of our hands 8And in Thy righteousness Thou visitest the sons of men. 9He that doeth righteousness layeth up life for himself with the Lord; And he that doeth wrongly forfeits his life to destruction; 10for the judgments of the Lord are (given) in righteousness to (every) man and (his) house Unto whom art Thou good, O God, except to them that call upon the Lord? 11He cleanseth from sins a soul when it maketh confession, when it maketh acknowledgement; 12for shame is upon us and upon our faces on account of all these things. 13And to whom doth He forgive sins, except to them that have sinned? 14Thou blessest the righteous, and dost not reprove them for the sins that they have committed; And Thy goodness is upon them that sin, when they repent. 15And, now, Thou art our God, and we the people whom Thou hast loved Behold and show pity, O God of Israel, for we are Thine; And remove not Thy mercy from us, lest they assail us. 16for Thou didst choose the seed of Abraham before all the nations, And didst set Thy name upon us, O Lord, 17And Thou wilt not reject (us) for ever Thou madest a covenant with our fathers concerning us; 18And we hope in Thee, when our soul turneth (unto Thee) The mercy of the Lord be upon the house of Israel for ever and ever.

Psalm 10
A Hymn of Solomon

1Happy is the man whom the Lord remembereth with reproving, And whom He restraineth from the way of evil with strokes, That he may be cleansed from sin, that it may not be multiplied. 2He that maketh ready his back for strokes shall be cleansed, for the Lord is good to them that endure chastening. 3for He maketh straight the ways of the righteous, And doth not pervert (them) by His chastening. 4And the mercy of the Lord (is) upon them that love Him in truth, And the Lord remembereth His servants in mercy. 5for the testimony (is) in the law of the eternal covenant, The testimony of the Lord (is) on the ways of men in (His) visitation. 6Just and kind is our Lord in His judgments for ever, And Israel shall praise the name of the Lord in gladness. 7And the pious shall give thanks in the assembly of the people; And on the poor shall God have mercy in the gladness (?) of Israel; 8for good and merciful is God for ever, And the assemblies of Israel shall glorify the name of the Lord The salvation of the Lord be upon the house of Israel unto everlasting gladness!

Psalm 11
Of Solomon Unto expectation
1Blow ye in Zion on the trumpet to summon (the) saints, 2Cause ye to be heard in Jerusalem the voice of him that bringeth good tidings; for God hath had pity on Israel in visiting them. 3Stand on the height, O Jerusalem, and behold thy children, From the East and the West, gathered together by the Lord; 4From the North they come in the gladness of their God, From the isles afar off God hath gathered them. 5High mountains hath He abased into a plain for them; 6The hills fled at their entrance The woods gave them shelter as they passed by; 7Every sweet-smelling tree God caused to spring up for them, That Israel might pass by in the visitation of the glory of their God. 8Put on, O Jerusalem, thy glorious garments; Make ready thy holy robe; for God hath spoken good concerning Israel, for ever and ever. 9Let the Lord do what He hath spoken concerning Israel and Jerusalem; Let the Lord raise up Israel by His glorious name The mercy of the Lord be upon Israel for ever and ever.

Psalm 12
Of Solomon Against the tongue of transgressors
1O Lord, deliver my soul from (the) lawless and wicked man, From the tongue that is lawless and slanderous, and speaketh lies and deceit. 2Manifoldly twisted (?) are the words of the tongue of the wicked man, Even as among a people a fire that burneth up their beauty. 3So he delights to fill houses with a lying tongue, To cut down the trees of gladness which setteth on fire transgressors, 4To involve households in warfare by means of slanderous lips May God remove far from the innocent the lips of transgressors by (bringing them to) want And may the bones of slanderers be scattered (far) away from them that fear the Lord! 5In flaming fire perish the slanderous tongue (far) away from the pious! 6May the Lord preserve the quiet soul that hateth the unrighteous; And may the Lord establish the man that followeth peace at home. 7The salvation of the Lord be upon Israel His servant for ever; And let the sinners perish together at the presence of the Lord; But let the Lord's pious ones inherit the promises of the Lord.

Psalm 13
Of Solomon A Psalm of Comfort for the righteous
1The right hand of the Lord hath covered me; The right hand of the Lord hath spared us. 2The arm of the Lord hath saved us from the sword that passed through, From famine and the death of sinners. 3Noisome beasts ran upon them with their teeth they tore their flesh, And with their molars crushed their bones But from all these things the Lord delivered us, 4The righteous was troubled on account of his errors, Lest he should be taken away along with the sinners; 5for terrible is the overthrow of the sinner; But not one of all these things toucheth the righteous for not alike are the chastening of the righteous (for sins done) in ignorance, And the overthrow of the sinners 6Secretly (?) is the righteous chastened, Lest the sinner rejoice over the righteous. 7for He correcteth the righteous as a beloved son, And his chastisement is as that of a firstborn. 8for the Lord spareth His pious ones, And blotteth out their errors by His chastening for the life of the righteous shall be for ever; 9But sinners shall be taken away into destruction, And their memorial shall be found no more. 10But upon the pious is the mercy of the Lord, And upon them that fear Him His mercy.

Psalm 14
A Hymn of Solomon
1Faithful is the Lord to them that love Him in truth, To them that endure His chastening, To them that walk in the righteousness of His commandments, In the law which He commanded us that we might live. 2The pious of the Lord shall live by it for ever; The Paradise of the Lord, the trees of life, are His pious ones. 3Their planting is rooted for ever; They shall not be plucked up all the days of heaven for the portion and the inheritance of God is Israel. 4But not so are the sinners and transgressors, Who love (the brief) day (spent) in companionship with their sin; Their delight is in fleeting corruption, 5And they remember not God for the ways of men are known before Him at all times, And He knoweth the secrets of the heart before they come to pass. 6Therefore their inheritance is Sheol and darkness and destruction, And they shall not be found in the day when the righteous obtain mercy; 7But the pious of the Lord shall inherit life in gladness.

Psalm 15

A Psalm of Solomon with a Song

1When I was in distress I called upon the name of the Lord, I hoped for the help of the God of Jacob and was saved; 2for the hope and refuge of the poor art Thou, O God. 3(a) for who, O God, is strong except to give thanks unto Thee in truth? 4And wherein is a man powerful except in giving thanks to Thy name? 5A new psalm with song in gladness of heart, The fruit of the lips with the well-tuned instrument of the tongue, The firstfruits of the lips from a pious and righteous heart□ 6He that offereth these things shall never be shaken by evil; The flame of fire and the wrath against the unrighteous shall not touch him, 7When it goeth forth from the face of the Lord against sinners, To destroy all the substance of sinners, 8for the mark of God is upon the righteous that they may be saved Famine and sword and pestilence (shall be) far from the righteous, 9for they shall flee away from the pious as men pursued in war; But they shall pursue sinners and overtake (them), And they that do lawlessness shall not escape the judgment of God; As by enemies experienced (in war) shall they be overtaken, 10for the mark of destruction is upon their forehead. 11And the inheritance of sinners is destruction and darkness, And their iniquities shall pursue them unto Sheol beneath. 12Their inheritance shall not be found of their children, 13for sins shall lay waste the houses of sinners And sinners shall perish for ever in the day of the Lord's judgment, 14When God visiteth the earth with His judgment. 15But they that fear the Lord shall find mercy therein, And shall live by the compassion of their God; But sinners shall perish for ever.

Psalm 16

A Hymn of Solomon for Help to the Pious

1When my soul slumbered (being afar) from the Lord, I had all but slipped down to the pit, When (I was) far from God, 2my soul had been well nigh poured out unto death, (I had been) nigh unto the gates of Sheol with the sinner, 3when my soul departed from the Lord God of Israel □Had not the Lord helped me with His ever lasting mercy. 4He pricked me, as a horse is pricked, that I might serve Him, My savior and helper at all times saved me. 5I will give thanks unto Thee, O God, for Thou hast helped me to (my) salvation; And hast not counted me with sinners to (my) destruction. 6Remove not Thy mercy from me, O God, Nor Thy memorial from my heart until I die. 7Rule me, O God, (keeping me back) from wicked sin, And from every wicked woman that causeth the simple to stumble. 8And let not the beauty of a lawless woman beguile me, Nor any one that is subject to (?) unprofitable sin. 9Establish the works of my hands before Thee, And preserve my goings in the remembrance of Thee. 10Protect my tongue and my lips with words of truth; Anger and unreasoning wrath put far from me. 11Murmuring, and impatience in affliction, remove far from me, When, if I sin, Thou chastenest me that I may return (unto Thee). 12But with goodwill and cheerfulness support my soul; When Thou strengthenest my soul, what is given (to me) will be sufficient for me. 13for if Thou givest not strength, Who can endure chastisement with poverty? 14When a man is rebuked by means of his corruption, Thy testing (of him) is in his flesh and in the affliction of poverty. 15If the righteous endureth in all these (trials), he shall receive mercy from the Lord.

Psalm 17

A Psalm of Solomon with Song of the King

1O Lord, Thou art our King for ever and ever, for in Thee, O God, doth our soul glory. 2How long are the days of man's life upon the earth? As are his days, so is the hope (set) upon him. 3But we hope in God, our deliverer; for the might of our God is for ever with mercy, 4And the kingdom of our God is for ever over the nations in judgment. 5Thou, O Lord, didst choose David (to be) king over Israel, And swaredst to him touching his seed that never should his kingdom fail before Thee. 6But, for our sins, sinners rose up against us; They assailed us and thrust us out; What Thou hadst not promised to them, they took away (from us) with violence. 7They in no wise glorified Thy honorable name; They set a (worldly) monarchy in place of (that which was) their excellency; 8They laid waste the throne of David in tumultuous arrogance But Thou, O God, didst cast them down and remove their seed from the earth, 9In that there rose up against them a man that was alien to our race. 10According to their sins didst Thou recompense them, O God; So that it befell them according to their deeds. 11God showed them no pity; He sought out their seed and let not one of them go free. 12Faithful is the Lord in all His judgments Which He doeth upon the earth. 13The lawless one laid waste our land so that none inhabited it, They destroyed young and old and their children together. 14In the heat of His anger He sent them away even unto the west, And (He exposed) the rulers of the land unsparingly to derision. 15Being an alien the enemy acted proudly, And his heart was alien from our God. 16And all things [whatsoever he did in] Jerusalem, As also the nations [in the cities to their gods.] 17And the children of the covenant in the midst of the mingled peoples [surpassed them in evil.] There was not among them one that wrought in the midst of Jerusalem mercy and truth. 18They that loved the synagogues of the pious fled from them, As sparrows that fly from their nest. 19They wandered in deserts that their lives might be saved from harm, And precious in the eyes of them that lived abroad was any that escaped alive from them. 20Over the whole earth were they scattered by lawless (men). 21for the heavens withheld the rain from dropping upon the earth, Springs were stopped (that sprang) perennial(ly) out of the deeps, (that ran down) from lofty mountains for there was none among them that wrought righteousness and justice; From the chief of them to the least (of them) all were sinful; 22The king was a transgressor, and the judge disobedient, and the people sinful. 23Behold, O Lord, and raise up unto them their king, the son of David, At the time in the which Thou seest, O God, that he may reign over Israel Thy servant 24And gird him with strength, that he may shatter unrighteous rulers, 25And that he may purge Jerusalem from nations that trample (her) down to destruction Wisely, righteously 26he shall thrust out sinners from (the) inheritance, He shall destroy the pride of the sinner as a potter's vessel with a rod of iron he shall break in pieces all their substance, 27He shall destroy the godless nations with the word of his mouth; At his rebuke nations shall flee before him, And he shall reprove sinners for the thoughts of their heart. 28And he shall gather together a holy people, whom he shall lead in righteousness, And he shall judge the tribes of the people that has been sanctified by the Lord his God. 29And he shall not suffer unrighteousness to lodge any more in their midst, Nor shall there dwell with them any man that knoweth wickedness, 30for he shall know them, that they are all sons of their God And he shall divide them according to their tribes upon the land, 31And neither sojourner nor alien shall sojourn with them any more He shall judge peoples and nations in the wisdom of his righteousness Selah. 32And he shall have the heathen nations to serve him under his yoke; And he shall glorify the Lord in a place to be seen of (?) all the earth; 33And he shall purge Jerusalem, making it holy as of old 34So that nations shall come from the ends of the earth to see his glory, Bringing as gifts her sons who had fainted, 35And to see the glory of the Lord, wherewith God hath glorified her And he (shall be) a righteous king, taught of God, over them, 36And there shall be no unrighteousness in his days in their midst, for all shall be holy and their king the anointed of the Lord. 37for he shall not put his trust in horse and rider and bow, Nor shall he multiply for himself gold and silver for war, Nor shall he gather confidence from (?) a multitude (?) for the day of battle. 38The Lord Himself is his king, the hope of him that is mighty through (his) hope in God < > All nations (shall be) in fear before him, 39for he will smite the earth with the word of his mouth for ever. 40He will bless the people of the Lord with wisdom and gladness, 41And he himself (will be) pure from sin, so that he may rule a great people He will rebuke rulers, and remove sinners by the might of his word; 42And (relying) upon his God, throughout his days he will not stumble; for God will make him mighty by means of (His) holy spirit, And wise by means of the spirit of understanding, with strength and righteousness. 43And the blessing of the Lord (will be) with him he will be strong and stumble not; 44His hope (will be) in the Lord who then can prevail against him? (He will be) mighty in his works, and strong in the fear of God, 45(He will be) shepherding the flock of the Lord faithfully and righteously, And will suffer none among them to stumble in their pasture. 46He will lead them all aright, And there will be no pride among them that any among them should be oppressed. 47This (will be) the majesty of the king of Israel whom God knoweth; He will raise him up over the house of Israel to correct him. 48His words (shall be) more refined than costly gold, the choicest; In the assemblies he will judge the peoples, the tribes of the sanctified. 49His words (shall be) like the words of the holy ones in the midst of sanctified peoples. 50Blessed be they that shall be in those days, In that they shall see the good fortune of Israel which God shall bring to pass in the gathering together of the tribes. 51May the Lord hasten His mercy upon Israel! May He deliver us from the uncleanness of unholy enemies! The Lord Himself is our king for ever and ever.

Psalm 18

A Psalm of Solomon of the Lord's Annointed

1Lord, Thy mercy is over the works of Thy hands for ever; Thy goodness is over Israel with a rich gift. 2Thine eyes look upon them, so that none of them suffers want; 3Thine ears listen to the hopeful prayer of the poor Thy judgments (are executed) upon the whole earth in mercy; 4And Thy love (is) toward the seed of Abraham, the children of Israel Thy chastisement is upon us as (upon) a first-born, only-begotten son, 5To turn back the obedient soul from folly (that is wrought) in ignorance. 6May God cleanse Israel against the day of mercy and blessing, Against the day of choice when He bringeth back His anointed. 7Blessed shall they be that shall be in those days, In that they shall see the goodness of the Lord which He shall perform for the generation that is to come, 8Under the rod of chastening of the Lord's anointed in the fear of his God, In the spirit of wisdom and righteousness and strength; 9That he may direct (every} man in the works of righteousness by the fear of God, That he may establish them all before the Lord, 10A good generation (living) in the fear of God in the days of mercy Selah. 11Great is our God and glorious, dwelling in the highest. 12(It is He) who hath established in (their) courses the lights (of heaven) for determining seasons from year to year, And they have not turned aside from the way which He appointed them 13In the fear of God (they pursue) their path every day, From the day God created them and for evermore. 14And they have erred not since the day He created them Since the generations of old they have not withdrawn from their path, Unless God commanded them (so to do) by the command of His servant.

The Testaments of The 12 Patriarchs

From The Apocrypha and Pseudepigrapha of the Old Testament by R. H. Charles, vol. II, Oxford Press
The Apocrypha and Pseudepigrapha of the Old Testament, edited by R.H. Charles (1913 edition)

THE TESTAMENT OF REUBEN, THE FIRST-BORN SON OF JACOB AND LEAH

1 1 The copy of the Testament of Reuben, even the commands which he gave his sons before he 2 died in the hundred and twenty-fifth year of his life. Two years after the death of Joseph his 3 brother, when Reuben fell ill, his sons and his sons' sons were gathered together to visit him. And 4 he said to them: My children, behold I am dying, and go the way of my fathers. And seeing there Judah, and Gad, and Asher, his brethren, he said to them: Raise me up, that I may tell to my brethren and to my children what things I have hidden in my heart, for behold now at length 5 I am passing away. And he arose and kissed them, and said unto them: Hear, my brethren, and 6 do ye, my children, give ear to Reuben your father in the commands which I give unto you. And behold I call to witness against you this day the God of heaven, that ye walk not in the sins of 7 youth and fornication, wherein I was poured out, and defiled the bed of my father Jacob. And I tell you that he smote me with a sore plague in my loins for seven months; and had not my father 8 Jacob prayed for me to the Lord, the Lord would have destroyed me. For I was thirty years old 9 when I wrought the evil thing before the Lord, and for seven months I was sick unto death. And 10 after this I repented with set purpose of my soul for seven years before the Lord. And wine and strong drink I drank not, and flesh entered not into my mouth, and I eat no pleasant food; but I mourned over my sin, for it was great, such as had not been in Israel.

2 1 And now hear me, my children, what things I saw concerning the seven spirits of deceit, when 2 I repented. Seven spirits therefore are appointed against man, and they are the leaders in the works 3 of youth. [And seven other spirits are given to him at his creation, that through them should be 4 done every work of man. The first is the spirit of life, with which the constitution (of man) is 5 created. The second is the sense of sight, with which ariseth desire. The third is the sense of hearing, with which cometh teaching. The fourth is the sense of smell, with which tastes are given 6, 7 to draw air and breath. The fifth is the power of speech, with which cometh knowledge. The sixth is the sense of taste, with which cometh the eating of meats and drinks; and by it strength is 8 produced, for in food is the foundation of strength. The seventh is the power

of procreation and 9 sexual intercourse, with which through love of pleasure sins enter in. Wherefore it is the last in order of creation, and the first in that of youth, because it is filled with ignorance, and leadeth the youth as a blind man to a pit, and as a beast to a precipice.

3 1 Besides all these there is an eighth spirit of sleep, with which is brought about the trance of 2 3 nature and the image of death. With these spirits are mingled the spirits of error.] First, the spirit of fornication is seated in the nature and in the senses; the second, the spirit of insatiableness, 4 in the belly; the third, the spirit of fighting, in the liver and gall. The fourth is the spirit of 5 obsequiousness and chicanery, that through officious attention one may be fair in seeming. The fifth is the spirit of pride, that one may be boastful and arrogant. The sixth is the spirit of lying, 6 in perdition and jealousy to practise deceits, and concealments from kindred and friends. The seventh is the spirit of injustice, with which are thefts and acts of rapacity, that a man may fulfill the desire of his heart; for injustice worketh together with the other spirits by the taking of gifts. 7, 8 And with all these the spirit of sleep is joined which is (that) of error and fantasy.] And so perisheth every young man, darkening his mind from the truth, and not understanding the law of 9 God, nor obeying the admonitions of his fathers as befell me also in my youth. And now, my children, love the truth, and it will preserve you: hear ye the words of Reuben your father. 10 Pay no heed to the face of a woman, Nor associate with another man's wife, Nor meddle with affairs of womankind. 11 For had I not seen Bilhah bathing in a covered place, I had not fallen into this great iniquity. 12 For my mind taking in the thought of the woman's nakedness, suffered me not to sleep until I had 13 wrought the abominable thing. For while Jacob our father had gone to Isaac his father, when we were in Eder, near to Ephrath in Bethlehem, Bilhah became drunk and was asleep uncovered in her 14 chamber. Having therefore gone in and beheld nakedness, I wrought the impiety without her 15 perceiving it, and leaving her sleeping I departed. And forthwith an angel of God revealed to my father concerning my impiety, and he came and mourned over me, and touched her no more.

4 1 Pay no heed, therefore, my children, to the beauty of women, nor set your mind on their affairs; but walk in singleness of heart in the fear of the Lord, and expend labour on good works, and on study and on your flocks, until the Lord give you a wife, whom He will, that ye suffer not as I did. 2 For until my father's death I had not boldness to look in his face, or to speak to any of my brethren, 3 because of the reproach. Even until now my conscience causeth me anguish on account of my 4 impiety. And yet my father comforted

me much and prayed for me unto the Lord, that the anger of the Lord might pass from me, even as the Lord showed. And thenceforth until now I have 5 been on my guard and sinned not. Therefore, my children, I say unto you, observe all things 6 whatsoever I command you, and ye shall not sin. For a pit unto the soul is the sin of fornication, separating it from God, and bringing it near to idols, because it deceiveth the mind and understanding, 7 and leadeth young men into hades before their time. For many hath fornication destroyed; because, though a man be old or noble, or rich or poor, he bringeth reproach upon 8 himself with the sons of men and derision with Beliar. For ye heard regarding Joseph how he guarded himself from a woman, and purged his thoughts from all fornication, and found favour in 9 the sight of God and men. For the Egyptian woman did many things unto him, and summoned 10 magicians, and offered him love potions, but the purpose of his soul admitted no evil desire. Therefore 11 the God of your fathers delivered him from every evil (and) hidden death. For if fornication overcomes not your mind, neither can Beliar overcome you.

5 1 For evil are women, my children; and since they have no power or strength over man, they use 2 wiles by outward attractions, that they may draw him to themselves. And whom they cannot 3 bewitch by outward attractions, him they overcome by craft. For moreover, concerning them, the angel of the Lord told me, and taught me, that women are overcome by the spirit of fornication more than men, and in their heart they plot against men; and by means of their adornment they deceive first their minds, and by the glance of the eye instill the poison, and then through the accomplished 4 act they take them captive. For a woman cannot force a man openly, but by a harlot's 5 bearing she beguiles him. Flee, therefore, fornication, my children, and command your wives and your daughters, that they adorn not their heads and faces to deceive the mind: because every woman 6 who useth these wiles hath been reserved for eternal punishment. For thus they allured the Watchers who were before the flood; for as these continually beheld them, they lusted after them, and they conceived the act in their mind; for they changed themselves into the shape of men, and 7 appeared to them when they were with their husbands. And the women lusting in their minds after their forms, gave birth to giants, for the Watchers appeared to them as reaching even unto heaven.

6 1 Beware, therefore, of fornication; and if you wish to be pure in mind, guard your senses from every 2 woman. And command the women likewise not to associate with men, that they also may be pure 3 in mind. For constant meetings, even though the ungodly deed be not wrought, are to them an 4 irremediable disease, and to us a destruction of Beliar and an eternal

reproach. For in fornication 5 there is neither understanding nor godliness, and all jealousy dwelleth in the lust thereof. Therefore, then I say unto you, ye will be jealous against the sons of Levi, and will seek to be exalted 6 over them; but ye shall not be able. For God will avenge them, and ye shall die by an evil death. 7 For to Levi God gave the sovereignty [and to Judah with him and to me also, and to Dan and 8 Joseph, that we should be for rulers]. Therefore I command you to hearken to Levi, because he shall know the law of the Lord, and shall give ordinances for judgement and shall sacrifice for all Israel until the consummation of the times, as the anointed High Priest, of whom the Lord spake, 9 I adjure you by the God of heaven to do truth each one unto his neighbour and to entertain love 10 each one for his brother. And draw ye near to Levi in humbleness of heart, that ye may receive 11 a blessing from his mouth. For he shall bless Israel and Judah, because him hath the Lord chosen to 12 be king over all the nation. And bow down before his seed, for on our behalf it will die in wars visible and invisible, and will be among you an eternal king.

7 1, 2 And Reuben died, having given these commands to his sons. And they placed him in a coffin until they carried him up from Egypt, and buried him in Hebron in the cave where his father was.

THE TESTAMENT OF SIMEON, THE SECOND OF JACOB AND LEAH.

1 1 The copy of the words of Simeon, the things which he spake to his sons before he died, in the 2 hundred

and twentieth year of his life, at which time Joseph, his brother, died. For when Simeon was sick , his sons came to visit him, and he strengthened himself and sat up and kissed them, and said:--

2 1 Hearken, my children, to Simeon your father, And I will declare unto you what things I have in my heart. 2 I was born of Jacob as my father's second son; And my mother Leah called me Simeon, Because the Lord had heard her prayer. 3 Moreover, I became strong exceedingly; I shrank from no achievement, Nor was I afraid of ought. 4 For my heart was hard, And my liver was immovable, And my bowels without compassion. 5, 6 Because valour also has been given from the Most High to men in soul and body. For in the time of my youth I was jealous in many things of Joseph, because my father loved him beyond 7 all. And I set my mind against him to destroy him, because the prince of deceit sent forth the spirit of jealousy and blinded my mind, so that I regarded him not as a brother, nor did I spare even 8 Jacob my father. But his God and the God of his fathers sent forth His angel, and delivered him 9 out of my hands. For when I went to Shechem to bring ointment for the flocks, and Reuben to Dothan, where were our necessaries and all our stores, Judah my brother sold him to the Ishmaelites. 10 And when Reuben heard these things he was grieved, for he wished to restore him to his father. 11 But on hearing this I was exceedingly wroth against Judah in that he let him go away alive, and 12 for five months I continued wrathful against him. But the Lord restrained me, and withheld from 13 me the power of my hands; for my right hand was half withered for seven days. And I knew, my children, that because of Joseph this had befallen me, and I repented and wept; and I besought the Lord God that my hand might be restored, and that I might hold aloof from all pollution and envy 14 and from all folly. For I knew that I had devised an evil thing before the Lord and Jacob my father, on account of Joseph my brother, in that I envied him.

3 1 2 And now, my children, hearken unto me and beware of the spirit of deceit and envy. For envy ruleth over the whole mind of a man, and suffereth him neither to eat nor to drink, nor to do any 3 good thing. But it ever suggesteth (to him) to destroy him that he envieth; and so long as he that 4 is envied flourisheth, he that envieth fadeth away. Two years therefore I afflicted my soul with fasting in the fear of the Lord, and I learnt that deliverance from envy cometh by the fear of God. 5 For if a man flee to the Lord, the evil spirit runneth away from him, and his mind is lightened. 6 And henceforward he sympathiseth with him whom he envied and forgiveth those who are hostile to him, and so ceaseth from his envy.

4 1 And my father asked Concerning me, because he saw that I was sad; and I said unto him, I am 2 pained in my liver. For I mourned more than they all, because I was guilty of the selling of Joseph. 3 And when we went down into Egypt, and he bound me as a spy, I knew that I was suffering justly, 4 and I grieved not. Now Joseph was a good man, and had the Spirit of God within him: being compassionate and pitiful, he bore no malice against me; but loved me even as the rest of his 5 brethren. Beware, therefore, my children, of all jealousy and envy, and walk in singleness of soul and with good heart, keeping in mind Joseph your father's brother, that God may give you also grace and glory, and blessing upon your heads, even as ye saw in 6 Joseph's case. All his days he reproached us not concerning this thing, but loved us as his own 7 soul, and beyond his own sons glorified us, and gave us riches, and cattle and fruits. Do ye also, my children, love each one his brother with a good heart and the spirit of envy will withdraw from 8 you. For this maketh savage the soul and destroyeth the body; it causeth anger and war in the mind, and stirreth up unto deeds of blood, and leadeth the mind into frenzy, and suffereth not prudence to act in men; moreover, it taketh away sleep, [and causeth tumult to the soul and trembling to the body]. 9 For even in sleep some malicious jealousy, deluding him, gnaweth and with wicked spirits disturbeth his soul, and causeth the body to be troubled, and waketh the mind from sleep in confusion; and as a wicked and poisonous spirit, so appeareth it to men.

5 1 Therefore was Joseph comely in appearance and goodly to look upon, because no wickedness 2 dwelt in him; for some of the trouble of the spirit the face manifesteth. And now, my children, Make your hearts good before the Lord, And your ways straight before men. And ye shall find grace before the Lord and men. 3 Beware, therefore, of fornication, For fornication is mother of all evils, Separating from God, and bringing near to Beliar. 4 For I have seen it inscribed in the writing of Enoch that your sons shall be corrupted in fornication, 5 and shall do harm to the sons of Levi with the sword. But they shall not be able to withstand Levi; 6 for he shall wage the war of the Lord, and shall conquer all your hosts. And they shall be few in number, divided in Levi and Judah, and there shall be none of you for sovereignty, even as also our father prophesied in his blessings.

6 1, 2 Behold I have told you all things, that I may be acquitted of your sin. Now, if ye remove from you your envy and all stiff-neckedness, As a rose shall my bones flourish in Israel, And as a lily my flesh in Jacob, And my odour shall be as the odour of Libanus; And as cedars shall holy ones be multiplied from me forever, And their branches shall stretch afar off. 3 Then shall

perish the seed of Canaan, And a remnant shall not be unto Amalek, And all the Cappadocians shall perish, And all the Hittites shall be utterly destroyed. 4 Then shall fail the land of Ham, And all the people shall perish. Then shall all the earth rest from trouble, And all the world under heaven from war. 5 Then the Mighty One of Israel shall glorify Shem, For the Lord God shall appear on earth, And Himself save men. 6 Then shall all the spirits of deceit be given to be trodden under foot, And men shall rule over wicked spirits. 7 Then shall I arise in joy, And will bless the Most High because of his marvellous works, [Because God hath taken a body and eaten with men and saved men].

7 1 And now, my children, obey Levi and Judah, and be not lifted up against these two tribes, for 2 from them shall arise unto you the salvation of God. For the Lord shall raise up from Levi as it were a High-priest, and from Judah as it were a King [God and man], He shall save all [the Gentiles 3 and] the race of Israel. Therefore I give you these commands that ye also may command your children that they may observe them throughout their generations.

8 1 And when Simeon had made an end of commanding his sons, he slept with his fathers, being an 2 hundred and twenty years old. And they laid him in a wooden coffin, to take up his bones to 3 Hebron. And they took them up secretly during a war of the Egyptians. For the bones of Joseph 4 the Egyptians guarded in the tombs of the kings. For the sorcerers told them; that on the departure of the bones of Joseph there should be throughout all the land darkness and gloom, and an exceeding great plague to the Egyptians, so that even with a lamp a man should not recognize his brother.

9 1, 2 And the sons of Simeon bewailed their father. And they were in Egypt until the day of their departure by the hand of Moses.

THE TESTAMENT OF LEVI, THE THIRD SON OF JACOB AND LEAH

1 1 The copy of the words of Levi, the things which he ordained unto his sons, according to all that 2 they should do, and what things should befall them until the day of judgement. He was sound in health when he called them to him; for it had been revealed to him that

he should die. And when they were gathered together he said to them:

2 1, 2 I, Levi, was born in Haran, and I came with my father to Shechem. And I was young, about

3 twenty years of age, when, with Simeon, I wrought vengeance on Hamor for our sister Dinah. And when I was feeding the flocks in Abel-Maul, the spirit of understanding of the Lord came upon me, and I saw all men corrupting their way, and that unrighteousness had built for itself walls, and lawlessness 4 sat upon towers. And I was grieving for the race of the sons of men, and I prayed to the 5 Lord that I might be saved. Then there fell upon me a sleep, and I beheld a high mountain, and 6 I was upon it. And behold the heavens were opened and an angel of God said to me, Levi enter 7 And I entered from the first heaven, and I saw there a great sea hanging. 8 And further I saw a second heaven far brighter and more brilliant, for there was a boundless light also therein. 9 And I said to the angel, Why Is this so? And the angel said to me, Marvel not at this, for thou shalt see another heaven more brilliant and incomparable. 10 And when thou hast ascended thither, Thou shalt stand near the Lord, And shalt be His minister, And shalt declare His mysteries to men, And shall proclaim concerning Him that shall redeem Israel. 11 And by thee and Judah shall the Lord appear among men Saving every race of men. 12 And from the Lord's portion shall be thy life, And He shall be thy field and vineyard, And fruits, gold, and silver.

3 1 Hear, therefore, regarding the heavens which have been shown to thee. The lowest is for this cause gloomy unto thee, in that it beholds all the unrighteous deeds of men. 2 And it has fire, snow, and ice made ready for the day of judgement, in the righteous judgement of God; for in it are all the spirits of the retributions for vengeance on men. 3 And in the second are the hosts of the armies which are ordained for the day of judgement, to work vengeance on the spirits of deceit and of Beliar. And above them are the holy ones. 4 And in the highest of all dwelleth the Great Glory, far above all holiness. 5 In [the heaven next to] it are the archangels, who minister and make propitiation to the Lord for all the sins of ignorance of the righteous; Offering to the Lord a sweet- smelling savour, a reasonable and a bloodless offering. 7 And [in the heaven below this] are the angels who bear answers to the angels of the presence of the Lord. 8 And in the heaven next to this are thrones and dominions, in which always they offer praise to God. 9 When, therefore, the Lord looketh upon us, all of us are shaken; yea, the heavens, and the earth, and the abysses are shaken at the presence of His majesty. 10

But the sons of men, having no perception of these things sin and provoke the Most High.

4 1 Now, therefore, know that the Lord shall execute judgment upon the sons of men. Because when the rocks are being rent, And the sun quenched, And the waters dried up, And the fire cowering, And all creation troubled, And the invisible spirits melting away; And Hades taketh spoils through the visitations of the Most High, Men will be unbelieving and persist in their iniquity. On this account with punishment shall they be judged. 2 Therefore the Most High hath heard thy prayer, To separate thee from iniquity, and that thou shouldst become to Him a son, And a servant, and a minister of His presence. 3 The light of knowledge shalt thou light up in Jacob, And as the sun shalt thou be to all the seed of Israel. 4 And there shall be given to thee a blessing, and to all thy seed, Until the Lord shall visit all the Gentiles in His tender mercies for ever. 5 And therefore there have been given to thee counsel and understanding, That thou mightst instruct thy sons concerning this; 6 Because they that bless Him shall be blessed, And they that curse Him shall perish.

5 1 And thereupon the angel opened to me the gates of heaven, and I saw the holy temple, and upon 2 a throne of glory the Most High. And He said to me: Levi, I have given thee the blessings of the 3 priesthood until I come and sojourn in the midst of Israel. Then the angel brought me down to the earth, and gave me a shield and a sword, and said to me: Execute vengeance on Shechem because 4 of Dinah, thy sister, and I will be with thee because the Lord hath sent me. And I destroyed at 5 that time the sons of Hamor, as it is written in the heavenly tables. And I said to him: I pray 6 thee, O Lord, tell me Thy name, that I may call upon Thee in a day of tribulation. And he said: I am the angel who intercedeth for the nation of Israel that they may not be smitten utterly, 7 for every evil spirit attacketh it. And after these things I awaked, and blessed the Most High, and the angel who intercedeth for the nation of Israel and for all the righteous.

6 1 And when I was going to my father, I found a brazen shield; wherefore also the name of the 2 mountain is Aspis, which is near Gebal, to the south of Abila And I kept these words in my 3 heart. And after this I counselled my father, and Reuben my brother, to bid the sons of Hamor not to be circumcised; for I was zealous because of the abomination which they had wrought on 4, 5 my sister. And I slew Shechem first, and Simeon slew Hamor. And after this my brothers 6 came and smote that city with the edge of the sword. And my father heard these things and was wroth, and he was grieved in that they had received the circumcision, and after that had been 7 put to death,

and in his blessings he looked amiss upon us. For we sinned because we had done 8 this thing against his will, and he was sick on that day. But I saw that the sentence of God was for evil upon Shechem; for they sought to do to Sarah and Rebecca as they had done to Dinah our 9 sister, but the Lord prevented them. And they persecuted Abraham our father when he was a stranger, and they vexed his flocks when they were big with young; and Eblaen, who was born in his 10 house, they most shamefully handled. And thus they did to all strangers, taking away their 11 wives by force, and they banished them. But the wrath of the Lord came upon them to the uttermost.

7 1 And I said to my father Jacob: By thee will the Lord despoil the Canaanites, and will give 2 their land to thee and to thy seed after thee. For from this day forward shall Shechem be 3 called a city of imbeciles; for as a man mocketh a fool, so did we mock them. Because also 4 they had wrought folly in Israel by defiling my sister. And we departed and came to Bethel.

8 1, 2 And there again I saw a vision as the former, after we had spent there seventy days. And I saw seven men in white raiment saying unto me: Arise, put on the robe of the priesthood, and the crown of righteousness, and the breastplate of understanding, and the garment of truth, and the plate of faith, and the 3 turban of the head, and the ephod of prophecy. And they severally carried (these things) and put (them,) on me, and said unto me: From henceforth become a priest of the Lord, thou and thy seed for 4, 5 ever. And the first anointed me with holy oil, and gave to me the staff of judgment. The second washed me with pure water, and fed me with bread and wine (even) the most holy things, and clad 6, 7 me with a holy and glorious robe. The third clothed me with a linen vestment like an ephod. The 8, 9 fourth put round me a girdle like unto purple. The fifth gave me a branch of rich olive. The sixth 10 placed a crown on my head. The seventh placed on my head a diadem of priesthood, and filled my 11 hands with incense, that I might serve as priest to the Lord God. And they said to me: Levi, thy 12 seed shall be divided into three offices, for a sign of the glory of the Lord who is to come. And the 13 first portion shall be great; yea, greater than it shall none be. The second shall be in the priesthood. 14 And the third shall be called by a new name, because a king shall arise in Judah, and shall 15 establish a new priesthood, after the fashion of the Gentiles [to all the Gentiles]. And His presence is beloved, as a prophet of the Most High, of the seed of Abraham our father. 16 Therefore, every desirable thing in Israel shall be for thee and for thy seed, And ye shall eat everything fair to look upon, And the table of the Lord shall thy seed apportion. 17 And some of them shall be high priests, and judges, and scribes; For

by their mouth shall the holy place be guarded. 18, 19 And when I awoke, I understood that this (dream) was like the first dream. And I hid this also in my heart, and told it not to any man upon the earth.

9 1, 2 And after two days I and Judah went up with our father Jacob to Isaac our father's father. And my father's father blessed me according to all the words of the visions which I had seen. And 3 he would not come with us to Bethel. And when we came to Bethel, my father saw a vision 4 concerning me, that I should be their priest unto God. And he rose up early in the morning, 5 and paid tithes of all to the Lord through me. And so we came to Hebron to dwell there. 6 And Isaac called me continually to put me in remembrance of the law of the Lord, even as the 7 angel of the Lord showed unto me. And he taught me the law of the priesthood, of sacrifices, 8 whole burnt-offerings, first-fruits, freewill-offerings, peace-offerings. And each day he was instructing me, and was busied on my behalf before the Lord, and said to me: Beware of the spirit of 10 fornication; for this shall continue and shall by thy seed pollute the holy place. Take, therefore, to thyself a wife without blemish or pollution, w bile yet thou art young, and not of the race of 11 strange nations. And before entering into the holy place, bathe; and when thou offerest the 12 sacrifices wash; and again, when thou finishest the sacrifice, wash Of twelve trees having leaves 13, offer to the Lord, as Abraham taught me also. And of every clean beast and bird offer a 14 sacrifice to the Lord. And of all thy first-fruits and of wine offer the first, as a sacrifice to the Lord God; and every sacrifice thou shalt salt with salt.

10 1 Now, therefore, observe whatsoever I command you, children: for whatsoever things I have 2 heard from my fathers I have declared unto you. And behold I am clear from your ungodliness and transgression, which ye shall commit in the end of the ages [against the Saviour of the world, Christ, acting godlessly], deceiving Israel, and stirring up against it great evils from the 3 Lord. And ye shall deal lawlessly together with Israel, so He shall not bear with Jerusalem because of your wickedness; but the veil of the temple shall be rent, so as not to cover your 4 shame. And ye shall be scattered as captives among the Gentiles, and shall be for a reproach 5 and for a curse there. For the house which the Lord shall choose shall be called Jerusalem, as is contained in the book of Enoch the righteous.

11 1,2 Therefore when I took a wife I was twenty-eight years old, and her name was Melcha. And she conceived and bare a son, and I called his name Gersam, for we were sojourners in our land 3, 4 And I saw concerning him, that he would not be in the first rank, And Kohath was born in the 5 thirty-fifth year of

my life, towards sunrise. And I saw in a vision that he was standing on high 6 in the midst of all the congregation, Therefore I called his name Kohath [which is, beginning of 7 majesty and instruction]. And she bare me a third son, in the fortieth year of my life; and since his mother bare him with difficulty, I called him Merari, that is, 'my bitterness,' because he also was 8 like to die. And Jochebed was born in Egypt, in my sixty-fourth year, for I was renowned then in the midst of my brethren.

12 1, 2 And Gersam took a wife, and she bare to him Lomni and Semei. And the sons of Kohath, 3, 4 Ambram, Issachar, Hebron, and Ozeel. And the sons of Merari, Mooli, and Mouses. And in the ninety-fourth year Ambram took Jochebed my daughter to him to wife, for they were born in one 5 day, he and my daughter. Eight years old was I when I went into the land of Canaan, and eighteen years when I slew Shechem, and at nineteen years I became priest, and at twenty-eight years I took 6 a wife, and at forty-eight I went into Egypt. And behold, my children, ye are a third generation. 7 In my hundred and eighteenth year Joseph died.

13 1 And now, my children, I command you: Fear the Lord your God with your whole heart, And walk in simplicity according to all His law. 2 And do ye also teach your children letters, That they may have understanding all their life, Reading unceasingly the law of God. 3 For every one that knoweth the law of the Lord shall be honoured, And shall not be a stranger whithersoever he goeth. 4 Yea, many friends shall he gain more than his parents, And many men shall desire to serve him, And to hear the law from his mouth. 5 Work righteousness, therefore, my children, upon the earth, That ye may have (it) as a treasure in heaven. 6 And sow good things in your souls, That ye may find them in your life. But if ye sow evil things, Ye shall reap every trouble and affliction. 7 Get wisdom in the fear of God with diligence; For though there be a leading into captivity, And cities and lands be destroyed, And gold and silver and every possession perish, The wisdom of the wise nought can take away, Save the blindness of ungodliness, and the callousness (that comes) of sin. 8 For if one keep oneself from these evil things, Then even among his enemies shall wisdom be a glory to him, And in a strange country a fatherland, And in the midst of foes shall prove a friend. 9 Whosoever teaches noble things and does them, Shall be enthroned with kings, As was also Joseph my brother.

14 1 Therefore, my children, I have learnt that at the end of the ages ye will transgress against the Lord, stretching out hands to wickedness [against Him]; and to all the Gentiles shall ye become a scorn. 2 For our

father Israel is pure from the transgressions of the chief priests [who shall lay their hands upon the Saviour of the world]. 3 For as the heaven is purer in the Lord's sight than the earth, so also be ye, the lights of Israel, (purer) than all the Gentiles. 4 But if ye be darkened through transgressions, what, therefore, will all the Gentiles do living in blindness? Yea, ye shall bring a curse upon our race, because the light of the law which was given for to lighten every man this ye desire to destroy by teaching commandments contrary to the ordinances of God. 5 The offerings of the Lord ye shall rob, and from His portion shall ye steal choice portions, 6 eating (them) contemptuously with harlots. And out of covetousness ye shall teach the commandments of the Lord, wedded women shall ye pollute, and the virgins of Jerusalem shall ye defile: and with harlots and adulteresses shall ye be joined, and the daughters of the Gentiles shall ye take to wife, purifying them with an unlawful purification; and your union shall be like unto Sodom and 7 Gomorrah. And ye shall be puffed up because of your priesthood, lifting yourselves up against 8 men, and not only so, but also against the commands of God. For ye shall contemn the holy things with jests and laughter.

15 1 Therefore the temple, which the Lord shall choose, shall be laid waste through your uncleanness, 2 and ye shall be captives throughout all nations. And ye shall be an abomination unto them, and ye 3 shall receive reproach and everlasting shame from the righteous judgement of God. And all who hate 4 you shall rejoice at your destruction. And if you were not to receive mercy through Abraham, Isaac, and Jacob, our fathers, not one of our seed should be left upon the earth.

16 1 And now I have learnt that for seventy weeks ye shall go astray, and profane the priesthood, and 2 pollute the sacrifices. And ye shall make void the law, and set at nought the words of the prophets by evil perverseness. And ye shall persecute righteous men, and hate the godly the words of the 3 faithful shall ye abhor. [And a man who reneweth the law in the power of the Most High, ye shall call a deceiver; and at last ye shall rush (upon him) to slay him, not knowing his dignity, taking 4 innocent blood through wickedness upon your heads.] And your holy places shall be laid waste 5 even to the ground because of him. And ye shall have no place that is clean; but ye shall be among the Gentiles a curse and a dispersion until He shall again visit you and in pity shall receive you [through faith and water].

17 1 And whereas ye have heard concerning the seventy weeks, hear also concerning the priesthood. 2 For in each jubilee there shall be a priesthood. And in the first jubilee, the first who is anointed to the priesthood shall be great, and shall speak to God as to a father. And his priesthood shall be perfect with the Lord, [and in the day of his gladness shall he arise for the salvation of the world]. 3 In the second jubilee, he that is anointed shall be conceived in the sorrow of beloved ones; and his 4 priesthood shall be honoured and shall be glorified by all. And the third priest shall be taken hold 5 of by sorrow. And the fourth shall be in pain, because unrighteousness shall gather itself against 6 him exceedingly, and all Israel shall hate each one his neighbour. The fifth shall be taken hold of 7 by darkness Likewise also the sixth and the seventh. And in the seventh shall be such pollution 8 as I cannot express before men, for they shall know it who do these things. Therefore shall they 9 be taken captive and become a prey, and their land and their substance shall be destroyed. 10 And in the fifth week they shall return to their desolate country, and shall renew the house of the 11 Lord. And in the seventh week shall become priests, (who are) idolaters, adulterers, lovers of money, proud, lawless, lascivious, abusers of children and beasts.

18 1 And after their punishment shall have come from the Lord, the priesthood shall fail. 2 Then shall the Lord raise up a new priest. And to him all the words of the Lord shall be revealed; And he shall execute a righteous judgement upon the earth for a multitude of days. 3 And his star shall arise in heaven as of a king. Lighting up the light of knowledge as the sun the day, And he shall be magnified in the world. 4 He shall shine forth as the sun on the earth, And shall remove all darkness from under heaven, And there shall be peace in all the earth. 5 The heavens shall exult in his days, And the earth shall be glad, And the clouds shall rejoice, [And the knowledge of the Lord shall be poured forth upon the earth, as the water of the seas; And the angels of the glory of the presence of the Lord shall be glad in him. 6 The heavens shall be opened, And From the temple of glory shall come upon him sanctification, With the Father's voice as from Abraham to Isaac. 7 And the glory of the Most High shall be uttered over him, And the spirit of understanding and sanctification shall rest upon him [in the water]. 8 For he shall give the majesty of the Lord to His sons in truth for evermore; And there shall none succeed him for all generations for ever. 9 And in his priesthood the Gentiles shall be multiplied in knowledge upon the earth, And enlightened through the grace of the Lord: In his priesthood shall sin come to an end, And the lawless shall cease to do evil. [And the just shall rest in him.] 10 And he shall open the gates of paradise, And shall remove the threatening sword against Adam. 11 And he shall give to the saints to eat from the tree of life, And the spirit of holiness shall be on them. 12 And Beliar shall be bound by him, And he shall give power to His children to tread upon the evil spirits. 13 And the Lord shall rejoice in His

children, And be well pleased in His beloved ones for ever. 14 Then shall Abraham and Isaac and Jacob exult, And I will be glad, And all the saints shall clothe themselves with joy.

19 1 And now, my children, ye have heard all; choose, therefore, for yourselves either the light or the 2 darkness, either the law of the Lord or the works of Beliar. And his sons answered him, saying, 3 Before the Lord we will walk according to His law. And their father said unto them, The Lord is witness, and His angels are witnesses, and ye are witnesses, and I am witness, concerning the word 4 of your mouth. And his sons said unto him: We are witnesses. And thus Levi ceased commanding his sons; and he stretched out his feet on the bed, and was gathered to his fathers, after he had 5 lived a hundred and thirty-seven years. And they laid him in a coffin, and afterwards they buried him in Hebron, with Abraham, Isaac, and Jacob

THE TESTAMENT OF JUDAH, THE FOURTH SON OF JACOB AND LEAH

1 1, 2 The copy of the words of Judah, what things he spake to his sons before he died. They gathered 3 themselves together, therefore, and came to him, and he said to them: Hearken, my children, to Judah your father. I was the fourth son born to my father Jacob; and Leah my mother named 4 me Judah, saying, I give thanks to the Lord, because He hath given me a fourth son also. I was 5 swift in my youth, and obedient to my father in everything. And I honoured my mother and my 6 mother's sister. And it came to pass, when I became a man, that my father blessed me, saying, Thou shalt be a king, prospering in all things.

2 1, 2 And the Lord showed me favour in all my works both in the field and in the house. I know that 3 I raced a hind, and caught it, and prepared the meat for my father, and he did eat. And the roes I used to master in the chase, and overtake all that was in the plains. A wild mare I overtook, and 4 caught it and tamed it. I slew a lion and plucked a kid out of its mouth. I took a bear by its paw 5 and hurled it down the cliff, and it was crushed. I outran the wild boar, and seizing it as I ran, 6 I tore it in sunder. A leopard in Hebron leaped upon my dog, and I caught it by the tail, and 7 hurled it on the rocks, and it was broken in twain. I found a wild ox feeding in the fields, and seizing it by the horns, and whirling it round and stunning it, I cast it from me and slew it.

3 1 And when the two kings of the Canaanites came sheathed in armour against our flocks, and much people with them, single-handed I rushed upon the king of Hazor, and smote him on the greaves 2 and dragged him down, and so I Slew him. And the other, the king of Tappuah, as he sat upon his 3 horse, [I slew, and so I scattered all his people. Achor the king] a man of giant stature I found, hurling javelins before and behind as he sat on horseback, and I took up a stone of sixty pounds 4 weight, and hurled it and smote his horse, and killed it. And I fought with (this) other for two 5 hours; and I clave his shield in twain, and I chopped off his feet, and killed him. And as I was 6 stripping off his breastplate, behold nine men his companions began to fight with me. And I wound my garment on my hand; and I slung stones at them, and killed four of them, and the rest fled. 7 And Jacob my father slew Beelesath, king of all the kings, a giant in strength, twelve cubits high. 8, 9 And fear fell upon them, and they ceased warring against us. Therefore my father was free from 10 anxiety in the wars when I was with my brethren. For he saw in a vision concerning me that an angel of might followed me everywhere, that I should not be overcome.
4 1 And in the south there came upon us a greater war than that in Shechem; and I joined in battle array with my brethren, and pursued a thousand men, and slew of them two hundred men and 2, 3 four kings. And I went up upon the wall, and I slew four mighty men. And so we captured Hazor, and took all the spoil.

5 1 On the next day we departed to Aretan, a city strong and walled and inaccessible, threatening us 2 with death. But I and Gad approached on the east side of the city, and Reuben and Levi on the 3 west. And they that were upon the wall, thinking that we were alone, were drawn down against 4 us. And so my brothers secretly climbed up the wall on both sides by stakes, and entered the city, 5 while the men knew it not. And we took it with the edge of the sword. And as

for those who had taken refuge in the tower, we set fire to the tower and took both it and them. 6 And as we were departing the men of Tappuah set upon our spoil, and delivering it up to our sons we fought with them as far as Tappuah. 7 And we slew them and burnt their city, and took as spoil all that was in it.

6 1, 2 And when I was at the waters of Kozeba, the men of Jobel came against us to battle. And we fought with them and routed them; and their allies from Shiloh we slew, and we did not leave 3 them power to come in against us. And the men of Makir came upon us the fifth day, to seize our spoil; and we attacked them and overcame them in fierce battle: for there was a host of mighty 4 men amongst them, and we slew them before they had gone up the ascent. And when we came to 5 their city their women rolled upon us stones from the brow of the hill on which the city stood, And I and Simeon hid ourselves behind the town, and seized upon the heights, and destroyed this city also.

7 1 And the next day it was told us that the king of the city of Gaash with a mighty host was coming 2 against us. I, therefore, and Dan feigned ourselves to be Amorites, and as allies went into their 3 city. And in the depth of night our brethren came and we opened to them the gates; and we destroyed all the men and their substance, and we took for a prey all that was theirs, and their three 4 walls we cast down. And we drew near to Thamna, where was all the substance of the hostile kings. Then being insulted by them, I was therefore wroth, and rushed against them to the summit; and 6 they kept slinging against me stones and darts. And had not Dan my brother aided me, they would 7 have slain me. We came upon them, therefore, with wrath, and they all fled; and passing by 8 another way, they besought my father, and he made peace with them. And we did to them no hurt, 9 and they became tributary to us, and we restored to them their spoil. And I built Thamna, and my 10 father built Pabael. I was twenty years old when this war befell. And the Canaanites feared me and my brethren.

8 1, 2 And I had much cattle, and I had for chief herdsman Iram the Adullamite. And when I went to him I saw Parsaba, king of Adullam; and he spake unto us, and he made us a feast; 3 and when I was heated he gave me his daughter Bathshua to wife. She bare me Er, and Onan and Shelah; and two of them the Lord smote: for Shelah lived, and his children are ye.

9 1 And eighteen years my father abode in peace with his brother Esau, and his sons with us, after 2 that we came from Mesopotamia, from Laban. And when eighteen years were fulfilled, in the fortieth year of my life, Esau, the brother of my father, came upon us with a mighty and strong 3 people. And Jacob smote Esau

with an arrow, and he was taken up wounded on Mount Seir, and 4 as he went he died at Anoniram. And we pursued after the sons of Esau. Now they had a city with walls of iron and gates of brass; and we could not enter into it, and we encamped around, and 5 besieged it. And when they opened not to us in twenty days, I set up a ladder in the sight of all and with my shield upon my head I went up, sustaining the assault of stones, upwards of three 6, 7 talents weight; and I slew four of their mighty men. And Reuben and Gad slew six others. Then they asked from us terms of peace; and having taken counsel with our father, we received them as 8 tributaries. And they gave us five hundred cors of wheat, five hundred baths of oil, five hundred measures of wine, until the famine, when we went down into Egypt.

10 1 And after these things my son Er took to wife Tamar, from Mesopotamia, a daughter of Aram. 2 Now Er was wicked, and he was in need concerning Tamar, because she was not of the land 3 of Canaan. And on the third night an angel of the Lord smote him. And he had not known her according to the evil craftiness of his mother, for he did not wish to have children by her. In the days of the wedding-feast I gave Onan to her in marriage; and he also in wickedness knew her not, 5 though he spent with her a year. And when I threatened him he went in unto her, but he spilled the seed on the ground, according to the command of his mother, and he also died through wickedness. 6 And I wished to give Shelah also to her, but his mother did not permit it; for she wrought evil against Tamar, because she was not of the daughters of Canaan, as she also herself was.

11 1 And I knew that the race of the Canaanites was wicked, but the impulse of youth blinded my 2 mind. And when I saw her pouring out wine, owing to the intoxication of wine I was deceived, and 3 took her although my father had not counselled (it). And while I was away she went and took for 4 Shelah a wife from Canaan. And when I knew what she had done, I cursed her in the anguish of 5 my soul. And she also died through her wickedness together with her sons.

12 1 And after these things, while Tamar was a widow, she heard after two years that I was going up 2 to shear my sheep, and adorned herself in bridal array, and sat in the city Enaim by the gate. For it was a law of the Amorites, that she who was about to marry should sit in fornication seven days 3 by the gate. Therefore being drunk with wine, I did not recognize her; and her beauty deceived 4 me, through the fashion of her adorning. And I turned aside to her, and said: Let me go in unto thee. And she said: What wilt thou give me? And I gave her my staff, and my girdle, and the 5 diadem of my kingdom in pledge. And I went in unto

her, and she conceived. And not knowing 6 what I had done, I wished to slay her; but she privily sent my pledges, and put me to shame. And when I called her, I heard also the secret words which I spoke when lying with her in my drunkenness; 7 and I could not slay her, because it was from the Lord. For I said, Lest haply she did it in 8 subtlety, having received the pledge from another woman. But I came not again near her while 9 I lived, because I had done this abomination in all Israel. Moreover, they who were in the city said there was no harlot in the gate, because she came from another place, and sat for a while in the 10, 11 gate. And I thought that no one knew that I had gone in to her. And after this we came into 12 Egypt to Joseph, because of the famine. And I was forty and six years old, and seventy and three years lived I in Egypt.

13 1 And now I command you, my children, hearken to Judah your father, and keep my sayings to 2 perform all the ordinances of the Lord, and to obey the commands of God. And walk not after your lusts, nor in the imaginations of your thoughts in haughtiness of heart; and glory not in the deeds 3 and strength of your youth, for this also is evil in the eyes of the Lord. Since I also gloried that in wars no comely woman's face ever enticed me, and reproved Reuben my brother concerning Bilhah, the wife of my father, the spirits of jealousy and of fornication arrayed themselves against me, until I lay with Bathshua the Canaanite, and Tamar, who was espoused to my sons. For I said to my father-in-law: I will take counsel with my father, and so will I take thy daughter. And he was unwilling, but he showed me a boundless store of gold in his daughter's behalf; for he was 5 a king. And he adorned her with gold and pearls, and caused her to pour out wine for us at the 6 feast with the beauty of women. And the wine turned aside my eyes, and pleasure blinded my 7 heart. And I became enamoured of and I lay with her, and transgressed the commandment of the 8 Lord and the commandment of my fathers, and I took her to wife. And the Lord rewarded me according to the imagination of my heart, inasmuch as I had no joy in her children.

14 1 And now, my children, I say unto you, be not drunk with wine; for wine turneth the mind away 2 from the truth, and inspires the passion of lust, and leadeth the eyes into error. For the spirit of fornication hath wine as a minister to give pleasure to the mind; for these two also take away the 3 mind of man. For if a man drink wine to drunkenness, it disturbeth the mind with filthy thoughts leading to fornication, and heateth the body to carnal union; and if the occasion of the lust be 4 present, he worketh the sin, and is not ashamed. Such is the inebriated man, my children; for he 5 who is drunken reverenceth no man. For, lo, it made me also to err, so that I was not ashamed of the

multitude in the city, in that before the eyes of all I turned aside unto Tamar, and I wrought 6 a great sin, and I uncovered the covering of my sons' shame. After I had drunk wine I reverenced 7 not the commandment of God, and I took a woman of Canaan to wife. For much discretion needeth the man who drinketh wine, my children; and herein is discretion in drinking wine a man 8 may drink so long as he preserveth modesty. But if he go beyond this limit the spirit of deceit attacketh his mind, and it maketh the drunkard to talk filthily, and to transgress and not to be ashamed, but even to glory in his shame, and to account himself honourable.

15 1 He that committeth fornication is not aware when he suffers loss, and is not ashamed when put 2 to dishonour. For even though a man be a king and commit fornication, he is stripped of his 3 kingship by becoming the slave of fornication, as I myself also suffered. For I gave my staff, that is, the stay of my tribe; and my girdle, that is, my power; and my diadem, that is, the glory of my 4 kingdom. And indeed I repented of these things; wine and flesh I eat not until my old age, nor 5 did I behold any joy. And the angel of God showed me that for ever do women bear rule over 6 king and beggar alike. And from the king they take away his glory, and from the valiant man his might, and from the beggar even that little which is the stay of his poverty.

16 1 Observe, therefore, my children, the (rights limit in wine; for there are in it four evil spirits--- of 2 lust, of hot desire, of profligacy of filthy lucre. If ye drink wine in gladness, be ye modest in the fear of God. For if in (your) gladness the fear of God departeth, then drunkenness ariseth and 3 shamelessness stealeth in. But if ye would live soberly do not touch wine at all, lest ye sin in words of outrage, and in fightings and slanders, and transgressions of the commandments of God, 4 and ye perish before your time. Moreover, wine revealeth the mysteries of God and men, even as I also revealed the commandments of God and the mysteries of Jacob my father to the Canaanitish 5 woman Bathshua, which God bade me not to reveal. And wine is a cause both of war and confusion.

17 1 And now, I command you, my children, not to love money, nor to gaze upon the beauty of women; because for the sake of money and beauty I was led astray to Bathshua the Canaanite. 2, 3 [For I know that because of these two things shall my race fall into wickedness. For even wise men among my sons shall they mar, and shall cause the kingdom of Judah to be diminished, which 4 the Lord gave me because of my obedience to my father. For I never caused grief to Jacob, my 5 father: for all things whatsoever he commanded I did. And Isaac, the father of my father,

blessed 6 me to be king in Israel, and Jacob further blessed me in like manner. And I know that from me shall the kingdom be established.

18 1 And I know what evils ye will do in the last days.] 2 Beware, therefore, my children, of fornication, and the love of money, and hearken to Judah your father. 3 For these things withdraw you from the law of God, And blind the inclination of the soul, And teach arrogance, And suffer not a man to have compassion upon his neighbour 4 They rob his soul of all goodness, And oppress him with toils and troubles, And drive away sleep from him, And devour his flesh. 5 And he hindereth the sacrifices of God; And he remembereth not the blessing of God, He hearkeneth not to a prophet when he speaketh, And resenteth the words of godliness. 6 For he is a slave to two contrary passions, And cannot obey God, Because they have blinded his soul, And he walketh in the day as in the night.

19 1 My children, the love of money leadeth to idolatry; because, when led astray through money, men name as gods those who are not gods, and it causeth him who hath it to fall into madness 2 For the sake of money I lost my children, and had not my repentance, and my humiliation, and 3 the prayers of my father been accepted, I should have died childless. But the God of my fathers 4 had mercy on me, because I did it in ignorance. And the prince of deceit blinded me, and I sinned as a man and as flesh, being corrupted through sins; and I learnt my own weakness while thinking myself invincible.

20 1 Know, therefore, my children, that two spirits wait upon man the spirit of truth and the spirit 2 of deceit. And in the midst is the spirit of understanding of the mind, to which it belongeth to turn whithersoever it will. 3 And the works of truth and the works of deceit are written upon the hearts of men, and each one of them the Lord knoweth. 4 And there is no time at which the works of men can be hid; for on the heart itself have they been 5 written down before the Lord. And the spirit of truth testifieth all things, and accuseth all; and the sinner is burnt up by his own heart, and cannot raise his face to the judge.

21 1 And now, my children, I command you, love Levi, that ye may abide, and exalt not yourselves 2 against him, lest ye be utterly destroyed. For to me the Lord gave the kingdom, and to him the 3 priesthood, and He set the kingdom beneath the priesthood. To me He gave the things upon the 4 earth; to him the things in the heavens. As the heaven is higher than the earth, so is the priesthood of God higher than the earthly kingdom, unless it falls away through sin from the Lord and is 5 dominated by the earthly kingdom. For the angel of the Lord said unto me: The Lord chose him

rather than thee, to draw near to Him, and to eat of His table and to offer Him the first-fruits of the choice things of the sons of Israel; but thou shalt be king of Jacob. 6 And thou shalt be amongst them as the sea. For as, on the sea, just and unjust are tossed about, some taken into captivity while some are enriched, so also shall every race of men be in thee: some shall be impoverished, being taken captive, and others grow rich by plundering the possessions of others. 7 For the kings shall be as sea-monsters. They shall swallow men like fishes: The sons and daughters of free men shall they enslave; Houses, lands, flocks, money shall they plunder: 8 And with the flesh of many shall they wrongfully feed the ravens and the cranes; And they shall advance in evil, in covetousness uplifted, 9 And there shall be false prophets like tempests, And they shall persecute all righteous men.

22 1 And the Lord shall bring upon them divisions one against another. And there shall be continual wars in Israel; 2 And among men of another race shall my kingdom be brought to an end, Until the salvation of Israel shall come, Until the appearing of the God of righteousness, That Jacob [and all the Gentiles] may rest in peace. 3 And He shall guard the might of my kingdom for ever; For the Lord sware to me with an oath that He would not destroy the kingdom from my seed for ever.

23 1 Now I have much grief, my children, because of your lewdness and witchcrafts, and idolatries which ye shall practise against the kingdom, following them that have familiar spirits, diviners, and 2 demons of error. Ye shall make your daughters singing girls and harlots, and ye shall mingle in 3 the abominations of the Gentiles. For which things' sake the Lord shall bring upon you famine and pestilence, death and the sword, beleaguering by enemies, and revilings of friends, the slaughter of children, the rape of wives, the plundering of possessions, the burning of the temple of God,] the 4 laying waste of the land, the enslavement of yourselves among the Gentiles. And they shall make some of you eunuchs for their wives. 5 Until the Lord visit you, when with perfect heart ye repent and walk in all His commandments; and He bring you up from captivity among the Gentiles.

24 1 And after these things shall a star arise to you from Jacob in peace, And a man shall arise [from my seed], like the sun of righteousness, walking with the sons of men in meekness and righteousness; And no sin shall be found in him. 2 and the heavens shall be open unto him, To pour out the spirit, (even) the blessing of the Holy Father; 3 And He shall pour out the spirit of grace upon you; And ye shall be unto Him sons in truth, And ye shall walk in His commandments first and last. 4 [This Branch of God Most High, And this Fountain

giving life unto all.] 5 Then shall the sceptre of my kingdom shine forth; And from your root shall arise a stem; 6 And from it shall grow a rod of righteousness to the Gentiles, To judge and to save all that call upon the Lord.

26 1 And after these things shall Abraham and Isaac and Jacob arise unto life, and I and my brethren shall be chiefs of the tribes of Israel: Levi first, I the second, Joseph third, Benjamin fourth, 2 Simeon fifth; Issachar sixth, and so all in order. And the Lord blessed Levi, and the Angel of the Presence, me; the powers of glory, Simeon; the heaven, Reuben; the earth, Issachar; the sea, Zebulun; the mountains, Joseph; the tabernacle, Benjamin; the luminaries, Dan; Eden, Naphtali; the sun, Gad; the moon, Asher. 3 And ye shall be the people of the Lord, and have one tongue; And there shall be there no spirit of deceit of Beliar, For he shall be cast into the fire for ever. 4 And they who have died in grief shall arise in joy , And they who were poor for the Lord's sake shall be made rich, And they who are put to death for the Lord's sake shall awake to life. 5 And the harts of Jacob shall run in joyfulness, And the eagles of Israel shall fly in gladness; And all the people shall glorify the Lord for ever.

26 1 Observe, therefore, my children, all the law of the Lord, for there is hope for all them who hold 2 fast unto His ways. And he said to them: Behold, I die before your eyes this day, a hundred and 3 nineteen years old. Let no one bury me in costly apparel, nor tear open my bowels, for this 4 shall they who are kings do; and carry me up to Hebron with you. And Judah, when he had said these things, fell asleep; and his sons did according to all whatsoever he commanded them, and they buried him in Hebron, with his fathers.

THE TESTAMENT OF ISSACHAR, THE FIFTH SON OF JACOB AND LEAH.

1 1 The copy of the words of Issachar. For he called his sons and said to them: Hearken, my children, to Issachar your father; Give ear to the words of him who is beloved of the Lord. 2, 3 I was born the fifth son to Jacob, by way of hire for the mandrakes. For Reuben my brother 4 brought in mandrakes from the field, and Rachel met him and took them. And Reuben wept, and 5 at his voice Leah my mother came forth. Now these (mandrakes) were sweet-smelling apples 6 which were produced in the land of Haran below a ravine of water. And Rachel said: I will not give them to thee, but they shall be to me instead of children. For the Lord hath despised me, 7 and I have not borne children to Jacob. Now there were two apples; and Leah said to Rachel: 8 Let it suffice thee that thou hast taken my husband: wilt thou take these also? And Rachel said 9 to her: Thou shalt have Jacob this night for the mandrakes of thy son. And Leah said to her: 10 Jacob is mine, for I am the wife of his youth. But Rachel said: Boast not, and vaunt not thyself; for he espoused me before thee, and for my sake he served our father fourteen years. 11 And had not craft increased on the earth and the

wickedness of men prospered, thou wouldst not now see the face of Jacob.

2 1 Then appeared to Jacob an angel of the Lord, saying: Two children shall Rachel bear, inasmuch 2 as she hath refused company with her husband, and hath chosen continency. And had not Leah my mother paid the two apples for the sake of his company, she would have borne eight sons; for this reason she bare six, and Rachel bare the two: for on account of the mandrakes the Lord 3 visited her. For He knew that for the sake of children she wished to company with Jacob, and not for lust of pleasure. For on the morrow also she again gave up Jacob. Because of the mandrakes; 5 therefore, the Lord hearkened to Rachel. For though she desired them, she eat them not, but offered them in the house of the Lord, presenting them to the priest of the Most High who was at that time.

3 1 When, therefore, I grew up, my children, I walked in uprightness of heart, and I became a husbandman for my father and my brethren, and I brought in fruits from the field according to 2, 3 their season. And my father blessed me, for he saw that I walked in rectitude before him. And 4 I was not a busybody in my doings, nor envious and malicious against my neighbour. I never slandered any one, nor did I censure the life of any man, walking as I did in singleness of eye. 5 Therefore, when I was thirty-five years old, I took to myself a wife, for my labour wore away my strength, and I never thought upon pleasure with women; but owing to my toil, sleep overcame me. 6 And my father always rejoiced in my rectitude, because I offered through the priest to the Lord 7 all first-fruits; then to my father also. And the Lord increased ten thousandfold His benefits in my 8 hands; and also Jacob, my father, knew that God aided my singleness. For on all the poor and oppressed I bestowed the good things of the earth in the singleness of my heart.

4 1 And now, hearken to me, my children, And walk in singleness of your heart, For I have seen in it all that is well-pleasing to the Lord. 2 The single-(minded) man coveteth not gold, He overreacheth not his neighbour, He longeth not after manifold dainties, He delighteth not in varied apparel. 3 He doth not desire to live a long life, But only waiteth for the will of God. 4 And the spirits of deceit have no power against him, For he looketh not on the beauty of women, Lest he should pollute his mind with corruption. 5 There is no envy in his thoughts, [No malicious person maketh his soul to pine away,] Nor worry with insatiable desire in his mind. 6 For he walketh in singleness of soul, And beholdeth all things in uprightness of heart, Shunning eyes (made) evil through the error of the world, Lest he should see the perversion of any of the commandments of the Lord.

5 1 Keep, therefore, my children, the law of God, And get singleness. And walk in guilelessness, Not playing the busybody with the business of your neighbour, 2 But love the Lord and your neighbour, Have compassion on the poor and weak. 3 Bow down your back unto husbandry, And toil in labours in all manner of husbandry, Offering gifts to the Lord with thanksgiving. 4 For with the first-fruits of the earth will the Lord bless you, even as He blessed all the saints 5 from Abel even until now. For no other portion is given to you than of the fatness of the earth, 6 whose fruits are raised by toil. For our father Jacob blessed me with blessings of the earth and of 7 first-fruits. And Levi and Judah were glorified by the Lord even among the sons of Jacob; for the Lord gave them an inheritance, and to Levi He gave the priesthood, and to Judah the kingdom. 8 And do ye therefore obey them, and walk in the singleness of your father; [for unto Gad hath it been given to destroy the troops that are coming upon Israel].

6 1 Know ye therefore, my children, that in the last times Your sons will forsake singleness, And will cleave unto insatiable desire; And leaving guilelessness will draw near to malice; And forsaking the commandments of the Lord, They will cleave unto Beliar. 2 And leaving husbandry, They will follow after their own wicked devices, And they shall be dispersed among the Gentiles. And shall serve their enemies. 3 And do you therefore give these commands to your children, that, if they sin, they may the more 4 quickly return to the Lord; For He is merciful, and will deliver them, even to bring them back into their land.

7 1 Behold, therefore, as ye see, I am a hundred and twenty-six years old and am not conscious of committing any sin. 2 Except my wife I have not known any woman. I never committed fornication by the uplifting of my eyes. 3 I drank not wine, to be led astray thereby; I coveted not any desirable thing that was my neighbour's. 4 Guile arose not in my heart; A lie passed not through my lips. 5 If any man were in distress I joined my sighs with his, And I shared my bread with the poor. I wrought godliness, all my days I kept truth 6 I loved the Lord; Likewise also every man with all my heart. 7 So do you also these things, my children, And every spirit of Beliar shall flee from you, And no deed of wicked men shall rule over you; And every wild beast shall ye subdue, Since you have with you the God of heaven and earth (And) walk with men in singleness of heart. 8 And having said these things, he commanded his sons that they should carry him up to Hebron, and bury him there in the cave with his fathers. And he stretched out his feet and died, at a good old age; with every limb sound, and with strength unabated, he slept the eternal sleep.

THE TESTAMENT OF ZEBULUN, THE SIXTH SON OF JACOB AND LEAH.

1 1 The copy of the words of Zebulun, which he enjoined on his sons before he died in the 2 hundred and fourteenth year of his life, two years after the death of Joseph. And he said to them: 3 Hearken to me, ye sons of Zebulun, attend to the words of your father. I, Zebulun, was born a good gift to my parents. For when I was born my father was increased very exceedingly, both in flocks 4 and herds, when with the straked rods he had his portion. I am not conscious that I have sinned 5 all my days, save in thought. Nor yet do I remember that I have done any iniquity, except the sin of ignorance which I committed against Joseph; for I covenanted with my brethren not to tell 6 my father what had been done. But I wept in secret many days on account of Joseph, for I feared my brethren, because they had all agreed that if any one should declare the secret, he should be slain. 7 But when they wished to kill him, I adjured them much with tears not to be guilty of this sin.

2 1, 2 For Simeon and Gad came against Joseph to kill him, and he said unto them with tears: Pity me, my brethren, have mercy upon the bowels of Jacob our father: lay not upon me your hands 3 to shed innocent blood, for I have not sinned against you. And if indeed I have sinned, with chastening chastise me, my

brethren but lay not upon me your hand, for the sake of Jacob our 4 father. And as he spoke these words, wailing as he did so, I was unable to bear his lamentations, and began to weep, and my liver was poured out, and all the substance of my bowels was loosened. 5 And I wept with Joseph, and my heart sounded, and the joints of my body trembled, and I was 6 not able to stand. And when Joseph saw me weeping with him, and them coming against him to 7 slay him, he fled behind me, beseeching them. But meanwhile Reuben arose and said: Come, my brethren, let us not slay him, but let us cast him into one of these dry pits, which our fathers digged 8 and found no water. For for this cause the Lord forbade that water should rise up in them, in order that Joseph should be preserved. And they did so, until they sold him to the Ishmaelites.

3 1, 2 For in his price I had no share, my children. But Simeon and Gad and six other of our brethren took the price of Joseph, and bought sandals for themselves, and their wives, and their children, 3 saying: We will not eat of it, for it is the price of our brother's blood, but we will assuredly tread it under foot, because he said that he would be king over us, and so let us see what will become of 4 his dreams. Therefore it is written in the writing of the law of Moses, that whosoever will not raise 5 up seed to his brother, his sandal should be unloosed, and they should spit in his face. And the brethren of Joseph wished not that their brother should live, and the Lord loosed from them the 6 sandal which they wore against Joseph their brother. For when they came into Egypt they were unloosed by the servants of Joseph outside the gate, and so they made obeisance to Joseph after the 7 fashion of King Pharaoh. And not only did they make obeisance to him, but were spit upon also, 8 falling down before him forthwith, and so they were put to shame before the Egyptians. For after this the Egyptians heard all the evils that they had done to Joseph.

4 1 And after he was sold my brothers sat down 2 to eat and drink. But I, through pity for Joseph, did not eat, but watched the pit, since Judah feared lest Simeon, Dan, and Gad should rush 3 off and slay him. But when they saw that I did not eat, they set me to watch him, till he was 5 sold to the Ishmaelites. And when Reuben came and heard that while he was away (Joseph) had been sold, he rent his garments, (and) mourning, said: How shall I look on the face of my father 6 Jacob? And he took the money and ran after the merchants, but as he failed to find them he returned grieving. But the merchants had left the broad road and marched through the Troglodytes by a short cut. 7 But Reuben was grieved, and eat no food that day. Dan therefore came to him and said: 8, 9 Weep not, neither grieve; for we have found what we can say to our

father Jacob. Let us slay 10 a kid of the goats, and dip in it the coat of Joseph; and let us send it to Jacob, saying: Know, is 11 this the coat of thy son? And they did so. For they stripped off from Joseph his coat when they were selling him, and put upon him the garment of a slave. Now Simeon took the coat, and would not give it up, for he wished to rend it with his sword, as he was angry that Joseph lived and that 12 he had not slain him. Then we all rose up and said unto him: If thou givest not up the coat, we 13 will say to our father that thou alone didst this evil thing in Israel. And so he gave it unto them, and they did even as Dan had said.

5 1 And now, my children, I bid you to keep the commands of the Lord, and to show mercy to your neighbours, and to have compassion towards all, not towards men only, but also towards, beasts. 2 For all this thing's sake the Lord blessed me, and when all my brethren were sick, I escaped without 3 sickness, for the Lord knoweth the purposes of each. Have, therefore, compassion in your hearts, my children, because even as a man doeth to his neighbour, even so also will the Lord do to him. 4 For the sons of my brethren were sickening and were dying on account of Joseph, because they 5 showed not mercy in their hearts; but my sons were preserved without sickness, as ye know. And when I was in the land of Canaan, by the sea-coast, I made a catch of fish for Jacob my father; and when many were choked in the sea, I continued unhurt.

6 1 I was the first to make a boat to sail upon the sea, for the Lord gave me understanding and 2 wisdom therein. And I let down a rudder behind it, and I stretched a sail upon another upright 3 piece of wood in the midst. And I sailed therein along the shores, catching fish for the house of my father until we came to Egypt. 4, 5 [And through compassion I shared my catch with every stranger. And if a man were a stranger, or sick, or aged, I boiled the fish, and dressed them well, and offered them to all men, as every man 6 had need, grieving with and having compassion upon them. Wherefore also the Lord satisfied me with abundance of fish when catching fish; for he that shareth with his neighbour receiveth manifold 7 more from the Lord.] For five years I caught fish [and gave thereof to every man whom I saw, 8 and sufficed for all the house of my father]. And in the summer I caught fish, and in the winter I kept sheep with my brethren.

7 1 [Now I will declare unto you what I did. I saw a man in distress through nakedness in winter time, and had compassion upon him, and stole away a garment secretly from my father's house, and 2 gave it to him who was in distress. Do you, therefore, my children, from that which God bestoweth upon you, show compassion and mercy without hesitation to all men,

and give to every man with 3 a good heart. And if ye have not the wherewithal to give to him that needeth, have compassion for 4 him in bowels of mercy. I know that my hand found not the wherewithal to give to him that needed, and I walked with him weeping for seven furlongs, and my bowels yearned towards him in compassion.

8 1 Have, therefore, yourselves also, my children, compassion towards every man with mercy, that the 2 Lord also may have compassion and mercy upon you. Because also in the last days God will send 3 His compassion on the earth, and wheresoever He findeth bowels of mercy He dwelleth in him. For in the degree in which a man hath compassion upon his neighbours, in the same degree hath the 4, 5 Lord also upon him.] And when we went down into Egypt, Joseph bore no malice against us. To whom taking heed, do ye also, my children, approve yourselves without malice, and love one 6 another; and do not set down in account, each one of you, evil against his brother. For this breaketh unity and divideth all kindred, and troubleth the soul, and weareth away the countenance.

9 1 Observe, therefore, the waters, and know when they flow together, they sweep along stones, trees, 2 earth, and other things. But if they are divided into many streams, the earth swalloweth them up, 3, 4 and they vanish away. So shall ye also be if ye be divided. Be not ye, therefore, divided into two heads, for everything which the Lord made hath but one head, and two shoulders, two 5 hands, two feet, and all the remaining members. For I have learnt in the writing of my fathers, that Ye shall be divided in Israel, And ye shall follow two kings, And shall work every abomination. 6 And your enemies shall lead you captive, And ye shall be evil entreated among the Gentiles, With many infirmities and tribulations. 7 And after these things ye shall remember the Lord, and repent, [And He shall cause you to return]; for He is merciful and compassionate. And He setteth not down in account evil to the sons of men, because they are flesh, And the spirits of deceit deceive them in all their deeds. 8 And after these things there shall arise unto you the Lord Himself, the light of righteousness, [And healing and compassion shall be in His wings. He shall redeem all the captivity of the sons of men from Beliar; And every spirit of deceit shall be trodden down]; And he shall bring back all the Gentiles into zeal for Him. And ye shall return unto your land. And ye shall see Him in Jerusalem, for His name's sake. 9 And again through the wickedness of your works shall ye provoke Him to anger, And ye shall be cast away by Him unto the time of consummation.

10 1 And now, my children, grieve not that I am dying, nor be cast down in that I am coming to my 2 end. For

I shall rise again in the midst of you, as a ruler in the midst of his sons; and I shall rejoice in the midst of my tribe, as many as shall keep the law of the Lord, and the commandments 3 of Zebulun their father. But upon the ungodly shall the Lord bring eternal fire, and destroy them 4, 5 throughout all generations. But I am now hastening away to my rest, as did also my fathers. But 6 do ye fear the Lord our God with all your strength all the days of your life. And when he had 7 said these things he fell asleep, at a good old age. And his sons laid him in a wooden coffin. And afterwards they carried him up and buried him in Hebron, with his fathers.

THE TESTAMENT OF DAN, THE SEVENTH SON OF JACOB AND BILHAH.

1 1 The copy of the words of Dan, which he spake to his sons in his last days, in the hundred and 2 twenty-fifth year of his life. For he called together his family, and said: Hearken to my words, ye 3 sons of Dan; and give heed to the words of your father. I have proved in my heart, and in my whole life, that truth with just dealing is good and well pleasing to God, and that lying and anger 4 are evil, because they teach man all wickedness. I confess, therefore, this day to you, my children, 5 that in my heart I resolved on the death of Joseph my brother, the true and good man. [And 6 I rejoiced that he was sold, because his father loved him more than us.] For the spirit of jealousy 7 and vainglory said to me: Thou thyself also art his son. And one of the spirits of Beliar stirred me up, saying: Take this sword, and with it slay Joseph: so shall thy father love thee when he is dead. 8 Now this is the spirit of anger that persuaded me to crush Joseph as a leopard crusheth a kid. 9 But the God of my fathers did not suffer him to fall into my hands, so that I should find him alone and slay him, and cause a second tribe to be destroyed in Israel.

2 1 And now, my children, behold I am dying, and I tell you of a truth, that unless ye keep yourselves from the spirit of lying and of anger, and love truth and longsuffering, ye shall perish. 2 For anger is blindness, and does not suffer one to see the face of any man with truth. 3 For though it be a father or a mother, he behaveth towards them as enemies; though it be a brother, he knoweth him not; though it be a prophet of the Lord, he disobeyeth him; though 4 a righteous man, he regardeth him not; though a friend, he doth not acknowledge him. For the spirit of anger encompasseth him with the net of deceit, and blindeth his eyes, and through lying 5 darkeneth his mind, and giveth him its own peculiar vision. And wherewith encompasseth it his eyes? With hatred of heart, so as to be envious of his brother.

3 1 For anger is an evil thing, my children, for it troubleth even the soul itself. And the body of the angry man it maketh its own, and over his soul it getteth the mastery, and 3 it bestoweth upon the body power that it may work all iniquity. And when the body does all 4 these things, the soul justifieth what is done, since it seeth not aright. Therefore he that is wrathful, if he be a mighty man, hath a threefold power in his anger: one by the help of his servants; and a second by his wealth, whereby he persuadeth and overcometh wrongfully; and thirdly, having his 5 own natural power he worketh thereby the evil. And though the wrathful man be weak, yet hath 6 he a power twofold of that which is by nature; for wrath ever aideth such in lawlessness. This spirit goeth always with lying at the right hand of Satan, that with cruelty and lying his works may be wrought.

4 1, 2 Understand ye, therefore, the power of wrath, that it is vain. For it first of all giveth provocation by word; then by deeds it strengtheneth him who is angry, and with sharp losses disturbeth his 3 mind, and so stirreth up with great wrath his soul. Therefore, when any one speaketh against you, be not ye moved to anger, [and if any man praiseth you as holy men, be not uplifted: be not moved 4 either to delight or to disgust]. For first it pleaseth the hearing, and so maketh the mind keen to perceive the grounds for provocation; and then being enraged, he thinketh that he is justly angry 5 If ye fall into any loss or ruin, my children, be not afflicted; for this very spirit maketh (a man) 6 desire that which is perishable, in order that he may be enraged through the affliction. And if ye suffer loss voluntarily, or involuntarily, be not vexed; for from vexation ariseth wrath with lying. 7 Moreover, a twofold mischief is wrath with lying; and they assist one another in order to disturb the heart; and when the soul is continually disturbed, the Lord departeth from it, and Beliar ruleth over it.

5 1Observe, therefore, my children, the commandments of the Lord, And keep His law; Depart from wrath, And hate lying, That the Lord may dwell among you, And Beliar may flee from you. 2 Speak truth each one with his neighbour. So shall ye not fall into wrath and confusion; But ye shall be in peace, having the God of peace, So shall no war prevail over you. 3 Love the Lord through all your life, And one another with a true heart. 4 I know that in the last days

ye shall depart from the Lord, And ye shall provoke Levi unto anger, And fight against Judah; But ye shall not prevail against them, For an angel of the Lord shall guide them both; For by them shall Israel stand. 5 And whensoever ye depart from the Lord, ye shall walk in all evil and work the abominations of the Gentiles, going a-whoring after women of the lawless ones, while with all wickedness the spirits 6 of wickedness work in you. [For I have read in the book of Enoch, the righteous, that your prince is Satan, and that all the spirits of wickedness and pride will conspire to attend constantly on the sons of Levi, to cause them to sin before the Lord. 7 And my sons will draw near to Levi. And sin with them in all things; And the sons of Judah will be covetous, Plundering other men's goods like lions.] 8 Therefore shall ye be led away [with them] into captivity, And there shall ye receive all the plagues of Egypt, And all the evils of the Gentiles. 9 And so when ye return to the Lord ye shall obtain mercy, And He shall bring you into His sanctuary, And He shall give you peace. 10 And there shall arise unto you from the tribe of [Judah and of] Levi the salvation of the Lord; And he shall make war against Beliar. And execute an everlasting vengeance on our enemies; 11 And the captivity shall he take from Beliar [the souls of the saints], And turn disobedient hearts unto the Lord, And give to them that call upon him eternal peace. 12 And the saints shall rest in Eden, And in the New Jerusalem shall the righteous rejoice, And it shall be unto the glory of God for ever. 13 And no longer shall Jerusalem endure desolation, Nor Israel be led captive; For the Lord shall be in the midst of it [living amongst men], And the Holy One of Israel shall reign over it [in humility and in poverty; and he who believeth on Him shall reign amongst men in truth].

6 1, 2 And now, fear the Lord, my children, and beware of Satan and his spirits. Draw near unto God and unto the angel that intercedeth for you, for he is a mediator between God and man, and for the 3 peace of Israel he shall stand up against the kingdom of the enemy. Therefore is the enemy eager 4 to destroy all that call upon the Lord. For he knoweth that upon the day on which Israel shall 5 repent, the kingdom of the enemy shall be brought to an end. For the very angel of peace shall 6 strengthen Israel, that it fall not into the extremity of evil. And it shall be in the time of the lawlessness of Israel, that the Lord will not depart from them, but will transform them into a nation 7 that doeth His will, for none of the angels will be equal unto him. And His name shall be in every place in Israel, and among the Gentiles. 8 Keep, therefore, yourselves, my children, from every evil work, And cast away wrath and all lying, And love truth and long-suffering. 9 And the things which ye have heard from your father, do ye also impart to your children [that the Saviour of the Gentiles may receive you; for he is true

and long-suffering, meek and lowly, and 10 teacheth by his works the law of God]. Depart, therefore, from all unrighteousness, and cleave unto the righteousness of God, and your race will be saved for ever. And bury me near my fathers.

7 1, 2 And when he had said these things he kissed them, and fell asleep at a good old age. And his sons buried him, And after that they carried up his bones, and placed them near Abraham, and 3 Isaac, and Jacob. [Nevertheless, Dan prophesied unto them that they should forget their God, and should be alienated from the land of their inheritance and from the race of Israel, and from the family of their seed.]

THE TESTAMENT OF NAPHTALI, THE EIGHTH SON OF JACOB AND BILHAH.

1 1 The copy of the testament of Naphtali, which he ordained at the time of his death in the hundred 2 and thirtieth year of his life. When his sons were gathered together in the seventh month, on the 3 first day of the month, while still in good health, he made them a feast of food and wine. And after 4 he was awake in the morning, he said to them, I am dying; and they believed him not. And as he 5 glorified the Lord, he grew strong and said that after yesterday's feast he should die. And he began 6 then to say: Hear, my children, ye sons of Naphtali, hear the words of your father. I was born from Bilhah, and because Rachel dealt craftily, and gave Bilhah in place of herself to Jacob, and she 7 conceived and bare me upon Rachel's knees, therefore she called my name Naphtali. For Rachel loved me very much because I was born upon her lap; and when I was still young she was wont 8 to kiss me, and say: May I have a brother of thine from mine own womb, like unto thee. Whence 9 also Joseph was like unto me in all things, according to the prayers of Rachel. Now my mother was Bilhah, daughter of Rotheus the brother of Deborah, Rebecca's nurse, who was born on one and 10 the self-same day with Rachel. And Rotheus was of the family of Abraham, a Chaldean, God 11 fearing, free-born, and noble. And he was taken captive and was bought by Laban; and he gave him Euna his handmaid to wife, and she bore a daughter, and called her name Zilpah, after the name 12 of the village in which he had been taken captive. And next she bore Bilhah, saying: My daughter hastens after what is new, for immediately that she was born she seized the breast and hastened to suck it.

2 1 And I was swift on my feet like the deer, and my father Jacob appointed me for all messages, 2 and as a deer did he give me his blessing. For as the potter

knoweth the vessel, how much it is to contain, and bringeth clay accordingly, so also doth the Lord make the body after the likeness of 3 the spirit, and according to the capacity of the body doth He implant the spirit. And the one does not fall short of the other by a third part of a hair; for by weight, and measure, and rule was all the 4 creation made. And as the potter knoweth the use of each vessel, what it is meet for, so also doth the Lord know the body, how far it will persist in goodness, and when it beginneth in evil. For 5 there is no inclination or thought which the Lord knoweth not, for He created every man after His own image. 6 As a man's strength, so also is his work; and as his mind, so also is his skill; and as his purpose, so also is his achievement; and as his heart, so also is his mouth; as his eye, so also is his sleep; as his soul, so also is his word, either in the law of the Lord or in the works of Beliar. 7 And as there is a division between light and darkness, between seeing and hearing, so also is there a division between man and man, and between woman and woman; and it is not to be said that the 8 one is like the other either in face or in mind. For God made all things good in their order, the five senses in the head, and He joined on the neck to the head, adding to it the hair also for comeliness and glory, then the heart for understanding, the belly for excrement, and the stomach for (grinding), the windpipe for taking in (the breath), the liver for wrath, the gall for bitterness, the spleen for laughter, the reins for prudence, the muscles of the loins for power, the lungs for drawing 9 in, the loins for strength, and so forth. So then, my children, let all your works be done in order 10 with good intent in the fear of God, and do nothing disorderly in scorn or out of its due season. For if thou bid the eye to hear, it cannot; so neither while ye are in darkness can ye do the works of light.

3 1 Be ye, therefore, not eager to corrupt your doings through covetousness or with vain words to beguile your souls; because if ye keep silence in purity of heart, ye shall understand how to hold 2 fast the will of God, and to cast away the will of Beliar. Sun and moon and stars change not their 3 order; so do ye also change not the law of God in the disorderliness of your doings. The Gentiles went astray, and forsook the Lord, and changed their order, and obeyed stocks and stones, spirits of 4 deceit. But ye shall not be so, my children, recognizing in the firmament, in the earth, and in the sea, and in all created things, the Lord who made all things, that ye become not as Sodom, which 5 changed the order of nature. In like manner the Watchers also changed the order of their nature, whom the Lord cursed at the flood, on whose account He made the earth without inhabitants and fruitless.

4 1 These things I say unto you, my children, for I have read in the writing of Enoch that ye yourselves also shall depart from the Lord, walking according to all the lawlessness of the Gentiles, and 2 ye shall do according to all the wickedness of Sodom. And the Lord shall bring captivity upon you, and there shall ye serve your enemies, and ye shall be bowed down with every affliction and 3 tribulation, until the Lord have consumed you all. And after ye have become minished and made few, ye shall return and acknowledge the Lord your God; and He shall bring you back into your 4 land, according to His abundant mercy. And it shall be, that after that they come into the land of 5 their fathers, they shall again forget the Lord and become ungodly. And the Lord shall scatter them upon the face of all the earth, until the compassion of the Lord shall come, a man working righteousness and working mercy unto all them that are afar off, and to them that are near.

5 1 For in the fortieth year of my life, I saw a vision on the Mount of Olives, on the east of Jerusalem, 2 that the sun and the moon were standing still. And behold Isaac, the father of my father, said to us; Run and lay hold of them, each one according to his strength; and to him that seizeth them 3 will the sun and moon belong . And we all of us ran together, and Levi laid hold of the sun, and Judah outstripped the others and seized the moon, and they were both of them lifted up with them. 4 And when Levi became as a sun, lo, a certain young man gave to him twelve branches of palm; 5 and Judah was bright as the moon, and under their feet were twelve rays. [And the two, Levi and 6 Judah, ran, and laid hold of them.] And 10, a bull upon the earth, with two great horns, and an 7 eagle's wings upon its back; and we wished to seize him; but could not. But Joseph came, and 8 seized him, and ascended up with him on high. And I saw, for I was there, and behold a holy writing appeared to us, saying: Assyrians, Medes, Persians, [Chaldeans,] Syrians, shall possess in captivity the twelve tribes of Israel.

6 1 And again, after seven days, I saw our father Jacob standing by the sea of Jamnia, and we were 2 with him. And behold, there came a ship sailing by, without sailors or pilot; and there was written 3 upon the ship, The Ship of Jacob. And our father said to us: Come, let us embark on our ship. 4 And when he had gone on board, there arose a vehement storm, and a mighty tempest of wind; and 5 our father, who was holding the helm, departed from us. And we, being tossed with the tempest, were borne along over the sea; and the ship was filled with water, (and was) pounded by mighty waves, 6 until it was broken up. And Joseph fled away upon a little boat, and we were all divided upon nine 7 planks, and Levi and Judah were together. And we were all scattered unto the ends of the earth. 8, 9 Then Levi, girt about with sackcloth, prayed for us all unto the Lord. And when the storm ceased, the ship

reached the land as it were in peace. And, 10, our father came, and we all rejoiced with one accord.

7 1 These two dreams I told to my father; and he said to me: These things must be fulfilled in their season, after that Israel hath endured many things. 2 Then my father saith unto me: I believe God that Joseph liveth, for I see always that the Lord numbereth him with you, 3 And he said, weeping: Ah me, my son Joseph, thou livest, though I behold thee not, and thou seest not Jacob that begat thee. 4 He caused me also, therefore, to weep by these words, and I burned in my heart to declare that Joseph had been sold, but I feared my brethren.

8 1 And lo! my children, I have shown unto you the last times, how everything shall come to pass in 2 Israel. Do ye also, therefore, charge your children that they be united to Levi and to Judah; For through them shall salvation arise unto Israel, And in them shall Jacob be blessed. 3 For through their tribes shall God appear [dwelling among men] on earth, To save the race of Israel, And to gather together the righteous from amongst the Gentiles. 4 If ye work that which is good, my children, Both men and angels shall bless you; And God shall be glorified among the Gentiles through you, And the devil shall flee from you, And the wild beasts shall fear you, And the Lord shall love you, [And the angels shall cleave to you]. 5 As a man who has trained a child well is kept in kindly remembrance: So also for a good work there is a good remembrance before God. 6 But him that doeth not that which is good, Both angels and men shall curse, And God shall be dishonoured among the Gentiles through him, And the devil shall make him as his own peculiar instrument, And every wild beast shall master him, And the Lord shall hate him. 7 For the commandments of the law are twofold, And through prudence must they be fulfilled. 8 For there is a season for a man to embrace his wife, And a season to abstain therefrom for his prayer. 9 So, then, there are two commandments; and, unless they be done in due order, they bring very 10 great sin upon men. So also is it with the other commandments. Be ye therefore wise in God, my Children, and prudent, understanding the order of His commandments, and the laws of every word, that the Lord may love you.

9 1 And when he had charged them with many such words, he exhorted them that they should 2 remove his bones to Hebron, and that they should bury him with his fathers. And when he had 3 eaten and drunken with a merry heart, he covered his face and died. And his sons did according to all that Naphtali their father had commanded them.

THE TESTAMENT OF GAD THE NINTH SON OF JACOB AND ZILPAH.

1 1 The copy of the testament of Gad, what things he spake unto his sons, in the hundred and twenty 2 fifth year of his life, saying unto them: Hearken, my children, I was the ninth son born to Jacob, 3 and I was valiant in keeping the flocks. Accordingly I guarded at night the flock; and whenever the lion came, or the wolf, or any wild beast against the fold, I pursued it, and overtaking (it) 4 I seized its foot with my hand and hurled it about a stone's throw, and so killed it. Now Joseph my brother was feeding the flock with us for upwards of thirty days, and being young, he fell sick 5 by reason of the heat. And he returned to Hebron to our father, who made him lie down near him, 6 because he loved him greatly. And Joseph told our father that the sons of Zilpah and Bilhah were slaying the best of the flock and eating them against the judgement of Reuben and Judah. 7 For he saw that I had delivered a lamb out of the mouth of a bear, and put the bear to death; but 8 had slain the lamb, being grieved concerning it that it could not live, and that we had eaten it. And 9 regarding this matter I was wroth with Joseph until the day that he was sold, And the spirit of hatred was in me, and I wished not either to hear of Joseph with the ears, or see him with the eyes because he rebuked us to our faces saying that we were eating of the flock without Judah. For whatsoever things he told our father, he believed him.

2 1 I confess now my sin, my children, that oftentimes I wished to kill him, because I hated him from 2 my heart. Moreover, I hated him yet more for his dreams; and I wished to lick him out of the land of the living, even as an ox licketh up the grass of the field. 3 Therefore I and Simeon sold him to the Ishmaelites [for thirty pieces of gold, and ten of them we hid, and showed the twenty to our brethren] 4 And thus through covetousness we were bent on slaying him. 5 And the God of my fathers delivered him from my hands, that I should not work lawlessness in Israel.

3 1 And now, my children, hearken to the words of truth to work righteousness, and all the law of the Most

High, and go not astray through the spirit of hatred, for it is evil in all the doings of 2 men. Whatsoever a man doeth the hater abominateth him: and though a man worketh the law of the Lord, he praiseth him not; though a man feareth the Lord, and taketh pleasure in that which is 3 righteous, he loveth him not. He dispraiseth the truth, he envieth him that prospereth, he welcometh evil-speaking, he loveth arrogance, for hatred blindeth his soul; as I also then looked on Joseph.

4 I Beware, therefore, my children of hatred; for it worketh lawlessness even against the Lord Himself. 2 For it will not hear the words of His commandments concerning the loving of one's neighbour, 3 and it sinneth against God. For if a brother stumble, it delighteth immediately to proclaim it to all men, and is urgent that he should be judged for it, and be punished and be put to death. 4 And if it be a servant it stirreth him up against his master, and with every affliction it deviseth against 5 him if possibly he can be put to death, For hatred worketh with envy also against them that prosper: so long as it heareth of or seeth their success, it always languisheth. 6 For as love would quicken even the dead, and would call back them that are condemned to die, so hatred would slay the living, and those that had sinned venially it would not suffer to live. 7 For the spirit of hatred worketh together with Satan, through hastiness of spirit, in all things to men's death; but the spirit of love worketh together with the law of God in long-suffering unto the salvation of men.

5 1 Hatred, therefore, is evil, for it constantly mateth with lying, speaking against the truth; and it maketh small things to be great, and causeth the light to be darkness, and calleth the sweet bitter, and teacheth slander, and kindleth wrath, and stirreth up war, and violence and all covetousness; 2 it filleth the heart with evils and devilish poison. These things, therefore, I say to you from experience, my children, that ye may drive forth hatred, which is of the devil, and cleave to 3 the love of God. Righteousness casteth out hatred, humility destroyeth envy. For he that is just and humble is ashamed to do what is unjust, being reproved not of another, but of his own heart, 4 because the Lord looketh on his inclination. He speaketh not against a holy man, because the fear 5 of God overcometh hatred. For fearing lest he should offend the Lord, he will not do wrong to any 6, 7 man, even in thought. These things I learnt at last, after I had repented concerning Joseph. For true repentance after a godly sort [destroyeth ignorance, and] driveth away the darkness, and 8 enlighteneth the eyes, and giveth knowledge to the soul, and leadeth the mind to salvation. And 9 those things which it hath not learnt from man, it knoweth through repentance. For God brought upon me a disease of the liver; and had not the prayers of Jacob my father succoured me, it had 10 hardly failed but my spirit had departed, For by what things a man transgresseth, by the same also 11 is he punished. Since, therefore, my liver was set mercilessly against Joseph, in my liver too I suffered mercilessly, and was judged for eleven months, for so long a time as I had been angry against Joseph.

6 1 And now, my children, I exhort you, love ye each one his brother, and put away hatred from 2 your hearts, love one another in deed, and in word, and in the inclination of the soul. For in the presence of my father I spake peaceably to Joseph; and when I had gone out, the spirit of hatred darkened my mind, and stirred up my soul to slay him. 3 Love ye, therefore, one another from the heart; and if a man sin against thee, cast forth the poison of hate and speak peaceably to him, and in thy soul hold not guile; and if he confess and repent, forgive him. 4 But if he deny it, do not get into a passion with him, lest catching the poison from thee he take 5 to swearing and so thou sin doubly. [Let not another man hear thy secrets when engaged in legal strife, lest he come to hate thee and become thy enemy, and commit a great sin against thee; for 6 ofttimes he addresseth thee guilefully or busieth himself about thee with wicked intent.] And though he deny it and yet have a sense of shame when reproved, give over reproving him. For he who denieth may repent so as not again to wrong thee; yea, he may also honour thee, and [fear 7 and] be at peace with thee And if he be shameless and persist in his wrong-doing, even so forgive him from the heart, and leave to God the avenging.

7 1 If a man prospereth more than you, do not be vexed, but pray also for him, that he may have 2 perfect prosperity. For so it is expedient for you. And if he be further exalted, be not envious of him, remembering that all flesh shall die; and offer praise to God, who giveth things good and 3 profitable to all men. Seek out the judgements of the Lord, and thy mind will rest and be at peace. 4 And though a man become rich by evil means, even as Esau, the brother of my father, be not jealous; 5 but wait for the end of the Lord. For if he taketh away (from a man) wealth gotten by evil 6 means He forgiveth him if he repent, but the unrepentant is reserved for eternal punishment. For the poor man, if free from envy he pleaseth the Lord in all things, is blessed beyond all men, because 7 he hath not the travail of vain men. Put away, therefore, jealousy from your souls, and love one another with uprightness of heart.

8 1 Do ye also therefore tell these things to your children, that they honour Judah and Levi, for from 2 them shall the Lord raise up salvation to Israel. [For I know that at the last your children shall depart from

Him, and shall walk in all wickedness, and affliction and corruption before the Lord.] 3 And when he had rested for a little while, he said again; My children, obey your father, and bury 4, 5 me near to my fathers. And he drew up his feet, and fell asleep in peace. And after five years they carried him up to Hebron, and laid him with his fathers.

THE TESTAMENT OF ASHER, THE TENTH SON OF JACOB AND ZILPAH.

1 1 The copy of the Testament of Asher, what things he spake to his sons in the hundred and 2 twenty-fifth year of his life. For while he was still in health, he said to them: Hearken, ye children of Asher, to your father, and I will declare to you all that is upright in the sight of the Lord. 3 Two ways hath God given to the sons of men, and two inclinations, and two kinds of action, and 4 two modes (of action), and two issues. Therefore all things are by twos, one over against the 5 other. For there are two ways of good and evil, and with these are the two inclinations in our 6 breasts discriminating them. Therefore if the soul take pleasure in the good (inclination), all its 7 actions are in righteousness; and if it sin it straightway repenteth. For, having its thoughts set upon righteousness, and casting away wickedness, it straightway overthroweth the evil, and uprooteth 8 the sin. But if it incline to the evil inclination, all its actions are in wickedness, and it driveth away the good, and cleaveth to the evil, and is ruled by Beliar; even though it work what is good, 9 he perverteth it to evil. For whenever it beginneth to do good, he forceth the issue of the action into evil for him, seeing that the treasure of the inclination is filled with an evil spirit.

2 1 A person then may with words help the good for the sake of the evil, yet the issue of the action 2 leadeth to mischief. There is a man who showeth no compassion upon him who serveth his turn in 3 evil; and this thing hath two aspects, but the whole is evil. And there is a man that loveth him that worketh evil, because he would prefer even to die in evil for his sake; and concerning this it is clear that it hath two aspects, but the whole is an evil work. 4 Though indeed he have love, yet is he wicked who concealeth what is evil for the sake of the good name, but the end of the action tendeth unto evil. 5 Another stealeth, doeth unjustly, plundereth, defraudeth, and withal pitieth the poor: this too 6 hath a twofold aspect, but the whole is evil. He who defraudeth his neighbour provoketh God, and sweareth falsely against the Most High, and yet pitieth the poor: the Lord who commandeth the 7 law he setteth at nought and provoketh, and yet he refresheth the poor. He defileth the soul, and maketh gay the body; he killeth many, and pitieth a few: this, too, hath a twofold aspect, but the 8 whole is evil. Another committeth adultery and fornication, and abstaineth

from meats, and when he fasteth he doeth evil, and by the power of his wealth overwhelmeth many; and notwithstanding his excessive wickedness he doeth the commandments: this, too, hath a twofold aspect, but the 9 whole is evil. Such men are hares; clean,- like those that divide the hoof, but in very deed are 10 unclean. For God in the tables of the commandments hath thus declared.

3 1 But do not ye, my children, wear two faces like unto them, of goodness and of wickedness; but 2 cleave unto goodness only, for God hath his habitation therein, and men desire it. But from wickedness flee away, destroying the (evil) inclination by your good works; for they that are double-faced serve not God, but their own lusts, so that they may please Beliar and men like unto themselves.

4 1 For good men, even they that are of single face, though they be thought by them that are double 2 faced to sin, are just before God. For many in killing the wicked do two works, of good and evil; 3 but the whole is good, because he hath uprooted and destroyed that which is evil. One man hateth the merciful and unjust man, and the man who committeth adultery and fasteth: this, too, hath a two fold aspect, but the whole work is good, because he followeth the Lord's example, in that he 4 accepteth not the seeming good as the genuine good. Another desireth not to see a good day with them that riot, lest he defile his body and pollute his soul: this, too, is double-faced, but the whole is 5 good. For such men are like to stags and to hinds, because in the manner of wild animals they seem to be unclean, but they are altogether clean; because they walk in zeal for the Lord and abstain from what God also hateth and forbiddeth by His commandments, warding off the evil from the good.

5 1 Ye see, my children, how that there are two in all things, one against the other, and the one is hidden by the other: in wealth (is hidden) covetousness, in conviviality drunkenness, in laughter 2 grief, in wedlock profligacy. Death succeedeth to life, dishonour to glory, night to day, and darkness to light; [and all things are under the day, just things under life, unjust things under 3 death;] wherefore also eternal life awaiteth death. Nor may it be said that truth is a lie, nor 4 right wrong; for all truth is under the light, even as all things are under God. All these things, therefore, I proved in my life, and I wandered not from the truth of the Lord, and I searched out the commandments of the Most High, walking according to all my strength with singleness of face unto that which is good.

6 1 Take heed, therefore, ye also, my children, to the commandments of the Lord, following the truth 2 with

singleness of face. For they that are double-faced are guilty of a twofold sin; for they both do the evil thing and they have pleasure in them that do it, following the example of the spirits of 3 deceit, and striving against mankind. Do ye, therefore, my children, keep the law of the Lord, and give not heed unto evil as unto good; but look unto the thing that is really good, and keep it in all 4 commandments of the Lord, having your conversation therein, and resting therein. For the latter ends of men do show their righteousness (or unrighteousness), when they meet the angels of the 5 Lord and of Satan. For when the soul departs troubled, it is tormented by the evil spirit which also it served in lusts and evil works. 6 But if he is peaceful with joy he meeteth the angel of peace, and he leadeth him into eternal life.

7 1 Become not, my children, as Sodom, which sinned against the angels of the Lord, and perished for 2 ever. For I know that ye shall sin, and be delivered into the hands of your enemies; and your land shall be made desolate, and your holy places destroyed, and ye shall be scattered unto the four 3 corners of the earth. And ye shall be set at nought in the dispersion vanishing away as water. Until the Most High shall visit the earth, coming Himself [as man, with men eating and drinking, and breaking the head of the dragon in the water. He shall save Israel and all the Gentiles [God speaking in 4 the person of man]. [Therefore do ye also, my children, tell these things to your children, that they 5 disobey Him not. For I have known that ye shall assuredly be disobedient, and assuredly act ungodly, not giving heed to the law of God, but to the commandments of men, being corrupted 6 through wickedness. And therefore shall ye be scattered as Gad and Dan my brethren, and ye shall 7 know not your lands, tribe, and tongue. But the Lord will gather you together in faith through His tender mercy, and for the sake of Abraham, Isaac, and Jacob.]

8 1 And when he had said these things unto them he commanded them, saying: Bury me in Hebron. 2 And he fell asleep and died at a good old age. And his sons did as he had commanded them, and they carried him up to Hebron, and buried him with his fathers.

THE TESTAMENT OF JOSEPH, THE ELEVENTH SON OF JACOB AND RACHEL.

1 1 The copy of the Testament of Joseph. When he was about to die he called his sons and his brethren together, and said to them:-- 2 My brethren and my children, Hearken to Joseph the beloved of Israel; Give ear, my sons, unto your father. 3 I have seen in my life envy and death, Yet I went not astray, but persevered in the truth of the Lord. 4 These my brethren hated me, but the Lord loved me: They wished to slay me, but the God of my fathers guarded me: They let me down into a pit, and the Most High brought me up again. 5 I was sold into slavery, and the Lord of all made me free: I was taken into captivity, and His strong hand succoured me. I was beset with hunger, and the Lord Himself nourished me. 6 I was alone, and God comforted me: I was sick, and the Lord visited me: I was in prison, and my God showed favour unto me; In bonds, and He released me; 7 Slandered, and He pleaded my cause; Bitterly spoken against by the Egyptians, and He delivered me; Envied by my fellow-slaves, and He exalted me.

2 1, 2 And this chief captain of Pharaoh entrusted to me his house. And I struggled against a shameless woman, urging me to transgress with her; but the God of Israel my father delivered me from 3 the burning flame. I was cast into prison, I was beaten, I was mocked; but the Lord granted me to find mercy in the sight of the keeper of the prison. 4 For the Lord doth not forsake them that fear Him, Neither in darkness, nor in bonds, nor in tribulations, nor in necessities. 5 For God is not put to shame as a man, Nor as the son of man is he afraid, Nor as one that is earth-born is He [weak or] affrighted. 6 But in all those things doth He give protection, And in divers ways doth He comfort, (Though) for a little space He departeth to try the inclination of the soul. 7 In ten temptations He showed me approved, And in all of them I endured; For endurance is a mighty charm, And patience giveth many good things.

3 1 How often did the Egyptian woman threaten me with death! How often did she give me over to punishment, and then call me back and threaten me, and when I was unwilling to company with 2 her, she said to me: Thou shalt be lord of me, and all that is in my house, if thou wilt give thyself 3 unto me, and thou shalt be as our master. But I remembered the words of my father, and going 4 into my chamber, I wept and prayed unto the Lord. And I fasted in those seven years, and I appeared to the Egyptians as one living

delicately, for they that fast for God's sake receive beauty of face. 5 And if my lord were away from home, I drank no wine; nor for three days did I take my food, but 6 I gave it to the poor and sick. And I sought the Lord early, and I wept for the Egyptian woman of Memphis, for very unceasingly did she trouble me, for also at night she came to me under pretence of visiting me. 7 And because she had no male child she pretended to regard me as a son, and so I prayed to the Lord, and she bare a male child. 8 And for a time she embraced me as a son, and I knew it not; but later, she sought to draw me 9 into fornication. And when I perceived it I sorrowed unto death; and when she had gone out, I came to myself, and lamented for her many days, because I recognized her guile and her deceit. 10 And I declared unto her the words of the Most High, if haply she would turn from her evil lust.

4 1 Often, therefore, did she flatter me with words as a holy man, and guilefully in her talk praise my 2 chastity before her husband, while desiring to ensnare me when we were alone. For she lauded me openly as chaste, and in secret she said unto me: Fear not my husband; for he is persuaded concerning 3 thy chastity: for even should one tell him concerning us, he would not believe. Owing to all these things I lay upon the ground, and besought God that the Lord would deliver me from her 4 deceit. And when she had prevailed nothing thereby, she came again to me under the plea of 5 instruction, that she might learn the word of God. And she said unto me: If thou willest that I should leave my idols, lie with me, and I will persuade my husband to depart from his idols, and 6 we will walk in the law of thy Lord. And I said unto her: The Lord willeth not that those who reverence Him should be in uncleanness, nor doth He take pleasure in them that commit adultery, 7 but in those that approach Him with a pure heart and undefiled lips. But she held her peace, 8 longing to accomplish her evil desire. And I gave myself yet more to fasting and prayer, that the Lord might deliver me from her.

5 1 And again, at another time she said unto me: If thou wilt not commit adultery, I will kill my 2 husband by poison; and take thee to be my husband. I therefore, when I heard this, rent my garments, and said unto her: Woman, reverence God, and do not this evil deed, lest thou be 3 destroyed; for know indeed that I will declare this thy device unto all men. She therefore, being 4 afraid, besought that I would not declare this device. And she departed soothing me with gifts, and sending to me every delight of the sons of men.

6 1, 2 And afterwards she sent me food mingled with enchantments. And when the eunuch who brought it came, I looked up and beheld a terrible man giving me with the dish a sword, and 3 I perceived that (her) scheme was to beguile me. And when he had gone out I wept, nor did 4 I taste that or any other of her food. So then after one day she came to me and observed the food, 5 and said unto me: Why is it that thou hast not eaten of the food? And I said unto her: It is because thou hast filled it with deadly enchantments; and how saidst thou: I come not near to 6 idols, but to the Lord alone. Now therefore know that the God of my father hath revealed unto me by His angel thy wickedness, and I have kept it to convict thee, if haply thou mayst see and repent. 7 But that thou mayst learn that the wickedness of the ungodly hath no power over them that worship God with chastity, behold I will take of it and eat before thee. And having so said, I prayed thus: The God of my fathers and the angel of Abraham, be with me; and ate. 8 And when she saw this she fell upon her face at my feet, weeping; and I raised her up and admonished her. And she promised to do this iniquity no more.

7 1 But her heart was still set upon evil, and she looked around how to ensnare me, and sighing deeply she became downcast, though she was not sick. 2 And when her husband saw her, he said unto her: Why is thy countenance fallen? And she said unto him: I have a pain at my heart, and the groanings of my spirit oppress me; and so 3 he comforted her who was not sick. Then, accordingly seizing an opportunity, she rushed unto me while her husband was yet without, and said unto me: I will hang myself, or cast myself over a cliff, 4 if thou wilt not lie with me. And when I saw the spirit of Beliar was troubling her, I prayed unto 5 the Lord, and said unto her: Why, wretched woman, art thou troubled and disturbed, blinded through, sins? Remember that if thou kill thyself, Asteho, the concubine of thy husband, thy rival, 6 will beat thy children, and thou wilt destroy thy memorial from off the earth. And she said unto me: Lo, then thou lovest me; let this suffice me: only strive for my life and my children, and 7 I expect that I shall enjoy my desire also. But she knew not that because of my lord I spake 8 thus, and not because of her. For if a man hath fallen before the passion of a wicked desire and become enslaved by it, even as she, whatever good thing he may hear with regard to that passion, he receiveth it with a view to his wicked desire.

8 1 I declare, therefore, unto you, my children, that it was about the sixth hour when she departed from me; and I knelt before the Lord all day, and all the night; and about dawn I rose up, weeping 2 the while and praying for a release from her. At last, then, she laid hold of my garments, forcibly dragging me to have connexion with her. 3 When, therefore, I saw that in her madness she was holding fast to my garment, I left it behind, and fled away naked. 4 And holding fast to the garment she falsely accused me, and when her

husband came he cast me into prison in his house; and on the morrow he scourged me and sent me into Pharaoh's prison. 5 And when I was in bonds, the Egyptian woman was oppressed with grief, and she came and heard how I gave thanks unto the Lord and sang praises in the abode of darkness, and with glad voice rejoiced, glorifying my God that I was delivered from the lustful desire of the Egyptian woman.

9 1 And often hath she sent unto me saying: Consent to fulfill my desire, and I will release thee from thy bonds, and I will free thee from the darkness. And not even in thought did I incline unto 2 her. For God loveth him who in a den of wickedness combines fasting with chastity, rather than the man who in kings' chambers combines luxury with licence. And if a man liveth in chastity, and desireth also glory, and the Most High knoweth that it is expedient for him, He bestoweth this 3 also upon me. How often, though she were sick, did she come down to me at unlooked for times, 5 and listened to my voice as I prayed! And when I heard her groanings I held my peace. For when I was in her house she was wont to bare her arms, and breasts, and legs, that I might lie with her; for she was very beautiful, splendidly adorned in order to beguile me. And the Lord guarded me from her devices.

10 1, 2 Ye see, therefore, my children, how great things patience worketh, and prayer with fasting. So ye too, if ye follow after chastity and purity with patience and prayer, with fasting in humility of 3 heart, the Lord will dwell among you, because He loveth chastity. And wheresoever the Most High dwelleth, even though envy, or slavery, or slander befalleth (a man), the Lord who dwelleth in him, for the sake of his chastity not only delivereth him from evil, but also exalteth him even as me. 4, 5 For in every way the man is lifted up, whether in deed, or in word, or in thought. My brethren knew how my father loved me, and yet I did not exalt myself in my mind: although I was a child, 6 I had the fear of God in my heart; for I knew that all things would pass away. And I did nor raise myself (against them) with evil intent, but I honoured my brethren; and out of respect for them, even when I was being sold, I refrained from telling the Ishmaelites that I was a son of Jacob, a great man and a mighty.

11 1 Do ye also, my children, have the fear of God in all your works before your eyes, and honour 2 your brethren. For every one who doeth the law of the Lord shall be loved by Him. And when I came to the Indocolpitae with the Ishmaelites, they asked me, saying: Art thou a slave? And 3 I said that I was a home-born slave, that I might not put my brethren to shame. And the eldest of them said unto me: Thou art not a slave, for even thy appearance doth make it manifest. But 4 I said that I was their slave. Now when

we came into Egypt they strove concerning me, which of 5 them should buy me and take me. Therefore it seemed good to all that I should remain in Egypt 6 with the merchant of their trade, until they should return bringing merchandise. And the Lord 7 gave me favour in the eyes of the merchant, and he entrusted unto me his house. And God blessed 8 him by my means, and increased him in gold and silver and in household servants. And I was with him three months and five days.

12 1 And about that time the Memphian woman, the wife of Pentephri, came down in a chariot, with 2 great pomp, because she had heard from her eunuchs concerning me. And she told her husband that the merchant had become rich by means of a young Hebrew, and they say that he had assuredly 3 been stolen out of the land of Canaan. Now, therefore, render justice unto him, and take away the youth to thy house; so shall the God of the Hebrews bless thee, for grace from heaven is upon him.

13 1 And Pentephris was persuaded by her words, and commanded the merchant to be brought, and said unto him: What is this that I hear concerning thee, that thou stealest persons out of the land 2 of Canaan, and sellest them for slaves? But the merchant fell at his feet, and besought him, saying: 3 I beseech thee, my lord, I know not what thou sayest. And Pentephris said unto him: Whence, then, is the Hebrew slave? And he said: The Ishmaelites entrusted him unto me until they should return. 4 But he believed him not, but commanded him to be stripped and beaten. And when he persisted 5 in this statement, Pentephris said: Let the youth be brought. And when I was brought in, I did 6 obeisance to Pentephris (for he was third in rank of the officers of Pharaoh). And he took me apart 7 from him, and said unto me: Art thou a slave or free? And I said: A stave. And he said: 8 Whose? And I said: The Ishmaelites. And he said: How didst thou become their slave? And 9 I said: They bought me out of the land of Canaan. And he said unto me: Truly thou liest; and strightway he commanded me to be stripped and beaten.

14 1 Now the Memphian woman was looking through a window at me while I was being beaten, for her house was near, and she sent unto him saying: Thy judgement is unjust; for thou dost punish 2 a free man who hath been stolen, as though he were a transgressor. And when I made no change in my statement, though I was beaten, he ordered me to be imprisoned, until, he said, the owners 3 of the boy should come. And the woman said unto her husband: Wherefore dost thou detain the 4 captive and well-born lad in bonds, who ought rather to be set at liberty, and be waited upon? For 5 she wished to see me out of a desire of sin, but I was ignorant concerning all these

things. And he said to her: It is not the custom of the Egyptians to take that which belongeth to others before 6 proof is given. This, therefore, he said concerning the merchant; but as for the lad, he must be imprisoned.

15 1 Now after four and twenty days came the Ishmaelites; for they had heard that Jacob my father 2 was mourning much concerning me. And they came and said unto me: How is it that thou saidst that thou wast a slave? and lo, we have learnt that thou art the son of a mighty man in the land of 3 Canaan, and thy father still mourneth for thee in sackcloth and ashes. When I heard this my bowels were dissolved and my heart melted, and I desired greatly to weep, but I restrained myself, that I should not put my brethren to shame. And I said unto them, I know not, I am a slave. 4, 5 Then, therefore, they took counsel to sell me, that I should not be found in their hands. For they feared my father, lest he [should come and] execute upon them a grievous vengeance. For they had 6 heard that he was mighty with God and with men. Then said the merchant unto them: Release 7 me from the judgement of Pentiphri. And they came and requested me, saying: Say that thou wast bought by us with money, and he will set us free.

16 1 Now the Memphian woman said to her husband: Buy the youth; for I hear, said she, that they are selling him. 2 And straightway she sent a eunuch to the 3 Ishmaelites, and asked them to sell me. But since the eunuch would not agree to buy me (at their price) he returned, having made trial of them, and he made known to his mistress that they asked a large price for their slave. 4 And she sent another eunuch, saying: Even though they demand two minas, give them, do not spare the gold; only buy the boy, and bring him to me. 5 The eunuch therefore went and gave them eighty pieces of gold, and he received me; but to the Egyptian woman he said: I have given a hundred. 6 And though I knew (this) I held my peace, lest the eunuch should be put to shame.

17 1 Ye see, therefore, my children, what great things I endured that I should not put my brethren to 2 shame. Do ye also, therefore love one another, and with long-suffering hide ye one another's 3 faults. For God delighteth in the unity of brethren, and in the purpose of a heart that takes 4 pleasure in love. And when my brethren came into Egypt they learnt that I had returned their 5 money unto them, and upbraided them not, and comforted them. And after the death of Jacob my father I loved them more abundantly, and all things whatsoever he commanded I did very 6 abundantly for them, And I suffered them not to be afflicted in the smallest matter; and all that 7 was in my hand I gave unto them. And their children were my children, and my children as their servants; and their

life was my life, and all their suffering was my suffering, and all their sickness 8 was my infirmity. My land was their land, and their counsel my counsel. And I exalted not myself among them in arrogance because of my worldly glory, but I was among them as one of the least.

18 1 If ye also, therefore, walk in the commandments of the Lord, my children, He will exalt you there, 2 and will bless you with good things for ever and ever. And if any one seeketh to do evil unto you, 3 do well unto him, and pray for him, and ye shall be redeemed of the Lord from all evil. [For], behold, ye see that out of my humility and long -suffering I took unto wife the daughter of the priest of Heliopolis. And a hundred talents of gold were given me with her, and the Lord made 4 them to serve me. And He gave me also beauty as a flower beyond the beautiful ones of Israel; and He preserved me unto old age in strength and in beauty, because I was like in all things to Jacob.

19 1 Hear ye, therefore, me vision which I saw. 2 I saw twelve harts feeding. And nine of them were dispersed. Now the three were preserved, but on the following day they also were dispersed. 3 And I saw that the three harts became three lambs, and they cried to the Lord, and He brought them forth into a flourishing and well watered place, yea He brought them out of darkness into light. 4 And there they cried unto the Lord until there gathered together unto them the nine harts, and they became as twelve sheep, and after a little time they increased and became many 5 flocks. And after these things I saw and behold, twelve bulls were sucking one cow, which produced a sea of milk, and there drank thereof the twelve flocks and innumerable herds. 6 And the horns of the fourth bull went up unto heaven and became as a wall for the flocks, and in the midst of the two horns there grew 7 another horn. And I saw a bull calf which surrounded them twelve times, and it became a help to the bulls wholly. 8 And I saw in the midst of the horns a virgin [wearing a many-coloured garment, and from her] went forth a lamb; and on his right (was as it were a lion; and) all the beasts and all the reptiles rushed (against him), and the lamb over 9 came them and destroyed them. And the bulls rejoiced because of him, and the cow [and the 10 harts] exulted together with them. And these 11 things must come to pass in their season. Do ye therefore, my children, observe the commandments of the Lord, and honour Levi and Judah; for from them shall arise unto you [the Lamb of God, who taketh away the sin of the world] one who saveth [all the Gentiles and] Israel. 12 For His kingdom is an everlasting kingdom, which shall not pass away; but my kingdom among you shall come to an end as a watcher's hammock, which after the summer disappeareth.

20 1For I know that after my death the Egyptians will afflict you, but God will avenge you, and will 2 bring you into that which He promised to your fathers. But ye shall carry up my bones with you; for when my bones are being taken up thither, the Lord shall be with you in light, and Beliar shall be in darkness with the Egyptians. 3 And carry ye up Asenath your mother to the Hippodrome, and near Rachel your mother bury her. 4, 5 And when he had said these things he stretched out his feet, and died at a good old age. And all Israel mourned for him, and all Egypt, with a great mourning. 6 And when the children of Israel went out of Egypt, they took with them the bones of Joseph, and they buried him in Hebron with his fathers, and the years of his life were one hundred and ten years.

THE TESTAMENT OF BENJAMIN, THE TWELFTH SON OF JACOB AND RACHEL

1 1 The copy of the words of Benjamin, which he commanded his sons to observe, after he had lived 2 a hundred and twenty-five years. And he kissed them, and said: As Isaac was born to Abraham 3 in his old age, so also was I to Jacob. And since Rachel my mother died in giving me birth, I had 4 no milk; therefore I was suckled by Bilhah her handmaid. For Rachel remained barren for twelve years after she had borne Joseph; and she prayed the Lord with fasting twelve days, and she 5 conceived and bare me. For my father loved Rachel dearly, and prayed that he might see two 6 sons born from her. Therefore was I called Benjamin, that is, a son of days.

2 1 And when I went into Egypt, to Joseph, and my brother recognized me, he said unto me: 2 What did they tell my father when they sold me ? And I said unto him, They dabbled thy coat with blood and sent it, and said: Know whether this be thy son's coat. 3 And Joseph said unto me: Even so, brother, the Canaanite merchants stole me by force, 4 And it came to pass that as they went on their way they concealed my garment, as though a wild beast had met 5 me and slain me. And so his associates sold me to the Ishmaelites. 6 And they did not lie in saying this. For he wished to conceal from me the deeds of my brethren. And he called to him his brethren and said: 7 Do not tell my father what ye have done unto me, but tell him 8 as I have told Benjamin. And let the thoughts among you be such, and let not these things come to the heart of my father.

3 1 Do ye also, therefore, my children, love the Lord God of heaven and earth, and keep His commandments, following the example of the good and holy man Joseph. 2 And let your mind be unto good, even as ye know me; for he that hath his mind right seeth 3 all things rightly. Fear ye the Lord, and love your neighbour; and even though the spirits of Beliar claim you to afflict you with every evil, yet shall they not have dominion over you, even 4 as they had not over Joseph my brother. How many men wished to slay him, and God shielded him! For he that feareth God and loveth his neighbour cannot be smitten by the spirit of 5 Beliar, being shielded by the fear of God. Nor can he be ruled over by the device of men or beasts, for he is helped by the Lord through the love which he hath towards his neighbour. 6 For Joseph also besought our father that he would pray for his brethren, that the Lord would 7 not impute to them as sin whatever evil they had done unto him. And thus Jacob cried out: My good child, thou hast prevailed over the bowels of thy father Jacob. And he embraced him, and kissed him for two hours, saying: 8 In thee shall be fulfilled the prophecy of heaven [concerning the Lamb of God, and Saviour of the world], and that a blameless one shall be delivered up for lawless men, and a sinless one shall die for ungodly men [in the blood of the covenant. for the salvation of the Gentiles and of Israel, and shall destroy Beliar and his servants].

4 1 See ye, therefore, my children, the end of the good man? Be followers of his compassion, therefore, 2 with a good mind, that ye also may wear crowns of glory. For the good man hath not 3 a dark eye; for he showeth mercy to all men, even though they be sinners. And though they devise with evil intent concerning him, by doing good he overcometh evil, being shielded by God: 4 and he loveth the righteous as his own soul. If any one is glorified, he envieth him not; if any one is enriched, he is not jealous; if any one is valiant, he praiseth him; the virtuous man he laudeth, on the poor man he hath mercy; on the weak he hath compassion; unto God he singeth praises. 5 As for him who hath the fear of God, he protecteth him as with a shield; him that loveth God he helpeth; him that rejecteth the Most High he admonisheth and turneth back; and him that hath the grace of a good spirit he loveth as his own soul.

5 1 If, therefore, ye also have a good mind, then will both wicked men be at peace with you, and the profligate will reverence you and turn unto good; and the covetous will not only cease from 2 their inordinate desire, but even give the objects of their covetousness to them that are afflicted. If 3 ye do well, even the unclean spirits will flee from you; and the beasts will dread you. For where there is reverence for good works and light in the mind, even darkness fleeth away from him 4 For if any one does violence to a holy man, he repenteth; for the holy man is merciful to his reviler, and holdeth his peace. 5 And if any one betrayeth a righteous man, the righteous man prayeth: though for a little he be humbled, yet not long after he appeareth far more glorious, as was Joseph my brother.

6 1 The inclination of the good man is not in the power of the deceit of the spirit of Beliar, for the 2 angel of peace guideth his soul. And he gazeth not passionately upon corruptible things, nor 3 gathereth together riches through a desire of pleasure. He delighteth not in pleasure, [he grieveth for not his neighbour], he sateth not himself with luxuries, he erreth not in the uplifting of the eyes, 4 the Lord is his portion. The good inclination receiveth not glory nor dishonor from men, and it knoweth not any guile, or lie, or fighting or reviling; for the Lord dwelleth in him and lighteth up his 5 soul, and he rejoiceth towards all men alway. The good mind hath not two tongues, of blessing and of cursing, of contumely and of honor, of sorrow and of joy, of quietness and of confusion, of hypocrisy and of truth, [of poverty and of wealth]; but it hath one disposition, uncorrupt and pure, concerning all 6 men. It hath no double sight, nor double hearing; for in everything which he doeth, or speaketh, or 7 seeth, he knoweth that the Lord looketh on his soul. And he

cleanseth his mind that he may not be condemned by men as well as by God. And in like manner the works of Beliar are twofold, and there is no singleness in them.

7 1 Therefore, my children, I tell you, flee the malice of Beliar; for he giveth a sword to them that obey him. 2 And the sword is the mother of seven evils. First the mind conceiveth through Beliar, and first there is bloodshed; secondly ruin; thirdly, tribulation; fourthly, exile; fifthly, dearth; sixthly, panic; seventhly, destruction. 3 Therefore was Cain also delivered over to seven vengeances by God, for in every hundred years the Lord brought one plague upon him. 4 And when he was two hundred years old he began to suffer, and in the nine-hundredth year he was destroyed. For on account of Abel, his brother, with all the evils was he judged, but Lamech with seventy times seven. 5 Because for ever those who are like Cain in envy and hatred of brethren, shall be punished with the same judgment.

8 1 And do ye, my children, flee evil-doing, envy, and hatred of brethren, and cleave to goodness 2 and love. He that hath a pure mind in love, looketh not after a woman with a view to fornication; for he hath no defilement in his heart, because the Spirit of God resteth upon him. 3 For as the sun is not defiled by shining on dung and mire, but rather drieth up both and driveth away the evil smell; so also the pure mind, though encompassed by the defilements of earth, rather cleanseth (them) and is not itself defiled.

9 1 And I believe that there will be also evil-doings among you, from the words of Enoch the righteous: that ye shall commit fornication with the fornication of Sodom, and shall perish, all save a few, and shall renew wanton deeds with women; and the kingdom of the Lord shall not be among, you, for straightway He shall take it away. 2 Nevertheless the temple of God shall be in your portion, and the last (temple) shall be more glorious than the first. And the twelve tribes shall be gathered together there, and all the Gentiles, until the Most High shall send forth His salvation in the visitation of an only 3 begotten prophet. [And He shall enter into the [first] temple, and there shall the Lord be treated with outrage, and He shall be lifted up upon 4 a tree. And the veil of the temple shall be rent, and the Spirit of God shall pass on to the Gentiles 5 as fire poured forth. And He shall ascend from Hades and shall pass from earth into heaven. And I know how lowly He shall be upon earth, and how glorious in heaven.]

10 1 Now when Joseph was in Egypt, I longed to see his figure and the form of his countenance; and through the prayers of Jacob my father I saw him,

while awake in the daytime, even his entire figure exactly as he was. 2 And when he had said these things, he said unto them: Know ye, therefore, my children, that I am dying. 3 Do ye, therefore, truth and righteousness each one to his neighbour, and judgement unto confirmation, and keep the law of the Lord and his commandments. 4 For these things do I leave you instead of inheritance. Do ye also, therefore, give them to your 5 children for an everlasting possession; for so did both Abraham, and Isaac, and Jacob. For all these things they gave us for an inheritance, saying: Keep the commandments of God, until the Lord 6 shall reveal His salvation to all Gentiles. And then shall ye see Enoch, Noah, and Shem, and Abraham, and Isaac, and Jacob, rising on the right hand in gladness. 7 Then shall we also rise, each one over our tribe, worshipping the King of heaven, [who appeared upon earth in the form of a man in humility. And as many as believe on Him on the earth 8 shall rejoice with Him]. Then also all men shall rise, some unto glory and some unto shame. And the Lord shall judge Israel first, for their unrighteousness; [for when He appeared as God in the flesh to deliver them they believed Him 9 not]. And then shall He judge all the Gentiles, [as many as believed Him not when He appeared 10 upon earth]. And He shall convict Israel through the chosen ones of the Gentiles, even as He reproved Esau through the Midianites, who deceived their brethren, [so that they fell into fornication, and idolatry; and they were alienated from God], becoming therefore children in the portion of them that fear the Lord. 11 If ye therefore, my children, walk in holiness according to the commandments of the Lord, ye shall again dwell securely with me, and all Israel shall be gathered unto the Lord.

11 1 And I shall no longer be called a ravening wolf on account of your ravages, but [a worker of the Lord, distributing food to them that work what is good. 2 And there shall rise up from my seed in the latter times one] beloved of the Lord, [hearing upon the earth His voice] and a doer of the good pleasure of His will, [enlightening with new knowledge all the Gentiles, even the light of knowledge, bursting in upon Israel for salvation and tearing away from them like a wolf, and giving to the synagogue of the Gentiles. 3 Until the consummation of the age shall he be in the synagogues of the Gentiles, and among their 4 rulers, as a strain of music in the mouth of all. And he shall be inscribed in the holy books, both 5 his work and his word, and he shall be a chosen one of God for ever. And through them he shall go to and fro as Jacob my father, saying: He shall fill up that which lacketh of thy tribe].

12 1 And when he finished his words, he said: I command you, my children, carry up my bones out of Egypt, and bury me at Hebron, near my 2 fathers. So Benjamin died a hundred and twenty-five years old, at a good old age, and they 3 placed him in a coffin. And in the ninety-first year from the entrance of the children of Israel into Egypt, they and their brethren brought up the bones of their fathers secretly during the Canaanitish war; and they buried them in Hebron, 4 by the feet of their fathers. And they returned from the land of Canaan and dwelt in Egypt until the day of their departure from the land of Egypt.

The Testament of Abraham

Translated by W.A. Craigie. From Ante-Nicene Fathers, Vol. 9. Edited by Allan Menzies. (Buffalo, NY: Christian Literature Publishing Co., 1896.)

Version 1

1. Abraham lived the measure of his life, nine hundred and ninety-five years, and having lived all the years of his life in quietness, gentleness, and righteousness, the righteous one was exceeding hospitable; for, pitching his tent in the cross-ways at the oak of Mamre, he received every one, both rich and poor, kings and rulers, the maimed and the helpless, friends and strangers, neighbors and travelers, all alike did the devout, all-holy, righteous, and hospitable Abraham entertain. Even upon him, however, there came the common, inexorable, bitter lot of death, and the uncertain end of life. Therefore the Lord God, summoning his archangel Michael, said to him: Go down, chief-captain Michael, to Abraham and speak to him concerning his death, that he may set his affairs in order, for I have blessed him as the stars of heaven, and as the sand by the sea-shore, and he is in abundance of long life and many possessions, and is becoming exceeding rich. Beyond all men, moreover, he is righteous in every goodness, hospitable and loving to the end of his life; but go, archangel Michael, to Abraham, my beloved friend, and announce to him his death and assure him thus: You shall at this time depart from this vain world, and shall quit the body, and go to your own Lord among the good.

2. And the chief-captain departed from before the face of God, and went down to Abraham to the oak of Mamre, and found the righteous Abraham in the field close by, sitting beside yokes of oxen for ploughing, together with the sons of Masek and other servants, to the number of twelve. And behold the chief-captain came to him, and Abraham, seeing the chief-captain Michael coming from afar, like to a very comely warrior, arose and met him as was his custom, meeting and entertaining all strangers. And the chief-captain saluted him and said: Hail, most honored father, righteous soul chosen of God, true son of the heavenly one. Abraham said to the chief-captain: Hail, most honored warrior, bright as the sun and most beautiful above all the sons of men; you are welcome; therefore I beseech your presence, tell me whence the youth of your age has come; teach me, your suppliant, whence and from what army and from what journey your beauty has come hither. The chief-captain said: I, O righteous Abraham, come from the great city. I have been sent by the great king to take the place of a good friend of his, for the king has summoned him. And Abraham said, Come, my Lord, go with me as far as my field. The chief-captain said: I come; and going into the field of the ploughing, they sat down beside the company. And Abraham said to his servants, the sons of Masek: Go to the herd of horses, and bring two horses, quiet, and gentle and tame, so that I and this stranger may sit thereon. But the chief-captain said, Nay, my Lord, Abraham, let them not bring horses, for I abstain from ever sitting upon any four-footed beast. Is not my king rich in much merchandise, having power both over men and all kinds of cattle? But I abstain from ever sitting upon any four-footed beast. Let us go, then, O righteous soul, walking lightly until we reach your house. And Abraham said, Amen, be it so.

3. And as they went on from the field toward his house, beside that way there stood a cypress tree, and by the command of the Lord the tree cried out with a human voice, saying, Holy, holy, holy is the Lord God that calls himself to those that love him; but Abraham hid the mystery, thinking that the chief-captain had not heard the voice of the tree. And coming near to the house they sat down in the court, and Isaac seeing the face of the angel said to Sarah his mother, My lady mother, behold, the man sitting with my father Abraham is not a son of the race of those that dwell on the earth. And Isaac ran, and saluted him, and fell at the feet of the Incorporeal, and the Incorporeal blessed him and said, The Lord God will grant you his promise that he made to your father Abraham and to his seed, and will also grant you the precious prayer of your father and your mother. Abraham said to Isaac his son, My son Isaac, draw water from the well, and bring it me in the vessel, that we may wash the feet of this stranger, for he is tired, having come to us from off a long journey. And Isaac ran to the well and drew water in the vessel and brought it to them, and Abraham went up and washed the feet of the chief captain Michael, and the heart of Abraham was moved, and he wept over the stranger. And Isaac, seeing his father weeping, wept also, and the chief captain, seeing them weeping, also wept with them, and the tears of the chief captain fell upon the vessel into the water of the basin and became precious stones. And Abraham seeing the marvel, and being astonished, took the stones secretly, and hid the mystery, keeping it by himself in his heart.

4. And Abraham said to Isaac his son: Go, my beloved son, into the inner chamber of the house and beautify it. Spread for us there two couches, one for me and one for this man that is guest with us this day. Prepare for us there a seat and a candlestick and a table with abundance of every good thing. Beautify the chamber, my son, and spread under us linen and purple and fine linen. Burn there every precious and excellent incense, and bring sweet-smelling plants from the garden and

fill our house with them. Kindle seven lamps full of oil, so that we may rejoice, for this man that is our guest this day is more glorious than kings or rulers, and his appearance surpasses all the sons of men. And Isaac prepared all things well, and Abraham taking the archangel Michael went into the chamber, and they both sat down upon the couches, and between them he placed a table with abundance of every good thing. Then the chief captain arose and went out, as if by constraint of his belly to make issue of water, and ascended to heaven in the twinkling of an eye, and stood before the Lord, and said to him: Lord and Master, let your power know that I am unable to remind that righteous man of his death, for I have not seen upon the earth a man like him, pitiful, hospitable, righteous, truthful, devout, refraining from every evil deed. And now know, Lord, that I cannot remind him of his death. And the Lord said: Go down, chief-captain Michael, to my friend Abraham, and do whatever he says to you, and eat with him whatever he eats. And I will send my Holy Spirit upon his son Isaac, and will put the remembrance of his death into the heart of Isaac, so that even he in a dream may see the death of his father, and Isaac will relate the dream, and you shall interpret it, and he himself will know his end. And the chief-captain said, Lord, all the heavenly spirits are incorporeal, and neither eat nor drink, and this man has set before me a table with abundance of all good things earthly and corruptible. Now, Lord, what shall I do? How shall I escape him, sitting at one table with him? The Lord said: Go down to him, and take no thought for this, for when you sit down with him, I will send upon you a devouring spirit, and it will consume out of your hands and through your mouth all that is on the table. Rejoice together with him in everything, only you shall interpret well the things of the vision, that Abraham may know the sickle of death and the uncertain end of life, and may make disposal of all his possessions, for I have blessed him above the sand of the sea and as the stars of heaven.

5. Then the chief captain went down to the house of Abraham, and sat down with him at the table, and Isaac served them. And when the supper was ended, Abraham prayed after his custom, and the chief-captain prayed together with him, and each lay down to sleep upon his couch. And Isaac said to his father, Father, I too would fain sleep with you in this chamber, that I also may hear your discourse, for I love to hear the excellence of the conversation of this virtuous man. Abraham said, Nay, my son, but go to your own chamber and sleep on your own couch, lest we be troublesome to this man. Then Isaac, having received the prayer from them, and having blessed them, went to his own chamber and lay down upon his couch. But the Lord cast the thought of death into the heart of Isaac as in a dream, and about the third hour of the night Isaac awoke and rose up from his couch, and came running to the chamber where his father was sleeping together with the archangel. Isaac, therefore, on reaching the door cried out, saying, My father Abraham, arise and open to me quickly, that I may enter and hang upon your neck, and embrace you before they take you away from me. Abraham therefore arose and opened to him, and Isaac entered and hung upon his neck, and began to weep with a loud voice. Abraham therefore being moved at heart, also wept with a loud voice, and the chief-captain, seeing them weeping, wept also. Sarah being in her room, heard their weeping, and came running to them, and found them embracing and weeping. And Sarah said with weeping, My Lord Abraham, what is this that you weep? Tell me, my Lord, has this brother that has been entertained by us this day brought you tidings of Lot, your brother's son, that he is dead? Is it for this that you grieve thus? The chief-captain answered and said to her, Nay, my sister Sarah, it is not as you say, but your son Isaac, methinks, beheld a dream, and came to us weeping, and we seeing him were moved in our hearts and wept.

6. Then Sarah, hearing the excellence of the conversation of the chief-captain, straightway knew that it was an angel of the Lord that spoke. Sarah therefore signified to Abraham to come out towards the door, and said to him, My Lord Abraham, do you know who this man is? Abraham said, I know not. Sarah said, You know, my Lord, the three men from heaven that were entertained by us in our tent beside the oak of Mamre, when you killed the kid without blemish, and set a table before them. After the flesh had been eaten, the kid rose again, and sucked its mother with great joy. Do you not know, my Lord Abraham, that by promise they gave to us Isaac as the fruit of the womb? Of these three holy men this is one. Abraham said, O Sarah, in this you speak the truth. Glory and praise from our God and the Father. For late in the evening when I washed his feet in the basin I said in my heart, These are the feet of one of the three men that I washed then; and his tears that fell into the basin then became precious stones. And shaking them out from his lap he gave them to Sarah, saying, If you believe me not, look now at these. And Sarah receiving them bowed down and saluted and said, Glory be to God that shows us wonderful things. And now know, my Lord Abraham, that there is among us the revelation of some thing, whether it be evil or good!

7. And Abraham left Sarah, and went into the chamber, and said to Isaac, Come hither, my beloved son, tell me the truth, what it was you saw and what befell you that you came so hastily to us. And Isaac answering began to say, I saw, my Lord, in this night the sun and the moon above my head, surrounding me with its rays and giving me light. As I gazed at this and rejoiced, I

saw the heaven opened, and a man bearing light descend from it, shining more than seven suns. And this man like the sun came and took away the sun from my head, and went up into the heavens from whence he came, but I was greatly grieved that he took away the sun from me. After a little, as I was still sorrowing and sore troubled, I saw this man come forth from heaven a second time, and he took away from me the moon also from off my head, and I wept greatly and called upon that man of light, and said, Do not, my Lord, take away my glory from me; pity me and hear me, and if you take away the sun from me, then leave the moon to me. He said, Suffer them to be taken up to the king above, for he wishes them there. And he took them away from me, but he left the rays upon me. The chief-captain said, Hear, O righteous Abraham; the sun which your son saw is you his father, and the moon likewise is Sarah his mother. The man bearing light who descended from heaven, this is the one sent from God who is to take your righteous soul from you. And now know, O most honored Abraham, that at this time you shall leave this worldly life, and remove to God. Abraham said to the chief captain O strangest of marvels! And now are you he that shall take my soul from me? The chief-captain said to him, I am the chief-captain Michael, that stands before the Lord, and I was sent to you to remind you of your death, and then I shall depart to him as I was commanded. Abraham said, Now I know that you are an angel of the Lord, and wast sent to take my soul, but I will not go with you; but do whatever you are commanded.

8. The chief-captain hearing these words immediately vanished, and ascending into heaven stood before God, and told all that he had seen in the house of Abraham; and the chief-captain said this also to his Lord, Thus says your friend Abraham, I will not go with you, but do whatever you are commanded; and now, O Lord Almighty, does your glory and immortal kingdom order anything? God said to the chief-captain Michael, Go to my friend Abraham yet once again, and speak to him thus, Thus says the Lord your God, he that brought you into the land of promise, that blessed you above the sand of the sea and above the stars of heaven, that opened the womb of barrenness of Sarah, and granted you Isaac as the fruit of the womb in old age, Verily I say unto you that blessing I will bless you, and multiplying I will multiply your seed, and I will give you all that you shall ask from me, for I am the Lord your God, and besides me there is no other. Tell me why you have rebelled against me, and why there is grief in you, and why you rebelled against my archangel Michael? Do you not know that all who have come from Adam and Eve have died, and that none of the prophets has escaped death? None of those that rule as kings is immortal; none of your forefathers has escaped the mystery of death. They have all died, they

have all departed into Hades, they are all gathered by the sickle of death. But upon you I have not sent death, I have not suffered any deadly disease to come upon you, I have not permitted the sickle of death to meet you, I have not allowed the nets of Hades to enfold you, I have never wished you to meet with any evil. But for good comfort I have sent my chief-captain Michael to you, that you may know your departure from the world, and set your house in order, and all that belongs to you, and bless Isaac your beloved son. And now know that I have done this not wishing to grieve you. Wherefore then have you said to my chief-captain, I will not go with you? Wherefore have you spoken thus? Do you not know that if I give leave to death and he comes upon you, then I should see whether you would come or not?

9. And the chief-captain receiving the exhortations of the Lord went down to Abraham, and seeing him the righteous one fell upon his face to the ground as one dead, and the chief-captain told him all that he had heard from the Most High. Then the holy and just Abraham rising with many tears fell at the feet of the Incorporeal, and besought him, saying, I beseech you, chief-captain of the hosts above, since you have wholly deigned to come yourself to me a sinner and in all things your unworthy servant, I beseech you even now, O chief-captain, to carry my word yet again to the Most High, and you shall say to him, Thus says Abraham your servant, Lord, Lord, in every work and word which I have asked of you you have heard me, and hast fulfilled all my counsel. Now, Lord, I resist not your power, for I too know that I am not immortal but mortal. Since therefore to your command all things yield, and fear and tremble at the face of your power, I also fear, but I ask one request of you, and now, Lord and Master, hear my prayer, for while still in this body I desire to see all the inhabited earth, and all the creations which you established by one word, and when I see these, then if I shall depart from life I shall be without sorrow. So the chief-captain went back again, and stood before God, and told him all, saying, Thus says your friend Abraham, I desired to behold all the earth in my lifetime before I died. And the Most High hearing this, again commanded the chief-captain Michael, and said to him, Take a cloud of light, and the angels that have power over the chariots, and go down, take the righteous Abraham upon a chariot of the cherubim, and exalt him into the air of heaven that he may behold all the earth.

10. And the archangel Michael went down and took Abraham upon a chariot of the cherubim, and exalted him into the air of heaven, and led him upon the cloud together with sixty angels, and Abraham ascended upon the chariot over all the earth. And Abraham saw the world as it was in that day, some ploughing, others

driving wains, in one place men herding flocks, and in another watching them by night, and dancing and playing and harping, in another place men striving and contending at law, elsewhere men weeping and having the dead in remembrance. He saw also the newly-wedded received with honor, and in a word he saw all things that are done in the world, both good and bad. Abraham therefore passing over them saw men bearing swords, wielding in their hands sharpened swords, and Abraham asked the chief-captain, Who are these? The chief-captain said, These are thieves, who intend to commit murder, and to steal and burn and destroy. Abraham said, Lord, Lord, hear my voice, and command that wild beasts may come out of the wood and devour them. And even as he spoke there came wild beasts out of the wood and devoured them. And he saw in another place a man with a woman committing fornication with each other, and said, Lord, Lord, command that the earth may open and swallow them, and straightway the earth was cleft and swallowed them. And he saw in another place men digging through a house, and carrying away other men's possessions, and he said, Lord, Lord, command that fire may come down from heaven and consume them. And even as he spoke, fire came down from heaven and consumed them. And straightway there came a voice from heaven to the chief-captain, saying thus, O chief-captain Michael, command the chariot to stop, and turn Abraham away that he may not see all the earth, for if he behold all that live in wickedness, he will destroy all creation. For behold, Abraham has not sinned, and has no pity on sinners, but I have made the world, and desire not to destroy any one of them, but wait for the death of the sinner, till he be converted and live. But take Abraham up to the first gate of heaven, that he may see there the judgments and recompenses, and repent of the souls of the sinners that he has destroyed.

11. So Michael turned the chariot and brought Abraham to the east, to the first gate of heaven; and Abraham saw two ways, the one narrow and contracted, the other broad and spacious, and there he saw two gates, the one broad on the broad way, and the other narrow on the narrow way. And outside the two gates there he saw a man sitting upon a gilded throne, and the appearance of that man was terrible, as of the Lord. And they saw many souls driven by angels and led in through the broad gate, and other souls, few in number, that were taken by the angels through the narrow gate. And when the wonderful one who sat upon the golden throne saw few entering through the narrow gate, and many entering through the broad one, straightway that wonderful one tore the hairs of his head and the sides of his beard, and threw himself on the ground from his throne, weeping and lamenting. But when he saw many souls entering

through the narrow gate, then he arose from the ground and sat upon his throne in great joy, rejoicing and exulting. And Abraham asked the chief-captain, My Lord chief-captain, who is this most marvelous man, adorned with such glory, and sometimes he weeps and laments, and sometimes he rejoices and exults? The incorporeal one said: This is the first-created Adam who is in such glory, and he looks upon the world because all are born from him, and when he sees many souls going through the narrow gate, then he arises and sits upon his throne rejoicing and exulting in joy, because this narrow gate is that of the just, that leads to life, and they that enter through it go into Paradise. For this, then, the first-created Adam rejoices, because he sees the souls being saved. But when he sees many souls entering through the broad gate, then he pulls out the hairs of his head, and casts himself on the ground weeping and lamenting bitterly, for the broad gate is that of sinners, which leads to destruction and eternal punishment. And for this the first-formed Adam falls from his throne weeping and lamenting for the destruction of sinners, for they are many that are lost, and they are few that are saved, for in seven thousand there is scarcely found one soul saved, being righteous and undefiled.

12. While he was yet saying these things to me, behold two angels, fiery in aspect, and pitiless in mind, and severe in look, and they drove on thousands of souls, pitilessly lashing them with fiery thongs. The angel laid hold of one soul, and they drove all the souls in at the broad gate to destruction. So we also went along with the angels, and came within that broad gate, and between the two gates stood a throne terrible of aspect, of terrible crystal, gleaming as fire, and upon it sat a wondrous man bright as the sun, like to the Son of God. Before him stood a table like crystal, all of gold and fine linen, and upon the table there was lying a book, the thickness of it six cubits, and the breadth of it ten cubits, and on the right and left of it stood two angels holding paper and ink and pen. Before the table sat an angel of light, holding in his hand a balance, and on his left sat an angel all fiery, pitiless, and severe, holding in his hand a trumpet, having within it all-consuming fire with which to try the sinners. The wondrous man who sat upon the throne himself judged and sentenced the souls, and the two angels on the right and on the left wrote down, the one on the right the righteousness and the one on the left the wickedness. The one before the table, who held the balance, weighed the souls, and the fiery angel, who held the fire, tried the souls. And Abraham asked the chief-captain Michael, What is this that we behold? And the chief-captain said, These things that you see, holy Abraham, are the judgment and recompense. And behold the angel holding the soul in his hand, and he brought it before the judge, and the judge said to one

of the angels that served him, Open me this book, and find me the sins of this soul. And opening the book he found its sins and its righteousness equally balanced, and he neither gave it to the tormentors, nor to those that were saved, but set it in the midst.

13. And Abraham said, My Lord chief-captain, who is this most wondrous judge? And who are the angels that write down? And who is the angel like the sun, holding the balance? And who is the fiery angel holding the fire? The chief-captain said, Do you see, most holy Abraham, the terrible man sitting upon the throne? This is the son of the first created Adam, who is called Abel, whom the wicked Cain killed, and he sits thus to judge all creation, and examines righteous men and sinners. For God has said, I shall not judge you, but every man born of man shall be judged. Therefore he has given to him judgment, to judge the world until his great and glorious coming, and then, O righteous Abraham, is the perfect judgment and recompense, eternal and unchangeable, which no one can alter. For every man has come from the first-created, and therefore they are first judged here by his son, and at the second coming they shall be judged by the twelve tribes of Israel, every breath and every creature. But the third time they shall be judged by the Lord God of all, and then, indeed, the end of that judgment is near, and the sentence terrible, and there is none to deliver. And now by three tribunals the judgment of the world and the recompense is made, and for this reason a matter is not finally confirmed by one or two witnesses, but by three witnesses shall everything be established. The two angels on the right hand and on the left, these are they that write down the sins and the righteousness, the one on the right hand writes down the righteousness, and the one on the left the sins. The angel like the sun, holding the balance in his hand, is the archangel, Dokiel the just weigher, and he weighs the righteousnesses and sins with the righteousness of God. The fiery and pitiless angel, holding the fire in his hand, is the archangel Puruel, who has power over fire, and tries the works of men through fire, and if the fire consume the work of any man, the angel of judgment immediately seizes him, and carries him away to the place of sinners, a most bitter place of punishment. But if the fire approves the work of anyone, and does not seize upon it, that man is justified, and the angel of righteousness takes him and carries him up to be saved in the lot of the just. And thus, most righteous Abraham, all things in all men are tried by fire and the balance.

14. And Abraham said to the chief-captain, My Lord the chief-captain, the soul which the angel held in his hand, why was it adjudged to be set in the midst? The chief-captain said, Listen, righteous Abraham. Because the judge found its sins. and its righteousnesses equal,

he neither committed it to judgment nor to be saved, until the judge of all shall come. Abraham said to the chief-captain, And what yet is wanting for the soul to be saved? The chief-captain said, If it obtains one righteousness above its sins, it enters into salvation. Abraham said to the chief-captain, Come hither, chief-captain Michael, let us make prayer for this soul, and see whether God will hear us. The chief-captain said, Amen, be it so; and they made prayer and entreaty for the soul, and God heard them, and when they rose up from their prayer they did not see the soul standing there. And Abraham said to the angel, Where is the soul that you held in the midst? And the angel answered, It has been saved by your righteous prayer, and behold an angel of light has taken it and carried it up into Paradise. Abraham said, I glorify the name of God, the Most High, and his immeasurable mercy. And Abraham said to the chief-captain, I beseech you, archangel, hearken to my prayer, and let us yet call upon the Lord, and supplicate his compassion, and entreat his mercy for the souls of the sinners whom I formerly, in my anger, cursed and destroyed, whom the earth devoured, and the wild beasts tore in pieces, and the fire consumed through my words. Now I know that I have sinned before the Lord our God. Come then, O Michael, chief-captain of the hosts above, come, let us call upon God with tears that he may forgive me my sin, and grant them to me. And the chief-captain heard him, and they made entreaty before the Lord, and when they had called upon him for a long space, there came a voice from heaven saying, Abraham, Abraham, I have hearkened to your voice and your prayer, and forgive you your sin, and those whom you think that I destroyed I have called up and brought them into life by my exceeding kindness, because for a season I have requited them in judgment, and those whom I destroy living upon earth, I will not requite in death.

15. And the voice of the Lord said also to the chief-captain Michael, Michael, my servant, turn back Abraham to his house, for behold his end has come near, and the measure of his life is fulfilled, that he may set all things in order, and then take him and bring him to me. So the chief-captain, turning the chariot and the cloud, brought Abraham to his house, and going into his chamber he sat upon his couch. And Sarah his wife came and embraced the feet of the Incorporeal, and spoke humbly, saying, I give you thanks, my Lord, that you have brought my Lord Abraham, for behold we thought he had been taken up from us. And his son Isaac also came and fell upon his neck, and in the same way all his men-slaves and women-slaves surrounded Abraham and embraced him, glorifying God. And the Incorporeal one said to them, Hearken, righteous Abraham. Behold your wife Sarah, behold also your beloved son Isaac, behold also all your men-servants and maid-servants round about you. Make disposition

of all that you have, for the day has come near in which you shall depart from the body and go to the Lord once for all. Abraham said, Has the Lord said it, or do you say this of yourself? The chief-captain answered, Hearken, righteous Abraham. The Lord has commanded, and I tell it you. Abraham said, I will not go with you. The chief-captain, hearing these words, straightway went forth from the presence of Abraham, and went up into the heavens, and stood before God the Most High, and said, Lord Almighty, behold I have hearkened to Your friend Abraham in all he has said to You, and have fulfilled his requests. I have shown to him Your power, and all the earth and sea that is under heaven. I have shown to him judgment and recompense by means of cloud and chariots, and again he says, I will not go with you. And the Most High said to the angel, Does my friend Abraham say thus again, I will not go with you? The archangel said, Lord Almighty, he says thus, and I refrain from laying hands on him, because from the beginning he is Your friend, and has done all things pleasing in Your sight. There is no man like him on earth, not even Job the wondrous man, and therefore I refrain from laying hands on him. Command, therefore, Immortal King, what shall be done.

16. Then the Most High said, Call me hither Death that is called the shameless countenance and the pitiless look. And Michael the Incorporeal went and said to Death, Come hither; the Lord of creation, the immortal king, calls you. And Death, hearing this, shivered and trembled, being possessed with great terror, and coming with great fear it stood before the invisible father, shivering, groaning and trembling, awaiting the command of the Lord. Therefore the invisible God said to Death, Come hither, you bitter and fierce name of the world, hide your fierceness, cover your corruption, and cast away your bitterness from you, and put on your beauty and all your glory, and go down to Abraham my friend, and take him and bring him to me. But now also I tell you not to terrify him, but bring him with fair speech, for he is my own friend. Having heard this, Death went out from the presence of the Most High, and put on a robe of great brightness, and made his appearance like the sun, and became fair and beautiful above the sons of men, assuming the form of an archangel, having his cheeks flaming with fire, and he departed to Abraham. Now the righteous Abraham went out of his chamber, and sat under the trees of Mamre, holding his chin in his hand, and awaiting the coming of the archangel Michael. And behold, a smell of sweet odor came to him, and a flashing of light, and Abraham turned and saw Death coming towards him in great glory and beauty. And Abraham arose and went to meet him, thinking that it was the chief-captain of God, and Death beholding him saluted him, saying, Rejoice, precious Abraham, righteous soul, true friend

of the Most High God, and companion of the holy angels. Abraham said to Death, Hail you of appearance and form like the sun, most glorious helper, bringer of light, wondrous man, from whence does your glory come to us, and who are you, and whence do you come? Then Death said, Most righteous Abraham, behold I tell you the truth. I am the bitter lot of death. Abraham said to him, Nay, but you are the comeliness of the world, you are the glory and beauty of angels and men, you are fairer in form than every other, and do you say, I am the bitter lot of death, and not rather, I am fairer than every good thing. Death said, I tell you the truth. What the Lord has named me, that also I tell you. Abraham said, For what are you come hither? Death said, For your holy soul am I come. Then Abraham said, I know what you mean, but I will not go with you; and Death was silent and answered him not a word.

17. Then Abraham arose, and went into his house, and Death also accompanied him there. And Abraham went up into his chamber, and Death went up with him. And Abraham lay down upon his couch, and Death came and sat by his feet. Then Abraham said, Depart, depart from me, for I desire to rest upon my couch. Death said, I will not depart until I take your spirit from you. Abraham said to him, By the immortal God I charge you to tell me the truth. Are you death? Death said to him, I am Death. I am the destroyer of the world. Abraham said, I beseech you, since you are Death, tell me if you come thus to all in such fairness and glory and beauty? Death said, Nay, my Lord Abraham, for your righteousnesses, and the boundless sea of your hospitality, and the greatness of your love towards God has become a crown upon my head, and in beauty and great peace and gentleness I approach the righteous, but to sinners I come in great corruption and fierceness and the greatest bitterness and with fierce and pitiless look. Abraham said, I beseech you, hearken to me, and show me your fierceness and all your corruption and bitterness. And Death said, You can not behold my fierceness, most righteous Abraham. Abraham said, Yes, I shall be able to behold all your fierceness by means of the name of the living God, for the might of my God that is in heaven is with me. Then Death put off all his comeliness and beauty, and all his glory and the form like the sun with which he was clothed, and put upon himself a tyrant's robe, and made his appearance gloomy and fiercer than all kind of wild beasts, and more unclean than all uncleanness. And he showed to Abraham seven fiery heads of serpents and fourteen faces, (one) of flaming fire and of great fierceness, and a face of darkness, and a most gloomy face of a viper, and a face of a most terrible precipice, and a face fiercer than an asp, and a face of a terrible lion, and a face of a cerastes and basilisk. He showed him also a face of a fiery scimitar,

and a sword-bearing face, and a face of lightning, lightening terribly, and a noise of dreadful thunder. He showed him also another face of a fierce stormy sea, and a fierce rushing river, and a terrible three-headed serpent, and a cup mingled with poisons, and in short he showed to him great fierceness and unendurable bitterness, and every mortal disease as of the odor of Death. And from the great bitterness and fierceness there died servants and maid-servants in number about seven thousand, and the righteous Abraham came into indifference of death so that his spirit failed him.

18. And the all-holy Abraham, seeing these things thus, said to Death, I beseech you, all-destroying Death, hide your fierceness, and put on your beauty and the shape which you had before. And straightway Death hid his fierceness, and put on his beauty which he had before. And Abraham said to Death, Why have you done this, that you have slain all my servants and maidservants? Has God sent you hither for this end this day? Death said, Nay, my Lord Abraham, it is not as you say, but on your account was I sent hither. Abraham said to Death, How then have these died? Has the Lord not spoken it? Death said, Believe, most righteous Abraham, that this also is wonderful, that you also were not taken away with them. Nevertheless I tell you the truth, for if the right hand of God had not been with you at that time, you also would have had to depart from this life. The righteous Abraham said, Now I know that I have come into indifference of death, so that my spirit fails, but I beseech you, all-destroying Death, since my servants have died before their time, come let us pray to the Lord our God that he may hear us and raise up those who died by your fierceness before their time. And Death said, Amen, be it so. Therefore Abraham arose and fell upon the face of the ground in prayer, and Death together with him, and the Lord sent a spirit of life upon those that were dead and they were made alive again. Then the righteous Abraham gave glory to God.

19. And going up into his chamber he lay down, and Death came and stood before him. And Abraham said to him, Depart from me, for I desire to rest, because my spirit is in indifference. Death said, I will not depart from you until I take your soul. And Abraham with an austere countenance and angry look said to Death, Who has ordered you to say this? You say these words of yourself boastfully, and I will not go with you until the chief-captain Michael come to me, and I shall go with him. But this also I tell you, if you desire that I shall accompany you, explain to me all your changes, the seven fiery heads of serpents and what the face of the precipice is, and what the sharp sword, and what the loud-roaring river, and what the tempestuous sea that rages so fiercely. Teach me also the unendurable

thunder, and the terrible lightning, and the evil-smelling cup mingled with poisons. Teach me concerning all these. And Death answered, Listen, righteous Abraham. For seven ages I destroy the world and lead all down to Hades, kings and rulers, rich and poor, slaves and free men, I convoy to the bottom of Hades, and for this I showed you the seven heads of serpents. The face of fire I showed you because many die consumed by fire, and behold death through a face of fire. The face of the precipice I showed you, because many men die descending from the tops of trees or terrible precipices and losing their life, and see death in the shape of a terrible precipice. The face of the sword I showed you because many are slain in wars by the sword, and see death as a sword. The face of the great rushing river I showed you because many are drowned and perish snatched away by the crossing of many waters and carried off by great rivers, and see death before their time. The face of the angry raging sea I showed you because many in the sea falling into great surges and becoming shipwrecked are swallowed up and behold death as the sea. The unendurable thunder and the terrible lightning I showed you because many men in the moment of anger meet with unendurable thunder and terrible lightning coming to seize upon men, and see death thus. I showed you also the poisonous wild beasts, asps and basilisks, leopards and lions and lions' cubs, bears and vipers, and in short the face of every wild beast I showed you, most righteous one, because many men are destroyed by wild beasts, and others by poisonous snakes, serpents and asps and cerastes and basilisks and vipers, breathe out their life and die. I showed you also the destroying cups mingled with poison, because many men being given poison to drink by other men straightway depart unexpectedly.

20. Abraham said, I beseech you, is there also an unexpected death? Tell me. Death said, Verily, verily, I tell you in the truth of God that there are seventy-two deaths. One is the just death, buying its fixed time, and many men in one hour enter into death being given over to the grave. Behold, I have told you all that you have asked, now I tell you, most righteous Abraham, to dismiss all counsel, and cease from asking anything once for all, and come, go with me, as the God and judge of all has commanded me. Abraham said to Death, Depart from me yet a little, that I may rest on my couch, for I am very faint at heart, for since I have seen you with my eyes my strength has failed me, all the limbs of my flesh seem to me a weight as of lead, and my spirit is distressed exceedingly. Depart for a little; for I have said I cannot bear to see your shape. Then Isaac his son came and fell upon his breast weeping, and his wife Sarah came and embraced his feet, lamenting bitterly. There came also his men slaves and women slaves and surrounded his couch,

lamenting greatly. And Abraham came into indifference of death, and Death said to Abraham, Come, take my right hand, and may cheerfulness and life and strength come to you. For Death deceived Abraham, and he took his right hand, and straightway his soul adhered to the hand of Death. And immediately the archangel Michael came with a multitude of angels and took up his precious soul in his hands in a divinely woven linen cloth, and they tended the body of the just Abraham with divine ointments and perfumes until the third day after his death, and buried him in the land of promise, the oak of Mamre, but the angels received his precious soul, and ascended into heaven, singing the hymn of thrice holy to the Lord the God of all, and they set it there to worship the God and Father. And after great praise and glory had been given to the Lord, and Abraham bowed down to worship, there came the undefiled voice of the God and Father saying thus, Take therefore my friend Abraham into Paradise, where are the tabernacles of my righteous ones, and the abodes of my saints Isaac and Jacob in his bosom, where there is no trouble, nor grief, nor sighing, but peace and rejoicing and life unending. (And let us, too, my beloved brethren, imitate the hospitality of the patriarch Abraham, and attain to his virtuous way of life, that we may be thought worthy of the life eternal, glorifying the Father, Son and Holy Ghost; to whom be glory and power forever. Amen.).

Version 2

1. It came to pass, when the days of the death of Abraham drew near, that the Lord said to Michael: Arise and go to Abraham, my servant, and say to him, You shall depart from life, for lo! The days of your temporal life are fulfilled: so that he may set his house in order before he die.

2. And Michael went and came to Abraham, and found him sitting before his oxen for ploughing, and he was exceeding old in appearance, and had his son in his arms. Abraham, therefore, seeing the archangel Michael, rose from the ground and saluted him, not knowing who he was, and said to him: The Lord preserve you. May your journey be prosperous with you. And Michael answered him: You are kind, good father. Abraham answered and said to him: Come, draw near to me, brother, and sit down a little while, that I may order a beast to be brought that we may go to my house, and you may rest with me, for it is toward evening, and in the morning arise and go wherever you will, lest some evil beast meet you and do you hurt. And Michael enquired of Abraham, saying: Tell me your name, before I enter your house, lest I be burdensome to you. Abraham answered and said, My parents called me Abram, and the Lord named me Abraham, saying: Arise and depart from your house, and from your kindred, and go into the land which I shall show unto you. And when I went away into the land which the Lord showed me, he said to me: Your name shall no more be called Abram, but your name shall be Abraham. Michael answered and said to him: Pardon me, my father, experienced man of God, for I am a stranger, and I have heard of you that you went forty furlongs and brought a goat and slew it, entertaining angels in your house, that they might rest there. Thus speaking together, they arose and went towards the house. And Abraham called one of his servants, and said to him: Go, bring me a beast that the stranger may sit upon it, for he is wearied with his journey. And Michael said: Trouble not the youth, but let us go lightly until we reach the house, for I love your company.

3. And arising they went on, and as they drew near to the city, about three furlongs from it, they found a great tree having three hundred branches, like to a tamarisk tree. And they heard a voice from its branches singing, Holy are you, because you have kept the purpose for which you were sent. And Abraham heard the voice, and hid the mystery in his heart, saying within himself, What is the mystery that I have heard? As he came into the house, Abraham said to his servants, Arise, go out to the flocks, and bring three sheep, and slay them quickly, and make them ready that we may eat and drink, for this day is a feast for us. And the servants brought the sheep, and Abraham called his son Isaac, and said to him, My son Isaac, arise and put water in the vessel that we may wash the feet of this stranger. And he brought it as he was commanded, and Abraham said, I perceive, and so it shall be, that in this basin I shall never again wash the feet of any man coming to us as a guest. And Isaac hearing his father say this wept, and said to him, My father what is this that you say? This is my last time to wash the feet of a stranger? And Abraham seeing his son weeping, also wept exceedingly, and Michael seeing them weeping, wept also, and the tears of Michael fell upon the vessel and became a precious stone.

4. When Sarah, being inside in her house, heard their weeping, she came out and said to Abraham, Lord, why is it that you thus weep? Abraham answered, and said to her, It is no evil. Go into your house, and do your own work, lest we be troublesome to the man. And Sarah went away, being about to prepare the supper. And the sun came near to setting, and Michael went out of the house, and was taken up into the heavens to worship before God, for at sunset all the angels worship God and Michael himself is the first of the angels. And they all worshipped him, and went each to his own place, but Michael spoke before the Lord and said, Lord, command me to be questioned

before your holy glory! And the Lord said to Michael, Announce whatsoever you will! And the Archangel answered and said, Lord, you sent me to Abraham to say to him, Depart from your body, and leave this world; the Lord calls you; and I dare not, Lord, reveal myself to him, for he is your friend, and a righteous man, and one that receives strangers. But I beseech you, Lord, command the remembrance of the death of Abraham to enter into his own heart, and bid not me tell it him, for it is great abruptness to say, Leave the world, and especially to leave one's own body, for you created him from the beginning to have pity on the souls of all men. Then the Lord said to Michael, Arise and go to Abraham, and lodge with him, and whatever you see him eat, eat also, and wherever he shall sleep, sleep there also. For I will cast the thought of the death of Abraham into the heart of Isaac his son in a dream.

5. Then Michael went into the house of Abraham on that evening, and found them preparing the supper, and they ate and drank and were merry. And Abraham said to his son Isaac, Arise, my son, and spread the man's couch that he may sleep, and set the lamp upon the stand. And Isaac did as his father commanded him, and Isaac said to his father, I too am coming to sleep beside you. Abraham answered him, Nay, my son, lest we be troublesome to this man, but go to your own chamber and sleep. And Isaac not wishing to disobey his father's command, went away and slept in his own chamber.

6. And it happened about the seventh hour of the night Isaac awoke, and came to the door of his father's chamber, crying out and saying, Open, father, that I may touch you before they take you away from me. Abraham arose and opened to him, and Isaac entered and hung upon his father's neck weeping, and kissed him with lamentations. And Abraham wept together with his son, and Michael saw them weeping and wept likewise. And Sarah hearing them weeping called from her bed-chamber, saying, My Lord Abraham, why is this weeping? Has the stranger told you of your brother's son Lot that he is dead? Or has anything else befallen us? Michael answered and said to Sarah, Nay, Sarah, I have brought no tidings of Lot, but I knew of all your kindness of heart, that therein you excel all men upon earth, and the Lord has remembered you. Then Sarah said to Abraham, How dare you weep when the man of God has come in to you, and why have your eyes shed tears for today there is great rejoicing? Abraham said to her, How do you know that this is a man of God? Sarah answered and said, Because I say and declare that this is one of the three men who were entertained by us at the oak of Mamre, when one of the servants went and brought a kid and you killed it, and said to me, Arise, make ready that we may eat with these men in our house. Abraham answered and said, You have perceived well, O woman, for I too, when I washed his feet knew in my heart that these were the feet which I had washed at the oak of Mamre, and when I began to enquire concerning his journey, he said to me, I go to preserve Lot your brother from the men of Sodom, and then I knew the mystery.

7. And Abraham said to Michael, Tell me, man of God, and show to me why you have come hither. And Michael said, Your son Isaac will show you. And Abraham said to his son, My beloved son, tell me what you have seen in your dream today, and wast frightened. Relate it to me. Isaac answered his father, I saw in my dream the sun and the moon, and there was a crown upon my head, and there came from heaven a man of great size, and shining as the light that is called the father of light. He took the sun from my head, and yet left the rays behind with me. And I wept and said, I beseech you, my Lord, take not away the glory of my head, and the light of my house, and all my glory. And the sun and the moon and the stars lamented, saying, Take not away the glory of our power. And that shining man answered and said to me, Weep not that I take the light of your house, for it is taken up from troubles into rest, from a low estate to a high one; they lift him up from a narrow to a wide place; they raise him from darkness to light. And I said to him, I beseech you, Lord, take also the rays with it. He said to me, There are twelve hours of the day, and then I shall take all the rays. As the shining man said this, I saw the sun of my house ascending into heaven, but that crown I saw no more, and that sun was like you my father. And Michael said to Abraham, Your son Isaac has spoken truth, for you shall go, and be taken up into the heavens, but your body shall remain on earth, until seven thousand ages are fulfilled, for then all flesh shall arise. Now therefore, Abraham, set your house in order, and your children, for you have heard fully what is decreed concerning you. Abraham answered and said to Michael, I beseech you, Lord, if I shall depart from my body, I have desired to be taken up in my body that I may see the creatures that the Lord my God has created in heaven and on earth. Michael answered and said, This is not for me to do, but I shall go and tell the Lord of this, and if I am commanded I shall show you all these things.

8. And Michael went up into heaven, and spoke before the Lord concerning Abraham, and the Lord answered Michael, Go and take up Abraham in the body, and show him all things, and whatsoever he shall say to you do to him as to my friend. So Michael went forth and took up Abraham in the body on a cloud, and brought him to the river of Ocean.

12. And after Abraham had seen the place of judgment, the cloud took him down upon the firmament below, and Abraham, looking down upon the earth, saw a man committing adultery with a wedded woman. And Abraham turning said to Michael, Do you see this wickedness? But, Lord, send fire from heaven to consume them. And straightway there came down fire and consumed them, for the Lord had said to Michael, do whatever Abraham shall ask you to do for him. Abraham looked again, and saw other men railing at their companions, and said, Let the earth open and swallow them, and as he spoke the earth swallowed them alive. Again the cloud led him to another place, and Abraham saw some going into a desert place to commit murder, and he said to Michael, Do you see this wickedness? But let wild beasts come out of the desert, and tear them in pieces, and that same hour wild beasts came out of the desert, and devoured them. Then the Lord God spoke to Michael saying, Turn away Abraham to his own house, and let him not go round all the creation that I have made, because he has no compassion on sinners, but I have compassion on sinners that they may turn and live, and repent of their sins and be saved.

8. And Abraham looked and saw two gates, the one small and the other large, and between the two gates sat a man upon a throne of great glory, and a multitude of angels round about him, and he was weeping, and again laughing, but his weeping exceeded his laughter seven-fold. And Abraham said to Michael, Who is this that sits between the two gates in great glory; sometimes he laughs, and sometimes he weeps, and his weeping exceeds his laughter seven-fold? And Michael said to Abraham, Do you not know who it is? And he said, No, Lord. And Michael said to Abraham, Do you see these two gates, the small and the great? These are they which lead to life and to destruction. This man that sits between them is Adam, the first man whom the Lord created, and set him in this place to see every soul that departs from the body, seeing that all are from him. When, therefore, you see him weeping, know that he has seen many souls being led to destruction, but when you see him laughing, he has seen many souls being led into life. Do you see how his weeping exceeds his laughter? Since he sees the greater part of the world being led away through the broad gate to destruction, therefore his weeping exceeds his laughter seven-fold.

9. And Abraham said, And he that cannot enter through the narrow gate, can he not enter into life? Then Abraham wept, saying, Woe is me, what shall I do? For I am a man broad of body, and how shall I be able to enter by the narrow gate, by which a boy of fifteen years cannot enter? Michael answered and said to Abraham, Fear not, father, nor grieve, for you shall enter by it unhindered, and all those who are like you. And as Abraham stood and marveled, behold an angel of the Lord driving sixty thousand souls of sinners to destruction. And Abraham said to Michael, Do all these go into destruction? And Michael said to him, Yea, but let us go and search among these souls, if there is among them even one righteous. And when they went, they found an angel holding in his hand one soul of a woman from among these sixty thousand, because he had found her sins weighing equally with all her works, and they were neither in motion nor at rest, but in a state between; but the other souls he led away to destruction. Abraham said to Michael, Lord, is this the angel that removes the souls from the body or not? Michael answered and said, This is death, and he leads them into the place of judgment, that the judge may try them.

10. And Abraham said, My Lord, I beseech you to lead me to the place of judgment so that I too may see how they are judged. Then Michael took Abraham upon a cloud, and led him into Paradise, and when he came to the place where the judge was, the angel came and gave that soul to the judge. And the soul said, Lord have mercy on me. And the judge said, How shall I have mercy upon you, when you had no mercy upon your daughter which you had, the fruit of your womb? Wherefore did you slay her? It answered, Nay, Lord, slaughter has not been done by me, but my daughter has lied upon me. But the judge commanded him to come that wrote down the records, and behold cherubim carrying two books. And there was with them a man of exceeding great stature, having on his head three crowns, and the one crown was higher than the other two. These are called the crowns of witness. And the man had in his hand a golden pen, and the judge said to him, Exhibit the sin of this soul. And that man, opening one of the books of the cherubim, sought out the sin of the woman's soul and found it. And the judge said, O wretched soul, why do you say that you have not done murder? Did you not, after the death of your husband, go and commit adultery with your daughter's husband, and kill her? And he convicted her also of her other sins, whatsoever she had done from her youth. Hearing these things the woman cried out, saying, Woe is me, all the sins that I did in the world I forgot, but here they were not forgotten. Then they took her away also and gave her over to the tormentors.

11. And Abraham said to Michael, Lord, who is this judge, and who is the other, who convicts the sins? And Michael said to Abraham, Do you see the judge? This is Abel, who first testified, and God brought him hither to judge, and he that bears witness here is the teacher of heaven and earth, and the scribe of righteousness, Enoch, for the Lord sent them hither to

write down the sins and righteousnesses of each one. Abraham said, And how can Enoch bear the weight of the souls, not having seen death? Or how can he give sentence to all the souls? Michael said, If he gives sentence concerning the souls, it is not permitted; but Enoch himself does not give sentence, but it is the Lord who does so, and he has no more to do than only to write. For Enoch prayed to the Lord saying, I desire not, Lord, to give sentence on the souls, lest I be grievous to anyone; and the Lord said to Enoch, I shall command you to write down the sins of the soul that makes atonement and it shall enter into life, and if the soul make not atonement and repent, you shall find its sins written down and it shall be cast into punishment. And about the ninth hour Michael brought Abraham back to his house. But Sarah his wife, not seeing what had become of Abraham, was consumed with grief, and gave up the ghost, and after the return of Abraham he found her dead, and buried her.

13. But when the day of the death of Abraham drew near, the Lord God said to Michael, Death will not dare to go near to take away the soul of my servant, because he is my friend, but go and adorn Death with great beauty, and send him thus to Abraham, that he may see him with his eyes. And Michael straightway, as he was commanded, adorned Death with great beauty, and sent him thus to Abraham that he might see him. And he sat down near to Abraham, and Abraham seeing Death sitting near to him was afraid with a great fear. And Death said to Abraham, Hail, holy soul! Hail, friend of the Lord God! Hail, consolation and entertainment of travelers! And Abraham said, You are welcome, servant of the Most High. God. I beseech you, tell me who you are; and entering into my house partake of food and drink, and depart from me, for since I have seen you sitting near to me my soul has been troubled. For I am not at all worthy to come near you, for you are an exalted spirit and I am flesh and blood, and therefore I cannot bear your glory, for I see that your beauty is not of this world. And Death said to Abraham, I tell you, in all the creation that God has made, there has not been found one like you, for even the Lord himself by searching has not found such an one upon the whole earth. And Abraham said to Death, How dare you lie? For I see that your beauty is not of this world. And Death said to Abraham, Think not, Abraham, that this beauty is mine, or that I come thus to every man. Nay, but if any one is righteous like you, I thus take crowns and come to him, but if it is a sinner I come in great corruption, and out of their sin I make a crown for my head, and I shake them with great fear, so that they are dismayed. Abraham therefore said to him, And whence comes your beauty? And Death said, There is none other more full of corruption than I am. Abraham said to him, And are

you indeed he that is called Death? He answered him and said, I am the bitter name. I am weeping....

14. And Abraham said to Death, Show us your corruption. And Death made manifest his corruption; and he had two heads, the one had the face of a serpent and by it some die at once by asps, and the other head was like a sword; by it some die by the sword as by bows. In that day the servants of Abraham died through fear of Death, and Abraham seeing them prayed to the Lord, and he raised them up. But God returned and removed the soul of Abraham as in a dream, and the archangel Michael took it up into the heavens. And Isaac buried his father beside his mother Sarah, glorifying and praising God, for to him is due glory, honor and worship, of the Father, Son and Holy Ghost, now and always and to all eternity. Amen.

THE BOOK OF CREATION
OR
SEPHER YETZIRAH

W.W. Wescott, tr. (1887)

CHAPTER 1

1. In two and thirty most occult and wonderful paths of wisdom did JAH the Lord of Hosts engrave his name: God of the armies of Israel, ever-living God, merciful and gracious, sublime, dwelling on high, who inhabiteth eternity. He created this universe by the three Sepharim, Number, Writing, and Speech.

2. Ten are the numbers, as are the Sephiroth, and twenty-two the letters, these are the Foundation of all things. Of these letters, three are mothers, seven are double, and twelve are simple.

3. The ten numbers formed from nothing are the Decad: these are seen in the fingers of the hands, five on one, five on the other, and over them is the Covenant by voice spiritual, and the rite of Circumcision, corporeal (as of Abraham).

4. Ten are the numbers of the ineffable Sephiroth, ten and not nine, ten and not eleven. Learn this wisdom, and be wise in the understanding of it, investigate these numbers, and draw knowledge from them, fix the design in its purity, and pass from it to its Creator seated on his throne.

5. These Ten Numbers, beyond the Infinite one, have the boundless realms, boundless origin and end, an abyss of good and one of evil, boundless height and depth, East and West, North and South, and the one only God and king, faithful forever seated on his throne, shall rule over all, forever and ever.

6. These ten Sephiroth which are ineffable, whose appearance is like scintillating flames, have no end but are infinite. The word of God is in them as they burst forth, and as they return; they obey the divine command, rushing along as a whirlwind, returning to prostrate themselves at his throne.

7. These ten Sephiroth which are, moreover, ineffable, have their end even as their beginning, conjoined, even as is a flame to a burning coal: for our God is superlative in his unity, and does not permit any second one. And who canst thou place before the only one?

8. And as to this Decad of the Sephiroth, restrain thy lips from comment, and thy mind from thought of them, and if thy heart fail thee return to thy place; therefore is it written, "The living creatures ran and returned," and on this wise was the covenant made with us.

9. These are the ten emanations of number. One is the Spirit of the Living God, blessed and more than blessed be the name of the Living God of Ages. The Holy Spirit is his Voice, his Spirit, and his Word.

10. Second, from the Spirit he made Air and formed for speech twenty-two letters, three of which are mothers, A, M, SH, seven are double, B, G, D, K, P, R, T, and twelve are single, E, V, Z, CH, H, I, L, N, S, O, Tz, Q, but the spirit is first among these. Third, Primitive Water. He also formed and designed from his Spirit, and from the void and formless made earth, even as a rampart, or standing wall, and varied its surface even as the crossing of beams. Fourth, from the Water, He designed Fire, and from it formed for himself a throne of honor, with Auphanim, Seraphim, Holy Animals, and ministering Angels, and with these he formed his dwelling, as is written in the text "Who maketh his angels spirits and his ministers a flaming fire." (Psalm civ. 4.)

11. He selected three letters from the simple ones, and sealed them as forming his great Name, I H V and he sealed the universe in six directions.

Five.- He looked above, and sealed the height, with I H V.

Six.- He looked below, and sealed the deep, with I V H.

Seven.- He looked forward, and sealed the East, with H I V.

Eight.-He looked backward, and sealed the West, with V H I.

Nine.- He looked to the right, and sealed the South, with V I H.

Ten.-He looked to the left, and sealed the North, with H V 1.

12. These are the ten ineffable existences, the spirit of the living God, Air, Water, Fire, Height and Depth, East and West, North and South.

CHAPTER II

1. The foundations are the twenty-two letters, three mothers, seven double, and twelve single letters. Three mothers, namely A, M, SH, these are Air, Water, and Fire: Mute as Water, Hissing as Fire, and Air of a spiritual type, is as the tongue of a balance standing

erect between them pointing out the equilibrium which exists.

2. He hath formed, weighed, transmuted, composed, and created with these twenty-two letters every living being, and every soul yet uncreated.

3. Twenty-two letters are formed by the voice, impressed on the air, and audibly uttered in five situations, in the throat, guttural sounds; in the palate, palatals; by the tongue, linguals; through the teeth, dentals; and by the lips, labial sounds.

4. These twenty-two letters, the foundations, He arranged as on a sphere, with two hundred and thirty-one modes of entrance. If the sphere be rotated forward, good is implied, if in a retrograde manner evil is intended.

5. For He indeed showed the mode of combination of the letters, each with each, Aleph with all, and all with Aleph. Thus in combining all together in pairs are produced these two hundred and thirty-one gates of knowledge. And from Nothingness did He make something, and all forms of speech and every created thing, and from the empty void He made the solid earth, and from the non-existent He brought forth Life.

He hewed, as it were, immense column or colossal pillars, out of the intangible air, and from the empty space. And this is the impress of the whole, twenty-one letters, all from one the Aleph.

CHAPTER III
1. The three mother letters A, M, SH are the foundations of the whole; and resemble a Balance, the good in one scale, the evil in the other, and the oscillating tongue of the Balance between them.

2. These three mothers enclose a mighty mystery, most occult and most marvelous, sealed as with six rings, and from them proceed primeval Fire, Water, and Air; these are subsequently differentiated into male and female. At first existed these three mothers, and there arose three masculine powers, and hence all things have originated.

3. The three mothers are A, M, SH; and in the beginning as to the Macrocosm the Heavens were created from Fire;nthe Earth from primeval Water; and the Air was formed from the Spirit, which stands alone in the midst, and is the Mediator between them.

4. In the Year or as regards Time, these three mothers represent Heat, Cold, and a Temperate climate, the heat from the fire, the cold from the water, and the temperate state from the spiritual air which again is an equalizer between them.

These three mothers again represent in the Microcosm or Human form, male and female; the Head, the Belly, and the Chest; the bead from the fire, the belly from water, and the chest from the air lieth between them.

5. These three mothers did he create, form, and design, and combine with the three mothers in the world, and in the year, and in Man, both male and female.

He caused Aleph to reign in the air, and crown it, and combined one with the other, and with these he sealed the Air in the world, the temperate climate of the year, and the chest (the lungs for breathing air) in man; the male with A, M, SH, the female with SH, M, A. He caused Mem to predominate in Water, and crowned it, and combined it with others, and formed Earth on the world, cold in the year, and the fruit of the womb in mankind, being carried in the belly.

He caused Shin to reign in Fire and crowned it, and he combined one with the other, and sealed them, as heaven in the universe, as heat in the year, and as the head of Man and Woman.

CHAPTER IV
1. There were formed seven double letters, Beth, Gimel, Daleth, Kaph, Pe, Resh, Tau, each has two voices, either aspirated or softened. These are the foundations of Life, Peace, Riches, Beauty or Reputation, Wisdom, Fruitfulness, and Power. These are double, because their opposites take part in life, opposed to Life is Death; to Peace, War; to Riches, Poverty; to Beauty or Reputation, Deformity or Disrepute; to Wisdom, Ignorance; to Fruitfulness, Sterility; to Power, Slavery.

2. These seven double letters point out the dimensions, East, West, height, depth, North, South, with the holy temple in the middle, sustaining all things.

3. These seven double letters He formed, designed, created, and combined into the Stars of the Universe, the days of the week, the orifices of perception in man; and from them he made seven heavens, and seven planets, all from nothingness, and, moreover, he has preferred and blessed the sacred Heptad.

4. From two letters, or forms He composed two dwellings; from three, six; from four, twenty-four; from five, one hundred and twenty; from six, seven hundred and twenty; from seven, five thousand and forty; and from thence their numbers increase in a manner beyond counting; and are incomprehensible. These seven are Planets of the Universe, the Sun,

Venus, Mercury, Moon, Saturn, Jupiter, and Mars; the seven days are the days of creation; and these an the seven gateways of a man, two eyes, two ears, two nostrils and a mouth, through which he perceives by his senses.

SUPPLEMENT TO CHAPTER IV
(Found in some editions)
He caused and produced Beth, predominant in wisdom, crowned, combined, and formed the Moon in the Universe, the first day of the week, and the right eye, of man.

Gimel, predominant in health, crowned, . combined and formed Mars in the Universe, the second day of the week, and the right ear in man.

Daleth, predominant in fertility, crowned, combined, and formed the Sun in the Universe, the third day of the week, and the right nostril in man.

Kaph, predominant in life, crowned, combined, and formed Venus in the Universe, the fourth day of the week, and the left eye of man.

Pe, predominant in power, crowned, combined, and formed Mercury in the Universe, the fifth day of the week, and the left ear in man.

Resh, predominant in peace, crowned, combined, and formed Saturn in the Universe, the sixth day of the week, and the left nostril in man.

Tau, predominant in beauty, crowned, combined and formed Jupiter in the Universe, the seventh day in the week, and the mouth of man.

By these seven letters were also made seven worlds, seven heavens, seven lands, seven seas, seven rivers, seven deserts, seven days (as before), seven weeks from Passover to Pentecost, and every seventh year a jubilee.

CHAPTER V
1. The simple letters are twelve, namely: He, Vau, Zain, Heth, Teth, Yod, Lamed, Nun, Samech, Oin, Tzaddi, and Quoph; they represent the fundamental properties, eight, hearing, smell, speech, desire for food, the sexual appetite, movement, anger, mirth, thought, sleep, and work. These symbolize also twelve directions in space: northeast, southeast, the east above, the east below, the northwest, southwest, the west above, the west below, the upper south, the lower south, the upper north, the lower north. These diverge to all eternity, and an as the arms of the universe.

2. These twelve letters, he designed, formed, combined, weighed, and changed, and created with them the twelve divisions of the heavens (namely, the zodiacal constellations), the twelve months of the year, and the twelve important organs of the frame of man, namely the right and left hands, the right and left feet, two kidneys, the liver, the gall, the spleen, the intestines, the gullet, and the stomach.

3. Three mothers, seven double and twelve simple, these are the twenty-two letters with which I H V H Tetragrammaton, that is our Lord of Hosts, exalted, and existed in the ages, whose name is Holy, created three fathers, fire and spirit and water, progressing beyond them, seven heavens with their armies of angels; and twelve limits of the universe.

SUPPLEMENT TO CHAPTER V
(Found in some Versions)
1. God produced He, predominant in Speech, crowned, combined, and formed Aries in the world, Nisan in the year, and the right foot of man.

2. God produced Vau, predominant in Mind, crowned, combined, and formed Taurus in the world, Yiar in the year, and the right kidney of man.

3. God produced Zain, predominant in movement, crowned, combined, and formed Gemini in the world, Sivan in the year, and the left foot of man.

4. He produced Heth, predominant in Sight, crowned, combined, and formed Cancer in the world, Tammuz in the year, and the right hand of man.

5. He produced Teth, predominant in Hearing, crowned, combined, and formed Leo in the world, Ab in the year, and the left kidney in man.

6. He produced Yod, predominant in Labor, crowned, combined, and formed Virgo in the world, Elul in the year, and the left hand of man.

7. He produced Lamed, predominant in sexual desire, crowned, combined, and formed Libra in the world, Tisri in the year, and the gall in man.

8. He produced Nun, predominant in smell, crowned, combined, and formed Scorpio in the world, Marchesvan in the year, and the intestines in man.

9. He produced Samech, predominant in sleep, crowned, combined, and formed Sagittarius in the world, Kislev in the year, and the stomach of man.

10. He produced Oin, predominant in Anger, crowned, combined, and formed Capricornus in the world, Tebet in the year, and the liver in man.

11. He produced Tzaddi, predominant in Taste, crowned, combined, and formed Aquarius in the world, Sebat in the year, and the gullet in man.

12. He produced Quoph, predominant in Mirth, crowned, combined, and formed Pisces in the world, Adar in the year, and the spleen in man.

CHATER VI

1. In proof of these things, and witnessing faithfully are the Universe, the Year of time, and Man himself, the Microcosm. He fixed these as testimonies of the Triad, the Heptad, and the Dodecad; the twelve constellations rulers of the world, the Dragon (THELE) Tali which environs the universe, and the microcosm, man.

The triad, fire, water, and air; the fire above, the water below, and the air in the midst. The proof of which is that air is a participator with both.

2. Tali, the Dragon, is above the Universe, as a king on his throne; the sphere in the year as a king in his State, the Heart of man as a king in warfare.

And our God made the states of opposition, good and evil, good from the good, and evil from the evil. Happiness is reserved for the just, and misery for the wicked ones.

3. And out of the triad one stands apart; and in the heptad there are two triads, and one standing apart. The dodecad symbolizes war, the triad of amity, the triad of enmity, three which are life-giving, three which are death-dealing, and God, the faithful king, rules over all from the throne of his sanctity.

One above three, three above seven, and seven above twelve, and all are linked together, and one with another.

4. After that our father Abraham had seen, and pondered over, investigated, and understood these things, he designed, engraved, and composed them, and received them into his power (hands). Then the Lord of all appeared unto him, made a covenant with him, and kissed his head, and naming him after his own name, called him his friend; and as it is written, completed a covenant with him and with his seed forever, who then believed on God, the Tetragrammaton, and it was imputed to him for righteousness.

God ordained a covenant between the toes of his feet, that of circumcision; and a covenant between the fingers of his hands, that of the Tongue. He bound the essences of the twenty-two letters on his tongue, and God disclosed to him the secrets of them. God has carried these through waters, He has borne them aloft through fire, and He has stamped them in the storms of the air; He has distributed them among the seven stars, and has assigned them to twelve celestial constellations. Amen.

THE THIRTY-TWO PATHS OF WISDOM
APPENDIX TO THE SEPHER YETZIRAH

The First Path is called the Admirable or the Concealed Intelligence (The Highest Crown) - for it is the Light giving the power of comprehension of that First Principle which has no beginning, and it is the Primal Glory, for no created being can attain to its essence.

The Second Path is that of the Illuminating Intelligence it is the Crown of Creation, the Splendor of the Unity, equaling it, and it is exalted above every bead, and named by the Kabbalists the Second Glory.

The Third Path is the Sanctifying Intelligence, and is the basis of foundation of Primordial Wisdom, which is called the Former of faith, and its roots, Amen; and it is the parent of Faith, from which virtues doth Faith emanate.

The Fourth Path is named Measuring, Cohesive, or Receptacular; and is so called because it contains all the holy powers, and from it emanate all the spiritual virtues with the most exalted essences: they emanate one from the other by the power of the primordial emanation (The Highest Crown), blessed be it.

The Fifth Path is called the Radical Intelligence, because it is itself the essence equal to the Unity, uniting itself to the BINAH or Intelligence which emanates from the primordial depths of Wisdom or CHOCHMAH.

The Sixth Path is called the Intelligence of the Mediating Influence, because in it are multiplied the influxes of the emanations; for it causes that affluence to flow into all the reservoirs of the Blessings, with which these themselves are united.

The Seventh Path is the Occult Intelligence, because it is the Refulgent Splendor of all the Intellectual virtues which are perceived by the eyes of intellect, and by the contemplation of faith.

The Eighth Path is called Absolute or Perfect, because it is the means of the primordial, which has no root by which it can cleave, nor rest, except in the hidden places Of GEDULAH. Magnificence, which emanate from its own proper essence.

The Ninth Path is the Pure intelligence so called because it purifies the Numerations, it proves and corrects the designing of their representation, and disposes their unity with which they are combined without diminution or division.

The Tenth Path is the Resplendent Intelligence, because it is exalted above every bead, and sits on the throne of BINAH (the Intelligence spoken of in the Third Path). It illuminates the splendor of all lights, and causes a supply of influence to emanate from the Prince of countenances.

The Eleventh Path is the Scintillating Intelligence because it is the essence of that curtain which is placed close to the order of the disposition, and this is a special dignity given to it that it may be able to stand before the Face of the Cause of Causes.

The Twelfth Path is the Intelligence of Transparency, because it is that species of Magnificence., called CHAZCHAZIT, which is named the place whence issues the vision of those seeing in apparitions. (That is, the prophecies by seers in a vision.)

The Thirteenth Path is named the Uniting Intelligence and is so called because it is itself the essence of Glory. It is the Consummation of the Truth of individual spiritual things.

The Fourteenth Path is the Illuminating Intelligence, and is so called because it is itself that CHASHMAL which is the founder of the concealed and fundamental ideas of holiness and of their stages of preparation.

The Fifteenth Path is the Constituting Intelligence, so called because it constitutes the substance of creation in pure darkness, and men have spoken of these contemplations; it is that darkness spoken of in scripture, Job xxxviii. 9, "and thick darkness a swaddling band for it."

The Sixteenth Path is the Triumphal or Eternal Intelligence, so called because it is the pleasure of the Glory, beyond which is no other Glory like to it, and it is called also the Paradise prepared for the Righteous.

The Seventeenth Path is the Disposing Intelligence, which provides Faith to the Righteous, and they are clothed with the Holy Spirit by it, and it is called the Foundation of Excellence in the state of higher thing.

The Eighteenth Path is called the House of Influence (by the greatness of whose abundance the influx of good things upon created beings is increased) and

from the midst of the investigation the arcana and hidden senses are drawn forth, which dwell in its shade and which cling to it, from the cause of all causes.

The Nineteenth Path is the Intelligence of all the activities of the spiritual beings, and is so called because of the affluence diffused by it from the most high blessing and most exalted sublime glory.

The Twentieth Path is the Intelligence of Will, and is so called because it is the means of preparation of all and each created being, and by this intelligence the existence of the Primordial Wisdom becomes known.

The Twenty-first Path is the Intelligence of Conciliation, and is so called because it receives the divine influence which flows into it from its benediction upon all and each existence.

The Twenty-second Path is the Faithful Intelligence, and is so called because by it spiritual virtues are increased, and all dwellers on earth are nearly under its shadow.

The Twenty-third Path is the Stable Intelligence, and it is so called because it has the virtue of consistency among all numerations.

The Twenty-fourth Path is the Imaginative Intelligence, and it is so called because it gives a likeness to all the similitudes, which are created in like manner similar to its harmonious elegancies.

The Twenty-fifth Path is the Intelligence of Probation, or is Tentative, and is so called because it is the primary temptation, by which the Creator (blessed be He) trieth all righteous persons.

The Twenty-sixth Path is called the Renovating Intelligence, because the Holy God (blessed be He) renews by it, all the changing things which are renewed by the creation of the world.
The Twenty-seventh Path is the Exciting Intelligence, and it is so called bemuse by it is created the Intellect of all created beings under the highest heaven, and the excitement or motion of them.

The Twenty-eighth Path is the Natural Intelligence, and is so called because through it is consummated and perfected the nature of every existent being under the orb of the Sun, in perfection.

The Twenty-ninth Path is the Corporeal Intelligence, so called because it forms every body which is, formed beneath the whole set of worlds and the increment of them.

The Thirtieth Path is the Collecting Intelligence, and is so called because Astrologers deduce from it the judgment of the Stars, and of the celestial signs, and the perfections of their science, according to the rules of their revolutions.

The Thirty-first Path is the Perpetual Intelligence; and why is it so called? Because it regulates the motions of the Sun and Moon in their proper order, each in an orbit convenient for it.

The Thirty-second Path is the Administrative Intelligence, and it is so called because it directs and associates, in all their operations, the seven planets, even all of them in their own due courses.

END OF THE SEPHER YETZIRAH

THE ACTS OF PAUL AND THECLA

CHAPTER I

1:1 When Paul went up to Iconium, after his flight from Antioch, Demas and Hermogenes became his companions, who were then full of hypocrisy.

1:2 But Paul looking only at the goodness of God, did them no harm, but loved them greatly.

1:3 Accordingly he endeavoured to make agreeable to them all the oracles and doctrines of Christ, and the design of the Gospel of God's well-beloved Son, instructing them in the knowledge of Christ, as it was revealed to him.

1:4 And a certain man named Onesiphorus, hearing that Paul was come to Iconium, went out speedily to meet him, together with his wife Lectra, and his sons Simmia and Xeno, to invite him to their house.

1:5 For Titus had given them a description of Paul's personage, they as yet not knowing him in person, but only being acquainted with his character.

1:6 They went in the king's highway to Lystra, and stood there waiting for him, comparing all who passed by, with that description which Titus had given them.

1:7 At length they saw a man coming (namely Paul), of a low stature, bald (or shaved) on the head, crooked thighs, handsome legs, hollow-eyed; had a crooked nose; full of grace; for sometimes he appeared as a man, sometimes he had the countenance of an angel. And Paul saw Onesiphorus, and was glad.

1:8 And Onesiphorus said: Hail, thou servant of the blessed God. Paul replied, The grace of God be with thee and thy family.

1:9 But Demas and Hermogenes were moved with envy, and, under a show of great religion, Demas said, And are not we also servants of the blessed God? Why didst thou not salute us?

1:10 Onesiphorus replied, Because I have not perceived in you the fruits of righteousness; nevertheless, if ye are of that sort, ye shall be welcome to my house also.

1:11 Then Paul went into the house of Onesiphorus, and here was great joy among the family on that account: and they employed themselves in prayer, breaking of bread, and hearing Paul preach the word of God concerning the temperance and the resurrection, in the following manner:

1:12 Blessed are the pure in heart; for they shall see God.

1:13 Blessed are they who keep their flesh undefiled (or pure); for they shall be the temple of God.

1:14 Blessed are the temperate (or chaste); for God will reveal himself to them.

1:15 Blessed are they who abandon their secular enjoyments; for they shall be accepted of God.

1:16 Blessed are they who have wives, as though they had them not; for they shall be made angels of God.

1:17 Blessed are they who tremble at the word of God;

for they shall be comforted.

1:18 Blessed are they who keep their baptism pure; for they shall find peace with the Father, Son, and Holy Ghost.

1:19 Blessed are they who pursue the wisdom (or doctrine) of Jesus Christ; for they shall be called the sons of the Most High.

1:20 Blessed are they who observe the instructions of Jesus Christ; for they shall dwell in eternal light.

1:21 Blessed are they, who for the love of Christ abandon the glories of the world; for they shall judge angels, and be placed at the right hand of Christ, and shall not suffer the bitterness of the last judgment.

1:22 Blessed are the bodies and souls of virgins; for they are acceptable to God, and shall not lose the reward of their virginity; for the word of their (heavenly) Father shall prove effectual to their salvation in the day of his Son, and they shall enjoy rest for evermore.

CHAPTER II

2:1 While Paul was preaching this sermon in the church which was in the house of Onesiphorus, a certain virgin, named Thecla (whose mother's name was Theoclia, and who was betrothed to a man named Thamyris) sat at a certain window in her house.

2:2 From whence, by the advantage of a window in the house where Paul was, she both night and day heard Paul's sermons concerning God, concerning charity, concerning faith in Christ, and concerning prayer;

2:3 Nor would she depart from the window, till with exceeding joy she was subdued to the doctrines of faith.

2:4 At length, when she saw many women and virgins going in to Paul, she earnestly desired that she might be thought worthy to appear in his presence, and hear the word of Christ; for she had not yet seen Paul's person, but only heard his sermons, and that alone.

2:5 But when she would not be prevailed upon to depart from the window, her mother sent to Thamyris, who came with the greatest pleasure, as hoping now to marry her. Accordingly he said to Theoclia, Where is my Thecla?

2:6 Theoclia replied, Thamyris, I have something very strange to tell you; for Thecla, for the space of three days, will not move from the window not so much as to eat or drink, but is so intent on hearing the artful and delusive discourses of a certain foreigner, that I perfectly admire, Thamyris, that a young woman of her known modesty, will suffer herself to be so prevailed upon.

2:7 For that man has disturbed the whole city of Iconium, and even your Thecla, among others. All the women and young men flock to him to receive his doctrine; who, besides all the rest, tells them that there is but one God, who alone is to be worshipped, and that we ought to live in chastity.

2:8 Notwithstanding this, my daughter Thecla, like a spider's web fastened to the window, is captivated by the discourses of Paul, and attends upon them with prodigious eagerness, and vast delight; and thus, by attending on what he says, the young woman is seduced. Now then do you go, and speak to her, for she is betrothed to you.

2:9 Accordingly Thamyris went, and having saluted her, and taking care not to surprise her, he said, Thecla, my spouse, why sittest thou in this melancholy posture? What strange impressions are made upon thee? Turn to Thamyris, and blush.

2:10 Her mother also spake to her after the same manner, and said, Child, why dost thou sit so melancholy, and, like one astonished, makest no reply?

2:11 Then they wept exceedingly: Thamyris, that he had lost his spouse; Theoclia, that she had lost her daughter; and the maids, that they had lost their mistress; and there was an universal mourning in the family.

2:12 But all these things made no impression upon Thecla, so as to incline her so much as to turn to them, and take notice of them; for she still regarded the discourses of Paul.

2:13 Then Thamyris ran forth into the street to observe who they were who went into Paul, and came out from him; and he saw two men engaged in a very warm dispute, and said to them;

2:14 Sirs, what business have you here? and who is that man within, belonging to you, who deludes the minds of men, both young men and virgins, persuading them, that they ought not to marry, but continue as they are?

2:15 I promise to give you a considerable sum, if you will give me a just account of him; for I am the chief person of this city.

2:16 Demas and Hermogenes replied, We cannot so exactly tell who he is; but this we know, that he deprives young men of their (intended) wives, and virgins of their (intended) husbands, by teaching, There can be no future resurrection, unless ye continue in chastity, and do not defile your flesh.

CHAPTER III

3:1 Then said Thamyris, Come along with me to my house, and refresh yourselves. So they went to a very splendid entertainment, where there was wine in abundance, and very rich provision.

3:2 They were brought to a table richly spread, and made to drink plentifully by Thamyris, on account of the love he had for Thecla and his desire to marry her.

3:3 Then Thamyris said, I desire ye would inform me what the doctrines of this Paul are, that I may understand them; for I am under no small concern about Thecla, seeing she so delights in that stranger's discourses, that I am in danger of losing my intended wife.

3:4 Then Demas and Hermogenes answered both

together, and said, Let him be brought before the governor Castillius, as one who endeavours to persuade the people into the new religion of the Christians, and he, according to the order of Caesar, will put him to death, by which means you will obtain your wife;

3:5 While we at the same time will teach her, that the resurrection which he speaks of is already come, and consists in our having children; and that we then arose again, when we came to the knowledge of God.

3:6 Thamyris having this account from them, was filled with hot resentment:

3:7 And rising early in the morning he went to the house of Onesiphorus, attended by the magistrates, the jailer, and a great multitude of people with staves, and said to Paul;

3:8 Thou hast perverted the city of Iconium, and among the rest, Thecla, who is betrothed to me, so that now she will not marry me. Thou shalt therefore go with us to the governor Castillius.

3:9 And all the multitude cried out, Away with this imposter (magician), for he has perverted the minds of our wives, and all the people hearken to him.

CHAPTER IV

4:1 Then Thamyris standing before the governor's judgment-seat, spake with a loud voice in the following manner.

4:2 O governor, I know not whence this man cometh; but he is one who teaches that matrimony is unlawful. Command him therefore to declare before you for what reason he publishes such doctrines.

4:3 While he was saying thus, Demas and Hermogenes (whispered to Thamyris, and) said; Say that he is a Christian, and he will presently be put to death.

4:4 But the governor was more deliberate, and calling to Paul, he said, Who art thou? What dost thou teach? They seem to lay gross crimes to thy charge.

4:5 Paul then spake with a loud voice, saying, As I am now called to give an account, O governor, of my doctrines, I desire your audience.

4:6 That God, who is a God of vengeance, and who stands in need of nothing but the salvation of his creatures, has sent me to reclaim them from their wickedness and corruptions, from all (sinful) pleasures, and from death; and to persuade them to sin no more.

4:7 On this account, God sent his Son Jesus Christ, whom I preach, and in whom I instruct men to place their hopes as that person who only had such compassion on the deluded world, that it might not, O governor, be condemned, but have faith, the fear of God, the knowledge of religion, and the love of truth.

4:8 So that if I only teach those things which I have received by revelation from God, where is my crime?

4:9 When the governor heard this, he ordered Paul to be bound, and to be put in prison, till he should be more at leisure to hear him more fully.

4:10 But in the night, THecla taking off her earrings, gave them to the turnkey of the prison, who then opened the doors to her, and let her in;

4:11 And when she made a present of a silver looking-glass to the jailer, was allowed to go into the room where Paul was; then she sat down at his feet, and heard from him the great things of God.

4:12 And as she perceived Paul not to be afraid of suffering, but that by divine assistance he behaved himself with courage, her faith so far increased that she kissed his chains.

CHAPTER V

5:1 At length Thecla was missed, and sought for by the family and by Thamyris in every street, as though she had been lost, but one of the porter's fellow-servants told them, that she had gone out in the night-time.

5:2 Then they examined the porter, and he told them, that she was gone to the prison to the strange man.

5:3 They went therefore according to his direction, and there found her; and when they came out, they got a mob together, and went and told the governor all that happened.

5:4 Upon which he ordered Paul to be brought before his judgement seat.

5:5 Thecla in the mean time lay wallowing on the ground in the prison, in that same place where Paul had sat to teach her; upon which the governor also ordered her to be brought before his judgement-seat; which summons she received with joy, and went.

5:6 When Paul was brought thither, the mob with more vehemence cried out, He is a magician, let him die.

5:7 Nevertheless the governor attended with pleasure upon Paul's discourses of the holy works of Christ; and, after a council called, he summoned Thecla, and said to her, Why do you not, according to the law of the Iconians, marry Thamyris?

5:8 She stood still, with her eyes fixed upon Paul; and finding she made no reply, Theoclia, her mother, cried out, saying, Let the unjust creature be burnt; let her be burnt in the midst of the theatre, for refusing Thamyris, that all women may learn from her to avoid such practices.

5:9 Then the governor was exceedingly concerned, and ordered Paul to be whipt out of the city, and Thecla to be burnt.

5:10 So the governor arose, and went immediately into the theatre; and all the people went forth to see the dismal sight.

5:11 But Thecla, just as a lamb in the wilderness looks every way to see his shepherd, looked around for Paul;

5:12 And as she was looking upon the multitude, she saw the Lord Jesus in the likeness of Paul, and said to herself, Paul is come to see me in my distressed circumstances. And she fixed her eyes upon him; but he instantly ascended up to heaven, while she looked on him.

5:13 The the young men and women brought wood and straw for the burning of Thecla; who, being brought naked to the stake, extorted tears from the governor, with surprise beholding the greatness of her beauty.

5:14 And when they had placed the wood in order, the people commanded her to go upon it; which she did, first making the sign of the cross.

5:15 Then the people set fire to the pile; though the flame was exceeding large, it did not touch her, for God took compassion on her, and caused a great eruption from the earth beneath, and a cloud from above to pour down great quantities of rain and hail;

5:16 Insomuch that by the rupture of the earth, very many were in great danger, and some were killed, the fire was extinguished, and Thecla was preserved.

CHAPTER VI

6:1 In the mean time Paul, together with Onesiphorus, his wife and children, was keeping a fast in a certain cave, which was in the road from Iconium to Daphne.

6:2 And when they had fasted for several days, the children said to Paul, Father, we are hungry, and have not wherewithal to buy bread ; for Onesiphorus had left all his substance to follow Paul with his family.

6:3 Then Paul, taking off his coat, said to the boy, Go, child, and buy bread, and bring it hither.

6:4 But while the boy was buying the bread, he saw his neighbour Thecla and was surprised, and said to her, Thecla, where are you going?

6:5 She replied, I am in pursuit of Paul, having been delivered from the flames.

6:6 The boy then said, I will bring you to him, for he is under great concern on your account, and has been in prayer and fasting these six days.

6:7 When Thecla came to the cave, she found Paul upon his knees praying and saying, O holy Father, O Lord Jesus Christ, grant that the fire may not touch Thecla; but be her helper, for she is thy servant.

6:8 Thecla then standing behind him, cried out in the following words: O sovereign Lord, Creator of heaven and earth, the Father of thy beloved and holy Son, I praise thee that thou hast preserved me from the fire, to see Paul again.

6:9 Paul then arose, and when he saw her, said, O God, who searchest the heart, Father of my Lord Jesus Christ, I praise thee that thou has answered my prayer.

6:10 And there prevailed among them in the cave an entire affection to each other; Paul, Onesiphorus and all that were with them being filled with joy.

6:11 They had five loaves, some herbs and water, and they solaced each other in reflections upon the holy works of Christ.

6:12 Then said Thecla to Paul, If you be pleased with it, I will follow you withersoever you go.

6:13 He replied to her, Persons are now much given to

fornication, and you being handsome, I am afraid lest you should meet with greater temptation than the former, and should not withstand, but be overcome by it.

6:14 Thecla replied, Grant me only the seal of Christ, and no temptation shall affect me.

6:15 Paul answered, Thecla, wait with patience, and you shall receive the gift of Christ.

CHAPTER VII

7:1 Then Paul sent back Onesiphorus and his family to their own home, and taking Thecla along with him, went for Antioch;

7:2 And as soon as they came into the city, a certain Syrian, named Alexander, a magistrate, in the city, who had done many considerable services for the city during his magistracy, saw Thecla and fell in love with her, and endeavoured by many rich presents to engage Paul in his interest.

7:3 But Paul told him, I know not the woman of whom you speak, nor does she belong to me.

7:4 But he being a person of great power in Antioch, seized her in the street and kissed her; which Thecla would not bear, but looking about for Paul, cried out in a distressed loud tone, Force me not, who am a stranger; force me not, who am a servant of God; I am one of the principal persons of Iconium, and was obliged to leave that city because I would not be married to Thamyris.

7:5 Then she laid hold on Alexander, tore his coat, and took his crown off his head, and made him appear ridiculous before all the people.

7:6 But Alexander, partly as he loved her, and partly being ashamed of what had been done, led her to the governor, and upon her confession of what she had done, he condemned her to be thrown among the beasts.

CHAPTER VIII

8:1 Which when the people saw, they said: The judgments passed in this city are unjust. But Thecla desired the favour of the governor, that her chastity might not be attacked, but preserved till she should be cast to the beasts.

8:2 The governor then inquired, Who would entertain her; upon which a certain very rich widow, named Trifina, whose daughter was lately dead, desired that she might have the keeping of her; and she began to treat her in her house as her own daughter.

8:3 At length a day came, when the beasts were to be brought forth to be seen; and Thecla was brought to the amphitheatre, and put into a den in which was an exceeding fierce she-lion, in the presence of a multitude of spectators.

8:4 Trifina, without any surprise, accompanied Thecla, and the she-lion licked the feet of Thecla. The title written which denotes her crime was: Sacrilege. Then the woman cried out, O God, the judgments of this city are unrighteous.

8:5 After the beasts had been shewn, Trifina took Thecla home with her, and they went to bed; and behold, the daughter of Trifina, who was dead, appeared to her mother, and said; Mother, let the young woman, Thecla, be reputed by you as your daughter in my stead; and desire her that she should pray for me, that I may be translated to a state of happiness.

8:6 Upon which Trifina, with a mournful air, said, My daughter Falconilla has appeared to me, and ordered me to receive you in her room; wherefore I desire, Thecla, that you would pray for my daughter, that she may be translated into a state of happiness, and to life eternal.

8:7 When Thecla heard this, she immediately prayed to the Lord, and said: O Lord God of heaven and earth, Jesus Christ, thou Son of the Most High, grant that her daughter Falconilla may live forever. Trifina hearing this groaned again, and said: O unrighteous judgments! O unreasonable wickedness! that such a creature should (again) be cast to the beasts!

8:8 On the morrow, at break of day, Alexander came to Trifina's house, and said: The governor and the people are waiting; bring the criminal forth.

8:9 But Trifina ran in so violently upon him, that he was affrighted, and ran away. Trifina was one of the royal family; and she thus expressed her sorrow, and said; Alas! I have trouble in my house on two accounts, and there is no one who will relieve me, either under the loss of my daughter, or my being able to save Thecla. But now, O Lord God, be thou the helper of Thecla thy servant.

8:10 While she was thus engaged, the governor sent one of his own officers to bring Thecla. Trifina took her by the hand, and, going with her, said: I went with Falconilla to her grave, and now must go with Thecla to the beasts.

8:11 When Thecla heard this, she weeping prayed, and said: O Lord God, whom I have made my confidence and refuge, reward Trifina for her compassion to me, and preserving my chastity.

8:12 Upon this there was a great noise in the amphitheatre; the beasts roared, and the people cried out, Bring in the criminal.

8:13 But the woman cried out, and said: Let the whole city suffer for such crimes; and order all of us, O governor, to the same punishment. O unjust judgment! O cruel sight!

8:14 Others said, Let the whole city be destroyed for this vile action. Kill us all, O governor. O cruel sight! O unrighteous judgment.

CHAPTER IX

9:1 Then Thecla was taken out of the hand of Trifina, stripped naked, had a girdle put on, and thrown into the place appointed for fighting with the beasts: and the lions and the bears were let loose upon her.

9:2 But a she-lion, which was of all the most fierce, ran to Thecla, and fell down at her feet. Upon which the multitude of women shouted aloud.

9:3 Then a she-bear ran fiercely towards her; but the she-lion met the bear, and tore it to pieces.

9:4 Again, a he-lion, who had been wont to devour men, and which belonged to Alexander, ran towards her; but the she-lion encountered the he-lion, and they killed each other.

9:5 Then the women were under a greater concern, because the she-lion, which had helped Thecla, was dead.

9:6 Afterwards they brought out many other wild beasts; but Thecla stood with her hands stretched towards heaven, and prayed; and when she had done praying, she turned about, and saw a pit of water, and said, Now it is a proper time for me to be baptized.

9:7 Accordingly she threw herself into the water, and said, In thy name, O my Lord Jesus Christ, I am this last day baptized. The women and the people seeing this, cried out, and said, Do not throw yourself into the water. And the governor himself cried out, to think that the fish (sea-calves) were like to devour so much beauty.

9:8 Notwithstanding all this, Thecla threw herself into the water, in the name of our Lord Jesus Christ.

9:9 But the fish (sea-calves,) when they saw the lighting and fire, were killed, and swam dead upon the surface of the water, and a cloud of fire surrounded Thecla, so that as the beasts could not come near her, so the people could not see her nakedness.

9:10 Yet they turned other wild beasts upon her; upon which they made a very mournful outcry; and some of them scattered spikenard, others cassia, other amomus [a sort of spikenard, or the herb of Jerusalem, or ladies-rose], others ointment; so that the quantity of ointment was large, in proportion to the number of people; and upon this all the beasts lay as though they had been fast asleep, and did not touch Thecla.

9:11 Whereupon Alexander said to the Governor, I have some very terrible bulls; let us bind her to them. To which the governor, with concern, replied, You may do what you think fit.

9:12 Then they put a cord round Thecla's waist, which bound also her feet, and with it tied her to the bulls, to whose privy-parts they applied red-hot irons, that so they being the more tormented, might more violently drag Thecla about, till they had killed her.

9:13 The bulls accordingly tore about, making a most hideous noise, but the flame which was about Thecla, burnt off the cords which were fastened to the members of the bulls, and she stood in the middle of the stage, as unconcerned as if she had not been bound.

9:14 But in the mean time Trifina, who sat upon one of the benches, fainted away and died; upon which the whole city was under a very great concern.

9:15 And Alexander himself was afraid, and desired the governor, saying: I entreat you, take compassion on me and the city, and release this woman, who has fought with the beasts; lest, both you and I, and the whole city be destroyed:

9:16 For if Caesar should have any account of what has passed now, he will certainly immediately destroy the city, because Trifina, a person of royal extract, and a relation of his, is dead upon her seat.

9:17 Upon this the governor called Thecla from among the beasts to him, and said to her, Who art thou? and what are thy circumstances, that not one of the beasts will touch thee?

9:18 Thecla replied to him; I am a servant of the living God; and as to my state, I am a believer on Jesus Christ his Son, in whom God is well pleased; and for that reason none of the beasts could touch me.

9:19 He alone is the way to eternal salvation, and the foundation of eternal life. He is a refuge to those who are in distress; a support to the afflicted, hope and defence to those who are hopeless; and, in a word, all those who do not believe on him, shall not live, but suffer eternal death.

9:20 When the governor heard these things, he ordered her clothes to be brought, and said to her put on your clothes.

9:21 Thecla replied: May that God who clothed me when I was naked among the beasts, in the day of judgment clothe your soul with the robe of salvation. Then she took her clothes, and put them on; and the governor immediately published an order in these words; I release to you Thecla the servant of God.

9:22 Upon which the women cried out together with a loud voice, and with one accord gave praise unto God, and said: There is but one God, who is the God of Thecla; the one God who hath delivered Thecla.

9:23 So loud were their voices that the whole city seemed to be shaken; and Trifina herself heard the glad tidings, and arose again, and ran with the multitude to meet Thecla; and embracing her, said: Now I believe there shall be a resurrection of the dead; now I am persuaded that my daughter is alive. Come therefore home with me, my daughter Thecla, and I will make over all that I have to you.

9:24 So Thecla went with Trifina, and was entertained there a few days, teaching her the word of the Lord, whereby many young women were converted; and there was great joy in the family of Trifina.

9:25 But Thecla longed to see Paul, and inquired and sent everywhere to find him; and when at length she was informed that he was at Myra, in Lycia, she took with her many young men and women; and putting on a girdle, and dressing herself in the habit of a man, she went to him in Myra in Lycia, and there found Paul preaching the word of God; and she stood by him among the throng.

CHAPTER X

10:1 But it was no small surprise to Paul when he saw her and the people with her; for he imagined some fresh trial was coming upon them;

10:2 Which when Thecla perceived, she said to him: I have been baptized, O Paul; for he who assists you in preaching has assisted me to baptize.

10:3 Then Paul took her, and led her to the house of Hermes; and Thecla related to Paul all that had befallen her in Antioch, insomuch that Paul exceedingly wondered, and all who heard were confirmed in the faith, and prayed for Trifina's happiness.

10:4 Then Thecla arose, and said to Paul, I am going to Iconium. Paul replied to her: Go, and teach the word of the Lord.

10:5 But Trifina had sent large sums of money to Paul, and also clothing by the hands of Thecla, for the relief of the poor.

10:6 So Thecla went to Iconium. And when she came to the house of Onesiphorus, she fell down upon the floor where Paul had sat and preached, and mixing her tears with her prayers, she praised and glorified God in the follwing words:

10:7 O Lord the God of this house, in which I was first enlightened by thee; O Jesus, son of the living God, who wast my helper before the governor, my helper in the fire, and my helper among the beasts; thou alone art God forever and ever. Amen.

10:8 Thecla now (on her return) found Thamyris dead, but her mother living. So calling her mother, she said to her: Theoclia, my mother, is it possible for you to be brought to a belief, that there is but one Lord God, who dwells in the heavens? If yo desire great riches, God will give them to you by me; if you want your daughter again, here I am.

10:9 These and many other things she represented to her mother, [endeavouring] to persuade her [to her opinion]. But her mother Theoclia gave no credit to the things which were said by the martyr Thecla.

10:10 So that Thecla perceiving she discoursed to no purpose, signing her whole body with the sign [of the cross], left the house and went to Daphine; and when she came there, she went to the cave, where she had found Paul with Onesiphorus, and fell down on the ground; and wept before God.

10:11 When she departed thence, she went to Seleucia, and enlightened many in the knowledge of Christ.

10:12 And a bright cloud conducted her in her journey.

10:13 And after she had arrived at Seleucia she went to a place out of the city, about the distance of a furlong, being afraid of the inhabitants, because they were worshippers of idols.

10:14 And she was led [by the cloud] into a mountain called Calamon, or Rodeon. There she abode many years, and underwent a great many grievous temptations of the devil, which she bore in a becoming manner, by the assistance which she had from Christ.

10:15 At length, certain gentlewomen hearing of the virgin Thecla, went to her, and were instructed by her in the oracles of God, and many of them abandoned this world, and led a monastic life with her.

10:16 Hereby a good report was spread everywhere of Thecla, and she wrought several [miraculous] cures, so that all the city and adjacent countries brought their sick to that mountain, and before they came as far as the door of the cave, they were instantly cured of whatsoever distemper they had.

10:17 The unclean spirits were cast out, making a noise; all received their sick made whole, and glorified God, who had bestowed such power on the virgin Thecla;

10:18 Insomuch that the physicians of Seleucia were now of no more account, and lost all the profit of their trade, because no one regarded them; upon which they were filled with envy, and began to contrive what methods to take with this servant of Christ.

CHAPTER XI

11:1 The devil then suggested bad advice to their minds; and being on a certain day met together to consult, they reasoned among each other thus: The virgin is a priestess of the great goddess Diana, and whatsoever she requests from her, is granted, because she is a virgin, and so is beloved by all the gods.

11:2 Now then let us procure some rakish fellows, and after we have made them sufficiently drunk, and given them a good sum of money, let us order them to go and debauch this virgin, promising them, if they do it, a larger reward.

11:3 (For they thus concluded among themselves, that if they be able to debauch her, the gods will no more regard her, nor Diana cure the sick for her.)

11:4 They proceeded according to this resolution, and the fellows went to the mountain, and as fierce as lions to the cave, knocking at the door.

11:5 The holy martyr Thecla, relying upon the God in whom she believed, opened the door, although she was before apprized of their design, and said to them, Young men, what is your business?

11:6 They replied, Is there any one within, whose name is Thecla? She answered, What would you have with her? They said, We have a mind to lie with her.

11:7 The blessed Thecla answered: Though I am a mean old woman, I am the servant of my Lord Jesus Christ; and though you have a vile design against me, ye shall not be able to accomplish it. They replied: It is impossible but we must be able to do with you what we have a mind.

11:8 And while they were saying this, they laid hold on her by main force, and would have ravished her. Then she with the (greatest) mildness said to them: Young men have patience, and see the glory of the Lord.

11:9 And while they held her, she looked up to heaven and said; O God most reverend to whom none can be likened; who makest thyself glorious over thine enemies; who didst deliver me from the fire, and didst not give me up to Thamyris, didst not give me up to Alexander; who deliveredst me from the wild beasts; who didst preserve me in the deep waters; who hast everywhere been my helper, and hast glorified thy name in me;

11:10 Now also deliver me from the hands of these wicked and unreasonable men, nor suffer them to debauch my chastity which I have hitherto preserved for thy honour; for I love thee and long for thee, and worship thee, O Father, Son, and Holy Ghost, for evermore. Amen.

11:11 Then came a voice from heaven, saying, Fear not, Thecla, my faithful servant, for I am with thee. Look and see the place which is opened for thee: there thy eternal abode shall be; there thou shalt receive the beatific vision.

11:12 The blessed Thecla observing, saw the rock opened to as large a degree as that a man might enter in; she did as she was commanded, bravely fled from the vile crew, and went into the rock, which instantly so closed, that there was not any crack visible where it had opened.

11:13 The men stood perfectly astonished at so prodigious a miracle, and had no power to detain the servant of God; but only, catching hold of her veil, or hood, they tore off a piece of it;

11:14 And even that was by the permission of God, for the confirmation of their faith who should come to see this venerable place, and to convey blessings to those in succeeding ages, who should believe on our Lord Jesus Christ from a pure heart.

11:15 Thus suffered that first martyr and apostle of God, and virgin, Thecla; who came from Iconium at eighteen years of age; afterwards, partly in journeys and travels, and partly in a monastic life in the cave, she lived seventy-two years; so that she was ninety years old when the Lord translated her.

11:16 Thus ends her life.

11:17 The day which is kept sacred to her memory, is the twenty-fourth of September, to the glory of the Father, and the Son, and the Holy Ghost, now and for evermore. Amen.

The Gospel of Judas

This is the proclamation, which was secretly revealed to Judas Iscariot by Jesus during that eight-day period that included (that was) the three days before he (Jesus) celebrated Passover (one translator has "celebrated his passion / suffering).

Note: The proclamation is not the logos, word or Christ for the orthodox church. The word here is a proclamation of judgment as in a court verdict.

1. Jesus appeared on earth to perform miracles and wondrous acts in order to save humanity.
Because some conducted themselves in a righteous way and others continued in their sins, he decided to call the twelve disciples.

2. He began to talk to them about the mysteries that lay beyond this world and what would happen at this world's end (at the end). He often changed his appearance and was not seen as himself but looked like a child (some translators have apparition or spirit) when he was with his disciples.

3. He came upon his disciples in Judea once when they were sitting together piously (training their piety – training in godliness). As he got closer to the disciples he saw they were sitting together, giving thanks and saying a prayer over the bread (Eucharist / thanksgiving). He laughed.

4. The disciples asked Him, "Rabbi, why are you laughing at our prayer of thanks? Have we not acted appropriately?"
He said, "I am not laughing at you. It is just that you are not doing this because you want to. You are doing this because your god (has to be / will be) praised."

5. They said, "Rabbi, you are the (earthly / only) son of our god."
Jesus answered, "How do you know me? (Do you think you know me?) I say to you truly, no one among you in this generation (in this race) will understand me."

6. His disciples heard this and became enraged and began mumbling profanities and mocking him in their hearts. When Jesus saw their inability (to understand what he said to them (their stupidity), he said,) "Why did you get so upset that you became angry? Your god, who is inside of you, (and your own lack of understanding guides you and) have instigated this anger in your (mind / soul). (I challenge) any man among you to show me who is (understanding enough) to bring out the perfect man and stand and face me."

7. They all said, "We are strong enough."
But in their (true being) spirits none dared to stand in front of him except for Judas Iscariot. Judas was able to stand in front of him, but even he could not look Jesus in the eyes, and he turned his face away.

Note: It is uncertain as to the reason Judas did not look at Jesus. It was a custom of respect not to look a superior in the eyes. Either Judas was unable to look at Jesus or was constrained by the position of Jesus as his Rabbi.

8. Judas said to Him, "I know who you are and where you came from. You are from the everlasting (eternal) aeon (realm or kingdom) of Barbelo (Barbelo's everlasting kingdom). I am not worthy to speak the name of the one who sent you."

9. Jesus knew that Judas was capable of understanding (showing forth / thinking about) something that was glorious, so Jesus said to him, "Walk away (step a distance away) from the others and I will tell you about the mysteries of God (the reign of God / kingdom of God).

10. It is possible for you to get there, but the path will cause you great grief because you will be replaced so that the twelve may be complete with their god again."
Judas asked him, "When will you tell me how the great day of light will dawn for this generation (race)? When will you explain these things?"
But as he asked these things, Jesus left him.

11. At the dawn of the next day after this happened, Jesus appeared to his disciples.
They asked Him, "Rabbi, where did you go and what did you do when you left us?"
Jesus said to them, "I went to another generation (race) that is a greater and holier generation (race)."

12. His disciples asked him, "Lord, what is this great race that is superior to us and holier than us, that is not now in this realm (kingdom)?"
When Jesus heard this, he laughed and said to them, "Why are you thinking in your hearts about the mighty and holy race (generation)? So be it - I will tell you. No one born in this age (realm / aeon) will see that (generation / race), and not even the multitude (army) of angels (controlling) the stars will rule over that generation (race), and no mortal (corruptible) person can associate (belong) with it.

13. That generation does not come from (a realm) which has become (mortal / corrupted). The

generation of people among (you) is from the generation of humanity (of inferior / without) power, which (cannot associate with the) other powers (above) by (whom) you rule / are ruled."

When (the /his) disciples heard this, they were all troubled in (their heart/spirit). They were speechless (could not utter a word).

Note: This begins a distinction drawn between the generation or race of mankind, which is inferior, decaying, and unenlightened, and the "great generation or race," which is enlightened, incorruptible, and eternal. There are only two races; those who have gnosis and those who do not. Interestingly, Jesus does not place the disciples in the great generation.

14. On another day Jesus came up to (them). They said to (him), "Rabbi, we have seen you in a (dream), because we all had weighty (dreams about a night you were taken away / arrested)."
(He said), "Why have (you come to me when you have) gone into hiding?"

15. They said, "There was (an imposing building with a great altar in it and twelve men, (which we would say were) the priests, and there was a name, and a crowd of people waiting (enduring because of their perseverance) at that altar, (for) the priest (to come and receive) the offerings. (However) we kept waiting (we were tenacious also)."
(Jesus asked), "What were (the priests) like?"
    They said, "Some (of them would fast) for two weeks; (others would) sacrifice their own children, others their wives, (all the while) in praise (offered in) humility with each other; some have sex with other men; some murder; some commit a plethora of sins and acts of crime. And the men who stand in front of the altar call upon your (name / authority), and in all the acts springing from their lack of knowledge (lack of light), the sacrifices are brought to completion (by their hands) (the alter remained full through their handiwork of slaughtering the sacrifices)."
After they said these things they became uneasy and quiet.

16. Jesus asked them, "Why are you bothered? So be it, I tell you that all the priests who have stood before that altar call upon my name. I have told I you many times that my name has been written on the (judgment) of this race (and on) the stars through the human generations. In my name (these people) have planted barren trees, (and have done so) without any honor."
17. Jesus said to them, "You are like those men you have seen conducting the offerings at the altar. That is the god you serve, and the twelve men you have seen represent you. The cattle you saw that were brought for sacrifice represent the many people you have led (will lead) astray before that altar. (You) will stand (lead / represent) and use my name in that way, as will the generations of the pious and you all will remain loyal to "him." (Some translations have- "The lord of chaos will establish his place in this way.") After "him" another man will lead from (the group of fornicators), and another (will lead at the alter from those who) murder children, and another from those who are homosexuals, and (another) those who fast, and (one will stand from) the rest of those who pollution themselves and who are lawlessness and who sin, and (from) those who say, 'We are like the angels'; they are the stars that (make everything happen / bring everything to an end).

18. It has been said to the human generations, 'Look, God has received your sacrifice from the hands of a priest.' But the priest is a minister of error (minister in error / ministers but is in sin). But it is the Lord, the Lord of all (the fullness of the divine), who commands, 'On the last day (of time) they will be shamed (some have - "at the end of days").'"

Note: Jesus tells the disciples that they are loyal to the wrong god. He goes on to say that they are the ones who murder, fornicate, and sin. Furthermore, Jesus tells them that they will lead people into a spiritual slaughter like the cattle they saw sacrificed in their dream. At this time the 12 included Judas. This, along with other such verses has led many scholars to conclude that the Gospel of Judas was not depicting Judas to be the sanctified person the original translators thought him to be.

19. Jesus (told them), "Stop (sacrificing that which) you have (and stop hovering) over the altar. The priests are over your stars and your angels. They have already come to their end there. So let them (be entrapped / quarrel / fight) before you, and leave them alone. (Do not be tainted by this generation but instead eat the food of knowledge given to you by the great one.)

Note: We will see "stars" referred to often in the text. They are used to symbolize two unique concepts. It was thought that in the creation of the cosmos, luminaries were created which were powers controlling each person's destiny. It was also thought that each person was assigned a star as his or her eternal home or resting place. A good person would ascend to his or her own star to rule and rest. Thus, stars were conscious powers, carrying out orders from God, and also were places of destiny for those who escape the material plane.

20. A baker cannot feed all creation under (heaven). And (they will not give) to them (a food) and (give)

to (those of the great generation the same food).
Jesus said to them, "Stop struggling with (against) me. Each of you has his own star, and every (Lines are missing here. Text could read " person has his own destiny." Or possibly, "person who does well will dwell and rest on their star").
(All things happen in their own season and all seasons are appointed. And in (the season) which has come (it is spring) for the tree (of paradise) of this aeon / age (and it will produce) for a time (then wither) but he has come to water God's paradise, and (also water this generation) that will last, because (he) will not corrupt / detour) the (path of life for) that generation, but (will guide it) from eternity to eternity."

21. Judas asked him, "Rabbi, what kind of fruit does this generation produce?"
Jesus answered, "The souls of every human generation will die. However, when these people (of this kingdom) have completed the time in the kingdom and the living breath leaves them, their bodies will die but their souls will continue to be alive, and they will ascended (be lifted up / be taken up)."
Judas asked, "What will the remainder of the human generations do?"
Jesus said, "It is not possible to plant seeds in (rocky soil) and harvest its fruit. (This is also the way (of) the (corrupted) race (generation), (the children of this kingdom) and corruptible Sophia / wisdom) (is / are) not the hand that has created mortal people, so that their souls ascend to the eternal realms above. Amen, I say, (that no) angel (or / of) power will be able to see that (kingdom of) these to whom (belong that) holy generations (above)."
    After Jesus said this, he departed.

22. Judas said, "Rabbi, you have listened to all of those others, so now listen to me too. I have seen a great vision."

23. When Jesus heard this, he laughed and said to him, "You (are the) thirteenth spirit (daemon), why are you trying so hard / why do you excite yourself like this? However, speak up, and I will be patient with you."
Judas said to him, "In the vision I saw myself and the twelve disciples were stoning me and persecuting me very badly / severely / strongly. And I (was following you and I) arrived at a place where I saw (a large house in front me), and my eyes could not (take in / comprehend) its size. Many people were surrounding it, and the house had a roof of plants (grass / green vegetation), and in the middle of the house (there was a crowd) (and I was there with you), saying, 'Rabbi, take me in (the house) along with

these people.'"

24. He responded and said, "Judas, your star has misled you. No person of mortal birth is worthy to enter the house you have seen. It is a place reserved for the saints. Not even the sun or the moon or day (light) will rule there. Only the saints will live there, in the eternal kingdom with the holy angels, always (some have the text as – "will be firmly established with the holy angels forever"). Look, I have explained to you the mysteries of the kingdom and I have taught you about the error of the stars; and (I have) sent it (on its path) on the twelve ages (aeons)."

Note: The Lost Book of Enoch tells of stars, which are the guiding forces of man and nature, erring. They become misplaced and out of order. They had to be placed or directed back into their proper paths. See The Lost Book of Enoch, by Joseph Lumpkin.

Note: There are 12 Astrological Ages. The 12 signs of the zodiac make up a 360-degree ecliptic path around the Earth, and takes 25,920 years to make the Precession of the Equinoxes. Each sign is comprised of 30 degrees of celestial longitude. Each degree of the precession is equal to 72 Earth years, and each year is equal to 50 seconds of degrees of arc of celestial longitude. In a 24 hour Earth day, the Earth rotates the entire 360 degrees of the ecliptic, allowing a person to see all 12 signs.

25. Judas said, "Rabbi, could it be that my (spiritual) seed will conquer the rulers of cosmic power (could also be rendered: "is under the control of the archons or rulers of cosmic power"?)"

26. Jesus answered and said to him, "Come (with me so) that I (may show you the kingdom you will receive. I will show you what is to come of you and this generation), but you will be grieved when you see the kingdom and all its race (of people)."
When Judas heard Him he said to him, "What good is it if I have received it seeing that you have set me apart from that race?"
Jesus answered him and said, "You will become the thirteenth, and you will be cursed by the other generations, and you will come to rule over them. In the last days they will curse your ascent to the holy (race / kingdom)."

Note: I have chosen the word, "daemon" and not "demon" because the meaning of the text is unclear. A daemon is a divinity or supernatural being of a nature between gods and humans. In verse 24 Jesus tells Judas that he will never be worthy to enter the house, which symbolizes the eternal kingdom. Later in verse 26 Jesus seems to indicate that Judas will be cursed by the other disciples but will be raised to enter the holy generation in the last days. It is possible the interim time will be spent in what the Bible calls, "his own place."

27. Jesus said, "(Follow / come with me), so that I may teach you the (secrets) that no person (has) ever seen.

Note: This begins a creation myth based on certain Sethian Gnostic cosmology. The telling of the story appears to be an attempt to link the Gnostic cosmology to the teachings of Jesus in order to add validity and authority to the creation story and entities as well as assisting in the propagation of the sect.

There is a great and limitless kingdom, whose scope no generation of angels has seen (and in it) The Great Invisible (Spirit) is, and no angel's eye has ever seen, no thought of the heart (mind) has ever understood it, and no name can be assigned it (it cannot be named).

28. "And a brightly glowing cloud appeared there. The Great Spirit said, 'Let an angel come into being as my assistant (attendant / helper).'
"A great angel, the enlightened, divine, Self-Generated (Self-Created) one emerged from the cloud. Because of him, four other angelic lights (luminaries), (Harmozel, Oroiael, Daveithai, and Eleleth) began to exist from another cloud, and they became assistants (helpers / attendants) to the Self-Generated angel (messenger). The Self-Created one proclaimed, 'Let (there) come into being (a star / Adam),' and it (he) came into being (at once). He (created) the first star (luminary / bright, shining being) to reign over him.

Note: Here we have a garbled text, the translation of which can go one of two ways. The words missing in the middle of the text could be Adam, who is also known as Adamas, or it could refer to a star, since the next reference is to a luminary. The direction of the text is unclear except that it is agreed that the word "it" is used in the text.

He said, 'Let angels (messengers) begin existence to adore (worship) (him),' and an innumerable plethora became existent. He said, '(Let there be) an aeon of light,' and he began existence. He created the second star to rule over him, to render service together with the innumerable plethora of angels. That is how he created the rest of the aeons of light. He made them rulers over them, and he created for them an innumerable plethora of angels to assist them.

29. "Adamas (Adam) was in the first luminous cloud (the initial divine expression) that no angel has ever seen, including all those called 'God.' He (was the one) that (created the enlightened aeon and beheld) the image and produced him after the likeness of

(this) angel. He made the incorruptible (generation) of Seth appear (from) the twelve (aeons and) the twenty-four (stars / angelic lights / luminaries). He made seventy-two angelic lights appear in the imperishable generation, as the will of the Spirit dictated. The seventy-two angelic lights themselves made three hundred sixty angelic lights appear in the immortal race, by following the will of the Spirit, that their number should be five for each.

Note: Seth is the son of Adam and was considered to be divine as Adam was divine. Seth produced "that incorruptible generation." He was thought to have received the knowledge that would bring freedom from the material realm, and thus, salvation.

30. "The twelve realms (aeons) of the twelve angelic lights make up / appoint their Father, with six heavens for each aeon, so that there are seventy-two heavens for the seventy-two angelic lights, and for each (there are five) skies, (producing all) three hundred sixty (skies for the stars). They were given authority and a innumerable host of angels, for glory and adoration (worship), (and then he gave the) virgin (pure spirits), for glory and worship of all the aeons and the heavens and their firmaments (skies).

Note: The numbers assigned to the various aeons, angels, and stars have significance in both biblical number symbolism and Pythagorean numerology.
> *One – Unity, sovereign, God, causality.*
> *Two – Duality and / or merging.*
> *Three - Spiritually complete, fullness, creation.*
> *Four – Foundations, systems, order.*
> *Five – Spirit, grace, movement.*
> *Six - Mankind.*
> *Seven – God, wisdom, knowledge, perfection.*
> *Twelve – Law, rule, authority.*
> *Thirteen – Cursed, beyond or without law.*
> *Twenty-four – Heavenly government, elders, a system. Duality within the system.*
> *Seventy-two – Both elements of two and seven as well as the element of completion.*
> *Three hundred and sixty – Elements of three and six as well as the meaning of a full cycle such as a yearly cycle. An end, and a new start.*

31. The totality (gathering) of those immortals is called the cosmos, that is to say perdition / decay / corruption, by the Father and the seventy-two angelic lights / luminaries who are with the Self-Created one and his seventy-two aeons. In the cosmos the first human appeared with his incorruptible powers.

Note: This first human is Adamas or Adam. It should be noted that the name "Adam" can also be rendered as "Man" in Hebrew.

32. And the aeon that appeared with his generation and the aeon in whom are the cloud of knowledge and the angel, is called El.

Note: El was the name of a Semitic god who was chief among the pantheon of gods affecting nature and society. He is father of the divine family and president of the divine assembly on the 'mount of assembly', the equivalent of Hebrew har mo'ed, which became through the Greek transliteration Armageddon. In Canaanite mythology he is known as 'the Bull', symbolizing his strength and creative force. He is called 'Creator of Created Things' which is how rivers were also metaphorically thought of. In the Biblical Garden of Eden a river flowed to form the four rivers, Tigris, Euphrates, Gihon and Pishon."
El expressed the concept of ordered government, justice and creation. The Bible never stigmatizes the Canaanite worship of El, whose authority in social affairs was recognized by the Patriarchs. His consort was Asherah, the mother goddess, represented in Canaanite sanctuaries by a natural tree (Hebrew ashera) such as the tree of life.

33. (He created the) aeon, (after that) (El) said, 'Let twelve angels come into being (in order to) rule over chaos and the (cosmos / perdition).' And look, from the cloud {called Sophia} there appeared an (angel / aeon) whose face flashed with fire and whose appearance was defiled with blood. His name was Nebro, meaning "rebel." Another angel, Saklas, also came from the cloud. So Nebro created six angels — as well as Saklas — to be assistants, and these produced twelve angels in the heavens, with each one receiving a piece of the heavens.

Note: Nebro may be a female demon who mates with Saklas; others call Nebro by the name "Yaldaboth (child of chaos) Yaldaboth and Saklas are both names given to the insane or deficient deity that created the physical world. Also the reading could be influenced by the fact that in some mythologies Nebro is a head demon and Saklas is a head angel. Nebro has the same meaning as Nimrod, which is "rebel."

The Jews and Greeks of the day were literalists. Each and every word of the scriptures was taken at face value. Therefore, the god who created Adam and Eve was a limited and tangible god. He walked and talked and asked questions, the answers to which he did not seem to know. By building a creation story that includes Saklas the problems were solved. Now the references to multiple gods were answered and when god said let "us" create man, the references could be to Saklas and his helpers. Since the Saklas deity was limited and restricted it left the Supreme God to be "God."

34. "The twelve rulers (aeons) spoke with the twelve angels: 'Let each of you (receive a portion) and let

them (that are in this) generation (be ruled by these) angels':

The first is Seth, who is called Christ. The (second) is Harmathoth, who is (head ruler of the underworld). The (third) is Galila. The fourth is Yobel. The fifth (is) Adonaios. These are the five who ruled all of the underworld, and primarily over chaos.

Note: These five names are probably associated with the five planets known at the time the Gospel of Judas was written. They were placed on their paths and courses to keep order and give light, both real and spiritual.

35. "Then Saklas said to his angels, 'Let us create a human being in the similitude and after the figure / image / representation (of the Supreme God) .' They fashioned Adam and his wife Eve, who is called Zoe / life when she was still in the cloud.

Note: Zoe is another name for Eve in the Septuagint.

36. For it is this name (life) that all the generations seek the man, and each of them calls the woman by these names. Now, Sakla did not command (as he was instructed) but (he commanded) the generations (of man to live so long / for a defined period of time), (but he did created them in his (Saklas') likeness). And the (ruler Saklas) said to Adam, 'You shall live long, with your children.'"

37. Judas said to Jesus, "(What length) is the long span of time that humans will live?"
Jesus said, "Why are you curious about this? Adam and his generation has lived his lifespan in the place where he received his kingdom, with his longevity bestowed by his ruler (as numbered with his ruler)."

38. Judas said to Jesus, "Does the human spirit die?"
Jesus said, "This is why God (the god of this realm) ordered Michael to loan spirits to people so that they would serve (be in servitude), but the Great One commanded Gabriel to give spirits to the great generation (race) which had no ruler over it (a generation that cannot be dominated). He gave the spirit and the soul. Therefore, the (remainder / mountain) of souls (loaned will come back to the god of this realm in the end).

Note: This passage indicates two lines of creation. For those people created by the god of this world the angel Michael was commanded to temporarily assign souls to his creation. To keep their souls they were enslaved to worship the god of this world. In contrast, the Great One commanded Gabriel to give souls to those of the great generation for eternity.

39. "(There was no) light (in this world to shine) around (the people to) allow (the) spirit (which is) within you all to dwell in this (body) among the generations of angels. But God caused knowledge to be (given) to Adam and those with him, so that the kings of chaos and the underworld might not oppress them with it."

Note: The word rendered as "rule" by most translators has the connotation of oppression.

40. Judas said to Jesus, "So what will those generations do?"
Jesus said, "Truthfully, I tell you all, that for all of them the stars bring matters to completion (heavenly apocalypse). When Saklas completes the span of time assigned for him, their first star will appear with the generations, and they will finish what they said they would do. Then they will (have illicit sex in my name and kill (sacrifice) their children and they will fast, and they will kill their wives in praise offered in humility with each other; some have sex with other men; some will murder, some commit a plethora of sins and acts of crime all in my name, and Saklas will destroy) your star over the thirteenth aeon."

41. After that Jesus (laughed).

Note: Jesus seems to find humor in the misguided judgments or concepts of the disciples. He laughs, as if shaking his head in disbelief of the error, then attempts to give insight and correction.

(Judas asked), "Rabbi, (why do you laugh at us)?"
(He) answered (Judas and said), "I am not laughing (because of you) but at the error of the stars, because these six stars wander about with these five warriors and they all will be destroyed along with their creations."

Note: The six stars were those who, along with Saklas or yaldaboth, created man and the cosmos. The five warriors refer to the five known planets at the time of the writing of the text. These planets were also connected with pagan worship and deities.

42. Judas said to Jesus, "Look at what those who have been baptized in your name do?"
Jesus said, "Truthfully I tell (you), this baptism done in my name (are done by those who do not know me. They sacrifice in vain to the god of this world. I baptized no one, for those baptized here have their hope here and those who follow me need no baptism for they will come) to me. In truth (I) tell you, Judas, (those offering) sacrifices to Saklas (do not offer

sacrifice to the Great) God (but instead worship) everything that is evil.
"But you will exceed all of them. For you will sacrifice the man (the body that clothes / bares / contains me).

Note: Gnostic theology sets up a duality between the material world and the spiritual world. Since the god that created the material world was flawed, cruel, and insane, anything produced in that environment must be corrupted and opposed to the spiritual world. In this belief system the killing of Jesus' body was a good thing since it would free his spirit and unite it with the "Great One." Looked at from this angle, Judas was assisting Jesus in showing mankind the way. This line of reasoning must be taken as metaphorical. Some authors have suggested that Jesus had become entombed in his body and was asking Judas to free him. This cannot be so since Jesus comes and goes from the Holy Race or Generation above at will. Neither is Jesus touting mass suicide. Gnostic lived long lives and propagated their faith. The message here is that to remain detached from the material or corporeal and to strive to receive the knowledge here will free you in the life to come.

Already your horn has been raised, your anger has been ignited, your star has shown brightly, and your heart has (prevailed / been made strong / pure).

Note: The symbol horn is a phallic symbol but also a symbol of strength in much the way a rhino's horn is a sign of power and might.

Note: Although the lines added to the first half of this verse are tenuous, the information that is available establishes Judas' place according to this story. It does, however, open some questions. What was Judas' anger directed against? Was he sacrificing Jesus because he was angry at the established religion of the day? Was it this anger that made his heart strong or pure? Was anger his motivating force? If so, it harmonizes well with certain readings of the canonical gospels, which may indicate Judas wanted to expedite Jesus' kingdom so he would have a place of authority therein.

43. "Truly (I tell you,) your last (act will become that which will free this race but it will) grieve (you and will anger this generation and) the ruler, since he will be destroyed. (And then the) image of the great race of Adam will be raised high, for before heaven, earth, and the angels, that race from the eternal realms, exists (existed). Look, you have been told everything. Lift up your eyes and look to the cloud and the light within it and the stars around it. The star that leads the way is your star (you are the star)."

44. Then, Judas raised his eyes and saw the radiant cloud, and entered it. Those standing below him heard a voice coming from the cloud, saying, (The return of the) great race (is at hand and the image of the Great One will be established in them because of Judas' sacrifice).

Note: This is the same cloud mentioned in verse 24. By entering the cloud Judas became one with the primal causality or "Great One / Supreme God." The Gnosis was imparted to him and he knew the mysteries. He then had understanding and strength to do what he was asked to do. This amounts to a transfiguration for Judas, much like that of Jesus. In the same manner, a voice from heaven announced his destiny.

45. (But the scribes waited for Judas, hoping to place a price on the head of Jesus.) Their high priests whispered that he had gone into the guest room for his prayer. But some scribes were there watching closely in order to arrest Jesus during the prayer, for they were afraid of the people, since he was accepted by everyone as a prophet. They approached Judas and said to him, "Why are you here? You are Jesus' disciple." Judas answered them in the way they wished. And he was given an amount of money and he handed Jesus over to them.

Note: We read of Judas' entrance into the radiant cloud and then his transaction with the scribes but there is no transition. It is possible the cloud is a metaphor for divine knowledge of the primal causality or Great God that produced Barbelo. See verse 28.

Note: The actual betrayal of Jesus by Judas is drastically downplayed. Only one paragraph is devoted to the actual act. Within this single paragraph no details are offered.
        The gospel is constructed to give the reason for the betrayal. Building the rational of the act becomes far more important than the act itself, given the fact that it was the body that clothed Jesus that was destroyed and not the inner spirit. Shedding the body fulfilled destiny and freed the Christ spirit.
        This was done as a demonstration of Jesus' belief in the immortal and eternal realm, which lay beyond human senses. The lesson of the Gospel of Judas and of Gnosticism in general had to do with reaching inside to gain knowledge of the unseen spiritual world. The orthodox church taught that only through martyrdom or the blessing of the church could one pass into the spiritual realm. Jesus was teaching another way. His death was the only way to exemplify his faith and show his disciples there was more than they could see in the material world. According to the Gnostic texts, the death of Jesus did not bring salvation. His life and death taught and provided knowledge, that if understood, would free the human race of its chains and allow it to ascend to the immortal realm.

This ends the Gospel of Judas.

Introduction to Gad the Seer

The Book of Gad the Seer was presumed lost until 1757, when Jacob Van Dort, a converted Jew, met with the patriarch of the Cochin Jews in India. Van Dort copied the text in Hebrew from the patriarch and translated the book into Dutch. He then gave it to the head of the Dutch East India company in Sri Lanka. After that, the book was translated into German and sent to be published by Johann G. Eichhorn. The original Hebrew copy found its way into the Vatican Library where it was forgotten.

The book surfaced again in the early 1900's and is now held in the University Library at Cambridge.
According to Solomon Schechter, the manuscript obtained by the University is a copy from the document purporting to be from the Vatican in Rome. The late linguistic forms and features of the Hebrew manuscript, as well as its substantial similarity with some medieval Kabbalistic literature and some aspects of Christianity, indicate a relatively late date. Schechter regards it therefore as not dating back to antiquity. However, according to Professor Meir Bar Ilan, although some linguistic aspects of the Hebrew manuscript are of late date, there is evidence that the book originated in approximately the 1st or 2nd century A.D.

The text is said to have been written by the Prophet Gad, which is mentioned at 1 Chronicles (1 Chronicles 29:29). The passage reads: "Now the acts of David the king, first and last, behold, they are written in the book of Samuel the seer, and in the book of Nathan the prophet, and in the book of Gad the seer."

The prophet, Nathan and the seer, Gad lived at the same time under the reign of King David. Therefore, this little book gives us fresh insight into the Jewish world of that time.

The original manuscript was believed by the Black Jews of Cochin of India to be an authentic and sacred manuscript. The Cochin Jews (also known as Malabar Jews or Kochinim Jews) are the oldest group of Jews in India, with roots that are claimed to date back to the time of King Solomon. The Cochin Jews settled in the Kingdom of Cochin in South India, now part of the state of Kerala. Mention is made of the Jews in southern India by Benjamin of Tudela as early as the 12th century. They are known to have developed Judeo-Malayalam, a dialect of Malayalam language.

Following their expulsion from Iberia in 1492 by the Alhambra Decree, a few families of Sephardi Jews eventually made their way to Cochin in the 16th century. They became known as Paradesi Jews (or

Foreign Jews). The European Jews maintained some trade connections to Europe, and their language skills were useful. Although the Sephardim spoke Ladino (i.e., Spanish or Judeo-Spanish), in India they learned Judeo-Malayalam from the Malabar Jews. The two communities retained their ethnic and cultural distinctions. In the late 19th century, a few Arabic-speaking Jews, who became known as Baghdadi, also immigrated to southern India, and joined the Paradesi community.

After India gained its independence in 1947 and Israel was established as a nation, most of the Malabar Jews made Aliyah and emigrated from Kerala to Israel in the mid-1950s. In contrast, most of the Paradesi Jews (Sephardi in origin) preferred to migrate to Australia and other Commonwealth countries, similar to the choices made by Anglo-Indians.
(Author's note: The phrase "made Aliyah" traditionally means "the act of going up" or immigration of Jews from a place of dispersion among Gentiles back to the geographical holy land of Israel, most of which is represented by the modern day nation state of Israel.)

Most of their synagogues still exist in Kerala. Among the 8 synagogues that survived till the mid-20th century, only the Paradesi synagogue still has a regular congregation. It is believed the Cochin Jews have additional texts, which were considered lost. At this time, the search continues for other texts.

About the Translation

By comparing and contrasting major translations of the text, we have endeavored to produce the most accurate and readable English version. A scholarly edition of the book was published in August 2015, edited by Professor Meir Bar Ilan of Bar Ilan University. Extra Oil Ministries published The Words of Gad the Seer on January 5, 2020, and The Ancient Book of Gad the Seer was published by Ken Johnson on Oct 27, 2016. While attempting to render a more accurate translation, there were decisions that haunted us. What to do with the name Yahweh? Some translators rendered this name as "The Lord". Others rendered the name Yahweh. The issue is, "The Lord" is a title and Yahweh is the name God gave himself. It is said to mean, "I am" or "I am that I am". However, if Gad was written in the time of King David it was before the time Hebrew scribe had adopted the use of vowel marks. At the time of David, around 1000 BC, written Hebrew used no vowels. In keeping with this fact, we decided to render the name using a more authentic Hebrew name revealed to Moses in the book of Exodus. The name YHWH, consisting of the sequence of consonants Yod, Heh, Waw, and Heh. This is known as the tetragrammaton and is a transliteration into English, but it is the best we can do without resorting to Paleo-Hebrew (10,000BC – 200BC). When it seems appropriate to use the title, such as in phrase, "I am your Lord" or "the Lord of heaven and earth" we use the title, but in a phrase such as, " The Lord commanded" we chose to use the name YHWH. Other names or titles were used to describe attributes of God. El Shaddai is one of these titles, meaning God Almighty. It is also a name given to Abraham by God but seems to describe God's capacity. We believed keeping only the Hebrew title kept the average reader from the richness of the attribute being named, thus we rendered those into English.

Gad the Seer

1. The First Vision

1 In the thirty-first year of King David's reign in Jerusalem, which is the thirty-eighth year of David's reign, the Word of YHWH came to Gad the Seer in the month of Ziv(between mid April and mid May), near the stream of the Kidron Valley,
saying:

2 "Thus says YHWH: 'Go, gird your loins like a man and stand in
the middle of the stream, and cry in a loud voice:
"Wait and prepare! Wait and prepare! Wait and prepare, for there is
still a vision for the son of Jesse."

3 And while you are shouting turn and
face the Eastern Gate, on the east side of the city, and stretch forth your hands toward heaven.'"

4 And I did what I had been commanded for me to do.
5 And it came to pass when I finished crying out, I opened
my eyes and saw a yoke of oxen, led by a donkey and a
camel, coming up from the stream of Kidro. The donkey was on
the right side of the yoke and the camel on the left.

6 And a loud voice proceeded them, crying with a sorrowful voice:
7 "Seer, seer, seer, these are four mixtures that confuse the people of YHWH.
8 Because the unclean and the clean have been mixed, and the clean
was placed under the control of the unclean.
9 This mixture came from Seir [Edom] as a way to rule over them, and to increase their power
over the righteous ones,
10 so that they [Edom] can betray and destroy holiness, and crown wickedness, to set up unclean
matters in the guise of purity."
11And after the voice, there was a great quake that occurred, and it threw down the uncleanness and a breath like a whirlwind blew the donkey and the camel into the moon.
12 And the moon was opened and looked like a bow, with her circle divided, and both her
points reached to the Earth.

13 And then I saw the sun came out of heaven in the shape of a man, with a crown on his head, carrying on his right shoulder a lamb, despised and rejected.

14 And on the crown on his head three shepherds are seen, each one was bound with
twelve shackles
15 and the shackles were made of gold, plated with silver. And the voice of the Lamb was heard, loud and dreadful, like the voice of a lion roaring over his prey: "Woe to me! Woe to me! Woe to me! My image (form) has been cut down. My refuge has been lost.
15 My inheritance has ceased. It is fulfilled that I am turned over to My spoilers, and I was defiled until evening by the touch of the unclean."

16 And it came to pass when the voice of the Lamb stopped speaking, I saw a man dressed in linen coming with three vine branches and twelve palms in his hand.
17 And he took the Lamb from the hand of the sun and placed the crown on His head, and the vine-branches and palms on His heart.

18 And the man dressed in linen, cried aloud with a sound like a ram's horn (shofar), saying:
"What is here for you, impurity, and how did you get here, defilement?
19 Do you think you have carved out a place within the innocent or within My covenant that I have established with the vine-branches and palms?"

20 And I heard the Lamb's shepherd saying:
"There is a place with Me for the clean, but not for the unclean, for I am a holy God, and I cannot desire the unclean. I desire only the clean;
21 Although I created both with my hands, and My eyes are on them both equally.
22 But there is an advantage to the abundance of purity over the abundance of uncleanness, just like there is an advantage of a man over a shadow.
23 For the shadow does not exist without man, and only by the man's existence is the shadow given to both the weary and exhausted and to the clean and unclean.

24 For all gates of understanding are turned away since the death of the eight branches of the vine. (Author's Note: Other sources say Nine vine branches.)
25 As is found in words of righteousness in the book of truth, but because of the wanderings of the sheep, and their rest, and divisions,
26 understanding is stopped until I do greatly in keeping grace."

27 I saw that uncleanness was driven out from the moon and it was given over to a consuming wrath, ground into fine dust, and blown away by the unceasing wind.
28 And the day burns as a furnace to remove impurity and to erase the transgressions.
29 And the Lamb was established on the moon forever and ever.

30 And from the clean, the Lamb took the impurity that had been mixed with them and brought it as a peace offering sacrifice on the altar before Almighty God (El Shaddai), the jealous LORD of Hosts.

31And I heard those singing the song of the Lamb, saying:

32 "I shall give thanks unto You, O YHWH. Although You were angry with me, You forgave me and comforted me.

33 For YHWH is my strength and song, and He has become my redeemer.

34 I will sing unto the LORD, for He is highly exalted; He had thrown the horse and his rider into the Sea of Reeds.

35 Arise, understanding; arise, power; arise, kingship (Your kingdom);

36 arise, majesty and glory; arise and assist YHWH.

37 For God has saved one who had strayed and He has obliterated the impurity from the earth.

38 He fought my fight and brought into the light my righteousness by His help.

39 "My help comes from The Almighty (Shaddai) who made heaven and earth."

40 Truly, who is like You in glory and holiness, and is never unclean?

41 For You are great and exalted over everything. You spoke and it was done.

42 For You declared the end from the beginning, and You sealed everything by Your word. You turned my heart and convicted me.

43 For Your seal is upon me, my Lord, and these are the three vine-branches and twelve palms that are on my heart.

44 You glorified me, You removed the uselessness of fearing man, and You gave me a clean heart forever.

45 For that I will praise You at all times, and give thanks to You among all the nations, for You have fully redeemed me for my king and showed favor to the anointed one, David, and to his seed, forever and ever."

46 I heard a voice crying from heaven, saying:

47 "You are My Son, You are My firstborn, You are My first-fruits.

48 Have I not brought You up from beyond Shihor (the river of Egypt, possibly the Nile) to be My daily delight?

49 But You have thrown away My gifts and dressed the unclean with the clean, and that is why all these things have happened to You.

50 And who is like You among all the creatures on earth? For they lived in Your shadow
and by Your wounds they were healed.

51 Because of that, consider well that which is before You.

52 Because You have fulfilled the words of the shepherd all the days You have been under the sun and You did not leave them; therefore, all this honor shall be Yours."

53 And I, Gad, son of Ahimelech of the Jabez family, of the tribe of Judah, son of Israel, was amazed by the vision and could not contain my spirit.

54 And the one dressed in fine linen came down to me and touched me, saying: "Write these words and seal them with the seal of truth, for I AM who I AM is My name, and with My name you shall bless the entire house of Israel, for they are from the seed of faith.

55 In a little while you shall go, and be quietly gathered to your fathers, but at the end of days you shall see with your own eyes all these things, not as a vision, but in reality.

56 For in those days they shall not be called Jacob, but Israel; for no iniquity will be found in their remnant, for they will belong entirely to YHWH.

57 And these words will restore your life and spirit. And this shall be a sign for you, that when you enter the town, you will find My servant David and he will be reading these words from the Book of Covenant:

58 'And yet for all that, when they are in the land of their enemies, I will not reject them, neither will I despise them, to destroy them completely, and to break My covenant with them; for I am YHWH their God.'

59 And you shall tell him about the vision you have just seen; and when he sees you, he will be glad in his heart."

60And it came to pass, when I came to the house of David, the man of God, I found him dressed in linen and I told him of all my visions.

61 Then David spoke the words of this song unto YHWH, saying: "I love You, O LORD, my strength."

62 And he said to me: "YHWH has blessed you by revealing His secrets to your ears.

63 And I lifted my voice to YHWH and said: You are blessed by YHWH, for has not removed His covenant from you, for He is true, and His word is true, and His seal is firm."

2. The Second Vision

1 After these true things, I had a vision from God saying:

2 "Set your face eastward, northward, southward, and westward.

3 And whistle with your mouth as a bird whistles to its young and say: 'Four corners of the earth,
listen to the Word of YHWH.

4 Thus saith YHWH, who sits and dwells over the cherubim: 'Cast, Cast, Cast, Gather, Gather, Gather My seed that I have sown in you, for the time for planting has come.

5 For only a little while I shall collect My seed on My threshing floor.

6 And the threshing floor will be holy; not an unclean seed will not be found there.

7 Prior to those days My seed was mixed with lentils, and barley, and wheat, beans, and gourds.

8 And in the end of days the sower shall be true and the seed shall be true and from the seed all the land will be blessed.

9 Be joyful and glad, you remnant of Judah and you rejected of Israel, for salvation is with YHWH.

10 As you shall be a curse and worthless to all the families of the earth, so shall you be a blessing and grace forever.

11 At that time no cursed or unholy people will be found among you,

12 for everyone will join you in the covenant, the Law, testimonies, statutes, and ordinances.

13 And you and they shall have one God, one covenant, one law, one language, for all shall speak in the language of the Jews, the holy language.

14 Blessed are you, O Israel, who is like unto you? A people saved by YHWH, for He will go
before you to fight your wars with your enemies.

15 Woe to you, O Edom, that sits in the land of Kittim in the north of the sea.

16 For your destroyers will emerge from a terrible nation. They will not leave you a remnant.

17 For you have said: 'My throne is on high, and only I have a knowledge (other sources say "covenant) of the God of gods, for YHWH chose me instead of His holy people, for He hated them.

18 And His former people, despised and rejected, did not know YHWH because they did not know His image.

19 We are truly wise and intelligent; we know YHWH and His Laws, we know His image and presence.

20 But thus says YHWH: 'Because you rose up in pride to brag about the God of gods, know that you will perish because of your own cleverness.

21 For why would you put confidence in man, whose nostrils are filled with breath that came up one night and passes like a shadow the next day, placing him to sit beside God.

22 For it is not you whom I knew formerly, and where is the bill of divorce of My people, that you
said would be a prey; show it to Me!

23 Your corpses will fall among My people.'

24 O jealous Lord, come out; come out of your place and crush Edom. Consume them.

25 Come to Zerephath, come to Sepharad, come to Ashkenaz, come to (Togarmish) Garmania; they
shall come and fall into the deepest pit, in destruction, and in the shadow of death, for your mouth will fail you, and no one will help you.

26 At the end of days Michael the great prince will stand up in war like a whirlwind against Samael the prince of this world to put him under his feet, and by the breath the of the LORD he shall be devoured, for YHWH has spoken it.

27 At the end of days the robbed will overcome the robber, and the weak, the strong, truly and in righteousness.

28 Your God is your Savior, O Israel; with Him you will be saved, for He is a merciful God. He will not abandon you,

29 for you shall keep doing all that I commanded you according to the Law of Moses My servant.'

Chapter 3

1 At the time when the feast of Passover came, on the fifteenth of the first month, a Moabite shepherd came to David and spoke to him saying: "My lord the king, you have known that your servant has been loyal to Israel from my youth, and now take me away from dwelling among uncircumcised people and circumcise the flesh of my foreskin to take away my reproach, so that I can live among your people."

2 And David said: "YHWH does not desire your people, and He commanded, 'An Ammonite or a Moabite shall not enter into the assembly of YHWH forever.' And we cannot ask Him for your peace nor your prosperity; but how can I help you today?"

3 The servant answered: "Is it not it true that Ruth was of our people, and you are one of her children and descendants, and YHWH has chosen you and your descendants forever?"

4 Then David said: "You have given me words that defeat me (my argument). Stand here with me to seek an answer from the mouth of my Lord."

5 And David asked the LORD about the statement of the Moabite servant.

6 And David said: "O YHWH, LORD of Hosts, teach me wondrous things out of Your Law so that I may know how to rule for this servant, and what should be done with him."

7 And YHWH said to Nathan the prophet: "Go to David My servant, and tell him the message that I tell you."

8And Nathan went to David, to his chambers, saying: "This is what the Lord of Hosts says: 'I have

heard your prayer, so tell the Moabite: 'You are a Moabite man, not a Moabite woman, for I did not say a 'Moabite woman' and 'Ammonite woman,' because their women and daughters may belong to YHWH; however you are cursed by YHWH, and forbidden to enter the LORD's assembly."

9 When the Moabite heard the message of YHWH, he cried out and exclaimed: "I am

forbidden from entering the assembly of YHWH."

10 And David took him and appointed him a shepherd among king's shepherds, and he was there until the third year of the reign of King Solomon, then he died.

11 And he had a daughter whose name was Sephirah; she had a beautiful form and was very pretty to look upon. King Solomon took her to be his concubine, and she found grace and favor in his sight more than all the other concubines, and she became the chief of the concubines' residence.

12 And this became the statute in Israel forever.

Chapter 4

1 In those days a man from Bethlehem, the city of David, went to Jerusalem to pay the vow which he had vowed unto YHWH. His name was Zabad the Parhi, and he was of the family of the Perezites.

2 Zabad's father was very sick, even unto the point of death, so Zabad vowed:

"When YHWH heals my father of his sickness, I will weigh out two talents of silver and give them to the House of YHWH, into the hand of King David."

3 And it came to pass, when he was at the house of the shepherds (the place where sheering of sheep took place) along the way, he lost the pouch with the money in it and he was very distraught.

4 So when he came to the city of Jerusalem, into the inner city, and he wrote on all the gates these words:

5 "Anyone who finds a lost pouch with two talents of silver and brings it to me I will give him a

talent of silver as a reward."

6 Then a man from the tribe of Dan came and had in his hand the pouch with the silver talents that he found along the way and he gave it to the owner of the pouch.

7 And the Danite said to the Perezite: "Give me the talent of silver as you promised."

8 And the Zabad said: "No, there were actually three talents in my pouch and you have already stolen one talent. I was mistaken about the amount."

9 So both of them came and stood before the king. And the king said to the Zabad:

10 "Swear to me in the name of YHWH, that you truly had three talents of silver in your pouch." And Zabad swore to him by YHWH.

11 And the king said to the Danite: "Swear to me in the name of YHWH, that you only found two talents of silver the pouch." And he swore to him by YHWH.

12 And David said to Zabad: "Give the pouch with the talents back to the Danite, because this is his money that YHWH had hidden to be given to him by chance.

13 Now, go and write on the city gates: 'Whoever finds the pouch with three talents should bring it to me,' because this pouch is not yours."

14And David took the pouch with the talents of silver from the hand of the Perezite and gave it to the Danite.

15 And the Danite bowed his head and prostrated himself to the earth and said: "Long live my lord, King David, forever."

16 And all Israel heard of this judgment and they marveled and were happy because they saw that David was full of the wisdom of God.

Chapter 5

1 All the Philistines assembled themselves together to fight against Israel. There were multitudes of tribes of the Philistines. So many that they could not be numbered.

2 And David was very distressed because he was afraid of the Philistines.

3 And YHWH said to Gad: "Go and tell David My servant: 'Do not be worried about these

uncircumcised Philistines, because tomorrow I will give them and those who oppress you into your hand."

4 And David said to Gad: "I am not worthy of all the mercies that YHWH has shown to me, but blessed be the name of YHWH forever and ever."

5 That night, a chariot of fire (fire-angel or fire-rider) came from heaven and the rider held his drawn sword in his hand.

6 And he attacked the camp of the uncircumcised. It was such a great slaughter that none of them were left alive.

7 And it came to pass the next day they came to David saying: "Behold, all the Philistines have been killed by those who rose up against them and not a single one was left alive."

8 And David raised his voice and said: "Now I know that nothing can hinder YHWH. He can save us from many or few, and His salvation can be in a blink of an eye."

9 And he said: "Blessed are You, O LORD, who has been taking revenge for us on our enemies."

10 And he set up a pillar and called it the "Pillar of Vengeance" unto this day.

Chapter 6

1 YHWH said to Gad: "Go tell David My servant:

2 'Thus says YHWH: 'Let not the mighty man glory in his might.

3 But let him glory in this, that My help (strength) is with him.

4 Then you should go and fear not, for YHWH is with you.'"

5 And Gad came and told David what YHWH had said.

6 And David said to Gad: "I have known the help of the LORD from my youth.

7 For who struck down the lion and who struck down the bear? Who smote the Philistines? Who killed my enemies? Was it not the help of God?"

8 And when YHWH heard that, He was very pleased.

9 And He said: "Because David has acknowledged My help in his time of glory, My help will dwell in the house of David forever."

10 And Gad told David what YHWH said.

11 And David bowed down and prostrated himself before YHWH and said: "Blessed be the LORD for I have found favor in His eyes."

Chapter 7

1And again the anger of YHWH was kindled against Israel

2 and He moved Satan against David, saying: "Go, number (do a census on) Israel and Judah," to bring them the evil He spoke through Samuel the seer.

3 And the king said to Joab the captain (of the army) and to the princes of the people: "Go now through all the tribes of Israel, from Dan even to Beersheba, and number the people, and bring me word, that I may know the total of them."

4 And Joab said unto the king: "May the YHWH add to the people a hundredfold of how many they may be, and may the eyes of YHWH our God watch over them; but my lord the king, are they not
all my lord's servants? Why does my lord require this thing? And why should it be done? Will it not cause guilt (a trespass) against Israel? For YHWH has said: 'These cannot be numbered for the multitude.'"

5 Notwithstanding, the king's word prevailed against Joab and against the captains of the host. And Joab and the captains of the host departed from the presence of the king to number the people of Israel. 6 And they passed over the Jordan, and camped in Aroer, south of the town in the middle of the streams (rivers) of Gad, and toward Jazer.

7 And they came to Gilead, and then to the land of the Hittites, to Kadesh, and they came to Dan and Enan, and round about to Zidon.

8 And they came to the stronghold of Tyre, and to all the cities of the Hivites and the Canaanites. And they went out to the south of Judah, to Beersheba.

9 So when they had gone through all the land, they came to Jerusalem at the end of nine months and twenty days. But Joab did not number Levi and Benjamin, for the king's word was abominable to Joab.

10 And Joab gave the total of the number of the people to David. And all they of Israel were eight hundred thousand valiant men and three hundred thousand men that drew a sword, and in Judah there were four hundred and seventy thousand valiant men and thirty thousand men that drew a sword.

11 And THE LORD GOD was displeased with this act Israel had done, and He sent Gad the seer to David, saying:

12"Thus said YHWH: 'I am the King of Israel, and I am their portion. I am their great dread (fear), I am their fortress and might, and you know that it is not with a sword or a spear that I will save, nor is it by men of valor who draws a sword, for this is the way of the gentiles (heathens) that they depend on their might and their many warriors.

13 But you are not like that, for I am a warrior standing alone and there is no one with Me. Why would you do this evil to number your people? For this deed I will strike Israel, so that you will know that I am The LORD in the midst of the earth."

14 And David's heart was strongly grieved after that. And David said unto YHWH: "I have sinned greatly in what I have done, but now O LORD, I beg You, take away the iniquity of Your servant, for I have acted very foolishly."

15 And David rose up in the morning, and the Word of YHWH had already come to Gad the prophet, David's seer, saying:

16"Go and say unto David: 'Thus says YHWH: 'I offer you three things; choose one of them, that I may do it unto you."

17 So Gad came to David and told him, and said unto him: "Shall four years of famine come unto the land of Israel and three years in the land of Judah? Or will you flee three months before your enemies while they pursue you, as their swords overtake you? Or shall there be three days of the sword of YHWH, which is pestilence in your land, and the angel of YHWH will spoil all the land of Israel? Now consider these things and decide what to answer and I shall return the answer to Him who sent me."

18 And David said unto Gad: "I am in a great strait; let me fall, and let us fall now, into the hand of YHWH, for His mercies are great; and let me not fall into the hand of man."

19 So YHWH sent a pestilence upon Israel, beginning in the morning and continuing until to the time appointed; and there died of the people from Dan to Beersheba, seventy thousand men.

20 And God sent an angel to Jerusalem to destroy it; and he was destroying it when YHWH saw this and He changed His mind about the evil and said to the angel that was destroying the people: "It is enough; now stay your hand."

21 And the angel of YHWH was standing by the threshing floor of Ornan the Jebusite. And David lifted up his eyes and saw the angel of YHWH standing between the heaven and the earth, with a drawn sword in his hand and the sword was stretched out over Jerusalem. And David and the elders, who were clothed in sackcloth, fell upon their faces.

22 And David said unto God: "Is it not I that commanded the people to be numbered? And I that sinned and acted wickedly; but these sheep, what have they done? O YHWH, my God, let Your hand be against me and my father's house, but not against Your people, that they should be plagued. Shall not the judge of all the earth be just?"

23 And YHWH said: "They incited Satan against you to number them, saying thus: 'We will be like

all the nations,' but I am a God of justice; and I returned their high hearts (their self importance/ arrogance) into their own bosoms.

24 For a broken or a contrite heart I shall not despise forever."

25 And the angel of YHWH told Gad to tell David that David should go up and raise (build) an altar to YHWH on the threshing floor of Ornan the Jebusite.

26 And David went up and did according to the words of Gad which he spoke in the name of YHWH.

27 And Ornan was threshing wheat when he was looking, and he saw the king and his four sons with him.

28 And Ornan looked and saw David, and he went out of the threshing floor, and bowed down to David with his face to the ground.

29 Then David said to Ornan: "Sell me the place of this threshing floor, that I may build an altar to YHWH on it. You shall sell it to me for the full price, so that the plague may be stayed from the people."

30 And Ornan said unto David: "Take it and let my lord the king do that which is good in his eyes. See, I shall also give the oxen for burnt offering, and the threshing instruments for wood, and the wheat for the meal offering. I give it all."

31 And King David said to Ornan, "No, truly, I will buy it for the full price. I will not take that which is yours for YHWH, nor offer a burnt offering without paying for it."

32 So David gave Ornan six hundred shekels of gold for the place, and fifty shekels of silver, by weight for the cattle.

33 And David built an altar to YHWH there, and offered burnt offerings and peace offerings, and called upon YHWH, and He answered him from heaven by fire upon the altar of burnt offering.

34 Then YHWH commanded the angel and he put his sword back into its sheath, and the plague was stayed from Israel.

35 At that time, when David saw that YHWH had answered him in the threshing floor of Ornan the Jebusite, and God did not despise him, then he sacrificed to YHWH there for the rest of his life.

36 For David would no longer go and sacrifice to YHWH in the high place at Gibeon, where there was an altar to YHWH and a tabernacle which Moses made, because he was terrified and weakened because he had seen the sword of the angel of YHWH.

Chapter 8

1 YHWH appeared unto David is his old age and said to him: "Behold, I am with you, and I am your God, and behold, My covenant is with you; do not be afraid, nor discouraged, because your God is your helper."

2 And David bowed down to YHWH and rejoiced in his heart.

3 And YHWH said: "Speak these words in the hearing of My people and do so in My name that they may obey so that they will live. If they do, there shall be no more wrath upon them."

4 And YHWH put His words in his mouth.

5 Then David assembled all Israel in Jerusalem, and he made a pulpit of wood for himself and he stood on it in the audience of the people and addressed all the people. He opened his mouth and said:

6 "Listen, O Israel, your God and my God is one, the only one. There is none other like Him and there is no one like Him. He is unique. He is hidden from everyone; He was. He is. And He will always be. He fills His dwelling place (creation), but His dwelling place (creation) does not fill Him. He sees everything, but He is unseen; He knows the future and He can declare it, but to Him there is no end. He is the Almighty (omnipotent) God of truth. Entire worlds are filled with His glory.

7 He gave each person free choice. If a person wants to do good, he will be helped. If a person wants to do evil, the way will be available to him.

8 As for us, we will worship our God, our King, our Lord, and Savior, with love and awe. For your wisdom begins with the fear of The Lord, and in our discernment we depart from evil.

9 Remember and obey the Law of Moses, the man of God, so that your lives will be blessed all of your days.

10 Ask your fathers, and they will teach you, ask your elders, and they will tell you.

11 be strong and fearless. Do not simply listen to the Law, but you must obey it.

12 Hearing is like the seed. A deed is like the root. Faith is like a tree, and its fruit is righteousness.

13 What becomes of a rotten stinking seed if no root has come from it?

14 Therefore, hurry. Be quick to hear and act. For if you are a true seed, if you have belief and

righteousness, then YHWH will bless you all with peace.

15 Speak (conduct yourselves) with peace toward each other. Show love with your deeds. Do these things to mankind and those created in the image of YHWH like as you would with your own souls,

16 because it is a sign that you love the Creator, if you love His creation.

17 You cannot do the one thing without doing the other, so Love YHWH and also man so that it will be well with you all the days of your life."

18 David raised his voice, and spread his hands toward heaven, and said: "YHWH, my God, the God of the spirits of all flesh, God, merciful and gracious, guard (keep) Israel forever.

19 Save Your people, and bless Your inheritance, and tend to them, and tend to them forever."

20 And all the people shouted: "Amen! Amen!"

21 And David sent the people away and they went home peacefully.

Chapter 9

1 Hiram king of Tyre sent messengers unto David saying:

2 "I know (I have perceived) that YHWH your God is the one true God, so now be kind to me and truthful and teach me the Law of your God, for I will worship Him all the days of my life."

3 Then the messengers came to David with an offering in their hands for YHWH and for David. They told him everything that Hiram had said and presented him with the offerings.

4 And David sent a reply to Hiram (and he said):

5 "Go and tell my brother, Hiram: 'This is what David, your brother, says: 'Reverence (fear) YHWH, creator of heaven and fire, the sea and the earth, the wet and the dry, the heat and the cold, the stones and the vegetation, the living and the speaking,

6 the spheres of the heavenly abodes, the Pleiades and Orion, the sun and the moon, the things of substance and of spirit, the wandering stars (planets), the senses, and everything.

7 These were all created without a blemish by God Almighty (El Shaddai) whose name is YHWH.

8 If you do this and observe the commandments that were ordered to the children of Noah, your forefather, then God will bless you all the days of your life.

9 We are both His by our alliance; but we are different from you by the Law of truth, sealed by the seal of the Almighty (Shaddai), called the children of the God of Truth.

10 We must therefore obey the whole Law that THE NAME commanded of us, saying:

'And you shall be unto Me a kingdom of priests, and a holy nation. These are the words which you shall speak unto the children of Israel.'

11 But He has not dealt the same way with any other nation as He has with us. He did not choose us for any reason other than His great love for us."

12 The messengers then returned to Hiram their king and told him the words of King David had spoken to them.

13 And Hiram rejoiced with all his heart and called all his princes and servants together and said to them:

14 " Hear me you Tyrians and Sidonians, and listen to what I am about to declare.

15 Have reverence and be in aw (respect) for God Almighty (El Shaddai), who is the God of Israel. He made everything by speaking and by the breath of His mouth; and who will tell Him what He can do? For He is one (first, only).

16 Declare these things with me (Repeat): 'Blessed is YHWH the God of Israel who chooses His people. Blessed is David, His servant, king of His people, and blessed is Israel whom the LORD has chosen to be His inheritance.

17 I wish we were the servants of the children of Israel because they are called the children of the LORD, their God.'"

18 And all his princes and his servants replied: "Amen, thus it shall be done."

19 And Hiram lifted up his voice and said: "I have seen, but it is not now, I have witnessed, but it is not close, that there shall come forth from David a sun, and a moon shall rise out of the house of Judah, and shall smite all the children of Ham, and break down all the children of Japheth, and he will possess all the kingdoms of the world." For who is like YHWH, God above all gods?

20 And who is like Israel a people above the nations? May our end be like theirs."

21 When YHWH heard what Hiram had said, He was very pleased with him.

22 And YHWH said to Gad, the seer of David, the following words I have spoken to you:

23 "Go to my servant and tell him the message that I gave you."

24 And Gad, the one in whose hand was the word of YHWH, came to David, and said, "Thus says YHWH the God of Hosts: 'I have heard what Hiram, king of Tyre, has said and what his princes and servants have said, and I am very pleased.

25 Therefore I will give him and his people a heart of wisdom and understanding so they may prepare My house where I shall put My name (power), and that will cause his kingdom to spring forth, for I have chosen them and I will not reject (despise) them.'"

26 And David said to Gad: "Now I know with assurance that YHWH our God greatly rewards all His creatures and all the works He has created with goodness, because He is a God of mercy, who dwells on high and looks after the lowly, and he who is lowly will not be cast out from Him.
Blessed be YHWH forever; Amen, and Amen.

27 For as high heaven is above the earth, this is how great His mercy is toward them that fear Him and towards His works.

28 Bless YHWH, and all His works, in all of His dominion. Bless YHWH, O my soul. Hallelujah."

Chapter 10

1 At that tie David wrote this psalm of praise: I will exalt You, my God, O King; and I will bless Your name forever and ever.

2 Every day I will bless You, and I will praise Your name forever and ever.

3 Great is YHWH. He is to be praised highly. His greatness is unsearchable.

4 One generation shall praise Your works, and shall declare Your mighty acts to the next generation.

5 The glorious splendor of Your majesty, and Your wondrous works I will announce and repeat.

6 Men shall speak of the might of Your amazing works; and I will tell them about Your greatness.

7 They shall tell stories of Your splendid goodness, and they shall sing of Your righteousness.

8 The LORD is gracious and full of compassion, slow to anger, and full of mercy.

9 YHWH is good to all, and His tender mercies are even greater than all His works.

10 All Your creation shall thank You, O LORD; and Your saints bless You.

11 They shall speak of the glory of Your kingdom and talk of Your mighty power.

12 They will make known to the sons of men His mighty acts, and the majestic glory of His kingdom.

13 Your kingdom is everlasting, and Your dominion endures throughout all ages.
All Your enemies have fallen, O LORD, and all of their might has been consumed (amounted to nothing)

14 YHWH lifts all those who fall and raises up all those who are bowed down.

15 every eye waits for You; and You give them their food in due season.

16 With favor You open Your hands and satisfy the desire of every living thing.

17 YHWH is righteous in all His ways, and merciful in all His works.

18 YHWH is near to all who call upon Him in truth.

19 He will grant the desire of them that fear Him. He will hear their cry and save them.

20 The LORD preserves all that love Him: but the wicked He will entirely destroy.

21 My mouth shall declare the praise of YHWH. Let all flesh bless His holy name forever and endlessly.

Chapter 11

1 The Psalm of David praising YHWH on the day when Elhanan the son of Jair slew Lahmi the brother of Goliath the Gittite, and Jonathan the son of Shimea killed a man of great stature, saying: Blessed be YHWH my rock, who teaches my hands to war, and my fingers to battle.

2 He is my love and mercy, and my fortress, my high tower, and my deliverer; my shield (protector). It is in He whom I take refuge. It is He who subdues peoples under me.

3 O LORD, what is man, that You take knowledge of him? Or the son of man, that You regard him?

4 Man is like a single breath: his days are as a shadow that passes away.

5 O LORD, make low (bow) Your heavens, and come down touch the mountains so that they smoke.

6 Throw out lightning and scatter them. Shoot Your arrows and make them fall.

7 Stretch out Your hand from above and rescue me. Deliver me out of many waters, out of the hand of foreigners;

8 whose mouths speak lies, and whose right hand is a right to lie.

9 O God, I will sing to You a new song: I will sing praise to You. On a psaltery (harp) made with ten strings I shall sign praises to you.

10 You give salvation to kings, You who rescues Your servant David from an evil sword.

11 Rescue me, and deliver me from the hand of foreigners, whose mouths speak lies, and whose right hand is a right of falsehood.

12 Our sons are like plants, grown up in their youth and our daughters are cornerstones, carved in the form of the temple.

13 May our storehouses be full with all manner of food; may our sheep increase by a thousand times and by ten thousands in our streets.

14 May our oxen be strong to labor. No breaks (in our walls), No intrusions. No outcries in our streets.
15 Happy is the people that live like this. Happy is the people whose God is YHWH.
16 Happy is he who waits (anticipates) the time there will be good to all Israel forever.

Chapter 12

1 These are the words of David, that he spoke to YHWH and all of Israel before his death. And David said:
2 "God, You are holy and mighty, the beginning and only one, guileless, fully righteous, amazing,
3 dreadful, benefactor of the miserable, beloved, our Father (ancient), God Almighty (El Shaddai).
4 Holy One, have mercy upon the vine, which is Your good inheritance.
5 Will you answer us in the day as we call upon You?
6 My Lord, hear my prayer and supplication, for (we know) You hear every word and the prayers of all people;
7 Listen and accept the cry of Your people with mercy,
8 for they are Your flock and Your inheritance.
9 Send out Your light and truth to help them.
10 Give them one heart to worship You, one shoulder to serve you as a single body, so they will be one in Your hand.
11 And do not lose any of them, for Your name is one, as our fathers and mothers are one.
12 And because of that I say, hear O Israel, YHWH is our God. YHWH is one.
13 Do not turn to the idols, for they are empty (false) and will completely pass away.
14 Cling only to God, for only He can be your fear and fortress.
15 He can defeat enemies. Enemies of the spirit and enemies in the flesh shall be put them under your feet.
16 He will bring you into the New Jerusalem that is hidden until the future comes,
17 where you will see God face to face, and you will be in the presence of the living God. And you are one people if you grow in faith. And the gates of your understanding will be filled.
18 Blessed is the eye that has seen all these things.
19 But if you lack faith, you will be overcome by the gates of impurity.
20 So cleanse and purify yourself before the LORD, your king, and it will be good for you all the days of your life."

21 And David died in the afternoon on the Sabbath day, in the fortieth year of his reign over Judah and Israel.
22 He was seventy years old when he died, and he was buried with great honor in the city of David.

23 And the rest of the deeds of David the King, during his mighty reign and the deeds done in the time that passed with him, Israel, and all the kingdoms of the land are written in the Book of Samuel the Seer and in the Book of Nathan the Prophet.

Chapter 13

1 Now, Solomon was able to strengthen his kingdom, because YHWH his God was with him, and greatly magnified him.
2 After this, David's daughter, Tamar, sister of Absalom, left and fled to the house of the king of Geshur, and she spent a year and eight months in palace of the king, which was also her mother's house.
3 And King Solomon did not know that her leaving, because she went secretly, and she concealed herself from the king, the people.

4 And King Solomon said: "whoever finds Tamar, my sister from my father, and brings her to me, I shall pay a reward consisting of wages, changes of clothing and fifty shekels of gold."
5 And so the king's servants searched for her throughout all the land, but they could not find her,
6 because she was hiding at her mother's home in Geshur, which was the home of the king, her mother's father.
7 And there was a friend of the king, whose name was Pirshaz, and he loved the young woman very much, for she had a beautiful form (body) and was very pretty.
8 In those days the king of Geshur went to see King Solomon, as all the kings of the lands do.
9 King Solomon inquired of him, saying: "Is it well with you?" and he said: "It is well."
10 And he (Solomon) said: "Is it well with the wife of my father, David in your house?" And he said: "It is well." And then King Solomon cunningly asked: "Is it well with Tamar, my sister?" And he lied to him, saying: "I do not know, for I have never met her."
11 And it came to pass when the king of Geshur was in Jerusalem, his friend, Pirshaz, came to Tamar's room, saying to her: "Lay with me."
12 But Tamar refused him, saying: "Let us not do this lustful (reckless) thing, because I am a king's daughter."
13 However he would not listen to her, because he was burning with lust.
14 And Tamar knew her strength (to fight him off) was growing weak, so she slyly said: "My lord, listen to the words of your maidservant.
15 Behold, I play the harp, so first, rest your head in my lap and listen to my song.

16 And after I play the song of my heart, then I will do all your heart's desire." And Pirshaz listened to Tamar, and he lay in her bosom.

17 And as Tamar took the harp and began to play beautifully, she said in her heart: "YHWH, king of my father David, Your servant,

18 send Your light and Your truth to hold me, and do not allow the desires of this wicked, uncircumcised, unclean man to be fulfilled.

19 For You know what is in my heart, so do not let this daughter of David, Your servant, commit sin.

20 My loving Father, my loving Father, my loving Father! Look at this reproach of your daughter

21 I go before Almighty God's (El Shaddai's) throne of glory and beg mercy and to the God of Hosts to help me by His strength.

22 For He does not want the sin of unclean fellows and His desire is to help those who have been robbed to overcome the strong men.

23 I beg You, O LORD, save me now. I beg You, O YHWH, let me prosper.

24 I call on You this day because I am frightened; please answer me, and do not let this unclean man cause me to lose holy seed by this corrupt act, for You are a holy God, and my trust is in You."

25 And YHWH heard the voice of David's daughter, and God caused Pirshaz to fall into a deep sleep. He fell asleep on her bosom while she was playing the pleasant sounds of the harp.

26 And when Tamar saw that he had fallen asleep, she unsheathed the sword that was tied around his waist.

27 And she said: "LORD of Hosts, remember David my father, and give me strength like You did my father.

28 Help me as You helped the wife of Heber the Kenite, to rid the earth of sins and sinners, so all will know that You are the only LORD."

29 And she took the sword and plunged it through Pirshaz's heart, and Pirshaz fell to the ground dead.

30 And Tamar saw that Pirshaz was dead and she cried with a loud voice: "May all Your enemies and the enemies of Your people perish this way, O YHWH.

31 And now I have seen that You have heard my voice because of my father. You have resolved to not allow his daughter to be disgraced by this unclean man.

32 Blessed are You from everlasting to everlasting. Amen."

33 It was the time of the noon meal, and Pirshaz's servants came to call their master to the king's table.

34 But when they came to the inner chamber, they found Tamar with a bloody sword in her hand standing over the body of their master, and they saw Pirshaz was dead.

35 And they turned trembling to one another, saying: "What happened?" And they took Tamar and brought her to the king's ministers.

36 And the king's servants said to Tamar: "What have you done? You have killed the king's friend. You must know that our master, the king, will consider this a disgrace (foolish act)."

37 And Tamar said: "Should one deal with a king's daughter like a harlot? His blood is upon his own head, and I will be seen as guiltless and clean in the king's eyes."

38 And they took Tamar and put her in the hands of the captain (minister) of the prison.

39 And they sent a letter by couriers to their king who was still in Jerusalem stating that Tamar, the king's granddaughter had killed his friend, Pirshaz, and that Tamar was placed in prison until the time the king returned.

40 And the couriers came to Jerusalem and King Solomon's guards saw them. And the guards asked them: "Where are you from?"

41 And they said: "We come from Geshur to bring letters to our master the king."

42 And the guards stopped them and brought them to King Solomon.

43 And King Solomon said: "You came here to spy out the land. Give me your king's letters and I will see if you are committing sin against me or not."

44 And King Solomon took the letters and gave them to the sons of Shisha, the king's scribes, to be read.

45 And they read them and it was written that Tamar had killed Pirshaz and that she had been placed in prison.

46 And King Solomon called Ahishar, who was head of the household, and said: "Put these uncircumcised men in prison and bring the king of Geshur to me."

47 And he did according as he had been commanded. And the king of Geshur was brought before King Solomon and he bowed his head toward the ground.

48 And King Solomon said: "Why have you wrong me by lying to me about Tamar my sister being with you? You told me that you had never seen her in all your life.

49 As YHWH lives, who has redeemed David, my father, out of all evil, this day you shall die."

50 And King Solomon called Benaiah, the son of Jehoiada, and said to him: "Go, and throw down the king of Geshur and his couriers." And he executed them, and they all died, because they had lied to King Solomon.

51 And they buried them in a cave in front of the Fish Gate.

52 This is why the name of the cave in front of the Fish Gate is the called Cave of the "Uncircumcised Ones", to this day.

53 And Solomon sent Benaiah, the son of Jehoiada, and said, "Take ten thousand men of valor from Judah and go to Geshur and bring back Tamar, my father's daughter. Destroy the royal palace, but take care not to

harm Tamar's mother, for she was your master's (King David's) wife."

55 And they departed and did all that King Solomon had commanded, and they presented Tamar before King Solomon.

56 And Tamar bowed down to the ground, before the king, and said: "Let my lord the king, my brother, live forever."

57 And King Solomon asked her: "Why did you flee to Geshur?"

58 And she answered: "I was living in my brother Absalom's house, and I felt empty and anguished because of what my brother Amnon had done to me. So, I decided to go to my mother's house so I would not be disgraced in the eyes of the sons of my king.

59 And King Solomon asked her: "Why did you kill Pirshaz?" And she explained what that uncircumcised man did to her, and what she did to him in revenge.

60 And King Solomon said: "You are blessed by YHWH. He has blessed you with discretion. You were wise. You acted (appropriately), and you were victorious."

61 Then King Solomon spoke so all of his servants could hear, saying: "Has anyone found such a woman of wisdom and strength?" And he said: "Daughter, God is gracious unto you.

62 From this day forward you shall not be called my sister, but my daughter, because of your wisdom." 63 And King Solomon gave his daughter Tamar to Abinadab's son to be his wife, and she found favor in her husband's eyes, and he loved her very much.

64 He was an officer over all the region of Dor.

65 And King Solomon changed the name of Tamar his daughter to Taphath (meaning to distill), for stacte (a sweet spice used for making incense), for it was the first of the incense. And this was her name the rest of her life.

Chapter 14

1 And it came to pass on the first day of the seventh month, at the beginning of the year, in the four hundred and seventy-eighth year after the children of Israel came out of the land of Egypt, in the second year of King Solomon's reign over Israel, I had a vision from YHWH, when I was in the river Gihon.

(Author's Note: the river Gihon is one of four said to branch from the river in Eden. Ethiopians hold that the river Gihon is the Blue Nile.)

2 And I raised my eyes, and saw the heavens rolled back like a scroll, and I saw the glory of YHWH, seated high above on a throne, which was very tall.

3 And here was the appearance of the throne: It had twelve stairs leading up to the throne. There were six

made of gold and six of silver. And there was a square back to the throne, which looked like a sapphire stone.

4 And at its right side were three smaller thrones and at its left side were four smaller thrones. And they were near the (great) throne, like the seven that see the king's face. And the thrones were covered with gold and silver and precious stones.

5 And the glory of YHWH appeared like a rainbow, which is His covenant.

6 And the host of heaven were standing before Him on His right hand and on His left, and Satan was not standing by them, but behind them.

7And then a man dressed in fine linen brought before the glory of YHWH three books, which contained the records of every person.

8 And he read from the first book and it contained the righteous deeds of His people, and YHWH said, "These shall have eternal life."

9 And Satan said, "Who are these guilty people?" And the man dressed in fine linen shouted at
Satan and it sounded like a ram's horn., and he said, "Silence! This day is holy to our Lord."

10 And then he read from the second book, and it contained the unintentional sins of His people. And the LORD said, "Set that book aside, but save it until one third of the month passes, to see what they will do."

11 And he read from the third book, and it contained the wicked deeds of His people.

12 And YHWH said to Satan, "These are your share. Take them and do what you desire to (with) them."

13 And Satan took the wicked to a waste land to destroy them there.

14 And the man dressed in fine linen shouted and it sounded like a ram's horn, saying:

15 "Blessed are the people who know the joyful shout and who walk in the light of Your
countenance, O LORD!"

16 And I heard the voice of the host of heaven rejoicing and saying, "Lord of Justice, Lord of the hosts, the whole heaven and earth is full of Your glory."

17 And I was amazed by the vision because I did not know what YHWH was going to do with me.

18 Then one of the cherubs flew up to me and he put an olive branch in my mouth, and said, "Look! This has touched your mouth, and your iniquity is taken away, and your sin are atoned for (paid for, forgiven).

19 And this law that you have seen in the statutes of Israel, it is the law of God to Abraham, and it brought peace to Isaac your father.

20 (With it) YHWH will bless your people in the time of trials (temptations) with everlasting peace."

21 And I said, "Amen. May the YHWH our God do this for us forever and ever."

22 And the angel answered, "Amen and Amen."